REVIEW OF RESEARCH IN EDUCATION

Review of Research in Education is published annually on behalf of the American Educational Research Association, 1430 K St., NW, Suite 1200, Washington, DC 20005, by SAGE Publications, 2455 Teller Road, Thousand Oaks, CA 91320. Send address changes to AERA Membership Department, 1430 K St., NW, Suite 1200, Washington, DC 20005.

Member Information: American Educational Research Association (AERA) member inquiries, member renewal requests, changes of address, and membership subscription inquiries should be addressed to the AERA Membership Department, 1430 K St., NW, Suite 1200, Washington, DC 20005; fax 202-238-3250; e-mail: members@aera.net. AERA annual membership dues are $180 (Regular Members), $150 (Affiliate Members), $110 (International Affiliates), and $55 (Graduate Students and Student Affiliates). **Claims:** Claims for undelivered copies must be made no later than six months following month of publication. Beyond six months and at the request of the American Educational Research Association, the publisher will supply missing copies when losses have been sustained in transit and when the reserve stock permits.

Subscription Information: All non-member subscription inquiries, orders, back-issue requests, claims, and renewals should be addressed to SAGE Publications, 2455 Teller Road, Thousand Oaks, CA 91320; telephone (800) 818-SAGE (7243) and (805) 499-0721; fax: (805) 375-1700; e-mail: journals@sagepub.com; http://www.sagepublications.com. **Subscription Price:** Institutions: $356; Individuals: $68. For all customers outside the Americas, please visit http://www.sagepub.co.uk/customercare.nav for information. **Claims:** Claims for undelivered copies must be made no later than six months following month of publication. The publisher will supply missing copies when losses have been sustained in transit and when the reserve stock will permit.

Abstracting and Indexing: Please visit http://rre.aera.net and, under the "More about this journal" menu on the right-hand side, click on the Abstracting/Indexing link to view a full list of databases in which this journal is indexed.

Copyright Permission: Permission requests to photocopy or otherwise reproduce copyrighted material owned by the American Educational Research Association should be submitted by accessing the Copyright Clearance Center's Rightslink® service through the journal's website at http://rre.aera.net. Permission may also be requested by contacting the Copyright Clearance Center via its website at http://www.copyright.com, or via e-mail at info@copyright.com.

Advertising and Reprints: Current advertising rates and specifications may be obtained by contacting the advertising coordinator in the Thousand Oaks office at (805) 410-7763 or by sending an e-mail to advertising@sagepub.com. To order reprints, please e-mail reprint@sagepub.com. Acceptance of advertising in this journal in no way implies endorsement of the advertised product or service by SAGE or the journal's affiliated society(ies). No endorsement is intended or implied. SAGE reserves the right to reject any advertising it deems as inappropriate for this journal.

Change of Address: Six weeks' advance notice must be given when notifying of change of address. Please send old address label along with the new address to ensure proper identification. Please specify name of journal.

International Standard Serial Number ISSN 0091-732X
International Standard Book Number ISBN 978-1-5063-7630-1 (Vol. 40, 2016, paper)
Manufactured in the United States of America. First printing, December 2016.

Printed on acid-free paper

REVIEW OF RESEARCH IN EDUCATION

Education Research:
A Century of Discovery

Volume 40, 2016

Patricia A. Alexander, Editor
University of Maryland

Felice J. Levine, Editor
American Educational Research Association

William F. Tate IV, Editor
Washington University in St. Louis

AMERICAN
EDUCATIONAL
RESEARCH
ASSOCIATION

Review of Research in Education

Education Research: A Century of Discovery

Volume 40

EDITORS

PATRICIA A. ALEXANDER
University of Maryland

FELICE J. LEVINE
*American Educational
Research Association*

WILLIAM F. TATE IV
Washington University in St. Louis

AMERICAN EDUCATIONAL RESEARCH ASSOCIATION

Tel: 202-238-3200 Fax: 202-238-3250
http://www.aera.net/pubs

Felice J. Levine
Executive Director

Martha Yager
Managing Editor

John Neikirk
Director of Publications

Jessica Sibold
Publications Associate

Contents

Cover image © Exarte Design

Introduction

Education Research: A Century of Discovery

Patricia A. Alexander
University of Maryland

Felice J. Levine
American Educational Research Association

William F. Tate IV
Washington University in St. Louis

When we assumed the role of editors of this centennial volume of the *Review of Research in Education*, we were both honored and humbled by the task before us. Since its inception almost 40 years ago, *RRE* has served the field as an annual peer-reviewed journal on specific topical issues with invited authors. This particular volume of *RRE* was to hold a unique place among these annual publications of the American Educational Research Association. Specifically, the 2016 volume was conceived as an examination of a century of discipline-defining work that has arisen within this multidisciplinary and diverse community of scholars.

In essence, the goal for the centennial volume was to publish chapters with a retrospective and prospective viewpoint on subject matter of critical import to education research. More precisely, we wanted chapters that would contribute to cumulative knowledge, capture research developments and findings of sustained significance, and address research innovations anchored in their time or place, which could ultimately shape directions of scholarly promise and potential for the future. Moreover, this volume was conceived as an opportunity through the lens of analytic research reviews to assess and acknowledge the contributions of education research scholars, past and present, alongside of those from related disciplines, in the pursuit of greater understanding about educational policies and practices in the past century.

THE PROCESS

To ensure that this vision of a unique and influential volume was achieved, we, as editors, first reached out to AERA members to solicit their ideas for chapters that

Review of Research in Education
March 2016, Vol. 40, pp. ix–xviii
DOI: 10.3102/0091732X16682960
© 2016 AERA. http://rre.aera.net

addressed a body of research they regarded as being of profound and enduring importance to education policy and practice. In that call for submissions, and in keeping with the complementary themes of retrospection and prospection, we asked that the proposed chapters not only capture the significant research contributions on education and learning of the past century but also look ahead to the most challenging issues and promising directions for the next century. The call was wide open to syntheses and analyses of empirical, theoretical, or methodological lines of research or the interplay between and among them in substantive areas of scientific and scholarly inquiry in the field. The call also invited consideration of research issues across substantive domains, levels of analysis, and modes of inquiry, including the very best thinking and scholarship across the subject areas of AERA's divisions and Special Interest Groups.

We made it clear that proposals related to historical developments in education research, the sociology of science/scholarship, or the infrastructure or infrastructural developments of the field were welcome. Furthermore, the open call for proposals encouraged ideas for chapters from seasoned and emerging scholars on wide-ranging issues and areas of specialization related to education and learning. As editors, we sought proposals that afforded critical examinations of the state of the knowledge situated in the emergence and transformation of work in a given area, broader historical issues that may have affected scientific and scholarly developments, and the challenges, opportunities, uncertainties, or controversies that may have shaped a topic or be of relevance looking ahead.

We recognized that the effort and expertise required of potential authors to achieve our stated expectations would be significant. Nonetheless, we were convinced that this scope was requisite, to dignify a century of educational inquiry. Thus, within the call, we encouraged scholars with a passion for critically examining topics, synthesizing and integrating bodies of knowledge, and reflectively assessing what is known and weighing the issues that should drive future research to accept the challenge. We were not disappointed. In fact, the response to that initial call was overwhelming—itself a tribute to the many contributions AERA members have made and are making to education research writ large. Specifically, we received well over 100 proposals for this centennial volume, covering an unbelievable range of relevant and timely topics from members across the globe. Our editorial task was then to systematically and meticulously review each of these submissions and to select those that would ultimately grace the pages of this special *RRE* edition. Following months of review and deliberation, we identified the proposals that we felt covered critical topics or issues and that offered the multidisciplinary and historical perspective we regarded as invaluable for this once-in-a-century volume.

As a next step in the process, we surveyed the contents of the selected proposals to ascertain whether any topics and issues fundamental to education research over the past century had inadvertently been overlooked. For example, we could not envision a compilation of the most significant work of the past 100 years without sufficient consideration of race and culture or learning or without reviews of research in core academic domains such as mathematics and science. Thus, we solicited chapters in essential areas from scholars long identified with these foundational domains of research, who could provide the retrospective and prospective look at the topics we sought. Although the coverage in this volume is not exhaustive, and not all topics we hoped to cover yielded research reviews (e.g., research on human development or higher education), we are pleased with how much territory this work covers. The result of this two-phase process is 22 chapters that constitute this centennial edition of *RRE*.

ORGANIZATION OF THE VOLUME

While embracing the theoretical and methodological variation that was both inevitable and desirable for the chapters found in this volume, we felt it important to retain some level of consistency across the contributions. In effect, we wanted the resulting work to be a coherent volume that would prove invaluable to anyone seeking to understand key areas of education research retrospectively and prospectively. The consistency that we sought was both structural and procedural in nature. Structurally, we asked the contributing authors to survey the 100 years of pertinent research, even as they focused on contemporary outcomes and future concerns. Such a historical lens was central to this volume. In addition, given the interdisciplinary and cross-disciplinary nature of the reviews populating this volume, we asked the contributors to acknowledge differing orientations or frameworks that have shaped their respective literatures over the century and to explore those differing orientations or frameworks critically. Finally, as the title of the volume suggests, we wanted these scholars to anticipate the future in their domains, using past trends and emergent issues as a foundation for projecting the next century of educational inquiry. Procedurally, we asked the authors to articulate the process by which they identified the works reviewed in their chapters. We considered this disclosure necessary to establish the evidentiary basis for whatever trends, claims, or insights authors would be advancing in their individual chapters.

We have organized the chapters that resulted from this two-phase process into four clusters representing significant and somewhat distinct domains of inquiry. The chapters in each cluster combined provide both depth of knowledge on topics and a sense of the development of research over time in addressing issues critical to the education research enterprise.

The Research Enterprise and the Doing of Education Research

Specifically, we open the volume with six chapters that expressly explore the research enterprise and the very process of engaging in education research. The chapter by Nancy Beadie leads off this collection of reviews by investigating the rise of social science research over the decades. Ultimately, it is her contention, grounded in the historical evidence, that social science research pertaining to educational concerns has continued to develop even in the face of what she describes as the "peculiarly decentralized and racialized structure" that has characterized educational policy and authority within the United States (p. 2). This historical analysis is followed by a very specific look at the scholarship that has populated AERA journals over their existence.

The authors of the second chapter in our initial cluster adopted a very different research methodology. Specifically, by means of a very precise analysis of the contents of *Review of Educational Research* and the *American Educational Research Journal* from 1931 to 2014, Raf Vanderstraeten, Frédéric Vandermoere, and Maarten Hermans focus on three trends of the past that speak as well to the future of publications in these and other prestigious journals. Those interrelated trends relate to (a) changes in the structures of authority and authorship, (b) the national versus global orientation of the articles, and (c) the citation networks exposed within these publications and the interdisciplinary links that they suggest.

Continuing with this theme of what is researched and what is ultimately published in education-related journals, Amy Stuart Wells and Allison Roda interrogate the literature to understand the potential impact of policy on the questions posed within education research. Their particular interest in this policy–research relation centers on the changing character of research dealing with equity and educational opportunity. It is the authors' contention that a key to understanding how racial politics and racial policy have influenced education research in the United States over the past century lies in the contrast between a contextual versus a deficit framing of race and education issues.

The next two chapters focus on issues of educational assessment. Eva Baker, Greg Chung, and Li Cai set out to capture the course that achievement testing has followed over the past 100 years. In the retrospective portion of their chapter, the authors examine two parallel purposes of assessment (i.e., measuring effects of education and identifying individual differences). They also take on the thorny issue of the effects of policy on assessment practices. Prospectively, Baker et al. consider the future of educational assessment in terms of the convergence of assessment purposes, the role of innovative learning technology, and the effects of new psychometric challenges.

Larry Hedges, Terri Pigott, Joshua Polanin, Ann Marie Ryan, Charles Tocci, and Ryan Williams similarly investigate the subject of student achievement. Their interest, however, is the effects of school resources on student achievement. In their chapter, they directly confront the challenges of addressing this critical question by means of a meta-analytic approach, as had been done in the recent past, due to the tremendous methodological diversity and inconsistency within the literature. Alternatively, the authors suggest what they call a "collaborative approach" as a mechanism for more effectively exploring the relation between school resources and student achievement. This approach brings together both historical narrative and meta-analysis to better unearth reliable evidence about the interplay between resources and achievement.

We close the first section with a chapter by Jeanne Century and Amy Cassata, who take on the question of implementation research, which they describe as the study of *whether* and *how* the multitude of educational interventions and related theories have had any enduring effects on students and on their academic success. The authors argue that there are basic questions that drive implementation research, such as: What are we doing? Is it working? For whom? Where? When? How? And why? They also contend that such an examination of the many interventions already introduced into schools and classrooms is paramount for future intervention development and for the advancements in student learning and performance that are the very goals of such interventions.

The Contexts of Education

The chapters in the next cluster of this volume share thoughtful consideration of the settings or contexts in which education operates. The section begins with David Gamson and Emily Hodge's inquiry into school districts in the United States and how the institutional form of districts has changed dramatically since the early 19th century. What the authors establish in their extensive review is how the definition of what constitutes a district, along with the criteria as to what constitutes an effective district, has shifted markedly over the past two centuries. Nonetheless, these administrative units remain the primary agent of local control and the principal unit for educational decision making.

In a chapter on urban school privatization, Janelle Scott and Jennifer Jellison Holme apply what they refer to as an "urban political economy framework" to explore how the demographics of school systems and the individual schools that form those systems have become comingled with property values in metropolitan areas. The undesirable outcome of this phenomenon is a growing racial and economic divide between urban and suburban districts. The growing divide has resulted in what the authors characterize as a decrement in property values and corresponding deterioration in the infrastructure of schools, especially for certain cities in the United States. They conclude that such undesirable conditions must be addressed by policy and research if the next century is to ensure greater economic equity in urban districts.

Catharine Biddle and Amy Price Azano carry the exploration of educational contexts away from cities and into rural settings. The focus in their chapter is on shifts in demographics, migratory patterns, economic conditions, and social changes in rural America over the past century. The authors also consider how scholarly interest in rural education research has fluctuated over this time frame. To illustrate the points raised, the authors review research on rural teacher preparation, recruitment, and retention as a case study of the "rural school problem."

The perspective that Shaun Dougherty and Allison Lombardi offer on the context of education is different from the administrative or geographic contexts in the preceding chapters. In this instance, the authors situate education in the workplace. Specifically, in their investigation into vocational education, Dougherty and Lombardi bring the long-standing debate over the purpose of education to the forefront. From their historical analysis, the authors demonstrate how the relation between schools and the workplace has changed over the past 100 years. They then complement that historical portrayal with a survey of the literature on career and technical education and draw on the survey results to articulate recommendations for the future of vocational education.

The last chapter in this section offers a sociocultural perspective on educational context. Barbara Rogoff, Maureen Callanan, Kris Gutiérrez, and Frederick Erickson set out to demonstrate in their review that informal learning, while retaining its fundamental nature, manifests differently when nested in diverse contexts. For instance, whether informal learning occurs within family or community settings or is part of innovative schools and classrooms, it entails meaningful activities that draw on learners' interests and personal choices, and the process of acquiring knowledge occurs in nondidactic ways.

The Process and Substance of Learning

Rather than address the "where" of education, the chapters that populate the third section are more concerned with the "what" of education. To initiate this focus, P. Karen Murphy and Stephanie Knight take on the general topic of advances in the science of learning over the past 100 years. Their systematic review not only interrogates the way in which learning has been defined within the literature, focusing on AERA journals as the principal data source, but also examines how beliefs about knowledge and knowing (i.e., epistemic beliefs) have changed over time and how such beliefs are ultimately reflected in the nature of investigations of learning that have been undertaken, including in classrooms.

What follows is an in-depth exploration of epistemic beliefs and, more specifically, of what William Sandoval, Jeffrey Greene, and Ivar Bråten term *epistemic cognition*. In keeping with the prior chapter, these authors contend that one of the goals of education is to promote reflection on knowledge and processes of knowing. Epistemic cognition, according to the authors, refers to the thinking that people do about what and how they know. In this critical analysis of the research on epistemic cognition, Sandoval et al. attend to what they call "fault lines" within the growing literature. The fault lines include the variability in how this construct is conceptualized and operationalized, as well as the differing accounts of how learners' epistemic cognition is presumed to develop.

The next three chapters in this section review school subject matter domains—mathematics, science, and literacy. Alan Schoenfeld offers a history of the developments and transformation that have occurred in the research on mathematics education across the past century. Schoenfeld argues through his analysis that the core nature of mathematics as an academic domain has sometimes led to broader trends in the education research literature.

Marcia Linn, Libby Gerard, Camillia Matuk, and Kevin McElhaney take a similarly deep dive into a century of research on science education. They illustrate how technological advances, scientific discoveries, and concomitant developments in science learning and teaching have fueled changes in research over the decades. To encapsulate these changes in the landscape of science education research, the authors focus on the literature pertaining to school-aged populations (i.e., 5- to 17-year-olds). They conclude with recommendations for guiding future research and practice in science learning and science teaching.

George Hruby, Leslie Burns, Stergios Botzakis, Susan Groenke, Leigh Hall, Judson Laughter, and Richard Allington focus on another field that is foundational to formal education—literacy—and they do so in a distinctive way. In particular, they examine how the constructs of motivation and engagement have been embedded in publications in literacy journals and handbooks over the past century. Drawing, as well, on related histories in literacy, education, psychology, and philosophy, the authors craft a narrative history of what they term *engaged literacies*: that is, a history of students' active engagement in their own literacy learning.

Moving beyond subject matter domains, David Osher, Yael Kidron, Marc Brackett, Allison Dymnicki, Stephanie Jones, and Roger Weissberg offer an analytic overview of school-based social-emotional learning. Through their interdisciplinary review of the literature, Osher et al. demonstrate that concern for social-emotional learning has a long and storied history. They also establish that interest is growing in this domain of research, fueled, in part, by the growing influence of such related issues as bullying prevention, prevention of drug use and abuse, and emotional intelligence. Based on their trend analysis, the authors offer recommendations for future research and practice in this school-related domain.

The Changing Attention to Diversity and Differences

In the last group of chapters, the contributing authors consider the timely and profound topics of diversity and learner differences as those topics play out in academic contexts. The first of these contributions, by Lucy Bailey and Karen Graves, affords a critical analysis of the relation between gender and education. The authors focus on what they describe as the "broad patterns and key developments" in the research on gender and education that have emerged across the decades. The authors' mission in this review was to understand how events and tensions that occurred over time helped shape these emerging patterns. They also sought to capture the diversity that is a hallmark of the research on gender and education.

The ensuing chapter, by Jennifer Langer-Osuna and Na'ilah Suad Nasir, looks at yet another arena of education research that has remained both foundational and provocative—race and education. The enticing perspective that the authors bring to this subject centers on the intersection of race, culture, and identity. They chronicle a history of dehumanization that has occurred for marginalized populations and the countermanding efforts of scholars of color to humanize those very same populations. The outcome of these continuing tensions within the social science literature is the emergence of a research literature on cultural identity, which the authors discuss both in contemporary terms and in terms of future directions for research and practice.

Jeanne Powers, Gustavo Fischman, and David Berliner, likewise, seek to bring to the surface a sometimes unseen or disregarded force shaping education and educational outcomes—poverty. By identifying two historical events as catalyzing forces—the 100-year anniversary of AERA and the 50-year anniversary of the infamous Coleman Report (Coleman et al., 1966)—the authors interrogate the interrelations of poverty, inequality, and schooling. They effectively reveal how these interrelations have manifested in the nexus between education research and educational policy. What we come to see in this penetrating review is how poverty has maintained a place in the science of education and how its place is often contentious and undervalued. Nonetheless, as the authors make apparent, poverty will continue to exert its effects on student learning and education in the years to come, and that influence can no longer be overlooked or disregarded.

The last two chapters in this section turn attention from diversity between groups or segments of society to differences that also exist at the level of individual learners. Alfredo Artiles, Sherman Dorn, and Aydin Bal systematically trace the evolution of disability over the past 100 years as a socially, historically, and spatially constructed notion. Their examination of the rich literature is divided into three historical periods: prior to 1960, 1960 to 1990, and 1990 to the present time. In capturing the character of these periods as it relates to the study of disabilities, the authors synthesize and critique not only the academic literature but also legal and social writings of relevance. Artiles et al. bring their chapter to a close by calling for interdisciplinary research programs that allow for a bicultural orientation to the future study of disabilities, which they rightly depict as a dynamic and complex phenomenon.

In the concluding chapter in this volume, Doris Luft Baker, Deni Lee Basaraba, and Paul Polanco undertake a critical analysis of a topic that has grown appreciably in significance over past decades—the education of learners whose mother language differs from the language of schooling. More specifically, the authors address two associated issues: bilingualism and bilingual education. Framing their analysis within the historical and sociopolitical history of bilingualism, the authors concentrate on two time periods. Their account of the first period, covering 1985 to 2003, expressly weighs the effects that bilingual education in the United States has had on the achievement of English learners. Their account of the second period involves the analysis of research on bilingual education conducted since 2003. What the authors seek to demonstrate in the more recent research is the growing evidence that bilingualism can be cognitively and neurologically advantageous to learners in ways not readily captured in the past.

CONCLUDING THOUGHTS: IN PRAISE AND IN HOPE

In the opening sentence of this introduction, we described ourselves as both honored and humbled by the task of editing this once-in-a-century edition of the *Review of Research in Education*. Yet, in reality, we did not, nor could we, accomplish this weighty task were it not for the contributions of so many in the education research community and in the wider community of scholars who were willing to give of their time and their expertise to this project. Among those many contributors were the more than 100 established and emerging scholars who responded to our call for proposals. We were truly heartened that interest in this project was so strong. We were also awed by the realization that, over the past century, scholars representing such diverse education research fields, disciplines, and traditions had built an impressive wealth of knowledge about learners, learning, and the educational enterprise.

Our thanks, as well, go to the authors of the 22 chapters that constitute this centennial volume. Their commitment to the goals of this publication, the care and diligence they displayed in their survey of the literature, and their subsequent analyses of the resulting sources, along with their patience and thoughtfulness in responding to comments and recommendations, were exceptional. Moreover, all those contributing to this publication, ourselves included, owe a tremendous debt of gratitude to the members of the editorial board. Those scholars are to be lauded not only for the thoroughness and perspicacity of their reviews but also for the importance they clearly placed on providing authors with the critical guidance they needed to ensure that their chapters were of the highest quality possible. Please review the list and note our heartfelt thanks to each and all.

Finally, there are members of the AERA organization and SAGE Publishing who have labored tirelessly and conscientiously to bring our vision for the volume to fruition. We are perhaps most beholden to John Neikirk, director of publications for AERA, who kept us informed and on-task throughout our editorship and who was always there to answer our questions or to lend a hand. The volume also reflects the expertise of Martha Yager, AERA's managing editor, who copyedited many of the chapters and provided authors with detailed comments and recommendations. Jessica Sibold, AERA's publications associate, provided exceptional help, from administrative to copyediting assistance. Finally, we could not have completed this special edition of *RRE* without the support of Sara Sarver, the production editor manager at SAGE Publishing, who worked patiently with us to guarantee that the volume was ultimately issued in this centennial year.

Thus, to all these individuals, from proposers, authors, and reviewers to AERA and SAGE staff, who made this centennial volume the publication that we had initially envisioned, we say, "Thank you." Moreover, to the members of the AERA community, the international community of education researchers, and all those who delve into the contents of this special edition, we express our fervent hope that our efforts as editors have resulted in a publication worthy of its unique place in AERA's history.

REFERENCE

Coleman, J. S., Campbell, E. Q., Hobson, C. J., McPartland, J., Mood, A. M., Weinfeld, F. D., & York, R. L. (1966). *Equality of educational opportunity*. Washington, DC: U.S. Government Printing Office.

I. The Research Enterprise and the Doing of Education Research

Chapter 1

The Federal Role in Education and the Rise of Social Science Research: Historical and Comparative Perspectives

NANCY BEADIE
University of Washington

Studies of the rise of social science research in education typically focus on the Progressive Era, from 1890 to 1930, the period in which the American Educational Research Association (AERA) was founded. As central as this story is to the intellectual history of education as a field, however, it obscures an earlier set of events that arguably is even more important to understanding why AERA and the larger progressive education research enterprise of which it was a part developed when and how they did. That episode was the major but ultimately failed effort of the 1870s and 1880s to establish a national education system in the United States. This chapter focuses on the use of social science research in this earlier episode of education reform. It reveals how the rise of education research during the Progressive Era, and ultimately the founding of AERA, responded to the failure of this earlier effort in multiple ways. More precisely, it shows how social science research in education developed historically in relation to the peculiarly decentralized and racialized structure of education authority and policy in the United States.

S tudies of the rise of social science research in education typically focus on the Progressive Era, from 1890 to 1930. Whether understood intellectually, as the product of university-based investigations in the emerging field of psychology circa 1890, or institutionally, as the product of school-based efforts to systematically survey and administer growing school systems and student populations in the early 1900s, the roots of social science research in education are generally identified as belonging to the larger Progressive Era project of using science and education to direct social change (Lagemann, 2000; Kimball, 1992). More specifically, scholars

Review of Research in Education
March 2016, Vol. 40, pp. 1–37
DOI: 10.3102/0091732X16668506
© 2016 AERA. http://rre.aera.net

have traced the origins of the American Educational Research Association (AERA) to a temporary convergence of interest between school-based administrators and university-based researchers in the 1910s and 1920s (Mershon & Schlossman, 2008). Building on the already widespread city and state school survey movement, as well as on the developing field of psychological testing and diagnosis, a group of school-based researchers in the Department of Superintendence of the National Education Association (NEA) founded the National Association of Directors of Educational Research in 1916. Expanding in the 1920s to more fully embrace university-based researchers and reflect the concurrent growth and development of university-based schools and colleges of education, the organization was renamed twice, becoming the AERA in 1928, at the close of the Progressive Era.

As central as this story is to the intellectual history of education as a field and to the institutional history of AERA as an organization, however, it obscures an earlier episode in the history of education reform and the politics of knowledge in the United States that arguably is even more important to understanding *why* AERA and the larger progressive education research enterprise of which it was a part developed when and how they did. That episode, investigated by an earlier generation of scholars but now largely forgotten by educators and even by educational historians, is the major but ultimately failed effort of the 1870s and 1880s to establish a national education system in the United States. In a formidable campaign that drew on data, analysis, and arguments conceived and prosecuted by leaders of the new and newly self-conscious social sciences, as represented by the American Social Science Association (ASSA) and the NEA, Congress came closer than it has ever come, then or since, to establishing a national system of funding and oversight of schooling throughout the country. A reexamination of this substantial national effort in light of recent scholarship in the history of education reveals how the rise of education research during the Progressive Era responded to the failure of this earlier effort in multiple ways. More precisely, it shows how social science research in education has developed historically in relation to the peculiarly decentralized and racialized structure of educational authority and policy in the United States.

This chapter focuses on the use of social science research in this earlier episode of education reform. Specifically, it revisits Gordon C. Lee's 1949 policy study *The Struggle for Federal Aid, First Phase*, published by the Bureau of Publications at Teachers College as part of its formidable series of doctoral research studies, *Contributions to Education* (No. 957). Conducted under the sponsorship of George S. Counts, with additional guidance from Freeman Butts and "constant interest and support" from "fellow student, Lawrence A. Cremin" (Lee, 1949, p. viii), Lee's study reviewed and analyzed 20 bills aimed at providing general federal aid for "common schools" introduced in Congress between 1870 and 1890. As indicated by the title of his study, Lee (and perhaps the Teachers College faculty and students with whom he worked) regarded his investigation as a guide to success for a "second phase" of the struggle for federal aid being conducted in his own post–World War II context. Both implicitly and explicitly, Lee framed his historical analysis as an investigation of historical precedents and lessons for this second phase.

Lee (1949) chose the language of his title carefully. Concerned with the politics of education in his own time, he used the language of "federal aid to education" in describing the object of legislation in the 1870s and 1880s, rather than the language of "establishing a national education system." This distinction was itself political, however. As Lee himself documented, members of Congress who supported such legislation and those who opposed it did so with different visions of its purpose and likely outcomes. Some clearly envisioned the establishment of a national education system as the ultimate and desirable aim of such legislation, and others quite clearly opposed such legislation for fear of just such an outcome. A central point of the present chapter is that the question of whether or how far the United States could or should go in establishing a national education system was open to debate in the 1870s and 1880s as it had never been before and, arguably, has never been since. The commonplace assumptions of the 20th century about the "limits" of federal authority in education were not yet a settled question. Lee's choice of wording reflected how that question came out by the end of the 1880s, and thus the lessons he wanted his readers to draw for the legislative battles of his own time. But his words also obscured some important dimensions of the earlier debate. Even as Lee completed his study in the spring of 1948, a bill that would have established general federal aid for education was approved by the Senate. Although that particular piece of legislation did not ultimately pass Congress, it was part of an intense and continuous period of congressional activity around the issue of federal aid for education, in the decade or so immediately following World War II, that rivaled the period following the Civil War. This period of intense activity eventually led to the passage of the National Defense Education Act in 1958, as well as, somewhat less directly, the Elementary and Secondary Education Act of 1965 (Urban, 2010). Lee's study thus provides a powerful pivot point for understanding the larger history of the federal role in education and the rise of social science research.

What follows is a multilayered reassessment of Lee's (1949) account in light of more recent literature in the history of education, comparative policy history, and social science history. The chapter is organized in five parts: (a) a discussion of the distinctively decentralized structure of U.S. education in comparative historical perspective; (b) a brief history of 19th-century efforts to establish a national education system in the United States, based on Lee's account; (c) a brief history and a critical analysis of the role of professional associations and social science research in promoting such legislation; (d) a discussion of lessons from this history as articulated by Lee and as reassessed in light of more recent scholarship; and (e) an assessment of the significance of professional associations such as AERA and of social science research in national education policymaking.

THE STRUCTURE OF U.S. EDUCATION AUTHORITY IN COMPARATIVE HISTORICAL PERSPECTIVE

A close look at 19th-century efforts to establish a national system of education in the United States yields important insights into the enduringly peculiar political logic of U.S. education reform and the role of social science research in that politics. Such a focus also places the project of nation building at the center of the account in a way that invites comparison with other nations. Comparative history highlights the distinctively decentralized structure of education authority in the United States (Beadie, 2010b, 2016; Caruso, 2010; Lindert, 2004; Miller, 1998; Sabato, 2001). As contrasted with most nations of Europe, Asia, and Latin America, the United States administers virtually every aspect of curriculum policy, accreditation, certification, and hiring at the state and local levels, rather than national. How and why did this decentralized system develop?

Historians of education have described the development of this distinctively decentralized structure in the United States. They have located its roots in the three or four decades before the Civil War, when Northern and Western states first established state school funds, state boards of education, state superintendents of education, state-based systems of taxation for education, and state constitutional provisions in support of schools (Kaestle, 1983; Tyack, James, & Benavot, 1987). Structured from the start to recognize, incorporate, and institutionalize already existing traditions of local school organization and funding, these systems operated with a high degree of local autonomy through the Antebellum Era (Beadie, 2010a).

Beginning in the Progressive Era, the significance of state government in education substantially increased (Steffes, 2012). As scholars working in the tradition of legal history have repeatedly noted (Hutt, 2012; Provasnik, 2006; Richardson, 1994, 1999), a substantial shift in the intervention of state governments in education occurred after 1890. Typified by the spread of compulsory attendance laws and, more importantly, by the determination of courts to enforce such laws, this shift encompassed an increasing willingness on the part of state legislatures, state courts, and state departments of education to assert public power over children and households through the agency of schools, to use state financial leverage to strengthen state supervision of teachers and standardization of curriculum and operations, and to broaden the purview of schools as official state agencies in matters of public health, labor regulation, child welfare, immigration, and "juvenile delinquency" (Steffes, 2012).

By this account, then, public education in the United States developed throughout as a distinctively state-based structure in a federated political system. For the most part, however, this account of the decentralized structure of education in the United States skips over the period from the beginning of the Civil War in 1860 to the rise of progressivism in 1890. As a result, it also skips over a period when education very much *was* a central focus of national policy in the United States, as a few scholars of congressional political history have noted (Hoffer, 2007; McAfee, 1998). During that period, as Peter Lindert (2004) has documented, systematic national-level investment in mass education increased substantially in many countries, including France, Japan, Germany, and England. Although the precise pattern of system development varied country by country, increases in national-level investment in schooling were generally associated with development of national-level capacity along one or more axes of educational standardization, such as facilities development and inspection, institutional accreditation, teacher certification, curriculum standardization, achievement examination, credentialization, and/or student admission, promotion, and attainment. Congressional leaders in the United States were very conscious of these contemporary developments in other countries and invoked concern about the competitive advantage that such systems conferred on those nations when promoting the development of a national education system in the United States.

Despite the aspirations of some lobbyists and the concerted efforts of some congressional leaders, however, the United States has never developed the kind of centralized national capacity for education funding or standardization that was developed by many other nations during this period. From a certain perspective it can be argued, as I have at length elsewhere (Beadie, in press), that the United States pursued its own distinctively "extragovernmental" model of system development at the national level. The result, however, is best described as a national system of policymaking rather than a *national education system* in the sense typically implied by that phrase. Even as compared with other federated systems developed during the same period, such as that of Canada, it lacks the infrastructure for effecting basic forms of standardization. And, perhaps more important, it lacks a formal mechanism by which the people who are responsible for schooling at state and local levels can directly influence the formulation of policy at the federal level.

The fact that U.S. efforts to establish a national education system failed at precisely the same time that similar efforts in other nations succeeded is intriguing and provides an important leverage point for analyzing the U.S. case. The failure of the U.S. effort should not be regarded as a foregone conclusion. This was the period, after all, of the Morrill Land Grant Act (1862), which dedicated shares of federal public lands to the support of agricultural and mechanical education in the states. It was the period in which Congress established the National Bureau of Education (1867, discussed further below), and the Bureau of Refugees, Freedmen, and Abandoned Lands, commonly known as the Freedmen's Bureau (1865), which for a brief 5- to 7-year period distributed federal subsidies to designated schools providing basic education to newly freed slaves. More broadly, this was the period of Southern Reconstruction (1867–1877), when Congress together with freedmen in secessionist Southern states established the first state systems of universal common education. It was also the period in which Congress developed a national system of Native American boarding schools (1875–1890), arguably the only truly national education system ever operated in the United States. During the same period (1875–1890), Congress considered multiple constitutional amendments that variously would have forbidden the use of public funds to support religious schools and required states to maintain public schools for all on an equitable, nondiscriminatory basis. In this context, the failure of the United States to establish a national education system despite multiple concerted attempts cannot simply be assumed; it must be examined.

Historians of education have provided major comprehensive accounts of the extent and limits of federal support for freedmen's schools during Southern Reconstruction (Anderson, 1988; Butchart, 2010; Williams, 2005) and of the development and consequences of the federal system of Native American boarding schools (Adams, 1995; Lomawaima, 1994). For the most part, however, these efforts have been understood as specialized policies focused on particular populations rather than as part of a broader national policy focus on education. A signal exception is Sarah Manekin's 2009 prizewinning dissertation, *Spreading the Empire of Free Education, 1865–1905*, which traces connections between specific individuals, organizations, and strategies involved in U.S. education policy from the Reconstruction South to the Native American West, to the National Bureau of Education, and eventually to colonial Puerto Rico. Her study indicates that the grounds for understanding these and other projects as part of a larger national education policy are many and substantial. More recently, Clif Stratton (2016) examines connections among such policies and the content of citizenship education and Americanization in multiple colonial and imperial contexts in his book *Education for Empire.*

The present chapter examines the ways in which early social science research undergirded the formulation of this larger national project. In the process, it situates the history of education and education research as part of a larger literature in policy history dedicated to uncovering the invisible but nonetheless powerful ways that national social policy has been constructed and prosecuted in the United States, despite its formally decentralized federalist structure. Scholars of the new statism in American history have documented the development of a diffuse model of national governance and policymaking in the United States. This literature, which ranges across a wide array of policy areas, from water rights to welfare, highlights the interactive roles that state governments, universities, and a variety of nongovernmental organizations, including private corporations, allied philanthropists, professional societies, and federated citizen groups, have played in forging policies that are truly national in scope despite the formal weakness of centralized national authority (Baldwin, 2005; Balogh, 2009; Clemens, 1997; Loss, 2012; Novak, 2008).

In particular, the historical sociologist Elisabeth Clemens (1997) has described the rise of "interest group politics" as a historical phenomenon. In her account, the now-familiar practice of organizing politically around specific issues or policy demands was not a timeless characteristic of the American political system but a particular historical innovation that developed after 1890 in critical response to the calcification of the two-party system. Understanding the phenomenon in relation to the rise of bureaucratic administrative authority during the same period, Clemens's study highlights the roles of various voluntary organizations in putting pressure on the legislative process and administrative structures. Framed as an attempt to understand the relative success of women's groups, agrarian groups, and labor groups in effecting reforms despite their relative lack of formal political power, Clemens's formulation explains how some pressure groups proved more successful at certain times than others. For example, in her analysis, the relative success of women's groups in winning a range of policy measures in the Progressive Era derived precisely from the fact that the absence of formal political power forced them to excel in developing extrapartisan methods of mobilizing public opinion and putting pressure on legislative and administrative systems.

Viewed from the perspective of Clemens's (1997) analysis, Lee's (1949) study of the struggle for federal aid to education provides both an example to be studied and a challenge of chronology and conceptualization. Throughout his study, Lee focused his analysis on the political dynamics of popular, professional, political, and press support and opposition for various federal aid measures. As part of his analysis, he discussed many of the very same farmer, labor, and women's groups that also figure prominently in Clemens's study. Moreover, Lee's frame of analysis was precisely that of interest group politics. Repeatedly in his account, Lee noted that the practice of pressure group politics was insufficiently developed in the 1870s and 1880s, effectively implying that this state of nascent development explains the ultimate failure of federal aid legislation in the late 19th century. In many respects, his study reads as a guide to more thorough and complete exercise of such political strategies in the legislative battles ahead.

That Lee should have invoked interest group politics in his 1949 study makes sense given Clemens's (1997) account. According to Clemens, political scientists first recognized and normalized the phenomenon as a feature of the American political system circa 1950. Published in 1949, Lee's analysis can be seen as representative of this frame of analysis. At the same time, Lee's account also challenges the chronology and conceptualization of Clemens's account in some ways. For starters, it pushes the story of how such politics developed back at least 20 years. It also poses the question of what role professional organizations played in the development of this new politics, a question Clemens does not specifically recognize or address.

In many ways, Lee stood too far inside the logic of interest group politics himself to be able to answer this question. He clearly saw his purpose in 1948 as that of advising professional educators of the role that "public and professional interest" would have to play in his own time for federal aid legislation to be successful in the future. Nonetheless, the evidence that Lee provided suggests that two professional organizations in particular were significant in formulating the arguments, marshaling the supportive data, and mobilizing support for the 19th-century effort to establish a national education system in the United States: the NEA, founded in 1857, and the ASSA, founded in 1865 (Haskell, 1977; Mattingly, 1975).

A BRIEF HISTORY OF 19TH-CENTURY EFFORTS TO ESTABLISH A NATIONAL EDUCATION SYSTEM

In Lee's (1949) assessment, the late 19th-century effort to establish federal aid for education could be divided into three main stages. Lee's account of these stages highlights important shifts in the logic of proposed federal legislation over the period from 1870 to 1890, summarized below. As part of his discussion, Lee also analyzed the levels and sources of "public and professional interest" mobilized in support of, or opposition to, the bills. These assessments are also summarized below.

Stage 1: The Hoar Bill (1870–1871)—Compelling "Delinquent States"

To appreciate the changing logic of federal education legislation, it helps to be aware of the specific context in which the first of the federal education bills was proposed in the House of Representatives. Recall that at the end of the Civil War, in 1865, a central governance issue was the basis on which the secessionist Southern states would regain representation in Congress. Under the terms of the Congressional Reconstruction Act of 1867, Confederate states were essentially treated as federal territories operated under military rule, much like the territories of the West. To regain political representation, secessionist states had to write new constitutions and apply for readmission in a process similar to that followed by new Western states.

By this means, the Reconstruction Congress, Republican leaders, and Southern Black convention delegates together effectively forced the South to accept the normative standard of constitutional provisions for education that had been worked out by states of the West and Midwest before the Civil War. The now nearly universal normative standard included government provision of a system of public schools, fully funded through tax support, nonsectarian in governance and instruction, and open to "all." By July 1870, all the secessionist states had been readmitted to Congress with new constitutions that included provisions requiring establishment of state systems of universal common education.[1]

Once the normative principle of state-based systems of common education had been established in the South, however, Congress still confronted the dual challenge of Southern poverty and White resistance to funding a universal system and ensuring equal access to schooling. The first bill proposing federal funding and oversight of education aimed directly at addressing these problems.

Introduced in the House of Representatives on February 25, 1870, as the last secessionist states were being readmitted to Congress and the funding of the Freedmen's Bureau was scheduled to run out, the first of these bills was the Hoar Bill, sponsored by George F. Hoar, Republican of Massachusetts.[2] The Hoar Bill essentially sought to enforce the education provisions that had been written into the new Southern constitutions and to establish the kind of educational oversight and support provided by the Freedmen's Bureau on a more permanent basis. Accordingly, the basic logic of implementation was more stick than carrot. The Hoar Bill would

> compel to be done what the States will not do and to do for them what they cannot do. . . . It must provide a good and universal system of common school education in those states which do not provide it . . . [but] only where dominant power refuses to do so by local authority. (Lee, 1949, p. 43)

More precisely, the legislation would enforce common school provisions in "delinquent states," by making available "under federal auspices" universal instruction in arithmetic, reading, and writing whenever states failed to do so. Such federal provisions would be funded by a combination of taxes on "delinquent" states and sale of public lands.

As analyzed by Lee (1949), the Hoar Bill was noteworthy not only for being the first measure of its kind to receive congressional consideration but also for being the most "drastic" and "extreme" of any of the bills to be considered. According to the bill's title, its purpose was "to establish a national system of education." The "extremity" that Lee implicitly critiqued in his account lay in the assertion of federal authority over education that the bill proposed to exercise. Referred to in some quarters as a system of "national compulsory education," the bill was, in short, an enforcement provision *but with the compulsion focused on state governments rather than on individuals.*

The language of state "delinquency" that the Hoar Bill used as the basic structure of its proposed system of federal aid for education fit the logic of a nation asserting its authority over territories, which the secessionist states effectively were during the immediate post–Civil War period. It also fit the logic of some theories of American statecraft at the time, which sanctioned the use of federal power when local power failed. The language of state "delinquency" did not fit the traditional logic of sovereign states that underlay U.S. federalism, however. The historical significance of the Hoar Bill lies in what it reveals about the fundamental limits of federalism for effecting a policy based primarily on enforcement of federal authority over the states. In this way, the Hoar Bill also illuminates the problem that subsequent bills tried to solve.

In Lee's (1949) analysis, these fundamental limits of federalism made the introduction of the Hoar Bill politically frivolous. After due discussion of various responses to the bill, Lee suggested that it received relatively little attention, with much of the attention being negative. Significantly, some of the strongest opposition came from professional educators, led by the NEA, apparently concerned about potential loss of local school autonomy and control. Implying that the proposal was too radical for the time, even among Republicans, Lee portrayed prevailing popular and professional sentiment as favoring (continued) aid for Southern education in the manner of the Freedmen's Bureau but rejecting general federal authority over education as inimical to republican principles.

Stage 2: The Perce and Burnside Bills (1872–1880)—Distributing Public Benefits

The next major federal education bills discussed by Lee reflected the fundamentally changed reality of a Congress with all the former secessionist states readmitted, albeit some with Republican representatives, both White and Black. Focusing his discussion on the two bills (of a total of 11 proposed) that not only made it to the floor but actually passed in either the Senate or the House in that period, Lee reviewed the terms of the Perce Bill of 1872 and the Burnside Bill of 1879. Both of these bills framed their purpose as that of establishing "an education fund" rather than "a national system of education," as the earlier Hoar Bill had. In both cases, the fund was to be capitalized through the sale of public lands, the proceeds of which would thereby "forever be consecrated and set apart for the education of the people."

In taking this approach to school support, the Perce and Burnside Bills drew on a long tradition of state-based systems of education funding, as well as on federal precedents for the allocation of public lands. Since the late 18th century, states from Connecticut to Georgia had used the proceeds from the sale of public lands to capitalize school and literary funds, which then typically were allocated to localities by application and/or on a matching basis. Also since the late 18th century, the federal government had dedicated portions of the public lands it controlled to support schooling in the territories of the West, as well as (later) for agricultural and industrial education in the land grant universities sponsored by the Morrill Act. As much a matter of land policy as school policy, such provisions ostensibly promoted White settlement by conferring public benefits on settler communities, even as they appropriated Native American land to do so. They also provided political cover for the often large-scale transfer of public wealth to private hands through discounted sales to land speculators, timber and mining companies, and railroads.

More important over the long term than the source of funding specified by the Perce and Burnside bills was the shift the bills marked in the basic structural logic of the policy, from one of enforcement to one of incentives. The logic of incentives meant that instead of detailing the conditions under which the federal government could assume control of state common schools, the legislation spelled out the conditions that states had to meet to qualify for a distribution of public benefits. In addition to this shift in logic, the Perce Bill eventually included two amendments representing compromises with respect to the principles on which funds would be distributed. The first compromise was that funds would *not* be withheld from states with segregated school systems, an arrangement that endured in every subsequent bill considered by Congress. The second compromise was the determination that funds should be distributed according to rates of illiteracy in each state rather than by the total size of the general population or the population of school-age youth. This provision also had a long-lasting impact, becoming a blueprint for subsequent bills. Substantively, it meant that more funding would go where it was most needed. Thus, Alabama, with a high illiteracy rate, would get more funding than Massachusetts, with a low illiteracy rate. Politically, these differential effects would presumably help garner support from Southern states.[3]

In Lee's (1949) analysis, the ultimate significance of the Perce and Burnside bills lay in the compromises they represented. Lee made much of the fact that these and subsequent federal education bills "discarded" the "extreme policies underlying the Hoar bill." Nonetheless, despite their noncoercive logic and their generous terms of eligibility and distribution for Southern states, the measures of the 1870s failed to mobilize sufficient organized support on the part of citizen or professional groups. Surveying first the activities of agricultural and labor interests as represented in the 1870s by the Grange and the Knights of Labor, Lee concluded that while both organizations formally espoused principles and platforms favoring the advancement of education for their members and constituents, neither organization undertook any organized activity on the part of either piece of legislation. Turning then to the actions of professional educators, Lee noted that from the start, the NEA and U.S. Commissioner of Education John Eaton were among the most vehement promoters of federal aid to common education under the terms of these bills, implying that Eaton together with NEA may have been important in suggesting the basic funding structure of the 1870s legislation. At the same time, Lee also highlighted opposition to any federal aid, not only among Catholic leaders and educators but also among some leaders of the education establishment, especially leaders of private institutions, such as President Charles Eliot of Harvard University, who argued "repeatedly, and with great vehemence," that any such program of federal subsidies for education "saps the foundations of public liberty" by undermining local responsibility and initiative (Lee, 1949, p. 66).

Stage 3: The Blair Bill (1882–1890)—Eliminating "Deficiencies of the People"

The Blair Bill was in many respects more ambitious and serious than its predecessors, in terms of both the scale of its appropriations and the distribution of its benefits. Labeled "a bill to aid in the establishment and temporary support of common schools," it provided a substantial influx of federal funding over a 10-year period to ensure the establishment of a solid and comprehensive common school system throughout the country. Thereafter, federal funding would taper off, with the systems presumably sustained primarily by state and local funding.

As compared with previous efforts, the Blair Bill represented a middle ground between a logic of enforcement and a logic of incentives. Like the legislative proposals of the 1870s, the Blair Bill operated through the systematic distribution of public benefits in the form of federal funds. However, the source of the funding was different. Instead of deriving from the sale of public lands, from which income could be slow to accumulate and initially small in amount, the funding would be appropriated directly from the general treasury on an annual basis. As a result, the amount of funding distributed under the Blair Bill was calculated to be more substantial and immediate, and thus to offer a more powerful incentive.

This power, in turn, conferred greater leverage for enforcing certain standards and conditions of schooling. As in the case of the 1870s proposals, states would have to meet certain eligibility criteria to receive funds. Authority to determine eligibility would ultimately lie with the commissioner of education, also as in previous proposals. In the case of the Blair Bill, however, the criteria of eligibility were more extensive and the principles and details of administration were more fully worked out, thereby effectively strengthening the bill's enforcement powers. In this respect, the Blair Bill embodied a logic of compliance familiar to federal funding provisions in our own time (Kaestle & Lodewick, 2007; Nelson, 2005).

To appreciate the significance of the Blair Bill (and of its ultimate failure), it is essential to know what these eligibility requirements were. A key provision of the bill, highlighted by Lee (1949), was the requirement that each state provide "by law" a "system of free common schools for all of its children of school age, without distinction of race or color." Specifically, no distinction by race or color should exist in "either the raising or distribution of school revenues or in the school facilities provided."

This criterion appeared not only as a statement of principle but also as part of the detailed specifications regarding the process of reporting. A second key provision of the bill concerned the issue of reporting. It required that states and territories report not only basic statistics on numbers of schools, school attendance rates, and moneys raised and expended but also evidence of nondiscrimination. Similarly, a separate section of the bill specified that recipient states and territories were to distribute the moneys raised for common school purposes—whether at the local, state, or national level—"equally for the education of all the children, without distinction of race or color." As noted earlier, these specifications, like those of the 1870s legislation, did not preclude segregation. Indeed, they seem to have assumed it. Nonetheless, with these specifications the authors of the bill endeavored to guarantee a degree of equity in school funding greater than was ever attempted thereafter.

A third provision of the bill, which Lee (1949) enumerated but did not elaborate on, concerned curriculum. Unlike most state legislation at the time, which before the Progressive Era tended to concentrate on structural issues of fund distribution, oversight, and reporting rather than on curriculum (Tyack et al., 1987), the Blair Bill explicitly defined the content of common education that was qualified to receive public funds in the states.[4] The curriculum of schools eligible for public funds was to include "the art of reading, writing, and speaking the English language, arithmetic, geography, the history of the United States, and such other branches of useful knowledge as may be taught under local laws." These specifications constituted a solid academic curriculum. They went beyond the most rudimentary literacy education to compose what might be considered more broadly an "education for citizenship."

This provision thus pointedly distinguished the education to be supported by federal funds from a more narrowly "industrial" education. The fact that the proposed legislation did indeed aim at ensuring an academic education for all children within the states is further illuminated by another provision of the bill, which distinguished the type of schooling required for federally subsidized education in the *territories* from that required in the *states*. As contrasted with the states, territories were authorized to apply federal funds for support of industrial education as well as for common education.

To appreciate this distinction, it is important to recognize that at the time of the bill's most serious consideration, in the mid-1880s, the territories of the United States included much of the trans-Mississippi West. The last territory to achieve statehood before the Blair Bill's introduction was Colorado, in 1876, which thereby joined the western states of California (1849), Oregon (1857), and Nevada (1864). Much of the rest of the West, however, would not achieve statehood until the very end of the period under consideration here, or substantially thereafter.[5]

The fact that the Blair Bill so deliberately encompassed education in the territories signals the truly national (rather than simply federal) scope and intention of the legislation. It further begins to suggest how, even as it attended to the unfinished business of Southern Reconstruction, the Blair Bill reached beyond that agenda to address additional issues, including those that Western historian Elliott West (2003) calls

"Greater Reconstruction," or Reconstruction of the Western territories acquired from 1848 forward. Part of that project included the territorial and political integration, or disposition, of the diverse peoples who lived in the West.

Specifically, what the curricular provisions of the Blair Bill indicate is that its authors envisioned Native American education as part of the federally funded system authorized by the bill. The practice of providing industrial education to Native Americans as a means of acculturation and accommodation to European systems of property-based household production dated back at least to the treaty agreements of the 1820s. However limited the implementation and success of these early provisions, the same basic idea effectively became the core curriculum of the federal system of Native American boarding schools developed concurrently with the Blair Bill in the 1880s (Adams, 1995; Lomawaima, 1994).

As elsewhere in his study, Lee focused most of his discussion of the Blair Bill on assessing the support for and opposition to the bill, and thus on political lessons that could be learned for future legislative campaigns. In his assessment, "No previous education legislation had elicited anything remotely comparable to the volume of public demand for congressional action as was stimulated by these proposals during the 1880s" (Lee, 1949, p. 94). Lee based his assertion in part on his analysis of the petitions received by Congress in support of the legislation between 1881 and 1891. Broken down by region, year, and type of petitioner (citizen, state government, educational organization, business group, reform group, religious organization), Lee's evidence allowed him to make a number of claims about the support that the iterations of the Blair Bill received over time.

With respect to region, Lee reported that "the largest number of citizen petitions was sent from the South," although his data suggest that Southern citizen action in support of the bill was somewhat stronger at the beginning of the decade, in 1881–1882, than at the end. Meanwhile, citizen action in the North and the Midwest peaked toward the later periods of the bill's consideration, in 1886–1887 and 1887–1888 (Lee, 1949, pp. 94–95). With regard to organizational petitions, Lee's data show that a number of state associations of school teachers and administrators were important sources of support, especially in the South. Southern state governments also actively petitioned Congress for the measure, particularly in the early years of the campaign (1882–1883).

With respect to formal organizations of farm, labor, business, reform, and religious groups, Lee (1949) found relatively little evidence of active support, with a few key exceptions. Considering not only the record of petitions received but also the official and formal endorsements of various national organizations, Lee determined, for example, that the Northern and Southern farmers' alliances of the 1880s, like the Grange of the 1870s, expressed general support for public education, including specific references to the value of "moral, manual and intellectual training that inculcate the essential dignity and necessity of honest labor," but took no position on the Blair Bill.

Organized labor, by contrast, did take a positive stand in the 1880s. By comparison with its relative silence on the legislation of the 1870s, the Knights of Labor formally memorialized Congress in 1886 that "the cause of education [should] be promoted by passage of the Blair education Bill." In addition, the Knights of Labor maintained a lobbying organization in Congress throughout the 1880s, which "kept a close watch on the Blair Education Bill." Similarly, the American Federation of Labor, founded in 1886, took a strong stand in favor of federal aid for education, both specifically in the form of the Blair Bill and more broadly for "universal compulsory education." Business groups, meanwhile, seem to have taken a more laissez-faire approach to the prospect of federal aid for education; with very few exceptions, they neither actively supported nor opposed such legislation.

Beyond organized labor, another national organization that took an active role in promoting the Blair Bill was the Women's Christian Temperance Union (WCTU). Founded in 1874, the WCTU became active in the battle for federal aid for education in 1886. According to Lee (1949), from 1886 to 1890, petitions from the national and local headquarters of the WCTU were "constantly placed before Congress." Among religious organizations, Protestant denominations generally supported the legislation, which included strong antisectarian provisions, while Catholics, accordingly, strongly opposed it, since antisectarian provisions were generally perceived as inimical to Catholic interests.

When it came to organized pressure in support of the Blair Bill, however, by far the most active group was the NEA. According to Lee (1949, p. 97), "Memorials from the National Education Association [in support of the Blair Bill] were continuous until 1890." Founded in 1857, the NEA from the start oriented its activity toward national policy. An early focus was promoting the establishment of a federal education department, a goal that was at least partly accomplished with the founding of the Bureau of Education in 1867, though without the status as a cabinet-level department that its promoters would have preferred (D. Warren, 1974). Working closely with the commissioner of education once the bureau was established, especially with John Eaton, who served as commissioner from 1870 to 1886, the NEA assumed an important role throughout the 1870s and 1880s in shaping legislative proposals and lobbying members of Congress in support of certain provisions.

In the 1870s, as noted earlier, the NEA strongly supported proposed legislation that would have devoted proceeds from the sale of federal public lands to support common education in the states, a position that the organization reiterated in 1881. By 1882, however, the association had "swung its support to the principle of direct financial assistance" represented by the Blair Bill, sending a strong unequivocal statement to every member of Congress in 1882, the first year the bill was introduced, declaring "that in the opinion of the Association, it is the *duty* of the Congress of the United States, to make liberal appropriation from the national treasury for the support of the schools in the states" (Lee, 1949, pp. 105–106).

Lee (1949) presents the support of the NEA and that of the ASSA for the Blair Bill as essentially independent of the proposed legislation. From the record of the campaign for the bill collected by Senator Henry W. Blair himself, however, it would seem more accurate to say that the distinct but complementary leadership of the

NEA and the ASSA together effectively designed the national campaign in favor of the Blair Bill, from its inception in 1882 through it final demise in 1890.[6]

THE ROLE OF PROFESSIONAL ASSOCIATIONS AND SOCIAL SCIENCE IN THE CAMPAIGN TO PASS THE BLAIR BILL

Born of similar impulses but different networks, the NEA and the ASSA were both rooted in the practical work of government. The origins of the NEA lay in the National Teachers Association (NTA), an organization founded in Philadelphia in 1857 by men who were already engaged in the work of cultivating and strengthening the teaching corps for the expanding common school systems of their states through the promotion, development, and administration of normal schools, teachers' institutes, teacher journals, and associated systems of teacher credentialing. Initially composed of 43 men from 13 states, the organization imagined itself from the start as a translocal professional body that would give leading members of already existing state-level teacher organizations the opportunity to trade professional knowledge, concerns, and ideas with their counterparts in other states—and to help build the capacity for systematic support of such work at the federal level (Wesley, 1957).

Although cosmopolitan by standards of the day, the NTA was far from the only translocal network of "schoolmen" active in the Antebellum Era (Mattingly, 1975). In the decade following the founding of the NTA, however, the disunion of the country paradoxically provided new opportunities for national consolidation of leadership and influence in the field of education, as the secession of Southern states in 1860, their defeat in the Civil War, and their continuing disbarment from Congress for 3 to 5 years following the war, made possible the enactment of several education acts at the federal level that representatives from Southern states had previously opposed, including a proposal to establish a federal department of education to collect and publish education data from the states and territories of the nation. This idea, which by most accounts originated with Henry Barnard and a few other close colleagues in 1837, influenced the first collection of data on education and illiteracy of the national population in the U.S. Census in 1840. Barnard himself continued to advocate for the idea through his work as state superintendent of education, first for Connecticut, then for Rhode Island, and eventually through his founding and editorship of the *American Journal of Education*, which, beginning in 1855, collected and published education data, legislation, and news from throughout the nation (D. Warren, 1974).

Building on the same wave of thinking as the *American Journal of Education* and many of the same networks within the states, the NTA focused, from its founding in 1857, on lobbying for a federal department of education. Thus, when Barnard became the first U.S. commissioner of education in 1867, the new department was already in direct communication with the NTA and its members. The establishment and funding of the Department of Education (soon demoted to the status of a bureau within the Department of the Interior) created, in turn, a need for a more fully national body of state-level leaders and policymakers to advise, support, and implement the data collection process. Responding to this new national context, the NTA merged with three other interstate organizations to form the renamed NEA in 1870. In this way, the National Bureau of Education and the NEA were effectively cocreated in the years surrounding the Civil War. Moreover, the development of social science data and knowledge about education and the development of national education policy were at the core of the work of both organizations from the start. Consolidated apparently at the suggestion of John Eaton, the new commissioner of education, in 1870, just as the last secessionist Southern state was readmitted to the Union and the question of whether the Freedmen's Bureau should be renewed or replaced by some larger national apparatus was being debated in Congress, the NEA purposefully developed itself as a national policy organization. From that point forward, it worked closely with commissioners of education and education-minded members of Congress to provide the intellectual and political manpower for identifying categories and strategies of education policymaking at the national level.[7]

The NEA did not fulfill this function alone, however. Even as the lobbying efforts of its parent organization came to fruition in 1867 with the establishment of a federal department of education, Henry Barnard, in his new role as commissioner of education, formally presented his plans for the department at a meeting of the ASSA. Founded in Boston in 1865 by a group of 100 institutional leaders and reformers, the ASSA, like the NTA/NEA, had roots in the practical responsibilities of state-level leaders charged with designing, legislating, and administering the work of state-level institutions and organizations. In the case of the ASSA, however, the institutional locations of its members were different and more various. The early ASSA was organized into four departments representing four main professional domains and branches of government activity, each with its own vice president. The four departments were Jurisprudence, Health, Education, and Finance, the last including subsections on Trade and Social Economy. Reflecting this broad scope, members had diverse institutional affiliations. The core membership and leadership of the organization included directors of the various reformatories, asylums, prisons, orphanages, and institutions for the feeble-minded that had been founded in several states over the previous two or three decades with some combination of philanthropic and state support. Another group of members consisted of doctors and social reformers concerned with issues of urban sanitation, public health, and disease prevention, while a third group consisted of a mix of political economists and businessmen concerned with issues of trade, tariffs, currency, and labor (Haskell, 1977).

Finally, the single largest group of ASSA members, according to the historian Thomas Haskell (1977), consisted of professional educators. As compared with membership of the NTA/NEA, however, the professional educators who constituted the core leadership of the ASSA's "Education Department" had quite different institutional affiliations. Instead of coming primarily from the leadership of state normal schools and common school systems, as did NTA/NEA members, the professional educators of the ASSA came primarily from the presidencies and professorships of colleges and universities. That the presidents of leading colleges and universities should have concerned themselves with the practical work of government in this way is not strange when one remembers that, at the time, the concluding experience of a BA degree was typically a course in moral philosophy and political economy taught by the college president, which took up just such matters of education, labor, charity, trade, and finance as became the core work of the ASSA. The most common and influential textbooks for such courses in the North by the 1850s, moreover, were those written by Francis Wayland Sr. of Brown University, and carried on by his sons, Francis Wayland Jr. and Heman Lincoln Wayland, after their father's death in 1865 (the year the ASSA was founded). Francis and Heman were founding members and subsequent presidents of the ASSA. Also important in the early history of the ASSA were presidents of the new "modern" universities emerging in the decade immediately following the Civil War, including Andrew Dickson White of Cornell, William Barton Rogers of MIT, James Angell of the University of Michigan, and Daniel Coit Gilman of Johns Hopkins.

These institutional affiliations, in turn, shaped the types of issues with which the ASSA was most concerned. With early sponsorship from the Massachusetts Board of Charities and other leadership coming from New England colleges and universities, the early ASSA was simultaneously more geographically parochial and more intellectually ambitious than the NEA, seeking to link institutions of learning and networks of college-educated doctors, lawyers, ministers, and educators more directly and powerfully to the work of government. Like the NEA, the ASSA emphasized statistics as one means of making this work more scientific and authoritative and its results more effective. Modeled in part on the British National Association for the Promotion of Social Science, founded in 1857, and informed by ties with leading members of the American Statistical Association, founded in 1839, the ASSA promoted the systematic collection, analysis, and dissemination of data on all aspects of national life, with the aim of influencing legislation to improve economy and society. Beyond this generally positive orientation to the culture of empiricism and the value of science for the practical work of public administration, the ASSA also exhibited a broader, intellectual interest in how far the traditional domains of mental and moral philosophy and political economy might come to parallel those of natural science. This broad intellectual interest directly shaped how the ASSA framed educational issues. At the very first meeting of the ASSA, in October 1865, for example, the one formal paper presented was, according to Haskell (1977, p. 111), a "plea for an inductive science of education." Strangely enough, the author of the paper, William P. Atkinson, was a professor of English and history at the just-opened Massachusetts Institute of Technology. What he chiefly had in mind was not the future behavioral psychology of G. Stanley Hall (though he did gesture toward the need for a more empirical "science of the mind"), or the basic learning of young children, but a more modern and scientific history for the education of professionals that was grounded not in the rote learning of classical rhetoric but in direct analysis of the evidentiary record of past societies and governments. Such knowledge, he believed, might become a useful and solid training for professional civil service, a notion that he explored 2 years later in a paper titled "Competitive Examinations for the Civil Service" (Haskell,

1977, p. 112). The vision that Atkinson articulated of a professional civil service certified in definite bodies of scientific and historical knowledge and methods of analysis became a central mission for the ASSA in subsequent years and the chief object of its lobbying efforts.

What the ASSA brought to the specific project of federal aid for education in the 1870s and 1880s, then, was something quite different from what the NEA brought to the project, though the interests of the two organizations temporarily dovetailed in what proved to be critical ways. While members of the NTA/NEA were concerned primarily with the explicit objects of the legislation—that is, with the categories and amounts of federal funding that would be allocated for support of common education—the ASSA brought two other somewhat broader concerns and domains of expertise to the business of forging federal education legislation, which, as we will see, would have an important impact on the way the legislation was formulated and promoted rhetorically in Congress and more broadly to the public. The first of these was a body of expertise in what it called "jurisprudence," but that can more fruitfully be understood as the philosophy of law, or ideas about the proper role of public law in regulating and structuring society. The central thrust and significance of this intellectual domain are reflected in the title of the first formal paper from the Department of Jurisprudence presented to the ASSA in 1867: "The Sphere of Law in Social Reform." The second distinctive concern that the ASSA brought to the project of promoting federal aid for education was civil service reform. That agenda would be embodied in part by the Pendleton Civil Service Reform Act of 1883, which established a system of civil service examinations for government service, limited the number and types of jobs that could be allocated on the basis of political appointment and patronage, and restricted the direct solicitation of party contributions from government officials. More broadly, however, the idea of civil service reform can be understood as an effort to take the politics out of government administration and establish a more merit-based system of governance, leadership, and policymaking. Although this project would seem to bear only a tangential relationship to that of ensuring universal access to common education, it in fact had a significant and far-reaching influence on the rhetorical logic and long-term impact of the campaign for passage of the Blair Bill in the 1880s.

A close look at the elements of this campaign illuminates the distinct but complementary roles that the NEA and ASSA played in the strategic development and promotion of the Blair Bill. The efforts of the NEA and ASSA focused first, on formulating an *argument* for the federal aid bill that would overcome frequent objections to the constitutionality of federal involvement in education; second, on marshaling *statistical data* in support of that argument; and third, on *mobilizing support* for the bill throughout the nation. Together, these elements of the Blair Bill campaign constituted an essential logic that in many ways continues to shape federal education legislation and the role of social science research in education to this day. Specifically, the Blair Bill campaign reveals *how social science data and arguments were used to address the problem of federalism.*

In the mid-1880s it seemed possible, even likely, that some version of the Blair Bill would eventually pass. In 1887, in what appears in retrospect as a last-ditch attempt to bring it to fruition, the bill's chief sponsor, Senator Henry W. Blair of New Hampshire, published a densely packed pamphlet of material including congressional committee reports, departmental studies, speeches, endorsements, transcripts of debates, texts of various versions of the bill, data, and analysis in support of the bill. From this material it is possible to see the role that the new and newly self-conscious social sciences played in the effort to establish a federal role in education in the 1880s (Blair, 1887).

Formulating an Argument

The basic argument in support of a federal role in education that Eaton, Blair, and their compatriots in the NEA and ASSA formulated was that such intervention was necessary for the preservation of the state itself. As Senator Blair stated the point in the Report of the Committee on Education and Labor, submitted in 1886,

Our leading proposition is that the General Government possesses the power and has imposed upon itself the duty of educating the people of the United States *whenever for any cause those people are deficient in that degree of education which is essential to the discharge of their duties as citizens* [italics added] either of the United States or of the several States wherein they chance to reside. (Blair, 1887, p. 5)

Here we see that a *deficiency of the people*, rather than a deficiency of the states, provided the foremost justification for federal intervention in education under the terms of the Blair Bill. This move was useful because it provided a logic for confronting and potentially circumventing the claims of state precedence and sovereignty over education that had stymied efforts at establishing a national system of education previously. It did so first by raising the stakes of the debate. A focus on a *deficiency of the people* made the problem not merely one of enforcing the will or power of the federal government over the states but also one of ensuring the survival of the government itself. A deficiency of the people effectively threatened the very survival of government, or more precisely of *self*-government, because

government for the people by the people implies that degree of popular intelligence which will enable the masses of men to comprehend the principles and to direct the administration of government in such ways as to promote the general welfare. (Blair, 1887, p. 5)

Second, a focus on the people rather than the states helped address a basic theoretical problem of federalism by shifting the locus of authority away from the nation state and toward the people themselves. Once a deficiency of the people was recognized, the question was who or what was responsible for addressing that deficiency, and under what authority. Again, the answer was "the people." This emphasis on the role of "the people" in republican government continued throughout the report, with a number of implications. One important dimension of the report's argument was its appeal to "the people" as the original and ultimate authorizing power for *both* federal and state governments. In this formulation, neither the state nor the federal government necessarily assumed precedence: Both were essentially responsible to the people, but the "general" government had the authority and even the duty to step in where more local powers failed. Drawing on prewar theories of the state that had been used to justify the use of federal power to prosecute the Civil War, the report cited Daniel Webster and the legal theorist John Bouvier to assert that residents of the several states *and territories* essentially constituted one body politic, "united together in one community for the defense of their rights." An essential such right was that of self-defense or self-preservation, including the right to constitute and maintain the state itself.

By this logic of a unitary people, Blair and his Committee on Education and Labor endeavored to confront and ultimately circumvent objections to federal intervention in education in the states. The allocation of certain functions to state government was by this logic itself a decision of the people. It was the people who "distributed the functions of government between the national and the sectional or the State authorities." But this distribution was not necessarily permanent. The people "have retained in themselves the initial exercise of all power through the ballot," and "the ballot is the republican form of government both in the nation and in the State." Although it might be preferable for a local power to assume the duty of qualifying the citizen to bear his or her responsibilities to the nation and the state, in a matter so essential as the preservation of the nation itself, "it is the right and duty of the whole to preserve the whole, and the right and duty of the whole to preserve the whole implies the preservation of all the parts by that whole, to the existence of which all the parts are necessary." More specifically,

the right to educate the child throughout the nation is the right to preserve the Government and the nation. That right cannot be curtailed. It is geographically coextensive with the jurisdiction of the Government itself, and self-preservation compels its exercise by the National Government whenever there is failure for any reason on the part of the parent and the State. (Blair, 1887, p. 5)

To further reinforce this line of argument, the report made extensive reference to the comprehensive education measures of other nations. Citing first of all the case of France, and then also Belgium, Italy, England, Scotland, Ireland, Prussia, Russia, Austria, and Japan, authors of the report recounted recent increases in the liberality of other countries, especially in Europe, in support of mass education, with particular attention to the goal of making universal the ability to read and write. As the report itself noted, quoting extensively from the U.S. Commissioner of Education, the high levels of investment in common education in other countries were absolutely concurrent with the U.S. effort to establish a national education system and with the Blair Bill itself. Comparative historical analysis reinforces this picture. In France, for example, beginning in the 1870s, a major increase in national education funding had occurred, and in 1882 national legislation substantially accelerated that support. Similarly, Belgium increased its national investment in education by leaps and bounds in the 1860s and 1870s and then again nearly doubled its expenditures between 1878 and 1882 (Lindert, 2004). Even "pagan people, like the Japanese" were "realizing [their] innate possibilities" through investment in mass education (Blair, 1887, p. 6).

The overall point of this analysis was both normative and competitive. Although, from the perspective of some historians and theorists of American statehood, the argument offered by authors of the committee report might have appeared somewhat novel and controversial, from an international perspective, the argument for education as a means of national self-preservation appeared increasingly normative. Other nations were "accelerating their pace" in mass education, while in the United States the pace was stagnant, or perhaps even declining. "Five years will educate a generation substantially," the report noted, "and it will not be long ere the Latin and the Saxon of Europe will reach and pass his kindred on this side of the Atlantic if a relative improvement shall not be here maintained." Moreover, the domain of this competition was not merely domestic but imperial and commercial. Great Britain in its wisdom had not only established a national education system within domestic borders in 1870 but also extended that system to its colonies, which now existed "on every vacant lot on the globe. . . . Wherever among these upheaving populations she sends her ships she carries her institutions and her laws," with the result that she had now "annexed the world" (Blair, 1887, pp. 6–7).

Marshaling Data, or the "Rhetoric of Statistics"

Having thus articulated both a legal logic and a normative context for establishing a national education system, the report then turned to examining the actual conditions of education in the United States. Making great use of the newly flourishing arts of data collection as practiced by the Bureau of the Census and the Commissioner of Education, Blair and his colleagues effectively laid out the case that there was indeed a deficiency of the people, and that this deficiency threatened the very survival of republican government. They did so primarily by presenting data. Promising to "give the country the cold steel of reliable statistics," they proclaimed such information to be "more eloquent than any other possible statement," demanding "the profoundest study of every citizen of the land."

It was in this presentation of data that the logical link between literacy and suffrage was made most clearly and strongly. Up to this point, the discussion had been framed more broadly in terms of education and citizenship. Recall that the jurisdiction of the committee was education and labor and that the subject of the report and of the Blair Bill itself was national aid to education. When it got to the section titled "Actual State of Education in This Country," however, the report reframed the discussion to focus more specifically on literacy and suffrage, explaining that while basic literacy would seem a rather low standard of qualification for a person to "discharge his duty as a sovereign," the "line of lowest qualification has been fixed as by common consent in the preparation of official data at that level" (Blair, 1887, p. 7).

This use of statistics on illiteracy to cement the case for national aid for education began right away with the presentation of data in Table 1 in the Blair Bill, which appeared under a section titled "Condition of the Suffrage." A close look at the introduction of data in this section illustrates how and why a focus on literacy and suffrage proved useful for addressing the politics of federalism. The actual content of the table, not clearly identified in the table itself, was a report of the number of persons over the age of 21 who could not write, broken down by state and race. In other words, the table provided no data on suffrage. It was preceded, however, by a discussion that extrapolated from the data an *estimate* of the number and proportion of illiterates who were *voters*. "It is the rule to estimate one voter for every five persons in the community," the authors explained. Given this rule, they continued, "The voting population of the country" could be estimated to be 10 million in 1880. Extrapolating from this premise, then, the authors used data from the table to estimate the proportion of the nation's voters who were illiterate. Concluding dramatically, that "one voter in five cannot write his name," the authors parsed out the statistical basis of that claim as follows:

The total number over twenty-one years of age who cannot write is 4,201,263, of whom 2,056,463 are white and 2,137,900 are colored, including about 200,000 Indians and 100,000 Asiatics. Assuming one half of these to be females, and therefore to have no souls, and not only to be without but to be unfit to exercise the suffrage, and making allowance for the unnaturalized citizens, there will remain 2,000,000 of illiterate voters about equally divided between the white and colored races. (Blair, 1887, p. 7)

Having now established the number and racialized distribution of this estimated illiteracy among voters, the authors went on to assess the "danger" that such a distribution represented:

One voter in five cannot write his name. He casts a ballot whose contents are to him unknown except from hearsay. He cannot tell the Constitution of his country from the code of Draco. He is the prey of the demagogue or the victim of prejudice, but he holds the balance of power in almost every state and in the nation at large. (Blair, 1887, p. 7)

Finally, and still before inserting the actual table, the authors of the report made one more important discursive move. They challenged the reader of that time (and, presumably, of the future) to see the problem of illiterate voters not simply as a Southern problem but also as a national problem. They did this first by highlighting the number of illiterates living in the North and implying that illiterates throughout the nation together constituted a kind of class with a potentially independent power to influence affairs of state. The last statement the reader encountered before the actual table was this set of admonishments:

Follow down these columns so pregnant with the demonstration of danger and dishonor to the Republic.
The illiterate voters of Maine, New Hampshire, Massachusetts, and Connecticut, of New York, New Jersey, Pennsylvania, Ohio, in short of every Middle, Southern and most of the Western States, have power, if combined to decide any political issue that is now, or for years is likely to be, pending between political parties. They represent ten of our fifty millions of people. (Blair, 1887, p. 7)

With this artful preemptive move, the authors effectively shifted focus away from Blacks in the South—where it would otherwise have surely landed, with Alabama at the top of the table's alphabetical list. (The data on Alabama showed an illiterate "colored" population of more than 200,000, over 3 times that of illiterate Whites in that state.) Instead of stopping there, the reader was challenged to "follow down the columns" and find the nearly 200,000 illiterates in New York, the same number in Pennsylvania, and the more than 100,000 illiterates in each of the states of Massachusetts, Ohio, and Illinois, most of them White. This preemptive shift of focus away from the South was then further reinforced by a visual detail of the table itself, which reported its results very simply in three columns: "White, Colored*, and Total." The arresting detail was the asterisk, which appeared right away at the top of the table, in the column heading. Proceeding to the asterisk at the bottom of the table, the reader could see that the figures in the "Colored*" column included "Indians and Asiatics" (Blair, 1887, pp. 7–8). The reader was reminded, in other words, that racialized illiteracy existed not only in the South but also in the West, and that such issues were matters of concern not only in the states but also in the territories, and thus in the nation at large.

Subsequent portions of the report's text and, indeed, of the legislation itself, as well as of other materials collected in the Blair Bill pamphlet, reinforced the visual cues from Table 1 in the Blair Bill. Together they convey a heightened sense of the scale and ambition of the Blair Bill. Although clearly still rooted in the problems of Southern Reconstruction, the national system of education envisioned in the Blair Bill went well beyond the South to embrace other projects as well. Blair and his colleagues made those other dimensions of their national education project explicit in other sections of the committee report. In a section devoted, for example, to analyzing the proportion of children enrolled in school as compared to the proportion of those of school age, the authors commented that soon there would be more children out of school than in it, and went on to admonish,

As we are constantly pointing pathetically at the unfortunate South, so we of the all-wise all-perfect, all-conquering North may well study the condition of our cities, which are as great a source of danger as the ignorant rural population of the South. (p. 11)

Several paragraphs later, they made a similar point with respect to Whites in the West, noting that the highest rate of illiteracy among Whites was in New Mexico, at 45% (Blair, 1887, p. 11). Of course, the reference was primarily to Spanish-speaking New Mexicans illiterate in English but defined as citizens by the Treaty of Guadalupe Hidalgo.[8] Also noteworthy in this passage, however, as throughout all the tables of statistics and associated documents, was the fact that Blair and his allies everywhere included the *territories* as well as the *states* in the national system of education that they envisioned. Commensurate, perhaps, with the imperial and colonial projects of Great Britain and other European nations that they invoked as models, this national system of education was colonial as well as domestic in ambition and scope.

In this respect the Blair Bill represented a truly *national* rather than simply federal vision of the education problem, as well as of the country itself. The trans-Mississippi West was significant to this vision precisely because at that time it consisted primarily of territories, *not* states. By articulating a vision of national education that encompassed the territories as well as the states, and by defining the problem of education in the territories in terms that made it the same as that of the post-Reconstruction South (that is, a problem of racialized illiteracy, or deficiency of the people), Blair and associates offered a vision of the country as a modern, amalgamated, imperial nation, rather than a federation of independent states.[9]

Mobilizing Support

Blair and his allies in the NEA and ASSA pulled out all the stops in prosecuting their campaign for establishing a national system of aid for education. In 1882 and again in 1883, they convened a "National Education Assembly" in Atlantic City for the purpose of marshaling public opinion behind the idea of federal assistance to public education. The assembly, ostensibly composed of "Christian educators and statesmen irrespective of section, Church, or party," included strong representation from Southern states, thereby perhaps partly explaining the relatively large number of petitions that Congress received from Southern citizen and education groups in those years (Lee, 1949, pp. 107–108). In 1882, 1884, and again in 1886 and 1887, sponsors of the Blair Bill solicited and published numerous endorsements, memorials, and petitions from state officials, representatives, citizen groups, and other organizations, and from around the country. One of the objectives, no doubt, of assembling and publishing the contents of Blair's 1887 pamphlet was to present in one place the cumulative record of this support (Blair, 1887).

The leadership of organizations such as the NEA and ASSA, meanwhile, who had been closely allied with provisions of the Blair Bill from the beginning, referred directly to data on illiteracy and to the link between literacy and suffrage as indicative of the need for national aid for education. The NEA, for example, included its own data on rates of illiteracy by race and by levels of state expenditure for education in its memorial in support of the 1882 Blair Bill, perhaps thereby outlining the strategy that the Senate committee subsequently took up and developed more fully in 1884 and 1886. The group's leadership then closed its final appeal to Congress by framing the threat of illiteracy in both religious and political terms:

In the name of the millions of Christian citizens whom we represent we earnestly urge Congress to help qualify the Ignorant voters who are intrusted largely by Congressional action with the ballot for the duties with which they are charged, believing the power to do this is co-ordinate with the power that enfranchised them. (Blair, 1887, p. 17)

Similarly, in his capacity as president of the ASSA, Francis Wayland (the younger), joined by the association's influential founding secretary, Frank B. Sanborn, presented a formal appeal and resolution by calling the attention of the Senate and

House of Representatives to the necessary link between literacy and voting. The appeal began with a long preamble as follows:

The American Social Science Association, impressed with the danger involved in the existence of a large number of illiterate voters in the population of this country, as revealed in the last census, for the proper enlightenment of which class of voters many of the States are unable to make adequate provisions, and believing that a Government resting on the suffrage of the majority of the people cannot preserve itself from corrupt influence nor secure a high degree of civil freedom unless education is generally diffused among all classes of voters; . . .

Their preamble then continued and closed by laying out the grounds for federal intervention in education that essentially became the blueprint for the Senate committee's subsequent arguments:

And further believing it to be within the constitutional power of Congress to provide in this manner for the safety of the Republic, and that the enfranchisement of the freedmen imposes an especial obligation upon the Government to qualify them for a safe discharge of the new duties devolved upon them, [the American Social Science Association] would earnestly pray that your honorable body will take prompt and efficient measures to avert these dangers; that money raised from such sources as your honorable body may in its wisdom deem best shall be distributed, for a limited period, to the common schools of the States and Territories, on the basis of illiteracy, and in such manner as shall not supersede nor interfere with local efforts, but rather stimulate the same and render them more efficient; said moneys to be distributed under such guarantees as shall secure their application to the objects therein named, with equal justice to all classes of citizens. (Blair, 1887, p. 23)

In the end, however, as we know, Blair and his associates failed in their effort. After a decade-long campaign and repeated introduction in Congress, the Blair Bill went down to clear defeat in early 1890. The consequences were many and significant—arguably much greater than has yet been fully assessed by scholars or than can be fully outlined in this chapter. For the present, however, two main sets of lessons from this history will be considered: the lessons drawn by Lee in 1949, and the lessons we might draw after reconsidering his analysis in light of more recent historical scholarship.

LESSONS FROM THE HISTORY OF 19TH-CENTURY EFFORTS TO ESTABLISH A NATIONAL SYSTEM OF EDUCATION

In a two-part conclusion to his study, Lee (1949) first provided an overview of his findings regarding 19th-century efforts to establish federal aid for education. He then followed with a section titled "The Contemporary Significance of the Early Attempts to Grant Federal Aid to the Common Schools," in which he delineated lessons for his own time.

The main lesson Lee (1949) drew from this analysis was the essential immutability of the constraints to which the 19th-century legislation responded. In the first point of his enumerated summary of significance, Lee effectively naturalized such conditions as fundamentally inherent to the American system of government. "There exists among the American people," he declared, "a powerful and lasting tradition of states' rights and local prerogative." Accepting the reality of this tradition was, in his analysis, the first step in making contemporary use of the lessons from history. In deference to that reality, the question for his own time was how best to keep federal involvement in education "within proper bounds and limits." Specifically, the record of the 1870s and 1880s indicated the unlikelihood of passage of federal aid legislation "which embodies *any* federal controls other than details of fiscal administration" (Lee, 1949, pp. 166–167).

As an analysis of the realpolitik of his own time, Lee's (1949) assessment may well have been justified, as is illustrated by the ultimate defeat of the eminently noncontrolling general aid legislation under consideration at the time of his writing. As an assessment of the historical significance of the 19th-century campaign, however, Lee's characterization of the states' rights tradition of U.S. education as immutable fails to recognize the extent to which that "tradition" was actively being created both *during* and *through* the 19th-century campaign for federal aid.

Lee's (1949) assumptions regarding the immutability of local and state limitations on federal power led him to characterize the Hoar Bill's effort to enforce the educational provisions of Southern state constitutions as essentially frivolous. At one point, Lee further suggested that Hoar himself was not seriously interested in education per se, but in some other purpose. This assessment of the weak political prospects of the Hoar Bill was no doubt true to some extent, though Hoar's "other purpose" may have been a genuine concern for political equality for African Americans, for which he consistently advocated throughout his long political career (as he also did for that of Native Americans, Chinese immigrants, women, and eventually Cubans and Filipinos). The Hoar Bill certainly agitated the fundamental problem of federalism that would be vociferously debated over the next 20 years (Hoffer, 2007) and eventually decided, by 1890, largely in favor of state's rights. No doubt, given the terms of Reconstruction, the bill's prospects for passage even in a modified form were dim after the readmission of the last of the Southern states in July 1870. In addition, it is fair to ask, as Lee did, whether at that important political moment, when Radical Republicans still dominated Congress, a more moderate proposal, acceptable to more Northern educators if not to White Southerners, might have achieved what no subsequent federal education bill could.

Nonetheless, to really come to terms with the significance of the historical moment, it is essential to point out that all historical evidence suggests that some sort of compulsion was indeed *necessary* for anything like universal common school systems to be established in the South. However limited the funding, support, and oversight provided by the Freedmen's Bureau, and however essential the initiative and self-help of Black communities (along with missionary organizations and mission-minded individuals) were to the development of Black education in the South in the immediate postwar period (Anderson, 1988; Foner, 2005; Span, 2009; Williams, 2005), the scholarship also shows how absolutely devastating the withdrawal of federal funding, enforcement, and protection was for schools and educators of all kinds after 1870. As has been documented with numerous examples by Williams (2005) and Butchart (2010), acts of terrorism against schools, schoolteachers, and Black education were ubiquitous throughout this period. Teachers, according to one correspondent from Alabama, were "advertized as subjects of assassination," and hundreds of schoolhouses were burned. The withdrawal of federal support meant the abandonment of Black education to such fates. As Butchart (2010, p. 172) noted, "The freed people understood the link between political efficacy and literacy, and even as early as 1870 they knew that they had been betrayed."

A close look at the dynamics between congressional and state action in this period suggests that the step-by-step compromises and failures of federal legislation and enforcement were read very closely within states and responded to accordingly. In 1872, just 2 months after the Perce Bill passed in the House of Representatives, with its compromise principle that states with segregated schools systems would still be eligible for federal funds, the border state of West Virginia, which had not been under military rule, effectively sent up a trial balloon by approving a new state constitution that *required* racial segregation in its schools. West Virginia thus became the second state (after Tennessee, which had been admitted to Congress before the requirements of the Reconstruction Act) to include such a provision in its constitution.[10] Within 5 years, five more states had revised their constitutions to require racial segregation in public schools. The remaining Southern and border states followed.[11]

More broadly, a reassessment of provisions of the Blair Bill reveals the complex and highly contingent context into which such legislation proposed to intervene. Scholarship in the history of education reveals that the decade of the 1880s was precisely when the future contours of education for Native Americans in the West and African Americans in the South were most hotly contested by reformers and policymakers. At that time, the subject was still open to debate.

With respect to Native Americans, this policy debate took shape at the first meetings of the Indian Rights Association in 1882, the very year that the Blair Bill was first introduced in Congress. The following year, in 1883, the first of the Lake Mohonk Conferences brought together reformers seeking an alternative to the militarized approach to federal Indian policy and the dependent, and often degraded, status of Native American life on reservations. In the meantime, in 1879, Richard Pratt's experiment with the federal off-reservation boarding school at Carlisle, Pennsylvania, commenced, followed by the founding of the second federally sponsored institution, Chemawa Indian School, in Forest Grove, Oregon. Four more schools were founded in 1884, the year the Blair Bill received its first favorable vote in the Senate.[12]

Throughout this period, according to Adams (1995, p. 58), policymakers continued to debate the role that off-reservation boarding schools should play in federal Indian policy, with reformers promoting a general program of education expansion for Native American populations rather than a specific institutional model. Real and substantial alternatives to a federal system already existed, moreover, among the sovereign nations of Indian territory, which had been developing their own schools and schools systems under their own authority since the 1830s (Steineker, 2016; Wickett, 2000). In Adams's analysis, it was not until the mid-1880s that policymakers became committed to the idea that some sort of boarding school experience (whether on- or off-reservation) would be an essential part of a broader national education policy for Native Americans, combined with a system of Native American day schools. Reflecting this policy trajectory, attendance rates at both boarding and day schools increased substantially after 1880 and especially between 1885 and 1890. It was not until 1887—as Henry Blair made his last-ditch effort to save his bill in Congress—that a somewhat settled national education policy for Native Americans became linked to the Indian land allotment policy in the Dawes Act.

Similarly, in his detailed analysis of the development of Black education in the South, Anderson (1988) emphasizes that the model of education that would be promoted for African Americans remained very open to debate through the 1880s and well into the 1890s. Although the Hampton Institute had been founded in 1868, under the auspices of the American Missionary Association, it was not until the early 1870s, after the demise of the Freedmen's Bureau, that Armstrong wrested pedagogical control of Hampton from Lucelia and Philomea Williams, who had been operating it on a liberal model (Butchart, 2010, pp. 90–91). Even after Armstrong assumed leadership of the institution, the industrial model of education for which it became known took time to be established. The heart of Hampton's manual labor program, according to Anderson, was established in 1879, when Armstrong created the night school with Booker T. Washington as principal (Anderson, 1988, p. 54). Washington then went on to establish a similar program at the newly founded Tuskegee Institute in Tuskegee, Alabama, in 1881.

According to Anderson (1988), "The most significant expansion of industrial education in black normal schools and colleges occurred during the 1880s" (p. 66), in large part through the influence of the Slater Fund. Other philanthropists, such as Robert Ogden and Peabody, also became associated with the Hampton–Tuskegee model of industrial education during this period. Despite the growing ties between Armstrong, Washington, and business philanthropists, however, the missionary model of liberal education remained influential. Moreover, missionary advocates remained strong and effective advocates for liberal education and strong critics of the system of industrial education for African Americans throughout the 1880s and well into the 1890s and beyond. As recounted by Anderson, missionary leaders attacked the "reviving Negrophobia" and the self-interested promotion of manual labor education by industrial philanthropists at a meeting of the ASSA in 1895 (Anderson, 1988, pp. 66–68).

In this context, the curricular provisions of the Blair Bill, which specified that states receiving federal funds must provide a strong curriculum of academic study for all students equally, "without distinction of race or color," stand out as a deliberate intervention in an ongoing debate. Moreover, the fact that this definition of "common education" was explicitly distinguished from the industrial education to which funds could be applied in the territories suggests that the somewhat unusual decision to detail the contents of common education was in fact a deliberate effort to ensure that the system of common schools established in the South with federal aid would indeed be "education for citizenship."

Drawing on student accounts from correspondence, memoirs, and oral histories, Adams (1995), Anderson (1988), Lomawaima (1994), and others have amply detailed the experience of industrial education at Hampton and various Native American boarding schools in strikingly similar terms. In both contexts, the domestic work required to support the institution, including laundry, kitchen work, cleaning, sewing and mending of uniforms, and the agricultural and mechanical work necessary to feed the occupants and maintain the institution's operations, filled most hours of the day for both female and male students, leaving little if any time for study and then typically of only the most rudimentary skills. Moreover, as Anderson thoroughly documented, and an earlier literature also established (Bond, 1934; DuBois, 1910, 1935; Woodson, 1933), after 1900 the industrial model became "the" model promoted by educators and philanthropists through the "Southern movement" conducted by the Southern and general education boards, though often resisted by African American students, parents, leaders, and communities. When it comes to African American education, however, this eventuality was as much a *result* as a precondition of the failed campaign for a national education system.

The one place where Lee (1949) directly addressed these racial dynamics was in the penultimate paragraph of his conclusion and thus of the study as a whole. Acknowledging the antidemocratic position of "those who maintain a 'morality of white supremacy,'" Lee engaged the question of whether, in his own time, federal legislation should include mandates that disqualified from federal aid any states "in which racial segregation [was] a legally established practice." Taking the position that no such mandates should be included, Lee offered several explanatory arguments. Starting with a statement about the limits of the law as a means of changing social attitudes, he articulated a logic of gradualism in improving Black school conditions, saying that a "growing social consciousness, supported by progressive tendencies of contemporary judicial decision, is gradually producing reform in the established pattern of race relationships, notably in the area of educational equalization" (pp. 169–170).

As we know from the work of Anderson (1988) and Margo (1990), however, the gap between funding for Black and White schooling in the South *began* in 1890, when the Blair Bill finally failed. In the period from 1870 to 1890, levels of funding for Black and White schools in the South, though low, were essentially equal. Similarly, it was only after it became clear that no federally funded national campaign to promote or guarantee universal literacy would be conducted that Southern states decided to make literacy a qualification for Black suffrage (Whites were largely exempted from meeting such qualifications), a condition that itself eventually reinforced and widened the gap in school funding. Furthermore, it was only after Southern states had perfected this strategy for suppressing Black education without federal response that *Plessy v. Ferguson* confirmed it as constitutional. Hence, when

Lee (1949) himself concluded that the attitudes of those "who maintain a morality of 'white supremacy' would be unlikely to be changed by federal mandates" and that any legislation which would be inapplicable to states with racial segregation "would be ineffective," he was addressing a reality that had been institutionalized in the 60 years *since* the final failure of the Blair Bill in 1890.

Lee's (1949) study is invaluable as a record of the legislative efforts and actions on federal aid for education from 1870 to 1890. Despite the fact that the study was conceived and executed in the interest of future success for a comparable legislative effort, it exhibits admirable detachment in its evaluation of factors that contributed to or inhibited the "struggle" and the relative success or failure of various strategies. Nonetheless, of course, the context of the study's creation did color its analysis in certain respects—chiefly, perhaps, with regard to the strength of its hopes. Shaped by a faith in future success, as well as by lingering assumptions of progress, Lee's account insufficiently reckoned with the consequences and significance of past failures, which in many ways created and explained the conditions of his present that he regarded as normal. The very fact of Lee's self-conscious effort to mobilize professionals in support of federal legislation derived from the failure of the earlier effort to empower the Bureau of Education with the authority to provide national direction in education itself. Similarly, the very virulence of the "states' rights" dynamic in education, which Lee had taken pains to recognize in the past in order to better strategize around it in the future, was confirmed, strengthened, and indeed stimulated by the ultimate failure of the Hoar, Perce, Burnside, and Blair bills of the 1870s and 1880s.

THE SIGNIFICANCE OF PROFESSIONAL ASSOCIATIONS AND SOCIAL SCIENCE RESEARCH IN NATIONAL EDUCATION POLICY

Substantively, the failure of the Blair Bill and of the larger campaign for a national system of education meant that the authority to define the terms of access to, and the regulation of, both education and suffrage returned to the states. But more than that, authority returned to the states with a new level of permission to discriminate in the distribution of both education and suffrage and, more specifically, to use educational qualifications as a *means* of discrimination with respect to voting rights. In other words, the final failure of the Blair Bill had effects well beyond the simple absence of its promised provisions. It took a set of issues about the extent and limits of federal authority in education and suffrage and settled them, and it settled them in favor of state prerogative. In a few Western states, such as Wyoming, this new permissiveness led to state provisions that expanded access to political rights for some—especially women—at the same time as it also emboldened some Western states to restrict access for others—for example, Chinese in Oregon and California, Indians in Washington, and citizens not fully literate in English in Oklahoma and Arizona (Beadie, 2016; Beadie et al., 2016; Bottoms, 2013). In the South, by comparison, the defeat of the Blair Bill spelled out a more fully restrictive logic. Note that it was only *after* the final defeat of efforts to achieve universal literacy through a federal system of funding for education for all that Southern states undertook literacy-based approaches to disfranchisement. And, as the historians Jim Anderson (1988) and Robert Margo (1990) have amply demonstrated, it was only after disfranchisement that Southern states began radically undermining principles of equal funding for Black schools.

Although it would certainly be an overstatement to say that the failure of the Blair Bill somehow *caused* the rise of suffrage restrictions in the South and some areas of the West, the failure of the bill and of the larger campaign of which it was a part did play a more central role in constructing the suffrage restrictions of Jim Crow than has generally been recognized (Beadie, 2016). As the legal scholar Alfred Avins (1965) pointed out in a somewhat curious 1965 *Washington Law Review* article on literacy tests, some radical Republicans in Congress recognized and worried from the outset of Reconstruction about the potential for education to become a proxy for race in the restriction of Black voting rights.[13] During debates over the first Civil Rights Bill of 1866 and the 14th Amendment, these Congressmen cautioned their colleagues about the educational loopholes that insufficiently strong civil rights provisions would leave for Southern states to exclude Blacks from voting. In 1866, for example, Congressman John Farnsworth of Illinois noted,

A State may enact that a man shall not exercise the elective franchise except he can read and write, making that law apply equally to the whites and blacks, and then may also enact that a black man shall not learn to read and write, exclude him from their schools, and make it a penal offense to instruct or to teach him, and thus prevent his qualifying to exercise the elective franchise according to the State law. (Avins, 1965, p. 438)

Similarly, Congressman Hamilton Ward of New York anticipated that Southern states would

readily publish some ground of exclusion from suffrage other than of "race or color." They may require them to read and write, and yet keep alive the black code against disseminating knowledge among them. Indeed, they may require them to have a collegiate education, or something else equally absurd. (Avins, 1965, p. 438)

Concerns like these were precisely what led radical Republicans to argue (unsuccessfully), first, that the right of suffrage should be unconditionally guaranteed by the federal government; second, that equal access to education should be guaranteed in a federal civil rights bill; and third, that a system of federal aid and oversight of universal common education should be established at the national level. Thus, in 1890, when the last of these efforts failed, the rhetorical and conceptual ground had already been laid for using literacy as a qualification for suffrage. In other words, the same logic once used to promote the success of the Blair Bill was inverted by defeat into a logic justifying contingencies exactly the opposite of those intended. If federally funded common education was *necessary* to ensure the literacy required for suffrage— and ultimately to ensure the very survival of self-government—then the failure to provide such federal support required *restriction* of suffrage based on literacy. In this way, the rhetoric used to legitimate a federal system of support for universal education and thereby prevent education from being used as a proxy for race doubled back on itself. It became a tool for legitimating exactly the suffrage restrictions the originators had hoped to prevent.[14]

Moreover, and perhaps more important, as Congressmen Farnsworth and Ward had recognized, the failure of the Blair Bill and the consequent return of state responsibility, power, and prerogative in education effectively provided an incentive for White supremacists to limit Black access to education as a *means* of limiting Black access to voting rights. In this way, the inability of the federal government to legislate in the domain of education and the disability of non-Whites as voters were co-constructed after 1890. The failed Blair Bill campaign was in effect the "lost wax" of state literacy restrictions on voting and unequal state education provisions that structured the Jim Crow edifice.[15]

The value of looking closely at this consequential defeat is that it illuminates some of the historical pitfalls of federalism that still plague efforts at national education policymaking in the United States today. In particular, the campaigns of the 1870s and 1880s show how traditional limits on federal authority over the states contribute to shaping policies framed in terms of deficiencies of the *people* rather than deficiencies of the states. In the process, it also shows how the difficulties of forging grand bargains across states can lead to policies solicitous of local and regional prejudice, and how those same dynamics can incentivize sponsors of such policies to lump together quite different populations and issues in one racialized problem or class. Finally, a close look at the campaigns for a national system in the 1870s and 1880s shows how the search for a usable national discourse of education reform can double back on itself and effectively reproduce the very problems it once was intended to solve. Or, to use the more recently salient language of Gloria Ladson-Billings (2006), the case of 19th-century efforts to establish a federal system of education shows how the historical limits of federalism repeatedly transform the "education debt" into an "achievement gap."

Finally, to return to the analysis by Elisabeth Clemens (1997), the case of the 19th-century campaign to secure federal funding for education illuminates the peculiar historical role and significance of professional associations like the NEA, the ASSA, and eventually, the AERA, in a national context of decentralized government authority. According to Lee (1949), the federal assistance question of the 1870s and 1880s marked the *beginning* of effective legislative activity within the education profession. In his analysis, however, the education profession during the 1870s and 1880s was extremely weak as a pressure group on the national scale. In particular, he critiqued professional educators of the past as "utterly unable to unite in recognizing the urgent necessity of federal aid." Using that critique as a point of departure for addressing the professional educators of his own time, Lee then went on to advise that "no federal legislation is likely to be enacted without aggressive professional organization representing approximate solidarity of professional support for such legislation" (p. 167). In effect, we can say that Lee was right. What the NEA and the ASSA did in the 1870s and 1880s was to work closely with the commissioner of education and members of Congress to shape legislation, formulate arguments, collect and interpret data, and mobilize "public and professional interest" in support of a national system of education. With the failure of the Blair Bill and the consequent stimulation of administrative power at the state level, the capacity to redefine educational issues in national terms became even more crucial. In effect, the culture of expertise became a substitute for federal authority itself. The significance of professional associations and social science research came to lie in their intellectual and organizational capacity to categorize education conditions in ways that turned them into politically action-able national "problems." Following the pattern laid down during the Blair Bill campaign, social science data and research would repeatedly be turned to as the means of redefining as "deficiencies of the people" what were really "deficiencies of the states."

ACKNOWLEDGMENT

Deep thanks to Karen Graves for encouraging this project.

NOTES

[1]The exception was Tennessee, which had been readmitted to Congress under President Andrew Johnson and before the Congressional Reconstruction Act of 1867. Tennessee had thus not been forced to accept the several requirements imposed on the other secessionist states, including provisions for a universal system of free common education.

[2]The last secessionist state to be readmitted was Virginia, in July 1870.

[3]Alabama's illiteracy rate was 29% in 1880; Massachusetts' was 4%, as reported in Blair (1887, p. 10).

[4]Although a few states specified state-level adoption of textbooks and thereby effectively specified the content of curriculum, state constitutions and laws actually said little, if anything, about the content of state-supported common education until the Progressive Era. The meaning of "common" was generally assumed rather than described.

[5]North Dakota, South Dakota, Montana, Idaho, Washington, and Wyoming were granted statehood in 1889–1890; Utah in 1896; Oklahoma and Indian Territory in 1906; Arizona and New Mexico in 1912; Alaska in 1958; and Hawaii in 1959.

[6]The bureau's only tool for promoting education in the states was the collection and diffusion of statistical data. Eaton began to build the reputation of the bureau by working closely with professional education associations, most notably the NEA, and building amicable relations with the U.S. Congress. Eaton was able to publish and distribute to the public a variety of circulars with information on several subjects (Sniegoski, 1995). For more on the later history of the NEA, see Urban (2000).

[7]One could say that the roots of the idea for the National Center for Education Statistics lie in this 35-year effort by Henry Barnard and others to develop a capacity at the national level for collecting and publishing education statistics, ultimately resulting in the founding of the National Bureau of Education in 1867 and the further development of its information-gathering capacity under Commissioner John Eaton.

[8]For accounts of the actual education conditions in New Mexico, Texas, and elsewhere in the Southwest at the time, see McDonald (2001, 2004) and Blanton (2004).

[9]For a fuller discussion of issues of education in the states and territories of the West during this period, see Beadie et al. (2016), a historiographical essay that focuses on the history of education from the perspective of the North American West, as well as other articles on

the same topic published in the same special issue of *History of Education Quarterly* (August 2016). For incisive analysis of the interaction between the West and South in Reconstruction era policymaking in Congress, see Anderson (2007); see also Bottoms (2013), West (2003), Wickett (2000).

[10]"Constitution of West Virginia—1872," Article XII, Section 8: "White and colored persons shall not be taught in the same school" (Thorpe, 1909, vol. 7, 4061).

[11]See Thorpe (1909), passim. Significantly, these first Jim Crow provisions for education were adopted in border and secessionist states where Blacks were a numerical minority, both in the general population and among the electors and officials at the state and federal levels. By comparison, the few states with large or majority Black populations—Florida, South Carolina, and Louisiana—did not constitutionally require racial segregation until the 1880s and 1890s, when Jim Crow provisions dramatically reducing Black suffrage were put into effect. Also noteworthy is the way in which the provisions developed as part of a give-and-take response to legislative efforts and failures in Congress.

[12]These included Chilocco Indian School in Oklahoma and others in Kansas, Nebraska, and New Mexico (Adams, 1995). In addition, see Adams (1988), Lomawaima (1994), Lomawaima and McCarty (2006), Child (1998), Gilbert (2010), Gram, (2015), K. Warren (2010), Reddick (2000), and Collins (2000).

[13]Avins's (1965) article is curious in that it was presented as an argument *against* the Voting Rights Act of 1965, which was signed into law the year the article was published. The main thrust of the argument is that since some congressional Republicans opposed, or were reluctant to support, the 14th Amendment (because it insufficiently guaranteed suffrage rights and allowed literacy restrictions on suffrage), clearly the "original intent" of the amendment was not to guarantee those rights. Thus, the elements of the Voting Rights Act that forbade the use of literacy tests to restrict suffrage were unconstitutional. According to the footnotes, the material in the article came from the legislative history appendices that Avins wrote for the U.S. Supreme Court in *Katzenbach v. Morgan*, a case involving the abolishment of a literacy test under the terms of the Voting Rights Act, also argued in 1965.

[14]For a thorough account of Jim Crow suffrage restrictions, including literacy tests, see Perman (1984, 2001).

[15]The metaphoric reference here is to the "lost-wax" casting process for creating bronze sculptures. In lost-wax casting, an original artwork is sculpted in wax and covered by a fireproof mold. The mold is then heated until the wax melts and is "lost," allowing the sculptor to create a more permanent work by filling the same mold with hot metal. Similarly, in this case, the Blair Bill campaign sculpted a rhetorical connection between voting and literacy that was "lost" when the bill did not pass but left behind a mold into which Southern politicians poured the material to construct a more substantial Jim Crow edifice.

REFERENCES

Adams, D. W. (1995). *Education for extinction: American Indians and the boarding school experience, 1875–1928*. Lawrence: University Press of Kansas.

Adams, D. W. (1988). Fundamental considerations: The deep meaning of Native American schooling, 1880–1900. *Harvard Education Review, 58*(1), 1–29.

Anderson, J. D. (1988). *The education of Blacks in the South, 1860–1935*. Chapel Hill: University of North Carolina Press.

Anderson, J. D. (2007). Race-conscious educational policies versus a color-blind Constitution: A historical perspective. *Educational Researcher, 36*, 249–257.

Anderson, J. D. (2015). A long shadow: The American pursuit of political justice and education equality. *Educational Researcher, 44*, 319–335.

Avins, A. (1965). Literacy tests, the Fourteenth Amendment, and District of Columbia voting: The original intent. *Washington University Law Repository, 1965*, 429–462.

Baldwin, P. (2005). Beyond weak and strong: Rethinking the state in comparative policy history. *Journal of Policy History, 17,* 12–33.

Balogh, B. (2009). *A government out of sight: The mystery of national authority in nineteenth-century America.* Cambridge, England: Cambridge University Press.

Beadie, N. (2010a). *Education and the creation of capital in the early American republic.* New York, NY: Cambridge University Press.

Beadie, N. (2010b). Education, social capital and state formation in comparative historical perspective: Preliminary investigations. *Paedagogica Historica, 46*(1–2), 15–32.

Beadie, N. (2016). War, education and state formation: Problems of territorial and political integration in the United States, 1848–1912. *Paedagogica Historica, 52*(1–2), 58–75.

Beadie, N. (in press). The history of national education systems: North America. In J. Rury & E. Tamura (Eds.), *The Oxford handbook of the history of education.* Oxford, England: Oxford University Press.

Beadie, N., Williamson-Lott, J., Bowman, M., Frizell, T., Guzman, G., Hyun, J., . . . Yoshida, L. (2016). Gateways to the West, Part I: Education in the shaping of the West. *History of Education Quarterly, 56,* 418–444.

Blair, H. (1887). *National aid in the establishment and temporary support of common schools: The Education Bill.* New York, NY: American News Co. Retrieved from https://babel.hathitrust.org/cgi/pt?id=loc.ark:/13960/t49p3sv5v;view=1up;seq=1

Blanton, C. (2004). *The strange career of bilingual education in Texas, 1836–1981.* College Station: Texas A&M University Press.

Bond, H. M. (1934). *The education of the Negro in the American social order.* New York, NY: Prentice Hall.

Bottoms, M. D. (2013). *An aristocracy of color: Race and Reconstruction in California and the West, 1850–1890.* Norman: University of Oklahoma Press.

Butchart, R. (2010). *Schooling the freed people: Teaching, learning, and the struggle for Black freedom, 1861–1876.* Chapel Hill: University of North Carolina Press.

Caruso, M. (2010). Latin American independence: Education and the invention of new polities. *Paedagogica Historica, 46,* 409–417.

Child, B. J. (1998). *Boarding school seasons: American Indian families, 1900–1940.* Lincoln: University of Nebraska Press.

Collins, C. C. (2000). The broken crucible of assimilation: Forest Grove Indian School and the origins of off-reservation boarding school education in the West. *Oregon Historical Quarterly, 101,* 466–507.

Clemens, E. (1997). *The people's lobby: Organizational innovation and the rise of interest group politics in the United States, 1890–1925.* Chicago, IL: University of Chicago.

DuBois, W. E. B. (1910). Reconstruction and its benefits. *American Historical Review, 14,* 781–799.

DuBois, W. E. B. (1935). *Black Reconstruction in America, 1860–1880.* New York, NY: Simon & Schuster.

Foner, E. (2005). *Forever free: The story of emancipation and Reconstruction.* New York, NY: Vintage.

Gilbert, M. S. (2010). *Education beyond the mesas: Hopi students at Sherman Institute, 1902–1929.* Lincoln: University of Nebraska.

Gram, J. R. (2015). *Education at the edge of empire: Negotiating Pueblo identity in New Mexico's Indian boarding schools.* Seattle: University of Washington Press.

Haskell, T. (1977). *The emergence of professional social science: The American Social Science Association and the 19th-century crisis of authority.* Urbana: University of Illinois Press.

Hoffer, W. (2007). *To enlarge the machinery of government: Congressional debates and the growth of the American state, 1858–1891.* Baltimore, MD: Johns Hopkins University Press.

Hutt, E. (2012). Formalism over function: Compulsion, courts, and the rise of educational formalism in America. *Teachers College Record, 114*(1), 1–27.

Kaestle, C. (1983). *Pillars of the republic: Common schools and American society, 1780–1860.* New York, NY: Hill & Wang.

Kaestle, C., & Lodewick, A. (2007). *To educate a nation: Federal and national strategies of school reform.* Lawrence: University of Kansas Press.

Kimball, B. (1992). *The "true professional ideal" in America: A history.* Cambridge, MA; Blackwell.

Ladson-Billings, G. (2006). From the achievement gap to the education debt: Understanding achievement in U.S. schools. *Educational Researcher, 35*(7), 3–12.

Lagemann, E. C. (2000). *An elusive science: The troubling history of education research.* Chicago, IL: University of Chicago Press.

Lee, G. C. (1949). *The struggle for federal aid, first phase: A history of the attempts to obtain federal aid for the common schools, 1870–1890.* New York, NY: Bureau of Publications, Teachers College, Columbia University.

Lindert, P. (2004). *Growing public: Social spending and economic growth since the eighteenth century.* Cambridge, England: Cambridge University Press.

Lomawaima, K. T. (1994). *They called it prairie light: The story of Chilocco Indian School.* Lincoln: University of Nebraska.

Lomawaima, K. T., & McCarty, T. (2006). *"To remain an Indian": Lessons in democracy from a century of North American education.* New York, NY: Teachers College Press.

Loss, C. P. (2012). *Between citizens and the state: the politics of American higher education in the 20th century.* Princeton, NJ: Princeton University Press.

Manekin, S. (2009). *Spreading the empire of free education, 1865–1905* (Unpublished doctoral dissertation). University of Pennsylvania, Philadelphia.

Margo, R. A. (1990). *Race and schooling in the South, 1880–1950: An economic history.* Chicago, IL: University of Chicago Press.

Mattingly, P. (1975). *The classless profession: American schoolmen in the nineteenth century.* New York: New York University Press.

McAfee, W. (1998). *Religion, race and Reconstruction: The public school in the politics of the 1870s.* Albany: State University of New York.

McDonald, V. (2001). Hispanic, Latino, Chicano, or "Other"? Deconstructing the relationship between historians and Hispanic-American educational history. *History of Education Quarterly, 41,* 365–413.

McDonald, V. (2004). *Latino education in the United States: A narrated history from 1513–2000.* New York, NY: Palgrave MacMillan.

Mershon, S., & Schlossman, S. (2008). Education, science, and the politics of knowledge: The American Educational Research Association, 1915–1940. *American Journal of Education, 114,* 307–340.

Miller, P. (1998). *Transformations of patriarchy in the West, 1500–1900.* Bloomington: Indiana University.

Nelson, A. (2005). *The elusive ideal: Equal educational opportunity and the federal role in Boston's schools, 1950–1985.* Chicago, IL: University of Chicago Press.

Novak, W. J. (2008). The myth of the "weak" American state. *American Historical Review, 113,* 752–772.

Perman, M. (1984). *The road to redemption: Southern politics, 1869–1879.* Chapel Hill: University of North Carolina Press.

Perman, M. (2001). *The struggle for mastery: Disfranchisement in the South, 1888–1908.* Chapel Hill: University of North Carolina Press.

Provasnik, S. (2006). Judicial activism and the origins of parental choice: The Court's role in the institutionalization of compulsory education in the United States, 1891–1925. *History of Education Quarterly, 46,* 311–347.

Reddick, S. (2000). The evolution of Chemawa Indian School: From Red River to Salem, 1825–1885. *Oregon Historical Quarterly, 101,* 444–465.

Richardson, J. G. (1999). *Common, delinquent, and special: The institutional shape of special education.* New York, NY: Falmer Press.

Richardson, J. G. (1994). Common, delinquent and special: On the formalization of common schooling in the United States. *American Educational Research Journal, 31,* 695–723.

Sabato, H. (2001). Political citizenship in nineteenth-century Latin America. *American Historical Review, 106,* 1290–1315.

Sniegoski, S. J. (1995). *John Eaton, U.S. Commissioner of Education, 1870–1886.* Washington, DC: Government Printing Office.

Span, C. M. (2009). *From cotton field to schoolhouse: African American education in Mississippi, 1862–1875.* Chapel Hill: University of North Carolina Press.

Steffes, T. L. (2012). *School, society, and state: A new education to govern modern America, 1890–1940.* Chicago, IL: University of Chicago Press.

Steineker, R. F. (2016). "Fully equal to that of any children": Experimental Creek education in the Antebellum Era. *History of Education Quarterly, 56,* 273–300.

Stratton, C. (2016). *Education for empire: American schools, race and the paths of good citizenship.* Oakland: University of California Press.

Thorpe, F. N. (1909). *The federal and state constitutions, colonial charters, and other organic laws of the states, territories, and colonies of the United States of America* (Vols. 1–7). Washington, DC: Government Printing Office.

Tyack, D., James, T., & Benavot, A. (1987). *Law and the shaping of public education, 1785–1954.* Madison: University of Wisconsin Press.

Urban, W. (2000). *Gender, race and the National Education Association: Professionalism and its limitations.* New York, NY: RoutledgeFalmer.

Urban, W. (2010). *More than science and Sputnik: The National Defense Education Act of 1958.* Tuscaloosa: University of Alabama.

Warren, D. (1974). *To enforce education: A history of the founding years of the United States Office of Education.* Detroit, MI: Wayne State University Press.

Warren, K. (2010). *The quest for citizenship: African American and Native American education in Kansas, 1880–1935.* Chapel Hill: University of North Carolina Press.

Wesley, E. B. (1957). *NEA: The first one hundred years: The building of the teaching profession.* New York, NY: Harper & Brothers.

West, E. (2003). Reconstructing race. *Western Historical Quarterly, 34*(1), 6–26.

Wickett, M. R. (2000). *Contested territory: Whites, Native Americans and African Americans in Oklahoma, 1865–1907.* Baton Rouge: Louisiana State University Press.

Williams, H. A. (2005). *Self-taught: African American education in slavery and freedom.* Chapel Hill: University of North Carolina Press.

Woodson, C. G. (1933). *The mis-education of the Negro.* New York, NY: Associated Publishers.

Chapter 2

Scholarly Communication in AERA Journals, 1931 to 2014

RAF VANDERSTRAETEN
Ghent University and University of Chicago

FRÉDÉRIC VANDERMOERE
University of Antwerp

MAARTEN HERMANS
University of Leuven

Scientific disciplines build on social structures, such as scholarly associations and scholarly journals, that facilitate the formation of communities of specialists. Analyses of such social structures can thus also be used to shed light on the morphogenesis of scientific specializations. The authors analyze how two journals of the American Educational Research Association, the Review of Educational Research *and the* American Educational Research Journal, *organized communication around education in the period between 1931 and 2014. The authors focus on three interrelated aspects: (a) the changing structures of authority and authorship, (b) the national-versus-global orientation of these journals and of the association, and (c) the features of the citation networks of both journals and the ties between education research and other fields of research, especially psychology and sociology. The authors' analyses of these interrelated aspects of the communication process enable them to provide an outline of the morphology of the community of education researchers and to raise reflectivity about the social conditions that control education research.*

The 19th- and 20th-century rise of disciplinary specializations within the field of science depended on two kinds of social structures. The level of structural support for scientific research increased markedly after the expansion and reformation of the university system, which was first realized in Germany (in the so-called

Review of Research in Education
March 2016, Vol. 40, pp. 38–61
DOI: 10.3102/0091732X16678836
© 2016 AERA. http://rre.aera.net

Bildungsuniversität) but quickly spread to other countries. New occupational roles in universities increased the time available for scientific research, and scholars became able to make careers in research. But the rise of scientific specializations also depended on the formation of specialized scientific communities—networks of individual specialists. Such communities built (and still build) on social structures that enable the intensification of interaction, the development of shared expertise, the articulation of conventionalized problems and approaches, and so on (see Abbott, 2001; Hoskin, 1993; Jacobs, 2013; Oleson & Voss, 1979; Turner, 1980).

Seen in this light, scholarly associations may play an important role in bringing communities of specialists together. The American Educational Research Association (AERA) is one example of a much broader development. Well before the establishment of AERA, several disciplinary associations had already been founded, such as the American Philological Association (1869), the American Chemical Association (1876), the American Psychological Association (1892), and the American Sociological Association (1905). Other national or global learned societies emerged in more recent years, such as the Society for the History of Technology (1958) and the American Society for Environmental History (1977). With varying success, these associations have enabled regular interaction among their specialists—for example, within the frame of annual conferences or committee meetings. Many of them have also published their own specialized journals, handbooks, and book series. Seen in this light, we may ask how AERA has been able to promote and organize scientific communication to enhance and ensure the continuity of specialized scholarly communication about education.

AERA was originally known as the National Association of Directors of Educational Research (NADER). Membership in NADER was highly restricted. Institutional position was the primary criterion; active membership was reserved for directors of education research units and their immediate assistants (who were working primarily in city public schools). In light of the growing public interest in research and education, this policy changed shortly after World War I, when the association opened active membership to anyone who displayed the ability to conduct "research investigations and experimentations." As Mershon and Schlossman (2008) point out in their review of AERA's early history, "The criterion for inclusion became demonstrated competence as a researcher—and the primary indicator of that competence was written work . . . that the members of the policy-making Executive Committee could assess" (p. 319). The more inclusive name Educational Research Association of America, which was adopted in 1922, reflected this shift in membership policy. Under its new name, the association asserted the claim to represent the interests of all U.S. education researchers. This claim did not change 6 years later, when the association again changed its name, becoming AERA.

In the course of its history, AERA has launched several major scholarly journals. With support from the National Education Association (NEA), AERA established the *Review of Educational Research* (*RER*) in 1930. *RER* was AERA's only journal during the Great Depression years and in the period during and after World War II.

But in the 1960s and 1970s, AERA expanded rapidly. In 1964, the *American Educational Research Journal* (*AERJ*) appeared. *Educational Researcher* (*ER*), emanating from AERA's member newsletter, was first published in 1972. One year later, the first volume of the annual *Review of Research in Education* (*RRE*) appeared, and two additional specialized journals came out in the latter half of the 1970s: the *Journal of Educational and Behavioral Statistics* (*JEBS*; formerly *Journal of Educational Statistics*), in 1976, and *Educational Evaluation and Policy Analysis* (*EEPA*), in 1979. Most recently, in 2015, AERA launched *AERA Open*, an open-access online journal. In short, AERA's journals have been facilitating communication in an expanding field of research for about one century (see Levine & Hill, 2015). Analyses of the forms and formats of the communication processes in these journals may hence allow us to discern some basic characteristics of the evolution of the field of education research.[1]

In more general terms, we think of scientific communities as precariously constructed and historically contingent networks of specialists. They depend on social contexts that support the development of particular interests. They may also cease to exist when the communication among the specialists is discontinued (see Fisher, 1966; Lenoir, 1997). Or stated differently, these networks depend on regular communication among their members. Publication venues, such as scholarly periodicals, channel this communication process. They do not just enable the formation of networks of specialists or sustain communication during the intervals between annual conferences or meetings, they also allow separating a small body of legitimate scholarly work from other, "unscientific" enterprises. These journals, taken as a whole, control and steer the communication process among specialists (e.g., Abbott, 1999; Bazerman, 1988; Gross, Harmon, & Reidy, 2002; Stichweh, 1991, 1994). Exactly because of their significance for this communication process, we may also use the history of these journals to shed light on the "morphogenesis" of their specializations or disciplines.[2]

In this chapter, our focus is on the changing forms and formats of communication in the AERA journals. To avoid overburdening the reader, we pay particular attention to AERA's oldest journals, *RER* and *AERJ*; however, it is worth noting that the data we gathered for the other AERA journals confirmed our analyses based on these two. Using historical–sociological analyses of *RER* and *AERJ* for the period 1931 to 2014, we focus on three aspects of the communication process in the field of education. First, we consider the shifting conventions and expectations regarding authorship and editorship, as well as changing forms of authority and inclusion in authorial roles. Second, we consider the changing position of the AERA journals in the scientific world. Although AERA is a national organization, its journals are highly visible at the global level. We pay particular attention to changing forms of openness toward "our foreign friends" (*AERJ*, 1973, p. 175). Third, we examine the citation networks of the AERA journals. These networks consist of ties to other journals in the field of education and to journals in other fields, especially psychology and sociology. Analyses of the structure of these networks allow us to shed light on the degree of interdisciplinarity among the AERA journals and in the field of education research overall. This in turn enables us to provide an outline of the morphology of the scientific community and to raise reflectivity about the social conditions that control education research.

The following analyses build on two types of material. On the one hand, we present a body of quantitative material on all the articles published in *RER* and *AERJ*. Because the coverage of the content of the older volumes of the AERA journals is often incomplete in the existing bibliographical databases, we composed our own data set, collected by examining each issue of the journals themselves. To calculate the citation networks of these journals, we relied on the "relatedness" data included in Web of Science.

On the other hand, we examined all editorial documents that appeared in AERA journals between 1931 and 2014. These documents frequently include reflections on the contemporary situation of education research in the United States; at times, they also offer thoughts on the history or the future of the field and/or its journals. We did not have access to the archives of the AERA journals, but we believe that the published editorial material from these journals will allow us to provide a thick description of the evolution of the forms and formats of scholarly communication in the field of education.

Participation in the community of American education researchers depends on a variety of often unarticulated rules and expectations. In this chapter, we try to show how the history of two of AERA's flagship journals sheds light on the ways in which communication among the members of this community has taken and takes place. It is therefore important to keep in mind that the forms and formats of communication affect the way research is conducted. In a kind of feedback loop, publications or publication possibilities exercise pressure on how research is imagined. We hope that our historical and sociological analyses of AERA's journals and of the field of education research will stimulate critical reflection on the directions in which education research and a number of adjacent academic specializations are currently developing.

EDITORS AND AUTHORS

In its first decades, *RER* was not what we would now call a "traditional" journal: It did not publish original research papers. Rather, it was conceived as a periodical reference work, regularly summarizing recent research on "the whole field" of education (*RER*, 1931, p. 2).[3] It was to appear five times per year, with each issue devoted to a specific topic. The editors presented a cycle of 15 topics to be addressed over a 3-year period; these topics related largely to contemporary challenges of schooling and school administration. *RER*'s first volumes dealt with topics such as the curriculum, teacher personnel, school organization, finance and business administration, tests of personality and character, tests of intelligence and aptitude, and school buildings, grounds, equipment, apparatus, and supplies. The last topic of the first cycle was "methods and technics of educational research."

For almost four decades, *RER* stayed close to its ambition to treat "the whole field" by means of a cyclical coverage of all important topics in education. Curriculum, for example, was the topic of the first and 12 subsequent issues that appeared every 3 to 5 years until 1970 (see also *RER*, 1999, pp. 347–363). But *RER*'s topic cycle also changed over time—especially in response to the expansion and diversification of research interests in the field. Over the years, more emphasis was also put on research methods to help education researchers cope with a proliferation of quantitative and qualitative techniques (e.g., *RER*, 1939, p. 451; *RER*, 1956, pp. 323–343).

It is clear that *RER*'s original aim was to disseminate the results of scientific research to a broader audience: "to review earlier studies" and "to summarize the literature" for an audience of "teachers, administrators, and general students of education" (*RER*, 1931, p. 2). This editorial strategy was characterized by a hierarchical structure. An issue editor and a committee of experts were assigned for each issue to solicit and review all manuscripts, and often to author several review articles themselves. Authority and authorship were thus closely connected: Issue editors and authors were chosen because of their authority on the topics, but inclusion in *RER* also granted the issue editors and authors considerable authority. Interestingly, some authorship problems appeared. Authorship was not easily extended to a group of specialists. Several authors of *RER* articles were aided by "assistants." Sometimes authors published "in cooperation with" others—but those other contributors were not identified as full coauthors. In 1935 and 1936, moreover, errata had to be published to add coauthors to reviews that had appeared in print in previous issues. While this illustrates that the attribution of authorship could be contested (no other errata appeared in the early volumes), *RER* did, in the first decades of its existence, entrust only a few scholars with reviewing the relevant research. Or stated somewhat differently, *RER* entrusted and *authorized* only a few scholars to summarize and review what was considered to be the relevant research and hence to speak to the broader community of people interested in education and the results of education research.

Already, from the 1930s onward, questions and tensions emerged regarding the proper readership of *RER*. In 1938 and 1939, for example, the editorial board adopted five new topics to be covered in 3-year cycles. In an editorial foreword, it was underlined that the new organization would give due attention to instructional areas and therefore be of benefit to practitioners in schools rather than to researchers in universities: "The new subject matter issues do not fall so readily into the accustomed areas of specialization of university research workers," the editors wrote (*RER*, 1940, p. 75). As no scholars specialized in such instructional areas, these journal issues would be "much more difficult to prepare." But, the editors added, "It is hoped that they will render a larger service to a greater number of users and thus justify the increased effort that they call for" (p. 75). In the following decades, however, AERA increasingly oriented itself to the growing community of education researchers instead of to practitioners.

Beginning in 1970, *RER* adopted a different editorial policy in which each issue was expected to include unsolicited reviews on topics of the authors' choice. The incoming editor, Gene V. Glass, stated "the new editorial policy" as follows:

The purpose of the *Review* has always been the publication of critical, integrative reviews of published education research. *In the opinion of the Editorial Board, this goal can now best be achieved by pursuing a policy of publishing unsolicited reviews of research on topics of the contributor's choosing.* . . . The reorganization of the *Review of Educational Research* is an acknowledgment of a need for an outlet for reviews of research that are initiated by individual researchers and shaped by the rapidly evolving interests of these scholars. (*RER*, 1970, p. 323)

The last issue that reflected the old editorial policy appeared in 1971.[4]

At that time, the landscape of scholarly publishing in the field of education had already changed. In 1964, AERA began publishing *AERJ*, with a mission to publish "original reports of experimental and theoretical studies in education." In the rapidly expanding field of scientific journals, *AERJ* was a "traditional" journal that put emphasis on the presentation of novel findings. Its establishment was an indication of the fact that AERA aspired to a more active, innovative role at the level of scholarly communication about education (see *AERJ*, 1966, pp. 211–221; *AERJ*, 1968, pp. 687–700). In 1967, AERA also became an autonomous organization of scholars and researchers, independent of NEA. In the same period of time, moreover, the *RER* editors put forward different expectations regarding the content and orientation of its articles. *RER* shifted its emphasis from summaries or reviews to critical evaluations; it now explicitly required its authors to provide an overview of the strengths and short-comings of the existing knowledge base. Articles now had to advance research on the topics they discussed. Glass wrote, "It is hoped that the new editorial policy of the *Review*, with its implicit invitation to all scholars, will contribute to the improvement and growth of disciplined inquiry on education" (*RER*, 1970, p. 324). No doubt, these new expectations corresponded with changes in the composition of AERA's membership and *RER*'s readership base. In the 1960s and 1970s, this community was no longer a small world with a few leading scholars, who were in a position to survey the relevant research and disseminate its results to a broader audience of interested laypeople. In light of the professionalization of research, *RER*, rather, had to attract the attention of other researchers. Its readership came to consist mainly of specialists, who did not need a popularizing review to learn about developments in their field of research. The *raison d'être* of *RER*—as well as of *AERJ* and the other AERA journals that were established in the 1970s (i.e., *ER, RRE, JEBS,* and *EEPA*)—lay in the presentation of findings that were relevant primarily to the community of researchers. Seen in this light, the new editorial policy expressed by *RER* disqualified most of the journal's own early educational publications as either unoriginal or not properly scientific.

In the same editorial, Glass also indicated that "the role played by the *Review* in the past [would] be assumed by an *Annual Review of Research in Education*, which AERA [was] planning" (*RER*, 1970, p. 323). The first volume of the *RRE* appeared only 3 years later. *RRE* solicited reviews in particular research areas. In this regard, the "Statement From the Editor" accompanying the first issue of the *RRE* was reminiscent of the old editorial policy of *RER*: "The more important areas will appear periodically but not necessarily regularly. Some areas, relatively dormant or unproductive, may not appear for years" (*RRE*, 1973, p. vii; see also *ER*, 1976, No. 11, p. 10). However, the *RRE* editor also took pains to underline that the new venue would orient itself toward a community of scholars, who would read it to inform themselves about ongoing education research. "Summaries of research studies are valuable and appropriate, but too much summary distracts from criticism and perspective" (*RRE*, 1973, p. vii). And he added, "Many conceive of reviewing as the summarizing of research studies and trends in order to inform readers and keep them abreast of their fields. Such an annotated bibliographic approach can have little impact, however" (*RRE*, 1973, p. vii).

It is clear that *RRE*, like the other AERA journals in that period of rapid expansion of the field, was prompted to reflect on the impact it could have on the work of education researchers. Also illustrative in this regard is the first issue of *AERJ*, which published a critical review by Benjamin Bloom on what had been accomplished in education research during the past quarter of a century:

Approximately 70,000 studies were listed in the *Review of Educational Research* over the past 25 years. Of these 70,000 studies, I regard about 70 as being crucial for all that follows. That is, about 1 out of 1,000 reported studies seem to me to be crucial and significant, approximately 3 studies per year. (*AERJ*, 1964, p. 218)[5]

While the forms and formats of communication changed, the overall publication output certainly did not decrease during this period. The expression "publish or perish," which became more widely used in the 1960s and 1970s, signaled the institutionalization of a "communication imperative" in science. Publications were now increasingly perceived as indices of full membership in the scientific community (see De Solla Price, 1963).

Against this background, it is interesting to point to a concomitant development at the level of the authorial roles. Figure 1 displays the evolution of the number of authors or coauthors per published article in *RER* and *AERJ*. It is clear that single-authored articles were the norm for a relatively long time. In 1931, all but two *RER* articles were single-authored (although "assistants" contributed to four of these articles). Forty years later, the majority of the articles in *RER* were still written by single authors. But the expectations and conventions quickly changed after that. In the case of *RER*, which adopted a new editorial policy in the 1970s, the average number of authors per article increased from 1.05 in 1931 to 1.21 in 1970 and 3.28 in 2014 (with a standard deviation of 1.45). In the case of *AERJ*, there was a relatively steady increase in the number of coauthored articles; the average changed from 1.42 in 1965 to 2.30 in 1990 and 3.22 in 2014 (with a standard deviation of 2.12). In 2014, only about one in six *RER* or *AERJ* articles was single-authored. Coauthored, if not multiple-authored, publications have now become the norm. For sure, research-intrinsic developments influenced this evolution—as empirical research is often carried out in teams. But the new communication formats also allow more researchers to participate in scholarly communication in education journals. This change may thus also be seen as a corollary of the expansion of the community of education researchers.

FIGURE 1
Yearly Average Number of Authors Per Article, 1931 to 2014

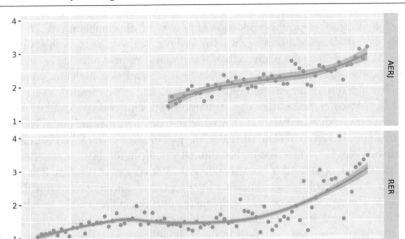

Not unimportantly, new forms of peer review (blind and double-blind) were introduced during this period. In a peer-review system, acceptance for publication in journals is to be governed by authors' scholarship, that is, manuscripts are to be evaluated impartially by referees—other scholars or peers—as acceptable for publication. Blind review was expected to replace the former system of invited submissions. In a number of fields, the introduction of the double-blind peer-review system has gone along with standardization (see Bazerman, 1988; Gross et al., 2002). Such standardization can also be observed in *RER* and *AERJ* in the 1970s. Shortly before the introduction of *RER*'s new editorial policy, for example, broad editorial guidelines were formulated: "There are no restrictions on the size of the manuscripts nor on the topics reviewed" (e.g., *RER*, 1969, inside cover). One decade later, much more detailed instructions were common in all AERA journals. Potential authors were referred to the publication manual of the American Psychological Association, which included detailed guidelines on manuscript structure and content, writing styles, and so forth. Manuscripts also needed to be accompanied by an abstract of 100 to 150 words. Page limitations were introduced. To enable blind review, the list of authors had to be typed on a separate sheet (e.g., *RER*, 1980, p. 201; *AERJ*, 1980, pp. 1, 125). As more emphasis was placed on individual scholarship, the community of education researchers increasingly defined and regulated the forms and formats of the communications or contributions that could be made.

No doubt, the new system required socialization processes on the part of editors, reviewers, and authors. In a somewhat unconventional "Message From the Editors," written shortly after the introduction of the peer-review system, the *AERJ* editors stressed the decisive role of the assessments of the various reviewers and tried to respond to "some irate colleagues" (*AERJ*, 1973, p. 176). The editors of the AERA journals, they stated, do "*not* meet or work as a group, even though all are doing what they can to contribute to the production of fine, worthwhile publications. They certainly do *not* 'conspire' for or against any authors, subjects, or types of study" (p. 176). Moreover, "frequent phone calls or letters to the editorial office do *not* facilitate the review process. Once a manuscript has been sent out to consultants, editors do not have any further information until the reviews and recommendations are back" (p. 176). Moreover, "the editors are *not* monsters with sinister motives, out to get this author or insult that scholar . . . [They make mistakes but] they are not so bad as to justify unbridled invectives and tirades on the part of some of our fellow educational researchers" (p. 177). As is clear in this editorial statement, the distribution of authority had to be renegotiated in the expanding field of education research. The "gatekeepers" had difficulty communicating the norms and conventions of this field of research. The development of the discipline required discipline of all its members.[6]

Such historical developments are not unique to the field of education research. Similar trends have been observed in other disciplinary specializations and other scientific communities. In fields such as physics, biology, mathematics, and information sciences, scholarly articles written by only one author have become highly exceptional. At the same time, it can be argued that these trends are quite pronounced in the field of education research (see Vanderstraeten, 2011). Building on Michel Foucault (1995), we might even speak of the "disappearance" and "effacement" of the author. It has become increasingly difficult to identify the "real" author or originator of a particular publication. As a consequence of the institutionalization of a broad range of norms and conventions that bear on publications, the "subjectivity" of the author tends to get lost in the process of scholarly communication.[7] Perhaps it is one of the contradictions of postmodern society that publication in scholarly journals has become *more* important for purposes of evaluating individual researchers and research groups.

NATIONAL AND GLOBAL AUDIENCES

Another central aspect of the development of scholarly journals and associations is their position in the social and scientific worlds. Although AERA was founded as a national organization, it has become a leader at the global level. It counts more than 25,000 members, with a good number outside the United States. Its journals are highly visible at the global level, if one takes, for example, the Thomson Reuters Web of Science impact factor as a proxy of global visibility.[8] In the 2014 index, *RER* ranked first in the Education and Educational Research category, which consisted of 224 peer-reviewed journals from around the world. The other AERA journals also ended up relatively high in this index: *ER* was ranked 9th; *AERJ*, *RRE*, *EEPA*, and *JEBS* were 13th, 22nd, 25th, and 50th, respectively. In this section, we present analyses of the ways that "the rest of the world" has been represented in AERA's two

FIGURE 2
Yearly Proportion of Authors With Non-U.S. Affiliations, 1931 to 2014

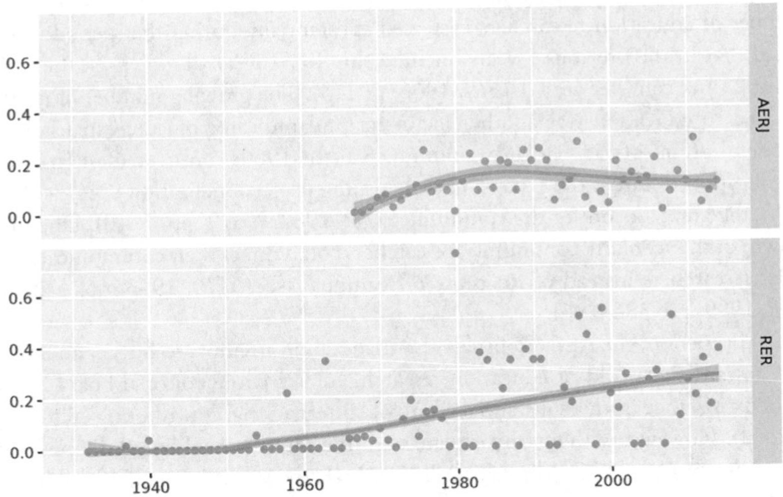

flagship journals in the course of the last century. We also point to the core position of American associations and journals, such as AERA and its journals, in the contemporary world of science.

Figure 2 presents a historical overview from 1931 to 2014 of the geographical locations of the researchers who actively contributed to scholarly communication in *RER* and *AERJ*. This figure displays, more particularly, data on the institutional affiliations of the first authors of all the articles published in these journals through 2014. For *RER*, the data again clearly show the difference between the old and new editorial policies. The first contribution *not* written by a U.S. author appeared in 1934, in the first issue devoted to the topic of "history of education and comparative education." In 1939, the next issue devoted to that topic included two contributions not written by U.S. authors. In 1957 and 1962, *RER* published two other issues on "education in countries other than the USA," in which its editors invited a relatively large number of "foreigners" to comment on the state of, and the main challenges for, the educational systems in their home countries. As long as the editors solicited chapters from individual authors, however, they largely relied on scholars from the United States. They invited non-U.S. scholars to write only on topics on which their authority was undisputed. As shown by the AERA membership lists published yearly in *RER*, the association and its journal were long directed primarily to people working in the U.S. context (see also *RER*, 1956, p. 208).

But the field of education research was a clear beneficiary of the expansion of the American system of higher education in the 1950s and 1960s. Benjamin Bloom, in his presidential address presented at the AERA Annual Meeting in 1966, provided a short overview of this rapid expansion. "From the level of support of 1960," Bloom estimated, the growth in federal funding of education research and development had been "of the order of 2,000 per cent" (*AERJ*, 1966, p. 211). In the United States, the number of education researchers increased substantially during that period; Bloom noted that in the previous 5 years, membership in AERA had grown "at the rate of about 25 per cent per year" (*AERJ*, 1966, p. 213). The growing number of journals devoted to education was another factor in (and indicator of) the expansion and "academization" of the scholarly community. If the 1960s constituted a Renaissance in education research, the expansion and ensuing professionalization of research also drove the amateurs out of the community (*ER*, 1982, No. 9, pp. 7, 10). Due to the growth of the scholarly community, researchers could direct their communications to other researchers instead of to "those off campus" (see *AERJ*, 1973, pp. 173–177; *RER*, 1999, pp. 384–396).

In this period, the AERA journals also made some attempts to further an orientation toward the world of education research. In 1964, the editorial board of *RER* invited assistance from a substantial group of "international contributing editors" (27 in total). However, without any explanation, the international board disappeared 5 years later (under Glass's editorship). In 1973, the new editors of *AERJ* published a message to specify their aims or missions: "These missions may be somewhat novel to the *AERJ* and our efforts may cause a little confusion in some quarters" (*AERJ*, 1973, p. 173). They listed three aims: covering the entire field of education research, introducing peer review for all submitted articles, and broadening the perspective "from the United States to the whole world," thus diminishing the "provincialism" of American education researchers (p. 175). The last aim was also expressed in more general terms by the *AERJ* editors:

We feel the urgent need to open our vista to what the rest of the world has to teach us. . . . Sooner or later, we hope that the AERA will recognize the necessity of such a broadened perspective and spearhead an effort for establishment of something like a World Congress of Educational Research. (*AERJ*, 1973, p. 175)

The data presented in Figure 2 make clear that the globalization of the AERA journals took off during this period. The geographical location of the authors widened.[9] In the case of *AERJ*, the share of articles written by "our foreign friends" increased from 2.0% in 1968 to 10.7% in 2013. In the case of *RER*, this share increased from 2.8% in 1968 to 37.0% in 2013. As Figure 2 shows, however, the fluctuations from year to year and the variations between the journals were relatively large, indicating the instability of the underlying trend. (It should not come as a surprise that globalization of authorship was more pronounced in the case of *RER*, which did not have a national index and attempted to cover the entire field of education research. *AERJ*, by contrast, explicitly presented itself as an American journal.)

From the late 1970s onward, one finds echoes of these broader aims. A new journal, *Issues in Education*, which was sponsored by members of Divisions A (Administration), F (History and Historiography), and G (Social Context of

Education), and which had the explicit aim of broadening the publication program of AERA, was published in 1983. However, only three volumes of the journal appeared. Confronted with the consequences of the economic and fiscal crisis of the 1970s, AERA choose not to sponsor *Issues* as a separate association journal.[10] Instead, the association decided to create two sections within *AERJ*, one focusing on "Studies of Teaching and Learning" and one focusing on "Social and Institutional Analysis of Education." The second section was presented as the successor of *Issues*. In the first introduction to the Social and Institutional Analysis of Education section, the editor presented a quite pessimistic historical summary. Looking back at what had been published in *AERJ* in the 1970s and 1980s, he concluded that "the contents of *AERJ* . . . seem, on the whole, similar to what was published before the attempt to change the journal [in 1973]" (*AERJ*, 1990, p. 4). A few exceptions were granted—but just as a relatively narrow thematic orientation was said to prevail (one on work that "conformed to the dictates of psychological science"), it was stated that "the international emphasis . . . [has] gradually faded from the pages of *AERJ*" (pp. 2, 4). As Figure 2 shows, however, the proportion of authors with non-U.S. affiliations increased gradually through the late 1980s. Perhaps the pessimistic historical summary had to support the case of the new *AERJ* section.[11]

But what currently motivates non-U.S. scholars to contribute to the journals and meetings of the AERA? Why do AERA and its journals no longer have to invest much effort to be attractive to educational specialists from "the rest of the world"? Although we cannot present data about the participation of American education researchers in non-American associations and journals, it is clear that the globalization of the field of education research has taken place in uneven and asymmetrical ways. The core position of several AERA journals within the world of education research is supported by the instruments that are used to measure "impact" or visibility within scientific communication processes. In quite a number of other countries, the journal rankings and impact factors of Web of Science have become important elements in evaluation assessments. That policy orientation prompts researchers from those countries to submit their work to top-ranked journals, such as *RER, AERJ*, and some other AERA journals. Seen in this light, the American education research arena has, in recent decades, become more globalized because of changing norms and structural pressures in other parts of the scholarly world.

We may conclude that, over the past few decades, AERA has become both a national and a global association of education research specialists. Like few other national associations of scholars specialized in education, it is able to regulate communication in national and global networks. Not many other national associations or journals of education attract participants or potential authors from so many parts of the world. Paradoxically, the increase in contributions by non-U.S. scholars is an indication of U.S. dominance in the world of education research. In the current World of Science, the rankings and impact factors have put AERA and its journals, when taken together, in a central and dominant position.

Globalization has taken other forms, too. For example, professional associations and journals with a regional focus have expanded rapidly in recent years—among them several European associations and journals (e.g., the *European Journal of Education*, the *European Journal of Teacher Education*, and *Higher Education in Europe*). Interestingly, however, AERA's format has been imitated in Europe. To enhance communication among European scholars, the European Educational Research Association was founded in 1994; its main journal, the *European Educational Research Journal*, was first published in 2002. Such isomorphic processes are another clear indication of AERA's leading position and that of its journals in the contemporary world of education research.[12] Current forms of globalization go hand-in-hand with increased stratification among journals and other media in scientific communication.

CITATION NETWORKS

In the preceding sections, we have looked at changing forms of authority and changing structures in the world of educational science.[13] In this section, we pay further attention to how *RER* and *AERJ* position themselves within the worldwide Web of Science. We complement the foregoing historical analyses with analyses of the relevant citation environment of these two AERA journals. As we have seen, *RER* originally aimed at disseminating research findings to an American audience of educational practitioners and policymakers (see *RER*, 1931, p. 2). But the expansion of the system of higher education in general, and of the field of education research in particular, has changed the forms and structures of communication in the field. Scholarly publications have become embedded within networks of related scholarly publications. All published work is expected to interact with preceding work, by incorporating arguments developed in other publications; at the same time, however, new publications are expected to lay claim to new knowledge, to invite responses, and thereby advance research. Interestingly, some of the changed expectations were already discussed in an early reflective *AERJ* article, which looked critically at the first *AERJ* issues:

As an instrument of communication, a journal is a *receiver* of information to the extent that its articles cite articles published in other journals; it is a source of information to the extent that its articles are cited as bibliographical references in other journals. Assuming that a journal should serve more than an archival function, the latter is the more important index of a journal's impact. (*AERJ*, 1968, p. 694)

There are a number of ways to sketch the networks within which the AERA journals participate. To provide some context, Figure 3 first looks at some network characteristics of all journals in the fields of education, psychology, and sociology that are included in Web of Science. More particularly, Figure 3 visually represents the relation between the density of their networks and the total number of journals in their one-step neighborhoods from 2003 to 2013. A network's density is the

FIGURE 3
Average Citation Neighborhood Density and Size of Education, Sociology, and Psychology Journals, 2003 to 2013

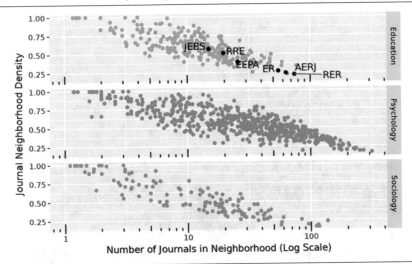

number of ties in the network, expressed as a proportion of the number possible. Not surprisingly, network density is highly correlated with the absolute number of journals in the network: Densities are lower in large networks than in small ones. The number of ties that a journal has to others does not keep pace with the number of other journals available. In this regard, the divergences between the disciplinary specializations represented in Figure 3 are small. To identify the AERA journals, we used black dots.[14] In comparison with other journals, both *RER* and *AERJ* are well connected with other Web of Science journals in terms of their absolute number of ties, while their network density is not particularly distinctive. In comparison with other education journals, they have a very large number of journals in their one-step neighborhood. Their position vis-à-vis other journals might be seen to reflect their generalist nature: Both journals succeed in bringing a wide variety of research to the fore. (It should not come as a surprise that specialist journals, such as *JEBS* and *EEPA*, have fewer peers. *RRE* can also be seen as a specialist journal, as each annual issue is devoted to a particular theme.)

In addition, Figures 4 and 5 portray the citation environments of *RER* and *AERJ*. These networks are based on the relatedness data from the Social Sciences Edition of the Journal Citation Reports (JCR, which is part of the Thomson Reuters Web of Science). Compared with density, the relatedness factor allows for more detailed analyses of citation networks. Relatedness data are calculated by means of an algorithm proposed by Pudovkin and Garfield (2002). They express the relationship (R) between two journals (x and y) as follows:

FIGURE 4
Journal Citation Environment of the *Review of Educational Research*, 2003 to 2013

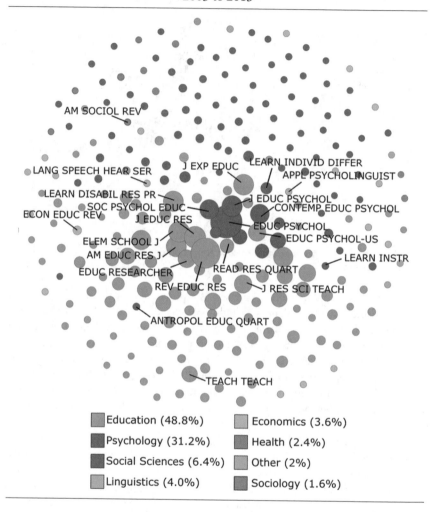

Education (48.8%)   Economics (3.6%)
Psychology (31.2%)   Health (2.4%)
Social Sciences (6.4%)   Other (2%)
Linguistics (4.0%)   Sociology (1.6%)

$$R_{(x>y)} = C_{(x>y)} * 10^6 / (P_y * Rf_x),$$

where $C_{x>y}$ refers to the number of citations from the citing journal x to the cited journal y, P_y refers to the total number of papers published in journal y, and Rf_x refers to the number of references cited in journal x. We collected the relatedness scores for *RER* and *AERJ*, as well as the relatedness scores for all the other journals in their respective environments. We also collected these data in two directions: We

FIGURE 5
Journal Citation Environment of the *American Educational Research Journal*, 2003 to 2013

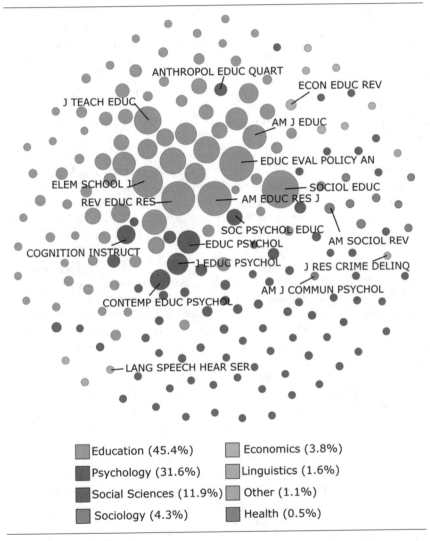

Education (45.4%) Economics (3.8%)

Psychology (31.6%) Linguistics (1.6%)

Social Sciences (11.9%) Other (1.1%)

Sociology (4.3%) Health (0.5%)

worked with cited data (i.e., in-degrees or citations) and citing data (i.e., out-degrees or references). In addition, to take random fluctuations into account, we calculated the average relatedness scores for the entire period for which the JCR data are currently available, that is, the period 2003 to 2013. Based on previous experience, we feel safe in arguing that this method allows for a detailed sketch of the relevant citation networks of *RER* and *AERJ* (Vandermoere & Vanderstraeten, 2012; Vanderstraeten & Vandermoere, 2015).[15] In Figures 4 and 5, for purposes of clarity in a limited space, we use the Web of Science abbreviations of journal titles.

As can be seen in the results presented in Figures 3 to 5, the AERA journals are connected with a broad range of other Web of Science journals. We might add, moreover, that both *AERJ* and *RER* systematically have larger incoming scores (at the citation level) than outgoing scores (at the reference level). Specifically, in 82% of the cases for *AERJ* and in 93% of the cases for *RER*, the in-degree is larger than the out-degree. Stated differently, *RER* and *AERJ* are more frequently cited in the other journals than the other journals are cited in *RER* and *AERJ*. This confirms the prestigious and central positions that the two journals occupy in the field of education research, to which we referred earlier.

To bring some order into these chaotic network structures, we have grouped the journals in categories. For each of the journals linked to *AERJ* and *RER*, we more particularly looked at their JCR subject categories (see the appendix). By using these categories, we obtained an overview of the broader, disciplinary and interdisciplinary environments of both core journals (see Silva, Rodrigues, Oliveira, & Costa, 2013). *AERJ* and *RER* are linked to 31 and 36 subject categories, respectively. To some degree, the colors used in Figures 4 and 5 reflect this diversity.[16] Not surprisingly, other journals in the subject category "Education and Educational Research" are highly interrelated with both *RER* and *AERJ*. But the two AERA journals are also strongly linked with journals in the categories "Educational Psychology" and "Developmental Psychology." Other psychological subcategories include "Experimental Psychology," "Social Psychology," and "Applied Psychology." After psychology, *AERJ* and *RER* are linked mainly with journals in sociology, followed by journals in economics and linguistics. Other common subject categories are "Special Education," "Rehabilitation," and "Family Studies." Overall, the categorized data presented in the appendix confirm the network data in Figures 4 and 5. The citation networks of *AERJ* and *RER* are broad and far reaching. They include journals not only in the adjacent disciplines and subdisciplines but also in other interdisciplinary categories, such as "Social Issues," "Urban Studies," and "Interdisciplinary Social Sciences." Viewing the field in this light, we can concur with a recent observation by the sociologist Jerry Jacobs: "The field of education should be absolved from the charge of intellectual remoteness" (Jacobs, 2013, p. 119; see also Graff, 2015).

The interdisciplinary communication networks in which both *RER* and *AERJ* are situated comprise two pairs of major subdisciplinary specializations: (a) psychology and educational psychology and (b) sociology and sociology of education. But in their relationships with these other specializations, *AERJ* and *RER* distinguish themselves from one another: While the input of studies in sociology seems to be stronger in the case of *AERJ*, the input of studies in psychology is stronger in the case of *RER*. The same holds true, but to a lesser extent, at the level of the subdisciplines. Although educational psychology and sociology of education are strongly connected to both *AERJ* and *RER*, the sociological specialization in education connects more strongly with *AERJ*, and the psychological specialization connects more strongly with *RER*. In the AERA journals, the dependence of education research and AERA on psychology and statistical methodology has been criticized on more than one occasion (e.g., *RER*, 1956, pp. 205–209; *AERJ*, 1966, pp. 223–229; *AERJ*, 1974, pp. 41–49; *AERJ*, 1990, pp. 1–8; *RER*, 1999, pp. 384–396; *RER*, 1999, pp. 397–405). As mentioned before, in 1990 *AERJ* was split into two sections—"Social and Institutional Analysis" and "Teaching, Learning, and Human Development"—in order to complement the journal's traditional focus on teachers and students. Our analyses suggest that *AERJ* strengthened the interdisciplinary orientation of the community of education researchers. But the question remains whether the "newly integrated *AERJ*" will be able to give ample attention to the social and historical aspects of education.

In the labyrinth of journals, one can also detect other differences. Journals in the field of educational psychology clearly outnumber those focusing on educational sociology or the sociology of education. Accordingly, a separate subject category, "Educational Psychology," has been added to the JCR of Web of Science. No such category exists for Sociology of Education. The few journals that explicitly mention this orientation in their titles (such as *Sociology of Education*) most strongly connect with generalist education research journals (such as *AERJ*) or generalist sociology journals (such as the *American Sociological Review*). In contrast, journals in the field of educational psychology (such as *Educational Psychologist*) most strongly connect with *RER* or with other journals specializing in educational psychology (e.g., *Contemporary Educational Psychology*, *Journal of Educational Psychology*, *Educational Psychology Review*). Thus, there seems to be a difference in the extent to which educational psychologists and educational sociologists relate to their respective specializations and disciplines. Not coincidentally, the label "educational sociology" is much less used than "sociology of education." Educational psychologists, it seems, now identify first of all with scholars who share an interest in educational psychology. Educational sociologists, on the other hand, might identify first and foremost with the discipline of sociology.

Over the years, education researchers have often reinterpreted psychological and sociological paradigms in terms amenable to their own research interests. From a sociological point of view, it might be added that the importance that education researchers attach to psychology (and, to a lesser extent, sociology) is linked to their position in an academic setting where psychology (and sociology) is often perceived to be the more prestigious disciplines. The low level of connection with journals in other fields of study, such as history and philosophy, not only reflects some biases of the JCR of Web of Science but, in our view, is also a result of the declining reputation of those fields of study within science overall.

With the growth of the scientific community, more specialized subdisciplinary affiliations also acquired greater weight. In the second half of the 1970s, at the end of a period of rapid expansion, AERA established more specialized journals such as *JEBS* and *EEPA*, hence contributing to trends toward increasing differentiation. It seems fair to say, however, that affiliations at the disciplinary level have not disappeared. Journals such as *RER* and *AERJ* publish research that is, in principle, directed toward the whole community of education researchers. Through the editorial policies of its generalist journals, AERA provides and upholds an orientation that is both more general than the subdisciplinary specializations and more specific than much of the research that is borrowed from other disciplines, such as psychology and sociology. In such policies, the association may, moreover, bring other considerations to bear, such as practical relevance for teachers, school administrators, or decision makers. Intangibles, such as the nature or identity of the discipline, are conditioned by these complex networks.

CONCLUSION

Many specialized scientific communities emerged and expanded in the course of the 19th and 20th centuries. Important opportunity structures for such collective efforts were provided by the expanding universities, which offered a widening range of career possibilities. Specialized journals also became the main vehicle for the scholarly claims of research specialists. They became media of scholarly publication par excellence. In addition, the scientometric instruments that have been developed in recent decades have strengthened the relevance of journals in ongoing scientific communication processes. The web of science, as it is now commonly depicted, consists mainly of publications in scholarly journals.

Education research was a clear beneficiary of the rapid postwar expansion of the university system, especially in the United States. The growth of the number of scholars interested in education has been reflected in the growth of the number of specialized journals. During the second half of the 20th century, there have emerged a substantial number of other cognate scholarly journals and learned societies. On the foregoing pages, we have also seen that the more decentralized communication structures, which AERA adopted in the postwar decades, allowed for the active participation of a larger community of specialists. At the same time, however, the journals developed regulatory norms and mechanisms, which disciplined the members of the entire scholarly community (see also *RER*, 1999, p. 399). The figures presented on the foregoing pages indicate how the AERA journals *RER* and *AERJ* organized communication around education in the period between 1931 and 2014. In particular, we have focused on some interrelated aspects: the structures of authority and authorship, the national versus global orientation of these journals, and the features of their citation networks. While there are differences in scale between *RER* and *AERJ*, the evolutions that we were able to discern in the forms and formats of communication are consistent for both journals. The longitudinal data that we gathered for all other AERA journals point in the same directions.

In the course of the past two centuries, scientific publication has become an imperative, interfering in every research process. During the last few decades, researchers have also become subject to structural pressures that call for regular or frequent publications. The institutionalization of the publication imperative ("publish or perish") even discredits research that has not yet led to this kind of scholarly output. As long as no results are published, it is even difficult—both institutionally and psychologically—to close particular research projects. Researchers gain the freedom to do something else, to move to new research projects, only after they have been able to communicate the results of previous commitments to their peers by means of publications. Seen from this perspective, the changing forms and formats of scholarly communication in the AERA journals also shed light on the evolution of the expectations regarding how education research is to be conducted.

APPENDIX

To offer a better overview of the citation environments of *RER* and *AERJ*, these tables present the JCR subject categories in which the journals linked to *RER* and *AERJ* are grouped by Web of Science. The tables include the number of journals in each subject category and the relative weight (in a percentage) of each subject category in the citation environment of *RER* and *AERJ*.

Journals Linked to *RER:* Web of Science Subject Categories for 2014

JCR Subject Category	Number of Journals	Percentage
Education & Educational Research	107	30.57
Psychology, Educational	40	11.43
Psychology, Developmental	24	6.86
Education, Special	18	5.14
Psychology, Experimental	17	4.86
Psychology, Multidisciplinary	16	4.57
Linguistics	12	3.43
Rehabilitation	13	3.71
Psychology, Applied	11	3.14
Psychology, Social	9	2.57
Social Sciences, Interdisciplinary	9	2.57
Sociology	9	2.57
Management	8	2.29
Economics	6	1.71
Family Studies	5	1.43
Psychology, Clinical	5	1.43
Psychology, Mathematical	5	1.43
Public, Environmental & Occupational Health	5	1.43
Information Science & Library Science	4	1.14
Social Work	4	1.14
Ergonomics	2	0.57
Ethnic Studies	2	0.57

(continued)

APPENDIX (CONTINUED)

JCR Subject Category	Number of Journals	Percentage
Hospitality, Leisure, Sport & Tourism	2	0.57
Nursing	2	0.57
Social Issues	2	0.57
Social Sciences, Mathematical Methods	2	0.57
Urban Studies	2	0.57
Business	1	0.29
Communication	1	0.29
Health Policy & Services	1	0.29
Industrial Relations & Labor	1	0.29
Law	1	0.29
Psychiatry	1	0.29
Public Administration	1	0.29
Women's Studies	1	0.29
Anthropology	1	0.29
Total	350	100.00

Journals Linked to *AERJ*: Web of Science Subject Categories for 2014

JCR Subject Category	Number of Journals	Percentage
Education & Educational Research	78	30.47
Psychology, Educational	35	13.67
Psychology, Developmental	20	7.81
Sociology	13	5.08
Psychology, Multidisciplinary	12	4.69
Psychology, Experimental	8	3.13
Psychology, Social	8	3.13
Social Sciences, Interdisciplinary	8	3.13
Economics	7	2.73
Education, Special	7	2.73
Psychology, Applied	7	2.73
Rehabilitation	7	2.73
Family Studies	6	2.34
Linguistics	6	2.34
Psychology, Mathematical	5	1.95
Social Sciences, Mathematical Methods	4	1.56
Ethnic Studies	3	1.17
Urban Studies	3	1.17
Criminology & Penology	2	0.78
Demography	2	0.78

(continued)

APPENDIX (CONTINUED)

JCR Subject Category	Number of Journals	Percentage
Political Science	2	0.78
Public Administration	2	0.78
Social Issues	2	0.78
Social Work	2	0.78
Health Policy & Services	1	0.39
Industrial Relations & Labor	1	0.39
Management	1	0.39
Psychiatry	1	0.39
Psychology, Clinical	1	0.39
Public, Environmental & Occupational Health	1	0.39
Women's Studies	1	0.39
Total	256	100.00

NOTES

[1]AERA also invested in other types of publications (see *ER*, 1976, No. 11, pp. 9–13). It sponsored the *Encyclopedia of Educational Research*, which first appeared in 1941, and collaborated with Phi Delta Kappa to publish a dictionary of educational terms (the first edition appeared in 1945). In more recent years, AERA has sponsored book series and book publications on a more systematic basis, as listed on the AERA website under Publications. Here, we deal only with the AERA journals. Because we use these journals as source materials, we cite them by referring to the journal, publication year, and page numbers.

[2]The National Society for the Study of Education (NSSE; originally the National Society for the Scientific Study of Education) is commonly perceived to be the oldest association devoted to education research in the United States; its first yearbook appeared in 1902 (Tyack & Hansot, 1982). But the NSSE was dissolved in 2008, shortly after it had celebrated its centenary. In our reading, some of the persistent crises in the NSSE resulted from the fact that it was unable to develop the tools (such as periodicals) to bring a community of specialists together on a regular and continuous basis.

[3]NADER sustained itself through a quarterly internal newsletter, the *Educational Research Bulletin*. Educational Research Association of America's main publication was the *Journal of Educational Research* (*JER*), which carried a mixture of articles, editorial commentaries, and news items. *JER* kept a distance from the world of science; it intended to "emphasize applications rather than abstractions, and practice rather than theory. . . . Research for the sake of research we shall leave for others" (*JER*, 1920, p. 1). In the late 1920s, conflicts with the publisher over the ownership of *JER* severely weakened AERA. With support from the NEA, AERA could again strengthen its organization and create a new journal: *RER* (see Mershon & Schlossman, 2008, pp. 326–327).

[4]By 1970, the limitations of the old editorial policy had already been discussed in various editorials. Since the 1970s, the policy of publishing unsolicited manuscripts has not changed substantially. Occasionally, *RER* still publishes solicited reviews of particular issues, studies, or books (see also *RER*, 1972, p. i). Over the past decades, however, only two issues have been entirely devoted to a special topic.

[5]A few years later, as a reaction to perceived information overload, which resulted from the expansion of the field, the Education Resources Information Center (ERIC) was established. After almost half a century, the ERIC database includes indexing for over 1,000 journals.

[6]Of course, it can also be argued that the complaints of the "irate colleagues" were indicative of the tensions that surrounded the rise of less hierarchical, less centralized structures in the expanding field of education research.

[7]As we will see in the final empirical section of this chapter, the increasing use of references to other literature (citations) is also an indication of the depersonalization of science. Texts build on the authority of other texts—texts that have also gone through the double-blind peer-review system.

[8]Of course, it should be taken into account that Web of Science originated in the United States. Although in recent years attempts have been made to include more non-Anglo-Saxon journals and to provide better coverage of the global scientific communication system, Web of Science is clearly biased in favor of the Anglo-Saxon world. We are aware of the limitations of its database, but it is also worth underlining that the widespread use of this database is indicative of the hegemony of Anglo-Saxon journals and Anglo-Saxon research.

[9]Fred Kerlinger was affiliated with the University of Amsterdam when the first issue of *RRE* appeared under his editorship (1973).

[10]Another AERA journal founded in the 1980s, *Contemporary Education Review*, was also discontinued after a few years.

[11]In recent years, the *AERJ* editors also called for perspectives that would "blend the methods and foci of the two sections of *AERJ*" (*AERJ*, 2012, p. 6). Thus, it is no surprise that a "newly integrated *AERJ*" has appeared—no longer divided into two sections with distinct programs and concerns.

[12]Another isomorphic initiative is the World Education Research Association, which was founded in 2009 by a number of education research associations from around the world "to transcend what any one association can accomplish in its own country, region, or area of specialization" (*ER*, 2009, p. 388; see also *ER*, 2009, pp. 650–651). For a discussion of the growing international scope of education research, see Levine and Hill (2015). For a discussion of the relevance of national and international audiences for processes of scientific specialization, see Vanderstraeten and Vandermoere (2015).

[13]Of course, our approach has been selective. We have dealt with a few aspects of the forms of inclusion in these communication processes but left out several others. Our database does not yet allow us to comment on aspects related to social background, race, or gender characteristics of the authors represented in the AERA journals. We hope that more encompassing analyses of forms of inclusion and exclusion will soon follow.

[14]We calculated yearly averages for the period 2003 to 2013 to smooth out short-term fluctuations and highlight longer term trends. Journals attributed by Web of Science to more than one subject field (such as education and psychology) appear only once in Figure 3; we used only the subject field they are first attributed to. Journals for which this attribution changed over time are classified according to the last available classification.

[15]It should be kept in mind that this database includes only part of the scientific literature: Articles in journals included in Web of Science. But we should not overlook the fact that publications in high-ranked periodicals have become the canonical form of scientific communication in a wide variety of disciplinary specializations, including education research (see Gross et al., 2002).

[16]However, a journal may belong to more than one subject category. The total number for the subject categories is higher than the total number of journals in the network. In our figures, we depart from the journals, not from the subject categories. For reasons of clarity, we have also focused at the disciplinary level, thereby amalgamating different Web of Science categories for subdisciplinary specializations.

REFERENCES

Abbott, A. (1999). *Department and discipline: Chicago sociology at one hundred.* Chicago, IL: University of Chicago Press.

Abbott, A. (2001). *Chaos of disciplines.* Chicago, IL: University of Chicago Press.

Bazerman, C. (1988). *Shaping written knowledge: The genre and activity of the experimental article in science.* Madison: University of Wisconsin Press.

De Solla Price, D. J. (1963). *Little science, big science.* New York, NY: Columbia University Press.

Fisher, C. S. (1966). The death of a mathematical theory: A study in the sociology of knowledge. *Archive for History of Exact Sciences, 3,* 137–159.

Foucault, M. (1995). *Dits et écrits I* [Said and written, Vol. 1]. Paris, France: Gallimard.

Graff, H. J. (2015). *Undisciplining knowledge: Interdisciplinarity in the twentieth century.* Baltimore, MD: Johns Hopkins University Press.

Gross, A. G., Harmon, J. E., & Reidy, M. (2002). *Communicating science: The scientific article from the 17th century to the present.* Oxford, England: Oxford University Press.

Hoskin, K. W. (1993). Education and the genesis of disciplinarity: The unexpected reversal. In E. Messer-Davidow, D. R. Shumway, & D. J. Sylvan (Eds.), *Knowledges: Historical and critical studies in disciplinarity* (pp. 271–304). Charlottesville, VA: University Press of Virginia.

Jacobs, J. A. (2013). *In defense of disciplines: Interdisciplinarity and specialization in the research university.* Chicago, IL: University of Chicago Press.

Lenoir, T. (1997). *Instituting science: The cultural production of scientific disciplines.* Stanford, CA: Stanford University Press.

Levine, F. J., & Hill, L. D. (2015). The field of educational research. In J. D. Wright (Ed.), *International encyclopedia of the social and behavioral sciences* (Vol. 7, pp. 279–288). Oxford, England: Elsevier.

Mershon, S., & Schlossman, S. (2008). Education, science, and the politics of knowledge: The American Educational Research Association, 1915–1940. *American Journal of Education, 114,* 307–340.

Oleson, A., & Voss, J. (1979). *The organization of knowledge in modern America, 1860–1920.* Baltimore, MD: Johns Hopkins University Press.

Pudovkin, A. I., & Garfield, E. (2002). Algorithmic procedure for finding semantically related journals. *Journal of the American Society for Information Science and Technology, 53,* 1113–1119.

Silva, F. N., Rodrigues, F. A., Oliveira, O. N., & Costa, L. (2013). Quantifying the interdisciplinarity of scientific journals and fields. *Journal of Informetrics, 7,* 469–477.

Stichweh, R. (1991). *Der frühmoderne Staat und die europäische Universität* [The early-modern state and the European university]. Frankfurt, Germany: Suhrkamp.

Stichweh, R. (1994). *Wissenschaft, Universität, Professionen: Soziologische Analysen* [Science, university, professions: Sociological analyses]. Frankfurt, Germany: Suhrkamp.

Turner, R. S. (1980). The Prussian universities and the concept of research. *Internationales Archiv für Sozialgeschichte der deutschen Literatur, 5,* 68–93.

Tyack, D. B., & Hansot, E. (1982). *Managers of virtue: Public school leadership in America, 1820–1980.* New York, NY: Basic Books.

Vandermoere, F., & Vanderstraeten, R. (2012). Disciplinary networks and bounding: Scientific communication between science and technology studies and history of science. *Minerva, 50,* 451–470.

Vanderstraeten, R. (2011). Scholarly communication in education journals. *Social Science History, 35,* 109–130.

Vanderstraeten, R., & Vandermoere, F. (2015). Disciplined by the discipline: A social-epistemic fingerprint of the history of science. *Science in Context, 28,* 195–214.

Chapter 3

The Impact of Political Context on the Questions Asked and Answered: The Evolution of Education Research on Racial Inequality

AMY STUART WELLS
Teachers College, Columbia University

ALLISON RODA
Molloy College

This chapter examines how the larger political context and policies enacted at different points in American history have affected the questions education researchers asked and answered. The authors argue that while education researchers are often quick to consider how their research should shape policy, they are less likely to contemplate the possible effect of policies on their scholarship. To examine whether the policy–research relationship is indeed bidirectional, the authors conducted a thorough content analysis of six of the most prominent education research journals, some of which date back to the late 19th and early 20th centuries. The goal was to consider how shifts in racial politics and educational policies may have influenced what was studied, particularly research that examined the role of race and ethnicity in education. The authors looked for shifts between education research examining race and education within a broader social context and research focused on the personal and familial deficits of individual students or families. They argue that if these shifts in research are somewhat synchronized with shifts in racial politics and policies in the United States, this is a potential indicator of the impact that the larger political milieu may have had on education research over the last 100 years. Consideration of this research–policy relationship may raise the awareness of education researchers in terms of the origins of the questions they will ask and answer in the American Educational Research Association's second century.

The relationship between education research and education policy has always been tenuous, with researchers constantly bemoaning the lack of impact their

Review of Research in Education
March 2016, Vol. 40, pp. 62–93
DOI: 10.3102/0091732X16681758
© 2016 AERA. http://rre.aera.net

work has on related policy decisions (Lagemann, 2000; Weiss, 1977, 1991). The topic less often discussed, however, is the opposite effect, or the impact of policy decisions, and of the larger political context of those decisions, on education research. In this chapter, we provide an initial analysis of what that impact could be by focusing on the relationship between policy discourse and research related to racial inequality across several decades to consider whether the effects flow in both directions.

To facilitate more bidirectional exploration of the research–policy connection, we reviewed the education research published in the most prominent journals over the last century to consider how shifts in political discourse on racial inequality and the related educational policies implemented *may have* affected the education research questions that were asked and answered. While we are not claiming that there is a clear causal link between the policy context and the research, we do think it is important to ponder the possible impact of researchers' larger context on how they understand what needs to be studied, not to mention what research is funded (see Banks, 1993). According to Aaron's (1978) analysis of the role of research during the Great Society era, "The findings of social sciences seemed to come after, rather than before, changes in policy, which suggests that political events may influence scholars more than research influences policy" (p. 9).

If Aaron's (1978) inference is correct—or at least partially so—what does this say about the role of education research in either challenging or perpetuating inequality across policy regimes and contexts? We ask this question, in particular, as it relates to issues of race and ethnicity in education and the research that examines disparate educational experiences and outcomes of students across racial lines. We argue, therefore, that if we consider the arguments of critical race theorists (Bell, 1995; Crenshaw, Gotanda, Peller, & Thomas, 1995; Delgado & Stefancic, 2012), who see issues of race and power embedded in the legal system, and critical policy theorists in education (Ball, 1997; Ladson-Billings & Tate, 1995; Lipman, 1998, 2004; Marshall, 2005; Yasso, 2005), who excavate assumptions about race and poverty that are embedded in educational mandates and laws, then this policy-to-research impact may not be so farfetched. Indeed, if the mandates and laws that shape educational practices and fund much of the education research are molded from racially problematic assumptions, then it is highly probable that much of the research shares at least some of these same assumptions.

We believe that helping education researchers think about the policy–research nexus as bidirectional allows them to question how this relationship might have shifted their gaze away from more critical research questions that are worth exploring. In fact, as we explain below, our study of 100 years of education research strongly suggests that in the past 10 to 15 years, more education researchers are asking these critical questions of the policy world and our field. New critical research on issues of race and education may, in fact, help lead many American Educational Research Association (AERA) members from a place of thinking "within the box" of education policy to imagining a world with a more compassionate and healing set of educational policies that are well grounded in solid research evidence on the multiple causes of racial inequality.

For this review of research, therefore, we conducted a detailed content analysis of six of the most widely cited education research journals published in the first 100 years of the AERA. We selected these journals based on their relatively rigorous peer-review process and their status in the field. These publications have published work by some of the most revered researchers in the field, and thus, they represent the valued knowledge in education research.

Four of these journals are published by AERA, and we reviewed them from the time they were first published, in the late 1960s or early 1970s, through 2014. In addition to our thorough content analysis of these four most-cited AERA journals, we reviewed articles in two non-AERA journals—the *American Journal of Education* and *Sociology of Education*—that began publication prior to the 1960s, allowing us to examine education research publications across most of the last 100 years.

This careful and labor-intensive content analysis of six education research journals over several decades was aimed at finding peer-reviewed, published research on issues of race and education across time. In other words, we wanted to see whether and when education researchers changed the ways they wrote about these issues over the last century, as the larger political discourse on race and inequality changed. We were particularly attuned to how researchers were writing about broader issues of structural inequality and cultural dominance and their impact on students' educational experiences over time. Thus, we were analyzing whether researchers used a *contextual framework* for studying issues of race and education, as opposed to explaining racial disparities in educational outcomes as the result of Black and Latino students' *personal and familial deficits*. The contrast between a *contextual* and a *deficit* framing of issues of race and education is important in efforts to understand the effect of politics on research because of what we know from the research about how the politics of race in the United States changed over the 20th and early 21st centuries. Indeed, what is remarkable about U.S. racial politics is the way in which it fluctuates between framing racial inequality in terms of a history of systemic racism and framing it more simply in terms of cultural or behavioral deficiencies of individual members of a racial/ethnic minority (J. D. Anderson, 2007; Lopez, 2014).

The central question explored in this review, therefore, is the extent to which this fluctuation in the larger political discourse on racial inequality and the effect it has had on educational policy has also had an impact on education research. Our content analysis of six prominent journals over the last 100 years suggests that the changing political context has an impact on the questions asked and answered, suggesting that the research–policy relationship in the field of education is bidirectional. The point of doing this review is to encourage researchers to think more critically about the relationship between the rhetoric and the research, allowing us to reframe our scholarship more independently from rhetorical policy discourse and more tightly connected to the needs of the field. We can hope that such reframing will enhance the agency of education researchers vis-à-vis the politics, which could, ironically enough, have the potential to strengthen the impact of the research on the policy.

THE BIDIRECTIONAL RESEARCH–POLICY CONNECTION

We begin our review of research by examining the "research utilization" or "uses of research" literature, which explores the relationship between social science research and public policy. In the applied and professional fields, such as education, researchers' commitment to speak to policymakers is of utmost significance (Finnigan & Daly, 2014; Lagemann, 2000; Weiss, 1977, 1991; Weiss & Bucuvalas, 1980). As a result, the research-to-policy relationship is closely examined in education and related fields, but as we note, far less has been written about the impact of policy on research (Whitty, 2006).

According to Weiss and Bucuvalas (1980), over the last century, most of the discussion about research utilization has focused on questions about how to *increase* the use of social science research in governmental bodies. Lagemann (2000) notes that beginning in the Progressive Era, American reformers have had faith in the power of social science research to further their causes. But between the Progressive Era and the late 1970s, when Weiss and Bucuvalas (1980) were writing their analysis of government officials, they found that these officials were often advised to heed the wisdom that social scientists offered. This was also the era in which the federal government, in particular, began funding more social science research, especially in the field of education.

The influence of researchers on policymaking appears to have hit its peak in the 1960s, at the time of the Great Society programs (Lagemann, 2000). This was the era in which government support for social science research expanded, as did the contributions of research findings to the development and enactment of many government programs, including Medicare, equal employment opportunity, legal services for the poor, urban aid, community mental health centers, and several other programs, including educational programs designed to redress historically based racial inequalities (Aaron, 1978). Weiss and Bucuvalas (1980) describe this era as a time when many programs designed to address the nation's social problems were "being based on social science research, or at least on social science concepts and values" (p. 6).

Lagemann (2000) has also written about this Great Society era and how education and social science researchers were conducting studies that profoundly enriched the policymaking process in education. Yet, as we quoted Aaron (1978) saying above, the research, in turn, was affected by the subsequent policies that emerged. In other words, as the federal government's role in K–12 public education policy and funding grew exponentially, the influence of these more centralized policies on education called for research that examined their impact.

As part of the new federal role in education, authorities in Washington became more involved in education research. Much of the research had to do with the evaluation of new federal programs, which became a major growth industry beginning in the late 1960s. (Lagemann, 2000, p. 162)

After this tighter relationship between the researchers and the policymakers developed in the 1960s, however, came a period of disillusionment with the research and the programs it fostered to address poverty, discrimination, and other problems. Aaron (1978) noted a distinct shift between the early 1960s and late 1970s in the relationship between the research and political action, as the social science research on the causes of poverty became more complex and thus less conclusive (Kantor & Lowe, 2014).

According to Weiss and Bucuvalas (1980), as the American economy slowed in the late 1970s, economists were seen to be fallible creatures. Meanwhile, many of the vaunted social programs created with input from social scientists were falling far short of expectations. Thus, Weiss and Bucuvalas (1980) noted, a certain ambivalence came to prevail in Washington agencies about the contributions of social science research to the development of social welfare policy and programs.

Similarly, Lagemann (2000) wrote about the retrenchment of the federal role in education during the 1970s, even as researchers were engaged in studies that would have profoundly enriched our knowledge and understanding of the shortcomings of federal education programs. She connected this political retrenchment to the concept of "anti-educationalism," which she derived from Hofstader's concept of anti-intellectualism, or skepticism toward intellect and a preference for more instrumental knowledge. Lagemann (2000) argued that anti-educationalism is an extension of anti-intellectualism, but focused more directly on the presumed lack of knowledge, skill, ambition, and competence needed and possessed by educators and education researchers (Lagemann, 2000).

Coinciding with Lagemann's (2000) chronology of educational policy and research, Aaron (1978) documented a change of heart in the political world between the early 1960s and the 1970s, regarding the perceived role of education in reducing poverty. In the early 1960s, he wrote that education was seen as an all-powerful transformer of the economic potential of poor children. But by the early 1970s, it was seen as an ineffective instrument that had few, if any, predictable consequences on poor children's earning potential. Such perspectives, Lagemann (2000) noted, supported arguments that excellence could be achieved in education without major investments in personnel, research, materials, and equipment.

Lagemann (2000) connected this anti-educationalism perspective to a sharp decline in federal funding for education research. She noted, for instance, that after the 1970s, although much remained to be learned from the research, the politics of that time jeopardized federal activities in education, especially those related to education research. "In no other way were antieducationist attitudes more starkly revealed than in congressional debates about legislation pertaining to education research" (Lagemann, 2000, p. 185).

What followed this era of backlash against the field, beginning with the report *A Nation at Risk* (National Commission on Excellence in Education, 1983) during the Reagan administration, was an accountability movement within the educational policy world that both pushed for the use of "evidence" in instructional decision making (see Finnigan & Daly, 2014) and grotesquely narrowed the measures that counted as evidence in evaluating academic achievement and success, for schools and individual students (Wells & Holme, 2005). In this context, systematically conducted education research that asks not only "what works" but also "why," "how," "for whom," and "under what conditions" is less valued. Such research is less likely to be supported, or taken up into a policy context driven by short-term test scores and easy-to-report data that can be collected and analyzed by "researchers" with no expertise in education or research (DeBray, Scott, Lubienski, & Jabbar, 2014; Lagemann, 2000).

In the current context, therefore, the old school "knowledge utilization" or "uses of research" literature seems somewhat quaint, harkening back to a time when researchers truly believed they could speak "truth to power" and that power would listen.

The Impact of Context on Researchers

The question of the impact of the political and policy context on scholarship is answered in part by examining the U.S. Department of Education's priorities for funding education research, and how that has changed over time, through congressional elections and presidential administrations (Lagemann, 2000; Weiss & Bucuvalas, 1980). Beyond federal funding per se, we argue that there may well be larger ripple effects on the questions that many researchers ask and answer as the policies shift in sync with the political context and the ways that the "problems" to be solved in education are defined in the media and public opinion.

In Aaron's (1978) analysis of the relationship between politics and professors, he pointed out the various ways in which researchers are influenced by prevailing political interests and preconceptions. He stated that research agendas are certainly "not immune to currents of intellectual fashion, which are related to prevailing political moods" (p. 157).

The argument that prevailing political moods can affect research agendas certainly fits with research on how all people—not just researchers—come to make sense of the world around them and how the larger context of their sense-making matters. For instance, in the literature on qualitative research methods, scholars note that the social context affects people's understanding of their reality. This is why qualitative researchers study how people make sense of particular phenomena across different contexts (see Merriam & Tisdell, 2016). Similarly, some research has more directly examined the relationship between context and meaning making, including a study by Xu and Garland (2010) that looked at the connection between people's understanding of income inequality and their context. They found that people living in states with greater income inequality perceived more inequality than those living in more equal states.

Similarly, reflexive sociology explains how our understanding of the social context in which we live and make decisions affects our thoughts, judgments, and classifications. According to Bourdieu, social structures such as racial segregation lead "a double life"—existing *first* in the unequal distribution of *material resources* and *second* in the systems of *classifications or templates* for the conduct, thoughts, feelings, and judgments of social agents (Bourdieu & Wacquant, 1992). In other words, researchers' understandings of the right questions to ask and answer exist both in real, measurable "tangible factors," such as research funds, and in the "intangible factors" or thoughts, judgments, and classifications of what the problems that need studying are (see also Burawoy, 2009).

Researchers, therefore, like those they research, are strongly influenced by the cultural and political contexts in which they live. In writing about this relationship between the context of researchers and the scholarship they produce about race more specifically, Banks (1995) argued that "knowledge reflects both the reality observed" by the researcher and "the subjectivity of the knower" (p. 15).

For instance, Banks (1995) noted that a researcher's location in the social structure, which is partially based on relations of race, social class, and gender, frames what he or she sees and views as significant. Banks used a historical case study of the construction and reconstruction of race between the late 19th century and the 1940s to document the ways in which the social, cultural, political, and historical contexts in which researchers are embedded influence our social locations and thus, the knowledge we construct and reconstruct. Similarly, Ladson-Billings (2012) wrote that, even beyond the social location of individual researchers, the different social science disciplines that contribute to the field of education have a history of racialized understandings that influence both research and practice.

In connecting the research with the policy context, Stevens (2007) analyzed how sociologists in England studied racial/ethnic inequalities in secondary education between 1980 and 2005. He concluded that the development of particular research traditions can be explained by pointing to more general developments in the social policy and intellectual climate in England. He wrote that research on race/ethnicity, and on educational inequality, more specifically, appears to be informed by developments in social policy. Stevens (2007) cited a set of policy reports released during the 1980s in England that put issues of racial and ethnic minority students' disadvantages, especially racism and discrimination, firmly on the agenda of English education research. "As a result," Stevens (2007) noted, in that era, "English educational research focused its attention increasingly on processes of racism and discrimination in schools" (p. 171).

In other words, Stevens (2007) found that the broader social, political, and intellectual context of these researchers influenced the framework, including the questions they asked and answered when conducting their research. Similarly, Aaron (1978), in his study of the use of social science research in the development of programs to address poverty, lack of education, and unemployment, concluded that in many cases, social science findings came *after*, rather than *before*, changes in policy, which "suggests that political events may influence scholars more than research influences policy" (p. 9).

Furthermore, in writing about the shift in public attitudes regarding the role of the federal government in solving poverty and other social problems in the early 1970s, Aaron (1978) viewed the research of that era as both part of the rationale for the shift *and* a reflection of the shift. He argued that prevailing political interests and preconceptions influenced the topics that researchers chose to study during that era—most notably, disillusionment about the potential good to be achieved by government.

In the U.S. context, many argue that the backlash against government antipoverty programs that Aaron (1978) discussed was related to racial politics. For instance, an argument that poor people of color—the so-called "undeserving" poor—were the primary recipients of these social welfare policies, even if that was not the case, allowed conservative politicians to use racial politics as a way to garner votes from the White working class (see Edsall & Edsall, 1992).

It is also important to remember that this backlash, discussed in more detail below, came in the aftermath of the controversial and infamous 1965 report issued by then Assistant Secretary of Labor Daniel Patrick Moynihan, titled, *The Negro Family: The Case for National Action.* Moynihan drew heavily from social science research and, in fact, made an argument in the report that research should play a more prominent role to address ongoing racial inequality. The problem with the report was its strong focus on the dissolution of the Negro family and its relationship to a culture of poverty that he claimed developed from the abundance of single-mother-headed households in the Black community. Even though Moynihan couched this concern in a context of structural inequalities and several historical factors well beyond the control of individual Black families, the takeaway from the report and the media coverage of it focused primarily on dysfunction within the Black community.

The response to this perception created a powerful chilling effect on the social science community (Gergen & Bauer, 1968). According to Wilson (1990), the acrimonious debate that emerged after African Americans' response to the report intimidated social scientists, especially liberal scholars.

In the aftermath of this controversy and in an effort to protect their work from the charge of racism or of 'blaming the victim,' liberal social scientists tended to avoid describing any behavior that could be construed as unflattering or stigmatizing to racial minorities. (Wilson, 1990, p. 6)

A major problem with the Moynihan report, therefore, was that this chilling effect on social science research created a knowledge-based vacuum, allowing the "culture of poverty" argument to run amok. And as we know, this argument did indeed enjoy a powerful resurgence in the late 1970s and 1980s. We also know that the culture of poverty claim was as much about race as it was about poverty, and that it was part of a larger backlash against the social welfare policies of the 1960s and early 1970s.

Wilson (1990) documents the longevity of this chilling effect on social science research, lasting until at least the early 1990s, despite the growing problems of urban poverty concentration, joblessness, and other social dislocations in the inner-city ghetto that were progressing during that period, the 1970s and 1980s. This dearth of systematic empirical research on urban poverty, in particular, hindered the development of thoughtful policy solutions to worsening conditions in many inner-city neighborhoods.

Thus, if social scientists ignore the process by which the larger society produces subjectivity and influences the construction of knowledge, we are unlikely to interrogate established knowledge that contributes to the oppression of marginalized and victimized groups (Banks, 1995).

Our goal in the next two sections of this review of research, however, is to do the exact opposite of *ignoring* the process by which the larger society produces subjectivity and thus influences the construction of knowledge about race and education. We begin with a description of the key findings from our review of the education research published over the last 100 years, followed by our analysis of the research on the political context in which this education research was being conducted.

THE ITERATIVE RELATIONSHIP BETWEEN CONTEXT AND QUESTIONS: RACIAL POLITICS AND EDUCATION RESEARCH OVER FOUR DECADES

In order to analyze the relationship between the larger political context and the focus and content of education research over the last 100 years, we conducted a thorough content analysis of six peer-reviewed journals and a brief review of literature on racial politics in the United States over the past century. We began by reviewing four of the most frequently cited education research journals according to the 2014 Journal Citation Reports. These four journals—(a) *Review of Educational Research* (*RER*), (b) *Educational Researcher* (*ER*), (c) *Review of Research in Education* (*RRE*), and (d) *American Educational Research Journal* (*AERJ*)—are all published by AERA. Two of them—*RER* and *RRE*—publish comprehensive reviews of research in a particular area. *Educational Researcher*, meanwhile, is sent to all members of AERA and publishes articles on salient issues for education researchers. *AERJ* publishes some the most widely recognized empirical research in the field. All four of these journals were ranked in the top 15 journals (out of 219) for citations in the Education and Educational Research categories of the Journal Citation Reports.

Unfortunately, of these four AERA journals, only *RER* has been published for more than 52 years. Thus, in order to discuss these themes going back further in the history of education research, we added two older, also widely read journals to our analysis: the *American Journal of Education* (formerly known as *School Review Journal*), which began publication in 1867, and *Sociology of Education* (formerly known as the *Journal of Educational Sociology*), which was first published in the 1920s (see Table 1 for a list of journals reviewed and their initial publication dates).

Thus, to explore our thesis about the ways in which research on the social context of racial inequality in education *responds* to the policy context, we conducted content analyses of the articles published by *AERJ*, *American Journal of Education*, *ER*, *RER*,

TABLE 1

Journals Reviewed and Their Initial Publication Dates

Titles of Journals Reviewed	Year First Published
American Educational Research Journal	1964
American Journal of Education (formerly *School Review Journal*)	1867
Educational Researcher	1972
Review of Educational Research	1931
Review of Research in Education	1973
Sociology of Education (formerly *Journal of Educational Sociology*)	1927

RRE, and *Sociology of Education* from 1867 to 2014. As we noted above, extensive content analysis was aimed at mapping published research on issues of race and education across time as the larger political discourse on race and inequality changed. To do this, we analyzed whether or not researchers used a *contextual framework for studying* issues of race and education, as opposed to framing racial disparities in educational outcomes as the result of Black and Latino students' personal and familial deficits to explain achievement gaps. As stated, this contrast between a *contextual* and a *deficit* framing of issues of race and education is key to understanding the effect of politics and policy on education research, as the politics of race in the United States has changed dramatically in terms of how issues of racial inequality are framed.

The first step of our review entailed using the advanced search function for each of the six journals to come up with a list of feature articles that contained the search terms "racial equity" or "equal educational opportunity," especially as the latter related to race. This process required methodically reviewing each journal and listing any articles related to issues of race and education in an Excel file, with the citation information and the abstract. The Excel file was broken down by journal and included the following information for each article: the topic; publication date, volume, and number; authors' full names; full title; and full abstract. Book reviews, editorials, commentaries, and response papers were excluded from analysis. A total of approximately 14,000 articles across the six journals were reviewed.

Next we categorized each of the articles into two distinct ways of framing issues of racial inequality in education: (a) A *contextual* way of framing racial inequality in terms of the larger social context and student disadvantages, including racial bias and other socioeconomic variables that affect student learning, or (b) a *deficit* framing of racial inequality in terms of students' differentiated educational outcomes, namely, achievement gaps usually narrowly measured by standardized tests, with only individualistic explanation as to why. In other words, we were trying to distinguish the researchers who considered factors related to social structures and systemic racism for at least some of the differences in students' educational experiences.

The frequencies of articles that fit within the first topic area, on the social context of racial inequality in education, were calculated for further analysis according to

FIGURE 1
Articles on the Social Context of Racial Inequality in Education

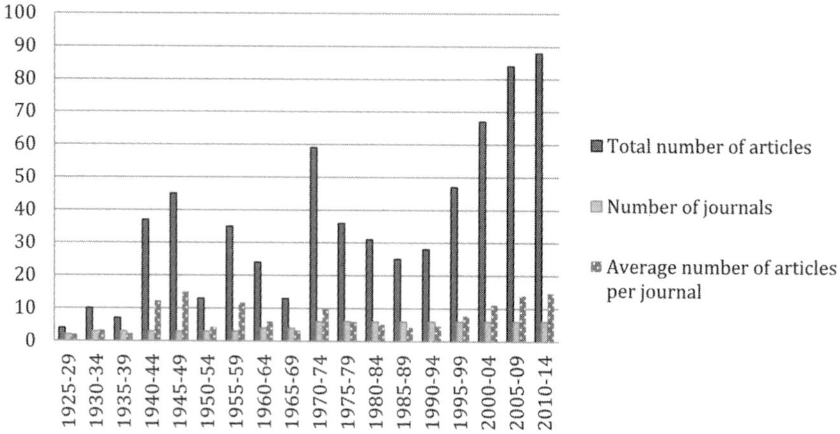

their chronology. Out of 14,000 total articles searched, 647 articles fit the topic of interest during the 100-year time period (see Figure 1). Finally, both authors read the abstracts and frequently the full text of the articles in order to cite examples and support the themes that were emerging. Our guiding question, therefore, was what impact did political shifts have on the questions asked and answered in the research? Were there certain periods in which education researchers placed less focus on these critical contextual factors and the belief systems that justified them?

As we illustrate in Figure 1, in these six journals there has been wide variation over time in the number of articles published that discuss the social context of racial inequality. For the years we studied in which all six of these journals were published (1970–2014), a total of 148 research/feature articles were published each year. Thus, over each of the 5-year periods we examined, these six journals published a total of 780 articles combined.

Looking more closely at the ebb and flow over time, several trends in our detailed content analysis stand out, leading us to argue that while more analysis is needed, the research–policy relationship in the field of education appears to be bidirectional. Thus, we see dips in the average number of articles per journal on the social context of racial inequality during historical moments when the politics and policies were counter to such a framing. For instance, in the late 1930s and early 1950s and then again from the late 1970s through the 1990s, the average number of articles per journal that focused on the context of racial disparities in education declined, coinciding with a sharp political shift in the United States in how politicians were defining the nature and causes of ongoing racial inequality (Murray, 1984; Quadagno, 1994).

Meanwhile, we see an increase in the number of articles on the social context of racial inequalities in the 1940s, the late 1950s, and the early 1970s, followed by a steep decline in the number of such articles in the late 1970s through the 1980s and well into the 1990s. There were two inexplicable dips in the number of articles focused on the social context of educational inequality in the early 1950s, in the years leading up to the *Brown* decision and in the late 1960s, as some of the most important federal legislation in the field of public education designed to ameliorate unequal social contexts was being passed. But these dips were short-lived and may have had more to do with uncertainty regarding policy than with a distinct split from it.

In fact, as we discuss in the following two sections—the first covering the period from the 1920s to the 1970s and the second covering the 1970s through 2014— there is ample evidence that the relationship between the research and the larger social–political context in which it was produced flows in both directions. We demonstrate this finding by interspersing the content analysis of education research published in these top journals with a review of political and historical research on racial politics in the United States during different eras of the last 100 years covered by the content analysis.

Pre–Civil Rights Era to the Late 1970s: The Ebb and Flow of Research on Racial Inequality

In analyzing the journal content in the early to mid-20th century, we were able to examine only three journals that began publication prior to 1964 and only four that began before the 1970s. But even within this limited number of publications, *we saw a notable dearth of research on the social context of racial inequalities in education prior to the 1940s.* In fact, most of the "research" on issues of race and education in the 1930s was descriptive analysis of the social assimilation or social betterment of marginalized racial/ethnic groups, including Jews, Native Americans, and "Negroes." The bulk of this early literature was published in the *Journal of Educational Sociology* (now *Sociology of Education*) and included a special issue in 1933 focused on the Tuskegee Institute and its role in educating Negroes. The backdrop to many of these articles was a discussion—or at least an acknowledgment—of racial oppression and ongoing inequality. Still the analysis remained highly functional and pragmatic in a manner that generally oversimplified the insidious nature of the systems of oppression in the United States.

For instance, in a 1938 article in the *Journal of Educational Sociology* on health education among Negroes, health was defined as

the quality of life that renders the individual fit to live most and serve best. Its principle involves keeping the body and mind at the highest levels in order to give and take the best that life has to offer. (Nathan, 1938, p. 532)

The article discussed the relationship between the conditions in which Negros lived and their health problems, demonstrating how several contextual factors, including poverty, poor housing, lack of medical care, prejudice, and ignorance, all accounted for the health plight of the Negro. But the authors also noted that virtually all the causes of diseases in the Negro community could be traced back *either* to ignorance on the part of members of the community *or* to poverty. This either–or framework struck us as odd, given that the lack of public health information in communities without economic resources.

Similarly, a 1939 article, also in the *Journal of Educational Sociology*, examined vocational education and guidance for Negro students. The author noted that these Negro youth were an "ambitious lot" but, at the same time, were bewildered by the "morass of social and economic confusion and the impasse presented to them as a group" (Patterson, 1939, p. 298). Yet the author also claimed these students were unable to make a decision regarding their vocational choice and that, when they did make a decision, it often represented a "stereotyped veering in the direction of the usual professions without the slightest notions of their probabilities of success" (Patterson, 1939, p. 298).

This author called for more counseling at the precollegiate stage to help convey the facts to Negro youth about their vocational possibilities. Never mentioned in this article was the larger context of Jim Crow in the South and a national trend of racial discrimination and violence. And this article was not unique.

To the extent that "context" is discussed at all in education research during this pre-1940s era, it was mostly connected to issues of poverty and the problems of poor families and students. Absent from most of the education research articles of that time was discussion of severe racial segregation in housing and schools, in both the North and the South, or the rampant lynching and assaults suffered by Black workers at the hands of working-class White workers competing for good jobs.

For instance, as Gilmore (2008) and other scholars noted of this time, although violence, oppression, and discrimination against Blacks, in particular, was rampant, there was little discussion of racial injustice in the media or on the part of political leaders (see also Gilmore, 2008; Klarman, 2004). Derrick Bell (2004) refers to this post–Reconstruction Era segregation as affecting virtually every aspect of Black's lives. "Blacks deprived of the law's protection were vulnerable to economic exploitation and physical intimidation. Violence included literally thousands of lynching and pogroms by white mobs" (p. 81).

The researchers publishing in the limited number of education research journals of this time made no direct connections to this larger context that we could see. Indeed, many of the early 20th-century education research articles that examined issues of race and education focused primarily on the benign topic of social mobility as a marker of equality and not, for the most part, on the complicated nature of the structural and cultural factors that worked against that mobility. For instance, one 1929 article in the *Journal of Educational Sociology* examined the social assimilation of the American Indian. The purpose of this study was to interpret and evaluate the cultural relations between Indians and dominant Euro-Americans within U.S. territories. The author acknowledged that the character of the Indians had been misrepresented by Euro-Americans who held extreme attitudes, "ranging from warlike hatred to philanthropic zeal, or even to total indifference" (see Blackmar, 1929, p. 7). The author's solution to this misrepresentation, however, appears to be assimilating Native Americans to the more Americanized "language and domestic science, family improvement, and religious life" in preparation for independent life.

By the 1940s and 1950s, however, as the U.S. came out of World War II and into the Cold War, the content analysis shows that education researchers were looking more closely at the causes of ongoing racial inequality. For example, in the 1950s, articles in what was then called *The School Review* (now the *American Journal of Education*) examined everything from racial differences in educational attainment to racial prejudice in schools and cultural sensitivity related to students' racial/ethnic backgrounds and how those affected their experiences in schools.

Indeed, one of the articles published in the *School Review* in 1946 proclaimed that issues of intercultural understanding across racial and ethnic groups constituted the dominant area of educational sensitivity at that time. Citing the end of World War II and the manner in which the world is more connected on a global level—referred to as the "shrinking world"—the author calls on educators and education researchers to focus on helping students learn to get along across cultural boundaries. When talking about the importance of this educative work on the domestic front in the United States, the author notes:

A war was fought to safeguard our shores from invasion and to preserve or restore the democratic way of life in the far corners of the world. Our present sense of moral obligation for perfecting that way of life in our own country as a beacon light to the rest of the world plays no small role in making intercultural and international relations the dominant area of educational sensitivity in our schools today. (E. L. Anderson, 1946, p. 378)

Noting the need and desire to improve the democratic way of life in the United States and to expand Americans' concept of democracy here to include social and economic democracy for members of all racial and ethnic "minority" groups, E. L. Anderson (1946) admitted our own shortcomings as a nation in exemplifying to the world the democratic way of life. He saw the growing popularity of curriculum and educational materials to further students' intercultural understanding as a clear sign that the field of education, with the support of key researchers writing for this issue of his journal, was taking a lead in the effort to further the democratic way of life in the United States and thus enhance our political credit on the world stage.

What E. L. Anderson (1946) and several other researchers during the 1940s and into the 1950s were doing was drawing more attention to issues of race and racial inequality within the educational system. By placing their research in the larger political context of the post–World War II era and the Cold War against the Soviet Union and other communist countries, these researchers were writing about their own version of what Derrick Bell (1980, 2004) came to call the "interest-convergence principle," which was his explanation for how and why the civil rights movement in the United States, including the Supreme Court ruling in *Brown v. Board of Education*, occurred when it did and not at an earlier stage in American history. Bell (2004) defines the principle of "interest convergence" as follows: "The interest of blacks in achieving racial equality will be accommodated only when it converges with the interests of whites" (p. 69). In other words, E. L. Anderson (1946) and Bell (1980) both made strong arguments that without the Cold War and American politicians' profound fear of being accused of human rights abuses by the Soviet Union, many civil rights gains in the United States would not have occurred when they did, despite ample evidence that racial violence and atrocities had been rampant in the first part of the 20th century.

Bell's (1980, 2004) interest convergence argument is critical to understanding the context–research relationship we are developing in this chapter, for two reasons:

1. He applies a parallel argument about the impact of the larger political context on federal judges and their rulings to the one we are making about the impact of the policy context on researchers. What was different in 1954, Bell argues, from the situation in prior years of Jim Crow and racial violence was that the broader political context of the country at the time of the Cold War ensured that White policymakers saw economic and political advantages to abandoning segregation.
2. The larger political context that Bell argues influenced the U.S. Supreme Court and the American public in the late 1940s and early 1950s no doubt also had a broader impact on educators and education researchers. If a growing number of White Americans—particularly those who lived in the North and were not poor—were suddenly increasingly aware of how problematic Southern racial segregation was to the United States' standing in the world, no doubt there were education researchers who were part of that population. It is hard to believe that they were not when we look at the content analysis.

Education Research in the Era of School Desegregation, Mid-1950s to Late 1970s

In the aftermath of the *Brown v. Board of Education* Supreme Court decision, much of the research related to race and education published in the late 1950s and through the 1960s focused on school desegregation policy, especially student outcomes and implementation. Much like the federal court cases that were ordering local education officials to dismantle de jure segregation in student assignment plans, the researchers were similarly obsessed with how to desegregate school districts that were resisting such efforts.

In addition, some of the research began examining so-called second-generation school desegregation issues. These second-generation concerns included the resegregation of students into separate and unequal classrooms and the sociocultural issues within desegregated schools and classrooms when students of color were not reflected in the curriculum or they were disciplined unfairly. For instance, during the 1960s, there were several articles in both the *American Educational Research Journal* and

Sociology of Education on so-called sociocultural or multicultural issues, which included analyses of curriculum and classroom climates. The overarching questions many researchers were asking during this time, therefore, was whether the school desegregation policies that began with *Brown v. Board of Education* were fulfilling their promise. The journal content analysis, therefore, does not contradict Bell's interest convergence argument; rather, it suggests that the larger context in which school desegregation policy was created—for example, the Cold War and the sense of shame it created in the United States about racial inequality—also affected the research community, as growing numbers of education researchers sought to understand whether educational policy lived up to its promise to move the nation beyond Jim Crow.

This research focus on school desegregation implementation continued, with some ebb and flow, into the mid-1970s. Interestingly enough, there were fewer research articles on school desegregation—and on the social context of race and education more generally—during the late 1960s than in the 1940s, the late 1950s, and the 1970s (see Figure 1). There may be several reasons for this drop in the number of articles in the 1960s related to the larger policy context in which education researchers were working. For instance, we know despite the fact that the *Brown* decision was rendered in 1954, very few schools or students were actually desegregated until the late 1960s or early 1970s (see Bell, 2004; Orfield, 1988; Wells, 2009). In fact, many of the relatively few articles published on the context of racial inequality in education during the late 1960s discussed the lack of progress toward desegregation.

In *Sociology of Education*, for instance, a series of articles published in the 1960s discussed ongoing segregation in several school systems in the northern, Midwestern, and western United States, including Gary (Indiana), New York City, New Rochelle (New York), and San Francisco. Authors often analyzed the legal, historical, and political context of school desegregation in these non-Southern areas, and often voiced frustration with the lackluster implementation of desegregation. In addition, several articles during that era also focused on the 1966 Coleman report and/or the 1968 U.S. Commission on Civil Rights report, both of which documented the obvious: that very little meaningful desegregation had been implemented by the mid- to late 1960s. Yet since the federal government had commissioned both of these reports, which were research-based examinations of the issues related to race, segregation, and education, they serve as illustrations of the iterative relationship between researchers and the policy context in which they function.

Subsequently, the spike in articles on the role of social context in racial inequality in U.S. public education in the early 1970s also clearly demonstrated how researchers responded to the belated implementation of school desegregation policy in the late 1960s. Indeed, the vast majority of the early to mid-1970s articles explore issues related to racial/ethnic differences in achievement and social development and the impact of a school's racial/ethnic makeup on those outcomes. For instance, a 1971 article in *AERJ*, titled "Self-Concept and Ethnic Group Membership Among Public School Students," examined the relationship between ethnic group membership of students in public schools in which they were minorities and the impact of that experience on the students' self-concept (Zirkel & Moses, 1971). The study symbolized a large body of research from that era in which education researchers were attempting to understand the relationship between educational policy and students' experiences in segregated versus desegregated settings (see, e.g., St. John, 1971).

Interestingly enough, many of the subsequent policy recommendations found in this and other articles of the same era speak to issues that should have shaped educational policy over the past 35 years. Clearly, however, that was not the case, as educational policy headed in the opposite direction (see McGuinn, 2006). But what is also clear is that the policies of the late 1960s and early 1970s—particularly federal court school desegregation orders—had a profound impact on education research, fostering a large body of work on how and why to desegregate schools.

The Post–Civil Rights Era: The Policy and Research on Neo-Plessism

Several journalists and political scientists have documented the evolution of racial politics in this country beginning in the mid- to late-1970s, all revealing important common themes across their analyses (Black & Black, 2003; Edsall & Edsall, 1992; Gitlin, 2007). While the implications of the political shift that occurred at that time have been discussed in terms of public policies in general and educational policies more specifically, we know of no other examination of its impact on education research. As we noted above, the 15-year period from 1975 until the early 1990s marked a low point in the number of education research articles published on the contextual issues contributing to racial inequality in public schools, and we believe this is related in some measure to the political discourse on racial inequality at that time.

We begin this examination of the changing "common sense" regarding the role of the government in solving social problems (such as racial inequality in schools and communities) with an acknowledgment of the larger political, social, and economic context of that sense making. For instance, we know that by the late 1970s, the United States was experiencing rising inflation, high unemployment, an oil shortage that led to long lines and high prices at gas stations, and the Iranian hostage crisis. At the same time, U.S. manufacturers were facing international competition from countries with lower labor costs, leading to a strong sense of insecurity about America's ability to compete (Edsall & Edsall, 1992; Reich, 2007). Within the social and political realm, the country was becoming more politically divided, as the civil rights coalitions were breaking down due to a growing number of Blacks becoming disillusioned with "liberal" policies that failed to address racial inequality and segregation, especially in the North (Bell, 2004; Orfield & Eaton, 1996). Meanwhile, the more conservative Sun Belt states were growing in population and political influence, becoming the incubators of the New Right (see Black & Black, 2003; Frank, 2005) that is still so clearly affecting our political debates and outcomes today.

The end result was a huge jump in political support for so-called "anti-redistributive racial politics," which portrays all government programs as taking money out of the pockets of hardworking Americans via taxes and giving it to the undeserving poor, who are more likely than not portrayed as lazy Blacks even though there were far more poor Whites at the time. This political backlash against taxes and the subsequent "redistribution" of tax revenue to be spent on people who did not "deserve" to be supported contributed to a larger frustration with all government programs and the sorts of bureaucracies and regulations that came with them. This in turn reignited a powerful antigovernment (particularly anti–federal government), ideology and the call for more states' rights and less federal regulation of everything from civil rights to the environment to labor rights. Related to this growing support for deregulation was a growing faith in the free market as a good substitute for government programs in addressing human needs and lifting all boats (Chubb & Moe, 1990; Edsall & Edsall, 1992; Frank, 2005; Friedman, 1962).

This confluence of factors and historic events created the context that led to massive reform of the country's social welfare and educational policies. It was, we argue, the rhetoric and ideology of the former that shaped the latter and the larger "common sense" understanding of the causes and potential solutions to inequality. Such changes in understanding of the problems to be solved by public policy, we contend, may well have had direct and indirect effects on the way in which researchers studied these problems and the public policies designed to correct them.

Thus, we believe that the declining number of race-conscious articles in the late 1970s and the lack of articles through the 1980s and well into the 1990s was most likely responsive to the changing rhetoric—for example, a study of the debate about the relationship between intelligence and race or quantitative research examining the impact of school desegregation policy, usually measured in terms of test score data, were the increasingly popular topics to be explored. Furthermore, many of these articles were framed as a response to Jensen's problematic 1969 article on the relationship between genetics and IQ, which, much like Charles Murray's 1984 book on welfare (described below) contributed to an anti-equity politics by implying there was no point in focusing on inequalities in children's environments since intelligence and the "Negro IQ deficit" was primarily to be explained by genetic factors. Thus, to the extent that Jensen's research was influencing the policy debate and framework, the policies and the research of that framework affected the subsequent education research. For instance, across several issues of the *RRE* from 1969 to 1971, Light and Smith (1971) debated with Shockley (1971) over the accuracy of Jensen's claim. Light and Smith (1971) put forth an empirically based argument that Jensen was wrong and that many environmental factors contribute to students' achievement levels, but Shockley (1971) disagreed with their analysis.

Still these articles and this debate illustrate the difficulty researchers had at that time presenting evidence about the social context of students' lives and how that context affected student achievement, particularly for students of color who experienced systemic racism. Other articles in the six journals during the subsequent 15-year low point (1975–1990) of publications on these contextual issues were testimony to the lack of thoughtful political discourse on racial inequality at that time. For instance, many of these articles focused on efforts to garner attention for cultural issues and ethnic identity or provided a critique of the cultural deficit models as a way of understanding the achievement gap. Still there was a definite shift in focus, even in these race-conscious articles, toward the problem of the achievement gap, even when the authors were trying to discredit the often problematic and racialized explanations of the gap.

A good example of this more defensive stance on issues of race and education is found in a 1982 *RER* article published by Shade, in which she tries to shift the focus on individual differences between students based on race to reconnect the issues of race with cultural ethnicity and its relationship to the "psychological, cognitive and behavioral strategies" for learning that different students used. This article points out the mismatch between school culture and the cultural frameworks that African American students grew up with and adopted. While Shade (1982) danced dangerously close to a cultural deficit model argument, she differentiated her perspective, calling it a stylistic approach to learning that required identification of diverse learning styles within an educational setting. In doing this, Shade (1982) shifted the focus from IQ to culture as a lens for examining the gaps in achievement in a way that represented the intent of many of the race-conscious articles published during this era. A discussion of that larger social context of racial inequality or the cultural biases of the instruments used to measure intelligence was mostly absent from the policy discourse and the education research of this era.

The Changing Understanding of What Needs to Be "Fixed": A New Common Sense

In thinking about the relationship between the political context and the education research on race and education in the 1980s and 1990s, it is important to consider the ideological dimension of the shift in racial politics during that time. For instance, the interest convergence theory noted above evolved into a post–Cold War political alliance, providing a new context for the research during the 1980s and 1990s. Rather than framing the government as the solution, as it had been during the civil rights era, this new era saw the rise of neoliberal or free market ideology, which shifted perceptions about the role of government vis-à-vis free enterprise, framing the latter as the engine of societal well-being. This shift in favor of the market and away from government programs recentered economic and political power upward, leading to greater income inequality. It also fostered an ideological orientation that rejected the idea of "public," collective action to address social problems. The new orientation instead privileged individualism and market solutions for society's ills (Covington, 1997; Echaveste & Scott, 2011).

In this post–civil rights era, corporations, foundations, and individual donors made significant investments across organizations to build a conservative political movement to counter the civil rights, feminist, disability, and labor movements (Echaveste & Scott, 2011; Rich, 2004). According to Echaveste and Scott (2011), this conservative movement helped create the "common sense" notion that inequality was caused by individual choices; it also helped undermine, and in many cases, reverse, the gains of the progressive rights movements by successfully capitalizing on fissures related to race, gender, social class, religion, and identity.

As a result, following the momentary progressive cohesion in the 1960s and early 1970s, the cross-racial networks that had been critical to progressive politics were being splintered, resulting in the pursuit of sometimes competing goals in the late 1970s and early 1980s. Often, this splintering played out over identity politics, which conservatives and neoliberals capitalized on to advance a narrow policy agenda that embraced the language of individual empowerment and rejected government programs designed to help the nonrich, along with the progressive tax policies that forced the rich to help pay for such programs (Duggan, 2003; Lopez, 2014).

This dramatic political shift toward the right was fostered by a politics of strong distrust in government and thus toward public policies and programs—from welfare to the U.S. Post Office, to public schools. It was also fostered by the argument that everyone employed by the government, including teachers, was underworked and overpaid. The racial overtones of this shifting perception are too often ignored. But as Lopez (2014) noted, by the 1980s, progressive politics that would have supported programs and policies to help the nonrich in general was "despised by a large group of voters as a sop to minorities and an infringement on the rights of Whites" (p. 71).

The racial politics of this era and how it shaped the antigovernment—and thus the anti–public education—rhetoric is well documented in the history of welfare reform (Zucchino, 1997), an area of public policy with strong parallels to educational policy during that era. In other words, what had been seen as much-needed government-funded "programs" when they helped Whites became "welfare" when extended across the color line. Echoing many themes in our most recent presidential election, Lopez (2014) writes that "racial attacks on liberalism shifted the enemy of the middle class from big money to lazy minorities, thereby reframing government programs that helped to build the nation into welfare for undeserving groups" (paraphrasing Phillips, 2014, p. 31).

While we are not arguing that most education researchers bought into the racial politics and conservative ideology of the era, that context had an impact on public policy, including education policy, which, in turn, affected what could be studied (and what many people thought "should" be studied). Thus, the broader reverberation of the politics of the welfare queen myth was reflected in the federal budgets of the 1980s and the sharp cuts in funding for social welfare policies, including public education. Arguing that the free market was a better provider of solutions to social and economic problems than the government, President Ronald Reagan pushed for drastic cuts in federal funding for social welfare and educational programs, particularly those targeted for urban areas. This resulted in a cut of $1.8 billion to budgets of larger cities (Lopez, 2014; Zucchino, 1997).

One of the mechanisms for cutting federal funding was the creation of "block grant" programs that consolidated several remaining Great Society programs into one block of funding that was far smaller than the total of the prior amounts spent on those programs. Block grants were also less likely to support the most disadvantaged children and families because they left more discretion to the state and local officials who often had a history of not serving low-income communities of color. In 1981, the federal block grants represented a 21% reduction in federal funding for all the programs enveloped in the grants (Brown, 2003).

In 1981, Congress passed Reagan's proposed Omnibus Budget Reconciliation Act, which dramatically affected educational programs targeted to poor students, as well as welfare programs by eliminating work incentives that had permitted recipients to retain a portion of their earnings while still receiving support. As a result, hundreds of thousands of working-poor households were forced off welfare, and others lost badly needed income, as federal funds for programs targeted at poor students were cut (Cross, 2014; Katz, 1996). Drawing on the political momentum of the welfare queen myth that Reagan had circulated, a central assumption of these policies was that the "undeserving poor" were gaming the system. Bolstering this increasingly popular framing of poor people as simply lazy and waiting for a government handout was the 1984 book written by Charles Murray titled *Losing Ground.* This book became the bible of welfare reformers and others who wanted to cut federally funded programs, organized around Murray's central premise that "We tried to provide more for the poor and produced more poor instead" (p. 9).

This way of framing people in poverty—particularly Black people—as undeserving of government support, together with the increasing role of a free-market, neoliberal ideology, set the stage for President Bill Clinton's 1992 campaign promise to "end welfare as we know it." By the 1994 midterm elections, the Republican-controlled Congress was devising its "Contract With America." The rhetoric surrounding that debate sometimes compared welfare recipients to "alligators" and "wolves." Then, in 1995, states seized the opportunity to launch demonstration projects to move Aid to Families with Dependent Children recipients from welfare to low-paying jobs (Katz, 1996). Twenty years after welfare reform, many states have used the changes in the federal law to shift welfare funds from serving the poorest families with the least access to decent-paying jobs to programs such as marriage counseling and college tuition grants that service a more middle- and upper-middle-class clientele. The result is that cash assistance aid to poor families now reaches about 25% of the families it supported 20 years ago as poverty rates have remained high ("A welfare check," 2016).

This was the era in which education research on the contextual explanations of racial disparities all but disappeared. Published in its stead was research on Black students' aptitude or the test score outcomes of students in desegregated schools (see, e.g., Hannafin, 1983, or Torrey, 1983). The focus of the research was shifting almost entirely in the direction of student "outcomes"—student achievement measured by test scores and dropout rates—and away from contextual explanations for why such outcomes may look different across racial lines.

The Rise of the Tough Love Education Policies: When "Excellence" Became the Only Route to Equity

As the backlash against policies that redistributed opportunities and resources to people of color evolved from the mid-1970s into the 1980s and 1990s, the parallel between education policies and social welfare policies remained strong, and a new wave of educational reform emerged. Thus, both the welfare recipients and the public school educators and students in low-performing schools (and by association, the students' parents) were portrayed as "problems" to be fixed. In other words, the solution to poverty and to achievement gaps in education was to fix the victims of inequality—students, educators, and parents in low-income communities—regardless of the larger context of economic, social, and political factors that continued to disadvantaged them after tough love policies were passed (Carter & Welner, 2013; Darling-Hammond, 2010; Ladson-Billings, 2006).

Related to this decontextualized way of thinking about public education and the achievement gap is the free-market, antigovernment ideology noted above. Proponents of this free-market, antigovernment rhetoric argue that the best way to improve public education is to force schools to compete for "customers" by providing their parents with more choice in where their children attend school (see Chubb & Moe, 1990; Ravitch, 2010). Deregulation and the introduction of more private service providers are also said to be needed, to supplant the bureaucratic public education system and infuse it with competition, high-stakes incentive systems, and consumer choice (Wells, 2007). Thus, the question we explore in the last section of this chapter is whether this shift in commonsense understandings about the problems and solutions in public education affected the research questions asked and answered.

Much like the welfare reform efforts described above, a series of events in the early 1980s changed the common sense about what was wrong with public education and the role the federal government should play in it. For instance, the Education Consolidation and Improvement Act was a reauthorization of the Elementary and Secondary Education Act of 1965, including the largest federally funded education program, Title 1. Under the Education Consolidation and Improvement Act of 1981, Title 1 became Chapter One, and remained the largest federal program for elementary and secondary education, continuing to provide compensatory education in reading and math to disadvantage students. For instance, this act reduced the funding for compensatory education while supposedly "streamlining" the implementation process, a claim that was never proved (Cross, 2014).

At the same time, the guidelines shifted to target the money toward *"low-achieving" students in poor schools* instead of to *poor students*. Thus, Chapter One was intended to support special compensatory services for low-achieving students in schools with high concentrations of poor children. Districts were then able to provide special services to low-achieving poor and nonpoor children in schools with above-average concentrations of poverty (Cross, 2014).

This helps contextualize the shift in the education research that we reviewed toward more narrow studies of student achievement rates, and dropout rates measured in terms of outcomes, and not, for the most part, the process by which students drop out of schools (see Fine, 1991, for an exception). Another focus of many research articles published in these journals, during the 1980s in particular, was a decontextualized comparison of public and private schools and of students' outcomes by race and class within each. This line of research was no doubt fueled by—and in turn fueled—the push for school vouchers that was raging at that time (see Keith & Page, 1985).

Similarly, one seminal edited book on the Black–White test score gap (Jencks & Phillips, 1998) played a pivotal role that no doubt influenced thousands of education researchers in the years after the book was released. Although the volume included contributors who wrote about the broader societal issues of racial inequality, the preponderance of the evidence brought to bear on those issues examined more individual factors—such as psychological and cultural factors. The researchers who contributed to this large volume undoubtedly had a profound impact on what was published in the 1990s in the six top education research journals that we reviewed. Meanwhile, the pattern noted above regarding the ideology of the "undeserving poor," which legitimized massive welfare reform in the 1990s, played out in a similar but more surreptitious fashion in education reform. While not as vitriolic as the debate over welfare queens, the discourse of federal education policy reform was framed around the inefficiencies and failures of the government-run public education system. The 1983 report *A Nation at Risk*, released by the National Commission for Excellence in Education, underscored this paradigm shift and created a new "common sense" of educational policy moving forward (Bell, 1988; Ravitch, 2010).

In particular, the members of the commission critiqued the lower expectations that they saw manifested in declining homework time for high school seniors and lower average "achievement" as measured by standardized tests (National Commission on Excellence in Education, 1983). Despite the fact that these critiques were made with little solid evidence and were subsequently refuted (see Berliner & Bidwell, 1995), they became part of a new common sense about what was "wrong" with public education in America and what was needed to resurrect it (see McGuinn, 2006). This rhetoric, in turn, led to the rise of the accountability movement in education, the next iteration of the "boot strap" mentality that put the burden of solving inequality on individual educators and students.

But not far below these explicit critiques of the public education bureaucracy was a backlash against Great Society educational programs that had been framed by a more contextual way of understanding inequality in education. In the post-1980s, programs like school desegregation and bilingual education that were targeted toward the most disadvantaged by assuring their access to schools and programs were being cut back and often replaced with accountability reforms that placed tremendous pressure on educators to produce similar results in unequal contexts or face punitive measures. Much like the work requirements of welfare policies that were strongly enforced regardless of the job market or the quality of the job training available to welfare recipients, the federal educational policies began linking federal funding to student "outcomes," narrowly measured by standardized tests (McGuinn, 2006; Ravitch, 2010; Wells & Holme, 2005).

Throughout the 1980s and 1990s, a string of laws were passed, including the 1988 reauthorization of the Elementary and Secondary Education Act, called the Hawkins-Stafford Bill, which directly linked Title I funding to students' achievement levels as defined by the states, which were required to identify schools where students were not achieving as expected. In 1994, President Clinton signed the Goals 2000 legislation that provided states with support for upgrading their school accountability systems and focusing almost exclusively on student outcomes, despite valiant efforts on the part of civil rights advocates to include "opportunity to learn" standards, which would have required schools, communities, and perhaps researchers to more carefully examine the nature of unequal educational opportunities.

These 1990s policies prodded and then required the states to construct elaborate accountability systems of standards and tests in order to receive the federal education funding that they had come to rely on. They laid the groundwork for the federal government to pass a more invasive federal policy that would not only require states to establish accountability systems but also would institute a set of sanctions for schools, districts, and states that failed to meet their achievement goals. President George W. Bush wholeheartedly supported this bipartisan legislation due to its embodiment of the "common sense" about a tough-love, free-market accountability system as the solution to poverty, inequality, and lack of excellence (Horn & Willburn, 2013; McGuinn, 2006).

Thus, from the early 1980s through the No Child Left Behind (NCLB) era, which ended in 2015 with the passage of the Every Student Succeeds Act, a dramatic shift in the federal role in public education occurred. In many ways, NCLB completed the evolution of the federal role in schooling, away from enforcing local compliance with civil rights laws and providing additional funding to poor students and schools, toward enforcing "excellence" measured by narrow standardized tests as the main "output" (DeBray, 2005; Horn & Willburn, 2013; McGuinn, 2006; Rothstein, Jacobsen, & Wilder, 2008).

This shift in the role of the federal government in public education required a shift in the policymakers' and the general publics' understanding of the "problems" to be solved by education policy—and a shift in their understanding of the causes of the problems. In other words, this dramatic swing in educational policy focus "from an emphasis on equalizing inputs to an emphasis on equalizing outcomes" led to arguments that equality of educational opportunity would be achieved not by ensuring disadvantaged students greater access to high-achieving schools or compensatory resources but rather by ensuring that all public schools were accountable for producing the same student outcomes across highly unequal contexts (Darling-Hammond, 2010; Ladson-Billings, 2012). In an era of "accountability," the argument went, educational equity could be achieved via "separate but more equal" schools. Sheer will, hard work, and an eye on reaching the state standards and achievement goals as measured primarily by standardized tests was all that was needed. According to President George W. Bush, NCLB was designed to attack "the soft bigotry of low expectations" ("Bush Warns Against," 1999).

Although we are not arguing that education researchers were ensconced in this "boot strap" ideology, the research published in the six journals during this period strongly suggests an emphasis on the problems in education as being vested in local communities and schools and not as much in the larger society in which the schools exist. We see, for instance, in the late 1980s and early 1990s, a sharp decline in the number of articles that examined the social context of racial inequality and a growing number of articles looking at very micro-level solutions to racial achievement gaps.

Thus, educational reform for the last 30 years has been strongly grounded in neoliberal ideology centered on individual responsibility, the backlash against redistributive government programs and equity-minded policies of the 1960s and 1970s, and tough love accountability. This trend led to a set of public policies that ignored the larger context of the labor market, the nature of poverty, ongoing segregation, and racial inequality, not to mention the impact of heavy-handed and narrowly defined accountability measures on curriculum and teaching in low-income schools with low test scores (Braun, Wang, Jenkins, & Weibaum, 2006; Lee & Wong, 2004; Rothstein et al., 2008; Wells, 2014; White, 2014). Clearly the shift had an impact on the type of education research that was deemed important and valuable in the policy world. We know it affected the type and amount of education research that was funded directly by the federal government (Lagemann, 2000).

A Slow Resurgence of the Research on Racial Inequality: Bringing Context Back

By the mid- to late-1990s, as the total number of articles addressing issues of race and the context of racial inequality began to increase, the published research in the six journals we studied shifted in large part toward a micro-level focus on racial identity, culturally relevant pedagogy, sociolinguistics, parent–school relationships, and resilience on the part of students of color. The more macro-level, policy-oriented articles examined issues such as the lack of implementation of multicultural education or school desegregation policy.

In more recent years, beginning in the early 2000s, we see evidence that education researchers may well be affected by the larger social context in a very different way. Here we see researchers ahead of what will hopefully be the next shift in the policy discourse to refocus on societal explanations for the so-called achievement gap, well ahead of projected changes in educational policy to address racial inequality more directly (see Hannah-Jones, 2016). This resurgence of research and academic writing on the broader, societal causes of racial inequality in the U.S. education system seems to have begun at about the time of the 50th anniversary of the *Brown v. Board of Education* Supreme Court decision in 2004 and snowballed since. It may also reflect the changing racial demographics of the education research community, as the more racially and ethnically diverse and biracial millennial generation enters the academy (AERA, 2016). Whatever the cause, this scholarship, we argue, may in fact be shifting the research–policy relationship in a new, more proactive direction, with the researchers out ahead of the politics. If this is indeed the case, we may see a more progressive educational policy agenda in the coming years.

In many of the articles published in these journals during this era, researchers were framing their analysis in the context of policy discourse and policy development that was ignoring these insights. For instance, in a 1995 issue of the *AERJ*, two articles— one written by Gloria Ladson-Billings and the other by Marilyn Cochran-Smith— argue in favor of teaching that connects with students' cultural understandings of the world. Building on the arguments central to the Shade (1982) article discussed above, these two 1995 articles are, to a large extent, a response to the way in which school desegregation policy has been implemented—that is, primarily on a superficial level that has focused almost exclusively on getting the right mix of students in a school without paying attention to the culture or norms of the school. This powerful theme of bringing a more culturally based focus into the discussion of race, diversity, and teaching made a lot of sense in terms of what had been ignored for too long in the field of education—namely, the role of culture in learning and student engagement.

These 1990s publications suggest an increasing degree of frustration and push-back against the prevailing policy context, steeped in the power of *A Nation at Risk* and subsequent reports that framed the problems in the field of education in terms of a lack of accountability for student outcomes in a lackluster system. Ignored in this context was the systemic inequality in which the schools existed and the structural and cultural implications of that context for how students, educators, parents, and schools were valued and how achievement was measured. We see evidence that by the 1990s a growing number of researchers and journal editors were pushing back against the dominant policy framework. By the early 2000s, the push-back was expanding to include more articles and journal pages.

The Research Out in Front of the Discourse on Issues of Race and the Context of Inequality

Indeed, by the first 5 years of the 2000s, it was far less evident that the policy milieu was having the same impact on research as was suggested by the data from 1975 to 1990. Instead, we see evidence, beginning with a series of articles published in conjunction with the 50th anniversary of *Brown v. Board of Education*, that the education research community began resisting the "tough love accountability" narrative of the policy world, to argue that context and broader societal issues of racial inequality permeate the educational system. A good example of the resistance is illustrated in a 2003 article in *Educational Researcher* by Stepick (2003), who highlighted the contradictions of educational policy with regard to race and racialized achievement gaps. Stepick wrote that while policymakers are quick to implement high-stakes testing for K–12 students, the harshest consequences of which are borne by minority students, the policymakers simultaneously attack race-conscious policies, such as affirmative action, that could help these students. Meanwhile, Stepick (2003) issued a rallying cry for education researchers to reveal this inherent contraction by demonstrating that the problems "confronting minority students are far more complex and profound than performance on standardized tests" (p. 3).

Similarly, in a 2010 chapter in *RRE*, Will Jordon wrote that defining "equity" as simply closing the achievement gap between White students and students of color—as measured almost exclusively by test scores—is problematic in the context of a multicultural society in which one's social class strongly influences life chances. Jordon reexamined equity by situating the issue of concept within an analysis of broader social forces that cultivate inequality, including employment, housing, criminal justice, and so forth, "so that educational inequality is part and parcel of overarching social ills" (p. 142).

The spike in the number of articles focused on racial inequality and its relationship to social context since 2000 in these top education research journals, as illustrated in Table 1, is impressive, to say the least. The articles that appear in 2004 and shortly thereafter in one of the many special issues published in conjunction with the 50th anniversary of *Brown v. Board of Education* are an important part of this story, but they are certainly not the only factor. Even prior to 2004, the number of articles related to social context and racial inequality were on the rise, and the increase continued after the anniversary, with the peak 5-year period thus far being 2010 to 2015.

Other factors at play, we believe, are the changing demographics of the education research community, which, we noted above, means that more of the authors, reviewers, and editors of these leading journals are scholars of color (AERA, 2016). Another fact, based on our content analysis, appears to be utter frustration with an educational policy milieu in which the problems and solutions continue to run contrary to thoughtful scholarship on educational inequality and the contextual variables that influence it. The Jordon (2010) article is but one example of this, as we see ample evidence that education researchers are trying to have a more profound effect on the way policymakers and the general public understand the problems to be solved in our field. This is also, we believe, a sign of a broader push-back against the ways in which the knowledge of our field and the understanding of teaching as a profession have been minimized, at best, and outright ignored, at worst in politics and policy.

CONCLUSION: POTENTIAL OF SOCIAL SCIENCE AND EDUCATION RESEARCH TO SHAPE THE POLICY AGENDA

We want to conclude this review of research in education by returning to the wisdom and insight of Weiss and Bucuvalas, who, in their 1980 book *Social Science Research and Decision-Making*, explained the ways in which social science research supplies more than data. They noted that research also supplies "perspective on events, generalizations about cause and effect, theories about the ways in which people and institutions interact," and understandings of the construction of social, political, and economic systems. To the extent that such research-based understandings affect the choices of those in positions of authority, Weiss and Bucuvalas (1980) wrote, they can "substantially influence not only discrete decisions but the whole framework within which issues are defined and policy responses considered" (p. 2).

The need for a new framework for education policymaking has never been more apparent. The demographics of the U.S. population—especially the school-age population—are changing rapidly. As of September 2014, the percentage of the U.S. K–12 public school population that is White non-Hispanic fell below 50% for the first time ever in our nation's history. Just 35 years ago, students enrolled in U.S. public schools were 79% percent White non-Hispanic. Our nation is undergoing a demographic sea change, and our public schools are at the forefront of this change, with an overall student population that is now about 30% Hispanic, 16% Black, and more than 5% Asian/Pacific Islander. At the same time, opposition to the "colorblind" or "postracial" rhetoric of the last 35 years of educational policy discourse is rising, especially in the aftermath of Ferguson and the rise of the Black Lives Matter movement.

The implications of this turning tide for education research are unknown. One hopeful sign is that policymakers are showing more interest in what the research says is found in the newly passed Every Student Succeeds Act, which allows more leeway for the states to develop accountability systems and school improvement plans. The new law uses the term *evidence-based* to describe requirements for every aspect of these plans, from parent engagement to early childhood programs. This wording suggests that the federal government wants states to pay attention to research and that the research may have had some impact on how the law was written and how states and districts proceed. If our content analysis of six leading journals in education is any indicator of how the knowledge of the field is advancing, the research could encourage local and state policymakers to consider broader contextual issues, such as racial inequality, as critical factors in the effort to close achievement gaps. At the same time, the results of the 2016 presidential election suggest that more progressive approaches to addressing the changing demographics of our student population face an uphill battle. Research on topics such as the educational benefits of diverse schools and classrooms (see Wells, Fox, & Cordovo-Coba, 2016) can not only, hopefully, influence a national debate on issues of changing demographics, but it can also help inform grassroots efforts to embrace diverse schools and communities.

This centennial *RRE* chapter is intended to empower education researchers who focus on issues of racial inequality to contemplate collectively how their research could substantially influence not only discrete decisions but, as Weiss and Bucuvalas (1980) argue, "the whole framework within which issues are defined and policy responses considered" (p. 2). This kind of collective contemplation could be an important goal for AERA in its second century.

ACKNOWLEDGMENT

We would like to thank Thomas Geib, a graduate student at Teachers College, Columbia University, for his research assistance on the content analysis of the journal articles.

REFERENCES

Aaron, H. J. (1978). *Politics and the professors: The great society in perspective.* Washington, DC: Brookings Institution Press.

American Educational Research Association. (2016). *AERA by the numbers.* Retrieved from http://www.aera.net/About-AERA/Who-We-Are/AERA-By-The-Numbers

Anderson, E. L. (1946). The dominant area of educational sensitivity. *The School Review, 54*(7), 377–388.

Anderson, J. D. (2007). Race conscious education policies versus a "colorblind constitution": A historical perspective. *Educational Researcher, 36*(5), 249–257.

A welfare check. (2016, July 16). In PRX (Producer), *Reveal* [Audio podcast]. Retrieved from http://www.wnyc.org/story/a-welfare-check.

Ball, S. (1997). Policy sociology and critical social research: A personal review of recent education policy and policy research. *British Educational Research Journal, 23*, 257–274.

Banks, J. A. (1993). Multicultural education: Developments, dimensions, and challenges. *Phi Delta Kappan, 75*(1), 22–28.

Banks, J. A. (1995). The historical reconstruction of knowledge about race: Implications for transformative teaching. *Educational Researcher, 24*(2), 15–25.

Bell, D. A. (1980). *Brown v. Board of Education* and the interest-convergence dilemma. *Harvard Law Review, 93*, 518–533. Retrieved from http://hartfordschools.org/files/Equity%20Page/Interest_Convergence_by_Bell.pdf

Bell, D. A. (1995). Who's afraid of critical race theory? *University of Illinois Law Review, 1995,* 893–910.

Bell, D. A. (2004). *Silent covenants: Brown v. Board of Education and the unfulfilled hopes for racial reform.* New York, NY: Oxford University Press.

Bell, T. H. (1988). *Thirteenth man: A Reagan Cabinet memoir.* New York, NY: The Free Press.

Berliner, D. C., & Bidwell, B. J. (1995). *The manufactured crisis: Myths, fraud, and the attack on America's public schools.* New York, NY: Basic Books.

Black, E., & Black, M. (2003). *The rise of Southern Republicans.* Cambridge, MA: Belknap Press.

Blackmar, F. W. (1929). The social assimilation of the American Indian. *Journal of Educational Sociology, 3*(1), 7–19.

Bourdieu, P., & Wacquant, L. (1992). *An invitation to reflexive sociology.* Chicago, IL: University of Chicago Press.

Braun, H., Wang, A., Jenkins, F., & Weibaum, E. (2006). The Black-White achievement gap: Do state policies matter? *Education Policy Analysis Archives, 14*(8), 1–110.

Brown, M. (2003). Ghettos, fiscal federalism, and welfare reform. In S. F. Schram, J. Sass, & R. C. Fording (Eds.), *Race and the politics of welfare reform* (pp. 47–71). Ann Arbor: University of Michigan Press.

Burawoy, M. (2009). The extended case method: Race and class in Postcolonial Africa. In *The extended case method: Four countries, four decades, four great transformations and one theoretical tradition* (pp. 1–72). Berkeley: University of California Press.

Bush warns against the "soft bigotry of low expectations." (1999, September 22). *Education Week.* Retrieved from http://www.edweek.org/ew/articles/1999/09/22/03bushs1.h19.html?querystring=soft%20bigotry

Carter, P. L., & Welner, K. (Eds.). (2013). *Closing the opportunity gap: What Americans must do to give every child an even chance.* New York, NY: Oxford University Press.

Chubb, J. E., & Moe, T. M. (1990). *Politics, markets and America's schools.* Washington, DC: Brookings Institution Press.

Cochran-Smith, M. (1995). Color blindness and basket making are not the answers: Confronting the dilemmas of race, culture, and language diversity in teacher education. *American Educational Research Journal, 32*, 493–522.

Covington, S. (1997). *Moving a public policy agenda: The strategic philanthropy of conservative foundations.* Washington, DC: National Committee for Responsive Philanthropy.

Crenshaw, K., Gotanda, N., Peller, G., & Thomas, K. (Eds.). (1995). *Critical race theory: The key writings that formed the movement.* New York, NY: New Press.

Cross, C. T. (2014). *Political education: National policy comes of age* (2nd ed.). New York, NY: Teachers College Press.

Darling-Hammond, L. (2010). *The flat world and education: How America's commitment to equity will determine our future.* New York, NY: Teachers College Press.

DeBray, E. (2005, March). *Partisanship and ideology in the ESEA reauthorization in the 106th and 107th Congresses.* Paper presented at the Wilson Center for Scholars Symposium Panel on ESEA at 40. Retrieved from http://www.wilsoncenter.org/sites/default/files/debray.doc

DeBray, E., Scott, J., Lubienski, C., & Jabbar, H. (2014). Intermediary organizations in charter school policy coalitions: Evidence from New Orleans. *Educational Policy, 28,* 175–206.

Delgado, R., & Stefancic, J. (2012). *Critical race theory: An introduction.* New York: New York University Press.

Duggan, L. (2003). *The twilight of equality? Neoliberalism, cultural politics, and the attack on democracy.* Boston, MA: Beacon Press.

Echaveste, M., & Scott, J. (2011). *How are Americans fighting inequality?* (White paper). New York, NY: Ford Foundation Building Knowledge for Social Justice Political Movements Working Group.

Edsall, T. B., & Edsall, M. (1992). *Chain reaction: The impact of race, rights and taxes on American Politics.* New York, NY: W. W. Norton.

Fine, M. (1991). *Framing dropouts: Notes on the politics of an urban high school.* New York: State University of New York Press.

Finnigan, K. S., & Daly, A. J. (Eds.). (2014). *Using research evidence in education: From the schoolhouse door to Capitol Hill.* New York, NY: Springer.

Frank, T. (2005). *What's the matter with Kansas? How conservatives won the Heart of America.* New York, NY: Holt.

Friedman, M. (1962). *Capitalism and freedom.* Chicago, IL: University of Chicago Press.

Gergen, K. J., & Bauer, R. A. (Eds.). (1968). *The study of policy formation.* New York, NY: Free Press.

Gilmore, G. E. (2008). *Defining Dixie: The radical roots of civil rights.* New York, NY: W. W. Norton.

Gitlin, T. (2007). *The bulldozer and the big tent: Blind Republicans, lame Democrats, and the recovery of American ideals.* New York, NY: Wiley.

Hannafin, M. J. (1983). Fruits and fallacies of instructional systems: Effects of an instructional systems approach on the concept attainment of Anglo and Hispanic students. *American Educational Research Journal, 20*(2), 237–249.

Hannah-Jones, N. (2016, June 9). Choosing a school for my daughter in a segregated city. *The New York Times Magazine.* Retrieved from http://www.nytimes.com/2016/06/12/magazine/choosing-a-school-for-my-daughter-in-a-segregated-city.html?_r=0

Horn, J., & Willburn, D. (2013). Where have we been and where are we going with educational assessment in U.S. schools. In *The mismeasure of education.* London, England: Information Age.

Jencks, C., & Phillips, M. (Eds.). (1998). *The Black-White test score gap.* Washington, DC: Brookings Institution Press.

Jordon, W. L. (2010). Defining equity: Multiple perspectives to analyzing the performance of diverse learners. *Review of Research in Education, 34,* 142–178.

Kantor, H., & Lowe, R. (2014). Educationalizing the welfare state and privatizing education: The evolution of social welfare policy since the New Deal. In P. Carter, & K. Welner (Eds.), *Closing the opportunity gap: What Americans must do to give every child an even chance* (pp. 25–39). New York, NY: Oxford University Press.

Katz, M. B. (1996). *In the shadow of the poorhouse: A social history of welfare in America.* New York, NY: Basic Books.

Keith, T. Z., & Page, E. B. (1985). Do Catholic high schools improve minority student achievement? *American Educational Research Journal, 22*, 337–349.

Klarman, M. J. (2004). *From Jim Crow to civil rights: The Supreme Court and the struggle for racial equality.* Oxford: Oxford University Press.

Jensen, A. (1969). How much can we boost IQ and achievement? *Harvard Educational Review, 39*(1), 1–123.

Ladson-Billings, G. (1995). Toward a theory of culturally relevant pedagogy. *American Educational Research Journal, 32*(3), 465–491.

Ladson-Billings, G. (2006). From the achievement gap to the education debt: Understanding achievement in U.S. schools. *Educational Researcher, 35*(7), 3–12.

Ladson-Billings, G. (2012). Through a glass darkly: The persistence of race in education research & scholarship. *Review of Research in Education, 41*(4), 115–120.

Ladson-Billings, G., & Tate, W. F. (1995). Toward a critical race theory in education. *Teachers College Record, 97*, 47–68.

Lagemann, E. C. (2000). *An elusive science: The troubling history of education research.* Chicago, IL: University of Chicago Press.

Lee, J., & Wong, K. K. (2004). The impact of accountability on racial and socioeconomic equity: Considering both school resources and achievement. *American Educational Research Journal, 41*, 797–832.

Light, R. J., & Smith, P. V. (1971). Statistical issues in social allocation models of intelligence: A review and a response. *Review of Educational Research, 41*, 351–367.

Lipman, P. (1998). *Race, class, and power in school restructuring.* Albany: State University of New York Press.

Lipman, P. (2004). *High stakes education: Inequality, globalization, and urban school reform.* New York, NY: Routledge.

Lopez, I. H. (2014). *Dog whistle politics: How coded racial appeals have reinvented racism and wrecked the middle class.* Oxford, England: Oxford University Press.

McGuinn, P. J. (2006). *No Child Left Behind and the transformation of federal education policy, 1965–2005.* Lawrence: University Press of Kansas.

Merriam, S. G., & Tisdell, E. J. (2015). *Qualitative research: A guide to design and implementation* (4th ed.). San Francisco, CA: Jossey-Bass.

Marshall, C. (Ed.). (2005). *Feminist critical policy analysis.* New York, NY: Routledge.

Moynihan, D. P. (1965). *The Negro family: The case for national action.* Washington, DC: Office of Policy Planning and Research, U.S. Department of Labor.

Murray, C. (1984). *Losing ground: American social policy, 1950–1980.* New York, NY: Basic Books.

Nathan, W. B. (1938). Health education among Negroes. *Journal of Educational Sociology, 11*(9), 532–542.

National Commission on Excellence in Education. (1983). *A nation at risk.* Washington, DC: U.S. Department of Education.

Orfield, G. (1988). Race and the liberal agenda: The loss of the integrationist dream. In M. Weir, A. S. Orloff, & T. Skocpol (Eds.), *The politics of social policy in the United States* (pp. 313–355). Princeton, NJ: Princeton University Press.

Orfield, G., & Eaton, S. E. (1996). *Dismantling desegregation: The quiet reversal of Brown v. Board of Education.* New York, NY: New Press.

Patterson, F. D. (1939). Vocational education and guidance for the Negro. *Sociology of Education, 12*(5), 298–307.

Quadagno, J. (1994). *The color of welfare: How racism undermined the war on poverty.* Oxford, England: Oxford University Press.

Ravitch, D. (2010). *The death and life of the great American school system: How testing and choice are undermining education.* New York, NY: Basic Books.

Reich, R. (2007). *Supercapitalism: The transformation of business, democracy, and everyday life.* New York, NY: Vintage.

Rich, A. (2004). *Think tanks, public policy, and the politics of expertise.* Cambridge: Cambridge University Press.

Rothstein, R., Jacobsen, R., & Wilder, T. (2008). *Grading education: Getting accountability right.* New York, NY: Teachers College Press & Economic Policy Institute.

Shade, B. J. (1982). Afro-American cognitive style: A variable in school success? *Review of Educational Research, 52,* 219–244.

Shockley, W. (1971). Models, mathematics, and the moral obligation to diagnose the origin of Negro IQ deficits. *Review of Educational Research, 41,* 369–377.

Stepick, A. (2003). Confronting structure and revealing diversity for Latino students. *Educational Researcher, 32*(7), 39–42.

St. John, N. (1971). Thirty-six teachers: Their characteristics and outcomes for Black and White pupils. *American Educational Research Journal, 8,* 635–648.

Stevens, P. (2007). Researching race/ethnicity and educational inequality in English secondary schools: A critical review of the research literature between 1980 and 2005. *Review of Educational Research, 77,* 147–185.

Torrey, J. W. (1983). Black children's knowledge of standard English. *American Educational Research Journal, 20*(4), 627–643.

Weiss, C. (1977). Research for policy's sake: The enlightenment function of social science research. *Policy Analysis, 3*(4), 531–545.

Weiss, C. (1991). Policy research as advocacy: Pro and con. *Knowledge & Policy, 4*(1/2), 37–56.

Weiss, C., & Bucuvalas, M. J. (1980). *Social science research and decision-making.* New York, NY: Columbia University Press.

Wells, A. S. (2007). Charter schools. In G. Ritzer (Ed.), *The Blackwell Encyclopedia of Sociology.* Oxford, UK: Blackwell.

Wells, A. S. (2009). Our children's burden: A history of federal education policies that ask (now require) our public schools to solve societal inequality. In M. A. Rebell, & J. Wolff (Eds.), *NCLB at the crossroads: Re-examining America's commitment to closing our nation's achievement gaps* (pp. 1–42). New York, NY: Teachers College Press.

Wells, A. S. (2014, Winter). *Seeing past the "colorblind" myth of education policy: Why policymakers should address racial/ethnic inequality and support culturally diverse schools* (Peer reviewed Policy Brief). Boulder, CO: National Education Policy Center.

Wells, A. S., Fox, L., & Cordova-Cobo, D. (2016). *How racially diverse schools and classrooms can benefit all students.* New York, NY: The Century Foundation. Retrieved from http://apps.tcf.org/how-racially-diverse-schools-and-classrooms-can-benefit-all-students

Wells, A. S., & Holme, J. J. (2005). No accountability for diversity: Standardized tests and the demise of racially mixed schools. In J. C. Boger, & G. Orfield (Eds.), *School resegregation: Must the South turn back?* (pp. 187–211). Chapel Hill: University of North Carolina Press.

White, T. (2014). *Culture, power, and pedagogy in market-driven times: Embedded case studies of teaching in four charter schools in New York City* (Dissertation). Teachers College, Columbia University, New York, NY.

Whitty, G. (2006). Education(al) research and educational policy making: Is conflict inevitable? *British Educational Research Journal, 32,* 159–176.

Wilson, W. J. (1990). *The truly disadvantaged: The inner city, the underclass, and public policy.* Chicago, IL: University of Chicago Press.

Xu, P., & Garand, J. C. (2010). Economic context and Americans' perceptions of income inequality. *Social Science Quarterly, 91,* 1220–1241.

Yasso, T. J. (2005). Whose culture has capital? A critical race theory discussion of community cultural wealth. *Race Ethnicity and Education, 8*(1), 69–91.

Zirkel, P. A., & Moses, G. (1971). Self-concept and ethnic group membership among public school students. *American Educational Research Journal, 8,* 253–265.

Zucchino, D. (1997). *Myth of the Welfare Queen: A Pulitzer Prize-Winning Journalist's portrait of women on the line.* New York, NY: Simon & Schuster.

Chapter 4

Assessment Gaze, Refraction, and Blur: The Course of Achievement Testing in the Past 100 Years

Eva L. Baker
Gregory K. W. K. Chung
Li Cai
University of California, Los Angeles

This chapter addresses assessment (testing) with an emphasis on the 100-year period since the American Education Research Association was formed. The authors start with definitions and explanations of contemporary tests. They then look backward into the 19th century to significant work by Horace Mann and Herbert Spencer, who engendered two parallel purposes for assessment: evaluating effects of education and identifying individual differences. The authors consider the interplay of these orientations over the years. After discussing policy impacts on assessment, they discuss the evolution of the concept of validity as it relates to changing rationales for testing. To enrich the reader's comprehension, the authors also discuss perspectives on innovation in technology and in quantitative analysis. They conclude with questions that summarize current concerns with assessment. Finally, they consider future prospects for assessment. They foresee the continued convergence of assessment purposes, innovative learning technology, and new psychometric challenges.

We write this chapter on the topic of educational assessment to celebrate the centennial year of the American Education Research Association (AERA). At the outset, we recognize that the field of *assessment* or *testing* (we use the terms synonymously) is too expansive to tackle as a whole, so we limit the discussion in a number of ways. We confine our principal focus to achievement testing in U.S. elementary and secondary education. Common reasons for this form of testing are to determine students' status and progress, to certify their competencies, or to enable learners, teachers, and policymakers to improve the learning process and outcomes.

Review of Research in Education
March 2016, Vol. 40, pp. 94–142
DOI: 10.3102/0091732X16679806
© 2016 AERA. http://rre.aera.net

Summary data from individual students provide indicators used to monitor and judge the progress and effectiveness of institutions.

It is increasingly clear that assessment has a strong social component at its core. Information derived from testing is valued in a modern information society. For many decades, testing has responded to and enacted combinations of political, policy, and technical purposes in its inception, application, expansion, and criticism.

CHAPTER CONTENT, STRUCTURE, AND PERSPECTIVES

In this chapter we give an extended overview of testing, beginning with a general discussion of tests to describe and explain their essential characteristics. Next, we consider why tests are used and consider common contemporary purposes. We show in a historical section how social context influences assessment development and why assessments continue to matter. In that section we describe two approaches to testing: (a) the improvement of education and (b) the study of individual and group mental capacity. The two approaches use assessment as a way to improve society but by different means. Studies of mental capacity by psychologists from an early time created methods still in use today. Throughout this overview, we also consider the roots of contemporary uses of achievement as they now affect teaching and learning. To signal shifts in assessment development or applications, we describe selected events and influential researchers. Over the years, we examine differences in assessment purposes and resultant trade-offs with regard to depth and breadth of content, the quality of inferences, the assessments' operational utility, and costs. Nonetheless, in recognition of our limitations as historians, we commend to the interested reader excellent chronicles of testing by Cremin (1961, 1964), Cronbach and Suppes (1969), Kliebard (1975, 1997), and Tyack and Cuban (1995). We conclude with a brief treatment of validity issues, persistent questions, and speculation on the future of testing.

To augment the overarching commentary on U.S. testing, we add perspectives from two important subfields of assessment: (a) quantitative methods applied to characterize and improve test properties; and (b) technologies developed for test design, administration, scoring, and interpretation.

To structure the complex story of testing, we borrow from two literary narratives, each illustrating how different points of view radically affect the interpretations of events and concepts. Kurosawa's landmark film *Roshamon* (Jingo & Kurosawa, 1950) and the novel series *The Alexandria Quartet* by Lawrence Durrell (1960) depict events seen through the eyes of four different narrators, each with only a limited view and interpretation. In each of these classics, nuanced meaning is found only at its completion when the viewers or readers themselves construct an integrated understanding of the depicted content. By analogy, we offer the perspectives of technology and of quantitative methods for this testing overview, and we consider their development over time. Although we tried to prepare an integrated chapter, we finally recognized that separate treatments of these two areas paradoxically resulted in a more coherent

overall story. The fields of quantitative methods and technology also relate reciprocally to educational policy, responding to the pull of identified requirements and
generating innovations to push ensuing policy and practice. Push-and-pull analogies
in research and development are found in work by Glennan and Melmed (1996), Di
Stefano, Gambardella, and Verona (2012), and E. L. Baker (2003). We turn now to
defining the term *test.*

What Is a Test?

This section is included especially for nonspecialist readers to provide common
background. In contemporary media, tests are often described by their formats (see
Strauss, 2013). Are examinees presented with short or extended problems? Do they
respond by selecting among multiple options or do they construct their answers?
Surface features, because they can be easily grasped, may draw much of the heat of
popular critiques of testing, particularly if the formats are thought to be artificial (see
Bracey, 1995; FairTest, 2007). Here, we suggest a more comprehensive definition,
actually an amalgam drawn from revisions of the *Standards for Educational and
Psychological Testing* (AERA, American Psychological Association [APA], & National
Council on Measurement in Education [NCME], 1985, 1999, 2014). We offer this
construction:

A test or an assessment consists of a *systematic* method of gaining a *sample of information* about people or
programs so as to draw *inferences* about examinees' knowledge, characteristics, or propensities.

The use of the term *sample* clarifies that tests usually represent only a small
portion of possible content and tasks theoretically drawn from a larger domain of
interest. Descriptions of test topics may be general or very specific, such as reading
comprehension, mathematics ability, essay writing, or knowledge of electromagnetism in simple circuits. Contemporary achievement tests used in schools are, for
the most part, intended to reflect the goals of curricula found at different grade
levels in elementary and secondary schools. The topics of English language (reading and writing) and mathematics have been staples of tests since the beginning of
school assessment.

Test composition, task or item design, and sampled content and skills depend first
on test purposes as well as other constraints, such as the intention to sample content
broadly or to concentrate more deeply on fewer topics, the time allowed for test
administration, the ages of the examinees, and cost constraints.

Because tests always are given to more than one examinee, *systematic*, or standardized, procedures strive for uniformity in material, in sampling of content, in administrative routines, and in scoring practices, thus allowing legitimate comparisons of
examinees (AERA et al., 2014). Standardization is a matter of degree.

To support standardization, tests typically consist of a fixed number of questions
to be answered or tasks to be completed, within tightly controlled or more flexible

time periods. Student answers or products are scored by using prespecified procedures, one of the essential elements of standardization. Test answers can be scored as on/off or by a graduated system of correctness. Responses constructed by examinees, such as essays, solved problems, or more extended tasks like research products, have been characterized as subjective tests. Yet, to protect objectivity, these assessments are typically developed and evaluated using procedures such as explicated rubrics or scoring guides attending to important features or processes involved with the answers. Usually a team of raters is trained to understand and apply the scoring rubric; the raters are given practice until they reach acceptable agreement. In addition to the answer or product, answers to selected and constructed responses may also be scored to record or note the process by which the students arrive at their answers. Rubrics vary in their conception of performance as a "trait" (Graves, 1994), as a skill, or as evidence of knowledge and thinking (E. L. Baker, Aschbacher, Niemi, & Sato, 2005). Computerized scoring of constructed responses will be treated in the technology section of this chapter. Answers are summarized in a set of scores, and these may be again transformed through the scaling process, part of Angoff's (1971) definition of a test (p. 508). Scaling approaches are extensively treated in the quantitative section of this chapter. Although understood as an estimate of performance by test developers and scholars, lay users and others may treat results from a test as the operational meaning of the domain or construct of interest (Cronbach, 1971, p. 481). As a result, less informed consumers have been known to imbue test results with inappropriate precision, for instance, by believing that a student's intelligence as measured by a test score will always and forever remain as measured by that score.

Scholars have created conceptual frameworks to describe the testing process. Among the best known, evidence-centered design (ECD; Mislevy, Almond, & Lukas, 2004) uses logical argument as the principal approach to tie together the elements of test design, development, and quality. First, the developer articulates claims to be made through use of the test about learning or performance in a domain. The test and student results provide the evidence to investigate the claim. Specific attention is given to whether inferences about the motivating claims are supported by the evidence of test results. ECD combines technical design thinking with quantitative or other sources of evidence in a logical framework where validity and quality are incorporated as part of the design frame. We will return to the treatment of validity in a later section. From this initial discussion of testing, we move to the reasons for testing and comment on their relationship to educational practice.

Why Do We Test?

We focus first on contemporary purposes before we treat the historical background of testing. Today, educational policy provides the rationale for most *external testing*, that is, testing not constructed by classroom teachers. Results of achievement tests and assessments are supposed to answer serious questions about education and schooling.

- How are the students or schools doing?
- Are they meeting their goals or on track to reach prescribed levels of student attainment?
- How do students or schools compare to those educated in other settings?
- What side effects occur as a result of testing?
- What areas of performance can be improved?

As we have suggested, assessment results document the status and progress of students with respect to particular constructs, goals, or standards. In addition to describing achievement, many test results may lead to decisions about individuals or institutions (Cronbach & Suppes, 1969). When student achievement serves as a principal indicator of educational effectiveness in formal accountability systems or in the evaluation of competing educational interventions or systems (Popham, 1978; Scriven, 1967), decisions will be made based on results, such as changing instructional practices or obtaining curriculum and materials for the classroom, school, or system. Information about student background; prior performance, curriculum, or instructional exposure; participation; attendance; or the school's composition situates findings and interpretation of the meaning of student achievement results.

A related contemporary goal of testing is equity: the goal of enabling groups to attain comparable levels of educational achievement. Test fairness focuses on lack of bias in the testing process and does not guarantee equal outcomes (AERA et al., 2014, pp. 49–72). Questions such as the following are relevant:

- Are all students making comparable progress toward goals?
- Are identifiable subgroups of students (e.g., girls, poorer students, students in rural settings) achieving comparable levels of results in mathematics and other school subjects?
- Are similar opportunities to learn the content on the tests available to all student groups?

Evidence of extreme or persistent differences in progress or attainment leads to institutional changes in policy and practice. Recent accountability frameworks based on poor results (No Child Left Behind [NCLB], 2002) have triggered consequences, such as requirements to modify school organization, staffing, or pedagogy.

A final purpose of contemporary testing is to communicate the desired content of schooling to educators, students, and the public. This communication naturally occurs at different levels of specificity. For parents and educators alike, general curriculum goals or standards (or claims and targets) addressed by the test communicate the big picture about content and skills that students are intended to learn. Even more specific information is given by developers about tests themselves for use by educators (e.g., the Smarter Balanced Assessment Consortium, and the Partnership for Assessment of Readiness for College and Careers). This information may map tasks or items to standards, give specifications for various tasks and items, and present administration guides, sample exercises, and details of scoring and data interpretation. Technical reports that summarize the quality of evidence for items such as these are further detailed in the quantitative review in this chapter.

Current educational testing policy usually calls for multiple purposes to be accomplished through the use of achievement tests, such as the purposes of accountability and educational improvement (NCLB, 2002; Every Student Succeeds Act, 2015). In earlier periods, tests were often created for a single purpose.

We now go back to the beginnings of testing in order to inform contemporary understanding and highlight sources of continuing controversies about the purposes of assessments and the uses of their results.

LOOKING BACK AT THE SOURCES AND PURPOSES OF TESTING AND ASSESSMENT

Overview

This section considers social and intellectual contexts that affect research and testing programs. Our story begins even before AERA existed. Following our introduction, we summarize illustrative research and development in the first three decades of the 20th century. We then review policy initiatives in the 1950s and 1960s, which began the modern era of testing when schools became more responsible for achieving student outcomes. Finally, we discuss the recent major influences, especially the rise of the dual concerns of accountability and equity. We will describe assessment as used to identify individual differences in mental capacity or in aptitude for different subject matters, or as applied to school outcomes associated with learning. These purposes and rationales have coexisted throughout the past 100 years, resulting in a continuing debate about proper testing methods for various purposes.

Early School-Based Assessment

We start more than 150 years ago at the point of the great expansion of public schools, when the United States experienced its largest flow of immigration (U.S. Census Bureau, 1880). Education was of heightened importance as a means to address societal change. Coincident with immigration, Horace Mann was a leading voice for better schooling. Mann called for democratizing education by reorganizing schools (see M. Mann, 1867). He argued that a clear blueprint guiding all schools would open educational opportunities to allow children to thrive in a democracy. His common school specified curriculum and divided students into grade levels generally associated with their age. Although periodic testing already existed, examinations usually consisted of oral presentations or exhibitions by a few students. Mann suggested adding standard written examinations to determine the quality of learning and instruction and to compare different schools (see M. Mann, 1867). He also advocated the use of grade-by-grade examinations to determine which students were ready for promotion. The New York Regents Examinations, beginning in 1865, followed the general assessment plan recommended by Horace Mann (1846/1957). Nationwide, attempts to "standardize" the organization of schools to raise school quality continued, an endeavor prompting numerous study tours. In 1892, John Mayer Rice, after visiting many districts and schools, reported that he could place "no reliance" on claims of quality made by school superintendents (reported in Cremin, 1964). Rice chose spelling and developed short lessons and regular standard examinations. Another contemporary scholar, John Dewey, would rise to great prominence as an educational reformer. At the turn of the century, he also argued that schools should provide engaging opportunities for knowledge acquisition and specifically for civic learning to support democracy (Dewey, 1897). Dewey's views spread widely but, early in the century, had only limited impact on assessment in schools. These three innovators, grounded in school observation, regarded curriculum as a central feature for judging quality. However, the rise of science pushed testing in another direction.

Evolution and Mental Capacity

Our focus on achievement testing would properly relegate tests of mental capacity or intelligence to a minor role. Such tests cannot be readily dismissed, however, at least at the outset of systematic testing of individuals. The intellectual history of achievement and intelligence is entwined.

The publication of Darwin's (1859) *On the Origin of Species* in England exerted pervasive impact on intellectuals in the United States and abroad. Darwin hypothesized that heredity depended on variation, differentiation, and competition, features essential to the success of surviving species. Herbert Spencer (1867), an English social theorist, extrapolated Darwin's observations of animals to humans. He argued that a successful society required means to identify and sort individuals capable of different contributions in order to improve society. Spencer argued that the principle of "survival of the fittest" precluded significant interventions to improve the lives of the lower classes. Social Darwinists held that success was tied to genetic capacity. Individuals in lower classes would find their "natural place" in society. Darwin's findings were extended to apply both to individuals and to societies.

Sir Francis Galton, Darwin's cousin, was among the first to pursue the implications of natural selection applied to mental ability. To do so, he experimented with testing procedures to assess mental capacity. His studies used a variety of tasks, including physical observations and sensory discriminations, to classify the mental ability of individuals in different social strata. He analyzed thousands of cases; many of the subjects paid to be tested and were people of means. He applied the normal distribution to these results, developed percentiles to communicate relative performance, and used correlational techniques to relate results of mental tests to other variables. Predictably, he concluded that superior mental ability resided in upper-class males in England. Galton (1883) promoted eugenics, the philosophy of trying to perfect society by reducing the proportion of those of inferior capacity. This viewpoint influenced scores of psychologists. For instance, Karl Pearson (1901) developed many of his statistical tools to demonstrate how society needs to maintain its "efficiency by insuring that its numbers are substantially recruited from the better stocks." Galton and his colleagues inspired the branch of testing used by psychologists to examine individual differences in mental capacity. In the late 19th century, James McKeen Cattell, a student of Wundt, experimented in the United States with measuring mental processes, such as reaction times (Cattell, 1890). The implications of Galton's positions were to linger in U.S. testing for almost 100 years. As is well known, the use of eugenics in U.S. and German society resulted in unfathomable evil. Cronbach (1971) notes that until the 1950s, all forms of U.S. testing grew from a eugenics perspective.

Testing for Individual Differences

Educational measurement of mental capacity as intelligence is also dated to studies by Alfred Binet, who was commissioned to identify French children who were unable to profit from regular classroom instruction. Binet, with his colleague Theodore Simon, developed a test consisting of classroom tasks encountered at different grade levels (Binet & Simon, 1916). Binet and Simon's test—like those by Mann, Rice, and Dewey—was based on extensive classroom observations. It elicited responses to sensory, memory, rhyming, and comprehension tasks commonly found in schools of that time. Using a developmental approach, Binet and Simon standardized the tasks by averaging the performances by children of the same age. Binet and Simon's test was introduced in the United States in 1916 and, with numerous revisions by Lewis M. Terman (1917a, 1917b, 1925), given in U.S. schools until court decisions in the1970s restricted the administration of intelligence tests (*Larry P. v. Riles*, 1972/1974). Terman (1925) was responsible for a large study, *Genetic Studies of Genius*, following high-scoring examinees over decades to determine their societal contributions. Binet himself later argued that intellectual ability was a combination of genetics and experience (Selden, 1999).

E. L. Thorndike, Lewis B. Terman, Charles Spearman, and Robert Yerkes were all strongly influenced by Galton. They pursued the differential measurement of mental capacity in part to understand its nature and to make predictions of future societal contributions. Thorndike's interests in human abilities were wide ranging, including studies of twins (1915), memory (1910), and animals (1898). Though his attention was directed to mental capacities (Thorndike, 1904, 1919, 1927), he also examined components of those capacities in tests of school subjects. He investigated, for example, children's performance in arithmetic (1922b), algebra (1922a), reading (1917), writing (1911a), and science (1911b). Thorndike's general conclusions aligned with those of Spearman (1925), who argued that a general intelligence factor (*g* factor) lay at the heart of achievement in specific realms. Spearman (1927) used factor analysis, among other innovative methods, to explore intelligence. The early 20th-century view of the stability of general intelligence over test content, type, and setting has been supported more recently by Carroll (1993) and Jensen (1980), positions that provoked great controversy. The view of genetic stability is undergoing rapid revision in the 21st century.

Efficiency Influences on Testing

Franklin Winslow Taylor (1911) is best known for bringing science to the world of work in pursuit of efficiency. Noted as the first management consultant, Taylor sought to improve productivity through careful analyses of work tasks, assignment of tasks to individuals of appropriate ability, and measurement of the productivity of workers. His influence in education grew in part because Franklin Bobbitt was Taylor's student. Bobbitt, an expert in curriculum, sought to structure schools in an orderly manner so that each student could be educated to his capabilities (Bobbitt, 1924). He believed that schools should exist to fit individuals to the roles they would eventually undertake in the world of work. He argued that identifying school objectives and creating curriculum from job analyses were appropriate procedures and that each student should be given exactly what he needs to meet these objectives (Bobbitt, 1913). As World War I approached, new uses were found to fit individuals to tasks through testing.

Army Alpha Examinations

A major testing milestone was generated by the need of the United States to rapidly identify men fit to join the Army prior to World War I. The Army Alpha test, developed by Clarence S. Yoakum, Robert Yerkes, Lewis M. Terman, G. M. Whipple, Carl Brigham, and colleagues, claimed to measure mental capacity (Yerkes & Yoakum, 1920). Using group-testing procedures, they demonstrated that paper-and-pencil tests could be given efficiently (they tested more than 1.7 million candidates). The test sorted out the "feeble minded" and those otherwise unfit for service and found higher capacity examinees to assign to higher ranks and more complex roles (Yerkes, 1923, in Brigham, 1923, pp. 80–86). The Army beta examination was individually administered to illiterates. The impact of these tests was enormous and extended far beyond their original intended uses. Brigham (1923) described systematic differences in intelligence associated with background. Men from northern European backgrounds tested at the highest levels, followed by southern Europeans and Blacks. These findings directly influenced the quotas of the Immigration Act (1917) and were echoed in the popular press of the time and in immigration preferences regarding countries of origin. The findings were taken to support the view that intellectual differences were stable, inherited, and related to geographical region. Brigham (1930) later recanted his theory of racial differences. (Note that Yerkes, Brigham, and Terman, along with Thorndike, were members of the Eugenics Society.)

Standardized Testing in Schools: Individual Differences

Before World War I, Yerkes and Terman approached the General Education Board (GEB) to propose mental testing for schoolchildren. Funded by philanthropists, such as John D. Rockefeller Sr., the GEB focused on rural education and the importance of vocational training, particularly for students in the South. The GEB occasionally funded surveys, and Terman and Yerkes proposed to develop a broad system of tracking students in three tiers, using intelligence tests related to the Army Alpha test. Yerkes explained the Army program and his view that "low-grade" children received large amounts of attention and that "high-grade" children were being sacrificed (Whipple, 1921; Yerkes, 1919).

Under the auspices of the National Research Council (NRC), Yerkes, Terman, Thorndike, Haggerty, and Whipple were made members of a committee to develop the National Intelligence Test, a task completed in summer 1920. By spring of 1921, more than 200,000 tests had been sold and widely used, consistent with Taylor's (1911) scientific principles, to assign students to homogeneous groups by their mental capacity. A related study described by Buckingham (1920), and Buckingham and Monroe (1920), linked achievement tests in mathematics and literacy with a version of an intelligence test to compare schools in various regions and provide guidance in instruction to teachers.

School and Curriculum as Sources of Tests

Notwithstanding the relationship between mental capacity and subject matter proficiency, recall that Horace Mann's vision of schooling rested on the idea that curriculum and instructional practices could raise the quality of schools and of learning for diverse groups of children. By 1920, schooling was widely distributed through age 13 (U.S. Census Bureau, 1920). The expansion of schooling continued, and the Great Depression of 1929–1939 resulted in population movements toward urban centers, from the South to the North and from the Midwest to the West. Attendance in secondary schools increased because of limited economic opportunity for children, and consolidated schools were developed to deal with larger numbers of students. Stenquist (1933) described as "commonplace" uses of tests to manage the larger numbers of students in schools, to deny additional schooling to those who could not profit from it (a necessity because of the lack of funds for education), or to extend opportunity to proficient students. Few researchers experimented in educational programs intended to improve learning for all students (Washburne, 1940). Yet Dewey continued to grow in stature as a counterbalance to the efficiency movement, and he emphasized that learning was desirable for all students. Other progressive educators in 1932 began to study high schools. They investigated the effects of an alternative high school curriculum, one based more on demonstrated learning than mere attendance in prescribed courses. The intent was to implement a new curriculum in 30 schools for 4 years and follow students who attended university for 4 more years; hence the title *The Story of the Eight-Year Study* (Aiken, 1942). Although a number of educational experts were involved in its design, its largest impact grew from an approach to curriculum development and evaluation widely credited to Ralph W. Tyler (1931). The strategy was to use operational or behavioral statements of student outcomes, designed through a careful procedure known as the "Tyler Rationale" (for a summary, see Tyler, 1949). Tyler held that student evaluation should match the objectives to be measured rather than rely on more general ability tests. He also argued for the provision of "learning opportunities" to reflect both the objectives and the methods of student evaluation. Sets of materials guiding instruction were developed for high school courses. Intended to create aligned instructional systems, Tyler's work still supports a contemporary ideal.

Tyler's study concluded at the onset of World War II. Similar selection measures to the Army Alpha test were used in World War II; however, great emphasis was placed on training as well. Consequently, psychologists populated the Office of Special Services to conduct experiments in training (see Hovland, Lumsdaine, & Sheffield, 1949) and as a result explored different types of criterion measures.

At the conclusion of the war, behavioral approaches to training began to make their way into schools. Robert Gagné (1965) advocated task analyses using a psychological orientation, and Robert Glaser (1962) began postwar research on instruction. B. F. Skinner moved his studies of animal behavior to experiments in systematic instructional approaches (Holland & Skinner, 1961). Skinner and others invested in systematic approaches using assessment during the course of instructional programs (these activities are more completely described in the technology section of this chapter). These assessments were to allow the student to advance to the next phase of instruction. Other test developers, such as Lindquist, working from school and testing perspectives, focused attention on curriculum-relevant tests (Feldt, 1979). Based on the curriculum in Iowa, Lindquist and his colleagues created curriculum-based tests that used innovative methodology (Lindquist, 1951). Lindquist is credited with at least two long-running, research-based, and highly valued systems, the Iowa Tests of Basic Skills, focused on elementary learning, and the American College of Testing admission tests (Lindquist, 1970).

Around the same time, Benjamin Bloom and his colleagues began to systematize the measurement of university performance, a process that would have great impact on American public school testing. Their work produced the *Taxonomy of Educational Objectives: Vol. 1. The Cognitive Domain* (Bloom, Englehart, Furst, Hill, & Krathwohl, 1956), a six-level classification system focused on the cognitive demands of test items. Bloom's work resulted in a hothouse of activity matching test items to levels, and pushed the demand for tests that included items requiring more than recognition or recall from examinees. These efforts presaged continuing efforts to categorize test items according to the types of thinking they require (AERA et al., 2014; Cai, Baker, Choi, & Buschang, 2014; Herman & Linn, 2013; Webb, 2009). The *Taxonomy*'s companion volume—*The Affective Domain*—emphasized the development of attitudes, starting from receiving and awareness of relevant stimuli to the personal embodiment of values (Krathwohl, Bloom, & Masia, 1964, p. 34). The topics in this work have found their way into current discussions of measuring character and noncognitive outcomes.

Educational reform was directly bolstered by the National Defense Education Act of 1958, stimulated by the Soviet Union's Sputnik satellite launch. The act affected education through its investment in the development of new school curricula in math and science, support of teacher development, and the inauguration of graduate programs focused on improved learning and better testing. It brought the federal government more overtly into questions about the quality of education.

Evaluating Federal Programs

The next watershed event for testing was the enactment of the Elementary and Secondary Education Act (ESEA; 1965), a centerpiece of President Lyndon B. Johnson's "War on Poverty." ESEA focused attention on the learning of poor, mostly minority students who had not yet been successful in school. ESEA also spurred educational development and research on new approaches to learning and classroom instruction by investing in the Regional Educational Laboratories and the National Education Research and Development Centers in the same year. Two centers, one at the University of Wisconsin and the other at the University of Pittsburgh, developed school programs related to analyses of subject matter (i.e., mathematics) and used, at the outset, behavioral approaches (Glaser, 1966; Klausmeier, 1977). The work of these centers was highly significant in the development of curriculum-based assessments.

In addition, the need to evaluate ESEA studies of interventions such as Head Start and Follow-Through programs for young children stimulated the development of a new profession, that of educational evaluator.

Required Standardized Testing

Students receiving resources from Title I of the ESEA were to be tested annually in their schools. The assessments were selected from commercially available tests in mathematics and reading and were to be given only to students fitting Title I criteria. Through various reauthorizations, the types of tests changed. The Improving America's Schools Act (1994), a continuation of ESEA, required testing of all students based on standards, not only those intended to receive Title I resources. The expectation of testing every student included students learning English and those with disabilities, requirements that have continued in the most recent reauthorization (Every Student Succeeds Act, 2015).

One upshot of the federally inspired programs was the explosion of new business for testing companies. At about the same time, researchers focused on developing instructional programs that would work for poor as well as more advantaged students. In the course of their efforts, these researchers reconceived ways that assessment could be designed. Until that time, most tests' development usually followed the models set out to measure individual differences. Robert Glaser (1963) and, later, Popham and Husek (1971) pointed out the mismatch between tests developed to identify student differences and those that sought to determine instructional effects on the learning of students. This point of view had a number of facets. The first was that, as Tyler (1949) had earlier noted, tests to measure intended changes in behavior needed to map to the objectives and instruction in the educational system.

Glaser (1963) described the differences between norm-referenced and criterion-referenced tests in two ways: how the tests should be designed and how they should be reported. Instead of comparing individuals against normative performance, reports should be made in terms of attainment of the prespecified criterion. What followed was a period when norm-referenced tests were retrofitted with goals and criterion levels to change their reporting (Gay, 1980, pp. 195–196). In 1978, Popham and Ebel, at a presidential session of the AERA annual meeting, debated the value of norm-referenced tests versus criterion tests. One point of contention was the specificity or breadth of tests—whether they should be linked to clear goals or to the more general constructs, described by Ebel as the guiding source of test item development (Ebel & Popham, 1978). The core issue was the value of the assessments for given purposes. If assessments were to be used to evaluate deliberate instructional activities relevant to clear goals, then, to paraphrase Popham, it was only fair that teachers should have as much clarity as possible to enable them to choose their instruction wisely. Ebel argued that tests should be broadly related to general goals because teachers might interpret their charge differently. The argument, sometimes oversimplified in terms of depth versus breadth, has both technical and moral dimensions—the latter if teachers were held accountable but had only limited access to, or understanding of, test content to guide and improve their teaching. Cronbach and Snow (1977), reporting on a generally futile search for aptitude–treatment interactions, recommended that construct-based "general" measures are better suited to identifying student differences, perhaps as moderating variables, than domain-focused tests, which were more appropriate for evaluating performance.

Criterion-referenced tests picked up surplus meaning from their association with the minimum competency movement (Cohen & Haney, 1980, p. 9). These programs set specific goals with low expectations, tied diplomas to particular pass rates, and were thought to affect disproportionately disadvantaged students (Cuban, 1980, pp. 69–71). The judicial decision in the Florida functional literacy case (a minimum competency test) came down on the side of providing opportunity to learn (remember Tyler again) for students for whom test consequences were substantial (*Debra P. v. Turlington*, 1983).

Three Mitigations to Behaviorism

No doubt there still exists a continuum of specificity in test development, anchored by so-called narrowly construed domains, such as the set theory orientation of Hively, Patterson, and Page (1968) or more recent explicit approaches of parameterization described in the technology section of this chapter. These specify boundaries within which test items can be developed. At the other end of the continuum are tests where content is described in more general, topical terms.

Three interventions mitigated the specificity of tests derived from behaviorism: (a) standards, (b) cognitive psychology, and (c) performance assessment. In the first intervention, the concept of *standards* was imported from Great Britain in 1988 to substitute for the concepts of *goals* or *objectives* (Education Reform Act, 1988). The new standards were written more clearly than statements of abilities and more generally than lists of behavioral requirements. In the United States, the National Council of Teachers of Mathematics (1989) found a reasonable way to describe standards, augmenting them with examples to flesh out meaning, much as Bloom et al. (1956) had done three decades earlier.

The second intervention to moderate behaviorism has had a much larger impact on learning and assessment: *cognitive psychology*. We date cognitive psychology from the late 1950s; it flowered in the 1970s (linked with computer science) with seminal work by Bransford (1979), Newell, Shaw, and Simon (1959), and Wiener (1950). Cognitive learning theorists hypothesized learning processes as well as outcomes and proposed that new learning is constructed by the learner based on prior learning and task demands. This perspective was taken by Bloom (1976, p. 16). Cognitive approaches emphasized records of the learning process as central to the interpretation of attained outcomes. One strategy was to create tasks to elicit mental models of subject matter or processes (Johnson-Laird, 1983). This method led to an extended interest in differences among types of expertise, anchored by DeGroot's work with chess (see Chi, Glaser, & Farr, 1988, as a referent work). Studies of contrasts between expert and novice approaches to learning and their representations (or mental models) were undertaken by Ericsson and Smith (1991) and Rumelhart (1980). Finally, cognitive researchers also emphasized that knowledge is derived from the community in which learning occurs rather than being an isolated, individual accomplishment (Wenger, 1998).

The third important intervention to moderate the influence of "atomized" behavioristic measures was the use of *performance assessment* in large-scale environments. Performance assessment was developed as a means to embody the expectations of cognitive approaches to learning, at minimum supporting learner-constructed responses over multiple-choice. Early examples, imported from Great Britain and Australia, started with essays of various genres. Topics to stimulate content-rich writing were illustrated in an early international comparison of written composition skills (Purves & Takala, 1982). Essay writing was used as a measure in state assessments in the 1980s, incorporating genres of description, explanation, narration, and persuasion (Coffman, 1971). Performance assessment claimed to accommodate other, newer conceptions of learning with more complex sets of expectations (E. L. Baker, Freeman, & Clayton, 1991). These included decision making, team performance (Salas & Cannon-Bowers, 2001), and problem solving (Resnick, 1994; Wittrock & Baker, 1991). The roots of performance assessment could be traced to Dewey's recommendations for "records" of student growth, to complex tasks in the military (see Hovland et al., 1949), and to workplace requirements described in a report from the Secretary of Labor (Secretary's Commission on Achieving Necessary Skills, 1991). Earlier versions of teacher performance tasks had been developed by Popham (1969). The most well-developed performance tests integrated different sources of knowledge in multistepped tasks. More extended records of student work, either to show progress or to exhibit range of performance, were compiled in portfolios, borrowing from the arts (see, e.g., Braun, 2016). Technical work surrounding performance assessments and portfolios was conducted to guide their development, evaluation, and reporting (Junker, 2011; Linn, 1993; Resnick & Resnick, 1992; Shavelson, Baxter, & Pine, 1992). Although performance assessments and portfolios were much in vogue in the late 1980s and 1990s, public questions about appropriateness of the content of tasks, their technical quality, and the time and costs involved led to a reduction in the popularity of its use in large-scale assessment, except for essays and fairly routine problem solving. At the beginning of the 21st century, however, new predictions of needed skills and knowledge revived performance-based tasks, including collaborative problem solving (O'Neil & Chuang, 2008), teamwork (O'Neil, Chung, & Brown, 1997), and transfer or application of knowledge to new settings or problems (Cooper & Sweller, 1987; Bransford, Brown, & Cocking, 2000). One tactic to support the continued use of performance tests was to place them in classrooms where they were to function less as formal tests and more as integral parts of instruction or embedded in formative assessment (Black & Wiliam, 2009; Phelan, Choi, Vendlinski, Baker, & Herman, 2011). *Knowing What People Know* (NRC, 2001) was a compilation of assessment approaches appropriate to more complex formulations of learning, involving cognitive, performance, and formative concepts of assessment. These initial formulations were to be renewed later in the 21st century, when computers could offer platforms able to contain costs, collect data, and standardize administration as described in the technology section of this work. Not limited to local practices, assessment innovation developed in national and international comparative assessments.

National and International Comparisons

In addition to scale, both national and international assessments contended with the problems of relevance and fairness. Curricula differed across the United States and among countries. The approaches taken in national and international studies involved extensive review by stakeholders and greater description of test instruments and interpretations. These processes were to modify U.S. expectations for test specifications and descriptions.

In 1969, under the leadership of Ralph Tyler, the National Assessment of Educational Progress (NAEP) was born (Lagemann, 2002, p. 190). It was intended to monitor school learning nationwide (sampling limited subjects and grade levels) and to provide innovative models for how assessment might depart from historical forms. Therefore, it was prospective as well as descriptive in its intent. NAEP reports were aggregated by region in the United States to preclude comparisons of individual states. A study of NAEP by Wirtz and Lapointe (1984) suggested that NAEP needed revision to strengthen its impact on education. In the next decade, NAEP sampling and reporting were changed to allow state-by-state administration and comparisons, a process studied by a panel of the National Academy of Education (Glaser, Linn, & Bohrnstedt, 1997). NAEP's technical rigor was improved when the Educational

Testing Service was contracted for its administration. NAEP reports now include large-city school district data. Throughout its history, NAEP has juggled the desire for longitudinal data with a compelling need to be relevant to educational change. As a result, two separate streams of assessment have been in play: longitudinal studies to show progress over time and studies based on assessment frameworks using more contemporary school expectations.

NAEP has been touted as a way to establish comparability of assessments (NCLB, 2002). Kifer (2001, p. 79) and Linn (2003) have raised questions about the conceptual argument and practical utility of NAEP in this role.

International Comparisons

International comparisons of achievement in the United States and other countries date from before the 1960s, when cross-national studies in various subject matters were conducted by the International Association for the Evaluation of Educational Achievement (E. L. Baker & O'Neil, 2016). These studies were variously supported by international groups, foundations, and governments. The Trends in International Mathematics and Science Study and the Progress in International Reading Literacy Study were both used to create curriculum-relevant assessments that could compare students at specific ages (Beaton et al., 1996). A benefit of those studies was a methodology developed to compare the curricular offerings underlying the relative performance of nations (Schmidt, McKnight, & Raizen, 1997). Schmidt et al. (1997) famously noted that U.S. math content was "a mile wide and an inch deep," sparking reforms related to standards and instruction. The methods used in this work stimulated continued interest in the alignment of curriculum, instruction, and assessment (p. 122).

The Organisation for Economic Co-operation and Development produced a set of descriptive educational indicators. In 2001, it administered the first examination of the Programme for International Student Assessment (PISA; Organisation for Economic Co-operation and Development, n.d.) intended to measure "domain-independent" skills, such as problem solving, required for success in the global workforce. PISA's orientation reverted in part to school subjects, and like the International Association for the Evaluation of Educational Achievement, PISA issued reports ranking countries by their achieved test performance. Both international projects have had periods of strong impact—for instance, a call for educational reform (*Nation at Risk*; National Commission on Excellence in Education, 1983) compared U.S. data on instructional time compared to those in other countries. More recently, PISA studies of cognition and content have been supplemented by reports about self-concept and motivation to pursue scientific studies. Both sets of international research have provided methodological models and prodded U.S. educational test developers to improve their offerings. The middling status of U.S. students has generated criticism of these comparisons, for example, by Berliner and Glass (2014). Nonetheless, current discussions of test quality call for international benchmarking.

More Recent Adventures in Achievement Testing

The notion of voluntary national standards was pursued in the 1990s, and the report *Raising Standards for American Education* (National Council on Education Standards and Testing, 1992) echoed Tyler's recommendations for standards for content, assessments, opportunity to learn, and methods of accounting for societal and learner needs. In 2002, NCLB stipulated that states develop standards and create or find assessments to measure them. In the reforms supported by the Obama administration, the idea of voluntary national tests was resuscitated by a Federal competition for voluntary tests to be developed by State consortia. The major winners, Smarter Balanced Assessment Consortium and the Partnership for Assessment of Readiness for College and Careers, created tests for students intended to substitute for existing state assessments of English language arts and mathematics performance (see http://www.smarterbalanced.org/ and http://www.parcconline.org/). Given 3 years of federal support, and relying on commercial vendors for elements of development and administration, these consortia have gradually lost state membership as federal funds ended. Additional state consortia have been created to measure English language proficiency, for example, English Language Proficiency Assessment for the 21st Century and World-Class Instructional Design and Assessment. These and other tests to measure educational standards are expected to show their impact on student performance and graduates' college and career readiness, as well as relationships to NAEP and to benchmarks derived from international comparisons.

Through evolution of test purposes, concepts of validity similarly changed. Let us now turn to the topic of validity, telescoping its development related to the varied purposes of testing over the past 100 years.

VALIDITY

Changing Notions of Validity

As defined by the 1999 edition of *Standards for Educational and Psychological Testing* (AERA et al., 1999), "Validity refers to the degree to which evidence and theory support interpretations of test scores entailed by proposed uses of tests" (p. 9). As defined by Linn (2010), "Validity is the most important consideration in the evaluation of interpretations of education assessment results and the uses that are made of the results" (p. 181).

Validity relates to the quality of the inferences made using evidence obtained for the purposes the test is intended to serve. In the past, validity has sometimes been ascribed to properties of the test itself. For example, content-related evidence relies on the extent to which the tasks included on the test are judged by experts to be relevant to the test's claims (Cronbach & Quirk, 1971); it was one of the major sources of validity claims prior to the 1950s. This kind of evidence should answer the question, "Do the observations truly sample the universe of tasks . . . or of situations [that the test developer would like to observe]"? (Cronbach, 1971, p. 446). The term *face validity* referred to whether surface features of the test reflected the test title and purpose. As an exercise, we might consider whether Rice's formulations of spelling tests would be judged to exhibit content validity, that is, to include appropriate vocabulary for the grade levels tested. Content-related validity requires a systematic qualitative process. To make judgments of relevance and comprehensiveness of achievement tests, researchers need to compare the test to resources such as a network or map of content relationships, sometimes labeled an ontology (Mousavi, Kerr, & Iseli, 2013). Content for such representations may be drawn from textbooks and other expert sources of subject matter. Determining how test content is related or aligned to stated educational standards or domain definitions is also relevant in validity studies. Linn, Baker, and Dunbar (1991) and E. L. Baker, O'Neil, and Linn (1993) suggested additional validity criteria relevant to the assessment, including quality of content, cognitive demands, and (likely) transfer and generalizability. Content richness was investigated by Baxter and Glaser (1998). Other recent formulations focus on alignment (see Dwyer, 2005). Explicit qualitative studies have been used to address the content, cognitive, task, and linguistic features of tests of large-scale tests and of formative assessments in games. Other researchers continue to describe cognitive properties of tests to guide design and review as part of validity (Bennett, 2006; Darling-Hammond, 2009).

Another precursor to more modern conceptions of validity was *predictive validity*, that is, the extent to which performance on the target measure dependably predicts desired outcomes. This type of validity evidence suffers from a number of problems, including the quality of the criterion or predicted variable (Cronbach, 1971). For example, a recent study of posttraumatic stress disorder (E. L. Baker et al., 2015) relied for credibility on the criterion judgments of psychologists, who may disagree about the state of patients with various scores on the predictors. Predictive validity of school content might look at subsequent advanced language performance predicted by performance on a beginning-level test of a foreign language. In 1954, APA published *Technical Recommendations for Psychological Tests and Diagnostic Techniques* (APA, AERA, & NCME, 1954) where they used the term *criterion validity* to include predictive validity (relationship with performance obtained at a later time) and concurrent validity (relationships with measures or categories on the same topic available in the same general time period; see Cronbach, 1971, p. 477). For example, Galton's approach to test validity focused on the use of tests of mental capacity to separate examinees into their extant social groups, an example of concurrent validity. Examples of predictive validity are found in Terman's (1925) longitudinal study of subsequent accomplishments of gifted students. An example of concurrent validity in curriculum-based tests involved studies to determine if a new test mode—completion of knowledge maps—was related systematically to students' performance on content tests and essay papers in the same subject-matter domain (Chung, Delacruz, et al., 2003).

Construct validity was introduced in 1954 as one type of validity that depended on sets of relationships between the target test and other variables. Cronbach (1971, pp. 475–477) early favored a network approach of construct validity, where test results are hypothesized to sit in a set of structural relationships to other measures or judgments about the respondents. The theory in which tests claims were embedded would generate propositions and predictions about the relationships of test results to other evidence. Salient methods of studying construct validity empirically were described by Cronbach and Meehl (1955) and Campbell and Fiske (1959). Incorporation of these and other methods led to a continuing consensus on the unified concept of construct validity shown in successive versions of the *Standards for Educational and Psychological Testing* (AERA et al., 1985, 1999, 2014; APA, AERA, & NCME, 1974).

Starting with a theory of purposes of a test, the framer of a construct validity claim would identify evidence that supported or undermined the desired claims. Thus, a wide range of evidence could be brought into play, including evidence of hypothesized relationships, both positive and negative (convergent or discriminant validity). Construct validity reified the notion that validity depended on the inferences drawn from the test results in light of its purposes rather than in the physical test itself (Cronbach, 1971), Cronbach (in Wainer & Braun, 1988, pp. 4–5) argued that validation was not a "thumbs-up/thumbs-down" proposition but a matter of degree. Various scholars have sought to clarify the concept of validity (e.g., see Kane, McCaffrey, Miller, & Staiger, 2013). Cronbach (1971) referenced evaluation work by House (1980) focusing on evidentiary claims. Messick (1989), in his important chapter in *Educational Measurement*, summarized his position that specific test purposes (rather than a general use of the test) should be linked to the requirements for developing evidence. Messick advocated including in validity analyses not only the proposed interpretations flowing from the evidence but also the consequences attending to use of the interpretations in decision making. Referencing the quality of a test to the potential frailties of decision makers may seem like an extension beyond the bounds of strong argument, as it conjointly depends on the unpredictable quality of interpretation and of subjective decisions. The consequences argument may apply more as an imperative to developers and users, encouraging them to foresee both positive and negative outcomes that might occur as a consequence of the decisions made through interpretation of the evidence. The extension of a validity argument and relationships among evidence and interpretations have been analyzed and clarified by the widely used ECD approach, as earlier described (Mislevy et al., 2004; Mislevy, Steinberg, & Almond, 1999).

Social Context Again

New alignments of power have developed in the recent past to illustrate the complex relations of assessment policy, politics, and R&D, and we might add, commercial interests. Until the 1990s, most test offerings were developed and controlled by testing organizations, and some educational buyers had few choices. It is still true that there are only a few major testing organizations, but policy incentives and new technology have created a more diverse set of providers. In the 1990s, policymakers at the federal and state levels became far more active in specifying what was desired in an assessment and shortening the time lines for development and tryouts. The details of test delivery and validity claims were still left to the vendor, but accountability requirements for ESEA reauthorizations, first with the Improving America's Schools Act (1994) and then with NCLB (2002), resulted in a noticeable shift toward the policymakers as an audience for test results (see Council of Chief State School Officers, 2014; Darling-Hammond, Wilhoit, & Pittenger, 2014). Despite increased testing requirements, no dramatic growth has been observed in student outcomes. Yet there remains confidence that testing will work miracles and improve educational performance. This belief may be because tests are a relatively inexpensive intervention. Poor test results have been used to rationalize the introduction of desired interventions. If the attention garnered by the opt-out movement, supported by strong populist contingents in politics, signals a pervasive shift, then development and vetting of test purposes will in the future engage a broader swath of the public. Ideally, some redress and balance of power would be desirable across political, educator, parent, policy, and R&D communities. However, serious understanding of advantages of different assessment options testing requires a level of detail that may elude policymakers and the public at large. Instead, members of the test and assessment community must work harder to communicate benefits or pitfalls to these communities (see Doorey & Polikoff, 2016).

In this discussion, we described quantitative methods that were developed across decades, from Galton to the present, to support the interpretation of test findings. There were instances where methods drove test development rather than the inverse. We turn now to a discussion of the quantitative underpinnings of test quality to add a key and clear perspective on the use and interpretation of testing, test quality, and validity. This perspective includes more technical detail on procedures used to analyze, interpret, and explain tests. When perusing the next section, the reader should have in mind the purposes of the described testing programs.

TECHNICAL QUALITY FROM A STATISTICAL PERSPECTIVE

As we have noted, the early history of statistics is intertwined with that of psychology and especially of psychometrics, a specialized (in terms of the number of living psychometricians) and highly technical field of study that is chiefly concerned with the type of statistics for data arising from mental measurement (e.g., measurement of intelligence, personality, achievement). Out of this small field grew many important (but perhaps also widely misused) statistical tools that are routinely employed to safeguard the technical quality of educational assessment programs. While the legacy of psychometrics may correspond to certain distinct features of educational testing (e.g., the construction of long and homogeneous test forms, standardization, emphasis on comparability, preference for simple item scoring), today relatively few people in the general public or even the education research community are aware that many psychometric methods were developed for the largely social role of supporting efforts to promote fairer, less costly, more predictive, and more accessible assessments. The foregoing historical reviews section has already mentioned important activities and influences such as the creation of the Army's tests in both world wars, testing for intelligence, and college testing. This section, however, emphasizes not only the often serendipitous discovery of powerful ideas that improved psychometrics but also statistical sciences in general.

As an example, consider the publication of Spearman's (1904) seminal article that articulated the model and technique of factor analysis. It was based on the now rudimentary statistics of correlation coefficients and partial correlations, which owe much to the contributions of biometricians (e.g., Karl Pearson) who were Spearman's contemporaries. The context of intelligence testing was characteristic of turn-of-the century psychological research, but the introduction of the idea of the latent variable[1] as a key building block for multivariate statistics was sheer brilliance and perhaps an accident. This concept was a completely homegrown export from education and psychology to the rest of statistical science. Perhaps the idea of the latent variable was invented before its time, as it would take statisticians many decades to fully process the idea, though now it is regarded as routine, especially in Bayesian statistics.

The formalism of including latent variables in statistical models for educational assessment data persist to this day, but the world had to wait for the genius of Fisher (1925) to teach us the modern language of statistical modeling, estimation, and inference. As a consequence, for several decades (until the middle of the 20th century), psychometricians were working on ever more complicated test theories and the related statistical procedures without the necessary statistical tools.

Another difficulty that psychometricians have had to contend with for well over 100 years is that the data sets from educational and psychological assessments are large and inherently multivariate, and the technical work in psychometrics is only as good as the statistical computing tools that researchers have at their disposal. Modern information technology, therefore, exerts its influence on educational assessment not only on design and data collection (as is discussed later, in the technology section) but also on the foundations of technical quality analysis. As a concrete example, consider Jöreskog's (1967) central contributions to practical algorithms for conducting maximum likelihood factor analysis. It is perhaps not a coincidence that in the year before, FORTRAN 66 became standardized for the first time and the programming language spread in the scientific and engineering communities along with IBM's mainframe computers in the preceding decade. Consequently, as we review the statistical research on technical quality of educational assessment, we hope that readers will keep in mind that the major thrusts for development in technical approaches lie in the specification of statistical models that correspond to assessment design with a higher degree of fidelity and complexity (to more fully capture the nuances implied by the design) and with improvements in statistical estimation and inference aided by computing advances.

The Past

Classical Test Theory

One could probably place the beginning of classical test theory (CTT) around several events. First is the founding of the Psychometric Society in 1935, and the subsequent publication in *Science* of L. L. Thurstone's (1937) presidential address to the society on September 4, 1936, calling for quantification of psychology. Published around the same time was J. P. Guilford's (1936) book *Psychometric Methods*, which not only summarized contemporary work but also presaged item response theory (IRT), among other things. In 1937, Kuder and Richardson published their famous formula (KR-20) in the then nascent journal *Psychometrika*. Extended subsequently by Cronbach (1951), KR-20 provided a means to estimate reliability of measures with dichotomously scored items. Reliability estimation would prove to be central to both CTT and subsequent discussions of technical quality of educational assessments in general, as aptly demonstrated by the tens of thousands of citations to Cronbach's (1951) article introducing the alpha coefficient.

One of the most widely known equations (and the only equation in this section) from CTT describes the relationship between observed test score, true score, and (uncorrelated) error of measurement:

$$Y = T + E,$$

where Y stands for the observed score, T for the true score that is presumed to be the true status of the test taker, and E for error of measurement. The simplicity of this equation perhaps masks the fact that without some additional side conditions, Equation (1) does not fully describe a statistical model. Nevertheless, correlational statistical techniques such as regression and analysis of variance (ANOVA) were frequently used in CTT exercises. In terms of the variances, CTT derivations lead to a familiar ANOVA-type decomposition that essentially says the observed test score variance is equal to the true score variance plus the error variance. From this decomposition the reliability in CTT can be defined as a ratio of true score to total observed test score variance. Unfortunately, because the true score is not observed (it is a latent variable), the reliability coefficient cannot be directly computed. Methods to consistently estimate reliability therefore dominate CTT discussions. A number of technical approaches can be taken (e.g., replication, random sampling, parallel forms, split-half), with different assumptions and varying degrees of practical utility and popularity. The most straightforward is to assume the existence of a parallel test X, which has the same true score and same error variance as test Y. With this assumption, the observed correlation between X and Y can be shown to equal reliability. Other approaches are possible, such as the average split-half arguments embedded in Cronbach's (1951) alpha coefficient. A number of comprehensive volumes have been devoted to CTT since Gulliksen's (1950/2013) influential *Theory of Mental Tests* (Lord, Novick, & Birnbaum, 1968; Nunnally & Bernstein, 1967, 1978, 1994; and others).

In terms of support for item analysis and test construction, CTT continues to be useful to this day. Sample means, category proportions, and item–total correlations are important descriptive statistics that have clear CTT-based interpretations in item analysis. They serve as the first line of defense in virtually all psychometric analysis in educational assessment.

Generalizability Theory

Notwithstanding CTT's success in the practice of educational measurement as a basis of continued conceptual and statistical innovation, it outlived its usefulness the minute generalizability theory (GT) was introduced by Cronbach and associates in 1963. Two central conceptual innovations associated with GT also improved our understanding of the validity of tests.

The first has to with the idea that the task of the modeler is to attribute the observed item and score variances to different sources (facets) that might contribute to error variability, for example, items, forms, repeated occasions, or raters. A generalizability (G) study is conducted to disentangle as many facets as realistically feasible. Random effects ANOVA became the predominant statistical tool to estimate the components of variance associated with the facets and their interaction terms. Unlike CTT, the estimated variance components in the underlying random effects ANOVA for the G study afford direct assessment design–related interpretations. For instance, the relative magnitude of individual variance versus test item variance versus rater variance shows the test designer where to focus attention in order to produce a better test (e.g., create more discriminating items or train the raters to be more consistent).

The second conceptual innovation in GT is the recognition that the purpose of measurement must be made explicit before the analysis. GT makes distinctions between two types of decision based on test scores: *relative decisions* and *absolute decisions*. Relative decisions are norm referenced; absolute decisions are referenced to a criterion. Different decisions lead to different specifications of error terms and indices of reliability. Shavelson and Webb (1991) provided excellent introductions to these concepts. With the rise of performance assessments that require complex judgmental scoring processes, GT is routinely used in evaluation studies of test quality. Brennan (2001) thoroughly discussed the more recent development of generalizability applications.

A statistical issue with the current incarnation of GT and its software implementation has to do with the use of random effects ANOVA models for categorical item-level data. More appropriate random effects models in the generalized linear modeling tradition have been developed through recent statistical research (McCulloch, Searle, & Neuhaus, 2008). As will be discussed later, the extension to categorical data merges elements of IRT with GT. The unique and lasting impact of GT on psychometric thinking, however, remains prominent, even as the statistical machinery continues to improve.

Item Response Theory

The roots of IRT were planted in early 20th-century research on psychological scaling (e.g., Thurstone, 1925, 1927). Other quantitative researchers also dabbled in IRT from different starting points (e.g., Lazarsfeld, 1950; Tucker, 1946). In original work, Rasch (1960/1980) and followers developed a model that would bear his name. The Rasch model resembles the IRT models, but philosophical differences regarding the definition of measurement and the role of data analysis in test construction emerged as the two frameworks for item response modeling continued to develop. Bock and Jones (1968) summarized Thurstonian scaling methods and provided a comprehensive statistical framework, prompting continued development in IRT for decades. In the same year, Lord et al.'s (1968) landmark text introduced IRT in its modern form for the first time, including Allen Birnbaum's logistic substitution, which would lead to the three-parameter logistic IRT model (used, e.g., in the NAEP). It would take a few more years until Bock and Lieberman (1970) published their clarification of the core statistical issues in item parameter estimation. Samejima (1969) and Bock (1972) convincingly demonstrated that IRT is useful for items scored in more than two categories. Because of its flexibility and conceptual power, IRT has shifted to the center of educational measurement research and practice. Related developments in the implementation of large-scale computerized adaptive testing that rely heavily on IRT models gradually took hold in educational testing and beyond (e.g., the Armed Services Vocational Aptitude Battery, the Graduate Management Admission Test, and the National Institute of Health's Patient Reported Outcomes Measurement Information System; see Wainer et al., 2000).

The item characteristic curve is the key building block in IRT. In parametric IRT, the item characteristic curve is a model of the conditional probabilities of observed responses (e.g., correct vs. incorrect) given unobserved latent variable(s). The model involves item parameters that characterize the psychometric properties of the test item (e.g., difficulty, discriminability) and person parameters that characterize individual differences in proficiency, achievement, attitude, and so forth. This division of item- and person-specific influences in IRT also extends to its operational use in educational testing situations. Item pools are generally field tested, and the item parameters are estimated in a process commonly called *calibration*. Poorly performing items that negatively affect the test's quality can be removed as a result of item analysis. Scoring of individuals or adaptive administration of items makes extensive use of the calibrated item parameters. With the advent of more powerful computers capable of performing real-time statistical calculations needed for computerized adaptive testing, and with widespread and reliable network access, IRT-based adaptive tests delivered over the Internet are now within reach for K–12 educational assessments (e.g., the Smarter Balanced assessments).

Factor Analysis and Structural Equation Modeling

As mentioned earlier, an almost parallel line of development starting with Spearman's 1904 article led to a large body of literature on factor analysis and structural equation modeling (SEM). Thurstone's (1938) *Primary Mental Abilities* and his (1947) *Multiple Factor Analysis* proved to be the impetus to the subsequent work on intelligence, exploratory factor analysis, and factor rotation, which stood in contrast to Spearman's single factor theory and methods. Faster electronic computers quickly led to the transformation of exploratory factor analysis to general confirmatory factor analysis and SEM. Along the way, publications by Bentler and Weeks (1980), Bock and Bargmann (1966), Browne (1984), Jöreskog (1967, 1969), and Wiley, Schmidt, and Bramble (1973) had particularly prominent and lasting influences. Confirmatory factor analysis and SEM afforded the researcher the ability to specify statistical models that correspond directly to conceptual models of educational assessment. The models also provided natural goodness-of-fit indices (see Bentler & Bonett, 1980) that inform researchers of the degree to which a model is consistent with empirical observations. For instance, in a language proficiency test, the test design might prescribe several subdomains of language proficiency that must be assessed (e.g., listening, speaking, writing, reading), and in an SEM the researcher would be able to set up and test competing models of subdomain structures that reflect the test design or other prior theories. Part of the large contribution of quantitative analyses has been to invent some of the technologies that such analyses rely on. In the next section, we consider technology as it has affected perspectives in assessment related to learning, scoring, and innovative testing practices. As before, we take a historical approach. Technology, as we see in daily life, has the potential to change our experiences dramatically.

TECHNOLOGY TO IMPROVE QUALITY

The design and development of computer-based assessments have been directed at leveraging the unique capabilities of technology to create tasks that better represent the targeted construct (E. L. Baker, Chung, & Delacruz, 2008; E. L. Baker & Mayer, 1999; Bennett, 1999, 2015; Huff & Sireci, 2001; NRC, 2001; Sireci & Zenisky, 2006; Yang, Buckendahl, Juszkiewicz, & Bhola, 2002; Zenisky & Sireci, 2002). In this section we first identify validity issues and then provide examples of how knowledge and skills can be measured with technology-based tasks; we also describe tools that structure the assessment design task.

Validity Issues in Computer-Based Tasks

Ironically, modern technology has spurred research and development around complex, constructed-response tasks—the very kind of tasks and research eliminated by the introduction of scoring technology in testing (Lindquist, 1969). Two major validity issues arise in computer-based assessment tasks. The first is task design: Does the task require respondents to apply the targeted knowledge and skills in the intended way? This validity issue can be addressed by careful design. Baker's model-based assessment design process (E. L. Baker, 1997) and Mislevy's ECD process (Mislevy et al., 2004) are examples of design processes that can lead to assessments that require assessment designers to explicitly connect cognitive demands to task design, and task design to observable responses. Examples of tools intended to support assessment designers and teachers are presented later in this section.

The second major validity issue in computer-based assessment is scoring: How is performance scored, and to what extent do the scores reflect competency on the targeted knowledge and skills? What type of evidence would support or refute validity claims? As with any assessment task, scoring criteria need to exist. However, for computer-based tasks the challenge is greater because the scoring procedure needs to be implemented in an algorithm (i.e., software) and the algorithm must operate on data that may be of low information value, such as a button click. Thus, the challenge in algorithm development is the creation of meaningful measures that can yield scores on some performance dimension.

However, how to validate scores from a computer-based task remains unclear. Several techniques have been developed to validate scores. The first approach is to compare scores generated from automated scoring algorithms to scores assigned to the same response by human raters. High agreement between machine and human scores is taken as strong validity evidence. However, the automated scoring algorithm often uses machine learning techniques that rarely if ever mimic the human judgment process—a natural interpretation. The second technique is rule-based scoring, where algorithms reflect explicit criteria and award credit for accurate responses that can be identified a priori. An important shortcoming is that credit is awarded only to responses that can be identified in advance; appropriate responses that are not part of the rule set are ignored. This scoring approach penalizes creative solutions and requires a more expansive rule set as the solution space expands. The third technique compares respondents' responses against a reference (e.g., experts' responses) and is sensitive both to any peculiarities in the reference sample and to any definitional problems with the sample. In the following sections, to expand this discussion, we provide examples of computer-based tasks that illustrate complex performance demands, automated scoring approaches, and assessment design tools.

Complex Computer-Based Tasks and Automated Scoring

Computers allow the creation of tasks that can have different degrees of interactivity, deliver various media, require any combination of selected or constructed responses, and respond either in a predefined sequence or dynamically as a function of the students' responses. These capabilities enable assessment designers to create tasks that exercise students' higher order thinking and practices that are demanded by rigorous academic standards, colleges, and employers (National Assessment Governing Board, 2013; National Governors Association Center for Best Practices & Council of Chief State School Officers, 2010; Next Generation Science Standards Lead States, 2013; NRC, 2012).

Great variety of computer-based assessment tasks have developed over the past 20 years, including domain-independent methods to measure conceptual understanding through mapping (e.g., E. L. Baker, Niemi, & Herl, 1994; Herl, O'Neil, Chung, &

Schacter, 1999), problem solving (Vendlinski & Stevens, 2002), science inquiry (e.g., Bennett, Persky, Weiss, & Jenkins, 2007; Quellmalz et al., 2013), teamwork and collaborative problem solving (e.g., Chung, O'Neil, & Herl, 1999; O'Neil & Chuang, 2008; O'Neil, Chung, & Brown, 1997), interpersonal skills (e.g., O'Neil, Allred, & Dennis, 1997), and domain-dependent methods, including measurement of math reasoning (e.g., Bennett, Morley, & Quardt, 2000), Web searching (e.g., Klein, Yarnall, & Glaubke, 2002; Schacter, Herl, Chung, Dennis, & O'Neil, 1999), specific design skills (e.g., Bejar, 1991; Chung & Baker, 2003; Katz & James, 1998), and medical decision making (e.g., Clauser, 2000, Margolis & Clauser, 2006). Automated essay scoring has been under way for a number of years and is included because of its scoring methods and cost savings in comparison with other current methods (e.g., Burstein, Tetreault, & Madnani, 2013; Landauer, Laham, & Foltz, 2003; Page, 1966; Page & Petersen, 1995; Shermis, 2014). Automated scoring is likely to be improved dramatically, given advances in natural language processing.

Two examples illustrate how technology can be leveraged in the creation and scoring of tasks requiring performance. The first example, knowledge mapping (Lambiotte, Dansereau, Cross, & Reynolds, 1989; Novak & Gowin, 1984), requires students to create a network representation of their understanding of a domain in terms of concepts and relationships. This representation is consistent with how researchers' models suggested people represent their knowledge mentally (Minsky, 1968). The key scoring innovation was the use of expert performance as the referent against which to compare student responses (E. L. Baker, 1997; Chi et al., 1988), not what experts *say* should be competent performance or experts' rating of student performance. In numerous studies across age, content, and setting, scoring student knowledge maps using expert-based referents has been found to be sensitive to instruction, to discriminate between experts and novices, to discriminate between different levels of student prior knowledge, to relate moderately strongly to external essay-based measures of the same construct, to be sensitive to language proficiency, and to show reasonable technical properties (Chung, Baker, et al., 2003; Chung, Harmon, & Baker, 2001; Herl, Niemi, & Baker, 1996; Herl et al., 1999; Kim, Chung, & Delacruz, 2004; Klein, Chung, Osmundson, & Herl, 2002; Lee, 2000; National Assessment Governing Board, 2008; Osmundson, Chung, Herl, & Klein, 1999; Ruiz-Primo, Schultz, Li, & Shavelson, 2001; Schacter et al., 1999; Yin & Shavelson, 2004).

The second example of leveraging technology is simulation-based assessments. Typically, in such assessments the student interacts with the simulation to achieve some specified goal. Simulation-based assessments can be used to measure processes and domain-related understanding. For example, Bennett et al. (2007) required students to reason about the relations among buoyancy, mass, and volume. Evidence of student understanding was based on the correctness of student actions in the simulation, multiple-choice questions, and explanation essays. A Bayesian network analyzed the evidence to generate estimates of proficiency on science inquiry and science synthesis skills. Bennett et al.'s approach typifies K–12 science simulation-based assessments (National Center for Education Statistics, 2012; Quellmalz et al., 2013).

In other kinds of simulations that allow for responses not easily evaluated for correctness, a viable scoring approach is to model experts' scoring judgments. In this case, expert judgment is the gold standard against which to compare examinees' performance. For example, Clauser, Margolis, and Clauser (2016) describe a computer-based assessment of patient management skills. Medical school graduates were presented with a description of the patient's appearance and location in the hospital, initial vital signs, and history. Examinees then chose from four categories of actions such as requesting more comprehensive information about the patient's history or advancing the case through simulated time. Measurement of students' performance in these technologies was done with a regression model that used students' actions to predict their scores, or by scoring the students' actions against a set of rules extracted from a policy capture procedure from a panel of experts. Both types of scoring corresponded highly with human ratings of the same performance. Subsequent generalizability analyses demonstrated that these procedures were as generalizable across tasks as those produced by the expert raters (Clauser et al., 1995; Clauser, Harik, & Clyman, 2000; Clauser, Margolis, Clyman, & Ross, 1997; Clauser, Swanson, & Clyman, 1999; Dillon & Clauser, 2009; Margolis & Clauser, 2006). Modeling expert or rater judgments have been used successfully in a variety of other applications, including ones not related to simulations (e.g., Burstein et al., 2013; Koenig, Lee, Iseli, & Wainess, 2010; Williamson, Bejar, & Hone, 1999). For a comprehensive review of various simulation-based assessment systems, see Clauser et al. (2016) and Russell (2006). For discussions of the issues around the use of expert performance or judgment as the basis for scoring algorithms, see E. L. Baker, Linn, Abedi, and Niemi (1995), E. L. Baker and O'Neil (1996), E. L. Baker and Schacter (1996), Bennett (2006), Bennett and Bejar (1998), Bennett and Zhang (2016), and Burstein and Chodorow (1999).

Automated Support for Item Generation and Assessment Task Design

The desire to simultaneously increase the throughput and the quality of assessment development has led to the development of computer-based supports for item generation and task design (E. L. Baker, 2002; F. B. Baker, 1971, 1989; Chung, Delacruz, et al., 2003; Drasgow, Luecht, & Bennett, 2006; Gierl & Haladyna, 2013; Irvine & Kyllonen, 2002). Under traditional item development processes, items are individually created, reviewed, and formatted. With item models, however, a template is used to represent the item structure and variables used to represent parts of the item that can vary—the parameterization of the item. Specific values are substituted for the variables, thereby creating new items. Items created using this method all have the same general structure (Bejar et al., 2003; Gierl, Lai, Hogan, & Matovinovic, 2015; Gierl, Zhou, & Alves, 2008; Singley & Bennett, 2002). Gierl and colleagues (Gierl et al., 2008, Gierl et al., 2015) present item models with detailed examples illustrating how items can be parameterized and how item models can be created to align with standards. Parameterization allows linear programming methods to generate or select items that satisfy constraints on item design, content coverage, and even the physical layout of the test booklet (e.g., Cor, Alves, & Gierl, 2009; van der Linden, 2005; van der Linden & Diao, 2011).

Similarly, tools have been developed to support limited parameterization of assessment task design. For example, components of a task (which is parameterized) can include cognitive demand, prompt, and response mode, in addition to content. As in item modeling, task modeling would substitute sets of values for the corresponding parameters. For instance, the cognitive demand of conceptual understanding would ask for an explanation and specify an essay response format. One of the earliest tools was the Assessment Design and Delivery System (ADDS; E. L. Baker, 2002; Vendlinski, Baker, & Niemi, 2008). With ADDS, assessment designers (in this case, teachers) assembled assessments using assessment objects (e.g., new or preexisting prompts, information sources) that emphasized the principled structure of an assessment. Teachers who used ADDS, compared to teachers who did not, focused more on measuring conceptual knowledge and created more appropriate rubrics and coherent prompts that addressed critical ideas (Vendlinski, Niemi, & Wang, 2005). A similar tool, the Principled Assessment Designs for Inquiry system, uses wizards and templates to help structure the ECD process for designers (Mislevy et al., 2013; Mislevy & Riconscente, 2005). The anticipated development of technology as applied to assessment will play a major role in our thinking about the future of testing.

SUMMARY

This chapter began with a definition, explanations of assessment, and our historical treatment. This review illustrated the shifts and interactions among tests created primarily to measure curricula and those intended to differentiate among students. In other words, sometimes testing was intended to document and assist education and sometimes it focused on distinguishing more stable characteristics of individuals. To this day, these different origins emerge in validity claims and the methods marshaled to clarify the quality of target measures for given purposes. Major changes have occurred as well as a consequence of enacted policies and international comparisons. Among the most important is a focus on equity, that is, policy to reduce performance differences among identifiable student groups. Pursuit of equity extends far beyond test development and use to the educational and societal structures that affect students. In addition, a better understanding has developed about tests and assessments, to evaluate and improve effectiveness, whether in international (Volante, 2016), national, state, or local venues.

In current assessments, questions of alignment, first raised in Tyler's work, continue to be central. Alignment requires demonstrated connections among standards (goals), instruction/learning, and the tasks and items on the assessment. But alignment is only part of the story, as the breadth of standards limits the attention of any assessment to only a small part of potentially relevant performance. It is also important to assure that those psychometric analyses required for accountability reports do not mitigate the strength of the alignment linkage. In addition, claims for accountability assessments imply that tests can measure relevant educational changes to assess the effects of interventions in addition to the status of an educational system.

The problems of creating and enacting effective instructional improvement plans related to instruction are complicated by the details of alignment. For instance, it has been shown by Schmidt et al. (1997) that relevant content in materials is associated with better performance in cross-national studies, but getting operational at classroom levels is not simple.

To achieve continuing, instructionally relevant improvement, we would need to investigate the evidence for the instructional improvement claim of accountability tests. As recommended by Cronbach (1971), we would identify key evidence that could support the claim that test use improves instruction. To start, we would want evidence that teachers understood the meaning of goals, content, and assessments and that they could infer from student test results potentially missing subtasks or prerequisites that caused lower performance. It is unlikely that this level of information, or "usable knowledge" (the term used by Lindblom & Cohen, 1979), will be available from the results of annually administered assessments. A second cluster of evidence would include evidence that teachers had the pedagogical repertoire and resources to allow them to assist individual students with different types of knowledge or skill gaps. Determining instructional practices still presents significant practical and research problems, especially where standards are vague, numerous, or both. Finding scalable evidence that can be unobtrusively obtained remains a goal. Lacking strong evidence of instruction and assessment relationships, teachers must meet expectations without access to available tools and resources to enable them and their students to succeed.

We extend this summary by posing three questions inherent in our review that should be answered in order to assist the improvement of assessment practice and research.

- *How reasonable is it to expect current outcome measures to be useful for accountability and for instructional improvement purposes?*

Central to this question are the differences in the formulations of tests as either stable measures (all incorporating a large component of g) or malleable measures (see Cai, 2013) reflective of educational efforts, at system, school, and classroom levels. An answer is also contingent on decisions about depth, breadth, and clarity of test purposes. As we have noted a generally phrased test description gives educators greater license to address a wide range of potential goals but less likelihood of squarely hitting the measured outcomes. Even if the test description were clearly stated, we would need to understand how the design of the test and its tasks and items are sensitive to effects of instructional interventions. There are current trade-offs between high levels of accuracy and instructional sensitivity. If there is little validity evidence documenting that the test responds to intended differences among educational programs, then the use of such tests for accountability should be reconsidered until such evidence is available.

- *When are studies of test quality best fielded? If validity inferences are made before sufficient instructional resources are applied in the system, how useful are the interpretations for the future?*

This may seem like a simple question; it is not. When validity inferences are used from field trials and report data obtained from "uninstructed" individuals (e.g., before new state standards have been fully implemented), findings will generate different inferences than those from students who had been taught the new material. An obvious example is the failure to find multiple dimensions in analyses of complex tasks. If the new test is a pretest, desired multiple dimensions, reflecting sets of concepts and steps of procedure, may emerge only after relevant instructional components have been taught.

- *How should fairness and equality be addressed in inferences drawn from tests?*

If it has been shown that all students can understand the test content and format, the equity problem then moves away from tests alone. Student performance is an aggregate of effects—for instance, experiences, economics, neighborhood, and school staffing decisions as well as instructional efforts (Bloom, 1976, p. 18). Tying growth targets to schools with different socioeconomic profiles is a way to adjust for background, and while such comparable background data may be "fair" for accountability uses, it may over time limit student aspirations and thereby perpetuate achievement gaps.

Obviously, there are many more questions that could be raised about inferences and uses of testing. Let us shift to a more optimistic view in our speculation about how assessments may help learning.

CONVERGENCE IN THE FUTURE OF TESTING AND ASSESSMENT

Our review invokes both the background and the current status of important factors in theory, test development, application, and quality, and although we have kept the overall discussion of testing partially separate from technology and quantitative perspectives, it is absolutely clear that these fields will continue to converge to support future applications of achievement tests. In the past, decisions about test development and purposes were often made in the context of the available technology to support test design, use, and reporting. Technology can work further to raise the accessibility of tests for all students. Increasingly sophisticated statistical tools also allow greater opportunity to identify tests and components that best serve the needs of all. In our own work, we see greater integration among assessment purposes, technology, and statistical analyses, not only in the service of improved assessment but also for its integration and better imagination of instructional and learning processes.

There is no dispute that technological and quantitative innovations have fundamentally transformed our way of life (see Christensen, Horn, & Johnson, 2008). Central to this change is the ease with which information can now be created, accessed, and shared. Information technology creates tremendous momentum to disrupt existing practices and conventional wisdom. Although its presence on a global scale creates tensions, it well may attain the democratizing purposes of education, first identified by Horace Mann.

What Will Happen Next?

Members of the Gordon Commission have written about the positive change in expectations from assessment *of* education and learning to assessment *for* education and learning (Armour-Thomas & Gordon, 2013). To complete the Lincoln analogy (of the people . . .), we add assessment *by* education and learning systems as well. This Gordon Commission formulation resolves a number of conflicts in historical purposes and designs of testing and, when expanded, sets additional challenges. To use assessment in support of learning, we expect advances in design, in data quality and resulting trustworthy interpretations. The assessment-for-learning imperative will shift a greater burden away from annual tests, and ultimately fully supplant them.

Instructionally linked assessments would involve greater frequency of administration, related to smaller chunks of instruction, essentially a type of teacher-administered or (if computerized) teacher-supervised formative assessment. Here, the effectiveness claims are inferred from distributed assessments. Challenges to be met include (a) better task sampling, (b) more usable reports, and (c) evidence of comparability among tests intended assesses similar demands. In practice, teachers might choose from a menu of available assessment options or prefer to build their own assessments assisted by fully or partially automated systems for development, scoring, and reports. Challenges involve maintaining the perception of fairness that often accompanies standardized testing—for example, procedures for embedded exams would need to clarify the types of help teachers could legitimately give students. A very different hurdle is communicating to test-weary parents, students, and educators that more frequent testing is worthwhile and sustainable. Success will depend on the extent testing can be made more seamless with instruction. Unless totally managed by technology, these assessments invariably will place greater demands on teacher time and abilities.

The Role of Technology

Technology-based instruction with embedded assessments will provide both accountability and instructional process indicators. Much existing instructional technology pays little attention to the quality assurance of assessments used in instruction.

We can envision the application of a variety of assessments, some extended over time and others of shorter duration, combining across a year complex simulations, research projects, and games. Their integration with learning could entail new requirements for developers to create useful and understandable frameworks to connect inventive learning experiences and assessments, both of documented quality.

In a coherent assessment platform, student answers could be frequently arrayed and summarized, perhaps using advances in artificial intelligence or neural networks to display individual or common patterns of errors. A comprehensive system of assessment would adapt instruction to findings in real time.

Even greater use of available technology is envisioned by using the extensive data generated by students during learning sequences. "Big data" are used routinely in social media, commercial games, and Web searches to adapt responses to the user's interactions. Big data have also been incorporated in the analyses of interventions. Here, fine-grained interaction data gathered from digital sources are used to form next steps and can summarize individual and group progress at any point (Chung, 2014, 2015; U.S. Department of Education, 2012). Technology capability now exists to feasibly capture multiple levels of data that vary in frequency and granularity, such as grades measured once a semester, game players' behavior measured moment to moment, and still finer grained sensor-generated data in simulations, such as EEGs measured 256 times a second, or real-time changes in facial expression recorded by cameras. Advances in hardware and software capabilities, such as vision- or sensor-based measurement approaches, can assess content and progress in developing teamwork and problem solving. Process information, such as detecting confusion, frustration, and boredom, can be obtained from facial expressions, physiological responses, and posture (Bosch et al., 2015; Calvo & D'Mello, 2010; D'Mello, & Kory, 2015).

Software libraries will continue to grow and will provide ever more varieties of user interfaces that can be used to develop novel item types (Parshall, Harmes, Davey, & Pashley, 2010). The earlier described teacher-based formative assessment pales when compared to the power to be derived from computerized analyses of designed attributes or from data analytics over many trials and many students. How such data are communicated to teachers, together with teachers' greater abilities to respond, will shortly revolutionize the entire assessment design process. In the technical literature, one also sees the development of statistical models that could extract more fine-grained information from assessment data. Diagnostic classification modeling is one step in this direction, and interested readers could consult Rupp, Templin, and Henson's (2010) accessible introductory volume and Leighton and Gierl's (2007) volume. As advances in other fields continue, we expect to see continued cross-pollination of ideas and methods. For example, ontologies, borrowed from artificial intelligence, have been used to represent domain knowledge and to coordinate the design of assessment, instruction, and professional development activities (E. L. Baker, 2012; Chung, Delacruz, et al., 2003; McGuinness, 2003; Mislevy et al., 2010). Student modeling borrowed from intelligent tutoring systems has been used to model student understanding and estimate student proficiencies on assessment tasks (Almond, Mislevy, Steinberg, Yan, & Williamson, 2015; Behrens, Mislevy, Bauer, Williamson, & Levy, 2004; Gitomer, Steinberg, & Mislevy, 1995; Mislevy, Almond, Yan, & Steinberg, 1999).

New Psychometrics

As noted, we anticipate increasing amounts of data generated from digital interactions. While current educational data mining methods have been applied successfully to identify patterns and associations in voluminous data (Peña-Ayala, 2014; Romero, Ventura, Pechenizkiy, & Baker, 2010), very little research has been done to investigate the psychometric properties of such data. The data from digital learning environments (e.g., simulations and games) have complex nested structures (e.g., interaction nested within tasks, tasks within applications, applications within individuals, individuals within classrooms). Simulations and games can have open-ended and interactive task structures, multiple constructs required to explain behavior, and learning occurring during the task itself. These complexities need to be modeled; otherwise, results are likely to be overly optimistic (Cai, 2013; Junker, 2011; Levy, 2013; Mislevy, Behrens, DiCerbo, & Levy, 2012; Mislevy et al., 2014).

Finally, as we said at the outset, we expect technology to continue to link learning, instruction, and assessment. In 1925, Pressey achieved this integration using mechanical technology (Pressey, 1925, 1926, 1927, 1932). Pressey's "Automated Teacher" provided immediate feedback, rewarded success, was mastery-based, had increasing test item difficulty, and embraced the idea of individualized instruction. Nearly 100 years later, we continue to improve our understanding of every level of the learning stack: the type of telemetric data to gather (e.g., Chung, 2015), the type of processing algorithm to use for complex data (e.g., Wu et al., 2008), the psychometric modeling of interactive data (e.g., Almond et al., 2015), the design and validity of assessment tasks (e.g., E. L. Baker et al., 2008; Mislevy et al., 2014), and effective instructional practices (e.g., Hattie, 2008; Hattie & Timperley, 2007). The challenge is to anticipate and manage, for the good of learners, the impending wave of information.

CONCLUSION

We have taken a long look back, and then forward, encompassing more than 150 years of assessment literature. We have sorted through the many lessons that could be learned from this rich vein of work. Learning and teaching specialists, assessment designers, technologists, and psychometricans will form new collaborations rather than work as now in largely compartmentalized spaces. The historical uses of some tests of individual differences resulted in a moral chasm in the field and impossibly heavy consequences ensued for identified groups, including African Americans, waves of U.S. immigrants from places other than Northern Europe, and people with disabilities. Yet studies of individual differences may have benefit if they are turned to ways to improve and personalize learning. We are not yet there. We imagine through emerging and unexpected complex sensing technologies to learn evermore about individual differences. We need to consider with care whether they can or should be used in our goals to further important learning, student accomplishments, and expanded human potential.

NOTE

[1]A latent variable is an unobserved random variable, for example, math achievement.

REFERENCES

Aiken, W. M. (1942). *The story of the eight-year study: Vol. 1. Adventure in American education.* New York, NY: McGraw-Hill.

Almond, R. G., Mislevy, R. J., Steinberg, L. S., Yan, D., & Williamson, D. M. (2015). *Bayesian networks in educational assessment.* New York, NY: Springer.

American Educational Research Association, American Psychological Association, & National Council on Measurement in Education. (1985). *Standards for educational and psychological testing.* Washington, DC: American Educational Research Association.

American Educational Research Association, American Psychological Association, & National Council on Measurement in Education. (1999). *Standards for educational and psychological testing.* Washington, DC: American Educational Research Association.

American Educational Research Association, American Psychological Association, & National Council on Measurement in Education. (2014). *Standards for educational and psychological testing.* Washington, DC: American Educational Research Association.

American Psychological Association, American Educational Research Association, & National Council on Measurement in Education. (1954). Technical recommendations for psychological tests and diagnostic techniques. *Psychological Bulletin, 51*(2, Pt. 2, Suppl.), 1–38.

American Psychological Association, American Educational Research Association, & National Council on Measurement in Education. (1974). *Standards for educational and psychological testing.* Washington, DC: American Psychological Association.

American Recovery and Reinvestment Act of 2009, Pub. L. No. 111-5.

Angoff, W. H. (1971). Scales, norms, and equivalent scores. In R. L. Thorndike (Ed.), *Educational measurement* (pp. 508–600). Washington, DC: American Council on Education.

Armour-Thomas, E., & Gordon, E. W. (2013). *Toward an understanding of assessment as a dynamic component of pedagogy.* Princeton, NJ: Gordon Commission.

Baker, E. L. (1997). Model-based performance assessment. *Theory Into Practice, 36,* 247–254.

Baker, E. L. (2002). Design of automated authoring systems for tests. In National Research Council, Board on Testing and Assessment, Center for Education, Division of Behavioral and Social Sciences and Education (Eds.), *Technology and assessment: Thinking ahead: Proceedings from a workshop* (pp. 79–89). Washington, DC: National Academies Press.

Baker, E. L. (2003). *From usable to useful assessment knowledge: A design problem* (CSE Rep. No. 612). Los Angeles: University of California, National Center for Research on Evaluation, Standards, and Student Testing.

Baker, E. L. (2012). *Ontology-based educational design: Seeing is believing* (CRESST Resource Paper No. 13). Los Angeles: University of California, National Center for Research on Evaluation, Standards, and Student Testing.

Baker, E. L., Aschbacher, P. R., Niemi, D., & Sato, E. (2005). *CRESST performance assessment models: Assessing content area explanations* (CSE Rep. No. 652). Los Angeles: University of California, National Center for Research on Evaluation, Standards, and Student Testing.

Baker, E. L., Chung, G. K. W. K., & Delacruz, G. C. (2008). Design and validation of technology-based performance assessments. In J. M. Spector, M. D. Merrill, J. J. G. van Merrienboer, & M. P. Driscoll (Eds.), *Handbook of research on educational communications and technology* (3rd ed., pp. 595–604). Mahwah, NJ: Lawrence Erlbaum.

Baker, E. L., Freeman, M., & Clayton, S. (1991). Cognitive assessment of history for large-scale testing. In M. C. Wittrock & E. L. Baker (Eds.), *Testing and cognition* (pp. 131–153). Englewood Cliffs, NJ: Prentice Hall.

Baker, E. L., Lee, J. J., Rivera, N. M., Choi, K., Bewley, W. L., Stripling, R., . . . Redman, E. (2015). *Detection and computational analysis of psychological signals: Evaluation of VetGuard and SimSensei for veteran use* (Final Report). Los Angeles: University of California, National Center for Research on Evaluation, Standards, and Student Testing.

Baker, E. L., Linn, R. L., Abedi, J., & Niemi, D. (1995). Dimensionality and generalizability of domain-independent performance assessments. *Journal of Educational Research, 89,* 197–205.

Baker, E. L., & Mayer, R. E. (1999). Computer-based assessment of problem solving. *Computers in Human Behavior, 15,* 269–282.

Baker, E. L., Niemi, D., & Herl, H. (1994). Using Hypercard technology to measure understanding. In E. L. Baker & H. F. O'Neil, Jr. (Eds.), *Technology assessment in education and training* (Vol. 1, pp. 133–152). Hillsdale, NJ: Lawrence Erlbaum.

Baker, E. L., & O'Neil, H. F., Jr. (1996). Performance assessment and equity. In M. B. Kane & R. Mitchell (Eds.), *Implementing performance assessment: Promises, problems, and challenges* (pp. 183–199). Mahwah, NJ: Lawrence Erlbaum.

Baker, E. L., & O'Neil, H. F., Jr. (2016). The United States: The intersection of international achievement testing and educational policy development. In L. Volante (Ed.), *The intersection of international achievement testing and educational policy: Global perspectives on large-scale reform* (pp. 122–139). New York, NY: Routledge.

Baker, E. L., O'Neil, H. F. Jr., & Linn, R. L. (1993). Policy and validity prospects for performance-based assessment. *American Psychologist, 48*(12), 12–20.

Baker, E. L., & Schacter, J. (1996). Expert benchmarks for student academic performance: The case for gifted children. *Gifted Child Quarterly, 40,* 61–65.

Baker, F. B. (1971). Automation of test scoring, reporting, and analysis. In R. L. Thorndike (Ed.), *Educational measurement* (pp. 202–234). Washington, DC: American Council on Education.

Baker, F. B. (1989). Computer technology in test construction and processing. In R. L. Linn (Ed.), *Educational measurement* (pp. 409–428). Washington, DC: American Council on Education.

Baxter, G. P., & Glaser, R. (1998). Investigating the cognitive complexity of science assessments. *Educational Measurement: Issues and Practices, 17,* 37–45.

Beaton, A. E., Mullis, I. V. S., Martin, M. O., Gonzales, E. J., Kelly, D. L., & Smith, T. A. (1996). *Mathematics achievement in the middle school years.* Chestnut Hill, MA: TIMSS International Study Center, Boston College.

Behrens, J. T., Mislevy, R. J., Bauer, M., Williamson, D. M., & Levy, R. (2004). Introduction to evidence-centered design and lessons learned from its application in a global E-learning program. *International Journal of Testing, 4,* 295–301.

Bejar, I. I. (1991). A methodology for scoring open-ended architectural design problems. *Journal of Applied Psychology, 76,* 522–532.

Bejar, I. I., Lawless, R., Morley, M. E., Wagner, M. E., Bennett, R. E., & Revuelta, J. (2003). A feasibility study of on-the-fly item generation in adaptive testing. *Journal of Technology, Learning, and Assessment, 2*(3). Retrieved from http://www.jtla.org

Bennett, R. E. (1999). Using new technology to improve assessment. *Educational Measurement: Issues and Practice, 18*(3), 5–12.

Bennett, R. E. (2006). Moving the field forward: Some thoughts on validity and automated scoring. In D. M. Williamson, I. I. Behar, & R. J. Mislevy (Eds.), *Automated scoring of complex tasks in computer-based testing* (pp. 403–412). Mahwah, NJ: Lawrence Erlbaum.

Bennett, R. E. (2015). The changing nature of educational assessment. *Review of Research in Education, 39,* 370–407.

Bennett, R. E., & Bejar, I. I. (1998). Validity and automated scoring: It's not only the scoring. *Educational Measurement: Issues and Practice, 17*(4), 9–17.

Bennett, R. E., Morley, M., & Quardt, D. (2000). Three response types for broadening the conception of mathematical problem solving in computerized tests. *Applied Psychological Measurement, 24,* 294–309.

Bennett, R. E., Persky, H., Weiss, A. R., & Jenkins, F. (2007). *Problem solving in technology-rich environments: A report from the NAEP Technology-Based Assessment Project* (NCES 2007–466). Washington, DC: National Center for Education Statistics.

Bennett, R. E., & Zhang, M. (2016). Validity and automated scoring. In F. Drasgow (Ed.), *Technology and testing: Improving educational and psychological measurement* (pp. 142–173). New York, NY: Taylor & Francis.

Bentler, P. M., & Bonett, D. G. (1980). Significance tests and goodness of fit in the analysis of covariance structures. *Psychological Bulletin, 88,* 588–606.

Bentler, P. M., & Weeks, D. G. (1980). Linear structural equations with latent variables. *Psychometrika, 45,* 289–308.

Berliner, D. C., & Glass, G. V. (2014). *50 myths and lies that threaten America's public schools: The real crisis in education.* New York, NY: Teachers College Press.

Binet, A., & Simon, T. (1916). *The development of intelligence in children.* Baltimore, MD: Williams & Wilkins.

Black, P., & Wiliam, D. (2009). Developing the theory of formative assessment. *Educational Assessment, Evaluation, and Accountability, 21*(1) 5–31.

Bloom, B. S. (1976). *Human characteristics and school learning.* New York, NY: McGraw-Hill.

Bloom, B. S., Englehart, M. D., Furst, E. J., Hill, W. H., & Krathwohl, D. R. (1956). *Taxonomy of educational objectives: Vol. 1. The cognitive domain.* New York, NY: David McKay.

Bobbitt, J. F. (1913). *The supervision of city schools: Some general principles of management applied to the problems of city school systems* (Twelfth Yearbook of the National Society for the study of Education). Bloomington: IL: National Society for the Study of Education.

Bobbitt, J. F. (1924). *How to make a curriculum.* Boston, MA: Houghton Mifflin.

Bock, R. D. (1972). Estimating item parameters and latent ability when responses are scored in two or more nominal categories. *Psychometrika, 37,* 29–51.

Bock, R. D., & Bargmann, R. E. (1966). Analysis of covariance structures. *Psychometrika, 31,* 507–534.

Bock, R. D., & Jones, J. V. (1968). *The measurement and prediction of judgment and choice.* San Francisco, CA: Holden-Day.

Bock, R. D., & Lieberman, M. (1970). Fitting a response model for dichotomously scored items. *Psychometrika, 35,* 179–197.

Bosch, N., D'Mello, S., Baker, R., Ocumpaugh, J., Shute, V., Ventura, M., . . .Zhao, W. (2015). Automatic detection of learning-centered affective states in the wild. In *Proceedings of the 2015 ACM International Conference on Intelligent User Interfaces* (pp. 379–388). New York, NY: Association for Computing Machinery.

Bracey, G. W. (1995). *Final exam: A study of the perpetual scrutiny of American education.* Bloomington, IN: Technos Press.

Bransford, J. D. (1979). *Human cognition.* Belmont, CA: Wadsworth.

Bransford, J. D., Brown, A. L., & Cocking, R. R. (2000). *How people learn: Brain, mind, experience and school.* Washington, DC: National Academies Press.

Braun, H. (Ed.). (2016). *The challenges to measurement in an era of accountability.* New York, NY: Routledge.

Brennan, R. L. (2001). *Generalizability theory.* New York, NY: Springer.

Brigham, C. C. (1923). *A study of American intelligence.* Princeton, NJ: Princeton University Press.

Brigham, C. C. (1930). Intelligence tests of immigrant groups. *Psychological Review, 37,* 158–165.

Browne, M. W. (1984). Asymptotically distribution-free methods for the analysis of covariance structures. *British Journal of Mathematical and Statistical Psychology, 37,* 62–83.

Buckingham, B. R. (1920). A proposed index of efficiency in teaching United States history. *Journal of Educational Research, 1* 161–171.

Buckingham, B. R., & Monroe, W. S. (1920). A testing program for elementary schools. *Journal of Educational Research, 2,* 521–532.

Burstein, J. C., & Chodorow, M. (1999, June). *Automated essay scoring for nonnative English speakers.* Paper presented at Computer-Mediated Language Assessment and Evaluation of Natural Language Processing, joint symposium of the Association of Computational Linguistics and the International Association of Language Learning Technologies, College Park, MD.

Burstein, J. C., Tetreault, J., & Madnani, N. (2013). The E-rater® automated essay scoring system. In M. D. Shermis & J. Burstein (Eds.), *Handbook of automated essay scoring: Current applications and future directions* (pp. 55–67). New York, NY: Routledge.

Cai, L. (2013). Potential applications of latent variable modeling for the psychometrics of medical simulation. *Military Medicine, 178*(10 Suppl.), 115–120.

Cai, L., Baker, E., Choi, K., & Buschang, R. (2014, April). *Kentucky CRESST functional validity model.* Draft slides prepared for the Kentucky Department of Education, Frankfort, KY.

Calvo, R. A., & D'Mello, S. (2010). Affect detection: An interdisciplinary review of models, methods, and their applications. *IEEE Transactions on Affective Computing, 1,* 18–37.

Campbell, D. T., & Fiske, D. W. (1959). Convergent and discriminant validation by the multitrait-multimethod matrix. *Psychological Bulletin, 56,* 81–105.

Carroll, J. B. (1993). *Human cognitive abilities: A survey of factor-analytic studies.* Cambridge, England: Cambridge University Press.

Cattell, J. M. (1890). Mental tests and measurements. *Mind, 15,* 373–381.

Chi, M. T. H., Glaser, R., & Farr, M. (Eds.). (1988). *The nature of expertise.* Hillsdale, NJ: Lawrence Erlbaum.

Christensen, C., Horn, M., & Johnson, C. (2008). *Disrupting class: How disruptive innovation will change the way the world learns.* New York, NY: McGraw-Hill.

Chung, G. K. W. K. (2014). Toward the relational management of educational measurement data. *Teachers College Record, 116*(11), 1–16.

Chung, G. K. W. K. (2015). Guidelines for the design, implementation, and analysis of game telemetry. In C. S. Loh, Y. Sheng, & D. Ifenthaler (Eds.), *Serious games analytics: Methodologies for performance measurement, assessment, and improvement* (pp. 59–79). New York, NY: Springer.

Chung, G. K. W. K., & Baker, E. L. (2003). An exploratory study to examine the feasibility of measuring problem-solving processes using a click-through interface. *Journal of Technology, Learning, and Assessment, 2*(2), 1–30.

Chung, G. K. W. K., Baker, E. L., Brill, D. G., Sinha, R., Saadat, F., & Bewley, W. L. (2003). Automated assessment of domain knowledge with online knowledge mapping. *Proceedings of the IITSEC, 25,* 1168–1179.

Chung, G. K. W. K., Delacruz, G. C., Dionne, G. B., & Bewley, W. L. (2003). Linking assessment and instruction using ontologies. *Proceedings of the IITSEC, 25,* 1811–1822.

Chung, G. K. W. K., Harmon, T. C., & Baker, E. L. (2001). The impact of a simulation-based learning design project on student learning. *IEEE Transactions on Education, 44,* 390–398.

Chung, G. K. W. K., O'Neil, H. F. Jr., & Herl, H. E. (1999). The use of computer-based collaborative knowledge mapping to measure team processes and team outcomes. *Computers in Human Behavior, 15,* 463–494.

Clauser, B. E. (2000). Recurrent issues and recent advances in scoring performance assessments. *Applied Psychological Measurement, 24,* 310–324.

Clauser, B. E., Harik, P., & Clyman, S. G. (2000). The generalizability of scores for a performance assessment scored with a computer-automated scoring system. *Journal of Educational Measurement, 37,* 245–262.

Clauser, B. E., Margolis, M. J., & Clauser, J. C. (2016). Issues in simulation-based assessment. In F. Drasgow (Ed.), *Technology and testing: Improving educational and psychological measurement* (pp. 49–78). New York, NY: Taylor & Francis.

Clauser, B. E., Margolis, M. J., Clyman, S. G., & Ross, L. P. (1997). Development of automated scoring algorithms for complex performance assessments: A comparison of two approaches. *Journal of Educational Measurement, 34,* 141–161.

Clauser, B. E., Subhiyah, R. G., Nungester, R. J., Ripkey, D. R., Clyman, S. G., & McKinley, D. (1995). Scoring a performance-based assessment by modeling the judgments of experts. *Journal of Educational Measurement, 32,* 397–415.

Clauser, B. E., Swanson, D. B., & Clyman, S. G. (1999). A comparison of the generalizability of scores produced by expert raters and automated scoring systems. *Applied Measurement in Education, 12,* 281–299.

Coffman, W. E. (1971). On the reliability of ratings of essay examinations in English. *Research in the Teaching of English, 5,* 24–36.

Cohen, D., & Haney, W. (1980). Minimums, competency testing, and social policy. In R. M. Jaeger & C. K. Tittle (Eds.), *Minimum competency achievement testing: Motives, models, measures, and consequences* (pp. 5–22). Berkeley, CA: McCutchan.

Cooper, G., & Sweller, J. (1987). Effects of schema acquisition and rule automation on mathematical problem-solving transfer. *Journal of Educational Psychology, 79,* 347–362.

Cor, K., Alves, C., & Gierl, M. (2009). Three applications of automated test assembly within a user-friendly modeling environment. *Practical Assessment, Research & Evaluation, 14*(14), 1–23.

Council of Chief State School Officers. (2014). *Criteria for procuring and evaluating high-quality assessments.* Washington, DC: Author.

Cremin, L. A. (1961). *The transformation of the School: Progressivism in American Education, 1876–1957.* New York, NY: Vintage Books.

Cremin, L. A. (1964). The progressive heritage of the guidance movement. In F. Landy & L. Perry (Eds.), *Guidance in American education: Background and prospects* (pp. 11–19). Cambridge, MA: Harvard Education Press.

Cronbach, L. J. (1951). Coefficient alpha and the internal structure of tests. *Psychometrika, 16,* 297–334.

Cronbach, L. J. (1971). Test validation. In R. L. Thorndike (Ed.), *Educational measurement* (2nd ed., pp. 443–507). Washington, DC: American Council on Education.

Cronbach, L. J., & Meehl, P. E. (1955). Construct validity in psychological tests. *Psychological Bulletin, 16,* 281–302.

Cronbach, L. J., & Quirk, T. J. (1971). Test validity. In L. C. Deighton (Ed.), *Encyclopedia of education* (Vol. 9, pp. 165–175). New York, NY: Macmillan.

Cronbach, L. J., & Snow, R. E. (1977). *Aptitudes and instructional methods.* New York, NY: Irvington.

Cronbach, L. J., & Suppes, P. (1969). *Research for tomorrow's schools: Disciplined inquiry for education.* London, England: Macmillan.

Cuban, L. (1980). Policy implications of minimum competency testing. In R. M. Jaeger & C. K. Tittle (Eds.), *Minimum competency achievement testing: Motives, models, measures, and consequences* (pp. 69–71). Berkeley, CA: McCutchan.

Darling-Hammond, L. (2009). *The flat world and education: How America's commitment to equity will determine our future.* New York, NY: Teachers College Press.

Darling-Hammond, L., Wilhoit, G., & Pittenger, L. (2014): Accountability for college and career readiness: Developing a new paradigm. *Education Policy Analysis Archives, 22*(86). Retrieved from https://edpolicy.stanford.edu/sites/default/files/publications/accountability-college-and-career-readiness-developing-new-paradigm.pdf

Darwin, C. (1859). *On the origin of species by means of natural selection.* London, England: J. Murray.

Debra P. v. Turlington, 564 F. Supp. 177 (M.D. Fla. 1983).

Dewey, J. (1897). My pedagogic creed. *The School Journal, 54*(3), 77–80.

Dillon, G. F., & Clauser, B. (2009). Computer-delivered patient simulations in the United States Medical Licensing Examination (USMLE). *Simulation in Healthcare, 4,* 30–34.

Di Stefano, G., Gambardella, A., & Verona, G. (2012, October). Technology push and demand pull perspectives in innovation studies: Current findings and future research directions. *Research Policy, 41,* 1283–1295.

D'Mello, S. K., & Kory, J. (2015). A review and meta-analysis of multimodal affect detection systems. *ACM Computing Surveys, 47*(3), 1–46.

Doorey, N., & Polikoff, M. (2016). *Evaluating the content and quality of next generation assessments.* Washington, DC: Thomas B. Fordham Institute.

Drasgow, F., Luecht, R. M., & Bennett, R. (2006). Technology and testing. In R. L. Brennan (Ed.), *Educational measurement* (4th ed., pp. 471–516). Washington, DC: American Council on Education.

Durrell, L. (1960). *The Alexandria quartet.* London, England: Faber.

Dwyer, C. N. (2005). *Measurement and research in the accountability era.* Mahwah, NJ: Lawrence Erlbaum.

Ebel, R. L., & Popham, W. J. (1978). The 1978 annual meeting presidential debate. *Educational Researcher, 7*(11) 3–10.

Education Reform Act of 1988

Elementary and Secondary Education Act of 1965 as amended, 20 U.S.C. §241 (1974).

Ericsson, K. A., & Smith, J. (1991). Prospects and limits in the empirical study of expertise: An introduction. In K. A. Ericsson & J. Smith (Eds.), *Toward a general theory of expertise: Prospects and limits* (pp. 1–38). Cambridge, England: Cambridge University Press.

Every Student Succeeds Act of 2015, Pub. L. No. 114-95.

FairTest. (2007, August 17). *Multiple-choice tests.* Retrieved from http://www.fairtest.org/multiple-choice-tests

Feldt, L. S. (1979). Everet F. Lindquist 1901–1978: A retrospective review of his contributions to educational research. *Journal of Educational Statistics, 4,* 4–13.

Fisher, R. (1925). *Statistical methods for research workers.* Edinburgh, England: Oliver & Boyd.

Gagné, R. M. (1965). *The conditions of learning and theory of instruction* (1st ed.). New York, NY: Holt, Rinehart & Winston.

Galton, F. (1883). *Inquiries into human faculty and its development.* London, England: J. M. Dent.

Gay, L. R. (1980). *Educational evaluation and measurement: Competencies for analysis and application.* Columbus, OH: Merrill.

Gierl, M. J., & Haladyna, T. (Eds.). (2013). *Automatic item generation: Theory and practice.* New York, NY: Routledge.

Gierl, M. J., Lai, H., Hogan, J. B., & Matovinovic, D. (2015). A method for generating educational test items that are aligned to the Common Core State Standards. *Journal of Applied Testing Technologies, 16*(1), 1–18.

Gierl, M. J., Zhou, J., & Alves, C. (2008). Developing a taxonomy of item model types to promote assessment engineering. *Journal of Technology, Learning, and Assessment, 7*(2). Retrieved from http://ejournals.bc.edu/ojs/index.php/jtla/article/view/1629

Gitomer, D. H., Steinberg, L. S., & Mislevy, R. J. (1995). Diagnostic assessment of trouble-shooting skill in an intelligent tutoring system. In P. Nichols, S. Chipman, & R. Brennan (Eds.), *Cognitively diagnostic assessment* (pp. 73–101). Hillsdale, NJ: Lawrence Erlbaum.

Glaser, R. (Ed.). (1962). *Training research and education.* New York, NY: Columbia University Press.

Glaser, R. (1963). Instructional technology and the measurement of learning outcomes: Some questions. *American Psychologist, 18,* 519–521.

Glaser, R. (1966). *The program for individually prescribed instruction.* Pittsburgh, PA: University of Pittsburgh Press.

Glaser, R., Linn, R. L., & Bohrnstedt, G. (1997). *Assessment in transition: Monitoring the nation's educational progress.* Stanford, CA: The National Academy of Education.

Glennan, T. K., & Melmed, A. (1996). *Fostering the use of educational technology.* Washington, DC: Rand Critical Technology Institute.

Graves, D. H. (1994). *A fresh look at writing.* Portsmouth, NH: Heinemann.

Guilford, J. P. (1936). *Psychometric methods.* New York, NY: McGraw-Hill.

Gulliksen, H. (2013). *Theory of mental tests.* New York, NY: Routledge. (Original work published 1950)

Hattie, J. (2008). *Visible learning: A synthesis of meta-analysis relating to achievement.* New York, NY: Routledge.

Hattie, J., & Timperley, H. (2007). The power of feedback. *Review of Educational Research, 77,* 81–112.

Herl, H. E., Niemi, D., & Baker, E. L. (1996). Construct validation of an approach to modeling cognitive structure of U.S. history knowledge. *Journal of Educational Research, 89,* 206–218.

Herl, H. E., O'Neil, H. F. Jr., Chung, G. K. W. K., & Schacter, J. (1999). Reliability and validity of a computer-based knowledge mapping system to measure content understanding. *Computers in Human Behavior, 15,* 315–334.

Herman, J. L., & Linn, R. L. (2013). *On the road to assessing deeper learning: The status of Smarter Balanced and PARCC assessment consortia* (CRESST Report 823). Los Angeles: University of California, National Center for Research on Evaluation, Standards and Student Testing.

Hively, W., Patterson, H. L., & Page, S. A. (1968). "Universe defined" system of arithmetic achievement tests. *Journal of Educational Measurement, 5,* 275–290.

Holland, J. G., & Skinner, B. F. (1961). *The analysis of behavior.* New York, NY: McGraw-Hill.

House, E. R. (1980). *Evaluating with validity.* Beverly Hills, CA: Sage.

Hovland, C., Lumsdaine, A. A., & Sheffield, F. D. (1949). Experiments on mass communication: Studies in social psychology in World War II. *Journal of Applied Psychology, 34,* 139–141.

Huff, K. L., & Sireci, S. G. (2001). Validity issues in computer-based testing. *Educational Measurement: Issues and Practice, 20*(3), 16–25.

Immigration Act of 1917, Pub. L. No. 301, 39 Stat. 874.

Improving America's Schools Act of 1994, Pub. L. No. 108, Stat. 3518.

Irvine, S. H., & Kyllonen, P.C. (Eds.). (2002). *Item generation for test development.* Mahwah, NJ: Lawrence Erlbaum.

Jensen, A. R. (1980). *Bias in mental testing.* New York, NY: Macmillan.

Jingo, M. (Producer), & Kurosawa, A. (Director). (1950). *Rashomon* [Motion picture]. Kobe, Japan: Daiei.

Johnson-Laird, P. N. (1983). *Mental models: Toward a cognitive science of language, inference, and consciousness.* Cambridge, MA: Harvard University Press.

Jöreskog, K. G. (1967). Some contributions to maximum likelihood factor analysis. *Psychometrika, 32,* 443–482.

Jöreskog, K. G. (1969). A general approach to confirmatory maximum likelihood factor analysis. *Psychometrika, 34,* 183–202.

Junker, B. W. (2011). Modeling hierarchy and dependence among task responses in educational data mining. In C. Romero, S. Ventura, M. Pechenizkiy, & R. S. J. D. Baker (Eds.), *Handbook of educational data mining* (pp. 143–155). Boca Raton, FL: CRC Press.

Kane, T. J., McCaffrey, D. F., Miller, T., & Staiger, D. O. (2013). *Have we identified effective teachers? Validating measures of effective teachers using random assignment.* Seattle, WA: Bill & Melinda Gates Foundation.

Katz, I. R., & James, C. M. (1998). *Toward assessment of design skill in engineering* (GRE Research Report 97–16). Princeton, NJ: Educational Testing Service.

Kifer, E. (2001). *Large-scale assessment: Dimensions, dilemmas, and policy.* Thousand Oaks, CA: Corwin.

Kim, J.-O., Chung, G. K. W. K., & Delacruz, G. C. (2004, April). *Examining the sensitivity of knowledge maps using repeated measures: A growth modeling approach.* Paper presented at the annual meeting of the American Educational Research Association, San Diego, CA.

Klausmeier, H. J. (1977). IGE in elementary and middle schools. *Educational Leadership, 34,* 330–336.

Klein, D. C. D., Chung, G. K. W. K., Osmundson, E., & Herl, H. E. (2002). *Examining the validity of knowledge mapping as a measure of elementary students' scientific understanding* (CSE Tech. Rep. No. 557). Los Angeles, CA: University of California, National Center for Research on Evaluation, Standards, and Student Testing.

Klein, D. C. D., Yarnall, L., & Glaubke, C. (2002). Using technology to assess students' Web expertise. In H. F. O'Neil & R. S. Perez (Eds.), *Technology applications in education: A learning view* (pp. 305–322). Mahwah, NJ: Lawrence Erlbaum.

Kliebard, H. M. (1975). The rise of scientific curriculum making and its aftermath. *Curriculum Theory Network, 5*(1), 27–38.

Kliebard, H. M. (1997). The rise of scientific curriculum making and its aftermath. In D. J. Flinders, & S. J. Thornton (Eds.), *The curriculum studies reader* (pp. 31–44). New York, NY: Routledge. (Original work published 1975)

Koenig, A. D., Lee, J. J., Iseli, M. R., & Wainess, R. (2010). *A conceptual framework for assessing performance in games and simulations* (CRESST Report No. 771). Los Angeles, CA: National Center for Research on Evaluation, Standards, and Student Testing.

Krathwohl, D. R., Bloom, B. S., & Masia, B. B. (1964). *Taxonomy of educational objectives: The classification of educational goals.* New York, NY: David McKay.

Kuder, G. F., & Richardson, M. W. (1937). The theory of the estimation of test reliability. *Psychometrika, 2,* 151–160.

Lagemann, E. C. (2002). *An elusive science: The troubling history of education research.* Chicago, IL: University of Chicago Press.

Lambiotte, J. G., Dansereau, D. F., Cross, D. R., & Reynolds, S. B. (1989). Multi-relational semantic maps. *Educational Psychology Review, 1,* 331–367.

Landauer, T. K., Laham, D., & Foltz, P. W. (2003). Automated scoring and annotation of essays with the Intelligent Essay Assessor. In M. D. Shermis & J. Burstein (Eds.), *Automated essay scoring: A cross-disciplinary perspective* (pp. 87–112). Mahwah, NJ: Lawrence Erlbaum.

Larry P. v. Riles, 343 F. Supp. 1036 (N.D. Cal 1972)(order granting preliminary injunction) aff'd 502 F.2d 963 (9th Cir. 1974); 495 F. Supp. 926 (N. D. Cal. 1979) aff'd in part, rev'd in part sub. nom. Larry P. by Lucille P. v. Riles. 793 F.2d 969 (9th Cir. 1974).

Lazarsfeld, P. F. (1950) The logical and mathematical foundation of latent structure analysis. In S. A. Stouffer, L. Guttman, E. A. Suchman, P. F. Lazarsfeld, S. A. Star, & J. A. Clausen (Eds.), *Measurement and prediction* (pp. 362–412). New York, NY: Wiley.

Lee, J. J. (2000). *The impact of Korean language accommodations on concept mapping tasks for Korean American English language learners* (Unpublished doctoral dissertation). University of California, Los Angeles.

Leighton, J.. & Gierl, M. (Eds.). (2007). *Cognitive diagnostic assessment for education: Theory and applications.* Cambridge, England: Cambridge University Press.

Levy, R. (2013). Psychometric and evidentiary advances, opportunities, and challenges for simulation-based assessment. *Educational Assessment, 18,* 182–207.

Lindblom, C. E., & Cohen, D. K. (1979). *Usable knowledge: Social science and social problem solving.* New Haven, CT: Yale University Press.

Lindquist, E. F. (Ed.). (1951). *Educational measurement.* Washington, DC: American Council on Education.

Lindquist, E. F. (1969). The impact of machines on educational measurement. *National Society for the Study of Education, 68,* 351–369.

Lindquist, E. F. (1970). The Iowa testing program: A retrospective view. *Education, 81,* 7–23.

Linn, R. L. (1993). Educational assessment: Expanded expectations and challenges. *Educational Evaluation and Policy Analysis, 15,* 1–16.

Linn, R. L. (2003). Accountability: Responsibility and reasonable expectations. *Educational Researcher, 32*(7), 3–13.

Linn, R. L. (2010). Validity. In P. Peterson, E. Baker, & B. McGaw (Eds.), *International encyclopedia of education* (pp. 181–185). Oxford, England: Elsevier.

Linn, R. L., Baker, E. L., & Dunbar, S. B. (1991). Complex, performance based assessment: Expectations and validation criteria. *Educational Researcher, 20*(8), 15–21.

Lord, F. M., Novick, M. R., & Birnbaum, A. (1968). *Statistical theories of mental test scores.* Boston, MA: Addison-Wesley.

Mann, H. (1957). *The republic and the school: On the education of free men.* New York, NY: Teachers College Press. (Original work published 1846)

Mann, M. (Ed.). (1867). *Life and works of Horace Mann.* Cambridge, MA: Walker, Fuller.

Margolis, M. J., & Clauser, B. E. (2006). A regression-based procedure for automated scoring of a complex medical performance assessment. In D. M. Williamson, I. I. Behar, & R. J. Mislevy (Eds.), *Automated scoring of complex tasks in computer-based testing* (pp. 123–167). Mahwah, NJ: Lawrence Erlbaum.

McCulloch, C. E., Searle, S. R., & Neuhaus, J. M. (2008). *Generalized, linear, and mixed models* (2nd ed.). New York, NY: Wiley.

McGuinness, D. M. (2003). Ontologies come of age. In D. Fensel, J. Hendler, H. Lieberman, & W. Wahlster (Eds.), *Spinning the semantic web: Bringing the World Wide Web to its full potential* (pp. 171–194). Cambridge: MIT Press.

Messick, S. (1989). Validity. In R. L. Linn (Ed.), *Educational measurement* (3rd ed., pp. 13–103). New York, NY: Macmillan.

Minsky, M. (Ed.). (1968). *Semantic information processing.* Cambridge: MIT Press.

Mislevy, R. J., Almond, R. G., & Lukas, J. F. (2004). *A brief introduction to evidence-centered design* (CSE Tech. Rep. No. 632). Los Angeles: University of California, Los Angeles, National Center for Research on Evaluation, Standards, and Student Testing.

Mislevy, R. J., Almond, R. G., Yan, D., & Steinberg, L. S. (1999). Bayesian networks in educational assessment: Where do the numbers come from? In K. B. Laskey, & H. Prade (Eds.), *Proceedings of the fifteenth conference on Uncertainty in Artificial Intelligence* (pp. 437–446). San Francisco, CA: Morgan Kaufmann.

Mislevy, R. J., Behrens, J. T., Bennett, R. E., DeMark, S. F., Frezzo, D. C., Levy, R., . . . Winters, F. I. (2010). On the roles of external knowledge representations in assessment design. *Journal of Technology, Learning, and Assessment, 8*(2). Retrieved from http://ejour-nals.bc.edu/ojs/index.php/jtla/article/view/1621

Mislevy, R. J., Behrens, J. T., DiCerbo, K. E., & Levy, R. (2012). Design and discovery in educational assessment: Evidence-centered design, psychometrics, and educational data mining. *Journal of Educational Data Mining, 4*(1), 11–48.

Mislevy, R. J., Orange, A., Bauer, M. I., von Davier, A., Hao, J., Corrigan, S., . . . John, M. (2014). *Psychometric considerations in game-based assessment.* New York, NY: GlassLab Resarch, Institute of Play.

Mislevy, R. J., & Riconscente, M. (2005). *Evidence-centered assessment design: Layers, structures, and terminology* (PADI Technical Report No. 9). Menlo Park, CA: SRI International.

Mislevy, R. J., Schank, P., Feng, M., Fried, R., Chang, B., Snow, E., . . . Colker, A. (2013). *A "wizard" for authoring scenario-based tasks, using evidence-centered design principles and structures* (Large-Scale Assessment Technical Report No. 14). Menlo Park, CA: SRI International.

Mislevy, R. J., Steinberg, L. S., & Almond, R. G. (1999). *Evidence centered assessments design.* Princeton, NJ: Educational Testing Service.

Mousavi, H., Kerr, D., & Iseli, M. (2013). *Unsupervised ontology generation from unstructured text* (CRESST Report 837). Los Angeles: University of California, National Center for Research on Evaluation, Standards, and Student testing.

National Commission on Excellence in Education. (1983). *Nation at risk.* Washington, DC: Department of Education.

National Assessment Governing Board. (2008). *Science framework for the 2009 National Assessment of Educational Progress.* Washington, DC: Author.

National Assessment Governing Board. (2013). *Technology and engineering literacy framework for the 2014 National Assessment of Educational Progress.* Washington, DC: Author.

National Center for Education Statistics. (2012). *The nation's report card: Science in action: Hands-on and interactive computer tasks from the 2009 science assessment* (Report No. NCES 2012–468). Washington, DC: Institute of Education Sciences, U.S. Department of Education.

National Council of Teachers of Mathematics. (1989). *Curriculum and evaluation standards report.* Retrieved from http://www.mathcurriculumcenter.org/PDFS/CCM/summaries/standards_summary.pdf

National Council on Education Standards and Testing. (1992, January 24). *Raising standards for American education: A report to Congress, the Secretary of Education, the National Education Goals Panel, and the American People.* Washington, DC: Government Printing Office.

National Defense Education Act of 1958.

National Governors Association Center for Best Practices & Council of Chief State School Officers. (2010). *Common Core State Standards for mathematics.* Washington, DC: Authors.

National Research Council, Committee on the Foundations of Assessment. (2001). *Knowing what students know: The science and design of educational assessment* (J. Pellegrino, N. Chudowsky, & R. Glaser, Eds.). Washington, DC: National Academies Press.

National Research Council. (2012). *Education for life and work: Developing transferable knowledge and skills in the 21st century.* Washington, DC: National Academies Press.

Newell, A., Shaw, J. C., & Simon, H. A. (1959). Report on a general problem-solving program. In *Proceedings of the International Conference on Information Processing* (pp. 256–264). Paris, France: UNESCO House.

Next Generation Science Standards Lead States. (2013). *Next Generation Science Standards: For states, by states.* Washington, DC: National Academies Press.

No Child Left Behind Act of 2001, Pub. L. No. 107-110, §115, Stat. 1425 (2002).

Novak, J. D., & Gowin, D. B. (1984). *Learning how to learn.* New York, NY: Cambridge University Press.

Nunnally, J. C., & Bernstein, I. H. (1967). *Psychometric theory* (1st ed.). New York, NY: McGraw-Hill.

Nunnally, J. C., & Bernstein, I. H. (1978). *Psychometric theory* (2nd ed.). New York, NY: McGraw-Hill.

Nunnally, J. C., & Bernstein, I. H. (1994). *Psychometric theory* (3rd ed.). New York, NY: McGraw-Hill.

O'Neil, H. F. Jr., Allred, K., & Dennis, R. A. (1997). Validation of a computer simulation for assessment of interpersonal skills. In H. F. O'Neil (Ed.), *Workforce readiness: Competencies and assessment* (pp. 229–254). Mahwah, NJ: Lawrence Erlbaum.

O'Neil, H. F. Jr., & Chuang, S. H. (2008). Measuring collaborative problem solving in low-stakes tests. In E. L. Baker, J. Dickieson, W. Wulfeck, & H. F. O'Neil (Eds.), *Assessment of problem solving using simulations* (pp. 177–199). Mahwah, NJ: Lawrence Erlbaum.

O'Neil, H. F. Jr., Chung, G. K. W. K., & Brown, R. S. (1997). Use of networked simulations as a context to measure team competencies. In H. F. O'Neil (Ed.), *Workforce readiness: Competencies and assessment* (pp. 411–452). Mahwah, NJ: Lawrence Erlbaum.

Organisation for Economic Co-operation and Development. (n.d.). *Programme for International Student Assessment (PISA)—Results from PISA 2012: United States country note.* Retrieved from http://www.oecd.org/unitedstates/PISA-2012-results-US.pdf

Osmundson, E., Chung, G. K. W. K., Herl, H. E., & Klein, D. C. D. (1999). *Concept mapping in the classroom: A tool for examining the development of students' conceptual understandings* (CSE Technical Report No. 507). Los Angeles: University of California, National Center for Research on Evaluation, Standards, and Student Testing.

Page, E. B. (1966). The imminence of grading essays by computer. *Phi Delta Kappan, 47,* 238–243.

Page, E. B., & Petersen, N. S. (1995). The computer moves into essay grading: Updating the ancient test. *Phi Delta Kappan, 76,* 561–565.

Parshall, C. G., Harmes, J. C., Davey, T., & Pashley, P. J. (2010). Innovative items for computerized testing. In W. J. van der Linden & C. A. W. Glas (Eds.), *Elements of adaptive testing* (pp. 215–230). New York, NY: Springer.

Pearson, K. (1901). *National life from the standpoint of science.* London: Adam & Charles Black.

Peña-Ayala, A. (2014). Educational data mining: A survey and a data mining–based analysis of recent works. *Expert Systems With Applications, 41,* 1432–1462.

Phelan, J., Choi, K., Vendlinski, T., Baker, E., & Herman, J. (2011). Differential improvement in student understanding of mathematical principles following formative assessment intervention. *Journal of Educational Research, 104,* 330–339.

Popham, W. J. (1969, October). *Performance criteria: The role of the Instructional Objectives Exchange in describing and measuring learner performance.* Paper presented at the PLEDGE conference, San Dimas, CA.

Popham, W. J. (1978). The case for criterion referenced measurements. *Educational Researcher, 7*(11), 6–10.

Popham, W. J., & Husek, T. R. (1971). Implications of criterion-referenced measurement. In W. J. Popham (Ed.), *Criterion-referenced measurement: An introduction.* Englewood Cliffs, NJ: Educational Technology.

Pressey, S. L. (1925). A simple self-recording double-action multiple choice apparatus. *Psychological Bulletin, 25,* 111.

Pressey, S. L. (1926). A simple apparatus which gives tests and scores—and teaches. *School and Society, 23,* 373–376.

Pressey, S. L. (1927). A machine for automatic teaching of drill material. *School and Society, 25*, 549–552.

Pressey, S. L. (1932). A third and fourth contribution toward the coming "industrial revolution" in education. *School and Society, 36*, 668–672.

Purves, A. C., & Takala, S. (Eds.). (1982). *An international perspective on the evaluation of written composition.* Oxford, England: Pergamon Press.

Quellmalz, E. S., Davenport, J. L., Timms, M. J., DeBoer, G. E., Jordan, K. A., Huang, C.-W., & Buckley, B. C. (2013). Next-generation environments for assessing and promoting complex science learning. *Journal of Educational Psychology, 105*, 1100–1114. doi:10.1037/a0032220

Rasch, G. (1980). *Probabilistic models for some intelligence and achievement tests.* Chicago, IL: University of Chicago Press. (Original work published 1960)

Resnick, L. B. (1994). Performance puzzles. *American Journal of Education, 102*, 511–526.

Resnick, L. B., & Resnick, D. P. (1992). Assessing the thinking curriculum: New tools for educational reform. In B. R. Gifford, & M. C. O'Connor (Eds.), *Changing assessments: Alternative views of aptitude, achievement, and instruction* (pp. 37–75). Boston, MA: Kluwer Academic.

Romero, C., Ventura, S., Pechenizkiy, M., & Baker, R. S. J. D. (Eds.). (2010). *Handbook of educational data mining.* New York, NY: CRC.

Ruiz-Primo, M. A., Schultz, S. E., Li, M., & Shavelson, R. J. (2001). Comparison of the reliability and validity of scores from two concept-mapping techniques. *Journal of Research in Science Teaching, 38*, 260–278.

Rumelhart, D. A. (1980). Schemata: The building blocks of cognition. In R. Spiro, B. Bruce, & W. Brewer (Eds.), *Theoretical issues in reading comprehension* (pp. 33–58). Hillsdale, NJ: Lawrence Erlbaum.

Rupp, A. A., Templin, J., & Henson, R. A. (2010). *Diagnostic measurement theory, methods, and applications.* New York, NY: Guilford Press.

Russell, M. (2006). *Technology and assessment: The tale of two interpretations.* Greenwich, CT: Information Age.

Salas, E., & Cannon-Bowers, J. A. (2001). The science of training: A decade of progress. *Annual Review of Psychology, 52*, 471–499.

Samejima, F. (1969). *Estimation of latent ability using a response pattern of graded scores* (Psychometric Monograph No. 17). Richmond, VA: Psychometric Society. Retrieved from http://www.psychometrika.org/journal/online/MN17.pdf

Schacter, J., Herl, H. E., Chung, G. K. W. K., Dennis, R. A., & O'Neil, H. F. Jr. (1999). Computer-based performance assessments: A solution to the narrow measurement and reporting of problem-solving. *Computers in Human Behavior, 15*, 403–418.

Schmidt, W. H., McKnight, C. C., & Raizen, S. A. (1997). *A splintered vision: An investigation of U.S. science and mathematics education.* Dordrecht, Netherlands: Springer.

Scriven, M. (1967). *The methodology of evaluation* (AERA Monograph Series on Curriculum Evaluation No. 1). Chicago, IL: Rand McNally.

Secretary's Commission on Achieving Necessary Skills. (1991). *What work requires of schools: A SCANS report for America 2000.* Washington, DC: U.S. Department of Labor. Retrieved from http://www.academicinnovations.com/report.html

Selden, S. (1999). *Advances in contemporary educational thought: Vol. 23. Inheriting shame: The story of eugenics and racism in America* (J. F. Soltis, Ed.). New York, NY: Teachers College Press.

Shavelson, R. J., Baxter, G. P., & Pine, J. (1992). Performance assessments: Political rhetoric and measurement reality. *Educational Researcher, 21*(4), 22–27.

Shavelson, R. J., & Webb, N. M. (1991). *Generalizability theory: A primer* (Vol. 1). Thousand Oaks, CA: Sage.

Shermis, M. D. (2014). State-of-the-art automated essay scoring: Competition results and future directions from a United States demonstration. *Assessing Writing, 20*, 53–76.

Singley, M. K., & Bennett, R. E. (2002). Item generation and beyond: Applications of schema theory to mathematics assessment. In S. H. Irvine & P. C. Kyllonen (Eds.), *Item generation for test development* (pp. 361–384). Mahwah, NJ: Lawrence Erlbaum.

Sireci, S. G., & Zenisky, A. L. (2006). Innovative item formats in computer-based testing: In pursuit of improved construct representation. In S. M. Downing & T. M. Haladyna (Eds.), *Handbook of test development* (pp. 329–347). Mahwah, NJ: Lawrence Erlbaum.

Spearman, C. (1904). "General intelligence," objectively determined and measured. *American Journal of Psychology, 15*, 201–292.

Spearman, C. (1925). Some issues in the theory of "g" (including the law of diminishing returns). *Nature, 116*, 436–439.

Spearman, C. (1927). *The abilities of man: Their nature and measurement.* New York, NY: Macmillan.

Spencer, H. (1867). *The principles of biology* (Vol. 2). London: Williams & Norgate.

Stenquist, J. L. (1933). Recent developments in the uses of tests. *Review of Educational Research, 3*(1), 49–61.

Strauss, V. (2013, January 25). The real problem with multiple-choice tests. *The Washington Post.* Retrieved from https://www.washingtonpost.com/news/answer-sheet/wp/2013/01/25/the-real-problem-with-multiple-choice-tests/

Taylor, F. W. (1911). *The principles of scientific management.* New York, NY: Harper & Row.

Terman, L. M. (1917a). *The intelligence of school children.* Boston, MA: Houghton Mifflin.

Terman, L. M. (1917b). The mental powers of children and the Stanford revision and extension of the Binet-Simon intelligence scale. *Child, 7*, 287–290.

Terman, L. M. (1925). *Genetic studies of genius: Vol. 1. Mental and physical traits of a thousand gifted children.* Stanford, CA: Stanford University Press.

Thorndike, E. L. (1898). Animal intelligence: An experimental study of the associative processes in animals. *Psychology Review, 8*, 109.

Thorndike, E. L. (1913). *An introduction to the theory of mental and social measurements* (2nd ed.). New York, NY: Science Press. (Original work published 1904)

Thorndike, E. L. (1910). The relation between memory for words and memory for numbers and the relation between memory over short and memory over long intervals. *American Journal of Psychology, 21*, 487–488.

Thorndike, E. L. (1911a). A scale for measuring the merit of English writing. *Science, 33*, 935–938.

Thorndike, E. L. (1911b). Testing the results of the teaching of science. *School Science and Mathematics, 11*, 315–320.

Thorndike, E. L. (1915). The resemblance of young twins in handwriting. *American Naturalist, 49*, 377–379.

Thorndike, E. L. (1917). The psychology of thinking in the case of reading. *Psychology Review, 24*, 220–234.

Thorndike, E. L. (1919). Tests of intelligence: Reliability, significance, susceptibility to special training and adaptation to the general nature of the task. *School and Society, 9*, 189–195.

Thorndike, E. L. (1922a). The nature of algebraic abilities. *The Mathematics Teacher, 15*, 6–15.

Thorndike, E. L. (1922b). *The psychology of arithmetic.* New York, NY: Macmillan.

Thorndike, E. L. (1927). *The measurement of intelligence.* New York, NY: Bureau of Publications, Teacher's College, Columbia University.

Thurstone, L. L. (1925). A method of scaling psychological and educational tests. *Journal of Educational Psychology, 16*, 433–449.

Thurstone, L. L. (1927). The law of comparative judgment. *Psychological Review, 34*, 278–286.

Thurstone, L. L. (1937). Psychology as a quantitative rational science. *Science, 85*, 227–232.

Thurstone, L. L. (1938). *Primary mental abilities*. Chicago, IL: University of Chicago Press.

Thurstone, L. L. (1947). *Multiple factor analysis*. Chicago, IL: University of Chicago Press.

Tucker, L. R. (1946). Maximum validity of a test with equivalent items. *Psychometrika, 11*, 1–13.

Tyack, D., & Cuban, L. (1995). *Tinkering toward utopia: A century of public school reform*. Cambridge, MA: Harvard University Press.

Tyler, R. W. (1931). A generalized technique for constructing achievement tests. *Educational Research Bulletin, 10*, 199–208

Tyler, R. W. (1949). *Basic principles of curriculum and instruction*. Chicago, IL: University of Chicago Press.

U.S. Census Bureau. (1880). *Census of population and housing, 1880*. Retrieved from https://www.census.gov/prod/www/decennial.html

U.S. Census Bureau. (1920). *Census of population and housing, 1920*. Retrieved from https://www.census.gov/prod/www/decennial.html

U.S. Department of Education. (2012). *Enhancing teaching and learning through educational data mining and learning analytics* (Issue Brief). Washington, DC: Author.

van der Linden, W. J. (2005). *Linear models for optimal test design*. New York, NY: Springer.

van der Linden, W. J., & Diao, Q. (2011). Automated test-form generation. *Journal of Educational Measurement, 48*, 206–222.

Vendlinski, T. P., Baker, E. L., & Niemi, D. (2008). Templates and objects in authoring problem-solving assessments. In E. L. Baker, J. Dickieson, W. Wulfeck, & H. F. O'Neil (Eds.), *Assessment of problem solving using simulations* (pp. 309–333). Mahwah, NJ: Lawrence Erlbaum.

Vendlinski, T. P., Niemi, D., & Wang, J. (2005). Learning assessment by designing assessments: An on-line formative assessment design tool. In C. Crawford, R. Carlsen, I. Gibson, K. McFerrin, J. Price, & R. Weber (Eds.), *Proceedings of Society for Information Technology and Teacher Education international conference 2005* (pp. 228–240). Norfolk, VA: Association for the Advancement of Computing in Education.

Vendlinski, T. P., & Stevens, R. (2002). Assessing student problem-solving skills with complex computer-based tasks. *Journal of Technology, Learning, and Assessment, 1*(3), 1–20.

Volante, L. (Ed.). (2016). *The intersection of international achievement testing and educational policy: Global perspectives on large-scale reform*. New York, NY: Routledge.

Wainer, H., & Braun, H. I. (1988). *Test validity*. Hillsdale, NJ: Lawrence Erlbaum.

Wainer, H., Dorans, N., Eignor, D., Flaugher, R., Green, B., Mislevy, R., . . . Thissen, D. (Eds.). (2000). *Computerized adaptive testing: A primer* (2nd ed.). Hillsdale, NJ: Lawrence Erlbaum.

Washburne, C. W. (1940). *A living philosophy of education*. New York, NY: John Day.

Webb, N. M. (2009). The teacher's role in promoting collaborative dialogue in the classroom. *British Journal of Educational Psychology, 79*, 1–28.

Wenger, E. (1998). *Communities of practice: Learning, meaning, and identity*. Cambridge, England: Cambridge University Press.

Whipple, G. M. (1921). The national intelligence tests. *Journal of Educational Research, 4*, 16–31.

Wiener, N. (1950). *The human use of human beings*. Boston, MA: Houghton Mifflin.

Wiley, D. E., Schmidt, W. H., & Bramble, W. J. (1973). Studies of a class of covariance structure models. *Journal of the American Statistical Association, 68*, 317–323.

Williamson, D. M., Bejar, I. I., & Hone, A. S. (1999). "Mental model" comparison of automated and human scoring. *Journal of Educational Measurement, 36*, 158–184.

Wirtz, W., & Lapointe, A. E. (1984). Measuring the quality of education: A report on assessing educational progress. *Journal of Educational Measurement, 21*, 209–212.

Wittrock, M. C., & Baker, E. L. (Eds.). (1991). *Testing and cognition.* Englewood Cliffs, NJ: Prentice Hall.

Wu, X., Kumar, V., Quinlan, J. R., Ghosh, J., Yang, Q., Motoda, H., . . . Steinberg, D. (2008). Top 10 algorithms in data mining. *Knowledge and Information Systems, 14,* 1–37.

Yang, Y., Buckendahl, C. W., Juszkiewicz, P. J., & Bhola, D. S. (2002). A review of strategies for validating computer-automated scoring. *Applied Measurement in Education, 15,* 391–412.

Yerkes, R. (1919). The mental rating of school children. *National School Service, 1*(12), 6–7.

Yerkes, R. (1923). *Introduction to C. C. Brigham's A Study of American Intelligence.* Princeton, NJ: Princeton University Press.

Yerkes, R., & Yoakum, C. S. (1920). *Army mental tests.* New York, NY: Henry Holt.

Yin, Y., & Shavelson, R. J. (2004). *Application of generalizability theory to concept-map assessment research* (CSE Technical Report No. 640). Los Angeles: University of California, National Center for Research on Evaluation, Standards, and Student Testing.

Zenisky, A. L., & Sireci, S. G. (2002). Technological innovations in large-scale assessment. *Applied Measurement in Education, 15,* 337–362.

Chapter 5

The Question of School Resources and Student Achievement: A History and Reconsideration

LARRY V. HEDGES
Northwestern University

TERRI D. PIGOTT
Loyola University Chicago

JOSHUA R. POLANIN
Development Services Group, Inc.

ANN MARIE RYAN
CHARLES TOCCI
Loyola University Chicago

RYAN T. WILLIAMS
American Institutes of Research

One question posed continually over the past century of education research is to what extent school resources affect student outcomes. From the turn of the century to the present, a diverse set of actors, including politicians, physicians, and researchers from a number of disciplines, have studied whether and how money that is provided for schools translates into increased student achievement. The authors discuss the historical origins of the question of whether school resources relate to student achievement, and report the results of a meta-analysis of studies examining that relationship. They find that policymakers, researchers, and other stakeholders have addressed this question using diverse strategies. The way the question is asked, and the methods used to answer it, is shaped by history, as well by the scholarly, social, and political concerns of any given time. The diversity of methods has resulted in a body of literature too diverse and too inconsistent to yield reliable inferences through meta-analysis. The authors suggest that a collaborative approach addressing the question from a variety of disciplinary and practice perspectives may lead to more effective interventions to meet the needs of all students.

Review of Research in Education
March 2016, Vol. 40, pp. 143–168
DOI: 10.3102/0091732X16667070
© 2016 AERA. http://rre.aera.net

An enduring question in education research is how, and sometimes even whether, the resources provided to schools relate to student achievement. This issue can be summarized into a seemingly simple question: Does money matter to student outcomes? A close examination of the historical origins of this question as well as of recent studies that examine the influence of resources on student achievement highlights the tension between the competing priorities of efficiency and equity in U.S. public schooling. It also raises issues about the ways in which certain questions develop and become central to education research.

This chapter is organized into three sections. The first section presents a historical background of school resources and student achievement research. The second section is a report on the results of a systematic review of quantitative studies examining the relationship between per-pupil expenditure (PPE) and student achievement. This review updates work first conducted by Hanushek (1989) and later reanalyzed by Greenwald, Hedges, and Laine (1996) by incorporating relevant literature published since 1966. The concluding section draws from both the historical narrative and the meta-analysis to discuss the limitations of contemporary research into the relationship between resources and student achievement, and it suggests ways that the field might develop better, more valuable questions to pursue.

HISTORICAL BACKGROUND ON RESEARCH INTO SCHOOL RESOURCES AND STUDENT ACHIEVEMENT

Like Hanushek (1989), we consider *Equality of Educational Opportunity* (Coleman et. al., 1966), known as the "Coleman Report," a historical milestone. The Coleman Report marks the start of the current era of research into relationships between schooling inputs and outputs, a period characterized by the increasingly sophisticated use of inferential statistics with large-scale data sets. This chapter briefly reviews the 100-plus years leading up to the Coleman Report history to provide context for how statistical studies of educational resources and student achievement developed in relationship to contemporaneous scholarly and social concerns. The history is cleaved into three eras and organized around central questions posed in each of those eras: 1867 to 1891 (What is the state of U.S. schooling?), 1892 to 1965 (Can the field of education measurement assist in directing school resources in more efficient ways?), and 1966 to the present day (Can education measurement indicate if money matters?). Each period witnessed the introduction of new statistical methods and debates about the nature of schooling in a socioeconomically diverse, multilingual, and multiracial society; the purposes of public education; and which are the academic fields best equipped to answer questions about how resources relate to achievement.

What Is the State of U.S. Schooling? Collecting Data on U.S. Schools (1867–1891)

The U.S. Department of Education was formed in 1867 as part of the Reconstruction Acts passed by a Republican-controlled Congress. The Republicans, especially the radical faction lead by Charles Sumner and Thaddeus Stevens, held strong views on education, including the idea that widespread, publicly supported school systems were essential for the country. Indeed, Sumner noted the lack of public schools in the Southern states and insinuated that it was a cause of their recent "rebelliousness" (Tyack, James, & Benavot, 1987). While the "Radical Republicans" failed in their attempt to pass a federal law guaranteeing a public education to all citizens, they were able to establish the Department of Education to, in the words of Republican Congressman from Minnesota Ignatius Donnelly, "enforce education, without regard to race or color, upon the population of all such States that fall below a standard to be established by Congress" (quoted in Tyack et. al., 1987, p. 141).

An immediate problem facing their effort was that little was known about the state of American education nationally. To address this need, Congress provided the Department of Education with the purpose of

collecting such statistics and facts as shall show the condition and progress of education in the several States and Territories, and of diffusing such information respecting the organization and management of schools and school systems, and methods of teaching, as shall aid the people of the United States in the establishment and maintenance of efficient school systems, and otherwise promote the cause of education throughout the country. (quoted in W. V. Grant, 1993, p. 1)

At the time, the modern field of statistics was in its infancy, though advances in mathematics (Feinberg, 1992) and epidemiology (Freedman, 1999) were attracting wide interest for their potential use to describe phenomena and make predictions. The notion that statistical information and facts about education can help support efficient and widespread schooling represents the influence of Horace Mann. Sumner, a self-described friend of and regular correspondent with Mann, unsuccessfully ran for the Boston School Committee in 1855 following Mann's encouragement (Reese, 2013). A year later, Mann introduced the nation's first system of standard examinations in an effort to gather objective information about the comparative quality of Boston schools and whether or not students were qualified to graduate (Gallagher, 2003). Mann promoted this use of examinations and statistical information nationally, later connecting it to the abolition movement through advocacy for multiracial common schools. The support for abolition helped garner Mann the Free Soil Party's 1852 nomination for governor of Massachusetts. (The short-lived political party had been established in Massachusetts by Sumner; by 1856, it was folded into the nascent Republican Party.)

By the time the first national commissioner of education was installed in 1869, Sumner had been marginalized within his party. Sumner was unable to deter legislation from downgrading the Department of Education to the Office of Education within the Department of the Interior and cutting the office's staff from three clerks to two. Nonetheless, the Office of Education developed and distributed a survey in 1870 to solicit information ranging from student enrollment totals to school expenditures to numbers of teacher to tallies of high school graduates to attendance figures. These efforts were hamstrung by sizable gaps in basic information, such as complete lists of schools and colleges. But the office persisted, hiring its first statistician in 1872 and publishing its first public report in 1875. Although Senator Donnelly's vision for a vigorous, forceful federal role in education never found sufficient political backing, the Office of Education was able to meet its mandate by progressively expanding its survey scope and increasing the detail of published data. In 1890, the office inquired about the subject areas taken by students, sources of public revenue, and the value of facilities and physical equipment from both public and private schools (W. V. Grant, 1993). A basic yet robust statistical portrait of American education was emerging.

Can the Field of Education Measurement Assist in Directing School Resources in More Efficient Ways? (1892–1965)

The late 19th century marked the developmental period of education measurement, an era characterized by trial and error, experimentation, and wide-ranging uses of this new tool. Much like any new discipline, seemingly contradictory perspectives coexisted within it. The late 19th and early 20th centuries were also known as the Progressive Era, and the field of education measurement grew as part of broader progressive efforts to develop and use scientific and social scientific methods to solve social problems (Feinberg, 1992; Freedman, 1999). Some efforts embraced progressive education aimed at limiting opportunities (e.g., eugenics and IQ testing), and others attempted to expand education efforts to all students (e.g., early efforts to develop special education). In both cases, the main issues revolved around how schools could efficiently educate all children to become productive citizens in an era of compulsory mandates.

In the late 19th and early 20th centuries, district officials, researchers, and concerned citizens, almost exclusively businessmen, used or encouraged the use of descriptive statistics to investigate two central questions:

- How can one use statistics to understand what is happening in schools?
- How can one use information gleaned from statistical analyses to best direct resources?

Education measurement did not yet distinguish between theory and practice. Education researchers developed scientific methods for the explicit purpose of improving education, and they worked diligently to integrate their ideas into formal education policy with great immediacy. This urgency came about in large part from the perceived inefficiency of schools and the resulting need for reform.

Demands for school reform came from several sectors, with business and industry pushing schools to be more efficient as they engaged in scientific management, their own reform effort. This reform idea derived from concepts about industrial efficiency and scientific management put forth by Frederick Taylor and popularly known as Taylorism. The rise of the social efficiency movement in schools at the turn of the 20th century resulted in large part from Taylorism (Kliebard, 2004).

One of the more noted figures who attempted to bring Taylor's ideas of scientific management to education was Joseph Mayer Rice. Kliebard (2004) dubs Rice "the father of comparative methodology" (p. 19) as a result of his surveys of American schools that he started in 1891. He published his findings in the education journal *The Forum* beginning the next year. Trained as a physician, Rice devoted his work to understanding the status of American education—curriculum, teaching, and the performance of students. He became interested in comparing student performance and education conditions through administrative school surveys. Using the results of his surveys, Rice advocated for better education conditions for American students. According to Callahan (1962), Rice's use and application of statistics reflected limited knowledge and questionable results, although he was taken seriously at the time and considered a pioneer in the field of measurement.

Rice published an expanded version of his work in a 1913 book, *Scientific Management in Education*, in which he proposed holding administrators and teachers accountable for both defining education goals and measuring the results of their efforts on meeting those goals through scientific measurement (as cited in Kliebard, 2004). He grounded these ideas in industrialism and the social efficiency culture that had begun to seep into American education.

Taylorism made a large impression on early 20th-century education reformers. They saw its adherence to efficiency as a ripe solution to the challenges faced by school systems dealing with an expanding school population with a multitude of needs. Rice's surveys signaled the beginning of a broader trend. The school survey took hold in districts and found support not only from business interests but from academics and professional education associations as well (Ryan, 2011).

In the 1910s, the *American School Board Journal* promoted the use of school surveys to examine the return of investments in schools, the efficiency and quality of teachers, and, to some degree, the efficiency of students (Callahan, 1962). Much of the work around efficiency stemmed from Taylorism, but it also stemmed from the work of academics like Arthur C. Boyce of the University of Chicago's Department of Education, who was a colleague of Franklin Bobbitt (Callahan, 1962). Teachers voiced concern about these rating systems but had to accept them in most districts due to a lack of bargaining power. Callahan (1962) notes that there was little resistance to the movement to make schools more efficient from professional circles. Conducting full school and district surveys required public support, and to garner such support, school boards often enlisted the help of business groups or groups that represented taxpayers and appealed to the public's desire to use funds wisely to provide education resources. George D. Strayer, a professor of educational administration at Teachers College Columbia and a key figure in the survey movement, played a large role in developing and conducting district-wide surveys well into the 1930s. These surveys left a lasting impression on how district and school administrators approached their positions in schools, putting data about administrative and management concerns at the forefront (Callahan, 1962).

The heightened focus on the efficiency of schools, teachers, and eventually students and their achievement led in part to a movement toward standardizing education testing (Callahan, 1962). Statistics reflected the number of students who repeated grades or dropped out altogether, the chief concerns in larger districts, for example, in New York and Chicago, in the early 20th century (Tyack, 1974). A district's goal in collecting such statistics was to determine how schools would deal with "backward" children, or the "feeble-minded." For example, in 1899, the Chicago public schools established a Department of Child Study, which, in 1911, tagged "educational research" on to the department's name. By 1918, Chicago had an entire department devoted to standards and statistics (Ryan, 2011). Departments such as these coincided with a growing school population and compulsory school laws in order to manage and sort school populations. Simultaneously, calls for how to better differentiate curriculum increased. Many educators sought to meet the needs of their students better and put their hopes in the use of IQ and other testing, as well as stratified curriculum to prepare children for what they might be best "suited for" in life.

Gould (1996) examined the introduction of intelligence testing in the United States and its European origins. His seminal work, *The Mismeasure of Man*, addresses how key figures who introduced the field of measurement and testing to American education through the promotion of IQ testing and other standard forms of testing rejected the cautions of French psychologist Alfred Binet, who believed the "aim of his scale was to identify in order to help and improve, not to label in order to limit" (p. 182). Henry H. Goddard of the University of Chicago, Lewis M. Terman of Stanford University, and Robert M. Yerkes of Harvard University and then Yale University were early and renowned figures in the field of testing in the United States. These psychologists had a significant impact on the growth and use of measurement. Terman, more so than the others, was responsible for the growth of testing in schools and across districts with his development of the Stanford–Binet Scale. This instrument, although focused on measuring the "intelligence" of individual children, broadened into other tests designed to assess all children by the late 1910s and early 1920s (Gould, 1996). According to Gould (1996), researchers like Terman took more interest in the "science" of hereditarianism (eugenics) than in the burgeoning field of statistics. When confronted with information that contradicted his beliefs— for example, a "correlation of 0.4 between social status and IQ"—Terman advanced a multifaceted argument in support of nature over environment (Gould, 1996, p. 219). Terman ended up backpedaling on some of his earlier arguments, but not until the late 1930s, after eugenics had largely been discredited.

E. L. Thorndike, a professor at Teachers College Columbia and an influential psychologist in the early 20th century, adhered to eugenic beliefs of intelligence and had a heavy influence on ideas about the curriculum (Kliebard, 2004). Bobbitt and others who supported curriculum that would stratify American children and prepare them for their "station in life" based on IQ test results found confirmation in Thorndike's conclusions (Kliebard, 2004). Both Terman and Thorndike believed that intelligence was inherited and fixed, but other educators questioned that notion. Harold Rugg (1917) of Teachers College Columbia believed teachers could achieve societal change through education and that students could learn and grow through curriculum (Kliebard, 2004). In 1917, Rugg published a textbook on statistics for teachers with the hope that they would learn to use statistics as a tool of social science.

The educators in the Progressive Education Association reflected similar beliefs. The Progressive Education Association was one of the more prominent users of statistics during the World War II era. The Eight-Year Study (1932–1940), directed by Ralph Tyler of the Ohio State University, examined 30 schools (the final tally was 29), with 15 given curricular freedom and the remaining schools following traditional curricula. At the close of the study, almost 1,500 students had attended college from across the study group, with little difference in academic performance based on grade point average and other factors, with the students in experimental schools slightly edging out those in traditional schools (Kliebard, 2004). This comparative study, in which education researchers employed an experimental design, provided a good example of a large-scale investigation beyond a school survey.

Although the use of education statistics was primarily centered on how to better use resources and reduce waste in K–12 school districts, researchers began to see how statistics could be used to address unequal conditions in education more broadly. Organizations such as the National Association for the Advancement of Colored People pulled statistics to address issues of school segregation and to equalize resources in graduate education. In 1935, Charles Hamilton Houston of the National Association for the Advancement of Colored People began efforts to desegregate law schools, arguing that separate but equal law schools would become prohibitively expensive for states. He saw law school desegregation as a strategy to eventually call for equal schooling at other levels. In 1938, the Supreme Court ruled in the case of *State of Missouri ex rel. Gaines v. Canada* that the state must provide Gaines with an equal legal education. This case led to a series of cases brought by Thurgood Marshall, eventually leading to the landmark decision to desegregate schools with *Brown v. Board of Education* in 1954. The shift in thinking about how education measurement and statistics could be marshaled to support the cause to equalize and perhaps even garner resources for those denied equal access would shape the next period in the field of measurement.

Can Education Measurement Indicate if Money Matters? (1966–Present)

With the election of President John F. Kennedy, two ideas were paired as central to federal social policy: a strong belief in the value of scholarly research to effectively design social policies combined with a commitment to social welfare in the form of the expansion of civil rights and the alleviation of poverty (Featherman & Vinovskis, 2001, p. 49). In the 1960s, prominent academics from leading universities, particularly those with personal ties to members of the Kennedy and later the Johnson administrations, were sometimes directly consulted and often solicited to prepare reports in support of key policy initiatives (Halberstram, 1993). These tendencies led to the emergence of two parallel approaches to education policy, traditions that are still present today. The first is the "compensatory" approach, codified by Bloom, Davis, and Hess (1965), which primarily seeks to design and implement programs and policies that improve education for students in poverty and minority students. The second is the "efficiency" approach, embodied in the Coleman Report (Coleman et al., 1966), which seeks to evaluate programs and policies in order to promote the most effective and resource efficient among them.

The divergence began in the earliest weeks of the Johnson administration as the president and his aides began pressing Congress to enact comprehensive civil rights legislation. The Kennedy administration had proposed the Civil Rights Act, but Johnson saw the bill through to law in the wake of Kennedy's assassination. A small provision was written into early drafts requiring the federal government to conduct a thorough national assessment of educational opportunities for children from all backgrounds. After a flurry of negotiations, Section 402 of the Civil Rights Act read,

The Commissioner (of Education) shall conduct a survey and make a report to the President and the Congress within two years of the enactment of this title concerning the lack of availability of equal educational opportunity for individuals by reason of race, color, religion, or national origin in public educational institutions at all levels in the U.S., its territories, and possessions, and the District of Columbia.

The completed survey would come to be known as the Coleman Report (G. Grant, 1973).

After the passage of the Civil Rights Act, the Johnson administration began focus on comprehensive education legislation independent from the Coleman Report. John W. Gardner, president of the Carnegie Corporation and a psychologist by training, was tapped to form a commission to draft a new education bill. The Gardner Commission put forth a proposal to categorically direct federal education spending, with a significant entitlement program addressing the needs of children from poor families. This concept became the basic structure of the Elementary and Secondary Education Act of 1965, and the provision of aid directly to school districts educating children in poverty became Title I. Following the passage of the Elementary and Secondary Education Act, Gardner was appointed secretary of Health, Education, and Welfare (Thomas & Brady, 2005). In turn, he contracted with eminent education psychologist Benjamin Bloom to organize a conference and publish its proceedings to make recommendations as to how Title I monies might be invested.

Bloom and his colleagues at the University of Chicago hosted the 5-day Research Conference on Education and Cultural Deprivation in June 1965, recruiting 30 leading education scholars. The vast majority were psychologists, although several sociologists and two public schools officials were included. In the wake of the *Brown v. Board of Education* ruling, which drew heavily on the Clarks' "doll tests" (Clark &

Clark, 1947) to demonstrate the injury done by segregated schooling, cognitive psychology took a central position in discussions about desegregation and education policy. These issues were typically framed in terms of "cultural deprivation"; as Bloom et al. (1965) explain in the introduction to the conference proceedings, the cultural deprivation discourse rejected the idea of natural intelligence deficits among certain races in favor of emphasizing "homes which do not transmit the cultural patterns necessary for the types of learning characteristic of the school and the larger society" (p. 4). These problems were to be addressed through "compensatory education," which sought to "prevent or overcome earlier deficiencies in the development of each individual" (p. 6). Frank Reisman (1963), the conference's opening speaker, had previously argued that the goal of compensatory education was not "to train the disadvantaged to become 'good middle class' children" (p. 345) but rather to change the way schools and teachers engaged culturally deprived students and families in order to better equip these children for success in society using a variety of programs and curricular changes. Policy suggestions published in the conference proceedings (Bloom et. al., 1965) ranged from providing free breakfasts and annual physical examinations to increasing contact between home and school, to identifying appropriate curricula and pedagogies, to effectively educate "disadvantaged" youths. The compensatory approach sought to develop and install targeted programs aimed at improving the education outcomes of students in poverty and minority students.

David Seeley, assistant commissioner of education, was a listed observer at the conference. Seeley came to the Office of Education as a Yale-trained lawyer with a particular interest in modernizing the office's historic data collection and publication functions. In 1964, Seeley successfully lobbied the commissioner to hire Alexander Mood, a mathematician and former executive at the RAND Corporation, to apply his expertise in inferential statistics and computers as assistant commissioner for education statistics. One of Mood's first tasks was to contract a principal investigator for the Section 402 survey, and Mood's immediate recommendation was James Coleman (G. Grant, 1973). Mood had been impressed by Coleman's 1961 book, *The Adolescent Society*, in which Coleman and a team of researchers surveyed more than 4,000 students across nine Chicago area high schools. A 175-item questionnaire was paired with informal observation and interviews to present a portrait of the American teenager as overly influenced by peers, being steered away from academic and mature social responsibilities and toward superficial entertainments and immature peer relationships.

Coleman agreed to lead the survey notwithstanding the short time line to deliver a report (less than 2 years) and the office's numerous contentious relationships with state and district leaders across the country stemming from attempts to enforce desegregation orders. Despite these challenges, Coleman and his researchers were able to administer their survey to more than 650,000 teachers and students across more than 3,000 schools over 3 days in October 1965. Defining "equality of educational opportunity" as the "equality of results, given the same individual input" (Coleman et al., 1966, p. 14), the survey generated data about individual students, school contexts, and academic performance. This massive data set allowed the researchers to cultivate a variety of sample groups using results from the 1960 census and to apply a relatively new analytic method that was uncommon outside of economics: an input-output analysis.

Input-output analysis was developed by Soviet economists during the 1920s as a way to inform socialist economic planning. The codification and popularization of the method are attributed to Wasily Leontief, a Russian Jew who left the USSR for Germany in 1925 at age 19 with a master's degree in economics. After earning his doctorate in economics in Munich, Leontief fled rising anti-Semitism in Germany to take a position with the U.S. National Bureau of Economic Research in 1931. From 1932 through 1975, Leontief also held a faculty appointment at Harvard, where he taught input-output analysis to successive generations of economists (Kaliadina, 2006; Kaliadina & Pavlova, 2006). Carl Christ (1955) was one of Leontief's early acolytes, publishing an influential paper on input-output analysis in 1955 and becoming a colleague of Coleman at Johns Hopkins in 1959. The use of input-output concepts as part of the report's regression analysis was groundbreaking and its use was soon employed by other scholars (e.g., Entwisle & Conviser, 1969) to open new lines of inquiry. Yet the regression methods employed by Coleman were poorly equipped to provide causal inferences (Hoxby, 2016) and were better suited for measuring correlations between phenomena.

The Coleman Report was released on July 1, 1966. At more than 700 pages, its three major conclusions were that racial segregation was widespread in public schools, there were distinct disparities in academic achievement between racial groups, and school effects on student achievement were much smaller than variation in individual background, particularly social class (Gamoran & Long, 2006). The claim that "schools are not acting as a strong stimulus independent of the child's background, or the level of the student body" (Coleman et al., 1966, p. 311) was the result of regression analysis and became the report's most noteworthy argument. In the short term, the Coleman Report was ignored by the Johnson administration, whose major foci were school desegregation and poverty alleviation; was questioned by other academics; and was met with confusion by the news media, which found the report technical, dense, and difficult to summarize (G. Grant, 1973). The report had no notable policy influences until 1968, when Daniel Patrick Moynihan wrote a laudatory review in the *Harvard Educational Review*. Moynihan brought his enthusiasm for the report into the Nixon administration, where he arranged for Coleman to become advisor to the Cabinet Committee on Desegregation as well as a favored expert to testify for Congressional committees. The Coleman Report's findings became central to the Emergency School Aid Act of 1970, which initiated two key changes in federal education policy: a shift from punishing school districts that did not desegregate to rewarding districts that complied with desegregation mandates, and targeted cuts in education spending under the rationale that school effects are comparatively small

(G. Grant, 1973). Subsequent education policies under Nixon, Ford, and Reagan would adopt similar "efficiency" approaches, thereby establishing the Coleman Report as foundational to recent education policy and scholarship.

THE STUDY

The Coleman Report's conclusion that schools have a comparatively minor influence on student achievement spurred research activity around examining the relationship between school outcomes such as achievement and school inputs using input-output analysis, or education production functions. Perhaps most reflective of the efficiency mind-set in the post-Coleman era is the Reagan administration's report *A Nation at Risk* (1983) and ensuing budget cuts to the Department of Education. The report argued for a "back to basics" approach to education focused on streamlined academic inputs in hopes of raising student achievement in core subject areas. Left unaddressed were any compensatory concerns about racial or socioeconomic inequities and how these might be addressed through targeted program or differentiated curricular reforms.

Twenty years after the Coleman Report and during a renewed focus on efficiency in the 1980s, Eric Hanushek, an economist, reviewed the existing literature using educational production functions. Hanushek has a personal history with the Coleman Report; as a graduate student at Harvard, he participated in a yearlong series of weekly seminar meetings among researchers from various backgrounds to parse the report's data, methods, and findings. Hanushek (2016) has written that this experience set him on a path to researching education policy. He published a series of articles (1981, 1986, 1989, 1991) reviewing the educational production function literature, typically using ordinary least squares regression analysis to predict student achievement using a number of covariates, including measures of school inputs such as PPE. The assumption in these analyses is that student background variables such as race, prior achievement, and socioeconomic status can be adequately controlled so that one can infer a causal relationship among school resource inputs and student outcomes. Across these studies, Hanushek concludes that school resources do not have a consistent relationship with school achievement—essentially, that money does not matter for student outcomes.

Hanushek used a method of research synthesis called vote counting. Vote counting categorizes each study into groups depending on the direction and significance of the studies' conclusions. The analyses counted the numbers of studies that determined a positive relationship between school resources and achievement, no relationship between resources and achievement, and a negative relationship between school resources and achievement. Hanushek found insufficient evidence that a majority of studies determined a positive relationship between school resources and achievement. Since his research, methodological developments in meta-analysis have provided more robust and statistically defensible alternatives to vote counting. A series of papers by Larry Hedges, Robert Greenwald, and Richard Laine (Greenwald et al., 1996; Hedges, Laine, & Greenwald, 1994; Laine, Greenwald, & Hedges, 1995) used meta-analytic techniques to reexamine Hanushek's conclusions. These analyses synthesized the actual values for measures of the relationship between school resources and achievement, instead of characterizing the studies based on the direction of their results. Greenwald et al. (1996) found a small but consistent positive relationship between school resources and student achievement.

Although Greenwald et al.'s (1996) methods followed the most current guidelines for research synthesis at the time, the authors encountered a number of difficulties in analyzing the education production function literature. Two of the major issues were the diversity of models used across the studies and the number of models presented in each study. In the education production function literature, researchers do not have an agreed-on set of covariates that should be included. Thus, when predicting academic achievement, researchers control for a wide range of student and school characteristics such as gender, race, socioeconomic status, and prior achievement. Greenwald et al. included only studies that controlled for socioeconomic status or prior achievement in order to decrease the possibility that student background characteristics would confound the findings. Similarly, Hanushek's (1989) vote-counting method did not account for the influence of other covariates in the studies' models.

The second issue concerns dependencies among the estimates of the relationship between achievement and PPE within studies. Studies included in the review typically reported more than one education production function model. Greenwald et al. (1996) used the median regression coefficient within each study to ensure that the coefficients used in the analysis were computed from independent samples.

Twenty years have passed since Greenwald et al.'s (1996) work, and new meta-analytic techniques exist for handling some of the difficulties faced in the original work. The present study used a subset of a larger work to provide an update of the synthesis of education production function studies. We focused on the subset of studies measuring the impact of PPE on achievement. Hanushek (1989) includes other resources such as teacher/pupil ratio, teacher education, and teacher salary, as this line of research flows directly from the historical concerns around efficiency.

Method

Background

The present study builds on the systematic review conducted by Greenwald et al. (1996) that expanded Hanushek's (1989) article examining the relationship between school resources and student achievement. In addition to including the studies used by Hanushek, Greenwald et al. (1996) conducted a search of electronic databases in economics, education, and psychology and examined the references from several narrative reviews of this literature. The final sample of studies in Greenwald et al. included 29 studies from Hanushek's review and an additional 31 studies.

The present study was designed to update the Greenwald et al. (1996) review. We conducted a search of studies published since 1993, the last year of the search in Greenwald et al., to examine the relationship between school resources and student achievement. We used the same search terms as the original study did. The full dates of the search were from 1993 to 2014. Using the search terms, we identified studies that directly examined the relationships among school resources and student achievement. Our search did not identify any studies where school expenditures are used as control variable. A list of search terms used in the current study is provided in the appendix.

Inclusion Criteria

We generally followed Greenwald et al.'s (1996) inclusion criteria for the additional studies, although we also included unpublished research. We included studies

- conducted in the United States,
- where the outcome measure was some form of K–12 student academic achievement, and
- that included a measure of education expenditures, such as PPE or teacher salary.

We included unpublished research given the changes in systematic review practice since 1996. Current guidelines for systematic reviews such as those in Cooper (2009) include both published and unpublished research. We focused exclusively on studies that included a measure of PPE in the models examining correlates of academic achievement. All studies included used independent samples. In some cases, studies used the same database; we used only the study that included the most complete model for the analysis.

Coding

All studies included in our analysis were coded by three of the authors. Coding categories included type of publication, year of publication, and demographic characteristics of participants such as race, socioeconomic status, gender, and grade level. We coded every model within each study, recording descriptive statistics if provided, descriptions of each predictor variable and associated outcome variable, the estimated regression coefficients and their standard errors if provided, measures of the quality of the model such as R^2, and the level of the analysis, such as district or student level.

Analysis

The focus in the analysis was the synthesis of the regression coefficient for PPE, a measure of the relationship among school expenditures and academic achievement. The studies included used some form of regression analysis to predict academic achievement from a set of covariates, including PPE. Studies typically reported more than one regression model, resulting in dependencies among the coefficients within the studies. Greenwald et al. (1996) computed the median value of the PPE regression coefficient for each study reporting more than one regression model. Since 1996, researchers have developed more sophisticated meta-analytic strategies for handling dependent effect sizes within studies.

Becker and Wu (2007) outline three key difficulties in combining multiple regression slope estimates. First, all model outcomes must be measured on a common scale. Second, the slope estimate of interest (focal slope) is measured on a common scale across studies. Finally, each study estimates the partial relationship between the focal slope and the outcome using the model (i.e., includes an identical set of additional predictors). Maintaining these assumptions in any synthesis will almost always be impossible.

An alternative approach that requires few assumptions and no additional information is robust variance estimation. Hedges, Tipton, and Johnson (2010) and Tipton (2013) identify three important features of this estimator. First, and most important, the covariance structure of effect size estimates is not needed. Second, parameter estimates converge on the target parameter as the number of studies, not the number of cases within studies, rises. These authors show that accurate standard errors are produced with as few as 10 to 20 studies, and Tipton (2013) provides a small sample correction for cases with fewer than 10 studies. Third, the robust variance estimator is unbiased for any set of weights. Williams (2012) conducted a simulation study that examined using robust variance estimation in synthesizing sample-dependent focal slope estimates and as a means of synthesizing regression models across multiple samples. His results indicate that the robust variance estimator provides accurate standard errors across a wide range of circumstances. All analyses were conducted in R (R Development Core Team, 2008) using the *robumeta* package (Fisher & Tipton, 2014).

Several studies have also used a log-transformation of the PPE variable in the model, potentially creating difficulties in synthesizing the PPE coefficient across studies. To correct for this problem, we divided the PPE regression coefficient by the mean PPE reported within each study. All the regression models that were included in the analysis reported on the mean PPE and could be included in the analysis.

Results

Our analysis focused on the models that predict some measure of academic achievement, including a measure of PPE as a predictor and control for race and either socioeconomic status or prior achievement in some manner. The meta-analysis was conducted separately for studies conducted at the level of the district and studies conducted at the level of the student.

Figure 1 is a flowchart of the results of the search process for the studies included. We identified 2,641 potential studies in the search of studies conducted from 1993 to 2014. After screening titles and abstracts, we obtained 56 studies for full-text screening. We coded 35 studies from the full-text eligibility screening.

FIGURE 1
Results of Search

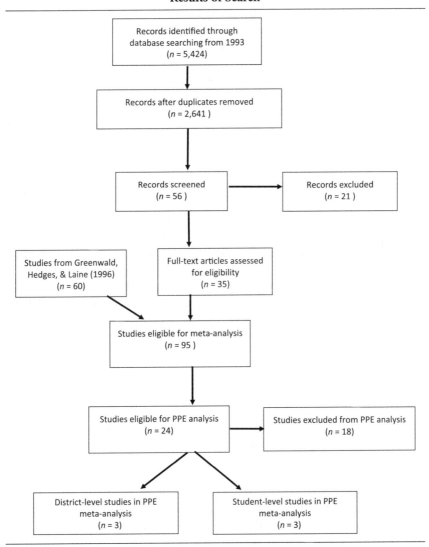

Of the 95 eligible studies (60 from Greenwald et al., 1996, plus 35 studies from our search), 24 included a measure of PPE as a covariate in a regression model predicting some form of academic achievement. The other 71 studies typically included some measure of teacher salary or administrative expenses rather than PPE. The majority of the 24 studies were published in journals in the field of economics. For a study to be eligible for our analysis, the regression model needed to include as a covariate a measure of students' race or the racial composition of the sample and a measure of either prior achievement or the socioeconomic status of the participants. We included the racial composition of the sample as a necessary covariate in our analysis in addition to those required by Greenwald et al. (1996). As displayed in Table 1, 12 of the 24 studies were missing the requisite control variables for inclusion in the meta-analysis. Eleven of these 12 studies were missing a control variable for racial background or composition in the sample, and most of them were also missing a measure of prior achievement as a covariate.

The second inclusion criterion for the meta-analysis concerned the information needed to synthesize the PPE coefficients across studies. We used Greenwald et al.'s (1996) strategy to synthesize the PPE coefficients across studies, which requires the mean value of the achievement outcome in the study. We used the half-standardized partial regression coefficient for PPE as our measure of effect size; we divided the estimate of the regression coefficient for PPE by the standard deviation of the achievement outcome variable. The half-standardized partial regression coefficient measures the number of standard deviations of change in achievement associated with a $1 change in PPE. As shown in Table 1, 3 of the 11 studies with the requisite control variables failed to provide the standard deviation of the achievement outcome variable.

The third inclusion criterion was related to a study's level of analysis. Most of the eight studies that reported on all requisite control variables and the standard deviation of the achievement outcome collected and analyzed data at the level of the school district or the student. Two studies, however, were at the school or classroom level. We decided not to conduct a separate analysis of these two studies, leaving us with six studies that met the following criteria:

1. A model that controls for race and either prior achievement or socioeconomic status
2. The reporting of the standard deviation of the outcome achievement measure
3. Data collected and analyzed at the student or district level

A list of ineligible studies is provided in Table 1.

Table 2 provides descriptions of the six studies included in the meta-analysis. Three of these studies included data at the level of the district, and three included data at the level of the student. All six studies focused on high school students, with one study also including achievement measures from middle schoolers. Two of the studies published used the Test of Economic Literacy as an outcome, with the remaining studies using either achievement or measures of readiness for college such as the SAT and ACT. Four of the studies used national samples of students, with two studies focused on single states (Virginia and Michigan).

In this discussion, we present the results of the robust variance meta-analytic model separately for the district- and student-level data set. For the three studies that included data at the district level, we could estimate 13 effect sizes. The results yielded a very

TABLE 1

Characteristics of Studies Excluded From the Meta-Analysis

Study	Race	Missing Control Variables		Missing Outcome *SD*	Analysis Not at Student or District Level
		Prior Achievement	Socioeconomic Status		
Baum (1986)		✓	✓		
Bieker and Anschel (1973)	✓				
Boser (2011)	✓	✓			
Deller and Rudnicki (1993)	✓	✓			
Gyimah-Brempong and Gyapong (1991)	✓				
Kiesling (1967)	✓		✓		
Nyhan (2001)	✓	✓			
Okpala, Okpala, and Smith (2001)	✓	✓			
Perl (1973)	✓	✓			
Ritzen and Winkler (1977)	✓				
Sander and Krautman (1991)	✓	✓			
Walberg and Fowler (1987)	✓	✓			
Dobbs (2012)		✓		✓	
Maynard and Crawford (1976)				✓	
Sebold and Dato (1981)				✓	
Dugan (1976)		✓			✓
Gross, Rainey, and Goldhaber (2006)		✓			✓

Note. The sources are listed in the order of their discussion in the text.

small, nonstatistically significant but positive effect size (b = .00114, SE = .000287, t = 3.97, p = .13, 95% confidence interval [CI; –.00159, .00387]). To put the mean effect size in context, every $1,000 increase in PPE would result in a 1.14 standard deviation increase in achievement. However, the confidence interval includes zero, indicating that, at the district level, PPE is not related to academic achievement. For the three studies that included data at the student level, we estimated eight effect sizes using the half-standardization procedures. The meta-analytic results again indicated a very small, nonstatistically significant but positive effect size (b = .000067, SE = .000035, t = 1.91, p = .29, 95% CI [–.0003, .00043]). Based on this very limited data set, one can conclude that PPE may not be related to academic achievement. In comparison, Greenwald et al. (1996) found a median PPE effect of 0.0003.

Summary of Findings

The models used in the education production function literature are diverse and limited our efforts to conduct a quantitative synthesis. Researchers focusing on the relationship between PPE and student achievement do not agree on a standard set of

TABLE 2

Characteristics of Studies Included in the Meta-Analysis

Study	Level of Analysis	No. of Models	Outcomes	Grade Levels	State	Control for Socioeconomic Status	Control for Prior Achievement	Control for Race
Grimes and Register (1990)	Student	3	Test of Economic Literacy	High school	National sample	Mother and father education	SAT	Student is Black or White/Other
Lopus (1990)	Student	2	Test of Economic Literacy	High school	National sample	Parent education	Pretest of Economic Literacy	Student is White or non-White
Ribich and Murphy (1975)	Student	3	Ninth-grade aptitude tests	High school	National sample	Socioeconomic Status	Ninth-grade tests	Student is non-White or Other
Jones and Zimmer (2001)	District	8	Seventh- and 10th-grade test scores	Middle and high school	Michigan	Median district income	No	Percentage of Black, Asian, Hispanic, American Indian
Register and Grimes (1991)	District	1	SAT and ACT	High school	National sample	Parents' occupation	Student grades	Percentage of non-White students
Unnever, Kerkhoff, and Robinson (2000)	District	4	Math scores in Grade 11, percentage of ninth graders who graduate high school, percentage of seniors aspiring to college	High school	Virginia	Average district income	Standardized fourth-grade test scores	Percentage of African American students

Note. The sources are listed in the order of their discussion in the text.

covariates, nor do they use similar measures of achievement. Of the identified 24 studies that examine PPE, half did not include any control for race in the model, a critical omission given the Coleman Report findings that inspired this area of research. The studies eligible for the analysis were all focused on students at the high school level and mostly focused on a single achievement measure such as economics or math. Generalizations from this set of studies to U.S. schools are thus not warranted.

Our major finding of a nonstatistical relationship between PPE and academic achievement is based on a small set of studies at both the district and the student levels. Although we are confident that our meta-analytic results are representative of the education production function literature, they are, as with all meta-analyses, not necessarily representative of the population of students or districts in the United States. Our finding, while statistically consistent with Hanushek's (1989) original argument, is not based on a strong evidence base. The studies identified for this review use narrow achievement measures, employ cross-sectional or short time frames, and use broad controls for race, socioeconomic status, and prior achievement. Jackson, Johnson, and Persico (2014) note that the research on educational production functions uses statistical methods (e.g., ordinary least squares) that cannot isolate the causal effects of PPE due to unresolved endogeneity biases.

Many research studies have examined school inputs and outputs, but the literature is too diverse and too inconsistent to employ meta-analysis to estimate a reliable effect. Even if we had been able to obtain a defensible estimate of the magnitude of the relationship between PPE and achievement, the studies included in the meta-analysis do not shed light on the underlying mechanisms of that relationship or how to use PPE to increase achievement. A more important finding of our synthesis is that most of the studies identified do not control for basic student background differences, highlighting a major flaw in this literature.

In these ways, the recent literature fits squarely in the tradition set out by the Coleman Report. It is a legacy that is both enlightening and confounding. The Coleman Report finds distinct disparities in academic achievement among racial groups, and yet the studies in our sample failed to account for race in their models. Since the Coleman Report came out, the broader education research field focused on student outcomes has recognized the importance of race, socioeconomic status, and prior achievement in understanding student performance. Furthermore, policymakers and researchers worked for years under the assumption that schools had little influence on student achievement; numerous scholars sought to test this proposition despite the methodology used in the Coleman Report, which was inadequate to justify the claims put forward (Hoxby, 2016). The question of whether monetary resources directly translate into achievement gains has not been addressed adequately in the literature, and may be impossible to explore given the complexity of schools and school districts and the critical importance of student background in examining student performance. Instead, researchers should reframe the question into one about how school resources could influence student outcomes across a wide range of school contexts and student needs.

One productive line of research centers on the impact of school finance reform. Prior to the 1970s, local property taxes funded most schools, leading to large within-state differences in PPE among districts (Howell & Miller, 1997; Hoxby, 1996). Since 1971, many states have implemented school finance reform through court or legislative action (Jackson et al., 2014). These efforts have been successful, to varying degrees, in equalizing school spending in low- and high-income districts. Jackson et al. (2014) show that low-income children born between 1955 and 1985 in districts that implemented school finance reform completed more years of education, earned higher incomes, and were less likely to experience poverty than poor children in districts that did not implement reform. Due to the broader set of outcomes Jackson et al. examine, their findings suggest room for new questions and research that examines how resources can be deployed to support student outcomes in a socioeconomically diverse, multilingual, and multiracial society.

CONCLUSION

The question of how resources relate to achievement is a recurring one in American education. It dates as far back as the 1867 law establishing the federal Department of Education to promote the "establishment and maintenance of efficient schools"; this question is also tied to debates about race, equity, and the purposes of schooling in American society. The way the question is asked and the methods used to answer it are shaped by history, as well as a reflection of the scholarly, social, and political concerns at any given time. There is no "best method" to answer the question unequivocally. Educators, researchers, policymakers, and other stakeholders should join forces to carefully consider what may be the best and most effective questions to ask in pursuit of shared goals in the interest of the education welfare of children and public education.

In examining the question of how resources have related to achievement over the past century and a half, one may conclude that responses have been driven by disciplines outside of education: Rice as a physician; Thorndike, Terman, and Bloom as psychologists; Coleman as a quantitative sociologist; and Hanushek as an economist. Most researchers had little relationship or intimate knowledge of the inner workings of schools. Rice attempted to understand the work of schools and how they used resources but did not have the perspective of a teacher or administrator. Psychologists focused on children and whether or not they *could* be taught—in other words, whether or not intelligence was fixed or malleable. Quantitative sociologists and economists created models and functions to isolate the impact of particular resources in relation to achievement. The Coleman Report narrowed the definition of equality of education opportunity in just this way: "equality of results, given the same individual input" (Coleman et al., 1966, p. 14). The result was to exclude or radically simplify the complex roles of social factors such as race, class, and gender that provide the inextricable context for schooling. The wide range of social scientists that focused on trying to ascertain whether or not one could tie student achievement to the resources devoted to a school or school district rarely included researchers from the field of education with substantial experience and familiarity with schools and school systems.

This lack of understanding the problem and its context on the part of those researching the perceived problem—a mismatch of resources and results—may have set up a situation where the research question was flawed. In the late 19th century, the focus was on understanding what kinds of schooling were available and where so that public education could be promoted nationally. The early 20th century brought the rise of efficiency and a new business model in the service of creating systems of public schools to educate all American youth. Resource achievement research has been conducted in the vein of this efficiency approach, which is characterized by evaluating the inputs and outputs of schooling. This approach was countered by a "compensatory" approach (Bloom et al., 1965), which focuses on identifying and implementing interventions for more equitable schooling with a secondary concern for efficiency (Coleman et al., 1966). Modern scholarly and political debates about education are often caught between these two approaches, whether aligning clearly with one side or attempting to argue an effective claim to both (e.g., Reading Recovery has been identified as a "what works" intervention, one reported to be highly efficient and highly effective in supporting literacy development for students in poverty and minority students; Institute of Education Sciences, 2013).

A critically important point to note is that the statistical models used to examine the relationship between school inputs and student outcomes are not consistent across studies and do not support causal inferences. Policy has been made on the basis of these studies without appreciation of their limitations despite prescient warnings (Murnane, 1991). Moreover, some policymakers seek research in support of their preexisting views without acknowledging the implications of selecting research for ideological purposes (Plank, 2011). Clearer measurement of education constructs, well-defined and articulated methods, and comprehensive results reporting are called for. Without such efforts, data will be limited and conclusions drawn will be suspect.

When one considers the questions that can be asked about education resources and student achievement, especially in this era of "big data," one must not confine consideration to a narrow sphere of experts, funders, and the various public and private entities that generate massive data sets. Researchers must continuously and vigorously engage with the stakeholders that will benefit from the work—policymakers, school districts, communities, and families of all backgrounds—to ensure that the questions asked have shared value in the pursuit of better education outcomes for all children. The history of this research, from the "Radical Republicans" of the late 1860s to the present, illustrates the dangers of failing to do so.

Modern researchers understand the value of asking complex, sophisticated questions and considering a range of factors in their attempts to understand school systems and student achievement. These questions must be generative. How does one reimagine research on school resources and student achievement as part of a concerted, deliberate collaboration among scholars, practitioners, policymakers, and communities? What processes can help researchers develop questions reflecting shared goals for the education welfare of children and in the best interests of school systems? Scholarship must be critical, research projects must be interdisciplinary, and engagements must be with a diverse range of stakeholders in public education. Researchers must endeavor to be rooted in the realities of those who understand schools at the ground level and those who work with students from all backgrounds and learning styles. They must build partnerships that allow them to ask questions about education that best serve all children in a diverse society.

APPENDIX
Search Terms Used
Input-Output and ERIC

- Administrator qualifications
- Class size
- Cost effectiveness
- Educational assessment
- Educational facilities
- Educational finance
- Educational resources
- Expenditure per student
- Outcomes of education
- Productivity and education
- Resource allocation
- School effectiveness
- Teacher education
- Teaching experience
- Teacher salaries

PsychInfo

- Academic achievement
- Educational aspirations
- Educational objectives
- Income
- School learning
- Classroom environment
- School administrators
- School counseling
- Student characteristics
- School environment
- School facilities

- Teacher characteristics
- Teacher education

EconLit/EconPapers

- Analysis of education
- Economics of education and capital and value of human life
- Economics of education and economics of discrimination and economics of minorities

ACKNOWLEDGMENTS

The meta-analysis reported in this chapter was partially supported by a grant from the National Science Foundation, NSF DRL-0723543

NOTE

The authors are listed in alphabetical order.

REFERENCES

References marked with an asterisk indicate studies included in the meta-analysis.

Baum, D. N. (1986). A simultaneous equations model of the demand for and production of local public services: The case of education. *Public Finance Quarterly, 14*, 157–178.

Becker, B. J., & Wu, M.-J. (2007). The synthesis of regression slopes in meta-analysis. *Statistical Science, 22*, 414–429

Bieker, R. F., & Anschel, K. R. (1973). Estimating educational production functions for rural high schools: Some findings. *American Journal of Agricultural Economics, 55*, 515–519.

Bloom, B., Davis, A., & Hess, R. (1965). *Compensatory education for cultural deprivation.* New York, NY: Holt, Rinehart & Winston.

Boser, U. (2011). *Return on educational investment: A district-by-district evaluation of U.S. educational productivity.* Washington, DC: Center for American Progress.

Callahan, R. E. (1962). *Education and the cult of efficiency: A study of the social forces that have shaped the administration of the public schools.* Chicago, IL: University of Chicago Press.

Christ, C. F. (1955). A review of input-output analysis. In *Input-output analysis: An appraisal* (pp. 137–182). Princeton, NJ: Princeton University Press.

Clark, K. B., & Clark, M. P. (1947). Racial identification and preference among Negro children. In E. L. Hartley (Ed.), *Readings in social psychology* (pp. 169–178). New York, NY: Holt, Rinehart & Winston.

Coleman, J. S. (1961). *The adolescent society: The social life of the teenager and its impact on education.* Glencoe, IL: Free Press.

Coleman, J. S., Campbell, E. Q., Hobson, C. J., McPartland, F., Mood, A. M., Weinfeld, F. D., & York, R. L. (1966). *Equality of educational opportunity.* Washington, DC: U.S. Government Printing Office. Retrieved from http://files.eric.ed.gov/fulltext/ED012275.pdf

Cooper, H. (2009). *Research synthesis and meta-analysis* (4th ed.). Thousand Oaks, CA: Sage.

Deller, S. C., & Rudnicki, E. (1993). Production efficiency in elementary education: The case of Maine public schools. *Economics of Education Review, 12*, 45–57.

Dobbs, R. A. (2012). *The No Child Left Behind Act (NCLB): A Texas economic analysis of accountability* (Unpublished doctoral dissertation). Texas Tech University, Lubbock.

Dugan, D. J. (1976). Scholastic achievement: Its determinants and effects in the education industry. In J. T. Froomkin, D. T. Jamison, & R. Radner (Eds.), *Education as an industry* (pp. 53–83). Cambridge, MA: National Bureau of Economic Research.

Entwisle, D. R., & Conviser, R. (1969). Input-output analysis in education. *High School Journal, 52*, 192–198.

Featherman, D. L., & Vinovskis, M. A. (2001). The growth and use of social and behavioral science in the federal government since World War II. In D. L. Featherman & M. A. Vinovskis (Eds.), *Social science and policy-making: A search for relevance in the twentieth century* (pp. 40–82). Ann Arbor: University of Michigan Press.

Feinberg, S. E. (1992). A brief history of statistics in three and one-half chapters: A review essay. *Statistical Science, 7*, 208–225.

Fisher, Z., & Tipton, E. (2014). Robumeta (Version 1.1) [Computer software]. Retrieved from http://cran.r-project.org/web/packages/robumeta/robumeta.pdf

Freedman, D. (1999). From association to causation: Some remarks on the history of statistics. *Journal de Societe Francaise de Statistique, 140*(5), 5–32.

Gallagher, C. J. (2003). Reconciling a tradition of testing with a new learning paradigm. *Educational Psychology Review, 15*(1), 83–99.

Gamoran, A., & Long, D. (2006). *"Equality of educational opportunity": A 40-year retrospective* (WCER Working Paper No. 2006–9). Madison: Wisconsin Center for Educational Research.

Gould, S. J. (1996). *The mismeasure of man.* New York, NY: Norton.

Grant, G. (1973). Shaping social policy: The politics of the Coleman Report. *Teachers College Record, 75*(1), 18–54.

Grant, W. V. (1993). Statistics in the U.S. Department of Education: Highlights from the past 120 years. In T. Snyder (Ed.), *120 years of American education: A statistical portrait* (pp. 1–4). Washington, DC: National Center for Education Statistics.

Greenwald, R., Hedges, L. V., & Laine, R. D. (1996). The effect of school resources on student achievement. *Review of Educational Research, 66*(3), 361–396.

*Grimes, P. W., & Register, C. A. (1990). Teachers' unions and student achievement in high school economics. *Journal of Economic Education, 21*, 297–306.

Gross, B., Rainey, L., & Goldhaber, D. (2006). *Seeing success: The impact of implementing model practices on student outcomes* (CPRE Working Paper No. 2006-2). Seattle, WA: Center on Reinventing Public Education.

Gyimah-Brempong, K., & Gyapong, A. O. (1991). Characteristics of education production functions: An application of canonical regression analysis. *Economics of Education Review, 10*, 7–17.

Halberstram, D. (1993). *The best and the brightest* (20th anniversary ed.). New York, NY: Ballantine.

Hanushek, E. A. (1981). Throwing money at schools. *Journal of Policy Analysis and Management, 1*, 19–41.

Hanushek, E. A. (1986). The economics of schooling: Production and efficiency in public schools. *Journal of Economic Literature, 24*, 1141–1177.

Hanushek, E. A. (1989). The impact of differential expenditures on school performance. *Educational Researcher, 18*(4), 45–65.

Hanushek, E. A. (1991). When school finance "reform" may not be good policy. *Harvard Journal on Legislation, 28*, 423–456.

Hanushek, E. A. (2016). What matters most for student achievement. *Education Next, 16*(2), 19–26.

Hedges, L. V., Laine, R. D., & Greenwald, R. (1994). Does money matter? A meta-analysis of studies of the effects of differential school inputs on student outcomes. *Educational Researcher, 23*(3), 5–14.

Hedges, L. V., Tipton, E., & Johnson, M. C. (2010). Robust variance estimation in meta-regression with dependent effect size estimates. *Research Synthesis Methods, 1*(1), 39–65.

Howell, P. L., & Miller, B. B. (1997). Sources of funding for schools. *The Future of Children, 7*(3), 39–50.

Hoxby, C. (1996). Are efficiency and equity in school finance substitutes or complements? *Journal of Economic Perspectives, 10*(4), 51–72.

Hoxby, C. (2016). The immensity of the Coleman data project. *Education Next, 16*(2), 65–69.

Institute of Education Sciences. (2013). *What Works Clearinghouse intervention report: Beginning reading: Reading recovery.* Washington, DC: U.S. Department of Education. Retrieved from http://ies.ed.gov/ncee/wwc/pdf/intervention_reports/wwc_readrecovery_071613.pdf

Jackson, C. K., Johnson, R., & Persico, C. (2014). *The effect of school finance reforms on the distribution of spending, academic achievement, and adult outcomes* (NBER Working Paper No. 20118). Cambridge, MA: National Bureau of Economic Research.

*Jones, J. T., & Zimmer, R. W. (2001). Examining the impact of capital on academic achievement. *Economics of Education Review, 20,* 577–588.

Kaliadina, S. A. (T. Babaskina & N. Pavlova, Trans.; C. Wittich, Ed.). (2006). W. W. Leontief and the repressions of the 1920s: An interview. *Economic Systems Research, 18,* 347–355.

Kaliadina, S. A., & Pavlova, N. (C. Wittich, Trans.). (2006). The family of W. W. Leontief in Russia. *Economic Systems Research, 18,* 335–345.

Kiesling, H. J. (1967). Measuring a local school government: A study of school districts in New York State. *Review of Economics and Statistics, 49,* 356–367.

Kliebard, H. M. (2004). *The struggle for the American curriculum, 1893–1958.* New York, NY: RoutledgeFalmer.

Laine, R. D., Greenwald, R., & Hedges, L. V. (1995). Money does matter: A research synthesis of a new universe of education production function studies. In L. O. Picus (Ed.), *Where does the money go? Resource allocation in elementary and secondary schools* (pp. 44–70). Newbury Park, CA: Corwin.

*Lopus, J. S. (1990). Do additional expenditures increase achievement in the high school economics class? *Journal of Economic Education, 21,* 277–186.

Maynard, R., & Crawford, D. (1976). School performance. In D. L. Bawden & W. S. Harrar (Eds.), *Rural income maintenance experiment: Final report* (Vol. 6, Pt. 2, pp. 1–104). Madison: University of Wisconsin, Institute for Research on Poverty.

Moynihan, D. P. (1968). Sources of resistance to the Coleman Report. *Harvard Educational Review, 38*(1), 23–35.

Murnane, R. (1991). Interpreting the evidence on: "Does money matter?" *Harvard Journal on Legislation, 28,* 457–464

Nyhan, R. C. (2001). The influence of class size on student achievement in Florida's elementary schools. In C. D. Herrington & K. Kasten (Eds.), *Florida 2001: Educational policy alternatives* (pp. 137–166). Tallahassee: Florida Institute of Education.

Okpala, C. O., Okpala, A. O., & Smith, F. E. (2001). Parental involvement, instructional expenditures, family socioeconomic attributes, and student achievement. *Journal of Educational Research, 95*(2), 110–115.

Perl, L. J. (1973). Family background, secondary school expenditure, and student ability. *Journal of Human Resources, 8,* 156–180.

Plank, D. N. (2011). Minding the gap between research and policy making. In C. F. Conrad & R. S. Serlin (Eds.), *The Sage handbook for research in education* (2nd ed.). Thousand Oaks, CA: Sage.

R Development Core Team (2008). R: A language and environment for statistical computing (Version 3.2.3) [Software]. Available from http://www.R-project.org.

Reese, W. J. (2013). *The testing wars in public schools: A forgotten history.* Cambridge, MA: Harvard University Press.

*Register, C. A., & Grimes, P. W. (1991). Collective bargaining, teachers, and student achievement. *Journal of Labor Research, 12,* 99–110.

Reisman, F. (1963). Research in review: The culturally deprived child: A new view. *Educational Leadership, February,* 337–347.

*Ribich, T. I., & Murphy, J. L. (1975). The economic returns to increased educational spending. *Journal of Human Resources, 10,* 56–77.

Ritzen, J. M., & Winkler, D. R. (1977). The revealed preferences of a local government: Black/White disparities in scholastic achievement. *Journal of Urban Economics, 4,* 310–323.

Rugg, H. O. (1917). *Statistical methods applied to education: A textbook for students of education in the quantitative study of school problems.* New York, NY: Houghton Mifflin.

Ryan, A. M. (2011). From child study to efficiency: District administrators and the use of testing in the Chicago Public Schools, 1899 to 1928. *Paedagogica Historica, 47,* 341–354.

Sander, W., & Krautman, A. C. (1991). Local taxes, schooling, and jobs in Illinois. *Economics of Education Review, 10,* 111–121.

Sebold, F. D., & Dato, W. (1981). School funding and student achievement: An empirical analysis. *Public Finance Quarterly, 9,* 91–105.

Thomas, J. Y., & Brady, K. P. (2005). The Elementary and Secondary Education Act at 40: Equity, accountability, and the evolving federal role in public education. *Review of Research in Education, 29,* 51–67.

Tipton, E. (2013). Robust variance estimation in meta-regression with binary dependent effects. *Research Synthesis Methods, 4,* 169–187.

Tyack, D. B. (1974). *The one best system: A history of American urban education.* Cambridge, MA: Harvard University Press.

Tyack, D. B., James, T., & Benavot, A. (1987). *Law and the shaping of public education, 1785–1954.* Madison: University of Wisconsin Press.

*Unnever, J. D., Kerkhoff, A. C., & Robinson, T. J. (2000). District variations in educational resources and student outcomes. *Economics of Education Review, 19,* 245–259.

U.S. National Commission on Excellence in Education. (1983). *A nation at risk: The imperative for educational reform: A report to the nation and the Secretary of Education, United States Department of Education.* Washington, DC: Author.

Walberg, H., & Fowler, W. (1987). Expenditure and size efficiencies of public school districts. *Educational Researcher, 16*(7), 5–13.

Williams, R. T. (2012). Using robust standard errors to combine multiple regression estimates with meta-analysis (Unpublished doctoral dissertation). Loyola University, Chicago, IL.

Chapter 6

Implementation Research: Finding Common Ground on What, How, Why, Where, and Who

JEANNE CENTURY
AMY CASSATA
University of Chicago

Over many decades, educators have developed countless interventions and theories about how to create lasting change. Implementation research is the study of these efforts with a set of basic questions: What are we doing? Is it working? For whom? Where? When? How? And, Why? In other words, implementation research is an endeavor to understand if and how educational efforts are accomplishing their goals. This chapter describes the landscape of implementation research, tracing it back to its historical roots and connecting it to other fields with the aim of identifying common threads across diverse efforts. The authors survey where the field is today and highlight different perspectives on complex questions that have long troubled researchers. They outline some of the sticky issues ahead and make a case for shared conceptual clarity and clearly communicated and understood language that will help researchers understand how various bodies of implementation research work are related. The authors conclude by describing the opportunity presented to the education research community in this moment: to capitalize on and learn from historical and contemporary work in education and other fields, and to identify connections across theories and approaches and find ways to collectively move forward toward the shared goal of making education better.

The field of education research is ultimately focused on one shared goal: making education better. Over many decades, we have developed countless interventions and theories about how to develop, enact, iterate, operationalize, institutionalize, and diffuse something that will yield the prize of successful, lasting change. Implementation research is the study of these efforts. It examines the products, strategies, processes, and theories that researchers, practitioners, policymakers, and other

Review of Research in Education
March 2016, Vol. 40, pp. 169–215
DOI: 10.3102/0091732X16665332
© 2016 AERA. http://rre.aera.net

stakeholders create by asking a set of basic questions: What are we doing? Is it working? For whom? Where? When? How? And Why? In other words, implementation research is an endeavor to better understand whether the field of education research is accomplishing its goal.

This chapter aims to describe a landscape of implementation research so that the field can identify and connect common threads across diverse efforts. "Implementation" has been referenced in education for decades (Berman, 1981; Fullan & Pomfret, 1977; Penuel, Fishman, Cheng, & Sabelli, 2011; Scheirer, Shediac, & Cassady, 1995; Spillane, Reiser, & Reimer, 2002). However, as a named field of scholarship in education, implementation research is relatively young. There are no journals focused solely on implementation research in education, nor are there consistent methods of inquiry. Indeed, one of the premier journals for implementation research in health care, *Implementation Science*, has been in circulation only since 2006. Moreover, as the study of implementation in education has evolved, the emergence of vastly different philosophical, theoretical, and practical orientations has made shared learning difficult.

In this chapter we do not argue for creating one approach for carrying out implementation research. We do, however, make a case for shared conceptual clarity and common (or at least clearly communicated and understood) language so that those working under the broad umbrella of implementation research can understand one another and how their various bodies of work relate.

For this chapter, we offer a working definition of *implementation research* as systematic inquiry regarding innovations enacted in controlled settings or in ordinary practice, the factors that influence innovation enactment, and the relationships between innovations, influential factors, and outcomes. In turn, we define *innovations* as programs, interventions, technologies, processes, approaches, methods, strategies, or policies that involve a change (e.g., in behavior or practice) for the individuals (end users) enacting them. To clarify further, an innovation can range from simple (e.g., tool or procedure) to complex (e.g., system-wide professional development or cross-system collaboration), and it can reside at one or more system levels (e.g., classroom, school, district, state). To communicate across domains and disciplines, we sometimes simply describe the innovation as "the it:" the object or focus of change in implementation research.

In this chapter, we examine work in education and other fields to identify how their driving questions about large-scale social innovation, improving education, and creating and sustaining change converge in the hybrid endeavor we are calling implementation research. We survey where the field is today, as evidenced in both theoretical and empirical literature, and highlight different perspectives on issues and complex questions that have long troubled researchers. We outline some of the sticky issues ahead and finish by describing the opportunity presented to the education research community in this moment: to capitalize on and learn from the historical and contemporary work of others so that we can identify connections across theories and approaches and find ways to collectively move forward toward our shared goal of making education better.

OUR APPROACH

Implementation research is not, in itself, a suitable topic for a traditional targeted systematic review. It is not the *subject* of empirical studies that can be found, evaluated, and synthesized. Nor is implementation research, itself, a specific innovation or even a genre of an innovation that can be tested as one might see in systematic reviews. It involves more than a single set of methodologies, and it includes many different theoretical approaches. The very qualities that make it a timely topic for this publication—its evolving nature, vague and overlapping definitions, diverse theoretical orientations, and widely varied applications—are the same qualities that make it a poor subject for a targeted search.

As a result, this chapter is a review in the most general sense, in that it provides an account of a particular body of literature (Sayfori, 2014). Under this general umbrella, we combine several of the focus areas and goals that characterize literature reviews as described by Cooper and Hedges (2009). More specifically, this chapter is informed by searches that focused on original and highly influential research as well as on systematic reviews, including a comprehensive review that we carried out in 2008 and a review conducted specifically for this chapter, targeting highly referenced works. This is a narrative synthesis in the sense that it seeks to tell a story—one of the growth and development of implementation research in education—yet not a synthesis in the sense of consolidating a set of findings (Popay et al., 2006).

In this narrative, we acknowledge that implementation research is carried out with different intentions, different approaches to inquiry, and different methodologies, and we aim to account for that diversity while also identifying common threads. We draw from others' reviews and writings, as well as from our own, to describe emerging conceptual frameworks and approaches. Unlike some other syntheses, ours does not seek to arrive at any definitive conclusions about a single innovation or type of innovation by using the findings of other works. Rather, it uses a combination of best evidence synthesis, systematic review, and narrative synthesis to provide the reader with a coherent and succinct snapshot of the past, present, and future of implementation research.

POSITIONING IMPLEMENTATION RESEARCH: LOOKING BEYOND FIDELITY

For many, implementation research is assumed to focus on establishing or evaluating *fidelity of implementation*, that is, the extent to which an innovation is enacted according to its intended model. This assumption is sometimes coupled with a view that implementation for educational improvement should entail replication of programs that demonstrate sufficient evidence of being potentially beneficial (Domitrovich & Greenberg, 2000; Downer & Yazejian, 2013; Durlak, 2010). While implementation research does include these views, its definition is far more wide-ranging. Current understandings of implementation research are now acknowledging decades-old observations: Contexts and conditions can affect innovation enactment in legitimate ways; replication is not always possible or even desirable; and improving education requires processes for changing individuals, organizations, and systems. These ideas are not new, but they are only now finding a place in the implementation research context.

Looking back 40 years, in the 1970s the seminal RAND Change Agent study (Berman & McLaughlin, 1978) shifted education reformers' mindsets with its conclusion that an innovation adoption decision alone was not reason enough to believe that the innovation had been or would be fully implemented (Short, 1973). Although this realization may seem obvious now (at least among implementation researchers), it was not so to many at the time. Solomon, Ferritor, Haern, and Myers (1973) made this then-new observation: "The fact that materials and strategies were prescribed does not guarantee that the teacher actually engaged children in the intended way" (p. 2). Accepting this fact called for recognition of the difference between dissemination and implementation. While "dissemination science" focuses on what creators of innovations do to *reach* potential adopters, *implementation science* focuses on what happens *once the innovation is in their hands* (Dearing & Kee, 2012). Simply put, implementation research (or what Dearing and Kee refer to as "implementation science") is not about the adoption decision alone; rather, it is about investigating what happens next—*what* is actually enacted, *how* an innovation is enacted, and *why* the contexts, conditions, characteristics, and other influences shape innovation enactment as they do.

In the decades since the educational policy implementation studies of the 1970s (Backer, 1991; Honig, 2006), rich and broadening perspectives on implementation research have grown in the medical and health literature. Implementation research in education has broadened as well, though in relative isolation from these other fields. Some studies have maintained a focus on questions of fidelity, replication, and outcomes (e.g., Hulleman & Cordray, 2009; T. Smith, Cobb, Farran, Cordray, & Munter, 2013; Strain & Bovey, 2011), while others have turned away from fidelity, to examine innovation adaptation, the reasons for adaptation, and the relationships between adaptation and student outcomes (e.g., Barab & Luehmann, 2003; Fogleman, McNeill, & Krajcik, 2011; Forbes & Davis, 2010). Other efforts—some rooted in the design experiments of the 1990s (e.g., A. L. Brown, 1992)—pursue questions of innovation creation and iteration more deeply (Bell, 2004; Collins, Joseph, & Bielaczyc, 2004; DeBarger, Choppin, Beauvineau, & Moorthy, 2013), while yet others pursue questions that embrace the notion of iterative design with broader change concerns.

Confrey, Castro-Filho, and Wilhelm (2000), for example, wrote that implementation research "models and documents the interrelations among system components identifying the catalysts and impediments to change" (p. 182). The design-based implementation research (DBIR) approach (Penuel et al., 2011) also focuses on more complex questions related to problem identification, innovation development and iteration, as well as developing theory and supporting system capacity for sustained change. These efforts represent a growing recognition that implementation research seeks to do more than answer questions pertaining to efficacy and fidelity; it includes questions about all aspects of the dynamic, complex implementation process.

Given the breadth of studies that fall under the implementation research umbrella, it is not surprising that disparities exist in the literature with respect to how implementation is defined. For example, Durlak (2015) defines implementation as "what a program looks like 'on the ground' when it is being conducted, as opposed to what a program looks like in theory or on the drawing board" (p. 1124) and, in doing so, maintains an innovation-focused definition of implementation. In contrast, Fixsen, Naoom, Blasé, Friedman, and Wallace (2005) describe implementation as a "specified set of [professional development] activities designed to put into practice an [intervention] activity or program of known dimensions" (as quoted in Dunst, Trivette, & Raab, 2013, p. 88). Other researchers understand implementation research to be like *translational research* in medicine, which seeks to move findings from clinical studies to practice settings or communities (Rubio et al., 2010). Still others focus on the dynamic nature of the innovation and the context. Berman (1981), for example, observed that implementation is "the adaptation of an innovative idea to its institutional setting" (p. 273), and Bryk et al. (2013) offer even more complexity by describing a nested innovation—a networked improvement community that is itself enacting innovations in different settings.

Notwithstanding these diverse purposes, theoretical orientations, and methods, we are beginning to see some convergence on the idea that implementation research as an area of inquiry includes the study of the innovation implementation (on-the-ground enactment and/or participation by the end user), the conditions and contexts that affect implementation (influential factors), and the aligned outcomes at a grain size commensurate with the innovation and its components (Century & Cassata, 2014; Durlak, 2010; Downer & Yazejian, 2013). Bringing conceptual clarity to these three key elements—the innovation, the influential factors, and the aligned outcomes—is at the heart of facilitating the field's movement forward.

WHY STUDY IMPLEMENTATION?

In brief, implementation research seeks to shed light on what an innovation can and should be (innovation design, development, testing, and improvement), what happens during and after innovation enactment (whether it worked and how, why, and where), and what we can learn through these inquiries about improving education (Domitrovich & Greenberg, 2000; Fullan & Pomfret, 1977). Under this broad umbrella, researchers then have varied interests and perspectives that we have grouped into five main categories (see Table 1). These categories are neither mutually exclusive nor bound to any particular theoretical orientation.

TABLE 1
Reasons to Study Implementation and Example Purposes

Reasons to Study Implementation	Example Purposes
1 Inform innovation design and development	Examine the creation of the innovation, qualities of the innovation, and characteristics of the innovation
	Understand feasibility and usability
	Create an innovation customized for a time, place, and context
2 Understand whether (and to what extent) the innovation achieves desired outcomes for the target population	Examine efficacy and effectiveness
	Explore emerging outcomes
	Identify system changes
	Ascertain outcomes for students, teachers, school and out-of-school settings, district, state, and other systems
3 Understand relationships between influential factors, innovation enactment, and outcomes	Examine why users enact/participate in innovations as they do
	Understand influences of adaptations
	Explore relationships between innovation characteristics, user characteristics, organizational characteristics, innovation enactment, and outcomes
	Explore moderating and mediating factors that influence how, why, when, where, and with whom an innovation is effective
4 Improve innovation design, use, and support in practice settings	Adjust innovation for local context
	Develop needed supports
	Improve outcomes
5 Develop theory	Improve understanding of change
	Inform understanding of specific innovation components that are "key" to success
	Inform innovation design

First, implementation research asks questions that inform innovation design and development. That is, it examines questions about what the innovation could and/or should be, the extent to which an innovation is feasible in particular settings, and its utility from the perspective of the end users (Berman, 1981; Lynch & O'Donnell, 2005; Penuel & Fishman, 2012). Findings from these questions can help innovation developers—whether curriculum writers, researchers, policymakers, practitioners, or a combination thereof—make informed choices about innovation components; identify the supports that may be needed prior to, during, and after innovation implementation; and identify innovation elements that are more or less challenging for end users (Penuel, Phillips, & Harris, 2014; Rohrbach, Grana, Sussman, & Valente, 2006).

Second, implementation research pursues questions about whether the innovation achieves its desired outcomes. Some studies focus on evaluating efficacy and effectiveness in particular contexts to establish evidence of "what works" through rigorous (often experimental or quasi-experimental) innovation testing. These studies seek to make causal claims about innovation impacts, which requires establishing the extent to which the innovation was actually enacted in the treatment and comparison conditions (Basch, 1984; Cohen, 1975; Dhillon, Darrow, & Meyers, 2015; Domitrovich & Greenberg, 2000; Moncher & Prinz, 1991; L. Peterson, Homer, & Wonderlich, 1982; Rohrbach et al., 2006; Solomon et al., 1973; Song & Herman, 2010; Wolery, 2011). In these cases, implementation data can confirm the integrity of experimental designs and enable statistical analyses of relationships between levels of implementation and outcomes (e.g., Darrow, 2013; Durlak, 2015; Gresham, Gansle, Noell, Cohen, & Rosenblum, 1993). L. Peterson et al. (1982) succinctly refer to this as "assessment of the independent variable" (p. 479).

Questions of "does it work" need not be limited to experimental or quasi-experimental designs, however. Some innovations, such as those that are complex, place-based, or perhaps system-embedded, are not good fits for an efficacy/effectiveness orientation that functions under more constrained conditions or seeks to make claims of generalizability. For example, one might consider DBIR, with its specified characteristics and system-level outcomes to be, in itself, an innovation. Within that innovation resides an effort to solve a "persistent problem of practice" (Penuel et al., 2011). The solution to the problem of practice may (or may not be) one or more other innovations that reside within the larger innovation of the DBIR structure. In this case, the question of effectiveness is twofold: Is there a meaningful solution to the problem of practice, and in turn, was the DBIR approach a powerful mechanism for realizing that solution? For dynamic and complex innovation approaches such as this, implementation research can examine success using qualitative, mixed-methods, and multidimensional research designs.

Third, implementation research asks questions that examined why the innovation works, for whom, where, when, and under what conditions. In other words, these studies explore relationships between influential factors (e.g., characteristics of the user, the organization, the external environment, or the innovation itself) and innovation enactment, with some also examining associated relationships to outcomes. In such studies, innovation enactment might be considered the dependent variable. Other studies with this orientation may test more complex theories, for example, by treating influential factors as moderating or mediating variables that influence innovation enactment and have indirect effects on intended outcomes.

Fourth, implementation research questions stem from the desire to improve the innovation and, in turn, the intended outcomes (Domitrovich & Greenberg, 2000). For studies on clearly bounded interventions (e.g., curriculum materials or professional development models) that have undergone efficacy testing, this type of implementation research shifts from establishing internal validity toward understanding what Wolery (2011, p. 156) called the "transportability" of the innovation and its use in the complex world of real-life settings (Berman, 1981; Domitrovich & Greenberg, 2000; Scheirer et al., 1995). Some studies targeting improvement seek to identify and establish support systems for innovation implementation, while others involving more complex or multilayered innovations give more attention to innovation design iteration. Ultimately, the goal of this kind of research is to improve the innovation design, the support strategies, and other elements of the context, to better realize the intended innovation outcomes.

Fifth, implementation research informs theory development. Implementation research informs a wide range of theoretical questions, from how to bring about deep, lasting change to how to understand the most essential elements of an innovative curriculum. Although the theoretical orientations, methodologies, and purposes of research described above vary widely, all nonetheless fall under the broad implementation research banner. Further, all share the goal of ultimately addressing the perennial and confounding fact that even when efficacy is established, implementers (end users) do not necessarily embrace innovations in any broad or sustainable way (Dearing, 2009; Dearing & Kee, 2012). This challenge stands for the simplest and the most complex innovations. In 1977, Fullan and Pomfret wrote, "By investigating implementation directly . . . we can begin to identify some of the most problematic aspects of bringing about change" (p. 337). The field has repeatedly confirmed that bringing about change is not as simple as finding what works. As Dearing (2009) succinctly states, "We assume that evidence matters in the decision making of potential adopters" (p. 509). Although evidence is likely to matter to some extent, many other things matter too. Implementation research reveals what they are.

LITERATURES THAT INFORM IMPLEMENTATION RESEARCH

Implementation research has roots in many varied and overlapping fields, a few of which we touch on here. Each offers a different view on two inextricably tied questions: (a) How do ideas (as manifested in innovations) spread? and (b) Why do people choose (or choose not) to embrace them?

Diffusion Theory and Dissemination

Diffusion theory can be traced to the 1800s with the work of two contributing founders: the French sociologist Gabriel Tarde and the German sociologist Georg Simmel. Tarde explained diffusion as "a societal-level phenomenon of social change" (Dearing & Kee, 2012, p. 60). His views of diffusion were influenced by practical observations and his belief that societal changes resulted from individuals' desires to imitate inspirational and original ideas (Green, Ottoson, García, & Hiatt, 2009; Kinnunen, 1996). Like Tarde, Simmel focused on individual actions but, in particular, theorized that they are affected by external conditions (Dearing, 2008). Both scholars are acknowledged as among the first to ask questions pertaining to *how* and *why* innovations spread from one individual or societal context to another (Dearing & Kee, 2012).

The 1920s and 1930s saw more anthropologists exploring diffusion (Backer, 1991; Green et al., 2009). As Dearing and Kee (2012) explained, anthropologists' work "focused not only on spread of innovations, but also on how cultures in turn shaped those innovations by giving them new purposes and by adapting them to suit local needs—the beginnings of what we now call implementation science" (p. 61).

Moving ahead to the 1940s, any account of the influence of diffusion on implementation research would be incomplete without mention of the Ryan and Gross report (1943) on the diffusion of farmers' use of hybrid corn. Their study set the stage for many diffusion studies to follow, including those that would inform Everett Rogers's (1962) seminal work *Diffusion of Innovations*. Rogers's work brought varied perspectives together in demonstrating how "macrolevel processes of system change could be linked to microlevel behavior" (Dearing & Kee, 2012, p. 63).

Diffusion theory informs implementation research by examining individual decision making and the attributes of an innovation that affect that decision making. It has highlighted the pervasive but not always accepted view that individual behavior change is slow and sometimes "discontinuous" over time (Rohrbach et al., 2006). This phenomenon continues to stymie those who seek to design implementation research studies today.

If diffusion research is the study of the *natural* spreading of innovations, dissemination research then is focused on conscious, active efforts to spread new knowledge or information to potential new adopters (Green et al., 2009). Dissemination activities include clearinghouses, special publications, and other methods for getting information about an innovation to audiences. These activities are, in turn, distinct from implementation activities that happen *after* the information is provided (Backer, 1991). The first instances of explicit authorization in support of dissemination in education in this country came with several broad policy initiatives, including the national Defense Education Act of 1958, the Elementary and Secondary Education Act of 1965, and the creation of the National Institute of Education, which in 1972 included dissemination as one of its priorities (Love, 1985). Other dissemination models included the creation of ERIC (Education Research Information Center) and the regional laboratory system (Louis, 1992). And yet, even though dissemination activities were popularly supported in the 1960s and 1970s, there was little evidence that dissemination actually resulted in behavior change (i.e., ongoing implementation) on the part of end users (Greco & Eisenberg, 1993; Grimshaw, 1999).

Knowledge Utilization and Technology Transfer

In the 1970s, scholars recognized that the concepts of *diffusion and dissemination*, and the related concept of *knowledge utilization*, were distinct, even though individuals casually used the terms interchangeably (Green et al., 2009). Whereas studies concerned with diffusion and dissemination targeted the use of *innovations*, studies focused on knowledge utilization were concerned with the use of knowledge of *all kinds* (Green et al., 2009). The knowledge utilization lens involves asking questions about the *ways* that knowledge gets used and how it can better be brought into use. Lehming and Kane (1981) define "knowledge" as information from research, practice, or both and suggest that it can reside in ideas, theories, explanations, advice, or "things" (p. 11). It is these *things* that are of interest in implementation research; they are the innovations that implementation researchers study.

Best, Hiatt, and Norman (2008) suggest that knowledge utilization can be broken down into two steps: the "imparting of research knowledge from producers to potential users" (dissemination) and "knowledge uptake—that is, the acquisition and review of research knowledge and its utilization" (p. 321). Implementation research brings a parallel perspective. In the case of an externally created innovation (from the end user perspective), implementation represents knowledge uptake as manifested in enacting an innovation that embodies a "set" of knowledge that originated from the innovation developers. In other cases, implementation focuses on co-creation of knowledge through collaborative innovation development (DeBarger et al., 2013). Other studies examine what happens when end users not involved in the development of an innovation enact that innovation, taking into account their previous knowledge (what some might call an influential factor) as they make sense of the new knowledge operationalized in the innovation (Coburn & Talbert, 2006; Penuel et al., 2014).

To complicate the lexicon further, knowledge utilization is sometimes confused with *knowledge transfer* and *technology transfer*. Similar to the concept of dissemination, knowledge transfer is defined as "a process of transmitting or conveying information from the developer, organizer or interpreter of research to the potential users" (Love, 1985, p. 344). Technology transfer, then, is exactly what it sounds like: a process of dissemination of technology, equipment, and devices or of technical information (Backer, 1991; Love, 1985). Twenty years ago, Hutchinson and Huberman (1994) considered the technology transfer perspective to be antiquated in the context of understanding innovation implementation. They saw what Short (1973) saw more than 20 years earlier: that researchers have unrealistic expectations about the contributions that research makes to practice. Short posited that "the relationship of research to practice is not a one-to-one relationship; rather it appears to be a process involving a series of complexly interrelated steps, still only partially understood" (p. 242).

Individual, Organizational, and Educational Change

Questions pertaining to change lie squarely at the heart of implementation research: What does it take for people, organizations, and systems to change? Oancea and Pring's (2008) observation illuminates the complexity of this question:

To ask why a person acts in the way he or she does is logically very different from asking why the lights failed or why such a person has "flu"—a different sort of explanation is required—one in terms of intentions and motives. (p. 31)

Thirty years prior, Berman and McLaughlin (1976) noted that effective implementation depends on individuals' and organizations' capacity for and receptivity to change and their joint process of adapting an innovation to meet local needs. Enacting new knowledge as manifested in new practices or programs in educational settings requires individual and organizational change that might be mechanically difficult and, more important, psychologically threatening (Backer, 1991).

Individual Change

Just as Tarde's early 19th-century work on diffusion entailed looking at individual motives for embracing new ideas (Dearing & Kee, 2012), some scholars examine educational change through the lens of the individual end user. Theories of change emphasizing the key role of end users who bring their own information and expertise to a situation gained prominence in the 1970s (Hutchinson & Huberman, 1994). One of the most widely referenced models is Hall and Loucks's (1978b) concerns-based adoption model that describes and explains the process of change experienced by teachers who implement instructional innovations (Anderson, 1997). This model is grounded in the assertion that change is a very personal experience requiring developmental growth (Hord, Rutherford, Huling-Austin, & Hall, 1987). Cohen and Ball (1990) also affirmed that teachers' practices are shaped by their many personal experiences over time and that changing those practices is no trivial matter, asserting that "changing one's teaching is not like changing one's socks" (Cohen & Ball, 1990, p. 334). Fullan (2007) points to the potential discomfort associated with change that individuals may experience, noting that "even changes that do not seem to be complex to their promoter, may raise numerous doubts and uncertainties on the part of those not familiar with them" (p. 45).

As Hord et al. (1987) suggested 30 years ago, change is enacted by individuals, and individuals each bring their own experiences to the process of change. Coburn and Talbert (2006) emphasize the important role that enactors' prior beliefs and experiences play in innovation implementation. Similarly, S. Peterson (2013) suggests that educational change is a collaborative practice of meeting people where they are. Other models of individual change have put forward the notion of *sense-making* as a lens through which to understand innovation implementation. Spillane et al. (2002), for example, note that the adaptations during implementation are the result of "human sense-making" (p. 419), that is, the ways that the innovation user constructs understanding of the innovation in practice informed by prior experience. Increasingly, implementation research is embracing these long-standing perspectives that recognize the important role of the individual in any change effort.

Organizational Change and Educational Change

The literature on organizational change comes from many disciplines, including health, business, and law—with many theories and research approaches seeking to find answers to similar challenges in how to bring about large-scale change behaviors (Burnes, 2005; House, 1981; Inbar, 1996; Rohrbach et al., 2006) or "transfer capabilities" (Szulanski, 1996, p. 27). Most of this literature carries a common theme: that organizational systems within which innovations exist (in the case of education, schools, and school systems) are complex and constantly changing. With this acknowledgement, the organizational change literature points toward the challenge that implementation researchers face in making sense of that complexity. As Meyer and Goes (1988) observe, "From both the theoretical and practical perspectives, our cumulative knowledge of why and how organizations adopt and implement innovations is considerably less than the sum of its parts" (p. 897).

Given that educational change theories are closely tied to organizational theories, it is not surprising that they, too, overlap and, to some extent, lack coherence. Some focus on systemic change, others on piecemeal change, and still others on phases of change (Joseph & Reigeluth, 2010). There are theories about "change agents," "planned change," "systemic change," "conditions of change," and more (Ellsworth, 2000; Fullan, as cited in Anson, 1994; Leithwood & Montgomery, 1980; Miles, 1998; Sikorski, 1976; Yin, Quick, Bateman, & Marks, 1978). Clark and Guba (1965) wrote about models and processes of change in education over 50 years ago, using many of these same words; yet the challenge of bringing consistency to the dialogue persists.

Sashkin and Egermeier's (1993) comprehensive review of educational change models identifies three perspectives on bringing about change. The first is a *rational-scientific* model that focuses on dissemination of new techniques to the end user. One might place the National Diffusion Network of the 1970s and the What Works Clearinghouse of today in this group. Second, there is a *political* perspective (top-down) that focuses on achieving change through policies. For example, the focus on systemic change in the 1990s (e.g., M. Smith & O'Day, 1991) sought to bring coherency to elements of the system rather than emphasize any single innovation (Knapp, 1997). Third is a *cultural perspective*, one that seeks to make change by influencing individual values. Given that these models are not mutually exclusive and overlap, implementation research can be situated within or across any of these orientations.

Many who take part in the educational change discourse lament the stubbornness of the system in relentlessly retaining the status quo. Elmore (1996) discusses the notion that what passes for change is not really change at all; that is, changes take place at a surface level but never really penetrate to "the core of educational practice" (p. 2) in any way that will endure. Similarly, Coburn (2003) offers an alternative view of scaling change as one that eschews breadth for depth, or what she calls "deep and consequential change in classroom practice" (p. 4). Tyack and Cuban (1995), in their seminal *Tinkering Toward Utopia*, put it well: "To bring about improvement at the heart of education—classroom instruction . . . has proven to be the most difficult kind of reform" (p. 135). Implementation research, in its current form, is shaped by the long-standing histories of preceding fields that sought to address these concerns.

RECENT HISTORY: APPROACHES, FRAMEWORKS, AND METHODS

With these literatures as a backdrop, we now provide an overview of the state of implementation research today. Our literature search involved three distinct approaches. We began by revisiting a comprehensive, systematic review that we had conducted in 2008 to identify factors that affect the implementation, spread, and sustainability of innovations (Century, Cassata, Rudnick & Freeman, 2012). For this chapter, we revisited that work (using the Web of Science database) with a 100-year historical lens by conducting backward and forward citations of the most highly referenced works to date, paying particular attention to references published in the education literature.

Next, to identify key empirical research approaches and analytic strategies, (because a comprehensive review was beyond the scope of this chapter), we identified highly cited articles that included practice recommendations and preliminary guidelines for implementation research (e.g., Dane & Schneider, 1998; Durlak & DuPre, 2008; Dusenbury, Brannigan, Falco, & Hansen, 2003; Mowbray, Holter, Teague, & Bybee, 2003; O'Donnell, 2008), and conducted a forward search in Web of Science to locate empirical education research studies that referenced one or more of these seminal works.

Finally, we reviewed the recent "gray literature" from growing professional organizations in and outside of education (including the American Educational Research Association, the Global Implementation Initiative, the National Implementation Research Network, and the Society for Implementation Research Collaboration). We located relevant conference presentations, report briefs, webinars, and other, more ephemeral sources disseminated through organizational websites and at professional meetings from 2011 to the present.

Theoretical Frameworks for Implementation Research

Implementation research, by our working definition, is the systematic inquiry of innovations enacted in controlled settings or in ordinary practice, the factors that influence innovation enactment, and relationships between innovations, influential factors, and outcomes. Thus, frameworks that inform the organization of implementation research address two main concerns—how to conceptualize and describe the innovation itself, and how to identify and organize the contexts, conditions, and characteristics that influence innovation enactment (influential factors). These two fundamental concepts—(a) characteristics of the innovation and (b) influential factors—are basic elements of varied theories of change and a key part of most recent research syntheses or metaframeworks depicting innovations in context (e.g., Domitrovich et al., 2008; Donaldson, 2001; Hulleman, Rimm-Kaufman, & Abry, 2013; Moulin, Sabater-Hernandez, Fernandez-Llimos, & Benrimaj, 2015).

Conceptual frameworks enable researchers to effectively communicate about implementation phenomena with other researchers, practitioners, developers, and policymakers. Moreover, they provide a starting point for the sometimes obscured but substantial challenge of knowing exactly where to the draw the conceptual boundary between an innovation itself and the contexts that influence its enactment. As established earlier, change is complex: Numerous multilevel, interacting, and dynamic variables work together to produce desired outcomes. Thus, the wily line that distinguishes innovation from context can be hard to pin down, but doing so, informed by a theoretical orientation, is a necessary step for researchers seeking to specify analytic models that explore the complex relationships between innovations, contexts, and outcomes.

In the sections that follow, we first discuss the challenge of, and approaches to, defining the innovation. We then outline theoretical frameworks for organizing and describing influential factors in innovation enactment. We end this section by revisiting considerations for distinguishing innovation from context.

Conceptualizing the Innovation

It is now widely accepted that educational innovations are (or at least should be) developed according to implicit or explicit theories of change and that they contain multiple elements (i.e., features, building blocks, ingredients) designed to produce desired outcomes in a given context. At the same time, researchers acknowledge that all innovation elements are not created equal: Some are *core components* (also known as *essential components, critical components*, or *active ingredients*) that are theorized or empirically determined to be the key contributors to outcomes of interest and primary mechanisms for change (Abry, Rimm-Kaufman, Larsen, & Brewer, 2013; Damschroder et al., 2009; Darrow, 2013; Domitrovich et al., 2008; Fixsen et al., 2005; Greenhalgh, Robert, MacFarlane, Bate, & Kyriakidou, 2004). For this reason, core components are often considered indispensable in practice (Damschroder et al., 2009; Greenhalgh et al., 2004), *at least until empirical data prove otherwise*. The remaining innovation components, in theory, are considered to be nonessential "related components" (Hall & Loucks, 1978a) or part of the "adaptable periphery" (e.g., Damschroder et al., 2009).

Identifying "core" components. Describing innovation components is challenging, even when working with the developers themselves (Hall & Loucks, 1978a; Leithwood & Montgomery, 1980; Meyers, Durlak, & Wandersman, 2012). This is true for relatively simple innovations as well as for complex and multifaceted innovations. It is not uncommon for developers to be unsure about which elements are indeed most critical (Remillard, 2005; Ruiz-Primo, 2005), and there is a tendency for innovation creators to identify the majority of components as "very important" (Mowbray et al., 2003) and to hold holistic views of their innovations (i.e., as "packages"), leading to component descriptions that lack specificity (Cohen, 1975; Harn, Parisi, & Stoolmiller, 2013; Leithwood & Montgomery,1980). For these reasons, researchers are encouraged to use multifaceted approaches to identifying innovation components that combine information from developers and other experts, from end users, from observations of innovations in practice, and from reviews of artifacts, such as practice guides and other program materials (e.g., Century, Rudnick, & Freeman, 2010; Leithwood & Montgomery, 1980; Mowbray et al., 2003).

Some researchers who have focused on conducting comparison studies suggest that identified core components should be further classified into two categories originally described by Waltz, Addis, Koerner, and Jacobson (1993): "unique" (i.e., innovation-specific) and "necessary but not unique." This perspective acknowledges that many innovations and business-as-usual educational practices may have some degree of component overlap (Century et al., 2010; Michie, Fixsen, Grimshaw, & Eccles, 2009; Nelson, Cordray, Hulleman, Darrow, & Sommer, 2012), in particular, with components representing general quality of instruction or good teaching practice. Identifying and measuring the enactment of the unique core components in both the treatment and comparison groups, while also taking into account the enactment of nonunique (shared) components, are key to determining differences in innovations (Darrow, 2013; Nelson et al., 2012).

Other studies are less focused on making comparisons between different innovation enactments and are more concerned with understanding the operation and evolution of innovations in natural settings. In these studies, it is still essential to articulate innovation components in order to measure, analyze, and understand their relationships to one another and to outcomes. Moreover, specific descriptions of innovation components afford the potential of enabling synthesis of studies that examine innovations with common components, leading to a cumulative knowledge base.

The extent to which innovation components should or can be described at a meaningful level of specificity is shaped by the innovation itself and by its underlying theory of action. Policy reforms, for example, have varied levels of specificity (Desimone, 2002) and often are vaguely stated (Cohen & Ball, 1990), leading to assortments of implementation on the ground. As Berman and McLaughlin (1978) observed decades ago, policy in operation can look very different in different contexts. In brief, if the field is to learn about improving education through implementation studies, it is essential to be able to answer the question: *implementation of what?*

Organizing core components. As part of identifying and organizing innovation core components, researchers must decide on the appropriate level of detail with which the components should be described. For instance, in a classroom-level curricular innovation, core components may include specific teacher practices (e.g., *guiding students' learning by taking into account students' ideas*); larger, more abstract categories of practice (e.g., *supporting student learning*); or even more abstract constructs (e.g., *instructional transactions*; Ruiz-Primo, 2005). In comparison, in a school-wide innovation, core components may include decision-making activities (e.g., *staff participate in decision making*), leadership activities (e.g., *school leaders model instructional practice*), or larger constructs that subsume multiple components (e.g., *staff foundations*; LaForce, Noble, King, Holt, & Century, 2014). In a district-level innovation, core components may be much broader in nature, reflecting district-wide activities (e.g., *professional development*). Finally, there are innovations that cut across multiple levels of the education system and have process-oriented components (e.g., *collaborative planning groups*).

Abry, Hulleman, and Rimm-Kaufman (2015) suggest that researchers, as a rule of thumb, identify the "kernels" of an innovation—the "fundamental units that cannot be further reduced while retaining their impact" (p. 334). Others suggest that once identified, specific innovation components should be organized according to the latent constructs they represent, so that those constructs, even if operationalized differently, can be measured in both the treatment and comparison conditions (Nelson et al., 2012). Another consideration might be the level of the outcome and alignment between the innovation component and that outcome (e.g., professional development elements may align with teacher outcomes; elements of system-level processes may align with system-level outcomes).

In recent years, researchers have begun to make the conceptual distinction between core components that are *structural* in nature (i.e., those that provide a format and organizational structure for the innovation) and those that represent *processes* such as specific teacher and student interactions, participation in decision-making processes, and innovation codevelopment (e.g., S. A. Brown, Pitvorec, Ditto, & Kelso, 2009; Century & Cassata, 2014; Harn et al., 2013; McKenna, Flower, & Ciullo, 2014; Odom et al., 2010; O'Donnell, 2008; Ruiz-Primo, 2005). The structure/process approach to categorizing educational innovation components can be traced back to a seminal publication by Mowbray et al. (2003), whose review of implementation research studies challenged the field to rigorously measure processes as well as the more easily captured structural innovation elements. Their work suggested the importance of doing more than noting the presence of a structure; researchers need to understand what happens *within* structures to draw conclusions about innovation enactment and outcomes.

Conceptualizing Factors Influencing Innovation Implementation

Conceptualizing the innovation specifies the "what" of change; conceptualizing the range of influences on innovation enactment specifies the "why" and the "how." For several decades, education researchers have sought to identify variables that influence how and why educational innovations are enacted in practice settings. As referenced earlier, in the 1960s and 1970s, educational innovations were seen as replicable "technologies" that would easily transfer once providers had knowledge that they "work." Then large-scale evaluations brought to light the influence of administrative structures, material resources, and problem-solving strategies on implementation (Berman & McLaughlin, 1976; Fullan & Pomfret, 1977). Concurrently, curriculum implementation research illuminated the needs and concerns of individual practitioners as they attempted to enact changes in their practice (e.g., Ball & Cohen, 1996; Buttolph, 1992; Hall & Loucks, 1978b; Sieber, 1981). Berman (1981, p. 279) was among those documenting these phenomena and published a preliminary categorization of factors affecting the educational change process, calling on the field to develop a "taxonomy of contextual conditions" to guide the design of empirical studies examining the individual and interacting spheres of influence. In introducing his preliminary taxonomy, he spoke about the importance of categorizing different types of variables in order to clarify their status in the educational change process.

Spheres of influence. Since that time, numerous studies have generated lists of factors that may support or inhibit educational and other social innovation enactments.

These factors converge across multiple disciplines, including school psychology, health, education, and prevention science. Greenhalgh et al. (2004) were among the first to organize influential factors into a comprehensive framework, creating a model that categorized them into layers or spheres of influence: the individual, the organization, the external environment, and the attributes of the innovation itself. Many similar frameworks and research reviews have since been published (e.g., Century & Cassata, 2014; Chambers, Glasgow, & Stange, 2013; Durlak & DuPre, 2008; Fixsen et al., 2005; Hall & Hord, 2015; Michie et al., 2009; Remillard, 2005; Rohrbach et al., 2006; Sanetti & Kratochwill, 2009; Weiss, Bloom, & Brock, 2013). Moulin et al. (2015) recently located, reviewed, and compared 49 such frameworks across disciplines. The Consolidated Framework for Implementation Research (CFIR) is a particularly well-developed and widely cited framework synthesizing the many influences on implementation identified through theory and empirical research in the health services sector. The CFIR includes a companion website with an online menu of constructs and measurement resources for researchers and evaluators (see http://cfirguide.org).

Characteristics of individual end users: The characteristics of individual end users cited in the literature generally fall into two categories: (a) *characteristics of the individual in relation to the innovation* (e.g., level of understanding, expertise, prior experience, beliefs, values, attitudes, motivation, or self-efficacy) and (b) *characteristics of the individual that exist independently of the innovation* (e.g., willingness to try new things, organizational skills, classroom management style, or views about teaching and learning in general). While research has emphasized the importance of individual competence and skills in enacting the innovation (e.g., Hall & Loucks, 1975; Mowbray et al., 2003), there is also a long-standing awareness that innovation use is more than a matter of skill or even self-efficacy. As early as 1950, Caswell urged researchers to consider "psychological factors in change" (p. 69), reminding them that trying out something new always involves an element of uncertainty and risk. This perspective emphasizes that individual innovation users are not passive recipients; in attempting new practices, they actively interpret and make decisions about their use by drawing on prior beliefs and experiences (Ball & Cohen, 1996; Greenhalgh et al., 2004; Penuel et al., 2014). Over several decades, research has noted the highly personal transformational process that takes place during innovation implementation, beginning with a sense of readiness, or a perception that one is willing and able to change (Buttolph, 1992; S. Peterson, 2013). While individual characteristics independent of the innovation are generally not emphasized in theory, preliminary research suggests they are potentially important influential factors (Hill, Blazar, & Lynch, 2015).

Organizational and environmental factors: The next spheres of influence are not always as clear. Depending on the innovation, the boundary of "inside the organization" and "outside the organization" may vary (Damschroder et al., 2009). However, in the context of classroom-level interventions, organizational factors often refer to school- or district-level influences (Snyder et al., 1992). Some organizational factors pertain to characteristics of the setting itself (e.g., class size, resources, physical space, scheduling, organizational structure; Hall & Hord, 2015; Macklem, 2014), while others involve the organizational administration, management, and decision-making processes that individuals in the organization (i.e., school or district) engage in related to innovation adoption and use (Fullan & Pomfret, 1977). The collective attitudes and behaviors of people within the organization (e.g., morale, vision, trust, collaboration, identity, commitment), which some refer to as aspects of organizational culture, are also considered important organizational influences (Maitlis & Sonenshein, 2010; Rohrbach et al., 2006). Environmental factors are those considered "outside the organization" (e.g., government agencies, economic conditions, shifting social priorities, or professional community networks). These elements of the broader context exert indirect influence on innovation implementation (Ball & Cohen, 1996; Fixsen et al., 2005; Fullan & Pomfret, 1977; Snyder et al., 1992).

Attributes of the innovation: The innovation attributes themselves can also influence innovation implementation. Innovations can have *actual* attributes (objective characteristics) and *perceived* attributes (subjective user perceptions about the innovation). These attributes, however, have not consistently been differentiated in the literature. Some researchers equate innovation attributes with objective characteristics such as number of components (complexity), specification, scope of effort, empirical evidence of effectiveness, design features, and cost (e.g., Berman, 1981; Century et al., 2012; Damschroder et al., 2009; Fullan & Pomfret, 1977; Snyder et al., 1992). The degree of specification—the explicitness with which an intervention (in whole or in part) is articulated for the end user—varies widely (Cohen & Ball, 1999; Desimone, 2002). While some interventions (e.g., curricula, technology, training materials) provide "blueprints" or detailed plans for end users, other types of interventions (e.g., policies, design principles, or goal statements) are much more ambiguous in comparison, leaving their operationalization more subject to the influence of the local context.

Other researchers consider innovation attributes to include not only objective features but also subjective judgments such as level of attractiveness of the materials, ease of use, familiarity, perceived relevance, and perceived advantage over current practice (e.g., Dearing, 2009; Rohrbach et al., 2006). Adaptability, or the extent to which an innovation may be flexibly enacted to fit the circumstances, may be subjective (depending on the skills, knowledge, and attitudes of the provider) or objective (in cases where flexibility is built into innovations by design). While both categories of factors are potentially important, researchers should note that the subjective factors will vary by different end user populations.

Implementation support strategies. In addition to the factors explained above, there is consensus in the field that deliberate, planned support for innovation users and their organizations is vital to change efforts (Forman et al., 2013; Hall

& Hord, 2015; Peters, Adam, Alonge, Agyepong, & Tran, 2013). The variety of these supports is broad, encompassing operational planning, resource provision, professional development, mentoring, strategic planning, evaluative processes, and other strategies that support ongoing implementation and improvement. Supports may be provided by innovation developers or intermediary organizations (also called *change agents, change facilitators, technical assistance providers,* or *purveyors*) or may come from within the enacting organization. In the literature, this factor category is described in various ways, including *implementation drivers* (Fixsen et al., 2005), *implementation-level activities* (Darrow, 2013), *support systems* (Domitrovich et al., 2008; Meyers et al., 2012), *strategies* (Moulin et al., 2015), and *implementation practices* (Dunst et al., 2013). In this chapter, we use the term *implementation support strategies* to highlight the primary purpose of supporting end users as they put an innovation into practice (Fullan & Pomfret, 1977). While implementation support strategies are often considered key variables in theories of change (e.g., Dunst et al., 2013; Fixsen et al., 2005; Meyers et al., 2012; Weiss et al., 2013), they are not present in all innovations. Moreover, they do not align cleanly with particular "spheres of influence," usually falling into the organizational or environmental groups.

Ultimately, implementation support strategies are designed according to underlying theories or best practices for facilitating individual and organizational learning and change. For this reason, researchers have begun to emphasize the importance of understanding the extent to which implementation support strategies were carried out as intended as part of interpreting observed effects (e.g., Dunst et al., 2013; Meyers et al., 2012; Nelson et al., 2012; Weiss et al., 2013).

Implementation over time. A final set of theories about factors influencing innovations focuses on implementation phases or stages. In general, these theories differ from others we have outlined because they bring a longer term view of implementation, depicting a developmental arc from the first moment of innovation adoption to a point at which the innovation has (potentially) become routine. Time-related theories are often cited in research exploring factors that influence an innovation's propensity to be sustained over time in a particular context. Such theories include views of innovation implementation from the perspectives of both the individual end user and the other individuals in the organization, as they move through developmental stages from awareness to initial adoption, to sophisticated innovation use.

Moulin et al. (2015), for example, in their synthesis of existing frameworks, explicitly note the nonlinear and recursive nature of the implementation process and the possibility of different contextual variables that come into play at different points in time. Hall and Loucks (1975) focus on the individual's evolution, moving from routine, mechanical use to more flexible and adaptive use with increasing skills and competence. Other frameworks theorize that whole organizations experience similar phases, progressing through awareness, then start-up activities (e.g., planning and securing resources), initial implementation, skilled implementation, and ultimately, routine practice (e.g., Berman & McLaughlin, 1976; Fixsen et al., 2005; Yin et al., 1978).

In effect, studies that examine innovation endurance are concerned with implementation over time. In such studies, the duration of the time horizon combines with the study's theoretical orientation to inform the study focus. In the shorter term, for example, studies may focus on the extent to which innovation structures are present. As the time horizon lengthens, however, research questions shift, reflecting a deeper concern for the changes that reside at the heart of lasting educational improvement. Adelman and Taylor (2003) speak about the presence of the "valued functions" that reside within the innovation structures and giving attention to ways those functions can endure even as the innovation structures come and go. Others assert that for change to be truly permanent and meaningful, it must take deep hold at the core of practice (Coburn, 2003; Elmore, 1996). Thus, implementation research studies concerned with questions about innovation endurance focus on questions of *what* is lasting: whether the innovation is changing, how it is changing, and why.

Distinguishing the Innovation From Context

The diversity of theoretical orientations that researchers bring to implementation research warrants an embrace of different research models, designs, and methods. Still, those engaged in a shared research endeavor need to establish shared conceptual understanding that transcends the different orientations (Bell, 2004; Coburn, 2003). The literature reveals an emerging consensus toward this goal, at the largest grain size, in designating variables as innovation core components or as contextual factors, and in specifying the level of contextual influence (i.e., innovation, individual, organizational, environmental). Then, within broad conceptual frameworks describing the phenomena under study (i.e., the innovation, its component parts, and categories of influence), researchers can hone in on a variety of specific innovation-related and contextual variables according to their particular research questions and theoretical orientation.

Still, even with a commitment to identifying the innovation and the influential factors, the lines that distinguish them are not always clear. Depending on the theory of change, the same innovation elements may be considered *part of* the innovation, *external to* the innovation, or even *outcomes* of the innovation. For example, some support strategies might be considered innovations (or innovation elements) in themselves, enacted to enhance the behaviors and skills of practitioners delivering service to target recipients. More specifically, a school district may establish district coaching to support teachers' implementation of a new instructional resource. The district (or researchers studying the phenomena, or both) may view the instructional resource as the innovation, with the coaching strategy acting as an influential factor (an implementation support strategy). Other districts or researchers, however, might view the coaching strategy *and* the instructional resource as key elements in a larger, systemic innovation. In the latter case, the coaching strategy is an innovation element, not an influential factor.

The challenge also applies to distinguishing between influential factors and outcomes. For example, teacher characteristics (e.g., beliefs about how students learn, values about education, attitudes about the subject matter, interpersonal skills) are often identified as key mediating or moderating variables that support or inhibit innovation enactment (e.g., Dane & Schneider, 1998; Domitrovich et al., 2008; Hulleman et al., 2013; Macklem, 2014; Ruiz-Primo, 2005). That is, they are considered influential factors. In some cases, however, individual attitudes, perceptions, and skills are explicitly targeted as desired outcomes of innovation enactment and theorized to change as a result of innovation use or participation.

The evident complexity of innovation enactment, its influences, and the multiple functions that variables play at different points in the implementation process challenge us as a field to find ways to communicate about our work in a clear and unambiguous manner. Having both clear language to discuss the innovation elements and shared conceptual understanding about the categories of influential factors will enable researchers to study implementation of their innovations of interest with the methodologies they embrace while being able to meaningfully share findings with one another.

MEASUREMENT AND ANALYSIS OF INNOVATION IMPLEMENTATION

Perspectives on Measurement

For the purpose of this chapter, we use the definition of *measurement* provided by Zeller and Carmines (1980)—"the process of linking abstract concepts to *empirical indicants*" (p. 2)—which involves operationalizing abstract concepts so that they may be observed. Thus, here we discuss the ways the determination of innovation components, influential factors, and innovation enactment may be operationalized for the purpose of systematic measurement. In this process, the translation from abstract concept to operational definition does not dictate a single methodological orientation or research method. Peters et al. (2013, p. 2), in outlining a set of key principles for implementation research, emphasize that the research question, typically organized around a theory of change or specific research objective (i.e., to explore, describe, influence, explain, or predict), drives the specific methods used and assumptions taken. Research questions and associated objectives may be shaped by the five purposes for studying implementation outlined earlier (see Table 1). Peters et al. describe a wide range of qualitative and quantitative research methods, including randomized controlled trials (RCTs), participatory action research, and mixed methods, that can be used to achieve these very different purposes.

Implementation research measurement has been informed by two main perspectives. First, studies conducted with the objectives of designing and developing innovations and establishing their efficacy and effectiveness are frequently driven by an interest in *evaluating fidelity of implementation* of the innovation—that is, the extent to which the innovation (i.e., its core components) was enacted as intended. In comparison, a second perspective resides in studies driven by the goals of innovation improvement and exploring relationships between innovations, contextual factors, and outcomes. These studies are less concerned with evaluating fidelity and more concerned with *describing implementation as conducted* (i.e., what actually happened), the extent to which desired outcomes are achieved, and why. They focus on questions such as the following: Is the innovation (i.e., its core components) being used, how is it being used, and to what extent? What is being adapted or modified from the original model? Why?

Research coming from the first perspective (fidelity of implementation) asks, "Was the innovation enacted *as intended* (i.e., compared to an ideal standard)?" In the context of design and feasibility studies for example, understanding fidelity of implementation even at the level of an individual component can inform developers (whether external to the setting, internal to the setting or a combination) about the innovation's potential to be enacted by the intended user. For experimental or quasi-experimental designs underlying efficacy or effectiveness studies, documenting fidelity of implementation in the treatment group is necessary to determine whether the treatment group indeed received the intended treatment (the innovation). Similarly, fidelity levels may be measured in the control or comparison condition (to the extent that common core components are identified) and then used to determine whether the two groups are sufficiently differentiated (Mowbray et al., 2003; Nelson et al., 2012; O'Donnell, 2008).

Research coming from the second perspective (describing implementation as conducted) may also examine relationships between implementation and outcomes without necessarily comparing it to a theoretical ideal. Such studies may seek to describe the extent and nature of innovation use in practice, including adaptations and omission of core components, and explore the contextual factors that support or inhibit innovation use. Rather than bringing an evaluative view to the innovation enactment, some studies that examine implementation as conducted bring a more descriptive and explanatory approach to the inquiry. Documenting implementation as conducted enables researchers to understand the ways that innovations are operationalized in practice, the influential factors that affect that practice (Hamilton & Feldman, 2014), the different patterns of practice, or "configurations" (Hall & Loucks, 1978a), and in some studies, the relationships between these patterns and outcomes. Researchers using this approach can also catalogue the nature of the adaptations that end users make to better describe the range of beneficial, acceptable (i.e., aligned with program goals and theory), or unacceptable adaptations (Durlak & DuPre, 2008; Hall & Loucks, 1978a; Moore, Bumbarger, & Cooper, 2013; O'Donnell, 2008; Penuel et al., 2014).

These two perspectives provide complementary and useful information about the status of and mechanisms driving innovation effectiveness. The first (fidelity of implementation) has been the primary focus of quantitative measurement in education to date, due in part to the recent predominance of RCT research designs. Fidelity of implementation is hypothesized to mediate the effect of random assignment to treatment or control and is important for understanding the mechanisms by which an innovation achieves its effects (Hansen, 2014). The second (implementation as conducted) involves descriptive or correlational analyses crucial for identifying critical components, specifying ranges of acceptable adaptation, and identifying key supportive and inhibiting contextual factors—data that can inform innovation improvement and endurance.

Notwithstanding the value of studying implementation as conducted and the wide range of implementation research purposes, the next section focuses on emerging understandings of fidelity and evolving strategies for fidelity measurement. The attention given to fidelity here is not intended to emphasize its importance over other perspectives but rather is a reflection of its dominance in the literature targeting implementation measurement.

Conceptualizing Fidelity of Innovation Implementation

While terminology varies across studies, fidelity criteria are generally related to which and how many core components are used, how much of the innovation is delivered and/or received, how well the innovation is delivered, and the level of participant engagement in the innovation (Sanetti & Kratochwill, 2009). Some authors suggest that in addition to these criteria, innovations come with expectations for how, when, and by whom each service should be provided, which may also be evaluated as part of fidelity measurement (e.g., Macklem, 2014; Sanetti & Kratochwill, 2009; Weiss et al., 2013).

Still, the most widely cited criteria for fidelity measurement are attributed to Dane and Schneider (1998), who conducted a literature review that identified five "aspects of program integrity," which they labeled *adherence, exposure, quality of delivery, participant responsiveness*, and *program differentiation*. The first four criteria describe ways the innovation may be enacted or engaged in by *users and/or recipients*; program differentiation describes a manipulation check carried out *by the researcher* to ensure that subjects in each experimental condition received only planned interventions (to safeguard against diffusion of treatments). At the time, Dane and Schneider established these categories as provisional, indicating that uniform definitions were needed; yet, 15 years later, Darrow (2013) noted that while the five aspects of implementation identified by Dane and Schneider (1998) are often cited, "individual interpretations and lack of consensus around those categories exist" (p. 1140). Multiple authors have suggested their own definitions, many of which continue to vary across studies or lack the level of detail needed to guide researchers in what, exactly, should be measured.

Hansen (2014) explains that the language of fidelity assessment is neither universally applied nor universally understood: "Even the most basic of terms—fidelity, adherence, dosage, engagement, program differentiation, and adaptation—may have one meaning for an evaluation staff and a very different meaning for practitioners" (p. 336). For example, across studies in the education literature, definitions of adherence capture the general concept of "doing what was expected or as intended," but as operationalized this may involve doing specified program activities (e.g., Benner, Nelson, Stage, & Ralston, 2011; Macklem, 2014), doing them at the recommended quantity (e.g., Abry et al., 2015; Moore et al., 2013), and doing them fully (e.g., Zucker, Solari, Landry, & Swank, 2013). Similarly, "exposure" has been operationalized in two ways: as the *amount of innovation received* from the perspective of the recipients (i.e., students, learners; e.g., Domitrovich et al., 2008; Dusenbury et al., 2003; Weiss et al., 2013) and as the *amount of innovation delivered* from the perspective of the end users (Durlak & DuPre, 2008; O'Donnell, 2008; Ruiz-Primo, 2005). In measuring quality, some researchers have measured end user characteristics (which we suggest fall into the spheres of influence), such as enthusiasm, interpersonal style, preparedness, and level of skill as indicators of quality (e.g., Domitrovich et al., 2008; Lynch & O'Donnell, 2005; Macklem, 2014; Pence, Justice, & Wiggins, 2008), while other researchers have focused on innovation use and on "how well" the innovation is delivered (e.g., Abry et al., 2015; Benner et al., 2011; Zucker et al., 2013). Participant responsiveness is sometimes defined as a measure of recipient (learner) participation and engagement (e.g., Lynch & O'Donnell, 2005) and sometimes as the interest and attention of both the end users *and* the recipients (e.g., Carroll et al., 2007).

Mowbray et al. (2003) and O'Donnell (2008) have encouraged researchers to consider the fidelity of implementation of process-related components (i.e., users and recipient behaviors and interactions) as well as structural components (i.e., innovation-specific materials, resources, and activities). Since that time, the field has increasingly acknowledged this view, resulting in hybrid models that organize Dane and Schneider's (1998) fidelity criteria into a larger "structure" and "process" framework. More specifically, researchers have created measures of "fidelity to structure" that generally align with the concepts of adherence and exposure, while "fidelity to process" generally aligns with the concepts of quality and participant responsiveness (e.g., Benner et al., 2011; McKenna et al., 2014; O'Donnell, 2008). Although placing Dane and Schneider's (1998) criteria into a structure/process framework provides a richer representation of enacted practice, given the lack of clear definitions and varied interpretations, this approach does not resolve problems of clarity and consensus.

The need for our field to establish clearly understood language regarding fidelity of implementation has been discussed by many researchers over the past decade (e.g., Century & Cassata, 2014; Greenhalgh et al., 2004; Irwin & Supplee, 2012; O'Donnell, 2008; Sanetti & Kratochwill, 2009). The need remains, and is as urgent as ever. The Department of Education's Institute of Education Sciences (IES) 2015 funding solicitation asks researchers not only to provide evidence regarding the impact of innovations but also to describe *sufficient implementation* for achieving beneficial effects so that those effects can be generalized to new contexts. However, as illustrated above, determining what constitutes sufficient implementation is largely a matter of perspective. As of this writing, the field has no agreed-on, systematic way to do so.

The Process of Innovation Implementation Measurement

Several step-by-step guidelines and resources now exist to assist researchers seeking to measure implementation (e.g., Hall & Loucks, 1978a; Mowbray et al., 2003; Nelson et al., 2012; O'Donnell, 2008). As previously noted, these guidelines are discussed almost exclusively in studies focused on measuring fidelity of implementation rather than implementation as conducted, and relate primarily to quantitative data sources. They describe key decisions that researchers must make in the process of developing, administering, and using implementation measures:

1. Identifying and operationally defining the core components of a given innovation model
2. If relevant to the study, determining fidelity benchmarks, or expectations for component enactment (typically determined by innovation developers)
3. Developing a theoretical model linking core components (and mediating variables) to outcomes in a causal chain
4. Specifying the methods and data sources used to measure each core component
5. Selecting an appropriate time frame for data collection
6. Ensuring the data collected are reliable and valid
7. Determining how the data will be summarized and/or reduced for analysis

While an extensive review of each of these decisions is beyond the scope of this chapter, we summarize a few key areas of consensus below.

Data Sources

A range of data sources can be used for implementation measurement, including expert observations, user interviews and self-reported surveys, and collection of institutional records (Hansen, 2014; Scheirer & Rezmovic, 1983). For decades, direct observation conducted by expert raters has been considered the preferred method for assessing innovation implementation (Durlak, 2010; Fullan & Pomfret, 1977; Leithwood & Montgomery, 1980; Ruiz-Primo, 2005). While experts can potentially work with any data source (including interviews, videos, logs, and other documents), observations by expert raters have generally been regarded as the most direct measures of practice, the most rigorous, and the most objective with respect to implementation quality, compared to self-reported data. Domitrovich, Gest, Jones, Gill, and DeRousie (2010) note that unlike researcher observation, users' reports via surveys or interviews may be inaccurate, for example, if their concerns about social desirability lead them to inflate their ratings. Furthermore, if the majority of respondents report their implementation at very high levels, variability in practice is not captured and the resulting data are not useful for outcome analysis.

However, with all of their advantages, observations are acknowledged to present clear practical challenges. They are expensive, often not feasible with large samples, and can be time-consuming (Domitrovich et al., 2010; Fullan & Pomfret, 1977). In addition, while observations can capture program elements with less potential bias than self-report measures, many innovation components are less observable and are difficult to assess (Fullan & Pomfret, 1977; Ruiz- Primo, 2005; Snyder et al., 1992) or not observable at all. Moreover, observations may not capture core components with enough precision (Leithwood & Montgomery, 1980), and the people being observed may act differently with the knowledge of being observed (McKenna et al., 2014). For these reasons, the use of a multimethod, multi-informant approach is recommended, including using observations to confirm self-reports (Domitrovich et al., 2008; McKenna et al., 2014; Mowbray et al., 2003; Nelson et al., 2012; Snyder et al., 1992). In some cases, self-report methods may be preferred, for example, in measuring provider knowledge, understanding, and other individual user characteristics (Fullan & Pomfret, 1977) or in documenting how often users completed specific activities or lessons (Durlak, 2010). Furthermore, in cases where analysis requires statistical power, self-report may be the only practical way to obtain a sufficient data set.

Instrument Validation

Recommendations in the literature encourage researchers to ensure that the measures used to assess fidelity are reliable and valid (Mowbray et al., 2003; Nelson et al., 2012; O'Donnell, 2008). However, recent reviews from the school psychology and health education fields reveal that psychometric properties of fidelity measures are rarely provided (Dusenbury et al., 2003; Schulte, Easton, & Parker, 2009). When researchers do report psychometric data, they typically report assessment of interrater or interobserver agreement, assessment of intraclass correlations among raters, examination of the internal structure of the data through measures of internal consistency or confirmatory factor analysis, and test-retest reliability (Mowbray et al., 2003; Scheirer & Rezmovic, 1983; Schulte et al., 2009). In turn, researchers most frequently report validation strategies such as establishing face validity, concurrent validity (comparing differences in fidelity scores among known groups), convergent validity (comparing data collected across multiple data sources), and predictive validity (examining relationships between fidelity of implementation and expected participant outcomes; Mowbray et al., 2003).

Timing of Data Collection

While there is limited research on how many time points are needed to capture changes in implementation, the consensus is that innovation implementation is dynamic and should be measured on multiple occasions (Durlak, 2010; Harn et al., 2013; Odom et al., 2010). Empirical data support this view; analytic strategies such as linear growth modeling and growth curve modeling have been used to illustrate changes in implementation status over time (Clements, Sarama, Wolfe, & Spitler, 2015; Domitrovich et al., 2010). In addition, decisions about data collection timing require careful consideration of the nature of the innovation itself, as researchers need to be able to capture all innovation core components, including those that happen frequently as well as those that happen only occasionally (Domitrovich et al., 2010). Finally, it is important to take into account the presence of contextual factors surrounding the innovation, including training, which may indicate whether and how much change can be expected over time (Durlak, 2010).

Data Reduction

The literature presents two primary approaches to data reduction consistent with the two main approaches to quantitative measurement of innovation implementation: (a) seeking to create *fidelity indices*, or variables summarizing the degree of deviation from, or convergence with, the innovation model across items (the predominant approach in the literature) and (b) seeking to create measures that represent the extent of component use without reference to fidelity criteria. While the first approach creates measures that represent distance from the ideal (i.e., the difference between what was enacted and what should have been enacted), the second approach creates measures that represent the absolute extent or degree of enactment. Research studies may use data measuring the extent or degree of enactment to *discover what is ideal*, for example, by examining relationships between variation in component enactment (in terms of quantity or quality) and outcomes.

Fidelity indices approach. In creating fidelity indices, researchers measure core component enactment with respect to one or more predetermined criteria such as component presence, quantity, or quality of delivery and/or receipt (e.g., Hord et al., 1987; Ruiz-Primo, 2005). Researchers create indices with varying levels of specificity. It is common for researchers to create fidelity indices representing the innovation as a whole through a "composite fidelity score" (e.g., Abry et al., 2015; Aladjem et al., 2006; Blakely et al., 1987; Pas & Bradshaw, 2012). Hulleman and Cordray (2009) demonstrated multiple ways these indices can be created, including a proportion score in which achieved fidelity is divided by maximum possible fidelity, a binary score that involves assigning a dichotomous *yes* or *no* value for fidelity, and an average score in which higher scores represent more or better fidelity. However, the more general the index, the less nuanced information is available with which to understand implementation. In recent years, more detailed approaches for creating fidelity indices have emerged, such as creating multiple fidelity indices for different core components (Abry et al., 2015; Aladjem et al., 2006) and creating separate indices to represent fidelity to "structural" and "process" aspects of the innovation (Odom et al., 2010).

Component approach. The component approach to data reduction creates indices that represent the degree of core component implementation without making the comparison between what was enacted and what was intended. This approach is useful for empirically determining which aspects of materials are linked to learning outcomes, that is, "for testing theories about what are the 'active ingredients'"

(Penuel et al., 2014, p. 773), as well as for answering the question of "how much" enactment is enough, so that we can create meaningful thresholds for the necessary presence and amounts of components (Abry et al., 2015). Some studies using the component approach provide descriptive reports of implementation (listing the components that were implemented most and least), while other studies explore relationships between component enactment and learning outcomes (e.g., Fogleman et al., 2011) or between component enactment and influential contextual factors (e.g., Stein & Kaufman, 2010). It is important to note that reporting implementation as enacted does not *preclude* the comparison of implementation as enacted to previously designated benchmarks or recommendations, although this type of reporting is less common (see Agodini et al., 2009, p. 41, as an example).

Analyzing the Implementation Process

In general, implementation analyses in the literature to date have focused on fidelity of implementation for three purposes: (a) discriminating between the treatment and control groups, (b) exploring relationships between variation in fidelity of implementation and learner outcomes, and (c) exploring relationships between variation in fidelity of implementation and contextual factors.

Discriminating Between Treatment and Control Group

With educational innovations, even when there is randomization, one cannot always assume there is a clear differentiation between treatment and control groups. Furthermore, the treatment group may deviate from protocol in a beneficial way (sometimes called *positive infidelity*; Cordray & Hulleman, 2009). For these reasons, several researchers have recommended computing the difference between fidelity in treatment and control groups (Durlak & DuPre, 2008; Mowbray et al., 2003; O'Donnell, 2008). Some researchers have conducted significance tests as a basic way to examine differences in fidelity scores between treatment and comparison conditions (O'Donnell, 2008), while others have devised more sophisticated methods to capture the differences. For example, the *achieved relative strength index* is a measure of intervention strength representing the standardized difference in the extent to which teachers enact core intervention components in the treatment and control conditions (Cordray, Pion, Brandt, Molefe, & Toby, 2012; Hulleman & Cordray, 2009).

Relating Fidelity of Implementation to Outcomes

Researchers have employed a range of linear modeling approaches for exploring relationships between fidelity and learner outcomes. For example, correlational analyses explore the nature of association between fidelity variables and outcomes (e.g., Odom et al., 2010), while multiple regression analyses assess the relative contribution of multiple fidelity variables to variation in outcomes (e.g., Benner et al., 2011). In contexts where study participants are nested (e.g., students within classrooms or groups), multilevel modeling approaches assess the extent to which fidelity (as one source of between-teacher variation) explains variation in student outcomes (e.g., Odom et al., 2010; Zvoch, 2012). Within the context of experimental designs, replacing the causal variable, or "intent to treat" (a dichotomous variable representing the treatment or control group as randomized), with a fidelity index score computed for each group estimates the effects of "treatment on the treated," as recommended by Cook (2005; e.g., Davidson, Fields, & Yang, 2009; Justice, Mashburn, Pence, & Wiggins, 2008; T. Smith et al., 2013). Structural equation modeling approaches, while less common, may be used to estimate mediated or indirect effects of the innovation treatment through fidelity indices (e.g., Abry et al., 2013; Gennetian, Bos, & Morris, 2002). Although none of these analyses enable causal conclusions, they do provide important information for understanding the content within the "black box" of observed causal effects.

Mediation analyses are particularly useful for analyzing the impacts of multilevel, complex interventions where multiple components are placed together and theorized to work in a causal chain to influence outcomes. Mediating variables are those affected by the innovation and that, in turn, affect the outcome of interest (Donaldson, 2001; Raudenbush & Bloom, 2015). The relationship between mediator and outcome is indirect, in that the mediating variable is a precursor to the outcome variable of interest. In theory, hypothesized mediating relationships can be tested through pilot studies and small-scale data collection, repeating the process until the developer decides the innovation is worthy of full-scale implementation. The goal of repeated analysis is to find a parsimonious model that accounts for a large percentage of variance in the desired outcome variables. Still, researchers who are focused on such approaches face a conundrum because the limited empirical data available during innovation development do not typically provide enough statistical power to analyze mediating relationships. Donaldson (2001) suggests that even with limited resources, descriptive quantitative or qualitative data on enactment of the variables of interest can be used to gauge mechanisms by which innovations appear to work, resulting in immediate information to guide program development and hypotheses that can be tested in larger scale studies. These issues are of less concern for studies focused on complex, place-based innovations and studies not seeking to establish causal findings.

Relating Contextual Factors to Implementation

Analyses examining factors that influence fidelity of implementation reside one step to the left in the causal chain leading to outcomes; the contextual factor variables become independent variables, and the implementation variables become dependent variables. Such analyses are sometimes carried out to supplement the initial findings from RCTs by describing for whom or under what conditions under which the innovation "worked," to uncover the best strategies for supporting optimal implementation, or to discover the influence of variation in context on implementation in a scale-up or sustainability study. These mostly exploratory analyses generally fall into two categories: those that examine short-term or immediate influences on implementation (e.g., Kurki, Boyle, & Aladjem, 2006; McCormick, Steckler, & McLeroy, 1995; Penuel, Fishman, Yamaguchi, & Gallagher, 2007) and those that examine long-term influences supporting sustained implementation over time (e.g., Clements et al., 2015; Lieber et al., 2010; McIntosh et al., 2013). Notably, in addition to quantitative studies, there are numerous examples of qualitative and mixed-methods studies that examine the influence of supportive or inhibiting factors on innovation implementation and sustainability (e.g., Billing, Sherry, & Havelock, 2005; Century & Levy, 2002; Lieber et al., 2009; Rijsdijk et al., 2014).

The influence of contextual factors may also be examined in terms of moderating variables in a theory of change. Moderating variables affect the direction or strength of relationships between predictor variables and outcomes by reducing, enhancing, or changing their influence (Fairchild & MacKinnon, 2009). Moderator effects are often referred to as interaction effects, where the effect of one variable depends on the levels of the other variables in the analysis. Moderator variables by definition must be uninfluenced by the innovation and observable prior to engaging in the innovation (Raudenbush & Bloom, 2015). Demographic characteristics of participants, such as gender, race, ethnicity, and socioeconomic status, are often included as moderating variables. Subgroup analysis can explore questions about for whom an innovation is most effective, and in what kinds of sites innovations work best. However, from a quantitative perspective, Fairchild and MacKinnon (2009) caution that, as in mediation analysis, the statistical power required to detect interaction effects often requires a sample size greater than typically available during innovation development.

MAKING NEW HISTORY: SEIZING THE OPPORTUNITY TO ACCUMULATE KNOWLEDGE

Looking at the current state of the literature in the context of a long and varied history, it is clear that although the field of education has made good progress, there is far to go. This section identifies decades-old needs and challenges that have yet to be resolved, new challenges ahead, and considerations for implementation research that we, as a field, must address.

Resolving the Fidelity-Adaptation Debate

Despite enduring challenges, there is a clear consensus that measuring innovation implementation provides one important avenue for understanding the education improvement process. In a review of over 200 experimental intervention studies, Sanetti, Gritter, and Dobey (2011) found that between 2008 and 1995, the proportion of studies reporting quantitative fidelity measurement increased threefold. Funding agencies increasingly require researchers to include fidelity data in innovation development and evaluation work (e.g., Stockard, 2010; U.S. Department of Education, IES, 2015; U.S. Department of Education, IES, & National Science Foundation, 2013). Furthermore, over the past 5 years, multiple professional development workshops and webinars on the topic of implementation measurement have been offered to education researchers, sponsored by organizations such as the Society of Research on Educational Effectiveness, the Global Implementation Initiative, and the National Implementation Research Network.

Profidelity Perspective

Underlying the rationale for measuring *fidelity* of implementation, in particular, is the view that once an innovation is found to be efficacious, future implementations should not deviate from the established "proven" or "evidence-based" model (which we will refer to as the *profidelity* view). This perspective recommends that users should be provided with supports that ensure that fidelity of implementation is sufficiently high. This profidelity stance has been extensively documented and referenced for decades as the dominant perspective on how end users should approach the use of novel practices and strategies that are identified as evidence-based (Blakely et al., 1987; Penuel et al., 2014; Snyder et al., 1992). In short, some of the literature embraces the assumption that more fidelity is better (Buxton et al., 2015; Cho, 1998; Macklem, 2014; Moore et al., 2013), and the default rule of thumb has been that "it is best not to tinker with the prescribed formula"—a conclusion drawn from the absence, rather than the presence, of empirical evidence about what types of adaptations are beneficial or harmful (Halle, Metz, & Martinez-Beck, 2013; Moore et al., 2013, p. 149). The profidelity position tends to view the educational improvement process as linear and rational, concerned with faithful implementation and minimizing variation and deviation from efficacious innovation models (Snyder et al., 1992).

Pro-Adaptation Perspective

Yet, for as long as the profidelity view has existed within the field, there has also existed an alternative perspective supported by assertions in the change and knowledge utilization literature. In this perspective, the innovation user's adaptations of innovation elements (rather than strict adherence to them) is key to reproducing positive outcomes from one context to another and bringing about ongoing improvement. We call this the *pro-adaptation* perspective. More specifically, this perspective holds that adaptations from an original innovation model may add effective strategies, make the innovation more contextually relevant (e.g., McGrew, Bond, Dietzen, & Salyers, 1994; Sanetti & Kratochwill, 2009), or establish that components once considered core to the innovation are not, in fact, vital (Harn et al., 2013; Macklem, 2014). Over the years, researchers have stated that variation within and across sites and over time is expected (Berman, 1981), that perfect implementation is never obtained (Durlak, 2010; Moore et al., 2013), and that adaptation is the natural tendency of implementers and of the change process (Dearing, 2009; Hall & Hord, 2015).

Pro-adaptation advocates contend that a strict fidelity perspective is an "outsider's perspective," in which the developer is deemed the best person to dictate what implementation should look like (Buxton et al., 2015). Others identify end users as the active agents, focusing on their need to be responsive to their context and to act in keeping with the personal meaning-making that guides their decisions (Berman & McLaughlin, 1976; Buttolph, 1992; Buxton et al., 2015; Penuel et al., 2014). Furthermore, Blakely et al. (1987) reported many studies finding that local buy-in of end users was enhanced by enabling program adaptation; in turn, their buy-in helped maintain ongoing program operations. It is also well documented that developers themselves (or other intermediary organizations) may alter their innovations to ensure success in a new context if they believe the new iteration is a better fit—a process known as "mutual adaptation" (Berman & McLaughlin, 1976; Dearing, 2009; Dusenbury et al., 2003). The adaptation perspective suggests that the success and eventual sustainability of an innovation may depend on its potential for use in a variety of ways (Buxton et al., 2015; Leithwood & Montgomery, 1980).

Mitigating the Artificial Divide

Between the extreme profidelity and pro-adaptation points on the spectrum, there is, of course, a middle ground that asserts that different kinds of adaptations are acceptable depending on their extent of alignment with or deviation from program theory. This view considers adaptations acceptable to a certain point (sometimes called the "point" or "zone" of "drastic mutation"), as long as they are congruent with the goals and principles of the designers (Coburn, 2003; Hall & Loucks, 1978a; Kelly et al., 2000; Penuel & Fishman, 2012). DeBarger et al. (2013) use the term *productive adaptations* because such adaptations respond to the demands of the context and are consistent with the innovation's core design principles. The authors note that productive adaptations may themselves be evidence-based, emerging from the tacit knowledge of the practitioners, which has developed through careful observations of their learners.

In reality, there is simply not enough information to determine which innovation components are *truly* critical to an innovation's effects, how much of a particular component is "good enough," or how much adaptation is acceptable. With the many interacting variables at play within educational innovations, the answer is almost certainly, "It depends." Some researchers have suggested that certain types of innovations, such as those that are less specified or less structured in nature, may inherently demand more interpretation by the provider (and in turn, more adaptation; Cohen & Ball, 1990), while innovations that are well structured and well specified are better suited to implementing with fidelity (Berman, 1981; O'Donnell, 2008). Other researchers point to the importance of understanding *why* adaptations are made, *where* implementation challenges come from, and how the nature of an adaptation matters for outcomes, before making a priori judgments about their appropriateness (DeBarger et al., 2013; Remillard, 2005). And perhaps most important, others highlight the need to understand the relative contributions of different innovation components and how different levels of component enactment are related to outcomes (Abry et al., 2015; Damschroder et al., 2009; Durlak, 2015; Odom, 2009).

Finding Clear Language and Shared Conceptual Understanding

As education researchers, we need only look at our history to ascertain what we need to change moving forward. We have already established a lack of consensus in the ways that fidelity of implementation data are described and reported in education research literature (Dane & Schneider, 1998; Darrow, 2013; Downer & Yazejian, 2013; Missett & Foster, 2015; Mowbray et al., 2003; O'Donnell, 2008; Sanetti et al., 2011; Scheirer & Rezmovic, 1983). These reviews, spanning several domains, reveal inconsistency in terms of operationally defining fidelity of implementation, data sources used, and analytic strategies. More recent reviews also reveal a tendency for researchers to measure structural aspects of implementation (e.g., adherence or quantity) rather than quality (e.g., Downer & Yazejian, 2013; Sanetti et al., 2011) and failure to analyze fidelity data in relation to measured innovation outcomes (Downer & Yazejian, 2013; Missett & Foster, 2015).

Now, there is momentum toward convergence in three areas: (a) the importance of identifying core components, (b) categories of influential factors, and (c) the definition of fidelity of implementation (enactment of an innovation compared to a model or theoretical ideal). However, given that the conversations underlying these points of agreement have taken place over decades, we need to find ways to move more quickly, more coherently, and more collaboratively. We still have far to go with regard to describing innovations and the factors that influence them, reconciling intersections of theoretical frameworks, and moving forward with consistent or complementary terminology, measures, and analytic strategies. The work of the past 100 years, accelerated by the increased focus on implementation in the past 20 years, gives us much to build on; it is there for the taking. With greater clarity about language and shared conceptual frameworks, we will be able to compare results and accumulate knowledge about the innovations we are studying and their abilities to generate desired outcomes for learners (Century & Cassata, 2014; Darrow, Goodson, & Boulay, 2014).

BROADENING OUR CONCEPTION OF EVIDENCE

It may be easier to progress toward agreement on common frameworks and processes than on some of the thornier, more philosophical issues, such as the fidelity-adaptation debate and the closely related question, *what is evidence*? These two issues are, in fact ultimately linked. The reasoning in favor of enacting innovations with fidelity is that once there is evidence that an innovation works, we must try to replicate the effects (Chambers et al., 2013). In contrast, some argue for a broader definition of legitimate, credible evidence and assert that because schools are social systems within which knowledge is socially constructed, school improvement should not focus on strict replication (Cousins & Leithwood, 1983, as cited in Helmsley Brown, & Sharp, 2003, p. 14).

Evidence Is Relative to Context

While one may assume that innovations designated as "evidence-based" are indisputably of value, in reality, evidence is relative. There are two important caveats to the "evidence-based" designation. First, evidence established in an efficacy study is grounded on the assumption that the intervention will be implemented with the experimental (treatment) group in the ideal manner. Second, RCT evidence, by its nature, is *relative* to what was happening in the control or comparison group in a particular study (Gennetian et al., 2002). Given that effectiveness studies often compare treatment to business-as-usual conditions, we need to acknowledge that what is effective now may not continue to be effective in 5 years—even if enacted in the ideal over time—if the business-as-usual condition undergoes a change (Lemons, Fuchs, Gilbert, Fuchs, 2014).

Second, the widely recognized reality that actual implementation is *always* different from the theoretical ideal is a reminder that evidence coming out of efficacy and effectiveness studies, while informative, is not definitive. Chambers et al. (2013) question why we "reify early phase interventions tested in the most artificial settings" (p. 3), pointing out that doing so leads to an overreliance on quality assurance practices and, in turn, to missed opportunities for ongoing improvement through innovation customization and optimization. With innovation use in ordinary settings as the end goal in mind, education research will benefit from a shift in the conception of educational innovations as static "evidence-based entities" to be replicated, toward the recognition that innovation enactment is a dynamic process influenced by and adapted to the local context.

Even within the medical field, the push to replicate treatments is criticized. Naylor (1995) refers to the grey zones of practice where good clinical medicine blends "the art of uncertainty with the science of probability" (p. 841). Good clinicians use what Feinstein and Horwitz (1997) call "soft" information (e.g., severity and nature of the symptoms, associated diseases, rate of symptom growth) to make decisions; the authors assert that "a good clinician constantly uses this 'soft' information for diverse clinical decisions" (p. 531). Soft information is like the factors that affect implementation—the very kind of information that implementation research seeks to capture. While RCTs provide clinicians with information that is helpful for the average patient, the information will not apply to all patients (Feinstein & Horwitz, 1997). There simply is not an "average" patient. Nor, we assert, is there an average teacher, school, district, or system.

In medical clinical settings, "what works" is a matter of judgment that weighs, judges, and considers RCT findings in context (Morrison, 2001). The same is true in education, where scholars increasingly recognize that "evidence" means different things to different innovation enactors (Coburn & Talbert, 2006). Sanderson (2003) argues that "the question for teachers is not simply 'what is effective,' but rather, more broadly it is, 'what is appropriate for these children in these circumstances'" (as quoted in Oancea & Pring, 2008, p. 23).

Embracing Complexity

Research in highly controlled settings is driven by the desire to reduce variability in order to draw clear conclusions about results. As acknowledged earlier, there is a place for this kind of study in the spectrum of implementation research. However, when moving from highly controlled conditions to ordinary settings, rather than try to *manage* the many influences that shape an end user's implementation, the field needs to *embrace* that complexity. To truly understand how an innovation will be effective in a new context and/or over time, we need techniques that illuminate the ways that innovations are associated with desired outcomes by recognizing and accounting for complexity rather than reducing it (Burns & Knox, 2011; Snyder, 2013). To do otherwise denies the reality of complex social systems, where individuals interact, feedback loops exist, one action influences another, and individuals in the system are in constant development as a function of their ongoing experiences.

Designs that isolate, decontextualize, and simplify issues of complexity decrease the applicability of implementation research results. "The key problems of today are 'wicked'" (Kessler & Glasgow, 2011, p. 638), and to solve them, we need to put all of our methodologies to work and recognize that some questions of implementation research can be fully addressed only with all of the techniques we have on hand and those not yet developed. The evidence-based movement carries the suggestion that solving problems of educational improvement is akin to a linear algorithm or technical fix. In such a paradigm, the problem space is knowable, all variables in the model that contribute to the outcome can be defined, and variables are treated largely as independent of one another (Preskill, Gopal, Mack, & Cook, 2014; Snyder, 2013). Yet educational innovations of any type are, in reality, much more complex. In systems, independent variables are not all knowable and do not behave uniformly at all times; rather, both end users and innovations are co-evolving (Nespor, 2002; Preskill et al., 2014). New innovation designs and associated analytic approaches that account for this complexity may provide much-needed insight into what it truly takes to realize lasting educational change.

Technological advances in data analysis emerging in the life sciences, economics, and systems science have something to offer education researchers, who seek to solve equally but differently complex problems (Lemke & Sabelli, 2008). For example, Burke et al. (2015) outline three nascent methodological approaches for implementation research—system dynamics modeling, agent-based modeling, and social network analysis—that may capture the complexity of the problem space of educational innovations. These methods enable modeling aspects of complex systems such as delays between cause and effect, nonlinear relationships between variables, and unanticipated outcomes—analyses that are limited by those using traditional methodological approaches. While such methods are not appropriate for the purpose of predicting what will happen, they are useful for describing and theorizing what has happened or what is happening currently, and for providing a useful paradigm for understanding the complex landscape where we work to improve education

(Morrison, 2010). A commitment to looking beyond the current borders of education research will be essential for the creation of new approaches to managing and analyzing implementation data in increasingly meaningful ways.

Accumulating Knowledge

A commitment to embracing complexity, hand in hand with the field's convergence on a component approach to describing innovations and frameworks for organizing influential factors, can enable us to accumulate knowledge and move toward our ambitious shared goal of making education better. Innovations today are commonly viewed as proprietary packages, but they share many of the same essential elements. Research that views innovations as combinations of components can contribute to learning not only about a specific innovation but also about its components. Mowbray et al. (2003) suggest an empirical approach of deconstructing innovation models and systematically testing the impact of key ingredients across sites. Similarly, Abry et al. (2015) envision a future where "evidence of active ingredients accumulates" and contributes to unified theories of change (p. 334). Similarly, the field can accumulate knowledge about the role of influential factors, ranging from characteristics of the innovation itself to organizational and environmental forces.

LOOKING FORWARD, LEARNING FROM THE PAST

We might do well to learn from the fields of medicine, public health, health care, psychology, prevention science, and other psychosocial disciplines, where the implementation research movement is alive and well. In the past 10 years alone, two cross-disciplinary communities of implementation researchers (the Society for Implementation Research Collaboration and the Global Implementation Initiative) were founded; an open-access peer-reviewed journal, *Implementation Science*, was launched; a yearly conference focusing on dissemination and implementation was instituted; and initiatives were launched to locate, catalogue, and rate measures associated with the CFIR framework (Damschroder et al., 2009). This is a pivotal time when the field can continue to diverge or decide to come together with coherency. Change is about changing mindsets (Joseph & Reigeluth, 2010). As Coburn wrote about rethinking scale in 2003, "scaling up" is more than a process of spreading an activity structure; it is also about spreading underlying beliefs and norms. In the field of education research, it is time that we put our own findings into practice to change ourselves.

REFERENCES

Abry, T., Hulleman, C. S., & Rimm-Kaufman, S. E. (2015). Using indices of fidelity to intervention core components to identify program active ingredients. *American Journal of Evaluation, 36,* 320–338. doi:10.1177/1098214014557009

Abry, T., Rimm-Kaufman, S. E., Larsen, R., & Brewer, A. (2013). The influence of fidelity of implementation on teacher-student interaction quality in the context of a randomized controlled trial of the Responsive Classroom approach. *Journal of School Psychology, 51,* 437–453.

Adelman, H., & Taylor, L. (2003). On sustainability of project innovations as systemic change. *Journal of Educational and Psychological Consultation, 14,* 1–25.

Agodini, R., Harris, B., Atkins-Burnett, S., Heaviside, S., Novak, T., & Murphy, R. (2009). *Achievement effects of four early elementary school math curricula: Findings from first graders in 39 schools* (NCEE 2009-4052). Washington, DC: National Center for Education Evaluation and Regional Assistance, Institute of Education Sciences, U.S. Department of Education. Retrieved from http://ies.ed.gov/ncee/pubs/20114001/pdf/20114001.pdf

Aladjem, D., LeFloch, K., Zhang, Y., Kurki, A., Boyle, A., Taylor, J., . . . Fashola, O. (2006). *Models matter—The final report of the National Longitudinal Evaluation of Comprehensive School Reform* (U.S. Department of Education PR/Award Number R306S0000012). Washington, DC: American Institutes for Research. Retrieved from http://eric.ed.gov/?id=ED499198

Anderson, S. (1997). Teacher change: Revisiting the concerns-based adoption model. *Curriculum Inquiry, 27,* 331–367.

Anson, R. (1994). *Systemic reform: Perspectives on personalizing education* (OR-94-3308). Washington, DC: Office of Research, Office of Educational Research and Improvement.

Backer, T. (1991). Knowledge utilization: The third wave. *Knowledge: Creation, Diffusion, Utilization, 12,* 225–240.

Ball, D., & Cohen, D. (1996). What is: Or might be: The role of curriculum materials in teacher learning and instructional reform? *Educational Researcher, 25*(9), 6–8.

Barab, S. A., & Luehmann, A. L. (2003). Building sustainable science curriculum: Acknowledging and accommodating local adaptation. *Science Education, 87,* 454–467.

Basch, C. (1984). Research on disseminating and implementing health education programs in schools. *Journal of School Health, 54*(6), 57–66.

Bell, P. (2004). On the theoretical breadth of design-based research in education. *Educational Psychologist, 39,* 243–253. doi:10.1207/s15326985ep3904_6

Benner, G., Nelson, J., Stage, S., & Ralston, N. (2011). The influence of fidelity of implementation on the reading outcomes of middle school students experiencing reading difficulties. *Remedial and Special Education, 32,* 79–88.

Berman, P. (1981). Educational change: An implementation paradigm. In R. Lehming & M. Kane (Eds.), *Improving schools* (pp. 253–286). London, England: Sage.

Berman, P., & McLaughlin, M. W. (1976). Implementation of educational innovation. *Educational Forum, 40,* 345–370.

Berman, P., & McLaughlin, M. W. (1978, May). *Federal programs supporting educational change: Vol. 8. Implementing and sustaining innovations* (Prepared for the U.S. Office of Education Department of Health, Education, and Welfare). Retrieved from https://www.rand.org/content/dam/rand/pubs/reports/2006/R1589.8.pdf

Best, A., Hiatt, R. A., & Norman, C. D. (2008). Knowledge integration: Conceptualizing communications in cancer control systems. *Patient Education and Counseling, 71,* 319–327. doi:10.1016/j.pec.2008.02.013

Billing, S., Sherry, L., & Havelock, B. (2005). Challenge 98: Sustaining the work of a regional technology integration initiative. *British Journal of Educational Technology, 36,* 987–1003.

Blakely, C. H., Mayer, J. P., Gottschalk, R. G., Schmitt, N., Davidson, W. S., Roitman, D. B., . . . Emshoff, J. G. (1987). The fidelity-adaptation debate: Implications for the implementation of public sector social programs. *American Journal of Community Psychology, 15,* 253–268. doi:0091-0562/87/0600-0253

Brown, A. L. (1992). Design experiments: Theoretical and methodological challenges in creating complex interventions in classroom settings. *Journal of the Learning Sciences, 2,* 141–178.

Brown, S. A., Pitvorec, K., Ditto, C., & Kelso, C. R. (2009). Reconceiving fidelity of implementation: An investigation of elementary whole-number lessons. *Journal for Research in Mathematics Education, 40,* 363–395.

Burke, J. G., Lich, K. H., Neal, J. W., Meissner, H. I., Yonas, M., & Mabry, P. L. (2015). Enhancing dissemination and implementation research using systems science methods. *International Journal of Behavioral Medicine, 22,* 283–291.

Burnes, B. (2005). Complexity theories and organizational change. *International Journal of Management Reviews, 7*(2), 73–90.

Burns, A., & Knox, J. (2011). Classrooms as complex adaptive systems: A relational model. *Electronic Journal for English as a Second Language, 15*(1), 1–25.

Buttolph, D. (1992). A new look at adaptation. *Knowledge: Creation, Diffusion, Utilization, 13,* 460–470.

Buxton, C. A., Allexsaht-Snider, M., Kayumova, S., Aghsaleh, R., Choi, Y.-J., & Cohen, A. (2015). Teacher agency and professional learning: Rethinking fidelity of implementations as multiplicities of enactment. *Journal of Research in Science Teaching, 52,* 489–502. doi:10.1002/tea.21223

Carroll, C., Patterson, M., Wood, S., Booth, A., Rick, J., & Balain, S. (2007). A conceptual framework for implementation fidelity. *Implementation Science, 2,* 40. doi:10.1186/1748-5908-2-40

Caswell, H. L. (1950). *Curriculum improvement in public school systems.* New York, NY: Bureau of Publications, Teachers College, Columbia University.

Century, J., & Cassata, A. (2014). Conceptual foundations for measuring the implementation of educational innovations. In L. Sanetti & T. Kratochwill (Eds.), *Treatment integrity: A foundation for evidence-based practice in applied psychology* (pp. 81–108). Washington, DC: American Psychological Association.

Century, J., Cassata, A., Rudnick, M., & Freeman, C. (2012). Measuring enactment of innovations and the factors that affect implementation and sustainability: Moving toward common language and shared conceptual understanding. *Journal of Behavioral Health Services & Research, 39,* 343–361.

Century, J., & Levy, A. (2002). *Research the sustainability of reform: Factors that contribute to or inhibit program endurance* (Cross-site report). Newton, MA: Center for Science Education, Education Development Center.

Century, J., Rudnick, M., & Freeman, C. (2010). A framework for measuring fidelity of implementation: A foundation for shared language and accumulation of knowledge. *American Journal of Evaluation, 31,* 199–218.

Chambers, D., Glasgow, R., & Stange, K. (2013). The dynamic sustainability framework: Addressing the paradox of sustainment amid ongoing change. *Implementation Science, 8,* 117.

Cho, J. (1998, April). *Rethinking curriculum implementation: Paradigms, models, and teachers' work.* Paper presented at the annual meeting of the American Educational Research Association, San Diego, CA. Retrieved from http://files.eric.ed.gov/fulltext/ED421767.pdf

Clark, D., & Guba, E. (1965). *An examination of potential change roles in education.* Washington, DC: National Education Association, Center for the Study of Instruction. Retrieved from http://eric.ed.gov/?id=ED043226

Clements, D., Sarama, J., Wolfe, C., & Spitler, M. E. (2015). Sustainability of a scale-up intervention in early mathematics: A longitudinal evaluation of implementation fidelity. *Early Education and Development, 26,* 427–449. doi:10.1080/10409289.2015.968242

Coburn, C. E. (2003). Rethinking scale: Moving beyond numbers to deep and lasting change. *Educational Researcher, 32*(6), 3–12.

Coburn, C. E., & Talbert, J. E. (2006). Conceptions of evidence use in school districts: Mapping the terrain. *American Journal of Education, 112,* 469–495.

Cohen, D. K. (1975). The value of social experiments. In A. M. Rivlin & P. M. Timpane (Eds.), *Planned variation in education: Should we give up or try harder?* (pp. 147–175). Washington, DC: Brookings Institution Press.

Cohen, D. K., & Ball, D. L. (1990). Relations between policy and practice: A commentary. *Educational Evaluation and Policy Analysis, 12,* 331–338.

Cohen, D. K., & Ball, D. L. (1999). *Instruction, capacity, and improvement* (CPRE Research Reports). Retrieved from http://repository.upenn.edu/cpre_researchreports/8

Collins, A., Joseph, D., & Bielaczyc, K. (2004). Design research: Theoretical and methodological issues. *Journal of the Learning Sciences, 13,* 15–42.

Confrey, J., Castro-Filho, J., & Wilhelm, J. (2000). Implementation research as a means to link systematic reform and applied psychology in mathematics education. *Educational Psychologist, 35,* 179–191. doi:10.1207/S15326985EP3503_4

Cook, T. D. (2005). Emergent principles for the design, implementation and analysis of cluster-based experiments in social science. In R. Boruch (Ed.), *Place randomized trials: Experimental tests of public policy* (pp. 176–198). Thousand Oaks, CA: Sage.

Cooper, H., & Hedges, L. V. (2009). Research synthesis as a scientific process. In H. Cooper, L. Hedges, & J. Valentine (Eds.), *The handbook of research synthesis and meta-analysis* (pp. 3–16). New York, NY: Sage.

Cordray, D. S., & Hulleman, C. (2009, June). *Assessing intervention fidelity: Models, methods and modes of analysis.* Paper presented at the Institute of Education Sciences 2009 Research Conference, Washington, DC. Retrieved from https://ies.ed.gov/director/conferences/09ies_conference/presentations/transcripts/presentation5.pdf

Cordray, D., Pion, G., Brandt, C., Molefe, A., & Toby, M. (2012). *The impact of the Measures of Academic Progress (MAP) program on student reading achievement* (NCEE 2013-4000). Washington, DC: National Center for Educational Evaluation and Regional Assistance, Institute of Education Sciences, U.S. Department of Education.

Damschroder, L., Aron, D., Keith, R., Kirsh, S., Alexander, J., & Lower, J. (2009). Fostering implementation of health services research findings into practice: A consolidated framework for advancing implementation science. *Implementation Science, 4,* 50.

Dane, A. V., & Schneider, B. H. (1998). Program integrity in primary and early secondary prevention: Are implementation effects out of control? *Clinical Psychology Review, 18,* 23–45. doi:0272-7358/98

Darrow, C. L. (2013). The effectiveness and precision of intervention fidelity measures in preschool intervention research. *Early Education and Development, 24,* 1137–1160. doi:10.1080/10409289.2013.765786

Darrow, C. L., Goodson, B., & Boulay, B. (2014, March). *Systematizing the measurement and reporting of intervention delivery in education research.* Poster presented at the Spring Conference of the Society for Research on Educational Effectiveness, Washington, DC. Retrieved from https://www.sree.org/conferences/2014s/program/downloads/abstracts/1090.pdf

Davidson, M., Fields, M., & Yang, J. (2009). A randomized trial study of a preschool literacy curriculum: The importance of implementation. *Journal of Research on Educational Effectiveness, 2,* 177–208.

Dearing, J. W. (2008). Evolution of diffusion and dissemination theory. *Journal of Public Health Management & Practice, 14,* 99–108.

Dearing, J. W. (2009, June 5). Applying diffusion of innovation theory to intervention development. *Research on Social Work Practice, 19,* 503–518. doi:10.1177/1049731509335569

Dearing, J. W., & Kee, K. F. (2012). Historical roots of dissemination science. In R. Brownson, G. Colditz, & E. Proctor (Eds.), *Dissemination and implementation research in health: Translating science to practice* (pp. 55–71). Oxford, England: Oxford University Press.

DeBarger, A., Choppin, J., Beauvineau, Y., & Moorthy, S. (2013). Designing for productive adaptations of curriculum interventions. *Yearbook of the National Society for the Study of Education, 112*, 298–319.

Desimone, L. (2002). How can comprehensive school reform models be successfully implemented? *Review of Educational Research, 72*, 433–479.

Dhillon, S., Darrow, C., & Meyers, C. (2015). Introduction to implementation fidelity. In C. Meyers & W. C. Brandt (Eds.), *Implementation fidelity in education research: Designer and evaluator considerations* (pp. 8–22). New York, NY: Routledge.

Domitrovich, C. E., Bradshaw, C. P., Poduska, J. M., Hoagwood, K., Buckley, J. A., Olin, S., & Ialongo, N. (2008). Maximizing the implementation quality of evidence-based preventive interventions in schools: A conceptual framework. *Advances in School Mental Health Promotion, 1*(3), 6–28.

Domitrovich, C. E., Gest, S. D., Jones, D., Gill, S., & DeRousie, R. M. S. (2010). Implementation quality: Lessons learned in the context of the Head Start REDI trial. *Early Childhood Research Quarterly, 25*, 284–298. doi:10.1016/j.ecresq.2010.04.001

Domitrovich, C. E., & Greenberg, M. (2000). The study of implementation: Current findings from effective programs that prevent mental disorders in school-aged children. *Journal of Educational and Psychological Consultation, 11*, 193–221.

Donaldson, S. I. (2001). Mediator and moderator analysis in program development. In S. Sussman (Ed.), *Handbook of program development for health behavior research and practice* (pp. 470–500). Thousand Oaks, CA: Sage.

Downer, J., & Yazejian, N. (2013). *Measuring the quality and quantity of implementation in early childhood interventions* (OPRE Research Brief OPRE 2013-12). Washington, DC: U.S. Department of Health and Human Services. Retrieved from http://www.research-connections.org/childcare/resources/25564/pdf

Dunst, C., Trivette, C., & Raab, M. (2013). An implementation science framework for conceptualizing and operationalizing fidelity in early childhood intervention studies. *Journal of Early Intervention, 35*(2), 85–101.

Durlak, J. A. (2010). The importance of doing well in whatever you do: A commentary on the special section, "Implementation Research in Early Childhood Education." *Early Childhood Research Quarterly, 25*, 348–357. doi:10.1016/j.ecresq.2010.03.003

Durlak, J. A. (2015). Studying program implementation is not easy but it is essential. *Prevention Science, 16*, 1123–1127.

Durlak, J. A., & DuPre, E. P. (2008). Implementation matters: A review of research on the influence of implementation on program outcomes and the factors affecting implementation. *American Journal of Community Psychology, 41*, 327–350. doi:10.1007/s10464-008-9165-0

Dusenbury, L., Brannigan, R., Falco, M., & Hansen, W. B. (2003). A review of research on fidelity of implementation: Implications for drug abuse prevention in school settings. *Health Education Research, 18*, 237–246.

Ellsworth, J. (2000). *Surviving change: A survey of educational change models.* Washington, DC: Office of Educational Research and Improvement. Retrieved from http://eric.ed.gov/?id=ED443417

Elmore, R. F. (1996). Getting to scale with good educational practice. *Harvard Educational Review, 66*(1), 1–26.

Fairchild, A., & MacKinnon, D. P. (2009). A general model for testing mediation and moderation effects. *Prevention Science, 10*(2), 87–99.

Feinstein, A., & Horwitz, R. (1997). Problems in the "evidence" of "evidence-based medicine." *American Journal of Medicine, 103*, 529–535.

Fixsen, D. L., Naoom, S. F., Blasé, K. A., Friedman, R. M., & Wallace, F. (2005). *Implementation research: A synthesis of the literature.* Tampa, FL: University of South

Florida, Louis de la Parte Florida Mental Health Institute, The National Implementation Research Network (FMHI Publication #231). Retrieved from http://nirn.fpg.unc.edu/resources/implementation-research-synthesis-literature

Fogleman, J., McNeill, K. L., & Krajcik, J. (2011). Examining the effect of teachers' adaptations of a middle school science inquiry-oriented curriculum unit on student learning. *Journal of Research in Science Teaching, 48*, 149–169.

Forbes, C. T., & Davis, E. A. (2010). Curriculum design for inquiry: Preservice elementary teachers' mobilization and adaptation of science curriculum materials. *Journal of Research in Science Teaching, 47*, 365–387.

Forman, S. G., Shapiro, E. S., Codding, R. S., Gonzales, J. E., Reddy, L. A., Rosenfeld, S. A., . . . Stoiber, K. C. (2013). Implementation science and school psychology. *School Psychology Quarterly, 28*(2), 77–100.

Fullan, M. (1994). Coordinating top-down and bottom-up strategies for educational reform. In R. Anson (Ed.), *Systemic reform: Perspectives on personalizing education* (pp. 1–7). Washington, DC: Office of Educational Research and Improvement.

Fullan, M. (2007). *The new meaning of educational change.* New York, NY: Teachers College Press.

Fullan, M., & Pomfret, A. (1977). Research on curriculum and instruction implementation. *Review of Educational Research, 47*, 335–397.

Gennetian, L., Bos, J., & Morris, P. (2002). *Using instrumental variables analysis to learn more from social policy experiments* (MDRC Working Paper on Research Methodology). New York, NY: Manpower Demonstration Research Corporation. Retrieved from http://mdrc.org/sites/default/files/full_599.pdf

Greco, P., & Eisenberg, J. (1993). Changing physicians' practices. *New England Journal of Medicine, 329*, 1271–1274.

Green, L. W., Ottoson, J. M., García, C., & Hiatt, R. A. (2009). Diffusion theory and knowledge dissemination, utilization, and integration in public health. *Annual Review of Public Health, 30*, 151–174. doi:10.1146/annurev.publhealth.031308.100049

Greenhalgh, T., Robert, G., MacFarlane, F., Bate, P., & Kyriakidou, O. (2004). Diffusion of innovations in service organizations: Systematic review and recommendations. *Milbank Quarterly, 82*, 581–629.

Gresham, F., Gansle, K., Noell, G., Cohen, S., & Rosenblum, S. (1993). Treatment integrity of school-based behavioral intervention studies: 1980–1990. *School Psychology Review, 22*, 254–272.

Grimshaw, J. (1999). Getting evidence into practice. *Effective Health Care, 5*, 1–16.

Hall, G. E., & Hord, S. (2015). *Implementing change: Patterns, principles and potholes* (4th ed.). New York, NY: Pearson.

Hall, G. E., & Loucks, S. F. (1975). Levels of use of the innovation: A framework for analyzing innovation adoption. *Journal of Teacher Education, 26*(1), 52–56.

Hall, G. E., & Loucks, S. F. (1978a). *Innovation configurations: Analyzing the adaptations of innovations* (Procedures for Adopting Educational Innovations Program, Research and Development Center for Teacher Education, University of Texas at Austin). Washington, DC: National Institute of Education. Retrieved from http://eric.ed.gov/?id=ED189074

Hall, G. E., & Loucks, S. F. (1978b). Teacher concerns as a basis for facilitating and personalizing staff development. *Teachers College Record, 80*(1), 36–53.

Halle, T., Metz, A., & Martinez-Beck, I. (Eds.). (2013). *Applying implementation science in early childhood programs and systems.* Baltimore, MD: Paul H. Brookes.

Hamilton, J., & Feldman, J. (2014). Planning a program evaluation: Matching methodology to program status. In J. M. Spector, M. D. Merrill, J. Elen, & M. J. Bishop (Eds.), *Handbook of research on educational communications and technology* (pp. 249–256). New York, NY: Springer.

Hansen, W. B. (2014). Measuring fidelity. In Z. Sloboda & H. Petras (Eds.), *Defining prevention science* (pp. 335–359). New York, NY: Springer.

Harn, B., Parisi, D., & Stoolmiller, M. (2013). Balancing fidelity with flexibility and fit: What do we really know about fidelity of implementation in schools? *Exceptional Children, 79,* 181–193.

Helmsley Brown, J., & Sharp, C. (2003). The use of research to improve professional practice: A systematic review of the literature. *Oxford Review of Education, 29,* 449–471.

Hill, H. C., Blazar, D., & Lynch, K. (2015). Resources for teaching: Examining personal and institutional predictors of high-quality instruction. *AERA Open, 1*(4), 1–23. doi:10.1177/2332858415617703

Honig, M. (2006). Complexity and policy implementation: Challenges and opportunities for the field. In M. Honig (Ed.), *New directions in education policy implementation: Confronting complexity* (pp. 1–23). Albany: State University of New York Press.

Hord, S. M., Rutherford, W. L., Huling-Austin, L., & Hall, G. E. (1987). *Taking charge of change.* Alexandria, VA: ASCD. Retrieved from http://files.eric.ed.gov/fulltext/ED282876.pdf

House, E. (1981). Three perspectives on innovation: Technological, political and cultural. In R. Lehming & M. Kane (Eds.), *Improving schools* (pp. 17–41). London, England: Sage.

Hulleman, C. S., & Cordray, D. S. (2009). Moving from the lab to the field: The role of fidelity and achieved relative intervention strength. *Journal of Research on Educational Effectiveness, 2,* 88–110. doi:10.1080/19345740802539325

Hulleman, C. S., Rimm-Kaufman, S. E., & Abry, T. (2013). Innovative methodologies to explore implementation: Whole-part-whole—construct validity, measurement, and analytical issues for intervention fidelity assessment in education research. In T. Halle, A. Metz, & I. Martinez-Beck (Eds.), *Applying implementations science in early childhood programs and systems* (pp. 65–93). Baltimore, MD: Brookes.

Hutchinson, J. R., & Huberman, M. (1994). Knowledge dissemination and use in science and mathematics education: A literature review. *Journal of Science Education and Technology, 3*(1), 27–47.

Inbar, D. (1996). *Planning for innovation in education.* Paris, France: UNESCO, International Institute for Educational Planning. Retrieved from http://unesdoc.unesco.org/images/0011/001119/111952Eb.pdf

Irwin, M., & Supplee, L. (2012). Directions in implementation research: Methods for behavioral and social science. *Journal of Behavioral Health Services & Research, 39*(4), 399–342.

Joseph, R., & Reigeluth, C. (2010). The systemic change process in education: A conceptual framework. *Contemporary Educational Technology, 1,* 97–117.

Justice, L., Mashburn, A., Pence, K., & Wiggins, A. (2008). Experimental evaluation of a preschool language curriculum: Influence on children's expressive language skills. *Journal of Speech, Language, and Hearing Research, 51,* 983–1001.

Kelly, J., Heckman, T., Stevenson, L., Williams, P., Hays, R., Leonard, N., . . . Neumann, M. (2000). Transfer of research-based HIV prevention interventions to community service providers: Fidelity and adaptation. *AIDS Education and Prevention, 12*(Suppl. 5), 87–98.

Kessler, R., & Glasgow, R. E. (2011). A proposal to speed translation of healthcare research into practice: Dramatic change is needed. *American Journal of Preventative Medicine, 40,* 637–644.

Kinnunen, J. (1996). Gabriel Tarde as a founding father of innovation diffusion research. *ACTA Sociologica, 39,* 431–442.

Knapp, M. S. (1997). Between systemic reforms and the mathematics and science classroom: The dynamics of innovation, implementation and professional learning. *Review of Educational Research, 67,* 227–266.

Kurki, A., Boyle, A., & Aladjem, D. (2006). Implementation: Measuring and explaining the fidelity of CSR implementation. *Journal of Education for Students Placed at Risk, 11,* 255–277.

LaForce, M., Noble, E., King, H., Holt, S., & Century, J. (2014). *The 8 elements of inclusive STEM high schools.* Chicago, IL: Outlier Research & Evaluation, CEMSE | University of Chicago. Retrieved from http://d30clwvkkpiyjx.cloudfront.net/S3/Elements_Findings.pdf

Lehming, R., & Kane, M. (Eds.). (1981). *Improving schools: Using what we know.* Beverly Hills, CA: Sage.

Leithwood, K., & Montgomery, D. (1980). Evaluating program implementation. *Evaluation Review, 4,* 193–214.

Lemke, J. L., & Sabelli, N. H. (2008). Complex systems and educational change: Toward a new research agenda. *Educational Philosophy and Theory, 40*(1), 112–123. doi:10.1111/j.1469-5812.2007.00401.x.

Lemons, C., Fuchs, D., Gilbert, J., & Fuchs, L. (2014). Evidence-based practices in a changing world: Reconsidering the counterfactual in education research. *Educational Researcher, 43,* 242–252.

Lieber, J., Butera, G., Hanson, M., Palmer, S., Horn, E., Czaja, C., . . . Odom, S. (2009). Factors that influence the implementation of a new preschool curriculum: Implications for professional development. *Early Education and Development, 20,* 456–481.

Lieber, J., Hanson, M., Butera, G., Palmer, S., Horn, E., & Czaja, C. (2010). Do preschool teachers sustain their use of a new curriculum? *NHSA Dialog, 13,* 248–252.

Louis, K. S. (1992). Comparative perspectives on dissemination and knowledge use policies: Supporting school improvement. *Knowledge, 13,* 287–304.

Love, J. (1985). Knowledge transfer and utilization in education. *Review of Research in Education, 12,* 337–386.

Lynch, S., & O'Donnell, C. (2005, April). *"Fidelity of implementation" in implementation and scale-up research designs: Applications from four studies of innovative science curriculum materials and diverse populations.* Paper presented at the annual meeting of the American Educational Research Association, Montreal, Quebec, Canada. Retrieved from http://dodk12grants.org/Docs/AERA_GWU_Fidelity_4.12.05.pdf

Macklem, G. L. (2014). *Preventive mental health at school: Evidence-based services for students.* New York, NY: Springer Science and Business Media. doi:10.1007/978-1-4614-8609-1_10

Maitlis, S., & Sonenshein, S. (2010). Sensemaking in crisis and change: Inspiration and insights from Weick. *Journal of Management Studies, 47,* 551–580.

McCormick, L., Steckler, A., & McLeroy, K. (1995). Diffusion of innovations in schools: A study of adoption and implementation of school-based tobacco prevention curricula. *American Journal of Health Promotion, 9,* 210–219.

McGrew, J., Bond, G., Dietzen, L., & Salyers, M. (1994). Measuring the fidelity of implementation of a mental health program model. *Journal of Consulting and Clinical Psychology, 62,* 670–678.

McIntosh, K., Mercer, S., Hume, A., Frank, J., Turri, M., & Mathews, S. (2013). Factors related to sustained implementation of schoolwide positive behavior support. *Exceptional Children, 79,* 293–311.

McKenna, J., Flower, A., & Ciullo, S. (2014, April). Measuring fidelity to improve intervention effectiveness. *Intervention in School and Clinic, 50,* 15–21. doi:10.1177/1053451214532348

Meyer, A., & Goes, J. (1988). Organizational assimilation of innovations: A multilevel contextual analysis. *Academy of Management Journal, 31,* 897–923.

Meyers, D., Durlak, J., & Wandersman, A. (2012). The quality implementation framework: A synthesis of critical steps in the implementation process. *American Journal of Community Psychology, 50,* 462–480.

Michie, S., Fixsen, D., Grimshaw, J., & Eccles, M. (2009). Specifying and reporting complex behavior change interventions: The need for a scientific method. *Implementation Science, 40*(4), 1–6. doi:10.1185/1748-59098-4-40

Miles, M. (1998). Finding keys to school change: A 40-year odyssey. In A. Lieberman (Ed.), *The roots of educational change: International handbook of educational change* (pp. 37–69). Dordrecht, Netherlands: Springer.

Missett, T., & Foster, L. (2015). Searching for evidence-based practice: A survey of empirical studies on curricular interventions measuring and reporting fidelity of implementation published during 2004–2013. *Journal of Advanced Academics, 26,* 96–111.

Moncher, F., & Prinz, R. (1991). Treatment fidelity in outcome studies. *Clinical Psychology Review, 11,* 247–266.

Moore, J., Bumbarger, B., & Cooper, B. (2013). Examining adaptations of evidence-based programs in natural contexts. *Journal of Primary Prevention, 34,* 147–161.

Morrison, K. (2001). Randomised controlled trials for evidence-based education: Some problems in judging "what works." *Evaluation & Research in Education, 15*(2), 69–83.

Morrison, K. (2010). Complexity theory, school leadership and management: Questions for theory and practice. *Educational Management Administration & Leadership, 38,* 374–393. doi:10.1177/1741143209359711

Moulin, J., Sabater-Hernandez, D., Fernandez-Llimos, F., & Benrimaj, S. (2015). A systematic review of implementation frameworks of innovations in healthcare and resulting generic implementation framework. *Health Research Policy and Systems, 13,* 16.

Mowbray, C., Holter, M., Teague, G., & Bybee, D. (2003). Fidelity criteria: Development, measurement and validation. *American Journal of Evaluation, 24,* 315–340.

Naylor, C. D. (1995). Grey zones of clinical practice: Some limits to evidence-based medicine. *The Lancet, 345*(8953), 840–842.

Nelson, M., Cordray, D., Hulleman, C., Darrow, C., & Sommer, E. (2012). A procedure for assessing intervention fidelity in experiments testing educational and behavioral interventions. *Journal of Behavioral Health Services & Research, 39,* 374–396.

Nespor, J. (2002). Networks and contexts of reform. *Journal of Educational Change, 3,* 365–382.

Oancea, A., & Pring, R. (2008). The importance of being thorough: On systematic accumulations of "what works" in education research. *Journal of Philosophy of Education, 42*(Suppl. 1), 15–39.

Odom, S. (2009). The tie that binds: Evidence-based practice, implementation science, and outcomes for children. *Topics in Early Childhood Special Education, 29*(1), 53–61.

Odom, S., Fleming, K., Diamond, K., Lieber, J., Hanson, M., Butera, G., . . . Marquis, J. (2010). Examining different forms of implementation in early childhood curriculum research. *Early Childhood Research Quarterly, 25,* 314–328.

O'Donnell, C. (2008). Defining, conceptualizing, and measuring fidelity of implementation and its relationship to outcomes in K–12 curriculum intervention research. *Review of Educational Research, 78,* 33–84.

Pas, E. T., & Bradshaw, C. P. (2012). Examining the association between implementation and outcomes: State-wide scale-up of school-wide positive behavior intervention and supports. *Journal of Behavioral Health Services & Research, 39,* 417–433. doi:10.1007/s11414-012-9290-2

Peile, E. (2004). Reflections from medical practice: Balancing evidence-based practice with practice-based evidence. In G. Thomas & R. Pring (Eds.), *Evidence-based practice in education* (pp. 102–118). Maidenhead, England: Open University Press.

Pence, K., Justice, L., & Wiggins, A. (2008). Preschool teachers' fidelity in implementing a comprehensive language-rich curriculum. *Language, Speech, and Hearing Services in Schools, 39,* 329–341.

Penuel, W. R., & Fishman, B. J. (2012). Large-scale science education intervention research we can use. *Journal of Research in Science Teaching, 49,* 281–304. doi:10.1002/tea.21001

Penuel, W. R., Fishman, B. J., Cheng, B. H., & Sabelli, N. (2011). Organizing research and development at the intersection of learning, implementation, and design. *Educational Researcher, 40,* 331–337. doi:10.3102/0013189X11421826

Penuel, W. R., Fishman, B. J., Yamaguchi, R., & Gallagher, L. (2007). What makes professional development effective? Strategies that foster curriculum implementation. *American Educational Research Journal, 44,* 921–958.

Penuel, W. R., Phillips, R. S., & Harris, C. J. (2014). Analysing teachers' curriculum implementation from integrity and actor-oriented perspectives. *Journal of Curriculum Studies, 46,* 751–777. doi:10.1080/00220272.2014.921841

Peters, D. H., Adam, T., Alonge, O., Agyepong, I. A., & Tran, N. (2013). Implementation research: What it is and how to do it. *British Medical Journal, 347,* 1–7. doi:10.1136/bmj.f6753

Peterson, L., Homer, A., & Wonderlich, S. (1982). The integrity of independent variables in behavior analysis. *Journal of Applied Behavior Analysis, 15,* 477–492.

Peterson, S. (2013). Readiness to change: Effective implementation processes for meeting people where they are. In T. Halle, A. Metz, & I. Martinez-Beck (Eds.), *Applying implementation science in early childhood programs and systems* (pp. 43–64). Baltimore, MD: Brookes.

Popay, J., Roberts, H., Sowden, A., Petticrew, M., Arai, L., Rodgers, M., & Duffy, S. (2006). *Guidance on the conduct of narrative synthesis in systematic reviews: A product from the ESRC methods programme* (Version 1). Lancaster, England: Lancaster University. doi:10.13140/2.1.1018.4643

Preskill, H., Gopal, S., Mack, K., & Cook, J. (2014). *Evaluating complexity: Propositions for improving practice.* Retrieved from http://www.fsg.org/publications/evaluating-complexity

Raudenbush, S. W., & Bloom, H. S. (2015). *Learning about and from variation in program impacts using multi-site trials* (MDRC Working Papers on Research Methodology). Retrieved from http://www.mdrc.org/sites/default/files/learning_about_and_from_variation.pdf

Remillard, J. (2005). Key concepts in research on teachers' use of mathematics curricula. *Review of Educational Research, 75,* 211–246.

Rijsdijk, L. E., Bos, A. E. R., Lie, R., Leerlooijer, J. N., Eiling, E., Atema, V., . . . Ruiter, R. A. C. (2014). Implementation of The World Starts With Me, a comprehensive rights-based sex education programme in Uganda. *Health Education Research, 29,* 340–353. doi:10.1093/her/cyt108

Rogers, E. M. (1962). *Diffusion of innovations.* New York, NY: Free Press of Glencoe.

Rohrbach, L. A., Grana, R., Sussman, S., & Valente, T. W. (2006). Type II translation: Transporting prevention interventions from research to real-world settings. *Evaluation & the Health Professions, 29,* 302–333. doi:10.1177/0163278706290408

Rubio, D. M., Schoenbaum, E. E., Lee, L. S., Schteingart, D. E., Marantz, P. R., Anderson, K. E., . . . Esposito, K. (2010). Defining translational research: Implications for training. *Academic Medicine, 85,* 470–475. doi:10/1097/ACM.0b013e3181ccd618

Ruiz-Primo, M. (2005, April). *A multi-method and multi-source approach for studying fidelity of implementation.* Paper presented at the annual meeting of the American Educational Research Association, Montreal, Quebec, Canada. Retrieved from http://files.eric.ed.gov/fulltext/ED492864.pdf

Ryan, B., & Gross, N. C. (1943). The diffusion of hybrid seed corn in two Iowa communities. *Rural Sociology, 8,* 15–24.

Sanetti, L., Gritter, K., & Dobey, L. (2011). Treatment integrity of interventions with children in the school psychology literature from 1995 to 2008. *School Psychology Review, 40,* 72–84.

Sanetti, L., & Kratochwill, T. (2009). Toward developing a science of treatment integrity: Introduction to the special series. *School Psychology Review, 38*, 445–459.

Sashkin, M., & Egermeier, J. (1993). *School change models and processes: A review and synthesis of research and practice.* Washington, DC: Office of Educational Research and Improvement. Retrieved from http://eric.ed.gov/?id=ED362960.pdf

Sayfori, N. (2014). An alternative method of literature review: Systematic review in English language teaching research. *Procedia: Social and Behavioral Sciences, 98*, 1693–1697.

Scheirer, M. A., & Rezmovic, E. (1983). Measuring the degree of program implementation: A methodological review. *Evaluation Review, 7*, 599–633.

Scheirer, M. A., Shediac, M. C., & Cassady, C. E. (1995). Measuring the implementation of health promotion programs: The case of the Breast and Cervical Cancer Program in Maryland. *Health Education Research, 10*, 11–25.

Schulte, A., Easton, J., & Parker, J. (2009). Advances in treatment integrity research: Multidisciplinary perspectives on the conceptualization, measurement, and enhancement of treatment integrity. *School Psychology Review, 38*, 460–475.

Short, E. C. (1973). Knowledge production and utilization in curriculum: A special case of the general phenomenon. *Review of Educational Research, 43*, 237–301.

Sieber, S. (1981). Knowledge utilization in public education. In G. Thomas & R. Pring (Eds.), *Evidence-based practice in education* (pp. 115–167). Maidenhead, England: Open University Press.

Sikorski, L. (1976). *Factors influencing school change* (Final report). San Francisco, CA: Far West Lab for Educational Research and Development. Retrieved from http://eric.ed.gov/?id=ED129622

Smith, M., & O'Day, J. (1991). *Putting the pieces together: Systemic school reform* (CPRE policy brief). New Brunswick, NJ: Consortium for Policy Research in Education. Retrieved from http://eric.ed.gov/?id=ED343215

Smith, T., Cobb, P., Farran, D., Cordray, D., & Munter, C. (2013). Evaluating math recovery: Assessing the causal impact of a diagnostic tutoring program on student achievement. *American Educational Research Journal, 50*, 397–428.

Snyder, S. (2013). *The simple, the complicated, and the complex: Educational reform through the lens of complexity theory* (OECD Education Working Papers, No. 96). Paris: OECD Publishing. Retrieved from http://dx.doi.org/10.1787/5k3txnpt1lnr-en

Snyder, J., Bolin, F., & Zumwalt, K. (1992). Curriculum implementation. In P. W. Jackson (Ed.), *Handbook of research on curriculum: A project of the American Educational Research Association* (pp. 402–435). New York, NY: Macmillan.

Solomon, W., Ferritor, D., Haern, J., & Myers, E. (1973). *The development, use, and importance of instruments that validly and reliably assess the degrees to which experimental programs are implemented.* St. Ann, MO: CEMREL. Retrieved from http://eric.ed.gov/?id=ED129914

Song, M., & Herman, R. (2010). Critical issues and common pitfalls in designing and conducting impact studies in education: Lessons learned from the What Works Clearinghouse (Phase 1). *Educational Evaluation and Policy Analysis, 32*, 351–371. doi:10.3102/0162373710373389

Spillane, J., Reiser, B., & Reimer, T. (2002). Policy implementation and cognition: Reframing and refocusing implementation research. *Review of Educational Research, 72*, 387–431.

Stein, M. K., & Kaufman, J. (2010). Selecting and supporting the use of mathematics curricula at scale. *American Educational Research Journal, 47*, 663–693.

Stockard, J. (2010). An analysis of the fidelity implementation policies of the What Works Clearinghouse. *Current Issues in Education, 13*(4). Retrieved from http://cie.asu.edu/ojs/index.php/cieatasu/article/view/398

Strain, P., & Bovey, E. H. (2011). The LEAP model of early intervention for young children with autism spectrum disorders. *Special Education, 31*, 133–154.

Szulanski, G. (1996). Exploring internal stickiness: Impediments to the transfer of best practice within the firm. *Strategic Management Journal, 17*, 27–43.

Tyack, D., & Cuban, L. (1995. *Tinkering toward utopia: A century of public school reform.* Cambridge, MA: Harvard University Press.

U.S. Department of Education, Institute of Education Sciences. (2015). *Request for applications: Education research grants* (CFDA No. 84.305A). Retrieved from http://ies.ed.gov/funding/pdf/2016_84305A.pdf

U.S. Department of Education, Institute of Education Sciences, & National Science Foundation. (2013). *Common guidelines for education research and development.* Retrieved from http://ies.ed.gov/pdf/CommonGuidelines.pdf

Waltz, J., Addis, M., Koerner, K., & Jacobson, N. (1993). Testing the integrity of a psychotherapy protocol: Assessment of adherence and competence. *Journal of Consulting and Clinical Psychology, 61*, 620–630.

Weiss, M., Bloom, H., & Brock, T. (2013). *A conceptual framework for studying the sources of variation in program effects* (MDRC Working Papers on Research Methodology). Retrieved from http://www.mdrc.org/sites/default/files/a-conceptual_framework_for_studying_the_sources.pdf

Wolery, M. (2011). Intervention research: The importance of fidelity measurement. *Topics in Early Childhood Special Education, 31*, 155–157.

Yin, R., Quick, S., Bateman, P., & Marks, E. (1978). *Changing urban bureaucracies: How new practices become routinized.* Santa Monica, CA: RAND. Retrieved from http://www.rand.org/pubs/reports/R2277.html

Zeller, R. A., & Carmines, E. G. (1980). *Measurement in the social sciences: The link between theory and data.* Cambridge, England: Cambridge University Press.

Zucker, A. A., Solari, E. J., Landry, S. H., & Swank, P. R. (2013). Effects of a brief tiered language intervention for prekindergarteners at risk. *Early Education and Development, 24*, 366–392.

Zvoch, K. (2012). How does fidelity of implementation matter? Using multilevel models to detect relationships between participant outcomes and the delivery and receipt of treatment. *American Journal of Evaluation, 33*, 547–565. doi:10.1177/1098214012452715

II. The Contexts of Education

Chapter 7

Education Research and the Shifting Landscape of the American School District, 1816 to 2016

David A. Gamson

The Pennsylvania State University

Emily M. Hodge

Montclair State University

Despite decades of critiques and scores of innovations designed to abolish or weaken it, the school district remains a central institution of the American educational system. Yet, although the district remains the primary agent of local democratic control and serves as the main unit for educational decisions, relatively little attention has been given to the historical evolution of the school district as an institutional form. Reformers and researchers alike often hold misperceptions and inaccurate assumptions about the nature of the school district's development, precisely because the district has been understudied. The authors of this chapter offer a first step toward correcting that oversight by broadening our attention span, providing a solid historical overview of how the district has developed over the past two centuries, and exploring how scholars have analyzed districts at different points in our past. They focus on how the definition of what constitutes a school district has changed over time and on how perceptions of what it has meant to be a good or effective district has shifted throughout our history. They argue that the district has never been a static institution, that its changing forms and functions deserve greater recognition, and that conflicts regarding school districts often reflect deep and enduring frictions that are endemic to American social structures.

Throughout its long lifespan, the American school district has been praised and lambasted, consolidated and reorganized, centralized, decentralized, and recentralized; yet, despite its many shifts in fortune, it has remained steadfastly in place, altered perhaps, but essentially intact. Scholars and reformers have differed in their appraisals of this longevity. Some critics see it as a sign of the district's intransigence;

Review of Research in Education
March 2016, Vol. 40, pp. 216–249
DOI: 10.3102/0091732X16670323
© 2016 AERA. http://rre.aera.net

others treat it as a testament to its vitality. Several generations of reformers have seen the district as obsolete and ripe for termination; others seek to strengthen it through robust attention to its role in improving instructional practice.

Whatever one's view, few would deny that the school district has played an important role in our educational past and present. Today, nearly 50 million American children are educated in, at last count, 13,515 "regular" public school districts (Snyder, de Brey, & Dillow, 2016). The district remains the primary platform on which we sort out local educational politics, school building construction, leadership, enrollment, governance, and busing and transportation. Yet, despite widespread recognition of the district's core duties, explaining the precise nature of the role that the district has played in our educational history has proved challenging, partly because we do not regularly pause to reflect on it. In fact, even though the district often serves as the point of focus for our data collection, as the unit of analysis for political and historical studies, or as the primary agency of local democratic control, it has rarely been a subject of inquiry itself.

Indeed, little attention has been devoted to the historical evolution of the school district as an institutional form. Certainly, researchers have written a great deal about districts, directly and indirectly, but these writings have never been woven into any kind of extended explanatory narrative. While we cannot undertake a complete version of that task here (see Gamson & Hodge, in press), we can highlight some of the biggest thematic shifts. The general goals of this chapter are to take a first step toward providing a solid historical overview of how the school district has developed over time, to explore how scholars have analyzed districts at different points in our past, and to do so in a way that integrates these two strands—the history and the research literature. In other words, we look at the historical and institutional development of local school systems alongside the literature produced about school districts during each historic period. In so doing, we hope to slightly broaden how scholars conceive of the "literature review," for we suggest that the evolution of school districts can best be understood by blending the stages of scholarship with the historical developments that surrounded them. To our knowledge, no one has taken quite this approach before, and this centennial issue of *Review of Research in Education* offers an excellent opportunity to look back on the district with this somewhat novel analytic lens.

As most students of American education will immediately recognize, any reflective investigation into school districts can easily expose an array of issues that involve core perceptions about our national educational enterprise. After all, through the district flows a wealth of standard scholarly concerns: power and privilege, expertise and authority, funding and equity, segregation and desegregation, centralization and decentralization, and instruction and community participation, among many others. Alertness to these themes is essential as we catalogue decades of research on school districts. Moreover, as we hope to show, tracing the history of scholarship on districts offers unique insight into the changing nature of education research itself. In fact, as we shall demonstrate, districts have often been directly interconnected with educational scholarship since the earliest investigations of the 19th and early 20th centuries. The sporadic research attention given to districts since then has meant that many of the earlier interconnections between districts and education research have been forgotten or overlooked.

We recognize at the outset that what precisely defines a school district varies significantly depending on perspective. The term *district* can refer to a school board, a collection of schools, a geographic demarcation, a legal entity, a bargaining unit, a central office, a set of enrollment boundaries—the list goes on. We cannot feasibly incorporate all versions or visions of a district into a short review; rather, we hope to paint with a broad brush the historical treatments of school districts and thereby help inform current and future research discussions.

Most database searches of literature pertaining to American school districts yield thousands of sources—for instance, 62,000 in JSTOR; 112,113 in WorldCat, 1.5 million in Penn State's LionSearch—far too many to reasonably review or integrate into a cogent essay. Rather than conducting a meta-analysis, we have made a careful selection of significant articles in particular areas of district research. In the process, we developed a multilayered approach to finding, collecting, and discussing the research included herein. Many of the historical studies were identified over a multiyear period of research on the history of school districts (Gamson & Hodge, in press). There is a rich historical tradition of studying the development of individual school districts (R. D. Cohen, 1990; Mirel, 1993; Raftery, 1992; Zilversmit, 1993), and these works helped inform our analysis. However, we did not attempt a review, per se.

We used, as a starting point, seminal research pieces in both education policy and the history of education as a springboard into more thorough investigations of the literature on districts, which brought us to influential examples of primary source material. We drew on several excellent studies and literature reviews that included one or more aspects of district-related reform (Alsbury, 2008; Campbell, Cunningham, Nystrand, & Usdan, 1990; Fuhrman & Elmore, 1990; Hallinger, 2013; Land, 2002; Lopate, Flaxman, Bynum, & Gordon, 1970; MacIver & Farley, 2003; Marsh, 2002; Marsh et al., 2005; Rorrer, Skrla, & Scheurich, 2008; Trujillo, 2013). Finally, our three anonymous reviewers offered healthy lists of suggestions regarding scholars and studies that we had previously overlooked. Taken together, the studies we include offer something of a representative (but by no means complete) sample that illustrates significant analytical perspectives regarding local control and local educational agencies throughout the nation's educational past.

As a way to focus our discussion, we developed a set of central questions to help guide our approach. First, how has the idea, or definition, of what a school district is changed over time, and why have discussions of districts periodically resulted in controversy? Second, what has it meant to be a good or effective district through history, and how has district quality been assessed, measured, or determined? And, finally, as the district has developed over time, how have researchers and practitioners articulated what they see as its appropriate role?

In addition to our general purpose for this chapter, we also have specific goals. First, we seek to adjust and broaden the usual time span of research on school districts. Recent literature on the subject usually begins with the reforms and writings of the 1980s or 1990s; we believe this restricted time frame robs us of a deeper understanding of how districts have developed in this nation over the past 100—if not 200—years. Second, we suggest that many of the key assumptions researchers make about districts are not informed by the historical record, and thus are unintentionally misinformed, misleading, or both. (We provide a brief synopsis of these perspectives after this introduction.) Third, we attempt to better understand the connections between the school district and instructional improvement, a relationship that many researchers now believe should be the core consideration of school reform efforts. And finally, by examining a longer time period, we hope to highlight how many of the current tensions in education policy and the challenges affecting school districts today echo those faced by districts in the 19th and 20th centuries. We see the current conflicts regarding districts not so much as the result of recent conditions or political divides as they are deep and enduring frictions that are endemic to American social structures and cultural institutions through history.

Historians and other scholars often use the technique of dividing the past into discrete time periods that correspond to changes within their domain of concern. In the case of education, these may be developments in curriculum, in theories of learning, or in testing and assessments. We have developed our own periodization here, identifying four periods between 1816 and the present: 1816 to 1916, 1916 to 1954, 1954 to 1990, and 1990 to 2016. However, our divisions should be understood more as an organizational device than as an analytic taxonomy that seeks to define district development through distinct developmental eras. Our general approach, we recognize, also has a number of limitations, and we wish to offer a preemptive acknowledgment that we have committed multiple sins of omission due to space considerations. However, we hope that a broad, long-term historical vantage point allows us to place in relief many of the struggles that school districts contend with today, even if we are forced to pass over a number of significant concerns that have inhabited the literature, including themes such as local politics or the ongoing role of school boards.

Before we commence on our own chronological survey, we think it worthwhile to summarize some of the standard narratives evident in relatively recent literature about the school district. Although this account essentially leapfrogs ahead of our historical sections by distilling more contemporary views on districts, it is precisely these common current perceptions and research assumptions that motivated our original interest in taking on this essay. Collectively, then, this catalogue of common beliefs provides a necessary foundation to our chapter.

RECENT VIEWS ON THE SCHOOL DISTRICT

Standard narratives on the school district have taken a variety of forms; most notable among them are three common perspectives. The first is the belief that district governance and local control serve as an embodiment of educational democracy. Second is the idea that districts have remained organizationally static ever since they were established in their modern form in the early 20th century (another variant of this view is that the district serves as an example of a retrograde institution, given its 19th-century origin). Third is the notion that districts are monolithic bureaucracies that are pathologically flawed and completely incapable of reinvigoration or reinvention. These conceptual categories are not mutually exclusive, and many critics of public education often amalgamate a combination of the three. We recognize that these are simplified representations of standard views: Many researchers and reformers hold more sophisticated and nuanced understandings. Therefore, as we provide some brief illustrations of these common views below, we simultaneously demonstrate how they overlap, intermingle, or conflict. Again, the purpose is to develop an appreciation for some of the more significant shared beliefs about districts.

In the popular imagination, the school district is often seen as the epitome of democratic governance of education, as the "crucible of democracy" (Iannaccone & Lutz, 1995). While scholars have acknowledged the power of this concept, especially in explaining the persistence of local control, they have often taken a critical stance on just how democratic the district truly is, rightly acknowledging the ways in which schools and school districts were organized to privilege White students through testing and tracking (Callahan, 1962; Katz, 1975; Oakes, 1985; Spring, 1972) and how district boundary lines segregated students (Bischoff, 2008). McDermott (1999) argues that districts not only fail to live up to their billing as forums for political participation but also impede pursuit of the educational equity that Americans profess to desire. In other words, the quintessentially democratic educational institution can be employed to achieve distinctly undemocratic ends.

At the advent of the 20th century, as we discuss in more detail later, researchers celebrated the growth of large modern school districts, especially those located in cities, and they presented city school systems as exemplary blueprints for other districts to copy—a deliberate effort to help diffuse innovation (Cubberley, 1916a). By the 1960s, however, the notion of the urban school district as a model for others to emulate had begun to crumble, as scholars, educators, and public intellectuals severely critiqued the urban districts as flawed structures that undermined educational opportunity (Bowles & Gintis, 1975; Gittell, 1965; Greer, 1972; Kozol, 1967; Schrag, 1967), alienated students and teachers alike, and were unresponsive to community concerns (Rogers, 1968). One of the most widely used historical metaphors is Tyack's (1974) notion of the district as the "one best system," the organizational model established by "administrative progressive" reformers during the early 20th century. These reformers ultimately established an interlocking directorate of elite educators who convinced locals to replace older forms of governance with centralized school districts that were "professionalized."

Since the 1970s, many scholars have used the notion of one best system as a way to explain both system and student failure. As Chubb and Moe (1990) put it, "We believe existing institutions cannot solve the problem, because they *are* the problem—and that the key to better schools is institutional reform" (p. 3). Despite a history of heated conflicts, the authors wrote,

The "one best system" has consistently stood above it all. It has provided the framework of democratic institutions with which demands are expressed, problems identified, solutions explored, and policy responses chosen. It has structured criticism and reform—but it has never been their target. (p. 6)

Others saw district structure as less of a problem, depicting school and district leaders as beleaguered, hamstrung by the emergence of a new array of forces—mandates and regulations that originated outside the district, such as union contracts, federal categorical programs, and state requirements (Ravitch, 1983; Zeigler, Tucker, & Wilson, 1977).

Throughout the 1960s and 1970s, and into the 1980s, reformers tended to sidestep the district as a unit of change, and researchers often followed suit, analyzing the role played by the schools, the states, or, increasingly, the federal government. When districts were discussed, researchers depicted them as resistant implementers, adaptive adopters, or mere compliance monitors (Berman & McLaughlin, 1977, 1978, 1979). Although the War on Poverty held great hope for the positive impact of large-scale federal funding through the Elementary and Secondary Education Act of 1965, the Coleman report (Coleman et al., 1966), along with the decades of "school effects" literature that followed, cast a great deal of doubt on the ability of educational institutions to enhance the academic achievement of children (Berends & Rand, 2002; Raudenbush & Willms, 1995; Teddlie & Stringfield, 1993).

Given the modest hopes that researchers had for increasing student achievement in poor and minority communities, some scholars were surprised to find that handfuls of schools in poor neighborhoods yielded assessment scores significantly higher than those of other schools located in similar circumstances (Edmonds, 1979). The "effective schools" movement that followed focused on identifying the specific characteristics of the schools that appeared to be inordinately successful. Some researchers tried to extend the lessons learned to create "effective school districts," but the results were disappointing (Purkey & Smith, 1985). In the 1980s and 1990s, several new types of school reform organizations—the Coalition of Essential Schools, the Accelerated School Project, and Success for All, among others—emerged as an outgrowth of the belief that the most effective unit of change was the school rather than the district (Levin, 1988; McQuillan & Muncey, 1994; Slavin, 1996).

In the 1990s, a variety of systemic reform approaches discounted districts. Advocates of systemic reform suggested that districts should avoid "usurping" the authority of schools or states, and the standards-based reform movement designated the state as the appropriate level of the system to leverage change (Smith & O'Day, 1991). Supporters of charter schools, voucher programs, restructuring, and site-based management all saw avoiding districts as fundamental to success. In an influential 1995 RAND report, Paul Hill asked, "Why has a decade of work on school reform produced so little?" Part of the answer, he said, lay in "school governance." First, he argued, "The seeds of today's disappointments were sown when educational reformers of the 19th century defined a public school as an institution financed, owned, and managed by a local agency of government." Second, "Public management of education has created a governance system divorced from public needs and democratic change, a system incapable of renewing itself" (Hill, 1995, p. ix).

Even researchers who have worked directly with districts, who are sympathetic to their plight, and have distinctive visions for how districts can foster systemwide instructional improvement, nevertheless may kindle misconceptions about what districts have or have not done in the past. As one set of researchers concisely captures the sentiment, "School district central offices have operated for most of their history in ways distinctly different from what efforts to improve teaching and learning across an entire district demand" (Honig, Copland, Rainey, Lorton, & Newton, 2010, p. 8).

To summarize: By the beginning of the 21st century, many (but by no means all) researchers saw school districts as outdated institutions that were no longer capable of adapting to new circumstances or leading their schools toward necessary improvements. Although views have varied quite a bit in recent decades, the American school district has generally been treated with wariness, suspicion, or scorn. When researchers or reformers engage with districts, it is often with a sense of trepidation. We have done our best above to capture some of the mainstream lines of research, sentiment, and argumentation. Of course, this is not the whole story.

1816 TO 1916: FROM DISTRICT SCHOOL TO SCHOOL DISTRICT

The idea of democratic local governance has a long history in our nation, but the policies designed to translate that core notion into practical plans have not always been easy to formalize. Although a few "founding fathers" sketched out plans for the establishment of state school systems, there was little desire among the new American citizens or their legislatures for the additional taxation that would come with such ventures, and none of the early state plans succeeded. As Dewey (1927) later put it: "The imagination of the founders did not travel beyond what could be accomplished and understood in a congeries of self-governing communities." Between the 1780s and the 1820s, as the states established their constitutions, they slowly began to erect the legal scaffolding of what would become state school systems. It took decades, however, for many of the state legislatures to pass the necessary enabling legislation (Bell, 1853; "Common School Laws . . . ," 1849; Curtin, 1855; Davidson, 1896; "Statutes of the State of New-York . . . ," 1847).

The characteristic school of the first decades of the 19th century was known as the "district school," usually a one-room schoolhouse, organized and controlled by a small locality and financed by a combination of property taxes, tuition, and state aid (Kaestle, 1983). School patrons selected a small group of board members or trustees to hire a teacher and oversee the school building. Each school, in other words, constituted its own district, and it was rare for much thought to go into issues of governance. Although would-be reformers often complained about the wretched quality of instruction, Kaestle (1983) points out that district schools served local communities quite well, as the chief goal was to provide children with rudimentary instruction at a low cost, all under firm community control. Americans have had a tendency to romanticize these early efforts at self-governance, for they evoke images of a different kind of society—close-knit and harmonious—but the historical records demonstrate that harmony was hardly ubiquitous, and schooling was rarely seen as a major local priority throughout much of the century.

To understand the educational change that began in the 1820s and 1830s, it is necessary to recognize that American society began to transform itself rather quickly. Urbanization took place at a faster rate between 1820 and 1860 than in any other period in U.S. history (Tyack, 1974). The household, once the main unit of production, was soon bypassed by a rapidly expanding economy, and self-reliance and voluntary services no longer met the needs or desires of mushrooming villages. Rudimentary academic skills no longer sufficed for the intensified competition of capitalist markets. Descriptions of schools from the 1830s and beyond (in local, state, and national publications) clearly illustrate how both local and state leaders struggled to improve instruction, modernize school buildings, attach more gravitas to the work of school governance, and enhance public support for education.

All this matters because, first, the standard local educational arrangements became less and less tenable as the need for more complex skills increased. Second, as educational leaders began to run up against the limits of their own knowledge and experience, they felt the need to solicit advice from, or simply communicate with, a broader range of school leaders throughout their own states and in others. Published annual reports became one device for this networking, and as the cost of printing dropped throughout the 19th century, educational journals became an increasingly popular mechanism for intellectual engagement. The articles contained in these journals were not necessarily "research" in the sense that we think of it today, but they were certainly scholarly, for they contained the writings and expositions of some of the most notable educators of the day on educational principles, practices, and philosophies. In some states, the state office of education produced a *Common Schools Journal* (Connecticut) or *District School Journal* (New York), or something similar.

The *American Journal of Education* commenced publication in 1826. It captured the spirit of the age in its opening issue by explaining that the fields of science and literature had their own periodicals, already

contributing incalculably to the dissemination of knowledge and taste. But education—a subject of the highest practical importance to every school, every family, and every individual in the community—remains unprovided with one of these popular and useful vehicles of information. ("Prospectus," 1826, p. 1)[1]

The journal announced its intention to furnish "*a record of facts*" (italics in the original) about the past and present state of education, collected through diligent inquiry; to offer a comparison of "the merits of various systems of instruction" in the United States and foreign countries; and to report the results of experimentation alongside discussions tracing the causes of failure or success.

With this new outward-focused, cosmopolitan attitude, the "district school" became more and more a main source of irritation and embarrassment. As one county deputy superintendent in New York State reported, "In almost every instance where a small district is found, we find a backward, ignorant and indolent school, if we find any at all" (Burgess, 1843, p. 89). The school terms lasted only 4 to 6 months, he explained, and the teachers—usually hired on the cheap—were often incompetent and did the children "more hurt than good." What "little truth they inculcate is so mixed with error" (p. 90), he concluded, that the pupil never quite recovered: "A mind that has been thus filled, seldom sees things in their true light ever afterward; a mist enshrouds the mind which is seldom entirely dissipated" (p. 90).

One finds similarly stinging assessments all the way from the 1830s through the 1890s and beyond. In 1879, the Ohio State Commissioner of the Common Schools listed some of the other states—New Hampshire, Rhode Island, Maine, and Wisconsin among them—that also critiqued the "incubus," the "wastefulness," and the "evils" of the district system (Burns, 1879, pp. 52–53). Such a system, complained its detractors, made it virtually impossible to properly and systematically govern, supervise, or improve the schools of any state.

Creating New Institutions

As the late historian Michael Katz (1971) has reminded us, the creation of institutions preoccupied early 19th-century Americans, whether they were building banks, railroads, political parties, factories, hospitals, or schools. Americans confronted the inappropriateness of traditional organizational arrangements, and their attempts to find a suitable fit between the form and context of social life, he says, stimulated a prolonged national debate about what forms these institutions should take. Katz's analysis is especially helpful in reminding us that there was nothing inevitable about the kind of education system that developed in the United States. His article was written during the years when "revisionist" scholars fiercely debated the core character of American schools: Did schools serve to equalize educational opportunity and enhance social mobility, revisionists asked, or were they racially discriminatory, imposing a class bias on the public schools? (cf. Katz, 1987; Ravitch, 1978). Katz (1971) wrote that Americans had considered four alternative models for the organization of schooling that competed for prominence during the first half of the 19th century. He labeled these models *paternalistic voluntarism*, *democratic localism*, *corporate voluntarism*, and *incipient bureaucracy*. Because each model represents tendencies that, we suggest, still exist in American thought about educational organizations, we discuss each briefly. Alert readers may recognize remarkable similarities between these long-ago governance efforts and tendencies of school reformers of today.

Paternalistic voluntarism represented the effort by the wealthy to educate the "unchurched poor." These reformers liked to think of themselves as "humble gleaners in the wide field of benevolence," volunteers who as unpaid but talented amateurs could guide schooling without the need for an extensive organization or professional staff. Perhaps the best example of this mode of thinking was the Free Public School Society of New York. After running several schools in New York City for some years, the society convinced the New York state legislature to give them control of all New

York schools in 1825. As seemingly benevolent as was this form of volunteerism, it still represented a class system of education, for it served as the vehicle enabling one class to civilize the other and thereby ensure that society would remain tolerable, orderly, and safe. The society offered mass education on the cheapest possible scale. This was education for the poor, not for the children of society members. Critics of paternalistic voluntarism believed the local district schools provided a much better option, arguing that the society was "a private corporation," providing an important governmental function "without a direct and immediate responsibility to the people," and that it ignored diversity in favor of enforcing a uniformity on all children, no matter their background or religious differences (Katz, 1971, p. 302).

Democratic localism attempted to extend and expand the vision of the district school across states and into urban environments. Advocates wanted to retain an important principle that they believed was transgressed by voluntarists, namely, the operation of schools by local districts in which the "whole control" of education remained "to the free and unrestricted action of the people themselves." City schools could follow the model by dividing municipalities into wards for the operation of schools block by block, if necessary. Democratic localists were opposed to the creation of state boards or state systems of education; in 1840, one legislative committee in Massachusetts called for the abolition of the new State Board of Education, created just 3 years earlier and presided over by Horace Mann as its secretary, arguing that "the commencement of a system of centralization and monopoly of power in a few hands, [is] contrary in every respect, to the true spirit of our democratical institutions" (as quoted in Katz, 1971, p. 306). Rather than enforcing education on an unwilling people, which would lead only to "reluctance and suspicion" (Katz, 1971, p. 308), democratic localists believed in the power that could be leveraged when communities determined to establish their own schools without external coercion.

Corporate voluntarism was focused on single institutions to be run by self-perpetuating boards of trustees (i.e., not elected) and financed by endowments or tuition. Corporate voluntarism stressed disinterested, enlightened, and continuous management, an approach they believed would keep the schools out of politics. This model was the quintessence of *noblesse oblige* and tended to be used primarily by private academies and colleges.

Finally, *incipient bureaucracy* was the model that ultimately triumphed. Democratic localists were the chief hindrance to its rapid adoption, but the localists stumbled over too many obstacles, especially in cities, where small ward districts often led to unnecessary duplications and were thus depicted as inefficient. Moreover, establishing small wards often created visible inequalities across wards in the same geographic area. As state superintendent of the common schools in Connecticut, Henry Barnard argued in 1865 that an "immediate union of all the districts" represented the "first great step" in urban school reform. The hallmarks of incipient bureaucracy were centralization, supervision, and professionalization. City schools also served the purpose of protecting poor children from poverty, vice, and "the temptations of the streets." Barnard, like many of his contemporaries, saw cities as the breeding ground for "poverty, ignorance, profligacy, and irreligion" (as quoted in Katz, 1971, pp. 309–310) and saw the schools as offering a necessary corrective. The resulting urban school systems thereby took on brand new duties well beyond strict academics, the like of which they had never shouldered before.

Critics of school districts today often incorrectly believe that incipient educational bureaucracies were directly modeled on 19th-century factories or on an imported, rigid Prussian system. Neither conception is accurate, for at least two reasons. First, bureaucracy borrowed one important dimension from the democratic localists by continuing the tradition of local school boards that were publicly elected. Second, the bureaucratic pedagogical approach was meant to be a departure from the rote memorization and recitation that characterized so much of education in the other three models. Educators like Mann and Barnard ultimately wanted students to internalize a love of learning. Classroom instructors, as explained in the journal *Massachusetts Teacher* in 1848, should endeavor to excite student curiosity; pupils should work "voluntarily, cheerfully, with hope" (Katz, 1971, p. 320–321).

Districts and Education Research From the 1880s to 1916

In the decades that followed, educators produced a great deal of writing about matters of educational policy, practice, curriculum, funding, administration, organization, and learning, many of the topics of obvious importance today. However, little of the great bulk of 19th-century writing would be considered research by today's standards. Indeed, the various societies that were established to address the major educational questions of the day operated according to a different logic. For example, the National Education Association (NEA) served as the major national organization in education, and its National Council on Education, established in 1880, set as its goal the consideration and discussion of educational questions of public importance. A former president of the NEA remarked that the council's duty would be to establish "correct opinions" and to combat and overthrow "heresies and false notions of education" ("Discussion of Mr. Bicknell's paper . . . ," 1880, p. 17). As Wesley (1957) has explained, educators in the 19th century had a naïve faith in the value of intellectual exchange and the efficacy of discussion; thus, they founded a number of organizations dedicated to wringing wisdom from debate and unity from a diversity of ideas.

One example of the kinds of debate captured in the NEA's proceedings comes from a discussion in 1890 that struck at the heart of what it meant to be a district superintendent. Attendees at the meeting hotly debated whether the role of the superintendent should be primarily that of a business executive or a pedagogical leader. The school chief of Providence, Rhode Island, worried about the dangers of the superintendent's becoming "a businessman, a manager of affairs, rather than continu[ing] to maintain the attitude of the scholar, and becom[ing] more and more the teacher" ("City School Systems: Discussion," 1890, p. 463). The superintendent of the Denver schools openly disagreed, arguing that the superintendent's duties properly focused on expenditures, the construction of schoolhouses, and appropriations for furniture and supplies. He worried that the superintendent would "be incompetent intelligently to participate in the business affairs of the corporation, whose executive officer he is or should be" ("City School Systems: Discussion," 1890, p. 464). It is worth noting that these discussions took place well before the 1910s, the period when business values suffused educational organizations (Callahan, 1962).

In addition to their grand debates, educators also understood the great value in the collection of information and statistics to better guide some educational decisions and to influence communities and school patrons. Many of the first state superintendents were essentially charged by their legislatures with the collection of statistics; the federal Office of Education, not established until 1867, also collected statistics and disseminated information about practices, innovations, and developments both within and outside the United States. In 1885, Philbrick published the first aggregation of national data on city school systems from throughout the country, which provided a solid foundation for other studies of urban districts in the years that followed.

In the early 1890s, Joseph Rice conducted a novel series of observations in the schools of 36 cities, startling the world of education with his frank descriptions of the rigid, and often inhumane, pedagogical practices he said characterized instruction in many urban systems. Rice described teachers conducting formal recitations with immobile students, an approach he described as "unscientific and mechanical." Such methods, Rice (1893) said, meant that "the aim of the instruction is limited mainly to drilling facts into the minds of children, and to hearing them recite lessons that they have learned by heart from textbooks" (p. 20). Rice raised the ire of practitioners again later in the decade when he argued that subject matter tests could be used to compare the efficiency of school systems in various cities. Instead of embracing Rice's proposals, practitioners attacked him for the temerity he demonstrated in presuming to dictate practice through the findings of mere quantitative studies (Wesley, 1957).

It was not until around the turn of the century that data began to make a significant difference in the standard practices of the day. Many urban school systems found themselves with an abundance of older children still stuck in the earlier grades. The surplus of overage students swiftly became a distressing national situation, especially in rapidly growing areas, because year after year, more pupils accumulated in the lower grades, unable to pass their promotion exams. New York City School Superintendent William Maxwell (New York City Public Schools, 1904) was among the first to draw public attention to these concerns, when in 1904 he published city school figures showing that a full 39% of students were above the normal age for their grades. Maxwell's report sent a jolt through the education world.

In a follow-up investigation into the problem of overage students in some 30 other cities, Ayres (1909) estimated that just over one third of the total elementary school population enrolled in all city school systems was overage—an astonishing finding. This was not at all a problem concerning just a few children, Ayres explained: "It is one affecting most intimately perhaps 6,000,000 children in the United States" (p. 4). The source of the problem, Ayres and others concluded, was that the standard curriculum of the day was too difficult for most students. Researchers across the country began to believe that the solution was to differentiate the curriculum.

1916 TO 1954: THE RISE OF THE PROFESSIONAL SCHOOL DISTRICT AND EDUCATION RESEARCH

The year 1916 must have been an exciting one for American educators because there was a palpable sense of transformation in the air. In fact, the middle years of the 1910s brought forth significant change, not just in education but across several dimensions of American life. Historian Henry May (1959/1994) depicts the mid-1910s as pivotal years in American culture, marking the Victorian past from the modern present—"the first years of our own time," he called them. Indeed, the 1910s were one of the most productive periods in 20th-century educational thought, sparking a massive amount of experimentation and investigation; it is not surprising that the American Educational Research Association (AERA) was established during this era, when education research as we now know it began to flourish (Bobbitt, 1913, 1918; Brown, 1915; Deffenbaugh, 1916; Graham, 1967; Hanus, 1913; Judd, 1925; Munro, 1917; Snedden & Allen, 1908; Wiebe, 1967).

Our previous section looked at school districts in their inchoate organizational forms in the 19th century. This section examines the early 20th-century apotheosis of the large urban school district, the components of districts that focused on curriculum and instruction, and the concerns that were raised by observers of districts. It was during this four-decade period when much of the school district as we think of it today was developed, when some of the strengths of that district structure emerged, and when concerns, tensions, and paradoxes about that structure also first appeared.

By the late 19th century, school officials at the local, state, and federal levels had become rather skilled at the collection of data concerning American public schools. They knew, for example, how many teachers were employed in South Carolina and how much they were paid, the number of schoolhouses in California, the enrollment in the schools of Minnesota, and the per-pupil expenditure in the counties of Maine. They could also distinguish between expenditures in White and African American schools in the southern and border states (and some northern states), between the conditions of rural and urban schools, and between the numbers of schools in the far west territories. The collection of data regarding the status of schools, students, and expenses was of incalculable value to understanding the status quo, but it did not yet point the way to the future action, even in places where the differences were extreme. In other words, the 1826 hope of the editor of the *American Journal of Education* remained unrealized; an accumulated record of facts did not necessarily yield evidence of success and failure, nor did it necessarily yield insightful analyses. In part, this was because academics and school leaders alike still subscribed to the older mode of policy arrived at via discussion. Nevertheless, it was during the 1910s and the years that followed that education research moved well beyond the simple collection of statistics; and much of the new research had to do with districts. As we have seen,

Rice, Maxwell, and Ayres had all used the district as their point of departure—especially its incarnation in city school systems.

Education research developed in various directions in the United States, and districts continued to play an integral role in the shifting conceptualizations of research. As described in the previous section, some of the early steps in research were taken by Maxwell in his aggregation of numbers of overage students in New York and by Ayres (1909) in his follow-up study. It is unlikely that individual districts with large numbers of overage students were unaware of enrollment imbalances, yet they did not appear to comprehend the extent of the problem nor did they take immediate action to rectify the situation. The growing size of districts created both serious dilemmas and new opportunities, and the standard approaches to addressing educational conundrums no longer worked.

The year 1916 marked a striking transition, not only for the founding of AERA but for other significant reasons as well. Two exceedingly influential books published in 1916 represented the disparate reactions to the problems that educators perceived in American education: John Dewey's (1916) *Democracy and Education* and Ellwood P. Cubberley's (1916a) *Public School Administration*. As we know, Dewey has had a remarkable influence on American educational thought over the past century (Westbrook, 1991), but Cubberley's book clearly had the more immediate impact on day-to-day educational practice in schools and districts (Lagemann, 2000; Zilversmit, 1993).

Cubberley, dean of the Stanford University School of Education, and other like-minded academics at the University of Chicago, the University of Wisconsin, Harvard University, and Teachers College have been depicted by historians as quintessential administrative progressives (Ryan, 2011; Tyack, 1974) or as scientific managers and social efficiency experts (Kliebard, 1995), all focused on establishing large, efficient district bureaucracies, systems that ultimately sorted children into differentiated curricular tracks. Scholars assert that these efforts were part of a broad social, political, and economic movement—the Progressive Era—that expected expertise to simultaneously abolish civic corruption, displace ward boards, and professionalize all aspects of public life. At the same time, Cubberley (1909), like many of his White, middle-class contemporaries, held unsavory views on immigrants, believing that the new arrivals from southern Europe were "illiterate, docile, [and] lacking in self-reliance and initiative" (p. 15)—and he argued that Americans should give up the "exceedingly democratic idea that all are equal" (pp. 56–57). Such sentiments caused the administrative progressives to be labeled as discriminatory, racist, and classist by later generations of scholars. Nevertheless, through writings, lectures, teachings, and numerous evaluations, Cubberley (along with other leading scholars in the new field of educational administration) was remarkably successful in convincing local leaders to consolidate smaller wards into single, unified school districts. Cubberley (1916a) believed that these reforms were a continuation of the work of the advocates of incipient bureaucracy, such as Mann and Barnard.

To Cubberley and other prominent academics of the time, such as George Strayer (Teachers College), Charles Judd (University of Chicago), and Lewis Terman

(Stanford University), the quality of any district could be judged by how closely it adhered to the organizational structure and administrative ethos of the newly reorganized urban school districts. "Nearly all of the important progress which has been made in education in America in the past quarter century has been made in our cities," proclaimed Cubberley in 1915 (p. 95). City school systems, he believed, were the true laboratories of progressive educational experimentation. "It is the cities which have perfected their administrative organization and developed an administrative machinery capable of handling educational business on a large scale," he wrote a year later. "It is in the cities, too, that the large problems of public school organization and administration have been worked out and the fundamental administrative principles we now follow have been established" (Cubberley, 1916b, p. 10). The city, it seemed, offered a fertile environment for realizing the American dream of universal democratic education.

One of the great qualities of the "city school system" (as it was called at the time) was the "unity of the work" (Cubberley, 1916a), the fact that it could be managed as a unit—all essential tasks were run through a small central board and a single administrative office, overseeing budgeting, finance, records and reports, attendance, school facilities, research and testing, curriculum, and the supervision of teachers. Such practices, stressed Cubberley (1916a), conformed to "the best principles of corporation control" (p. 435). Scholars were to make much of these corporate origins later in the century (Bowles & Gintis, 1975; Callahan, 1962). Through the early 20th century, however, the "educational department" of the district had often been relegated to second-class, or merely comparable, status in relation to other district departments. Urged on by the administrative progressives, districts began to merge the educational functions with those of business and finance so that the superintendent had full purview over where and how funds were allotted in the service of instruction and curriculum.

From our vantage point today, it can be tempting to presume that reformers in the early 20th century were rather provincial in their views, that they assigned to the school district old-fashioned top-down administrative edicts, that they failed to foresee the depersonalization that would accompany the growth of corporate and business values, and that they had little savvy or understanding when it came to emphasizing instructional improvement. It is also commonly assumed today that districts were not originally organized to undertake district-wide pedagogical change. But the historical record gives us a different view. Indeed, the district as established in the early 20th century was designed to accomplish a number of tasks, many of them mundanely bureaucratic, to be sure, but others focused directly on curriculum development and instructional improvement (it can be difficult at times to tease apart the curriculum work from work that related directly to the enhancement of instruction). If we are to do justice to early 20th-century educators' perspectives, we must recognize that progressive educators saw the two dimensions of curriculum and instruction as intertwined. Moreover, a close look at some of their writings demonstrates that their views were a bit more sophisticated, and decidedly less top-down, than we might have imagined. For example, in his commentary about the proper role of the superintendent, Cubberley (1916a) betrayed a remarkable sensitivity to what would later be called "instructional leadership":

> The superintendent who is essentially an office superintendent, who from his office chair promulgates and enforces a uniformity throughout the school system, who inspects rather than supervises, and who controls by rules and regulations rather than by developing initiative and strength on the part of those under him, will in time develop a school system so uniform that progress will become difficult, a supervisory force which lacks initiative and keeps close to old and well-established paths, and a teaching force wanting in personal strength and professional enthusiasm. One type of superintendent produces a live school system; the other a dead one. Regulations "from the office" and the enforcement of the letter of the law kill; it is the spirit and the personal touch which give life. (p. 180)

Cubberley even implored superintendents to encourage a certain self-reliance in the teaching force and to judiciously foster the kind of "personal liberty" that would stimulate individual initiative and personal growth. The fact that these kinds of sentiments never became deeply embedded in the culture of the American school district should not blind us to the fact that instructional improvements—through administrative encouragement and teacher autonomy—were once believed, by those who designed the systems, to be as important as organizational structure.

Not only do the years between 1913 and 1918 seem significant in retrospect, but educators at the time were also aware of the monumental changes afoot. Speaking at the 1925 NEA annual meeting, for example, University of Chicago professor Charles Judd recounted one 1915 session of the American Council of Education—the elite discussion group established by the NEA—that had featured a fierce debate about testing and measurement. According to Judd (1925), the clash at that meeting essentially constituted the last stand of "the forces of conservatism" against the science-minded progressives. And Judd viewed the battle as the culmination of the educational investigations and reformist agitation evident since the 1890s:

> There can be no doubt as we look back on that council meeting that one of the revolutions in American education was accomplished by that discussion. Since that day tests and measures have gone quietly on their way, as conquerors should. Tests and measures are to be found in every progressive school in the land. The victory of 1915 slowly prepared during the preceding twenty years was decisive. (pp. 806–807)

Moreover, Judd (1915) had reported immediately after the 1915 meeting how pleased he was to find an active interconnection between research and practice: "The most gratifying result of a year's work on reading tests is the fact that a variety of different kinds of work along this line has been undertaken by a number of school superintendents and special students of education" (p. 561). Here was the kind of close collaboration between practitioners—teachers and principals—and university-based researchers that educators and policymakers have so often called for. In fact, a close link between researchers and district practitioners characterized much of the work in the early 20th century and was in some ways a continuation of the close contact that university faculty and urban district superintendents had maintained since the latter decades of the 19th century. Importantly, as we look back, there were several avenues for collaboration between researchers and district leaders.

One good, though ultimately misguided, example of how researchers cultivated relationships with districts is the work that Stanford University's Lewis Terman undertook with districts that were experimenting with intelligence testing in the early 1920s, when he worked directly with the districts. In a contribution to the volume *Intelligence Tests and School Reorganization* (Terman et al., 1922), Terman asserted that the development of differentiated courses of instruction was "one of the most urgent needs in education today." The book also demonstrated how quickly districts across the country created a new role in the central office: director of research. For example, it included studies from Oakland and Los Angeles in California, as well as from Des Moines, Iowa, and the small city of Miami, Arizona. In many places, experimentation or implementation of IQ tests drove districts to reorganize their curriculum work across all schools.

The Role of the Central Office in the Improvement of Curriculum and Instruction

Although the early 20th-century adoption of IQ testing and business-oriented practices by school districts has traditionally drawn a good deal of researchers' attention (Oakes, 1985), these were far from the only reforms that district leaders implemented during the first half of that century. A number of practitioners and researchers pursued the kind of instructional improvement that Cubberley had articulated (albeit briefly) in 1916. In fact, just as discussions about the appropriateness of business attitudes in school leadership predated the scientific management movement, the enhancement of instruction had long been a major topic at many educational association meetings throughout the 19th century; it simply has not been well researched.

In the 1920s, leaders in newly reorganized districts renewed the challenge of instructional improvement by coupling it with curricular modernization. Building on the successful work of curriculum revision in Los Angeles (Bobbitt, 1922), St. Louis (Cocking, 1928), Denver (Cuban, 1993; Newlon & Threlkeld, 1926), and Winnetka, Illinois (Zilversmit, 1993), many other districts undertook district-wide curriculum revision projects that included both administrators and teachers. Although the tenor, quality, and inclusiveness of these efforts varied a great deal across districts, the early developers were remarkably influential in setting off a nationwide effort to modernize curricula across grade levels and subject areas in city after city. These efforts were characterized by focused attention to revising the curriculum so that it might become more "progressive" and child-centered, to folding classroom teachers into the process of remaking the curriculum, and—importantly— to the improving quality of instruction. Here, too, despite beliefs to the contrary, we find concerted efforts to use the leverage of the school district, its schools, and its central office, to simultaneously enhance teaching, learning, and curriculum.

Throughout the 1920s and 1930s, many districts across the country established some kind of curriculum revision program; one study (Bruner, 1937) reported that roughly 70% of cities with populations above 25,000 had ongoing revision programs, even during some of the worst years of the Great Depression. Other studies tended to confirm these findings (Trillingham, 1934). Bruner (1937) reported that between approximately 1920 and 1937, some 10,000 general courses of study (district curricula) and roughly 30,000 subject-specific curricula had been produced.

The curriculum revision efforts of districts across the country proved challenging to manage, but Caswell (1950) was clear that the district central office should carry out the bulk of the coordination and leadership as a means to connect curriculum development with instructional improvement. The authors listed a set of principles intended to guide action, whereby they identified a range of areas in which the district leadership should be directly involved. "The central office staff," the authors explained, "should provide leadership in a continuing analysis of curriculum problems and needs and in the formulation of a comprehensive program to meet them"; they should "foster a sense of group purpose among the instructional workers in a school system [and] stimulate creative leadership among the entire teaching force"; and they should "provide for the coordination of the activities of various instructional workers so that a unified curriculum is developed" (p. 72). Later, follow-up studies by McNally and Passow (1960) reinforced the findings of the Caswell studies and discussed how efforts earlier in the century had "laid the groundwork for the modern curriculum movement in which the local school system play[ed] the lead role" (p. 32).

What Did It Mean to Be a Good School District at Midcentury?

At the same time that the curriculum revision activities were underway, other researchers advocated alternate methods for identifying high-quality school districts. In the 1930s and 1940s, Paul Mort, at Teachers College, along with colleagues, students, and members of the Metropolitan School Study Council, undertook a series of studies on school district administration, ultimately formulating what was considered to be an important measure of the effectiveness of school systems. Mort and Cornell (1941) argued that the quality of school districts could be measured by their "adaptability" to change. Among the variables they identified as indicating the capacity for improvement were curricular innovations, new types of classes, and new classroom structures. Using an "adaptability index," the researchers found correlations between a district's adaptability rating and such characteristics as financial policies and district size.

Although scholars have depicted the 1960s as the period when researchers first began to challenge the notion that large school districts were more efficient and effective, we can find warnings embedded in the literature considerably earlier. In 1940, Cillié conducted a study of centralization and decentralization in school districts and argued that immense size—such as that of the New York City school system at the time—was related to inflexibility and powerlessness at all levels of the system.

Mort and Vincent (1946) looked directly at the problems increasingly faced by large city schools systems, the same kind that Cubberley and others had once argued enhanced professionalization and the quality of school districts. According to Mort and Vincent (1946),

Education in many ways is hampered in the large city, . . . because here, as nowhere else among American schools, education is centrally controlled. . . . You have no voice, no control, your questions go unanswered, your demands on the local administrator are parried by: "I'm sorry, but that matter is completely out of my hands; you will have to go to headquarters." But you can never get close enough to the man at headquarters who makes the decisions, and you give up. (p. 88)

Mort and Cornell (1941) argued that to be maximally effective, districts should include no more than 100,000 students. Later studies by Leggett and Vincent (1947) and a meta-analysis by Ross (1958) confirmed that estimate. In the 1960s, researchers returned to these themes.

It makes sense that we find deliberations about what makes for ideal district size, because the 1930s, 1940s, and 1950s marked renewed interest in research attention to district consolidation (cf. Dawson, 1934). During the worst years of the Great Depression, the commissioner of education convened meetings on proper district size and organization, primarily as a way to combat the shrinking educational coffers at every level of the system. Many of these efforts paused during World War II, but after the war researchers returned to the task. In 1946, through joint efforts at the Rural Education Project at the University of Chicago and the NEA, they redoubled their efforts and established the National Commission on School District Reorganization, which issued several reports, among them *Your School District* (National Commission on School District Reorganization, 1948), with the explicit charge of determining what constituted district quality. A "strong" district has at least 1,200 students, the commission stated, and it identified an enrollment of 10,000 as being a more ideal minimum; a "satisfactory" district had at least one elementary school with sufficient students for at least one teacher per grade (National Commission on School District Reorganization, 1948, p. 10).

Despite studies that questioned the role of size, reformers of the time continued to push for district reorganization and consolidation (National Commission on School District Reorganization, 1948). Although administrative reformers had made some progress during the previous decades, by the late 1940s there still remained some 103,000 local school districts (down from an estimated 200,000) scattered quite unevenly around the country; 15 of those were in Delaware, whereas Illinois had more than 10,000. The commission (National Commission on School District Reorganization, 1948) made several other points that may seem unusual for the time, including the contention that there never had been, nor should be, any kind of one best system. "One thing is perfectly clear: school organization in our country has never been static. Scarcely anyone believes that there is any one kind of local school administration unit that is superior to all other[s]" (p. 14).

Meanwhile, the commission matter-of-factly provided statistics on the supervisors who served counties in states throughout the country, listing the number of White and "Negro" supervisors, without additional comment. In fact, most elite academics, even those writing reports on and conducting surveys of school systems of the South, ignored the segregation that persisted throughout the country. With only a few exceptions (e.g., Washburne's 1942 survey of Louisiana schools), surveys described in business-like fashion the numeric tables of the inequitable funds that went to African American schools, perhaps along with mentions of the poor conditions of the buildings, statistics on the number of classrooms that were overcrowded, and the lack of proper books or materials.

DISTRICT STRUCTURE, ORGANIZATION, REORGANIZATION, AND DESEGREGATION: 1954 TO 1990

Although state-level rationales for district reorganization and consolidation between 1945 and 1960 typically focused on efficiency, local resistance to district reorganization was often influenced by race, not just loss of local control. In the wake of the 1954 *Brown* school desegregation decision, district reorganization efforts of the 1960s intersected with increasingly forceful Supreme Court desegregation mandates in the *Green* (1968) and *Swann* (1971) decisions. Districts in both the North and the South frequently used local control as a rationale to resist district consolidation and desegregation. Desegregation mandates were often treated with open resistance in the South and covert resistance in the North. However, in the South, despite massive resistance, district reorganization resulted in county-wide desegregation of school districts; eventually, the South became the most desegregated region of the country (Boger & Orfield, 2005). In the North, the reorganization and consolidation of small, fragmented districts were also influenced by race, though there was no "massive resistance" as there was in Virginia (Lassiter & Lewis, 1998). For example, Pennsylvania's *School District Reorganization Act of 1963* (Act 299) required each county to consolidate its school districts so that each district would serve at least 4,000 students (Lundin, 1973). However, a study of racial demographics before and after district consolidation in the Pittsburgh, Harrisburg, and Philadelphia metropolitan areas (each containing many small, fragmented districts required to merge with each other) found that, overall, school districts sought out mergers with demographically similar districts—reducing segregation very little if at all (Lundin, 1973).

There was some interest in metropolitan approaches to desegregation and district governance at the federal level—indeed, the 1968 yearbook of the National Society for the Study of Education was titled *Metropolitanism* and focused on metropolitan and regional concepts of school governance, such as education parks and interdistrict transfer plans. However, metropolitan desegregation efforts were hampered by the *Milliken v. Bradley* (1974) decision, ruling that the outlying suburbs of Detroit had no obligation to remedy the segregation in the city of Detroit, thereby solidifying fragmented district boundary lines in the North. The construction of interstate highways and inner- and outer-ring suburbs also exacerbated between-district segregation by creating more small, fragmented districts (Jackson, 1985; Massey & Denton, 1993).

Despite nominally desegregated districts, district boundary lines that stratified students along the lines of race and class became the norm in the wake of *Milliken*, with the few exceptions being the controlled choice plans in city-county districts such as Louisville-Jefferson County, Kentucky, and Charlotte-Mecklenburg County,

North Carolina (Siegel-Hawley, 2013), and the interdistrict transfer plans in cities such as St. Louis, Missouri (Wells & Crain, 1997), and Rochester, New York (Finnigan et al., 2015). The majority of recent school segregation is due to between-district segregation, rather than within-district segregation (Bischoff, 2008).

From our 21st-century perspective, reorganization seems to be an example of successful reform. After all, the number of school districts in the country plummeted from roughly 130,000 in the 1930s to approximately 55,000 in the mid-1950s, to under 18,000 by the 1970s; but, as always, success is in the eye of the beholder. As with many reform movements, the people most intimately involved with the innovation constantly perceived the distance between that which has been accomplished and that which remained to be done. Many reorganizers were vexed by the lack of local willingness to embrace their seemingly rational reforms. But it was their inability to understand the reasons behind local resistance that was often their undoing.

The second half of the 20th century is the story of states slowly wresting more and more power and responsibility from their local school districts, as standards-based reforms expected state educational agencies not only to administer money and collect data but also to take increasing responsibility for the quality of education (Massell, 1998).

A RENEWED FOCUS ON THE ROLE OF THE DISTRICT IN INSTRUCTIONAL IMPROVEMENT: 1990 TO 2016

By the mid-1990s, reformers were paying relatively little attention to the school district as an important factor in policy implementation. In fact, some reformers called for sidestepping the district central office entirely and focusing on the school as the unit of change. For example, the Cross City Campaign for Urban School Reform's 1995 report, *Reinventing Central Office: A Primer for Successful Schools*, recommended "a fundamental revision of urban public school systems, one that shifts virtually all funds and most authority to the schools and dismantles centralized, bureaucratic structures" (Berne et al., 1995, p. 3). Because of conceptions like this, education researcher James Spillane (1996) felt compelled to title a study of the implementation of reading policy in Michigan "School Districts Matter." Flagging how the district had not figured prominently in recent reform proposals, Spillane noted that district administrators' understandings of policy were critical in how they perceived policy problems and shaped their own solutions. Indeed, during the mid-1990s, much of the policy talk swirled around notions of "bottom-up" (school or classroom) reforms versus "top-down" (state or federal) reforms. School districts were not considered a key part of systemic reform; they did not play a pivotal role in decentralization efforts, and they were not necessarily involved in state efforts to boost the curriculum by means of academic standards.

Similarly, Spillane and Thompson (1997) drew attention to the idea that capacity at the local level means more than the capacity of teachers within the local educational agency (LEA), but also includes the capacity of the LEA itself. In other words, district administrators, coaches, and teacher leaders shape the policy understandings available to teachers. As a consequence, Spillane and Thompson (1997) argue that "LEAs' capacity to support ambitious instruction consists to a large degree of LEA leaders' ability to learn new ideas from external policy and professional sources and to help others within the district learn these ideas" (p. 187). These two articles on the role of the school district and the LEA (Spillane, 1996; Spillane & Thompson, 1997) represent a key turning point in the literature on school districts. They offer important new conceptions of the critical role of the school district in instructional improvement, which have inspired and driven a new generation of research literature over the past decade and a half.

Spillane's work points to the need to focus on district-level implementation and district actors' understanding of policy to achieve greater coherence across the policy system. Spillane ultimately concludes that districts matter in at least three key ways.

First, when district staff understand policy differently than state policymakers, those inconsistencies can undermine state policymakers' efforts. Spillane found that when states ignored districts, it did not prevent the districts from getting involved in instructional policymaking; it just made coherence more difficult.

Second, because districts are often responsible for instructional guidance through professional development, curriculum guidelines, and teacher supervision, they have a great deal of influence over the message that school practitioners receive about instructional policy. For example, in Spillane's study, the notions about teaching reading that were communicated in the districts' instructional guidance tools varied considerably across districts and were not necessarily consistent with state policymakers' reform ideas. When, for instance, district central office administrators initiated policies that supported rather traditional notions about instruction, the resources they mobilized limited the opportunities for teachers to comprehend the state-level reform messages.

Third, districts matter because they influence state-level efforts to increase the coherence of the instructional signals that are sent to school practitioners from within the school system. In Spillane's (1996) study, "the district's instructional policies conveyed one set of ideas about instruction to teachers, whereas state policy conveyed an altogether different message" (p. 85). Moreover, districts can find and utilize resources outside the traditional state jurisdictions, and these resources may have information similar to or different from that presented by the state.

Spillane's conclusion that districts matter in these ways is consistent with reform notions that had been building up for years prior to his study. One of those notions was that meaningful and complex policy—the kind that can help improve instruction—departs sharply from existing practice (e.g., D. K. Cohen & Barnes, 1993). Another was the idea of alignment in systemic reform—that instruction can best be accomplished in a coherent policy system with alignment in messages about instruction across levels of the system.

It should be noted, first, that for Spillane and for many of the studies that followed, it was not the district per se that was the focus of inquiry. Rather, the primary concern was how teachers and leaders in any given school or system were able to learn together and pursue ambitious instructional reform, as it was only through the combined effort that improvement could take place. Taken together, these articles (Spillane, 1996; Spillane & Thompson, 1997) offered an alternative viewpoint, in contrast to the literature that called for the abolition of districts or characterized them as befuddled bureaucracies unable to undertake change. Second, these two articles highlighted the necessity of collaborative policymaking—the understanding that educational policymaking is not a zero-sum game and that collaboration is necessary to fundamental change. Third, these articles concentrated attention on instructional improvement, a focus that became more important in the No Child Left Behind decade that followed, as researchers continued to dig deeper into the kinds of environments that provide the necessary conditions for continued educational enhancement at the district level.

Spillane's focus on the ways that district administrators were making sense of policy ushered in a new wave of research on school districts, with several strands: (a) the critical role of districts in instructional reform, (b) the importance of sense-making by district and other local actors in policy implementation, (c) district administrators' use of evidence to make decisions, (d) distributed leadership, and (e) the flow of information, trust, and advice through district communication networks.

The Role of Districts in Instructional Reform

Building on Spillane (1996) and Spillane and Thompson's (1997) findings on the importance of districts as gatekeepers of knowledge about reform, researchers came to a new appreciation of the role of the district in instructional reform. Gradually, school districts—when effectively run—came to be considered sites of powerful instructional change (e.g., MacIver & Farley, 2003), and a great deal of literature focused on identifying the elements of district leadership relevant to instructional improvement. By 2003, Togneri and Anderson's (2003) report *Beyond Islands of Excellence: What Districts Can Do to Improve Instruction and Achievement in All Schools* took for granted that districts can and should play a leading role in improving student learning (or at least, student achievement). Togneri and Anderson (2003) studied five high-poverty districts with rapidly improving test scores and narrowed achievement gaps, in order to identify the characteristics of effective districts (as in the effective schools research of the 1970s, but at the district level). These characteristics were sustained reform, data-driven decision making, a focus on instruction, and coherence in district curriculum and professional development. Finally, Togneri and Anderson recommended building principal capacity in instructional leadership while also distributing instructional leadership across content experts and mentor teachers.

Along the same lines, research studying urban districts' partnerships with intermediary organizations whose work revolved around ambitious instruction also suggested that building the capacity of administrators in district central offices would help create coherence (Marsh et al., 2005). Other research investigating the role of the district in instructional improvement used in-depth, single-district case studies to identify the factors associated with systemwide improvement (e.g., Supovitz, 2006). Building on the theme of the importance of the central office in instructional improvement, the Wallace Foundation sponsored a series of reports on improving school leadership, one of which concluded that "central office transformation" was an essential element of improving instruction in urban schools (Honig et al., 2010). Central office transformation that supports instructional improvement involves processes such as creating strong partnerships between the central office and school principals and reorienting the work of the central office to focus on supporting instruction (Honig et al., 2010).

More recently, Marsh and Wohlstetter (2013) picked up the theme of districts as important sites for reform, examining how some traditional school districts (among other nonsystem actors) have pushed back against reforms usually considered to be top-down, or taken the lead in implementing large-scale reforms ahead of states. For instance, Marsh and Wohlstetter point to the "CORE districts" in California, a group of mostly urban districts that independently petitioned the U.S. Department of Education for a waiver from the requirements of No Child Left Behind, as an example of districts taking the lead in shaping policy. The Wallace Foundation similarly acknowledged that school districts'

role has long been underappreciated: bypassed by reformers who believe the antidote to mediocre schools is to free them to manage their own improvement efforts with a minimum of regulatory interference, and scorned by those who regard districts and their employees as money-draining bureaucrats more interested in rules than school renewal. (Mitgang, 2013, p. 8)

However, this report also notes that districts shape principal pipelines, training, and ongoing professional development; thus, partnering with districts to improve principal preparation is an important part of any effort to improve instruction (Mitgang, 2013).

How District and School Administrators Make Sense of Policy

Building on Spillane's research on how district actors understand policy, a growing body of research began to use conceptual frameworks that integrated cognitive and sociocultural perspectives of policy implementation with organizational theory (e.g., Coburn, Toure, & Yamashita, 2009; Honig, 2003, 2008; Honig & Coburn, 2008). These frameworks differ in the extent to which they place more emphasis on the social aspects of meaning making, on the way that new knowledge is integrated with preexisting beliefs, and on the way that evidence can be used for rhetorical and political purposes. In general, however, this literature demonstrated how central office administrators, like other street-level bureaucrats, actively interpret policy and make decisions in ways that are consistent with their worldviews, backgrounds and experiences, and contexts, in a framework sometimes called *sense-making* (Coburn, 2005; Spillane, Reiser, & Reimer, 2002). Research using a sense-making perspective has also investigated how school leaders understand and enact policy, and how those understandings shape the policy messages available to teachers (Coburn, 2005; Spillane et al., 2002).

How District Administrators Use Evidence to Make Decisions

One strand of recent district-related research using sociocultural and organizational theories such as sense-making focuses on how central offices and district administrators use evidence to make decisions. For example, Coburn et al. (2009) analyzed a midsize district's instructional decisions over a 3-year period, finding that central office staff tended to interpret problems in ways consistent with their existing worldviews. Then, district staff marshaled evidence to justify their framing of a particular problem and solution, and to convince others of that solution. Similarly, Honig and Coburn's (2008) review of research on how district administrators used evidence found that district officials sometimes directly applied evidence to school improvement, but often used evidence to gather political support from different stakeholders for a particular initiative. In other instances, district offices used evidence to systematically examine and improve their own operation. Honig et al. (2010), in a study of three urban districts seeking to transform their central offices, found that one critical dimension was the "use of evidence throughout the central office to support continual improvement of work practices and relationships with schools" (p. ix). Honig and Coburn (2008) also found that although administrators have relied on school-level and student-level data as well as research evidence, they have also frequently relied on practitioner knowledge to make decisions.

How Leadership Responsibilities Are Distributed Across Networks of District Actors

A distinct, though related, strand of literature on district decision making focuses on "distributed leadership," or how leaders (broadly construed) and others interact in particular situations and contexts (Spillane, 2005; Spillane, Halverson, & Diamond, 2004). While the concept of distributed leadership is commonly invoked to describe how leadership responsibilities can be spread across teachers, coaches, and other individuals, rather than simply principals and superintendents, Spillane (2005) pointed out that distributed leadership is the practice of decision making as a dynamic interaction between leader, follower, and situation. Borrowing from organizational sociology, Spillane (2005) classified key aspects of the situation as *structures*, *routines*, and *tools*. For example, a school leader might create structures like professional learning communities governed by particular routines and protocols, and these communities might use the tool of student assessment data in particular ways that lead toward school improvement (Feldman & Pentland, 2003). Other research on distributed leadership suggests that teacher leaders can play an integral role in supporting district reform because of their personal relationships with other teachers (Firestone & Martinez, 2007).

Trust, Advice, and Information Flow Across Networks of District Actors

A final line of research that builds on sociocultural and organizational views of knowledge about policy and district reform is research using the tools of social network analysis to study district reform. Scholars interested in how policy is translated into practice in districts have increasingly used social network analysis to study how information, trust, and advice flow between actors within a district (e.g., Coburn, Russell, Kaufman, & Stein, 2012; Daly & Finnigan, 2010; Finnigan, Daly, & Che, 2013). Research in this vein often relies on questionnaires filled out by, or interviews with, teachers, coaches, and administrators within a school district, asking them with whom they talk about a policy or whom they perceive as having expertise about a particular reform (Moolenaar, 2012). The questionnaire and interview data can then be used to visually represent the presence or absence of social ties between actors within and between schools and central offices. These studies have emphasized the importance of the relational aspects of instructional improvement, such as trust and school climate (Finnigan & Daly, 2012; Spillane & Kim, 2012). Because individuals are often critical to information flow and policy knowledge, turnover—especially among school and district leaders—can be a significant barrier to sustainability of reform (Daly, Finnigan, & Liou, 2016). As part of the new literature on how districts can support instructional improvement, research using social network analysis finds that district policy can enable reform by providing the conditions that facilitate social interaction, as well as conditions that support consistent understandings of policy across administrators, coaches, and teachers (Coburn et al., 2012; Coburn & Russell, 2008; Daly & Finnigan, 2011).

CONCLUSION

Although few would consider the American school district a nimble institution, it is, and clearly has been, a dynamic one, changing form and function over the past 200 years. Once the most local of organizations—especially in its initial incarnation as the "district school" in the 19th century—the school district has transformed over time as the general purposes of education have broadened through the past century. Although researchers have become less sanguine than they were a century ago about the ability of the district to assist in educational improvement, we must also recognize that over the same period districts have been asked to devote increasing attention to populations that had previously been ill served or underserved, not only by public schools but also by a whole range of public institutions. Therefore, researchers and reformers alike should continue to look for ways that local districts can proactively adapt to changing circumstances while also fostering the kind of powerful instructional practice that will ensure future student learning, especially for children living in poverty.

We have seen that early 20th-century researchers believed that districts constituted the laboratories of democracy. Therefore, it is striking to observe that, in recent years, certain terms have rarely been associated with districts, such as *invent, experiment, propose, innovate,* and *originate.* The absence of an innovative attitude may reflect the many resource constraints on districts today, along with an ongoing history of mandates, compliance issues, and shifts in authority and flexibility. Nevertheless, if we want to enhance and build on the kinds of district-oriented instructional improvement that have engaged researchers and practitioners since the

1990s, we must look for ways to recapture the spirit of innovation that once characterized our school districts.

Based on the twists and turns of education history, we suggest several areas of research that might be productively pursued in the future. First, researchers might once again return to the question of what constitutes an optimal size range for school districts. Recent years have seen an interest in small schools and charter schools, but we know little about what benefits smaller districts might bring.

Second, if districts are no longer the originators of innovative practices and experimentation, researchers might ask where new ideas come from and how to help foster the spirit of innovation that is so critical to productive institutional growth. Is it possible that current efforts at uniformity, through projects like the Common Core State Standards and the associated assessments, have dampened efforts at creative invention?

Third, we might ask, what precisely is it about districts that has allowed them to persist for so long? Are there unrecognized strengths in districts that might be enhanced and developed?

Fourth, what role might teachers continue to play in ongoing district reform? Might the curriculum revision efforts that began in the 1920s offer one model for folding teachers into district-wide improvement efforts? Are there lessons here for how to successfully spread ambitious instructional practices within and across districts?

Finally, if state policymaking is not a zero-sum game (Marsh, 2002), then how might states reconsider the optimal role they can play in developing policies that will foster productive district improvement?

Although researchers are fully aware that districts are embedded within a larger frame of governmental agencies, it can be easy to forget that reality, especially when we are deeply engaged in local district research. Kaestle (1983) reminds us that the history of American federalism is one of constantly evolving relationships between local, state, and federal governments, "conditioned but not mechanically determined by technological, economic, political, constitutional, and cultural changes" (p. 224). We should expect that contestations about power, privilege, and instructional and organizational form will persist, periodically shifting in form and focus but never completely disappearing. Thus, as education researchers, we need to reenvision how the changing nature of the school district might best be harnessed in the service of improving student learning in the future.

NOTE

[1]Note that the *American Journal of Education* of 1826 is not the same *American Journal of Education* published by the University of Chicago Press today—that *American Journal of Education* began as *The School Review* in 1893.

REFERENCES

Alsbury, T. L. (2008). *The future of school board governance: Relevancy and revelation.* New York, NY: Rowman & Littlefield.

Ayres, L. P. (1909). *Laggards in our schools: A study of elimination and retardation in city school systems.* New York, NY: Russell Sage Foundation.

Barnard, H. (1865). Sixth annual report of the Superintendent of Common Schools to the General Assembly of Connecticut for 1851. *American Journal of Education, 5,* 293–310.

Bell, S. N. (1853). *A digest of the laws of New-Hampshire pertaining to common schools: With legal decisions, forms, prepared at the request of the secretary of state, agreeably to a resolution of the Legislature, passed June session, 1853.* Concord, NH: G. P. Lyon.

Berends, M., & Rand, E. (2002). *Challenges of conflicting school reforms: Effects of New American Schools in a high-poverty district* (Vol. 1). Santa Monica, CA: RAND.

Berman, P., & McLaughlin, M. (1977). *Federal programs supporting educational change: Vol. 7. Factors affecting implementation and continuation.* Santa Monica, CA: RAND.

Berman, P., & McLaughlin, M. (1978). *Federal programs supporting educational change: Vol. 8. Implementing and sustaining innovations.* Santa Monica, CA: RAND.

Berman, P., & McLaughlin, M. (1979). *An exploratory study of school district adaptation.* Santa Monica, CA: RAND.

Berne, R., Fine, M., Fruchter, N., Lauber, D., Lewis, H., Palaich, R., & Stillwell, T. (1995). *Reinventing central office: A primer for successful schools.* Chicago, IL: Cross City Campaign for Urban School Reform.

Bischoff, K. (2008). School district fragmentation and racial residential segregation: How do boundaries matter? *Urban Affairs Review, 44,* 182–217.

Bobbitt, J. F. (1913). The supervision of city schools. In S. C. Parker (Ed.), *The National Society for the Study of Education: Twelfth yearbook, Part 1* (pp. 7–96). Chicago, IL: University of Chicago Press.

Bobbitt, J. F. (1918). *The curriculum.* New York, NY: Houghton Mifflin.

Bobbitt, J. F. (1922). *Curriculum-making in Los Angeles.* Chicago, IL: University of Chicago Press.

Boger, J. C., & Orfield, G. (Eds.). (2005). *School resegregation: Must the South turn back?* Chapel Hill: University of North Carolina Press.

Bowles, S., & Gintis, H. (1975). Capitalism and education in the United States. *Socialist Revolution, 5,* 101–138.

Brown, E. E. (1915). Educational progress of the past fifteen years. *National Education Association Journal of Proceedings and Addresses,* 48–54.

Bruner, H. B. (1937). *Criteria for evaluating course-of-study materials.* New York, NY: Bureau of Publications, Teachers College, Columbia University.

Burgess, A. (1843). Allegany County. In *Annual report of the Superintendent of Common Schools of the State of New York with the reports of the Deputy Superintendents made to the legislature, Jan. 13, 1843* (pp. 76–91). Albany, NY: Thurlow Weed, Printer to the State.

Burns, J. J. (1879). *Twenty-fifth annual report of the State Commissioner of the Common Schools to the General Assembly of the state of Ohio for the school year ending August 31, 1878.* Columbus, OH: Nevins & Meyers.

Callahan, R. E. (1962). *Education and the cult of efficiency: A study of the social forces that have shaped the administration of the public schools.* Chicago, IL: University of Chicago Press.

Campbell, R. F., Cunningham, L. L., Nystrand, R. O., & Usdan, M. D. (1990). *The organization and control of American schools* (6th ed.). New York, NY: Merrill Macmillan.

Caswell, H. L. (1950). *Curriculum improvement in public school systems.* New York, NY: Bureau of Publications, Teachers College, Columbia University.

Chubb, J. E., & Moe, T. M. (1990). *Politics, markets, and America's schools.* Washington, DC: Brookings Institution Press.

Cillié, F. S. (1940). *Centralization or decentralization? A study in educational adaptation* (No. 789). New York, NY: Columbia University Press.

City school systems: Discussion. (1890). *National Education Association Journal of Proceedings and Addresses*, 460–468.

Coburn, C. E. (2005). Shaping teacher sensemaking: School leaders and the enactment of reading policy. *Educational Policy, 19*, 476–509.

Coburn, C. E., & Russell, J. L. (2008). District policy and teachers' social networks. *Educational Evaluation and Policy Analysis, 30*, 203–235.

Coburn, C. E., Russell, J. L., Kaufman, J. H., & Stein, M. K. (2012). Supporting sustainability: Teachers' advice networks and ambitious instructional reform. *American Journal of Education, 119*, 137–182.

Coburn, C. E., Toure, J., & Yamashita, M. (2009). Evidence, interpretation, and persuasion: Instructional decision making at the district central office. *Teachers College Record, 111*, 1115–1161.

Cocking, W. D. (1928). *Administrative procedures in curriculum making for public schools*. New York, NY: Bureau of Publications, Teachers College, Columbia University.

Cohen, D. K., & Barnes, C. A. (1993). Pedagogy and policy. In D. Cohen (Ed.), *Teaching for understanding: Challenges for policy and practice* (pp. 207–239). San Francisco, CA: Jossey-Bass.

Cohen, R. D. (1990). *Children of the mill: Schooling and society in Gary, Indiana, 1906–1960*. Bloomington: Indiana University Press.

Coleman, J. S., Campbell, E. Q., Hobson, C. J., McPartland, J., Mood, A. M., Weinfeld, F. D., & York, R. L. (1966). *Equality of educational opportunity*. Washington, DC: U.S. Government Printing Office. Retrieved from http://eric.ed.gov/?id=ED012275

Common school laws, being the acts in relation to common schools passed by the last General Assembly, at the session begun and held on the 6th Day of November, 1848, and ended on the 10th day of January, 1849. (1849). (Printed at the Gazette Office [Arkansas]). Retrieved from https://babel.hathitrust.org/cgi/pt?id=loc.ark:/13960/t77s8fm85;view=1up;seq=7

Cuban, L. (1993). *How teachers taught: Constancy and change in American classrooms, 1890–1990*. New York, NY: Teachers College Press.

Cubberley, E. P. (1909). *Changing conceptions of education*. Boston, MA: Houghton Mifflin.

Cubberley, E. P. (1915). Organization of public education. In *Proceedings and addresses of the Fifty-Third Annual Meeting and International Congress on Education* (pp. 91–96). Chicago, IL: University of Chicago Press.

Cubberley, E. P. (1916a). *Public school administration: A statement of the fundamental principles underlying the organization and administration of public education*. New York, NY: Houghton Mifflin.

Cubberley, E. P. (1916b). State and county school administration: Changes in practices and principles of action during the past quarter of a century. *School Board Journal, 52*(3), 10.

Curtin, A. G. (1855). *The common school laws of Pennsylvania, and decisions of the superintendent: With explanatory instructions and forms*. Harrisburg, PA: A. Boyd Hamilton, State Printer. Retrieved from https://babel.hathitrust.org/cgi/pt?id=uc1.31175035157208;view=1up;seq=3

Daly, A. J., & Finnigan, K. S. (2010). A bridge between worlds: Understanding network structure to understand change strategy. *Journal of Educational Change, 11*, 111–138.

Daly, A. J., & Finnigan, K. S. (2011). The ebb and flow of social network ties between district leaders under high-stakes accountability. *American Educational Research Journal, 48*, 39–79.

Daly, A. J., Finnigan, K. S., & Liou, Y. (2016). How leadership churn undermines learning and improvement in low-performing school districts. In A. J. Daly & K. S. Finnigan (Eds.), *Thinking and acting systematically: Improving school districts under pressure* (pp. 189–213). Washington, DC: American Educational Research Association.

Davidson, W. J. (Ed.). (1896). *Kentucky common school laws.* Louisville, KY: G. G. Fetter. Retrieved from https://babel.hathitrust.org/cgi/pt?id=uc2.ark:/13960/t7kp7x 52x;view=1up;seq=7

Dawson, H. A. (1934). *Satisfactory local school units: Functions and principles of formation, organization, and administration.* Nashville, TN: Division of Surveys and Field Studies, George Peabody College for Teachers.

Deffenbaugh, W. S. (1916). City schools of tomorrow. In *School administration progress of twenty-five years* (pp. 69–79). Milwaukee, WI: Bruce.

Dewey, J. (1916). *Democracy and education: An introduction to philosophy of education.* New York, NY: Macmillan.

Dewey, J. (1927). *The public and its problems.* New York, NY: Henry Holt.

Discussion of Mr. Bicknell's paper on a national council of education, and resolution thereon. (1880). *Circulars of Information of the Bureau of Education,* 1880(2), 15–19. Proceedings of the Department of Superintendence of the National Education Association, at its meeting in Washington, D.C., February 18–20, 1880. In *Addresses and Journal of Proceedings of the National Education Association,* 1880.

Edmonds, R. (1979). Effective schools for the urban poor. *Educational Leadership, 37*(1), 15–24.

Feldman, M. S., & Pentland, B. T. (2003). Reconceptualizing organizational routines as a source of flexibility and change. *Administrative Science Quarterly, 48,* 94–118.

Finnigan, K. S., & Daly, A. J. (2012). Mind the gap: Organizational learning and improvement in an underperforming urban system. *American Journal of Education, 119,* 41–71.

Finnigan, K. S., Daly, A. J., & Che, J. (2013). Systemwide reform in districts under pressure: The role of social networks in defining, acquiring, using, and diffusing research evidence. *Journal of Educational Administration, 51,* 476–497.

Finnigan, K. S., Holme, J. J., Orfield, M., Luce, T., Diem, S., Mattheis, A., & Hylton, N. D. (2015). Regional educational policy analysis: Rochester, Omaha, and Minneapolis' interdistrict arrangements. *Educational Policy, 29,* 780–814.

Firestone, W. A., & Martinez, C. M. (2007). Districts, teacher leaders, and distributed leadership: Changing instructional practice. *Leadership and Policy in Schools, 6*(1), 3–35.

Fuhrman, S. H., & Elmore, R. F. (1990). Understanding local control in the wake of state education reform. *Educational Evaluation and Policy Analysis, 12*(1), 82–96.

Gamson, D., & Hodge, E. (in press). *The shifting landscape of the American school district: Race, class, geography, and the perpetual reform of local control, 1935–2015.* New York, NY: Peter Lang.

Gittell, M. (1965). A pilot study of Negro middle class attitudes toward higher education in New York. *Journal of Negro Education, 34,* 385–394.

Graham, P. A. (1967). *Progressive education: From Arcady to academe.* New York, NY: Teachers College Press.

Greer, C. (1972). *The great school legend: A revisionist interpretation of American public education.* New York, NY: Basic Books.

Hallinger, P. (2013). A conceptual framework for systematic reviews of research in educational leadership and management. *Journal of Educational Administration, 51,* 126–149.

Hanus, P. H. (1913). Improving school systems by scientific management: Underlying principles. *National Education Association Journal of Proceedings and Addresses,* 247–259.

Hill, P. T. (1995). *Reinventing public education.* Santa Monica, CA: RAND.

Honig, M. I. (2003). Building policy from practice: District central office administrators' roles and capacity for implementing collaborative education policy. *Educational Administration Quarterly, 39,* 292–338.

Honig, M. I. (2008). District central offices as learning organizations: How sociocultural and organizational learning theories elaborate district central office administrators' participation in teaching and learning improvement efforts. *American Journal of Education, 114,* 627–664.

Honig, M. I., & Coburn, C. (2008). Evidence-based decision making in school district central offices: Toward a policy and research agenda. *Educational Policy, 22,* 578–608.

Honig, M. I., Copland, M. A., Rainey, L., Lorton, J. A., & Newton, M. (2010). *Central office transformation for district-wide teaching and learning improvement.* Seattle: Center for the Study of Teaching and Policy, University of Washington.

Iannaccone, L., & Lutz, F. W. (1995). The crucible of democracy: The local arena. In J. Scribner & D. Layton (Eds.), *The study of educational politics: The 1994 commemorative yearbook of the Politics of Education Association, 1969–1994* (pp. 39–52). Washington, DC: Falmer.

Jackson, K. T. (1985). *Crabgrass frontier: The suburbanization of the United States.* New York, NY: Oxford University Press.

Judd, C. H. (1915). Reading tests: Report of the committee on tests and standards of efficiency in schools and systems. *National Education Association Journal of Proceedings and Addresses,* 561–565.

Judd, C. H. (1925). The curriculum: A paramount issue. *National Education Association of the United States Addresses and Proceedings,* 806–807.

Kaestle, C. F. (1983). *Pillars of the republic: Common schools and American society, 1780–1860* (1st ed.). New York, NY: Hill & Wang.

Katz, M. B. (1971). From voluntarism to bureaucracy in American education. *Sociology of Education, 44,* 297–332.

Katz, M. B. (1975). *Class, bureaucracy, and the schools.* New York, NY: Praeger.

Katz, M. B. (1987). *Reconstructing American education.* Cambridge, MA: Harvard University Press.

Kliebard, H. M. (1995). *The struggle for the American curriculum, 1893–1958.* New York, NY: Routledge-Falmer.

Kozol, J. (1967). *Death at an early age: The destruction of the hearts and minds of Negro children in the Boston public schools.* Boston, MA: Houghton Mifflin.

Lagemann, E. C. (2000). *An elusive science: The troubling history of education research.* Chicago, IL: University of Chicago Press.

Land, D. (2002). Local school boards under review: Their role and effectiveness in relation to students' academic achievement. *Review of Educational Research, 72,* 229–278.

Lassiter, M. D., & Lewis, A. (Eds.). (1998). *The moderates' dilemma: Massive resistance to school desegregation in Virginia.* Charlottesville: University of Virginia Press.

Leggett, S. F., & Vincent, W. F. (1947). *A program for meeting the needs of New York City schools.* New York, NY: Public Education Association.

Levin, H. M. (1988). *Accelerated schools for at-risk students* (CPRE Research Report Series RR-010). Philadelphia, PA: Center for Policy Research in Education.

Lopate, C., Flaxman, E., Bynum, E. M., & Gordon, E. W. (1970). Decentralization and community participation in public education. *Review of Educational Research, 40,* 135–150.

Lundin, G. E. (1973). *School district reorganization in Pennsylvania between 1963 and 1971 and its effect on racial balance* (Unpublished doctoral dissertation). University of Pittsburgh, PA.

MacIver, M. A., & Farley, E. (2003). *Bringing the district back in: The role of the central office in improving instruction and student achievement.* Baltimore, MD: Center for Research on the Education of Students Placed at Risk, Johns Hopkins University.

Marsh, J. A. (2002). How districts relate to states, schools, and communities: A review of emerging literature. In A. M. Hightower, M. S. Knapp, J. A. Marsh, & M. W. McLaughlin (Eds.), *School districts and instructional renewal* (pp. 25–40). New York, NY: Teachers College Press.

Marsh, J. A., Kerr, K. A., Ikemoto, G. S., Darilek, H., Suttorp, M., Zimmer, R. W., & Barney, H. (2005). *The role of districts in fostering instructional improvement: Lessons from three urban districts partnered with the Institute for Learning.* Santa Monica, CA: RAND.

Marsh, J. A., & Wohlstetter, P. (2013). Recent trends in intergovernmental relations: The resurgence of local actors in education policy. *Educational Researcher, 42,* 276–283.

Massell, D. (1998). *State strategies for building local capacity: Addressing the needs of standards-based reform* (CPRE Policy Briefs). Philadelphia, PA: Consortium for Policy Research in Education.

Massey, D., & Denton, N. A. (1993). *American apartheid: Segregation and the making of the underclass.* Cambridge, MA: Harvard University Press.

May, H. F. (1994). *The end of American innocence: A study of the first years of our own time, 1912–1917.* New York, NY: Columbia University Press. (Original work published 1959)

McDermott, K. A. (1999). *Controlling public education: Localism versus equity. Studies in government and public policy.* Lawrence: University Press of Kansas.

McNally, J. J., & Passow, A. H. (1960). *Improving the quality of public school programs: Approaches to curriculum development.* New York, NY: Teachers College Press.

McQuillan, P. J., & Muncey, D. E. (1994). "Change takes time": A look at the growth and development of the Coalition of Essential Schools. *Journal of Curriculum Studies, 26,* 265–279.

Mirel, J. (1993). *The rise and fall of an urban school system: Detroit, 1907–81.* Ann Arbor: University of Michigan Press.

Mitgang, L. (2013). *Districts matter: Cultivating the principals urban schools need.* New York, NY: Wallace Foundation.

Moolenaar, N. M. (2012). A social network perspective on teacher collaboration in schools: Theory, methodology, and applications. *American Journal of Education, 119*(1), 7–39.

Mort, P. R., & Cornell, F. G. (1941). *American schools in transition: How our schools adapt their practices to changing needs. A study of Pennsylvania.* New York, NY: Teachers College Press.

Mort, P. R., & Vincent, W. S. (1946). *A look at our schools.* New York, NY: Cattell.

Munro, W. (1917). *The government of American cities.* New York, NY: Macmillan.

National Commission on School District Reorganization. (1948). *Your school district: The report of the National Commission on School District Reorganization.* Washington, DC: Department of Rural Education, National Education Association of the United States.

New York City Public Schools. (1904). *Seventh annual report of the city superintendent of schools.* New York, NY: Department of Education.

Newlon, J. H., & Threlkeld, A. L. (1926). The Denver curriculum-revision program. In *The foundations and technique of curriculum construction, Part I. Curriculum-making: Past and present: The twenty-sixth yearbook of the National Society for the Study of Education* (pp. 229–240). Bloomington, IL: Public School.

Oakes, J. (1985). *Keeping track.* New Haven, CT: Yale University Press.

Philbrick, J. D. (1885). *City school systems in the United States.* Washington, DC: U.S. Bureau of Education, Government Printing Office.

Prospectus. (1826). *American Journal of Education, 1*(1), 1.

Purkey, S. C., & Smith, M. S. (1985). School reform: The district policy implications of the effective schools literature. *Elementary School Journal, 85,* 353–389.

Raftery, J. R. (1992). *Land of fair promise: Politics and reform in Los Angeles schools, 1885–1941.* Stanford, CA: Stanford University Press.

Raudenbush, S. W., & Willms, J. D. (1995). The estimation of school effects. *Journal of Educational and Behavioral Statistics, 20,* 307–335. doi:10.2307/1165304

Ravitch, D. (1978). *The revisionists revised: A critique of the radical attack on the schools.* New York, NY: Basic Books.

Ravitch, D. (1983). *The troubled crusade: American education, 1945–1980.* New York, NY: Basic Books.

Rice, J. M. (1893). *The public-school system of the United States.* New York, NY: Century.

Rogers, D. (1968). *110 Livingston Street: Politics and bureaucracy in the New York City schools.* New York, NY: Random House.

Rorrer, A. K., Skrla, L., & Scheurich, J. J. (2008). Districts as institutional actors in educational reform. *Educational Administration Quarterly, 44,* 307–357. doi:10.1177/00131 61X08318962

Ross, D. H. (Ed.). (1958). *Administration for adaptability.* New York, NY: Metropolitan School Study Council.

Ryan, A. M. (2011). From child study to efficiency: District administrators and the use of testing in the Chicago public schools, 1899 to 1928. *Paedagogica Historica, 47,* 341–354.

Schrag, P. (1967). *Village school downtown: Politics and education. A Boston report.* Boston, MA: Beacon Press.

Siegel-Hawley, G. (2013). Mitigating *Milliken?* School district boundary lines and desegregation policy in four southern metropolitan areas, 1990–2010. *American Journal of Education, 120,* 391–433.

Slavin, R. E. (1996). *Every child, every school: Success for all.* Thousand Oaks, CA: Corwin Press.

Smith, M. S., & O'Day, J. (1991). Systemic school reform. In S. H. Fuhrman & B. Malen (Eds.), *The politics of curriculum and testing: The 1990 yearbook of the Politics of Education Association* (pp. 233–267). Bristol, PA: Falmer.

Snedden, D. S., & Allen, W. H. (1908). *School reports and school efficiency.* New York, NY: Macmillan.

Snyder, T. D., de Brey, C., & Dillow, S. A. (2016). *Digest of education statistics 2014* (NCES 2016-006). Washington, DC: National Center for Education Statistics, Institute of Education Sciences, U.S. Department of Education.

Spillane, J. P. (1996). School districts matter: Local educational authorities and state instructional policy. *Educational Policy, 10*(1), 63–87.

Spillane, J. P. (2005). Distributed leadership. *Educational Forum, 69,* 143–150.

Spillane, J. P., Halverson, R., & Diamond, J. (2004). Theory of leadership practice: A distributed perspective. *Journal of Curriculum Studies, 36*(1), 3–34.

Spillane, J. P., & Kim, C. M. (2012). An exploratory analysis of formal school leaders' positioning in instructional advice and information networks in elementary schools. *American Journal of Education, 119,* 73–102.

Spillane, J. P., Reiser, B. J., & Reimer, T. (2002). Policy implementation and cognition: Reframing and refocusing implementation research. *Review of Educational Research, 72,* 387–431.

Spillane, J. P., & Thompson, C. L. (1997). Reconstructing conceptions of local capacity: The local education agency's capacity for ambitious instructional reform. *Educational Evaluation and Policy Analysis, 19,* 185–203.

Spring, J. (1972). *Education and the rise of the corporate state.* Boston, MA: Beacon.

Statutes of the State of New-York relating to common schools: Including Title II, of Chapter XV, Part I, of the revised statutes, as amended by the Act Chapter 480, Laws of 1847. (1847). Albany, NY: C. Van Benthuysen, Public Printer.

Supovitz, J. A. (2006). *The case for district-based reform: Leading, building and sustaining school improvement.* Cambridge, MA: Harvard Education Press.

Teddlie, C., & Stringfield, S. (1993). *Schools make a difference: Lessons learned from a 10-year study of school effects.* New York, NY: Teachers College Press.

Terman, L. M., Dickson, V. E., Sutherland, A. H., Franzen, R. H., Tupper, C. R., & Fernald, G. M. (1922). *Intelligence tests and school reorganization.* Yonkers-on-Hudson, NY: World Book Company.

Togneri, W., & Anderson, S. E. (2003). *Beyond islands of excellence: What districts can do to improve instruction and achievement in all schools: A leadership brief.* Alexandra, VA: Learning First Alliance.

Trillingham, C. C. (1934). *The organization and administration of curriculum programs.* Los Angeles: University of Southern California Press.

Trujillo, T. (2013). The reincarnation of the effective schools research: Rethinking the literature on district effectiveness. *Journal of Educational Administration, 51,* 426–452.

Tyack, D. B. (1974). *The one best system: A history of American urban education* (Vol. 95). Cambridge, MA: Harvard University Press.

Washburne, C. (1942). *Louisiana looks at its schools: A summary report of the Louisiana educational survey.* Baton Rouge: Louisiana Educational Survey Commission.

Wells, A. S., & Crain, R. L. (1997). *Stepping over the color line: African-American students in White suburban schools.* New Haven, CT: Yale University Press.

Wesley, E. B. (1957). *NEA: The first hundred years, the building of the teaching profession.* New York, NY: Harper.

Westbrook, R. B. (1991). *John Dewey and American democracy.* Ithaca, NY: Cornell University Press.

Wiebe, R. H. (1967). *The search for order, 1877–1920.* New York, NY: Hill & Wang.

Zeigler, H., Tucker, H. J., & Wilson, L. A. (1977). Communication and decision making in American public education: A longitudinal and comparative study. In J. D. Scribner (Ed.), *The politics of education: The seventy-sixth yearbook of the National Society for the Study of Education* (pp. 218–254). Chicago, IL: University of Chicago Press.

Zilversmit, A. (1993). *Changing schools: Progressive education theory and practice.* Chicago, IL: University of Chicago Press.

Chapter 8

The Political Economy of Market-Based Educational Policies: Race and Reform in Urban School Districts, 1915 to 2016

Janelle Scott
University of California, Berkeley

Jennifer Jellison Holme
The University of Texas at Austin

The authors situate the emergence and effects of contemporary market-based reforms within a framework of urban political economy that centers on racial inequality. They discuss how and why market-based reforms have evolved alongside racialized political and economic trends that have transformed cities over the past century, and they critically evaluate the research literature in light of such trends. The authors argue that deterioration of the urban core's infrastructure, schools, and housing has created ripe conditions for market-oriented reforms to take root. They also argue that these reforms have exacerbated divides in increasingly unequal and bifurcated cities. The authors conclude that these intersections and interactions between market-based reforms and urban contexts must be addressed by policy and research.

In 2015, a group of African American parents and community members in the Bronzeville neighborhood on the South Side of Chicago staged a 34-day hunger strike. The 15 hunger strikers were protesting the Chicago Public Schools' (CPS) decision to close the only remaining comprehensive high school on the South Side of Chicago, preferring that it instead be reopened as a school focused on green science and technology. The CPS reasoned that the school was underperforming and that the neighborhood lacked sufficient numbers of children to populate the school. But these activists feared that Dyett High School would undergo a fate experienced by dozens of schools in their region: takeover and closure by the CPS and conversion to a charter school operated by a private charter management organization.

In 2013 alone, the CPS had closed nearly 50 schools on the South Side. After increased national and international scrutiny, the CPS agreed to reopen the school,

Review of Research in Education
March 2016, Vol. 40, pp. 250–297
DOI: 10.3102/0091732X16681001
© 2016 AERA. http://rre.aera.net

not as a science-focused high school, but rather one that centered on the arts. The strikers declared a provisional victory in that they had succeeded in securing a community voice, resisting another district takeover, and keeping another school that served African American and Latino students in Chicago from being contracted out (Cholke, 2015). The new Dyett High School opened in 2016. According to Jitu Brown, one of the leaders of the strike and national director of the Journey for Justice Alliance, the move by the district echoed other actions in similar urban spaces:

In Chicago, New Orleans, Camden, Philadelphia, Newark, DC, Detroit and scores of other cities where the schools serve primarily children of color, a common denominator is that we don't have voting rights. Our silence is demanded, while school boards in over 94% of America's cities are elected. We have no direct way to hold officials accountable for the policies they set. Here is what we know; nationally, only 1 out of 5 charters outperform traditional public schools, but we see across this country the starving of neighborhood schools while charters and contract schools are expanded. We know that in Chicago since 2002, only 18% of the schools that replaced closed schools perform well. In New York under Bloomberg, after closing nearly 160 schools, only 13% of Black and Brown children graduated college and career ready. As if "accountability to the public" is the problem with public education. (Brown, 2015, p. 1)

The impasse between the strikers and the CPS reflected a broader dynamic underway in urban school districts across the United States: rapidly gentrifying cities with vast wealth inequality, market-oriented school policies aimed at increasing school choice and private operation of district schools, and hypersegregation within cities and across metropolitan areas. We deploy the terms *market-oriented policies* and *market-based policies* to refer to education policies that incorporate elements of capitalism into their design. These include charter schools, vouchers, merit pay for teachers and students, mayoral control, contracting, school closures, and the use of high-stakes standardized assessments to judge student learning and school and system quality (Persson, 2015).

Market-oriented policies have been established, even flourished, in the very contexts in which people of color were spatially marginalized through private and public policies across the last century. Over the past several decades in Chicago, for example, state and city divestment in public housing, coupled with redevelopment that rendered alternatives unaffordable, had displaced thousands of African American residents. Ewing (2015), writing about the Dyett standoff, noted this connection:

Perhaps the demographic changes that drove enrollment numbers down at schools like Dyett—indeed, the very "utilization crisis" itself—did not arise by happenstance but through the machinations of where and how Black people in Chicago have been allowed to live in the course of the last hundred years. (p. 7)

Indeed, as African Americans migrated from the American South into cities like Chicago, they were often faced with violence, redlining, and restrictive covenants that segregated them into densely populated parts of the city (Ewing, 2015). By the 1970s, when industry and related job opportunities dissipated, these racially segregated sections of cities became even more vulnerable. In addition, states often dramatically reduced funding to cities as White and middle-class residents fled to the suburbs (Davis, 2014). As desegregation mandates were vacated or rendered difficult to implement because of demographic shifts in school districts, school choice policies expanded by the 2000s. These social convergences have created fertile soil in which school choice and privatization have taken root in many urban school districts, including Detroit, Newark, New Orleans, Philadelphia, Washington, D.C., and Los Angeles (Garnett, 2014; Turque, 2008).

THE CONTEMPORARY POLICY LANDSCAPE OF URBAN MARKET REFORMS

As in Chicago, education policies that incorporate elements of the market, such as competition, school closures, school choice, merit pay, high-stakes accountability, and private contracting, have grown across the United States over the past six decades, especially in urban school districts. Such policies include charter schools, vouchers, tuition tax credit plans, and online or virtual schools (National Center for Education Statistics, 2011).[1] In addition, the private, for-profit, and nonprofit educational management and provider sectors have grown apace with these policy developments, with school district leaders contracting with the private sector for an increasing number of services formerly delivered by school districts (Burch, 2009).

These policies have coincided with demographic and sociopolitical shifts that have resulted in urban schools that enroll predominantly children living in poverty and children of color. At the same time, policies have produced a decline in school integration plans and rising state disinvestment in public K–12 and higher education. Education donors and philanthropies, seeking to radically alter the operation of public schools and public school systems, have invested hundreds of millions of dollars in legislative advocacy, school board elections, and the production of research evidence in order to implement market reforms across the nation's largest urban school districts (Reckhow, Henig, Jacobsen, & Litt, 2016; Scott & Jabbar, 2014; Tompkins-Stange, 2016).

The adoption and implementation of these policies has been controversial, not simply because they alter longstanding governance structures, the influence of teachers' unions, and classroom practices but also because they directly affect children and communities that have long been the least well served by public and private institutions. These communities have typically sought redress through the mechanisms of the state: litigation, democratic participation, and elections. Neoliberal educational reforms, however, often disrupt traditional pathways to community engagement and reshape them along individualistic dimensions of parental choice, and receive significant funding from venture philanthropies and conservative legislative networks such as the American Legislative Exchange Council (G. Anderson & Donchik, 2016; Pedroni, 2007).

In many ways, these policies serve as a rejection of the common school ideal. Policymakers, donors, and advocates have reframed urban public education as primarily a private good, where school quality is best determined by parents and delivered not through traditional school district oversight but rather through a panoply of diverse school providers who compete for students and students' data (Labaree, 1997). In addition, advocates, supported by venture philanthropies and donors, have called for a reimagining of school districts to serve as managers of diverse portfolios of schools—some traditional, some operated by management organizations, others online, for example—rather than functioning to operate schools as a unified system (Bulkley, Henig, & Levin, 2010; Tompkins-Stange, 2016).

The politics that created these system transformations are complex. A core group of philanthropies have invested millions of dollars into these urban districts on the condition that they expand market-oriented education policies (Henig, 2013; Reckhow, 2013; Scott, 2009; Zehr, 2011; Zeichner & Peña-Sandoval, 2015). Many market reform advocates claim that these urban district transformations are aligned with goals for empowerment and equality of opportunity, and a number of advocates of color have aligned with these reform efforts, while tens of thousands of parents have enrolled their children in charter and voucher schools (Pattillo, 2015; Pedroni, 2007; Scott, 2011b). At the same time, fierce resistance from communities of color has also emerged over issues of access, governance, and voice as policy makers have adopted and implemented these policies (Buras, 2011; Scott, 2011c; Scott & Fruchter, 2009).

While parents, advocacy groups, and philanthropic organizations have embraced many elements of these market-oriented policies, the transformations are not simply reflections of policymaker or citizen preferences. They are also connected to broader social, political, ideological, and economic trends, particularly the globalization, gentrification, spatial segregation, and job market bifurcation that have increasingly characterized urban areas, especially in the past two decades (Lipman, 2002, 2004; Sassen, 2011).

As we illustrate in this chapter, however, these trends also have deeper roots, emanating from shifts in urban space that began in the early part of the 20th century. Revealing these roots requires a focus on the political economy of urban education, with an explicit focus on the centrality of race and educational justice (Brayboy, Castagno, & Maughan, 2007). These transformations over the past century have had consequences for the structure and governance of school systems, the racial and socioeconomic segregation of schools within cities, the growing racial segregation into surrounding and more remote suburbs, and the changing face of teaching and leadership in schools and within school systems. An empirical and conceptual analysis requires an intersectional understanding of the issues connected to urban education policy in the 21st century (G. Anderson & Donchik, 2016; G. Anderson & Scott, 2012; G. Orfield, 2001).

The expansion of market-oriented policies in the midst of these spatial alterations requires a review of the literature that broadens the theoretical terrain in which choice and competition take center stage. A number of scholars have examined the sociology of markets through institutional, network, or economic analysis, producing important conceptual advances and empirical findings on the structure and dynamics of spatial and political shifts (Fligstein & Dauter, 2007). Our review builds upon this work while also echoing Rury and Mirel (1997) in its conclusion that the political economy of urban school districts and market reforms requires a more explicit focus on the racialized history of urban space to fully capture the effects of efforts to improve or transform schools and in order to evaluate those efforts. This broader lens should incorporate and account for political, economic, and sociological contexts.

In this chapter, we situate the emergence and effects of contemporary market-based reforms within a framework of urban political economy. Our analysis is grounded by the seminal *Review of Research in Education* piece published in 1997 by John Rury and Jeffrey Mirel, titled "The Political Economy of Urban Education." Our framework, like that of Rury and Mirel (1997), highlights the interrelationships between power, race, politics, urban space, and educational reform. We discuss how and why market-based reforms have evolved, given sociopolitical, racial, and economic trends over the past century, and we critically evaluate the research literature in light of such trends. We start our analysis just 15 years after the turn of the 20th century in order to provide a background on the historical context and the political economy of urban space, and to provide a broader overview of the evolution of cities alongside the development of schooling in the United States.

This review examines the transformations in metropolitan areas and how the demographics of schools and school systems have reflected the growing racial and economic divide between cities and suburbs. In addition, as the U.S. population becomes more racially and ethnically diverse (U.S. Census Bureau, 2012), yet deeply unequal in social and economic opportunity, challenges emerge in terms of generating broad-based consensus about the need to provide sufficient state support to all public schools. In our analysis, we argue that the trends that left the urban core's infrastructure, schools, and housing to deteriorate have created ripe conditions for market-oriented reforms to take root. We also argue that these reforms have exacerbated divides in increasingly unequal cities. While Rury and Mirel (1997) concluded that schools could not be reformed without attending to the crisis-facing cities, we argue that the fate of cities is also shaped by school reform and, in particular, marketization in education. We conclude that these intersections and interactions must be addressed by policy and research in ways that center the unresolved issues of racial inequality and educational justice.

FRAMEWORK AND METHOD

Our framework for reviewing the literature on the changing dynamics of urban space and suburban space incorporates research on economic and racial segregation, globalization, and disinvestment and reinvestment in urban cores. As noted, we draw heavily from Rury and Mirel's (1997) chapter in the *Review of Research in Education*. When we were doctoral students, we read this piece closely. It greatly informed our choices of dissertation topics and has continued to inform our work on desegregation, school choice, and the politics of education. Rury and Mirel provided an analytic framework through which the 1990s crisis of academic failure, segregation, and concentrated poverty facing urban schools could be understood. In their analysis, they critiqued much of existing education research for "too often accept[ing] the urban environment as a given natural setting, rather than one that has itself been determined by larger economic and political processes" (p. 85). To fully understand the dynamics of urban educational inequality, Rury and Mirel argued that researchers needed to employ a broad theoretical lens, drawing from multiple disciplines, including economic, sociological, and political perspectives. Their project ultimately sought to examine the "political and economic forces that have shaped urban schools, drawing on extant research literature on urban education and related social science disciplines to identify and discuss them" (p. 49).

In the nearly two decades since this seminal publication, market-oriented reforms have greatly expanded in scope and in number; new advocacy organizations have emerged; school desegregation plans have been vacated; and cities have undergone significant spatial, economic, political, and demographic transformations. In addition, wealth inequality in the United States has reached Depression Era levels (Hacker & Pierson, 2010). Within this widening economic inequality, African Americans have been especially affected. They were specifically targeted by the subprime mortgage schemes that decimated their accumulated wealth during the Great Recession of 2008 (Pedroni, 2011), and have been slower than other racial groups to enjoy the subsequent economic recovery. In addition, many cities are undergoing major demographic shifts, as younger, Whiter, and more highly educated transplants move into the city centers abandoned by their parents and grandparents (Lipman, 2011). Public education in these settings has been characterized by a rise in school closures, in the growth of charter schools, and in rates of racial, socioeconomic, and linguistic segregation. School closures, teacher layoffs, and charter school growth have been largely concentrated in African American and Latino neighborhoods, triggering a spate of civil rights complaints and community outcry (Otterman, 2011; Pappas, 2012; Trujillo, 2016). We apply a political economy analysis to the emergence of these trends in contexts of these and other significant urban transformations. We examine developments in urban space, school desegregation, and educational markets over the past century, but focus our review of education research, in particular, on the past several decades in light of the rapid shifts in these areas.

To construct our review, we analyzed three broad areas of scholarship, drawing on traditional scholarly databases (e.g., JSTOR, ERIC, Sociological Abstracts), as well as our own knowledge of the research in these areas as reflected within our own scholarship. We also considered reports produced by research organizations, think tanks, and news media. We first examined the literature on the changing dynamics of urban space, exploring interrelated issues of economic and racial segregation, globalization, and disinvestment and reinvestment in urban cores. Second, we examined literature that describes how these dynamics have shaped districts and urban school district reform. We therefore examined the policy efforts to address the challenges created by the broader political and economic trends, and how and why market-based reforms emerged in the midst of such efforts. Third, we reviewed the literature on the outcomes and effects of market-based reforms, particularly for urban schools, and the implications of those reforms for urban political dynamics. In that final review area, we attended to research that examined not only academic effects but also social and political ones. We drew from recent literature on the trends and politics of inequality and the changing dynamics of urban space. In the process, we explored research on the interrelated issues of economic and racial segregation, globalization, and disinvestment and reinvestment in urban core.

THE POLITICAL ECONOMY OF URBAN SCHOOLING

In the next section, we detail the elements of the economy framework that we employ to review the literature on the changing dynamics of urban space, and to situate the emergence of market-based reforms. Our framework on the political economy of urban schools draws from conceptual insights from several scholarly traditions, including education, economics, sociology, critical geography, and public policy. We then, in the subsequent section, develop our analysis of the literature on the political economy of urban school privatization.

Urban Political Economy

Urban political economy frameworks emerged in the 1970s as a challenge to the ecological theories of urban development that had been set forth by scholars in the Chicago School of Sociology (Kleniewski & Thomas, 2011). The urban ecological frameworks developed by theorists such as Robert Park and Ernest Burgess in the 1920s sought to explain urban life through a perspective that emphasized the interdependence of geographic areas within cities, and the functional role of the spatial concentration of populations. Under this perspective, the urban environment evolved naturally and became spatially differentiated in a way that reflected the different functions of cities and groups. This spatial differentiation was not just efficient; it also promoted group cohesion and interdependence (Logan & Molotch, 2007). In the ecological perspective, as Logan and Molotch (2007) wrote, "The result is an optimal ordering of human settlement, in which the only real interests are the shared ones of keeping the market system functioning smoothly. Inequality is inevitable, but benign" (p. 6).

Over time, theorists began to question this benevolent view of markets and urban space. Some scholars argued for the need to give greater credence to the role of political, business, and governmental actors in shaping the patterns that ecologists viewed as "natural" outgrowths of intergroup competition. The urban political economy perspective thus broadened the ecological perspective on cities to focus on understanding how metropolitan environments were shaped by powerful actors, government, and the macroeconomy (Kleniewski & Thomas, 2011).

The urban political economy framework has its roots in a Marxian framework, which regards the built environment as the product of the processes of capitalism and also as a vehicle for capital accumulation in its own right. Marxian theorists argued that capitalism controlled the dynamics of urban geography. For example, Engels

rejected the notion that urban land use was simply a matter of the process of bidding for land in an impersonal marketplace. Instead, he pointed us toward a more fundamental mechanism of the social, economic, and political domination of one social class over another. To Engels, the economic and social relations of the workplace, in which the employers dominated the workers, formed a foundation for all other aspects of life, including urban patterns. (Kleniewski & Thomas, 2011, p. 34)

Similarly, theorist David Harvey argued that "the surface appearance of conflicts around the built environment—the struggles against the landlord or against urban renewal—conceals a hidden essence that is nothing more than the struggle between capital and labor" (Logan & Molotch, 2007, p. 11). While the Marxian framework provides a way to understand the built environment as a manifestation of broader political and economic conflicts, it also, like the ecology framework, can be overly reductionist, viewing cities as purely shaped by the interests of capital, and tends to be silent on the centrality of race and racism in political and economic processes. This perspective also gives little credence to how people actively participate in these constructions. Indeed, some argue that this perspective verges on functionalism, and "avoids working through how human activities actually give social structures their reality" (Logan & Molotch, 2007, p. 10).

Urban political economists Logan and Molotch (2007) argue for what they call a middle ground: They argue that political economic analysis must incorporate micropolitical (individual, institutional actors) and macropolitical perspectives, understanding the role of human actors not just as mindless agents of capital but as individuals and collectives actively negotiating, creating, and often reproducing the unequal environment in which they are embedded. "The reality of places is constructed through political action, with the term *political* encompassing both individual and collective efforts, through both informal associations and institutions of government and the economy" (Logan & Molotch, 2007, p. 48). Political economy analyses, they argue, therefore incorporate a multilayered analysis of global economic forces, governmental actors (federal, state, and local), local actors who interact with these processes and shape them—and the built environment—for their own gain. The built environment reinforces systems of hierarchy within broader society: Just as individuals with power and status (often structured by unequal markets, via racism, inheritance, etc.) use those attributes to secure advantages for themselves within the marketplace, they are able to take advantage of inequality in social space to further their status. In this conception, the dynamics of social reproduction happen *through* space, as space reinforces the stratification that exists among individuals.

Spatial theorists have further developed these ideas in recent years. These scholars have placed a stronger emphasis on the built environment's role in shaping social outcomes. Edward Soja (2010), for example, argues that social reproduction is accomplished through "spatial causality." In this construct, geographic spaces—especially patterns of racial and economic isolation—are not a mere reflection of material inequality (i.e., income, wealth, capital accumulation). Rather, according to this theory, these patterns themselves actively *reproduce* inequality through their effects on the distribution of opportunity and resources. The notion that space, race and racism, and the economy work in concert to shape the geographic distribution of opportunity has been applied by many urban theorists, such as Drier, Mollenkopf, and Swanstrom (2014), as well as educational scholars such as Jean Anyon (1997) and William Tate (2008).

Political Economy and Education

Education research has often treated schooling as largely disconnected from broader social structures and economic dynamics. Despite growth in the number of education scholars engaging issues of political economy, education scholars tend, for the most part, not to acknowledge these contextual considerations unless their work is explicitly focused on the political dynamics of education. Nearly 20 years ago in this journal, Rury and Mirel (1997) critiqued much of existing education research for its failure to incorporate a political economy approach. They argued that education research "too often accepted the urban environment as a given natural setting, rather than one that has itself been determined by larger economic and political processes" (p. 85). They argued that education researchers must engage in an analysis of the dynamics of power and wealth in urban contexts; examine the "spatial relationships that have shaped existing conceptions of city schools;" and understand the "historical forces that have brought the schools to their present state" (p. 50). Rury and Mirel conducted a review of research and theory on urban schooling from 1961, when Conant wrote one of the first inquiries into the crisis of urban schools (*Slums and Suburbs*), to 1997, a period of approximately 35 years. In their review, they were "concerned with the forces of historical change that have affected city schools and ways in which the research community has thought about them" (p. 50).

Rury and Mirel (1997) argued that a political economy of urban education must, at its core, examine "the essential social and economic dimensions of the city itself, the fundamental processes that contribute to the peculiar spatial configuration of people and relationships that we know as cities and their environs" (p. 98). They insisted that understanding the spatial configuration of cities and schools was not enough: They believed researchers must also examine the role that political forces and political interests have played in these configurations. They concluded that the school desegregation literature had come the closest to this type of work because that literature had brought to bear *both* "social and political forces shaping the development of urban education at a particular point in time" (p. 77). A political economy of education must therefore consider how urban schools, and school reform efforts, are "situated within a larger web of social, economic, and political forces" (p. 98).

Rury and Mirel (1997) described the origins of contemporary market-based reforms, noting that they emerged in the 1990s as a package of policies (decentralization, development of site-based governance councils) that were concerned with changing the governance structures of urban schools. The authors explain:

While these policies differ greatly in many of their key provisions, all share several assumptions about the problems of urban education and about some of the solutions to those problems. These include: (a) bureaucratic control of urban public schools has been one of the main causes of the deterioration of education in these schools; (b) people closest to the educational process (building administrators, teachers, or parents) should have the greatest amount of control over school policy and practice; and (c) shifting control of education from centralized bureaucracies to schools or parents will lead to improved educational outcomes for students. (pp. 89–90)

Their assessment of these reforms' potential to redress inequality, including school choice, is that such policies would fail to produce equitable schools and school systems because their policy framework did not attend to forces shaping the urban systems that they were trying to reform. They write that

focusing on questions of school organization and competitive mechanisms for allocating resources within urban school systems probably will not resolve the problems of big city schools. If indeed the crisis in urban education is largely a product of the general crisis of the cities themselves, the solution to the crisis probably lies outside of the schools altogether. (Rury & Mirel, 1997, p. 97)

Rury and Mirel's (1997) argument is that school systems will be subject to the political and social forces facing cities; unless those forces are addressed, school reform, including market-based reforms, will be unlikely to address core problems facing urban education. Analyses of market-based reforms therefore, must address "the ways in which identifiable social and economic interests employ the political domain to define the spatial distribution of educational activities" (Rury & Mirel, 1997, p. 98).

Since Rury and Mirel's 1997 publication, the state of economic inequality has exceeded that of the late 1920s, just before the stock market crash that led to the Great Depression (Saez & Zucman, 2016). The increase in wealth inequality aligns with heightened racial, gender, linguistic, and political inequality as well. Moreover, the global economic crisis of 2008, which was catalyzed by the implosion of Lehman Brothers, triggered mass home foreclosures and short sales and erased decades of accumulated wealth through the vacating of property values, with particularly devastating impacts on middle-class families and especially African American families and people of color whose banks targeted with subprime loans (Pew Research Center, 2011, 2012). These rapid economic shifts have altered the ability of states to fund their public schools or to provide adequate social services at the very time when families and communities are experiencing historical rates of unemployment, housing, and food insecurity.

It is no coincidence that markets in education expanded alongside this rapid rise in inequality. The significant political and economic developments since Rury and Mirel's 1997 publication warrant revisiting the urban political economy perspective for which they argued, to better illuminate the underlying reasons for, and effects of, the significant expansion of markets in education. In addition, we cast our gaze to the period of rapid centralization and school district consolidations just after the turn of the 20th century, which led to the establishment of the large urban school districts that are currently being challenged by the spread of market-oriented reforms. We include a race-centered analysis that helps explain the persistence of racialized patterns of inequality despite the embrace of reforms that, in theory, are aimed at ameliorating educational disparity.

AN URBAN POLITICAL ECONOMY OF MARKET-BASED REFORMS IN EDUCATION: 1915 TO 2015

In the sections that follow, we construct a political economy of urban school marketization through our systematic review of the literature on the changing dynamics of urban space and the evolution of market-based reforms. For the present journal volume marking the centennial of the American Educational Research Association (AERA), we aim to capture significant developments in scholarship and reform in the past 100 years. We consider how education researchers have attended to the relationship between space, political economy, race, and schooling over time.

We divide our review of the literature into four chronological eras. As noted, our aim is to construct a political economy of market-based reform while also centering race; in doing so, we are concerned primarily with political and economic dimensions of cities, the spatial configuration of populations, how these dynamics affect urban school systems, and how race factors into spatial and educational inequality. We therefore chose to focus on particular eras on the basis of significant trends and/or changes in urban demography and space, identified through our review of the literature. Each era covers a 20- to 35-year period. The first is from 1915 to 1944, a period that began in the middle of a major growth period for cities (Hobbs & Stoops, 2002; Massey & Denton, 1998) and ended with the creation of one of the largest federal programs, the 1944 Veterans Administrations program, that actively sponsored residential segregation (Jargowsky, 2015; Massey & Denton, 1998). The second period is from 1945 to 1970, the beginning of the era of mass suburbanization—an era that ended with a deepening city–suburban divide (Massey & Denton, 1998). The third period, from 1970 to 1990, was marked by further suburban expansion, an increase in income inequality, and a rise in concentrated poverty (Hobbs & Stoops, 2002; Jargowsky, 2015). In the fourth period, from 1990 to 2015, metropolitan areas saw significant growth in suburban diversity while urban cores saw contradictory trends: emerging gentrification and, first, a decrease (1990–2000), then an increase (2000–2013) in concentrated poverty and concentrated affluence (Frey, 2011; Jargowsky, 2015; Kneebone & Garr, 2010).

While our division of eras is specific with regard to years, our review of the developments and literature on the corresponding changes is fluid, as the changes unfolded over many years and often across eras. We believe the understanding of the urban spatial dynamics of today is deeply rooted in the urban political dynamics of the early 20th century, particularly in the governmental and business response to growing diverse and urban populations. Therefore, we consider the development and impact of market-based reforms from approximately 1916 forward, through the 100 years marked by AERA's centennial.

1915 to 1944: Industrialization, Corporatization, and School Choice for Elites

Changing Dynamics of Urban Space

From the roaring 1920s through the Great Depression, urban spaces saw massive and significant changes. Cities, especially in the North, experienced growing immigration, brought on by changing global conditions and the growing industrial economy (Tyack, 1974, 1993; Tyack & Cuban, 1995). The African American population exploded in the 1920s in many Northern cities, as industries lured workers North (often as strike breakers), with worker demand heightened due to the curtailment of European immigration. The first great migration of African Americans from the rural South into Northern and Midwestern cities was also propelled by the changes in technology that reduced the need for farm labor, and the boll weevil infestation that devastated many efforts at sharecropping in the South (Wilkerson, 2010). This migration was also fueled by brutal racism under Jim Crow and by de jure and de facto segregation and racism in the South that maintained systems of racial subjugation for African Americans (Massey & Denton, 1998). Residential segregation in cities grew sharply in this era, as the Black population was forced into tight and restricted quarters through a combination of racially restrictive covenants, violence, and realtor discrimination. Indeed, African Americans who attempted to live in residences in White neighborhoods were met with racialized violence. According to Ewing (2015),

Between 1917 and 1921 in Chicago, fifty-eight bombs struck the homes of Black residents, bankers who loaned them mortgages, and real-estate agents who sold them property—a rate of one bombing every twenty days in a period of under four years. (p. 8)

As Shedd (2015) notes, schooling in these cities typically paralleled these spatial inequalities:

Before court-mandated desegregation in the 1950s, Chicago schools were intensely segregated, and the Chicago public school system's policies during the first half of the twentieth century reinforced racial and ethnic inequality in myriad ways. African American public school students confronted educational institutions vastly different from those of their White immigrant counterparts. (pp. 22–23)

The urban landscape became even more deeply divided as the Great Depression brought about a significant crisis in housing markets, and a concurrent questioning of capitalism as a system. The government sought to shore up the housing market through a series of policies that created what researcher Paul Jargowsky (2015) calls the "architecture of segregation," laying the foundation for contemporary metropolitan spatial inequality. These policies centered on government-sponsored racially biased real estate appraisal systems, which encoded the racial bias in the real estate industry at the time, deeming neighborhoods that were racially diverse or transitioning as "risky" (encoded on real estate appraisal maps in the color red), and rendering them ineligible for loans (Massey & Denton, 1998). This rating system was adopted by the private banking industry and shaped lending practices for decades in the private housing market, depriving neighborhoods of color of capital, denying families of color wealth-building opportunities through home ownership, and driving spatial stratification in metropolitan areas for decades.

School Reform and Marketization

As urban school populations grew larger and more diverse, educational reformers, propelled by business interests, instituted an array of policies to ensure that schools maintained the increasingly stratified social systems that were being implemented in housing and employment. During this era, school bureaucracies became stronger and more centralized, driven in part by business elites who sought to apply principles of business management to make schools mirror corporate—particularly manufacturing—operations. Indeed, businesses played a strong role in the development of what Tyack (1974) refers to as the "administrative progressive" era, during which business and professional elites sought to reshape a system dominated by ward politics into a system that more closely mirrored corporate operations. These elites "planned to delegate almost total administrative power to an expert superintendent and his staff so that they could reshape the schools to fit the new economic and social conditions of an urban-industrial society" (Tyack, 1974, p. 126).

"Scientific" innovations in testing and measurement provided the logics to segregate and track students by race and poverty. The centralization movement advocated by the administrative progressives also diminished the number of school board members, who were business and professional men (Tyack, 1974, p. 127). Education research during this era focused on school district reorganization and the merits of corporate-style management (see, e.g., Cubberly, 1916). For African Americans in cities, these alterations served to establish separate and unequal schooling in the North, West, and East that they had hoped to leave in the South, and conditions that would lead to the current marketization of schooling for their descendants:

Undoubtedly, though they came with the hope for economic prosperity, they were also looking for that portion of the American dream that has always had a special salience for Black people: a quality education. What they found in the nineteen-twenties was physical, psychic, and structural violence that pinned them into place. What their descendants found in the two thousands was displacement, first from their homes, then from their schools. (Ewing, 2015, p. 18)

Corporate elites influenced not only the governance structure of schools but also the internal operation of many schools with the establishment of vocational education programs, along with academic tracking programs that slotted students toward presumed destinations within the economy (Tyack, 1974). These systems were designed, in part, in response to the waves of new immigrants and the growing diversity of urban districts and the desire to socialize them into U.S. institutions (Oakes, 1985). Moreover, the rise of educational "science" during this era facilitated the tracking efforts, for the results of the newly developed tests purported to measure intelligence mapped onto existing assumptions about which racial, ethnic, and immigrant groups were deserving of higher order instruction. These tracks were often racially and economically stratified, with students of color relegated to the lowest rungs of the academic ladder (Oakes, 1985). Indeed, as Bartlett, Frederick, Gulbrandsen, and Murillo (2002) wrote of corporations' influence in education in this era: "The advent of tracking in the early 20th century to prepare immigrant students for working-class jobs and the consolidation of schools along the factory model are the most spectacular examples of their sway" (p. 1). Research in this era was focused on improving academic tracking systems (see, e.g., Parker & Russell, 1953).

Thus, during this period, corporate power translated into what could be termed "corporatization" of education. While markets were not a central feature of this philosophy, school choice did become a core feature of urban education policy, made available to Whites through transfer policies created by school boards (dominated by White elites) that allowed White parents to transfer their children out of schools that were growing more racially diverse (Miner, 2013). These school board policies, together with the gerrymandering of attendance boundaries and race-based school construction decisions exacerbated the growing residential segregation (Clotfelter, 2004; Ryan, 2011). At the same time, Black segregated schools were overcrowded, and Black schools were put on double-shift schedules to accommodate overenrollment (see Miner, 2013; Neckerman, 2007). Thus, choice in education during this era was tied directly with the tensions resulting from the changing urban political landscape, employed as a tool by elites to maintain power (Shedd, 2015). In the South, schooling for African Americans was subject to the generosity of Northern philanthropists, whose generosity was limited to the development of schooling that prepared African American students for trades (J. Anderson, 1988).

In this era, the color lines that were growing more rigid in housing and employment were also inscribed increasingly in education policy. At the same time, the housing policies that were enacted in this era set in motion for decades a growing stratification of urban space which, decades later, created prime conditions for markets in education.

1945 to 1970: Metropolitan Stratification, Deindustrialization, and Desegregation

Changing Dynamics of Urban Space

The foundation of geographic segregation laid down by the federal government, banks, and the real estate industry in response to growing urban diversity in the 1930s resulted in massive reorganization of urban space in the 1940s through the 1960s. The redlining system was applied on a massive scale through the 1934 Federal Housing Administration program, and later through the 1944 Veteran's Administration loan program, fueling the flight of middle-class White families out of cities, while leaving families of color trapped in urban cores, and stripping racially diverse neighborhoods of capital and depriving families of color access to wealth (Oliver & Shapiro, 1997). This growing segregation established geopolitical divides, untying the fate of urban residents of color and White suburban middle-class families (Ryan, 2011). As Richard Thompson Ford (1994) writes, these dynamics created both racial and political cleavages between cities and suburbs, and created new sub-urban power bases within state legislatures that would later be in charge of developing reform—particularly market-based reforms—for urban cores from which they were politically and economically removed. These realignments would eventually have a significant influence on the shape of market-based reforms in the 2000s and 2010s.

These city–suburban economic and political divisions were exacerbated by state laws permitting suburbs to incorporate into separate, autonomous cities and school districts, instead of being annexed by cities as they had in the past (Drier et al., 2014; Jackson, 1987). As a result, White families who fled to the suburbs effectively moved across political lines, to one of dozens of suburban districts outside urban cores, tak-ing their tax dollars with them. Thus, it was during this era, that a deep, vast system of competition in education began to flourish: The result of this competition was that suburban school systems gained middle-class families, resources, and wealth, while urban school systems were left with growing levels of need and fewer resources with which to meet it. These are the underlying dynamics through which the later educa-tional marketplace would unfold.

School Reform and Marketization in Education

As middle-class Whites fled to suburban schools, civil rights activists at the same time fought in court to address the segregationist practices of the urban school districts that middle-class Whites were fleeing, such as the gerrymandering of attendance zones and discriminatory school choice policies. While courts handed down desegregation orders in many northern, urban school districts in this era, it was simply too little, too late, because there were few Whites left in these systems. In the South, resistance was rampant, and school choice became a key tool used by White elites to avoid integra-tion. In Virginia, the state resisted desegregation by closing public schools, instead creating a tuition voucher program available only to Whites to attend segregated White schools (Alexander & Alexander, 2005; Reed, 2014; Ryan, 2011).

Milton Friedman's initial call for tuition vouchers in the mid-1950s came during this time (Ryan, 2011). Friedman argued that while education was a public good and thus required public funding, government did not have to actually provide educa-tional services. Instead, the government could give parents money in the form of a voucher to be used at any school, with minimal oversight and regulation. However, Ryan (2011) argues that because this call for vouchers came at a time when many states were advocating the use of vouchers for resistance to desegregation, Friedman's proposal politically "went nowhere for decades" (p. 203).

In the 1960s, under pressure from the civil rights movement, the federal govern-ment sought to address the inequalities generated by the capitalist system, and specifically spatial and economic inequalities generated by New Deal policies (Quadagno, 1994), through targeted, strategic taxing and spending policies. Such Keynesian policies were embodied in the Elementary and Secondary Education Act (ESEA) of 1965, which infused billions of dollars into the public education system (Kantor & Lowe, 1995). Enacted just 1 year after Congress passed the landmark 1964 Civil Rights Act, in a time of federal legislative and judicial efforts to redistribute resources and opportunity and to remedy historical de jure segregation in housing, education, and labor, ESEA provided for targeted funding to high-poverty schools to compensate for the concentrated effects of poverty. For many scholars, 1965 signals a pivotal moment in U.S. race relations, as legislative progress took place while urban uprisings broke out, and a political backlash from suburban voters challenged efforts to fully desegregate America's schools (Edsall & Edsall, 1992; G. Orfield, 1988, 1995).

As part of the Johnson administration's War on Poverty, ESEA was intended to address poverty not by directly intervening in the labor market (i.e., through policies of full employment or income redistribution) or changing the structure of the capitalist system, but rather by helping "those on the bottom of society acquire the skills and attitudes they needed to compete more successfully in it" (Kantor, 1991, p. 58). Thus the focus came to be addressing the growing concentration of poverty in urban cores through increased funding for low-income students for programs and interventions that would provide the skills for low-income children to help themselves. Although these policies also came with strings attached to prevent districts from discriminating, they did not challenge the broader underlying economic and racial separation between cities and suburbs (Kantor & Lowe, 2013).

During this era, there emerged growing frustration with what was perceived as unresponsive urban bureaucracies. This frustration emerged among those concerned with economic efficiency as well as those concerned with civil rights. For example, in 1961, Theodore Shultz, at the American Economic Association, advanced the notion of human capital in the context of the efficiency of modern state bureaucracies. While early theorists such as Adam Smith had previously engaged the human capital concept and its relation to the state, Shultz and other researchers, such as Gary Becker, helped stimulate a series of research reports focused on education's contribution to human capital. For advocates of greater spending on public education, Engel (2000) argues, the human capital concept was quite powerful.

It provided an empirical and quantitative rationale in terms of economic growth, the ultimate goal of a market economy. It justified government action on the basis of arguments consistent with the principles of market ideology. Money for the schools could be regarded not as consumption spending but as an investment in human resources that would pay off in the future. (Engel, 2000, p. 25)

Milton Friedman's *Capitalism and Freedom* (1962) further influenced thinking about markets and education. In this publication, Friedman called for the establishment of a voucher system, which he viewed as a way to make public education bureaucracies more responsive to the liberty of parents. The invisible hand of the market would create pricing that reflected a mutually beneficial exchange for buyers and consumers. There remained a role for government, but that role, according to Friedman, was to be restricted to four primary areas of activity. These included the military, the criminal justice system, the production of public goods that the market would not produce, and the protection of the mentally ill and children (Engel, 2000). Friedman allowed that government should play a small role in schooling; society needed minimal levels of literacy in a democracy, in his vision. He argued, however, that government should provide schooling for communities unable to provide it for themselves. This would lower the tax burden on parents and cut back on administration.

Friedman argued that the government's role in education was justified by the neighborhood effect—the notion that everyone benefits from having children educated. Government could require a minimum amount of schooling to meet this goal. Yet Friedman balked at subsidies for vocational education that could prepare workers to make money. Friedman argued that there was no convincing rationale for preserving the state's operation of public schools; rather, he argued, they should simply provide baseline funding. Vouchers should be given to parents so they could buy educational services from a variety of nonprofit and for-profit providers, whose costs parents could supplement. Requiring parents to provide educational subsidies, Friedman reasoned, would also ensure that family planning happened in accordance with family resources. Under this vision,

> The role of the government would be limited to insuring that the schools met certain minimum standards, such as the inclusion of a minimum content in their programs, much as it now inspects restaurants to insure that they maintain minimum sanitary standards. (Friedman, 1962, p. 89)

Friedman made no mention of race or racism beyond acknowledging the existence of "Negro" neighborhoods. Friedman also found fault with increasing expenditures for teaching of subjects he regarded as frivolous. Parents under a voucher system could spend additional money, as they deemed appropriate. And teacher salaries could be made more flexible and responsive to market demands. Current compensation structures, he argued, served to attract to teaching the "dull, mediocre, and uninspiring" (Friedman, 1962, p. 96).

Policy scholars have traced the influence of Friedman's ideas over time (Engel, 2000; Henig, 1990). As Henig (1990) notes,

> By the early 1970s, much of the theoretical infrastructure for privatization had been put into place. There were three elements to this infrastructure: first, a revisionist interpretation of the origin and maintenance of the welfare state that accounted for government programs and regulations by self-interested bureaucrats and politicians rather than pursuit of a public interest or democratic pressures; second, a formalized theory; and third, in vouchers, a proposed mechanism for moving away from governmental provision of services without necessarily denouncing governmental responsibility. (p. 656)

These ideas were further supported by a 1970 publication by Christopher Jencks on school vouchers. Yet these efforts produced just one small voucher program, the Alum Rock Voucher Demonstration Program in California, in 1972, which lasted just 5 years (Wells, 1993). The program provided low-income students with public funding to exit their neighborhood schools.[2] Unlike Friedman's conservative, libertarian approach to vouchers, Jencks and others attempted to forge a progressive route that would use vouchers as a means to provide better educational opportunities for students than had previously been available through their home school districts, allowing them to exercise a modicum of consumer power despite their otherwise limited economic resources. Although the program was intended to include private schools, political resistance resulted in a program that was limited to public schools. The program had mixed results in terms of student achievement, however, and publicly funded voucher plans did not reappear until two decades later. Ryan and Heise (2002) argue that repeated political efforts to expand and enact voucher programs for private schools after this were unsuccessful in large part due to the city–suburban divide—such programs did not have the support of suburbanites, who felt vouchers were irrelevant to their children as they were highly satisfied with the level of education and did not want children from cities entering suburban schools (Ryan, 2011; Ryan & Heise, 2002). This early experiment with vouchers, however, demonstrated the linkages between the state, urban political economies, and race. It pointed to the enduring tensions between market policy tools and progressive government regulations and funding—the very mechanisms that set the boundaries of the market—and showed how the resulting policies can result in outcomes that aim to counter the inequities that accumulate when markets play out without intentional structuring by government.

Another form of market strategy during this era was the use of performance contracting for Title I and other instructional services in several urban and rural school districts. Title I funds allocated to high-poverty school districts through the 1965 ESEA were meant to alleviate the concentrated effects of poverty on students through compensatory services (Ascher, Fruchter, & Berne, 1996). The idea appealed to members of the U.S. Office of Education, including Leon Lessinger, then associate commissioner of education, who thought it would be a way to ensure accountability for school performance. The first site of performance contracting was Texarkana. Some felt that African American students, before they could be integrated with Whites, needed intensive academic remediation. Dorsett Educational Systems, Inc., was hired to provide direct instruction to 350 students, both Black and White. The company's contract stipulated that it would have students gain one grade level after 80 hours of instruction; bonuses would be awarded if the students made larger gains. Using what they termed Rapid Learning Centers, students were promised stickers, radios, and even televisions for outstanding performance (Ascher, 1996). The educational delivery models were flawed and had negative results:

Dorsett's contract with the district had dispensed with some tasks that had been written into the ESEA proposal, including developing study habits and improving grooming. Moreover, Dorsett was not offering instruction in science and social studies, as it had initially promised the district. The fact that the company's fees were tied to students' test score gains made these two subjects the focus of its efforts. In fact, at the end of the year, while RLC [Residential Learning College] students tested above those in a control group in some areas, their scores were deemed invalid because the RLC students were found to have been exposed to most of the test questions. The discouragement, even disgust of students who had worked all year to improve their performance became evident when many failed to pick up their radios and the prize television lay unclaimed. (Ascher, 1996, p. 616)

Class sizes were generally larger in performance contracting settings, and there was a tendency to hire unlicensed teachers. Moreover, Ascher (1996) found that despite a larger social agenda of empowerment for minority and low-income communities in the 1960s and 1970s, performance contracting was never aimed at increasing the voices and participation of these communities. "Rather, accountability was described in terms of companies and school districts" (p. 620). In addition, the rote instructional strategies were quite different from the kinds of alternative and progressive education that many suburban and urban schools serving primarily White and wealthier communities were offering.

By 1968, in the South, desegregation policies became relatively effective at achieving integration, particularly after the U.S. Supreme Court decision in *Green v. County School Board of New Kent County* (1968), and later the 1971 *Swann v. Charlotte-Mecklenburg Board of Education* decision. These orders were particularly effective because districts in the South were often countywide, incorporating both cities and suburbs, thus providing few escape routes for resistant Whites. However, Northern desegregation efforts were more limited and less effective, because in the North segregation was most often de facto and more difficult to prove, and because districts often covered just the urban core (suburbs were excluded from those remedies).

In this era, as a result, the increasingly stratified school systems became key drivers in the shaping of urban spaces: Affluent suburban districts lured White and middle-class families out of the urban core with the promise of increased housing wealth for those families who could gain access to "desirable" school districts (Holme, 2002). In the meantime, urban core school systems grew more racially isolated, with higher concentrations of poverty, and reduced tax bases.

1971 to 1990: Deindustrialization, Concentrated Poverty, and Deregulation

Changing Dynamics of Urban Space

The city–suburban racial separation that emerged in the 1950s and 1960s grew into a very deep economic chasm in the 1970s and 1980s in the North and Midwest, as deindustrialization stripped urban cores of high-wage manufacturing jobs (Wilson, 1987). The job losses, accompanied by ongoing intense housing segregation during this era that locked people of color into urban cores (including realtor discrimination, redlining, lack of affordable housing in suburbs, etc.) led to massive rises in urban unemployment and poverty rates in urban centers for families of color (Wilson, 1987; also see Miner, 2013, for a discussion of Milwaukee.) The middle class began to shrink significantly, and income inequality began to grow (Massey & Fischer, 2003). As a result of these trends, the proportion of people living in concentrated poverty census tracts, primarily in urban cores, grew significantly between 1970 and 1990 (Jargowsky, 2003). Moreover, the concentration of poverty affected Blacks disproportionately during this time (Massey & Fischer, 2003).

As the geographic concentration of poverty rose, so did concentrated affluence. Indeed, according to Massey and Fischer (2003),

Within the 30 largest metropolitan areas, the geographic concentration of poverty rose by 20 percent between 1970 and 1980 and the spatial concentration of affluence grew by 13 percent. Between 1980 and 1990 the concentration of poverty rose by another 10 percent and that of affluence by 21 percent in the ten largest metropolitan areas. (p. 3)

While these trends would moderate somewhat in the 1990s, this was primarily due to the dislocation of low-income families to low-income suburbs (Briggs, 2005). Income segregation would again rise sharply in the 2000s, as we will discuss later.

School Reform and Marketization

Federal efforts to address these divides, through programs such as ESEA, tinkered at the margins of, but did not directly challenge, capitalist and geopolitical dynamics (Kantor & Lowe, 1995). Such programs were unable to address the significant demographic shifts that left urban schools facing growing concentrations of poverty and weakening tax bases, rendering them largely powerless to "compete" with suburban systems, which continued to lure families out of urban cores.

Indeed, in this era, the racial and economic divide between urban and suburban schools grew more pronounced, especially in the North. This was due, in part, to increased residential sorting of families, as the level of "between-district" segregation grew (Clotfelter, 2004; Reardon & Owens, 2014). The growing inequality was also the result of two significant U.S. Supreme Court decisions that cemented the educational inequities resulting from these growing divides: First, the 1973 decision in *San Antonio Independent School District v. Rodriguez* blocked efforts to address finance inequities between urban and suburban schools, and the 1974 decision in *Milliken v. Bradley* ultimately ended efforts by attorneys to draw suburbs into the desegregation remedies.

In the South, however, the trends were somewhat different: Integration progressed significantly in the 1970s and 1980s in many Southern cities, primarily the result of significant differences in the political geography of the region. As noted previously, Southern school districts frequently encompass entire counties, giving suburban Whites and middle-class families nowhere to flee if they want to avoid public school integration. As a result, as the North was growing more segregated, Southern school districts became significantly *more integrated* during this time period (Clotfelter, 2004). Indeed, as G. Orfield (1993) noted, comparing Northern and Southern integration:

The fact that the school district serving Charlotte, N.C. happened to cover a county of 528 square miles while the Boston school district was only one twelfth as large in a much bigger metropolitan area explains a great deal about the kind of desegregation the two cities experienced. (p. 9)

A great deal of research on school desegregation emerged during this period, focusing on the politics of school integration (see, e.g., Crain, 1969; G. Orfield, 1978), the problem of White flight (see, e.g., Armor & Schwarzbach, 1978), and the need for metropolitan integration plans (see, e.g., G. Orfield, 1996).

Despite the setbacks, during this time period, some locales began using school choice to directly challenge patterns of segregation, and prevent White flight. Indeed, since 1980, most school desegregation plans have focused heavily on the use of school choice strategies (Wells, 1993). Chief among these plans were magnet schools, which sought to use specialized programs to recruit students from different backgrounds. Federal funding supported these efforts in 1976 through the Emergency School Aid Act, which was the Nixon administration's method of providing Southern districts "carrots" to encourage rather than force integration.

Desegregation assistance funding, however, fell dramatically in the 1980s, when government programs were consolidated and funding reduced (Wells, 1993). Other types of policies implemented in this era were controlled choice plans (i.e., in Cambridge, Massachusetts), and interdistrict choice-based desegregation plans designed to address city–suburban segregation by allowing transfers across district lines (Finnigan et al., 2015). Each of these diversity-based choice policies incorporated many equity-minded elements, such as diversity targets, information campaigns, transportation, and mechanisms for parent involvement. Research on these programs focused on academic outcomes as well as social outcomes (interracial attitudes, prejudice, self-esteem; see, e.g., Stephan, 1978) and the effects of school culture on racial dynamics (Schofield, 1989). Despite some gains achieved by choice-based integration in the North and Midwest, efforts at desegregation were unable to address the accelerating macrolevel competition between city and suburban school systems, which contributed to growing levels of city–suburban racial segregation in the 1970s and 1980s and increasing housing segregation in urban cores (Massey & Denton, 1998; G. Orfield, 1993).

Another aspect of this period of declining desegregation policies and rising market-oriented education policies was the rise of national-level conservative think tanks and advocacy groups (Rich, 2001, 2004). Funded by wealthy donors and foundations such as Bradley, Olin, Scaife, and Smith Richardson, these organizational "idea brokers" were generally opposed to the increased role of government, particularly in the realm of social equality policies like desegregation, workplace discrimination, and affirmative action. They provided philosophical arguments and research reports to support policies that reduced the role of the state in the provision of public services (Kumashiro, 2008; J. A. Smith, 1991; Snider, 1989).

It was in this context that the charter proposals and early voucher proposals of the 1990s took root, with many market-oriented funders interested in moving the ideas of conservative think tanks (e.g., the Heritage Foundation and the American Enterprise Institute) into the public sphere through incremental implementation. This included targeted voucher programs for children living in poverty or for special education students, for example. The theory of action was that incremental implementation would eventually lead to universal implementation (Bolick, 1998; Cohen, 2007). Indeed, researchers have found synergy between the funders of conservative think tanks and those of new civil rights organizations, staffed by African American or Latino leaders, that advocate for school choice in communities of color (Miller, 2003; People for the American Way, 2001). The impact of all of this activity, Cohen (2007) argues, can be seen in electoral politics: Candidates and the public increasingly favor vouchers.

Support for school vouchers, school choice, and education tax credits does not exist simply because of the hopes, aspirations, disappointments and frustrations of school children's parents. Their awareness of school privatization options is supported by an array of advocacy institutions, think tanks and scholarship organizations that function to create a consciousness that there are alternatives to traditional public schools. (Cohen, 2007, p. 30)

As we will discuss further, foundations and think tanks have played a large role in determining the research evidence produced on the very reforms that these idea brokers helped to inform (Lubienski, Weitzel, & Lubienski, 2009).

1990 to 2016: Increasing Inequality and Rapid Growth in Market Reforms

Changing Dynamics of Urban Space

Education researchers, demographers, social critics, and economists have documented and decried the unprecedented and growing wealth inequality in the United States and other industrialized societies. By every indicator of inequality, the top 1% of Americans possesses inordinate wealth, while the middle class has shrunk significantly, and poverty—especially among children—is growing at ever more alarming rates. In fact, increasing social inequality has resulted in the largest wealth gap since before the Great Depression (Hacker & Pierson, 2010). It has resulted in a bifurcation of wealth, high unemployment, and an ever-diminishing social safety net. The "Occupy" movements of 2011 were formed in response to the sense that the wealth held by the top 1% of the population was primarily to blame for the relative economic constraints on the other 99% of the population, who were cut off from educational, social, and economic mobility. More recently, in 2016, the Black Lives Matter movement has foregrounded economic and educational justice in its policy platform (https://policy.m4bl.org). Many economists predict that since the 2008 global economic crisis and subsequent Great Recession, most families will never recover the loss of wealth that resulted from the plummeting of housing values and the widespread foreclosure crisis (Judson, 2012).

Growing inequality, as researchers have shown, has been inscribed in the social geography of U.S. metropolitan areas. As income inequality has risen, researchers have documented a concurrent rise in residential segregation by income (Reardon & Bischoff, 2011), as the affluent and poor live residentially more isolated from one another than at any point in the past 40 years. Researchers have also found persistent levels of racial segregation in many contexts. In the past decade, however, there have been some reversals of past trends in urban cores, as gentrification has drawn middle- and upper middle-class professionals into redeveloped downtowns. These trends are built on the urban racial politics of the past—occurring in communities that were previously segregated and denied capital, creating contexts ripe for redevelopment for the benefit of the affluent (powell & Spencer, 2002). It is in these contexts that the very rich and the very poor live proximally, yet with very different services, experiences, and access to political power (Sassen, 2011). Indeed, the "good news" of lower poverty rates in urban areas due to gentrification serves to mask a growing crisis in urban school districts. For example, in Detroit, New Orleans, Philadelphia, and Milwaukee, schools districts became even more poor in terms of student populations, as schools continued a steady decline in enrollment and as infrastructure continued to age, leading to layoffs, school closures, and even bankruptcy and state receivership (Cucchiara, 2013; Holme, Finnigan & Diem, 2016; Lipman, 2011).

At the same time, these trends are causing low-income people to be displaced into older suburbs, which are often as segregated and high poverty as the cities that they left, and which lack infrastructure, adequate tax bases, and access to transit and jobs (Drier et al., 2014; M. Orfield, 2002). A new framework of urban political economy needs therefore to look beyond the old definition of an "urban education crisis" to reframe inequality as a metropolitan-level phenomenon, with an understanding that the poor are more dispersed across jurisdictions, and often more isolated, than in the past.

Public health researchers have argued that this inequality is harmful not only for those lacking adequate resources but for society as a whole. Specifically, they note lack of trust, a decline in longevity, high rates of incarceration, lower rates of school completion, and higher incidences of violent crime in countries where the gap between the rich and others is particularly acute (Wilkinson & Pickett, 2009). This inequality has particular implications for the lives of children, as the number of children living in poverty in the United States has spiked to unprecedented levels. Because inequality is also linked to the ability to assert political power, the political leadership at the national, state, and local levels tends to reflect these broader economic trends.

Moreover, as wealth is concentrated in the hands of a few, the wealthy are able to influence social policy by supporting elected officials, funding think tanks and advocacy groups, engaging lobbying firms, and establishing their own philanthropic foundations to implement their preferred policies (Reich, 2008; Rich, 2004; Scott, 2009). Given ample evidence that socioeconomic inequality has reached historic levels, and with particular stratified effects on communities of color, education research needs to grapple with trends and their implications for schooling (Reardon, 2011; Reardon & Bischoff, 2011).

School Reform and Marketization

The politics of education and privatization in education has been driven by, and interacted with, these trends. As urban school systems and some inner-ring suburbs remain underresourced and segregated, with associated declines in student performance, they also face increasing demands from policymakers, particularly for improved performance on standardized assessments, to which they must respond or face high-stakes sanctions such as school closure, conversion to charter schools, or reconstitution.

Yet the accountability systems installed have not yielded the intended gains, nor have they turned around urban schools. Instead, these systems have created a way of labeling districts as failing and thus providing a rationale for significant state intervention and removal from public control. For example, urban schools are handed over to private, nonprofit, or for-profit management organizations; elected school boards are eradicated; mayoral offices assume control of schools; public schools are converted to charter schools; and new charter schools are founded (Buras, 2012; Lipman, 2011; Pedroni, 2011). Green, Baker, Oluwole, and Mead (2016) posit that the relatively unregulated growth of charter schools constitutes educational "reverse redlining," in which communities of color are vulnerable to a "charter school bubble" that the authors argue is rife with fraud and exclusionary admissions practices and results in the segregation of students of color into predatory schools operated by private managers. In addition, many researchers have noted the rise of the education reform and advocacy sector, a well-funded coalition positioned against what they see as the deep pockets of teachers unions (McGuinn, 2012; Scott, 2011a). There has been significant philanthropic involvement and influence within these organizations and coalitions by venture philanthropies, intermediary organizations, and advocacy groups seeking to shape education law and social policies more broadly such as the American Legislative Exchange Council (G. Anderson & Donchik, 2016; Reckhow, 2013; Saltman, 2010; Scott, 2009; Tompkins-Stange, 2016).

These elite networks are accompanied by support from African American and Latino parents who are clamoring for better schooling options than exist within struggling school districts. New civil rights organizations have emerged—largely funded by venture philanthropies such as the Eli and Edythe Broad Foundation and the Walton Family Foundation—to lobby for the expansion of market-based reforms. Cohen and Lizotte (2015) attribute the embrace of market-based reforms from communities of color not only to those communities' dissatisfaction with school district bureaucracies and teachers unions but also to decades of advocacy aimed at reframing equity in individualized terms of parental choice.

In this section, we describe the rapid rise of marketization and privatization in education from the 1990s through 2016. We begin by describing the origins of the privatization movement in the 1990s; we then discuss the political dynamics of those reforms, review the research on the reforms, and conclude with emerging evidence about how the reforms are reshaping urban space.

Deregulation and privatization. At the same time that inequality grew during this period, public sector reforms, including education, have been characterized by deregulation, decentralization, and, increasingly, privatization. As Henig (1990) notes, privatization moved from "pragmatic adjustment" in the Reagan era to "partisan program(s)" by the 1990s (p. 663). Under the Reagan administration, a rollback of redistributive programs began, and the antigovernment rhetoric that characterized the subsequent reforms took hold. According to Edsall and Edsall (1992), "the issues of race and taxes fostered the creation of a middle-class, anti-government, property-holding, conservative identification among key White voters who had previously seen their interests as aligned with a downwardly redistributive federal government" (p. 11). These voters expressed a loss of control over social choices and frustration with many redistributive policies established in the 1960s and 1970s. Increasingly, many White and middle-class citizens perceived a loss of control over their social choices and became resentful toward "big" government. To regain citizen control, in their view, was to remove government from the lives of citizens, setting the stage for the rapid privatization of public services (Lipman, 1998, 2004).

The privatization of public education followed this broader series of deregulatory actions that eased restrictions over the private sector's provision of public services (Donahue, 1989). Deregulation involved the easing and removal of codified rules, decentralization and redistribution of power and decision making.

During this era, conservatives and libertarians, and many progressives, embraced aspects of the deregulation, decentralization, and privatization of public education, often linking their support to educational equity for students "trapped" in urban schools. For example, Bolick (1998) argued, "School choice should be the empowerment movement's most urgent priority, for it offers the most immediate prospect for expanding educational opportunities for children who need them most desperately" (p. 62). Chubb and Moe (1990) argued in their seminal work, *Politics, Markets, and America's Schools,* that when schools fail to meet students' needs, parents should be permitted to "shop with their feet," by choosing a school that does. Schools that failed to respond to parental preferences would be forced "out of business."

Tuition tax credits, vouchers, and charter schools were popular manifestations of this ideology, as states began enacting laws in support of the new approach. Related policy proposals emerged at this time, when many urban districts had become racially isolated and resource-strapped. Many commentators characterized these districts as dysfunctional and unresponsive, leading to a "crisis" in urban schooling, though many disputed the roots of this crisis as not being rooted in the failures of public bureaucracies, as critics framed it, but rather in the devolution of state support for civil rights provisions (Kantor & Brenzel, 1993). In market rhetoric, for example, popularized by the Washington, D.C.–based Center for Education Reform, "strong" charter schools legislation provides the most deregulation, allowing for unfettered charter school growth, and places less emphasis on redistribution, quality, equity, and public accountability (Scott & Barber, 2001).

While many voucher programs were proposed in the 1980s, it was not until 1989 that the first publicly funded voucher program was passed by the Wisconsin legislature. The program targeted the Milwaukee Public Schools, which had experienced large increases in poverty and struggling performance alongside the steep manufacturing job losses and population losses (of primarily middle-class Whites) in the 1970s and 1980s (Miner, 2013). The program was limited to students residing within the Milwaukee city limits and was targeted at low-income students (Witte, 1995). In 1995, a similar program was implemented in Cleveland, although it differed in that it included parochial schools. The Cleveland voucher program also permitted Cleveland students to attend school in surrounding suburban school districts. No surrounding public school districts participated in the voucher program, even though such schools would have stood to gain up to three times the funding that religious schools received. Researchers have found that students receiving vouchers were less likely to be poor and African American than the broader Cleveland school population (70% vs. 83%; Metcalf, 2001; Ryan & Heise, 2002). Choices within Cleveland included public schools, public school with tutoring, religious school, nonreligious private school, community school, or magnet school. The Supreme Court upheld the constitutionality of the Cleveland voucher program in the *Zelman v. Simmons-Harris* ruling (2002). As of 2016, 15 states have enacted school voucher laws, and there were several privately funded programs in existence as well.

Charter schools also emerged during this era, in the early 1990s. First enacted in Minnesota in 1991, charter school legislation had passed in 43 states by 2016, enrolling some 2.5 million children in roughly 6,500 schools. Originators of the charter schools concept imagined the reform as a means for teachers and school-site administrators to assume greater power over the schooling environments for which they were being held accountable (Budde, 1988). In the most idealized conception, charter schools were to be the vehicles of a new, revitalized, local participatory democracy, with teachers, parents, community members, and policymakers deliberating about the purposes and possibilities of public education (Nathan, 1996; S. Smith, 2001). Charter schools tended to be concentrated in urban school districts, and they enrolled a disproportionate number of African American and Latino students, although evidence of racial segregation and other stratification within and across this sector quickly emerged, challenging the remaining voluntary and court-ordered efforts to desegregate schools (Themba, 2001).

These market-oriented reforms took hold in a sharply different urban context than when vouchers were first proposed by Friedman in the 1950s and 1960s, and by Jencks in the 1960s and 1970s. As noted, the social geography of metropolitan areas had changed, resulting in dramatic increases in concentrated poverty in urban cores by the early 1990s when these reforms were again proposed (Jargowsky, 2003). Yet the strong economy of the 1990s brought unemployment rates down during the course of the decade, bringing a drop in the concentration of poverty to some degree in some of the urban cores. This overall positive trend, as Drier et al. (2014) wrote, masked growing inequality:

The booming economy of the 1990s pulled many people up; poor people benefitted from the tight labor markets of the late 1990s. At the same time, however, the gap between those at the top and the bottom widened—and increasingly, rich and poor lived in different neighborhoods. (p. 49)

These trends of rising and falling fortunes in the 1990s, which were highly circumscribed by race and place, contributed to new political alignments in education policy. Increasingly, support for market-oriented reforms—particularly charter schools and vouchers—emanated from leaders and advocates of color, who saw these policies as ways to regain control over schooling for African American and Latino children. And yet another layer of market-oriented policies emerged: the increasing presence of private sector providers, such as educational management and charter school organizations that replaced school district functions in the operation of charter schools (Bennett, 2008).

The racial and spatial politics of school choice. The market-based empowerment arguments rely on powerful, normative ideals: democracy, choice, equality, and innovation. Many of these values echo the ideals of the civil rights movement, ideals that were themselves based on the founding principles of American democracy (King, 1967). Thus, alliances were forged between politically conservative market advocates and low-income communities of color, and rifts have emerged between leading civil rights groups over the issue of school choice (Apple & Oliver, 1996; Carl, 1996, 2011; DeBray-Pelot, Lubienski, & Scott, 2007). Lewis and Nakagawa (1995), commenting on this phenomenon, wrote:

In the current educational arena the conflict between middle-class and lower-class minorities is exacerbated. The inclusionary ideal of the 1960s opened the system up to many Black professionals, drawing them inside the bureaucracy. The outsiders pushing for more reform today are business groups and reform organizations. They call for grassroots decision-making, bypassing the Black middle-class school professionals. They accept budgetary limits. In cities with large minority populations, the result is a handicapped system of governance, where black school professionals have little capacity to harness and articulate the interests of the poor, let alone improve the capacity of the schools to do their job. The dispersal of power makes a clear statement of goals and the exercise of leadership difficult. (p. 17)

In a context of segregated, underresourced, schooling, charter school management organizations and charter school founders target low-income, often African American and Latino communities in troubled urban school districts (Hernández, 2016). The growth of charter schools has provided families with options but has also further destabilized school districts financially given the loss of students, leading to the phenomenon of school closures and consolidations being resisted by parents and communities left behind by charter school growth in places like Chicago, New York, Detroit, and Philadelphia (Arsen, DeLuca, Ni, & Bates, 2015). In 2016, the National Association for the Advancement of Colored People and the Black Lives Matter movement issued calls for a moratorium on the growth of charter schools due to concerns about segregation, privatization, harsh disciplinary practices, and transparency. Yet many parents and charter advocates in and for these communities feel that the traditional and new civil rights organizations, such as the Black Lives Matter movement are out of sync with the schooling preferences of all families, but especially of poor people of color (Holt, 2000). Constituencies holding this view include communities and grassroots activists of color, hedge fund investors, philanthropic supporters, education reform and advocacy groups. These stakeholders view school choice as a primary mechanism for community empowerment through parents being able to exert their preferences (Holt, 2000; Scott, 2013; Wilgoren, 2000). Yet the research is clear that many influential market advocates supporting charter school and school choice reforms have a different vision for public education than do those who support the reform in the hope of community or professional empowerment, and are often seeking to expand private sector involvement in the delivery of core educational services through contracting with state and local agencies (Burch, 2009; Molnar, 1996). This involvement shifts the very meaning of the notion of "public" in public schools. For example, Green and McCall (1998) found that many charter schools, when faced with requests to share their enrollment or financial records often argued that they are not subject to public records requests because their boards are private. These dynamics require researchers to examine the privatization aspects of school choice policies in light of highly unequal urban political economies. According to Fuller (2000),

Any analysis of the charter uprising must recognize the heavy-duty political and corporate forces that have grown stronger over the past decade. And charter activists are rooted in this wider school choice movement, which focuses not only on opening school choice options for families but also on business options for private firms that increasingly create and manage charters. (p. 23)

To the extent that charter schools legislation has devolved governance from centralized agencies, and to the extent that deregulation has failed to provide adequate resources for schools to operate autonomously, charter school reform has paved the way for the rapid introduction of the private sector in educational management and governance (Wells & Scott, 2001). Thus, in charter school reform, we find community control advocates intersecting with market advocates and forming alliances to start and run charter schools in the context of highly unequal political urban economies (Galster & Killen, 2010).

The political economy of evidence production on market-oriented reforms. The close connection between shifts in urban space and the expansion of market-based reforms raise questions about the interaction between markets and their connections to, and effects on, urban space. However, much of the empirical research on school choice policies tends to be narrowly focused on questions of effectiveness. Given the national emphasis on "what works," this focus is not surprising and, in fact, offers an important strand of evidence. It is notable, however, that much of the evidence on the effectiveness of charter schools concludes that there exist subtle and overt creaming, cropping, and other activities aimed at generating students who are likely to perform better than their peers on standardized assessments. For example, researchers investigating the effectiveness of the widely touted Knowledge is Power

Program charter school network have found that these schools tend to have high rates of attrition at the elementary and secondary levels, particularly for African American boys (David, Woodworth, Grant, Lopez-Torkos, & Young, 2006; Vasquez Heilig, Williams, McNeil, & Lee, 2011; Miron, Urschel, & Saxton, 2011).

Across school choice research, researchers have found evidence that choice schools tend to underenroll special education students and English language learners, and that they overenroll girls (Buckley & Sattin-Bajaj, 2011; Corcoran & Jennings, 2015; Government Accountability Office, 2012; Lacireno-Paquet, Holyoke, Moser, & Henig, 2002; Miron, 2014; Vasquez Heilig, Holme, LeClair, Redd, & Ward, in press). Researchers have found that some of these schools engage in general selective behavior through school location decisions or marketing and communications strategies, for example (Henig & MacDonald, 2002; Jabbar, 2015; Jennings, 2010; Lubienski, Gulosino, & Weitzel, 2009). In addition, given the location decisions of charter school founders, coupled with distinct "no excuses" pedagogies in many urban charter schools emphasizing high expectations, a longer school day and year, and strict discipline policies, students of color in charter schools tend to have disproportionate rates of expulsions and suspensions than their Asian and White charter school counterparts (Hirji, 2014; Miron, Urschel, & Mathis, 2010; Taylor, Cregor, & Lane, 2014; Tough, 2006, 2008).

There exists, however, disagreement about the issue of selectivity and student achievement in charter school and choice policies in the literature (Zimmer & Guarino, 2013). Other researchers find no evidence of selection in the sector (Buckley & Schneider, 2005; Nichols-Barrer, Gleason, Gill, & Tuttle, 2015). National studies, such as the ones produced by Stanford University's Center for Research on Education Outcomes (CREDO), tend to find mixed results across the in states with charter schools in terms of student performance (CREDO, 2009, 2013; Woodworth et al., 2015), despite the general evidence about selectivity in enrollments (Welsh, Duque, & McEachin, 2015). The question of the educational effectiveness of vouchers also tends to show mixed results. Like the research on charters, these results often are distilled through debates on the appropriate metrics and controls to determine causal effects on student test score performance across schools (Goldie, Linick, Jabbar, & Lubienski, 2014).

Researchers, however, have also examined school choice effects beyond test score performance by examining how these schools function within a political economy of market-oriented reforms. The research literature on market-based reforms (like the policymakers themselves) has tended to overlook the political and economic forces that are at work in the contexts where these reforms are being implemented. Indeed, the evidence on the efficacy of market reforms as measured by accountability, democratic participation, and community engagement has found that the terrain in which school choice operates is highly circumscribed by the broader unequal political economy (see, e.g., CREDO, 2009, 2013; Jabbar, 2014; Ni, 2009; Ni & Arsen, 2010; Scott, 2011a; Wells, 2002).

One strand of this work has examined the policy networks that have shaped the development and implementation of school choice policies in urban school districts, helping identify a tightly connected, elite policy and planning community across funders, educational reform advocacy organizations, policymakers, think tanks, and alternative teacher programs such as Teach For America (Kretchmar, Sondel, & Ferrare, 2014; McGuinn, 2012; Scott, 2009). Related to this strand of research is the question of democratic participation in charter schools, given the role of private organizations that frequently operate schools serving large concentrations of students of color. This research finds that parents and community members are often frustrated by their lack of voice and their limited influence on the schools they have chosen (Bulkley, 2005; Scott, 2011c; Wexler & Huerta, 2000; Whitty, 1997).

Another research strand focuses on the politics of evidence on market reforms. These scholars have found that the research on school choice and other market reforms tends to be highly politicized, and that foundations that are funding organizations to implement or advocate for market reforms are often also funding researchers to determine the reforms' effectiveness (Lubienski, Scott, & DeBray, 2014; Scott & Jabbar, 2014). Other researchers have focused on how market education policies inform the behavior and work of teachers and school leaders, finding that many school-based actors have focused on narrow roles for parents; on singular purposes of schooling, such as academic achievement or job preparation; and on parents as choosers and fundraisers (Becker, Nakagawa, & Corwin, 1997; Hemphill, 2008; Woods & Woods, 2004, 2005). Yet another strand has examined how parents navigate choice systems, finding that they often traverse a complex terrain in which their abilities to realize their choice in schools is constrained by structural, geographic, institutional, cultural, and linguistic barriers (Bell, 2007, 2009; Jessen, 2011; Pattillo, 2015; Pattillo, Delale-O'Connor, & Butts, 2014; Payne & Knowles, 2009; Pedroni, 2007; Wilson-Cooper, 2005). Without a regulatory framework that facilitates equitable and diverse access—like the framework that exists for active desegregation plans that utilize choice mechanisms (Chavez & Frankenberg, 2009)—many researchers have found that charter schools reflect, rather than interrupt, patterns of urban racial segregation (Cobb & Glass, 1999; Frankenberg & Lee, 2003; Frankenberg, Siegel-Hawley, & Wang, 2010, 2011; Garcia, 2008a, 2008b).

Markets, urban space, and stratification. As our review of the research evidence has indicated, market-based reforms have not, on the whole, improved performance in choice or traditional public schools. These reforms have also coincided with—and even reified—the hyperresegregation of public education, especially in urban and suburban school districts, leading to social costs for surrounding schools and school districts (Koedel, Betts, Rice, & Zau, 2010).

Research also finds that market-based reforms not only affect school systems and students; they also have an impact on the urban landscape in which they have been created and implemented. Some research into interactions between schools, markets, and the social geography of cities focused on school choice via the housing market and labor markets, revealing that patterns of racial segregation are replicated in the growth of school choice policies (Sharkey, 2013). Conversely, families living in "high-opportunity" neighborhoods are able to enjoy quality public services and public education (Turner, Nichols, Comey, Franks, & Price, 2012). Research by Holme (2002), Lareau (2003), and Bischoff (2008) has found that when parents with resources use residential choice to sort themselves into schools and districts, these choices often deepen racial and economic stratification resulting in identifiable racial achievement gaps (Bifulco & Ladd, 2007). In addition, Andre-Bechely (2005) found that White middle-class parents in an urban California school district utilized their more elite social networks to game public school choice systems in ways that inadvertently advantaged their children over children of color, whose families lacked access to the strategies and information shared within these racially stratified networks. Deregulatory school choice policies that provide minimal regulation and incentives for school desegregation, transportation, and resource equity contribute to these parental selection dynamics.

More recently, researchers have focused on the relationship between gentrification and market-based reforms. This research has found that cities have sought to remake themselves into centers for technological and artistic innovation, and that private and public policymakers have sought in some contexts to use public schools as ways to attract elite parents to particular parts of the city (see, e.g., Cucchiara, 2008, 2013; Lipman, 2011). For example, Cucchiara's (2013) study of Philadelphia illustrated how school choice and urban revitalization were closely and explicitly interconnected: Schools were used as a tool to lure elites back into the urban core, and once there, the schools privileged those families, marginalizing others. As Cucchiara (2016) writes, in

a city hoping to promote urban revitalization by attracting and retaining professional families to its downtown, the result was a set of "advantaging mechanisms" that worked both tangibly and intangibly to benefit more affluent families and neighborhoods, while marginalizing or excluding other groups. (p. 125)

In addition, as gentrification tends to be concentrated in small, isolated pockets of cities—where other neighborhoods are declining at the same time—gentrifiers often concentrate in the elite schools within the city where other White and upper middle-class families are sending their children (see, e.g., Posey-Maddox, 2014).

As cities continue to gentrify, researchers continue to establish the relationship between school choice, race, and demographic shifts (Jordan & Gallagher, 2015; Stein, 2015). As Jordan and Gallagher (2015) point out, in gentrifying areas or areas that are beginning gentrification,

School-choice policies might play an increasingly important role in patterns of development by influencing which city neighborhoods these families deem most desirable, changing the distribution of public education resources, and introducing uncharted opportunities for alleviating or exacerbating inequality.

Yet Mickelson's (2001, 2003) longstanding research in Charlotte-Mecklenburg has demonstrated that in the aftermath of the granting of unitary status after the vacating of the *Swann* decision, and the subsequent implementation of a school choice plan with no provisions for equity or integration, this formerly desegregated school system rapidly resegregated along race and class lines. Mickelson concluded that without policy instruments to curtail the tendency for White families to select into majority-White and advantaged schools, school choice would continue to create separate and unequal schooling that mapped onto housing patterns in the countywide school district.

Emerging research has illustrated other ways markets can have effects on local communities by creating perceptions of differential school quality through marketing and public relations. For example, Hernández (2016) found that marketing by charter management organization schools can contribute to negative perceptions of low-income communities as a whole. Hernández (2016) writes that "these discursive patterns and characterizations of racial groups often tap into urban imaginaries such as the pathologized urban jungle, thus reifying widely held stereotypes about racial groups and spaces without implicating race specifically" (p. 59). Middle-class families engaging in school choice polices are inclined to choose away from schools enrolling large numbers of children of color or children living in poverty (Kimelberg & Chase, 2012). These images and narratives have implications not only for education policymaking but also can have implications for urban policy and urban geography more broadly.

In addition, evidence indicates that urban school districts are facing vast teacher shortages. The teachers who remain often struggle to afford the rising housing costs of the cities in which they work, and the numbers of African American teachers in particular, have declined precipitously over the past decade as market reforms, school closures, and urban gentrification have been on the rise (Albert Shanker Institute, 2016). Meanwhile, less experienced White teachers often staff urban charter schools that serve predominantly poor students of color, and these schools experience even higher rates of teacher turnover than do similar traditional public schools. African American and Latino teachers and leaders struggle to gain a foothold in this new political terrain; despite their deep expertise in meeting the pedagogical and cultural needs of the students served by new schools (Henry & Dixson, 2016; Siddle-Walker, 2012). These dynamics are intimately linked to the political economy of urban education, in which race and inequality characterize schooling opportunities, much as they did when the AERA was founded in 1916.

DISCUSSION

An urban political economy framework—incorporating the social and geographic landscape of space and the racialized politics that drive it—helps illuminate how and why market-based reforms have taken deeper roots in these evolving urban contexts, and how these reforms, when layered on the existing inequality, can magnify social, economic, and spatial divisions. Over the past several decades, much of the education policy scholarship has narrowly focused on questions of educational effectiveness, to the detriment of considering the broader context in which educational interventions operate. As Tate (2008) argued in his AERA presidential address, prevailing theories and methods can inadvertently serve to silence the experiences of the families, students, and communities that are most vulnerable to social inequality. Focusing on the role of technology industries in two cities, Tate issued a call to researchers to broaden their frameworks to understand the connections between educational opportunity and the urban context. He explained, "As a result of ideological commitments to social evaluation and reform, our education research community has a civic responsibility to better understand how science and related industries influence the geography of opportunity in our cities and metropolitan regions" (Tate, 2008, p. 397).

We extend Tate's framing to consider the context of market reforms in an urban political economy characterized by racial segregation and economic inequality. The framework of the "geography of opportunity" highlights how political decisions and policies have, over time, created unequal opportunity structures in which people live, work, and go to school—which then have profound effects on individual life chances (Galster & Killen, 2010; powell, Heller, & Bundalli, 2011; Rosenbaum, 1995). Our review leads us to conclude that the very processes that created the conditions for market-based reforms to take hold in urban school districts also ripened the ability of private sector actors to secure contracts over the provision of local school operations, district functions, and policy decisions for poor students. As our review has illustrated, decades of disinvestment in the urban core and the weakening of meaningful civil rights policies helped propel these changes, with significant impacts on urban school systems, including loss of enrollment, state divestment in school funding for urban school districts, and increasing racial and ethnic segregation.

The urban political economy framework highlights the limitations of market-based reforms to systemically lift up and improve urban school districts if they are not accompanied by explicit policy mechanisms to redress the tendency of wealthy and advantaged families to select into schools that primarily serve their children. Our review of the literature indicates that market-based reforms can perpetuate and reify social, political, and economic inequality unless strong regulations allow for more equitable implementation. Because research on market-based reforms in urban school districts shows that current policies have emerged out of the convergence of racialized economic and political decisions that isolate those living in poverty, these policies tend to relegate their schooling options in ways that benefit wealthier urban citizens. In addition, although the majority of the U.S. teaching force is White, African American teachers and teachers of color tend to be concentrated in schools serving poor children of color, adding another layer of segregation to schooling, and making these teachers most affected by school closures, a lack of sufficient resources, and the proliferation of charter schools. According to the Albert Shanker Institute (2016), which examined data from the Schools and Staffing Survey and the Teacher Follow-Up Survey in nine cities in traditional public schools and in the charter sector, these same urban school districts are undergoing significant losses in teachers of color:

When examining teacher diversity trends over the course of the 10 years in our study—from 2002 to 2012—a number of disquieting trends become evident. In every one of the nine cities studied, the Black share of the teacher workforce declined, at rates from the very small to the quite large—from roughly 1 percent in Boston's charter sector and Cleveland's district sector, to more than 24 percent in New Orleans (combined sectors) and nearly 28 percent in Washington, D.C. (combined sectors). Losses in the population (i.e., number) of Black teachers were even greater, ranging from a low of 15 percent in New York City (combined sectors) to a high of 62 percent in New Orleans (combined sectors). The available evidence suggests that seniority-based layoffs played little or no role in these declines. (Albert Shanker Institute, 2016, p. 2)

A political economy framework helps illustrate how broader racial and economic stratification has emerged under market-oriented reforms, with elite and well-funded, desirable schools accessible to some, while traditional public schools and many choice schools struggle to stay afloat and to provide quality schooling, and diversity in the teacher force rapidly declines. The effects of these reform efforts for urban students and the urban educational systems in which they are situated have often been unintended: little growth in achievement, growing segregation, and loss of teachers who are more likely to share students' racial, ethnic, and linguistic backgrounds.

Our review raises questions about the degree to which these reforms have moved public education even further away from the common school ideal. We began this chapter with an anecdote about the 2015 hunger strike to keep a school open on Chicago's South Side. These activists deeply understood the political economy of urban schooling and its relationship to market-oriented education reforms. Jitu Brown (2015) explained that the CPS's refusal of their request to keep Dyett school open as a green technology academy, while privileging wealthier parts of the city, was a part of this dynamic:

Education experts from across the country and CPS itself, acknowledged that it was the best plan for Bronzeville's children. The mayor of this city and his education chair Alderman Will Burns blocked this plan because of politics. I was one of 12 people who reluctantly launched a 34 day hunger strike on August 17, 2015 not to run a charter school; or land contracts, but for CPS to finally value Black children in Bronzeville like they do children in Lincoln Park. What was burned on our memory was that on the 25th day of our hunger strike, Rahm Emanuel and Forest Claypool awarded Lincoln Elementary, a well-resourced school in Lincoln Park a $21 million dollar annex. They held a ribbon cutting ceremony while we starved in Washington Park.

Market-based reforms in urban schools have emerged out of the convergence of these economic and political trends. Indeed cities, working to remake themselves as spaces welcoming to young, wealthy residents, have increasingly adopted school reform policies emphasizing charter schools and private management (Lipman, 2002). Under the Obama administration, federal education policy has followed these patterns established at the beginning of the last century, most recently with the reauthorization of the ESEA, referred to as the Every Student Succeeds Act. Every Student Succeeds Act devolves more authority and autonomy to the states and also provides significant support for charter schools and charter school management organizations.

A faith in market approaches to school improvement, structure, and governance remains remarkably persistent even in the face of mixed empirical evidence of these policies' effectiveness, and strong evidence that they result in greater sorting, stratification, and segregation. Even as urban spaces have undergone significant alterations—changing from thriving centers of industry, to centers of industrial decline, to hubs of finance, technology, and artistic expression—the children of those made poor by these economic alterations have rarely been well served systemically. The effects of reform efforts for urban students and the urban educational systems in which they are situated typically are framed in terms of results on standardized assessments and fail to account for the broader effects on teachers, surrounding schools, communities, parental and student engagement, and increased racial, linguistic, and economic segregation.

Nearly 20 years ago, Rury and Mirel (1997), suggested that school reform would be limited insofar as the cities in which schools were situated were stratified. They argued that schools "are likely to prove highly resistant to change until the deteriorating and often oppressive quality of their urban environment is altered in fundamental ways" (p. 98). This review of the literature on the evolution of cities and city schools leads us to extend and broaden Rury and Mirel's assessment, to argue that the economy of marketization illustrates how schools—to the extent to which they are themselves stratified and unequal—can also powerfully shape the urban environment in ways that deepen inequality. Indeed, the economic and structural shifts affecting cities over the last century, by fueling segregation and concentration of poverty in urban schools, created ripe conditions for the expansions of markets in education, as we have illustrated. These markets have resulted in some schools' posting often isolated gains in achievement, but have also resulted in greater school segregation and a decline in the ability of the most economically marginalized citizens to participate democratically in their children's education, because of the eradication of democratic processes such as local school board elections.

As school closures and the fiscal effects of the growth of charter schools have constrained urban school districts financially, opportunities have been created for elites to remake urban space and public schools. For example, researchers have found that political donations for urban school board elections have grown significantly, with national market reform advocates supporting local elections, often from out of state (Reckhow et al., 2016). This money has the potential to usurp local preferences for school board representation in typically low-spending elections. Indeed, recent research suggests that school choice is increasingly allowing elite families to reclaim cities within pockets of affluence (Posey-Maddox, 2014). In this way, schools—and markets in education, in particular—are active players in the remaking of urban space (see Lipman, 2011) This review of the literature indicates that in order to redress the current patterns of segregation and inequality, education policies must move beyond individual parental choice as a driver to school improvement, and instead attend to these interactions in concert with housing, transit, and economic development policy.

DIRECTIONS FOR FUTURE RESEARCH

Our review suggests at least four directions for the next era of research on the political economy of schooling. First, as we noted previously, the research literature on market-based reforms, has (like the policymakers themselves) tended to overlook the political and economic forces that are at work in the contexts in which these reforms are being implemented. Research on market-based reforms should consider how these reforms are driven by, and interact with, those forces. In particular, the growing role of private sector actors from foundations and advocacy organizations acting as de facto public policymakers requires more robust theories of the policy-making process, and of philosophical considerations about the implications of such shifts for democratic participation and civic engagement in an era of vast, racialized wealth inequality.

Second, education researchers should resist examining school districts in isolation from one another; inequality plays out across often multiple jurisdictions; and school reforms often have "ripple effects" that go outside school district boundaries. Families seeking better schooling frequently attempt to enroll their children in high-achieving and well-resourced suburban school districts using falsified addresses, only to find that many of these districts employ investigators to ensure that such families are removed from those schools (Spencer, 2015). The role of suburban school districts in helping to maintain patterns of racial segregation has been at issue since at least the 1974 *Milliken* decision, and it continues to have relevance in this era of market-based educational reforms.

Third, education researchers should broaden and deepen existing research on successful education policies that increase student learning and equality of opportunity. This work, underway in comparative international contexts, points to the importance of redressing inequality, shunning marketized approaches, and making significant investments in teacher preparation and professional development (Adamson, Åstrand, & Darling-Hammond, 2016; Kirp, 2013; Powers, Fischman, & Berliner, 2016).

Researchers should also incorporate longer term measures when evaluating policy success. An example of this type of approach is Rucker Johnson's (2015) study of the long-term effects of school desegregation, which followed the life trajectories of children born between 1948 and 1968; he found that school desegregation had positive effects on long-term educational attainment, labor market outcomes, family income, and health outcomes for African American students.

As teachers in suburban, rural, and urban schools alike are finding themselves in classrooms in which children lack sufficient food, shelter, medical and mental health care, and lack pedagogical and other supports to learn how to teach in ways that respond to their students' social challenges and build on their unique strengths and existing "funds" of knowledge nested within communities and families (Moll, Amanti, Neff, & González, 1992; Valenzuela, 1999). Policymakers demand that teachers, rather than these broader macro-level dynamics, are the cause for the racial achievement gap, and much of the professional development targeted at teachers aims to help them close it (Lashaw, 2010). While improving student learning is an important goal that joins many reformers across ideological differences, unyoked to deeper understandings of the multigenerational effects of poverty and inequality on communities, policy efforts aimed at improving learning can result in reforms that neglect more effective, interconnected interventions in housing, labor, and health (Johnson, 2016). Narrow educational policies can also widen within and between-school stratification (Anyon, 2005; Kantor, & Lowe, 2013; Rothstein, 2004).

Finally, it would be fruitful for researchers to attend to the role of current and historical social movements in pressuring policymakers to make urban education and city life more equitable through housing, labor, and economic policies such as raising the minimum wage, investing in transportation, or rent stabilization. These movements will likely become more active, interconnected, and complex in the aftermath of the 2016 U.S. presidential election. Researchers should also attend to how grassroots organizations, national coalitions, progressive arms of teachers' unions, and parental activists are working to remake and resist many market-based reforms in light of the growing evidence of their equality of opportunity limitations. These social movements stand to mobilize support for a revitalized public education sector of which choice policies can play a more equitable role. Such mobilization can help researchers and the public reimagine schooling systems that could move American urban school districts closer to the common school ideals that shaped the original purposes of public education in a diverse and democratic society.

NOTES

[1]Policies that include accountability considerations are not inherently market based. We include in our definition the use of accountability metrics to reward or sanction schools, teachers, or school systems as being market-based reforms.

[2]See, for example, Wortman, Reichardt, and St. Pierre (1978).

REFERENCES

Adamson, F., Åstrand, B., & Darling-Hammond, L. (Eds.). (2016). *Global education reform: How privatization and public investment influence education outcomes.* New York, NY: Routledge.

Albert Shanker Institute. (2016). *The state of teacher diversity in American education.* Washington, DC: Author.

Alexander, K., & Alexander, K. (2005). Vouchers and the privatization of American education: Justifying racial resegregation from *Brown* to *Zelman. University of Illinois Law Review, 2004,* 1131–1154.

Anderson, G., & Donchik, L. M. (2016). Privatizing schooling and policymaking: The American Legislative Exchange Council and new political and discursive strategies of education governance. *Educational Policy, 30,* 322–364. doi:10.1177/0895904814528794

Anderson, G., & Scott, J. (2012). Toward an intersectional understanding of social context and causality. *Qualitative Inquiry, 18,* 674–685.

Anderson, J. (1988). *The education of Blacks in the south, 1860–1935.* Chapel Hill: University of North Carolina Press.

Andre-Bechely, L. (2005). *Could it be otherwise? Parents and the inequalities of public school choice.* New York, NY: Routledge.

Anyon, J. (1997). *Ghetto schooling: A political economy of urban educational reform.* New York, NY: Teachers College Press.

Anyon, J. (2005). *Radical possibilities.* New York, NY: Routledge.

Apple, M., & Oliver, A. (1996). Becoming right: Education and the formation of conservative movements. *Teachers College Record, 97,* 419–445.

Armor, D. J., & Schwarzbach, D. (1978). *White flight, demographic transition, and the future of school desegregation.* Santa Monica, CA: RAND.

Arsen, D., DeLuca, T., Ni, Y., & Bates, M. (2015). *Which districts get into financial trouble and why: Michigan's story* (Working Paper #51). East Lansing, MI: Education Policy Center.

Ascher, C. (1996, May). Performance contracting: A forgotten experiment in school privatization. *Phi Delta Kappan,* 615–621.

Ascher, C., Fruchter, N., & Berne, R. (1996). *Hard lessons: Public schools and privatization.* New York, NY: Twentieth Century Fund Press.

Bartlett, L., Frederick, M., Gulbrandsen, T., & Murillo, E. (2002). The marketization of education: Public schools for private ends. *Anthropology & Education Quarterly, 33*(1), 1–25.

Becker, H. J., Nakagawa, K., & Corwin, R. (1997). Parental involvement contracts in California charter schools: Strategy for educational improvement or method of exclusion? *Teachers College Record, 98,* 512–536.

Bell, C. A. (2007). Space and place: Urban parents' geographical preferences for schools. *Urban Review, 39,* 375–404.

Bell, C. A. (2009). All choices created equal? The role of choice sets in the selection of schools. *Peabody Journal of Education, 84,* 191–208.

Bennett, J. (2008). *Brand-name charters.* Retrieved from http://educationnext.org/brand-name-charters/

Bifulco, R., & Ladd, H. (2007). School choice, racial segregation, and test-score gaps: Evidence from North Carolina's charter school program. *Journal of Policy Analysis and Management, 26*(1), 31–56.

Bischoff, K. (2008). School district fragmentation and racial residential segregation: How do boundaries matter? *Urban Affairs Review, 44,* 182–217.

Black Lives Matter. (2016). *Black lives matter: Policy demands for Black power, freedom & justice.* Retrieved from https://policy.m4bl.org

Bolick, C. (1998). *Transformation: The promise and politics of empowerment.* Oakland, CA: Institute for Contemporary Studies.

Brayboy, B., Castagno, A., & Maughan, E. (2007). Equality and justice for all? Examining race in education scholarship. *Review of Research in Education, 31,* 159–194.

Briggs, X. D. (2005). Politics and policy: Changing the geography of opportunity. In X. D. Briggs (Ed.), *The geography of opportunity: Race and housing choice in metropolitan America* (pp. 310–342). Washington, DC: Brookings Institution Press.

Brown, J. (2015, October 21). *Fruit from a rotten tree: The truth about Barbara Byrd-Bennett & CPS.* Retrieved from http://www.progressillinois.com/quick-hits/content/2015/10/21/op-ed-fruit-rotten-tree-truth-about-barbara-byrd-bennett-cps

Buckley, J., & Sattin-Bajaj, C. (2011). Are ELL students underrepresented in charter schools? Demographic trends in New York City, 2006–2008. *Journal of School Choice, 5*(1), 40–65. doi:10.1080/15582159.2011.548242

Buckley, J., & Schneider, M. (2005). Are charter school students harder to educate? Evidence from Washington, D.C. *Educational Evaluation and Policy Analysis, 27,* 365–380. doi:10.3102/01623737027004365

Budde, R. (1988). *Education by charter: Restructuring school districts key to long-term continuing improvement in American education.* Retrieved from http://eric.ed.gov/?q=ED295298&id=ED295298

Bulkley, K. (2005). Losing voice? Educational management organizations and charter schools' educational programs. *Education and Urban Society, 37,* 204–234.

Bulkley, K., Henig, J., & Levin, H. (2010). *Between public and private: Politics, governance, and the new portfolio models for urban school reform.* Cambridge, MA: Harvard Education Press.

Buras, K. (2011). Race, charter schools, and conscious capitalism: On the spatial politics of Whiteness as property (and the unconscionable assault on Black New Orleans). *Harvard Educational Review, 81,* 296–330.

Buras, K. (2012). "It's all about the dollars": Charter schools, educational policy, and the racial market in New Orleans. In W. Watkins (Ed.), *The assault on public education: Confronting the politics of corporate school reform* (pp. 160–188). New York, NY: Teachers College Press.

Burch, P. (2009). *Hidden markets: The new education privatization.* New York, NY: Routledge.

Carl, J. (1996). Unusual allies: Elite and grass-roots origins of parent choice in Milwaukee. *Teaches College Record, 98,* 266–284.

Carl, J. (2011). *Freedom of choice: Vouchers in American education.* Santa Barbara, CA: Praeger.

Center for Research on Education Outcomes. (2009). *Charter school performance in Louisiana.* Palo Alto, CA: Stanford University.

Center for Research on Education Outcomes. (2013). *Charter school performance in Louisiana.* Palo Alto, CA: Stanford University.

Chavez, L., & Frankenberg, E. (2009). *Integration defended: Berkeley Unified's strategy to maintain school diversity.* Berkeley: Chief Justice Earl Warren Institute on Race, Ethnicity, and Diversity, University of California, Berkeley Law School.

Cholke, S. (2015). *Dyett hunger strike ends with dinner, declaration of victory.* Retrieved from http://www.dnainfo.com/chicago/20150922/kenwood/dyett-hunger-strike-ends-with-dinner-declaration-of-victory

Chubb, J. E., & Moe, T. M. (1990). *Politics, markets and America's schools.* Washington, DC: The Brookings Institute.

Clotfelter, C. T. (2004). *After Brown: The rise and retreat of school desegregation.* Princeton, NJ: Princeton University Press.

Cobb, C. D., & Glass, G. V. (1999). Ethnic segregation in Arizona charter schools. *Education Policy Analysis Archives, 7*(1), 1–40. Retrieved from http://olam.ed.asu.edu/epaa/v7n1/

Cohen, D., & Lizotte, C. (2015). Teaching the market: Fostering consent to education markets in the United States. *Environment and Planning, 47,* 1824–1841.

Cohen, R. (2007). *Strategic grantmaking: Foundations and the school privatization movement.* Washington, DC: National Committee for Responsive Philanthropy.

Corcoran, S., & Jennings, J. L. (2015). *The gender gap in charter school enrollment.* Retrieved from http://www.nyu.edu/projects/corcoran/papers/Corcoran%20Jennings%20-%20Gender%20Gap%20in%20Charter%20Enrollment%20(08_04_14).pdf

Crain, R. L. (1969). *The politics of school desegregation: Comparative case studies of community structure and policy-making.* New York, NY: Doubleday.

Cubberly, E. (1916). *Public school administration: A statement of the fundamental principles underlying the organization and administration of public education.* Cambridge, MA: Riverside Press.

Cucchiara, M. (2008). Re-branding urban schools: Urban revitalization, social status, and marketing public schools to the upper middle class. *Journal of Education Policy, 23,* 165–179.

Cucchiara, M. (2013). *Marketing schools, marketing cities: Who wins and who loses when schools become urban amenities.* Chicago, IL: University of Chicago Press.

Cucchiara, M. (2016). Thinking locally: Attending to social context in studies of marketing and education. *Peabody Journal of Education, 91,* 121–130.

David, J., Woodworth, K., Grant, E., Lopez-Torkos, A., & Young, V. (2006). *Bay Area KIPP schools: A study of early implementation: First year report 2004–2005.* Retrieved from https://www.sri.com/sites/default/files/publications/kippyear_1_report.pdf

Davis, O. (2014, May 28). The Newark school reform wars. *The Nation*. Retrieved from https://www.thenation.com/article/newark-school-reform-wars/

DeBray-Pelot, E., Lubienski, C., & Scott, J. (2007). The institutional landscape of interest-group politics and school choice. *Peabody Journal of Education, 82*, 204–230.

Donahue, J. D. (1989). *The privatization decision: Public ends, private means*. New York, NY: Basic Books.

Drier, P., Mollenkopf, J., & Swanstrom, T. (2014). *Place matters: Metropolitics for the 21st century*. Wichita: University of Kansas Press.

Edsall, T., & Edsall, M. (1992). *Chain reaction: The impact of race, rights and taxes on American politics*. New York, NY: W. W. Norton.

Engel, M. (2000). *The struggle for control of public education: Market ideology vs. democratic values*. Philadelphia, PA: Temple University Press.

Ewing, E. (2015, September 21). "We shall not be moved": A hunger strike, education, and housing in Chicago. *New Yorker*. Retrieved from http://www.newyorker.com/news/news-desk/we-shall-not-be-moved-a-hunger- strike-education-and-housing-in-

Finnigan, K. F., Holme, J. J., Diem, S. L., Orfield, M., Luce, T. M., Hylton, N., & Mattheis, A. (2015). Regional educational policy analysis: Rochester, Omaha, and Minneapolis' inter-district arrangements. *Educational Policy, 29*, 780–814.

Fligstein, N., & Dauter, L. (2007). The sociology of markets. *Annual Review of Sociology, 33*, 105–128.

Ford, R. T. (1994) The boundaries of race: Political geography in legal analysis. *Harvard Law Review, 107*, 1844–1921.

Frankenberg, E., & Lee, C. (2003). *Charter schools and race: A lost opportunity for integrated education*. Retrieved from http://epaa.asu.edu/ojs/index.php/epaa/article/view/260

Frankenberg, E., Siegel-Hawley, G., & Wang, J. (2010). *Choice without equity: Charter school segregation and the need for civil rights standards*. Retrieved from https://www.civilrightsproject.ucla.edu/research/k-12-education/integration-and-diversity/choice-without-equity-2009-report

Frankenberg, E., Siegel-Hawley, G., & Wang, J. (2011, January). Choice without equity: Charter school segregation. *Education Policy Analysis Archives, 19*(1). Retrieved from http://epaa.asu.edu/ojs/article/view/779/878

Frey, W. (2011, May). *Melting pot cities and suburbs: Racial and ethnic change in metro America in the 2000s*. Washington, DC: Brookings Institution Press.

Friedman, M. (1962). *Capitalism and freedom*. Chicago, IL: University of Chicago Press.

Fuller, B. (2000). The public square, big or small? Charter schools in political context. In B. Fuller (Ed.). *Inside charter schools: The paradox of radical decentralization* (pp. 12–65). Cambridge, MA: Harvard University Press.

Galster, G. C., & Killen, S. P. (2010). The geography of metropolitan opportunity: A reconnaissance and conceptual framework. *Housing Policy Debate, 6*(1), 7–43.

Garcia, D. R. (2008a). Academic and racial segregation in charter schools: Do parents sort students into specialized charter schools? *Education and Urban Society, 40*, 590–612.

Garcia, D. R. (2008b). The impact of school choice on racial segregation in charter schools. *Educational Policy, 22*, 805–829.

Garnett, N. (2014). *Disparate impact, school closures, and parental choice*. Retrieved from http://scholarship.law.nd.edu/law_faculty_scholarship/1135

Goldie, D., Linick, M., Jabbar, H., & Lubienski, C. (2014). Using bibliometric and social media analyses to explore the "echo-chamber" hypothesis. *Educational Policy, 28*, 281–305.

Government Accountability Office. (2012). *Charter schools: Additional federal attention needed to help protect access for students with disabilities*. Retrieved from http://www.gao.gov/products/gao-12-543

Green, v. County School Board of New Kent County, 391 U.S. 430 (1968).

Green, P., Baker, B., Oluwole, J., & Mead, J. (2016). Are we heading toward a charter school bubble? Lessons from the subprime mortgage crisis. *University of Richmond Law Review, 50*, 783. Retrieved from https://papers.ssrn.com/sol3/papers.cfm?abstract_id=2704305

Green, P. C., & McCall, D. (1998). Are charter schools sufficiently public to receive public funds? An analysis of Council of Organizations about Parochiaid v. Governor. *International Journal of Education Reform, 7*, 232–242.

Hacker, J., & Pierson, P. (2010). *Winner-take-all politics: How Washington made the rich richer—and turned its back on the middle class.* New York, NY: Simon & Schuster.

Hemphill, C. (2008). *Parent power and mayoral control: Avenues for parent and community involvement in New York City schools.* New York, NY: Commission on School Governance.

Henig, J. (1990). Privatization in the United States: Theory and practice. *Political Science Quarterly, 104*, 649–670.

Henig, J. R. (2013). *The end of exceptionalism: The changing politics of school reform.* Cambridge, MA: Harvard Education Press.

Henig, J. R., & MacDonald, J. A. (2002). Locational decisions of charter schools: Probing the market metaphor. *Social Science Quarterly, 83*, 962–980. doi:10.1111/1540-6237.00126.

Henry, K. L., & Dixson, A. D. (2016). Locking the door before we got the keys: Racial realities of the charter school authorization process in post-Katrina New Orleans. *Educational Policy, 30*, 218–240.

Hernández, L. (2016). Race and racelessness in CMO marketing: Exploring charter management organizations' racial construction and its implications. *Peabody Journal of Education, 91*, 47–63. doi:10.1080/0161956X.2016.1119566

Hirji, R. (2014, January 14). *Are charter schools upholding student rights?* Retrieved from http://apps.americanbar.org/litigation/committees/childrights/content/articles/winter2014-0114-charter-schools-upholding-student-rights.html

Hobbs, F., & Stoops, N. (2002). *Census 2000 special reports: Demographic trends in the 20th century.* Washington, DC: U.S. Census Bureau.

Holme, J. J. (2002). Buying homes, buying schools: School choice and the social construction of school quality. *Harvard Educational Review, 72*, 177–205.

Holme, J. J., Finnigan, K. S., & Diem, S. L. (2016). Challenging boundaries, changing fate? Metropolitan inequality and the legacy of Milliken. *Teachers College Record, 118*(3), 1–40.

Holt, M. (2000). *Not yet "free at last": The unfinished business of the civil rights movement.* Oakland, CA: Institute for Contemporary Studies.

Jabbar, H. (2014). *The rising tide: School choice and competition in post-Katrina New Orleans* (Unpublished doctoral dissertation). University of California, Berkeley.

Jabbar, H. (2015). Every kid is money: Market-like competition and school leader strategies in New Orleans. *Educational Evaluation and Policy Analysis, 37*, 638–659.

Jackson, K. (1987). *Crabgrass frontier: The suburbanization of the United States.* New York, NY: Oxford University Press.

Jargowsky, P. (2003). *Stunning progress, hidden problems: The dramatic decline of concentrated poverty in the 1990s.* Washington, DC: Brookings Institution, Center for Metropolitan and Urban Policy.

Jargowsky, P. (2015). *Architecture of segregation: Civil unrest, the concentration of poverty, and public policy.* New York, NY: Century Foundation.

Jencks, C. (1970) *Education vouchers: A report on financing education in payments to parents.* Cambridge, MA: Center for the Study of Public Policy.

Jennings, J. (2010). School choice or schools' choice? Managing in an era of accountability. *Sociology of Education, 83*, 227–247.

Jessen, S. B. (2011). *A year in the labyrinth: Examining the expansion of mandatory high school choice in New York City* (Unpublished doctoral dissertation). New York University, New York.

Johnson, R. C. (2015). *Long-run impacts of school desegregation & school quality on adult attainments* (NBER Working Paper No. 16664). Cambridge, MA: National Bureau of Economic Research. Retrieved from http://www.nber.org/papers/w16664

Johnson, R. C. (2016). *Can schools level the intergenerational playing field? Lessons from equal educational opportunity policies.* Retrieved from https://www.stlouisfed.org/~/media/Files/PDFs/Community%20Development/Econ%20Mobility/Sessions/JohnsonRPresentation508.pdf

Jordan, R., & Gallagher, M. (2015). *Does school choice affect gentrification? Posing the question and assessing the evidence.* Retrieved from http://www.urban.org/sites/default/files/alfresco/publication-pdfs/2000374-Does-School-Choice-Affect-Gentrification.pdf

Judson, (2012, February 21). Why inequality matters: The housing crisis, our justice system, and capitalism. *The Huffington Post.* Retrieved from http://www.huffingtonpost.com/bruce-judson/why-inequality-matters-th_b_1288132.html

Kantor, H. (1991). Education, social reform, and the state: ESEA and Federal education policy in the 1960s. *American Journal of Education, 100*(1), 47–83.

Kantor, H., & Brenzel, B. (1993). Urban education and the "truly disadvantaged": The historical roots of the contemporary crisis, 1945–1990. In M. Katz (Ed.), *The "underclass" debate: Views from history* (pp. 366–402). Princeton, NJ: Princeton University Press.

Kantor, H., & Lowe, R. (1995). Class, race, and the emergence of federal education policy: From the new deal to the great society. *Educational Researcher, 24*(3), 4–11, 21.

Kantor, H., & Lowe, R. (2013). Educationalizing the welfare state and privatizing education: The irony of recent school reform. In P. L. Carter & K. G. Welner (Eds.), *Closing the opportunity gap: What America must do to give every child an even chance* (pp. 25–39). New York, NY: Oxford University Press.

Kimelberg, S. M., & Chase, M. B. (2012). Attitudes toward diversity and the school choice process: Middle-class parents in a segregated urban public school district. *Urban Education, 48*, 198–231.

King, M. L. (1967). *Where do we go from here? Chaos or community?* New York, NY: Beacon Press.

Kirp, D. (2013). *Improbable scholars: The rebirth of a great American school system and a strategy for America's schools.* New York, NY: Oxford University Press.

Kleniewski, N., & Thomas, A. (2011). *Cities, change, and conflict: A political economy of urban life* (4th ed.). Belmont, CA: Wadsworth.

Kneebone, E., & Garr, E. (2010). *The suburbanization of poverty: Trends in metropolitan America, 2000 to 2008.* Washington, DC: Brookings Institution Press.

Koedel, C., Betts, J., Rice, L., & Zau, A. (2010). *The social cost of open enrollment as school choice policy.* Retrieved from https://economics.missouri.edu/working-papers/2009/wp0910_koedel.pdf

Kretchmar, K., Sondel, B., & Ferrare, J. J. (2014). Mapping the terrain: Teach for America, charter school reform, and corporate sponsorship. *Journal of Education Policy, 29*, 742–759.

Kumashiro, K. (2008). *The seduction of common sense: How the Right has framed the debate on America's schools.* New York, NY: Teachers College Press.

Labaree, D. F. (1997). Public goods, private goods: The American struggle over educational goals. *American Educational Research Journal, 34*, 39–81.

Lacireno-Paquet, N., Holyoke, T. T., Moser, M., & Henig, J. R. (2002). Creaming versus cropping: Charter school enrollment practices in response to market incentives. *Educational Evaluation and Policy Analysis, 24*, 145–158. doi:10.3102/01623737024002145

Lareau, A. (2003). *Unequal childhoods: Class, race, and family life.* Berkeley: University of California Press.

Lashaw, A. (2010). The radical promise of reformist zeal: What makes "inquiry for equity" plausible? *Anthropology & Education Quarterly, 41,* 323–340.

Lewis, D. A., & Nakagawa, K. (1995). *Race and educational reform in the American metropolis: A study of school decentralization.* Albany: State University of New York Press.

Lipman, P. (1998). *Race, class, and social power in school restructuring.* Albany: State University of New York Press.

Lipman, P. (2002). Making the global city, making inequality: The political economy and cultural politics of Chicago school policy. *American Educational Research Journal, 39,* 379–419.

Lipman, P. (2004). *High stakes education: Inequality, globalization and urban school reform.* New York, NY: Routledge.

Lipman, P. (2011). *The new political economy of urban education: Neoliberalism, race, and the right to the city.* New York, NY: Routledge.

Logan, J. R., & Molotch, H. L. (2007). *Urban fortunes: The political economy of place.* Berkeley: University of California Press.

Lubienski, C., Gulosino, C., & Weitzel, P. (2009). School choice and competitive incentives: Mapping the distribution of educational opportunities across local education markets. *American Journal of Education, 115,* 601–647.

Lubienski, C., Scott, J., & DeBray, E. (2014). The politics of research use in education policymaking. *Educational Policy, 28,* 131–144.

Lubienski, C., Weitzel, P., & Lubienski, S. T. (2009). Is there a "consensus" on school choice and achievement? Advocacy research and the emerging political economy of knowledge production. *Educational Policy, 23,* 161–193.

Massey, D., & Denton, N. (1998). *American apartheid: Segregation and the making of the underclass.* Cambridge, MA: Harvard University Press.

Massey, D. S., & Fischer, M. J. (2003). The geography of inequality in the United States: 1950–2000. *Brookings-Wharton Papers on Urban Affairs, 2003,* 1–40.

McGuinn, P. (2012). Fight club: Are advocacy organizations changing the politics of education? *Education Next, 12,* 25–31.

Metcalf, K. K. (2001). *Evaluation of the Cleveland Scholarship Program.* Bloomington: Indiana Center for Evaluation.

Mickelson, R. (2001). Subverting Swann: First and second generation segregation in Charlotte–Mecklenburg schools. *American Educational Research Journal, 38,* 215–252.

Mickelson, R. (2003). Academic consequences of desegregation and segregation: Evidence from the Charlotte–Mecklenburg Schools. *North Carolina Law Review, 81,* 1513–1562.

Miller, J. J. (2003). *Strategic investment in ideas: How two foundations changed America.* Washington, DC: Philanthropy Roundtable.

Miner, B. (2013). *Lessons from the heartland: A turbulent half-century of public education in an iconic American city.* New York, NY: New Press.

Miron, G. (2014). Charters should be expected to serve all kinds of students. *Education Next. 14*(4). Retrieved from http://educationnext.org/charters-expected-serve-kinds-students/

Miron, G., Urschel, J. L., & Mathis, W. J. (2010). *Schools without diversity: Education management organizations, charter schools, and the demographic stratification of the American school system.* Boulder, CO: Education and the Public Interest Center, Education Policy Research Unit.

Miron, G., Urschel, J. L., & Saxton, N. (2011). *What makes KIPP work? A study of student characteristics, attrition and school finance.* Retrieved from http://www.edweek.org/media/kippstudy.pdf

Moll, L. C., Amanti, C., Neff, D., & González, N. (1992). Funds of knowledge for teaching: A qualitative approach to connect households and classrooms. *Theory Into Practice, 31,* 132–141.

Molnar, A. (1996). *Giving kids the business: The commercialization of America's schools.* Boulder, CO: Westview Press.

Milliken v. Bradley, 418 U.S. 717 (1974).

Nathan, J. (1996). *Charter schools: Creating hope and opportunity for American education.* San Francisco, CA: Jossey-Bass.

National Center for Education Statistics. (2011). *State support for school choice and other options.* Retrieved from http://nces.ed.gov/programs/statereform/sss.asp

Neckerman, K. M. (2007). *Schools betrayed: Roots of failure in inner-city education.* Chicago, IL: University of Chicago Press.

Ni, Y. (2009). The impact of charter schools on the efficiency of traditional public schools: Evidence from Michigan. *Economics of Education Review, 28,* 571–584. doi:10.1016/j.econedurev.2009.01.003

Ni, Y., & Arsen, D. (2010). The competitive effects of charter schools on public school districts. In C. A. Lubienski & P. C. Weitzel (Eds.), *The charter school experiment: Expectations, evidence, and implications* (pp. 93–120). Cambridge, MA: Harvard Education.

Nichols-Barrer, I., Gleason, P., Gill, B., & Tuttle, C. C. (2015). Student selection, attrition, and replacement in KIPP middle schools. *Educational Evaluation and Policy Analysis, 38,* 5–20.

Oakes, J. (1985). *Keeping track: How schools structure inequality.* New Haven, CT: Yale University.

Oliver, M. L., & Shapiro, T. L. (1997). *Black wealth, White wealth: New perspectives on racial inequality.* New York, NY: Routledge.

Orfield, G. (1978). *Must we bus? Segregated schools and national policy.* Washington, DC: Brookings Institution Press.

Orfield, G. (1988). Race and the liberal agenda: The loss of the integrationist dream 1965–1974. In M. Weir, A. Orloff, & T. Skocpol (Eds.), *The politics of social policy in the United States* (pp. 314–355). Princeton, NJ: Princeton University Press.

Orfield, G. (1993). *The growth of segregation in American schools: Changing patterns of separation and poverty since 1968.* Cambridge, MA: Harvard Project on School Desegregation.

Orfield, G. (1995). *Metropolitan school segregation: Impacts on metropolitan society. Minnesota Law Review, 80,* 825–845.

Orfield, G. (2001). *Schools more separate: Consequences of a decade of resegregation.* Retrieved from http://eric.ed.gov/?id=ED459217

Orfield, M. (2002). *American metropolitics.* Washington, DC: Brookings Institute Press.

Otterman, S. (2011, February 3). Criticizing school closings, in a noisy annual ritual. *The New York Times.* Retrieved from http://www.nytimes.com/2011/02/04/nyregion/04panel.html

Pappas, L. (2012). School closings and parent engagement. *Peace and Conflict, 18,* 165–172.

Parker, J. C., & Russell, D. H. (1953). Ways of providing for individual differences. *Educational Leadership, 11,* 169–174.

Pattillo, M. (2015). Everyday politics of school choice in the Black community. *Du Bois Review, 12,* 41–71.

Pattillo, M., Delale-O'Connor, L., & Butts, F. (2014). High stakes choosing: How parents navigate Chicago Public Schools. In A. Lareau & K. Goyette (Eds.), *Choosing homes, choosing schools* (pp. 237–267). New York, NY: Russell Sage Foundation.

Payne, C., & Knowles, T. (2009). Promise and peril: Charter schools, urban school reform, and the Obama Administration. *Harvard Educational Review, 79,* 227–239.

Pedroni, T. C. (2007). *Market movements: African American involvement in school voucher reform.* New York, NY: Routledge.

Pedroni, T. C. (2011). Urban shrinkage as a performance of Whiteness: Neoliberal urban restructuring, education, and racial containment in the post-industrial, global niche city. *Discourse: Studies in the Cultural Politics of Education, 32,* 203–215.

People for the American Way. (2001). *Community voice or captive of the right? A closer look at the Black alliance for educational options.* Retrieved from http://www.pfaw.org/media-center/publications/community-voice-or-captive-right-closer-look-black-alliance-educational-op

Persson, J. (2015, September 22). *CMD publishes full list of 2,500 closed charter schools (with interactive map).* Retrieved from http://www.prwatch.org/news/2015/09/12936/cmd-publishes-full-list-2500-closed-charter-schools

Pew Research Center. (2011). *Twenty-to-one: Wealth gaps rise to record highs between Whites, Blacks, and Hispanics.* Washington, DC: Author.

Pew Research Center. (2012). *Fewer, poorer, gloomier: The lost decade of the middle class.* Washington, DC: Author.

Posey-Maddox, L. (2014). *When middle-class parents choose urban schools: Class, race, and the challenge of equity in public education.* Chicago, IL: University of Chicago Press.

powell, j. a., Heller, C. C., & Bundalli, F. (2011). *Systems thinking and race: Workshop summary.* Los Angeles: California Endowment.

powell, j. a., & Spencer, M. L. (2002.) Giving them the old "one-two": Gentrification and the k.o. of impoverished urban dwellers of color. *Howard Law Journal, 46,* 433–490.

Powers, J. M., Fischman, G. E., & Berliner, D. C. (2016). Making the visible invisible: Willful ignorance of poverty and social inequalities in the research-policy nexus. *Review of Research in Education, 40,* 744–776.

Quadagno, J. (1994). The *color of welfare: How racism undermined the war on poverty.* New York, NY: Oxford University Press.

Reardon, S. (2011). The widening socioeconomic status achievement gap: New evidence and possible explanations. In R. Murnane & G. Duncan (Eds.), *Whither opportunity: Rising inequality, schools, and children's life chances.* Washington, DC: Brookings Institution.

Reardon, S., & Bischoff, K. (2011). *More unequal and more separate: Growth in the residential segregation of families by income, 1970–2009.* New York, NY: Russell Sage Foundation.

Reardon, S. F., & Owens, A. (2014). 60 Years after Brown: Trends and consequences of school segregation. *Annual Review of Sociology, 40,* 199–218.

Reckhow, S. (2013). *Follow the money: How foundation dollars change public school politics.* New York, NY: Oxford University Press.

Reckhow, S., Henig, G., Jacobsen, R., & Litt, S. (2016). "Outsiders with deep pockets": The nationalization of local school board elections. *Urban Affairs Review.* Advance online publication. doi:10.1177/1078087416663004

Reed, D. (2014). *Building the federal schoolhouse: Localism and the American education state.* New York, NY: Oxford University Press.

Reich, R. (2008). *Supercapitalism: The transformation of business, democracy, and everyday life.* New York, NY: Vintage Books.

Rich, A. (2001). *U.S. think tanks and the intersection of ideology, advocacy, and influence.* Retrieved from http://www.nira.or.jp/past/publ/review/2001winter/rich.pdf

Rich, A. (2004). *Think tanks, public policy, and the politics of expertise.* Cambridge, MA: Cambridge University Press.

Rosenbaum, J. E. (1995). Changing the geography of opportunity by expanding residential choice: Lessons from the Gatreaux program. *Housing Policy Debate, 6,* 231–269.

Rothstein, R. (2004). *Class and schools: Using social, economic, and educational reform to close the Black-White achievement gap.* New York, NY: Economic Policy Institute & Teachers College Press.

Rury, J., & Mirel, J. (1997). The political economy of urban education. *Review of Research in Education, 22,* 49–110.

Ryan, J. (2011). *Five miles away, a world apart: One city, two schools, and the story of educational opportunity in modern America.* Cambridge, England: Oxford University Press.

Ryan, J. E., & Heise, M. (2002). The political economy of school choice. *Yale Law Journal, 111*, 2043–2136.

Saez, E., & Zucman, G. (2016) Wealth Inequality in the United States since 1913: Evidence from capitalized income tax data. *Quarterly Journal of Economics, 131*, 519–578.

Saltman, K. (2010). *The gift of education: Public education and venture philanthropy.* New York, NY: Palgrave Macmillan.

Sassen, S. (2011). *Cities in a world economy.* Thousand Oaks, CA: Sage.

Schofield, J. W. (1989). *Black and White in school: Trust, tension or tolerance?* New York, NY: Teachers College Press.

Scott, J. (2009). The politics of venture philanthropy in charter school policy and advocacy. *Educational Policy, 23*, 106–136.

Scott, J. (2011a). Market-driven education reform and the racial politics of advocacy. *Peabody Journal of Education, 86*, 580–599.

Scott, J. (2011b). School choice as a civil right: The political construction of a claim and implications for school desegregation. In E. Frankenberg & E. DeBray-Pelot (Eds.), *Integrating schools in a changing society: New policies and legal options for a multiracial generation* (pp. 32–51). Chapel Hill: University of North Carolina Press.

Scott, J. (2011c). When community control meets educational privatization: The search for empowerment in two African American charter schools. In D. Slaughter-Defoe, H. Stevenson, E. Arrington, D. Johnson, & S. Shange (Eds.), *Black educational choice in a climate of school reform: Consequences for K-12 student learning and development* (pp. 191–204). Santa Barbara, CA: ABC-CLIO.

Scott, J. (2013). School choice and the empowerment imperative. *Peabody Journal of Education, 88*, 60–73.

Scott, J., & Barber, M. (2001). *An alternative framework for policy analysis: Charter school legislation in California, Michigan, and Arizona* (Occasional Paper Number 40). New York, NY: Teachers College Press.

Scott, J., & Fruchter, N. (2009). Community resistance to school privatization: The case of New York City. In R. Fisher (Ed.), *The people shall rule: ACORN, community organizing, and the struggle for economic justice* (pp. 180–205). Nashville, TN: Vanderbilt University Press.

Scott, J., & Jabbar, H. (2014). The hub and the spokes: Foundations, intermediary organizations, incentivist reforms, and the politics of research evidence. *Educational Policy, 28*, 233–257.

Sharkey, P. (2013). *Stuck in place: Urban neighborhoods and the end of progress toward racial equality.* Chicago, IL: University of Chicago Press.

Shedd, C. (2015). *Unequal city: Race, schools, and perceptions of injustice.* New York, NY: Russell Sage Foundation.

Siddle-Walker, V. (2012). *Original intent: Black educators in an elusive quest for justice* (Annual Brown Lecture). Washington, DC: American Educational Research Association. Retrieved from http://www.aera.net/Newsroom/AERAiHighlightsiEnewsUpdate/AERA HighlightsNovember2012/SiddleWalkerPresents2012BrownLecture/tabid/14641 /Default.aspx

Smith, J. A. (1991). *The idea brokers: Think tanks and the rise of the new policy elite.* New York, NY: Free Press.

Smith, S. (2001). *The democratic potential of charter schools.* New York, NY: Peter Lang.

Snider, W. (1989, October 11). Conservatives' civil-rights agenda puts spotlight on choice. *Education Week.* Retrieved from http://www.edweek.org/ew/articles/1989/10/11/0909 0016.h09.html

Soja, E. W. (2010). *Seeking spatial justice.* Minneapolis: University of Minnesota Press.

Spencer, K. (2015, May 18). Can you steal an education? Wealthy school districts are cracking down on "education thieves." *The Hechhinger Report.* Retrieved from http://hechingerreport.org/can-you-steal-an-education/

Stein, M. (2015). Public school choice and racial sorting: An examination of charter schools in Indianapolis. *American Journal of Education, 121,* 597–627.

Stephan, W. (1978). School desegregation: An evaluation of predictions made in *Brown v. Board of Education. Psychological Bulletin, 85,* 217–238.

Tate, W. (2008). "Geography of opportunity": Poverty, place, and educational outcomes. *Educational Researcher, 37,* 397–411.

Taylor, J., Cregor, M., & Lane, P. (2014). *Not measuring up: Massachusetts' students of color and students with disabilities receive disproportionate discipline, especially in charter schools.* Retrieved from http://lawyerscom.org/wp-content/uploads/2014/11/Not-Measuring-up_-The-State-of-School-Discipline-in-Massachusetts.pdf

Themba, M. N. (2001, Fall). "Choice" and other White lies. *Rethinking Schools, 16.*

Tompkins-Stange, M. (2016). *Policy patrons: Philanthropy, education reform, and the politics of influence.* Cambridge, MA: Harvard University Press.

Tough, P. (2006, November 26). Can teaching poor children to act more like middle-class children help close the achievement gap? *The New York Times,* pp. 44–51, 69–72, 77.

Tough, P. (2008). *Whatever it takes: Geoffrey Canada's quest to change Harlem and America.* New York, NY: Mariner Books.

Trujillo, T. (2016). Restoring the commitment to equal education opportunity: New directions for ESSA's school improvement initiatives. *Education Law and Policy Review, 3,* 141–165.

Turner, M. A., Nichols, A., Comey, J., Franks, K., & Price, K. (2012). *Benefits of living in high-opportunity neighborhoods.* Washington, DC: Urban Institute.

Turque, B. (2008, August 3). Rhee details prescription for ailing schools to donors. *Washington Post.* Retrieved from http://www.washingtonpost.com/wp-dyn/content/article/2008/08/02/AR2008080201414.html

Tyack, D. (1974). *The one best system: A history of American urban education.* Cambridge, MA: Harvard University Press.

Tyack, D. (1993). School governance in the United States: Historical puzzles and anomalies. In J. Hannaway & M. Carnoy (Eds.), *Decentralization and school improvement: Can we fulfill the promise* (pp. 1–32). San Francisco, CA: Jossey-Bass.

Tyack, D., & Cuban, L. (1995). *Tinkering toward utopia: A century of public school reform.* Cambridge, MA: Harvard University Press.

U.S. Census Bureau. (2012). *U.S. Census Bureau projections show a slower growing, older, more diverse nation a half century from now.* Retrieved from https://www.census.gov/newsroom/releases/archives/population/cb12-243.html

Valenzuela, A. (1999). *Subtractive schooling: US-Mexican youth and the politics of caring.* Albany: State University of New York Press.

Vasquez Heilig, J., Holme, J. J., LeClair, A. V., Redd, L., & Ward, D. (in press). Separate and unequal? The problematic segregation of special populations in charter schools relative to traditional public schools. *Stanford Law & Policy Review.*

Vasquez Heilig, J., Williams, A., McNeil, L., & Lee, C. (2011). Is choice a panacea? An analysis of Black secondary student attrition from KIPP, other private charters and urban districts. *Berkeley Review of Education, 2,* 153–178.

Wells, A. S. (1993). *Time to choose: America at the crossroads of school choice policy.* New York, NY: Hill & Wang.

Wells, A. S. (Ed.). (2002). *Where charter school policy fails.* New York, NY: Teachers College Press.

Wells, A. S., & Scott, J. (2001) Privatization and charter school reform: Social, political and economic dimensions. In H. M. Levin (Ed.), *Privatizing education: Can the marketplace deliver a system of schools that offers freedom of choice, efficiency, equity, and social cohesion?* (pp. 234–262). Boulder, CO: Westview Press.

Welsh, R., Duque, M., & McEachin, A. (2015). School choice, student mobility and school quality: Evidence from post-Katrina New Orleans. *Education Finance and Policy*. Retrieved from http://www.rand.org/pubs/external_publications/EP50925.html

Wexler, E., & Huerta, L. A. (2000). An empowering spirit is not enough: A Latino charter school struggles over leadership. In B. Fuller (Ed.), *Inside charter schools: The paradox of radical decentralization* (pp. 98–123). Cambridge, MA: Harvard University Press.

Whitty, G. (1997). Creating quasi-markets in education: A review of recent research on parental choice and school autonomy in three countries. In M. Apple (Ed.), *Review of research in education* (Vol. 22, pp. 3–47). Washington, DC: American Education Research Association.

Wilgoren, J. (2000, October 9). Young Blacks turn to school vouchers as civil rights issue. *The New York Times*. Retrieved from http://www.nytimes.com/2000/10/09/us/young-blacks-turn-to-school-vouchers-as-civil-rights-issue.html

Wilkerson, I. (2010). *The warmth of other suns: The epic story of America's great migration.* New York, NY: Vintage Books.

Wilkinson, R., & Pickett, K. (2009). *The sprit level: Why greater equality makes societies stronger.* New York, NY: Bloomsbury Press.

Wilson, W. J. (1987). *The truly disadvantaged.* Chicago, IL: University of Chicago Press.

Wilson-Cooper, C. (2005). School choice and the standpoint of African American mothers: Considering the power of positionality. *Journal of Negro Education, 74*, 174–189.

Witte, J. (1995). The Milwaukee voucher experiment. *Educational Evaluation and Policy Analysis, 20*, 229–251.

Woods, P. A., & Woods, G. J. (2004). Modernising leadership through private participation: A marriage of inconvenience with public ethos. *Journal of Education Policy, 19*, 643–672.

Woods, P. A., & Woods, G. J. (2005, January). *Pressure and support the private way: Lessons from a public-private partnership case study.* Paper presented at the Private Sector Participation in Public Sector Education, London Institute of Education, England.

Woodworth, J. L., Raymond, M. E., Chirbas, K., Gonzalez, M., Negassi, Y., Snow, W., & Van Donge, C. (2015). *Online charter school study.* Palo Alto, CA: Center for Research on Education Outcomes.

Wortman, P., Reichardt, C., & St. Pierre, R. G. (1978). The first year of the education voucher demonstration. *Evaluation Quarterly, 2*, 193–214.

Zehr, M. A. (2011, March 21). New urban playbook: Hand over schools to charter operators. *Education Week*. Retrieved from http://www.edweek.org/ew/articles/2011/03/21/26detroit.h30.html

Zeichner, K., & Peña-Sandoval, C. (2015). Venture philanthropy and teacher education policy in the U.S.: The role of the New Schools Venture Fund. *Teachers College Record.* Retrieved from http://www.tcrecord.org/PrintContent.asp?ContentID=17539

Zelman v. Simmons-Harris, 536 U.S. 639 (2002).

Zimmer, R. W., & Guarino, C. M. (2013). Is there empirical evidence that charter schools "push out" low-performing students? *Educational Evaluation and Policy Analysis, 35*, 461–480. doi:10.3102/0162373713498465

Chapter 9

Constructing and Reconstructing the "Rural School Problem": A Century of Rural Education Research

CATHARINE BIDDLE
University of Maine

AMY PRICE AZANO
Virginia Tech

This chapter examines 100 years of rural education research in the context of the demographic, migratory, economic, and social changes that have affected rural America in the past century. The authors conducted a systematic review of the literature on rural teacher recruitment, retention, and training as a case study to examine the constancy and change in the construction of the "rural school problem," a concept drawn from early work by urban education reformers. They found that attention to rurality as a factor affecting education boomed in the first half of the 20th century thanks to a commitment to achieving a kind of modernity, an emphasis that waned in the second half of that century when modernity was believed to have been more or less achieved. Neoliberal economic policies and the precariousness of rural economies revived interest in the resilience and adaptability of rural America in the late 20th and early 21st centuries, however, leading to a renaissance in rural education research but one largely restricted to a few subfield journals. The authors discuss the implications of these trends for the future of rural education research, including the use of place as a lens for considering education.

The story of rural America in the 20th century is one of significant change, with regard to the physical landscapes, economic structures, migrations of populations, and diverse ways of rural life (Bailey, Jensen, & Ransom, 2014). The increasing trend toward a globalized, integrated world economy has had complex implications for many rural communities in the United States. Farming communities have seen the increasing consolidation of family farms on industrial agricultural models (Bonnano, 2014). Communities with economies based on resource extraction have experienced economic booms and busts as logging, energy, and manufacturing companies pursue

Review of Research in Education
March 2016, Vol. 40, pp. 298–325
DOI: 10.3102/0091732X16667700
© 2016 AERA. http://rre.aera.net

opportunities for cheaper production and labor abroad. New technological develop-ments, particularly in energy, have changed the intensity of the mark these industries leave on rural landscapes (Schafft & Biddle, 2014, 2015; Sherman, 2009). Global migration patterns and growing populations have led to expanding cultural and ethnic diversity in some rural places and suburbanization or urbanization in others (Bustamante, Brown, & Irby, 2010; D. S. Massey & Capoferro, 2008; Salaman, 2003). Some rural communities have experienced intense outmigration of young people in search of economic opportunity in the face of local economic decline (Carr & Kefalas, 2009; Corbett, 2007; Petrin, Schafft, & Meece, 2014). In many rural com-munities the local populations are aging more rapidly than in cities, as suburban and urban baby boomers relocate to amenity-rich rural places and the rural poor, unable to move, age in place (Glasgow & Berry, 2013).

The changing social circumstances of America's diverse and changing rural com-munities have created new opportunities and new challenges for rural schools and school districts. While the effects of these broad social forces have led to different outcomes in different communities, many rural communities have been marked by declining industries or boom-bust cycles of opportunity that complicate local oppor-tunities for recent graduates, the consolidation of long-time community institutions such as local schools, the aging of White populations, and the introduction of young, new-destination immigrants, often from the global south, with educational needs new to the communities they enter (Bustamante et al., 2010; McLaughlin, Shoff, & Demi, 2014). In many rural areas, schools have faced these challenges in the context of increasing fiscal constraints, as tax bases have eroded and state and federal budget cuts have had implications at the local level (Strange, Johnson, Showalter, & Klein, 2012). While schools everywhere are facing similar issues, rural schools often face the additional burden of being one the few local social institutions in sparsely populated communities, and sometimes also of serving as one of the largest employers.

Over the course of this century, educational reformers and researchers have tried to make sense of the unique educational needs of rural communities within these changing social and economic contexts. Just over a century ago, the U.S. Commission on Country Life (1909) issued a definitive report on the status of life in rural America. Charged by President Theodore Roosevelt with the task of outlining ways to make rural American life more attractive, the report detailed, among other topics, deficien-cies in the condition of country schools. Shortly after the report's release, Ellwood Cubberley (1912), a prominent education reformer, deplored the state of rural schools, referring to the issue as the "rural school problem" (p. 75), a term that came to frame the nationwide interest of the time in education reform specifically for rural places and people. Cubberley's lament was echoed by many of his contemporary progressive education reformers, until rural education eventually came to be seen as "the gravest of American problems" (Brooks, 1926, p. 155). Sixty years later, DeYoung (1987) described the zeitgeist of education reform from that era as "in essence based on a notion that rural ways of life were, and would increasingly become, archaic in an emerging urban and cosmopolitan America" (p. 124). It is possible to see this in the writings of Cubberley (1912), Foght (1912), Chase (1917), and others concerned about the provinciality of rural life and people, the administrative inefficiency of rural schools, and the lack of adequate preparation for rural teachers.

All research requires problem definition (Creswell, 2014; Kuhn, 1962; Maxwell, 2012), and the coalescing of research communities happens, in some sense, over agreement on the nature and scope of the problems to be addressed (Kuhn, 1962). Debates over parameters, term definitions, salient factors, and conceptual relationships dominate these kinds of discussions. As the field of education research has developed, agreement has fluctuated over whether the concept of place (the meaning that one gives to space)—rurality, in particular—is a valuable lens through which to view educational issues. However, the power of these largely urbanite educational reformers' acceptance of this construction of rurality itself as "a problem" still echoes in the field today. Although the nature of the rural problem as defined by Cubberley and other education reformers of his generation may have changed, education researchers and advocates throughout the past century have attempted to document the complexities of rural schools' adaptations to changing circumstances and to continue to educate rural youth for a future in which the sustainability of rural life is uncertain.

The purpose of the present review of the literature was to understand how education researchers in the past century have constructed the rural school problem through a case study of one recurring issue in the literature—rural teacher training, recruitment, and retention. In our review, we paid particular attention to how education researchers have couched rurality and defined or redefined the "rural school problem" over time. Tracing this lineage through this case is important to understanding the evolving relationship between attention to context and particularly spatial difference within the growing coherence of education research as a field in this century. We situate our discussion of these changes within the context of the social and economic forces affecting rural communities broadly throughout this time period, drawing on literature from sociology and rural sociology in order to better understand the sensitivity and responsiveness of education research to these social and economic changes.

THEORETICAL FRAMEWORK

To identify relevant literature and the most significant changes influencing the landscape of rural education research, we relied on a theoretical lens that allowed us to consider sociocultural change, the advent of rural education as a scholarly field, and the larger perspective of education research that contextualizes and nests these issues as symbols brought into dialogue with one another. Using symbolic interactionism (Blumer, 1969) and transactional theory, we considered how conceptions of rurality and rural education ascribe meanings to the very condition of rurality. Symbolic interactionism allowed us to understand the meaning making that occurs through social interaction and the subjective meaning one gives to abstract ideas (e.g., "rural") by examining how language is used to create discourse and interpretations (Blumer, 1969).

We also relied on transactional theory to understand the mutually shaping experience between the text (e.g., the literature on rural education research) and the reader (Rosenblatt, 1978, 1938/1983, 2005). Just as social interactions and meaning making are subjective, so too is reading. The reader does not come to a text devoid of experience; rather, the reader comes with his or her own unique experiences with language and the sociocultural contexts that have shaped those experiences. These histories inform the reader's understanding, and according to Rosenblatt (1978, 1938/1983, 2005), these transactions shape the reader and the text during the process of reading or, in this case, the research.

This theoretical frame allowed us to examine language and discourse as symbols and to understand not simply that change has occurred but also how change is brought into dialogue with education research.

METHOD

To explore the issue of how the "rural school problem" has been constructed in the past century by educationalists, we began by reviewing the literature published in two rural-specific journals, the *Journal of Research in Rural Education* and *The Rural Educator*. Through a content analysis of article titles and abstracts,[1] we were able to identify four of the most prevalent topical areas of study: (a) school improvement processes; (b) school-community relationships; (c) teacher recruitment, retention, and training; and (d) youth achievement, aspirations, and retention in school. From these, we chose teacher recruitment, retention, and training as a topical case study for our review, because we felt that it represented an issue most directly within the control of schools as institutions and would therefore provide the most fertile ground for an exploration of education researchers' social construction of rurality as it intersects with this educational focus of scholarly interest. Although we endeavored throughout our review to acknowledge the significant contributions of sociologists, rural sociologists, and anthropologists to our understanding in the past century of the dynamics of rural education within communities and used these contributions to frame our findings, the "rural school problem" as a concept emanated from educationalists. Therefore, we wanted to focus on the unique constructions and contributions of educationalists within the context of an education research field gaining coherence over the same time period (Lagemann, 2000). Although our case study approach did limit the volume of literature reviewed, it allowed us to provide a focused look at change in the relationship between an educational issue and perceptions of and interest in rurality over time.

Content analysis is a qualitative literacy research method in which text is examined for the recurring presence and intersecting relationships of themes, concepts, or words (Hoffman, Wilson, Martinez, & Sailors, 2011). This type of text analysis allowed us to infer and extract messages from the texts, seeking to understand how the texts were shaped by the author, intended audience, time period, and culture in which they were written (Hoffman et al., 2011). During a content analysis, recurring patterns provide the basis for interpretation and can "reveal the more subtle messages imbedded in a text" (Hoffman et al., 2011, p. 28).

Source Identification

We began our systematic review of the literature in 1911, directly after the convening of Theodore Roosevelt's Country Life Commission, which, as we and others have argued, drew unprecedented attention to the lifeways of rural Americans. Because many academic search engines do not archive journal articles prior to 1970, we relied on Google Scholar and JSTOR as the primary avenues for locating education research related to rural teacher preparation, retention, and training for the time period of 1911 to 1970. For the decades after 1970, we used ERIC (EBSCO) and JSTOR. Web of Science was also used, but this returned no new relevant results not found in other search engines. Through each, we conducted decade-by-decade searches using the terms "rural education," "rural teacher," "rural teacher" AND "training," "small schools" AND "teacher training" AND "rural," "rural teacher retention," "rural" AND "professional development," and "rural" AND "pre-service" OR "inservice," until we were satisfied that we were not seeing new, additional results. In sifting through the search results, reviewing article titles, abstracts, and in some cases, the full text of the article, we applied a number of winnowing criteria to our searches. Articles had to be English-language pieces published in academic or professional association journals, focused on the United States exclusively, and not summaries of conference proceedings or conference papers. We applied peer review as a criterion for articles published after 1970.[2] Books, unpublished dissertations, and government documents were excluded from consideration in order to ensure that we were comparing like material in our synthesis across the considerable time period encompassed in the review. We did this, in part, to ensure that the constructions of both rurality and the research problems being compared were developed within similar editorial constraints (i.e., a journal article length). The number of articles reviewed using these search strategies and criteria by decade is presented in Table 1.

Source Analysis

Once we identified articles through systematic searches ($n = 148$), we approached the analysis of articles to address the research questions of (a) how "the rural problem" had been constructed within the education research literature and (b) how and if those constructions had changed over time. Recognizing that authors might approach the contribution of rurality to rural teacher recruitment, retention, and training from a variety of perspectives, our analysis looked at the source material cross-sectionally as well as longitudinally. We chose the decade as a boundary for these analyses because of the likelihood that literature written within a specific decade would be written in dialogue with other recent literature of the time period. As with any relatively arbitrary demarcation of time, a limitation of this strategy was the way in which literature on either side of a decade demarcation might reflect the scholarly conversation happening around the turn of a decade rather than the one happening 10 years prior, but we felt that decades would assist us in identifying trends across time and, more importantly, provide like units of analysis for comparison. Consistent with content analysis, our reading of the texts involved inspecting patterns of the texts and "drawing on

TABLE 1
Results Reviewed by Decade

Decade	Relevant Results Reviewed
1910–1919	21
1920–1929	17
1930–1939	14
1940–1949	20
1950–1959	8
1960–1969	1
1970–1979	2
1980–1989	10
1990–1999	14
2000–2009	25
2010–2015	16

combinations of inductive, deductive, and abductive analytical techniques" (Hoffman et al., 2011, p. 29), or inferences throughout the coding process. In this sense, our methods represent content analysis as "the method of making inferences from texts and making sense of those interpretations in a context surrounding the text" (Hoffman et al., 2011, p. 30).

Within-Decade Analysis

To begin identifying trends within decades, we took articles from a single decade (1911–1920) and each approached the 23 articles we had identified for this time period separately to answer three questions: (a) What type of article is this (empirical, theoretical, opinion/advocacy)? (b) Broadly speaking, what is the takeaway or enduring message? (c) How is the "rural school problem" constructed? We each separately made notes about these articles, including the generation of possible descriptive codes, and then compared our notes and generated codes to identify commonalities and divergences in our reading of these articles.

Across-Decade Analysis

To begin our comparison of sources across decades, we examined articles from a single journal ($n = 10$), *Teachers College Record*, that was in existence for the entirety of the period studied. We determined that articles from this journal were appropriate for this type of longitudinal analysis because the journal spans education research subfields and has published scholarly articles on a broad variety of topics in education since 1900.

To complete our analysis, we divided the data corpus of 148 articles, each reading half of the articles per decade, to compare codes by decade. We completed a common read of 25% of the articles across all decades. We then wrote summative memos of potential groupings of time and themes to arrive at the synthesis presented in our findings.

FINDINGS

In examining the literature on rural teacher training, recruitment, and retention as a case study of the changing definition of the rural school problem over a century, we observed three distinct periods. In the following synthesis, we discuss these periods in the context of (a) the social and economic trends that defined rural America at those times, (b) the development of rural education research and education research as a field, and (c) the evolving conversation about the "rural school problem" with a focus on how this conversation manifested in scholars' writing about teacher recruitment, retention, and training.

Identifying and Defining the "Rural School Problem": 1909 to 1945

In 1909, Theodore Roosevelt's convocation of the Country Life Commission signified a formal symbol of growing interest in and attention to the reformation of rural life in the United States (DeYoung, 1987). There was interest in improving transportation to rural areas by expanding railroads and building better roads and to ensuring rural access to modern technology, such as electrification and the telephone. Advances in farming technology were of interest to reformers as well, with an emphasis on what could be achieved by applying steam and motorized power to labor previously done by humans and animals. There was a burgeoning sense, in this era, that progress, and in particular, new efficiencies, could be achieved through the proper application of technology and human organization (Bowers, 1971).

In keeping with the zeitgeist of the times, there was consistent and growing interest in rural school reform as urban education reformers and leaders of local rural school districts took note of the findings of the Country Life Commission. Universities and normal schools began to form rural education departments designed to address specifically the unique needs of rural school reform. One of the primary foci of university-based, urban education reformers was on differentiated teacher preparation to aid recruitment and retention of teachers in rural areas. These reformers also debated the effect of consolidation on promoting better instruction and development of teaching staff and the role of the community in supporting the isolated rural teacher. Over the next several decades, interest in these topics and others around rural education grew so strong and were so commonly discussed that, by 1944, the first White House Conference for Rural Education was convened and established educational rights for every rural child, including the right to a modern education in modern buildings; an education that bridges the gap between home and school; health services, vocational guidance, school lunches, and public transportation; and sufficiently prepared teachers and school leaders who understand rural life. The well-intended Charter of Rights of the Rural Child to Education (Dawson & Hubbard, 1944) was written as a pledge to rural schools and students to solidify the government's commitment to combating perceived inequities in rural schooling.

Defining a Rural School Reform Agenda by Defining the "Problem"

The literature of this period slowly defined many of the issues that constituted what reformers saw as "the rural school problem." Reformers of the time addressed the growing concerns of increasing youth outmigration to cities by describing (often in desperate tones) an urgent need to train rural teachers to better deliver an education. Fishpaw (1912) wrote in her definition of "the rural school problem,"

As the environment of the country child differs from that of the town and city, so the rural school problem differs. We must admit that organization supervision, consolidated schools, sanitary buildings and a well coordinated and properly correlated course of study are all necessary for the solution, but we may have all of these and fail unless the trained teacher is at the helm. (p. 79)

These efforts were infused by an awareness of the difficulty of recruiting teachers who could serve these dual roles, largely because of teachers' perceptions of the tradition-bound and parochial nature of rural America (Foght, 1912; Gray, 1916; Hillyer, 1916; Smart, 1919). Authors argued that rural school districts could not compete with the "physical comforts and the intellectual, spiritual, and social advantages of modern town life" (Hillyer, 1916, p. 31). Some authors described these needs as "puzzling educational problems" (Knight, 1920, p. 182; Shibley, 1917, p. 541), stating that "first-aid remedies" such as new gardens, new playgrounds, better seating arrangements, and better curriculum "would not work because rural schools have inadequate finances, in comparison with the city and town schools" (Shibley, 1917, p. 541). There was a hope that properly trained teachers could connect rural students to the natural charm of the rural environment and (in the hope of promoting a new generation interested in farming) prepare students to transcend the backwardness and parochialism assumed to be a part of their communities through exposure to high culture, assumed to be located in urban places (Smart, 1920).

In defining the parameters of the "rural school problem," these early writers and researchers found that the construction proved useful in building consensus for the need for reform. This utility can be seen throughout the 1920s and into the 1930s in the formation of professorships and academic departments devoted to rural education, the formation of a federal Department of Rural Education, and the brief establishment of the *Journal of Rural Education* (Carney, 1918, 1932; Knight, 1920; McCallister, 1938; Dawson & Hubbard, 1944). As the infrastructure for exploring rural education problems received institutional support, discrete categories in which to understand the particular challenges of rurality emerged: school buildings, community support, teacher training, curriculum for students. The literature of this time is unspecialized and intersectional, providing broad, sweeping overviews of the interconnections among these issues, while also trying to identify the unique contributions of their constituent parts. In the relatively new progressive tradition, consideration of this problem even stretched to debating the teacher's role in supporting the health and well-being of students and in promoting the economic development and education of their communities (Conaway, 1922). Henry Dewey (1910) identified the intersectional challenges of the rural context as a

lack of carefully-trained and experienced teachers, short terms of school, poorly constructed schoolhouses, insufficient equipment, annual or semi-annual change of teachers, enrollment too small for best results, many grades and small classes, limited social opportunities for teachers, inconvenient boarding places, teachers not in touch with life of community, and community not vitally interested in the schools. (p. 542)

The literature talks of rural as monolithic, with attention paid to the similarities of the challenges in bringing qualified teachers to these areas rather than the differentiated challenges, for example, in New England versus Appalachia versus the rural South or the West. This is not to say that the literature was uniform in its opinions, however. As "the rural school problem" became better defined and categorized, distinct lines of difference and debate around teacher recruitment, retention, and training also became more clearly defined.

Defining the Unique Responsibilities of the Rural Teacher

In the first part of the century, the image of the rural school depicted by reformers was largely consistent with what has become an enduring image of the one-room schoolhouse. However, the meaning imbued in this symbol seemed to vary depending on the agenda of the reformer. For some, the one-room schoolhouse, centered around a singular rural teacher, seemed to represent a defensible approach to the schooling of rural children, problematic only to its detractors (Gillette, 1912), while for others, particularly urban-based education reformers, that same schoolhouse seemed to represent the "poorest institution" (Inglis, 1921, p. 516), the antithesis of what was becoming "modern" education and symptomatic of the lag of rural schools behind their urban counterparts, with networks of teachers specializing in educating young people at particular ages overseen by an administrator trained in the new science of bureaucratic efficiency (Foght, 1912; Foote, 1923; Inglis, 1921). As these factions engaged, two key arguments begin to surface in the literature: one about the conditions necessary for proper instruction for rural children and the other about the adequacy of training and institutional support for rural teachers to create those conditions.

In regard to educating young people, scholars identified two main areas of need: one about the physical needs of rural schools (the adequacy of facilities) and the other about the content of the curriculum. Both of these issues, in the context of the one-room schoolhouse, were framed as questions of teacher responsibility and training. The problem with rural teacher recruitment and retention, Shibley (1917) wrote, was that "instructors [in training schools] are not properly trained in the subjects of rural schools and rural life—inseparable parts of each other" (p. 541). This problem was critical, he argued, because the isolation of rural teaching in one-room schoolhouses meant that rural teachers required more initial training and preparation than teachers in cities or towns. There is a tension in the literature of this time on focusing efforts on adequately preparing teachers for the challenges of the one-room schoolhouse versus pushing systematically for the consolidation of these outdated institutions in favor of more modern, consolidated schools with grade-level splits (Kephart, 1919). Underpinning this debate was how best to accomplish standardizing and improving education so that it could equal the education offered by urban communities. In other words, it was important, to use the phrasing of the United States Education Commissioner of the time, to focus on "a square deal for the country child" (Tigert, 1922, p. 354).

Reformers also questioned the relevance of the curriculum to promoting the best outcomes for rural youth living in rural contexts. Before John Dewey's pedagogical creed advocating for the school experience to be as relevant as real life, some rural reformers made similar arguments, stating that the rural school experience should reflect the aims of the community, with agriculture being a decided preoccupation of these arguments. The conflation of rural vocational life with farming is common in the reform literature of this period. The focus on the importance of agriculture reflected the economic positioning of some rural communities, although not all. An interesting feature of the arguments for curriculum relevant to farming was the emphasis that many reformers placed on the ways in which such a curriculum would stem youth outmigration by more deeply connecting youth to the vocational realities of their parents (Dewey, 1910). Reformers considered this notion important in large part because of the role they believed rural communities played in providing the nation with food and raw materials (Cherry, Holdford, & Alexander, 1936). However, at the same time, it was acknowledged that the lure of "modern town life" could not be avoided and that therefore education, with a broad base in music, art, and other aspects of modern culture, should be included in the curriculum so that farm children, on growing up, would not feel deprived (Dunn, 1923; Foght, 1912; Meredith, 1929). Teachers, therefore, needed to be well versed in the ins and outs of what was seen as traditional country life and also able to deliver a strong curriculum in urban high culture. Adequate and differentiated training for rural teachers was seen as the way to support the development of this broad knowledge base (Bunting & McGuffey, 1928; Burnham, 1915; Shibley, 1917).

Although normal schools had been the means for educating teachers, universities were defining education as a discipline and reconsidering their role in educating rural teachers. Over time, many normal schools were renamed universities as their purpose was developed and widened; Knight (1920) and others advocated for separate rural education departments at universities "to train rural school and rural life leaders" (p. 177). Carney (1918) posed the issue of preparing rural teachers as part of the "neglect and backwardness" (p. 147) of rural schooling, citing the fact that more than one-third of rural teachers "had no professional preparation whatever, and thousands are but seventh and eighth-grade graduates, without even a high school training" (p. 149). Carney's thinking mirrors initiatives at Teachers College to respond to the "rural life problem," stating the university commitment to respond to "one of the most vital and urgent issues of our national well-being" and advocating that any university wishing to "meet national demands in the field of education must focus a considerable share of its attention and service in the direction of rural school needs" (p. 149). Fourteen years later, Carney (1932) reflected on these efforts within the context of the Great Depression, noting some limited progress in teacher pay and preparation, for example, but citing a persistent gap between rural teacher qualifications and those of their urban counterparts.

The refrain of the time was the need for "carefully-trained and experienced teachers" in rural schools (Dewey, 1910), with Chase (1917) stating that "no part of our school system is in such need of teachers of training, ability, and experience as the rural schools" (p. 61). Advocacy for teacher training often included a discussion on incentivizing teachers to live and work in rural areas, and academics and school leaders used journal articles as a brainstorming forum of sorts. They (e.g., Gray, 1916) discussed the option of teacher cottages, explaining that housing would support recruitment and retention efforts. Several authors engaged in these conversations about incentives, pointing to the tension between teacher recruitment in rural areas and the draw of "modern" amenities (Fishpaw, 1912; Foght, 1912; Smart, 1920).

This attention culminated, to a certain extent, in the White House Conference on Rural Education, hosted by Eleanor Roosevelt, and inclusive of writers and thinkers about rural education at that time. The end product of the conference was the definition of the Charter of Rights for the Rural Child to Education (Dawson & Hubbard, 1944), which laid out the rights of rural children "to a satisfactory, modern, education" (p. 14), to qualified teachers, and to an education program that prepares them for life after school, vocational or otherwise, among other specified rights. Unbeknownst to the drafters of the charter, the end of the war was coming and with it a shift in the characterization of rural schools and the rural school problem.

The Adolescence of Education Research and the Decline of Attention to Rurality: 1945 to 1980

By the 1950s, one center of the "rural school problem" as it had been defined prior to World War II—the ongoing debate about school consolidation and the antiquity of one-room schoolhouses—had largely been won rhetorically. As more and more one-room schools were closed in favor of consolidated community schools, the administrative modernity described by urban education reformers who had set their sights on solving the rural school problem had, by most measures, prevailed (Stonecipher, 1947). At the same time, education as a scholarly discipline in the United States was itself changing as educationalists embraced postpositivism and began to enjoy unprecedented government support for the problems posed by the field, including a rise in support for evaluation of education policies (Travers, 1958). As a result, perceptions of both the uniqueness of rurality as an educational context and, in particular, the unique preparation needs of the rural teacher became subsumed in a larger discourse of education as an institutional phenomenon, rather than as a community-based, highly contextual one.

The Manpower Crisis and the Rebranding of the Rural Problem

The writing of the late 1940s and early 1950s reflects a slow shift from the debates that characterized the educational conversation prior to World War II. The debates that started to gain traction, however, were less of a departure from those of the previous era than a rebranding or repackaging of them for a new age. Teacher shortages in rural areas in the late 1940s were acute because many teachers had left the profession during the war to enroll in the military or to provide nonmilitary services (Eliassen & Anderson, 1945; Washington, 1947). Referred to as the "manpower crisis" (Eliassen & Anderson, 1945, p. 119) or the "manpower problem" (Patton, 1957, p. 14), this issue was linked to a variety of factors: the low status of teaching as a profession and associated issues such as low salaries; low entry requirements; high turnover (Eliassen & Anderson, 1952; Lester, 1946; Washington, 1947; J. B. White, 1947); population growth, in particular during the baby boom immediately following World War II; and a "dictatorship in school administration" brought about through consolidation (Eliassen & Anderson, 1952). Additionally, the lure of opportunities that had not been as widely available to women prior to the war, such as business and administration, became strong in the postwar era, drawing women who might have become teachers prior to the war (Patton, 1957). The shortage was felt most acutely in elementary schools with rapidly expanding enrollments due to the baby boom, and particularly so in rural schools already struggling to recruit to newly consolidated schools and requiring teacher certification in more than one subject area (Eliassen & Anderson, 1952). However, in a survey of teacher training institutions, Ferrell (1946) found that no institution had specific plans for rural-specific teacher recruitment.

A Decline in Interest in Differentiating Training for Rural Schools

Along with the triumph of administrative centralization represented by consolidation, the relationship between teacher training institutions and rural schools seems to have changed during the postwar period, with normal schools and universities beginning to move away from the rural focus that had characterized some of their work in the first half of the 20th century. Despite the declaration of the White House Charter on Rural Education (Dawson & Hubbard, 1944) that "every rural child has a right to teachers, supervisors, and administrators who know rural life, and who are educated to deal effectively with the problems peculiar to rural schools" (p. 14), a mere 10 years later, Robinson (1954) observed,

> Twenty years ago, 84% of the state teacher preparing institutions made some differentiation in the preparation of rural teachers. Ten years ago, 84% were offering rural sociology. At the moment, concern for rural education is at a low. One reason for this is that deans of schools of education seem to recognize but one difference between rural and urban schools, that of size. To them, reorganization of school districts is rapidly eliminating "the rural school problem." (pp. 30–31)

Ferrell (1946) made similar observations, reporting on findings from a survey of teacher training institutions that showed that "no curriculum distinction is made in the education of teachers for rural and urban schools in the institutions reporting" (p. 360), although some continued to provide opportunities for rural field experiences. Ferrell predicted, rightly, that the period of training for teachers would be lengthened and standardized in the postwar era. In the 1970s, however, renewed attention was paid to the idea that rural schools might require special efforts from the university in order to adequately train, recruit, and retain teachers, and the idea of the field-based professor or the field-based training and in-service center was raised in the scholarly community once again. Bruce, Hubright, and Yarbrough (1976), in their statement of the problem, echoed sentiments raised earlier in the century when they suggested, "Lacking any preparation for rural schools, many teachers from urban academic centers find them unattractive" (p. 452). Shifting demographics and population, they argued, require that greater attention be paid to issues of rural equity. Mancus and Rodriquez (1980) discussed the limited use in rural areas of teacher centers, mostly because of issues of access. "Because rural school problems are not as visible nationally and the number of teachers and children are not as great," they wrote, "the benefits of Teacher Centers have not reached more than a handful of communities" (p. 26).

The reduced interest in differentiating training for rural teachers may have been partially a function of the rise of postpositivism as a dominant lens for considering educational problems within the cohering field of education research in this period and also potentially a function of the growing coherence in institutional practice across the new landscape of consolidated schools (Lagemann, 2000). Lagemann (2000) argues that a preoccupation of university-based education researchers in the midcentury was raising the status of education as a discipline. In keeping with the spirit of the time in high-status social science research fields, such as sociology and economics, this was accomplished through an increased affinity for behaviorism and the insistence on the use of quantitative research methods with an eye toward creating knowledge that could be generalized to public schools across the country. Such behavior would explain the relative disappearance of explicit interest in and writing on rural education research within the field more broadly and on rural teacher training, recruitment, and retention specifically.

The Rise in Prominence of New Lenses for Examining Equity

These issues are reflected in the construction of scholarly problems around rural teacher recruitment, retention, and training through the use of new lenses for thinking about equity that had been overlooked or ignored in the previous decades. In the postwar period of the 1940s and 1950s, for example, new attention was paid to the intersection of rural inequity with regard to teacher quality and the inequity in teacher quality perpetuated by segregation (J. B. White, 1947). Although there had been explorations of these themes in previous decades, most notably in the *Journal of Negro Education*, the intersectionality of these issues had not been prominently foregrounded, and few comparisons of segregated schools had been made at all (see Brewton, 1943; Carney, 1932; Lee, 1944; McCallister, 1938).

In the 1970s, despite the paucity of literature discussing rural teachers, a few articles focused on the intersection between the special needs of certain marginalized populations and the challenges of meeting those needs in the rural context. Barnhardt (1974), for example, wrote about the challenges of implementing a teacher training program centered on teaching Alaskan Native students, looking carefully at the challenges associated with the remoteness of many Alaskan Native communities, as well as the unique historical and cultural concerns that might be important for teachers in these communities to better understand.

Exploring the Meaning of Rural Education Within a Globalizing World Economy: 1980 to 2015

In the late 20th century, the increased globalization of the U.S. economy, including the growth and domination of transnational supply chains in agricultural and other traditionally rural American industries, profoundly reorganized life not only in rural communities but in all communities (Bonnano, 2014; Heffernan, Hendrickson, & Gronski, 1999). The increasing emphasis on neoliberal economic policy, largely policies emphasizing free market decision making driven by bigger and bigger data, as well as the de-emphasis of the importance of antitrust regulations, resulted in the integration and internationalization of previously diverse and geographically bounded supply chains for food and natural resources (Constance, Hendrickson, Howard, & Heffernan, 2014). Although these trends were experienced everywhere in the United States, rural communities without the diversified local economies characteristic of many urban areas were particularly affected as the number of employers contracted and the relative negotiating power of the few companies left increased (Constance et al., 2014; Heffernan et al., 1999; Lobao & Stofferahn, 2007). More and more rural communities found themselves with reduced political power and beholden to the shifting sands of international company interests, leading to rising poverty (Sherman, 2014), community outmigration (particularly of youth seeking work; Corbett, 2007; Provasnik et al., 2007), and dependence on the cycles of boom-bust economies tied to global commodity prices (Schafft & Biddle, 2015).

With this shift in the national economic focus, the aims of school reform also shifted. Following the release of *A Nation at Risk* in 1983, there was an increased emphasis on the mobility of human capital and the preparation of young people for a geographically diffuse, ever-changing skills-based economy (Corbett, 2007; Eppley, 2015; Schafft, 2010; Schafft & Biddle, 2013). This emphasis intensified with the renewal of the Elementary and Secondary Education Act (No Child Left Behind) in 2001, with its emphasis on performance-based accountability, and the addition of college and career readiness under the Obama administration (Au, 2007). During this period, there was a resurgence in interest in rural education research and attention to differentiated rural teacher preparation, recruitment, and retention tinged with a tone of advocacy. For scholars interested in rural education, the policy and practice of education resulting from the confluence of decreased attention to rural communities and the political effects of the shift in educational purpose at the national level became, itself, the rural school problem. Corbett (2007) and Schafft (2010) suggest that, between the rapid globalization of the world economy and the resulting neoliberal shift of American educational policy, the resilience of rural communities, the necessity of their very existence, has never been tested in quite the way that it is being today.

The Crystallization of a Rural Education Research Community

In the early 1980s, the scholarly outlook toward prospects for rural communities was one of optimism, due largely to a demographic trend in migration patterns in the early 1970s in which rural population growth rates (4.2%) exceeded urban growth rates (2.9%) for the first time in the 20th century (Oelschlager & Guenther, 1983). Predictions in the literature of this time suggested that this switch would continue in the coming decades, and paved the way for strident insistence that rural education was an area that should hold wider scholarly and political interest (S. Massey & Crosby, 1983).

Around this time, a number of journals focusing exclusively on rural education were founded, including the *Journal of Research in Rural Education, The Rural Educator*, and the *Rural Special Education Quarterly.* Since their founding, these journals have published much of the American research using rurality as a salient analytical lens. From 1990 to 2015, only 15 out of the 55 articles found in search engines for our case study were published outside of these three journals. Furthermore, in a search of American Educational Research Association journals for this time period, only 9 articles contain "rural" in the title, and only 23 contain "rural" as part of their abstracts (as compared to 59 articles with "urban" in the title and 156 with "urban" in the abstract).

Increased Emphasis on Fiscal and Performance-Based Accountability

The demographic flip that informed interest in rural communities in the early 1980s had, by the end of the decade, been exposed as the demographic anomaly that it was. However, continuing into the 1990s and early 2000s, the problems articulated in many of the previous decades regarding rural teacher training, recruitment, and retention continued to attract scholarly attention: low salaries (Finson & Beaver, 1990; Jacobson, 1990; L. C. Miller, 2012), a lack of strong school leadership (Goodpaster, Adedokun, & Weaver, 2012; Haar, 2007), a lack of privacy (Maranto & Shuls, 2012), and the wide range of responsibilities required of a rural teacher outside of instruction (Berry & Gravelle, 2013; Finson & Beaver, 1990; LaChance, Benton, & Klein, 2007), as well as the need to serve as both a subject generalist and a specialist simultaneously. New factors affecting recruitment and retention were also identified, such as competition between new and veteran teachers (Huysman, 2008) and the rise of the use of distance learning technologies and school-university partnerships to combat teachers' feelings of professional isolation (Cegelka & Alvarado, 2000; Fry & Bryant, 2006; Gal, 1993; Love, Emerson, Shaw, & Leigh, 1996; Murry & Herrera, 1998). However, the meaning of the contribution of these factors to the "rural school problem" seemed to change within the context of a renewed emphasis on fiscal factors and, in the late 1990s and early 2000s, performance-based accountability. As standardizing expectations around student performance became a cornerstone measure by which to judge teacher effectiveness, rural education researchers increasingly perceived their role as making visible the differences between rural contexts for schooling and the urban and suburban contexts for which policymakers seemed to be crafting education policy (Sher, 1978). In the case of teacher recruitment, retention, and training, this took the form of a reinvigorated call for differentiated training for rural contexts. In 1983, S. Massey and Crosby wrote,

Why are programs to train teachers for service in rural schools so scarce? Part of the answer lies in the fact that rural communities are politically invisible and impotent. Rural residents are far more likely to suffer in silence than to demand attention from agencies and institutions ostensibly designed to serve them. (p. 266)

The specter of school consolidation in search of economic efficiencies and economies of scale played an important role in the literature of this period. This threat to the very existence of rural schools haunts discussions of rural school problems, as declining enrollments symptomatic of larger economic issues tied to population migration and globalization clearly affected the daily life of rural schools (Eppley, 2015; Schafft, 2010). Fears of closure and the attendant economic troubles for both schools and communities are suggested to affect teacher beliefs and satisfaction with their work (Edington, 1976; Eppley, 2015; Maranto & Shuls, 2012). Furthermore, dissatisfaction with value-added measures and evaluative systems, increasingly popular in the early 21st century, only invigorated advocacy for increased attention to the role of context in mediating student achievement (Goetz, 2005; Newton, Darling-Hammond, Haertel, & Thomas, 2010).

A (Re)new(ed) Emphasis on the Importance of Place as a Concept in Teacher Training

Despite the articulation of the unique educational needs of rural contexts, teacher training programs of this period, following the trends of the 1960s and 1970s, rarely dealt with rural topics (Campbell, 1986; Fickel, 2005). Much of the research looking specifically at the relationship between university training and preparation for rural schools advocates for the inclusion of some rural-specific component of the curriculum, though one study did find little difference in satisfaction with their training program between teachers with rural and urban placements (Horn, Davis, & Hilt, 1985). Rural science teachers, in particular, were argued to be particularly poorly served by this inattention to rural circumstance, as training for science in most training programs is so highly specialized to the discipline (Finson & Beaver, 1990).

With regard to teacher training, the concept of sensitivity to place was a way for scholars to advocate for training programs with both social and spatial sensitivity across the rural-urban continuum. Rural education researchers, as part of a coalescing group, continued to explore the meaning of rural field experiences for preservice teachers in changing their perceptions of rural places. A new practice—introduced into the scholarly conversation at this time—of naming cultural deficit models in research exposed the century-long trend of looking only at problems of rural communities, rather than at the opportunities. Particularly in the early 2000s, authors began to acknowledge a trend of portraying rural as the absence of urban amenities, of population, and of assets or culture. At the same time, a rising sensitivity to the concept of "a sense of place" or "place attachment" provided a way forward for those wishing to move away from deficit perspectives and also looking for a conceptual counter to the global rhetoric of both educational purpose and curriculum (Azano, 2011; Azano & Stewart, 2015; Eppley, 2009; C. Howley & Howley, 2014). Place-based pedagogies, for example, provide a lens through which the uniqueness of a learning context—rural or otherwise—can be examined and leveraged to increase curricular relevance (Azano & Stewart, 2015, 2016).

CONCLUSION: "RURAL SCHOOL PROBLEMS" IN THE SECOND CENTURY OF EDUCATION RESEARCH

Rural teacher recruitment, retention, and training—the case study that has been the topic of this review—shed light on several evolving relationships over the course of the past century: education researchers' changing perceptions of rural contexts; the manifestations of these changes as they relate to preparing, recruiting, and retaining the teacher labor force in these areas; and by extension, the changing nature of rurality itself during these periods. The patterns of interaction and constructed meaning that we have traced in these evolving relationships hold lessons for contemporary education researchers and directions for future scholarly work.

At the most basic level, the fluctuating prominence of rural education as a problem of the broader field, as exemplified in this case, demonstrates the changing attitude of education reformers and researchers to rurality over time and the different meanings ascribed to "rural problems" in different eras. When rural was painted as the antithesis to modernity, as the opposite of industrial progress, there was a movement among educationalists to create parity and equity between rural schools and town and city schools, which were equated with modernity. This was done, in part, because of a concern for the sustainability of rural areas—if education in these places could be considered equal to that in cities, then the out-migration that plagued rural communities could perhaps be reversed. The literature on rural reform from the first half of the 20th century is peppered with phrases that put the teacher at the center of this endeavor and emphasize preparing teachers for these premodern contexts and positioning them as the makers of a new, modern generation of rural citizens. However, the modernity conceived of by these reformers seems largely to have been a linear one that benchmarked progress by the number of consolidated schools, the proliferation of rural school supervisors, and the elimination of the one-room schoolhouse—not necessarily by real progress made in the efforts to prepare teachers.

After World War II, the achievement of many of the goals of this early period of rural reform, coupled with the status-seeking behavior of educational scientists, seems to have succeeded in eliminating the conversation on rural education as a unique educational context altogether. In the 1960s and 1970s, the little rural education reform conversation that persisted grappled with issues that brought into question the march toward modernity—for example, the suitability of modern rural schooling for Native populations (Barnhardt, 1974) or the necessity of buying into the new, liquid modernity introduced by neoliberal economic reform (Bauman, 2001; Corbett, 2007). After 1980, the increasing liquidity of a new globalized way of life brought into question the relevance of place as an analytic concept for thinking about education altogether, with ardent defenses of the importance of attention to rural education mounted by a newly crystallized rural scholarly community. However, this conversation has largely been contained to several subfield journals, while within the broader field of education research, rurality in this becomes one of many lenses through which to evaluate schooling, including increased attention paid to race, class, gender, ability, and many other previously marginalized perspectives.

Throughout the past century, concerns about equity around schooling in rural areas have been central to education researchers interested in rural contexts, although the nature of trenchant inequity has been deeply tied to the meanings ascribed to rurality and the definition of its problems. Moreover, the ways in which these "rural school problems" have been situated in the larger field of education research have perhaps become emblematic of rurality in general. Using symbolic interactionism (Blumer, 1969) as a lens, we wonder if readers' meaning-making has interpreted educational challenges in rural contexts as unsolvable rural problems. The language used to describe these rural challenges—for example, "teacher training, recruitment, and retention"—creates a discourse that might unintentionally position rural as the "cause" of the problem itself. If one replaces these unsolvable problems or symbols with new language, then meaning-making—or solutions—might follow. Rather than discourse around teacher training, then, researchers could use language around equity. Does place-based school funding continue to marginalize low-income communities? Do teachers in a given state receive equitable pay? If researchers become entrenched in thinking that it is not desirable for a teacher to live and work in a rural community, then they position rurality in deficient or undesirable ways. If, instead, researchers discuss pay equality for teachers, they can reposition rural education challenges by understanding how policy inequitably privileges place.

There is some evidence, perhaps, of history repeating itself in the current push for explicit attention to urban contexts and their unique needs in the current field. At one time, entire departments of rural education were maintained specifically to understand the unique rural social context and how to best enact formal educational structures within it. Educators and researchers believed, sincerely, that unique preparation was needed for these social contexts in order for teachers to successfully fulfill the promise of modern education for these communities. This belief is clearly no longer in evidence—despite documentation of the enduring problems of teacher recruitment, retention, and training in rural places, for example, little differentiated preparation is now believed necessary for these rural contexts at all.

In recent years, much research attention has been paid to the belief that preparation programs that uniquely address issues of the cultural and linguistic diversity of urban communities, racial difference between teachers and students, and the unique opportunities and challenges of urban educational environments will adequately allow schools to enact modern educational practices in urban settings. Again, the language itself becomes symbolic of our values in education. If researchers diminish the need for specialized training for rural teaching at the same time they increase the attention paid to specialized training in urban contexts, then they place a certain value on those different contexts. By understanding how this discourse symbolically positions place, researchers can better understand how education programs may in fact institutionally devalue the need for teachers trained to work in rural communities. We assert that a critical perspective is needed in training teachers for all contexts.

Our observations on the implications of this trend extend to a caution and a recommendation. First, the caution: Rurality, as a concept, has changed in meaning for reformers as the social and economic context itself has changed. The conflation of rurality and antimodernity in the early part of the century that once the problem of rural education's modern delivery was solved, attention to other persistent issues (e.g., teacher recruitment, retention, and training) also seemed to wane. The diverse needs of urban communities are similarly complex, and as social and economic systems continue to evolve in this 21st century, we caution education researchers interested in urban contexts to continue to document these complexities and not allow for the collapse of this term into any single dimension pegged to a singular conception of progress.

Second, we recommend that, as a field, we reevaluate education's relationship to marginalized places and spaces in a holistic and inclusive way. Within the current globalized context, it can be difficult to perceive the relevance of studying places or allowing geographic realities to foreground our understanding of the world. It is the fate of the postmodern individual to live both locally and globally, shaped both by "the constraints of the body . . . contextually situated in space and time" and "the intrusion of distance into local activities" (Giddens, 1991, p. 680). The lived realities of students, teachers, administrators, and community members happen within the context of a school, situated in a place, and in the current American system of public schooling, much of the local economic and social realities of that place determine the opportunities and constraints of local schooling.

However, in combating the perceived erasure of these contextual differences within education research concerned with "best practices" and "generalizability," there has been little unified effort among urban and rural education researchers to understand the similarities and differences of contextual opportunities and constraints in ways that embrace localized complexities but do not, ultimately, reify them. As marginalized places vie for power in our political system, there is a sense in the contemporary literature on rural education that attention to the urban context comes at the expense of attention to rural, and perhaps vice versa.

As the 21st century brings new social and economic changes for rural communities, it will be important for researchers to continue to critically evaluate these changes, to resist the collapse of rurality into one ascribed meaning, and to do so with broader attention to the similarities and differences of social and economic factors in other contexts and communities. To do this, the conversation about the political marginalization of place in a global context must be expanded. Advocacy for the importance of rural within education is not enough—researchers must find the intersection of rural realities with diverse sociospatial realities in the context of 21st-century globalization. It is in this intersection that researchers can move beyond defining and redefining "the rural school problem" and move to a place of promise that rural communities may offer in new or alternative ways forward in a context of global capitalism.

ACKNOWLEDGMENTS

The authors would like to thank Amber Gray, social science and humanities librarian at the University of Maine, for her assistance with this chapter.

NOTES

[1]We reviewed 485 *Journal of Research in Rural Education* article titles and abstracts from the founding of the journal in 1982 to June 2015. We reviewed 129 *Rural Educator* articles published between 2004 and 2013.

[2]Peer review was not a criterion in searches conducted for years prior to 1970 for two reasons. First, standards of peer review prior to this time period appear to be uneven and therefore would have excluded the majority, if not all, source material for these years. Second, academic search engine capabilities make the addition of peer review as a criterion difficult to apply. Searches both with and without peer review after 1970 were conducted to ensure that source material was not unsystematically excluded through the addition of this constraint.

REFERENCES

References marked with an asterisk indicate studies included in the review.

*Adams, B. L., & Woods, A. (2015). A model for recruiting and retaining teachers in Alaska's rural K–12 schools. *Peabody Journal of Education, 90*, 250–262.

*Aley, R. (1910). Rural school teachers in Indiana. *Journal of Education, 72*, 630–631.

*Allen, C. H. (1943). In-service education of teachers. *Review of Educational Research, 13*(3), 262–270.

*Anderson, E. W., & Eliassen, R. H. (1949). Supply and demand in teaching. *Review of Educational Research, 19*(3), 179–184.

*Anglin, J. M., & Piland, D. E. (1995). Reflections of a rural school student teacher. *The Rural Educator, 17*, 27–31.

*Askins, B., & Schwisow, J. A. (1988). A university-school partnership for providing in-service staff development to a rural school: The Greenwood experience. *Journal of Staff Development, 9*(4), 40–44.

Au, W. (2007). High-stakes testing and curricular control: A qualitative metasynthesis. *Educational Researcher, 36*, 258–267.

*Ayer, A. M. (1921). What rural teachers think of group teachers' meetings. *Journal of Rural Education, 1*, 20–23.

Azano, A. (2011). The possibility of place: One teacher's use of place-based instruction for English students in a rural high school. *Journal of Research in Rural Education, 26*(10), 1–12.

Azano, A. P., & Stewart, T. T. (2015). Exploring place and practicing justice: Preparing preservice teachers for success in rural schools. *Journal of Research in Rural Education, 30*(9), 1–12.

Azano, A. P., & Stewart, T. T. (2016). Confronting challenges at the intersection of rurality, place, and teacher preparation: Improving efforts in teacher education to staff rural schools with qualified teachers. *Global Education Review, 3*, 108–128.

Bailey, C., Jensen, L., & Ransom, E. (2014). *Rural America in a globalizing world: Problems and prospects for the 2010s.* Morgantown: West Virginia University Press.

*Barber, L. L. (1942). Beginning teachers in one-room schools: A problem in teacher-education. *Elementary English Review, 19*, 29–35.

*Barley, Z. A., & Beesley, A. D. (2007). Rural school success: What can we learn? *Journal of Research in Rural Education, 22*(1), 1–15.

*Barnhardt, R. (1974). Being a native and becoming a teacher. *Council on Anthropology and Education Quarterly, 5*(4), 13–19.

*Barrett, N., Cowen, J., Toma, E., & Troske, S. (2015). Working with what they have: Professional development as a reform strategy in rural schools. *Journal of Research in Rural Education, 30*(10), 1–18.

*Baughman, D. (1957). Will they be strangers in their own communities? *Educational Administration & Supervision, 43*, 182–192.

Bauman, Z. (2001). *Liquid modernity.* Cambridge, England: Polity.

*Beilin, H. (1956). Effect of changes in rural life upon teachers' attitudes toward the school program. *School Review, 64*, 181–186.

*Berry, A. B., & Gravelle, M. (2013). The benefits and challenges of special education positions in rural settings: Listening to the teachers. *The Rural Educator, 34*(2), 1–13.

*Beswick, K., & Jones, T. (2011). Taking professional learning to isolated schools: Perceptions of providers and principals, and lessons for effective learning. *Journal of Math Education Research, 23*, 83–105.

Blumer, H. (1969). *Symbolic interactionism: Perspective and method.* Berkeley: University of California Press.

Bonnano, A. (2014). Agriculture and food in the 2010s. In C. Bailey, L. Jensen, & E. Ransom (Eds.), *Rural America in a globalizing world: Problems and prospects for the 2010s* (pp. 3–15). Morgantown: West Virginia University Press.

*Borg, W. R. (1965). *Perceptions of the teacher's role in the small rural school.* Denver, CO: Western State Small Schools Project.

*Boschee, M. A. (1996). Perceived effects of training and compensation on rural and urban school based teacher educators. *The Rural Educator, 18*(1), 13–19.

Bowers, W. L. (1971). Country-life reform, 1900–1920: A neglected aspect of Progressive Era history. *Agricultural History, 45*, 211–221.

*Brewton, J. (1943). Teaching and learning in small, rural schools. *Peabody Journal of Education, 20*, 322–329.

*Brooks, T. D. (1926). Progressive trends in rural education: A. D. Mueller. *Elementary School Journal, 27*, 155–156.

*Brouillette, J. W., & Barrow, C. L. (1943). Some persistent problems of rural life and education in the South. *Peabody Journal of Education, 20,* 266–271.

*Bruce, W. C., Hubright, R. L., & Yarbrough, V. E. (1976). Decentralizing graduate education: A case for the field-based professor. *Phi Delta Kappan, 57*(7), 452–453.

*Bunting, R. L., & McGuffey, V. (1928). Preparation of rural teachers. *Teachers College Record, 29,* 716–727.

*Burkes, J. (1916). Rural supervision in Tennessee. *Journal of Education, 83,* 395–397.

*Burnham, E. (1915). A decade of progress in training rural teachers. *Elementary School Journal, 16,* 181–189.

*Burnham, E. (1920). What the Western State Normal School is doing in training rural teachers. *Journal of Rural Education, 2,* 298–304.

Bustamante, R., Brown, G., & Irby, B. (2010). Advocating for English language learners: U.S. teacher leadership in rural Texas schools. In K. Schafft, & A. Youngblood (Eds.), *Rural education for the 21st century: Identity, place and community in a globalizing world* (pp. 232–252). University Park: Pennsylvania State University Press.

*Campbell, M. K. (1986). Preparing rural elementary teachers. *Research in Rural Education, 3,* 107–110.

*Carney, M. (1918). The service of Teachers College to rural education. *Teachers College Record, 19,* 147–155.

*Carney, M. (1932). The pre-service preparation of rural teachers. *Teachers College Record, 34,* 110–118.

Carr, P., & Kefalas, M. (2009). *Hollowing out the middle: The rural brain drain and what it means for rural America.* Boston, MA: Beacon Press.

*Cegelka, P. A., & Alvarado, J. (2000). A best practices model for preparation of rural special education teachers. *Rural Special Education Quarterly, 19*(3–4), 15–29.

*Chase, W. O. (1917). Some suggestions for rural school improvement. *Journal of Education, 86*(3), 61–62.

*Cherry, A. M., Holdford, A. V., & Alexander, C. (1936). Guide to the literature on rural education. *Elementary School Journal, 36,* 748–759.

*Collins, E. A. (1940). Survey of in-service training. *Phi Delta Kappan, 23*(4), 126–127.

*Conaway, E. (1922). Better rural teachers. *Journal of Education, 95,* 488–489.

Constance, D. H., Hendrickson, M., Howard, P., & Heffernan, W. (2014). Economic concentration in the agrifood system: Impacts on rural communities and emerging responses. In C. Bailey, L. Jensen, & E. Ransom (Eds.), *Rural America in a globalizing world: Problems and prospects for the 2010s* (pp. 16–35). Morgantown: West Virginia University Press.

Corbett, M. (2007). *Learning to leave: The irony of schooling in a coastal community.* Halifax, Nova Scotia, Canada: Fernwood.

*Crabbe, A. L. (1924). A study in teacher transiency. *Peabody Journal of Education, 1,* 295–300.

*Crabbe, J. G. (1913). The normal school. *Journal of Education, 78,* 230–231.

Creswell, J. (2014). *Educational research: Planning, conducting and evaluating quantitative and qualitative research* (5th ed.). New York, NY: Pearson.

Cubberley, E. (1912). *Rural life and education.* Cambridge, MA: Riverside.

*Darlington, M. W. (1937). New venture in the rural school. *Phi Delta Kappan, 19*(8), 239–242.

*Davidson, I. (1921). Rural school supervision as an agency for improving rural schools. *Journal of Rural Education, 1,* 3–9.

Dawson, H. A., & Hubbard, F. W. (1944). *Proceedings from The White House Conference on Rural Education.* Washington, DC: National Education Association, Department of Rural Education.

*Dewey, H. B. (1910). Rural school possibilities. *Journal of Education, 72,* 541–542.

DeYoung, A. J. (1987). The status of American rural education research: An integrated review and commentary. *Review of Educational Research, 57*(2), 123–148.

*Dunn, F. (1923). The curriculum of the rural elementary school. *Teachers College Record*, *24*(2), 122–131.

*Dunn, F. (1930). Modern education in small schools. *Teachers College Record*, *32*(5), 411–423.

*Eargle, J. C. (2013). "I'm not a bystander": Developing teacher leadership in a rural school-university collaboration. *The Rural Educator*, *35*(1), 23–34.

Edington, E. (1976). *Strengthening the small rural school*. Austin, TX: Educational Laboratory.

*Edwards, N. (1939). Problems of rural education in the United States. *Elementary School Journal*, *40*, 106–112.

*Eggert, C. L. (1937). Modern trends in rural education. *Phi Delta Kappan*, *19*(8), 254–256.

*Eliassen, R. H., & Anderson, E. W. (1945). Teacher supply and demand: Investigations reported in 1944. *Educational Research Bulletin*, *24*(5), 119–126.

*Eliassen, R. H., & Anderson, E. W. (1952). Investigations in teacher supply and demand reported in 1951. *Educational Research Bulletin*, *31*(3), 67–74.

*Elsea, A. F. (1940). Modern rural school. *Phi Delta Kappan*, *23*(4), 124–125.

Eppley, K. (2009). Rural schools and the highly qualified teacher provision of No Child Left Behind: A critical policy analysis. *Journal of Research in Rural Education*, *24*(4), 1–11.

*Eppley, K. (2015). "Hey, I saw your grandparents at Walmart": Teacher education for rural schools and communities. *The Teacher Educator*, *50*(1), 67–86.

*Favrot, L. M. (1936). How the small rural school can more adequately serve its community. *Journal of Negro Education*, *5*, 430–438.

*Ferrell, D. T. (1946). Current practice in the education of teachers for rural children. *Peabody Journal of Education*, *23*, 360–363.

*Fickel, L. H. (2005). Teachers, tundra, and talking circles: Learning history and culture in an Alaska Native village. *Theory and Research in Social Education*, *33*, 476–507.

*Finson, K. D., & Beaver, J. B. (1990). Rural science teacher preparation: A re-examination of an important component of the educational system. *Journal of Science Teacher Education*, *1*(3), 46–48.

*Fishpaw, C. (1912). The training of rural teachers. *The Province of Education*, *33*, 79–83.

*Flynn, H. E. (1925). Teacher training in connection with high schools. *Journal of Education*, *101*, 331–332.

*Foght, H. (1912). The country school. *Annals of the American Academy of Political and Social Science*, *40*, 149–157.

*Foote, J. M. (1923). A comparative study of instruction in consolidated and one-teacher schools. *Journal of Rural Education*, *2*(8), 337–351.

*Fox, R. S. (Ed.). (1956). *Teaching in the small community* (National Education Association yearbook). Washington, DC: National Education Association, Department of Rural Education.

*Fry, S. W., & Bryant, C. (2006). Using distance technology to sustain teacher education for student teachers in isolated areas: The technology-supported induction network. *Journal of Computing and Teacher Education*, *23*(2), 63–69.

*Fulkerson, M. L. (1917). The Oregon normal school rural week. *Journal of Education*, *85*, 511–513.

*Gal, S. (1993). Teachers and teaching. *Journal of Rural Education Research*, *9*(1), 38–42.

Giddens, A. (1991). *Modernity and self-identity: Self and society in the late modern age*. Boston, MA: Pearson.

*Gillette, J. M. (1912). Conditions and needs of country life. *Annals of the American Academy of Political Science*, *40*, 3–11.

Glasgow, N., & Berry, E. H. (2013). *Rural aging in 21st century America*. Dordrecht, Netherlands: Springer.

Goetz, S. J. (2005). Random variation in student performance by class size: Implications for NCLB in rural Pennsylvania. *Journal of Research in Rural Education*, *20*(13), 1–8.

*Goodpaster, K. S., Adedokun, O. A., & Weaver, G. C. (2012). Teachers' perceptions of rural STEM Teaching: Implications for rural teacher retention. *The Rural Educator, 33*(3), 9–23.

*Graves, F. (1931). Teacher training. *Journal of Education, 113*, 53–54.

*Gray, A. A. (1916). The teacher's home. *Elementary School Journal, 17*, 201–208.

*Green, C. R., & Weiner, C. A. (1997). Arkansas evolution: The ruralization of Goodlad's professional development school. *The Rural Educator, 19*(2), 11–14.

*Haar, J. (2007). Retaining experienced, qualified teachers: The principal's role. *The Rural Educator, 28*(2), 28–34.

*Hammer, P. C., Hughes, G., McClure, C., Reeves, C., & Salgado, D. (2005). *Rural teacher recruitment and retention practices: A review of the research literature, National Survey of Rural Superintendents, and case studies of programs in Virginia*. Charleston, WV: Appalachia Educational Laboratory at Edvantia.

*Harmon, H., Gordanier, J., Henry, L., & George, A. (2007). Changing teaching practices in rural schools. *The Rural Educator, 28*(2), 8–12.

Heffernan, W., Hendrickson, M., & Gronski, R. (1999). *Consolidation in the food and agriculture system*. Washington, DC: National Farmers Union. http://www.foodcircles.missouri.edu/whstudy.pdf

*Heyl, H. (1940). Guidance of rural teachers. *Teachers College Record, 41*(4), 334–338.

*Hillkirk, K., Chang, B., Oettinger, L. A., Saban, A., & Villet, C. (1998). Supporting ongoing professional learning in rural schools. *The Rural Educator, 19(3)*, 20–24.

*Hillyer, T. A. (1916). The preparation of rural school teachers by state normal schools. *Journal of Education, 84*, 31–33.

Hoffman, J. V., Wilson, M. B., Martinez, R. A., & Sailors, M. (2011). Content analysis: The past, present, and future. In N. Duke, & M. Mallette (Eds.), *Literacy research methodologies* (2nd ed., pp. 28–49). New York, NY: Guilford Press.

*Holloway, D. (2002). Using research to ensure quality teaching in rural schools. *Journal of Research in Rural Education, 17*(3), 138–153.

*Horn, J. G., Davis, P., & Hilt, R. (1985). Importance of areas of preparation for teaching in rural /small schools. *Research in Rural Education, 3*(1), 23–29.

*Howley, A., & Howley, C. B. (2005). High-quality teaching: Providing for rural teachers' professional development. *Journal of Research in Rural Education, 26*(2), 1–5.

Howley, C., & Howley, A. (2014). Making sense of rural education research: Art, transgression, and other acts of terroir. In S. White, & M. Corbett (Eds.), *Doing educational research in rural settings: Methodological issues, international perspectives, and practical solutions* (pp. 7–25). New York, NY: Routledge.

*Huftalen, M. (1911). How the teacher can secure the confidence and co-operation of director and district. *Journal of Education, 73*, 510–511.

*Hunt-Barron, S., Tracy, K. N., Howell, E., & Kaminski, R. (2015). Obstacles to enhancing professional development with digital tools in rural landscapes. *Journal of Research in Rural Education, 30*(2), 1–14.

*Huysman, J. T. (2008). Rural teacher satisfaction: An analysis of beliefs and attitudes of rural teacher's job satisfaction. *Journal of Research in Rural Education, 29*(2), 31–38.

*Inglis, A. (1921). The one-teacher school. *Journal of Education, 94*, 516.

*Jacobson, S. L. (1990). Change in entry level salary and the recruitment of novice teachers. *Journal of Education Finance, 15*, 408–413.

*Jaggers, R. E. (1939). A desirable rural secondary school program. *Peabody Journal of Education, 16*, 404–409.

*Jones, R. (1944). The White House conference on rural education: A summary report. *High School Journal, 27*(5), 173–181.

*Kephart, A. P. (1919). Better teaching in rural schools. *High School Journal, 2*(5), 144–145.

*Kibbe, D. (1928). An analysis of the activities of rural-school supervisors. *Elementary School Journal, 28,* 346–352.

*King, C. (1988). Some basic understandings about rural education and staff development. *Journal of Staff Development, 9*(4), 8–11.

*Kleinfeld, J., Mcdiarmid, G. W., Grubis, S., & Parrett, W. (1983). Doing research on effective cross-cultural teaching: The teacher tale. *Peabody Journal of Education, 61*(1), 86–108.

*Knapczyk, D., Chapman, C., Rodes, P., & Chung, H. (2001). Teacher preparation in rural communities through distance education. *Teacher Education and Special Education, 24,* 402–407.

*Knight, E. W. (1920). The state university and rural schools. *High School Journal, 3*(6), 177–183.

Kuhn, T. (1962). *The structure of scientific revolutions.* Chicago, IL: University of Chicago Press.

*LaChance, A., Benton, C. J., & Klein, B. (2007). The school-based activity model: A promising alternative to professional development schools. *Teacher Education Quarterly, 34*(3), 95–111.

Lagemann, E. C. (2000). *An elusive science: The troubling history of education research.* Chicago, IL: University of Chicago Press.

*Lee, M. A. (1944). Improving the reading of the Negro rural teacher in the South. *Journal of Negro Education, 13*(1), 47–56.

*Lester, H. (1946). Social status of the teacher. *Review of Educational Research, 16*(3), 291–297.

*Lillehoj, C. J., Spoth, R., & Trudeau, L. (2002). Rural teacher training. *The Rural Educator, 24*(1), 3–12.

Lobao, L., & Stofferahn, C. W. (2007). The community effects of industrialized farming: Social science research and challenges to corporate farming laws. *Agriculture and Human Values, 25,* 219–240.

*Love, F., Emerson, P., Shaw, J., & Leigh, C. (1996). Evolution of professional development schools in a rural setting. *Contemporary Education, 67,* 210–212.

*Ludlow, B. L. (1998). Preparing special education personnel for rural schools: Current practices and future directions. *Journal of Research in Rural Education, 14*(2), 57–75.

*Lyons, T. (2008). More equal than others? Meeting the professional development needs of rural primary and secondary science teachers. *Teaching Science, 54*(3), 27–31.

*Mancus, D., & Rodriquez, R. C. (1980). Rural teacher centers: New roles for teacher educators. *The Rural Educator, 2*(2), 25–29.

*Maranto, R., & Shuls, J. (2012). How do we get them on the farm? Efforts to improve rural teacher recruitment and retention in Arkansas. *The Rural Educator, 34*(1) 32–41.

*Martin, L. E., Shafer, T., & Kragler, S. (2009). Blending together, step by step: Principal uses professional learning to combine two school cultures into one. *Journal of Staff Development, 30*(5), 20–24.

Massey, D. S., & Capoferro, C. (2008). The geographic diversification of American immigration. In D. S. Massey (Ed.), *New faces in new places: The changing geography of American immigration* (pp. 25–50). New York, NY: Russell Sage Foundation.

*Massey, S., & Crosby, J. (1983). Special problems, special opportunities: Preparing teachers for rural schools. *Phi Delta Kappan, 65,* 265–269.

Maxwell, J. A. (2012). *Qualitative research design: An interactive approach* (3rd ed.). Thousand Oaks, CA: Sage.

*McCallister, J. E. (1938). A venture in rural-teacher education among Negroes in Louisiana. *Journal of Negro Education, 7,* 132–143.

McLaughlin, D. K., Shoff, C. M., & Demi, M. A. (2014). Influence of perceptions of current and future community on residential aspirations of rural youth. *Rural Sociology, 79,* 453–477.

*Meredith, A. B. (1929). The preparation of teachers for rural schools. *Elementary School Journal, 29*, 344–350.

*Miller, C. L., & Gregg, H. D. (1932). The teaching staff. *Journal of Negro Education, 1*, 196–223.

*Miller, L. C. (2012). Situating the rural teacher labor market in the broader context: A descriptive analysis of the market dynamics in New York State. *Journal of Research in Rural Education, 27*(13), 1–32.

*Miretzky, D., & Stevens, S. (2012). How does location impact meaning and opportunity? Rural schools and the NCATE Diversity Standard. *Teachers College Record, 114*(5), 1–36.

*Mitchem, K., Wells, D., & Wells, J. (2003). Using evaluation to ensure quality professional development in rural schools. *Journal of Research in Rural Education, 18*(2), 96–103.

*Mollenkopf, D. L. (2009). Creating highly qualified teachers: Maximizing university resources to provide professional development in rural areas. *The Rural Educator, 30*(3), 34–39.

*Monk, D. H. (2007). Recruiting and retaining high-quality teachers in rural areas. *Future of Children, 17*(1), 155–174.

*Munsch, T. R., & Boylan, C. R. (2008). Can a week make a difference? Changing perceptions about teaching and living in rural Alaska. The *Rural Educator, 29*(2), 14–23.

*Murry, K., & Herrera, S. (1998). Crisis in the Heartland: Addressing unexpected challenges in rural education. *Journal of Research in Rural Education, 14*(1), 45–49.

Newton, X. A., Darling-Hammond, L., Haertel, E., & Thomas, E. (2010). Value-added modeling of teacher effectiveness: An exploration of stability across models and contexts. *Education Policy Analysis Archives, 18*(23), 1–27.

*Oelschlager, R., & Guenther, J. (1983). Rural school innovations, preparation, awareness and adoption. *NASSP Bulletin, 67*, 94–99.

*O'Hair, M., & Reitzug, U. C. (2006). Working for social justice in rural schools: A model for science education. *International Electronic Journal for Leadership in Learning, 10*(28), 1–11.

*Patton, J. G. (1957). Manpower problems in rural schools. *Teachers College Record, 59*(1), 14–20.

*Pavia, B. K. (1982). Dipping sheep and Shakespeare, or how an urbanite was kept down on the farm. *English Journal, 71*(2), 22–26.

Petrin, R., Schafft, K. A., & Meece, J. (2014). Educational sorting and residential aspirations among rural high school students: What are the contributions of schools and educators to the rural brain drain? *American Educational Research Journal, 51*(2), 294–326.

*Phelps, C. L. (1917). Training of rural teachers. *Elementary School Journal, 17*, 662–667.

Provasnik, S., Kewal Ramani, A., Coleman, M. M., Gilbertson, L., Herring, W., & Xie, Q. (2007). *Status of education in rural America* (NCES 2007-040). Washington, DC: National Center for Education Statistics.

*Reaves, W., & Larmer, W. G. (1996). The effective schools project: School improvement in rural settings through collaborative professional development. *The Rural Educator, 18*(1), 29–33.

*Reeves, F. W. (1935). Rural educational problems in relation to the new trends in population distribution. *Social Forces, 14*(1), 7–16.

*Rhoads, K. (2011). Despite rough seas, teachers in rural Maine swim together. *Journal of Staff Development, 32*(2), 22–26.

*Robertson-Kraft, C., & Duckworth, A. (2014). True grit: Trait-level perseverance and passion for long-term goals predicts effectiveness and retention among novice teachers. *Teachers College Record, 116*(3), 1–27.

*Robinson, W. M. (1954). Preparing teachers for rural schools. *Phi Delta Kappan, 36*(1), 29–31.

*Rose, C. E. (1917). The education of a rural teacher. *Journal of Education, 86*, 298.

Rosenblatt, L. M. (1978). *The reader, the text, the poem: The transactional theory of the literary work.* Carbondale: Southern Illinois University Press.

Rosenblatt, L. M. (1983). *Literature as exploration* (4th ed.). New York, NY: Modern Language Association. (Original work published 1938)

Rosenblatt, L. M. (2005). "Retrospect" from "Transactions with Literature." *Voices From the Middle, 12*(3), 13–19.

Salaman, S. (2003). *Newcomers to old towns: Suburbanization of the heartland.* Chicago, IL: University of Chicago Press.

*Sand, O. P. (1943). In-service training for rural teachers through professional reading. *Peabody Journal of Education, 20,* 336–343.

Schafft, K. A. (2010). Conclusion: Economics, community, and rural education: Rethinking the nature of accountability in the twenty-first century. In K. A. Schafft, & A. Youngblood Jackson (Eds.), *Rural education for the 21st century: Identity, place and community in a globalizing world* (pp. 275–289). University Park: Pennsylvania State University Press.

Schafft, K. A., & Biddle, C. (2013). Place and purpose in public education: District mission statements and educational (dis)embeddedness. *American Journal of Education, 120*(1), 55–76.

Schafft, K. A., & Biddle, C. (2014). Education and schooling in rural America. In C. Bailey, L. Jensen, & E. Ransom (Eds.), *Rural America in a globalizing world: Problems and prospects for the 2010s* (pp. 556–572). Morgantown: West Virginia University Press.

Schafft, K. A., & Biddle, C. (2015). Opportunity, ambivalence and the purpose of schooling in Pennsylvania's Marcellus Shale region. *Human Organization, 74*(1), 74–85.

*Scribner, J. P. (2003). Teacher learning in context: The special case of rural high school teachers. *Education Policy Analysis Archives, 11*(12), 1–23.

*Sears, J. B. (1917). The normal school and rural education in California. *Education, 37*(7), 410–426.

Sher, J. (1978). *Education in rural America: A reassessment of conventional wisdom.* Boulder, CO: Westview Press.

Sherman, J. (2009). *Those who work and those who don't: Poverty, morality, and family in rural America.* Minneapolis: University of Minnesota Press.

Sherman, J. (2014). Rural poverty: The Great Recession, rising unemployment, and the underutilized safety net. In C. Bailey, L. Jensen, & E. Ransom (Eds.), *Rural America in a globalizing world: Problems and prospects for the 2010s* (pp. 523–542). Morgantown: West Virginia University Press.

*Shibley, A. P. (1917). Improving the rural school: A program of progress. *Journal of Education, 85*(20), 541–542.

*Silver, S. (1987). Compliance with PL94-142 mandates: Implications for rural teacher training programs. *Research in Rural Education, 4*(3), 103–109.

*Smart, T. J. (1919). Training a socialized rural leadership. *American Journal of Sociology, 24*(4), 389–410.

*Smart, T. J. (1920). A program to meet the immediate shortage of rural teachers. *American Journal of Sociology, 25,* 456–468.

*Smith, F. (1921). The place of the city normal school in a state system of teacher training. *Journal of Education, 93,* 229–231.

*Stonecipher, E. E. (1947). A brief history of the one-teacher school. *Peabody Journal of Education, 25,* 130–138.

*Storer, J. H., & Crosswait, D. J. (1995). Delivering staff development to the small rural school. *Rural Special Education Quarterly, 14*(3), 23–30.

Strange, M., Johnson, J., Showalter, D., & Klein, R. (2012). *Why rural matters 2011–12: The condition of rural education in the 50 states.* Washington, DC: Rural School and Community Trust.

*Summerville, J., & Johnson, C. S. (2006). Rural creativity: A study of district-mandated online professional development. *Journal of Technology and Teacher Education, 14,* 347–361.

*Theobald, N. D. (1991). A persistent challenge: Staffing special education programs in rural schools. *Journal of Research in Rural Education*, 7(3), 39–50.

*Tigert, J. J. (1922). The need for educational equality. *Journal of Education*, 95, 354.

*Torrence, A. (1956). A study of the relationship of certain competencies to success in teaching vocational agriculture. *Journal of Experimental Education*, 25, 1–31.

Travers, R. (1958). *An introduction to educational research*. New York, NY: MacMillan.

U.S. Commission on Country Life. (1909, February). *Report of the Country Life Commission and Special Message from the President of the United States* (S. Doc. 705, 60th Congress, 2nd session). Washington, DC: Government Printing Office.

*Vaughn, M., & Saul, M. (2013). Navigating the rural terrain: Educators' visions to promote change. *The Rural Educator*, 34, 1–9.

*Washington, A. H. (1936). The American problem of rural education. *Journal of Negro Education*, 5, 420–429.

*Washington, A. H. (1940). Negro secondary education in rural areas. *Journal of Negro Education*, 9, 513–524.

*Washington, A. H. (1947). Rural education—To the teachers of rural America. *Journal of Negro Education*, 16, 100–104.

*Weiler, K. (2005). Mabel Carney at Teachers College: From home missionary to White ally. *Teachers College Record*, 107, 2599–2633.

*Wells, J. A. (1937). Adequate rural education: The backbone of the nation's progress. *Peabody Journal of Education*, 15, 144–147.

*Weltzin, F. (2015). Dare the teacher breathe? *The American Scholar*, 4, 214–222.

*White, J. B. (1947). A study of the teachers in the small rural schools of South Carolina. *Peabody Journal of Education*, 24, 266–275.

*White, S., & Kline, J. (2012). Developing a rural teacher education curriculum package. *The Rural Educator*, 33(2), 36–43.

*Wigle, S., & Sylvester, T. (1996). The professional knowledge base of rural inservice teachers. *The Rural Educator*, 17(3), 35–40.

*Winship, A. E. (1917). Rural school ideals. *Journal of Education*, 85, 286–287.

*Wofford, K. (1940). Education for teachers in the rural environment. *Teachers College Record*, 41, 323–333.

*Wood, M. B., Jilk, L. M., & Paine, L. W. (2012). Moving beyond sinking or swimming: Reconceptualizing the needs of beginning mathematics teachers. *Teachers College Record*, 114(8), 1–44.

Chapter 10

From Vocational Education to Career Readiness: The Ongoing Work of Linking Education and the Labor Market

SHAUN M. DOUGHERTY
ALLISON R. LOMBARDI
University of Connecticut

A long-standing debate has been waged over the past century or more about the purpose of education. Is the primary purpose to provide for the general edification of the individual, or must education have a pragmatic application that relates to one's intended role in the workforce? Public education's focus on these ends has evolved over time, often in relation to changing economic demands. Using a broad historical lens to examine recent developments, incorporating salient historical debates and social forces, the authors attempt to better understand how the relationship between education and preparation for the workforce has changed over time. They focus on the proliferation of federal innovations in this area over the past 100 years and consider persistent themes in philosophical and policy debates. They supplement this broad history and context with the results of a more focused survey of the literature in career and technical education, with search terms that yielded scholarship from the past 50 years. Drawing themes from this more recent literature, and in light of historical foci, the authors make recommendations for future directions of scholarship.

This year, which is the centennial of the American Educational Research Association, also marks a century since the first publication of John Dewey's (1916) *Democracy and Education*. Among other influences, this book is one of the first formal statements of the potential benefits of what is now known as career and technical education (CTE) made by American philosophers of education. The current focus on college and career readiness (CCR) in education policy emphasizes utilitarian

Review of Research in Education
March 2016, Vol. 40, pp. 326–355
DOI: 10.3102/0091732X16678602
© 2016 AERA. http://rre.aera.net

elements of education and the need for learning to relate to the world of work. This acknowledgement of the need for both general and specific forms of educational training evolved from a fundamental point of conflict about the purpose of education. Was education to provide for the general edification of the individual (Dewey, 1916)? Or must it have a pragmatic application that relates to the individual's role in the workforce (Lazerson & Grubb, 1974)? These two perspectives have, in some ways, offered a false dichotomy as to the purpose of education, though, as other scholars have pointed out, understanding the purpose of education and its impacts on social stratification and social dynamics is as important as the purported ends of public education (Bowles & Gintis, 1976; Dorn, 1996; Labaree, 1997; Loveless, 1999).

The role of public education in supporting the various articulated ends has evolved over time, often in relation to changing economic demands. Recently, economists have identified changes in the economy and labor market that demand modifications in how we educate, while still highlighting the persistent needs of those less fortunate or less attached to schooling or employment (Autor, Katz, & Kearney, 2006; Autor, Levy, & Murnane, 2003; Holzer, Linn, & Monthey, 2013). Such revelations are reminiscent of the turn of the past century and the development of CTE instruction in schools, as well as of the midcentury revival of CTE as a pathway out of poverty, particularly in American cities and rural areas (Conant, 1959).

Much of what was developed to offer CTE in secondary educational settings stems from governmental supports in education and the workforce. As with all things in education, much of this support and guidance has come at the state and local levels. However, for almost a full century, the federal government has provided funding to states in order to support the use of education to promote the development of a workforce that can fill the current and emerging labor needs of industry. Federal policy helped normalize spending and development of CTE programs, in part by requiring that states match federal outlays for CTE at least dollar for dollar.

Despite a century of policy and practice directed at building capacity and renewing the purpose of technical education, there is no less debate now than there was at the start of the 20th century about whether education is intended primarily to promote understanding of the liberal arts and generalized knowledge or to add specific job skills for employment in response to labor market demands (Grubb & Lazerson, 2005). At all times, the emphasis has remained on the role of education as an engine of economic growth and a mechanism to equalize individual opportunity (Goldin & Katz, 2008; Labaree, 1997). Issues of whether and how educational structures consider class, gender, race, and ability have long threads in the literature and history across most of this period (Anderson, 1988; Clifford, 1982). Specifically, there has been a continual need to recognize that career preparation may need to take into account structural differences in the resources available to certain groups in the larger population. Which groups have been emphasized and the policy solutions that have been offered have also differed over time. There has also been a clear recognition that the educational enterprise itself, while perhaps intended to reduce inequity, may have adopted elements of design and practice that reproduce social inequality (Bowles & Gintis, 1976; Dorn, 1996; Grubb & Lazerson, 1982), and that access to different types of educational opportunity may be incidentally or deliberately limited, based on the policies and programmatic structures of educational systems (Oakes, 1983, 1986; Oakes, Selvin, Karoly, & Guiton, 1992; Tyack, 1974).

Recent policy initiatives require that CCR be integrated in high schools for *all* students (U.S. Department of Education, 2010a, 2010b). The Common Core State Standards (CCSS) have been adopted by 42 states, the District of Columbia, and 4 territories. Thirty-seven states have defined college readiness, and 16 now require each high school student to complete a college preparatory curriculum resulting in an earned diploma (Mishkind, 2014). The Department of Defense Education Activity, 23 states, and the District of Columbia require schools to implement college and career readiness curricula aligned to the CCSS (Achieve, Inc., 2015). The content knowledge and skills associated with CCR are particularly important underlying goals of the CCSS (National Governors Association & Council of Chief State School Officers, 2010) and were incentivized via the Race to the Top Assessment Program (U.S. Department of Education, 2010b). Given the great variety in student interests and potential career paths, educators are faced with the daunting task of providing universal CCR for their students while at the same time personalizing career planning for each student, based on interests, skills, and performance to date. Thus, while CCR is the current policy priority, the concept of vocational education and preparation is not new.

Most recently, the passage of the Every Student Succeeds Act (ESSA), which is the latest iteration of the Elementary and Secondary Education Act, has provided for unprecedented incorporation of CTE, as well as recognition of its role in providing an appropriately balanced education (ESSA, 2015; Perkins Collaborative Resource Network, n.d.). This renewal comes even as individual states have already leveraged the CCR movement as a way to update their secondary school curricula and requirements (e.g., Arkansas' SmartCore requirements). ESSA and CCR are just the most recent domestic policy manifestations of the long-running linkages between public education and recognition of the need to prepare a workforce to meet the changing demands of the economy (Callahan, 1962; Grubb & Lazerson, 2004; Labaree, 1997; Lazerson & Grubb, 1974).

In this chapter, we first consider the history and development of CTE and its relationship to the concepts of contemporary notions of CCR. This examination includes a consideration of international trends as well as of the domestic federal legislation and policies that have influenced present-day CTE. Using a broad historical lens, recent developments, and incorporating salient historical debates and social forces, we attempt to better understand how the relationship between education and preparation for the workforce has changed over time, with a focus on the proliferation of federal innovations in this area over the past 100 years, as well as persistent themes in philosophical and policy debates. We then supplement this broad history and context with the results of a more focused survey of CTE literature, the terms of which yielded scholarship from the past 50 years. In this focused literature review, we point out trends in scholarship, synthesize subtopics that proved salient and notably absent and then consider these trends in light of the long-standing debates that have characterized technical education and the purpose of schooling more generally. We conclude with a consideration of limitations and recommendations for further scholarship and policymaking.

FOUNDATIONS AND ORIGINS OF CAREER-RELEVANT EDUCATION

The historical arc of formal education spans the apprentice and guild models of education for work in the 13th century, through the current system of increasingly differentiated structures for upper and postsecondary education worldwide (Bennett, 1926). The potential importance of developing specialized skills in education was formalized at least as recently as the 17th and 18th centuries, when philosophers such as Rousseau, Locke, and Adam Smith made sense of the role of formal education and training in terms of preparing individuals for increasingly specialized elements of working life (Bennett, 1926). This pragmatism was, at least in part, an acknowledgment of the monastic scholarship that aimed to perpetuate intellectual knowledge in the Dark Ages (Cahill, 1995), when guilds and apprenticeships were responsible for economic production. The evolution of the ideals of a common element of education for all, paired with specialized knowledge to support economic demand, is a duality that has persisted across the 20th century (and into the 21st) in the United States and elsewhere. How the acknowledgment of the dual purposes of education is translated into current educational systems has differed regionally. Whereas the central European nations have embraced a dual system that capitalizes on apprenticeships with employers in upper secondary school for the plurality of students, many British-influenced nations have favored longer stretches of compulsory general education with less investment in infrastructure to support apprenticeships or work-based learning (Hoffman, 2011). Despite differences in the ways that these systems have been operationalized, the scholarship and policy that are focused on understanding how best to develop a workforce with sufficient general and specific forms of skill (Becker, 1962) have been broad based and voluminous.

Philosophers in the 18th century observed the organization of the economy around them as well as the educational structures that supported that organization. Among other things, they acknowledged the role of apprenticeships and applied learning that led to the production of goods and services not otherwise made available by men of letters. This was no doubt made more salient as the feudal system dissolved and gave rise to what we now acknowledge as the foundations of our current capitalist economy. Around the world, the role and process of learning technical trades and methods of production became only more salient in the 19th century, as mechanization and forms of automated production were accelerated. In parallel, forms of mass education had evolved both nationally and internationally. There was a recognized disconnect between the common schools that provided general training in literacy and numeracy and the need for more technical training demanded by manufacturers and others in production (Bennett, 1937). There was also an acknowledgment that urbanization and poverty required that education be differentiated in ways that could serve the needs of people with less access to resources—a theme that arose then but continues to this day. The demand for education linked to work skill development, initially given names like *manual arts* or *vocational education*, gave rise to what we now know as CTE.[1] In the United States, central Europe, Scandinavia, and Russia, systems of technical education evolved (though on quite different trajectories and yielding quite different forms) to ensure that youth could gain both general training (in reading, writing, and arithmetic) and specific technical training (Bennett, 1937).

In the United States, the common school movement, the lobbying of manufacturers, and the influence of organized labor all contributed to a debate in the late 19th century about whether and how job training or the development of occupational skills should be a part of government-funded education (Lazerson & Grubb, 1974). Over a similar time period, the vocational education and training systems of Europe evolved in response to industrial demand and the growth of manufacturing industries (Wollschlager & Reuter-Kumpmann, 2004).

The timing of the engagement of national governments in the provision and support of vocational education differed, with some of the latest adoptions of formalized support for vocational education occurring in the United States with the passage of the Smith-Hughes Act of 1917.[2] In both domestic and European societies the impetus for federal involvement was the recognition that vocational training was related to economic growth, and the interest in growth and employment spanned state boundaries. The new law provided funding to states, with the idea that states would match federal funds to determine total expenditures on vocational education. It also, notably, included provisions that vocational education was to comprise only part of a student's school day, the rest of the time being spent in general education settings focused on developing skills for reading, mathematics, and citizenship. In the wake of Smith-Hughes, the National Association of State Directors of Career and Technical Education (now Advance CTE) was formed to coordinate efforts across state boundaries and to work in conjunction with localized industry. Such developments, and the reports from a 1936 advisory commission, shaped vocational education in the United States until the Vocational Education Act of 1963 and subsequent amendments to that act, in 1968. Whereas legislation preceding the Vocational Education Act of 1963 was concerned with providing a justification and model for federal funding of vocational education, the 1963 and 1968 acts focused on addressing forms of social inequality that had been identified and addressed, simultaneously, in other parts of the Great Society reforms. The passage of the Carl D. Perkins Act in 1984 was the first in a series of four federal authorizations to continue to fund what is now called CTE. Importantly, the most recent reauthorization of the Perkins Act, in 2006, declared a clear need to increase the focus of CTE on preparing students for postsecondary education. This postsecondary connection has existed for some time abroad, perhaps most notably in Switzerland, which despite having a dual system of secondary education still has clear pathways to postsecondary education (Hoffman, 2011).

As educational and economic needs evolved, so did the commitment of the U.S. federal and state governments to providing and funding education to prepare students for the workforce. The Perkins Act and its three subsequent reauthorizations, each of which further modified how and what was funded, are the most recent examples of these commitments. As the federal government's role and commitment evolved, so did the states' as they experimented with schooling models. In the post–World War II era, and especially in the 1960s and 1970s, this included the first instances of occupation-focused academies (e.g., in the Philadelphia school district; see Neubauer, 1986; Stern, 1992), as well as specialized CTE schools (Conant, 1959). More recently, these models include new waves of career academies, linked learning models (started in California and now just beginning to proliferate), and the formation of other specialized academies (e.g., see Jacoby & Dougherty, 2016; Visher & Stern, 2015). Changing funding commitments also precipitated a change in name: from *vocational education*—often viewed negatively, based on the perceived concentration of lower ability individuals in these programs—to *career and technical education*. The change was first codified in the 2006 reauthorization of Perkins, but the new term had come into broader use sometime between the 1998 reauthorization and 2006.

Tensions and Trade-Offs in the Debates Over Technical Education

The evolution of policies to fund and codify federal and state support for CTE tended to mirror philosophical debates about the contemporary purpose of schooling, as well as the empirical realities about how schooling was organized, implemented, and made available to all manner of students. In this section we review more of the observations and concerns that paralleled much of the legislative change that we highlighted earlier.

In his landmark, groundbreaking study of the American comprehensive high school, James Bryant Conant (1959) proposed a set of recommendations for reforming secondary education and in many ways set the tone for how schools were updated in the 1960s and beyond. Central to this work was an understanding that the need for completion of a high school degree had expanded, and was likely to become increasingly important (Conant, 1959, p. 6). His emphasis on the customization of education to suit individual needs and the importance of offering broad access to core academic coursework, as well as to electives (including vocational courses), helped codify the broad range of offerings that dominated the latter half of the 20th century and the beginning of the 21st.

The need for the further evolution of the American high school, and the role of offering diverse curricular options, was also met by a recognition that earlier efficiency movements born out of the early 20th century retained a strong hold on how schools were organized and administered (Callahan, 1962; Tyack, 1974). Callahan (1962) criticized the overly large role of notions of efficiency in education; at the same time, the holdover of Taylorism led to increased focus on work-related training in public education but at the risk of being too prescriptive and lessening the chance for real opportunity for learning and growth.

The Callahan critique of efficiency has also been advanced in several lines of argument that have problematized the notion that schooling should offer differentiated pathways from secondary education to postsecondary life. Whereas some pragmatists and others advancing notions of social efficiency have noted the importance of employability immediately after high school, others, such as Tyack (1974) and Bowles and Gintis (1976), have emphasized that the structure of schooling was created largely to facilitate the reproduction of social classes, rather than to spark upward mobility. This scholarship followed a decade of broad social movements and the Great Society reforms that were, in principle, aimed at reducing the social inequality that motivated the federal vocational policies of the 1960s. However, the critiques offered by these reforms suggested that education might acclimate students to remaining in their prior social class rather than provide them with an opportunity for upward mobility, long a purported goal of public education.

Concerns about education as a potential perpetrator of inequality were also evident in the earlier work of Conant (1959), where there was a clear indication that some of the inequality or limited options appeared to operate along gender and racial lines. A specific focus on the role of education in limiting professional options and social mobility was especially salient along racial lines, particularly for Black Americans in the South (Anderson, 1982). In particular, funneling of Black youth into vocational education was identified as a mechanism through which CTE was touted as improving the life outcomes of largely marginalized populations, while simultaneously being used to limit access or to track students based on racial stereotypes or law-based discrimination (Grubb & Lazerson, 1982).

The debate over whether the existence of CTE offered multiple educational pathways in secondary education or led to de facto tracking of students was accelerated by the scholarship of Jeannie Oakes and colleagues in the 1980s and 1990s. For instance, a study from Oakes (1983) demonstrated that access to particular vocational curricula (e.g., business versus building trades) differed systematically based on the racial composition of schools (predominantly White schools had more of the former). This finding echoed work by earlier historians of gender- and race-based distinctions in the offering and availability of CTE (see, e.g., Anderson, 1988; Clifford, 1982). Oakes's evidence in the 1980s harkened back to this earlier period and highlighted the question of whether vocational education was actually providing options to students or merely serving to reproduce existing social hierarchies. This critique was reminiscent of earlier social efficiency movements that actually justified the existence of differentiated learning opportunities in high schools based on the different work possibilities a student might face after formal schooling was complete (see discussion of David Snedden in the early 20th century by Bergen, 1981, among others). In later work, Oakes (1986) further advanced the same argument and later provided evidence of overrepresentation of low-income students and students of color in vocational coursework in high school (Oakes et al., 1992). In the latter work, Oakes et al. also documented the relative lack of resources provided for CTE as evidence that it was treated as a lower status pathway.

Throughout the 1990s, and amid broad policy concern regarding educational tracking, vocational education as a manifestation of such tracking remained salient (Gamoran & Mare, 1989; Oakes & Guiton, 1995). Though advocates of CTE, as well as those who pushed for the passage of the School to Work Opportunities Act of 1994, continued to highlight the importance of preparing students for the world of work, the debates continued regarding what was the most important role of education and whether it was being achieved (Labaree, 1997).

The Shift to "Vocationalized" Higher Education

Change and debate regarding the role of CTE in education and its connection to job preparation have not been confined to the K–12 realm. There has also been a shift in higher education that provides further context. In the past century, higher education degree programs have shifted to meet the demands of the labor market (Grubb & Lazerson, 2005). Higher education has undergone a "vocationalization" process, whereby institutions have shifted away from educating an elite few on intellectual, moral, and civic values and moved to expand offerings of "professional education" for the masses (Grubb & Lazerson, 2005). *Professional education* refers to the incorporation of professional schools that are more pragmatic in nature and address the ongoing and changing needs of the labor market: professions, such as nursing, teaching, agriculture, and business, to name a few. This evolution of higher education has influenced the larger picture of vocational education and the CCR movement of late. The rise of vocationalized higher education has increased the demand for more students to be college- and career-ready on graduation from high school. The term *college* is applied broadly to any type of postsecondary education, ranging from short-term certificate programs to 4-year degrees. Within the broad sectors of health care, education, and business, professionals with varying levels of education and skill sets are needed. Thus, the vast majority of students need some exposure and readiness to enter these fields. Importantly, students need this exposure in high school. The tech-prep programs of the late 1990s and early 2000s required the creation of articulation agreements between secondary and postsecondary schools and were an initial acknowledgment of the importance of finding policy solutions to facilitating this transition. Existing evidence suggests that the tech-prep policy did increase college going but with most of the increase occurring at 2-year rather than 4-year schools (Cellini, 2006).

Reviewing the history of CTE and the research literature in the field is particularly important as CTE is designed to serve as a productive setting for secondary students who may not thrive in traditional, comprehensive high schools. In fact, from its inception, CTE was designed to prepare youth for careers that required varying levels of education. The 2006 reauthorization of the Perkins Act emphasized the importance of access to CTE for special populations to promote self-sufficiency in adulthood, partly in response to evidence that traditional high schools might not be adequately serving students, especially those from low-income families, English language learners, and students with disabilities.

Though high school graduation rates have been trending positively across the nation (Stilwell & Sable, 2013), this has not been true for all groups of students (Doren, Murray, & Gau, 2014; Goodman, Hazelkorn, Bucholz, Duffy, & Kitta, 2011; Stilwell & Sable, 2013). Students with disabilities, English language learners, and students from low-income families have all experienced lower rates of academic success and attainment (Gregg, 2007; Hoxby & Turner, 2013; Kanno & Cromley, 2013; Welton & Martinez, 2013). This reality suggests that these students may stand to benefit most from programs or curricula designed to make them career ready and that traditional high school may be inadequate for certain disadvantaged subgroups of students. Thus, CTE is an important option for all students and may be especially beneficial to disadvantaged students. However, we find historical examples where these ends have been posited but not attained. Therefore, it is important to draw from the current CTE literature to determine what works for all student populations, particularly disadvantaged students.

A SYSTEMATIC REVIEW OF THE LITERATURE: TECHNICAL EDUCATION AND THE LABOR MARKET

In this section, we focus on identifying peer-reviewed scholarship that studied the linkages between formal secondary education and preparation for the world of work. By relying on a systematic search, we sought to separate our own prior knowledge and potential biases from the corpus of relevant literature on this topic. Our intention was to later synthesize the findings and relate them to the long history of scholarship in this area. First, we generated a relevant and appropriate subset of the larger literature on CTE, using prespecified but limited search terms; then, we used the results to point out historical trends and cycles in the focus on education for work, as well as systematic changes in focal populations, particularly historically disadvantaged groups. In so doing, and in putting the articles from this search in conversation with long-established debates in education policy related to technical education, we emphasize the extent to which empirical research on the connection between education and preparation for employment has changed over the past five or more decades. We conclude with a consideration of what changes are still needed, and we offer recommendations for furthering the understanding of how education for work is implemented and can be studied.

Method

To identify the relevant literature, we followed a clear set of procedures and coding schemes. In all instances the choices we made led to both intentional and unintentional narrowing of the scope of the search. However, given the stated focus on the intersection of schooling and preparation for work, we explicitly targeted literatures believed to overlap with both areas. First, we considered literatures that spanned social sciences broadly and that explicitly included education, as well as the disciplines of psychology, sociology, and economics. We searched the databases of ERIC, PsycInfo, and EconLit, where we found that the bulk of the literature related to vocational and technical education and work existed. Importantly, within these databases we further limited our search to peer-reviewed journals and books that indicated some degree of scholarly review.[3]

Within these databases, we narrowed our search terms to include the following: "vocational education," "career and technical education," "work," and "career." Initial searches on only the first two of these terms individually led to over 9,000 citations. Our focus on the intersection between (a) career vocational and technical education and (b) preparation for the workforce led us to employ one, then the other, of the first two terms ("vocational education" and "career and technical education"), followed in each case by both of the latter terms ("career" and "work") in both possible orderings. Thus, any article or book related to vocational or career and technical education that did not explicitly make reference to work or career was not included in the final results.[4] When we searched on "vocational education" followed by "work" and then "career," we found 541 articles. The analogous search that led with "career and technical education" yielded 428 results. Reversing the order of "career" and "work" in these compound searches further restricted the overall pool of citations, though we included any additional citations not present in the initial searches. This led to an initial pool of 650 unique peer-reviewed publications. Our citations span the years 1946 through 2015 and include several books on the history of education that discuss the emergence and development of CTE in the United States and in relation to industrializing European nations.[5]

From this initial list we narrowed the literature to focus exclusively on work that addressed secondary or upper secondary education (e.g., Grades 6–12). Though we included domestic and international literature, in all contexts this meant removing articles or studies that focused on college-level education or adult populations as revealed by an initial abstract review of all 650 sources. These criteria eliminated nearly 200 sources, suggesting there is a growing and rich literature on the linkages between college and preparation for work. An additional 74 articles were removed during full coding once we determined that they focused on nonsecondary student populations (college or adult). We removed another 14 articles that were duplicated citations, six articles that did not actually cover career or vocational education, and 55 articles that were not locatable through the University of Connecticut library system or interlibrary loan. Of these 55, the title or journal names revealed that 9 were international in scope and 10 addressed students with disabilities—specifically, visual impairment, deafness, and emotional disorders. Our final analytic sample included 301 articles or books that met our selection criteria and that spanned the middle of the 20th century through early 2015 (see online appendix, available in the online journal). The time span covered by the articles retained from our search was an unintended result of the search parameters, not an explicit restriction on the search.[6]

Our systematic review of the peer-reviewed articles and books focused on coding the data for 15 key characteristics, all of which were informed by our review of the historical literature as well as by our own prior work in this area. The categories for which we coded included whether an article was historical in focus, whether it was specific to the United States or another national context, and whether it had key sample characteristics indicating that it related to historically disadvantaged subgroups. The articles were assigned binary codes (1/0) for the following focuses as indicated by sample characteristics: male students, female students, Black or Latino students, students with disabilities, and students from families with lower incomes. Finally, we assigned binary codes for categories of programs according to whether they were curriculum-based, were situated in nonschool settings, included school-business partnerships, focused on particular occupations, addressed the transition process to postsecondary education or work, served disengaged youth, or addressed outcomes related to employment or high school completion. Though the initial search yielded a few articles prior to 1970, these articles were not available. Thus, based on our search terms, the included articles spanned the 1970s through the present and were representative of a broad range of themes and student populations, which we detail below.

Assessment of whether each of the 15 characteristics should be coded as equal to 1 was done in accordance with a series of nine decision rules that we established at the outset of coding (see the appendix for details) and then refined as we progressed through the pilot rounds and resolved disagreements. Each of the student subgroup categories (race, gender, disability, disengaged youth or dropouts, etc.) was coded as equal to 1 only if the article explicitly reported on that group. We accounted for whether an article addressed a particular program or intervention as follows: An article was coded as addressing a curriculum-based program if it was a CTE-focused intervention delivered in a dedicated class during the school day. We coded studies as addressing nonschool settings if they were operated outside of school hours (e.g., after school). School-business partnerships were coded as present if the program or intervention involved coordinated efforts between industry and school personnel in support of a CTE program. Occupation-based programs were those specific to a particular occupational field (e.g., construction, agriculture). Finally, with regard to student outcomes, we coded programs as emphasizing the transition from high school to postsecondary education if there was deliberate coordination or planning between employees at both levels and/or if programs to facilitate the transition were present (e.g., bridge programs, dual enrollment). Articles that looked at employment, wages, or job skills as an outcome were coded as having an employment focus. Articles that tracked school completion or high school graduation as a student outcome were coded as equal to 1 in that category.

We coded these characteristics as binary indicators of whether or not an article described each of the 15 dimensions (1 = *yes*, 0 = *no*). We both participated in the coding. First, we independently coded a subset of the articles (*n* = 7). Then the authors met to discuss any disagreements in order to reconcile and refine the coding instrument and/or decision rules. There were two rounds of this initial pilot process. In addition, 15% of the 300 articles were independently coded by both authors, and codes were later compared to calculate interrater reliability. Interrater reliability was calculated as a percentage of agreement, where the total number of agreed-on codes (numerator) was divided by the total number of possible codes (denominator). Among the 15% of articles that were double-coded, interrater reliability was calculated as 94%.[7]

Once all articles were coded, our initial analysis focused on summarizing areas of revealed emphasis, identifying trends and changes in CTE scholarship over time, and reconciling findings. In addition, we generated cross-tabulations of article content across coding categories, with an emphasis on overlaps that had been highlighted by prior policy or historical relevance. Within these cross-tabulations we conducted chi-square tests of independence (given our binary outcomes and our desire to limit parametric assumptions in analysis), to assess whether two coding categories in a given cross-tabulation were statistically dependent on one another.

Results

Our coding and analysis of the articles yielded several noteworthy trends. Scholarship relating to education and labor market preparation has increased in recent years, and the mix of topics covered has been highly focused on employment outcomes, transition to postsecondary education, international scholarship, and students with disabilities as a subgroup. We found interesting trends in topics over time, with regard to what was studied in this literature and time period and what was not.

Next, we report our findings, and in the discussion we consider how these trends related to long-standing historical trends and considerations in CTE policy.

Growth in CTE and Work Scholarship

In Panel A of Figure 1, we demonstrate the growth in scholarship on this topic over the past five decades. The trend is clear and is interrupted only by the fact that the current decade, which is incomplete, is on pace to eclipse the previous ones. Though we focus on our selected and coded articles here, in our initial search, which yielded roughly 9,000 hits, we saw nearly identical positive trends in scholarship on this topic across the same span of time. This mirrors growth in education-related scholarship more broadly, though particular areas of growth, which we highlight below, are especially noteworthy. We emphasize a few of these areas in Panels B through D in Figure 1, where we show trends in scholarly focus on students with disabilities, postsecondary transition, and scholarship outside the United States. In all

FIGURE 1
Trend in Scholarship Addressing the Intersection of Secondary Education and Preparation for Work Over Time

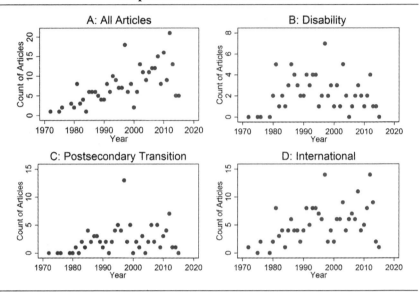

Note. Each point represents the count of articles published and reviewed in a given year.

cases there is a positive trend over time, though in the case of studies involving students with disabilities the trend is more parabolic. We discuss reasons for this below.

In addition to observing temporal trends in volume, we also summarize in Table 1 the topics covered across this body of literature, as derived from our adopted coding scheme. In the table we report proportions of articles focused on a particular theme, along with their standard deviations. About 30% of the articles we reviewed addressed students with disabilities; 20% reported specifically about differences by gender; about 12% focused on Black or Latino students, with a similar share on students from lower income families; and about 10% focused on students who were more likely to be disengaged from school (e.g., dropouts). Over 60% of the articles focused on employment as an explicit or desired outcome of CTE programs or concepts; nearly 30% addressed transitions to employment and postsecondary education; only 17% focused specifically on CTE in relation to completing high school (see Figure 2 for a comparison of trends in employment and graduation focus). Emphasis on postsecondary transitions also trended positively during this time (though at a slower pace than overall scholarship on CTE and its connection to work), following a general secular trend and policy emphasis on college going, as well as the recognition that postsecondary training is increasingly demanded in the labor market.

TABLE 1

Proportion of Coded Articles Addressing Attributes of Students, Programs, and Outcomes

Attribute	M	SD
Historical	0.164	0.371
U.S. focus	0.709	0.455
Male	0.220	0.415
Female	0.234	0.424
Students with disabilities	0.305	0.461
Black/Latino	0.120	0.325
Lower income	0.113	0.318
Curriculum-based programs	0.490	0.501
Nonschool settings	0.318	0.467
School-business partnerships	0.086	0.280
Occupation-specific programs	0.274	0.447
Secondary-postsecondary transition	0.318	0.467
Dropouts or disengaged youth	0.107	0.310
High school graduation	0.159	0.366
Employment	0.632	0.483

Note. The proportions were calculated as the total number of articles coded as equal to 1 for a given attribute, divided by the total of coded articles, 301.

FIGURE 2

Trends in Focus on Employment and High School Completion as Outcomes of Interest

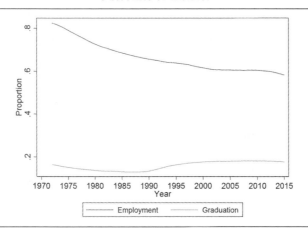

Note. Trends in the share of articles focusing on employment and high school completion as outcomes were smoothed using a localized polynomial smoothing option in Stata.

Disability Focus

In the 1980s and 1990s, growth in scholarship related to students with disabilities comprised 50% to 80% of all annual scholarship on this topic, and grew considerably faster than other scholarship related to CTE. In the early part of this time period, there was a massive growth in research related to students with disabilities, which constituted the clear majority of scholarship in the 1980s. This trend coincides with the passage of P.L. 94-142 in 1975 (Education of All Handicapped Children Act), which has since been reauthorized as the Individuals With Disabilities Education Improvement Act (IDEIA) of 2004. As part of the new law, children with disabilities had to be educated in public schools, and the legal mandate included transition planning for students exiting the K–12 system into the workforce. The share of this literature devoted to addressing students with disabilities has fallen off over time, largely due to the general increase in scholarship in CTE more broadly.

Among the articles about students with disabilities, more than three quarters focused on employment as an outcome, often including school-to-work transitions (e.g., Rusch, Hughes, Agran, Martin, & Johnson, 2009). Among the articles not addressing students with disabilities, only two thirds listed employment as a clear outcome. Results of a chi-square test of independence also supported the relationship between disability focus and employment outcomes ($p = .002$). Importantly, 43% of the scholarship that focused on students with disabilities also addressed the transition to postsecondary education, an association that is likewise statistically significant ($p = .001$). In contrast, only 25% of scholarship that is not disability-focused addresses the transition to postsecondary education.

The focus on employment outcomes, specifically school-to-work transitions, suggests that the vast majority of the programs described in the articles were geared toward preparing students with disabilities for low-wage work (e.g., Keim, Rak, & Fell, 1982; Sowers & Powers, 1989; Wisniewski, 1991). In fact, one particular study found that community business professionals may be less willing to partner with high schools to create meaningful work experiences for adolescents with disabilities, as opposed to their peers without disabilities, leaving this subgroup more limited options for work experience (Carter et al., 2009). Yet there are more students with disabilities in college settings now than ever before (Newman et al., 2011), and the types of disabilities represented are even more diverse (e.g., developmental disabilities, intellectual disabilities, and others). This increase represents a pivotal turning point for students with disabilities, as does more recent federal funding targeted toward building postsecondary programs for students with more severe disabilities (Think College, 2016). As more postsecondary programs become available for students with disabilities, it will be important to reconsider the secondary programs that are in place for this population. In other words, simply preparing all students with disabilities for low-wage work will no longer be sufficient.

In a similar vein, it is equally troubling that no articles in our review described the integration of technology tools into a curriculum, into an after-school program, or into a job setting for students with disabilities. As is the case for all students, technology skills are critical for students with disabilities in order to compete in the job market. These students tend to be unemployed more often than others and, when employed, tend to earn lower wages (Sanford et al., 2011). Thus, it is arguably more important to ensure that students with disabilities are exposed to technology tools prior to entering the workforce so that they may reasonably compete. Students with disabilities should not be left out of any efforts to integrate technology into the classroom.

Finally, the majority of studies that involved students with disabilities described some link to the transition planning process as facilitated by the individualized education program (IEP) as the driving force behind setting the course of study (e.g., Colley & Jamison, 1998; Everson, Zhang, & Guillory, 2001; Hutchinson, Versnel, Chin, & Munby, 2008; Kolstoe, 1981). In other words, if a specific skill was not mentioned as an IEP goal, then it was not a priority for students to learn each year. This finding is not surprising, considering that the IEP is the cornerstone of special education (Yell, 2016) and, as such, prioritizes any and all skill development among students with disabilities. The legally mandated IEP structure can work for or against students with disabilities with regard to ensuring they have opportunities to gain vocational skills needed to compete in the job market. As long as critical vocational skills are assessed for and integrated into the IEP goals, the structure can work quite well. However, it is up to the adults—that is, the special educators, career and technical educators, school counselors, and other professionals who might be members of an IEP team—to ensure that there is adequate alignment between the critical vocational skills that are measured and prioritized and the IEP process. Compliance with IDEIA does not necessarily ensure quality (Flannery, Lombardi, & Kato, 2015); educators can write compliant IEP goals that are not necessarily aligned to critical vocational skills or quality. As a result, students with disabilities may have measurably compliant IEP goals that remain focused on preparation for low-wage work, with scarce integration of technology tools. The existing special education system mandated by IDEIA will not necessarily prevent this from occurring.

Other Marginalized Populations

Given the historical focus of federal legislation and its relationship to ensuring educational access and economic mobility through CTE, we also generated cross-tabulations aimed at the overlap between disengaged students, lower income students, and the key outcomes of high school graduation, on one hand, and employment, on the other. As reported earlier, only about 10% of the articles we coded focused on students who were disengaged from school, and coverage of these topics has not trended as positively as in other areas, though it occupies a consistent share of total scholarship. However, there was a clear association between scholarship focused on disengaged students and whether the scholarship also used high school completion ($p = .000$) as an outcome. Similarly, there was a suggestive relationship ($p = .085$) between a focus on these students and whether employment was emphasized in the same set of articles.

Focus on high school completion among disengaged students was a clear theme, in part because there was broad recognition that, through much of this period, a high school diploma was an important minimum marker of attainment for accessing middle-class wages (Goldin & Katz, 2008). In our review the significant relationship between focus on disengaged students and focus on high school completion as an outcome spans the entire time period. An article from Tanzman (1972) early in this period adopted the optimistic view of CTE as a way to get would-be dropouts to learn a trade and complete high school, whereas research published in the past 20 years has recognized the changed employment landscape and erosion of high school completion as a sufficient educational credential (Raffo, 2006). Some of this research also emphasizes the potential for CTE to provide increased relevance for disengaged students, which could induce school completion while promoting the accumulation of relevant work skills; this effect is suggested by several articles from Europe and the United Kingdom, where youth unemployment has been consistently high (Beekhoven & Dekkers, 2005; DeLuca et al., 2010; Raffo, 2006). As with disengaged students, scholarship on students from lower income backgrounds also accounted for a modest 12% of CTE scholarship in our sample. Yet we again found evidence of a clear relationship between articles that emphasized lower income youth and high school graduation (p = .002) and suggestive evidence with employment outcomes (p = .06). These relationships suggest that literature related to CTE over the past five decades has continued to include discussion of how CTE can be applied to or designed for students whose families have fewer economic resources, or who are disengaged from schooling. Such a focus highlights the ways in which CTE was touted in the past as a path to economic mobility; it also raises concerns that CTE may also be used to track students based on these observable characteristics.

There is remarkably little scholarship that spans both disengaged students and students from lower income backgrounds, despite a long-running understanding in the broader education literature that these factors are correlated. In fact, in our review, only 6 of the 35 articles addressing low-income students also focused on disadvantaged students. Of particular interest in this overlap is Kim (2013), who sought to understand the career trajectories of school leavers who were employed. Kim (2013) used his qualitative data to develop typologies of career trajectories and found most school leavers in positions with low growth potential. However, he found that about a third of these students gained access to career ladders through work experience and training and that elements of socioeconomic status (e.g., access to computers) influenced whether a student ended up in this particular category. Also important in this small, overlapping literature is empirical evidence that when employers lack good information about students making the high-school-to-work transition, they are likely to revert to statistical discrimination (Mueller & Wolter, 2014). That is, in the absence of good information on academic or work-related skill (such as high school diplomas, test scores, or other credentials), employers used observable characteristics as proxies for human capital. Such an approach, if generalized in the United States, could have problematic implications, especially for students of color, thus emphasizing the importance of this small overlapping literature on lower income and disengaged students.

International Scholarship

Less than one third of all articles reviewed focused on a context outside the United States. Since 1980 the share of international scholarship on this topic has been fairly constant, with overall volume growing in step with CTE scholarship more broadly (see Figure 1, Panels A and D). Despite the reputation of central European models for having substantial linkages between employers and secondary education (e.g., apprenticeships), there is no difference between the domestic and international shares of articles that addressed school-business partnerships. A chi-square test of independence led us to conclude that whether an article focused on employment as an outcome was independent of whether the research took place in the United States or another nation ($p = .19$). The absence of such a relationship may be related to the fact that the international literature notably includes some work set in African and Middle Eastern nations, with more focus in those settings on the role of CTE education as a vehicle for economic growth. In this way, the contemporary literature on developing contexts is a reprisal of the work and policies of Western nations from the turn of the 20th century.

Of the 90 internationally coded articles, more than 20% focused on Anglo contexts (Canada, Britain, Australia, or New Zealand), nearly 15% focused on Germany or the former East and West Germany, and about 7% focused on the Middle East or Africa, with each of those emphasizing training or economic growth. For instance, an article situated in Lebanon focused on moving vocational training from a historically stigmatized pursuit to one that could promote academic and workforce success (Vlaardingerbroek & El-Masri, 2008). The authors highlighted that positive perceptions of vocational training had emerged, as there had been broader awareness and acknowledgment of the positive career outcomes for individuals who made the transition from purely academic training to a hybrid of academic and technical training. Such work is salient in its ability to map onto other contexts, such as the United States, where it is only recently that awareness has increased regarding the career trajectories that are possible through CTE. In Stuart (2012), the context was South Africa and the challenges associated with trying to replicate the central European model of vocational education and training, particularly toward the end of developing manufacturing skills. Each of these cases highlights some potential challenges of trying to grow or establish CTE in new contexts.

The international literature also highlighted the tensions between using vocational education for long-term skill development and using it only to ensure shorter term labor market preparation. Santa Cruz, Siles, and Vrecer (2011) linked tracking toward vocational training early in students' schooling to midcareer employment vulnerability, emphasizing a concern in the policy world that accumulation of specific skills in the short term could have longer term costs if it means having lower levels of generalizable skills or knowledge that could facilitate career changing. This concern is similar to that of recently published work from Hanushek, Schwerdt, Woessmann, and Zhang (2016), who found a similar trade-off existing for workers across 11 European countries. This line of scholarship relays the importance of the fact that secondary education programs can better prepare youth for the need for midcareer retraining by improving baseline "academic" or general skills. Other scholars of international CTE provided evidence, in a similar vein, of the growing importance of secondary credentials, of dwindling apprenticeships, and of perceptions that college preparation/readiness was increasingly vital for students who would have traditionally followed a vocational pathway (Kupfer, 2010). Niemeyer (2014) looked specifically at the case of Germany as an example of a system in transition, where the role of postsecondary education is growing.

International literature was focused less on the transition to postsecondary education (only 20% vs. 35% in the United States) and more on gender aspects (30% focusing explicitly on girls and women vs. 20% in the United States). Internationally oriented articles were much less focused on curriculum-based programs (28% vs. 53%, and a statistically significant association, $p < .000$) and were more likely to focus on specific occupations (36% vs. 24%, $p = .026$). In recent years, among articles that were set outside the United States, there was a more noteworthy uptick in the share of articles whose titles included the word *tracking* (Van Houtte & Stevens, 2009). In particular, in most instances the settings were European, which may reflect a growing emphasis on college going in those nations, and related reforms to detrack some of their systems (C. Hall, 2012).

Across the scholarship on vocational education outside the United States, there were several salient characteristics. First, in the literature we accessed there was a clear emphasis on European and Anglo contexts. Second, the literature was focused on details of vocational educational structure, the tradition of tracking, and the role of apprenticeships. There was a noteworthy and important rise in the frequency of discussion of tracking and of the need to move further toward college skill development, even among vocational education participants, as a way to hedge against career stagnation or midcareer job dislocation. This trend echoed a U.S. focus on the need to prepare for college and career and on the importance of strong academic and social skills as a means of reducing the risk of midcareer decline or job loss through technical change.

DISCUSSION

Our synthesis of the literature on CTE and preparation for work or career identified several trends or areas of focus. In most instances, these trends related directly to long-standing debates and focus on CTE and schooling as preparation for work. Equally clear were several noteworthy areas where students or topics were underrepresented. We highlight three notable trends that our review and analysis revealed and put them in conversation with the earlier literature on this topic: (a) students with disabilities have been studied disproportionately, while other historically marginalized groups (e.g., lower income students, students of color) have received less attention; (b) there has been increased attention on postsecondary transitions in the literature; and (c) employment remains a salient point of focus, as opposed to academic outcomes (e.g., achievement, graduation).

Marginalized Populations

While scholarship on students with disabilities has grown over the past five decades, focus on lower income students and students of color in this literature has not been as salient. The implications of this undercoverage relate directly to earlier scholarship on economic mobility and tracking for these groups, both of which are underemphasized in recent decades.

The absence of scholarship focusing on African American or Latino students, or on students from lower income families, suggests that we know little about whether or how these students may benefit from CTE exposure in high school, especially in more recent years. Importantly, these groups of students are often among those who are touted as potentially benefiting from an expanded focus on career readiness. Also important is that the most recent national statistics, as well as statistics from some states (Dougherty, 2015; National Center for Education Statistics [NCES], 2013), suggest that students of color and lower income students are overrepresented in CTE, a fact that was first unearthed by Oakes (1983). Investigation of such potential over-representation or tracking has garnered less scholarly attention in recent years (notable exceptions are C. Hall, 2012; and Lewis & Cheng, 2006, though the latter did not find evidence of race-based tracking in CTE). However, simply seeing that some groups of students are overrepresented makes understanding the potential influence of CTE on outcomes for these students of particular import. Interestingly, our initial cursory review of over 9,000 peer-reviewed sources that came from a larger source for work related to career and technical or vocational education showed a clear focus on both lower income youth and African American students in the first half of the 20th century, making the absence of this literature in the more recent scholarship more surprising (Anderson, 1982; Lazerson & Grubb, 1974).

The mountain of research exploring the experiences and outcomes of students with disabilities in CTE programs could inform and support the extension of these lines of inquiry with respect to students of color and lower income students in CTE. Specifically, thinking about what services and experiences can be built into high schools that can enable students to make the transition from secondary to postsecondary education or the workforce seems potentially valuable in communities where many students cannot afford to attend college outright or where college may not be an optimal placement for many (Sanford et al., 2011). There is existing evidence that students (with and without disabilities) earn higher wages after participating in CTE models such as school-to-work programs in the 1990s and career academies in the early 2000s (Bishop & Mane, 2004; Kemple & Willner, 2008; Neumark & Rothstein, 2006). Such results emphasize that exposure to these programs in high school could provide enhanced financial support while young people are working only or working while in college. There may also be a substantial pool of students who graduate from high school but whose academic skills are too high to qualify them for special education services and too low to set them up for success in college (Martorell & McFarlin, 2011). In such cases we must have a more robust understanding of how CTE exposure in high school could influence later outcomes, as well as the factors that influence whether and how these students access CTE while in high school.

Our review of the literature in the first half of the 20th century showed some clear evidence of focus on the potential for classed and discriminatory education systems (Bowles & Gintis, 1976; Dorn, 1996; Tyack, 1974). For instance, coverage of gender differences in CTE was not robust in the literature that we reviewed (it was stronger in the international articles), although there was ample scholarship on the role of vocational education in preparing women for vocations and secretarial work (Clifford, 1982; Goldin, 2006; Kopczuk, Saez, & Song, 2010), which was also noted as a feature of high schools in the late 1950s by Conant (1959). There is a parallel literature on the argument for vocational education in the segregated South as a means to economic self-sufficiency for Black Americans (Anderson, 1988; Bowles & Gintis, 1976; C. W. Hall, 1973). Both of these themes that are connected to historically marginalized populations echo the earlier sentiments that led to the adoption of federal investment and innovation with respect to CTE policy. The underrepresentation of these themes in more recent literature (at least as concerns direct connection to preparation for work) is perhaps emblematic of the continued wage and employment discrimination faced by these groups in schooling and the workforce. At the very least, the suppressed level of scholarship in CTE with respect to these populations of students is noteworthy.

Postsecondary Transitions

Increasing scholarship attending to postsecondary transitions reflects a broad secular focus on the importance of at least some postsecondary training in preparation for entering the workforce. This is reminiscent of Conant's (1959) observation of the importance of increasing the share of high school graduates more than 50 years ago, and it highlights the importance of continued research in this area, particularly with expansions of programs that are modified versions of tech-prep (Cellini, 2006) and emphasize postsecondary transition. Early-college high schools and structures that fuse high school and associate's degree credentials within a CTE context have been proliferating (Jacoby & Dougherty, 2016) but remain largely understudied. Initial evidence regarding the early-college high school, or 9–14 model, has been promising (Haxton et al., 2016), but evidence of replicated results and examinations in multiple contexts does not yet exist.

In addition, the fact that we removed nearly 200 articles from our initial search on the grounds that they focused exclusively on adult or postsecondary settings underscores that some scholarship on CTE in postsecondary settings is already under way. Recent work has looked at the impact of CTE programs in community colleges and found positive economic returns to certificates earned in these settings (Kurlaender, Huff-Stevens, & Gros, 2014; Xu & Trimble, 2016). However, overall scholarship on up-to-date delivery models for CTE in postsecondary settings is somewhat limited.

Employment

The idea that employment is an end of education or an impetus for education policy is not new. The advocacy for the Smith-Hughes Act by manufacturers, the space race and the push for economic competition with Russia during the Cold War, the Great Society reforms, and the recent use of PISA scores as a call to improve the nation's global competitiveness are all instances of emphasis on employment as a goal of education. In the context of this chapter, the overall prevalence of employment as an outcome in our literature review is at least partially driven by our focus on the linkages between education and preparation for the workforce and the search terms we employed. However, the fact that so many articles relied on this outcome as an element of study in their research also highlights the persistent pragmatic connection between education and employment.

The focus on employment as an outcome in the studies of CTE that we reviewed mirrors existing literature in labor economics that explores whether and how additional education is rewarded in the labor force (e.g., Angrist & Krueger, 1991). Emphasis on employment as an outcome in international contexts also highlights the potential for career-oriented education to provide a foundation for economic development and growth. In the late 19th and early 20th centuries, career-focused education was justified as part of an overall economic development plan (Lazerson & Grubb, 1974) and as a means to compete globally (Benavot, 1983); this, in turn, provided justification for the federal role in funding CTE. During the 1960s, vocational education was used as a motivation for helping lower income urban populations escape the "poverty trap," and in recent years it has been touted as an alternative (or concurrent complement) to college. That our review revealed such a tight linkage between employment and historically disadvantaged populations suggests that because these groups of students are not as well represented in the literature, there is room for more scholarship in the future.

Limitations

The primary limitation of this study of the CTE literature is its relatively narrow focus on the intersection of CTE exposure in secondary education and preparation for a career, a focus that undoubtedly masked rich variation in the scholarship related to CTE more generally. Our initial search for scholarship that addressed the topics of vocational education and CTE revealed more than 9,000 peer-reviewed articles or books spanning the years 1900 to 2015. Systematically culling a subset of these articles that also explored the connection with work or job preparation still resulted in a large volume of scholarship. A related limitation is that in choosing databases to search we may have inadvertently limited our access to the international literature from this period. Specifically, focusing on English-language publications alone limited the results of our search, suggesting that true comparative work would have to take a more nuanced and comprehensive approach to identifying the relevant international literature.

Despite our review of this substantial body of work, there remains opportunity to further review and synthesize the existing literature. In particular, our focus on studies situated in secondary education settings means that, at a minimum, the literature on postsecondary CTE exposure and both college and employment outcomes is ripe for analysis. The increased availability of longitudinal data systems, the richness of the National Student Clearinghouse data for covering college outcomes (Dynarski, Hemelt, & Hyman, 2015), and the increased emphasis on multiple measures of performance under ESSA provide ample motivation and possibility for extending such work.

CONCLUSION

The results of the historical analysis and systematic literature review that we have undertaken here reveal several key areas to consider in moving forward in scholarship and policy related to vocational education and career readiness. These key areas are (a) historically marginalized student subgroups, (b) transitions to postsecondary education, and (c) continued focus on employment as an outcome. Our synthesis highlights the need for a return to critical analysis of the ways in which CTE may or may not be paying off for lower income students, students of color, and women. Concerns about tracking, social reproduction, and the potential for heterogeneous access and impact may not be warranted but must be explored in ways that do not appear in the CTE literature for at least the past decade. In addition, the literature related to the role of CTE in facilitating the transition to postsecondary education and employment is in need of additional updating. While there is a growing interest in transition in general, it has been concentrated on students with disabilities, with less focus on typically developing peers. Furthermore, the recent proliferation of new or revamped CTE delivery models, particularly with respect to facilitating the transition to college, suggests that more research and evaluation of such models are needed.

In the next 10 years, the field needs more work to examine critically the new models of CTE delivery, the changes in program offerings (e.g., the addition of information technology, biotechnology, advanced manufacturing), and the mechanisms by which students have come to access them (selective admission, lotteries, school choice). Lessons from the shifting role of CTE in European economies and its implications for educational practice and policy should be salient in informing this future work (Hanushek et al., 2016; Kupfer, 2010; Niemeyer, 2014; Santa Cruz et al., 2011). In an era of large-scale longitudinal data systems, the ability to conduct high-quality impact analyses on such new (and old) programs is better than ever before, and the level of detail available in these data permits reexamination of questions of access to curriculum and potential renewed tracking, as well as impact of program participation on postsecondary enrollment and employment outcomes. Without continuous investigation, we risk lapsing back to the highly unequal systems of the past, particularly for the students who, historically, are least well served by our education system (Raffo, 2006). We also risk misunderstanding the effect of CTE on student outcomes, particularly over the long run (Hanushek et al., 2016).

As many states adopt (or have adopted) the CCSS and pivot to emphasize both college readiness and career readiness, it is an opportune time to study how policy and program shifts in these areas affect student experiences and outcomes. In light of our review, it will be particularly important to understand how these changes affect students with disabilities, students from lower income families, and students who exhibit signs of being disengaged with schooling. Furthermore, with CTE featured more prominently in ESSA, and as Congress continues to entertain a reauthorization of the Perkins Act, there is an opportunity to refocus the policy conversation on what is known in the literature and what sorts of policy or program adoption should be encouraged. Specifically, requirements of states regarding how and where they spend Perkins funds could create incentives for evaluation of those programs. The best innovations in scholarship connecting CTE participation and outcomes will undoubtedly come from the ability of researchers to connect education and labor market data and to critically examine the ways in which CTE access intersects with long-standing debates about whether and how CTE promotes long-term success and allows for social mobility, or reinforces inequalities in access and outcomes.

APPENDIX
Decision Rules: CTE Literature Search

All subgroup categories: Any reporting of listed subgroups (e.g., race, gender, disability) can be counted as a 1, including frequencies and percentages. Count all that apply.

Program/Intervention Characteristics

Curriculum based: The program or intervention is delivered as a curriculum, which might include lesson plans, activities, assignments, work products, and so on. The curriculum could be delivered in a dedicated class period or somewhere else (e.g., a resource room) and must be implemented during the school day. The curriculum includes specific career and tech education courses.

Nonschool setting: The program or intervention is delivered outside of the school building or school day (includes community-based settings, after-school programs, job shadowing, work experience, work-study, etc.).

School-business partnership: The program or intervention is a coordinated effort between school personnel and a business entity or corporation.

Occupation-based: The program or intervention is specific to a certain field (e.g., construction, agriculture). There is no mention of a partnership with a business or corporation.

Secondary-postsecondary transition: The program, intervention, or research study involves a coordinated effort between secondary and postsecondary systems and/or personnel (e.g., teachers, counselors), including transition planning. This includes bridge programs such as dual enrollment, where students can earn simultaneous credit and/or work with personnel from both systems.

Dropouts or disengaged youth: The focus of the program is on special populations that are at risk (e.g., high school dropouts, students at risk for dropout, disengaged youth). The program does not necessarily include students with disabilities.

School completion/high school graduation: The study addresses school completion and/ or high school graduation in some way (e.g., high school graduation is an independent or dependent variable in the study).

Employment: There is a focus on job skills, wages earned, employment/unemployment, or something else related to employment during or after high school.

ACKNOWLEDGMENTS

We would like to thank Shelley Goldstein of the University of Connecticut library system for important search assistance, as well as Monique Golden for her research support in the generation of the chapter. We are also indebted to three anonymous referees and to the thoughtful directives of the volume editors, who substantially shaped the final version. All errors and omissions are our own.

NOTES

[1]The name change from *vocational education* to *career and technical education* was first codified at the national level under the 2006 reauthorization of the Perkins legislation, though it had been in relatively broad use for several years prior.

[2]The earlier Morrill Act of 1861 arguably had moved in this direction with the establishment of land-grant universities, but the focus of Smith-Hughes was exclusively on secondary education.

[3]The search feature allowed us to select peer-reviewed sources and books as distinct categories of scholarship. These excluded dissertations, newspaper articles, and other popular media.

[4]This, we realize, eliminated some seminal pieces related to the study of CTE. However, in our historical review, as described at the beginning of this chapter, we leveraged other searches, prior knowledge, and seminal literature to later put our objective search in conversation with these weighty historical pieces.

[5]With the assistance of a research librarian, we compiled a spreadsheet that captures all of these search results and records the database, identifier, journal, title, ISSN, year, volume, issue, and the link to the electronic citation that includes an abstract.

[6]It should be noted that the passage of additional federal legislation that subsequently spurred greater investment by states in vocational and technical education in the 1960s likely spurred the more voluminous scholarship in this area after 1970.

[7]In the initial round of comparison, agreement was calculated at 87%. Among the 15% of all coded articles that were coded by both authors, roughly one third were coded identically as not fitting the scope of the study. In all instances, not fitting the scope of the study meant that the article was focused on adult populations or students in higher education, both of which were defined as outside the purview of this analysis.

REFERENCES

Achieve, Inc. (2015). *Closing the expectations gap: 2014 annual report on the alignment of state K–12 policies and practice with the demands of college and careers.* Retrieved from http://www.pathwaylibrary.org/ViewBiblio.aspx?aid=22696

Anderson, J. D. (1982). The historical development of Black vocational education. In H. Kantor & D. B. Tyack (Eds.), *Work, youth, and schooling: Historical perspectives on vocational education* (pp. 180–222). Stanford, CA: Stanford University Press.

Anderson, J. D. (1988). *The education of Blacks in the South, 1860–1935.* Chapel Hill: University of North Carolina Press.

Angrist, J., & Krueger, A. (1991). Does compulsory school attendance affect schooling and earnings? *Quarterly Journal of Economics, 106,* 979–1014.

Autor, D., Katz, L., & Kearney, M. (2006). The polarization of the U.S. labor market. *American Economic Review, 96,* 189–194.

Autor, D., Levy, F., & Murnane, R. (2003). The skill content of recent technological change: An empirical exploration. *Quarterly Journal of Economics, 118,* 1279–1333.

Becker, G. S. (1962). Investment in human capital: A theoretical analysis. *Journal of Political Economy, 70*(5), 9–49.

Beekhoven, S., & Dekkers, H. (2005). Early school leaving in the lower vocational track: Triangulation of qualitative and quantitative data. *Adolescence, 40,* 197–213.

Benavot, A. (1983). The rise and decline of vocational education. *Sociology of Education, 56*(2), 63–76.

Bennett, C. A. (1926). *History of manual and industrial education up to 1870.* Peoria, IL: Manual Arts Press.

Bennett, C. A. (1937). *History of manual and industrial education, 1870 to 1917.* Peoria, IL: Manual Arts Press.

Bergen, T. J. (1981). David Samuel Snedden: The ideology of social efficiency. *Journal of Thought, 16*(2), 91–102.

Bishop, J. H., & Mane, F. (2004). The impacts of career-technical education on high school labor market success. *Economics of Education Review, 23,* 381–402.

Bowles, S., & Gintis, H. (1976). *Schooling in capitalist America* (Vol. 57). New York, NY: Basic Books.

Cahill, T. (1995). *How the Irish saved civilization.* New York, NY: Doubleday.

Callahan, R. E. (1962). *Education and the cult of efficiency.* Chicago, IL: University of Chicago Press.

Carter, E., Trainor, A. A., Cakiroglu, O., Cole, O., Swedeen, B., Ditchman, N., & Owens, L. A. (2009). Exploring school-employer partnerships to expand career development and early work experiences for youth with disabilities. *Career Development for Exceptional Individuals, 32,* 145–159.

Cellini, S. R. (2006). Smoothing the transition to college? The effect of Tech-Prep programs on educational attainment. *Economics of Education Review, 25,* 394–411.

Clifford, G. J. (1982). "Marry, stitch, die, or do worse": Educating women for work. In H. Kantor & D. Tyack (Eds.), *Work, youth, and schooling: Historical perspectives on vocationalism in American education* (pp. 223–268). Stanford, CA: Stanford University Press.

Colley, D. A., & Jamison, D. (1998). Post-school results for youth with disabilities: Key indicators and policy implications. *Career Development for Exceptional Individuals, 21,* 145–160.

Conant, J. B. (1959). *The American high school today: A first report to interested citizens.* New York, NY: McGraw-Hill.

DeLuca, C., Hutchinson, N. L., deLugt, J. S., Beyer, W., Thornton, A., Versnel, J., . . . Munby, H. (2010). Learning in the workplace: Fostering resilience in disengaged youth. *Work, 36,* 305–319.

Dewey, J. (1916). *Democracy and education: An introduction to the philosophy of education.* New York, NY: Macmillan.

Doren, B., Murray, C., & Gau, J. (2014). Salient predictors of school dropout among secondary students with learning disabilities. *Learning Disabilities Research & Practice, 29*(4), 150–159.

Dorn, S. (1996). *Creating the dropout: An institutional and social history of school failure.* Westport, CT: Praeger.

Dougherty, S. M. (2015, February). *The effect of career and technical education on human capital accumulation: Causal evidence from Massachusetts.* Paper presented at the Association for Education Finance and Policy annual conference, Washington, DC.

Dynarski, S. M., Hemelt, S. W., & Hyman, J. M. (2015). The missing manual using National Student Clearinghouse data to track postsecondary outcomes. *Educational Evaluation and Policy Analysis, 37*(Suppl. 1), 53S–79S.

Everson, J. M., Zhang, D., & Guillory, J. D. (2001). A statewide investigation of individualized transition plans in Louisiana. *Career Development for Exceptional Individuals, 24*(1), 37–49.

Every Student Succeeds Act of 2015. 20 U.S.C. § 6301.

Flannery, K. B., Lombardi, A., & Kato, M. M. (2015). The impact of professional development on the quality of the transition components of IEPs. *Career Development and Transition for Exceptional Individuals, 38,* 14–24.

Gamoran, A., & Mare, R. D. (1989). Secondary school tracking and educational inequality: Compensation, reinforcement, or neutrality? *American Journal of Sociology, 94,* 1146– 1183.

Goldin, C. (2006). *The quiet revolution that transformed women's employment, education, and family* (No. w11953). Cambridge, MA: National Bureau of Economic Research.

Goldin, C. D., & Katz, L. F. (2008). *The race between education and technology.* Cambridge, MA: Harvard University Press.

Goodman, J. I., Hazelkorn, M., Bucholz, J. L., Duffy, M. L., & Kitta, Y. (2011). Inclusion and graduation rates: What are the outcomes? *Journal of Disability Policy Studies, 21,* 241– 252.

Gregg, N. (2007). Underserved and unprepared: Postsecondary learning disabilities. *Learning Disabilities Research & Practice, 22,* 219–228.

Grubb, W. N., & Lazerson M. (1982). Education and the labor market: Recycling the youth problem. In H. Kantor & D. Tyack (Eds.), *Work, youth, and schooling: Historical perspectives on vocational education* (pp. 110–141). Stanford, CA: Stanford University Press.

Grubb, W. N., & Lazerson, M. (2004). *The education gospel: The economic power of schooling.* Cambridge, MA: Harvard University Press.

Grubb, W. N., & Lazerson, M. (2005). Vocationalism in higher education: The triumph of the education gospel. *Journal of Higher Education, 76,* 1–25.

Hall, C. (2012). The effects of reducing tracking in upper secondary school evidence from a large-scale pilot scheme. *Journal of Human Resources, 47,* 237–269.

Hall, C. W. (1973). *Black vocational technical and industrial arts education: Development and history.* Chicago, IL: American Technical Society.

Hanushek, E. A., Schwerdt, G., Woessmann, L., & Zhang, L. (2016). General education, vocational education, and labor-market outcomes over the life-cycle. *Journal of Human Resources.* Advance online publication. doi:10.3368/jhr.52.1.0415-7074R

Haxton, C., Song, M., Zeiser, K., Berger, A., Turk-Bicakci, L., Garet, M. S., . . . Hoshen, G. (2016). Longitudinal findings from the Early College High School Initiative Impact Study. *Educational Evaluation and Policy Analysis, 38,* 410–430.

Hoffman, N. (2011). *Schooling in the workplace.* Cambridge, MA: Harvard Education Press.

Holzer, H. J., Linn, D., & Monthey, W. (2013). *The promise of high-quality career and technical education: Improving outcomes for students, firms, and the economy.* New York, NY: The College Board.

Hoxby, C., & Turner, S. (2013). *Expanding college opportunities for high-achieving, low income students* (SIEPR Discussion Paper No. 12-014). Stanford, CA: Stanford Institute for Economic Policy Research.

Hutchinson, N. L., Versnel, J., Chin, P., & Munby, H. (2008). Negotiating accommodations so that work-based education facilitates career development for youth with disabilities. *Work, 30,* 123–136.

Jacoby, T., & Dougherty, S. M. (2016). *The new CTE: New York City as laboratory for America.* New York, NY: The Manhattan Institute.

Kanno, Y., & Cromley, J. G. (2013). English Language Learners' access to and attainment in postsecondary education. *TESOL Quarterly, 47,* 89–121.

Keim, R., Rak, C., & Fell, G. (1982). Career awareness and developmental model to prepare the handicapped for employment. *Journal of Career Development, 8,* 263–272.

Kemple, J., & Willner, C. J. (2008). *Career academies: Long-term impacts on labor market outcomes, educational attainment, and transitions to adulthood.* New York, NY: MDRC.

Kim, K. (2013). Career trajectory in high school dropouts. *Social Science Journal, 50,* 306–312.

Kolstoe, O. P. (1981). Career education for the handicapped: Opportunities for the '80s. *Career Development for Exceptional Individuals, 4,* 3–12.

Kopczuk, W., Saez, E., & Song, J. (2010). Earnings inequality and mobility in the United States: Evidence from social security data since 1937. *Quarterly Journal of Economics, 125,* 91–128.

Kupfer, A. (2010). The socio-political significance of changes to the vocational education system in Germany. *British Journal of Sociology of Education, 31,* 85–97.

Kurlaender, M., Huff-Stevens, A., & Gros, M. (2014, July). *Career technical education and labor market outcomes: Evidence from California community colleges.* Paper presented at the conference Building Human Capital and Economic Potential, Madison, WI.

Labaree, D. F. (1997). Public goods, private goods: The American struggle over educational goals. *American Educational Research Journal, 34,* 39–81.

Lazerson, M., & Grubb, W. N. (1974). *American education and vocationalism: A documentary history, 1870–1970.* New York, NY: Teachers College Press.

Lewis, T., & Cheng, S. Y. (2006). Tracking, expectations, and the transformation of vocational education. *American Journal of Education, 113,* 67–99.

Loveless, T. (1999). *The tracking wars: State reform meets school policy.* Washington, DC: Brookings Institution Press.

Martorell, P., & McFarlin, I., Jr. (2011). Help or hindrance? The effects of college remediation on academic and labor market outcomes. *Review of Economics and Statistics, 93,* 436–454.

Mishkind, A. (2014). *Definitions of college and career readiness: An analysis by state* (College and Career Readiness and Success Center). Washington, DC: American Institutes for Research.

Mueller, B., & Wolter, S. C. (2014). The role of hard-to-obtain information on ability for the school-to-work transition. *Empirical Economics, 46,* 1447–1471.

National Center for Education Statistics. (2013). *Trends in CTE coursetaking.* Retrieved from http://nces.ed.gov/pubs2014/2014901.pdf

National Governors Association & Council of Chief State School Officers. (2010). *Common Core State Standards.* Washington DC: Author.

Neubauer, A. (1986). Philadelphia high school academies. *Educational Horizons, 65,* 16–19.

Neumark, D., & Rothstein, D. (2006). School-to-career programs and transitions to employment and higher education. *Economics of Education Review, 25,* 374–393.

Newman, L., Wagner, M., Knokey, A. M., Marder, C., Nagle, K., Shaver, D., & Schwarting, M. (2011). *The post–high school outcomes of young adults with disabilities up to 8 years after high school: A report from the National Longitudinal Transition Study–2 (NLTS–2)*. Menlo Park, CA: SRI International.

Niemeyer, B. (2014). Working the boundaries between education and work: Transformations of the German educational system reconsidered. *Globalisation, Societies and Education, 12*, 391–402.

Oakes, J. (1983). Limiting opportunity: Student race and curricular differences in secondary vocational education. *American Journal of Education, 91*, 328–355.

Oakes, J. (1986). Beneath the bottom line: A critique of vocational education research. *Journal of Vocational Education Research, 11*(2), 33–50.

Oakes, J., & Guiton, G. (1995). Matchmaking: The dynamics of high school tracking decisions. *American Educational Research Journal, 32*(1), 3–33.

Oakes, J., Selvin, M., Karoly, L. A., & Guiton, G. (1992). *Educational matchmaking: Academic and vocational tracking in comprehensive high schools* (R-4189-NCRVE/UCB). Santa Monica, CA: RAND. Retrieved from http://www.rand.org/pubs/reports/R4189.html

Perkins Collaborative Resource Network. (n.d.). *Legislation: Every Student Succeeds Act (ESSA)*. Retrieved from http://cte.ed.gov/legislation/about-essa

Raffo, C. (2006). Disadvantaged young people accessing the new urban economies of the post-industrial city. *Journal of Education Policy, 21*, 75–94.

Rusch, F. R., Hughes, C., Agran, M., Martin, J. E., & Johnson, J. R. (2009). Toward self-directed learning, post–high school placement, and coordinated support constructing new transition bridges to adult life. *Career Development for Exceptional Individuals, 32*, 53–59.

Sanford, C., Newman, L., Wagner, M., Cameto, R., Knokey, A. M., & Shaver, D. (2011). *The post-high school outcomes of young adults with disabilities up to 6 years after high school: Key findings from the National Longitudinal Transition Study-2 (NLTS2)*. Menlo Park, CA: SRI International.

Santa Cruz, I., Siles, G., & Vrecer, N. (2011). Invest for the long term or attend to immediate needs? Schools and the employment of less educated youths and adults. *European Journal of Education, 46*, 197–208.

Sowers, J. A., & Powers, L. (1989). Preparing students with cerebral palsy and mental retardation for the transition from school to community-based employment. *Career Development for Exceptional Individuals, 12*, 25–35.

Stern, D. (1992). *Career academies: Partnerships for reconstructing American high schools* (Jossey-Bass Education Series). San Francisco: Jossey-Bass.

Stilwell, R., & Sable, J. (2013). *Public school graduates and dropouts from the Common Core of Data: School Year 2009–10: First look (provisional data)*. Washington, DC: National Center for Education Statistics.

Stuart, J. D. (2012). An examination of factors in adapting a technical and vocational education and training programme within South Africa. *Human Resource Development International, 15*, 249–257.

Tanzman, J. (1972). A new approach to the world of work. *School Management, 16*(11), 30–32.

Think College. (2016). *College options for people with intellectual disabilities*. Boston: Institute for Community Inclusion, University of Massachusetts, Boston.

Tyack, D. B. (1974). *The one best system: A history of American urban education* (Vol. 95). Cambridge, MA: Harvard University Press.

U.S. Department of Education. (2010a). *Blueprint for reform*. Retrieved from http://www2ed.gov/policy/elsec/leg/blueprint/index.html

U.S. Department of Education. (2010b). *Race to the Top Assessment Program*. Retrieved from http://www2.ed.gov/programs/racetothetop-assessment/index.html

Van Houtte, M., & Stevens, P. A. (2009). Study involvement of academic and vocational students: Does between-school tracking sharpen the difference? *American Educational Research Journal, 46*, 943–973.

Visher, M. G., & Stern, D. (2015). *New pathways to careers and college: Examples, evidence, and prospects.* Oakland, CA: MDRC. Retrieved from http://www.mdrc.org/sites/default/files/New_Pathways.pdf

Vlaardingerbroek, B., & El-Masri, Y. H. (2008). Student transition to upper secondary vocational and technical education (VTE) in Lebanon: From stigma to success. *Journal of Vocational Education & Training, 60*, 19–33.

Welton, A. D., & Martinez, M. A. (2013). Coloring the college pathway: A more culturally responsive approach to college readiness and access for students of color in secondary schools. *Urban Review, 46*, 197–223.

Wisniewski, L. A. (1991). Work-experience and work-study programs for students with special needs: Quality indicators of transition services. *Career Development for Exceptional Individuals, 14*, 43–58.

Wollschlager, N., & Reuter-Kumpmann, H. (2004). From divergence to convergence: A history of vocational education and training in Europe. *European Journal: Vocational Training, 32*, 6–17.

Xu, D., & Trimble, M. (2016). What about certificates? Evidence on the labor market returns to nondegree community college awards in two states. *Educational Evaluation and Policy Analysis, 38*, 272–292.

Yell, M. L. (2016). *The law and special education* (4th ed.). Boston, MA: Pearson.

Chapter 11

The Organization of Informal Learning

Barbara Rogoff
Maureen Callanan
University of California, Santa Cruz

Kris D. Gutiérrez
University of California, Berkeley

Frederick Erickson
University of California, Los Angeles

Informal learning is often treated as simply an alternative to formal, didactic instruction. This chapter discusses how the organization of informal learning differs across distinct settings but with important commonalities distinguishing informal learning from formal learning: Informal learning is nondidactic, is embedded in meaningful activity, builds on the learner's initiative or interest or choice (rather than resulting from external demands or requirements), and does not involve assessment external to the activity. The informal learning settings discussed all have learning and innovation as goals, and they all include guidance to newcomers through social interaction and/or the structure of activities. Along with the features in common, the organization of informal learning also differs in important ways across settings as distinct as everyday family and community engagements that are not organized around instruction; voluntary settings with an instructional focus, such as after-school programs; innovative schools that emphasize children's initiative and choice; children's "underground" informal learning in schools; and institutions such as science centers that have an instructional as well as a voluntary leisure focus. These informal learning settings differ in extent of focus on and ways of including play, instruction, collaborative or solo activity, contribution to "real" productive goals, and connection with a larger community.

Here is a thought experiment. In 1998, in her courageous and bodacious way, Dr. Diana Slaughter-Defoe[1] issued a call to action. It got the attention of the other participants in a planning meeting for the initiation of the Developmental and Learning Sciences unit of the National Science Foundation (NSF).

Review of Research in Education
March 2016, Vol. 40, pp. 356–401
DOI: 10.3102/0091732X16680994
© 2016 AERA. http://rre.aera.net

She asserted that in 75 years, schools would no longer exist, and therefore research should be focusing on how to foster the learning of coming generations, without schools. She supported this claim with the observation that many people were learning a great deal via the Internet without needing a teacher as an intermediary or tests to motivate or assess them.[2] She also observed the growing interest and involvement in home schooling and charter schools, and a turn to private religious schools among various populations.

Once the participants had gotten over their shock at this idea, a lively discussion ensued. Participants chimed in with other evidence for her claim. They noted that mass, compulsory schooling had been in existence in the United States for only about a century and that it had been based in part on a model stemming from the organization of early factories, at the turn of the 20th century. The participants noted dramatic societal changes in the organization of work as well as access to information over the 20th century, with all signs suggesting a trajectory of rapid transformation in children's opportunities for learning continuing into the 21st century.[3]

In this chapter, we address Slaughter-Defoe's call to consider how children's learning can be supported, by examining the organization of several forms of informal learning. We believe that considering a variety of ways of organizing informal learning will provide inspiration for expanding the ways of supporting children's learning, both in schools and out. In particular, informal learning can provide guidance for getting beyond the factory model that has prevailed in schools in the 20th century and into the 21st century.

Even if schools themselves remain a societal institution, articulating other ways of supporting children's learning can develop a deeper conceptual understanding of learning itself. In addition, articulation of alternative approaches can provide practical ideas for improving the ways that society organizes support for children's learning. What is known about learning in informal settings can be instructive for new forms of learning and their organization in a range of learning environments, including schools as well as the out-of-school settings of children's lives, which provide learning opportunities during about 81% of U.S. children's waking hours (LIFE Center, Stevens, Bransford, & Stevens, 2005, from the NSF Center for Learning in Informal and Formal Environments).

WHAT *IS* INFORMAL LEARNING?
ISSUES OF LABELS AND DEFINITIONS

Researchers and practitioners involved in formal learning have perennially discussed their dissatisfaction with the label "informal" and with not having a single agreed-on definition of informal learning.

Regarding the common lament regarding the label "informal learning," we agree with the critics that it is unfortunate that this label does not focus on the processes involved but rather identifies these ways of learning as what they are *not*—"formal." However, no better alternative umbrella term for the various forms of informal learning has surfaced.

Often, informal learning has been defined simply as learning that occurs outside of schools. However, we believe that *how* learning is organized and supported is more important than *where* learning occurs. After all, schools themselves can be organized in informal ways (which we discuss later), and many settings outside of schools employ the factory model of instruction that is often found in schools (such as when parents didactically control children's learning).

The question "What IS informal learning?" often dominates discussions among informal learning researchers and practitioners. How is informal learning organized? What are its key features? The U.S. public can probably describe many aspects of how classroom instruction is organized, and in little children's pretend play, their portrayal of school uses the common, recognizable script, even among children attending an innovative school (Rogoff, Goodman Turkanis, & Bartlett, 2001). But there is little such awareness of the common features of informal learning. Indeed, the processes of informal learning are often taken for granted, perhaps in part because people do not have to work hard to learn in informal learning settings, unlike in factory model schooling (Paradise, 1998; Paradise & Rogoff, 2009). Informal learning can be "second nature" (Paradise & Rogoff, 2009), along the lines of children learning their first language. At the same time, informal learning can be an important part of designed settings that share a common view of learning and its organization.

The organization of informal learning has some shared features across many settings: It is nondidactic; is embedded in meaningful activity; builds on the learner's initiative, interest, or choice (rather than resulting from external demands or requirements); and does not involve assessment external to the activity. The informal learning settings examined in this chapter also all include guidance for learners, orienting them through social interaction and/or the structure of activities (to which the newcomers also contribute), and all include innovation of new knowledge and skills as well as learning of current knowledge and skills.

In addition to examining the common features by which informal learning is organized, we discuss the different ways of organizing informal learning in distinct settings—everyday family and community settings that are not organized around instruction; voluntary settings that have an instructional focus, such as after-school programs; innovative schools that emphasize children's initiative and choice; children's "underground" informal learning in schools; and institutional settings that have an instructional as well as a voluntary leisure focus, such as science centers. Informal learning in these settings differs in how and how much it includes play, instruction, collaborative or solo activity, contributions to "real" productive goals, and connections with a larger community. Who participates in these settings also tends to differ.

WHO ENGAGES IN INFORMAL LEARNING? CHILDREN AND ADULTS OF ALL BACKGROUNDS

In this chapter, we focus on the organization of children's informal learning with adults, although clearly, an enormous amount of informal learning occurs solo (Schugurensky, 2000) as well as in interactions *among* children and among adults. For example, children's games are passed down from children to children across centuries, and children's peer groups are the site of much learning about gender roles, interpersonal politics, and language (Goodwin, 1991; Opie & Opie, 1959).

Similarly, adult–adult informal learning contributes to a great deal of the learning in workplaces and in family groups. The importance of informal learning is recognized in U.S. industry and work teams and is the basis for many self-help groups as well as casual conversations among adults. Adult–adult informal learning encompasses a full range of information and skills, including scientific knowledge, pedagogy, language skills, parenting approaches, personal and spiritual development, medical support for oneself and one's family members, work skills, and how to get access to community resources.

For example, in two support groups of immigrant Latina mothers in North Carolina, the women exchanged advice, shared recipes and information on traditional medicine, and collectively used their personal life experiences as the basis for learning; as they engaged in projects, they chatted about where to get a good deal or how to download an upcoming episode of a *telenovela*. As one mother recounted,

Everyone can relax, can express herself, and you can say, "Do you all know where they do this or that? Someone called me and they asked me this. Does anyone know how this is done?" And so we proceed sharing information. (Fitts & McClure, 2015, p. 303)

Similarly, a group of Latina mothers in Texas shared their knowledge of herbs and traditional gardening methods—as well as information about how this knowledge was incorporated in schools in Latin America—with each other and with receptive teachers, who integrated their new knowledge into science, literacy, and social studies assignments (Bonilla, 2014).

A few other examples of informal learning among adults: African American women in a beauty parlor discussed personal experiences and current events, bringing newcomers into the rhetorically powerful and carefully reasoned sociolinguistic repertoire needed to participate appropriately in such conversations (Majors, 2015). In a Guatemalan weaving factory, novice adult weavers observed skilled weavers using a foot loom and began to weave when they felt confident after weeks of simply watching, listening to pointers volunteered by the skilled weaver, and helping with peripheral aspects of weaving such as fetching thread (Nash, 1967). When traditional Yucatecan (Mexican) women learn about aiding in childbirth through their problem-solving discussions of difficult cases with each other, their explanations are in the service of the ongoing activity, rather than lengthy explanations outside the context of the activity, as often occurs in didactic situations (Jordan, 1989).

Informal learning is organized similarly whether it occurs among adults, among children, or between children and adults:

- Informal learning is interactive and embedded in meaningful activity.
- Guidance is available to learners and their partners through social interaction and the structure of activities.

- Talk is conversational, not didactic.
- Involvement builds on individual initiative, interest, and choice.
- Assessment occurs in support of contributing to the activity, not for external purposes.
- Participants hone their existing knowledge and skills and also innovate, developing new ideas and skills.

Along with these common features that organize informal learning are important differences across settings:

- The extent to which they focus on play
- The extent to which they involve contributions to "real" productive goals
- The extent of focus on instruction or guidance
- The extent of role differentiation among participants
- The extent to which activities have collaborative versus individual goals
- The connection of the immediate activity with a larger community
- The specific cultural practices and topics of interest of the cultural communities engaged in the setting

WHO ENGAGES IN INFORMAL LEARNING? IT DEPENDS ON WHERE

This chapter discusses commonalities and distinctions in the organization of informal learning in quite different settings. We first examine key aspects of fostering learning in children's productive involvement in everyday family and community settings that are not organized around instruction. Next, we consider informal learning within compulsory schooling, in some innovative schools that emphasize children's initiative and choice and in children's "underground" informal learning in schools. We then turn to informal learning through voluntary involvement in settings that include an instructional focus, such as after-school programs. Finally, we examine key aspects of informal learning in leisure institutions that are voluntary, not compulsory, but have instructional goals, such as science centers. In each of these settings, we highlight how opportunities to learn are organized and fostered by adults and by the organization of the institutions and society itself.

The question "Who is involved in informal learning?" has both a general answer ("Everybody") and a specific answer ("It depends on the setting"). Adult–child informal learning settings vary in terms of which cultural, ethnic, and social class populations are more likely to be involved. These differences revolve around community and societal organization, especially in terms of which children are likely to be present and validated in the different informal learning settings.

Everyday family and community settings that are not designed around instruction. The voluminous literature on informal learning in children's productive involvement in everyday family and community settings not organized around instruction focuses especially on children in small face-to-face communities where children are involved in the wide range of community activities (Lancy, 2015; Rogoff, 2003). Children in such communities have more opportunities for informal learning because of their greater inclusion along with adults in the range of endeavors, although children everywhere can be involved in informal learning when they are included in the activities of their families and communities.

However, there may be differences across populations in the extent to which inclusion in family and community endeavors has the organization that we have described as characterizing informal learning. Specifically, research worldwide is not yet sufficient to determine whether the inclusion of children in family and community endeavors is collaborative and based on children's voluntariness and initiative, as has been found in Indigenous and Indigenous-heritage communities of the Americas (Alcalá, Rogoff, Mejía-Arauz, Coppens, & Dexter, 2014; Coppens, Alcalá, Mejía-Arauz, & Rogoff, 2014; Coppens, Alcalá, Rogoff, & Mejía-Arauz, 2016; de León, 2015; García, 2015; Lorente Fernández, 2015; Paradise & Rogoff, 2009). Further research is needed to examine whether children's collaborative initiative is characteristic of children's inclusion in informal learning in family and community endeavors in other communities, such as Indigenous-heritage communities on other continents, or other communities that include children in the range of family and community endeavors.

Innovative schools. Involvement in the other informal learning settings on which we focus also varies in who tends to be involved. Participation in innovative schools that emphasize children's initiative and choice within compulsory schooling probably varies with social class and ethnicity, although some innovative schools that allow for children's initiative and choice target children from underserved minority backgrounds (e.g., Brown & Campione, 1990; McCarty; 2002; Moll & Whitmore, 1993; Tharp & Gallimore; 1988).

Children's "underground" informal learning in schools. This kind of informal learning in schools likely occurs in all classrooms. However, it may be especially common in classrooms that are not organized collaboratively among adults and children.

After-school programs. The structure of after-school programs varies, and participation in after-school programs organized around informal learning varies based on such demographic features as whether a child's mother is employed full-time and whether the family has resources to choose after-school programs that are conducive to children wanting to be there (Cole & the Distributed Literacy Consortium, 2006).

Institutional settings that have an instructional as well as voluntary leisure focus, such as science centers and museums. Visits to museums are a common feature of everyday life for some families but not for others. In fact, while many modern museums engage in vigorous outreach to attract broad participation, visitors to most museums continue to be largely White (Levitt, 2015) and middle-class. This varies depending on the type of museum and the community context, however. Some individual museums have been successful in developing partnerships with local communities to better welcome visitors from diverse backgrounds (Farrell & Medvedeva, 2010; Stein, Garibay, & Wilson, 2008). In addition, teachers and students in school groups that visit science centers are more diverse, and programs designed for inclusion of children and youth from diverse backgrounds have been successful (Huerta Migus, 2015).

In focusing on the organization of informal learning in settings where children engage with adults, we believe that the insights available from these settings can transform the understanding of learning itself. In addition, the insights can help address ways that children's learning can be supported, to go beyond the factory model that has prevailed in formal schooling throughout the 20th century. We turn now to consider how learning is promoted in family and community settings that are not designed for instruction.

FOSTERING LEARNING IN CHILDREN'S PRODUCTIVE INVOLVEMENT IN EVERYDAY FAMILY AND COMMUNITY SETTINGS

For millennia, children have learned the skills, life ways, and philosophies of their communities informally, through their engagement in everyday family and community settings. Their elders may be generally interested in children learning through such informal modes of socialization. However, the immediate focus is not so much on instruction as on accomplishing the productive goal of the activity at hand, such as harvesting the corn or creating the computer program, organizing the festival or the club play, or persuading the authorities or writing the grant proposal. Learning occurs almost "by osmosis" (Azuma, 1994) in a purposeful incidental fashion while children are engaged with others in accomplishing a shared activity. This form of learning is ubiquitous, though often overlooked, including in societies with extensive Western schooling.

In this section, we first review the historical development of research interest in informal learning in family and community life. Much of the scholarship on this form of learning emerged as researchers (especially anthropologists) took note of the skills and activities of children in cultural communities other than their own, in places where schooling has not been prevalent.

Following this historical account of informal learning in family and community life, we turn to research and scholarship that further articulate the specific ways that this form of informal learning is structured. What are the key features of children's informal learning in families and communities? The second and third parts of this section discuss ethnographic and comparative characterizations of learning in communities where informal learning or Western schooling is prevalent. Completing the section is an examination of several conceptual frameworks that propose principles that underlie the contrasts between informal community learning and formal schooling.

The Historical Development of Ethnographies of Informal Childhood Learning

Research on informal learning first developed in ethnographic studies in small face-to-face communities, about a century ago. Thus, the study of informal learning approximately shares its time of origin with the American Educational Research Association and with the first Committee in Child Development at the National Academy of Sciences.

In the 1800s, studies of whole communities—"general ethnography"—did not include specific reference to child rearing or informal teaching and learning. The guide for observational field research, first published in England in 1874 by the British Association for the Advancement of Science, titled *Notes and Queries on Anthropology*, contained topic lists and questions for informants covering both physical anthropology and what would later be called cultural anthropology. But these did not focus on childhood.

In the second edition, this pattern continued (Garson & Read, 1892): Section 39 concerns initiation ceremonies; Section 66 concerns "education." In the latter section, education—considered as "training"—is discussed briefly and only in very general terms:

Education in its widest sense means training. . . . Physical training begins in early childhood, and those children's games which mimic the employments of their elders form a kind of education, later, when the youths associate with the men more serious instruction commences. Ordeals which lads, and sometimes girls, have to undergo at puberty, or before receiving full standing as adults or as warriors, though employed as tests of bravery and endurance, constitute a short but sharp training. (Garson & Read, 1892, p. 218)

It was not until the 1920s that ethnographers began to present specific descriptions of what and how children learned. This seems to have been due to three main influences from the early years of the 20th century. The first of these was the child study movement (e.g., Stern, 1911), which focused on childhood and children's development as a topic of scientific interest and of public policy concern. (By the mid-1920s, child development research centers had been established at universities throughout the United States, including at Yale, Iowa, Minnesota, and Berkeley.)

A second influence came from Freudian psychodynamic theory, which identified early childhood experience as an important influence on later personality development. (Freudian and other approaches to psychotherapy became increasingly well known in the 1920s.)

A third influence, from within American anthropology, came from the culture theory of Franz Boas and his students. Boas made strong claims for the shaping influence of culture and the importance of culture difference—the priority of nurture over nature. We learned to be human, he and his students argued, in culturally differing ways, and this warranted more detailed ethnographic attention to processes and contents of childhood socialization than had been the case in earlier observational research.

The first monograph-length study of informal learning was authored by Margaret Mead, a student of Boas. Titled *Coming of Age in Samoa: A Psychological Study of Primitive Youth for Western Civilization* (Mead, 1928), this was a study of adolescence that argued that what in Western societies was considered an inherently turbulent stage of development, marked by anxiety and conflict concerning sexuality, need not be a time of emotional upheaval. Adolescent sexual exploration could be stress-free and guilt-free, and indeed that was the case among the adolescent girls in Samoa that Mead had studied. It was culture that produced the turmoil of adolescence in modern Western societies, as Boas observed in his preface to the book.

Mead's study was widely read and was both controversial and influential. Published in the years after World War I, as deep doubts arose about what previously had been assumed to be the superiority of Western civilization, as Freud's critique of rationality was receiving increasing attention, and as the postwar generation of parents in America were wondering about the validity of their child-rearing practices (which their children were rebelling against), Mead's book touched nerves in both popular culture and social science.

Connections between anthropology and psychiatry increased in the 1930s, continuing in the years following World War II. Ruth Benedict (1934), Cora DuBois (1944), and their students were influenced by the psychiatrist Abram Kardner, among others. John Whiting published a monograph on child rearing in New Guinea titled *Becoming a Kwoma* (J. W. M. Whiting, 1940) that included close behavioral descriptions of child-rearing activity.

It became more and more common for general ethnographic reports to include a chapter on child rearing and/or childhood experience. For example, Firth's classic ethnography *We the Tikopia* (Firth, 1936) included a separate chapter on "household and family," followed by one on "personal relations in the family circle." Gregory Bateson and Margaret Mead (1942) used still photography and cinema film to show in great behavioral detail the teaching of dance to youth in Bali.

A subfield of "culture and personality" research developed in anthropology, attempting to discover general causal relations between specific early child-rearing practices (e.g., weaning and toilet training) and the development of adult temperamental dispositions, contrasting the consequences of severe practices with indulgent ones. These correlational studies were magisterially presented in a volume that appeared in the early 1950s, titled *Child Training and Personality* (J. W. M. Whiting & Child, 1953).

In 1954, George Spindler convened a conference on "anthropology and education" at Stanford University, and informal teaching and learning in settings outside school figured prominently in the papers and discussion at that meeting (Spindler, 1955). However, the focus of such informal education was primarily the socialization of temperament rather than informal cognition or development of skills.

In the late 1950s and early 1960s, the husband-and-wife team of John and Beatrice Whiting directed a large-scale comparative study of childhood socialization, based on yearlong visits by ethnographers to six small communities around the world, in the

Philippines, Kenya, Mexico, Japan, India, and the United States (B. B. Whiting & Whiting, 1975). A primary conclusion of the study was that latency (late childhood/ early adolescence) was a time in which older siblings were disposed to care for their younger siblings and tended to be given that responsibility by parents.

But the overall program of the "culture and personality" school faltered as time went on. By the mid-1960s it was apparent that clear patterns of correlation between early child-rearing practices and adult temperament could not be established—there were too many exceptions appearing empirically to the generalizations that were theoretically posited.

Moreover, new interests had developed in language and cognition and these began to influence the study of informal teaching and learning. Following the "cognitive turn" in psychology, cross-cultural studies began to focus on the socialization of specific aspects of thinking—for example, the work on memory and cognition by Sylvia Scribner and Mike Cole (1973, 1981), Jean Lave's (1977, 2011) research on the mathematics of tailoring, and Patricia Greenfield and Carla Childs's (1977) study of perceptual development in weaving. Much of this early work focused on how well people did on cognitive tests, but there was a growing interest in the socialization of learning.

Accompanying a "linguistic turn" in anthropology was growing interest in the ethnographic study of culturally differing ways of speaking—language function in language use (Gumperz & Hymes, 1964)—such as the talk of African American teenagers (Labov, 1972; Smitherman, 1977) and code-switching between one language and another (Gumperz & Hernandez-Chavez, 1971). However, the socialization processes by which these speech styles were learned were not the direct focus of the early ethnographers of speaking. An exception in one of the early studies was Albert's (1964) description of adolescent males in Burundi who rehearsed culturally valued oratorical practices as they stood on hillsides tending herds of cattle.

Soon ethnographers began to focus on socialization processes. Susan Philips (1972, 1983) reported on the childhood socialization of culturally distinctive ways of speaking by Native American children and the conflicts between those ways and what was expected by nonnative teachers in elementary school classrooms. Erickson and Mohatt (1982) extended that work, showing how a Native American early-grades teacher used "community" ways of speaking in her teaching and allowed students in her classroom to speak and interact in the stylistic ways they had learned at home. Heath (1983), in an influential study titled *Ways With Words*, also reported on the family socialization of speech styles in three communities in the Carolinas, to which early-grades teachers reacted differently in school classrooms.

Focusing even more directly on socialization processes, Ochs and Schieffelin (1984) studied in detail how culturally distinctive ways of speaking were socialized in interaction taking place between parents and children and among siblings (see also Schieffelin, 1990). Watson-Gegeo and Boggs (1977) discussed children's acquisition of a Hawaiian adult speech routine called "talk story."

Through their ethnographic studies of socialization of cognition and language in this era and since then, researchers often contrasted the family and community emphases on informal means of supporting children's learning with the ways that schooling was often organized. Research focusing on informal learning in communities where Western schooling is not prevalent has provided opportunities to see many taken-for-granted aspects of "informal" as well as "formal" learning (i.e., the way learning is often organized in Western schooling). The next section examines key features that have been identified in the socialization processes used in informal learning in family and community settings.

Ethnographic Characterizations of Informal Learning in Communities Where Schooling Has Not Been Prevalent

Some of the earliest descriptions of informal learning are quite compelling and informative, such as those of Meyer Fortes and Margaret Mead. In his classic 1938 account of learning among the Tallensi of Ghana, Fortes contrasted the form of instruction that occurs in "real situations" with formal school instruction, in which the utility of the information is often unknown:

A child repeating the multiplication table is participating in the practical activity appropriate to and defined by the school; but measured by the total social reality it is a factitious activity, a training situation constructed for that purpose. The Tallensi do not make systematic use of training situations. They teach through real situations which children are drawn to participate in because it is expected that they are capable and desirous of mastering the necessary skills. . . . Learning becomes purposive. Every advance in knowledge or skill is pragmatic, directed to achieve a result there and then, as well as adding to a previous level of adequacy. (Fortes, 1938/1970, pp. 37–38)

In any given social situation everybody takes it for granted that any person participating either already knows, or wants to know, how to behave in a manner appropriate to the situation and in accordance to his level of maturity. An effort to learn is thus evoked as an adaptation to the demands of a real situation. (Fortes, 1938/1970, p. 35)

Mead (1970) characterized traditional informal educational practices as taking for granted that children desire to learn ("steal" knowledge), in communities where children participate similarly in the same activities as other members of the community. She contrasted this with the organization of learning in Western schooling, in which adults wish to teach ("proselytize").

There are several striking differences . . . but perhaps the most important one is the shift from the need for an individual to learn something which everyone agrees he would wish to know, to the will of some individual to teach something that it is not agreed that anyone has any desire to know. (p. 3)

Many ethnographers have provided in-depth analyses of the type of informal learning they observed in families and communities and have especially emphasized the importance of observing and listening in on ongoing family and community activities (e.g., Bolin, 2006; Briggs, 1970; Cazden & John, 1971; Chisholm, 1996; Driver & Driver, 1963; Gaskins, 2000; Paradise, 1996; Philips, 1983; Rogoff, 1990;

Romney & Romney, 1966; Urrieta, 2013; Wilbert, 1979). For example, Navajo daughters learn to weave by being included in their mothers' weaving work, keenly watching. Their mothers do not teach them, "but one day a girl may say, 'I am ready. Let me weave'" (Collier, 1988, p. 262).

In an Athabascan (native Northern Canadian) community,

the ideal learning situation for a child or young person is to be able to hear the stories of elders. The ideal situation described is that of elders speaking to each other as narrator and audience with the child in a third, observational role. . . . Because the child is not directly required to respond to the narratives, his own autonomy is respected at a time in his life when it is likely to be highly vulnerable. While this three-party narrative situation may not always obtain, those who are able to learn in this way are regarded as very fortunate. (Scollon & Scollon, 1981, pp. 120–121)

Athabascan children also learn how to participate in complex narratives by solving riddles and learning to guess meanings in situations that require reading between the lines, anticipating outcomes, and communicating indirectly (Scollon & Scollon, 1981).

The importance of listening in on everyday conversation and "absorption in community life" for toddlers' language learning in an African American community in Louisiana was emphasized by Ward (1971, p. 37). Heath (1983) similarly reported that African American toddlers in a working-class community were always in the company of others and expected to be keen listeners and observers. At first they echoed and experimented with variations on the speech around them and were ignored, but gradually they began to participate in conversation.

Listening to everyday conversation and observing are similarly important in Kaluli language learning in Polynesia. Mothers encourage toddlers to take notice of ongoing events, and when engaging in a task they show the toddlers how it is to be done, without extensive explanation (Schieffelin, 1990).

The verbal environment of these children is rich and varied, and from the beginning, infants are surrounded by adults and older children who spend a great deal of time talking to each other. . . . [Toddlers'] actions are referred to, described, and commented upon by members of the household, especially older children, speaking to one another. . . . This talk about the activities and interests of toddlers is available for the toddlers to hear, though it is not addressed to or formulated for them. (Schieffelin, 1990, p. 73)

Ethnographic observations of informal learning, especially in Native American and Japanese settings, indicate that verbal explanations occur, but within the context of engaging in and supporting the process that is being learned (Cazden & John, 1971; de León, 2015; John-Steiner, 1984; Jordan, 1989; Kojima, 1986). In the words of Paradise and Rogoff (2009), "Guiding and directing comments augment rather than replace firsthand learning through observation and participation" (p. 120).

Storytelling, advising children on how to act, and correcting children with teasing are important forms of informal learning in many communities. These skilled verbal forms are contextualized, unlike explanations that occur outside the context of action. In storytelling, the setting and the drama of the story create the context;

when advising children (e.g., providing *consejos*), this is often done in the context of a concern raised by recent events (Delgado-Gaitan, 1994; Knight, Norton, Bentley, & Dixon, 2004; Valdes, 1996); in correcting children with teasing (*instructional ribbing*; Silva & Rogoff, 2016), a lighthearted comment draws the child's attention to misbehavior in the same moment and social context in which it arose (Eisenberg, 1986; Miller, 1982).

Comparisons of the Form of Interaction in Communities in Which Informal Learning or Western Schooling Is Prevalent

A number of studies have systematically compared the forms of interaction that are common in communities where informal learning is prevalent with the forms of interaction in communities in which extensive Western schooling has occurred for generations, such as middle-class European American communities. The findings have shown similarities in use of some informal learning processes as well as many important differences across such communities.

Some aspects of informal learning are common in all populations, including in highly schooled families. As parents and children converse, they adjust their ways of communicating in trying to reach mutual understanding, even in the simplest of interactions. This "mutual bridging of meanings" (Rogoff, 2003) provides opportunities to learn about language, communication, and the activity at hand but not necessarily with an intent to instruct. For example, in guiding children to produce culturally valued narratives, middle-class European American mothers encourage children's lengthy narratives, whereas Japanese mothers encourage children to produce concise accounts that trust listeners to make inferences (Minami & McCabe, 1995).

Structuring children's participation is also a ubiquitous feature of informal learning (Rogoff, 2003; B. B. Whiting, 1980). Children as well as adults determine what sorts of situations children are allowed or required to participate in. They determine whether children are present in family or community workplaces, whether children spend their days in preschools and schools, whether bedtime includes a story book, and what sorts of "screen time" are allowed and available. While engaging in activities together, children and adults also structure the extent and type of help provided to the learner.

Many other features of informal learning vary in prevalence and emphasis in different communities, and they often differ between homes and schools. Some common features of parent–child interaction in highly schooled European American families (and expected in textbooks on child development) are uncommon in many other communities around the world.

Middle-class parents often try to engage young children in mini lessons, shaping their behavior step by step and employing mock excitement and praise to motivate them (Dixon, LeVine, Richman, & Brazelton, 1984; Metge, 1984; Rogoff, Mejía-Arauz, & Correa-Chávez, 2015; Rogoff, Mistry, Göncü, & Mosier, 1993; B. B.

Whiting, 1996). In contrast, children who join in their family's ongoing work can see the importance as well as the success or failure of their efforts, without commentary; approval may be shown by allowing a child to engage in more difficult work or with less supervision (Jordan, 1989; B. B. Whiting & Edwards, 1988).

Highly schooled, middle-class U.S. adults often adapt conversation to child-centered topics, negotiating meaning and responding to children's initiations. In contrast, in Kaluli (New Guinean) and Samoan families, adults expect children to adapt to mature situations (Ochs & Schieffelin, 1984). Conversations focus on the activities of adults, with children joining mature activities, rather than adults becoming peers with children in child-focused conversations (Morelli, Rogoff, & Angelillo, 2003).

Studies of learning in communities where schooling and associated practices have not been prevalent often remark on the keen attention of the children, in comparison with children from communities where extensive schooling has been common for generations (Chavajay & Rogoff, 1999; Paradise & Rogoff, 2009; Rogoff et al., 1993). Young rural Senegalese children observed other people more than twice as much as middle-class European American children (Bloch, 1989). Guatemalan Mayan children attended closely to a nearby demonstration that did not include them, and so did Mexican-heritage U.S. children from traditional backgrounds, but European American and Mexican-heritage children from families with extensive Western schooling paid less attention to the nearby opportunity to learn (Correa-Chávez & Rogoff, 2009; López, Correa-Chávez, Rogoff, & Gutiérrez, 2010; Silva, Correa-Chávez, & Rogoff, 2010; Silva, Shimpi, & Rogoff, 2015).

These studies of children's attentiveness are accompanied by observations of cultural differences in their collaborative initiative in contributing to family endeavors (de Haan, 1999; López, Najafi, Rogoff, & Mejía-Arauz, 2012; Paradise & Rogoff, 2009). In family household work, Mexican children from families with Indigenous backgrounds generally show initiative in helping out collaboratively, whereas children from highly schooled families in Mexico and the United States often provide minimal help in family work, and when they do help, it is often under the control of adults who attempt to motivate them (Alcalá et al., 2014; Coppens et al., 2014; Coppens et al., 2016; Mejía-Arauz, Correa-Chávez, Keyser Ohrt, & Aceves-Azuara, 2015). In addition, very flexible, collaborative approaches with adults and with other children have been noted among Guatemalan Mayan, Navajo, and U.S. Mexican-heritage children from Indigenous backgrounds, compared with children from families with extensive Western schooling and associated practices (Alcalá & Rogoff, 2016; Chavajay & Rogoff, 2002; Ellis & Gauvain, 1992: López & Rogoff, 2016; Mejía-Arauz, Rogoff, Dexter, & Najafi, 2007; Ruvalcaba & Rogoff, 2016).

As can be seen, comparisons of communities in which informal learning or Western schooling is prevalent have found a number of differences in the ways that adults and children interact. Several teams of scholars have made progress in systematizing the features characterizing the kind of informal learning that is common in families and communities, especially in Indigenous-heritage communities.

Conceptual Frameworks Contrasting Key Features
of Informal Community Learning and Formal Schooling

Several frameworks have provided systematic articulations of the processes of informal learning in families and communities and contrasted them with the processes of Western schooling. Although the contrast is often made in seemingly dichotomous ways, informal learning and formal learning are not opposing approaches; individuals can and often do learn in more than one way, and any community employs multiple approaches (Greenfield & Lave, 1982; Maynard & Martini, 2005; Paradise & Rogoff, 2009; Scribner & Cole, 1973).

The conceptual frameworks overlap a great deal, perhaps because they generally rely on the same or similar ethnographic accounts and refer to each other. However, some differences between them may stem from differences between the communities where the specific authors have done their fieldwork.

Two early frameworks—Scribner and Cole (1973) and Greenfield and Lave (1982)—contrasted ethnographies of informal learning around the world (especially Latin America and Africa) with formal schooling. A more recent framework (Rogoff, 2014; Rogoff, Paradise, Mejía Arauz, Correa-Chávez, & Angelillo, 2003; Rogoff, Moore, Correa-Chávez, & Dexter, 2014) focuses on contrasts between a way of organizing learning that appears to be common in Indigenous-heritage communities of the Americas—Learning by Observing and Pitching In (LOPI)—and a more didactic way of organizing instruction that is common in schools—Assembly-Line Instruction (ALI).

Scribner and Cole's Framework

Scribner and Cole (1973) emphasized that school learning relies almost exclusively on language, especially language used out of the context of practical activities and concrete referents, whereas informal learning heavily employs demonstration without stating rules or principles. Scribner and Cole contrasted schooling's focus on instruction with informal learning's engagement in activities that are not "set aside solely to 'educate the child'" (p. 555). Furthermore, they indicated that, whereas schooling focuses primarily on cognition, in informal education, intellectual and emotional domains are fused.

It is worth noting, however, that one speculation reported by Scribner and Cole has not held up to scrutiny: At the time, many scholars erroneously assumed that informal learning would be conservative and traditionalist. But schooling does not lead to more generalized and creative use of knowledge than informal learning (Paradise & Rogoff, 2009; Scribner & Cole, 1981).

Greenfield and Lave's Framework

Greenfield and Lave (1982) described informal education as being embedded in observation and imitation of everyday life activities, with relatives demonstrating activities without (or with rare) explicit curriculum or pedagogy but with the goal of helping children learn to contribute to the family or their own welfare. They described formal education, in contrast, as taking place in institutional settings that are removed from everyday life, with specialized personnel presenting principles using a highly systematized and verbal curriculum and pedagogy that focuses on training as an end in itself.

Certain consequences would follow from those contrasts, according to Greenfield and Lave (1982). In informal education, the learner is likely to be highly motivated by the opportunity to make a genuine contribution to the family, through close participation and interaction in the sphere of adults, and by the assumption, shared with family and neighbors, that it is normal to learn the skill or information at hand. In contrast, in formal education, these are not sources of motivation: "Learning a multiplication table is not going to have immediate practical consequences for anybody" (p. 184).

Greenfield and Lave (1982) also discussed the complexities of whether informal education is oriented to preserving tradition rather than to encouraging change and innovation. According to Rosado-May, Urrieta, Dayton, and Rogoff (in press), this is not generally the case—for example, informal learning in Mayan communities includes innovating knowledge and skills, in order to contribute the resulting innovations for the benefit of the community.

Learning by Observing and Pitching In

LOPI—Learning by Observing and Pitching In to the activities of the family and community—is a conceptual framework developed by Rogoff and colleagues (Rogoff, 2014; Rogoff et al., 2003; Rogoff et al., 2007; Rogoff et al., 2015; Rogoff, Moore, et al., 2014; Paradise & Rogoff, 2009). Although LOPI likely occurs everywhere, it appears to be particularly central to the organization of learning in Indigenous-heritage communities of North and Central America and parts of South America. The LOPI framework bears some similarities with prior efforts to articulate the organization of informal learning in families, but it differs in some important ways, some of which may be particular to Indigenous communities of the Americas.

LOPI may also be common in locales other than the Americas, but Rogoff and colleagues call for empirical examination of patterns before generalizing worldwide. Other informal education approaches may be more common in other parts of the world. For example, LOPI's emphasis on keen observation occurs on many other continents, but its emphasis on collaboration and flexible leadership seems distinct from ethnographic reports from some other continents.

The seven facets of the LOPI prism contrast with the seven facets of Assembly-Line Instruction (Rogoff, 2014; Rogoff et al., 2015). It is important to note that ALI is not the same as schooling, although it often appears in that setting. LOPI and ALI are not opposites but two different systems (among many) with informative contrasts. Rogoff (2016) has argued that LOPI and ALI represent two distinct paradigms, reflected in each of the seven facets of the two approaches.

Facet 1 deals with the community organization of learning. In Learning by Observing and Pitching In, the community includes children and adults in the wide range of endeavors of families and the community, with children being contributors in the same "world" as adults, working for common goals.

In Assembly-Line Instruction, children are segregated for instruction into a bureaucratically controlled setting, apart from the ordinary activities of the community, creating a child world separate from adults.

Facet 2 deals with learners' motivation in the learning situation. In LOPI, children are interested in contributing to and being part of valued activities of their families and communities; other people are trying to accomplish a productive goal and may or may not regard guiding children as part of their purpose in the endeavor.

In ALI, the learner is motivated by extrinsic rewards (or by trying to avoid threats); an expert's primary goal of instructing includes sorting learners.

Facet 3 deals with the social organization of immediate face-to-face groups. In LOPI, groups engage collaboratively as an ensemble, with flexible leadership and fluid coordination among people; anyone may take initiative as they see a way to contribute.

In ALI, the organization of the group is unilateral—the expert controls the learner's pace, attention, and motivation in the attempt to "transmit" information; the expert divides the labor and does not collaborate with learners in the assigned tasks.

Facet 4 deals with the overall goal of learning. In LOPI, the overall goal is for learners to transform their participation in order to enhance their contributions and role in the community. The goal of learning includes learning to collaborate with consideration and innovation, as well as gaining task-specific information and skills.

In ALI, the overall goal is to transmit isolated pieces of information and skills, for the purpose of certification, which is prerequisite for learners' eventual inclusion in society.

Facet 5 deals with the means of learning. In LOPI, learning occurs by means of wide, keen attention and ongoing or anticipated contribution to the endeavor. Community expectations and people's instructing, counseling, and correcting may also be sources of guidance.

In ALI, learning is expected to occur through lessons, exercises, and tests that are outside the context of accomplishing something productive.

Facet 6 deals with the form of communication. In LOPI, communication builds on the participants' mutual endeavors, which allow concise and precise reference to the shared activity. This includes nonverbal conversation as well as verbal means of coordination, in addition to contextualized narratives and dramatization.

In ALI, communication employs a limited range of formats, especially explanations outside the context of the target activity, and quiz questions to which the questioner already knows the answers.

Facet 7 deals with assessment. In LOPI, assessment includes examining how and how well a learner is supported in the effort to contribute, as well as evaluating how and how well the learner is contributing to the endeavor. The assessment is done to aid the learners' contributions during the ongoing endeavor. Feedback for learners is available in the adequacy of their contribution and through other people's responses to their contribution, which may be accepted as part of the endeavor, corrected, or discarded.

In ALI, assessment aims to sort learners into categories of quality and to test their receipt of the instruction, separate from the learning process. Feedback comes from extrinsic rewards, praise or threats, and ranking against other learners.

When children whose learning has occurred largely in informal education participate in ALI-based formal schooling, the resulting challenges provide valuable insights into how informal learning operates in families and communities where schooling has not been prevalent. For example, Philips (1972, 1983) noticed that at home and in community settings, Warm Springs Indian children were not singled out by adults for attention and that social influence over them was exercised subtly and indirectly. In classrooms with White teachers, the Native American children were uncomfortable in large group instruction and when a teacher's questions were directed to them in front of other children; they tended to not respond. The children were much more comfortable in small groups, where they spoke in animated ways. (See also Erickson & Mohatt, 1982; Tharp & Gallimore, 1988.)

Noninterference is a principle of teaching in a number of Indigenous American communities that conflicts with the teacher control of ALI schooling (Scollon & Scollon, 1981). For example, the ideal role of Tzeltal (Mexican) parents is to support children's self-governance, including the right not to do as a parent asks (Paoli, 2003).

Some school settings have used learning approaches that are congruent with the informal learning approaches of Indigenous communities. A Yup'ik (Alaskan) teacher avoided "bubbly" praise and controlling via extensive explanation that she had seen used by European American teachers; she gave the children freedom to make decisions and to move around rather than attempting to force them to follow a teacher-controlled uniform pace (Mohatt & Sharp, 1998). In a Mazahua Indigenous community in Central Mexico, elementary school children freely moved around the classroom, worked together fluidly with each other and with the teacher, and ran the classroom responsibly when the teacher had to be away for a few days (Paradise, 1991).

The next section considers efforts to transform formal schooling through informal education–related approaches in order to escape the ALI approach. Some innovative schools have managed to do this. However, these efforts often involve challenges for adults in moving from one paradigm to another.

INFORMAL LEARNING IN SCHOOLS TRYING TO AVOID ASSEMBLY-LINE INSTRUCTION

Informal learning takes place in some schools that emphasize children's initiative and choice within compulsory formal schooling. Innovative schools often attempt to avoid the Assembly-Line Instruction model commonly found in formal schooling. A number of such schools emerged in the United States and the United Kingdom in the 1960s and 1970s (Firestone, 1977), explicitly aiming to create less adult-controlled didactic pedagogies.

Innovative schools have adopted a variety of informal approaches, given that there are many ways NOT to do ALI. Some of them, to avoid adult control of the classroom, have turned the control over to the children, switching from an adult-run model of learning to a child-run model of learning based on discovery and play, with adults relegated to the sidelines—after providing the children with some materials, the adults retreat (Rogoff, Matusov, & White, 1996).

Other innovative schools have created a collaborative organization, where children and adults together contribute to decision making regarding what is learned, how it is approached, when specific activities are undertaken, and how social relations in the classroom are organized. A group of parents, teachers, and children in an innovative kindergarten-to-sixth-grade public school articulated a collaborative philosophy, emphasizing the inclusion of both adults and children in decision making about classroom governance and curriculum (Rogoff et al., 2001). The adults participate in the activities along with the children. Although the adults often have a leadership role, this involves openness and flexibility to the ideas, interests, and learning opportunities offered by children.

Similarly, in Japanese preschools and elementary schools, observers report that children and adults collaborate skillfully and children have impressive responsibility for running the classroom (Lewis, 1995; Rogoff & Toma, 1997). (An interesting historical note is that Japanese elementary schooling was highly influenced a century ago by John Dewey, including from his visit to Japan in 1918 [Rogacheva, 2011]. Dewey, in turn, was inspired by his visits to small-scale Indigenous communities in Mexico in the early 1900s, where he observed community-based collaborations and learning resembling LOPI [Flores, Urrieta, Chamoux, Lorente Fernández, & López, 2015]!)

Informal learning also occurred in a U.S. dual-immersion elementary school classroom organized around a community-of-learners model, where students' seemingly off-task sense-making activity and use of Spanish, including everyday or informal Spanish, were not only allowed but were ratified and taken up in the official classroom space (Gutiérrez, Baquedano-Lopez, & Tejeda, 1999). This classroom had flexible participation structures such that children could choose where to sit, with whom to sit, and what language to speak. Although the second-/third-grade children often engaged in more responsive teacher-led instruction in which they could contribute freely, they also could challenge the topic and format and place their own interests at the center of the curriculum. It was in these informal learning spaces that the formation of deeper understandings began to develop.

Similarly, in a designed learning environment for secondary students from migrant farmworker backgrounds, a collective zone of proximal development was interactionally constituted. Traditional conceptions of academic instruction for youth from nondominant communities were contested and replaced with forms of learning that privilege and are contingent on students' sociohistorical lives, presently and historically (Gutiérrez, 2008). Students' everyday knowledge and ways of learning were reframed and understood as central to learning.

Some schools serving Indigenous students have developed innovative curricula that fit with informal learning approaches (Tharp & Gallimore, 1988). They have incorporated flexibility in adults' and children's roles; encouraged learner initiative, responsibility, and collaboration; incorporated family members; and involved children in community life (e.g., Ahkwesáhsne Mohawk Board of Education, 1994; Collier, 1988; Lipka, 1991).

It is important to note, however, that even when schools share some features with LOPI or other informal learning approaches, schooling is distinguished from settings in which learning situations involve children pitching in to accomplish productive activities. In school, the organizing purpose is to instruct children, not to accomplish other productive family or community endeavors. Robert Serpell (1996), like Margaret Mead, noted,

The educational philosophy underlying formal schooling is formalized as a deliberate undertaking, with an explicit purpose and design. The school's very *raison d'être* is to change the children who enter it. (p. 138)

Serpell (1996) contrasted this with the "implicit philosophy" of informal educational practices in an African community in Zambia:

If there were no child around to be educated, many if not all of these activities would still take place in the interactions between adults, albeit perhaps in a slightly different form. Individually and collectively, adult members of the community are aware that in the process of these activities they influence children's development, that the adult who performs these interventions is assuming some kind of responsibility for a change in the child's outlook. But in many cases the activity did not come into existence solely for that purpose. Even storytelling, which might appear to be a deliberately pedagogical activity, has a self-justifying celebratory quality that enables the storyteller to derive a reflexive satisfaction from its performance. It is thus less factitious than the educational activities of formal schooling, which are designed explicitly for the purpose of instruction." (p. 138)

Challenges for Schools Switching From Formal Instructional Models to Informal Learning Models

People who are familiar with only one learning paradigm often have difficulty understanding and learning to participate in another. For example, in an innovative elementary school, teachers as well as parent volunteers had difficulty moving to a collaborative informal learning model if their own schooling had been more along the lines of Assembly-Line Instruction (Rogoff et al., 2001). Teachers reflected on the difficulty of giving up "control" of the classroom, letting go of the techniques and philosophy that were emphasized in their teacher training (Steele, 2001).

Parent volunteers often began by moving to a children-run model, to avoid the adult-run model, and usually only after several years did they become familiar and comfortable with collaborating with the children, an approach that is not on the pendulum swing between adult control versus child control (Matusov & Rogoff, 2002). Rogoff (2001) reflected on the challenges for her as a parent volunteer in becoming a cooperative parent in a parent cooperative, even though she had studied collaborative adult–child interaction in a Mayan community in Guatemala for a decade. Other parent volunteers in this school reported similar difficulties in changing paradigms (Rogoff et al., 2001).

Valuable reflections on challenges of switching paradigms from an adult-run to an informal, collaborative approach were provided by an accomplished bilingual teacher who served as a research assistant in a project that required her to interact like an "auntie," inviting groups of three children to fold some origami figures and helping them fold the figures without trying to control their attention, motivation, or involvement (Paradise, Mejía-Arauz, Silva, Dexter, & Rogoff, 2014). This teacher was eager to experiment with the informal approach. With some practice, she was able to stop giving detailed explanations and to avoid explicit praise, in line with the script she was given as the research assistant. But she found it very difficult to stop trying to control the children's attention, although she switched to nonverbal means of calling their attention rather than statements such as "I'm waiting for Alex to pay attention . . ." She also continued to direct the pace of the children, breaking the activity into steps that she controlled. The teacher was fascinated by her difficulty in changing to an informal approach, and she spontaneously reflected on the deeply engrained efforts to control children stemming from classroom teachers' training and job experience.

UNDERGROUND INFORMAL LEARNING IN FORMAL SCHOOLING

Even in schooling that is as organized as ALI, important informal learning occurs, especially as children learn the implicit structure of classroom interaction. Some of the informal learning in formal learning settings such as school classrooms has been described as having to do with the "underlife" of the classroom and with the "hidden curriculum."

This perspective developed in the 1960s and 1970s in a critical and "revisionist" line of scholarship that questioned the previously taken-for-granted assumptions that schools were uniformly benign institutions, straightforwardly providing the opportunity to learn and reducing inequality in society (Young, 1971). Jackson (1968) pointed out that school experience for students involves learning to handle being treated as a member of a crowd and (analogous to the experience of being a soldier) spending a lot of time in boredom, waiting for something to happen. Adelman (1978) observed that school talk among students continually involves "muttering" mixed with "uttering"—that is, unofficial grousing off the record as well as officially sanctioned talk.

Drawing on Goffman (1961), Gutiérrez, Rymes, and Larson (1995) indicated that students construct and participate in the unsanctioned underlife in the classroom by employing strategies that are differentiated from teacher-dominated discourse: that is, strategies that undercut the roles students are expected to play. By creating a parallel script to the teachers' formal script, students engage in "counterscript," in which students assert unacknowledged cultural references and linguistic practices that are neither recognized nor included in the traditional teacher-led script, as students take stances against roles they are expected to play.

Student counterscript in classrooms involves a kind of informal learning insofar as counterscript exists as a sense-making space that necessarily draws on students' own everyday experiences that are both parallel and in tension with the dominant classroom norms (Gutiérrez et al., 1995). These ruptures help reposition students' knowledge and reorganize the participation structures, the division of labor, and the asymmetry in the classroom. Learning is side by side, where relationships and everyday knowledge are valued.

Implicit conventions for the conduct of interaction in everyday classroom life have been discussed as an "invisible culture" of social relations in the classroom (Merritt, 1998; Philips, 1983). The implicit conventions often are not taught or intended by teachers to be learned, but children learn them informally through their participation in classroom interactions. For example, in a preschool where children were not allowed to engage in or talk about popular culture, children learned, informally, that they could do so under some circumstances. When the researcher asked a 5-year-old boy if the children are allowed to play Pokémon at school, he replied "No, Ms. Allen's not OK with it." When the researcher asked if he could play it outside on the playground, the boy responded, "No, well, maybe, but it would have to be way out there. We can play anything we want to when they aren't looking" (Henward, 2015, p. 216).

In an example from another preschool with a similar rule, the teacher called attendance by asking the children to answer a question when she called their name. This day, she asked them to tell her what they want to be when they grow up. The first child to be called on responded, "Fireman," and the teacher said, "Good." Other children respond in turn with "poet," "pilot," "nurse," and so on. But then a 3-year-old replied, "Superhero." The teacher responded by asking if a superhero is a real thing, and the child said, "Yes." The teacher moved to the next child, looking annoyed. But the next child answered "Princess Belle." The teacher told her she couldn't be that, "You know that's not a real thing." The child modified: "I . . . I want to be a mother named Belle." Other children learned from this child's subversive tactic: "mermaid dolphin trainer," "GI Joe pilot." Children learn informally—underground in the classroom—both the teacher's ways of attempting to control them as well as ways they can resist (Henward, 2015, pp. 218–219).

Many aspects of the "hidden curriculum" of implicit messages in classrooms have been considered pernicious, in conflict with the aims of the manifest curriculum and undermining its accomplishment (Giroux & Penna, 1983). Such informal learning by students includes (1) learning to feel bad about not knowing how to read, (2) learning that it is more important to finish assigned work quickly than to do it accurately, (3) learning how to look as if you are paying attention when you are really not doing so, and (4) learning that advanced mathematics knowledge is not appropriate for girls.

Less pernicious are implicit conventions for the conduct of interaction in everyday classroom life. These have been discussed as an "invisible culture" of social relations in the classroom (Philips, 1983).

The importance of the "invisible culture" of classrooms was shown by Erickson and Mohatt (1982) in a study revealing how social control was exercised very differently in two adjoining first-grade classrooms on a Native American reservation in Northern Ontario. In one classroom, taught by a Native American teacher, social control was exercised very indirectly. During whole-group instruction, students were never called on to answer academic content questions individually—all content questions were addressed to the class as a whole, and the teacher avoided naming individual students while issuing classroom management directives ("Leroy, put the pencil down."). Overall, the teacher avoided directing the spotlight of public attention to individual students—avoiding even public positive reinforcement of students' desirable behavior as well as public negative reinforcement of negative behavior. (This indirection was characteristic of interaction in the children's everyday life outside school in family and community.) In the adjoining classroom, taught by a White teacher, social control was exercised much more directly, with content questions and management directives addressed to named individual students. In that classroom, the Native American children had to learn new cultural ways of interacting with an adult; this was not taught explicitly, for the most part, but children learned it informally.

In a study of a kindergarten/first-grade classroom in the United States, Erickson identified other aspects of "invisible culture," such as variability in turn-taking procedures in classroom discussion (Erickson, 1996, 2004). Despite an explicit "rule" that teacher dialogue with an individual student should not be interrupted by other students, such interruptions did happen and sometimes the interrupter succeeded in "stealing" the turn at talk with the teacher. Consequently, one of the interactional skills students needed to learn in that classroom was how to fend off the attempts by other students to interrupt and take away their turn. Acquisition of this interactional survival skill was done entirely informally by students, learning the "invisible culture" of formal schooling.

INFORMAL LEARNING IN VOLUNTARY INSTRUCTIONAL SETTINGS, SUCH AS AFTER-SCHOOL PROGRAMS

In this section, we examine the organization of informal learning in after-school settings, which are known to offer rich opportunities for students to engage in consequential learning, develop new identities, and construct new trajectories through participation in informal and hybrid settings. We discuss a family of design-based approaches (Cole & Engeström, 1993; Gutiérrez, 2016) that employ principles grounded in the conceptual frameworks discussed earlier in this chapter (Greenfield & Lave, 1982; Rogoff, 2003; Scribner & Cole, 1973). As we will elaborate, these contemporary designed environments engage youth in new forms of activity, while leveraging their histories of involvement in a range of valued family and community practices (Cole & the Distributed Literacy Consortium, 2006; Gutiérrez, 2008, 2016; Gutiérrez & Jurow, 2016; Vásquez, 2002).

However, before examining these long-standing innovative ecologies, it is important to situate their design in the history of research on informal learning in settings in which schooling was not prevalent or the norm (e.g., see Scribner & Cole, 1973). We summarize key principles learned from this antecedent work that have been instrumental in imagining and designing new forms of learning for underserved and immigrant youth and youth from nondominant communities.

Informal Learning in After-School Settings: Leveraging Family and Community Practices

Cole and the Distributed Literacy Consortium (2006) examined the socially and ideologically motivated rationale for bringing adults and children together in organized after-school settings since the late 19th century, drawing on Halpern's (2003) extensive review of after-school programs. Increased attention to and valuing of after-school programs occurred in the 1980s, with concern over children who were unsupervised or at home with siblings while adults were at work. Despite a lack of empirical research, the public discourse argued that these youth were particularly at risk (Cole & the Distributed Literacy Consortium, 2006). After-school programs have expanded significantly, ranging from early boys and girls clubs to technology-rich and STEM-oriented programs currently in vogue, while their original motivation has remained largely intact.

We focus on one long-standing after-school model that explicitly identifies informal learning as a key design principle to support ongoing interaction and joint activity among adults and children from diverse backgrounds. Using cultural historical approaches to learning and development, Peg Griffin and Michael Cole (1984, 1987) developed the Fifth Dimension model in the late 1980s to provide a range of innovative opportunities for informal learning with activities that adapt to the participants' interests and demands/constraints of the systems of which they were a part (Cole, 1996; Cole & the Distributed Literacy Consortium, 2006). These informal environments were intentionally organized "without imposing a school-like control structure" (Cole & the Distributed Literacy Consortium, 2006, p. 53).

Informal learning in after-school settings was inspired by the history of seminal work in informal settings indicating that learning has been organized in communities in ways that have worked for many generations, and as such, the social organization of learning is contiguous with experiences encountered in everyday life (Rogoff & Lave, 1984; Scribner & Cole, 1973, 1981). In contrast to solo or discovery learning, people learn through community participation, with children and youth integrated in their communities' activities. Here, learning is tied to practices that are historically and locally situated and that index individuals' and community-oriented values. In this way, knowledge and skills are deeply relational with a high positive social value and thus are bound up in meaningful relationships with the people in the teaching role.

The Fifth Dimension informal learning ecologies attend to dynamic and more symmetrical participant structures, in which adults are *amigas/amigos* working side-by-side with peers and youth. Since their inception, these sites have privileged hybrid language, such that youth could leverage their full linguistic repertoires to play and learn in intergenerational ensembles (Gutiérrez, Baquedano-Lopez, Alvarez, & Chiu, 1999; Gutiérrez & Rogoff, 2003). In these educationally rich after-school learning environments, children engage with technology, with special attention given to recruiting youth from nondominant communities and girls. Thus, these programs have had an explicit equity focus and have been designed to create a more robust and equitable educational pipeline for underserved youth.

A long-standing consortium of Fifth Dimension after-school programs, known as UC Links, was implemented across the entire university system of California as a coordinated educational response to a political problem: the short- and long-term effects of a California state law banning affirmative action (Proposition 187). An enduring consequence of this research-based and ecologically valid intervention has been the engagement of generations of youth in innovative technology-mediated learning activities, while providing a rich context of informal learning for novice teachers to learn jointly with youth across a range of practices (Stone & Gutiérrez, 2007; Underwood & Parker, 2014).

The voluntary nature of involvement in such after-school programs (as well as museums, community organizations, and summer camps) puts pressure on the organizers to move away from formal schooling approaches in order to attract children's participation. In addition, in line with the community-based informal learning approaches reviewed earlier in this chapter, Fifth Dimension programs focus on creating programs that are mutually beneficial to a broader community (including the research and instructional goals of universities; Cole & the Distributed Literacy Consortium, 2006).

The Social Organization of Informal Learning in After-School Settings

Reframing what counts as learning for youth generally not served well by traditional forms of learning in schooling institutions (Gutiérrez, 2008) is a central feature of robust learning environments such as those organized as Fifth Dimensions (Cole & the Distributed Literacy Consortium, 2006; Gutiérrez, Bien, & Selland, 2011; Vásquez, 2002) and summer learning institutes, such as the Migrant Student

Leadership Institute (MSLI; Vossoughi, 2011, 2014). These designed environments align with the principles and sensibilities of informal learning within cultural historical approaches to learning and development, and move beyond dichotomizing home/ school, the formal/nonformal. These are often hybrid settings that leverage principles from informal learning and, yet, share some features in common with the institutions in which they are often embedded (e.g., schools, libraries, universities, and boys and girls clubs). However, these programs take great care not to replicate school, especially the ways traditional schooling organizes learning and participation structures that reinforce hierarchies in relationships and in forms of knowledge.

Instead, these design experiments privilege learning over teaching, where shared practice is the object of activity. Adults or more experienced participants, then, are expected to employ a "light pedagogical touch" (Gutiérrez & Calabrese Barton, 2015) in which learning is a shared endeavor, with assistance readily available. With flexible and fluid participation structures and a division of labor that is collective and distributed, learning is emergent, contingent, and indeterminate. These fluid and flexible participation structures create more openings for a range of practices, including valued everyday and cultural practices, often not taken up in schools.

Collaborative approaches building on children's and youths' prior knowledge and ways of learning undergird the iterations of Fifth Dimension programs such as *La Clase Mágica* (Vásquez, 2002) and *Las Redes* (Gutiérrez, Baquedano-Lopez, Alvarez, & Chiu, 1999) and the MSLI (Espinoza, 2009; Gutiérrez, 2008; Vossoughi, 2014), a university-based, summer residential academic program for youth from migrant farmworker backgrounds. For example, these programs encourage the use of children's and youths' full linguistic tool kits to learn, with all participants drawing on home languages used by the youth to engage more fully in a range of innovative learning activity—such as learning from play and the playful imagination around gaming, making, and tinkering. As in everyday learning experiences, using English or a particular register is not the goal; instead, engagement in meaningful learning and accomplishing or completing a particular task with others is central to people's sustained involvement.

As in informal learning in children's families and communities, the range of everyday life experience provided abundant learning opportunities in the MSLI. The curriculum created openings for learning across all the spaces that the MSLI students and their teachers traversed on the University of California, Los Angeles (UCLA), campus—including opportunities to learn in the long walk from their dormitories to their classrooms. For example, racist taunts or other racializing experiences encountered by students were made the object of collective examination and learning in the classroom. In short, the UCLA campus was transformed into an open, unbounded learning ecology that brought together aspects of formal and informal learning in all its practices. Not only were there multiple ways of learning, learning opportunities followed youth across the practices that constituted MSLI. The study of learning across time and space in MSLI led to theoretical and methodological insights about the importance of attending to what and how people learn across the settings and practices of everyday life, what Gutiérrez (2008) terms "learning as movement."

Challenges for Informal Learning in After-School Settings

The informal learning environments of many after-school and community-based programs create learning environments not only for the children and youth but also for adults who may learn a more collaborative approach than they themselves experienced in school. As hybrid settings, these informal learning environments must be vigilant to the ways in which institutional practices and sensibilities seep in and can reinscribe traditional ways of participating and learning (DiGiacomo & Gutiérrez, in press; Mendoza, 2014).

Sometimes out-of-school settings are organized in ways that resemble the Assembly-Line Instruction approach common in schools, perhaps due to the adults' familiarity with this approach or concern with controlling children and youth. In after-school programs, adult volunteers often have challenges in moving away from an ALI model to more informal interactions with children (Chavajay, Angelillo, & Pease-Alvarez, 2005). Even when after-school settings are organized around more robust models of learning and equity, adults often default to their familiar notions of teaching and learning.

Although the activities of many after-school settings, such as "making and tinkering," involve a social organization that has the potential to support more symmetrical intergenerational relationships (DiGiacomo & Gutiérrez, 2015, in press), it is often difficult for teachers to disrupt default teaching scripts that privilege traditional forms of participation, support, and hierarchy. Of significance, traditional notions of how to organize teaching and learning and static views of cultural communities can reinforce and maintain reductive and inequitable pedagogies. In their expansive work and studies in an equity- and science-oriented maker space, Vossoughi, Hooper, and Escudé (2016) call for explicit attention to pedagogy in ways that foreground the generative role of elders and mentors in young people's development. In making, the familiar art, skill, and practice of teaching among adults and other educators makes the development of social relationships a primary rather than secondary aspect of making activity.

In designed out-of-school settings organized around the playful imagination, including making and tinkering environments, explicit learning is made the object or goal of the activity and happens as a result of participating in interest-driven and connected forms of learning (Ito et al., 2013). In designed hybrid learning environments that carefully and closely tie college students' learning with sense-making opportunities in informal settings with children and youth, college students write that they learn much more when they have the opportunity to work collaboratively with youth in authentic activity and engage in reflective practice (Gutiérrez & Vossoughi, 2010).

Explicit learning as a result of participating in interest-driven and connected forms of learning is also the goal of many voluntary public leisure institutions that have a focus on instruction, especially museums and science centers.

INFORMAL LEARNING IN VOLUNTARY LEISURE INSTITUTIONS WITH INSTRUCTIONAL FOCUS, SUCH AS MUSEUMS AND SCIENCE CENTERS

Science centers and hands-on museums embody an interesting combination of instructional goals and voluntary leisure focus. They are designed spaces, with goals of supporting both learning and personal interest. Many science centers and children's museums base their design on evidence about effective learning that includes providing opportunities for social collaboration, meaningful participation with authentic objects, and hands-on participation (Allen, 2004; Allen & Gutwill, 2016; Borun et al., 1998). Although museums are designed for learning, they are also "free choice" environments (Falk & Dierking, 2013) where visitors choose to go voluntarily, often as a form of entertainment or leisure activity, and where there is no formal assessment of their learning.

In this section, we consider research findings on what informal learning looks like in science centers and hands-on museums. We consider what effective informal learning in science centers has in common with the facets of the LOPI style of learning discussed earlier.

Although some children's museums and science museums had been in existence since before 1900, more of these museums appeared throughout the 1960s and 1970s, and they became more interactive and less focused on the display of artifacts. The focus on informal learning in museums emerged in the 1960s as part of a sense of dissatisfaction with school science learning and a belief in the importance of public understanding of science. In particular, Frank Oppenheimer, the founder of the Exploratorium in San Francisco, which opened in 1969, developed the idea of open-ended interaction with objects relevant to science and technology as a way to increase understanding and appreciation of science by nonscientists (Oppenheimer, 1968). Museum educators during these decades often borrowed ideas from school reform movements focused on inquiry and self-directed exploration (K. Crowley, personal communication, October 20, 2016).

These ideas inspired the types of experiences found in many discovery-based science museums and children's museums today. Practitioners in these museums and science centers have often articulated a constructivist approach that is very much in line with Oppenheimer's views (Hein, 1998). More recently, many museums and museum researchers became more heavily influenced by sociocultural approaches, taking a turn away from individual inquiry and instead seeing learning as socially constructed and embedded in practices of families and communities (K. Crowley, personal communication, October 20, 2016; Davidsson & Jakobsson, 2012).

The roots of learning research in museums and science centers integrated several traditions and disciplines, all with a common thread of viewing informal learning in museum settings as very different from school learning. One strand developed from in-house research and evaluation groups within museums, at the Exploratorium and other science centers (Allen & Gutwill, 2016; Borun et al., 1998; Duensing, 1999).

A second strand involves independent evaluation researchers hired by museums to evaluate their exhibits and programs, often with NSF funding (e.g., Bell, Lewenstein, Shouse, & Feder, 2009; Falk & Dierking, 2013; Garibay, 2011). A third strand of museum learning research emerged from developmental and educational psychologists branching out from research on children's learning in homes and other family settings, as they saw museums as a kind of natural laboratory to observe families interacting in spontaneous activity in a public space (Borun et al., 1998; Callanan, 2012; Callanan & Jipson, 2001; Haden, 2010; Knutson & Crowley, 2005).

We first focus on what informal learning means in the museum world, and on how science center spaces are designed to foster learning. Next, we compare ideals of informal learning in the museum world with the key features of LOPI. We then consider research showing that some parents and children organize their actions and interactions in science centers in ways that resemble Learning by Observing and Pitching In, whereas others organize their actions more in line with Assembly-Line Instruction.

How Museums Conceptualize and Support Informal Learning

A central question in the museum learning world involves defining informal learning and how it can be best supported. Museums are designed environments, as are school classrooms, but the definition of learning assumed by museum designers is usually quite different from that of schools. As discussed earlier, there are a variety of ways that informal learning differs from formal learning. While the labels "formal" and "informal" may imply that location is central, in fact many other aspects are arguably more important, such as whether didactic teaching is involved, how much free choice is involved, how meaningful the activity is, how socially collaborative it is, and whether assessment of learning occurs that has consequences for the learner (Callanan, Cervantes, & Loomis, 2011; Falk & Dierking 2013; Umphress, Miele, Simons, & Cohen, 2006).

Museum educators and museum exhibit designers often discuss learning in museums as being quite different from learning in schools. Much as in the alternative schools described earlier, museum designers often explicitly try to avoid ALI. An important voice in the museum field, George Hein (2005), argued,

> The *raison d'être* of the museum is education broadly defined. It's possible to have collections of objects, even collections carefully classified, organized and preserved, that are not primarily educational—the world includes many fine private collections and archives—but as soon as these are open to the public, the museum becomes an educational institution. (p. 357)

In his extensive writing, Hein (1998, 2005, 2012) has characterized museum learning using a constructivist philosophy, wherein visitors actively construct their own meaning based on their prior experiences, interests, and beliefs and on the social context of meaning making as it unfolds during their visit. In other words, Hein and other museum researchers have claimed that museums provide a setting for informal learning. The constructivist view espoused by Hein and others has been very influential in the design of hands-on museums such as the Exploratorium in San Francisco.

Sally Duensing (2000), a leading designer and educator during the formative decades of the Exploratorium, argued that museum exhibits are more effective as learning tools to the extent that they are "generative." That is, a generative exhibit provides deep, multiple opportunities for learners of any level of prior experience to extend an exhibit to create new experiences or expand the phenomena that the exhibit sparks.

As Allen and Gutwill (2016) point out, museum exhibits embody the learning theories and intentions of their designers, making museums different from natural (undesigned) environments like beaches or forests. Education and exhibit staff in hands-on science centers and children's museums often strive to create informal learning environments that deeply contrast with the assembly-line approach to learning (Hein, 1998, 2012). In designing exhibits and spaces, the goal is often to provide opportunities for informal learning that is self-driven and active.

One illustrative example comes from a team of researchers and exhibit designers at the Exploratorium (Allen & Gutwill, 2016; Humphrey & Gutwill, 2005) who aimed to explore and document the types of exhibit experiences that allow visitors to "drive the experience" for themselves. In an NSF-funded project, Gutwill and colleagues redesigned a set of existing exhibits to foster what they call "active prolonged engagement" (APE); they identified aspects of exhibit experiences that encouraged visitors not only to engage in hands-on exploration and scientific inquiry but also to stay engaged for a longer time than at typical exhibits, and to go beyond the exhibit instructions to come up with and test ideas of their own (similar to the "generative" exhibit idea of Duensing, 2000). The APE idea seems to resonate with philosophies of designers and educators at a number of other museums and science centers, showing some agreement with these goals across the field.

Another trend is the introduction of maker spaces and tinkering spaces in museums, as in after-school settings. In both museums and after-school programs, these activities have been adapted from do-it-yourself maker movements such as Maker Faires, including both computer hackers and artisans. The goal of maker and tinkering spaces in museums is to provide visitors with opportunities to engage in inquiry and to set their own agendas by actively engaging with materials and with other people (Bevan, Gutwill, Petrich, & Wilkinson, 2014). There is a conscious effort to train facilitators in these spaces to avoid unilateral direction and to instead develop an atmosphere of more fluid coordination of action.

Informal Learning in Science Centers and LOPI

Many aspects of informal learning in hands-on museums seem to have similarities with the LOPI approach. In other aspects the two are distinctive.

The hope in museums is that, like in LOPI, visitors' motive for learning in museums will be intrinsic, voluntary, and free choice. Children and other visitors are expected to engage with exhibits that are interesting to them, to avoid those that seem less interesting, and to engage in self-directed discovery as in the APE exhibits described above. There is no preset curriculum, and there is usually an intentionally flexible structure, with the understanding that visitors may attend exhibits in any order and that visitors with different background experiences will engage with the same exhibit in very different ways.

Also similar to LOPI, learning in museums involves communication that is in the context of current activity and assessment that is more connected to the learning activity rather than given at some later time. Frank Oppenheimer, the founder of the Exploratorium, famously said, "No one ever flunked a museum" (Semper, 1990, p. 52), highlighting a distinction between informal learning in museums as compared to school learning and, in particular, suggesting that assessment of learning is not a focus in museums.

There are, however, some distinctions between LOPI and museum learning. Whereas with LOPI the motive is to contribute to productive endeavors, in museums the goal is more about play and discovery without necessarily contributing to producing something useful. Museum designers often value collaboration as well, but there is some variability on this dimension, and some exhibits may be designed to be quite solitary.

At the same time, it is important to note that although LOPI is inherently collaborative, it also involves solo activities, as when children complete some part of a larger task on their own or practice what they observe on their own. But in LOPI, even solo activity is connected with family or community endeavors. For example, a U.S. 3-year-old emulated her mother's research work, which involved extensive transcription of tape-recorded conversations, in play:

"Each day I sit at the word processor, stopping and starting the tape recorder, tapping in the words and referring to the text. And now Lindsey has incorporated my behavior into her play. This morning I discovered her setting up her own office.

She had pulled her small director's chair up to her bed, which served as a desk. It held her "computer" (really a toy typewriter), as well as her small plastic tape recorder. She would play a section of *Star Wars*, and then stop the recording to bang out a message on the plastic keys of her typewriter. Back and forth she went between the recorder and her 'computer,' playing and typing, playing a new section and typing again, in a way more than a little reminiscent of my efforts at transcription." (Wolf & Heath, 1992, pp. 11–12)

The role of the community itself is more central to LOPI. In LOPI, the community integrates learners as productive contributors in the range of everyday community endeavors. In the museum "community," visitors generally do not contribute to the creation of the museum activities—as in school, they are recipients (indeed, just "visitors") and generally remove themselves from their usual lives to participate.

However, in some museums, visitors are invited to contribute comments on phenomena as part of an exhibition and to participate in the prototyping of exhibits, and encouraged to make regular visits. Indeed there is a move in the museum world toward finding ways to transform visitors into "participants," as in Simon's (2010) book, *The Participatory Museum*. Some museums also form partnerships with their local communities and adapt their programs to local goals and practices (Garibay, 2011).

Duensing (1999, 2013) uncovered a variety of ways that cultural values and assumptions influenced the adaptation of museum exhibits from the Exploratorium in San Francisco to museums in different communities around the world. Her work has highlighted the importance of the community contexts within which museums exist, and the (often hidden) assumptions about the nature of learning that guide the development and design of museums as informal learning environments.

A key difference with LOPI is that museums are less organic in their organization than are villages and towns; they are designed environments and formal organizations with accountability pressures and requirements set by other organizations. Despite many science center staff members' goals of making museum learning more LOPI-like in structure, there remains a dilemma for science centers that also want to connect with schools, and foster specific curricular (e.g., STEM) ideas, and with state and federal standards. Funding needs for science centers often push them in the direction of becoming more in line with school curricula and more assessment driven.

Despite the overall view of "ideal" informal learning in museums from the designers' perspective, as we will see, families vary in their goals and ways of participating. Some look more similar to ALI and others more similar to LOPI learning.

How Opportunities for Informal Learning in Science Centers Are Fostered by Parent–Child Interactions

Research has examined spontaneous styles of talk and activity in museum settings to ask how different families organize their learning, and how differently designed spaces foster learning activities (Callanan, 2012; Haden, 2010). Different families organize their action in diverse ways and with diverse roles in the informal learning setting of museums (Eberbach & Crowley, 2005; Zimmerman Reeve, & Bell, 2010). Within U.S. children's museums and science centers, visitors tend to vary in terms of ethnicity, race, and language spoken, although in many museums the visitor population is largely highly schooled and middle class or higher in socioeconomic background. Even within this relatively homogeneous sample, diversity of interaction style has been evident.

Across a large number of studies, research indicates that some families interact in museums in ways that seem closer to LOPI, whereas other families interact in ways that seem closer to ALI. Parents' likelihood of taking on a teacher-like didactic role, more in keeping with ALI, has been found to be related to parents' background as well as to aspects of the museum environment. For example, in one study, parents with more formal schooling were more likely to direct children's action (Siegel, Esterly, Callanan, Wright, & Navarro, 2007); in other studies, parents who value science or who talk about science as based on evidence (rather than settled facts) are likely to structure conversations with their children that are more collaborative and open-ended (Luce, Callanan, & Smilovic, 2013; Szechter & Carey, 2009). However, even parents who may take a directive approach at times usually give their children some choice about which exhibits to visit in the museum.

Aspects of the exhibits are also relevant to the ways that families structure their interaction. For example, exhibits that have clear built-in goals seem to elicit more directive teacher-like behavior from parents (Fung & Callanan, 2016). In contrast, exhibits that allow hands-on interaction and active engagement tend to invite more collaborative and fluid interaction with different family members taking different roles (Callanan, Martin, & Luce, 2016; Humphrey & Gutwill, 2005). Exhibit designs that encourage narrative reflection seem to foster deeper discussions of the conceptual ideas behind the exhibit (Haden, Cohen, Uttal, & Marcus, 2016; Solis, Diep, Castañeda, Martin, & Callanan, 2016). Duensing (1999, 2013) found intriguing differences in how museums in different cultural communities modified museum exhibits to better fit the interactional styles of the local community (e.g., modifying exhibits designed for solo use to accommodate groups, in Brazil), some of which relate to the collaborativeness emphasized in LOPI.

Despite these differences across parents and exhibits, it is important to point out that children attending with their families are learning in ways that bridge between home and museum. When interacting at a particular exhibit, parents tend to guide their children's attention in subtle ways (Crowley et al., 2001; Jant, Haden, Uttal, & Babcock, 2014). One way that parents often guide their children in museums is in the personal connections that they make for the children—bridging the activities at hand to the children's prior experiences or knowledge (Benjamin, Haden, & Wilkerson, 2010; Callanan et al., 2016). Family interactions in museums, then, involve both institutional and family contexts of informal learning.

Notably, the same situation may hold very different meaning for families from diverse cultural communities, perhaps related to the prevalence of formal schooling practices in the community and whether those practices lead to assumptions about learning in informal settings (Gaskins, 2008; Duensing, 1999, 2013). Gaskins (2008) found that parents' cultural background predicted the way they structured interactions in the museum—for example, Latino parents encouraged more collaborative interactions, in line with LOPI, compared to African American or European American parents. Tenenbaum and Callanan (2008) found that new immigrant Mexican parents generated fewer explanations than Mexican American parents in a museum setting, and yet the two groups explained equally in a museum-like task at home, perhaps reflecting the novelty of the museum setting for the immigrant families, many of whom had never been to a museum before. Considering the research findings on family interactions in museums, it is clear that the organization of learning for some families may be more like Learning by Observing and Pitching In, whereas for others it may be more like direct Assembly-Line Instruction.

CONSIDERING KEY FEATURES OF INFORMAL LEARNING ACROSS COMMUNITY AND DESIGNED SETTINGS

We conclude this chapter with our conjectures regarding the aspects of informal learning that are held in common, as well as those that vary, in these quite distinct settings: family and community productive endeavors, innovative schools and "underground" learning in schools, and designed voluntary institutions such as after-school programs and science centers.

Based on the ethnographic literature as well as research in hands-on science centers, Callanan et al. (2011) argued that what distinguishes informal from formal learning is that it is nondidactic, highly collaborative, embedded in meaningful activity, and initiated by the learner's interest or choice (rather than resulting from external demands or requirements) and does not involve assessment external to the activity.

In all the settings of informal learning that we have examined, informal learning is less constrained than the institutional structure of schooling. Schooling depends on legally prescribed compulsory attendance of all children and externally focused assessment to control and attempt to motivate children's compliance with instructional goals. In contrast, in all of the informal learning settings, learning is regarded as based on children's voluntary interest in engaging with the activities. Assessment is focused on social partners' or designers' evaluation of the success of the activities in engaging and supporting the learners' progress, and on the growth in learners' understanding and skill in the activity.

In all of the settings, innovation is valued. In family and community informal learning, the goal of contributing to the family and community includes coming up with new ideas and improved ways of doing things. In the designed voluntary settings of innovative informal schooling, informal after-school programs, and science centers, the emphasis on discovery and constructing knowledge includes valuing new ideas and ways of doing things. In the "underground" informal learning in schools, students' creative ways of addressing constraints are especially appreciated by their classmates, if not by their teachers.

Learning in informal settings is often more conceptual than in Assembly-Line Instruction, where superficial knowledge is often sufficient to get by. In informal learning settings, learners are motivated to be involved and need to understand the phenomena in order to contribute well. A common misconception that has been disproven is that informal learning is less general than formal instruction. In fact, most learning is somewhat specific to the contexts and problems that have been experienced, whether it is school learning or informal learning (Lave, 1985, 2011; Saxe, 2012; Scribner & Cole, 1981).

Accompanying the similarities across settings in the organization of informal learning, there are also important differences between informal learning in distinct settings:

Collaboration is a central feature of children's participation in family and community productive activities and in innovative schooling and after-school programs based on informal learning; however, collaboration is optional (though often desired) in science center settings, which often also involve solo exploration.

Connection with a larger community, in addition to the social interactions of face-to-face endeavors, is key to children's participation in family and community productive activities. It is also fostered in informally structured innovative schools and some after-school programs but is rare in science center informal learning settings.

Play is central as both a way of motivating involvement and a way of exploring, in science centers and often in after-school programs. Children learning in family and community endeavors also engage in play, particularly as they experiment with aspects of what they are learning in productive activities, but this is not a highlighted feature of learning by participation in family and community endeavors. Rather, in participating in family and community endeavors, learning is based more on observing and pitching in to ongoing productive activities. In innovative schools based on informal learning, play is an important feature, but it is often wedded to curricular goals rather than being a goal in itself.

In all of the informal learning settings that we have examined, learning is a goal. However, learning is more explicitly the goal in the designed settings and is a valued byproduct in learning while accomplishing family and community productive endeavors. In turn, contribution to "real" goals (outside of instruction and play) is central to learning in family and community endeavors and is possible but not key in innovative informal schooling, after-school programs, and science centers.

Like the goal of learning, guidance is a key feature of all the informal learning approaches. It occurs through suggestions and pointers and brief explanations in the context of shared activities as well as through the structure of the activities in which learners engage. However, a focus on instruction is more fully the purpose of the adults in innovative informal schooling, after-school activities, and museums. In family and community endeavors, adults have a central purpose of accomplishing the endeavor; they may go out of their way to include children and they value children's learning, but instruction is often not their primary goal of the moment. Nonetheless, they generally provide guidance through their inclusion of children and by orienting and supporting children's contributions to the activity.

In many ways, the practices involved in informal learning through children's engagement by observing and pitching in to family and community endeavors have inspired designed learning in innovative schools and after-school programs, and to some extent in museums and science centers. Our hope is that by articulating key features of informal learning across quite distinct settings, the insights available from the success of informal learning can inspire efforts to enhance children's (and adults') learning in formal schooling as well as in settings where informal learning is already employed. The models of informal learning available in these diverse settings can contribute to the improvement of all children's learning opportunities.

NOTES

Sally Duensing had hoped to join us in writing this chapter, contributing her deep knowledge of informal learning in the museum world. Unfortunately, she passed away, leaving us to try to carry forward her inclusive spirit of curiosity and generative approach to fostering learning.

[1]Now Diana Slaughter Kotzin.

[2]For a more recent take on a similar idea, see John Green's 2012 TED Talk on learning everything through the Internet, especially YouTube, at https://www.ted.com/talks/john_green_the_nerd_s_guide_to_learning_everything_online#t-168753.

[3]In recognition of the importance of informal learning, the NSF has, since somewhat prior to that 1998 meeting, invested in the study of informal learning. The NSF has funded several lines of grant making, including the Informal Science Education program (renamed Advancing Informal STEM Learning, or AISL) and national centers such as the Center for Informal Learning and Schools, run by the Exploratorium, the University of California, Santa Cruz, and King's College London; and the Center for Learning in Informal and Formal Environments, run by Stanford and the University of Washington.

REFERENCES

Adelman, C. (1978). *Uttering, muttering: Collecting, using, and reporting talk for social and educational research.* Norwich, England: Centre for Applied Research in Education.

Ahkwesâhsne Mohawk Board of Education. (1994). *How did it all start? The Ahkwesâhsne Science and Math Pilot Project narrative.* Cornwall, Ontario, Canada: Author.

Albert, E. (1964). Rhetoric, logic, and poetics in Burundi: Cultural patterning of speech behavior. *American Anthropologist, 66*(6), Pt. 2, 35–54.

Alcalá, L., & Rogoff, B. (2016). *Collaboration as shared thinking or dividing roles: Cultural differences.* Unpublished manuscript, University of California, Santa Cruz.

Alcalá, L., Rogoff, B., Mejía-Arauz, R., Coppens, A. D., & Dexter, A. L. (2014). Children's initiative in contributions to family work in Indigenous-heritage and Cosmopolitan communities in Mexico. *Human Development, 57,* 96–115.

Allen, S. (2004). Designs for learning: Studying science museum exhibits that do more than entertain. *Science Education, 88*(Suppl. 1), S17–S33.

Allen, S., & Gutwill, J. (2016). Exploring models of research-practice partnership within a single institution: Two kinds of jointly negotiated research. In D. M. Sobel & J. L. Jipson (Eds.), *Cognitive development in museum settings: Relating research and practice* (pp. 190–208). New York, NY: Psychology Press.

Azuma, H. (1994). Two modes of cognitive socialization in Japan and the United States. In P. M. Greenfield & R. R. Cocking (Eds.), *Cross-cultural roots of minority child development* (pp. 275–284). Hillsdale, NJ: Erlbaum.

Bateson, G., & Mead, M. (1942). *Balinese character: A photographic analysis.* New York: New York Academy of Sciences.

Bell, P., Lewenstein, B., Shouse, A., & Feder, M. (2009). *Learning science in informal environments: People, places, and pursuits.* Washington, DC: National Academies Press.

Benedict, R. (1934). *Patterns of culture.* New York, NY: Houghton Mifflin.

Benjamin, N., Haden, C. A., & Wilkerson, E. (2010). Enhancing building, conversation, and learning through caregiver-child interactions in a children's museum. *Developmental Psychology, 46,* 502–515.

Bevan, B., Gutwill, J., Petrich, M., & Wilkinson, K. (2014). Learning through STEM-rich tinkering: Findings from a jointly negotiated research project taken up in practice. *Science Education, 99,* 98–120.

Bloch, M. N. (1989). Young boys' and girls' play at home and in the community: A cultural-ecological framework. In M. N. Bloch & A. D. Pellegrini (Eds.), *The ecological context of children's play* (pp. 120–154). Norwood, NJ: Ablex.

Bolin, I. (2006). *Growing up in a culture of respect.* Austin: University of Texas Press.

Bonilla, C. M. (2014). Racial counternarratives and Latina epistemologies in relational organizing. *Anthropology & Education Quarterly, 45,* 391–408.

Borun, M., Dritsas, J., Johnson, J., Peter, N., Wagner, K., Fadigan, K., . . . Wenger, A. (1998). *Family learning in museums: The PISEC perspective.* Philadelphia, PA: The Franklin Institute.

Briggs, J. L. (1970). *Never in anger: Portrait of an Eskimo family.* Cambridge, MA: Harvard University Press.

Brown, A. L., & Campione, J. C. (1990). Communities of learning and thinking, or a context by any other name. In D. Kuhn (Ed.), *Developmental perspectives on teaching and learning thinking skills* (pp. 108–126). Basel, Switzerland: Karger.

Callanan, M. (2012). Conducting cognitive developmental research in museums: Theoretical issues and practical considerations. *Journal of Cognition and Development, 13,* 137–151.

Callanan, M., Cervantes, C., & Loomis, M. (2011). Informal learning. *WIREs Cognitive Science, 2,* 646–655.

Callanan, M., & Jipson, J. (2001). Explanatory conversations and young children's developing scientific literacy. In K. S. Crowley, C. Schunn, & T. Okada (Eds.), *Designing for science: Implications from everyday, classroom, and professional settings* (pp. 21–49). Mahwah, NJ: Erlbaum.

Callanan, M., Martin, J., & Luce, M. (2016). Two decades of families learning in a children's museum: A partnership of research and exhibit development. In D. Sobel & J. Jipson (Eds.), *Cognitive development in museum settings: Relating research and practice* (pp. 15–35). New York, NY: Routledge.

Cazden, C. B., & John, V. P. (1971). Learning in American Indian children. In M. L. Wax, S. Diamond, & F. O. Gearing (Eds.), *Anthropological perspectives on education* (pp. 252–272). New York, NY: Basic Books.

Chavajay, P., Angelillo, C., & Pease-Alvarez, L. (2005). Teachers, mentors, friends? Undergraduates' engagements with Latino children in an after-school program. In L. Pease-Alvarez & S. Schecter (Eds.), *Learning, teaching, and community: Contributions of situated and participatory approaches to education innovation* (pp. 151–169). Hillsdale, NJ: Erlbaum.

Chavajay, P., & Rogoff, B. (1999). Cultural variation in management of attention by children and their caregivers. *Developmental Psychology, 35,* 1079–1090.

Chavajay, P., & Rogoff, B. (2002). Schooling and traditional collaborative social organization of problem solving by Mayan mothers and children. *Developmental Psychology, 38,* 55–66.

Chisholm, J. S. (1996). Learning "respect for everything": Navajo images of development. In C. P. Hwang, M. E. Lamb & I. E. Sigel (Eds.), *Images of childhood* (pp. 167–183). Mahwah, NJ: Erlbaum.

Cole, M. (1996). *Cultural psychology: A once and future discipline.* Cambridge, MA: Harvard University Press.

Cole, M., & the Distributed Literacy Consortium. (2006). *The Fifth Dimension: An after-school program built on diversity.* New York, NY: Russell Sage Foundation.

Cole, M., & Engeström, Y. (1993). A cultural-historical approach to distributed cognition. In G. Salomon (Ed.), *Distributed cognitions: Psychological and educational considerations* (pp. 1–46). Cambridge, England: Cambridge University Press.

Collier, J., Jr. (1988). Survival at Rough Rock: A historical overview of Rough Rock Demonstration School. *Anthropology & Education Quarterly, 19,* 253–269.

Coppens, A. D., Alcalá, L., Mejía-Arauz, R., & Rogoff, B. (2014). Children's initiative in family household work in Mexico. *Human Development, 57,* 116–130.

Coppens, A. D., Alcalá, L., Rogoff, B., & Mejía-Arauz, R. (2016). Children's contributions in family work: Two cultural paradigms. In T. Skelton (General Ed.), *Geographies of children and young people: Vol. 5. Families, intergenerationality and peer group relations* (S. Punch & R. Vanderbeck, Vol. Eds., pp. 1–27). New York, NY: Springer.

Correa-Chávez, M., & Rogoff, B. (2009). Children's attention to interactions directed to others: Guatemalan Mayan and European American patterns. *Developmental Psychology, 45*, 630–641.

Crowley, K., Callanan, M., Jipson, J., Topping, K., Galco, J., & Shrager, J. (2001). Shared scientific thinking in everyday parent-child activity. *Science Education, 85*, 712–732.

Davidsson, E., & Jakobsson, A. (2012). *Understanding interactions at science centers and museums: Approaching sociocultural perspectives.* Rotterdam, Netherlands: Sense.

de Haan, M. (1999). *Learning as cultural practice.* Amsterdam, Netherlands: Thela Thesis.

de León, L. (2015). Mayan children's creation of learning ecologies by initiative and cooperative action. In M. Correa-Chávez, R. Mejía-Arauz, & B. Rogoff (Eds.), *Advances in child development and behavior: Vol. 49. Children learn by observing and contributing to family and community endeavors: A cultural paradigm* (pp. 153–184). Waltham, MA: Academic Press.

Delgado-Gaitan, C. (1994). Consejos: The power of cultural narratives. *Anthropology & Education Quarterly, 25*, 298–316.

DiGiacomo, D., & Gutiérrez, K. (2015). Relational equity as a design tool within making and tinkering activities. *Mind, Culture, & Activity, 22*(3), 1–15.

DiGiacomo, D., & Gutiérrez, K. (in press). Seven chilis: Making visible the complexities in leveraging cultural repertoires of practice in a designed teaching and learning environment. *Pedagogies.*

Dixon, S. D., LeVine, R. A., Richman, A., & Brazelton, T. B. (1984). Mother-child interaction around a teaching task: An African-American comparison. *Child Development, 55*, 1252–1264.

Driver, H., & Driver, W. (1963). *Ethnography and acculturation of the Chichimec-Jonaz of Northeast Mexico.* The Hague, Netherlands: Mouton.

DuBois, C. (1944). *The people of Alor: A socio-psychological study of an East Indian island.* Minneapolis: University of Minnesota Press.

Duensing, S. (1999). *Cultural influences on science museum practices: A case study* (Unpublished doctoral dissertation). University of Michigan, Ann Arbor.

Duensing, S. (2000). Using Gal'perin's perspectives to explore generative learning in informal science centers. *Human Development, 43*, 107–114.

Duensing, S. (2013). Cultural assumptions and social interactions in museums. Retrieved from http://www.legofoundation.com/it-it/research-and-learning/foundation-research/cultures-creativity

Eberbach, C., & Crowley, K. (2005). From living to virtual: Learning from museum objects. *Curator, 48*, 317–338.

Eisenberg, A.R. (1986). Teasing: Verbal play in two Mexicano homes. In B. B. Schieffelin & E. Ochs (Eds.) *Language socialization across cultures* (pp. 182–198). New York, NY: Cambridge University Press.

Ellis, S., & Gauvain, M. (1992). Social and cultural influences on children's collaborative interactions. In L. T. Winegar & J. Valsiner (Eds.), *Children's development within social context* (pp. 155–180). Hillsdale, NJ: Erlbaum.

Erickson, F. (1996). Going for the zone: The social and cognitive ecology of teacher-student interaction in classroom conversations. In D. Hicks (Ed.), *Discourse, learning, and schooling* (pp. 29–62). New York, NY: Cambridge University Press.

Erickson, F. (2004). *Talk and social theory: Ecologies of speaking and listening in everyday life.* Cambridge, England: Polity Press.

Erickson, F., & Mohatt, G. (1982). Cultural organization of participation structures in two classrooms of Indian students. In G. Spindler (Ed.), *Doing the ethnography of schooling: Educational anthropology in action* (pp. 132–174). New York, NY: Holt, Rinehart & Winston.

Espinoza, M. (2009). A case study of educational sanctuary in one migrant classroom. *Pedagogies, 4*(1), 44–62.

Falk, J., & Dierking, L. (2013). *The museum experience revisited.* Walnut Creek, CA: Left Coast Press.

Farrell, B., & Medvedeva, M. (2010). *Demographic transformation and the future of museums.* Washington, DC: American Association of Museums.

Firestone, W. A. (1977). The balance of control between parents and teachers in co-op free schools. *School Review, 85,* 264–286.

Firth, R. (1936). *We the Tikopia.* London, England: Allen & Unwin.

Fitts, S., & McClure, G. (2015). Building social capital in Hightown: The role of confianza in Latina immigrants' social networks in the New South. *Anthropology & Education Quarterly, 46,* 295–311.

Flores, R., Urrieta, L., Chamoux, M.-N., Lorente Fernández, D., & López, A. (2015). Using history to analyze the Learning by Observing and Pitching in practices of contemporary Mesoamerican societies. In M. Correa-Chávez, R. Mejía-Arauz, & B. Rogoff (Eds.), *Advances in child development and behavior: Vol. 49. Children learn by observing and contributing to family and community endeavors: A cultural paradigm* (pp. 315–340). Waltham, MA: Academic Press.

Fortes, M. (1970). Social and psychological aspects of education in Taleland. In J. Middleton (Ed.), *From child to adult: Studies in the anthropology of education* (pp. 14–74). Garden City, NY: National History Press. (Original work published 1938).

Fung, G., & Callanan, M. (2016). *Explaining and exploring: Parent-child interactions in a museum setting.* Unpublished manuscript, University of California, Santa Cruz.

García, F. A. (2015). Respect and autonomy in children's observation and participation in adults' activities. In M. Correa-Chávez, R. Mejía-Arauz, & B. Rogoff (Eds.), *Advances in child development and behavior: Vol. 49. Children learn by observing and contributing to family and community endeavors: A cultural paradigm* (pp. 137–152). Waltham, MA: Academic Press.

Garibay, C. (2011, February 28). Responsive and accessible: How museums are using research to better engage diverse cultural communities. *ASTC Dimensions, January-February 2011,* p. 4. Retrieved from http://astc.org/pubs/dimensions/2011/Jan-Feb/JanFeb11.pdf

Garson, J., & Read, C. (Eds.). (1892). *Notes and queries on anthropology* (2nd ed.). London, England: The Anthropological Institute.

Gaskins, S. (2008). The cultural meaning of play and learning in children's museums. *Hand to Hand, 22*(4), 1–11.

Gaskins, S. (2000). Children's daily activities in a Mayan village: A culturally grounded description. *Cross-Cultural Research, 34,* 375–389.

Giroux, H., & Penna, A. (1983). Social education in the classroom: The dynamics of the "hidden curriculum." In H. Giroux & D. Purpel (Eds.), *The hidden curriculum and moral education* (pp. 100–121). Berkeley, CA: McCutchan.

Goffman, E. (1961). *Asylums: Essays on the social situation of mental patients and other inmates.* New York, NY: Anchor.

Goodwin, M. H. (1991). *He-said-she-said: Talk as social organization among Black children.* Bloomington: Indiana University Press.

Greenfield, P., & Childs, C. P. (1977). Weaving, color terms and pattern representation: Cultural influences and cognitive development among the Zinacantecos of Southern Mexico. *Inter-American Journal of Psychology, 11,* 23–48.

Greenfield, P., & Lave, J. (1982). Cognitive aspects of informal education. In D. A. Wagner & H. W. Stevenson (Eds.), *Cultural perspectives on child development* (pp. 181–207). San Francisco, CA: Freeman.

Griffin, P., & Cole, M. (1984). Current activity for the future: The zo-ped. In B. Rogoff & J. V. Wertsch (Eds.), *Children's learning in the "zone of proximal development": New directions for child development* (pp. 45–63). San Francisco, CA: Jossey-Bass.

Griffin, P., & Cole, M. (1987). New technologies, basic skills, and the underside of education: What is to be done? In J. A. Langer (Ed.), *Language, literacy, and culture: Issues of society and schooling* (pp. 199–231). Norwood, NJ: Ablex.

Gumperz, J., & Hernandez-Chavez, E. (1971). Bilingualism, bidialectalism, and classroom interaction. In C. Cazden, V. John, & D. Hymes (Eds.), *The functions of language in the classroom* (pp. 84–108). New York, NY: Teachers College Press.

Gumperz, J., & Hymes, D. (Eds.). (1964). The ethnography of communication [Special issue]. *American Anthropologist, 66*(6), Pt. 2.

Gutiérrez, K. (2008). Developing a sociocritical literacy in the Third Space. *Reading Research Quarterly, 43*, 148–164.

Gutiérrez, K. (2016). Designing resilient ecologies: Social design experiments and a new social imagination. *Educational Researcher, 45*, 187–196.

Gutiérrez, K., Baquedano-Lopez, P., Alvarez, H., & Chiu, M. (1999). A cultural-historical approach to collaboration: Building a culture of collaboration through hybrid language practices. *Theory Into Practice, 38*(2), 87–93.

Gutiérrez, K., Baquedano-Lopez, P., & Tejeda, C. (1999). Rethinking diversity: Hybridity and hybrid language practices in the third space. *Mind, Culture, & Activity, 6*, 286–303.

Gutiérrez, K., Bien, A., & Selland, M. (2011). Polylingual and polycultural learning ecologies: Mediating emergent academic literacies for dual language learners. *Journal of Early Childhood Literacy, 11*, 232–261.

Gutiérrez, K., & Calabrese Barton, A. (2015). The possibilities and limits of the structure-agency dialectic in advancing science for all. *Journal of Research in Science Teaching, 52*, 574–583.

Gutiérrez, K., & Jurow, S. (2016). Social design experiments: Toward equity by design. *Journal of Learning Sciences, 25*, 565–598.

Gutiérrez, K., & Rogoff, B. (2003). Cultural ways of learning: Individual traits or repertoires of practice. *Educational Researcher, 32*, 19–25.

Gutiérrez, K., Rymes, B., & Larson, J. (1995). Script, counterscript, and underlife in the classroom: James Brown versus Brown v. Board of Education. *Harvard Educational Review, 65*, 445–471.

Gutiérrez, K., & Vossoughi, S. (2010). "Lifting off the ground to return anew": Documenting and designing for equity and transformation through social design experiments. *Journal of Teacher Education, 61*, 100–117.

Haden, C. (2010). Talking about science in museums. *Child Development Perspectives, 4*, 62–67.

Haden, C., Cohen, T., Uttal, D., & Marcus, M. (2016). Building learning: Narrating experiences in a children's museum. In D. M. Sobel & J. L. Jipson (Eds.), *Cognitive development in museum settings: Relating research and practice* (pp. 84–103). New York, NY: Psychology Press.

Halpern, R. (2003). *Making play work: The promise of after-school programs for low-income children.* New York, NY: Teachers College Press.

Heath, S.B. (1983). *Ways with words: Language, life, and work in communities and classrooms.* Cambridge, England: Cambridge University Press.

Hein, G. E. (1998). *Learning in the museum.* London, England: Routledge.

Hein, G. E. (2005). The role of museums in society: Education and social action. *Curator, 48*, 357–363.

Hein, G. E. (2012). *Progressive museum practice: John Dewey and democracy.* London, England: Routledge.

Henward, A. S. (2015). "She don't know I got it. You ain't gonna tell her, are you?" Popular culture as resistance in American preschools. *Anthropology & Education Quarterly, 46,* 208–223.

Huerta Migus, L. (2015). *Broadening access to out-of-school STEM learning environments* (Report commissioned by National Research Council Committee on Successful Out-of-School STEM Learning). Retrieved from http://sites.nationalacademies.org/cs/groups/dbassesite/documents/webpage/dbasse_089995.pdf

Humphrey, T., & Gutwill, J. (2005). *Fostering active prolonged engagement: The art of creating APE exhibits.* Walnut Creek, CA: Left Coast Press.

Ito, M., Gutiérrez, K., Livingstone, S., Penuel, W., Rhodes, J., Salen, K., . . . Watkins, C. (2013). *Connected learning: An agenda for research and design.* Irvine, CA: The Digital Media and Learning Research Hub Reports on Connected Learning.

Jackson, P. (1968). *Life in classrooms.* New York, NY: Holt, Rinehart, & Winston.

Jant, E., Haden, C., Uttal, D., & Babcock, E. (2014). Conversation and object manipulation influence children's learning in a museum. *Child Development, 85,* 2029–2045.

John-Steiner, V. (1984). Learning styles among Pueblo children. *Quarterly Newsletter of the Laboratory of Comparative Human Cognition, 6,* 57–62.

Jordan, B. (1989). Cosmopolitical obstetrics: Some insights from the training of traditional midwives. *Social Science & Medicine, 28,* 925–944.

Knight, M. G., Norton, N. E. L., Bentley, C. C., & Dixon, I. R. (2004). The power of Black and Latina/o counterstories: Urban families and college-going processes. *Anthropology and Education, 35,* 99–120.

Knutson, K., & Crowley, K. (2005). Museum as learning laboratory: Developing and using a practical theory of informal learning (Pt. 1 of 2). *Hand to Hand, 18,* 4–5.

Kojima, H. (1986). Child rearing concepts as a belief-value system of the society and the individual. In H. Stevenson, H. Azuma, & K. Hakuta (Eds.), *Child development and education in Japan* (pp. 39–54). New York, NY: Freeman.

Labov, W. (1972). *Language in the inner city: Studies in the Black English vernacular.* Philadelphia: University of Pennsylvania Press.

Lancy, D. F. (2015). *The anthropology of childhood: Cherubs, chattel, changelings* (2nd ed.). Cambridge, England: Cambridge University Press.

Lave, J. (1977). Tailor-made experiments and evaluating the intellectual consequences of apprenticeship training. *Quarterly Newsletter of the Institute for Comparative Human Development, 1,* 1–3.

Lave, J. (1985). Introduction: Situationally specific practice. *Anthropology & Education Quarterly, 16,* 171–176.

Lave, J. (2011). *Apprenticeship in critical ethnographic practice.* Chicago, IL: University of Chicago Press.

Levitt, P. (2015, November 9). Museums must attract diverse visitors or risk irrelevance. *The Atlantic.* Retrieved from http://www.theatlantic.com/politics/archive/2015/11/museums-must-attract-diverse-visitors-or-risk-irrelevance/433347/

Lewis, C. C. (1995). *Educating hearts and minds: Reflections on Japanese preschool and elementary education.* Cambridge, England: Cambridge University Press.

Lipka, J. (1991). Toward a culturally based pedagogy: A case study of one Yup'ik Eskimo teacher. *Anthropology & Education Quarterly, 22,* 203–223.

López, A., Correa-Chávez, M., Rogoff, B., & Gutiérrez, K. (2010). Attention to instruction directed to another by U.S. Mexican-heritage children of varying cultural backgrounds. *Developmental Psychology, 46,* 593–601.

López, A., Najafi, B., Rogoff, B., & Mejía-Arauz, R. (2012). Collaboration and helping as cultural practices. In J. Valsiner (Ed.), *The Oxford handbook of culture and psychology* (pp. 869–884). New York, NY: Oxford University Press.

López, A., & Rogoff, B. (2016). *Helping without being asked as a cultural practice.* Unpublished manuscript, University of California, Santa Cruz.

Lorente Fernández, D. (2015). Children's everyday learning by assuming responsibility for others: Indigenous practices as a cultural heritage across generations. In M. Correa-Chávez, R. Mejía-Arauz, & B. Rogoff (Eds.), *Advances in child development and behavior: Vol. 49. Children learn by observing and contributing to family and community endeavors: A cultural paradigm* (pp. 53–90). Waltham, MA: Academic Press.

Luce, M., Callanan, M., & Smilovic, S. (2013). Links between parents' epistemological stance and children's evidence talk. Invited submission for special section, "Children's Learning From Others." *Developmental Psychology, 49,* 454–461.

Majors, Y. (2015) *Shop talk: Lessons in teaching from an African American hair salon.* New York, NY: Teachers College.

Matusov, E., & Rogoff, B. (2002). Newcomers and oldtimers: Educational philosophies-in-action of parent volunteers in a community of learners school. *Anthropology & Education Quarterly, 33,* 415–440.

Maynard, A. E., & Martini, M. (Eds.). (2005). *Learning in cultural context: Family, peers and school.* New York, NY: Kluwer Academic/Plenum.

McCarty, T. L. (2002). *A place to be Navajo—Rough Rock and the struggle for self-determination in Indigenous schooling.* Mahwah, NJ: Erlbaum.

Mead, M. (1928). *Coming of age in Samoa: A psychological study of primitive youth for Western civilization.* New York, NY: William Morris.

Mead, M. (1970). Our educational emphases in primitive perspective. In J. Middleton (Ed.), *From child to adult: Studies in the anthropology of education* (pp. 1–13). Garden City, NY: Natural History Press.

Mejía-Arauz, R., Correa-Chávez, M., Keyser Ohrt, U., & Aceves-Azuara, I. (2015). Collaborative work or individual chores: The role of family social organization in children's learning to collaborate and develop initiative. In M. Correa-Chávez, R. Mejía-Arauz, & B. Rogoff (Eds.), *Advances in child development and behavior: Vol. 49. Children learn by observing and contributing to family and community endeavors: A cultural paradigm* (pp. 25–51). Waltham, MA: Academic Press.

Mejía-Arauz, R., Rogoff, B., Dexter, A., & Najafi, B. (2007). Cultural variation in children's social organization. *Child Development, 78,* 1001–1014.

Mendoza, E. (2014). *Disrupting common sense notions through transformative education. Understanding purposeful organization and movement toward mediated praxis* (Doctoral dissertation). Available from ProQuest Dissertation & Theses database. (UMI No. 3635879)

Merritt, M. (1998). Of ritual matters to master: Structure and improvisation in language development at primary school. In S. M. Hoyle & C. T. Adger (Eds.), *Kids talk: Strategic language use in later childhood* (pp. 134–150). New York, NY: Oxford University Press.

Metge, J. (1984). *Learning and teaching: He tikanga Maori.* Wellington, New Zealand: New Zealand Ministry of Education.

Miller, P. (1982). *Amy, Wendy, and Beth: Learning language in South Baltimore.* Austin: University of Texas Press.

Minami, M., & McCabe, A. (1995). Rice balls and bear hunts: Japanese and North American family narrative patterns. *Journal of Child Language, 22,* 423–445.

Mohatt, G. V., & Sharp, N. (1998). The evolution and development of a Yup'ik teacher. In J. Lipka (Ed.), *Transforming the culture of schools* (pp. 41–69). Mahwah, NJ: Erlbaum.

Moll, L. C., & Whitmore, K. F. (1993). Vygotsky in classroom practice: Moving from individual transmission to social transaction. In E. A. Forman, N. Minick, & C. A. Stone (Eds.), *Contexts for learning: Sociocultural dynamics in children's development* (pp. 19–42). New York, NY: Oxford University Press.

Morelli, G., Rogoff, B., & Angelillo, C. (2003). Cultural variation in young children's access to work or involvement in specialized child-focused activities. *International Journal of Behavioral Development, 27,* 264–274.

Nash, M. (1967). *Machine age Maya.* Chicago, IL: University of Chicago Press.

Ochs, E., & Schieffelin, B. B. (1984). Language acquisition and socialization: Three developmental stories and their implications. In R. Schweder & R. LeVine (Eds.), *Culture theory: Essays on mind, self, and emotion* (pp. 276–320). Chicago, IL: University of Chicago Press.

Opie, I., & Opie, P. (1959). *The lore and language of schoolchildren.* Oxford, England: Oxford University Press.

Oppenheimer, F. (1968). Rationale for a science museum. *Curator, 1,* 206–209.

Paoli, A. (2003). *Educación, autonomía, y lekil kuxlejalm* [Education, autonomy, and *lekil kuxlejal*]. Mexico City, Mexico: Universidad Autónoma Metropolitana.

Paradise, R. (1991). *El conocimiento cultural en el aula: Niños indígenas y su orientación hacia la observación* [Cultural knowledge in the classroom: Indigenous children and their orientation toward observation]. *Infancia y Aprendizaje, 55,* 73–85.

Paradise, R. (1996). Passivity or tacit collaboration: Mazahua interaction in cultural context. *Learning and Instruction, 6,* 379–389.

Paradise, R. (1998). What's different about learning in schools as compared to family and community settings? *Human Development, 41,* 270–278.

Paradise, R., Mejía-Arauz, R., Silva, K. G., Dexter, A. L., & Rogoff, B. (2014). One, two, three, eyes on me! Adults attempting control versus guiding in support of initiative. *Human Development, 57,* 131–149.

Paradise, R., & Rogoff, B. (2009). Side by side: Learning through observing and pitching in. *Ethos, 37,* 102–138.

Philips, S. (1972). Participant structures and communicative competence: Warm Springs children in community and classroom. In C. Cazden, V. John, & D. Hymes (Eds.), *Functions of language in the classroom* (pp. 370–394). New York, NY: Teachers College Press.

Philips, S. (1983). *The invisible culture: Communication in classroom and community on the Warm Springs Indian reservation.* New York, NY: Longman.

Rogacheva, E. (2011). International dimention of John Dewey's pedagogy: Lessons for tomorrow. In A.-T. Tymieniecka (Ed.), *Analecta Husserliana: The yearbook of phenomenological research* (Vol. 110, pp. 147–169). Dordrecht, Netherlands: Springer.

Rogoff, B. (1990). *Apprenticeship in thinking: Cognitive development in social context.* New York, NY: Oxford University Press.

Rogoff, B. (2001). Becoming a cooperative parent in a parent cooperative. In B. Rogoff, C. Goodman Turkanis, & L. Bartlett (Eds.), *Learning together: Children and adults in a school community* (pp. 145–155). New York, NY: Oxford University Press.

Rogoff, B. (2003). *The cultural nature of human development.* New York, NY: Oxford University Press.

Rogoff, B. (2014). Learning by Observing and Pitching in to family and community endeavors: An orientation. *Human Development, 57,* 69–81.

Rogoff, B. (2016). Culture and participation: A paradigm shift. *Current Opinion in Psychology, 8,* 182–189.

Rogoff, B., Goodman Turkanis, C., & Bartlett, L. (2001). *Learning together: Children and adults in a school community.* New York, NY: Oxford University Press.

Rogoff, B., & Lave, J. (Eds.). (1984). *Everyday cognition: Its development in social context.* Cambridge, MA: Harvard University Press.

Rogoff, B., Matusov, E., & White, C. (1996). Models of teaching and learning: Participation in a community of learners. In D. Olson & N. Torrance (Eds.), *Handbook of education and human development: New models of learning, teaching, and schooling* (pp. 388–414). London, England: Basil Blackwell.

Rogoff, B., Mejía-Arauz, R., & Correa-Chávez, M. (2015). A cultural paradigm—Learning by Observing and Pitching In. In M. Correa-Chávez, R. Mejía-Arauz & B. Rogoff (Eds.), *Advances in child development and behavior: Vol. 49. Children learn by observing and contributing to family and community endeavors: A cultural paradigm* (pp. 1–22). Waltham, MA: Academic Press.

Rogoff, B., Mistry, J., Göncü, A., & Mosier, C. (1993). Guided participation in cultural activity by toddlers and caregivers. *Monographs of the Society for Research in Child Development, 58* (8, Serial No. 236), v-vi, 1–174.

Rogoff, B., Moore, L., Correa-Chávez, M., & Dexter, A. (2014). Children develop cultural repertoires through engaging in everyday routines and practices. In J. E. Grusec, & P. D. Hastings (Eds.), *Handbook of socialization* (2nd ed., pp. 472–498). New York, NY: Guilford.

Rogoff, B., Moore, L., Najafi, B., Dexter, A., Correa-Chávez, M., & Solís, J. (2007). Children's development of cultural repertoires through participation in everyday routines and practices. In J. E. Grusec & P. D. Hastings (Eds.), *Handbook of socialization* (pp. 490–515). New York, NY: Guilford.

Rogoff, B., Paradise, R., Mejía Arauz, R., Correa-Chávez, M., & Angelillo, C. (2003). Firsthand learning through intent participation. *Annual Review of Psychology, 54,* 175–203.

Rogoff, B., & Toma, C. (1997). Shared thinking: Cultural and institutional variations. *Discourse Processes, 23,* 471–497.

Romney, K., & Romney, R. (1966). *The Mixtecans of Juxtlahuaca, Mexico.* New York, NY: John Wiley.

Rosado-May, F. J., Urrieta, L., Dayton, A., & Rogoff, B. (in press). The pedagogy and innovation involved in Indigenous Knowledge Systems. In N. S. Nasir, C. Lee, & R. Pea (Eds.), *Handbook of the cultural foundations of learning.* London, England: Routledge.

Ruvalcaba, O., & Rogoff, B. (2016). *Cultural differences in children's pair collaboration in computer programming: Fluid synchrony versus negotiating individual agendas.* Unpublished manuscript, University of California, Santa Cruz.

Saxe, G. (2012). *The cultural development of mathematical ideas.* New York, NY: Cambridge University Press.

Schieffelin, B. (1990). *The give and take of everyday life: Language socialization of Kaluli children.* Cambridge, England: Cambridge University Press.

Schugurensky, D. (2000). *The forms of informal learning: Towards a conceptualization of the field* (WALL Working Paper No. 19). Retrieved from https://tspace.library.utoronto.ca/bitstream/1807/2733/2/19formsofinformal.pdf

Scollon, R., & Scollon, S. (1981). *Narrative, literacy, and face in interethnic communication.* Norwood, NJ: Ablex.

Scribner, S., & Cole, M. (1973). The cognitive consequences of formal and informal education. *Science, 182,* 553–559.

Scribner, S., & Cole, M. (1981). *The psychology of literacy.* Cambridge, MA: Harvard University Press.

Semper, R. (1990). Science museums as environments for learning. *Physics Today, 43,* 50–56.

Serpell, R. (1996). Cultural models of childhood in Indigenous socialization and formal schooling in Zambia. In C. P. Hwang, M. E. Lamb, & I. E. Sigel (Eds.), *Images of childhood* (pp. 129–142). Mahwah, NJ: Erlbaum.

Siegel, D., Esterly, J., Callanan, M., Wright, R., & Navarro, R. (2007). Conversations about science across activities in Mexican-descent families. *International Journal of Science Education, 29,* 1447–1466.

Silva, K. G., Correa-Chávez, M., & Rogoff, B. (2010). Mexican heritage children's attention and learning from interactions directed to others. *Child Development, 81,* 898–912.

Silva, K. G., & Rogoff, B. (2016). *Teaching children through "little dramas": Opinions about instructional ribbing from US Mexican-heritage and European American mothers.* Unpublished manuscript, University of California, Santa Cruz.

Silva, K. G., Shimpi, P. M., & Rogoff, B. (2015). Young children's attention to what's going on: Cultural differences. In M. Correa-Chávez, R. Mejía-Arauz, & B. Rogoff (Eds.), *Advances in child development and behavior: Vol. 49. Children learn by observing and contributing to family and community endeavors: A cultural paradigm* (pp. 208–227). Waltham, MA: Academic.

Simon, N. (2010). *The participatory museum.* Santa Cruz, CA: Museum 2.0

Smitherman, G. (1977). *Talking and testifying: The language of Black America.* Detroit: Wayne State University Press.

Solis, G., Diep, M., Castañeda, C., Martin, J., & Callanan, M. (2016, June). *"He fell in and that's how he became a fossil": Parents' narratives and explanatory science talk during a museum visit.* Poster presented at Jean Piaget Society, Chicago, IL.

Spindler, G. (Ed.). (1955). *Education and anthropology.* Stanford, CA: Stanford University Press.

Steele, K. (2001). A new teacher learning to share responsibility with parents. In B. Rogoff, C. Goodman Turkanis, & L. Bartlett (Eds.), *Learning together: Children and adults in a school community* (pp. 138–144). New York, NY: Oxford University Press.

Stein, J., Garibay, C., & Wilson, K. (2008). Engaging immigrant audiences in museums. *Museums & Social Issues, 3,* 179–196.

Stern, W. (1911). The supernormal child. *Journal of Educational Psychology, 2,* 143–148.

Stevens, R., Bransford, J., & Stevens, A. (2005). *The LIFE Center's lifelong and lifewide diagram.* Retrieved from http://life-slc.org/about/about.htm

Stone, L., & Gutiérrez, K. (2007). Problem articulation and processes of assistance: An activity theoretic view of mediation in game play. *International Journal of Educational Research, 46,* 43–56.

Szechter, L., & Carey, E. (2009). Gravitating toward science: Parent-child interactions at a gravitational-wave observatory. *Science Education, 93,* 846–858.

Tenenbaum, H., & Callanan, M. (2008). Parents' science talk to their children in Mexican-descent families residing in the USA. *International Journal of Behavioral Development, 32,* 1–12.

Tharp, R. G., & Gallimore, R. (1988). *Rousing minds to life: Teaching, learning and schooling in social context.* Cambridge, England: Cambridge University Press.

Umphress, J., Miele, D., Simons, T., & Cohen, D. (2006, April). *Re-opening the debate: Introducing social prescription as the key to understanding informal learning.* Poster presented at the annual meeting of American Educational Research Association, San Francisco, CA.

Underwood, C., & Parker, L. (2014). University-Community Links: Collaborative engagement in extended learning. *International Journal for Research on Extended Education, 2,* 5–11.

Urrieta, L., Jr. (2013). Familia and comunidad-based saberes: Learning in an Indigenous heritage community. *Anthropology & Education Quarterly, 44,* 320–335.

Valdes, G. (1996). *Con respeto: Bridging the distances between culturally diverse families and schools.* New York, NY: Teachers College Press.

Vásquez, O. A. (2002). *La clase mágica: Imagining optimal possibilities in a bilingual community of learners.* Mahwah, NJ: Erlbaum.

Vossoughi, S. (2011). *On the formation of intellectual kinship: A qualitative case study of literacy, learning, and social analysis in a summer migrant education program* (Doctoral dissertation). Retrieved from ProQuest Dissertations & Theses Database. (UMI No. 3472609)

Vossoughi, S. (2014). Social analytic artifacts made concrete: A study of learning and political education. *Mind, Culture, and Activity, 21,* 353–373.

Vossoughi, S., Hooper, P., & Escudé, M. (2016). Making through the lens of culture and power: Toward transformative visions for educational equity. *Harvard Educational Review, 86*, 206–232.

Ward, M. C. (1971). *Them children: A study in language learning.* New York, NY: Holt, Rinehart & Winston.

Watson-Gegeo, K., & Boggs, S. (1977). From verbal play to talk story: The role of routines in speech events among Hawaiian children. In S. Ervin-Tripp & C. Mitchell-Kernan (Eds.), *Child discourse* (pp. 76–90). New York, NY: Academic Press.

Whiting, B. B. (1980). Culture and social behavior: A model for the development of social behavior. *Ethos, 8*, 95–116.

Whiting, B. B. (1996). The effect of social change on concepts of the good child and good mothering: A study of families in Kenya. *Ethos, 24*, 3–35.

Whiting, B. B., & Edwards, C. P. (1988). *Children of different worlds: The formation of social behavior.* Cambridge, MA: Harvard University Press.

Whiting, B. B., & Whiting, J. W. M. (1975). *Children of six cultures: A psycho-cultural analysis.* Cambridge, MA: Harvard University Press.

Whiting, J. W. M. (1940). *Becoming a Kwoma: Teaching and learning in a New Guinea tribe.* New Haven, CT: Yale University Press.

Whiting, J. W. M., & Child, I. L. (1953). *Child training and personality.* New Haven, CT: Yale University Press.

Wilbert, J. (1979). To become a maker of canoes: An essay on Warao enculturation. In J. Wilbert (Ed.), *Enculturation in Latin America* (pp. 303–358). Los Angeles: UCLA Latin America Center Publications.

Wolf, S. A., & Heath, S. B. (1992). *The braid of literature: Children's world of reading.* Cambridge, MA: Harvard University Press.

Young, M. F. D. (1971). *Knowledge and control: New directions for the sociology of education.* London, England: Macmillan.

Zimmerman, H. T., Reeve, S., & Bell, P. (2010). Family sense-making practices in science center conversations. *Science Education, 94*, 478–505.

III. The Process and Substance of Learning

Chapter 12

Exploring a Century of Advancements in the Science of Learning

P. Karen Murphy
Stephanie L. Knight
The Pennsylvania State University

The past century has yielded a plethora of advancements in the science of learning, from expansions in the theoretical frames that undergird education research to cultural and contextual considerations in educational practice. The overarching purpose of this chapter is to explore and document the growth and development of the science of learning using a tripartite approach. The authors first provide an overview of definitions of learning that have been forwarded in the extant literature, with particular emphasis on journals published by the American Educational Research Association. Next, they overview the epistemic frames that have undergirded investigations of learning during the past century. Finally, they explore the ways in which the nature of investigations of learning has transitioned over time and how these transitions have manifested themselves in settings such as classrooms. In reflecting on the maturation and adaptation of the science of learning over the past century, the authors conclude with thoughts on the future of the science of learning.

There is no question that schools, as sociopolitical institutions, exist for many reasons (National School Boards Association, 2014; Storr, 1976). Undoubtedly, one reason for the existence of educational institutions is the orchestration of opportunities for the growth of individuals and for the societies they inhabit (National School Boards Association, 2014). The growth to which we refer implies change—change in how individuals understand themselves, as well as in how they see, comprehend, and act in and on the world. In effect, the change of which we speak can be labeled *learning*. Thus, it is understandable that learning has been and remains a centerpiece of education research and practice since long before the birth of learning sciences or the establishment of the American Educational Research Association

Review of Research in Education
March 2016, Vol. 40, pp. 402–456
DOI: 10.3102/0091732X16677020

(AERA). Indeed, endeavors to understand learning date back to the pre-Socratic philosophers, as recorded in the ancient Greek fragments. For example, the pre-Socratic philosopher Heraclitus wrote about unceasing and ever-present change, which he conceived as the very foundation of the universe (Kirk, 1954). Furthermore, Heraclitus's contentions that one can never step in the same river twice and that the essence of an entity relies on its pairing with an opposite (e.g., to understand the meaning of "up," there must be "down"; "good" can be understood only in comparison with "evil") were echoed centuries later in the writings of William James (1890) and again in more contemporary research on antithetical reasoning (Alexander, Dumas, Grossnickle, List, & Firetto, 2016).

What is easily gleaned from centuries of writings is that the pursuit of deeper and more justified understandings of learning reveals underlying tensions or dualities, which still thread their way into the science of learning today. Be it Plato's rationalism, Aristotle's empiricism, or Descartes' mind–body dualism, scientists of learning must consciously or unconsciously wrestle with a host of ontological and epistemic issues about the very nature of learning, or what ultimately will stand as evidence that learning has occurred (Bredo, 2016). For instance, as we will discuss later in this chapter, there is the unresolved question of whether learning is in its essence an individual transformation or whether groups can learn. There is also the unresolved question of whether there must be some observable and documentable evidence of learning, or whether learning can remain forever buried in the mind or brain of the learner. Those committed to the science of learning cannot sidestep such fundamental questions. Consequently, as we attempt to chronicle the history of how learning has come to be understood over the past century, we must place such enigmatic concerns front and center in our analysis. It is important to understand that, by *science of learning*, we are referring to an accumulated body of knowledge about the nature and processes of student learning that has been derived through scientifically sound, empirical research. Thus, readers should be careful not to conflate our use of the term *science of learning* with *science learning* (i.e., learning in the content area of science). Rather, we mean to explore advancements in scientific understandings about student learning.

Arguably, the advancement of the science of learning over the past century has undergone adaptations somewhat like those that Darwin ascribed to the evolution of species. Some might aver that, metaphorically speaking, theoretical and empirical advancements pertaining to learning have been achieved through an evolutionary process. In this process, conceptual ideas or methodological approaches have been laid bare on the altar of science and their essence put to the test so that strengths could be built on and weaknesses culled and cast aside. But it remains open to debate what determines the viability of conceptual ideas and methodological approaches in the science of learning and how that occurs. It is clear, however, that there are documentable changes in how we define and theorize about learning.

In this chapter, we examine "adaptations" in the science of learning through a tripartite approach. First, we explore definitions of learning that have been forwarded in the extant literature, with a particular emphasis on journals published by AERA.

Second, we overview the various epistemic frames that have undergirded investigations of learning during the past century. Finally, we explore the ways in which investigations of learning have moved from primarily laboratory-based to more realistic settings such as classrooms, and how these moves were made manifest in learning settings such as classrooms. No doubt, maturation and adaptation of the science of learning should be reflected in ecologically valid settings where learning is expected to occur; that is, in settings such as classrooms.[1]

DEFINING LEARNING

A recurring challenge of any science, but particularly the social sciences, is the defining of key terminology (e.g., Alexander, Schallert, & Hare, 1991; Murphy & Alexander, 2000). Such well-defined terminology serves as shorthand for communication among community members, while at the same time allowing those from the outside to eavesdrop, metaphorically, on activities (Bruner, 1990; Pintrich, 1994). This is particularly important in scientific research focused on student learning, as there are a growing number of researchers and education stakeholders (e.g., school personnel and policymakers) whose interest in becoming lexically proficient in the nuances of learning-related terms varies tremendously. The issue of vernacular versus academic terminology is further complicated by the fact that conceptual understandings about learning appear to have undergone certain transformations or adaptations over time. However, unlike the evolution of species depicted by Darwin, the evolution of conceptions of learning is neither clear nor simple.

As Alexander and colleagues (Alexander et al., 1991; Alexander, Murphy, & Greene, 2012) have suggested, the field of learning has experienced an "unbridled spawning" of learning-related terms over the past century—far too many to synthesize within the present review. Alexander et al. (2012) described the proliferation of learning and learning-related terms as an exemplar of the incremental trends evident in educational psychology research. The concern raised by Alexander et al. (2012) was that while there is a burgeoning of learning-related terms, such terms often go undefined in the literature or seem to share conceptual space with associated ideas (e.g., Alexander et al., 1991; Murphy & Alexander, 2000). Furthermore, as eloquently articulated by Peirce (1878), what is needed are clear ideas, where "a clear idea is defined as one which is so apprehended that it will be recognized wherever it is met with, and so that no other will be mistaken for it" (p. 286).

There have been attempts over the past century to derive a unified definition or understanding of learning. In fact, a routine practice in the initial decades of the *Review of Educational Research* (*RER*) was to synthesize key understandings and discoveries in a major area of education research every three years. One of those areas was learning. For example, Brownell (1936) attempted to summarize core understandings about learning between 1933 and 1935. Brownell's synthesis quickly drew the reader to the importance of the muscular and neurological underpinnings of learning and the conception of learning as a change in the polarization patterns of resting neurons. Examinations of the highlights and importance of the neuronal discoveries were followed by an admission of bewilderment regarding the quibbling among proponents of behaviorism (Thorndike, 1911) and Gestalt theory (e.g., Ogden, 1926). In essence, Brownell suggested that despite the disagreement, both psychological schools were ardently tied to mechanistic methods of measuring learning, and both had become so overly consumed with testing their theory of learning that they had lost sight of studying learning per se.

Flashing forward more than 75 years, attempts to create unifying definitions are still met with harsh criticisms and rejection on theoretical and epistemic grounds. As a case in point, Alexander, Schallert, and Reynolds (2009) recently initiated a series of discussions at AERA's annual meeting. Their goal was to foster critical discussions about learning among adherents of diverse theoretical positions with the aim of unifying the increasingly fractured perspectives and understandings of learning—that is, finding common ground regarding learning (P. Alexander, personal communication, November 29, 2015). The fruit of this endeavor was the landscape model of learning (Alexander et al., 2009), where learning was defined as

a multidimensional process that results in a relatively enduring change in a person or persons, and consequently [in] how that person or persons will perceive the world and reciprocally respond to its affordances physically, psychologically, and socially. The process of learning has as its foundation the systemic, dynamic, and interactive relation between the nature of the learner and the object of the learning as ecologically situated in a given time and place as well as over time. (Alexander et al., 2009, p. 186)

There is little debate regarding the extent to which Alexander et al. found common ground, as it seems that key components from most major theories of learning were represented in the definition. Instead, the landscape model and accompanying definition of learning were strongly criticized by one scholar for being abstract, underspecified, and lacking in "teeth" (Graesser, 2009, p. 194). Simply put, Graesser accused Alexander et al. of failing to forward what Peirce (1878) referred to as a "clear idea." Graesser contended that the broadness of the definition rendered it impossible to distinguish cases of learning from cases of nonlearning, and he further argued that the principles on which the definition rested were untestable. It seems that in finding common ground regarding learning, Alexander et al. sacrificed necessary theoretical specificity, at least from Graesser's vantage point.

Our overarching goal in this review is to examine how learning has been defined both conceptually and operationally over the past century across the various sectors of education. Thus, our review entertains understandings of learning that are diverse in theoretical and empirical foundations, ranging from cognitive to sociocultural or contextual underpinnings, as well as those emanating from experimental and quasi-experimental studies, longitudinal research, large-scale secondary data analyses, and situated, design-based paradigms. In doing so, we will heed the lessons of the past. In essence, drawing on Darwin, we will attempt to delineate the adaptations apparent in the extant literature (i.e., observable artifacts), while forgoing attempts to settle longstanding debates, quibbles, or theoretical discord in hopes of finding common ground.

Conceptual Definitions of Learning

To undergird our understanding of how learning has been defined over the past century, we conducted an exhaustive review of AERA journals, with a particular emphasis on articles published in *RER* because it is the only journal that dates back almost a century (i.e., 1931 to the present).[2] Given the breadth and focus of this review, we began by searching all volumes of *RER* for articles that contained the word *learning* in the title, which resulted in 163 articles. Our next step was to download all of the selected articles and electronically search for any use of the term *learning*. The goal in searching for the term was to find and document explicit definitions of learning. Two coders trained by the first author of this chapter independently searched the 163 articles. Having individually examined each document, we reviewed the list of selected articles for possible inclusion. Discrepancies regarding inclusion were discussed until consensus was reached and a final reconciled list compiled. The only exclusions were articles that pertained to professional learning (e.g., training occurring in an employment setting; e.g., Kyndt & Baert, 2013; Webster-Wright, 2009) or articles in which learning was defined only in the context of a modifier (e.g., learning disability; e.g., Grotberg, 1965; Swanson & Hoskyn, 1998). Our justification was that these articles addressed special cases of learning and would, therefore, have limited generalizability beyond the specialized form of learning or setting.

These criteria resulted in a pool of 16 articles. As seen in Table 1, we recorded certain elements for each article: (a) author, (b) brief description of the topic or purpose, (c) explicit definition of learning, and (d) theoretical lens. When possible, we recorded direct quotes of the explicit definitions provided by the authors. When no direct quote was given by the authors, we extracted a definition based on textual content. As will be subsequently discussed, the *theoretical lens* refers to the discernable overarching framework assumed by the researchers (e.g., behavioral versus cognitive orientation).

Several key findings are evident across the articles and definitions listed in Table 1. First, despite the fact that theory building and empirical investigations of learning have been a central endeavor of AERA since its inception, with over 3,000 published entries, few authors in this sample included learning as a construct of interest (5.40%), and fewer still provided the readers with a "clear idea" of what learning means (0.53%). Certainly, as Graesser (2009) suggested, it may be the case that many other terms (e.g., *behavior, memory,* or *knowledge*) could serve as proxies or placeholders for learning. Nonetheless, it is worth noting that, on average, approximately two articles per year in *RER*'s history directly explored the topic of learning. Even more disheartening is that, of the 163 articles with learning in the title, only 16 included explicit definitions of the term.

Another key finding is a strong alignment between the publication dates, the historical timeline of learning theory, and the discernable theoretical lenses. As shown in Table 1, the earliest reviews of learning (Brownell, 1936; Mowrer, 1952) forward a behavioral/biological theoretical lens, followed by more cognitive views of learning (Belanger, 1969; Bereiter, 1985; Iran-Nejad, 1990; Kozma, 1991; Shuell, 1986, 1990), and then there is a transition from a cognitive lens to one more focused on the social or

TABLE 1
Explicit Definitions of Learning From the *Review of Educational Research*, 1931 to 2015

Author	Year	Topic/Purpose	Definition	Theoretical Lens
Brownell	1936	Discoveries about learning, 1933–1935	"Learning is a change in patterns of the polarization of resting neurons." (p. 282)	Behavioral/ biological
Trow	1945	Factors that influence learning	"Learning . . . could be viewed as acquired changes in the behavior probabilities of an individual brought about thru a definitely controlled environment." (p. 227)	1. Behavioral/ biological 2. Cognitive
Mowrer	1952	Learning theory from a historical perspective	"Two forms of learning exist and function, not side-by-side, but end-to-end: sign learning is the process whereby external events come to produce internal drive states, and solution learning is the process whereby internal drive states produce external, overt behavior." (p. 492)	Behavioral/ biological
Shaw	1967	Motivation in human learning	"[Learning can be defined as] memory, psychomotor tasks, problem solving, and achievement" (p. 563; e.g., amount of immediate recall and recall at two brief intervals following stimulus presentation, p. 574).	Cognitive
Belanger	1969	Application of theoretical and empirical understandings to learning in science	1. "Learning is change in behavior." (p. 377) 2. "Learning is internal processing/developmental change." (p. 378)	1. Behavioral/ biological 2. Cognitive
Rohwer	1971	The relationship among learning, race, and school success	"Learning is the process that mediates between differences in IQ and differences in school achievement." (p. 193)	Cognitive

(continued)

TABLE 1 (CONTINUED)

Author	Year	Topic/Purpose	Definition	Theoretical Lens
Bereiter	1985	The mental resources available to the learner in the building of new knowledge	Learning is the process of constructing knowledge and cognitive strategies by bootstrapping a number of cognitive resources.	Cognitive
Shuell	1986	Current thinking about learning within the framework of cognitive psychology	"[Learning consists of] changes in human performance, knowledge structures, and/or conceptions" (p. 411); "Three criteria for defining learning (see, e.g., Shuell & Lee, 1976): (a) a change in an individual's behavior or ability to do something, (b) a stipulation that this change must result from some sort of practice or experience, and (c) a stipulation that the change is an enduring one" (p. 412); "More domain specific than earlier learning theorists believed" (p. 427); "Viewed as being active, constructive, cumulative, and goal oriented" (p. 430)	Cognitive
Iran-Nejad	1990	The assumptions of learning and the active and dynamic self-regulation of learning	"Learning is internalization of externally available knowledge" (p. 573); "Creative reconceptualization of internal knowledge" (p. 573)	Cognitive
Shuell	1990	The stages and phases of the learning process and influential variables	"Learning is an active, constructive, cumulative, and goal-oriented process that involves problem-solving" (p. 532); "Occurs gradually over a period of time" (p. 540)	Cognitive

(continued)

TABLE 1 (CONTINUED)

Author	Year	Topic/Purpose	Definition	Theoretical Lens
Kozma	1991	Characteristics of media that influence cognitive representations	"Learning is viewed as an active, constructive process whereby the learner strategically manages the available cognitive resources to create new knowledge by extracting information from the environment and integrating it with information already stored in memory" (pp. 179–180); "School learning is acquiring an understanding of the relationship between various symbol systems and the real world they represent" (p. 195)	Cognitive
Aleven, Stahl, Schworm, Fischer, and Wallace	2003	Help-seeking and learning in interactive learning environments	"We define learning loosely as cognitive activities in which the processing of new information results in the acquisition of new skills or knowledge." (p. 279)	Cognitive
Paavola, Lipponen, and Hakkarainen	2004	Knowledge communities in relation to learning metaphors	1. *Acquisition metaphor*: "Learning is a matter of construction, acquisition, and outcomes, which are realized in the process of transfer." (p. 557)	1. Cognitive
			2. *Participation metaphor*: "Learning is a process of participation in various cultural practices and shared learning activities; focus is on activities more than products." (p. 557)	2. Contextual
			3. *Knowledge-creation metaphor*: "Learning is understood as a collaborative effort directed toward developing some mediated artifacts, broadly defined as including knowledge, ideas, practices, and material or conceptual artifacts." (pp. 569–570)	

(continued)

TABLE 1 (CONTINUED)

Author	Year	Topic/Purpose	Definition	Theoretical Lens
de Kock, Sleegers, and Voeten	2004	Scheme for learning environments in secondary education	1. "Learning is a social-interactive, contextual, constructive, self-regulated and reflective process." (p. 141)	1. Cognitive
			2. "Constructivism views learning as more than merely the reception or transmission of information; it is seen primarily as the active and personal construction of knowledge." (p. 146)	2. Contextual
			3. "Learning is a constructive, situated, and social activity; which has implications for the learning goals, the division of the roles between teachers and learners in the learning environment, roles of the learners in relation to each other, respectively." (p. 150)	
Nasir and Hand	2006	Sociocultural perspectives for integrating and research on race, culture, and learning	"Learning is constituted by changing relations in these social relationships and the social world" (p. 459); "Shifting relations between the individuals and the communities of practice in which they participate" (p. 462); "Learning is not only about taking on new knowledge structures, but it is about personal transformation—about becoming" (p. 467)	Contextual
Esmonde	2009	The use of cooperative groups to provide equitable opportunities	"Learning can be defined as a change in participation in a set of collective practices." (p. 1011)	Contextual

educational context (de Kock et al., 2004; Nasir & Hand, 2006; Paavola et al., 2004). Interestingly, several of the reviews of literature involved explicit attempts to delineate differences between the definitions and theoretical underpinnings of learning (e.g., Belanger, 1969; de Kock et al., 2004). Despite such attempts, our review revealed a substantive relation between the nature of the definition of learning and the theoretical positions expressed by the authors. This finding reinforces the presupposition of Hull (1935) that definitions of learning and theoretical framing are intimately linked.

The final trend emerging from these explicit definitions of learning is that there was very little consensus regarding what learning is or is not. In fact, the only definitional aspect of learning represented across all of these articles was the idea that *learning is change*, echoing Alexander et al.'s (2009) "common ground" definition. From the 1930s to the early 2000s, it seems that learning, and necessarily the science of learning, was seen as pertaining to human change—change apart from maturation. In some cases, the change is related to neuronal activation (Brownell, 1936) or behavior (e.g., Trow, 1945), whereas in others the focus is on internal reorganization of cognitive structures (e.g., Iran-Nejad, 1990) or changes in social and contextual interactions (e.g., Nasir & Hand, 2006). These definitional findings affirm Darwin's (1859) notion of adaptation, in that definitions of learning have retained the essential defining feature of the term (i.e., human change), while altering aspects or characteristics of the definition that increase likelihood of the term surviving.

Operational Definitions of Learning

Although conceptual understandings regarding the term *learning* can be gleaned from the reviews and syntheses appearing in *RER*, it is more challenging to get a sense of how the term has been operationalized within research investigations. To examine *learning in use*, we turned to AERA's flagship empirical journal, the *American Educational Research Journal* (*AERJ*), which published its first issue in 1964. Beginning with the year of the journal's inception, we hand-searched each article in the first volume of that year. Studies in which *learning*, as designated by the author, was a primary outcome were retained for further review. This selection procedure was followed in one volume of each subsequent decade of the journal (i.e., 1974, 1984, 1994, 2004, and 2014). The search revealed 39 articles in which learning was reported as an outcome of the investigation or a target of the research. Once the corpus was identified (see Table 2), the articles were coded for the following elements: (a) author; (b) publication year; (c) topic/purpose of the study; (d) whether the topic was domain general or domain specific; (e) theoretical lens as evident in the framing of the study; (f) participants under investigation; (g) setting, or where the study took place; (h) duration, or the time span for the investigation; and (i) actual learning outcome(s). In all cases, each article was dual-coded to ensure accuracy. Discrepancies were discussed until consensus was reached. The data in Table 2 represent the reconciled codings. Various trends were evident in the resulting data. In this chapter, we discuss the trends that substantively informed understanding of how the term *learning* has been operationally defined in *AERJ*.

TABLE 2

Operationalization of Learning From Selected Empirical Articles Published in the *American Educational Research Journal*, 1964 to 2015

Authors	Year	Topic/Purpose	Domain	Lens	Participants	Setting	Duration	Learning Outcome
Travers and Wagenen	1964	The influence of accuracy on students' observational learning	General	Behavioral/ biological	Fourth, fifth, and sixth graders (*n* = 136)	Classroom as laboratory	1 week (Monday, Tuesday, Wednesday, and Friday)	Lorge–Thorndike (Thorndike & Lorge, 1944), German noun battery stimulus response task
Bingham-Newman and Hooper	1974	Teaching students to complete Piagetian tasks through small-group training sessions	General	Cognitive	Preschool students (*n* = 60)	Classroom as laboratory	3-week instructional program	Peabody picture vocabulary; Piagetian assessment tasks: (a) relational terms task; (b) seriation measures; (c) classification measures; (d) conservation measures
Hosie, Gentile, and Carroll	1974	Extending the Premack Principle to human (i.e., student) learners	General	Behavioral/ biological	Experiment 1: sixth graders (*n* = 14); Experiment 2: fifth and sixth graders (*n* = 20)	Classroom as laboratory	Five sessions over several school days	Observation of time taken to complete the assignment (i.e., painting, modeling clay)

(continued)

TABLE 2 (CONTINUED)

Authors	Year	Topic/Purpose	Domain	Lens	Participants	Setting	Duration	Learning Outcome
Lintner and Ducette	1974	The influence of locus of control orientation and gender on students' responsiveness to praise	General	Behavioral/ biological	Third, fifth, and seventh graders ($n = 285$)	Classroom intervention	3 weeks	Observation and reading achievement (Gates–MacGinitie)
Thompson, Brassell, Persons, Tucker, and Rollins	1974	Comparing the differences in teachers' and students' behaviors for classrooms implementing a contingency management program and control classrooms	General	Behavioral/ biological	22 elementary school teachers and students	Classroom intervention	3-week baseline; 3-week trial	Observation: positive and negative behavior events by student and teacher
Benware and Deci	1984	Testing the effect of students' orientation to a task (i.e., active or passive) on the resulting motivation, engagement, conceptual learning, and rote learning	General	Cognitive	Undergraduate ($n = 43$)	Laboratory	3–5 hours	24-item exam to measure rote memory and conceptual understanding of the material

(continued)

413

TABLE 2 (CONTINUED)

Authors	Year	Topic/Purpose	Domain	Lens	Participants	Setting	Duration	Learning Outcome
Garner, Hare, Alexander, Haynes, and Winograd	1984	Testing the effect of a lookback strategy; compared to a control group, on students' lookbacks and question accuracy	General	Cognitive	Elementary and middle school students (n = 24)	University (reading clinic) intervention	3 days of training (2–3 hours total); 5-day delayed assessment	Video coding of strategic behaviors and recall
McCormick and Levin	1984	The effect of instructing students to use variations of the keyword mnemonic method as compared to letting students choose their own strategy on recall	General	Cognitive	Experiment 1: eighth graders (n = 220); Experiment 2: seventh and eighth graders (n = 82)	Classroom as laboratory	Experiment 1: 40 minutes; delayed test carried out 2 days later in Experiment 2	Experiment 1: 20 cued-recall questions on texts; Experiment 2: Name attribute matching test based on text information
Park	1984	The effect of identifying critical attributes along with prototype formation and elaboration on concept learning	General	Cognitive	12th graders (n = 68)	Classroom as laboratory	35-minute lesson and test; 1-week delayed test lasting 20 minutes	Posttest: 24 test items on concepts; delayed test: same items as posttest plus eight open-ended concept elaboration questions

(continued)

TABLE 2 (CONTINUED)

Authors	Year	Topic/Purpose	Domain	Lens	Participants	Setting	Duration	Learning Outcome
Peterson, Swing, Stark, and Waas	1984	Examining the relationship between students' self-reports and observers' judgments on students' learning	Specific (math)	Cognitive	Fifth graders ($n = 38$) and teacher ($n = 1$)	Classroom as laboratory	9-day instructional unit	55-item mathematics achievement test
Roberge and Flexer	1984	The influence of cognitive style (i.e., field dependence–independence) and cognitive development (i.e., high–low operational development) on students' reading achievement	General	Cognitive	Sixth, seventh, and eighth graders ($n = 450$)	Classroom as laboratory	Two testing sessions 1 week apart	Metropolitan Reading Achievement test
Seddon, Eniaiyeju, and Jusoh	1984	Using remedial instruction to teach struggling students to visualize the rotation of 3D diagrams	General	Cognitive	Experiment 1: high school students ($n = 245$); Experiment 2: undergraduates ($n = 252$)	Classroom intervention (Experiment 1); university intervention (Experiment 2)	Experiment 1: three 1-hour sessions; Experiment 2: approximately three 1-hour sessions	Experiments 1 and 2: rotation test and cues test

(continued)

TABLE 2 (CONTINUED)

Authors	Year	Topic/Purpose	Domain	Lens	Participants	Setting	Duration	Learning Outcome
Slavin and Karweit	1984	Testing the effect of mastery orientation, student teams, and a combination of the two on students' mathematics learning	Specific (math)	Contextual	Ninth graders ($n = 588$)	Classroom intervention	1 year (26 lesson sequences)	Comprehensive Test of Basic Skills: Mathematics
Talmage, Pascarella, and Ford	1984	Enhancing teachers' use of cooperative goal structuring strategies and the subsequent changes to the classroom learning environment and students' learning	General	Contextual	Elementary school students (1982; $n = 493$ to 587) and teachers ($n = 107$)	Classroom intervention	3-year longitudinal	Self-report cooperation score; observation of cooperative practices; standardized reading achievement; language arts achievement
Wixson	1984	Using postquestions after reading as a backward review of information to enhance students' delayed recall of questioned information	General	Cognitive	Fifth graders ($n = 172$)	Classroom as laboratory	Brief reading and testing session; delayed testing	Session 1: 15 questions on texts; delay: free recall of passage, 15 probing questions

(continued)

TABLE 2 (CONTINUED)

Authors	Year	Topic/Purpose	Domain	Lens	Participants	Setting	Duration	Learning Outcome
Alexander, Kulikowich, and Schulze	1994	Examining the effect of subject-matter knowledge on students' interest and recall	Specific (physics)	Cognitive	Undergraduate ($n = 163$); graduate ($n = 46$)	University as laboratory	1 hour	Cued recall
Bornholt, Goodnow, and Cooney	1994	Examining adolescents' gender differences in achievement, perceptions of achievement, and traditional gender stereotypes	Specific (English and math)	Contextual	High school students ($n = 663$)	Classroom as laboratory	40-minute lesson period	Test of Reading Comprehension Achievement; Progressive Achievement Test of Mathematics
Fuchs, Fuchs, Bentz, Phillips, and Hamlett	1994	Examining the effect of providing students with peer tutoring training and experience on the nature of students' interactions during tutoring and the quality of tutoring instruction	General	Contextual	Third, fourth, and fifth graders and their teachers ($n = 16$)	Classroom intervention	10 weeks	Student outcomes on worksheets, observational ratings of tutor/tutee exchanges

(continued)

TABLE 2 (CONTINUED)

Authors	Year	Topic/Purpose	Domain	Lens	Participants	Setting	Duration	Learning Outcome
Graesser and Person	1994	Investigating the quality and frequency of questions asked by students and tutors during tutoring sessions	General	Contextual	Experiment 1: undergraduate ($n = 27$); Experiment 2: seventh graders ($n = 13$)	Classroom (Experiment 2); university (Experiment 1) (tutoring session) as laboratory	Experiment 1: 8 weeks; Experiment 2: 4 weeks	Experiment 1: course exam scores and questions during tutoring; Experiment 2: questions during tutoring
King	1994	Testing the effect of teaching students to use explanations and two levels of questioning to enhance text comprehension	Specific (science)	Cognitive	Fourth graders ($n = 28$), fifth graders ($n = 30$), and their teachers ($n = 2$)	Classroom intervention	3 weeks	Lesson comprehension tests (science lesson), knowledge mapping, discussion analysis
Meloth and Deering	1994	The effects of a reward condition cooperative discussion and a strategic condition cooperative discussion on the talk and task content of the discussions	General	Contextual	Fourth and fifth graders ($n = 206$)	Classroom intervention	2 weeks	Discourse analysis of groups; social and behavioral observations; individual interviews

(continued)

TABLE 2 (CONTINUED)

Authors	Year	Topic/Purpose	Domain	Lens	Participants	Setting	Duration	Learning Outcome
Phelan, Yu, and Davidson	1994	Describe problems that students perceive as being powerful enough to influence their academic learning	General	Contextual	High school students ($n = 55$); a majority of the students were freshmen when the study began	Classroom as laboratory	2-year longitudinal	Interviews about learning, discourse analysis, self-report
Webb and Farivar	1994	Comparing the effects of cooperative learning instructional programs with and without academic helping skills on students' achievement and verbal interaction	Specific (math)	Contextual	Seventh graders ($n = 166$) and their teachers ($n = 2$)	Classroom intervention	11 weeks	Mathematics achievement test; small-group verbal interactions
Zimmerman and Bandura	1994	The influence of self-efficacy beliefs on academic attainment, regulation of writing, goals, and self-standards	Specific (writing)	Contextual	Undergraduate ($n = 95$)	University as laboratory	1 testing session	Final course grade

(continued)

TABLE 2 (CONTINUED)

Authors	Year	Topic/Purpose	Domain	Lens	Participants	Setting	Duration	Learning Outcome
Chin, Bell, Munby, and Hutchinson	2004	Examining Hung's theory of epistemological appropriation by analyzing the regulatory behaviors of a co-op supervisor and the subsequent influence on one students' learning, actions, and beliefs	General	Contextual	High school student ($n = 1$), her workplace supervisor ($n = 1$), and the dentist ($n = 1$)	Work site as laboratory	1 semester	Interviews and researchers' journal of changes in behavior and beliefs about learning in the workplace; performance assessments
Draper and Siebert	2004	Identifying the similarities and differences between instructional goals and practices of mathematics and literacy educators	General	Contextual	Undergraduate ($n = 25$)	University as laboratory	15-week semester	Field notes, classroom artifacts, discourse, shared understandings, teaching materials
Fuchs, Fuchs, Finelli, Courey, and Hamlett	2004	Examining the effect of schema-based transfer instruction on students' transfer of mathematics problem solving to real-life math problems	Specific (math)	Cognitive	Third graders ($n = 351$) and their teachers ($n = 24$)	Classroom intervention	16-week treatment	Transfer of math problem solving

(continued)

TABLE 2 (CONTINUED)

Authors	Year	Topic/Purpose	Domain	Lens	Participants	Setting	Duration	Learning Outcome
Magnuson, Meyers, Ruhm, and Waldfogel	2004	The influence of preschool education on students' success in kindergarten and the inequality between enrollment from advantaged and disadvantaged families	General	Contextual	Kindergarten students (*n* = 12,804)	Secondary data analysis	Secondary data analysis	Reading and math achievement and skills
Murphy and Alexander	2004	Examining the influence of persuasive texts on changes in readers' knowledge, beliefs, and interests, as well as the influence of individual differences on change	General	Cognitive	Undergraduate (*n* = 234); a majority of the students were third and fourth years	Laboratory	75 minutes	Perceived knowledge, demonstrated knowledge, and beliefs
Porat	2004	Examining the differential effect of comprehension based on students' political and social backgrounds	General	Contextual	12th graders (*n* = 11)	Classroom as laboratory	2 brief sessions	Oral summaries and 1-year delayed postnarratives

(continued)

421

TABLE 2 (CONTINUED)

Authors	Year	Topic/Purpose	Domain	Lens	Participants	Setting	Duration	Learning Outcome
Shapiro	2004	The importance of assessing prior knowledge rather than assuming negligible effects from fictitious content or from novice students	General	Cognitive	Undergraduate—Experiment 1: $n = 24$; Experiment 2: $n = 34$	University as laboratory	Experiment 1: 90 to 120 minutes; Experiment 2: four brief testing sessions	Experiments 1 and 2: factual knowledge; inferential reasoning based on texts being read
Tatsuoka, Corter, and Tatsuoka	2004	Examining the patterns of students' mastery of mathematics content and process subskills by country	Specific (math)	Cognitive	Eighth graders ($n = 51,435$)	Secondary data analysis	Secondary data analysis	Mathematics achievement
Wortham	2004	Describing the interrelationship between social identification and learning	General	Contextual	Ninth graders ($n = 19$)	Classroom as laboratory	1 year	Discourse analysis
Xue and Meisels	2004	The impact of early literacy instruction on teachers' ratings of students' achievement and students' cognitive test scores in kindergarten	Specific (language and literacy)	Cognitive	Kindergarten students ($n = 13,609$)	Secondary data analysis	Secondary data analysis	Cognitive test of language and literacy achievement; teacher ratings of students' skills, knowledge, and behaviors

(continued)

TABLE 2 (CONTINUED)

Authors	Year	Topic/Purpose	Domain	Lens	Participants	Setting	Duration	Learning Outcome
Claessens, Engel, and Curran	2014	Examining the relationship between advanced and basic academic content coverage and learning for students who did and did not attend preschool	Specific (reading and math)	Contextual	Kindergarten students ($n = 15,892$)	Secondary data analysis	Secondary data analysis	Language, literacy, and mathematics achievement
Ladd et al.	2014	Identifying specific students' collaborative skills and examining the relationship between those skills and students' social and academic competence	General	Contextual	Sample 1: third, fourth, and fifth graders ($n = 113$); Sample 2: third, fourth, and fifth graders ($n = 212$) and their teachers ($n = 11$)	Classroom as laboratory	Multiple testing sessions	Collaborative skill use, collaborative partner preference, teacher ratings of achievement (reading, arithmetic, spelling, oral language)
Lesaux, Kieffer, Kelley, and Harris	2014	Examining the effect of an academic vocabulary intervention on students' vocabulary knowledge, morphological awareness skills, and comprehension of expository texts	General	Cognitive	Sixth graders ($n = 2,082$) and their teachers ($n = 50$)	Classroom intervention	20 weeks	Gates–MacGinitie and researcher-made tests of vocabulary, word mastery, word association, reading comprehension, morphological awareness, and writing

(continued)

423

TABLE 2 (CONTINUED)

Authors	Year	Topic/Purpose	Domain	Lens	Participants	Setting	Duration	Learning Outcome
Niehaus and Adelson	2014	Examining the relationships between school support, parental involvement, and English language learners' academic/social–emotional outcomes	General	Contextual	Third graders (n = 1,020)	Secondary data analysis	Secondary data analysis	Reading and mathematics achievement scores
Rimm-Kaufman et al.	2014	Examining the efficacy of the Responsive Classroom intervention on students' reading and math achievement	Specific (reading and math)	Contextual	Second graders followed through fifth grade (n = 2,904) and their teachers (n = 276)	Classroom Intervention	3-year longitudinal	State standardized reading and mathematics achievement

Perhaps the most telling trend evident in the coded studies was that learning must be observable and enduring. Indeed, regardless of the topic/purpose, theoretical lens, participants, or setting of the study, researchers required that participants display some observable manifestation that endured long enough to be recorded. The nature of that manifestation varied considerably; it included records from stimulus response tasks (e.g., Travers & Wagenen, 1964), records of time spent working on tasks (e.g., Hosie et al., 1974), scores on achievement tests (e.g., Roberge & Flexer, 1984), responses to questions during tutoring sessions (e.g., Graesser & Person, 1994), and classroom artifacts and verbal discourse (e.g., Draper & Siebert, 2004). The duration also varied dramatically. For example, Murphy and Alexander (2004) had individual students read and respond to questions about various texts in a laboratory setting and made use of intervening tasks (i.e., long division problems) to clear working memory; the entire duration was only 75 minutes per student. The authors argued that the intervening task made it necessary for participants to have encoded their understandings in long-term memory and that retrieval was evidence of their learning.

By comparison, Rimm-Kaufman et al. (2014) implemented a 3-year longitudinal, multischool intervention of the Responsive Classroom curriculum. Their goal was to measure transfer effects on students' learning in reading and mathematics using students' scores from state standardized achievement tests. Clearly, this type of learning would necessarily need to be enduring. This trend suggests that learning refers not just to change, but change that is observable and enduring. We would contend that regardless of the theoretical or epistemic tenets undergirding a given study, the reality, as evident in these coded studies, is that the science of learning began as an empirical science and has remained so throughout the century.

The differences in the studies cited above are consistent with Newell's (1990) conceptualization of learning and human behavior as occurring along a continuum of time scales—time scales that tend to delineate boundaries between various research traditions. For example, the cognitive exploration by Murphy and Alexander (2004) represents a much more fine-grained level of examination than the "social-cultural-historical" investigation by Rimm-Kaufman et al. (2014), which is characterized by an increased time scale and a more coarse-grained level of analysis (Nathan & Alibali, 2010). Nathan and Alibali, like Newell, suggested that the time boundaries (e.g., preceding or following time scale) that define learning-specific theories promote a unified theory about the various ways that learning is manifested. The theoretical lenses that are elucidated later in this chapter provide a similar means of viewing learning that allows complementarity, rather than dissimilarity, to be a unifying factor across theories.

Another major finding evident in the *AERJ* studies sampled was that although the analytical techniques used to study learning became increasingly sophisticated—moving from simple mean difference tests to complex hierarchical linear models—the ways that learning was measured did not advance tremendously over the years after the inception of the journal. Researchers consistently made use of researcher-designed assessments of targeted areas of learning, such as measures of rote retention (Benware & Deci, 1984), attribute naming (McCormick & Levin, 1984), or gains in inferential reasoning (Shapiro, 2004). Similar trends were evident for the collection and coding of student discourse as a mechanism for gauging student learning, regardless of the theoretical lens or methodological orientation. Indeed, it seems that analysis of verbal discourse or talk as a proxy for learning has been as useful for those with a behavioral, quantitative approach (e.g., Travers & Wagenen, 1964) as it has been for those invoking a social–contextual, qualitative approach (e.g., Wortham, 2004).

Perhaps the most surprising trend in the nature of measurement has been the movement from techniques like classroom observation (e.g., Fuchs et al., 1994; Lintner & Ducette, 1974; Talmage et al., 1984) to some combination of classroom observation combined with standardized achievement outcomes (e.g., Peterson et al., 1984), and furthermore, to the use of proxies for learning such as standardized achievement scores (e.g., Bornholt et al., 1994; Ladd et al., 2014; Magnuson et al., 2004). In fact, as Table 2 substantiates, 15 of the 39 studies involved some type of standardized achievement test, and all studies in 2014 employed achievement test scores as a primary proxy for learning. Moreover, there is a parallel trend from consideration of domain-general assessments of the learning target (e.g., Piagetian assessment tasks; Bingham-Newman & Hooper, 1974) to more domain-specific outcome measures (e.g., mathematics achievement; Webb & Farivar, 1994).

Although one could propose many explanations for this domain-general to domain-specific trend, it seems plausible that at least three factors are at play. First, the nature of research funding is such that standardized assessments, particularly those that are domain-specific, psychometrically sound, and commercially available, are encouraged so that gains can be compared across studies. Second, sophisticated analytic techniques that account for unique characteristics of data (e.g., nested samples through multilevel modeling) require very large sample sizes to detect effects. Finally, there is a national and international trend toward learning comparisons on large-scale, standardized measures, which has given way to secondary data analyses (e.g., Claessens et al., 2014), as well as to a desire on the part of researchers to conduct investigations that employ standardized assessments such as learning metrics (e.g., Lesaux et al., 2014).

Also of note were the settings of the various charted studies. The vast majority of the studies were conducted either in an actual laboratory (e.g., Benware & Deci, 1984) or in laboratory-like settings in schools (e.g., Graesser & Person, 1994), classrooms (e.g., Park, 1984), preschools (e.g., Bingham-Newman & Hooper, 1974), universities (e.g., Alexander et al., 1994; Zimmerman & Bandura, 1994), or work sites (e.g., Chin et al., 2004), where the location was used in the very same way that an actual laboratory would function. The use of an elementary, secondary, or university classroom usually involved studies that were shorter in duration and excluded the teacher as a component of the research (e.g., Phelan et al., 1994;

FIGURE 1
Chart of Learning Outcomes From Articles Published in the *American
Educational Research Journal,* as Classified Into the Three Theoretical Lenses;
Articles Without a Learning Outcome Are Also Depicted for Reference

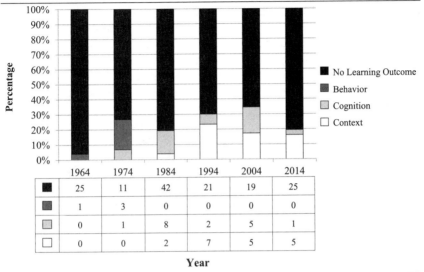

Porat, 2004). Moreover, most of these studies did not directly involve use of or modification of students' everyday curriculum materials. Rather, when instruction was involved, it was self-contained within a packet passed out to students (e.g., Wixson, 1984). By comparison, study settings classified as classroom intervention involved teachers and their students and some form of modification to existing classroom curriculum (e.g., Meloth & Deering, 1994; Slavin & Karweit, 1984; Thompson et al., 1974). We also classified two studies as university interventions (e.g., Garner et al., 1984; Seddon et al., 1984) because they were somewhat extended in duration, made use of ecologically valid materials, and were attempting remedial instruction at an alternative site.

The final trend worthy of note pertains to the theoretical underpinnings articulated in these empirical studies. To aid in interpretation, we created Figure 1, in which we present the percentage of articles reflecting the prominence of each theoretical emphasis by decade. What is evident is that the vast majority of articles published in *AERJ* do not appear to pertain to general learning, as indicated by the authors' outcome variable(s). Moreover, the trend from behavioral/biological theory to cognitive and then contextual frameworks generally parallels the chronological unfolding evident in the review articles charted for the conceptual definitions of learning (see Table 1).

When we analyzed the theoretical lenses in relation to the setting and duration, two additional trends emerged. Specifically, secondary analyses of data allowed researchers some latitude in determining the theoretical lens that would guide their studies (e.g., Niehaus & Adelson, 2014). For example, several secondary data analyses made use of the Early Childhood Longitudinal Study–Kindergarten database (U.S. Department of Education). In some cases, the authors cited cognitive underpinnings (e.g., Xue & Meisels, 2004), while others were more social or contextual in their theoretical leanings (e.g., Claessens et al., 2014), despite the fact that the authors made use of the very same data set.

The second trend to emerge was that all of the coding disagreements pertaining to theoretical lens identification were for classroom intervention studies. In fact, when assessing this trend, we were able to find multiple theoretical frameworks present for each of these studies. A case in point is a study by Fuchs et al. (2004) in which they tested the effects of schema-broadening instruction (SBI), with and without explicit strategies to solve real-life math problems, on third-grade students' mathematics problem solving. Thirty teachers were randomly assigned to a 16-week condition (i.e., control, SBI with strategies, SBI without strategies). The teacher played an instructional role, the strategies were embedded in the existing mathematics curriculum, and a variety of outcome measures were employed. In the researchers' theoretical framing, the SBI, learning strategies, and focus on transfer seems to have been derived from a cognitive framework, while the attention paid to the importance of contextual factors like "real-world" problem sets seemed to have more of a context-oriented frame. This is just one exemplar, but similar challenges were evident in other investigations with settings classified as intervention. One possible explanation is that affecting learning in classrooms requires that the researcher make use of theoretical weaving to account for the various factors that could affect learning as it unfolds in situ (Shulman, 1986a). We will return to this possibility in later sections of the chapter.

THEORETICAL LENSES AS LEARNING FILTERS

As is apparent in the preceding definitional review, learning is a complex construct for which theoretical understandings have evolved dramatically over the past century. Indeed, how one conceptualizes learning, makes predictions about learning outcomes, considers factors that affect learning, or designs approaches to improve learning are all guided by theory. By theory, we mean a scientifically rigorous, principled understanding or explanation for a given phenomenon (Popper, 1963). Such a principled understanding guides the questions asked, the hypotheses posed, the methods employed, and eventually, the interpretations made. Analogously, theory serves a researcher as a lens serves a photographer. There is no single lens that fits every photographer in every situation; different lenses offer distinct advantages and disadvantages. The photographer's choice of a lens determines the possible focal length (e.g., zoom vs. wide-angle) and depth of focus (e.g., sharp or blurry background). The photographer can also supplement the selected lens in a given situation to produce the desired effect (e.g., using a polarizing filter to alter reflections on water). Moreover, the photographer constrains the possible images to be captured, choosing a given setting depending on conditions.

FIGURE 2
Epistemic Frame Foci Based on the Philosophical and Psychological Theory on Knowledge and Learning

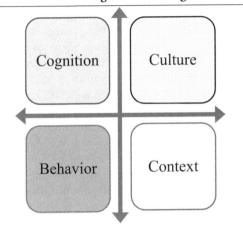

Similarly, theories serve to constrain all aspects of a given study or investigation. In so doing, a theory serves to filter researchers' understandings of learning. For instance, strict adherence to a behavioral lens will constrain an investigation such that cognitive processing is not considered. Again, it is not so much that cognitive processing is not occurring, but rather that the cognitive processes are not the focus for that researcher and are not measured. Arguably, researchers, just like photographers, select a given theoretical lens because they believe it will result in understandings that will optimize learning in a given setting under certain conditions.

Alexander and colleagues (Alexander, 2006, 2007; Murphy, Alexander, & Muis, 2012) have used the notion of *epistemic vector space* as a way to organize and position particular philosophical and psychological perspectives (i.e., lenses) and learning theories associated with knowledge and knowing (see Figure 2). The epistemic vector space is situated in a Cartesian coordinate plane whose axes align with two central epistemic questions: (a) What is the source of knowledge (i.e., where does it come from)? and (b) Where does knowledge ultimately reside? The X axis (horizontal), pertains to the source of knowledge, and the continuum ranges from the *individually informed* to the *socially derived*. Scholars positioned at one end of this continuum hold that knowledge is wholly created or constructed by the individual, whereas those positioned at the other end hold that knowledge originates from the physical, social, and cultural environment in which one exists.

The Y axis considers where knowledge ultimately resides, and the continuum ranges from *in the mind* (of the individual) to *in the environment*. Scholars aligning with the extreme mind view typically characterize the mind or brain as a repository of knowledge that can be later accessed or retrieved and made use of in a given situation or for a given task. At the opposite end of the continuum is the view that knowledge exists in the external world and is linked to some space, place, or time. Such a view suggests that individuals can interact with objects to be known, or participate in knowing with an object, but that they should not be thought of as repositories for such knowledge (Sfard, 1998). As is characteristic of any Cartesian plane, the horizontal and vertical axes meet at moderate positions of the continua, a theoretical middle ground. At this intersection, views of knowledge and knowing acknowledge that the individual is constantly interacting in a social world and that not only the individual mind but also the physical, social, and cultural environments can serve as receptacles of knowledge.

What is important to the present review on the topic of learning is the quadrants formed by the intersection of these two continua (see Figure 2). Each of the quadrants has particular foci associated with the continua (e.g., individual and mind), and the foci serve as a shared lens for filtering learning (e.g., cognition). In the present review, we will build on the epistemic frames forwarded by Murphy et al. (2012) by overviewing specific lenses that have served to filter how we view and investigate learning, as well as how we frame interventions and instruction. Specifically, the next section of this chapter provides an overview of three theoretical lenses: *behavioral/ biological, cognitive,* and *cultural/contextual.* As will be explained, we chose to combine Murphy et al.'s cultural and contextual quadrants because, like Vygotsky (1978), we posit that culture can be considered an aspect of the context of learning. For each lens, we will overview critical characteristics, including (a) chronological rise to prominence and key events, (b) exemplar theories of learning, (c) associated conceptions of learning, and (d) key theorists/researchers/proponents of the lens. For each section, we will also overview selected classical and contemporary empirical research articles exemplifying that particular lens. When possible, the article will be drawn from journals published by AERA. Finally, we will discuss implications and ramifications for each lens in terms of educational activities and events, because it is imperative to look not only at how a given lens has served to frame research but also at how it has shaped the learning fostered in real learning settings, such as classrooms, through such activities and events.

Behavioral/Biological Lens

The turn of the 20th century was the heyday of Wilhelm Maximilian Wundt's impassioned efforts to have psychology recognized as a branch of the natural sciences. Toiling away in his laboratory in Leipzig, Germany, Wundt studied human consciousness using as his primary methodology the subjective observation of one's experiences (i.e., introspective methods; Boring, 1957). Despite the popularity of introspection as a methodological approach by prolific scholars like G. Stanley Hall, James McKeen Cattell, Charles Judd, and William James, its use quickly played out as behaviorism established a foothold in psychology. The weakness of introspective methods was that they required an "experiencing subject," which no other branch of the natural sciences required (Klein, Mathieu, Gendlin, & Kiesler, 1970, p. 832). Their strength was their strict adherence to precise measurement and definitive methods (Walberg & Haertel, 1992).

Moreover, as was echoed by pragmatists like James, Dewey, and Peirce, deeply understanding that the psychological implications of a stimulus and its concomitant response required consideration of the stimulus and response as a circuit that extended beyond what could be observed (James, 1890; Murphy et al., 2012). Indeed, Dewey's (1896) *reflex arc* suggested that psychologists must also heed the underlying physiological mechanisms and the purpose or function of the stimulus and response interaction as situated within a particular context (James, 1890). To Dewey, a response to a given stimulus was a means to an end as realized within some environment. Although the pragmatists would continue to influence the evolution of a science of learning throughout the next century, their prominence at the turn of the 20th century was, arguably, short lived. Indeed, by 1916, when AERA came into existence, behaviorism had emerged as the dominant learning paradigm (Walberg & Haertel, 1992). The shift was nicely captured by Watson's (1929) contention that "the Behaviorist cannot find consciousness in the test-tube of his science" (p. 6).

Behaviorism is often regarded as a rather deterministic branch of psychology concerned with the experimental study of behavior (Cooper, Heron, & Heward, 2007). Within the behavioral/biological lens, the science of learning turns to the observable ways in which animals, including humans, adapt to their environment; that is, behaviorism explains learning in terms of environmental events (Skinner, 1948; Thorndike, 1913). Theories emanating from this lens share several assumptions (Gredler, 2001): (a) observable behavior should be the object of investigation, (b) the simplest forms of behavior should be investigated (e.g., physiological reflexes or observable emotional responses), and (c) behavioral change constitutes learning. Such an epistemic focus translates into a science of learning in which mental events, verbal reconstructions, or other unobservable changes are of little value and, in fact, distract from the science of learning (Watson, 1930).

As depicted in Figure 2, this behavioral lens necessarily has an epistemic focus on the individual, the environment, and on the ways in which such responses can be *conditioned*; that is, made to occur with predictability (Murphy et al., 2012). Despite its restrictive core assumptions, the reach of behaviorism has been relatively expansive (Figure 3), encompassing a number of theoretical variations, including classical conditioning (Pavlov, 1928; Watson, 1913), instrumental conditioning (Thorndike, 1911), drive reduction theory (Hull, 1935), and operant conditioning (Skinner, 1948). Each of these behavioral theories, indeed, sought to explain observable physical or biological behavior through experimental methods but differed in the type of behavior targeted (i.e., respondent vs. operant) and the associated form of conditioning employed (e.g., classical vs. instrumental). In the case of *respondent behavior*, the hypothesis is that the individual comes to react involuntarily to certain stimulations within a given environment. From a "learning" standpoint, in this theory, the existing association between stimulus and response becomes the basis for conditioning

FIGURE 3
Lenses and Their Concomitant Epistemic Foci That Serve to Filter Our
Understanding of Learning Through Theory, Research, and Instruction

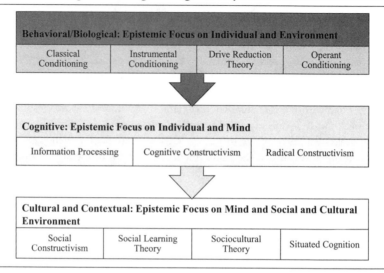

new behaviors in an individual. After repeated exposures, the new pairing becomes set in place—habituated, in effect.

The mechanistic orientation ascribed to the behavioral lens is clearly exemplified in Watson and Rayner's (1920) classical conditioning case of Little Albert and his emotional responses to particular stimuli. At the outset of this study, the researchers established that Albert was a healthy baby of normal weight and adequate temperament, who when initially confronted with small, white, furry objects (e.g., a mouse) showed no behavioral indications of fear (e.g., crying). Beyond the establishment of Albert's neutral emotional state, Watson made no mention of Albert's cognitive processing, gender, cultural background, or even the contextual nuances of the experiment. Rather, Watson's experimental concerns were focused only on the chronicling of Albert's altered responses when white objects were systematically paired with a loud, startling sound. As the conditioning took hold, Albert began to show the same fear reaction to various white objects that he displayed from that loud, startling noise. As a result, Watson surmised that Albert had *learned* to fear white things.

Little Albert's fear responses notwithstanding, human behaviors are not often involuntary or aligned with such basic human responses as fear. Indeed, as Thorndike, Hull, Skinner, and others argued, many behaviors manifest in response to environmental conditions (i.e., operant) and are systematically shaped by the consequences that result (Cooper et al., 2007). When those consequences are positive, the behavior is apt to increase, while negative consequences bring about a reduction or cessation of the behavior (Ferster & Skinner, 1957). This simple principle of learning is at the heart of not only operant conditioning (Skinner, 1935) but also instrumental conditioning (Thorndike, 1911) and drive reduction theory (Hull, 1935). As a case in point, consider Thorndike's experiment involving cats trapped in a puzzle box and their eventual escape. In this experiment, the cats take an instrumental role in their escape by coming to associate the striking of a lever with release over successive trials, an action that was initially trial and error in its performance. What is important about this experiment in terms of the epistemic lens is that Thorndike set out to establish a law that would apply not just to a cat in a puzzle box but to all of human learning. Be it a cat or a human, a puzzle box or a classroom, the principle of instrumental conditioning was seen to apply to any reinforced behavior.

Investigations employing operant conditioning continued to be published well into the latter half of the 20th century. For example, Thompson et al. (1974) conducted an experimental study rooted in Skinner's operant conditioning as applied to classroom management that was published in *AERJ* in the early 1970s. Specifically, Thompson and colleagues trained an entire school of teachers in the use of a contingency management program and compared their students' behavior over 3 weeks of implementation to a control school and its teachers. Like the pigeons and mice in Skinner's boxes, students in the treatment classrooms were reinforced in a highly prescribed manner, and the reinforcement gave way to improved on-task behavior and decreased unnecessary talking. The study results showed that a highly orchestrated classroom where student responses are systematically reinforced would predictably result in what behaviorists called "learning": the demonstration of desired prosocial behaviors in an academic context.

Cognitive Lens

During the mid-20th century, there was a growing dissatisfaction with the prevailing behavioral orientation to human learning and development—a dissatisfaction that ultimately resulted in the abandonment of behaviorism as the dominant lens. There appears to be no single cause for this theoretical shift; rather, the shift resulted from a confluence of factors that came to undermine a strict environmental view of learning. One of those factors was the "misbehavior" of species, including the human animal. Hints of this misbehavior were present even in the early conditioning experiments, as when Thorndike's Cats #11 and #13 apparently refused to play by the rules and decided to remain ensconced in the puzzle box. One of the more dramatic tests of animal misbehavior was documented by Tolman (1948) in his study of cognitive maps. In this now classic study, Tolman reported the actions of one rather infamous rat that chose to circumvent the training maze developed for his conditioning. Apparently calling up some form of cognitive map or mental model of the maze, this disobedient rat utilized an "escape hatch," popping open the top of the maze to circumvent the blocked route. Based on this and related observations, Tolman surmised that this rat and other animals do more than simply react to the "environments" that others orchestrate for them. Rather, they interject their own mental thoughts and models into those created spaces, and they also retain some control as to how they will respond to those environments—if they elect to respond at all.

In addition to documented misbehavior of species, there were other forces working to bring about the fading glory of behaviorism. Indeed, the emergence of computer technology was a monumental force, which continues to this day to refocus the lenses applied to human learning. Alan Turing devised the Turing machine, the prototype for the modern computer, in his efforts to break the seemingly unbreakable Enigma code developed by the Nazis during World War II. In conceptualizing this machine, Turing drew analogically on the workings of the human mind. Yet at some point during the 1950s, the computer-as-human-mind metaphor was reversed. That is to say, the computer—a machine invented for data input and output—became the metaphor for the human mind, particularly in the form of information-processing theory. The mind was the black box through which all human experiences were processed and interpreted. What responses might eventually emerge as outputs were the results of the cognitive machinations hypothesized to occur within the mind of the individual and the store of knowledge that already resided within the human "black box."

As with behaviorism, however, there was not one singular theory representing the cognitive lens. Various theoretical orientations fall within the cognitive realm, including information processing, cognitive constructivism, and radical constructivism. Yet as with the prior discussion of behaviorism, there are certain overarching assumptions around which these orientations cohere. Specifically, what all cognitive theories have in common is recognition that (a) the individual mind filters all sensory experiences, and thus all environments are uniquely experienced; (b) individuals retain a degree of free will and choice in what they attend to, and in how, or whether, they will respond to any given environment; and (c) "learning" from this vantage point signifies a change in the mind of the individual—a change that may or may not translate into immediately observable behavior. Indeed—regardless of whether its Tolman's (1948) vicarious trial-and-error analysis, Miller's (1956) channel capacity research, or J. Anderson's (1983) explorations of cognitive architecture—the theories falling within this lens have a central focus on the cognitive mechanisms that control the processing, construction, and use of knowledge.

We have already briefly introduced one cognitive frame that was strongly represented in education research well into the late 20th century: *information-processing theory* (Atkinson & Shiffrin, 1968). The tenets of this theory are nicely illustrated by the investigations into memory by Craik and Lockhart (1972). In their classic study, these researchers set out to demonstrate that how deeply or superficially individuals process the information in their environments serves to explain what they remember over time. The principle that Craik and Lockhart (1972) forwarded is that information that is only shallowly processed with limited attention will not be well remembered or long retained, as compared with information that is well attended to and deeply and elaborately processed. We find traces of this "levels of processing" argument woven through many longstanding and even contemporary models of human learning. Consider, for example, the current fascination with student engagement during instruction (e.g., Reeve, Jang, Carrell, Jeon, & Barch, 2004). As with Craik and Lockhart's (1972) levels of processing model, the contention of researchers and practitioners who study student participation is that students learn better when they engage more deeply, attempting to make sense of the material at hand.

Such attention to depth of processing is exemplified in King's (1994) contemporary intervention study published in *AERJ*. Specifically, King trained fourth- and fifth-grade students in how to generate and respond to questions about science content designed to elicit deeper cognitive processing and *knowledge construction* through elaboration. Students who were trained to ask deeper, more meaningful questions and to respond by linking to prior knowledge in an extended way exhibited substantively better knowledge acquisition, as evidenced in verbal and written artifacts as compared with both a treatment group trained to ask lower level questions and a business-as-usual control group. The filtering of the cognitive lens, as illustrated by King, shows a central focus on mechanisms for modifying the internal processing of information to increase knowledge building. The information that is filtered, although not ignored, has to do with the roles of contiguity and conditioning. In essence, the focus is altered from that of behavior as learning to behavior as representative of changes to internal cognitive structures and associated knowledge.

Contemporary to information processing theory—but more expressly influenced by biophysical understandings of human growth and development, as well as by the role the environment plays in experience—is the theory on human learning that has been labeled *cognitive constructivism*. Framed primarily around the extensive writings of Jean Piaget, who was initially trained as a biologist, this particular frame focuses on systematic transformations that occur in the mind as a consequence of the biological maturation of the human species, given appropriate experiences and the concomitant mental activities that align with particular stages of maturation. What Piaget investigated, and what draws cognitive constructivists' attention, is how cognitive maturation allows individuals to grasp certain understandings or to hold increasingly more complex and varied perspectives on ideas, events, or environments than was possible at earlier and less sophisticated stages of cognitive development. While cognitive constructivists, like information-processing theorists, focus their investigations on the mind of the individual and on the power of the mind to filter human experience, the aspect that differentiates them is this centering on biological/physiological aspects of humanness rather than on the internal machinations of the mind.

A more recent school of thought that still falls squarely within the cognitive realm is *radical constructivism*. Largely the brainchild of Ernst von Glasersfeld, radical constructivism has been described as an existential orientation to human learning (Woods & Murphy, 2002). That label seems aptly applied because at its core, radical constructivism attributes the greatest power to the individual, not only to shape his or her learning process but also to dictate what constitutes viable learning outcomes. Whereas behaviorists would contend that the highly orchestrated environment should translate into consistent and generalizable outcomes for anyone placed in that environment, radical constructivists hold an antithetical view. To be more precise, those situated within the radical constructivist frame see all of learning not just as idiosyncratic—a belief they share with other cognitivists—but as wholly in the mental purview of individual minds.

This truly radical cognitive perspective on learning is reflected in the writings of Martin Simon (1995). In his explorations of his own instructional practices in the teaching of mathematics, Simon describes how he operates under the expectation that his classroom of preservice teachers not only come into the educational context with unique experiences pertaining to mathematics learning and teaching but also they operate in that environment with no common or objective interpretations or reality. Thus, his pedagogical approach can take nothing as a given, even among a collection of students with some demographic similarities. Each student's learning path is entirely distinct and will remain so across the course of instruction. This is the antithesis of behaviorism or even cognitive constructivism, both of which presume some level of similarity either as a consequence of a consistent environment or biological determinism.

Cultural/Contextual Lens

What should become evident in the examination of the theoretical frames we have overviewed is that in the case of behaviorism and the family of cognitive theories, there is a strong focus on the person or individual learner, whether in actions or thinking. For instance, a question emanating from a behaviorally focused lens might be, "What configuration of reinforcements or punishments will result in the manifestation of desired behaviors or the cessation of unwanted actions for a targeted individual?" Alternatively, a question derived from a more cognitively focused lens might be, "What mental processes or developmental transformations promote the emergence of new understandings or knowledge stored in the individual mind?" In effect, the behavioral and cognitive lenses on learning inhabit the left side—which can be considered the more individualistic side—of the 2 × 2 epistemic vector space represented in Figure 2.

The other, more social lenses of learning are represented by the frames located on the right half of the epistemic vector space in Figure 2, where the influences of the individual are filtered to bring the power of the social into clear view. Specifically, the theories populating the social half of the vector model are much more invested in factors that reside outside the individual, whether mind or behavior (Figure 3). These factors take the form of social forces or cultural/contextual factors and consequently embrace the actions or learning of the collective. Beyond that shared foundation, there are important differences among these more cultural/contextual frames that merit attention. Specifically, the learning frames occupying the social half of the vector model tend to cluster into two discernible groups. Those that cluster toward the upper right quadrant of the vector model (i.e., social constructivism and social cognition) give more credence to cultural/contextual factors than prior theoretical frames, perceiving those factors as largely shaping the thinking and behavior of individual learners. Conversely, the theories found in the lower right quadrant (i.e., socioculturalism and situated cognition) set aside the focus on individuals and remain clearly centered on social or cultural groups (e.g., a peer network and/or ethnic group) as the unit of analysis, recognizing the context as inseparable from the ways in which these social or cultural groups learn. With this overview in place, we want to delve briefly into each of those theories that we have positioned within the broad cultural/contextual frame.

One of the theories that crossed the line from a more individualistic to a more social orientation to learning is *social constructivism*. As discussed, the focus on the individual mind and the mental processes afforded by cognitive frames proved an unsatisfying orientation to human learning for various theorists and researchers. Among those theorists and researchers was Lev Vygotsky (1962, 1978), who, along with a group of Russian scholars known as the Vygotsky Circle (e.g., Leontiev, 1977; Luria, 1931, 1933), took issue with the writings and research of their contemporary Jean Piaget for failing to acknowledge the power of social "others" to serve as critical catalysts for learning. These social constructivists faulted Piaget and other cognitive constructivists for neglecting the very social and collaborative nature of learning, mediated largely through language. Researchers with a social constructivist perspective maintained that learning cannot be separated from its social context and that social forces drive cognitive development rather than the reverse, as Piaget claimed (Vygotsky, 1978). For social constructivists, learning is more than mental assimilation and accommodation. Rather, it is the result of social interactions, as well as being the process by which learners are enculturated into knowledge communities.

The research that best represents the tenets of social constructivism is contained in a pair of case studies conducted in the early 1930s by Vygotsky's colleague Luria (1931, 1933). In this study, Luria interviewed Russian "peasants" (the term he used) and presented them with a series of items that they were asked to classify, while also providing the rationale for their classification (e.g., shapes, tools, or groups of people). The participants tended to group objects by their function in everyday activities, rather than by more abstract schemes. Luria concluded that cognition is taxonomic and guided by certain culturally derived criteria. By contrast, the thinking of the "peasants" Luria studied in Central Asia focused on contextualized activity that reflected the culture and history of the region. Luria's interpretation of their groupings reflected his own theoretical attunement to cultural/contextual influences.

Current education researchers from a social constructivist perspective tend to focus on learning and reasoning in collaborative groups and on the use of scaffolding, and they view instruction in terms of dialogue, argumentation, and problem-based learning (e.g., R. C. Anderson et al., 2001; Clarke, Resnick, & Rosé, 2016; Palincsar, 1986; Pea, 2004). In one such study, Jadallah et al. (2011) explored teacher roles in collaborative reasoning discussions through videotapes of 30 class discussions. The findings indicated that the teachers' scaffolding influenced children's talking and thinking both directly and indirectly. Students progressed from talking in response to the teacher's prompts to unprompted responses and even to prompting other students in turn.

Vygotsky and those ascribing to social constructivism were not alone in crossing the line into the cultural/contextual realm. For example, Albert Bandura (1976) felt that much of human learning came from observing and modeling others. Yet several aspects of Bandura's framing, often referred to as *social cognition*, can be distinguished from the orientation of social constructivism. For one, social cognition posits that not only does the environment affect human behavior but human behavior also affects the environment, through the process of reciprocal determinism. Moreover, this interplay of person, environment, and behavior can take place not only through direct human interactions but also by means of observation and vicarious or indirect reinforcement. As Bandura argued, learners are not the passive creatures depicted by behavioral frames. Rather, they act on the environment through psychological processes that are shaped by being astute observers of others whom they perceive as social models.

The Bobo doll experiment by Bandura, Ross, and Ross (1961) is a classic study that illustrates many of the elements of observational learning. In addition, it well represents the lens with an overt focus on the socially influenced and contextually bound nature of human learning. The researchers assigned nursery school children to one of three conditions. One group (i.e., aggressive model) watched a person display aggressive behavior toward toys, in particular a large doll referred to as Bobo. A second group (i.e., nonaggressive model) watched someone who played with tinker toys and ignored the Bobo doll, while the third group (i.e., control) had no model to observe. Then all the children were put in a room with interesting toys and told they could not play with them, in order to arouse mild aggression. Following several intervening steps, researchers found that children in the aggressive model group engaged in more imitative aggressive play, irrespective of their initial level of aggressive behavior, than did those in the other groups. The implications were that children learn from others through observation, imitation, and modeling.

In contrast to social constructivism and social cognition, which still attend to the workings of the individual mind, *socioculturalism* takes the social interactions of the cultural group as its point of focus. Therefore, this particular orientation moves into the vector space reserved for frames with a stronger social and environmental configuration. What matters is how social or cultural groups provide opportunities for growth or change (i.e., affordances) in individuals as they function in social settings, not the isolated functioning of the individual minds that constitute those groups. In effect, proponents of sociocultural theories, such as Lave and Wenger (1991) or Wertsch and Bivens (1992), diverge from both Vygotsky's and Bandura's notions of internalization of knowledge. Rather, sociocultural theorists and researchers advocate for a participatory model that involves increasing responsibilities for activities within a community of practice. From this perspective, learning becomes a process through which individuals reproduce social and cultural practices through their everyday participation in a particular community, by means of guided participation or apprenticeship with others in the community (Rogoff, 1990). In effect, learning becomes an act of enculturation, and culture is not merely a set of artifacts or structures that support learning, but a process in which learners engage.

It is not surprising that many drawn to this frame have been greatly influenced by sociological or anthropological research and the corresponding methodologies (see Shulman, 1986b). In fact, one of the earliest classic exemplars of a sociocultural frame is anthropologist Margaret Mead's (1928) study of adolescent females in Samoa. Mead employed an ethnographic approach in which she was totally immersed in the everyday life of the villagers. Her writings provided the detailed descriptions of the context and culture of Samoan society necessary for understanding female adolescence in that society, including the lives of villagers, their education, family life, social structures and mores, as well as the role of music, dancing, and singing in their culture. Mead's theoretical lens was finely focused on social and cultural practices as the vehicles for learning.

Much of the more recent research from a sociocultural perspective has focused on informal learning or learning outside of school (e.g., Saxe, 1994) and/or differences in influences related to in- and out-of-school learning (e.g., J. Gay & Cole, 1967; Lave, Murtaugh, & de la Rocha, 1984). For example, Saxe (1991) illustrated the influence of cultural practices and artifacts in his study of the body parts–counting system developed by the Oksapmin in Papua New Guinea, while Carraher, Carraher, and Schliemann (1985) analyzed the computational strategies used by youth involved in commercial transactions on the streets of Recife, Brazil. In both studies, computational strategies are different from those taught in school but result in superior performance in the specific context. Other studies that continue this ethnographic tradition include the work of Luis Moll with Mexican American families and cultures of practice in Arizona (Moll, 1992; Moll & Greenberg, 1990); Katherine Au with Hawaiian children learning to read using a "talk-story" approach (Au & Kawakami, 1985); Lave et al. (1984) with grocery shoppers performing mathematical operations in a supermarket; and J. Gay and Cole's (1967) comparison of the learning of Kpelle children in Liberia with that of American children.

An example of research from a sociocultural perspective that was highlighted in our review of AERA publications is a study by Phelan et al. (1994). The researchers wanted to explore the family, peer, and school issues that adolescents viewed as having an impact on their ability to engage optimally in school and learning activities. Specifically, over a 2-year period, the authors conducted a series of interviews with ethnically and academically diverse youth. Drawing on these interviews via qualitative methodologies, Phelan et al. richly described four categories of problems and pressures that affected students' participation, as well as the social, emotional, and educational consequences of those problems for the students.

One final theory occupies the lower right quadrant in our vector space model: *situated cognition*. Situated cognitivists, like socioculturalists, reject the more traditional views of learning that require the internalization of knowledge; instead, they employ a theoretical frame focused on contextualized social practices that must be investigated in situ. Despite these commonalties under the cultural/contextual umbrella, the two claims of inseparability and centrality of process take very different forms and degrees of strength in the two theories, when closely examined. A major difference between sociocultural learning theory and situated cognition theory is that, in the latter, knowledge resides in the nexus of the individual and the environment, in the "person-in-situation," and is not solely in the head of the individual or in the environment alone (Corno et al., 2002, p. 41). The situational context in which learning occurs informs what is learned. Authentic activity shapes an individual's intellectual tools and provides the experience needed for subsequent action (Brown, Collins, & Duguid, 1989).

The work of Sylvia Scribner provides a classic example of research conducted from a situated cognition perspective (see, e.g., Scribner, 1984a, 1984b). In her investigation of the Vai people of Liberia, Scribner explored questions about the social influences on literacy skills associated with reading and writing in their culture. First, using interviews and in-depth ethnographic studies, she examined the social organization of Vai literacy and how certain social practices presented different kinds of reading and writing tasks to individuals. Then she set up experiments to determine the processing skills associated with the different tasks and their general intellectual implications. The first set of tasks tested general hypotheses about literacy and investigated performance on cognitive tasks by schooled and unschooled literate Vai. The second set used hypotheses about literacy developed from the ethnographic observations to determine what skills were promoted by reading and writing tasks. In this manner, Scribner sought to understand the interrelationship between the social and psychological processes involved in literacy. Other situated cognition theorists have extended the theory and research through investigation of authentic activity and the use of cognitive apprenticeship to enable students to "acquire, develop, and use cognitive tools in authentic domain activity," employing situated modeling and scaffolding (Brown et al., 1989).

A recent example of an investigation, guided by a cultural/contextual lens and theoretically framed from a situated cognition perspective, was reported by Wortham (2004). Wortham used an ontological approach to investigate how learning and the development of social identity were intertwined through the use of curricular categories as tools to both identify students and understand curriculum. In this investigation, Wortham studied ninth-grade English and history classrooms taught by two female teachers and populated largely by African American female students. Wortham's interest was the identity development of one African American male. Discourse analysis was used to analyze classroom observations with audio recordings and field notes, as well as interviews with teachers and students. The aim of the teachers was to socialize students into the practice of generating rational arguments through argumentation and the use of evidence to support their arguments. Local models of identification and local models of the curriculum became intertwined through the personalization of discourse. The use of participant examples depicted the interrelation of identity and curriculum and how the focal male student struggled between being a good student and a respected male, categories that emerged as oppositional in the class.

IMPLICATIONS FOR TEACHING AND INSTRUCTION THROUGH EPISTEMIC LENSES

While theories of learning do not necessarily translate directly into education practice, they have been adapted and integrated for use in classrooms and other educational contexts, depending on the kind of outcome addressed (e.g., Woolfolk Hoy, Davis, & Anderman, 2013). For that reason, instructional applications often refer to multiple theories and are not clearly or simply defined by any one lens. Nevertheless, in this section, we provide prototypic examples of teaching and instructional practices that fit each of the three lenses we have discussed.

Behaviorally Framed Instruction

Behavioral learning theories have had considerable impact on classroom instruction, ranging from isolated behavioral management techniques using cuing or stimulus control to entire systems using reinforcement and conditioning as a basis for obtaining learning or managing behavior. Since the behavioral lens focuses on observable changes in behavior, with emphasis on the simplest unit and pairing of behavior with reinforcement, specific skills and actions of both students and teachers have received considerable attention within classrooms, particularly in special education settings and for use with technology. For example, the nature of teacher feedback to students, which can be viewed as a response to a particular stimulus that provides students with information, has been studied extensively as a discrete teacher behavior that affects student performance (Hattie & Timperley, 2007).

Behavioral approaches are particularly useful for learning explicit information or when change in specific behavior is desired, when change can be achieved through extrinsic motivation, or when automaticity of skills becomes the target. Early applications included token economy programs (Kazdin, 1977), which allowed students to earn tokens for academic work or positive behaviors that could be exchanged for some desired reward; contingency contract programs (Cantrell, Cantrell, Huddleston, & Wooldridge, 1969), which enabled students to obtain privileges or rewards for accomplishing specific goals; and mastery learning (Bloom & Carroll, 1971; Kulik, Kulik, & Bangert-Downs, 1990), which was based on students' meeting specific behavioral objectives at a specified level prior to continuing to the next unit. *Applied behavioral analysis* is a broad term for programs focusing on application of behavioral science in real-world settings, such as schools and clinics, to target change in the IQ and social skills of students diagnosed with a variety of disabilities and behavior disorders (Baer, Wolf, & Risley, 1968). Currently, applied behavioral analysis has been used successfully with children with autism (Virués-Ortega, 2010).

Perhaps the most pervasive application of behavioral research and theory, although it is often adapted to incorporate more current paradigms such as cognitive learning theory, is direct instruction as described by Rosenshine and Stevens (1986). During the 1970s and early 1980s, behavioral learning theory influenced approaches to research on teaching through the *process–product paradigm*, which focused on the relations between discrete observed teacher behaviors and students' performance, a proxy for learning favored by behaviorists in education in the form of standardized achievement tests of basic skills. The observed teacher behaviors that empirically related to student achievement were later synthesized into a generic approach, referred to as *direct instruction* or *active teaching* and studied experimentally (Gage, 1972; Rosenshine & Stevens, 1986).

Direct instruction approaches from this perspective are typically teacher-centered because the teacher controls the environment important in eliciting student behaviors and determines appropriate stimulus presentation and reinforcement. The teacher structures and sequences the learning content, which is usually presented in lecture or demonstration format; sets behavioral objectives that specify student performance; and provides opportunities for guided and independent practice with ample feedback, reinforcement, and correction. Madeline Hunter (1983) developed a seven-step direct instruction approach to teaching and lesson planning that was adopted by thousands of U.S. schools in the 1980s and 1990s; this program was based on the elements of effective teaching identified from process–product research. Research suggests that the direct instruction model is effective when using standardized tests of basic skills as outcome measures, particularly for elementary students in urban settings considered at risk of academic failure (Rosenshine & Stevens, 1986).

Widespread adoption of direct instruction in classrooms provided a test of the applicability of behavioral learning theory in practice and an example of the reciprocity of theory and practice. Criticism of the generic nature of the model, the emphasis on basic skills, the limited definition of learning, and the teacher-centered instructional strategies implemented in classrooms mirrored and influenced dissatisfaction with the value of a behavioral lens for explaining human learning. In particular, the goals and outcomes of teaching were scrutinized, and behavioral theories were deemed limited in their application (see, e.g., Kuhn, 2007). While some behavioral approaches have been modified to incorporate elements of emerging cognitive and contextual learning theories, others have persisted in special education settings. As advocacy for behavioral theories of learning waned, so did the instructional approaches they spawned.

Cognitively Based Teaching and Instruction

As we have argued, cognitive and behavioral learning views differ in their orientations and assumptions about the nature of learning. Cognitivists, whether from an information-processing, constructivist, or radical constructivist perspective, assume that mental processes are important in learning and can be studied empirically.

Furthermore, they see humans as active participants in cognition, with prior knowledge influencing subsequent knowledge construction. The change to a cognitive perspective shifts the goal of instruction toward the importance of attending to, organizing, elaborating, and remembering knowledge; focuses on the more complex concepts and skills involved in thinking, decision making, and problem solving; and examines the role of instruction in student use of tactics and strategies for learning (Woolfolk Hoy et al., 2013). The change in metaphors from *learning as response strengthening* to *learning as information processing* and *learning as knowledge construction* (Mayer, 1996) changed views of effective teaching from *teacher as dispenser of information* to *teacher as promoter of effective cognitive processing*. The importance of the domain-specific organization of subject matter in relation to cognitive processing and the need to explicitly teach cognitive strategies became paramount (Mayer, 2001).

As with behavioral applications, cognitive applications can be seen as influences on discrete teacher behaviors, whether integrated into existing lessons or implemented as larger scale programs in classrooms. For example, teachers may develop a signal such as a rhythmic tapping on the desk that alerts students to the need to pay attention to what is going to occur in class; they may ask students to recall what they know about a topic prior to beginning a lesson so students can build on prior knowledge; or they may integrate visual representations concurrently into texts so that information can be processed deeply without overloading working memory (Mayer, 2001). Teachers might also explicitly teach students memory, learning, and metacognitive strategies so that reading comprehension and problem-solving capabilities are enhanced (Pressley, 1986; Pressley, Goodchild, Fleet, Zajchowski, & Evans, 1989; Pressley, Levin, & Delaney, 1982).

Many of the teaching strategies from an information-processing perspective may appear similar to behavioral teaching strategies, but they are implemented for different reasons and for the purpose of developing complex concepts and processes as opposed to basic skills. The use of feedback (Hattie & Timperley, 2007) cited earlier (i.e., in the discussion of behaviorism as a reinforcement of a stimulus-response connection) appears from a cognitive perspective as a means of providing information to encourage more productive cognitive processing. The importance of practice for memorization to strengthen connections in behavioral applications appears in cognitive applications as a means of having students acquire automaticity to lessen demands on working memory.

An example of a more comprehensive program incorporating aspects of cognitive theory is Bransford and Stein's (1993) IDEAL model for problem solving. The IDEAL model is one of a group of general problem-solving programs (e.g., Newell & Simon, 1972; Polya, 1957) developed from early conceptualizations of cognitive theory with the idea that decontextualized problem-solving skills could be learned and transferred to contextualized problem solving. In this program, five steps are enacted to guide students: identify the problem, define the problem, explore solutions, act on strategies, and look back and evaluate the steps. However, the past 20 years of research have seen a shift in cognitive applications for learning complex content and skills to more domain-specific approaches that reflect current conceptualizations of cognitive learning theory (e.g., Bransford, Brown, & Cocking, 2000; Duschl, Schweingruber, & Shouse, 2007). Combined with the adoption of Shulman's (1986b) notion of pedagogical content knowledge in teaching and teacher education, applications from the cognitive perspective in classroom settings tend to be adapted to the particular content area of interest.

Culturally Enriched/Contextually Attuned Practices for Teaching and Instruction

While theories constituting a cultural and/or contextual lens on learning are relatively new, having emerged in the 1990s, they have had considerable influence on contemporary classroom instruction. Consequently, important reform elements for the development of 21st-century student skills and knowledge have emerged from these theories: (a) student-centered approaches, as opposed to teacher-centered ones influenced by behaviorism; (b) emphasis on group participation and classroom communities of learning (Brown & Campione, 1996); (c) inquiry and problem-based learning models (Cognition and Technology Group at Vanderbilt, 1993); (d) cognitive apprenticeships that scaffold student learning (Schoenfeld, 1998); and (e) the use of *culturally relevant (responsive) teaching strategies* (see, e.g., G. Gay, 2000; Ladson-Billings, 1994) or the more recent *culturally sustaining pedagogical practices* (Paris, 2012) to promote diverse literacies and viewpoints in classrooms.

Two models provide examples of the kinds of approaches supported by the four learning frames described previously within the culture/context lens. The first model, which emerged in the 1980s, serves as a bridge between cognitive theories and social cognition or social constructivist theories. *Reciprocal Teaching* (Palincsar & Brown, 1984) focuses on explicit instruction in four reading comprehension strategies: questioning, clarifying, summarizing, and predicting. The design of the research follows the cognitive training studies of the 1980s, with determination of improvement in strategy use, reading comprehension, and transfer after strategy training. However, the design of the delivery system was grounded in Vygotskian notions of the role of social interaction, dialogue, and scaffolding within the zone of proximal development. Teachers and students silently read a portion of text and then take turns generating summaries of what they have read, clarifying complex sections, and predicting what might occur next. The summarization serves as a self-review, which enhances metacognitive skills. The teacher first models the four strategies and then encourages students to participate at whatever level they can, providing guidance and feedback during the activity. Gradually, students assume the role of the teacher, asking questions as a teacher would, and serve as models in addition to the teacher for less skilled classmates. Studies of the impact of reciprocal teaching show improvement in reading comprehension, particularly for younger adolescents and students at lower levels of comprehension ability (Palincsar & Brown, 1984, 1986, 1989).

The second model, *funds of knowledge* (Moll, 1992, 2010; Moll, Amanti, Neff, & Gonzalez, 1992), draws primarily on sociocultural learning theories to connect families, students, and teachers with the aim of understanding how social, cultural, and linguistic resources mediate learning and how they can be applied to educational innovation. Moll suggests an approach that involves three primary activities: Teachers serve as coresearchers with university researchers conducting ethnographic research in their students' homes; teachers examine their classroom practices in relation to the findings from the research activity; and teachers participate in after-school study groups in which they develop classroom innovations based on what they have learned from the first two activities. Using interviews, field notes from home visits and observations, and collected artifacts, teachers investigate the social, political, and economic context of the region in which the students live, as well as the social and work histories of individual households. The historically and culturally developed body of knowledge and skills identified in the households, referred to as funds of knowledge, become the basis for innovative learning modules involving students in inquiry into their community and culture. As a result, teachers typically value the intellect of the student, connect families with classrooms, and affirm the value of the culture of the students.

What becomes evident in the preceding sections is that the evolution of the science of learning has had a tremendous impact on teaching and instructional practices. Indeed, just as definitions of learning have framed and been framed by various theoretical lenses, so to have teaching and instruction. As we have highlighted, the theoretical lenses that have driven research on learning have also been a strong force on everyday classroom practice. As a case in point, it is difficult to imagine an American elementary school classroom that fails to make use of some sort of token economy system to increase students' positive, prosocial behavior when that is the desired outcome. Similarly, almost every student leaves school with at least one useful memory mnemonic (e.g., Roy G. Biv: red, orange, yellow, green, blue, indigo, violet) emanating from the decades of research on cognition. Most teachers have also embraced Bandura (1976) and modeled some type of active learning for their students (e.g., worked examples in math problem solving).

What is perhaps even more important, however, is that few contemporary instructional applications of advancements in the science of learning claim a pure or singular theoretical underpinning. Rather, as the science of learning has evolved, intervention researchers have begun to blend or weave the theoretical roots emanating from various traditions to maximize the effects of an instructional intervention on students' learning as it unfolds in the multidimensional, dynamic nature of actual classrooms. There are numerous examples of this type of intervention: that is, intervention that draws on the very best of what is known about the science of learning across the various lenses (e.g., Flourishing Learning Youth, see Ebersöhn, 2015; Self-Regulated Strategy Development, see Harris et al., 2012; Quality Talk, see Murphy, Greene, & Firetto, 2015). What is articulated by Murphy (2015) and others (e.g., Greene, 2015; Harris, Graham, & Adkins, 2015; Star et al., 2015) in a recent special issue of *Contemporary Educational Psychology* is that the sustainability of instructional innovations rests in their feasibility and usefulness as well as their adaptability. In essence, each classroom is a unique place where many factors are at play, including the teacher, students, administrators, and parents, and each of these stakeholders plays a role in determining how learning will unfold (Ebersöhn, 2015). Thus, it is fundamental that instructional interventions must address the challenges faced by sociocultural groups in particular contexts, while simultaneously nurturing behavior, motivation, and cognition.

CLOSING THOUGHTS

In this chapter, we delved into the theoretical and empirical literature on the science of learning published over the past century with the purpose of understanding the following:

- How the term *learning* has been conceptually and operationally defined in select journals such as *RER* and *AERJ*, which are known to capture the science of learning from an educational vantage point
- The theoretical lenses that have guided research on learning
- The ways in which learning research has influenced educational practice

Importantly, given the vastness of the literature on learning, our review was not meant to be exhaustive but, rather, was targeted for the specific aforementioned purposes. Certainly, there are many more areas of learning that one could review, including informal learning, learning types (e.g., collaborative), and learning as maturation. Similarly, a multitude of education and education-related journals from a variety of areas pertaining to learning (e.g., mathematics, higher education, or education policy) could have yielded vastly different results or, at a minimum, offered more fodder for consideration. However, such explorations are beyond the scope of this systematic and interdisciplinary review. We encourage others to continue where our review leaves off.

Limitations notwithstanding, a number of key findings emerged from our extensive review. First, we found that the science of learning over the past century has been guided by three predominant theoretical lenses. We have characterized these lenses as behavioral/biological, cognitive, and cultural/contextual. In each case, the change to a new lens was intended to fill a gap in the understanding of the nature of learning, and was likely fueled by an inability to create sound explanatory frames for study findings. For example, Tolman's (1948) study highlighted cognitive maps in mice—cognitive maps that indicated latent learning. Behaviorism simply could not account for such findings. Similarly, reigning cognitive theories were not well suited for explaining the situated, everyday mathematics learning documented by Lave and Wenger (1991) or apprenticeship learning as described by Rogoff (1990). Indeed, such findings required changes in the very ontology of learning. The result of such explanatory needs was concomitant epistemological and methodological shifts.

Yet, even across these three lenses, we show critical commonalities. For one thing, learning was best understood as enduring change (Brownell, 1936; Iran-Nejad, 1990; Nasir & Hand, 2006). Regardless of the theoretical lens or the nuances of a given empirical study, we found that learning involved change in a target behavior, function, process, interaction, or discourse. As well, we found that change must endure long enough to be measured or captured by research (e.g., Draper & Siebert, 2004; Graesser & Person, 1994; Hosie et al., 1974; Roberge & Flexer, 1984; Travers & Wagenen, 1964). Furthermore, the concept of "learning as enduring change," whether by individuals or groups, has withstood the test of time. Nonetheless, while all theoretical lenses share this central tenet, there remains variability in its instantiation. Moreover, along with this definitional commonality, we determined that the epistemic practices of the science of learning seem to require *external* evidence of such change. For instance, the behaviorist wants to measure change in behavior, the cognitivist conducts digit span tasks to externalize changes in information processing, the social constructivist wants changes in verbal discourse, and the socioculturalist wants changes in societal or community practices. In short, internal, unobservable and, therefore, undocumentable changes fail to meet the epistemic requirements of the science of learning.

Along with these shared definitional and methodological attributions, we recognized that the enactment of these theoretical lenses within communities of practice, most notably schools and classrooms, has consequences for both the theories and the educational system (Murphy, 2015). For example, one only needs to scan the headlines to know that American public schools and education policy makers and administrators are consumed with measurable improvement in students' learning—learning that is most often operationalized as performance on standardized achievement tests. Indeed, policymakers, administrators, and educators, like learning scientists, fully embrace the notion of learning as enduring change. In many ways, teaching and instruction in classrooms is reflective of the operationalization of learning as enduring change, and seemingly also reflective of the theoretical frames that have guided research in the science of learning for the past century.

There are, however, two trends apparent in the literature on the science of learning that vary from the theoretical and empirical trends. First, instructional change that positively influences student learning seems to become part of the fabric of classroom practice and remains somewhat impervious to the tidal changes in laboratory research. As mentioned, behavioral frames have long been out of favor in education research, but many behavioral interventions (e.g., token economy systems) remain mainstays in pedagogy textbooks and classrooms. In some classrooms, depending on individual and cultural values and the kind of outcome desired, token economy systems provide an effective means for teachers to help students regulate their behavior.

The second trend pertains to the nature of the teaching and instructional interventions that are finding their way into classrooms. Specifically, although some interventions for educational practitioners have a strong influence from a given epistemic frame, many more appear to have integrated tenets from more than one theoretical lens (e.g., Murphy, Firetto, Wei, Li, & Croninger, 2016). Reciprocal teaching (Palincsar & Brown, 1984) serves as a robust exemplar of an intervention guided by multiple lenses, including comprehension strategies from cognitive theory, rehearsal and explicit instruction from behaviorism, and social interaction from the cultural/

contextual lens. A similar argument could be made for many of the studies listed in Table 2 that we coded as classroom interventions. It seems that in moving investigations of learning from the laboratory to the classroom, or to other settings where education occurs but that we did not study, there is the implicit acknowledgment that enhancing learning requires a tightly woven theoretical and empirical foundation—a foundation where the primary focus is on the enhancement of durable and positive changes in students' understandings rather than allegiance to a particular theoretical perspective, frame, or filter.

We opened this chapter with a reference to Darwin and the theory of evolution. In essence, what we witnessed in this investigation of the science of learning over a century is that educational evolution is not as clear or linear as its biological analog. In essence, there is no denying the documentable shifts in prevailing learning theories over the past 100 years, but one lens does not simply replace the next. There is no paradigmatic transformation when it comes to learning. Rather, many kinds of perspectives cohabit in education's ecosystem, and their crossbreeding appears evident, especially when classroom-based interventions are the focus. Thus, it remains for education researchers and education practitioners, who work directly with students, to understand the nuanced perspectives afforded by the various learning lenses and to draw on them in reasoned and reasonable ways, depending on the goals, domains, and tasks at hand.

NOTES

[1]Although learning can occur in a variety of settings, formal and informal, our review will focus primarily on more formal, structured learning settings (e.g., schools).

[2]A similar procedure was followed for the *Journal of Educational Research*, published by AERA from 1920 to 1928. During that period, the term *learning* was explicitly defined only once in *Journal of Educational Research*, when Goodenough (1925) characterized it through a behaviorist lens as a "function of time as well as of ability" (p. 298).

REFERENCES

Aleven, V., Stahl, E., Schworm, S., Fischer, F., & Wallace, R. (2003). Help seeking and help design in interactive learning environments. *Review of Educational Research, 73*, 277–320.

Alexander, P. A. (2006). Evolution of a learning theory: A case study. *Educational Psychologist, 41*, 257–264.

Alexander, P. A. (2007). Bridging cognition and socioculturalism within conceptual change research: Unnecessary foray or unachievable feat? *Educational Psychologist, 42*(1), 67–73.

Alexander, P. A., Dumas, D., Grossnickle, E. M., List, A., & Firetto, C. (2016). Measuring relational reasoning. *Journal of Experimental Education, 84*, 119–151.

Alexander, P. A., Kulikowich, J. M., & Schulze, S. K. (1994). How subject-matter knowledge affects recall and interest. *American Educational Research Journal, 31*, 313–337. doi:10.3102/00028312031002313

Alexander, P. A., Murphy, P. K., & Greene, J. A. (2012). Projecting educational psychology's future from its past and present: A trend analysis. In K. R. Harris, S. Graham, & T. Urdan (Eds.), *Educational psychology handbook: Vol. 1. Theories, constructs, and critical issues* (pp. 3–32). Washington, DC: American Psychological Association.

Alexander, P. A., Schallert, D. L., & Hare, V. C. (1991). Coming to terms: How researchers in learning and literacy talk about knowledge. *Review of Educational Research, 61*, 315–343.

Alexander, P. A., Schallert, D. L., & Reynolds, R. E. (2009). What is learning anyway? A topographical perspective considered. *Educational Psychologist, 44*, 176–192.

Anderson, J. (1983). *The architecture of cognition*. Cambridge, MA: Harvard University Press.

Anderson, R. C., Nguyen-Jahiel, K., McNurlen, B., Archodidou, A., Kim, S.-Y., Reznitskaya, A., . . . Gilbert, L. (2001). The snowball phenomenon: Spread of ways of talking and ways of thinking across groups of children. *Cognition and Instruction, 19*, 1–46. Retrieved from http://www.jstor.org/stable/3233905

Atkinson, R. C., & Shiffrin, R. M. (1968). Human memory: A proposed system and its control processes. In K. W. Spence & J. T. Spence (Eds.), *The psychology of learning and motivation* (Vol. 2, pp. 90–197). New York, NY: Academic Press.

Au, K. H., & Kawakami, A. J. (1985). Research currents: Talk story and learning to read. *Language Arts, 62*, 406–411.

Baer, D. M., Wolf, M. M., & Risley, T. R. (1968). Some current dimensions of applied behavior analysis. *Journal of Applied Behavior Analysis, 1*, 91–97.

Bandura, A. (1976). *Social learning theory*. Englewood Cliffs, NJ: Prentice-Hall.

Bandura, A., Ross, D., & Ross, S. A. (1961). Transmission of aggression through imitation of aggressive models. *Journal of Abnormal and Social Psychology, 63*, 575–582.

Belanger, M. (1969). Learning studies in science education. *Review of Educational Research, 39*, 377–395.

Benware, C. A., & Deci, E. L. (1984). Quality of learning with an active versus passive motivational set. *American Educational Research Journal, 21*, 755–765. doi:10.3102/00028312021004755

Bereiter, C. (1985). Toward a solution of the learning paradox. *Review of Educational Research, 55*, 201–226.

Bingham-Newman, A. M., & Hooper, F. H. (1974). Classification and seriation instruction and logical task performance in the preschool. *American Educational Research Journal, 11*, 379–393. doi:10.2307/1162791

Bloom, B. S., & Carroll, J. B. (1971). Mastery learning. In J. Block (Ed.), *Mastery learning: Theory and practice* (pp. 47–63). New York, NY: Holt, Rinehart, & Winston.

Boring, E. G. (1957). *A history of experimental psychology* (2nd ed.). New York, NY: Appleton-Century-Crofts.

Bornholt, L. J., Goodnow, J. J., & Cooney, G. H. (1994). Influences of gender stereotypes on adolescents' perceptions of their own achievement. *American Educational Research Journal, 31*, 675–692. doi:10.3102/00028312031003675

Bransford, J. D., Brown, A. L., & Cocking, R. R. (Eds.). (2000). *How people learn: Brain, mind, experience, and school*. Washington, DC: National Academies Press.

Bransford, J. D., & Stein, B. S. (1993). *The IDEAL problem solver: Guide for improving thinking, learning, and creativity* (2nd ed.). New York, NY: Freeman.

Bredo, E. (2016.) Philosophical perspectives in mind, nature, and educational psychology. In L. Corno & E. M. Anderman (Eds.), *Handbook of educational psychology* (3rd ed., pp. 3–15). New York, NY: Routledge.

Brown, A. L., & Campione, J. C. (1996). Psychological theory and the design of innovative learning environments: On procedures, principles, and systems. In L. Schauble & R. Glaser (Eds.), *Innovations in learning: New environments for education* (pp. 289–325). Mahwah, NJ: Lawrence Erlbaum.

Brown, J., Collins, A., & Duguid, P. (1989). Situated cognition and the culture of learning. *Educational Researcher, 18*(1), 32–42.

Brownell, W. A. (1936). Theoretical aspects of learning and transfer of training. *Review of Educational Research, 6*, 281–290.

Bruner, J. S. (1990). *Acts of meaning*. Cambridge, MA: Harvard University Press.

Cantrell, R. P., Cantrell, M. L., Huddleston, C. M., & Wooldridge, R. L. (1969). Contingency contracting with school problems. *Journal of Applied Behavior Analysis, 2*, 215–220.

Carraher, T. N., Carraher, D. W., & Schliemann, A. D. (1985). Mathematics in streets and in schools. *British Journal of Developmental Psychology, 3*, 21–29.

Chin, P., Bell, K. S., Munby, H., & Hutchinson, N. L. (2004). Epistemological appropriation in one high school student's learning in cooperative education. *American Educational Research Journal, 41*, 401–417. doi:10.3102/00028312041002401

Claessens, A., Engel, M., & Curran, F. C. (2014). Academic content, student learning, and the persistence of preschool effects. *American Educational Research Journal, 51*, 403–434. doi:10.3102/0002831213513634

Clarke, S. N., Resnick, L. B., & Rosé, C. P. (2016). Dialogic instruction: A new frontier. In L. Corno & E. M. Anderman (Eds.), *Handbook of educational psychology* (3rd ed., pp. 378–389). New York, NY: Routledge.

Cognition and Technology Group at Vanderbilt. (1993). Anchored instruction and situated cognition revisited. *Educational Technology, 33*(3), 52–70.

Cooper, J., Heron, T., & Heward, W. (2007). *Applied behavior analysis* (2nd ed.). Upper Saddle River, NJ: Prentice Hall.

Corno, L., Cronbach, L., Kupermintz, H., Lohman, D., Mandinach, E., Porteus, A., & Talbert, J. (2002). *Remaking the concept of aptitude: Extending the legacy of Richard E. Snow.* Mahwah, NJ: Lawrence Erlbaum.

Craik, F. I. M., & Lockhart, R. S. (1972). Levels of processing: A framework for memory research. *Journal of Verbal Learning and Verbal Behavior, 11*, 671–684.

Darwin, C. (1859). *On the origin of species by means of natural selection, or the preservation of favoured races in the struggle for life.* Retrieved from http://darwin-online.org.uk/content/frameset?pageseq=20&itemID=F373&viewtype=image

de Kock, A., Sleegers, P., & Voeten, M. J. M. (2004). New learning and the classification of learning environments in secondary education. *Review of Educational Research, 74*, 141–170.

Dewey, J. (1896). The reflex arc concept in psychology. *Psychological Review, 3*, 357–370.

Draper, R. J., & Siebert, D. (2004). Different goals, similar practices: Making sense of the mathematics and literacy instruction in a standards-based mathematics classroom. *American Educational Research Journal, 41*, 927–962. doi:10.3102/00028312041004927

Duschl, R., Schweingruber, H., & Shouse, A. (Eds.). (2007). *Taking science to school: Learning and teaching science in Grades K–8.* Washington, DC: National Research Council.

Ebersöhn, L. (2015). Making sense of place in school-based intervention research. *Contemporary Educational Psychology, 40*, 121–130.

Esmonde, I. (2009). Ideas and identities: Supporting equity in cooperative mathematics learning. *Review of Educational Research, 79*, 1008–1043.

Ferster, C. B., & Skinner, B. F. (1957). *Schedules of reinforcement.* New York, NY: Appleton-Century-Crofts.

Fuchs, L. S., Fuchs, D., Bentz, J., Phillips, N. B., & Hamlett, C. L. (1994). The nature of student interactions during peer tutoring with and without prior training and experience. *American Educational Research Journal, 31*, 75–103.

Fuchs, L. S., Fuchs, D., Finelli, R., Courey, S. J., & Hamlett, C. L. (2004). Expanding schema-based transfer instruction to help third graders solve real-life mathematical problems. *American Educational Research Journal, 41*, 419–445. doi:10.3102/00028312041002419

Gage, N. L. (1972). *Teacher effectiveness and teacher education: The search for a scientific basis.* Palo Alto, CA: Pacific Books.

Garner, R., Hare, V. C., Alexander, P. A., Haynes, J., & Winograd, P. (1984). Inducing use of a text lookback strategy among unsuccessful readers. *American Educational Research Journal, 21*, 789–798.

Gay, G. (2000). *Culturally responsive teaching: Theory, research, and practice.* New York, NY: Teachers College Press.

Gay, J., & Cole, M. (1967). *The new mathematics and an old culture: A study of learning among the Kpelle of Liberia.* New York, NY: Holt, Rinehart & Winston.

Goodenough, F. L. (1925). Efficiency in learning and the accomplishment ratio. *Journal of Educational Research, 12,* 297–300.

Graesser, A. C. (2009). Cognitive scientists prefer theories and testable principles with teeth. *Educational Psychologist, 44,* 193–197.

Graesser, A. C., & Person, N. K. (1994). Question asking during tutoring. *American Educational Research Journal, 31,* 104–137. doi:10.3102/00028312031001104

Gredler, M. (2001). *Learning and instruction: Theory into practice* (4th ed.). New York, NY: Prentice Hall.

Greene, J. A. (2015). Serious challenges require serious scholarship: Integrating implementation science into the scholarly discourse. *Contemporary Educational Psychology, 40,* 112–120. doi:10.1016/j.cedpsych.2014.10.007

Grotberg, E. H. (1965). Learning disabilities and remediation in disadvantaged children. *Review of Educational Research, 35,* 413–425.

Harris, K. R., Graham, S., & Adkins, M. (2015). Practice-based professional development and self-regulated strategy development for Tier 2, at-risk writers in second grade. *Contemporary Educational Psychology, 40,* 5–16.

Harris, K. R., Lane, K. L., Graham, S., Driscoll, S., Sandmel, K., Brindle, M., & Schatschneider, C. (2012). Practice-based professional development for self-regulated strategies development in writing: A randomized controlled study. *Journal of Teacher Education, 63,* 103–119.

Hattie, J., & Timperley, H. (2007). The power of feedback. *Review of Educational Research, 77,* 81–112.

Hosie, T. W., Gentile, J. R., & Carroll, J. D. (1974). Pupil preferences and the Premack principle. *American Educational Research Journal, 11,* 241–247.

Hull, C. L. (1935). The conflicting psychologies of learning: A way out. *Psychological Review, 42,* 491–516.

Hunter, M. (1983). *Mastery teaching.* El Segundo, CA: TIP.

Iran-Nejad, A. (1990). Active and dynamic self-regulation of learning processes. *Review of Educational Research, 60,* 573–602.

Jadallah, M., Anderson, R. C., Nguyen-Jahiel, K., Miller, B. W., Kim, I. H., Kuo, L. J., . . . Wu, X. (2011). Influence of a teacher's scaffolding moves during child-led small-group discussions. *American Educational Research Journal, 48,* 194–230.

James, W. (1890). *The principles of psychology.* New York, NY: Holt, Rinehart & Winston.

Kazdin, A. E. (1977). *The token economy: A review and evaluation.* New York, NY: Plenum Press.

King, A. (1994). Guiding knowledge construction in the classroom: Effects of teaching children how to question and how to explain. *American Educational Research Journal, 31,* 338–368. doi:10.3102/00028312031002338

Kirk, G. S. (1954). *Heraclitus: The cosmic fragments.* Cambridge, England: Cambridge University Press.

Klein, M. H., Mathieu, P. L., Gendlin, E. T., & Kiesler, D. J. (1970). *The experiencing scale: A research and training manual.* Madison: Wisconsin Psychiatric Institute.

Kozma, R. B. (1991). Learning with media. *Review of Educational Research, 61,* 179–211.

Kuhn, D. (2007). Is direct instruction an answer to the right question? *Educational Psychologist, 42,* 109–113.

Kulik, C., Kulik, J., & Bangert-Downs, R. (1990). Effectiveness of mastery learning programs: A meta-analysis. *Review of Educational Research, 60,* 265–299.

Kyndt, E., & Baert, H. (2013). Antecedents of employees' involvement in work-related learning: A systematic review. *Review of Educational Research, 83,* 273–313.

Ladd, G. W., Kochenderfer-Ladd, B., Visconti, K. J., Ettekal, I., Sechler, C. M., & Cortes, K. I. (2014). Grade-school children's social collaborative skills: Links with partner preference and achievement. *American Educational Research Journal, 51*, 152–183. doi:10.3102/0002831213507327

Ladson-Billings, G. (1994). *The dreamkeepers: Successful teachers of African American children.* San Francisco, CA: Jossey-Bass.

Lave, J., Murtaugh, M., & de la Rocha, O. (1984). The dialectic of arithmetic in grocery shopping. In B. Rogoff & J. Lave (Eds.), *Everyday cognition: Its development in social context* (pp. 67–94). Cambridge, MA: Harvard University Press.

Lave, J., & Wenger, E. (1991). *Situated learning: Legitimate peripheral participation.* Cambridge, England: Cambridge University Press.

Leontiev, A. N. (1977). Activity and consciousness (R. Daglish, Trans.). In *Philosophy in the USSR, problems of dialectical materialism* (pp. 180–202). Moscow: Progress.

Lesaux, N. K., Kieffer, M. J., Kelley, J. G., & Harris, J. R. (2014). Effects of academic vocabulary instruction for linguistically diverse adolescents: Evidence from a randomized field trial. *American Educational Research Journal, 51*, 1159–1194. doi:10.3102/0002831214532165

Lintner, A. C., & Ducette, J. (1974). The effects of locus of control, academic failure and task dimensions on a student's responsiveness to praise. *American Educational Research Journal, 11*, 231–239.

Luria, A. R. (1931). Psychological expedition to Central Asia. *Science, 74*, 383–384.

Luria, A. R. (1933). The second psychological expedition to Central Asia. *Science, 78*, 191–192.

Magnuson, K. A., Meyers, M. K., Ruhm, C. J., & Waldfogel, J. (2004). Inequality in preschool education and school readiness. *American Educational Research Journal, 41*, 115–157.

Mayer, R. E. (1996). Learners as information processors: Legacies and limitations of educational psychology's second metaphor. *Educational Psychologist, 31*, 151–161.

Mayer, R. E. (2001). *Multimedia learning.* New York, NY: Cambridge University Press.

McCormick, C. B., & Levin, J. R. (1984). A comparison of different prose-learning variations of the mnemonic keyword method. *American Educational Research Journal, 21*, 379–398. doi:10.3102/00028312021002379

Mead, M. (1928). *Coming of age in Samoa: A psychological study of primitive youth for Western civilization.* New York, NY: Morrow.

Meloth, M. S., & Deering, P. D. (1994). Task talk and task awareness under different cooperative learning conditions. *American Educational Research Journal, 31*, 138–165. doi:10.3102/00028312031001138

Miller, G. A. (1956). The magical number seven, plus or minus two: Some limits on our capacity for processing information. *Psychological Review, 63*, 81–97.

Moll, L. C. (1992). Bilingual classroom studies and community analysis: Some recent trends. *Educational Researcher, 21*(2), 20–24.

Moll, L. C. (2010). Mobilizing culture, language, and educational practices: Fulfilling the promises of Mendez and Brown. *Educational Researcher, 39*, 451–460.

Moll, L. C., Amanti, C., Neff, D., & Gonzalez, N. (1992). Funds of knowledge for teaching: Using a qualitative approach to connect homes and classrooms. *Theory Into Practice, 31*, 132–141.

Moll, L. C., & Greenberg, J. B. (1990). Creating zones of possibilities: Combining social contexts for instruction. In L. C. Moll (Ed.), *Vygotsky and education: Instructional implications and applications of sociocultural psychology* (pp. 67–94). New York, NY: Cambridge University Press.

Mowrer, O. H. (1952). Learning theory. *Review of Educational Research, 22*, 475–495.

Murphy, P. K. (2015). Marking the way: School-based interventions that "work." *Contemporary Educational Psychology, 40*, 1–4.

Murphy, P. K., & Alexander, P. A. (2000). A motivated exploration of motivation terminology. *Contemporary Educational Psychology, 25*, 3–53.

Murphy, P. K., & Alexander, P. A. (2004). Persuasion as a dynamic, multidimensional process: An investigation of individual and intraindividual differences. *American Educational Research Journal, 41*, 337–363. doi:10.3102/00028312041002337

Murphy, P. K., Alexander, P. A., & Muis, K. R. (2012). Knowledge and knowing: The journey from philosophy and psychology to human learning. In K. Harris, S. Graham, & T. Urdan (Eds.), *American Psychological Association handbook of educational psychology: Theories, constructs, and critical issues* (Vol. 1, pp. 189–226). Washington, DC: American Psychological Association. doi:10.1037/13273-008

Murphy, P. K., Firetto, C. M., Wei, L., Li, M., & Croninger, R. (2016). What REALLY works: Optimizing classroom discussions to promote comprehension and critical-analytic thinking. *Policy Insights from the Behavioral and Brain Sciences*. Advance online publication. doi:10.1177/2372732215624215

Murphy, P. K., Greene, J. A., & Firetto, C. M. (2015). *Quality talk: Developing students' discourse to promote critical-analytic thinking, epistemic cognition, and high-level comprehension* (Tech. Rep. No. 2). University Park: Pennsylvania State University.

Nasir, N. S., & Hand, V. M. (2006). Exploring sociocultural perspectives on race, culture, and learning. *Review of Educational Research, 76*, 449–475.

Nathan, M., & Alibali, M. (2010). Learning sciences. *Wiley Interdisciplinary Reviews: Cognitive Science, 3*, 329–345.

National School Boards Association. (2014). *The purpose of public education and the role of the school board*. Retrieved from http://www.nsba.org/sites/default/files/The%20 Purpose%20of%20Public%20Education%20and%20the%20Role%20of%20the%20 School%20Board_National%20Connection.pdf

Newell, A. (1990). *Unified theories of cognition*. Cambridge, MA: Harvard University Press.

Newell, A., & Simon, H. A. (1972). *Human problem solving*. Englewood Cliffs, NJ: Prentice Hall.

Niehaus, K., & Adelson, J. L. (2014). School support, parental involvement, and academic and social-emotional outcomes for English language learners. *American Educational Research Journal, 51*, 810–844. doi:10.3102/0002831214531323

Ogden, R. M. (1926). *Psychology and education*. New York, NY: Harcourt Brace.

Paavola, S., Lipponen, L., & Hakkarainen, K. (2004). Models of innovative knowledge communities and three metaphors of learning. *Review of Educational Research, 74*, 557–576.

Palincsar, A. S. (1986). The role of dialogue in providing scaffolded instruction. *Educational Psychologist, 21*, 73–98.

Palincsar, A. S., & Brown, A. L. (1984). Reciprocal teaching of comprehension-fostering and comprehension-monitoring activities. *Cognition and Instruction, 2*, 117–175.

Palincsar, A. S., & Brown, A. L. (1986). Interactive teaching to promote independent learning from text. *The Reading Teacher, 39*, 771–777.

Palincsar, A. S., & Brown, A. L. (1989). Classroom dialogues to promote self-regulated comprehension. In J. Brophy (Ed.), *Advances in research on teaching* (Vol. 1, pp. 35–67). Greenwich, CT: JAI.

Paris, D. (2012). Culturally sustaining pedagogy: A needed change in stance, terminology, and practice. *Educational Researcher, 41*, 93–97.

Park, O. (1984). Example comparison strategy versus attribute identification strategy in concept learning. *American Educational Research Journal, 21*, 145–162. doi:10.3102/ 00028312021001145

Pavlov, I. P. (1928). *Lectures on conditioned reflexes* (W. H. Gantt, Trans.). London, England: Allen & Unwin.

Pea, R. D. (2004). The social and technological dimensions of scaffolding and related theoretical concepts for learning, education, and human activity. *Journal of the Learning Sciences, 13*, 423–451.

Peirce, C. S. (1878). How to make our ideas clear. *Popular Science Monthly, 12*, 286–302.

Peterson, P. L., Swing, S. R., Stark, K. D., & Waas, G. A. (1984). Students' cognitions and time on task during mathematics instruction. *American Educational Research Journal, 21*, 487–515. doi:10.3102/00028312021003487

Phelan, P., Yu, H. C., & Davidson, A. L. (1994). Navigating the psychosocial pressures of adolescence: The voices and experiences of high school youth. *American Educational Research Journal, 31*, 415–447.

Pintrich, P. R. (1994). Continuities and discontinuities: Future directions for research in educational psychology. *Educational Psychologist, 29*, 137–148.

Polya, G. (1957). *How to solve it: A new aspect of mathematical method* (2nd ed.). Garden City, NY: Doubleday.

Popper, K. (1963). *Conjectures and refutations*. London, England: Routledge.

Porat, D. A. (2004). It's not written here, but this is what happened: Students' cultural comprehension of textbook narratives on the Israeli-Arab conflict. *American Educational Research Journal, 41*, 963–996.

Pressley, M. (1986). The relevance of the good strategy user model to the teaching of mathematics. *Educational Psychologist, 21*, 139–161.

Pressley, M., Goodchild, F., Fleet, J., Zajchowski, R., & Evans, E. D. (1989). The challenges of classroom strategy instruction. *Elementary School Journal, 89*, 302–342.

Pressley, M., Levin, J., & Delaney, H. (1982). The mnemonic key-word method. *Review of Educational Research, 52*, 61–91.

Reeve, J., Jang, H., Carrell, D., Jeon, S., & Barch, J. (2004). Enhancing students' engagement by increasing teachers' autonomy support. *Motivation and Emotion, 28*, 147–169.

Rimm-Kaufman, S. E., Larsen, R. A. A., Baroody, A. E., Curby, T. W., Ko, M., Thomas, J. B., . . . DeCoster, J. (2014). Efficacy of the Responsive Classroom approach: Results from a 3-year, longitudinal randomized controlled trial. *American Educational Research Journal, 51*, 567–603. doi:10.3102/0002831214523821

Roberge, J. J., & Flexer, B. K. (1984). Cognitive style, operativity, and reading achievement. *American Educational Research Journal, 21*, 227–236. doi:10.3102/00028312021001227

Rogoff, B. (1990). *Apprenticeship in thinking: Cognitive development in social context*. New York, NY: Oxford University Press.

Rohwer, W. D., Jr. (1971). Learning, race, and school success. *Review of Educational Research, 41*, 191–210.

Rosenshine, B., & Stevens, R. (1986). Teaching functions. In M. C. Wittrock (Ed.), *Handbook of research on teaching* (3rd ed., pp. 376–391). New York, NY: MacMillan.

Saxe, G. B. (1991). *Culture and cognitive development: Studies in mathematical understanding*. Hillsdale, NJ: Lawrence Erlbaum.

Saxe, G. B. (1994). Studying cognitive development in sociocultural context: The development of a practice-based approach. *Mind, Culture, and Activity, 1*, 135–137.

Schoenfeld, A. H. (1998). Toward a theory of teaching-in-context. *Issues in Education, 4*, 1–94.

Scribner, S. (1984a). Studying working intelligence. In B. Rogoff & J. Lave (Eds.), *Everyday cognition: Its development in social context* (pp. 9–40). Cambridge, MA: Harvard University Press.

Scribner, S. (1984b). The practice of literacy—Where mind and society meet. *Annals of the New York Academy of Sciences, 433*, 5–19.

Seddon, G. M., Eniaiyeju, P. A., & Jusoh, I. (1984). The visualization of rotation in diagrams of three-dimensional structures. *American Educational Research Journal, 21*, 25–38. doi:10.3102/00028312021001025

Sfard, A. (1998). On two metaphors for learning and the dangers of choosing just one. *Educational Researcher, 27*(3), 4–13.

Shapiro, A. M. (2004). How including prior knowledge as a subject variable may change outcomes of learning research. *American Educational Research Journal, 41*, 159–189.

Shaw, M. C. (1967). Motivation in human learning. *Review of Educational Research, 37*, 563–582.

Shuell, T. J. (1986). Cognitive conceptions of learning. *Review of Educational Research, 56*, 411–436.

Shuell, T. J. (1990). Phases of meaningful learning. *Review of Educational Research, 60*, 531–547.

Shuell, T. J., & Lee, C. Z. (1976). *Learning and instruction.* Monterey, CA: Brooks/Cole.

Shulman, L. S. (1986a). Paradigms and programs in the study of teaching: A contemporary perspective. In M. C. Wittrock (Ed.), *Handbook of research on teaching* (3rd ed., pp. 3–36). New York, NY: Macmillan.

Shulman, L. S. (1986b). Those who understand: Knowledge growth in teaching. *Educational Researcher, 15*(2), 4–14.

Simon, M. A. (1995). Reconstructing mathematics pedagogy from a constructivist perspective. *Journal for Research in Mathematics Education, 26*, 114–145. doi:10.2307/749205

Skinner, B. F. (1935). The generic nature of the concepts of stimulus and response. *Journal of General Psychology, 12*, 40–65.

Skinner, B. F. (1948). Superstition in the pigeon. *Journal of Experimental Psychology, 38*, 168–172.

Slavin, R. E., & Karweit, N. L. (1984). Mastery learning and student teams: A factorial experiment in urban general mathematics classes. *American Educational Research Journal, 21*, 725–736. doi:10.3102/00028312021004725

Star, J. R., Pollack, C., Durkin, K., Rittle-Johnson, B., Lynch, K., Newton, K., & Gogolen, C. (2015). Learning from comparison in algebra. *Contemporary Educational Psychology, 40*, 41–54. doi:10.1016/j.cedpsych.2014.05.005

Storr, R. J. (1976). The role of education in American history: A memorandum. *Harvard Educational Review, 46*, 331–354.

Swanson, H. L., & Hoskyn, M. (1998). Experimental intervention research on students with learning disabilities: A meta-analysis of treatment outcomes. *Review of Educational Research, 68*, 277–321.

Talmage, H., Pascarella, E. T., & Ford, S. (1984). The influence of cooperative learning strategies on teacher practices, student perceptions of the learning environment, and academic achievement. *American Educational Research Journal, 21*, 163–179. doi:10.2307/1162359

Tatsuoka, K. K., Corter, J. E., & Tatsuoka, C. (2004). Patterns of diagnosed mathematical content and process skills in TIMSS-R across a sample of 20 countries. *American Educational Research Journal, 41*, 901–926.

Thompson, M., Brassell, W. R., Persons, S., Tucker, R., & Rollins, H. (1974). Contingency management in the schools: How often and how well does it work? *American Educational Research Journal, 11*, 19–28. doi:10.3102/00028312011001019

Thorndike, E. L. (1911). *Animal intelligence: Experimental studies.* New York, NY: Macmillan.

Thorndike, E. L. (1913). *The psychology of learning.* New York, NY: Teachers College, Columbia University.

Thorndike, E. L., & Lorge, I. (1944). *The teacher's word book of 30,000 words.* New York, NY: Columbia University Press.

Tolman, E. C. (1948). Cognitive maps in rats and men. *Psychological Review, 55*, 189–208.

Travers, R. M. W., & Wagenen, R. K. V. (1964). Observational learning in a simulated recitation group. *American Educational Research Journal, 1*, 26–34.

Trow, W. C. (1945). Psychology of learning. *Review of Educational Research, 15*, 227–242.

Virués-Ortega, J. (2010). Applied behavior analytic intervention for autism in early childhood: Meta-analysis, meta-regression, and dose-response meta-analysis of multiple outcomes. *Clinical Psychology Review, 30*, 387–399.

Vygotsky, L. S. (1962). *Thought and language.* Cambridge: MIT Press.

Vygotsky, L. S. (1978). *Mind in society: The development of higher psychological processes.* Cambridge, MA: Harvard University Press.

Walberg, H. J., & Haertel, G. D. (1992). Educational psychology's first century. *Journal of Educational Psychology, 84*, 6–19.

Watson, J. B. (1913). Psychology as the behaviorist views it. *Psychological Review, 20*, 158–177.

Watson, J. B. (1929). *Behaviorism—The modern note in psychology.* Retrieved from http://psychclassics.yorku.ca/Watson/Battle/watson.htm

Watson, J. B. (1930). *Behaviorism.* Chicago, IL: University of Chicago Press.

Watson, J. B., & Rayner, R. (1920). Conditioned emotional reactions. *Journal of Experimental Psychology, 3*, 1–14.

Webb, N. M., & Farivar, S. (1994). Promoting helping behavior in cooperative small groups in middle school mathematics. *American Educational Research Journal, 31*, 369–395. doi:10.3102/00028312031002369

Webster-Wright, A. (2009). Reframing professional development through understanding authentic professional learning. *Review of Educational Research, 79*, 702–739.

Wertsch, J. V., & Bivens, J. A. (1992). The social origins of individual mental functioning: Alternatives and perspectives. *Quarterly Newsletter of the Laboratory of Comparative Human Cognition, 14*(2), 35–44.

Wixson, K. K. (1984). Level of importance of postquestions and children's learning from text. *American Educational Research Journal, 21*, 419–433.

Woods, B. S., & Murphy, P. K. (2002). Thickening the discussion: William James and contemporary educational psychology. *Educational Theory, 52*, 43–59.

Woolfolk Hoy, A., Davis, H., & Anderman, E. (2013). Theories of learning and teaching in TIP. *Theory Into Practice, 52*, 9–21.

Wortham, S. (2004). The interdependence of social identification and learning. *American Educational Research Journal, 41*, 715–750.

Xue, Y., & Meisels, S. J. (2004). Early literacy instruction and learning in kindergarten: Evidence from the early childhood longitudinal study—Kindergarten class of 1998–1999. *American Educational Research Journal, 41*, 191–229. doi:10.3102/00028312041001191

Zimmerman, B. J., & Bandura, A. (1994). Impact of self-regulatory influences on writing course attainment. *American Educational Research Journal, 31*, 845–862. doi:10.3102/00028312031004845

Chapter 13

Understanding and Promoting Thinking About Knowledge: Origins, Issues, and Future Directions of Research on Epistemic Cognition

WILLIAM A. SANDOVAL
University of California, Los Angeles

JEFFREY A. GREENE
University of North Carolina at Chapel Hill

IVAR BRÅTEN
University of Oslo

Epistemic cognition is the thinking that people do about what and how they know. Education has long been concerned with promoting reflection on knowledge and processes of knowing, but research into epistemic cognition began really in the past half century, with a tremendous expansion in the past 20 years. This review summarizes the broad range of psychological and education research that comprises the study of epistemic cognition, and it identifies various fault lines that currently prevent coherent synthesis of theoretical models and empirical findings. The fault lines include differences in how scholars conceptualize knowledge and cognition, and the contextual nature of epistemic cognition, with consequent differences in accounts of individual development, as well as in research methods. In the coming century, research that can integrate findings among individual, situative, and cultural accounts of cognition may enable the advancement of coherent models of epistemic cognition and its development and support improved educational efforts aimed at such development.

The most prominent and influential trend in the still-young 21st century is the Digital Age's rapid production and distribution of information (Leu, Kinzer, Coiro, Castek, & Henry, 2013). Unfortunately, this trend brings with it age-old concerns about the quality, veracity, and utility of information. Citizens of the modern world must have the dispositions, beliefs, and skills to think critically about others'

Review of Research in Education
March 2016, Vol. 40, pp. 457–496
DOI: 10.3102/0091732X16669319
© 2016 AERA. http://rre.aera.net

claims and the ability to make convincing claims of their own (Goldman et al., 2010; National Education Association, 2014). In a time of unprecedented information complexity, the evidence that people often do not think about that complexity in effective ways (Sinatra, Kienhues, & Hofer, 2014; Stanovich, 2010) has led to numerous calls for educators to prioritize teaching people how to discern positive contributions to human knowledge from opinion, dogma, and unsubstantiated or maliciously intended deceptions (Council of Chief State School Officers, 2010; NGSS Lead States, 2013).

The study of *epistemic cognition* concerns how individuals think about what they know, what knowledge is, how it can be used, and how they know what they know (Greene, Sandoval, & Bråten, 2016a; Kitchener, 1983). Questions about knowledge and knowing have, for most of history, been the purview of epistemology—the philosophical study of knowledge and its justifications. Over the past century, psychological inquiry into how individuals think about epistemic issues has steadily grown, as it has become apparent that epistemic cognition influences learning and reasoning. This review summarizes the broad areas of psychological and education research that have combined to define the area of research on epistemic cognition. This work has old roots in philosophical epistemology but has expanded tremendously in the past 50 years as its importance to education has been increasingly recognized. Our review identifies a number of fault lines in the various approaches to studying epistemic cognition. We characterize these fault lines and propose avenues toward their resolution that can productively guide research on epistemic cognition over the next century.

APPROACH TO REVIEW

The study of epistemic cognition is not a single, coherent field. Rather, scholars from educational and developmental psychology, disciplinary education, and the learning sciences all have been interested in how learners come to know and to think about knowledge. Reviewing the disparate breadth of relevant work presents unusual challenges. A straightforward review of the history of each field now considered relevant to epistemic cognition would be extremely lengthy, making it difficult to identify points of confluence, divergence, and incompatibility. Instead, we briefly review historical developments within these disparate fields to describe the origins of key conceptualizations and empirical findings relevant to epistemic cognition. We then shift away from this historical overview to draw out what we see as major fault lines running across the fields of epistemic cognition research. The fault lines represent obstacles to producing more integrated work on epistemic cognition—integration we believe necessary both to intellectual efforts to model epistemic cognition and to educational efforts to develop it. This approach will identify the major models of epistemic cognition applied to education, their conceptual and empirical strengths and weaknesses, and areas of scholarship that can strengthen and develop these models and their educational applications. We conclude by suggesting how the fault lines might be addressed in the coming century in ways that can support more integrative work across the many fields that concern themselves with epistemic cognition.

To gather material relevant to our review, we conducted a search within the following Thomson Reuters Web of Science databases: Social Sciences Citation Index; Conference Proceedings Citation Index—Social Sciences & Humanities; Book Citation Index—Social Sciences & Humanities. We used the search terms *personal epist**, *epistemic cognition*, and *epistem* belief**, which returned 294, 29, and 724 results, respectively. Thomson Reuters produced reference and citation data on each publication. We included in our review database all publications cited at least 10 times, resulting in 225 unique results. We expanded our results list by entering all chapters from three prominent texts on epistemic cognition: Bendixen and Feucht (2010), Hofer and Pintrich (2002), and Khine (2008). We also added Perry's (1970) seminal text on intellectual and ethical development. Finally, we included chapters from the new *Handbook of Epistemic Cognition* (Greene, Sandoval, & Bråten, 2016b). This resulted in a final database of 267 publications.

The Thomson Reuters index is a limited subset of all possible publications (e.g., it does not capture book chapters well), which may lead to misrepresentations of how the 267 publications influenced the field. Google Scholar captures a broader array of publications (e.g., book chapters, books, white papers), making it a useful comparison tool for evaluating publications' impact. Only 5 of our 267 publications were not located in Google Scholar. We calculated total citations and average citations per year and ordered rankings for each publication from both the Thomson Reuters and Google Scholar sources.

As expected, the Thomson Reuters data set was more conservative than the Google Scholar data set. Thomson Reuters indicated that our database of epistemic cognition literature averaged 44.75 citations per publication, with an *h*-index of 54. Google Scholar data resulted in 159.09 citations per publication, with an *h*-index of 101. These indices reflect the high volume of activity in epistemic cognition research. The values and ranks between data sets were highly correlated. The Pearson correlation for total citations between data sets was .966; the Pearson correlation for average citations per year was .928. Using Spearman's rho for ranked data, the correlation for total citations rankings was .903; and for the average citations per year rankings, the correlation was .834. All correlations were statistically significant at $p < .001$. Our hand review of the rankings across databases corroborated the high degree of statistical correlation between the two, as well as corroborating our own intuitions about influential publications. Therefore, when deciding on the most significant publications to include in our review, we consulted our citation rankings as well as our own sense of influential work.

ORIGINS OF RESEARCH ON EPISTEMIC COGNITION

The sections that follow provide a historical overview of various strands of scholarship on questions and concerns related to epistemic cognition, although some of the fields discussed below did not explicitly frame themselves in such terms. Given the number of fields in psychology and education addressing epistemic issues, we do not attempt a comprehensive review of any single one of them. Instead, we highlight research findings and conceptual models that have influenced research on epistemic cognition over time. These sections rely more heavily than later ones on secondary sources (i.e., prior reviews), where interested readers can find much more detail on any particular field.

Philosophical Epistemology

In many of the most cited sources in our database, the authors drew from philosophical epistemology to define epistemic cognition and determine its scope (Chinn, Buckland, & Samarapungavan, 2011; Greene, Azevedo, & Torney-Purta, 2008; Hofer & Pintrich, 1997; Muis, Bendixen, & Haerle, 2006). In the first sentence of their landmark review of epistemic cognition research, Hofer and Pintrich (1997) defined epistemology as "an area of philosophy concerned with the nature and justification of human knowledge" (p. 88). This definition guided their conceptualization of epistemic cognition, and many others as well (e.g., Greene et al., 2008; Muis et al., 2006). Chinn et al.'s (2011) recent argument for an expansion of the scope of epistemic cognition research was based on their review of contemporary philosophical epistemology, in which they found that "epistemologists view their field much more broadly" (p. 145) than previous education researchers had suggested. Clearly, philosophical epistemology has influenced, and continues to influence, education research on epistemic cognition.

It is far beyond the scope of this chapter to comprehensively review epistemology, a field with roots stretching back to Plato.[1] Instead, we describe how ideas from "traditional" epistemology (Rysiew, 2016) have informed the scope and foci of epistemic cognition research. Then, we discuss how more recent "naturalized" epistemology scholarship has pushed researchers to consider more social and situated views of epistemic cognition.

Traditional Epistemology

Epistemology (from the Greek, "study of knowledge") has, for most of its history, focused on the proper means of defining knowledge and discerning it from opinion, faith, and misinformation (Steup, 2014). Until the late 20th century, the predominant view of necessary and sufficient conditions for claiming knowledge was that the claim had to be a justified true belief (Chisholm, 1983): For a person to have knowledge, a proposition must be true, and the person must believe it to be true. Philosophers recognized that a person could have a true belief by chance, such as believing that this sentence was written on an Apple computer, while lacking any reasonable cause to make the claim. To avoid characterizing cases of true belief by chance or luck as knowledge, philosophers added that to know something, one had to be justified in that knowledge, for example, by seeing one of this chapter's authors typing on an Apple computer (i.e., justification by perception).

Debates in traditional epistemology have focused largely on the proper and sufficient means of justification, with some arguing for evidence (e.g., perception) as being sufficient (Conee & Feldman, 1985) and others arguing that justifications must come from processes that have been shown to reliably produce knowledge (e.g., testimony from a trusted source; Goldman, 1994). Gettier (1963) issued a major challenge to traditional epistemology when he showed that having a justified true belief alone was not a sufficient condition for knowledge, leading to increased focus on other means of justification or delimitation of knowledge (Moser & vander Nat, 1987). Another challenge to the justified true belief model came from radical skepticism, the idea that humans can never know anything with certainty, debated in epistemology since Plato. The details of Gettier's (1963) arguments and how they have been debated in the field are beyond the scope of this review (cf. Williams, 2001). The key point is that until fairly recently, the majority of education research on epistemic cognition, influenced by traditional epistemology, focused on when and how individuals recognize that knowledge claims are complex, evolving phenomena requiring justifications (e.g., Hofer & Pintrich, 1997; Kuhn, Cheney, & Weinstock, 2000), and which types of justifications are associated with positive academic outcomes (e.g., Bråten, Britt, Strømsø, & Rouet, 2011; Greene et al., 2008; Greene, Torney-Purta, & Azevedo, 2010).

Naturalized Epistemology

Many contemporary epistemologists continue to explore and debate traditional views of epistemology (e.g., strategic reliabilism; Bishop & Trout, 2008). Yet, partially in response to the seemingly intractable nature of Gettier problems and radical skepticism, relatively recently some philosophers have taken a different approach to epistemology (Chinn et al., 2011). One major area of scholarship is naturalized epistemology (Goldman, 1994; Kitcher, 1993; Kornblith, 1985; Quine, 1969). Adherents of this movement have argued that the field should move away from solely a priori theorizing about knowledge and knowing and, instead, bolster philosophical epistemology with findings from psychology and other sciences regarding the actual processes, cognitive and otherwise, that laypeople and experts use to make and evaluate knowledge. Rather than using abstract examples to explore their ideas (e.g., "this sentence was written on an Apple computer"), they study how disciplinary or domain ideas are justified (e.g., astronomers' decision-making processes that led them to change Pluto's status from a planet to a dwarf planet). Naturalized epistemology often intersects with social epistemology (Fuller, 1988), which is the study of how knowledge is constructed, substantiated, and communicated within and among communities. For example, communities cohere around particular epistemic practices to make and disseminate knowledge (e.g., peer review), and both philosophers and education researchers have begun studying how epistemic practices are adopted, or not, by people in those communities (Goldman, 1999; Kelly, 2014). Philosophical scholarship in naturalized epistemology, with its focus on how knowledge is determined and disseminated within and among communities of practice, coheres well with, and has informed, models of epistemic cognition based in the disciplines (e.g., Hammer & Elby, 2002) as well as those with a situated view (e.g., Chinn et al., 2011).

Philosophical Epistemology and Education

Traditional epistemology continues to influence education research on how people think about knowledge and justification (e.g., Barzilai & Weinstock, 2015; Muis & Duffy, 2013). Likewise, the naturalistic turn has changed and broadened philosophical epistemology in numerous ways, with similar effects appearing in epistemic cognition research. Questions about the development of epistemic cognition and the level of generality of means of justification have been approached, in part, by looking to studies of the knowledge work of particular disciplines (e.g., Duschl's, 2008, summary of these trends in science). Naturalized epistemology has also been used to argue for an expansion of the purview of epistemic cognition research beyond knowledge sources and justifications (Chinn et al., 2011), and to motivate study of specific forms of epistemic cognition in particular contexts, especially disciplinary learning (e.g., Kelly, 2016) and expert practice (Samarapungavan, Westby, & Bodner, 2006). The distinctions between traditional and naturalized epistemology mirror and inform fault lines between psychological and disciplinary approaches to epistemic cognition, specifically differences in emphasis between models of epistemic cognition focusing on epistemic beliefs or theories (e.g., Hofer & Pintrich, 1997) and those that focus on epistemic standards and practices in context (e.g., Chinn, Rinehart, & Buckland, 2014).

Education and Psychology

Education has always been concerned with how people come to understand the nature of knowledge and develop strategies to justify belief. Plato's *The Republic* (1991) outlined an epistemology of ideal knowledge and an educational model to obtain it; the Socratic dialogues articulated a view on how knowledge could be obtained and justified. In the modern era, Dewey (1910) expounded on the value of developing "scientific" habits of mind, and modern psychologists have routinely explored how insights from the study of knowledge generation and application are relevant in educational settings. Here we take a historical approach to highlight salient models, findings, and trends in broad strands of research related to epistemic cognition: personal epistemology research as it has been conducted within educational and developmental psychology, scholarship on epistemic aspects of cognitive development from developmental psychology, and disciplinary education research.

Personal Epistemology

The field of personal epistemology began with Perry's (1970) study of the changes in "intellectual development" of a sample of (male) Harvard students over their college careers. From this root have grown three prominent models of epistemic cognition that dominate the top 20 sources in our database, in terms of both total citations and average citations per year. Besides Perry's (1970) model, they are Kuhn et al.'s (2000) model of epistemological understanding, Schommer-Aikins's (2004) epistemological belief system, and Hofer and Pintrich's (1997) epistemological theories model. These models group into two classes, often called *developmental* (i.e., Kuhn et al., 2000;

Perry, 1970) and *dimensional* (i.e., Hofer & Pintrich, 1997; Schommer-Aikins, 2004). Developmental models characterize differences in epistemic cognition in terms of phases or stages, positing sequential movement from one stage to the next with concomitant changes to people's views of knowledge and knowing. Dimensional models, on the other hand, characterize people's views of knowledge and knowing in terms of multiple beliefs or theories, which can change independently from one another.

Perry (1970) described a scheme akin to a Piagetian stage model, with nine sequential positions grouped into four main stages, each of which included predictions about how college students would interpret all of their experiences, regardless of domain or discipline. People in the first stage of Perry's model were termed dualists, and they were posited to have an objective view of the world, believing that knowledge is factual, unchanging, and the property of experts who pass it along to others. Such views meant that dualists would not engage in critical thinking about knowledge or its sources. Through cognitive disequilibrium resulting from experiences in education and elsewhere, Perry argued that people eventually move into a multiplistic view, believing there are no objective standards for knowledge, making all views equally valid, akin to radical subjectivity. Some people, if they continue to encounter experiences fostering cognitive disequilibrium, were thought to move into the relativist category, acknowledging the contingent and contextual nature of knowledge and the necessity of using one's own logic and reasoning (i.e., critical thinking) to sort knowledge propositions from other types of claims. Perry's fourth category, commitment within relativism, largely concerns how individuals adopt particular values and identities that shape their reasoning. While Perry did little more to investigate or expand this model, his work inspired a number of other developmental models of epistemic cognition (e.g., Baxter Magolda, 1992; Belenky, Clinchy, Goldberger, & Tarule 1986; King & Kitchener, 1994).

Kuhn's (1991) work on informal reasoning about everyday problems resulted in a model that paralleled Perry's trajectory through objective and subjective views of knowledge. Absolutists view claims as facts that describe or explain a directly knowable, certain, and objective reality. These people do not see a need to think critically beyond determining which sources are expert and which knowledge claims match reality. Multiplists deny that reality can be directly knowable and view claims as subjective opinions, thus making critical thinking irrelevant. Finally, evaluativists share multiplists' view that reality is not directly knowable, but like Perry's committed relativists, they believe that critical thinking can be used to determine which claims are more justifiable than others. Kuhn's characterization of the stages of epistemic cognition development has informed numerous other publications in our database (e.g., Barzilai & Zohar, 2012). Another of Kuhn's major contributions to the field of epistemic cognition was to distinguish domains of value judgments (e.g., personal taste, aesthetics) from truth judgments (e.g., social and natural sciences) and provide evidence that developmental levels might vary across these domains.

In a major shift in conceptualization of epistemic cognition, Schommer (1990) proposed a model composed of multiple, somewhat independent belief dimensions, on which individuals might vary. These dimensions have naïve and sophisticated poles, with the assumption that more sophisticated beliefs are associated with better performance on various learning outcomes. The names of the dimensions have changed over time, but are most commonly referred to as *simple knowledge, certain knowledge, source of knowledge, ability to learn,* and *quick learning* (Schommer-Aikins, 2004). The latter two belief dimensions have proved controversial, as several authors have argued that they are not epistemic in nature but, rather, concern beliefs about learning (Greene et al., 2008; Hofer & Pintrich, 1997; Sandoval, 2009). The other three beliefs roughly translate the ideas characterizing developmental models of epistemic cognition (e.g., Kuhn et al., 2000; Perry, 1970) into somewhat independent dimensions. For example, absolutists in Kuhn et al.'s model could be described as believing knowledge to be simple and certain, with the source external to the self, whereas evaluativists would view knowledge as complex and dynamic, and deriving from the self. A key difference between developmental and dimensional models is that the former posit that these beliefs change in a systematic way, whereas the latter posit that people might develop asynchronously across these dimensions.

Another of Schommer's major influences on the field was her development of a self-report instrument for measuring epistemic beliefs that produced scores amenable to quantitative analyses. Her epistemological questionnaire (EQ) ignited an order-of-magnitude increase in scholarly publications about epistemic cognition, with many of the most cited empirical studies of epistemic cognition in our database including the EQ or some variant of it (e.g., Kardash & Scholes, 1996; Schommer, 1993; Sinatra, Southerland, McConaughy, & Demastes, 2003). These publications provided evidence of correlations between the various belief dimensions of epistemic cognition and numerous desirable educational outcomes including cognitive and metacognitive strategy use (Cano, 2005), reading comprehension (Kardash & Scholes, 1996), conceptual change (Qian & Alvermann, 1995), and academic performance (Schommer, 1993; Schommer, Crouse, & Rhodes, 1992). These findings suggested that interventions designed to facilitate students' adoption of adaptive epistemic beliefs (e.g., knowledge is complex and dynamic) might have concomitant positive effects on learning and performance (Conley, Pintrich, Vekiri, & Harrison, 2004).

Aside from Perry's (1970) initial text, the most cited publication in our data set, by a large margin, is Hofer and Pintrich's (1997) review of epistemic cognition models. Hofer and Pintrich synthesized and juxtaposed the prominent developmental and belief dimension models of epistemic cognition, finding a significant amount of coherence and overlap. They used this review to warrant their epistemological theories model, composed of four somewhat independent belief dimensions: *simple knowledge, certain knowledge, source of knowledge,* and *justification of knowledge.* They classified the first two dimensions as beliefs about the nature of knowledge and the latter two as beliefs about the nature of knowing; they characterized all four as personal theories. At that time in the literature, respondents who reported relying on authorities for justification were classified as naïve, but this characterization would be challenged in the early years of the 21st century. Hofer and Pintrich posited that change along these dimensions might be due to cognitive disequilibrium, but pointed to models of conceptual change (Posner, Strike, Hewson, & Gertzog, 1982) and sociocultural enculturation (Vygotsky, 1962) as promising analogs for epistemic development.

Dominant themes among the empirical studies of developmental and dimensional models of epistemic cognition in our database include findings that (a) epistemic cognition predicts academic performance (e.g., Cano, 2005; Schommer et al., 1992); (b) it correlates with other major constructs in education, such as implicit theories of intelligence and self-regulated learning (e.g., Bråten & Strømsø, 2005; Bromme, Pieschl, & Stahl, 2010); (c) there is questionable construct validity of scores from quantitative measures of epistemic cognition (e.g., DeBacker, Crowson, Beesley, Thoma, & Hestevold, 2008); and (d) there is a domain-specific and even task-specific aspect of epistemic cognition, according to a growing corpus of findings (e.g., Buehl, Alexander, & Murphy, 2002; Greene & Yu, 2014; Hofer, 2000, 2004; Muis et al., 2006). Influential conceptual expansions of epistemic cognition include elaborations of the relationships between epistemic cognition, metacognition, and self-regulated learning (e.g., Barzilai & Zohar, 2014; Greene, Muis, & Pieschl, 2010; Hofer, 2004); expanded models of epistemic cognition development (e.g., Bendixen & Rule, 2004); studies of how people evaluate sources of knowledge (e.g., Braasch, Bråten, Strømsø, Anmarkrud, & Ferguson, 2013; Porsch & Bromme, 2011); investigations of teachers' epistemic cognition (Bråten & Ferguson, 2015; Buehl & Fives, 2009, 2016; Fives & Buehl, 2008; Gregoire, 2003); and the expansion of Hofer and Pintrich's (1997) justification dimension to account for multiple means of warranting knowledge claims. This expansion has included the recognition that justification by authority is not necessarily naïve, and in fact is often availing and even necessary given the proliferation of knowledge claims in the modern world (Bromme, Kienhues, & Stahl, 2008; Chinn et al., 2011; Greene et al., 2008; Kitcher, 1993). Bråten et al. (2011) have demonstrated how models of multiple document comprehension can inform epistemic cognition research, particularly in terms of how people coordinate multiple means of justification.

Finally, Chinn and colleagues (Chinn et al., 2011; Chinn et al., 2014; Chinn & Rinehart, 2016) have argued that contemporary work in philosophical epistemology has a number of implications for models of epistemic cognition, including that (a) epistemic cognition is fundamentally a social phenomenon; (b) investigations of people's epistemic aims for a task are needed to contextualize and understand their actual epistemic cognition; (c) epistemic practices or reliable processes (e.g., experimental methods, sourcing) are key aspects of epistemic cognition; and (d) epistemic cognition is situated in context. Chinn and colleagues' incorporation of ideas from naturalized epistemology has challenged the traditional epistemology foundations of developmental and dimensional models. At the same time, the naturalistic turn has highlighted potentially generative connections between personal epistemology research and work in developmental psychology and disciplinary education.

Developmental Foundations of Epistemic Cognition

For many years after Perry's (1970) seminal work, epistemic cognition was presumed to develop only in adolescence or later. Burr and Hofer (2002), among others, have found evidence of epistemic cognition in young children, suggesting an early start to its development. Montgomery (1992) argued that as children pass cognitive developmental milestones in early childhood, they can be said to develop a "folk epistemology," an intuitive, perhaps naïve, way of thinking about what and how they and others know. Over the past three decades, developmental psychology research in several areas has expanded the view of antecedent foundations of epistemic cognition. Children develop and apply a range of strategies to evaluate their own and others' claims to knowledge, even though they may not understand them in explicitly epistemic terms. Our review suggests four major areas of development where connections to epistemic cognition have been made most clearly.

Theory of mind. Children's theory of mind involves the understanding that people can have mental states (e.g., beliefs, desires, goals, knowledge) that differ from others' mental states and differ also from reality (Wellman, 2011). Early research suggested that theory of mind did not develop until age 3 or later, but more recent evidence indicates even infants are able to display integral aspects of theory of mind (e.g., understanding other peoples' goals and perceptions and how they drive their behavior; Sodian & Kristen, 2016). These findings can illuminate investigations of young children's epistemic cognition, where researchers have found that 3-year-olds can exhibit evidence of a preabsolutist stage, called egocentric subjectivity. In this stage, children believe their perspective is the only one possible (Burr & Hofer, 2002; Wildenger, Hofer, & Burr, 2010). A key milestone in theory of mind development, and likely epistemic cognition as well, is children's understanding that other people may believe something to be true that the child knows is false. This understanding of false belief manifests around the fifth year of life, on average, and may serve as foundation for the kinds of source evaluations posited in many models of epistemic cognition. At a minimum, theory of mind and epistemic cognition share some common developmental foundations (e.g., attribution of mental states to others), suggesting the need for more research connecting these two areas of study (Hofer & Bendixen, 2012; Sodian & Kristen, 2016).

Causal reasoning. Children display an early, even immediate, ability to draw causal inferences about events they perceive and experience (e.g., what makes a marble roll in a straight or diagonal path). Inference develops into more systematic reasoning throughout childhood (Moshman & Tarricone, 2016). By 8 or 9 years of age, children distinguish inference from other sources of knowing, like guessing or direct perception (Pillow, Hill, Boyce, & Stein, 2000). Beyond early childhood, children also distinguish causal explanation from logical necessities or proofs (Moshman & Tarricone, 2016), and people's evaluations of causal explanations seem to shift over time from a reliance on causal mechanisms alone toward mechanisms with evidence

(Kuhn, 2001). Causal reasoning is clearly an antecedent to epistemic cognition. It may even be where epistemic cognition begins, as young children begin making justifications using perception and logic to decide, even if tacitly, which causal inferences are reliable and which are not.

Scientific thinking. The developmental study of "scientific" thinking began in the 1980s, following work with adults by Wason (1960) and others (Zimmerman, 2000). Historically, developmental psychology has framed scientific thinking in terms of hypothesis testing, experimental control of variables, and reasoning about correlation (a narrower notion of scientific thinking than is pursued in science education, see below). The biases displayed by adults to distort evidence and confirm already-held beliefs appear early in childhood and have been labeled as an inability to distinguish claims from evidence (Kuhn, Amsel, & O'Loughlin, 1988). Research suggests that a basic distinction between claims and the evidence that might bear on them, as distinct epistemic entities, emerges by school age (Ruffman, Perner, Olson, & Doherty, 1993; Sodian, Zaitchik, & Carey, 1991), but children's competence at evaluating specific claims or the quality of evidence for a specific claim depends on familiarity with the domain and other factors (Lehrer & Schauble, 2006; Sandoval, Sodian, Koerber, & Wong, 2014). Scientists themselves display the same sorts of biases related to evidence as do lay adults (Chinn & Brewer, 1993), suggesting that what develops is not a general sense of the nature of evidence or of its role in evaluating knowledge but competence within particular domains or topics. The crucial epistemic questions therefore seem to be how individuals and groups (e.g., disciplines) develop processes of justification, source evaluation, and so forth, as well as how those processes are communicated and refined.

Social cognition. Developmental psychologists have long been concerned with how children come to trust or mistrust particular sources of knowledge (for reviews, see Clément, 2016; Harris, 2007, 2012). Children are largely dependent on other people's testimony for gaining knowledge about the world (Fricker, 1995), hence the social nature of children's knowledge acquisition processes (Clément, 2016). Children's trust in others' testimony is not blind, however. It is based on basic evaluations of trustworthiness referring to features such as the accuracy, competence, coherence, audience reception, and benevolence of sources (Clément, 2016; Harris, 2012). For example, when two sources make conflicting claims about the name of an unfamiliar object, 3- and 4-year-olds have been found to display selective trust based on the accuracy of those sources in naming a familiar object in the past (Corriveau & Harris, 2009; Jaswal & Neely, 2006; Koenig, Clément, & Harris, 2004; Koenig & Harris, 2005). These early evaluations of testimony and source reliability likely form the foundation for evaluating trustworthiness of sources later in life. The importance of testimony as an essential, social source of knowledge has recently been emphasized in the field of epistemic cognition (Chinn et al., 2011), and critical source evaluation leading to selective trust in sources of knowledge has been found to facilitate students' understanding of multiple conflicting perspectives on controversial socioscientific issues (Braasch et al., 2013; Bråten, Strømsø, & Britt, 2009; Wiley et al., 2009).

Summary of Developmental Foundations of Epistemic Cognition

These areas of cognitive development appear to form the building blocks for epistemic cognition and highlight early competencies of children's thinking about knowledge and knowing that should be more thoroughly integrated into current models of epistemic cognition and research about them. Over the coming century, it should be quite fruitful for scholars across fields studying epistemic cognition to look at these, and perhaps other, aspects of cognitive development as essential facets of epistemic cognition. While some scholars of development (e.g., Kuhn, 2001) explicitly locate their research across psychology and education, a broader exchange of ideas across disciplines could inform conceptualizations of epistemic cognition and its development across both schooled and unschooled settings.

Disciplinary Education

Education in the disciplines of math, science, and history has been concerned with the epistemological aspects of these disciplines for decades. Historically, educational psychology research in school subjects has focused on epistemic beliefs and their relation to learning processes and academic outcomes (e.g., Depaepe, De Corte, & Verschaffel, 2016; Qian & Alvermann, 1995; Schommer et al., 1992). Researchers in the learning sciences have focused instead on relations between engagement in disciplinary practices (e.g., scientific inquiry, historical argument) and understanding of disciplinary knowledge and disciplinary epistemologies (e.g., Rosebery, Warren, & Conant, 1992; Schoenfeld, 1992; Wineburg, 1991). There are a number of recent reviews of research related to epistemic cognition in each of these disciplines, including the long-standing research on conceptions of the nature of science (Elby, Macrander, & Hammer, 2016; Lederman, 2007), and on epistemic cognition in mathematics (Depaepe et al., 2016; Muis, 2004) and history (VanSledright & Maggioni, 2016). Here we summarize trends from these disciplinary lines of research as they apply to the broader study of epistemic cognition.

One feature of epistemic cognition research in the disciplines is that it has been framed within discipline-specific epistemological concerns. Sometimes these overlap with the more general conceptions from personal epistemology research; for example, the concern in science education that students understand the tentativeness of science knowledge maps onto the general dimension of certainty of knowledge. Yet, within disciplinary education, the epistemologies of the disciplines are fleshed out more deeply and specifically than is typically the case in the psychology or personal epistemology literatures. Science educators link tentativeness to the theory-laden nature of observation in science (Lederman, 2007), while asserting that some claims are more certain than others (Osborne, Collins, Ratcliffe, Millar, & Duschl, 2003).

Historians locate uncertainty in the distance between the present and the past and the ambiguity of historical objects (VanSledright & Maggioni, 2016). In mathematics, the issue of certainty presents as whether one believes mathematical procedures are given or constructed (Depaepe et al., 2016).

The later half of the 20th century saw in all these academic disciplines a growing recognition that students need to learn the epistemology of a discipline in addition to its theories, concepts, and facts (Duschl, 2008; Schoenfeld, 1992; Wineburg, 1991). This concern has driven a range of efforts to assess students' understanding of specific epistemological conceptions within the disciplines, as well as to examine how constructs from personal epistemology relate to learning in the disciplines. At the same time, researchers have become increasingly interested in characterizing how conceptions of knowledge and knowing in the disciplines are related to particular sense-making practices in those disciplines. A range of studies have shed light on beliefs and thinking about knowledge and knowing as situated within disciplinary activities and, thus, peculiar to particular disciplines (e.g., Cobb, Stephan, McClain, & Gravemeijer, 2001; De Corte, Op't Eynde, Depaepe, & Verschaffel, 2010; diSessa, Elby, & Hammer, 2002; Greene & Yu, 2014; Hammer, 1994; Maggioni, VanSledright, & Alexander, 2009; Samarapungavan et al., 2006; Sandoval & Çam, 2011; Wineburg, 1991).

With respect to broader debates about the generality or specificity of epistemic cognition, research in the disciplines has made a strong case for disciplinary specificity tied directly to the obviously different epistemological perspectives among the disciplines. Empirical research on learning across disciplines is starting to show that students appreciate, for example, that evidence in science and history looks different (Herrenkohl & Cornelius, 2013). Likewise, across disciplines, elementary and high school students ask different types of questions when seeking to understand texts (Portnoy & Rabinowitz, 2014). For epistemic cognition research broadly, it is crucial to recognize that disciplines have developed their own epistemologies in response to the particular questions and problems of knowledge development they have faced. The likelihood of epistemic cognition predicting academic performance in these fields depends on the degree to which individuals can adopt and use discipline-specific epistemic norms and practices (Goldman, 2011; Greene, 2016).

The State of Epistemic Cognition Research

The past half-century has seen research on epistemic cognition grow immensely in a number of fields. The disparate roots of research into how people generate knowledge, interpret knowledge, and think about the nature of knowledge have begun, in the past 10 to 20 years, to converge in some ways. Current models are explicitly informed by relevant work in the field of philosophical epistemology (Chinn et al., 2011; Greene et al., 2008; Muis et al., 2006). Contemporary models of epistemic cognition also pay more attention to the antecedents and early forms of epistemic cognition suggested by work in developmental psychology (Burr & Hofer, 2002; Hofer & Pintrich, 1997). Earlier debates about the specificity or generality of epistemic beliefs have mostly given way to a recognition that epistemic cognition has contextual and disciplinary aspects that are only somewhat understood (Sandoval, 2012), creating a need to better explain both the extent and mechanisms of generalization of epistemic cognition. The historical trends in these fields are converging to create a broader conceptualization of epistemic cognition, albeit not without some growing pains (Chinn et al., 2011; Hofer & Bendixen, 2012; Sandoval, 2012). Conceptual expansion of the idea of epistemic cognition has brought with it questions about the appropriate boundaries of the concept (e.g., Alexander, 2016). We believe these questions are important. To answer them, researchers must begin to identify and wrestle with the differences in how they conceptualize, measure, and intervene in people's engagement with knowledge and knowing.

FAULT LINES

Given the variety of intellectual perspectives on phenomena of epistemic cognition, it is no surprise that as various communities of scholarship have come into closer contact around them, a range of fault lines have emerged. These characterize dilemmas that scholars from a variety of fields have recognized as needing some resolution to move toward coherent accounts of epistemic cognition and its possible development. We highlight some fault lines that derive from our analysis of the literature we have reviewed, acknowledging that others working in this area might see different issues.

Conceptualizations of Knowledge and Cognition

One of the major intellectual shifts in the social sciences over the past decades of the 20th century and into the 21st has been the cultural turn (Bruner, 1996). In psychology, education, and philosophy, there has been a shift from viewing thinking and knowing as fundamentally individual activities to viewing them as fundamentally social (e.g., naturalized epistemology; Goldman, 1994; Quine, 1969). This shift, however, has been taken up to different extents, and differences in where scholars, and even fields, see the locus of explanation of epistemic cognition on this individual–social continuum creates a tangle of empirical results and interpretations that have yet to be clarified.

Piaget's (1972) genetic epistemology and stage theory of development directly influenced epistemic cognition research from the start. This view of knowledge construction as an individual achievement continues to underlie much of the psychology research pertinent to epistemic cognition. The term *personal epistemology* as a moniker for this research itself conveys the assumption that persons construct epistemologies as part of their efforts to interpret the world around them. The constructivist abandons the idea that knowledge is an object in the world. Instead, "*knowledge* refers to conceptual structures that epistemic agents, given the range of present experience within their tradition of thought and language, consider *viable*" (Glasersfeld, 1989, p. 124). That is, while cultural traditions of thought and language may shape experience, individual epistemic agents build conceptual structures that can viably be considered knowledge. This is not to say that constructivists necessarily abandon the idea of an objective reality (see Phillips, 1995, for a discussion of variants of constructivism on this point), only that our knowledge of reality is constructed. The cognitive constructivism of Piaget locates that knowledge as a construct of individual minds.

Several models of epistemic cognition maintain this cognitive constructivism as the underlying definition of knowledge. Piagetian (e.g., King & Kitchener, 1994; Perry, 1970) and neo-Piagetian (e.g., Kuhn et al., 2000) models propose progressive trajectories that vary mainly in the generality they posit for the stages along the way. Belief systems models (e.g., Hofer, 2004; Schommer-Aikins, 2004) articulate dimensions of belief and their possible influences and interactions. All of these models share an assumption that cognitive representations (i.e., knowledge and belief) are constructed by individuals, via some level of reflection on experience, and then applied to subsequent experiences.

Sociocultural theories of cognition and development derived from Vygotsky (1962, 1978) locate the individual knower within a specific cultural and historical context, thereby framing knowledge as a cultural product and knowing as a cultural activity. Models of epistemic cognition that have been influenced by sociocultural perspectives vary in where they locate knowledge and knowing. What we can call a cognitive contextualist view (see especially the next section), attempts to account for how social factors influence individual knowledge construction, including individuals' ideas about knowledge and knowing. Bendixen and colleagues (Bendixen & Rule, 2004; Muis et al., 2006), for example, have proposed models that attempt to account for how environmental (i.e., social) factors and features of specific domains influence individual epistemic cognition. Muis et al. (2006) have proposed that general epistemic beliefs develop within the social and cultural context in which people grow up. Hammer and Elby (2002) have suggested that participation in culturally shaped patterns of activity lead to the construction of epistemic "resources," fine-grained cognitive structures tied closely to contexts of use. These contexts of use become bound into epistemological "frames" that organize the conditional activation of epistemic resources (Elby & Hammer, 2010). That is, in contrast to Muis et al. (2006), the epistemic resources model suggests that generalization is an outcome of repeated use.

A stronger social perspective on knowledge and knowing derives from situative perspectives on cognition (Engeström, 1987; Lave & Wenger, 1991), allied with the social epistemologists discussed above (Fuller, 1988; Goldman, 2011), who see knowledge as fundamentally a social construct and epistemology as a social phenomenon. The situative perspective takes as its base unit of analysis the individual-in-interaction, emphasizing features of interaction external to individuals and their minds. This interactional view on cognition sees knowledge as distributed among social and material resources and deployed within cultural activity. Thus, individuals' and groups' interpretations of the purpose of an activity are seen as shaping the epistemic cognition that might occur. Chinn and colleagues' (Chinn et al., 2011; Chinn et al., 2014) model thus highlights processes of epistemic cognition as tied to the epistemic aims an individual might pursue during activity, how those aims relate to nonepistemic aims, and how aims are related to reliable processes of knowledge development. These reliable processes are social in nature: They are social practices developed within particular communities to solve specific epistemic problems (Chinn & Rinehart, 2016). The situative perspective on epistemic cognition thus sees knowledge as reflected in practice—in how people accomplish activity—rather than as a mental representation of some aspect of reality that is then applied (Kelly, 2016).

In sum, the divergent perspectives on knowledge and cognition generally are reflected in current models of epistemic cognition, not surprisingly. The crucial difference among these perspectives with respect to epistemic cognition research is that they theorize knowledge itself, its development, and related concepts such as belief and the role of context, rather differently. Such differences have implications for the unit of analysis in epistemic cognition research (e.g., individuals' construction of knowledge propositions vs. the interplay of cultural forms of knowledge and individuals' practice) as well as for perspectives on how epistemic cognition develops (e.g., a focus on changes in individuals' conceptions of knowledge vs. changes in a community's norms and practices and individual participation in those). The parallels between personal epistemology and disciplinary education models of epistemic cognition, and traditional and naturalized epistemology, are clear.

Whether such differences are incommensurate is perhaps an ideological question. Packer and Goicoechea (2000) argued that cognitive constructivism and the situative perspective are ontologically incommensurate, whereas Greeno (2015) suggested they address different levels of explanation. It is clear, however, that broad differences in how knowledge and knowing are theorized produce differences in how issues of contextualization and generality are addressed in research on epistemic cognition. They lead to different explanations of the nature of developmental pathways for epistemic cognition. They also, naturally, produce differences in research methods for identifying, defining, and studying phenomena of epistemic cognition.

Generality and Context in Epistemic Cognition

Hofer and Pintrich (1997) noted that the developmental and belief system models they critiqued paid only marginal attention to the issue of domain specificity versus domain generality in personal epistemology, with an underlying assumption that beliefs and thoughts about knowledge and knowing were largely consistent across domains and disciplines. Hofer and Pintrich (1997) discussed the possibility that both domain-specific and domain-general beliefs about knowledge and knowing existed, while suggesting there might be specific ways of thinking about knowledge and knowing within academic disciplines that made general models of personal epistemology less applicable. The idea that epistemic cognition occurs at different levels of specificity, as well as the idea that there are discipline-specific forms of epistemic cognition, has gained empirical support and been reflected in models of personal epistemology and epistemic cognition. Articles on domain or disciplinary differences in epistemic cognition were frequent among the most cited sources in our data set (e.g., Buehl & Alexander, 2001; Hofer, 2000; Kuhn et al., 2000; Muis et al., 2006).

To study generality and context, researchers working within the belief system paradigm of personal epistemology conducted between-subjects investigations (e.g., Jehng, Johnson, & Anderson, 1993; Lonka & Lindblom-Ylänne, 1996), where students majoring in different domains were compared with respect to their epistemic beliefs. They also conducted within-subject investigations (e.g., Buehl et al., 2002; Hofer, 2000), where the same students were asked about their epistemic beliefs in different domains. In general, this work supported the idea that epistemic beliefs varied as a function of academic domain and, moreover, that such variation was related to perceptions of domain structuredness. That is, researchers found that students viewed knowledge as more certain and integrated, and that they more readily accepted experts as sources of knowledge, in well-structured domains, such as mathematics, than in ill-structured domains, such as history. At the same time, however, this line of research seemed to indicate that students' epistemic beliefs were not solely domain-specific, meaning that students could simultaneously hold both domain-specific and more domain-general or overarching beliefs about knowledge and knowing (Buehl & Alexander, 2001; Muis et al., 2006).

Recent research has started to target epistemic beliefs at a topic-specific level, that is, as beliefs about more delimited subject areas (e.g., World War II) that can be subsumed under an academic domain (e.g., history). This research has led to the use of topic-specific questionnaires (Bråten, Gil, Strømsø, & Vidal-Abarca, 2009; Stahl & Bromme, 2007; Trautwein & Lüdtke, 2007) or think-aloud methodology (Ferguson, Bråten, & Strømsø, 2012; Hofer, 2004; Mason, Ariasi, & Boldrin, 2011; Mason & Boldrin, 2008; Mason, Boldrin, & Ariasi, 2010) to assess students' beliefs about specific topics along different belief dimensions (e.g., the certainty and simplicity of knowledge). For example, such topic-specific epistemic beliefs have been shown to uniquely predict comprehension when students read texts about the same topics (Bråten & Strømsø, 2010; Bråten, Strømsø, & Samuelstuen, 2008; Strømsø, Bråten, & Samuelstuen, 2008).

In the past decade, the empirical work in personal epistemology summarized above has been reflected in theoretical frameworks that take the multilevel nature of epistemic beliefs into account. For example, in their theory of integrated domains in epistemology framework, Muis et al. (2006) posited that beliefs concerning the certainty, simplicity, and source of knowledge, as well as the justification for knowing, may exist at the level of general epistemic beliefs that develop in nonacademic contexts, domain-general academic beliefs that develop in educational contexts, and domain-specific academic beliefs that reflect the various domains of knowledge that students experience. Muis, Trevors, Duffy, Ranellucci, and Foy (2016) have acknowledged that an additional level of specificity may be required beyond the domain-specific level, such as topic-specific beliefs about knowledge and knowing. In a more parsimonious model, at least with respect to levels of specificity, Greene et al. (2008) proposed that beliefs regarding the simplicity and certainty of knowledge and the justification for knowing vary at a level between domain specificity and domain generality, mainly differentiated between well-structured (e.g., mathematics and physics) and ill-structured (e.g., history and literature) domains. In more recent work, Greene and Yu (2014) used qualitative interview data from novices and experts to critique prior conceptualizations of domain specificity in personal epistemology research; they called for greater attention to differences in knowledge and knowing across disciplines.

Although research has indicated that students' beliefs about knowledge and knowing are contextualized, in the sense that they differ across domains and topics within domains, this work is limited by the fact that it has essentially used the same questionnaires targeting the same belief dimensions across domains and topics. As a result, mean differences between scores on those dimensions across domains have been used to indicate domain specificity in epistemic beliefs, and correlations between scores on those dimensions across domains have been used to indicate domain generality in such beliefs (e.g., Buehl et al., 2002; Hofer, 2000; Muis et al., 2016). Also, most research using think-aloud methodology to assess a topic-specific level of epistemic cognition (e.g., Ferguson et al., 2012; Mason et al., 2011) has coded the resulting verbal protocols in terms of dimensions from epistemic belief system models, such as the Hofer and Pintrich (1997) multidimensional framework. Given that those measures presumed, a priori, the existence of a common set of dimensions or beliefs across domains, it could be argued that what has been captured within such research is not really domain- or discipline-specific epistemic beliefs and thinking but, rather, the extent to which scores on general belief dimensions vary across domains and disciplines (Elby et al., 2016; Hofer, 2006). To better understand patterns of epistemic beliefs and thinking within different disciplines, other approaches may be needed.

As indicated above, perspectives from disciplinary education suggest contextual differences both between and within disciplines. Researchers representing such perspectives argue that students' epistemic beliefs and thinking should be understood as situated within individual and collective disciplinary learning activities (Sandoval, 2012, 2015). Some research suggests that variations in epistemic aims and virtues may also be discipline specific or even situation specific. In an intriguing study in history, Gottlieb and Wineburg (2012) showed that historians' epistemic cognition, specifically the criteria they used for evaluating claims and evidence, depended on the relationships between the documentary material under consideration and the values and commitments of the historians. The same historians could switch their thinking between academically and religiously based forms of epistemic cognition, even within the same text. It seems highly unlikely that such disciplinary and situational variation can be captured by a small set of generally applicable dimensions, an assumption on which much research on the specificity-versus-generality issue within personal epistemology seems to rest (Greene & Yu, 2014).

Arguably, the theoretical framework best aligned with the discipline-specific, situated view discussed above is the contextualist resource framework of Hammer and Elby (2002; Elby & Hammer, 2010), which focuses on variations in epistemic cognition in response to situational demands. This means that learners are conceived of as responding adaptively or maladaptively to specific tasks by activating and deactivating existing fine-grained epistemic resources. According to Elby and Hammer (2010), the activation of fine-grained epistemic resources in a specific context over time may form a stable network with belief-like qualities, an "epistemological frame" that is typically activated in that context and sometimes even generalized across contexts.

Likewise, Chinn and colleagues (Chinn et al., 2011; Chinn et al., 2014; Chinn & Rinehart, 2016) have argued for a fine-grained, context-specific approach to epistemic cognition, where epistemic cognition varies across situations and may predict situation-specific patterns of learning. At the same time, Chinn et al.'s framework is a multicomponential model that expands on previous multidimensional personal epistemology models, with a fixed set of epistemic cognition components seen as applicable across disciplines and situations. How epistemic cognition plays out within those components is viewed as largely dependent on contextual factors, however, allowing for essential variability across and within specific disciplines.

Finally, Barzilai and Zohar's (2014) multifaceted framework, distinguishing between cognitive and metacognitive aspects of epistemic thinking, can be said to reflect recent developments toward further contextualization and situativity in epistemic cognition research. In particular, they proposed that the cognitive aspect of epistemic thinking, concerning specific information, knowledge claims, sources, and epistemic strategies, may be highly specific in the sense that it varies with task contexts. The metacognitive aspect of epistemic thinking, however, is viewed as having more pronounced domain-general qualities within this framework. Epistemic metacognition involves, among other things, knowledge about what makes a source reliable, but epistemic cognition involves using that knowledge to evaluate a particular source (see also Barzilai & Zohar, 2012).

In sum, a disciplinary view of epistemic cognition implies that general models of personal epistemology, as well as models that operate with a fixed set of dimensions across domains and disciplines, do not sufficiently capture important differences in the epistemic norms and practices across the disciplines. Such critiques imply the need for potentially extensive model revision, which can be interpreted as another fault line between the fields. To build theory bottom-up from such research, a first step could be to produce more local models applicable to a limited range of learners and contexts. In turn, such models might be combined to produce more overarching frameworks for epistemic cognition that are better grounded in actual knowledge construction and evaluation within the disciplines (Elby et al., 2016). Such models may then be used to identify commonalities or convergences in epistemic cognition across contexts.

Developmental Pathways

Despite the consistency of proposed developmental trajectories in models of epistemic cognition described earlier, evidence for a clear developmental pathway has been inconsistent, and multiple lines of evidence undermine the notion of omnibus stagelike epistemic worldviews (Hofer & Bendixen, 2012; Sandoval, 2012). This has led to proposals that people develop domain-specific epistemic theories (Hofer, 2006) that follow the general trend identified by Kuhn et al. (2000). This line of theorizing argues that such domain-specific theories develop at variable rates, dependent on personal experiences. Within domains, however, scholars such as Hofer, Kuhn, and others (e.g., Hallett, Chandler, & Krettenauer, 2002) have argued for recapitulation of the same developmental trend from absolutist to evaluativist.

A problem for developmental models is that "evidence for just about every conceivable sort of epistemic development has been shown to characterize persons of just about every conceivable age" (Chandler, Hallett, & Sokol, 2002, p. 161). This weight of competing evidence and interpretations about epistemic development led Chandler et al. (2002) to argue that epistemic development is recursive, that people pass through epistemic levels more than once within and across domains of epistemic cognition. At the moment, it is not clear what evidence can determine the viability of the developmental recursion hypothesis. Elby et al. (2016) argued that the recursion proposal is similar to the proposal of planetary "epicycles" as an effort to rescue Ptolemaic theories of celestial motion. They suggested that their epistemic resources model provides a more parsimonious account, arguing that development is nothing more or less than the construction and coordination of epistemic resources through experience in the contexts of activity in which their use is productive.

At issue is that what appears to be a broad developmental trend may be an artifact of researchers' own assumptions and efforts to document that trend. There is a need to account for a broad range of evidence that is at least potentially inconsistent with the reigning developmental hypothesis. Notions of epistemic development from Perry (1970) forward have been rooted in a distinction that sees development as a slow, broad, maturational process and learning as a more rapid, specific, enduring adaptation to environmental influences. This distinction is problematic for epistemic development for several reasons. First, epistemic change, whether characterized as development or not, may depend on systematic, organized schooling, which can hardly be said to be a natural maturational process. Second, describing epistemic change as independent of maturation seems to overlook the possibility that interventions to change epistemic cognition may be more or less successful depending on more general developing patterns of epistemic thinking in individuals. Finally, specific changes in epistemic cognition from particular interventions may generalize to influence epistemic developmental trajectories as described by Perry (1970) and other developmentalists (e.g., Baxter Magolda, 1992; King & Kitchener, 1994; Kuhn et al., 2000).

Much more conceptual and empirical work is needed to distinguish models and mechanisms of epistemic change from epistemic development, to the extent that scholars continue to see them as separate, albeit related, processes. Mechanisms of change have been proposed, from Hammer and Elby's model of activation of epistemic resources and their stabilization into epistemological frames from repeated activation in context (Elby & Hammer, 2010), to Bendixen and colleagues' constructs of epistemic doubt, volition, and resolution strategies (Bendixen & Rule, 2004; Muis et al., 2006). More work is needed to clarify proposed mechanisms of change, including how components of such mechanisms are involved in specific instances of epistemic change, as well as the ways in which changes in epistemic cognition may generalize. Research is needed that looks at epistemic cognition across multiple contexts over longer periods of time, to connect microgenetic processes to ontogenetic ones (Sandoval, 2014).

Research Design and Methods

Research methods and designs for capturing epistemic cognition vary a great deal across the fields engaged in this work, but can be roughly differentiated based on the assessment methods used, the contexts in which the work is done, and the kinds of epistemic cognition that are targeted. The most controversial type of assessment methods used are those that rely on self-report. The majority of self-report instruments require participants to rate their degree of agreement or disagreement with various statements by using Likert-type response scales. The first such instrument was Schommer's (1990) EQ, which was followed by various iterations and variations of that instrument (e.g., Epistemic Belief Inventory; Schraw, Bendixen, & Dunkle, 2002), as well as instruments that require participants to make semantic differential judgments, such as Connotative Aspects of Epistemological Beliefs (CAEB; Stahl & Bromme, 2007). These instruments, most commonly used by adherents of dimensional models of epistemic cognition (e.g., Hofer & Pintrich, 1997; Schommer-Aikins, 2004), have been criticized for their failure to replicate posited relations between items and proposed factors (Clarebout, Elen, Luyten, & Bamps, 2001; DeBacker et al., 2008) and for their reliance on response formats (i.e., Likert-type response scales) better suited for the measurement of attitudes than beliefs or practices (Carifio & Perla, 2007; Hofer & Sinatra, 2010).

Aside from psychometric concerns, self-report assessment methods have been criticized as inauthentic, requiring respondents to construct or make explicit aspects of their epistemic cognition that many scholars believe to be largely tacit, complex, and contextual (Chinn & Rinehart, 2016; Sandoval, 2012; Sinatra & Chinn, 2011). Finally, despite attempts to use self-report instruments to examine within-person differences in epistemic cognition across disciplines (e.g., Buehl et al., 2002; Greene et al., 2008), there are many researchers, predominantly those who study epistemic cognition within disciplinary education, who claim these instruments require assumptions that epistemic cognition is traitlike rather than a function of context (Elby & Hammer, 2010). To some degree, this claim about the inherent assumptions regarding the use of self-report instruments is borne out in practice: The vast majority of studies conducted with self-report instruments like the EQ or the Epistemic Belief Inventory involve designs where participants complete self-report instruments in artificial contexts (e.g., completing a survey individually, without being asked to engage in a learning task), as opposed to more authentic contexts that actually invoke epistemic cognition (e.g., arguing about the meaning of experimental data; Sandoval, 2012).

Various forms of semistructured interviews have been used to measure epistemic cognition, beginning with Perry's (1970) seminal work and continuing through many of the studies on developmental models of epistemic cognition (Mason, 2016). For example, such interviews were used extensively over the course of King and Kitchener's (2004) scholarship on their reflective judgment model; they involved presenting participants with ill-structured problems about which "reasonable people reasonably disagree" (p. 5), such as whether news reporting is accurate or chemical additives to food are safe. These interviews were concurrent, meaning that a scenario or example was presented to participants, who then had to respond to interview probes about it, often "without practice or even much time to collect their thoughts" (King & Kitchener, 2002, p. 57). Like the majority of research using self-report instruments, studies involving concurrent semistructured interviews tend to be conducted outside actual learning or practice contexts.

Recently, there has been an increase in the number of studies designed to capture aspects of developmental and dimensional models of epistemic cognition while in the context of thinking about everyday problems or scenarios. For example, there has been an increase in the use of concurrent think-aloud protocols (Ericsson & Simon, 1993) to surface participants' epistemic cognition as they engage in everyday epistemic tasks such as searching the Internet for information (e.g., Barzilai & Zohar, 2012; Ferguson et al., 2012; Greene, Yu, & Copeland, 2014; Hofer, 2004; Mason et al., 2010, 2011). Cognitive interviews have also been used to assess the ways in which people understand the items on survey instruments (Greene, Torney-Purta, Azevedo, & Robertson, 2010), as well as the ways in which their thinking might challenge assumptions of dimensional and developmental models of epistemic cognition (Greene & Yu, 2014; Muis, Duffy, Trevors, Ranellucci, & Foy, 2014). Importantly, however, the majority of this research involving concurrent measures of epistemic cognition has been conducted outside of formal learning (i.e., classrooms) or practice contexts.

On the other hand, many authors from a disciplinary education background have argued that epistemic cognition should be studied in authentic practice contexts, such as when students conduct experiments or construct models (Elby & Hammer, 2010; Kelly, 2016; Sandoval, 2005). Observation and discourse analysis are two predominant nonintrusive assessment methods that allow data collection while students engage in authentic tasks (Kelly, 2016). The data that arise from these techniques are often context-specific and interpreted solely within a single model of epistemic cognition, which makes it difficult to make inferences from them to other developmental or dimensional models (Sandoval, 2005).

Observation and discourse analysis can be done nonintrusively, but some researchers have argued that the addition of retrospective interviews to these designs can lead to more informed understanding of people's epistemic cognition (Chinn et al., 2011; Sandoval, 2005). For example, Pluta, Chinn, and Duncan (2011) assessed epistemic cognition by first asking participants to engage in scientific inquiry and then prompting them to reflect on their epistemic practices and ideals. Data from these retrospective interviews can be triangulated with observation and discourse analysis data gathered during practice to understand both enacted epistemic practices and the epistemic aims and ideals that students bring to those practices (e.g., Chinn & Rinehart, 2016; Sandoval, 2012). Hammer and Elby have studied their epistemological resources model by triangulating across observational studies of activity (Rosenberg, Hammer, & Phelan, 2006) and cognitive interview studies (diSessa et al., 2002).

There are a number of scholars who examine how people think about knowledge and knowing across and outside of formal learning contexts (Bricker & Bell, 2016). While these researchers may not identify their work as epistemic cognition research, this area of scholarship makes an important, unique contribution to the field. The models of epistemic cognition providing the foundation for this area of scholarship vary, from developmental models (e.g., Weinstock, 2011) to epistemological resources models (e.g., Bang & Medin, 2010). As would be expected given the research focus, these scholars study epistemic cognition in a wide variety of contexts, including courtrooms (Weinstock, 2016), Internet browsing (Strømsø & Bråten, 2010), and museums (Bell, Bricker, Reeve, Zimmerman, & Tzou, 2012). Capturing epistemic cognition in situ often requires open-ended assessment methods and nonintrusive research designs, such as observations and case studies, although some of this research includes interviews either during or after observing epistemic cognition in practice. Research across contexts has revealed how people enact epistemic cognition differently in response to these contexts (Goldman, 2011; Gottlieb & Wineburg, 2012). Greene (2016) argued that within-person differences in enacted epistemic cognition may be due, in part, to people's perceptions of the salient epistemic system, or systems, across contexts (Goldman, 2011). Students who are hesitant to enact epistemic practices in the classroom may do so eagerly in a museum, and their perceptions of the epistemic systems at play may hold the key to understanding these differences in performance across contexts. Scholarship on these contextual differences illustrates how multiple assessment methods are needed to capture not only how epistemic cognition happens but also how features of context are perceived as relevant (Bricker & Bell, 2016).

Our review of research designs and methods in epistemic cognition has revealed a number of trends concerning the assessment methods used, the contexts in which research is conducted, and the kinds of epistemic cognition under study. Continued psychometric problems with self-report methods of assessing epistemic cognition, coupled with the often-decontextualized or inauthentic contexts in which these data are gathered, and their presumptions of domain consistency or traitlike aspects of epistemic cognition, cast doubt on research findings from these studies. The growing acceptance that epistemic cognition is largely tacit, and that people's enactment of epistemic cognition can often be different from their expressed reconstruction of that cognition, has led an increasing number of researchers to pursue concurrent assessment methods (e.g., observations, discourse analysis, think-aloud protocols) that can be implemented in contexts where participants are asked to think about knowledge and knowing (e.g., inquiry activities, searching the Internet for information on controversial issues). Researchers' models of epistemic cognition seem to predict their choice of context, with adherents to dimensional or developmental models often investigating how people enact epistemic cognition outside of practice settings, and adherents to situative models of epistemic cognition more often using various kinds of inquiry contexts as research settings (Mason, 2016). An important question being studied by researchers of everyday epistemic cognition is the degree to which research in one of these contexts (e.g., classrooms, museums, courtrooms) can connect to, or inform, research in other contexts. Regardless of method, research design context, or underlying model, it is apparent to us that there is a clear need for research involving multiple, mixed methods of gathering data, across a variety of contexts, to understand how epistemic cognition is acquired, enacted, and changed (Chinn et al., 2011). Fault lines across methodology seem to be the most amenable to a "more is more" approach.

RESOLUTIONS LOOKING FORWARD

To close this review, we offer some possibilities for how current fault lines in research on epistemic cognition can be bridged. One possibility is to expand and coordinate across sites of intervention around epistemic cognition. A second is to carefully, and perhaps more openly, imagine possibilities for measuring or describing epistemic cognition in the many places where it occurs. Third, it seems clear that researchers working on questions of epistemic cognition must conscientiously cross disciplinary boundaries to synthesize and extend coherent and reliable findings and models. Addressing each of these possibilities, however, may require integrating conceptual perspectives on epistemic cognition.

Integrating Perspectives on Epistemic Cognition

A basic issue to resolve, from our reading of the many fields that now comprise epistemic cognition research, is the relation between traditional cognitive accounts focused on individual cognitive structures and processes and situative accounts of persons functioning within systems of cultural activity. Greeno (2015) argued for a notion of "integrative pluralism" that accepts that cognition can be seen as occurring, and thus modeled, at multiple levels. He asserted that models focused at different levels of aggregation can each advance understanding of important phenomena. Beyond mere pluralism, however, is the goal of integrating alternative conceptualizations. Greeno suggested that a single, unifying theory that accomplishes such integration is obviously desirable but not currently feasible. He argued instead for case studies that can integrate explanations for some aspects of functioning across cognitive and situative levels. Given the scope of contexts where epistemic cognition is now seen to occur and the various perspectives on how it happens, integration of findings from these myriad contexts should be a major focus of research in the coming century.

Progress toward an integrative pluralism of accounts of epistemic cognition can occur through an expansion of current trends in epistemic cognition research. Obviously, to integrate theoretical accounts across multiple levels of analysis requires an articulation of the levels. Greeno (2015) suggested there are at least three levels relevant to cognition generally: the individual, the individual-in-interaction, and the activity system(s) in which the interaction occurs. Much of the research comprising the data set for this review focuses on the individual, on characterizing the structure of epistemic beliefs and their function. Some of it attends more closely to individuals-in-interaction from a situative perspective, by attending to how material and social resources available within a given interaction mediate the epistemic cognition engaged by individuals. We think that relatively little epistemic cognition research to date focuses at the level of activity systems, in other words, at the level of communities of people and the practices collectively used to solve epistemic problems. There are studies of episodes of collective activity and its mediation (e.g., Kelly, 2016; Rosenberg et al., 2006). Muis and Duffy's (2013) construct of epistemic climate is an attempt to characterize an aspect of an intact activity system, a classroom, in relation to its influence on the epistemic cognition of actors in that activity system. Greene's (2016) discussion of interacting epistemic systems, and how they affect individuals in those systems, is another way of conceptualizing effects among different levels. We encourage more work at the activity system level as an avenue to increase our understanding of how particular communities of practice might structure epistemic cognition. Kelly (2016) points to sociological studies of science as a helpful analog for such work.

Integrating across levels of analysis further requires that individual researchers, or teams, are at least aware of, if not specifically attentive to, work and models at levels that are not familiar. For example, researchers focused on individual cognitive structures and their assessment should be mindful of how particular research settings may both shape the goals of participants and structure the social and material resources that might mediate epistemic cognition in that setting. Researchers looking at the participation of individuals in collective activity could consider how to trace the individual cognitive consequences from that participation. We see such efforts beginning to happen, and likely to continue, across sites of intervention and measurement of epistemic cognition.

Bridging Schooled and Unschooled Contexts

In the past decades, epistemic cognition researchers have made considerable headway in understanding how more adaptive epistemic cognition can be promoted at different educational levels (Bråten, 2016). In elementary classrooms, intervention work in science (e.g., Metz, 2011; Ryu & Sandoval, 2012), mathematics (e.g., Mason & Scrivani, 2004; Verschaffel et al., 1999), history (Nokes, 2014; VanSledright, 2002), and language arts (Reznitskaya et al., 2012) suggests how engagement in scaffolded disciplinary practices can change students' beliefs and thinking about knowledge and knowing in these disciplines. Moreover, many studies have tried to induce epistemic change in secondary and postsecondary classrooms, focusing on different disciplines (e.g., Bell, Matkins, & Gansneder, 2011; Hynd-Shanahan, Holschuh, & Hubbard, 2004; Muis & Duffy, 2013). Whether any changes brought about by such interventions affect people's beliefs and thinking about knowledge and knowing outside formal educational contexts is currently not known, however (see Bendixen, 2016; Muis, Trevors, & Chevrier, 2016).

One important aspect of epistemic cognition that is highly relevant outside school is how people evaluate conflicting knowledge claims about complex scientific and socioscientific issues (Bromme & Goldman, 2014; Tabak, 2016), for example, when searching for information on the Internet (Strømsø & Kammerer, 2016). In such instances, people's critical-analytic evaluation of sources becomes a key competence, yet this is a competence that many researchers, educators, and policymakers around the world feel is not adequately developed through schooling, not even at the secondary and postsecondary levels (Bråten & Braasch, in press). Some recent studies (e.g., Braasch et al., 2013; Kammerer, Amann, & Gerjets, 2015; Mason, Junyent, & Tornatora, 2014; Stadtler, Scharrer, Macedo-Rouet, Rouet, & Bromme, 2016) suggest that people's ability to cope with conflicting knowledge claims about scientific and socioscientific issues can be improved through brief source evaluation interventions. However, next to nothing is known about whether or how epistemic change resulting from participation in disciplinary practices in school can be brought to bear on students' judgments of disciplinary issues in everyday contexts, highlighting the issue of transfer across schooled and unschooled contexts. There is thus a clear need for future research that investigates and seeks to promote connections between epistemic cognition embedded within disciplinary practices in school and thinking about knowledge and knowing outside formal educational contexts. Such research should not be limited to the discipline of science, however.

For example, VanSledright and Maggioni (2016) suggested that citizens will have difficulties participating in genuine democratic discourse and making balanced decisions about the future without developing adaptive epistemic cognition within the discipline of history, involving the weighing of evidentiary support for conflicting accounts and using interpretive decision criteria (e.g., corroboration). To what extent promoting adaptive epistemic cognition through history education will actually contribute to critical, deliberate thinking about controversial social and political issues outside school (e.g., helping people avoid polarization) is an open question for future epistemic cognition researchers to address.

Until recently, epistemic cognition change has been seen as a progression from naïve to sophisticated general views on knowledge. It is now coming to be seen as appropriate adaptiveness to context. A reliance on authoritative sources, for example, is no longer seen as inherently inferior to other ways of knowing, given that much of what we learn comes from the testimony of others (Chinn et al., 2011). Teaching for adaptive epistemic cognition in a way that not only promotes disciplinary learning but also has consequences for how students engage and cope with controversial scientific and social issues outside school requires teachers who know the epistemologies of the disciplines they teach, the applicability of those disciplines to students' everyday lives, and pedagogies that promote connections between epistemic cognition in the discipline and in everyday life. One issue in need of much further research is the potential lack of calibration between teachers' own epistemic cognition and the epistemic aims (e.g., deep understanding) and reliable processes (e.g., reasoned argumentation; Chinn et al., 2014) they try to implement in their classrooms. This is an important issue because less adaptive epistemic cognition on the part of the teachers may interfere with teaching for adaptive epistemic cognition in students, highlighting the need to support the development of epistemic cognition among teachers participating in epistemic cognition interventions (Brownlee & Schraw, in press). An important goal for epistemic cognition researchers should be to develop empirically based, testable instructional models that can guide interventions for epistemic change (Bråten, 2016). Preferably, such instructional models should also take into consideration the need to help teachers develop their own epistemic cognition and describe how this can be effectively done.

Finally, more intervention work is needed that spans individual and social levels of intervention and coordinates between them. For example, research is needed regarding how to integrate reflection on one's own epistemic beliefs regarding particular disciplinary issues with collective reflection and argumentation as part of social disciplinary practices dealing with those issues. This implies that the effectiveness of epistemic cognition interventions would have to be evaluated quite broadly by attending to changes in disciplinary practices at the interpersonal level, in addition to individual belief change and potential interactions between those loci of intervention (e.g., Ryu & Sandoval, 2012).

Sites of Measurement

Many of the most cited publications we reviewed, from Hofer and Pintrich's (1997) article through more recent reviews and conceptual revisions of epistemic cognition (e.g., Barzilai & Zohar, 2014; Chinn et al., 2011), have lamented the poor reliability and lack of construct validity for scores from Likert-type scale instruments. Numerous studies have shown that the most frequently used self-report measures of epistemic cognition do not meet even minimal psychometric criteria, particularly in terms of configural invariance across samples and contexts (e.g., DeBacker et al., 2008). There appears to be a growing consensus that the ease of administering Likert-type scale assessments of epistemic cognition comes with concerns about the authenticity of whatever it is that those instruments purport to measure (Hofer & Sinatra, 2010; Sinatra, 2016). The field should no longer tolerate publications that utilize instruments with low reliability, poor data-model fit, or even worse, no investigation of construct validity at all. There is nothing innately flawed about quantitative methods of measuring epistemic cognition, but developing, testing, and refining such measures requires effort, time, patience, and persistence. Researchers interested in developing such measures should endeavor to understand and meet epistemic ideals for psychometric validity (e.g., Bandalos & Finney, 2010; Knapp & Mueller, 2010) and should fully report the evidence regarding such efforts in their empirical work. Editors, reviewers, and publishers should be critical of manuscripts that do not meet these ideals.

From our vantage point, epistemic cognition research needs a "right tool for the right job" perspective. People can self-report best about thoughts and attitudes that are explicit in their minds and that require little construction in the moment. Whether self-report instruments should use Likert-type scales or other forms of response (e.g., semantic differentials; Stahl & Bromme, 2007) is an open question. On the one hand, epistemic cognition phenomena that may be amenable to self-report assessments include epistemic metacognitive knowledge and epistemic aims (Barzilai & Zohar, 2014; Chinn et al., 2011). On the other hand, collecting data about what people do when enacting epistemic cognition requires that measurement occur in contexts where people actually enact epistemic cognition (Kelly, 2016). Analyzing data as people engage in epistemic practices, including observations of the practices used, as well as of the discourse between people (e.g., Herrenkohl & Cornelius, 2013; Ryu & Sandoval, 2012; Samarapungavan et al., 2006), can be a powerful way to understand not only people's epistemic cognition but also their perceptions of larger epistemic systems such as science or history (Goldman, 2011; Greene, 2016), as well as how those systems enculturate people to normative practices and knowledge (Kelly, 2014).

One benefit to observations is that they can be used to collect data without interfering in people's epistemic cognition. However, the bridge from observation data to research findings is inference, which often can be difficult to justify. The challenges of deriving and justifying inferences increase as researchers move from studying what people do (e.g., epistemic practices), to studying what they think but often do not verbalize (e.g., epistemic vices). Even more difficult are inferences about what people have learned but rarely reflect on (e.g., epistemic metacognitive skills, epistemic ideals), and what they feel but rarely think about (e.g., epistemic metacognitive experiences; Barzilai & Zohar, 2014; Chinn & Rinehart, 2016). Epistemic cognition phenomena that are rarely consciously invoked may be best measured by prompting individuals to surface and reflect on the otherwise nonconscious aspects of their epistemic cognition (e.g., "How did you feel when you realized that your views on evolution were being challenged?"). Regardless of whether researchers intervene into participants' epistemic cognition or not, these data can and should be usefully triangulated with data from semistructured interviews (e.g., Feucht & Bendixen, 2010), cognitive interviewing (e.g., Barzilai & Weinstock, 2015; Greene, Torney-Purta, Azevedo, et al., 2010; Muis et al., 2014), or cued reflection (e.g., Berland & Crucet, 2016; Ferguson, Bråten, Strømsø, & Anmarkrud, 2013), as well as data regarding the context in which the participants engaged in epistemic cognition (e.g., Kelly & Crawford, 1997).

Of course, the more unusual the context, the more the findings are encapsulated. Completing a survey before a class begins is not something that students do very often; therefore, it is not surprising that data from this context have shown only modest-to-small relationships with data drawn from more familiar contexts, such as grades in a class. What is needed is more description of the contexts in which epistemic cognition is measured, and more research that systematically varies context in investigations of the same epistemic cognition phenomena. Such studies would reveal how perceptions of contextual factors, such as epistemic climate (Feucht, 2010; Muis & Duffy, 2013), influence enacted epistemic cognition. Likewise, drawing from psychometrics research, there is a need for studies that assess the same epistemic cognition phenomena across contexts designed to elicit typical performance (e.g., casual browsing of the Internet for a question of curiosity) and maximal performance (e.g., heavily scaffolded or supported investigations of questions with serious implications, such as reviewing literature for a dissertation).

In sum, the field's growing recognition of the need for more attention to context and tools of measurement is not a sign of methodological or philosophical splintering, nor does it warrant calls for nihilism or methodological relativism. Rather, it represents the field's better understanding of the problem space and of the complexity of the phenomena under study. To borrow from Perry (1970), we suspect that in the coming years, the field will make commitments within methodological relativism, where different combinations of epistemic cognition phenomena and contexts will be addressed with different measurement tools, which will be seen as more or less useful depending on the circumstances.

Transdisciplinary Possibilities

Academic disciplines tend to fragment themselves in order to focus on specific questions and problems, and psychology and education are no different in this regard. Furthermore, education is a huge field informed by multiple disciplinary perspectives besides psychology, including anthropology, sociology, history, and more. These perspectives often clash around theories, methodologies, and ideologies. Nevertheless, it is clear that scholars working on issues of epistemic cognition recognize the need to bridge disciplinary boundaries, and this trend will, and should, continue. As we have shown in this review, perspectives from disciplinary education research have reframed questions of the general versus specific character of epistemic cognition. This has come from now well-established lines of communication between educational psychologists, disciplinary education researchers, and learning scientists working within those disciplines. The next step to take in this dialogue is to try to synthesize empirical results across subfields to scrutinize available models of epistemic cognition. A recent example of this effort includes a broad synthesis of research across the elementary grades in math, science, and social studies as those areas of teaching might bear on the theory of integrated domains in epistemology model of epistemic cognition (Bendixen, 2016), an effort notable for its attention to substantive differences among disciplines and their significance to modeling epistemic cognition broadly. More syntheses like these ought to be conducted in the coming century.

Extending this sort of synthesis requires several things. Fundamentally, it requires researchers to be knowledgeable about the many fields of research that bear on specific questions of epistemic cognition. This demands both training across disciplines that would seek to develop integrative specialists around particular aspects of epistemic cognition, and research collaborations that cross specializations and can produce the sorts of case studies that Greeno (2015) suggested. It may also be the case that epistemic cognition research needs particular lines of communication to become more open. For example, the links between relevant text comprehension research (e.g., Bråten, Strømsø, et al., 2009) and disciplinary education research are relatively weak, and the same is likely to be true for other subfields of epistemic cognition research. Finally, it is critical that integrative work explicitly tests predictions of various models of epistemic cognition against one another. Epistemic cognition research over the past century has seen only a profusion of possible models, with no real pruning of the contenders. While a single theory of epistemic cognition and its development seems infeasible now, the work of comparing the value of alternative models should be done.

CONCLUSION

Over the past century, epistemic cognition has moved from a latent concern to a buzzing, blooming field of research. Our review has traced the many historical lines of scholarship that have produced the buzz, and the emerging confluence of these lines into a broad, perhaps turbulent, stream of research. We are optimistic that recent trends of dialogue between the fields interested in epistemic cognition will expand over the next century to generate more integrative approaches to the study of epistemic cognition and better accounts of its development. Such trends must take into account multiple levels of analysis, the many forms and causes of development, and how the context in which research occurs can influence the types of epistemic cognition produced. Only then will the field have what it needs to effectively promote the kinds of thinking needed to successfully traverse the many challenges of the 21st century and beyond.

NOTE

[1]We also do not attempt any summary of history, philosophy, or sociology of science, or other disciplines, even though those fields have significantly influenced contemporary epistemology and the ways in which disciplinary education research frames and studies epistemological issues. (Interested readers can consult Chinn et al., 2011; Depaepe et al., 2016; Kelly, 2016; VanSledright & Maggioni, 2016.)

REFERENCES

Alexander, P. A. (2016). The arguments for and the reasoning about epistemic cognition. In J. A. Greene, W. A. Sandoval, & I. Bråten (Eds.), *Handbook of epistemic cognition* (pp. 100–110). New York, NY: Routledge.

Bandalos, D. L., & Finney, S. J. (2010). Factor analysis: Exploratory and confirmatory. In G. R. Hancock & R. O. Mueller (Eds.), *The reviewer's guide to quantitative methods* (pp. 93–114). New York, NY: Routledge.

Bang, M., & Medin, D. (2010). Cultural processes in science education: Supporting the navigation of multiple epistemologies. *Science Education, 94,* 1008–1026.

Barzilai, S., & Weinstock, M. (2015). Measuring epistemic thinking within and across topics: A scenario-based approach. *Contemporary Educational Psychology, 42,* 141–158.

Barzilai, S., & Zohar, A. (2012). Epistemic thinking in action: Evaluating and integrating online sources. *Cognition and Instruction, 30,* 39–85.

Barzilai, S., & Zohar, A. (2014). Reconsidering personal epistemology as metacognition: A multifaceted approach to the analysis of epistemic thinking. *Educational Psychologist, 49,* 13–15.

Baxter Magolda, M. B. (1992). *Knowing and reasoning in college: Gender-related patterns in students' intellectual development.* San Francisco, CA: Jossey-Bass.

Belenky, M. F., Clinchy, B. M., Goldberger, N. R., & Tarule, J. M. (1986). *Women's way of knowing: The development of self, voice, and mind*. New York, NY: Basic Books.

Bell, P., Bricker, L. A., Reeve, S., Zimmerman, H. T., & Tzou, C. (2012). Discovering and supporting successful learning pathways of youth in and out of school: Accounting for the development of everyday expertise across settings. In B. Bevan, P. Bell, R. Stevens, & A. Razfar (Eds.), *LOST opportunities: Learning in and out of school time* (pp. 119–140). London, England: Springer.

Bell, R. L., Matkins, J. J., & Gansneder, B. M. (2011). Impacts of contextual and explicit instruction on preservice elementary teachers' understandings of the nature of science. *Journal of Research in Science Teaching, 48,* 414–436.

Bendixen, L. D. (2016). Teaching for epistemic change in elementary classrooms. In J. A. Greene, W. A. Sandoval, & I. Bråten (Eds.), *Handbook of epistemic cognition* (pp. 281–299). New York, NY: Routledge.

Bendixen, L. D., & Feucht, F. C. (Eds.). (2010). *Personal epistemology in the classroom: Theory, research, and implications for practices*. Cambridge, England: Cambridge University Press.

Bendixen, L. D., & Rule, D. C. (2004). An integrative approach to personal epistemology: A guiding model. *Educational Psychologist, 39,* 69–80.

Berland, L., & Crucet, K. (2016). Epistemological trade-offs: Accounting for context when evaluating epistemological sophistication of student engagement in scientific practices. *Science Education, 100,* 5–29.

Bishop, M. A., & Trout, J. D. (2008). Strategic reliabilism: A naturalistic approach to epistemology. *Philosophy Compass, 3,* 1049–1065.

Braasch, J. L. G., Bråten, I., Strømsø, H. I., Anmarkrud, Ø., & Ferguson, L. E. (2013). Promoting secondary school students' evaluation of source features of multiple documents. *Contemporary Educational Psychology, 38,* 180–195.

Bråten, I. (2016). Epistemic cognition interventions: Issues, challenges, and directions. In J. A. Greene, W. A. Sandoval, & I. Bråten (Eds.), *Handbook of epistemic cognition* (pp. 360–371). New York, NY: Routledge.

Bråten, I., & Braasch, J. L. G. (in press). Key issues in research on students' critical reading and learning in the 21st century information society. In C. Ng & B. Bartlett (Eds.), *Improving reading engagement and achievement in the 21st century: International research and innovations*. Dordrecht, Netherlands: Springer.

Bråten, I., Britt, M. A., Strømsø, H. I., & Rouet, J.-F. (2011). The role of epistemic beliefs in the comprehension of multiple expository texts: Toward an integrated model. *Educational Psychologist, 46,* 48–70.

Bråten, I., & Ferguson, L. E. (2015). Beliefs about sources of knowledge predict motivation for learning in teacher education. *Teaching and Teacher Education, 50,* 13–23.

Bråten, I., Gil, L., Strømsø, H. I., & Vidal-Abarca, E. (2009). Personal epistemology across cultures: Exploring Norwegian and Spanish university students' epistemic beliefs about climate change. *Social Psychology of Education, 12,* 529–560.

Bråten, I., & Strømsø, H. I. (2005). The relationship between epistemological beliefs, implicit theories of intelligence, and self-regulated learning among Norwegian postsecondary students. *British Journal of Educational Psychology, 75,* 539–565.

Bråten, I., & Strømsø, H. I. (2010). When law students read multiple documents about global warming: Examining the role of topic-specific beliefs about the nature of knowledge and knowing. *Instructional Science, 38,* 635–657.

Bråten, I., Strømsø, H. I., & Britt, M. A. (2009). Trust matters: Examining the role of source evaluation in students' construction of meaning within and across multiple texts. *Reading Research Quarterly, 44,* 6–28.

Bråten, I., Strømsø, H. I., & Samuelstuen, M. S. (2008). Are sophisticated students always better? The role of topic-specific personal epistemology in the understanding of multiple expository texts. *Contemporary Educational Psychology, 33,* 814–840.

Bricker, L., & Bell, P. (2016). Exploring images of epistemic cognition across contexts and over time. In J. A. Greene, W. A. Sandoval, & I. Bråten (Eds.), *Handbook of epistemic cognition* (pp. 197–214). New York, NY: Routledge.

Bromme, R., & Goldman, S. (2014). The public's bounded understanding of science. *Educational Psychologist, 49*, 59–69.

Bromme, R., Kienhues, D., & Stahl, E. (2008). Knowledge and epistemological beliefs: An intimate but complicate relationship. In M. S. Khine (Ed.), *Knowing, knowledge, and beliefs: Epistemological studies across diverse cultures* (pp. 423–441). New York, NY: Springer.

Bromme, R., Pieschl, S., & Stahl, E. (2010). Epistemological beliefs are standards for adaptive learning: A functional theory about epistemological beliefs and metacognition. *Metacognition and Learning, 5*, 7–26.

Brownlee, J. L., & Schraw, G. (in press). Reflection and reflexivity: A focus on higher order thinking in teachers' personal epistemologies. In G. Schraw, J. L. Brownlee, L. Olafson, & M. Vanderveldt (Eds.), *Teachers' personal epistemologies: Theoretical and practical considerations.* Charlotte, NC: Information Age.

Bruner, J. (1996). *The culture of education.* Cambridge, MA: Harvard University Press.

Buehl, M. M., & Alexander, P. A. (2001). Beliefs about academic knowledge. *Educational Psychology Review, 13*, 385–418.

Buehl, M. M., Alexander, P. A., & Murphy, P. K. (2002). Beliefs about schooled knowledge: Domain specific or domain general? *Contemporary Educational Psychology, 27*, 415–449.

Buehl, M. M., & Fives, H. (2009). Exploring teachers' beliefs about teaching knowledge: Where does it come from? Does it change? *Journal of Experimental Education, 77*, 367–408.

Buehl, M. M., & Fives, H. (2016). The role of epistemic cognition in teacher learning and praxis. In J. A. Greene, W. A. Sandoval, & I. Bråten (Eds.), *Handbook of epistemic cognition* (pp. 247–264). New York, NY: Routledge.

Burr, J. E., & Hofer, B. K. (2002). Personal epistemology and theory of mind: Deciphering young children's beliefs about knowledge and knowing. *New Ideas in Psychology, 20*, 199–224.

Cano, F. (2005). Epistemological beliefs and approaches to learning: Their change through secondary school and their influence on academic performance. *British Journal of Educational Psychology, 75*, 203–221.

Carifio, J., & Perla, R. J. (2007). Ten common misunderstandings, misconceptions, persistent myths, and urban legends about Likert scales and Likert response formats and their antidotes. *Journal of Social Sciences, 3*, 106–116.

Chandler, M. J., Hallett, D., & Sokol, B. W. (2002). Competing claims about competing knowledge claims. In B. K. Hofer & P. R. Pintrich (Eds.), *Personal epistemology: The psychology of beliefs about knowledge and knowing* (pp. 145–168). Mahwah, NJ: Lawrence Erlbaum.

Chinn, C. A., & Brewer, W. F. (1993). The role of anomalous data in knowledge acquisition. *Review of Educational Research, 63*, 1–49.

Chinn, C. A., Buckland, L. A., & Samarapungavan, A. (2011). Expanding the dimensions of epistemic cognition: Arguments from philosophy and psychology. *Educational Psychologist, 46*, 141–167.

Chinn, C. A., & Rinehart, R. W. (2016). Epistemic cognition and philosophy: Developing a new framework for epistemic cognition. In J. A. Greene, W. A. Sandoval, & I. Bråten (Eds.), *Handbook of epistemic cognition* (pp. 460–478). New York, NY: Routledge.

Chinn, C. A., Rinehart, R. W., & Buckland, L. A. (2014). Epistemic cognition and evaluating information: Applying the AIR model of epistemic cognition. In D. N. Rapp & J. L. G. Braasch (Eds.), *Processing inaccurate information: Theoretical and applied perspectives from cognitive science and the educational sciences* (pp. 425–453). Cambridge: MIT Press.

Chisholm, R. (1983). *The foundations of knowing*. Minneapolis: University of Minnesota Press.

Clarebout, G., Elen, J., Luyten, L., & Bamps, H. (2001). Assessing epistemological beliefs: Schommer's questionnaire revisited. *Educational Research and Evaluation, 7*, 53–77.

Clément, F. (2016). Social cognition. In J. A. Greene, W. A. Sandoval, & I. Bråten (Eds.), *Handbook of epistemic cognition* (pp. 86–99). New York, NY: Routledge.

Cobb, P., Stephan, M., McClain, K., & Gravemeijer, K. (2001). Participating in classroom mathematical practices. *Journal of the Learning Sciences, 10*, 113–163.

Conee, E., & Feldman, R. (1985). Evidentialism. *Philosophical Studies, 48*, 15–35.

Conley, A. M., Pintrich, P. R., Vekiri, I., & Harrison, D. (2004). Changes in epistemological beliefs in elementary science students. *Contemporary Educational Psychology, 29*, 186–204.

Corriveau, K. H., & Harris, P. L. (2009). Choosing your informant: Weighing familiarity and recent accuracy. *Developmental Science, 12*, 426–437.

Council of Chief State School Officers. (2010). *Common Core State Standards for English language arts and literacy in history/social studies, science, and technical subjects*. Washington, DC: Author.

DeBacker, T. K., Crowson, H. M., Beesley, A. D., Thoma, S. J., & Hestevold, N. (2008). The challenge of measuring epistemological beliefs: An analysis of three self-report instruments. *Journal of Experimental Education, 76*, 281–312.

De Corte, E., Op't Eynde, P., Depaepe, F., & Verschaffel, L. (2010). The reflexive relation between students' mathematics-related beliefs and the mathematics classroom culture. In L. D. Bendixen & F. C. Feucht (Eds.), *Personal epistemology in the classroom: Theory, research, and implications for practice* (pp. 292–327). Cambridge, England: Cambridge University Press.

Depaepe, F., De Corte, E., & Verschaffel, L. (2016). Mathematical epistemological beliefs: A review of the research literature. In J. A. Greene, W. A. Sandoval, & I. Bråten (Eds.), *Handbook of epistemic cognition* (pp. 147–164). New York, NY: Routledge.

Dewey, J. (1910). *How we think*. Boston, MA: D. C. Heath.

diSessa, A., Elby, A., & Hammer, D. (2002). J's epistemological stance and strategies. In G. M. Sinatra & P. R. Pintrich (Eds.), *Intentional conceptual change* (pp. 237–290). Mahwah, NJ: Lawrence Erlbaum.

Duschl, R. A. (2008). Science education in three-part harmony: Balancing conceptual, epistemic and social goals. *Review of Research in Education, 32*, 268–291.

Elby, A., & Hammer, D. (2010). Epistemological resources and framing: A cognitive framework for helping teachers interpret and respond to their students' epistemologies. In L. D. Bendixen & F. C. Feucht (Eds.), *Personal epistemology in the classroom: Theory, research, and implications for practice* (pp. 409–434). Cambridge, England: Cambridge University Press.

Elby, A., Macrander, C., & Hammer, D. (2016). Epistemic cognition in science: Uncovering old roots to turn over new leaves. In J. A. Greene, W. A. Sandoval, & I. Bråten (Eds.), *Handbook of epistemic cognition* (pp. 113–127). New York, NY: Routledge.

Engeström, Y. (1987). *Learning by expanding: An activity-theoretical approach to developmental research*. Helsinki, Finland: Orienta-Konsultit.

Ericsson, K. A., & Simon, H. A. (1993). *Protocol analysis: Verbal reports as data* (2nd ed.). Cambridge: MIT Press.

Ferguson, L. E., Bråten, I., & Strømsø, H. I. (2012). Epistemic cognition when students read multiple documents containing conflicting scientific evidence: A think-aloud study. *Learning and Instruction, 22*, 103–120.

Ferguson, L. E., Bråten, I., Strømsø, H. I., & Anmarkrud, O. (2013). Epistemic beliefs and comprehension in the context of reading multiple documents: Examining the role of conflict. *International Journal of Educational Research, 62*, 100–114.

Feucht, F. C. (2010). Epistemic climate in elementary classrooms. In L. D. Bendixen & F. C. Feucht (Eds.), *Personal epistemology in the classroom: Theory, research, and implications for practice* (pp. 55–93). Cambridge, England: Cambridge University Press.

Feucht, F. C., & Bendixen, L. D. (2010). Exploring similarities and differences in personal epistemologies of U.S. and German elementary school teachers. *Cognition and Instruction, 28*, 39–69.

Fives, H., & Buehl, M. M. (2008). What do teachers believe? Developing a framework for examining beliefs about teachers' knowledge and ability. *Contemporary Educational Psychology, 33*, 134–176.

Fricker, E. (1995). Telling and trusting: Reductionism and anti-reductionism in the epistemology of testimony. *Mind, 104*, 393–411.

Fuller, S. (1988). *Social epistemology*. Bloomington: Indiana University Press.

Gettier, E. (1963). Is justified true belief knowledge? *Analysis, 23*, 121–123.

Glasersfeld, E. V. (1989). Cognition, construction of knowledge, and teaching. *Synthese, 80*, 121–140.

Goldman, A. I. (1994). Naturalistic epistemology and reliabilism. *Midwest Studies in Philosophy, 19*, 301–320.

Goldman, A. I. (1999). *Knowledge in a social world*. Oxford, England: Oxford University Press.

Goldman, A. I. (2011). A guide to social epistemology. In A. I. Goldman & D. Whitcomb (Eds.), *Social epistemology: Essential readings* (pp. 11–37). Oxford, England: Oxford University Press.

Goldman, S. R., Lawless, K. A., Gomez, K. W., Braasch, J., McLeod, S., & Manning, F. (2010). Literacy in the digital world: Comprehending and learning from multiple sources. In M. G. McKeown & L. Kucan (Eds.), *Bringing reading research to life* (pp. 257–284). New York, NY: Guilford.

Gottlieb, E., & Wineburg, S. (2012). Between veritas and communitas: Epistemic switching in the reading of academic and sacred history. *Journal of the Learning Sciences, 21*, 84–129.

Greene, J. A. (2016). Interacting epistemic systems within and beyond the classroom. In J. A. Greene, W. A. Sandoval, & I. Bråten (Eds.), *Handbook of epistemic cognition* (pp. 265–277). New York, NY: Routledge.

Greene, J. A., Azevedo, R., & Torney-Purta, J. (2008). Modeling epistemic and ontological cognition: Philosophical perspectives and methodological directions. *Educational Psychologist, 43*, 142–160.

Greene, J. A., Muis, K. R., & Pieschl, S. (2010). The role of epistemic beliefs in students' self-regulated learning in computer-based learning environments: Conceptual and methodological issues. *Educational Psychologist, 45*, 245–257.

Greene, J. A., Sandoval, W. A., & Bråten, I. (2016a). An introduction to epistemic cognition. In J. A. Greene, W. A. Sandoval, & I. Bråten (Eds.), *Handbook of epistemic cognition* (pp. 1–15). New York, NY: Routledge.

Greene, J. A., Sandoval, W. A., & Bråten, I. (Eds.). (2016b). *Handbook of epistemic cognition*. New York, NY: Routledge.

Greene, J. A., Torney-Purta, J., & Azevedo, R. (2010). Empirical evidence regarding relations among a model of epistemic and ontological cognition, academic performance, and educational level. *Journal of Educational Psychology, 102*, 234–255.

Greene, J. A., Torney-Purta, J., Azevedo, R., & Robertson, J. (2010). Using cognitive interviewing to explore primary and secondary students' epistemic and ontological cognition. In L. D. Bendixen & F. C. Haerle (Eds.), *Personal epistemology in the classroom: Theory, research, and implications for practice* (pp. 368–406). Cambridge, England: Cambridge University Press.

Greene, J. A., & Yu, S. B. (2014). Modeling and measuring epistemic cognition: A qualitative re-investigation. *Contemporary Educational Psychology, 39*, 12–28.

Greene, J. A., Yu, S. B., & Copeland, D. Z. (2014). Measuring critical components of digital literacy and their relationships with learning. *Computers & Education, 76*, 55–69.

Greeno, J. G. (2015). Commentary: Some prospects for connecting concepts and methods of individual cognition and of situativity. *Educational Psychologist, 50,* 248–251.

Gregoire, M. (2003). Is it a challenge or a threat? A dual-process model of teachers' cognition and appraisal processes during conceptual change. *Educational Psychology Review, 15,* 147–179.

Hallett, D., Chandler, M. J., & Krettenauer, T. (2002). Disentangling the course of epistemic development: Parsing knowledge by epistemic content. *New Ideas in Psychology, 20,* 285–307.

Hammer, D. (1994). Epistemological beliefs in introductory physics. *Cognition and Instruction, 12,* 151–183.

Hammer, D., & Elby, A. (2002). On the form of a personal epistemology. In B. K. Hofer & P. R. Pintrich (Eds.), *Personal epistemology: The psychology of beliefs about knowledge and knowing* (pp. 169–190). Mahwah, NJ: Lawrence Erlbaum.

Harris, P. L. (2007). Trust. *Developmental Science, 10,* 135–138.

Harris, P. L. (2012). *Trusting what you're told: How children learn from others.* Cambridge, MA: Harvard University Press.

Herrenkohl, L. R., & Cornelius, L. (2013). Investigating elementary students' scientific and historical argumentation. *Journal of the Learning Sciences, 22,* 413–461.

Hofer, B. K. (2000). Dimensionality and disciplinary differences in personal epistemology. *Contemporary Educational Psychology, 25,* 378–405.

Hofer, B. K. (2004). Epistemological understanding as a metacognitive process: Thinking aloud during online searching. *Educational Psychologist, 39,* 43–55.

Hofer, B. K. (2006). Domain specificity of personal epistemology: Resolved questions, persistent issues, new models. *International Journal of Educational Research, 45,* 85–95.

Hofer, B. K., & Bendixen, L. D. (2012). Personal epistemology: Theory, research, and future directions. In K. R. Harris, S. Graham, T. Urdan, C. B. McCormick, G. M. Sinatra, & J. Sweller (Eds.), *Educational psychology handbook: Vol. 1. Theories, constructs, and critical issues* (pp. 227–256). Washington, DC: American Psychological Association.

Hofer, B. K., & Pintrich, P. R. (1997). The development of epistemological theories: Beliefs about knowledge and knowing and their relation to learning. *Review of Educational Research, 67,* 88–140.

Hofer, B. K., & Pintrich, P. R. (Eds.). (2002). *Personal epistemology: The psychology of beliefs about knowledge and knowing.* Mahwah, NJ: Lawrence Erlbaum.

Hofer, B. K., & Sinatra, G. M. (2010). Epistemology, metacognition, and self-regulation: Musings on an emerging field. *Metacognition and Learning, 5,* 113–120.

Hynd-Shanahan, C., Holschuh, J. P., & Hubbard, B. P. (2004). Thinking like a historian: College students' reading of multiple historical documents. *Journal of Literacy Research, 36,* 141–176.

Jaswal, V. K., & Neely, L. A. (2006). Adults don't always know best: Preschoolers use past reliability over age when learning new words. *Psychological Science, 17,* 757–758.

Jehng, J. J., Johnson, S. D., & Anderson, R. C. (1993). Schooling and students' epistemological beliefs about learning. *Contemporary Educational Psychology, 18,* 23–35.

Kammerer, Y., Amann, D. G., & Gerjets, P. (2015). When adults without university education search the Internet for health information: The roles of Internet-specific epistemic beliefs and a source evaluation intervention. *Computers in Human Behavior, 48,* 297–309.

Kardash, C. M., & Scholes, R. J. (1996). Effects of preexisting beliefs, epistemological beliefs, and need for cognition on interpretation of controversial issues. *Journal of Educational Psychology, 88,* 260–271.

Kelly, G. J. (2014). The social bases of disciplinary knowledge and practice in productive disciplinary engagement. *International Journal of Education Research, 64,* 211–214.

Kelly, G. J. (2016). Methodological considerations for the study of epistemic cognition in practice. In J. A. Greene, W. A. Sandoval, & I. Bråten (Eds.), *Handbook of epistemic cognition* (pp. 392–408). New York, NY: Routledge.

Kelly, G. J., & Crawford, T. (1997). An ethnographic investigation of the discourse processes of school science. *Science Education, 81,* 533–559.

Khine, M. S. (Ed.). (2008). *Knowing, knowledge, and beliefs: Epistemological studies across diverse cultures.* Dordrecht, Netherlands: Springer.

King, P. M., & Kitchener, K. S. (1994). *Developing reflective judgment: Understanding and promoting intellectual growth and critical thinking in adolescents and adults.* San Francisco, CA: Jossey-Bass.

King, P. M., & Kitchener, K. S. (2002). The reflective judgment model: Twenty years of research on epistemic cognition. In B. K. Hofer & P. R. Pintrich (Eds.), *Personal epistemology: The psychology of beliefs about knowledge and knowing* (pp. 37–62). Mahwah, NJ: Lawrence Erlbaum.

King, P. M., & Kitchener, K. S. (2004). Reflective judgment: Theory and research on the development of epistemic assumptions through adulthood. *Educational Psychologist, 39,* 5–18.

Kitchener, K. S. (1983). Cognition, metacognition, and epistemic cognition. *Human Development, 26,* 222–232.

Kitcher, P. (1993). *The advancement of science.* New York, NY: Oxford University Press.

Knapp, T. R., & Mueller, R. O. (2010). Reliability and validity of instruments. In G. R. Hancock & R. O. Mueller (Eds.), *The reviewer's guide to quantitative methods* (pp. 337–342). New York, NY: Routledge.

Koenig, M., Clément, F., & Harris, P. L. (2004). Trust in testimony: Children's use of true and false statements. *Psychological Science, 10,* 694–698.

Koenig, M., & Harris, P. L. (2005). Preschoolers mistrust ignorant and inaccurate speakers. *Child Development, 76,* 1261–1277.

Kornblith, H. (Ed.). (1985). *Naturalizing epistemology.* Cambridge: MIT Press.

Kuhn, D. (1991). *The skills of argument.* Cambridge, England: Cambridge University Press.

Kuhn, D. (2001). How do people know? *Psychological Science, 12,* 1–8.

Kuhn, D., Amsel, E., & O'Loughlin, M. (1988). *The development of scientific thinking skills.* San Diego, CA: Academic Press.

Kuhn, D., Cheney, R., & Weinstock, M. (2000). The development of epistemological understanding. *Cognitive Development, 15,* 309–328.

Lave, J., & Wenger, E. (1991). *Situated learning: Legitimate peripheral participation.* Cambridge, England: Cambridge University Press.

Lederman, N. G. (2007). Nature of science: Past, present, and future. In S. K. Abell & N. G. Lederman (Eds.), *Handbook of research on science education* (pp. 831–879). Mahwah, NJ: Lawrence Erlbaum.

Lehrer, R., & Schauble, L. (2006). Scientific thinking and science literacy. In W. Damon, R. Lerner, K. A. Renninger, & I. E. Sigel (Eds.), *Handbook of child psychology: Vol. 4. Child psychology in practice* (6th ed., pp. 153–196). Hoboken, NJ: Wiley.

Leu, D. J., Kinzer, C. K., Coiro, J., Castek, J., & Henry, L. A. (2013). New literacies: A dual-level theory of the changing nature of literacy, instruction, and assessment. In D. E. Alvermann, N. J. Unrau, & R. B. Ruddell (Eds.), *Theoretical models and processes of reading* (6th ed., pp. 1150–1181). Newark, DE: International Reading Association.

Lonka, K., & Lindblom-Ylänne, S. (1996). Epistemologies, conceptions of learning, and study practices in medicine and psychology. *Higher Education, 31,* 5–24.

Maggioni, L., VanSledright, B., & Alexander, P. A. (2009). Walking the borders: A measure of epistemic cognition in history. *Journal of Experimental Education, 77,* 187–214.

Mason, L. (2016). Psychological perspectives on measuring epistemic cognition. In J. A. Greene, W. A. Sandoval, & I. Bråten (Eds.), *Handbook of epistemic cognition* (pp. 375–392). New York, NY: Routledge.

Mason, L., Ariasi, N., & Boldrin, A. (2011). Epistemic beliefs in action: Spontaneous reflections about knowledge and knowing during online information searching and their influence on learning. *Learning and Instruction, 21*, 137–151.

Mason, L., & Boldrin, A. (2008). Epistemic metacognition in the context of information searching on the Web. In M. S. Khine (Ed.), *Knowing, knowledge, and beliefs: Epistemological studies across diverse cultures* (pp. 377–404). New York, NY: Springer.

Mason, L., Boldrin, A., & Ariasi, N. (2010). Searching the Web to learn about a controversial topic: Are students epistemically active? *Instructional Science, 38*, 607–633.

Mason, L., Junyent, A. A., & Tornatora, M. C. (2014). Epistemic evaluation and comprehension of Web-source information on controversial science-related topics: Effects of a short-term instructional intervention. *Computers & Education, 76*, 143–157.

Mason, L., & Scrivani, L. (2004). Enhancing students' mathematical beliefs: An intervention study. *Learning and Instruction, 14*, 153–176.

Metz, K. E. (2011). Disentangling robust developmental constraints from the instructionally mutable: Young children's epistemic reasoning about a study of their own design. *Journal of the Learning Sciences, 20*, 50–110.

Montgomery, D. E. (1992). Young children's theory of knowing: The development of a folk epistemology. *Developmental Review, 12*, 410–430.

Moser, P., & vander Nat, A. (Eds.). (1987). *Human knowledge: Classical and contemporary approaches.* New York, NY: Oxford University Press.

Moshman, D., & Tarricone, P. (2016). Logical and causal reasoning. In J. A. Greene, W. A. Sandoval, & I. Bråten (Eds.), *Handbook of epistemic cognition* (pp. 54–67). New York, NY: Routledge.

Muis, K. R. (2004). Personal epistemology and mathematics: A critical review and synthesis of research. *Review of Educational Research, 74*, 317–377.

Muis, K. R., Bendixen, L. D., & Haerle, F. C. (2006). Domain-generality and domain-specificity in personal epistemology research: Philosophical and empirical reflections in the development of a theoretical framework. *Educational Psychology Review, 18*, 3–54.

Muis, K. R., & Duffy, M. C. (2013). Epistemic climate and epistemic change: Instruction designed to change students' epistemic beliefs and learning strategies and improve achievement. *Journal of Educational Psychology, 105*, 213–225.

Muis, K. R., Duffy, M. C., Trevors, G., Ranellucci, J., & Foy, M. (2014). What were they thinking? Using cognitive interviewing to examine the validity of self-reported epistemic beliefs. *International Education Research, 2*, 17–32.

Muis, K. R., Trevors, G., & Chevrier, M. (2016). Epistemic climate for epistemic change. In J. A. Greene, W. A. Sandoval, & I. Bråten (Eds.), *Handbook of epistemic cognition* (pp. 331–359). New York, NY: Routledge.

Muis, K. R., Trevors, G., Duffy, M., Ranellucci, J., & Foy, M. J. (2016). Testing the TIDE: Examining the nature of students' epistemic beliefs using a multiple methods approach. *Journal of Experimental Education, 84*, 264–288. doi:10.1080/00220973.2015.1048843

National Education Association. (2014). *Preparing 21st century students for a global society: An educators guide to the "Four Cs."* Washington, DC: Author.

NGSS Lead States. (2013). *Next Generation Science Standards: For states, by states: Vol. 1. The standards.* Washington, DC: National Academies Press.

Nokes, J. (2014). Elementary school students' roles and epistemic stances during document-based history lessons. *Theory & Research in Social Education, 42*, 375–413.

Osborne, J., Collins, S., Ratcliffe, M., Millar, R., & Duschl, R. A. (2003). What "ideas-about-science" should be taught in school science? A Delphi study of the expert community. *Journal of Research in Science Teaching, 40*, 692–720.

Packer, M. J., & Goicoechea, J. (2000). Sociocultural and constructivist theories of learning: Ontology, not just epistemology. *Educational Psychologist, 35*, 227–241.

Perry, W. G. (1970). *Forms of intellectual and ethical development in the college years: A scheme.* New York, NY: Holt, Rinehart & Winston.

Phillips, D. C. (1995). The good, the bad, and the ugly: The many faces of constructivism. *Educational Researcher, 24*, 5–12.

Piaget, J. (1972). *Principles of genetic epistemology: Selected works* (Vol. 7). New York, NY: Routledge.

Pillow, B. H., Hill, V., Boyce, A., & Stein, C. (2000). Understanding inference as a source of knowledge: Children's ability to evaluate the certainty of deduction, perception, and guessing. *Developmental Psychology, 36*, 169–179.

Plato. (1991). *The republic* (B. Jowett, Trans.). New York, NY: Vintage Books.

Pluta, W. J., Chinn, C. A., & Duncan, R. G. (2011). Learners' epistemic criteria for good scientific models. *Journal of Research in Science Teaching, 48*, 486–511.

Porsch, T., & Bromme, R. (2011). Effects of epistemological sensitization on source choices. *Instructional Science, 39*, 805–819.

Portnoy, L. B., & Rabinowitz, M. (2014). What's in a domain: Understanding how students approach questioning in history and science. *Educational Research and Evaluation, 20*, 122–145.

Posner, G. J., Strike, K. A., Hewson, P. W., & Gertzog, W. A. (1982). Accommodation of a scientific conception: Toward a theory of conceptual change. *Science Education, 66*, 211–227.

Qian, G., & Alvermann, D. E. (1995). Role of epistemological beliefs and learned helplessness in secondary school students' learning science concepts from text. *Journal of Educational Psychology, 87*, 282–292.

Quine, W. V. O. (1969). *Ontological relativity and other essays.* New York, NY: Columbia University Press.

Reznitskaya, A., Glina, M., Carolan, B., Michaud, O., Rogers, J., & Sequeira, L. (2012). Examining transfer effects from dialogic discussions to new tasks and contexts. *Contemporary Educational Psychology, 37*, 288–306.

Rosebery, A. S., Warren, B., & Conant, F. R. (1992). Appropriating scientific discourse: Findings from language minority classrooms. *Journal of the Learning Sciences, 2*, 61–94.

Rosenberg, S., Hammer, D., & Phelan, J. (2006). Multiple epistemological coherences in an eighth-grade discussion of the rock cycle. *Journal of the Learning Sciences, 15*, 261–292.

Ruffman, T., Perner, J., Olson, D. R., & Doherty, M. (1993). Reflecting on scientific thinking: Children's understanding of the hypothesis-evidence relation. *Child Development, 64*, 1617–1636.

Rysiew, P. (2016, Spring). Naturalism in epistemology. In E. N. Zalta (Ed.), *The Stanford encyclopedia of philosophy.* Retrieved from http://plato.stanford.edu/archives/spr2016/entries/epistemology-naturalized/

Ryu, S., & Sandoval, W. A. (2012). Improvements to elementary children's epistemic understanding from sustained argumentation. *Science Education, 96*, 488–526.

Samarapungavan, A., Westby, E. L., & Bodner, G. M. (2006). Contextual epistemic development in science: A comparison of chemistry students and research chemists. *Science Education, 90*, 468–495.

Sandoval, W. A. (2005). Understanding students' practical epistemologies and their influence on learning through inquiry. *Science Education, 89*, 634–656.

Sandoval, W. A. (2009). In defense of clarity in the study of personal epistemology. *Journal of the Learning Sciences, 18*, 150–161.

Sandoval, W. A. (2012). Situating epistemological development. In J. van Aalst, K. Thompson, M. J. Jacobson, & P. Reimann (Eds.), *The future of learning: Proceedings of the 10th International Conference of the Learning Sciences* (Vol. 1, pp. 347–354). Sydney, New South Wales, Australia: International Society of the Learning Sciences.

Sandoval, W. A. (2014). Science education's need for a theory of epistemological development. *Science Education, 98*, 383–387. doi:10.1002/sce.21107

Sandoval, W. A. (2015). Epistemic goals. In R. Gunstone (Ed.), *Encyclopedia of science education* (pp. 393–398). Dordrecht, Netherlands: Springer.

Sandoval, W. A., & Çam, A. (2011). Elementary children's judgments of the epistemic status of sources of justification. *Science Education, 95,* 383–408.

Sandoval, W. A., Sodian, B., Koerber, S., & Wong, J. (2014). Developing children's early competencies to engage with science. *Educational Psychologist, 49,* 139–152.

Schoenfeld, A. H. (1992). Learning to think mathematically: Problem solving, metacognition, and sense making in mathematics. In D. Grouws (Ed.), *Handbook for research on mathematics teaching and learning* (pp. 334–370). New York, NY: Macmillan.

Schommer, M. (1990). Effects of beliefs about the nature of knowledge on comprehension. *Journal of Educational Psychology, 82,* 498–504.

Schommer, M. (1993). Epistemological development and academic performance among secondary students. *Journal of Educational Psychology, 85,* 406–411.

Schommer, M., Crouse, A., & Rhodes, N. (1992). Epistemological beliefs and mathematical text comprehension: Believing it is simple does not make it so. *Journal of Educational Psychology, 84,* 435–443.

Schommer-Aikins, M. (2004). Explaining the epistemological belief system: Introducing the embedded systemic model and coordinated research approach. *Educational Psychologist, 39,* 19–29.

Schraw, G., Bendixen, L. D., & Dunkle, M. E. (2002). Development and evaluation of the Epistemic Belief Inventory (EBI). In B. K. Hofer & P. R. Pintrich (Eds.), *Personal epistemology: The psychology of beliefs about knowledge and knowing* (pp. 261–275). Mahwah, NJ: Lawrence Erlbaum.

Sinatra, G. M. (2016). Thoughts on knowledge about thinking about knowledge. In J. A. Greene, W. A. Sandoval, & I. Bråten (Eds.), *Handbook of epistemic cognition* (pp. 479–491). New York, NY: Routledge.

Sinatra, G. M., & Chinn, C. (2011). Thinking and reasoning in science: Promoting epistemic conceptual change. In K. Harris, C. B. McCormick, G. M. Sinatra, & J. Sweller (Eds.), *Critical theories and models of learning and development relevant to learning and teaching* (Vol. 1, pp. 257–282). Washington, DC: American Psychological Association.

Sinatra, G. M., Kienhues, D., & Hofer, B. K. (2014). Addressing challenges to public understanding of science: Epistemic cognition, motivated reasoning, and conceptual change. *Educational Psychologist, 49,* 123–138.

Sinatra, G. M., Southerland, S. A., McConaughy, F., & Demastes, J. W. (2003). Intentions and beliefs in students' understanding and acceptance of biological evolution. *Journal of Research in Science Teaching, 40,* 510–528.

Sodian, B., & Kristen, S. (2016). Theory of mind. In J. A. Greene, W. A. Sandoval, & I. Bråten (Eds.), *Handbook of epistemic cognition* (pp. 68–85). New York, NY: Routledge.

Sodian, B., Zaitchik, D., & Carey, S. (1991). Young children's differentiation of hypothetical beliefs from evidence. *Child Development, 62,* 753–766.

Stadtler, M., Scharrer, L., Macedo-Rouet, M., Rouet, J. F., & Bromme, R. (2016). Improving vocational students' consideration of source information when deciding about science controversies. *Reading and Writing, 29,* 705–729. doi:10.1007/s11145-016-9623

Stahl, E., & Bromme, R. (2007). The CAEB: An instrument for measuring connotative aspects of epistemological beliefs. *Learning and Instruction, 17,* 773–785.

Stanovich, K. E. (2010). *Decision making and rationality in the modern world.* New York, NY: Oxford University Press.

Steup, M. (2014, Spring). Epistemology. In E. N. Zalta (Ed.), *The Stanford encyclopedia of philosophy.* Retrieved from http://plato.stanford.edu/archives/spr2014/entries/epistemology/

Strømsø, H. I., & Bråten, I. (2010). The role of personal epistemology in the self-regulation of Internet-based learning. *Metacognition and Learning, 5,* 91–111.

Strømsø, H. I., Bråten, I., & Samuelstuen, M. S. (2008). Dimensions of topic-specific episte-mological beliefs as predictors of multiple text comprehension. *Learning and Instruction, 18*, 513–527.

Strømsø, H. I., & Kammerer, Y. (2016). Epistemic cognition and reading for understanding in the Internet age. In J. A. Greene, W. A. Sandoval, & I. Bråten (Eds.), *Handbook of epistemic cognition* (pp. 230–246). New York, NY: Routledge.

Tabak, I. (2016). Functional scientific literacy: Seeing science within the words and across the Web. In L. Corno & E. M. Anderman (Eds.), *Handbook of educational psychology* (3rd ed.). New York, NY: Routledge.

Trautwein, U., & Lüdtke, O. (2007). Predicting global and topic-specific certainty beliefs: Domain-specificity and the role of the academic environment. *British Journal of Educational Psychology, 77*, 907–934.

VanSledright, B. (2002). Fifth graders investigating history in the classroom: Results from a researcher-practitioner design experiment. *Elementary School Journal, 103*, 131–160.

VanSledright, B., & Maggioni, L. (2016). Epistemic cognition in history. In J. A. Greene, W. A. Sandoval, & I. Bråten (Eds.), *Handbook of epistemic cognition* (pp. 128–146). New York, NY: Routledge.

Verschaffel, L., De Corte, E., Lasure, S., Van Vaerenbergh, G., Bogaerts, H., & Ratinckx, E. (1999). Learning to solve mathematical application problems: A design experiment with fifth graders. *Mathematical Thinking and Learning, 1*, 195–229.

Vygotsky, L. S. (1962). *Thought and language*. Cambridge: MIT Press.

Vygotsky, L. S. (1978). *Mind in society: The development of higher psychological processes*. Cambridge, MA: Harvard University Press.

Wason, P. C. (1960). On the failure to eliminate hypotheses in a conceptual task. *Quarterly Journal of Experimental Psychology, 12*, 129–140.

Weinstock, M. (2011). Narrative and relational argument orientations: Knowledge-telling and knowledge-transforming in verdict justifications. *Thinking & Reasoning, 17*, 282–314.

Weinstock, M. (2016). Epistemic cognition in legal reasoning. In J. A. Greene, W. A. Sandoval, & I. Bråten (Eds.), *Handbook of epistemic cognition* (pp. 215–229). New York, NY: Routledge.

Wellman, H. M. (2011). Developing a theory of mind. In U. Goswami (Ed.), *The Wiley-Blackwell handbook of childhood cognitive development* (2nd ed., pp. 258–284). Oxford, England: Wiley-Blackwell.

Wildenger, L., Hofer, B. K., & Burr, J. E. (2010). Epistemological development in very young knowers. In L. D. Bendixen & F. C. Feucht (Eds.), *Personal epistemology in the class-room: Theory, research, and implications for practice* (pp. 220–257). Cambridge, England: Cambridge University Press.

Wiley, J., Goldman, S. R., Graesser, A. C., Sanchez, C. A., Ash, I. K., & Hemmerich, J. A. (2009). Source evaluation, comprehension, and learning in Internet science inquiry tasks. *American Educational Research Journal, 46*, 1060–1106.

Williams, M. (2001). *Problems of knowledge: A critical introduction to epistemology*. New York, NY: Oxford University Press.

Wineburg, S. (1991). Historical problem solving: A study of the cognitive processes used in the evaluation of documentary and pictorial evidence. *Journal of Educational Psychology, 83*, 73–87.

Zimmerman, C. (2000). The development of scientific reasoning skills. *Developmental Review, 20*, 99–149.

Chapter 14

Research in Mathematics Education

ALAN H. SCHOENFELD
University of California, Berkeley

As one of the three Rs, "'rithmetic" has always been central to education and education research. By virtue of that centrality, research in mathematics education has often reflected and at times led trends in education research. This chapter provides some deep background on epistemological and other issues that shape current research, with a primary focus on empirical research, which sprouted and flowered over the past 100 years or so—roughly coinciding with the existence of the American Educational Research Association as a professional organization. The author begins by tracing the growth and change in research in mathematics education and its interdependence with research in education in general over much of the 20th century, with an emphasis on changes in research perspectives and methods and the philosophical/empirical/disciplinary approaches that underpin them. He then turns to an overview of currently flourishing research and some indications of potentially productive arenas for future work.

Distilling a century of research in mathematics education into some 40 double-spaced pages calls for difficult decisions. Focusing on history alone would allow just four pages per decade, with no meaningful discussion of the field's extraordinary growth in recent decades. Even a focus on recent research would demand a bird's-eye view: Recent handbooks of research in mathematics education, such as English and Kirshner (2015) or Lester (2007), average 1,000 journal pages in length. Then, there is the issue of scope. What takes place in schools and classrooms is intimately connected to what happens in society at large. Where do we draw the line—at student thinking and learning, at the classroom door, at the school, at discussions of policy? Do we include the interactions of society and schooling? Politics, policy, and the social environment of education all shape what happens in mathematics classrooms.

Review of Research in Education
March 2016, Vol. 40, pp. 497–528
DOI: 10.3102/0091732X16658650
© 2016 AERA. http://rre.aera.net

Some issues, such as equity—or perhaps better put, inequity—cut across all disciplines. Here, I focus primarily on research on mathematics education, almost exclusively within the United States.

The first half of this review covers the grand sweep of research on mathematics education conducted in the United States over much of the 20th century.[1] The second half discusses selected contemporary issues and trends.

EPISTEMOLOGICAL UNDERPINNINGS

The roots of mathematics education lie in ancient philosophy. Plato's *Meno* (380 B.C.E.), for example, introduced the Socratic dialogue. In conversation, Socrates induces a slave to "recollect" a special case of the Pythagorean theorem. Their dialogue illustrates the idea of *anamnesis*—that the soul is eternal and all knowing, and that "recollecting" is all that is necessary for learning. The Platonic view of mathematics in the *Meno*—that mathematical knowledge is "out there" in an ideal form, perhaps to be revealed ("recollected" with guidance) but not discovered—echoes to this day. The idea of individuals building their own understandings, or of collectives constructing disciplinary practices, is not part of this picture. This is consequential, in that what one takes to be the nature of truth and what counts as evidence for it shape what one strives to describe and measure.

The conception of education research as an empirical discipline is much more modern. AERA's (American Educational Research Association) formation in 1916 reflected the coming of age of the empirical approach, in which data matter and are used to inform and shape policy. In the century since the founding of AERA, the scope of inquiry into education has expanded. While still grounded in epistemology (whether explicit or not) and shaped by social contexts, education research expanded inwardly to include the study of thinking and learning, and outwardly to include, for example, sociocultural characterizations of policies and their impact.

HISTORY OF MATHEMATICAL EDUCATION RESEARCH
The Early Years

Toward the turn of the 20th century, mass education was an elementary affair, focused for the most part on the three Rs. In 1890, only 6.7% of the 14-year-olds in the United States attended high school, and only 3.5% of the 17-year-olds graduated (Stanic, 1987, p. 150). The vast majority of schoolchildren studied arithmetic with a practical bent: The main focus of instruction was mastering arithmetic operations for the commercial marketplace. In contrast, the small fraction of the population that enrolled in high school (often *en route* to college) took courses in algebra, geometry, and physics.

The late 19th and early 20th centuries witnessed the beginnings of the profes-sionalization of education, as witnessed by the emergence of a number of societies devoted to the study of the field of education and to mathematics and mathematics education in particular. Here is a brief chronology of the emergence of relevant soci-eties. The American Mathematical Society (AMS) was founded in 1888, its focus being primarily the advancement of university mathematics. The National Society for the Study of Education (NSSE), founded by John Dewey, among others, in 1901, was an organization of "scholars, professional educators, and policy makers dedicated to the improvement of education research, policy, and practice" (NSSE, 2015). The Mathematical Association of America was established in 1915, in large measure as breakaway faction of the AMS, because the AMS had not proved hospitable to a mathematical/pedagogical focus (Mathematical Association of America, 2015).

This is AERA's centennial year. Founded in 1916, AERA is "concerned with improv-ing the educational process by encouraging scholarly inquiry related to education and evaluation and by promoting the dissemination and practical application of research results" (AERA, 2016). The NCTM was founded in 1920. As described on its website, the NCTM is "the public voice of mathematics education, supporting teachers to ensure equitable mathematics learning of the highest quality for all students through vision, leadership, professional development, and research" (NCTM, 2016).

The emergence of these societies represented, in large measure, a series of disci-plinary attempts to gain an orderly perspective on what had, hitherto, been a some-what unstructured educational context.[2] Yearbooks, presidential papers, and other documents provide a sense of the state of the art at the time. In mathematics and, as far as one can tell, across all disciplines, the focus was on what should be taught and how it should be taught—with little attention given to the learner. For example, NCTM's (1926/1995) first yearbook was published in 1926. David Eugene Smith (1925/1995) describes the early chaos:

No secondary school could adjust its work and its program to the requirements of several colleges without a sort of competence as a pedagogic acrobat that was rare to the point of non-existence. The situation would have been comic were it not so preposterous. (p. 1)

The need for order gave rise to the existence of the College Entrance Examination Board and, ultimately, to the growth of schools of education in the universities to provide agreed-upon backgrounds to teachers. Curricular concerns percolated down-ward, resulting in the rise of junior high schools and, ultimately, to the reshaping of elementary mathematics education. By 1926, mathematics curricular foci had shifted away from the abstract topics (e.g., methods of solving mixture problems, greatest common divisor, and Gregorian and Julian calendars) to the concrete—the arithme-tic of home and store, of maintaining a simple bank account, of balancing a check-book, and other practically oriented applications. This "uniformizing" of curriculum and assessments, with a focus on the practical, fed naturally into the measurement regime that typified the first half of the century.

Arithmetic and algebra are easy to proceduralize and measure. One can construct tests, define empirical standards, and see how students and teachers stack up; one can test varied methods of instruction and see which is better. This was the agenda laid out by Schorling (1926/1995), who documented the poor performance of students on a range of mathematical tasks and proposed the following five-point program for general improvement: (a) develop a consistent set of principles and methods for making progress; (b) specify goals clearly; (c) be *objective*, using empirical studies as the basis for specifying and refining curricula; (d) "employ certain well accepted principles from the psychology of drill"; and (e) "construct our teaching materials under precisely controlled and tested conditions" (p. 72). Each of these agenda items met with substantial elaboration.

Schorling (1926/1995) laid out 20 rules for drill in careful detail. Here are the first four, as presented in subheadings in Schorling's chapter: (a) Drill, to be effective, must be individual; (b) In general, there should be much practice for a few skills rather than a little practice for each of many; (c) A drill exercise must be specific; and (d) A drill exercise must provide a scoring technique so that the pupil may watch his or her daily growth.

Schorling's (1926/1995) chapter exemplifies the perspectives underlying the yearbook volume in which it appeared, and much of the spirit of the times. First, mathematics itself was taken to be largely procedural. The content to be learned was conceptualized as a set of operations that could be mastered and used reliably by students. Second, learning (and the minds that did it) were grossly underconceptualized, if they were conceptualized at all. The psychological underpinnings of learning were grounded primarily in associationist or behaviorist psychology.[3] These views proved fertile ground for empirical study. Indeed, one of the most telling comments in NCTM's first yearbook (1926) is a comment inserted by the editors to frame the chapter titled "Some Recent Investigations in Arithmetic":

Detailed investigations and controlled experiments are distinctly the product of the last quarter of a century. The yearbook would not be truly representative of the recent developments without a sampling of the newer types of materials that are developing to guide our practice. (p. 166)

Here we see the emergence of scientism, in the name of science—a phenomenon that would plague education research and practice through the entire 20th century and beyond. The trappings of science—"objective" measurement and "rigorous" methods—are easy to adopt, but they may miss the point entirely. The point here is that empiricism, while essential, can be problematic if not carefully used. What you choose to look at in the first place and how you think about, represent, and characterize what goes on in the minds of learners, are consequential.

We shall return to this issue in the discussion of more recent events, but it must be noted that the perspective described above was anything but anomalous. In the introduction to the 1930 yearbook of the NSSE, which was devoted to arithmetic, F. B. Knight (1930a) wrote:

There has been a conscious attempt to avoid the urging of any point of view not supported by considerable scientific fact. It has seemed preferable to proceed slowly and on sure ground, to be content with sane and moderate progress, rather than to expound a theory of instruction which, though supported by fine hopes and splendid aspirations, has as yet no basis in objective data. (p. 2)

Even so, comments by individual authors pointed to issues that would emerge more than half a century later as being central to the field's understandings of teaching and learning. For example, Knight (1930b) himself observed that "a mathematical description of an arithmetic process does not yield the kind of information about that process which is an essential basis for its instruction to children" (p. 162). This could be taken as a precursor of the concept of pedagogical content knowledge (Shulman, 1986), the idea that teachers' knowledge includes a range of ways to connect content to student understandings. Greene and Buswell (1930) characterize the limits of objective testing by indicating that although such tests may indicate what students failed to get correct, they do not indicate the cause of the errors. The authors give the example of a fifth-grade student who produced the answer 14 when asked to subtract 36 from 42:

Judging simply from his answer on a test paper, one would probably say that in addition to the error in the first combination the student had forgotten to borrow and had for this reason subtracted 3 from 4, getting 1 in the ten's place.[4] What the pupil actually did was this: "Thirty-two to forty-two is ten and four more (32 to 36) is fourteen." In such an example as this, simply observing the answer on a test paper does not help the teacher to understand the difficulty. Nothing short of a detailed individual diagnosis in which the teacher observes the mental processes of the pupil as he works would throw light on the real difficulties that are involved. (p. 275)

This last sentence is strikingly modern. It may not anticipate the systematicity of student errors revealed by later research (e.g., Brown & Burton, 1978), but it certainly points to the fact that individual students' thought patterns matter.

Similarly, objective measurement, properly employed, has always been a very useful tool. An example comes from AERA's first president, Frank Ballou, who was director of the Massachusetts Department of Educational Investigation and Measurement in Boston. In *Improving Instruction Through Educational Measurement*, Ballou (1916) suggested that (a) the goals for instruction should be established by a rational policy mechanism, (b) high-quality tests should be developed to capture student performance, (c) median performance might be considered a goal for all to achieve over time, and (d) schools whose performance was conspicuously low should be given guidance and resources for improvement (see Schoenfeld, 2016, for more details). But it should be noted that the understanding of what constituted school mathematics and what should be done to measure mathematics performance were considered unproblematic.

Part of what is interesting about education research in the early years is the question of just what was considered mainstream *research* and what was not. In general, classroom-based research was not (at least if it took place within a single classroom and without a control group). For that reason, it is worth stopping to examine Harold Fawcett's (1938) masterpiece, *The Nature of Proof*, which appeared in NCTM's year-book series. The series editor, W. D. Reeve (1938), noted,

The present study is one in which interest has already been aroused all over the country through the desires of teachers to find a way not only to teach the important facts of geometry but also to acquaint the pupil with the kinds of thinking one needs in life situations which can best be learned by a study of geometry. (p. v)

Fawcett's (1938) book represents a striking exception to the epistemological zeit-geist of the first half-century of education research, as well as to then-contemporary pedagogy. In today's language, Fawcett wanted students to experience geometry and geometric thinking as sense-making activities. Geometry was not about Platonic truths handed down from generation to generation to be memorized or mastered; it was a rational human creation in which people made carefully considered definitions, from which certain conclusions followed. Fawcett saw his task as being the initiation of students into this culture of *doing* mathematics. To introduce students to the need for precise definition, he opened the course with a wide-ranging discussion of the proposition that "awards should be granted for outstanding achievement in the school" (p. 30). The discussion quickly got muddled: Does performance on the foot-ball team count as an achievement? What would be outstanding in that case? If the award is given to a teacher, is the librarian eligible? It became clear to Fawcett's class over time that definitions needed to be made, but that the actual nature of the defini-tion could be somewhat arbitrary (one might consider librarians to be teachers, or not; one could consider a fly ball that hits the foul pole to be either fair or foul). However, once the definition is made, that is it; consequences follow directly from the way the definition is framed. Fawcett then turned to mathematics and had his students grapple with the issue of what definitions are and how they come about. He had his students define "adjacent angles"—a challenging task to accomplish precisely! So the class began, and it continued, as a deep exploration into geometric thinking and proving. The course description and its assessment (Fawcett employed multiple measures) were strikingly modern, in both epistemological and pedagogical terms.

Midcentury, Painted With a Broad Brush

The middle of the 20th century saw significant demographic, political, and cur-ricular changes—but, in large part, stasis with regard to the character of research in mathematics education. Demographic trends documented by the U.S. Census Bureau (2015) show significant increases in the number of 25-year-olds who graduated from high school, from nearly 25% in 1940 to more than 60% in 1974 (and 88% in 2014), with concomitant increases in college enrollment and graduation rates. What that meant in midcentury was that high school mathematics, once reserved for the elite, was now open to (some of) the masses.[5] That caused problems, requiring adjustments. Also, more advanced mathematics was pushed lower into the curriculum as the century passed. At midcentury, for example, calculus was often a course for college juniors, with "college algebra" and advanced geometry part of the freshman and sophomore curricula; today, high school seniors pursuing STEM (science, technology, engineering, and mathematics) careers are expected to take calculus. The steady compression of the curriculum consistently moved advanced topics into earlier grades.

And, of course, social context made a difference. Wars—whether hot, cold, or economic—focus attention on the mathematical and scientific preparedness of America's citizenry. After World War II broke out, the U.S. Office of Education and NCTM collaborated in an effort to characterize the level of mathematical competency that schools needed to provide, if students were to enter the military with adequate mathematical preparation (NCTM, 1943). Soviet success in launching Sputnik on October 4, 1957, marked the start of the space race and major efforts to rejuvenate STEM education, with coalitions of mathematicians, scientists, and educators banding together to create new curricula. A series of papers from a National Academy of Sciences (1997) symposium in recognition of the 40th anniversary of Sputnik's launch describes the impact. The science curricula were longer lived than the mathematics curricula, which came to be known collectively as the "New Math" in the 1960s. The new math was ultimately discredited in the public eye and replaced by the "back to basics" movement in the 1970s.

In short, what we see at midcentury is social, political, and curricular upheaval. What we see in mathematics education research is multivocal and nonconvergent. Two synoptic sources come from NCTM and NSSE. The very first sentence of NCTM's 21st yearbook (Fehr, 1953/1995a) announces improbable ambitions: "How does the human brain and nervous system acquire its store of knowledge?"[6] (p. vii). The first chapter, "Theories of Learning Related to the Field of Mathematics" (Fehr, 1953/1995b) begins with what is known about the physiology of the brain, but rapidly acknowledges "how the physical behavior of this vast network of nerves in the brain and nervous system produces the response $a^2 - b^2$ is $(a - b)(a + b)$ is totally unknown" (p. 2) and will be a long time coming. There are disquisitions on animal learning, conditioning, connectionism, field theories, and more; there are invocations of introspection and John Dewey's (1910) *How We Think* and Gestaltism, referencing Jacques Hadamard's (1949) *The Psychology of Invention in the Mathematical Field*. But one is left without much assistance regarding either how thinking and learning take place or how to improve them. In the rest of the yearbook, one finds chapters on motivation, sensory learning (a concept that is in some ways an antecedent of contemporary ideas on embodied cognition), the role of language, the role of drill, transfer, problem solving, and more. But productive suggestions grounded in actual observations of teaching and learning are not to be found.

The Gestaltists are a new entry in the historical mix. Hadamard (1949) and Wertheimer (1945) are the two primary mathematical exponents, building on and synergistic with efforts by Köhler (1947) and Duncker (1945). Hadamard's famous reflections on discovery (having immersed himself in a difficult problem and then put it aside for a while, he saw the elements of a solution in a flash, and verified them at leisure) were corroborated by anecdotal conversations with others and codified as a four-step model of problem solving: (a) preparation, which involves immersion in the problem; (b) incubation, which involves letting the subconscious mind work on the problem; (c) illumination or inspiration, which produces a solution; and (d) verification. I will turn to theoretical and methodological issues concerning all of the groups discussed here at the end of this section.

The 1951 NSSE yearbook, which focused on the teaching of arithmetic, paints a different picture of the same scene. Buswell (1951) addresses conflicts between adherents of associationism and Gestaltism as follows:

The very reason that there are conflicting theories of learning is that some theories seem to afford a better explanation of certain aspects or types of learning, while other theories stress the application of pertinent evidence or accepted principles to other aspects and types of learning. It should be remembered that the factual data on which all theories must be based are the same and equally accessible to all psychologists. Theories grow and are popularized because of their particular value in explaining the facts, but they are not always applied with equal emphasis to the whole range of facts. (p. 144)

Looking ahead to the conflicts that took place in the 1990s between perspectives on what counts in mathematics instruction (aka the math wars; see Schoenfeld, 2004), between phonics and whole language (aka the reading wars; see Pearson, 2004), and between some cognitive and situated learning theorists (see, e.g., Anderson, Reder, & Simon, 1996; Greeno, 1997), we see the wisdom of Buswell's perspective.

Likewise, in a remarkably prescient comment, Harold Fawcett (1951.) proposes that research on arithmetic should take place in "actual classroom situations under the direction of teachers interested in organizing their program in such a manner as to learn and record the thought processes of their students as their number concepts become enriched through guided experience," and that the sources of data should include accurate documentation of student thinking: "If a child could be encouraged to talk as he works, to 'think out loud,' and if a recording could be made, the results would be helpful" (p. 285). It would be some years before these became accepted as mainstream techniques.[7]

Our final stop in the midcentury time band is the 1970 NSSE yearbook (Begle, 1970). That yearbook is distinctive for the ways in which it highlights the multivocalism of the mathematics and mathematics education research communities at the time, demonstrates the ways in which curricular activities were shaped by aspects of the larger social context, and offers inklings of perspectives that would flower in the late 20th and early 21st centuries. At the same time, it is notable for the ways in which it reflects the dominant social narrative. The Sputnik era was concurrent with the civil rights era. A social history of the time, emphasizing the civil rights struggles of the 1950s and 1960s, tells a story very different from the one told by the yearbook (e.g., Martin, 2013). More generally, there is a vibrant literature both in mathematics education research (e.g., Berry, Ellis, & Hughes, 2014; Martin, 2012; Stinson & Bullock, 2012) and in education research more broadly that offers counternarratives to the mainstream story.

The NSSE yearbook reflects the American mathematical community's reaction to Sputnik. Post-Sputnik reform was undergirded by the desire to restructure education in ways that created a much more mathematically and scientifically literate populace. This, for mathematicians, meant focusing on mathematical structure. Armed with the idea of a "spiral curriculum" as advanced by Bruner (1960), mathematicians began "with the hypothesis that any subject can be taught effectively in some intellectually honest form to any child at any stage of development" (p. 33). They believed that "a curriculum as it develops should revisit basic ideas repeatedly, building upon them until the student has grasped the full formal apparatus that goes with them" (p. 13).

The NSSE yearbook focused on underlying issues of mathematical structure in all mathematical K–12 content areas. These included the study of sets, primes, and clock arithmetic in the early grades, and in algebra, the study of groups, fields, complex numbers, vector spaces, and a collection of vector-related topics that, today, are typically seen in collegiate linear algebra courses at the sophomore level. A significant part of the volume is devoted to elaborating on mathematical structure and how to implement and evaluate these new ideas. With one notable exception—a forward-looking chapter titled "Psychology and Mathematics Education," by Lee Shulman (1970)—students and student thinking did not receive major focal attention. Shulman indicated the fundamental importance of an epistemological stance in shaping how people go about their educational work. He observed that experimental psychology was not at a point where it could make direct contributions to the practice of education, because laboratory studies do not reflect the complexity of classroom learning environments. Echoing Buswell (1951), he noted that carefully conducted empirical studies were needed to resolve questions of what works best in what circumstances.

The Latter 20th and Early 21st Centuries: A New Field and an Explosion of Knowledge

Until the latter part of the 20th century, research in mathematics education was an orphan discipline, with neither an identity nor a home. It had roots in philosophy, although those were often not explicitly recognized; it was shaped by mathematicians and psychologists; it drew on empirical methods from the fields of statistics, measurement, and psychology. Historically, many education researchers focused on mathematics education, but those practitioners had no center of gravity—no professional organizations, no journals of their own. Then, just as education as a field had become professionalized in the early 20th century, mathematics education came together as a discipline in the 1960s and 1970s.

The premier American mathematics education research journal—*Journal for Research in Mathematics Education* (*JRME*)—was first published in 1970. Johnson, Romberg, and Scandura (1994) provide a retrospective of the conditions that led to its creation, which was, to put it simply, a long haul reflective of the state of the field. The article is well worth reading for the historical context; given the large number of high-quality mathematics education journals today, it may be as difficult for emerging researchers to imagine an intellectual universe without such journals as it is for teenagers to imagine a world without cell phones.

The emergence of *JRME* was part of the zeitgeist. *Educational Studies in Mathematics* published its first issue in 1968, and the first International Congress on Mathematics Education was held in Lyon, France, in 1969; the first issue of the *Zentralblatt für Didaktik der Mathematik* (now known as *ZDM*) was published in 1969. Mathematics education research now had a home base. It had one within AERA as well. The Special Interest Group for Research in Mathematics Education was one of the first to be founded after AERA established Special Interest Groups in 1971.

Much of the work done in the United States in the 1970s, however, was of the "scientific" type that dominated math-ed research in the earlier parts of the century: laboratory studies, controlled experiments, and factor analyses. Works such as Piaget's (1952) *The Child's Conception of Number* and his 1960 volume *The Child's Conception of Geometry* had yet to have much of an impact in the United States. Similarly, Jeremy Kilpatrick and Izsak Wirszup worked to bring the work of the Soviets to the attention of the mathematics education community in the United States (e.g., Kilpatrick & Wirszup, 1969, the first of 14 volumes translated from the Russian; Krutetskii, 1976), but the research community as a whole was not ready for that kind of work.

The years around 1980 proved to be a turning point for the field. In a review of research on problem solving, Kilpatrick (1978) decried the sterility of research conducted under the banner of "science," suggesting that less "rigor" and more creativity in research would be a good thing for the field. Similarly, in a review of a volume reporting problem-solving studies conducted between 1968 and 1977, Schoenfeld (1981) lamented the absence of theory in "Treatment A versus Treatment B" and factor-analytic statistical studies, and the insular character of research in mathematics education:

> The name Piaget is not to be found once in a set of references that is 31 pages long! There are any number of areas in problem solving in which it is difficult if not impossible to do good research unless one is familiar with related research in the "cognitive sciences." . . . Modeling techniques in artificial intelligence and information-processing psychology are more advanced than our own. Others may not directly address our most important questions, but they can provide us help along the way. (p. 389)

In 1980, the field's first de facto research handbook was published, marking the boundary between the precognitive and cognitive eras. In 487 pages, *Research in Mathematics Education* (Shumway, 1980) summarized the state of the art prior to 1980. For example, David Johnson (1980b), in his chapter "Types of Research," listed five basic categories of education research:

> *The survey* (to establish norms and baseline data . . .), *the experiment* (involves the careful control of variables in an experimental situation . . .), *the case study* (involves the intensive study of individuals or

situations . . .), *evaluation* (which, unlike those types considered up to this point, is primarily concerned with changes that occur over time . . .), and *philosophical or historical research*. (pp. 21–24)[8]

There are constraints even there: In "The Research Process," Johnson (1980a) focuses almost exclusively on statistical methods, with an emphasis on how to choose the right "instruments" to measure the right "variables" when doing statistical analyses. Neither of these two chapters, which serve as the research framing for the volume, discusses the study of mental processes.

THE COGNITIVE REVOLUTION

Shumway's (1980) volume represents the end of one era and the beginning of another—the era of the cognitive sciences in education. There is an interesting irony in the way that the cognitive sciences emerged, breaking the hold that behaviorism had on psychology.[9] A tenet of radical behaviorism (Skinner, 1945, 1958) was that constructs such as "mind" were unnecessary: What counted in explaining people's actions were characterizations of overt, scientifically describable behaviors.

That, precisely, is what artificial intelligence (AI) provided. Pioneering AI programs, such as Newell and Simon's (1972) General Problem Solver (GPS) solved "cryptarithmetic" problems, played chess, and proved theorems in logic. The irony is that the structure of the algorithms that GPS employed to solve problems was abstracted from systematic observations of human beings solving problems. That is, GPS's overt, scientifically describable problem-solving strategies came from abstractions of the same strategies in humans. Thus, the study of human thought processes was legitimized—in large measure by the creation of "machines who think" (e.g., McCorduck, 1979).

Mathematics education and AI made for a natural partnership. In the late 1970s, mathematics education was just emerging from the "back to basics" movement. Signaling a major change of course, NCTM's *An Agenda for Action* (1980) made its first recommendation as follows: "Problem solving must be the focus of school mathematics in the 1980s" (p. 2). The primary resource for thinking about problem solving was the work of George Pólya (1945), whose *How to Solve It* introduced the notion of "heuristic strategies"—patterns of productive thinking that often help one better understand and/or make progress toward the solution of a problem. Examples of heuristic strategies include drawing diagrams, solving easier related problems and exploiting either the methods or the results thereof, and establishing subgoals (trying to get part of the way to a solution and then moving on from there).

Although it worked at a much finer level of grain size than Pólya, AI had focused, successfully, on the use of certain problem-solving heuristics (Newell, 1983; Sleeman & Brown, 1982). Moreover, AI and cognitive science, more generally, offered mathematics educators a number of tools and methods that substantially expanded the math-ed repertoire. For example, protocol analysis—examining records of people solving problems "out loud" to look for patterns of behavior—became a tool available to the research community; so did the very idea of modeling people's mathematical behavior.

As one example of the intersection, Schoenfeld's (1985) research on mathematical problem solving was motivated directly by the desire to make Pólya-type heuristics implementable, using AI-like methods to delineate the mechanisms by which the strategies could be implemented. If protocol analysis could work with an eye toward machine implementation, why not use it with an eye toward human implementation? That was the idea behind a 10-year program of research and development, in which theoretical development and testing took place amid the dialectic between laboratory work and the ongoing development of my problem-solving courses, in what was effectively an early series of design experiments (Cobb, Confrey, diSessa, Lehrer, & Schauble, 2003; Schoenfeld, 2006). Once the door opened to looking closely at people's mathematical activity (whether in the laboratory or the classroom), a range of discoveries followed. There was the specification of problem-solving strategies to the point that they could be learned and used. There was the documentation of the fact that difficulties with monitoring and self-regulation (aspects of metacognition) could cause problem-solving failure, despite individuals having the knowledge to solve problems; and there was evidence that people's belief systems (about themselves and about what it meant to learn and do mathematics) shaped their mathematical behavior in fundamental ways. More broadly, the rapprochement between mathematics education research and work in the emerging cognitive sciences opened up a spectrum of research methods and foci that expanded the scope of the enterprise in tremendously productive ways. This was true in a broader sense as well: Research on reading and writing changed in comparable ways.

The world of mathematics education changed radically during the 1980s, as did education research in general. By the end of the decade, student thinking was a major focus of inquiry. Piagetian studies had entered the mainstream, with early beachheads established in the late 1960s and early 1970s (e.g., Ginsburg & Opper, 1969) and with methods such as the clinical interview coming into wide use (Ginsburg, 1981). The cognitive perspective was well established, with constructivist underpinnings and the understanding that investigations of student thinking in general required attention to the knowledge base, problem-solving strategies, metacognition, and belief systems (Schoenfeld, 1985; Silver, 1985). Moreover, there was the recognition that investigations into thinking and learning needed to be interdisciplinary—that mathematics education was part of a larger enterprise, cognitive science and education.[10]

By the mid-1980s, NCTM was in a position to take stock and establish a research agenda for the field. It held a series of conferences that led to a five-volume collection, with specific volumes devoted to the teaching and assessing of mathematical problem solving (Charles & Silver, 1988), effective mathematics teaching (Grouws, Cooney, & Jones, 1988), learning and teaching of algebra (Wagner & Kieran, 1988), and number concepts and operations in the middle grades (Hiebert & Behr, 1988), along with a volume setting a general agenda for mathematics education research (Sowder, 1989).

The developments in research in mathematics education beginning in the 1980s drew from and contributed to developments in research in education in general. The NCTM research-agenda volume on problem solving (Charles & Silver, 1988) provides a case example. Chapter topics include warrants for the study of mathematical epistemology (Greeno, 1988); treating mathematics as an ill-structured discipline (Resnick, 1988); treating problem solving as an everyday practice (Lave, Smith, & Butler, 1988); problem solving in contexts (Schoenfeld, 1988); metacognition (Campione, Brown, & McConnell, 1988); assessment (Marshall, 1988; Silver & Kilpatrick, 1988); reframing teaching as an act of problem solving (Carpenter, 1988); and studies of teachers' beliefs and conceptions (Thompson, 1988). Each of these chapters was part of something larger, which cut across all of research in education and, by the late 1980s and early 1990s, was flowering in multi- or interdisciplinary research in education.

The chapters by Greeno (1988) and Resnick (1988), for example, reflected attempts to understand authentic disciplinary practices and to conceptualize classroom activities that would enable students to engage in a wide range of disciplines, such as reading and writing, history, social studies, and science, in more authentic ways. (Resnick & Klopfer, 1989, offer characterizations of parallel attempts in a range of disciplines.) The chapter by Lave et al. (1988) was an early attempt to characterize learning environments in which mathematics was seen as something that developed and had meaning within real contexts. This was part of a larger movement toward exploring everyday cognition (Rogoff & Lave, 1984) and its flip side, the creation of learning environments for cognitive apprenticeship (Collins, Brown, & Newman, 1989). All of these were part of the emerging situative perspective (e.g., Greeno, Collins, & Resnick, 1996). Assessment was, at long last, being problematized; the challenge addressed by Marshall (1988) and Silver and Kilpatrick (1988) was, and is, to craft assessments that capture what it means to engage in a discipline. That issue is still very much with us (see, e.g., Ercikan, 2015).

Finally, studies of teachers and teaching, as reflected in the chapters by Carpenter (1988) and Thompson (1988), were leaving behind the counting and correlational techniques of earlier days (e.g., the "process–product paradigm," which sought correlations between teacher actions and student outcomes) and beginning to treat teachers as problem solvers and decision makers. Mathematics education was part and parcel of a huge expansion of research on teaching, as reflected in the third edition of the *Handbook of Research on Teaching* (Wittrock, 1986). The theme of teacher decision making would, like all of the themes highlighted here, become a mainstream topic in education research.

In sum, research in mathematics education underwent a major transformation over the 1980s and the beginning of the 1990s. Much was unsettled, but the field had broken free of the paradigmatic straightjackets that dominated NCTM's 1980 volume, *Research in Mathematics Education* (Shumway, 1980), and it was embarking on many new directions that flourish to this day. One indication of the growth of the field is the size of the 1992 *Handbook of Research on Mathematics Teaching and Learning* (Grouws, 1992), which is at least three times the size of its antecedent, containing 771 pages (8½" × 11") filled with small type. The coverage is far broader, including not only direct descendants of the topics in the earlier volume (history, epistemology, studies of teaching and learning) but also innovative expansions of those topics (e.g., studies of teaching including discussions of the culture of the mathematics classroom and of teacher beliefs, e.g., Thompson, 1984, 1988) and full-fledged discussions of "critical issues" that had barely been on the horizon as subjects of research a mere decade before—technology and mathematics education; ethnomathematics and everyday cognition; research on affect in mathematics education; mathematics and gender; race, ethnicity, social class, and achievement in mathematics; and theorizing assessment of students' knowledge in mathematics. All these chapters represented well-grounded but early explorations into new areas, which would flourish over the next two decades. But this was only the beginning.

Of fundamental importance is the fact that mathematics education had reached the point where research and practice could work together in productive dialectic. Research could inform practice in productive ways, and practice, in turn, could serve as the site for meaningful research. Prior to the 1980s, research and development had been at some remove—and, because of the differences in context, the results of laboratory research typically failed to apply meaningfully in classrooms. In addition, the statistical methods employed in classroom studies often failed to capture what really mattered. But over the latter part of the 20th century and into the 21st century, research in mathematics education, and in education in general, took place increasingly in "Pasteur's quadrant" (Stokes, 1997),[11] attending simultaneously to issues of foundational knowledge and considerations of use.

This dialectic played out in multiple ways as the field flowered. For example, early studies of children's developing understandings of addition and subtraction of whole numbers (see Carpenter, 1985) took place in the laboratory. Carpenter, Fennema, Franke, and colleagues reasoned that such knowledge, in the hands of teachers, could produce instruction that was more responsive to students' understandings. They produced Cognitively Guided Instruction, a professional development program for teachers that was "designed to help teachers understand student thinking and use this knowledge to make instructional decisions" (Carpenter & Fennema, 1992, p. 457), and which had significant positive impact on student learning (see, e.g., Carpenter & Fennema, 1992; Carpenter, Fennema, & Franke, 1996).

More broadly, studies of teacher knowledge and beliefs and of how they played out in instruction grew in scope and depth. Early pioneering studies by Thompson (1984, 1988; see Thompson, 1992, for a review) established the central, though subtle, role that teachers' beliefs about mathematics and mathematics teaching play in shaping their instructional practice. The works of Ball (1993, 1997) and Lampert (1985; see also Ball & Lampert, 1999) elaborated on the complexity of teaching, documenting both the knowledge and the subtlety of the decision making required.

Lampert's 2001 book *Teaching Problems and the Problems of Teaching* provides an extraordinarily rich characterization of the day-by-day, weekly, and yearly goals that teachers have for their students, and the knowledge and beliefs they bring to bear in the service of those goals. Teacher noticing (Mason, 2002; Sherin, Jacobs, & Philipp, 2010) became established as a line of inquiry. In a major cross-cultural study, Stigler and Hiebert (1999) provided evidence that teaching practices are much more closely related within a nation's borders than between nations. In sum, the field's understanding of teaching grew tremendously, in both scope and detail.

A watershed event, politically and intellectually, was the publication of the NCTM *Curriculum and Evaluation Standards for School Mathematics* in 1989. The standards were NCTM's attempt to enhance the quality of mathematics instruction nationwide. They were produced as a partial response to *A Nation at Risk: The Imperative for Educational Reform* (National Commission on Excellence in Education, 1983), an influential report that decried the state of American education in a time of economic crisis. An orchestrated response through federal agencies such as the National Science Foundation was not possible at the time (see Schoenfeld, 2004, for details), so it fell to the mathematics education research community to make change.

The NCTM standards represented a radical shift in the ways that curriculum specifications were put forward. Curriculum specifications in general were nothing new: Ever since the Committee of Ten (National Education Association, 1894) set forth desiderata for school curricula in a wide range of content areas, representatives of various fields have convened periodically to identify what should be taught. But all such documents prior to the publication of the NCTM standards focused on identifying the content that students should learn; for example, the Committee of Ten report had sections on arithmetic, concrete geometry, algebra, and formal geometry. The standards did, of course, list such content. But in addition, they focused heavily on the processes of doing mathematics in which students should engage to become mathematically proficient: mathematical problem solving, mathematical communication, mathematical reasoning, and making mathematical connections. Learning mathematics was redefined to mean learning the processes of doing mathematics as well as learning the content—a fundamental shift grounded in the work produced by the research community.

The Standards and Their Impact

The NCTM standards had tremendous impact, catalyzing what has been called the standards movement. The 1990s saw the creation of the *National Science Education Standards* (National Research Council, 1996), the *Standards for the English Language Arts* (National Council of Teachers of English, 1996), the *National Standards for History* (National Center for History in the Schools, 1996), and more. For better or for worse, the notion of standards became enshrined in law, both in the No Child Left Behind Act of 2001 and in Race to the Top, part of the American

Recovery and Reinvestment Act of 2009. Race to the Top gave rise to the Common Core State Standards for mathematics and English language arts (Common Core State Standards Initiative, 2010a, 2010b) and the *Next Generation Science Standards* (NGSS Lead States, 2013).

The standards movement took directions that were not predicted in 1989 with the publication of the original standards. NCTM (1989) defined "standard" as follows: "A standard is a statement that can be used to judge the quality of a mathematics curriculum or methods of evaluation. Thus, standards are statements about what is valued" (p. 2). The high-stakes accountability measures that were so central to No Child Left Behind and Race to the Top were not part of the original plan at all. Another unintended consequence was the math wars, which arose as part of a conservative backlash to the process-oriented parts of the NCTM *Standards* (these wars were part of the zeitgeist, parallel to the reading wars; see Schoenfeld & Pearson, 2009). What is interesting, and saddening, is that the math wars took place in the absence of data. The literature leading to the original *Standards* provided clear documentation of the difficulties caused by traditional curricula and noted the positive impact of instances of practice consistent with the ideas in the *Standards*—but, as there were no curricula designed along the lines of the *Standards*, the evidence in favor of such curricula was circumstantial. "Standards-based" curricula were developed and field tested during the 1990s, while the math wars raged. The first clear evidence emerged with the publication of Senk and Thompson (2003). All of the standards-based curricula examined by Senk and Thompson offered "balanced diets" of skills, concepts, and problem solving. Across the board, evaluations indicated that students who learned from these curricula did about as well on tests of skills as students who learned from more traditional, skills-oriented curricula—and they outperformed those students on tests of conceptual understanding and problem solving.

Continued Growth

By the 1990s, research in mathematics education had undergone a significant transformation and expansion, which has continued to the present. The *Second Handbook of Research on Mathematics Teaching and Learning* (Lester, 2007) grew to two large volumes, covering more territory in more depth. Some of the work was distinctively mathematical, but much of it reflected the expansion of education research as a whole. The section titles of this handbook illustrate the broad range of research in mathematics education now being conducted. Part I, on foundations, is general. The opening chapter, by Paul Cobb (2007), whose subtitle is "Coping With Multiple Theoretical Perspectives," addresses theoretical/epistemological pluralism by noting the contexts in which various approaches to studying human behavior—including experimental psychology, cognitive psychology, sociocultural theory, and distributed cognition—all contribute to our understanding. Silver and Herbst (2007) expand the discussion by considering the dialectic between theory making and issues of research and practice. They note that theories exist at various levels of detail and generality and that the enterprise of research in mathematics education includes the refinement and/or creation of "midrange" or "local" theories, sometimes suggested by and necessarily refined by empirical work (i.e., design experiments). Schoenfeld (2007) describes the huge expansion of research methods in recent decades (as exemplified, e.g., by the *Handbook of Complementary Methods in Education Research* [Green, Camilli, & Elmore, 2006], which contains chapters on 35 research methods) and discusses various meta-level considerations for their rigorous use.

Part II of the *Handbook* goes on to discuss research on teachers and teaching, including studies of teacher knowledge, affect, and belief; it includes a review of the literature on the complexities of classroom culture and practice. Here, the focus is on mathematics, but mathematics is a case in point: Teacher beliefs about students and about content are consequential no matter what the content. (Some of the foundational work on teacher knowledge and beliefs was discussed above.)

The Social/Sociopolitical Turn

Part III of the *Handbook* concerns influences on student outcomes. In this arena, we see perhaps the most dramatic change in the field—in what is seen to constitute the "outcomes" of instruction, and the range of factors that influences outcomes. This arena, reflecting the "social turn" in mathematics education research (Lerman, 2000) or, alternatively, the "sociopolitical turn" (Gutierrez, 2013), goes beyond the purely cognitive to examine the broad range of ways in which mathematics instruction has an impact on students, and the social and cultural issues that shape who students are, both inside and outside the classroom. Key arenas of growth include critical race theory (Ladson-Billings, 1995; Ladson-Billings & Tate, 2006; Tate, 1997), culturally relevant pedagogy (Gay, 2010; Ladson-Billings, 1997), and the funds of knowledge that students bring to instruction (Moll, Amanti, Neff, & Gonzalez, 1992), the very conception of equitable instruction (Bishop, Tan, & Barkatsas, 2015; Gutierrez, 2008; Nasir & Cobb, 2007; Secada, Fennema, & Adajian, 1995; Tate & D'Ambrosio, 1997), issues of power (Diversity in Mathematics Education Center for Learning and Teaching, 2007), and studies of identity (Boaler & Greeno, 2000; Gutierrez & Irving, 2012; Martin, 2009, 2013; Wenger, 1998). To sum things up in too small a nutshell: Different aspects of people's identities become manifest in different contexts, including mathematics classrooms; people bring with them knowledge, traditions, and a sense of self, which is in constant negotiation; classrooms are sites where much more than "content learning" takes place, including negotiations of self in context; and classrooms can be hospitable to the development of positive or negative mathematics identities, depending on what individuals bring to the environment, how it is perceived, and how they perceive what the environment has to offer them. And, as noted above, a larger framing (Berry et al., 2014; Martin, 2009, 2013; Stinson & Bullock, 2012) raises the fundamental questions of who has access to what kinds of mathematics in the first place. All of this is dynamic and constantly in flux; one can expect continued advances.

Rounding Out the *Handbook* to Set the Stage for a Comparison

Part IV of the 2007 *Handbook* describes advances in the understanding of the teaching and learning of specific mathematical topics, providing ample evidence of the field's growth. Part V deals with assessment, a field that has been revitalized by the need to assess the kinds of content and process understandings called for by evolving curricula. (This has been the case since the 1989 NCTM *Standards*, and is that much more critical given the high-stakes nature of the assessments used to evaluate performance on the Common Core State Standards. See below for an elaboration.) Part VI, the final section, deals with continuing and unresolved issues. Access and equity still need major attention; technology demanded attention in 2007 and is much more of an issue today; and there are, of course, issues of policy and the engineering of positive change in mathematics education.

CATCHING UP AND LOOKING FORWARD

It is interesting to compare the 1988 NCTM research-agenda volume on problem solving (Charles & Silver, 1988) and the 1989 NCTM *Standards* with the second *Handbook of Research on Mathematics Teaching and Learning* (Lester, 2007) and what has happened since then.

The volume by Charles and Silver (1988) made a case for the study of epistemology, which was partly reflected by the issues leading up to the 1989 NCTM *Standards*: The idea that both content *and* process count as part of doing mathematics in these standards represented a very significant epistemological shift. In 1989, explicit discussions of epistemology were rare in mathematics education circles, and the conversations were often at the level of grand theory—behaviorists versus constructivists, for example. By 1996, "theories of mathematical learning" had come to center stage (Steffe, Nesher, Cobb, Goldin, & Greer, 1996). The discussions of theory in the 2007 *Handbook* are far more nuanced and cover much more ground: anthropological, cognitive, situative, and sociological perspectives intersect and coexist. But the ground is constantly changing. For example, the term "embodied cognition" did not appear in the index of the 2007 *Handbook*; yet both embodied cognition (e.g., Nemirovsky & Ferrara, 2009) and embodied design (e.g., Abrahamson, 2009; Alibali & Nathan, 2012) are receiving increased attention in mathematics education. The role of discourse in interactions, and the relationships between communication and cognition (see, e.g., Sfard, 2008) increasingly are being explored and will, presumably, be themes in the third edition of the *Handbook*. But these are only two of many areas in which our knowledge is expanding. Consider, for example, the growth in our understandings of the social and sociopolitical "turns" described above. Periodic updates, compare-and-contrasts, and syntheses will be needed as the field's understandings of the foundations of thinking and learning—both physical and social—continue to evolve.

The situation with regard to research methods is far more dynamic. New theoretical orientations bring with them a plethora of methods, and with those, questions of robustness, connections to other methods, and problems of idiosyncrasy. A Google Scholar search on "design research methods mathematics" since the publication of the 2007 *Handbook* yields more than 65,000 results, including a number of research handbooks. A major challenge here is cumulativity. While every study has its own special features, researchers often design their own methods and measures, making it difficult to compare the results from different studies. To pick just one example of an emerging field that overlaps research in mathematics education, consider collaborative learning. The *International Handbook of Collaborative Learning* (Hmelo-Silver, Chinn, Chan, & O'Donnell, 2013) represents an attempt to bring some theoretical, methodological, and empirical order to an emerging field that is, perhaps, in a state similar to that of mathematics education a quarter century ago. Our toolkits and our findings are still expanding rapidly. This is healthy, of course, as we education researchers find richer ways to characterize thinking, teaching, learning, and learning environments. But attention needs to be given to ways to regularize data gathering, storage, and analysis within and across subfields of education, to facilitate making connections and building on what has been done.

Significant advances have been made in other areas that were hinted at in 1988 and that had gathered critical mass by 2007. Metacognition, a somewhat novel construct in the 1980s, has become recognized as a central aspect of cognition; the same can be said of belief systems. A theory of decision making, focusing on teachers but more generally applicable, has been developed (Schoenfeld, 2011).

This work, as well as the work on teaching and learning environments described below, is indicative of the fact that the field has now reached the stage where there is a fundamental and productive dialectic between theory and practice. Research is no longer typically conducted in the laboratory and then "applied" in classrooms. Rather, given that there are now tools for reliable naturalistic observations and programmatic interventions, classrooms can serve as laboratories. Research and development in mathematics education increasingly live in powerful synergy. Two examples concerning teaching involve the TeachingWorks project at the University of Michigan and the Teaching for Robust Understanding (TRU) framework developed by the Algebra Teaching Study and Mathematics Assessment Projects at the University of California at Berkeley, Michigan State University, and the University of Nottingham. The TeachingWorks project (2016) focuses on the "core work of teaching," with an emphasis on 19 "high-leverage" practices for beginning and early-career teachers, such as recognizing common patterns of students' thinking, conducting a whole class discussion, building relationships with students, choosing representations and examples, and assessing students' learning. Ongoing R&D serves to refine the practices and examine their impact. The TRU Framework is an analytic perspective that characterizes "what counts" in classrooms. TRU provides a theory-based language and tools for focusing on five comprehensive and consequential aspects the classroom environment: content; cognitive demand; access and equity; agency, authority, and identity; and formative assessment (Algebra Teaching Study of University of

California at Berkeley & Michigan State University, 2016, "Publications" and "Tools"; Mathematics Assessment Project [TRU Math Suite], 2016b). The key idea is that classrooms that do increasingly well along these five dimensions will increasingly produce students who are powerful thinkers and problem solvers (Schoenfeld, 2014). At the policy level, Cobb and colleagues (Cobb & Jackson, 2012; Cobb & Smith, 2008) have conducted design experiments aimed at bringing teacher support to scale.

It has taken some time for educational R&D to reach this point of research–practice dialectic, which requires projects of duration and scale (Burkhardt & Schoenfeld, 2003). Moreover, these projects represent just a small beginning in terms of addressing the major problems the nation faces in (re)building a teacher corps that is capable of supporting students equitably in the pursuit of meaningful mathematical knowledge and identities. Further explorations in the creation of contexts, cultures, and materials that support such growth are necessary.

Three major issues remain in our comparison of the late 1980s and the present: diversity, assessment, and technology. As discussed above, the field has made extraordinary progress in conceptualizing issues of diversity and equity. But there is so much more to be done. Gutierrez (2013) lays out some of the territory:

Taking the sociopolitical turn is a necessary chapter in mathematics education, as it is from the views of such groups that mathematics education will continue to grow and evolve (in ways that allow schooling to appropriately supplement what goes on elsewhere). With new conceptual tools in mind, we can begin to investigate questions such as these:

- How do mathematics education research, practice, and policy shape constructions of African American, Latin@, American Indian, poor, English learners, LGBTQ, and other marginalized learners? And, what are the ways in which such learners accommodate, resist, subvert, (re)signify, (re)produce, and transgress those constructions? . . .
- What are the strategies and experiences of learners who successfully negotiate the mathematics classroom and education as a broader social practice so that they maintain their cultural identities and fare well on standardized measures of (school) success? How can educators support these strategies of negotiation? . . .
- With respect to learning/doing mathematics, what do we need to understand about how learners are positioned and how they position themselves when they use their cultural/linguistic resources across multiple settings, both in and out of school? (p. 60)[12]

Assessment bifurcates into summative and formative types, and there have been advances in both. Part of the implementation of the Race to the Top initiative (The White House, 2009) involved the creation of two consortia to develop assessments consistent with the Common Core State Standards in mathematics and English language arts (Common Core State Standards Initiative, 2010a, 2010b). Both consortia, the Smarter Balanced Assessment Consortium (2012) and the Partnership for Assessment of Readiness for College and Careers (2012), crafted exams intended to reflect evolving conceptions of domain proficiency that go beyond traditional testing in what was tested and how scores would be reported.

Traditional summative examinations in mathematics reported one score only. That provided enough information to rank students and to inform programs about their level of success in general, but it did not indicate which aspects of instruction (or student thinking) were strong and which were in need of improvement. The Smarter Balanced content specifications (Smarter Balanced Assessment Consortium, 2012) initially called for reporting separate scores on four areas of proficiency: concepts and procedures, problem solving, communicating reasoning, and modeling and data analysis (problem solving and modeling have now been combined; Smarter Balanced Assessment Consortium, 2015). Although implementation is both a pragmatic and a political challenge, specs of this type, grounded in decades of research on mathematical cognition, represent a potential step forward. Much more work along these lines is needed, given the consequential character of high-stakes testing.

Formative assessment in the classroom (the ongoing assessment of student understanding, in enough time to respond productively in instruction) has been well theorized by Paul Black and Dylan Wiliam (1998a, 1998b, 2009). The challenge has been to support teachers in actually conducting such work. A significant step toward practicality—with full research documentation—was made by Swan (2006). The ideas in that volume were the models for a set of formative assessment lessons, which are available as free downloads from the Mathematics Assessment Project website (2016a, "Lessons" tab). To date, more than 5 million copies of the formative assessment lessons have been downloaded. Studies by the National Center for Research on Evaluation, Standards, and Student Testing (2015) and Research for Action (2015) document the kind of impact that research-based materials, refined through multiple design cycles, can have on teaching practices and student performance.

Last but not least, technology. Here, the story is not as clear, or as positive. The challenge in pragmatic terms is that technological change comes so rapidly that it is difficult for the research community (and practitioners!) to keep pace. Sowder's *Setting a Research Agenda* (1989) focuses on the emergence of microcomputers as educational tools and their potential—including, among other things, their capacity to display dynamic representations of mathematical objects such as functions and graphs. These ideas are reflected in the 1989 *Standards.* By the time NCTM issued the successor volume, *Principles and Standards for School Mathematics* (2000), the role of technology as an exploratory medium had been recognized (especially with regard to geometry). The 2007 *Handbook* chapter by Zbiek, Heid, Blume, and Dick (2007) expanded the frame, with the idea of "cognitive tools" as devices that could help link technical and conceptual activities, raising issues of mathematical and cognitive fidelity of the artifacts that were making their way into classrooms. It raised the questions of how to incorporate rapidly changing technologies into everyday classroom practice, and into the curriculum. Those were challenges in 2007.

Those challenges represented just the tip of the technological iceberg. The iPad was introduced in January 2010, and the commercial world moves at much greater speed than either the research community or the schools. An *Education Week* column by

Michelle Davis (2013) indicated the radical transformations taking place just 3 years after tablets entered the marketplace. Arizona's Vail school district was "curating" its own curriculum. Pearson planned to "tabletize" mathematics curricula, digitizing materials drawn from multiple sources; hard copy versions of those materials would not be available. Houghton Mifflin planned to build "highly modular" curricula, and McGraw-Hill planned for "blended" classrooms that used some text materials and some digital technology. The emergence of the Common Core State Standards for Mathematics created a major dilemma for school districts: There were no Common Core State Standards for Mathematics–based curricula available, so adaptations, cutting and pasting, and "curating" were the only options available. Needless to say, this kind of fast-paced change is challenging for teachers and schools—and for researchers, who are trying to understand and support those involved. The challenge will be to develop an understanding of the impacts of such changes at multiple levels (e.g., individual student learning, classroom dynamics, school culture, administrative decision making, and more) while at the same time deepening our theoretical understandings of learning and the environments that support it.

Where are we, then? To be sure, the growth in the field's understanding of issues in mathematics education, and in research in education as a whole, has been nothing short of phenomenal in recent decades. We have, collectively, built much more relevant and nuanced theoretical frameworks, a closer relationship between research and practice, and a collection of tools to use in making progress on challenging problems. At the same time, there is much to be done in the scholarly, practical, and sociopolitical arenas. Many of the scholarly challenges (e.g., with regard to the need for evolving theory and methods, equity, assessment, and technology) were listed above. The field has done excellent work theorizing equity, but there are major societal issues to be confronted in working on a broad equity agenda. We have made great progress in understanding teacher thinking and learning, but there is much to be done in supporting teacher growth—in developing and researching professional learning communities, for example, or in learning about practices such as lesson study (see, e.g., Fujii, 2014; Lewis, 2002; Takahashi, 2008) in ways that would enable more widespread use in the United States. We know a great deal more about formative and summative assessment than we did a few decades ago—but where are the resources for the development and study of curricula and assessments that represent our current understandings?

There are major theoretical and practical challenges related to "going to scale." What does it take for good ideas to make their way into practice? Given limited person-power and the huge challenges of curriculum and professional development, what kinds of support structures will enable ideas that work on a small scale to "travel" in practice and take root? And is there any way for research to make its way more sensibly into the political arena? All too often, as in the case of high-stakes testing, ideas that have superficial face validity are adopted and implemented, with sometimes foreseen and often unforeseen negative consequences. The connections between research and policy are always iffy, and not just in mathematics education—consider public health and science policy as other high-profile examples. Nonetheless, it would behoove us as math education researchers to position ourselves to have greater impact (see Burkhardt & Schoenfeld, 2003) and to seek more powerful interactions with policymakers.

As a longtime participant in mathematics education research and practice, I have been immensely gratified to see the tremendous expansion of the field's understandings, only a small part of which I have been able to chronicle here. I look forward to seeing progress on the many challenging issues that remain.

ACKNOWLEDGMENTS

I want to expresses my sincere gratitude to the volume editors and the four anonymous reviewers whose detailed and thoughtful comments on an earlier draft were of immeasurable help in improving the chapter.

NOTES

[1]Warrants for many of the historical claims made in this chapter come from various societies' yearbooks, in particular from the National Council of Teachers of Mathematics (NCTM). The reason is that research in mathematics education did not emerge as a discipline with its own scholarly identity until the last third of the 20th century. Before that, there were no journals focusing on research in mathematics education, and the "research" sections of many journals (e.g., NCTM's *Arithmetic Teacher* and *Mathematics Teacher*) often provided descriptions of research attempts as justifications for suggestions for improving practice. In contrast, yearbooks devoted to the state of the art provided synoptic descriptions and served, effectively, as occasional journals.

[2]Perhaps the most famous example is Abraham Flexner's (1910) call for the reform of medical teaching practice, which resulted in the formation of teaching hospitals and the restructuring of medical education. But Flexner (1916) had more arrows in his quiver, as indicated by his essay "A Modern School." Reform was in the air in the early 20th century.

[3]See, for example, Thorndike's (1911) discussion of the "Law of Effect" or Watson's (1913) "Psychology as the Behaviorist Views It."

[4]Perhaps another possibility would be that the student had subtracted the smaller digit from the larger in both the ones and tens columns (a common arithmetic "bug").

[5]Access and opportunity were, then and now, very unevenly distributed, with race, ethnicity, and socioeconomic status being major factors in those inequities.

[6]This appeal to brain research and its hard science underpinnings was hardly a random event. The lure of "brain-based" science and its educational applications has been with us for some time, as, for example, in the Decade of the Brain, announced by the Library of Congress in 1990.

[7]"Out loud" methods were used occasionally. However, battles raged in psychology and elsewhere about their legitimacy, in part because of earlier battles over the Gestaltists' use of introspection/retrospection, which had been discredited as being unreliable. To give but one example, Nobel Prize winner Herbert A. Simon, one of the founders of artificial intelligence, felt compelled to produce a number of publications (e.g., Ericsson & Simon, 1980, 1984) in defense of using verbal reports "as data."

[8]In this passage, Johnson also notes that in case studies "it is dangerous to state generalizations . . . since the samples are usually limited."

[9]George Miller (2003), one of the founders of the cognitive perspective, put it this way: "Psychology could not participate in the cognitive revolution until it had freed itself from behaviorism, thus restoring cognition to scientific respectability" (p. 141).

[10]As noted below, the field of cognitive science was coalescing at about that time. Volume 1 of the journal *Cognitive Science* was published in 1977, and the Cognitive Science Society was incorporated in 1979.

[11]Some researchers (e.g., Niels Bohr) focused on theory without much concern for practice, and some (e.g., Thomas Edison) focused on applications without much concern for theory. Louis Pasteur exemplified the conduct of theoretically sound work in the context of addressing very real problems (e.g., developing the germ theory of disease while fighting illness and contamination). Stokes (1997) named this theoretical/applied nexus "Pasteur's quadrant."

[12]Gutierrez lists 10 issues, developed in concert with the *JRME* editorial panel; these 3 issues are just a sample.

REFERENCES

Abrahamson, D. (2009). Embodied design: Constructing means for constructing meaning. *Educational Studies in Mathematics, 70,* 27–47.

Alibali, M., & Nathan, M. (2012). Embodiment in mathematics teaching and learning: Evidence from learners' and teachers' gestures. *Journal of the Learning Sciences, 21,* 247–286. doi:10.1080/10508406.2011.611446

American Educational Research Association. (2016). *Who we are.* Retrieved from http://www.aera.net/AboutAERA/WhoWeAre/tabid/10089/Default.aspx

American Recovery and Reinvestment Act of 2009, Pub. L. 111-5, 16 U.S.C. (2009).

Anderson, J., Reder, L., & Simon, H. (1996). Situated learning and education. *Educational Researcher, 25*(4), 5–11.

Ball, D. L. (1993). With an eye on the mathematical horizon: Dilemmas of teaching elementary school mathematics. *Elementary School Journal, 93,* 373–397.

Ball, D. L. (1997). What do students know? Facing challenges of distance, context, and desire in trying to hear children. In B. J. Biddle, T. L. Good, & I. Goodson (Eds.), *International handbook of teachers and teaching* (pp. 769–818). New York, NY: Macmillan.

Ball, D. L., & Lampert, M. (1999). Situating research within an education context: A case study in mathematics teaching and learning. In E. R. Lagemann & L. Shulman (Eds.), *Issues in education research: Problems and possibilities* (pp. 371–398). San Francisco, CA: Jossey-Bass.

Ballou, F. (1916). *Improving instruction through educational measurement.* Boston, MA: Department of Educational Investigation and Measurement.

Begle, E. G. (Ed.). (1970). *Mathematics education: The sixty-ninth yearbook of the National Society for the Study of Education.* Chicago, IL: National Society for the Study of Education.

Berry, R. Q., III, Ellis, M., & Hughes, S. (2014). Examining a history of failed reforms and recent stories of success: Mathematics education and Black learners of mathematics in the United States. *Race Ethnicity and Education, 17,* 540–568.

Bishop, A., Tan, H., & Barkatsas, T. (Eds.). (2015). *Diversity in mathematics education: Towards inclusive practices.* New York, NY: Springer.

Black, P., & Wiliam, D. (1998a). Assessment and classroom learning. *Assessment in Education, 5,* 7–74.

Black, P., & Wiliam, D. (1998b). *Inside the black box: Raising standards through classroom assessment.* London, England: School of Education, King's College London.

Black, P., & Wiliam, D. (2009). Developing the theory of formative assessment. *Educational Assessment, Evaluation and Accountability, 21,* 5–31.

Boaler, J., & Greeno, J. G. (2000). Identity, agency, and knowing in mathematics worlds. In J. Boaler (Ed.), *Multiple perspectives on mathematics teaching and learning* (pp. 171–200). Westport, CT: Ablex.

Brown, J. S., & Burton, R. R. (1978). Diagnostic models for procedural bugs in basic mathematical skills. *Cognitive Science, 2*, 155–192.

Bruner, J. (1960). *The process of education.* Cambridge, MA: Harvard University Press.

Burkhardt, H., & Schoenfeld, A. H. (2003). Improving educational research: Toward a more useful, more influential, and better funded enterprise. *Educational Researcher, 32*(9), 3–14.

Buswell, G. (1951). The psychology of learning in relation to the teaching of arithmetic. In N. B. Henry (Ed.), *The teaching of arithmetic: The fiftieth yearbook of the National Society for the Study of Education* (pp. 143–154). Chicago, IL: University of Chicago Press.

Campione, J., Brown, A., & McConnell, M. (1988). Metacognition: On the importance of understanding what you are doing. In R. Charles & E. Silver (Eds.), *The teaching and assessing of mathematical problem solving* (pp. 93–114). Reston, VA: National Council of Teachers of Mathematics.

Carpenter, T. P. (1985). Learning to add and subtract: An exercise in problem solving. In E. A. Silver (Ed.), *Teaching and learning mathematical problem solving: Multiple research perspectives* (pp. 17–40). Hillsdale, NJ: Lawrence Erlbaum.

Carpenter, T. P. (1988). Teaching as problem solving. In R. Charles & E. Silver (Eds.), *The teaching and assessing of mathematical problem solving* (pp. 187–202). Reston, VA: National Council of Teachers of Mathematics.

Carpenter, T. P., & Fennema, E. (1992). Cognitively guided instruction: Building on the knowledge of teachers. *International Journal of Educational Research, 17*, 457–470.

Carpenter, T. P., Fennema, E., & Franke, M. L. (1996). Cognitively guided instruction: A knowledge base for reform in primary mathematics instruction. *Elementary School Journal, 97*, 3–20.

Charles, R., & Silver, E. (Eds.). (1988). *The teaching and assessing of mathematical problem solving.* Reston, VA: National Council of Teachers of Mathematics.

Cobb, P. (2007). Putting philosophy to work: Coping with multiple theoretical perspectives. In F. Lester (Ed.), *Handbook of research on mathematics teaching and learning* (2nd ed., pp. 3–38). Charlotte, NC: Information Age.

Cobb, P., Confrey, J., diSessa, A., Lehrer, R., & Schauble, L. (2003). Design experiments in educational research. *Educational Researcher, 32*(1), 9–13.

Cobb, P., & Jackson, K. (2012). Analyzing educational policies: A learning design perspective. *Journal of the Learning Sciences, 21*, 487–521.

Cobb, P., & Smith, T. (2008). The challenge of scale: Designing schools and districts as learning organizations for instructional improvement in mathematics. In T. Wood, B. Jaworski, K. Krainer, P. Sullivan, & D. Tirosh (Eds.), *International handbook of mathematics teacher education* (Vol. 3, pp. 231–254). Rotterdam, Netherlands: Sense.

Collins, A., Brown, J. S., & Newman, S. (1989). Cognitive apprenticeship: Teaching the craft of reading, writing, and mathematics. In L. B. Resnick (Ed.), *Knowing, learning, and instruction: Essays in honor of Robert Glaser* (pp. 453–494). Hillsdale, NJ: Lawrence Erlbaum.

Common Core State Standards Initiative. (2010a). *Common Core State Standards for English Language Arts.* Retrieved from http://www.corestandards.org/the-standards

Common Core State Standards Initiative. (2010b). *Common Core State Standards for Mathematics.* Retrieved from http://www.corestandards.org/the-standards

Davis, M. (2013, February 6). "Big Three" publishers rethink K–12 strategies. *Education Week.* Retrieved from http://www.edweek.org/dd/articles/2013/02/06/02textbooks.h06.html

Dewey, J. (1910). *How we think.* Boston, MA: D. C. Heath.

Diversity in Mathematics Education Center for Learning and Teaching. (2007). Culture, race, power, and mathematics education. In Lester F. (Ed.), *Handbook of research on mathematics teaching and learning* (2nd ed., pp. 405–434). Charlotte, NC: Information Age.

Duncker, K. (1945). On problem-solving. *Psychological Monographs, 58*(5), 1–113.

English, L., & Kirshner, D. (Eds.). (2015). *Handbook of international research in mathematics education* (3rd ed.). New York, NY: Routledge.

Ercikan, K. (Ed.). (2015). Assessment of complex thinking [Special issue]. *Theory Into Practice, 54*, 179–277.

Ericsson, K. A., & Simon, H. A. (1980). Verbal reports as data. *Psychological Review, 87*, 215–251.

Ericsson, K. A., & Simon, H. A. (1984). *Protocol analysis: Verbal reports as data.* Cambridge: MIT Press.

Fawcett, H. P. (1938). *The nature of proof: A description and evaluation of certain procedures used in a senior high school to develop an understanding of the nature of proof. Thirteenth Yearbook of the National Council of Teachers of Mathematics.* New York, NY: Teachers College Bureau of Publications.

Fawcett, H. P. (1951). Proposal for research on problems of teaching and learning arithmetic. In N. B. Henry (Ed.), *The Teaching of Arithmetic : The fiftieth yearbook of the National Society for the Study of Education Part II* (pp. 278–291). Chicago, IL: University of Chicago Press.

Fehr, H. F. (Ed.). (1995a). *The learning of mathematics: Its theory and practice. Twenty-first yearbook of the National Council of Teachers of Mathematics.* Reston, VA: National Council of Teachers of Mathematics. (Original work published 1953)

Fehr, H. F. (1995b). Theories of learning related to the field of mathematics. In H. F. Fehr (Ed.), *The learning of mathematics: Its theory and practice. Twenty-first yearbook of the National Council of Teachers of Mathematics* (pp. 1–41). Reston, VA: National Council of Teachers of Mathematics. (Original work published 1953)

Flexner, A. (1910). *Medical education in the United States and Canada: A report to the Carnegie Foundation for the Advancement of Teaching.* New York, NY: Carnegie Foundation for the Advancement of Teaching.

Flexner, A. (1916). A modern school. *American Review of Reviews, 53*, 465–474.

Fujii, T. (2014). Implementing Japanese lesson study in foreign countries: Misconceptions revealed. *Mathematics Teacher Education and Development, 16*(1), 65–83.

Gay, G. (2010). *Culturally responsive teaching* (2nd ed.). New York, NY: Teachers College Press.

Ginsburg, H. (1981). The clinical interview in psychological research on mathematical thinking: Aims, rationales, techniques. *For the Learning of Mathematics, 1*(3), 4–11.

Ginsburg, H., & Opper, S. (1969). *Piaget's theory of intellectual development: An introduction.* Englewood Cliffs, NJ: Prentice Hall.

Green, J., Camilli, G., & Elmore, P. B. (Eds.). (2006). *Handbook of complementary methods in education research.* Washington, DC: American Educational Research.

Greene, C. E., & Buswell, G. (1930). Testing, diagnosis, and remedial work in arithmetic. In G. M. Whipple (Ed.), *Report of the Society's Committee on Arithmetic: The twenty-ninth yearbook of the National Society for the Study of Education* (pp. 269–318). Bloomington, IL: Public School.

Greeno, J. G. (1988). For the study of mathematics epistemology. In R. Charles & E. Silver (Eds.), *The teaching and assessing of mathematical problem solving* (pp. 23–31). Reston, VA: National Council of Teachers of Mathematics.

Greeno, J. G. (1997). On claims that answer the wrong questions. *Educational Researcher, 26*(1), 5–17.

Greeno, J. G., Collins, A., & Resnick, L. (1996). Cognition and learning. In D. Berliner & R. Calfee (Eds.), *Handbook of educational psychology* (pp. 15–46). New York, NY: Simon & Schuster/Macmillan.

Grouws, D. (Ed.). (1992). *Handbook of research on mathematics teaching and learning.* New York, NY: Macmillan.

Grouws, D., Cooney, T., & Jones, D. (Eds.). (1988). *Effective mathematics teaching.* Reston, VA: National Council of Teachers of Mathematics.

Gutierrez, R. (2008). A "gap-gazing" fetish in mathematics education? Problematizing research on the achievement gap. *Journal for Research in Mathematics Education, 39,* 357–364.

Gutierrez, R. (2013). The sociopolitical turn in mathematics education. *Journal for Research in Mathematics Education, 44,* 37–68.

Gutierrez, R., & Irving, S. E. (2012). *Latino/a and Black students in mathematics.* Chicago, IL: Jobs for the Future.

Hadamard, J. (1949). *The psychology of invention in the mathematical field.* Princeton, NJ: Princeton University Press.

Hiebert, J., & Behr, M. (Eds.). (1988). *Number concepts and operations in the middle grades.* Reston, VA: National Council of Teachers of Mathematics.

Hmelo-Silver, C., Chinn, C., Chan, C., & O'Donnell, A. (Eds.). (2013). *International handbook of collaborative learning.* New York, NY: Routledge.

Johnson, D. C. (1980a). The research process. In R. Shumway (Ed.), *Research in mathematics education* (pp. 29–46). Reston, VA: National Council of Teachers of Mathematics.

Johnson, D. C. (1980b). Types of research. In R. Shumway (Ed.), *Research in mathematics education* (pp. 20–28). Reston, VA: National Council of Teachers of Mathematics.

Johnson, D. C., Romberg, T. A., & Scandura, J. M. (1994). The origins of the JRME: A retrospective account. *Journal for Research in Mathematics Education, 25,* 560–582.

Kilpatrick, J. (1978). Variables and methodologies in research on problem solving. In L. L. Hatfield (Ed.), *Mathematical problem solving* (pp. 7–20). Columbus, OH: ERIC/SMEAC Center for Science, Mathematics, and Environmental Education.

Kilpatrick, J., & Wirszup, I. (Eds.). (1969). *Soviet studies in the psychology of learning and teaching mathematics: Vol. 1. The learning of mathematical concepts.* Stanford, CA: School Mathematics Study Group.

Knight, F. B. (1930a). Introduction. In G. M. Whipple (Ed.), *Report of the Society's Committee on Arithmetic: The twenty-ninth yearbook of the National Society for the Study of Education* (pp. 1–8). Bloomington, IL: Public School Publishing.

Knight, F. B. (1930b). Some considerations of method. In G. M. Whipple (Ed.), *Report of the Society's Committee on Arithmetic: The twenty-ninth yearbook of the National Society for the Study of Education* (pp. 145–268). Bloomington, IL: Public School Publishing.

Köhler, W. (1947). *Gestalt psychology.* New York, NY: Liveright.

Krutetskii, V. A. (1976). *The psychology of mathematical abilities in school children* (J. Teller, Trans.). Chicago, IL: University of Chicago Press.

Ladson-Billings, G. J. (1995). Toward a critical race theory of education. *Teachers College Record, 97,* 47–68.

Ladson-Billings, G. J. (1997). *The dreamkeepers: Successful teachers of African-American children.* San Francisco, CA: Jossey-Bass.

Ladson-Billings, G. J., & Tate, W. (2006). *Education research in the public interest: Social justice, action, and policy.* New York, NY: Teachers College Press.

Lampert, M. (1985). How do teachers manage to teach? Perspectives on problems in practice. *Harvard Educational Review, 55,* 178–194.

Lampert, M. (2001). *Teaching problems and the problem of teaching.* New Haven, CT: Yale University Press.

Lave, J., Smith, S., & Butler, M. (1988). Problem solving as everyday practice. In R. Charles & E. Silver (Eds.), *The teaching and assessing of mathematical problem solving* (pp. 61–81). Reston, VA: National Council of Teachers of Mathematics.

Lerman, S. (2000). The social turn in mathematics education research. In J. Boaler (Ed.), *Multiple perspectives on mathematics teaching and learning* (pp. 19–44). Westport, CT: Ablex.

Lester, F. (Ed.). (2007). *Second handbook of research on mathematics teaching and learning.* Charlotte, NC: Information Age.

Lewis, C. (2002). *Lesson study: A handbook of teacher-led instructional change.* Philadelphia, PA: Research for Better Schools.

Library of Congress. (1990). *Project on the Decade of the Brain.* Retrieved from http://www.loc.gov/loc/brain/home.html

Marshall, S. (1988). Assessing problem solving: A short-term remedy and a long-term solution. In R. Charles & E. Silver (Eds.), *The teaching and assessing of mathematical problem solving* (pp. 159–177). Reston, VA: National Council of Teachers of Mathematics.

Martin, D. B. (Ed.). (2009). *Mathematics teaching, learning, and liberation in the lives of Black children.* New York, NY: Routledge.

Martin, D. B. (2012). Learning mathematics while Black. *Educational Foundations* (Winter-Spring), 47–66.

Martin, D. B. (2013). Race, racial projects, and mathematics education. *Journal for Research in Mathematics Education, 44,* 316–333.

Mason, J. (2002). *Researching your own practice: The discipline of noticing.* New York, NY: Routledge.

Mathematical Association of America. (2015). *MAA history.* Retrieved from http://www.maa.org/about-maa/maa-history

Mathematics Assessment Project. (2016a). *Lessons.* Retrieved from http://map.mathshell.org/lessons.php

Mathematics Assessment Project. (2016b). *TRU math suite.* Retrieved from http://map.mathshell.org/trumath.php

McCorduck, P. (1979). *Machines who think: A personal inquiry into the history and prospect of artificial intelligence.* San Francisco, CA: Freeman.

Miller, G. (2003). The cognitive revolution: A historical perspective. *Trends in Cognitive Sciences, 7,* 141–144.

Moll, L., Amanti, C., Neff, D., & Gonzalez, N. (1992). Funds of knowledge for teaching: Using a qualitative approach to connect homes and classrooms. *Theory Into Practice, 31,* 132–141.

Nasir, N., & Cobb, P. (Eds.). (2007). *Improving access to mathematics: Diversity and equity in the classroom.* New York, NY: Teachers College Press.

National Academy of Sciences. (1997). *Reflecting on Sputnik: Linking the past, present, and future of educational reform.* Retrieved from http://www.nas.edu/sputnik/index.htm

National Center for History in the Schools. (1996). *National standards for history, basic edition.* Los Angeles, CA: Author.

National Center for Research on Evaluation, Standards, and Student Testing. (2015). *The implementation and effects of the Mathematics Design Collaborative (MDC): Early findings from Kentucky ninth grade Algebra 1 courses* (CRESST Report 845). Los Angeles, CA: Author.

National Commission on Excellence in Education. (1983). *A nation at risk: The imperative for educational reform.* Washington, DC: Government Printing Office. Retrieved from http://www.ed.gov/pubs/NatAtRisk/risk.html

National Council of Teachers of English. (1996). *Standards for the English language arts.* Urbana, IL: Author.

National Council of Teachers of Mathematics. (1943). Essential mathematics for minimum army needs. *Mathematics Teacher, 6,* 243–282.

National Council of Teachers of Mathematics. (1980). *An agenda for action: Recommendations for school mathematics of the 1980s.* Reston, VA: Author.

National Council of Teachers of Mathematics. (1989). *Curriculum and evaluation standards for school mathematics.* Reston, VA: Author.

National Council of Teachers of Mathematics. (1995). *First yearbook: A general survey of progress in the last twenty-five years.* Reston, VA: Author. (Original work published 1926)

National Council of Teachers of Mathematics. (2000). *Principles and standards for school mathematics.* Reston, VA: Author.

National Council of Teachers of Mathematics. (2016). *Mission.* Retrieved from https://www.nctm.org/About/

National Education Association. (1894). *Report of the Committee of Ten on secondary school studies with the reports of the conferences arranged by committee.* New York, NY: American Book Company.

National Research Council. (1996). *National science education standards.* Washington, DC: National Academies Press.

National Society for the Study of Education. (2015). *National Society for the Study of Education (About).* Retrieved from https://nsse-chicago.org/About.asp

Nemirovsky, R., & Ferrara, F. (2009). Mathematical imagination and embodied cognition. *Educational Studies in Mathematics, 70,* 159–174. doi:10.1007/s10649-008-9150-4

Newell, A. (1983). The heuristic of George Pólya and its relation to artificial intelligence. In R. Groner, M. Groner, & W. Bischof (Eds.), *Methods of heuristics* (pp. 195–243). Hillsdale, NJ: Lawrence Erlbaum.

Newell, A., & Simon, H. A. (1972). *Human problem solving.* Englewood Cliffs, NJ: Prentice Hall.

NGSS Lead States. (2013). *Next generation science standards: For states, by states.* Washington, DC: National Academies Press.

No Child Left Behind Act of 2001, Pub. L. 107-110, 20 U.S.C. (2001).

Partnership for Assessment of Readiness for College and Careers. (2012). *Model content frameworks: Mathematics Grades 3–11* (Version 2.0, Revised). Retrieved from http://www.parcconline.org/parcc-model-content-frameworks

Pearson, P. D. (2004). The reading wars. *Educational Policy, 18,* 216–252.

Piaget, J. (1952). *The child's conception of number.* London, England: Routledge & Kegan Paul.

Piaget, J. (1960). *The child's conception of geometry.* London, England: Routledge & Kegan Paul.

Pólya, G. (1945). *How to solve it.* Princeton, NJ: Princeton University Press.

Reeve, W. D. (1938). Editor's preface. In H. P. Fawcett (Ed.), *The nature of proof: A description and evaluation of certain procedures used in a senior high school to develop an understanding of the nature of proof. Thirteenth Yearbook of the National Council of Teachers of Mathematics* (p. v). New York, NY: Teachers College Bureau of Publications.

Research for Action. (2015). *MDC's influence on teaching and learning.* Philadelphia, PA: Author.

Resnick, L. (1988). Treating mathematics as an ill-structured discipline. In R. Charles & E. Silver (Eds.), *The teaching and assessing of mathematical problem solving* (pp. 32–60). Reston, VA: National Council of Teachers of Mathematics.

Resnick, L., & Klopfer, L. (1989). *Toward the thinking curriculum: Current cognitive research.* Alexandria, VA: Association for Supervision and Curriculum Development.

Rogoff, B., & Lave, J. (1984). *Everyday cognition: Its development in social context.* Cambridge, MA: Harvard University Press.

Schoenfeld, A. H. (1981). Review of John G. Harvey and Thomas A. Romberg's problem-solving studies in mathematics. *Journal for Research in Mathematics Education, 12,* 386–390.

Schoenfeld, A. H. (1985). *Mathematical problem solving.* Orlando, FL: Academic Press.

Schoenfeld, A. H. (1988). Problem solving in contexts. In R. Charles & E. Silver (Eds.), *The teaching and assessing of mathematical problem solving* (pp. 82–92). Reston, VA: National Council of Teachers of Mathematics.

Schoenfeld, A. H. (2004). The math wars. *Educational Policy, 18,* 253–286.

Schoenfeld, A. H. (2006). Design experiments. In P. B. Elmore, G. Camilli, & J. Green (Eds.), *Handbook of complementary methods in education research* (pp. 193–206). Washington, DC: American Educational Research Association.

Schoenfeld, A. H. (2007). Method. In F. Lester (Ed.), *Handbook of research on mathematics teaching and learning* (2nd ed., pp. 69–107). Charlotte, NC: Information Age.

Schoenfeld, A. H. (2011). *How we think.* New York, NY: Routledge.

Schoenfeld, A. H. (2014). What makes for powerful classrooms, and how can we support teachers in creating them? *Educational Researcher, 43,* 404–412. doi:10.3102/0013189X1455

Schoenfeld, A. H. (2016). 100 Years of curriculum history, theory, and research. *Educational Researcher, 45,* 105–111.

Schoenfeld, A. H., & Pearson, P. D. (2009). The reading and math wars. In G. Sykes, B. Schneider, & D. Plank (Eds.), *Handbook of education policy research* (pp. 560–580). New York, NY: Routledge.

Schorling, R. (1995). Suggestions for the solution of an important problem that has arisen in the last quarter of a century. In C. Austin, H. English, W. Betz, W. Eells, & F. Touton (Eds.), *National Council of Teachers of Mathematics' first yearbook: A general survey of progress in the last twenty-five years* (pp. 58–105). Reston, VA: National Council of Teachers of Mathematics. (Original work published 1926)

Secada, W., Fennema, E., & Adajian, L. B. (Eds.). (1995). *New directions for equity in mathematics education.* Cambridge, England: Cambridge University Press.

Senk, S., & Thompson, D. (Eds.). (2003). *Standards-based school mathematics curricula: What are they? What do students learn?* Mahwah, NJ: Lawrence Erlbaum.

Sfard, A. (2008). *Thinking as communicating.* Cambridge, England: Cambridge University Press.

Sherin, M., Jacobs, V., & Philipp, R. (Eds.). (2010). *Mathematics teacher noticing: Seeing through teachers' eyes.* New York, NY: Routledge.

Shulman, L. S. (1970). Psychology and mathematics education. In E. G. Begle (Ed.), *Mathematics education: The sixty-ninth yearbook of the National Society for the Study of Education* (pp. 23–71). Chicago, IL: National Society for the Study of Education.

Shulman, L. S. (1986). Those who understand: Knowledge growth in teaching. *Educational Researcher, 17*(1), 4–14.

Shumway, R. (Ed.). (1980). *Research in mathematics education.* Reston, VA: National Council of Teachers of Mathematics.

Silver, E. (Ed.). (1985). *Teaching and learning mathematical problem solving: Multiple research perspectives.* Hillsdale, NJ: Lawrence Erlbaum.

Silver, E., & Herbst, P. (2007). Theory in mathematics education scholarship. In F. Lester (Ed.), *Handbook of research on mathematics teaching and learning* (2nd ed., pp. 39–68). Charlotte, NC: Information Age.

Silver, E., & Kilpatrick, J. (1988). Testing mathematical problem solving. In R. Charles & E. Silver (Eds.), *The teaching and assessing of mathematical problem solving* (pp. 178–186). Reston, VA: National Council of Teachers of Mathematics.

Skinner, B. F. (1945). The operational analysis of psychological terms. *Psychological Review, 52,* 260–277.

Skinner, B. F. (1958). Teaching machines. *Science, 128,* 969–977.

Sleeman, D., & Brown, J. S. (1982). *Intelligent tutoring systems.* New York, NY: Academic Press.

Smarter Balanced Assessment Consortium. (2012). *Content specifications for the summative assessment of the Common Core State Standards for Mathematics.* Retrieved from http://www.smarterbalanced.org/smarter-balanced-assessments/

Smarter Balanced Assessment Consortium. (2015). *Mathematics summative assessment blueprint* (As of 02/09/15). Retrieved from http://www.smarterbalanced.org/wp-content/uploads/2015/08/Mathematics_Blueprint.pdf

Smith, D. E. (1995). A general survey of the progress of mathematics in our high schools in the last twenty-five years. In C. Austin, H. English, W. Betz, W. Eells, & F. Touton (Eds.), *National Council of Teachers of Mathematics' first yearbook: A general survey of progress in the last twenty-five years* (pp. 1–31). Reston, VA: National Council of Teachers of Mathematics. (Original work published 1926)

Sowder, J. (Ed.). (1989). *Setting a research agenda*. Reston, VA: National Council of Teachers of Mathematics.

Stanic, G. M. A. (1987). Mathematics education in the United States at the beginning of the twentieth century. In T. S. Popkewitz (Ed.), *The formation of school subjects: The struggle for creating an American institution* (pp. 147–183). New York, NY: Falmer.

Steffe, L., Nesher, P., Cobb, P., Goldin, G., & Greer, B. (1996). *Theories of mathematical learning*. Mahwah, NJ: Lawrence Erlbaum.

Stigler, J., & Hiebert, J. (1999). *The teaching gap*. New York, NY: Free Press.

Stinson, D. W., & Bullock, E. C. (2012). Critical postmodern theory in mathematics education research: A praxis of uncertainty. *Educational Studies in Mathematics, 80*(1–2), 41–55.

Stokes, D. E. (1997). *Pasteur's quadrant: Basic science and technical innovation*. Washington, DC: Brookings Institution Press.

Swan, M. (2006). *Collaborative learning in mathematics: A challenge to our beliefs and practices*. Leicester, England: National Institute for Advanced and Continuing Education and National Research and Development Centre for Adult Literacy and Numeracy.

Takahashi, A. (2008). *Beyond show and tell: Neriage for teaching through problem-solving—Ideas from Japanese problem-solving approaches for teaching mathematics*. Paper presented at the 11th International Congress on Mathematics Education (Section TSG 19: Research and Development in Problem Solving in Mathematics Education), Monterrey, Mexico.

Tate, W. F. (1997). Critical race theory and education: History, theory, and implications. *Review of Research in Education, 22*, 195–247.

Tate, W. F., & D'Ambrosio, B. (Eds.). (1997). Equity, mathematics reform, and research: Crossing boundaries in search of understanding [Special issue]. *Journal for Research on Mathematics Education, 28*, 649–782.

Thompson, A. (1984). The relationship of teachers' conceptions of mathematics and mathematics teaching to instructional practice. *Educational Studies in Mathematics, 15*, 105–127.

Thompson, A. (1988). Learning to teach mathematical problem solving: Changes in teachers' beliefs and conceptions. In R. Charles & E. Silver (Eds.), *The teaching and assessing of mathematical problem solving* (pp. 232–243). Reston, VA: National Council of Teachers of Mathematics.

Thompson, A. (1992). Teachers' beliefs and conceptions: A synthesis of the research. In D. Grouws (Ed.), *Handbook of research on mathematics teaching and learning* (pp. 127–146). New York, NY: Macmillan.

Thorndike, E. (1911). *Animal intelligence: Experimental studies*. New York, NY: Macmillan.

University of California at Berkeley & Michigan State University. (2016). *Algebra Teaching Study*. Retrieved from http://ats.berkeley.edu/tools.html

University of Michigan. (2016). *TeachingWorks*. Retrieved from http://www.teachingworks.org/work-of-teaching

U.S. Census Bureau. (2015). *Percentage of U.S. population age 25 and over by educational attainment, 1940–2014*. Retrieved from http://www.census.gov/hhes/socdemo/education/data/cps/historical/index.html

Wagner, S., & Kieran, C. (Eds.). (1988). *Research issues in the learning and teaching of algebra*. Reston, VA: National Council of Teachers of Mathematics.

Watson, J. B. (1913). Psychology as the behaviorist views it. *Psychological Review, 20*, 158–177.

Wenger, E. (1998). *Communities of practice. Learning, meaning and identity.* Cambridge, England: Cambridge University Press.

Wertheimer, M. (1945). *Productive thinking.* New York, NY: Harper & Row.

The White House. (2009). *Fact sheet: The Race to the Top.* Retrieved from https://www.whitehouse.gov/the-press-office/fact-sheet-race-top

Wittrock, M. (Ed.). (1986). *Handbook of research on teaching* (3rd ed.). New York, NY: Macmillan.

Zbiek, R., Heid, M. K., Blume, G., & Dick, T. (2007). Research on technology in mathematics education. In F. Lester (Ed.), *Handbook of research on mathematics teaching and learning* (2nd ed., pp. 1169–1207). Charlotte, NC: Information Age.

Chapter 15

Science Education: From Separation to Integration

MARCIA C. LINN
LIBBY GERARD
University of California, Berkeley

CAMILLIA MATUK
New York University

KEVIN W. MCELHANEY
SRI International

Advances in technology, science, and learning sciences research over the past 100 years have reshaped science education. This chapter focuses on how investigators from varied fields of inquiry who initially worked separately began to interact, eventually formed partnerships, and recently integrated their perspectives to strengthen science education. Advances depended on the broadening of the participants in science education research, starting with psychologists, science discipline experts, and science educators; adding science teachers, psychometricians, computer scientists, and sociologists; and eventually including leaders in cultural studies, linguistics, and neuroscience. This process depended on renegotiating power structures, deliberate funding decisions by the National Science Foundation and others, and sustained, creative teamwork. It reflects a growing commitment to ensure that all learners are respected and that all students learn to address the complex scientific dilemmas they face in their lives. This chapter traces the evolution of research on science education in the United States with a focus on 5- to 17-year-olds. It highlights trends in the view of the learner, the design of instruction, the role of professional development, and the impact of technology. The chapter closes with recommendations designed to realize the full potential of these advances.

Advances in technology, science, and learning sciences research over the past 100 years have reshaped science education. Opportunities are now rife to align

Review of Research in Education
March 2016, Vol. 40, pp. 529–587
DOI: 10.3102/0091732X16680788
© 2016 AERA. http://rre.aera.net

science instruction with the needs of citizens (National Science Foundation [NSF] Taskforce on Cyberlearning, 2008), especially given the growing urgency of the need for science literacy for all (Dewey, 1897; National Research Council [NRC], 2005, 2007; American Association for the Advancement of Science (AAAS; 2013a). These opportunities arise against the backdrop of expanding and multidisciplinary scientific knowledge, America's increasing cultural diversity, substantial changes in science education policies, and the systemic nature of science and education. Research in science education has increasingly integrated insights from diverse fields (e.g., science disciplines, psychology, technology, sociology; cultural studies) while also developing new research methods and more multidisciplinary organizational structures.

Through discussion of selected research, we analyze the shift within science education research from separate fields to integrated programs, with a focus on science learning in and out of school among 5- to 17-year-old students in the United States. We identify four periods (see Table 1 for a timeline of notable events over the past 100 years). The first period, from 1916 to 1960, starts with Dewey's (1916) call for inquiry learning and ends with the United States' initial response to the launch of the Sputnik satellite by the Soviet Union. This period is characterized by separate investigations from different fields of inquiry (such as psychology, physics, chemistry, biology, engineering, and psychometrics) into questions relevant to science education. The second period (1960–1980) is marked by the funding of new curriculum materials in response to Sputnik. It ends with the founding of the Cognitive Science Society. During this period, science education research is largely conducted by discipline experts who draw on the writings of Bruner (1960) as they construct curriculum materials. These discipline experts interact with science education researchers to evaluate their programs and with teachers to enact the materials. The third period (1980–1995) starts with the emergence of personal computers and a diversifying population and ends with the first international comparison test in science (Third International Mathematics and Science Study [TIMSS]; see Schmidt, Raizen, Britton, Bianchi, & Wolfe, 1997). During this period, those concerned with science education often formed partnerships and added experts in technology, professional development, and sociology to solve challenges in education. The call of the new NSF director to diversify the workforce led to a focus on meeting the needs of diverse learners. The final period (1995–2016) starts with the founding of NSF centers and includes the development of the field of the learning sciences. During this period, researchers integrated insights from new disciplines now seen as essential (such as linguistics and cultural studies) and broadened the contexts they considered (including out-of-school opportunities). Events over the past 100 years stimulated regular reformulation of the nature of science education as themes continuously emerged and reemerged, and ultimately became integrated into the complex whole of our current understanding of science education (Figure 1).

We explore the trends over the past 100 years from four perspectives: The view of the learner, the nature of instruction, the view of the teacher, and the impact of technological advances. We end by reflecting on remaining challenges for the upcoming years and offer recommendations based on our review.

TABLE 1

Notable Events in the History of Science Education

1916–1960 Separation Period: Growing emphasis on science education in science disciplines, psychology, and preparation of teachers

1916	*General Science Quarterly* founded to publish science education articles
1925	Radio broadcast of science classes for anyone within listening distance
1925	Classroom filmstrip projectors show science content
1928	National Association for Research in Science Teaching (NARST) is founded
	NARST purchases *General Science Quarterly* and renames it *Science Education*
1932	National Society for the Study of Education Yearbook features science education
1936	The Universal Turing Machine, by Alan Turing, gives rise to modern computing
1938	*American Biology Teacher* journal is founded
1940	50% of 17-year-olds graduate from high school
1944	National Science Teachers Association is founded
1945	Vannevar Bush proposes National Science Foundation (NSF) to President Truman
1947	National Society for the Study of Education Yearbook addresses science education in American schools
1952	IBM releases first mainframe computer
	The Federal Communications Commission allocates 242 television channels for educational programming
1953	NSF is established
1955	Half of American households own a television set and seven stations are allocated to educational programming
1956	Sputnik is launched by the Soviet Union
1957	Skinner Teaching Machine
1959	Xerox photocopier replaces mimeograph machines in schools

1960–1980 Interaction Period: NSF to Cognitive Science: Beginning interactions between natural scientists and psychologists, teachers

1960	NSF funding for education more than triples; curriculum materials published
	Overhead projectors invented
1963	NARST founds *Journal of Research in Science Teaching*
	Biological Sciences Curriculum Study published D
1964	American Association for the Advancement of Science establishes a Commission on Science Education
	BASIC designed by Kemeny and Kurtz
1967	Logo programming language developed by Bobrow, Feurzeig, Papert, and Solomon
1969	First Logo turtle robot
1970	National Assessment of Educational Progress measures science in Grades 4, 8, and 12
1971	Intel microprocessor is announced

(continued)

TABLE 1 (CONTINUED)

1972	Public Law 99-372, the NSF Authorization Act establishes NSF responsibility for science education
	1972 Scantron Corporation is founded
	Dynabook proposed as children's personal computer
1976	*Journal of Cognitive Science Society* founded
1977	Apple II Computer introduced with BASIC computer language software
1979	The Cognitive Science Society is founded

1980–1995 Partnership Period: Technology to International Assessment: Spurred by NSF funding natural scientists, science education researchers, and teachers form partnerships

1980	Time, Inc., launches *Discover Magazine*
	IBM PC introduced
	Data projectors
	PLATO system most used computer in classrooms
	First systems for wearable computing introduced
1981	NSF announces CSNET, precursor to the Internet
	First portable computer
1982	President Ronald Reagan's budget cuts NSF funding for education
	Commodore 64 introduced
	Apple Wheels for the Mind competition for computer donations
1983	*A Nation-At-Risk* published by the National Commission on Excellence in Education
1984	Macintosh computer introduced
1987	NSF upgrades science education in Grades K–12
1991	*Journal of the Learning Sciences* founded
1992	*Journal of Science and Technology Education* founded

1995–2015 Integration Period: Science Education Centers to Next Generation Science Standards (NGSS): Multidisciplinary centers encourage participation of all relevant stakeholders

1995	Third International Mathematics and Science Study
	NSF funds Center for Innovative Learning Technologies
1996	The National Research Council produces the National Science Education Standards
1998	Google is founded
1999	Interactive whiteboards introduced in science classrooms
	NetLogo is released
2001	Wikipedia is launched
2002	International Society of the Learning Sciences founded
	NSF funds Centers for Learning and Teaching
2003	NSF funds Science of Learning Centers
2006	*The International Journal of Computer-Supported Collaborative Learning* founded
2008	StarLogo released
2010	Apple iPad is released
2012	*NGSS. A framework for K–12 Science Education: Practices, Crosscutting Concepts, and Core Ideas*

(continued)

TABLE 1 (CONTINUED)

2013	NGSS Lead States. (2013). *Next Generation Science Standards: For States, By States*. Washington, DC: National Academies Press Year of the MOOC (Massive Open Online Courses), as declared by the *New York Times* (2012)

VIEW OF THE SCIENCE LEARNER

This section explores how the view of the science learner evolved over the past 100 years as researchers integrated perspectives from multiple disciplines. We focus on studies and perspectives that have had particular influence on the design of curriculum and instruction, teacher education, and technologies that support science education.

1916–1960: Multiple Perspectives on the Learner

Natural scientists typically viewed learners as absorbing information and designed lectures, demonstrations, and experiments to transmit information. Behaviorists reinforced the transmission view by studying stimulus–response connections and investigating memory and retrieval of information (e.g., Thorndike, 1912). Skinner's (1938) work on operant conditioning (building on Watson, 1913) emphasized reward for desired behavior and inspired programmed texts (Pressey, 1926). Cronbach (1963) argued that psychology research had minimal effects on science curriculum design; however, teacher preparation programs required psychology courses emphasizing behaviorism, and student assessments generally measured recall of details. Meanwhile Dewey (1916), a philosopher, distinguished acquiring facts from using the methods of science and called for emphasizing scientific reasoning in science instruction.

Research on human reasoning informed by the emergence of the first transistorized computers in the 1950s led to what has been called the cognitive revolution (e.g., Broadbent, 1958; Gardner, 1985; Proctor & Vu, 2006). Computers provided cognitivists with a helpful analogy for the human mind as an information processor, a view of thinking and human behavior that remains popular today.

Meanwhile Piaget (1930) studied how his own children developed scientific insights and posited a theory featuring developmental constraints. He described a stage of concrete operations where children do not initially conserve mass or volume but, rather, believe that balls of clay are bigger when deformed into a pancake and that there is more orange juice when it is poured from a wide to a narrow cylinder. By studying physical systems such as pendulums, balance beams, and shadows, he distinguished concrete from formal operations, showing that older children could control variables (Inhelder & Piaget, 1958/1972). In his genetic epistemology, Piaget (1952) articulated mechanisms of assimilation and accommodation culminating in equilibration to describe how children respond to new information and advance across

FIGURE 1
The Changing Relationships Between Science Learners, Teachers, Instruction, and Technology

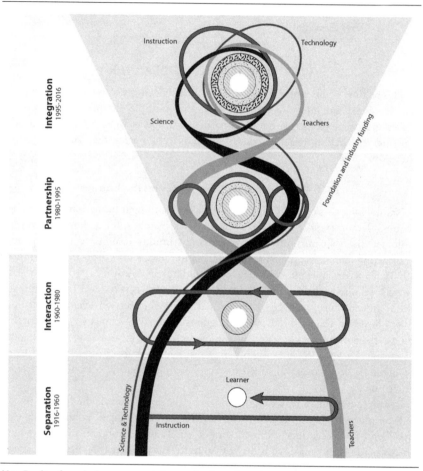

Note. Reading from the bottom toward the top, the figure shows how science and technology progressed in consistent synergy with one another throughout the century. In the Separation Period, science experts dictated the curriculum and teachers delivered it to students, with the goal of preparing future scientists. In the Interaction Period, science experts received funding from industries and foundations to design curriculum for teachers to deliver. In the Partnership Period, foundation-funded partnerships of discipline experts, teachers, technology experts, and science education researchers sought to prepare a broad audience of learners. In the Integration Period, funded centers promote integration of the views of discipline experts, teachers, technology experts, science education researchers, and sociocultural researchers to meet the needs of a diversifying student population, with an increasingly nuanced view of the learner, teacher, and curriculum.

stages. Flavell (1963) synthesized Piaget's developmental perspective, increasing its accessibility to educators.

1960–1980: Interacting Perspectives on Scientific Reasoning

In the 1960s, in response to the Soviet launch of Sputnik, the NSF funded natural scientists to lead curriculum reforms. Interactions with psychologists were spurred by an influential conference held at Woods Hole, Massachusetts, and captured in Bruner's (1960) *The Process of Education.* Bruner emphasized the generalizable science processes involved in problem solving, refuting developmental constraints, and asserting that any topic can be taught to learners of any age (Bruner, 1960, inspired by Polya, 1943).

The cognitive revolution continued in parallel with the development of curriculum materials. Vygotsky (1978) described the zone of proximal development as the progress that students make when given hints or social supports while solving difficult problems. Science education researchers documented the limits of science teachers' knowledge of disciplinary topics and conceptions of the nature of science (Kimball, 1968; Lederman, 1992).

Psychologists studied the development of logical reasoning, including ability to conduct and interpret controlled experiments, using tasks that did not require disciplinary knowledge. For example, Siegler and Liebert (1975) asked learners to determine how to set four binary switches to make an electric train run. In actuality, the train was operated by a researcher who would activate the train only when all 16 possible configurations had been tested by the learner. Students' prior knowledge of trains could not inform their hypotheses. Instead, they needed combinatorial reasoning to solve the problem. This experiment separated the role of prior scientific knowledge from the strategy of testing combinations. These studies were intended to characterize learners' development of logical strategies such as isolating variables or using combinatorial reasoning. However, lack of knowledge of the context could deter students from attempting a task that appeared to require specialized knowledge. In addition, logical strategies like combinatorial reasoning might benefit from instruction as well as development (Case, 1985; Duckworth, 1987).

Other investigators compared decontextualized versus context-rich isomorphic tasks. For example, the four-card problem (Wason, 1968, Wason & Johnson-Laird, 1972) asked students which card(s) they needed to turn over to test whether cards that had a number on one side and a letter on the other confirmed or falsified an abstract logical rule: If a card has a vowel on one side, then it has an even number on the other side. An isomorphic contextualized problem involved determining which people needed to be queried to determine whether people in a bar falsified the rule that one has to be older than 21 years to drink alcohol. The contextualized problem was much easier, yet did not completely clarify the role of domain knowledge in learners' reasoning processes (Tweney & Doherty, 1983).

Differential psychologists sought to identify components of reasoning, such as spatial abilities (French, Ekstrom, & Price, 1963). Spatial reasoning (essentially, the ability to interpret, generate, and recall spatial images) was thought to be important for scientific reasoning because many scientific phenomena cannot be observed with the naked eye. Psychologists (Liben, 1974; Sherman, 1967; Waddington, 1966), psychometricians (French et al., 1963; Lohman, 1988), and science educators (Linn, 1977; Pribyl & Bodner, 1987) studied spatial reasoning in abstract and scientific contexts. Cronbach and Snow (1977) studied aptitude treatment interactions to determine ways to create instruction that resonated with student characteristics. These studies revealed multiple dimensions of spatial reasoning. They showed that some spatial reasoning tasks correlated with scientific performance but did not establish the direction of causality, as both science topics and spatial reasoning were amenable to instruction.

1980–1995: Respecting and Building on Disciplinary Knowledge

In the early 1980s, psychologists and science education researchers delved into the relationship between learners' disciplinary knowledge and scientific reasoning. They explored multiple topics and varied problem contexts, such as testing hypotheses, designing experiments, and evaluating evidence. They generated evidence for a constructivist view of learners as actively making sense of the experiences they encountered. This view had roots in Piaget's (1952) genetic epistemology and Vygotsky's (1978) zone of proximal development.

Researchers found approaches to scientific tasks to be more consistent with learners' prior knowledge than with logical reasoning (e.g., Driver & Oldham, 1986; D. Kuhn, Amsel, & O'Loughlin, 1988; Linn, Clement, & Pulos, 1983; Schauble, Glaser, Raghavan, & Reiner, 1992; Tschirgi, 1980). Learners' reasoning approaches depended on numerous factors such as whether the learner was asked to describe a relationship between variables or to achieve a specific outcome (e.g., Schauble, Klopfer, & Raghavan, 1991; Vollmeyer, Burns, & Holyoak, 1996). Researchers demonstrated that prior knowledge could both foster and inhibit use of logical processes. Likewise, teachers' prior knowledge could foster or inhibit their use of inquiry teaching strategies (Blumenfeld et al., 1991). These studies underscored the interdependence of domain knowledge and scientific reasoning and provided a foundation for subsequent perspectives on integrating disciplinary knowledge and scientific practice. Detailed case studies of learners acquiring scientific ideas and generating explanations for phenomena clarified the nature of scientific knowledge and provided evidence for a constructivist view of learning (e.g., Baird, Fensham, Gunstone, & White, 1991). Other research cast doubt on the developmental constraints popularized by Piaget (Metz, 1995).

At the same time, Piaget's descriptions of student reasoning motivated researchers to look carefully at the concepts that students articulated. This resulted in a cottage industry focused on identifying student alternative ideas in a broad range of disciplines (Pfundt & Duit, 2009). Teachers elicited students' range of explanations (van

Zee & Minstrell, 1997). Some noted parallels between student ideas and ideas developing in the history of science (Wiser & Carey, 1983). Others noted characteristics of these ideas. For example, diSessa (1988) referred to student ideas as knowledge in pieces. He postulated a conception of phenomenological primitives (p-prims), deeply held ideas about science originating in everyday experiences. DiSessa illustrated how learners' failure to coherently explain everyday phenomena could be attributed largely to their incorrect application or overgeneralization of productive observations about science. For example, learners' understanding of force and motion in the everyday world are difficult to apply to environments without friction or gravity.

These studies supported multiple views of conceptual change. Some investigators described how learners abandon one idea in favor of a new one (Strike & Posner, 1985). Others depicted learners as holding coherent scientific theories that needed to be contradicted (S. Carey, 1985; Chi & Slotta, 1993; McCloskey, 1983; Vosniadou, 1994). DiSessa (1988) argued for supporting students to build on their intuitive ideas and spurred investigation of facets (Hunt & Minstrell, 1994) and knowledge integration (Linn, 1995; Linn, Songer, & Eylon, 1996; Songer & Linn, 1991). Studies of knowledge in pieces, facets, and knowledge integration continue to inform the design of innovations in classroom-based science instruction, assessment, professional development, and technology design.

Psychologists showed that memory demands (referred to as cognitive load) could inhibit reasoning enough to justify designing instruction that managed learners' short- and long-term memory (Chandler & Sweller, 1991; Sweller, 1988). Studies on learning from pictorial information accompanied by text (e.g., Mayer, 1989), audio narration (Mousavi, Low, & Sweller, 1995), or learning from computer-generated animations (e.g., Hegarty, Kriz, & Cate, 2003; Tversky, Morrison, & Betrancourt, 2002) demonstrated the importance of managing cognitive load.

Researchers sought to help students manage cognitive load and identified metacognition or awareness of one's own progress in learning as crucial (Flavell, 1971). In particular, learners' ability to self-monitor (Palincsar & Brown, 1984), self-explain (Chi & VanLehn, 1991), engage in intentional learning (Scardamalia & Bereiter, 1994), behave autonomously (Linn et al., 1996), and reflect back on what has been learned (Collins & Brown, 1988) or taught (Sweitzer & Anderson, 1983) gave rise to new possibilities for teaching, and for designing science instruction and teacher education. Metacognition represented a set of potentially generalizable learning skills necessary for lifelong learning. Metacognition informed new research on students' science epistemologies, such as students' view of the nature of scientific models (Grosslight, Unger, Jay, & Smith, 1991), the nature of scientific knowledge (S. Carey & Smith, 1993), and the purposes of scientific experiments (Schauble, Glaser, Duschl, Schulze, & John, 1995).

When standardized science tests such as the National Assessment of Educational Progress were first administered, in 1970 (Jones, 1988; Welsh, Kucinkas, & Curran, 1990), they revealed that students from families of low socioeconomic status and from some cultural groups were underperforming relative to White males. These results were often attributed to deficits of the learners. Yet many studies refuted the deficit idea, showing that question context (e.g., sailing vs. baseball) influenced the performance of cultural groups on items with similar reasoning requirements (Holland & Wainer, 1993). Professional development programs helped teachers guide students to connect their knowledge from everyday experiences to inquiry (Roseberry, Warren, & Conant, 1992).

Differential psychologists explored possible contributors to the deficit, including spatial reasoning. Research revealed correlations between science learning and various measures of spatial ability and also demonstrated the benefit of short exposure to spatial reasoning tasks to remediate performance (Lohman, 1988). Researchers also documented differences in exposure to spatial tasks and dramatic impacts of short training opportunities (e.g., Baenninger & Newcombe, 1989; Linn & Petersen, 1985; Maccoby & Jacklin, 1974). This research illustrated the importance of opportunity to learn and disputed the idea of inherent deficits.

1995–2016: Integrating Perspectives in the Learning Sciences

In the mid-1990s, science education's model of the learner was still largely derived from studies conducted in psychology laboratories rather than classrooms. New research methods led to fruitful, complex studies in classrooms. These studies revealed the important role of the learning context. For instance, students could simultaneously believe that in the real world, moving objects slow down to a stop, but in the physics classroom, objects remain in motion until acted on by an external force. These investigations brought together researchers from diverse fields such as psychology, sociology, technology, education, and design, as well as school-based teachers and administrators who all shared interests in learning and instruction. In addition, individuals from new, relevant fields, including sociocultural studies and neuroscience, contributed ideas that were integrated into investigations of learning. The complexity of learning, along with the advantages of combining multiple perspectives, gave rise to the learning sciences discipline. Those attracted to the learning sciences sought to explain learning in authentic settings, such as everyday problem solving, and to identify ways to build on the cultural commitments of all learners.

New methods for research were needed and emerged. A. L. Brown (1992) and Collins (1992) proposed increasing reliance on design-based research methodologies, which intertwine the design of learning environments and learning theories, use iterative cycles of design and enactment, result in relevant implications for practitioners, occur in authentic settings, and connect learning processes to learning outcomes (Design-Based Research Collective, 2003). Research extended beyond the classroom and into informal settings (NRC, 2009). Connections to diverse stakeholders at the district and community levels began to emerge (Fishman, Penuel, Allen, Cheng, & Sabelli, 2013).

Several new aspects of the learner model became increasingly prominent as learning studies occurred in authentic settings. Collaboration and the community-based practice of science, long observed in professional settings (T. S. Kuhn, 1962), became a central research theme in studies of classroom-based learning (A. L. Brown & Campione, 1994; Scardamalia & Bereiter, 1994). Learning in collaborative settings requires students to acquire an increasing awareness about the ideas of their peers (Clark & Jorde, 2004; Linn & Hsi, 2000) and to respect their peers' ideas in addition to those of their teacher (Cohen, 1994). Moreover, studies found that learners' cultural backgrounds and gender influenced collaborative behaviors (e.g., Bagno & Eylon, 1997; Burbules & Linn, 1991; Howe & Tolmie, 2003).

Research also uncovered the importance of motivating students by illustrating the relevance of science to students and building on the concerns of the students themselves. Researchers on motivation (e.g., Pintrich, Marx, & Boyle, 1993) made arguments for integrating affective and cognitive views on learning. Studies examining the intersection of science and language (e.g., B. A. Brown, 2006; O. Lee, 2005), culture (Polman & Pea, 2001), and identity (Barton, 1998) shed light on ways to increase the accessibility and relevance of science for learners from diverse backgrounds. Studies on learners' participation in community-based science (Bouillion & Gomez, 2001; Fusco, 2001), in addition to valuing and leveraging the ideas of others, helped focus learners on relevant community problems, further contributing to broadening participation in science.

Finally, learning sciences research strengthened connections across science knowledge, science practice, and other learning perspectives. For example, comprehensive programs often supported by NSF centers, such as ThinkerTools (B. Y. White & Frederiksen, 1998) and the Web-based Inquiry Science Environment (WISE; Linn & Eylon, 2011) were able to integrate science practices, metacognition, and science visualizations in the discipline of physics or physical science. Sandoval (2005) explored relationships between science inquiry and students' practical epistemologies. Research reviews have integrated classroom-based research studies focusing on specific practices of science, such as (a) argumentation (e.g., Bell & Linn, 2000), (b) explanation (e.g., Sandoval & Reiser, 2004), (c) modeling (e.g., Wu, Krajcik, & Soloway, 2001), (d) visualizing (e.g., McElhaney, Chang, Chiu, & Linn, 2015), collaborating (Kyndta et al., 2013), and (f) conducting experiments (e.g., Lehrer, Schauble, & Petrosino, 2001). These studies demonstrate the tight link between the practice of science and advances in students' conceptual views of science. These studies informed the science-as-practice perspective (Duschl, 2008), the Framework for K–12 Science Education (NRC, 2012), and the Next Generation Science Standards (NGSS; NGSS Lead States, 2013).

In summary, research on the science learner has progressed from separated disciplines to integrated research programs. Initially, psychologists studied learning from the standpoint of memorization and had minimal influence on either science educators or science discipline experts. The launch of Sputnik spurred interactions between science discipline experts who led reforms to the curriculum and psychologists, as well as science teachers, as discussed in the next section. In the 1980s, these interactions were often converted into partnerships where experts from multiple disciplines gained respect for each other, fostered in part by new NSF-funding programs requiring collaborations between discipline experts and science educators. This accompanied a weakening of the distinction between science reasoning or methods and scientific ideas. A plethora of empirical work focused on students' conceptual understanding, new reasoning tasks that sought to separate disciplinary and reasoning processes, and connections to spatial reasoning, as well as cognitive load. Starting in the mid-1990s, true integration of perspectives became more common. The audience for science education became more diverse, and the goals of educating all students to address personally relevant problems became more important. Sociocultural research perspectives were incorporated and respected as the field sought to prepare all students to tackle problems throughout their lives. This integration was in part stimulated by NSF funding for centers that involved multidisciplinary collaborations. Other factors included a focus on conducting research in classrooms, the emergence of computer technologies that could help monitor student progress, and research showing the importance of incorporating cultural perspectives into education research.

Much work is still needed to achieve a full integration of the perspectives relevant to the challenges facing science education today. We discuss some of these opportunities as we consider the historical development of science instruction in the following section.

SCIENCE INSTRUCTION

The trend from separation to integration of research on science instruction reflects the impact of NSF funding policies, along with shifts in the power structures among the participants. Science education was initially led by natural scientists, who often sought to prepare individuals like themselves. NSF funding for curriculum materials and for teacher institutes in the 1960s put natural scientists in charge. Funding for research on teaching and learning, starting in the 1980s, and for NSF centers, starting in 1995, called for collaborations where leadership was shared across natural scientists, psychologists, science educators, and often technology experts, as well as teachers. Importantly, in 1980, Erich Block, the eighth director of NSF, called for diversifying the workforce by broadening participation in science education, initiating a trend that is reflected in NSF guidelines for all funding today.

As researchers from distinct fields began to interact, form partnerships, and eventually integrate their perspectives, they reconceptualized science instruction. Initially, the science curriculum was designed to transmit science knowledge. As high school education became almost universal and science requirements for graduation expanded, the audience for secondary science courses broadened from an elite group of men (who were often admitted on passing entrance examinations) to a culturally diverse population who regularly questioned the value of their science courses. Instructional designers interacted with psychologists studying learning or child development, classroom teachers reported on student responses to the curriculum materials, and science education researchers documented the complexities of preparing teachers. They formulated views of instruction that recognized the role of the learner in making sense of science. New frameworks emerged to address the challenge of preparing diverse students to grapple with scientific problems they encounter in their lives. These instructional frameworks include communities of learners (e.g., A. L. Brown & Campione, 1994), science as practice (e.g., Duschl, 2008), and knowledge integration (e.g., Linn & Eylon, 2011).

This section articulates some of the persistent (and unresolved) dilemmas in science instruction and highlights how education researchers built on expertise from multiple research disciplines to integrate views of instruction.

Persistent Challenges in Science Instruction

During the past 100 years, some instructional challenges have resisted resolution. Perhaps the most prominent challenge concerns selecting topics to include in the curriculum. Each branch of science has representatives lobbying for the importance of topics from their field. From Philip Morrison's argument that "less is more" in the 1960s to the TIMSS analysis of the curriculum as "a mile wide and an inch deep" (Schmidt et al., 1997), the superficial coverage of topics has been unavoidable for curriculum designers and those setting standards. A related issue concerns controversial topics, such as evolution, that have been debated, banned, and voted out of the curriculum in some districts (Berkman & Plutzer, 2010; Pew Research Center, 2009), often when powerful interest groups have falsely portrayed uncertainty about a specific finding as doubt about established phenomena such as global warming or the health risks of smoking (Conway & Oreskes, 2010). Students have little chance to develop coherent understanding when confronted with more than 60 distinct topics in a single year. In contrast, the Japanese science curriculum is both frugal—often covering only eight topics in a year—and more coherent (Linn, Lewis, Tsuchida, & Songer, 2000).

Another persistent challenge concerns how to sequence science topics in the curriculum to ensure that students have the prerequisite knowledge, are developmentally ready to learn the material, and can integrate new ideas with prior knowledge. The National Society for the Study of Education devoted its 1932 yearbook to sequencing the science curriculum. Yet earth scientists complained that their discipline was neglected (E. B. Lewis, 2008). Bruner's (1960) spiral curriculum was designed to allow students to build on their prior coverage by revisiting topics. Analyses of this approach demonstrated that most textbooks failed to build on prior instruction and instead retaught the topic at the same level of detail (Schmidt et al., 1997). Efforts to address this challenge have resulted in the placement of complex topics at progressively earlier points in the curriculum. For example, the California standards (1998) placed the periodic table in Grade 3, far in advance of when students are most likely to grasp its basic meaning.

Few empirical studies support a specific sequence. Bruner's (1960) claim that students can learn any topic at any age further eroded support for specific sequences.

Bruner's claim revealed the need to specify a topic's level of detail or abstraction to analyze its role in a sequence. Simplifying a topic, even to the extent of neglecting key ideas, might pave the way for future understanding (Feynman, Leighton, & Sands, 1995; Linn & Muilenburg, 1996). Recently, researchers have sought evidence to distinguish among alternative enacted topic sequences to determine which are more effective learning progressions (e.g., Duncan, Rogat, & Yarden, 2009).

1916–1960: Separation of Curriculum and Instruction

Between 1916 and 1960, psychologists studying learning had little interaction with science education. A review of research in science education concluded that most research studies involved some form of survey of curriculum or of student reasoning (H. Smith, 1963). Vocabulary analyses revealed that texts frequently used words beyond the level of the students, possibly because textbooks were often written by natural scientists with the goal of transmitting scientific knowledge. For example, Millikan, a Nobel laureate, wrote with H. G. Gale (1906), many college texts as well as A Laboratory Course in Physics for Secondary Schools. Science assessments embedded in the textbooks typically called for memorizing and retrieving science information.

The audience for secondary science education was initially White and male, and many high schools had entrance examinations for admission prior to the growth of the high school in the 1930s (Goldin, 2008). Few non-White students attended beyond elementary school, and high schools were not available for non-Whites in the segregated South. In cities, immigrants were less likely to enroll than others. The emergence of high schools created a need for science teachers and a market for science textbooks. Schools often had a single science teacher who taught all science topics.

Surveys of syllabi and textbooks concluded that there was a great diversity of goals and topics taught across schools (H. Smith, 1963). Dewey (1916) called for replacing the emphasis on nature study in elementary education with attention to science methods. Others emphasized identifying key scientific concepts necessary for all learners. One high school biology teacher, Ella Thea Smith, who had trained as a botanist, wrote her own biology textbook after becoming frustrated by the mainly phylogenetic biology textbooks, such as Truman J. Moon's *Biology for Beginners* (Moon & Mann, 1933), that had separate sections on botany, zoology, and human physiology (Ladouceur, 2008). E. T. Smith's (1938) book, the first of its kind with a female lead author, was eventually published as *Exploring Biology*. It emphasized appreciation of nature and of natural cycles and processes across topics in biology.

During the separation period, researchers studied science reasoning and documented the plethora of student ideas about each science topic. They found that elementary students had multiple ideas about curricular topics such as magnetism, the moon, and atomic energy (Haupt, 1948; Young, 1958), consistent with Piaget's (1930) findings for conservation and experimentation. Surveys showed a disparity between the ideas of girls and boys that was attributed to cultural differentiation and expectations for the sexes starting at an early age (H. Smith, 1963). Curriculum developers rarely paid attention to these rich insights, focusing instead on transmitting information.

1960–1980: Interaction Led by Natural Scientists

With the Sputnik launch came a wake-up call to improve science education in the United States. Physics, biology, and chemistry professors secured substantial funding from NSF to create new curriculum materials and initiated interactions with science teachers, psychologists, and science educators.

New curriculum materials focused on preparing students to think like the scientists who designed them. Designers embraced Bruner's (1960) claim that it was possible to teach any topic to learners of any age. Chase and Simon's (1973) finding that the development of expertise requires 10,000 hours, reinforced the idea of pushing complex topics down into earlier grades (Goldstein, 1992). Not surprisingly, designers created instruction that was too difficult for most students and textbooks that could not be covered in the time allocated (Curtis, 1963). The main response to the difficulty of the texts was to create versions with reduced demands rather than seek ways to make the instruction effective for a broader range of learners. In addition, the designers often criticized the teachers for not successfully teaching the material in the texts (Welch, 1979).

Designers of elementary curriculum materials were more likely to interact with researchers on learning than were designers of secondary materials. For example, the Science Curriculum Improvement Study incorporated theoretical principles from the work of Piaget (Karplus, 1964). These curricula included instructional frameworks, such as the Science Curriculum Improvement Study learning cycle, involving exploration, invention, and discovery to guide use of kits of materials.

Classroom laboratory experiments involved more discovery than was typical with prior materials, yet were also focused on abstract ideas and principles. For example, Zacharias, the designer of Physical Science Study Committee, was particularly enthusiastic about the study of wave motion and admonished teachers to test their wave tanks in September so they would be ready for use (Goldstein, 1992). Designers, recognizing the visual nature of science, created filmstrips to illustrate scientific phenomena that were difficult to observe (Chemical Education Material Study, 1963).

Research using surveys and analyses of national tests compared performance of subgroups of students. Analysis of National Assessment of Educational Progress data from 1970 to 1980 interpreted findings that women took fewer science courses and were less successful than men as indicating a deficit in women (Mullis, Jenkins, & Lynn, 1988). Another approach explored aptitude–treatment interactions to find ways to support all learners (Cronbach & Snow, 1977). For example, research showed the advantage of instruction that strengthened areas of weakness such as spatial reasoning to help all learners.

During the interaction period, researchers compared student reasoning between typical and new curriculum materials (e.g., Wollman, 1977). Evaluations of the

NSF-funded curricula often showed advantages over typical instruction (Bowyer & Linn, 1978; Linn & Thier, 1975). A meta-analysis of these studies supported the value of asking students to generate explanations by showing that the innovative curricula did no harm to students' performance on state tests that primarily measured recall. In fact, these curricula led to higher scores on assessments with which they were aligned (Shymansky, Hedges, & Woodworth, 1990). Most interpretations of the results ascribed the effectiveness of the innovative curriculum to general features (e.g., hands-on activities) that were not sufficient to guide future design. A few studies offered more mechanistic accounts of the results, such as by demonstrating the value of generating explanations, consistent with psychology laboratory studies that identify an effect of generating explanations on learning (e.g., Slamecka & Graf, 1978).

1980–1995: Partnerships to Improve Science Instruction

The education directorate at NSF was established in 1975 and began a small research program around 1980. The Research in Teaching and Learning program, led by program officer Ray Hannapel, required proposers to form partnerships involving science educators, science discipline experts, and teachers. In 1984, taking advantage of the IBM PC (1981), the Commodore 64 (1982), and the Macintosh (1984), Andrew Molnar became director of the Applications of Advanced Technologies program. Applications of Advanced Technologies was the first NSF effort to support partnerships between researchers and developers. Molnar called for high-risk, high-gain initiatives. These research programs supported investigations of learning in and out of school and encouraged researchers to challenge the deficit model and address opportunity and inclination to learn.

In a review, Eylon and Linn (1988) delineated four emerging research traditions that engaged partnerships (concept learning, development, individual differences, and problem solving). Although most of the research was conducted in laboratories rather than classrooms, these traditions all offered some support for instruction that encouraged students to make sense of their multiple, often conflicting ideas. Work on concept learning continued to reveal the multiple, diverse ideas each student held about scientific phenomena (e.g., diSessa, 1988; McCloskey, 1983) and gave rise to conflicting instructional implications. Some viewed learners as holding fragmented ideas they could be motivated to sort out (e.g., Linn, 1995; J. P. Smith, diSessa, & Roschelle, 1993). Others saw students as having naïve, coherent theories that required refutation (Vosniadou & Brewer, 1992).

Researchers extended this focus to document how students' developing beliefs about their own learning were intertwined with beliefs about the epistemology of science (Hofer & Pintrick, 1997). Focusing on autonomy, intentionality, and agency, researchers recognized the value of encouraging students to monitor their own progress (A. L. Brown, 1987). For example, Chi and collaborators demonstrated the advantage of self-explanations (Chi, Bassok, Lewis, Reimann, & Glaser, 1989). They found that students who spontaneously explained to themselves while learning were more successful than those who did not explain, consistent with the generation effect. Connecting to theories of motivation, studies demonstrated that science materials created to engage students in personally relevant problems could promote autonomy and strengthen science understanding (Linn, 1995; Norman & Schmidt, 1992; Pintrich, 2003).

Research following the developmental tradition often involved designing instruction to resonate with Piaget's stages and build on student capabilities such as concrete operations (Case, 1985). Other research studied how instruction might take advantage of mechanisms of accommodation and assimilation by varying the context of the problem (e.g., Linn et al., 1983). Emerging research showed the value of students' learning from others (Scardamalia & Bereiter, 1994).

Researchers focusing on individual differences looked for explanations of differential performance on science assessments. They considered stereotype threat: where students' perceptions of the risk of conforming to stereotypes for their social group may raise anxiety and depress performance (Steele, 1997; Steele & Aronson, 1995). They found that spatial reasoning, important for science, was amenable to instruction, rather than an impediment to success (Harle & Towns, 1963; Linn & Petersen, 1985).

Researchers focusing on problem solving compared experts and novices. A key study of categorization of physics problems noted that students focused on superficial features, while experts categorized problems using abstract principles (Chi, Feltovich, & Glaser, 1981). This work suggested the importance of instruction that guides students to distinguish superficial from substantive problem features.

These studies suggested synergies between science reasoning and science ideas. Students advanced their reasoning and developed their identity as scientists by reasoning about their ideas. They needed science ideas to engage in complex reasoning. Thus, researchers argued that learning, including learning about how to guide one's own learning, was situated in the discipline (Lave & Wenger, 1991). Careful observation of apprenticeship programs revealed the importance of learning by distinguishing one's own ideas from those of more successful students (Collins, Brown, & Newman, 1989; Vygotsky, 1978). Furthermore, partnerships with social psychologists showed that students could develop an identity as a science learner by integrating their ideas about compelling dilemmas in science contexts (Markus & Nurius, 1986).

Partnerships of science educators, psychologists, discipline experts, and science teachers contributed to the emerging science of learning. The *Journal of the Learning Sciences* was founded in 1991, providing an outlet for detailed analysis of complex learning and promoting multidisciplinary collaboration. Early issues reported laboratory studies of students' learning from self-explanations in physics (Chi & VanLehn, 1991) and from insights into causal reasoning through the study of electrical circuits (Schauble et al., 1991). Studies during this period contributed to instructional frameworks that supported guiding students, both individually and collaboratively, to construct their own understanding (A. L. Brown & Campione, 1994; Scardamalia & Bereiter, 1994). These frameworks, when tested in classrooms, offered preliminary design principles to guide those creating instructional materials. For example, the knowledge integration framework articulated design principles in four categories: make science accessible, make thinking visible, enable students to learn from each other, and promote autonomy (Linn, 1995).

1995–2016: Learning Sciences and Science Education

The integration period featured efforts to take advantage of the culturally complex and broadening audience for science education and to bridge the widening achievement gap in America's cities. Determining ways to offer meaningful instruction to all learners motivated the integration of research on linguistic diversity (O. Lee, 2005), epistemological beliefs (Sandoval, 2012), and student identity (McNeill, Lizotte, Krajcik, & Marx, 2006; Sfard & Prusak, 2005). This effort accompanied a new understanding of the integral place of science in societal issues (Driver, Leach, Millar, & Scott, 1996; Millar, 1996; Millar & Hunt, 2001; Osborne, Duschl, & Fairbrother, 2002). Furthermore, contemporary problems, such as climate change, water shortages, energy depletion, and virus outbreaks, established the need to refocus science education on preparing students to become intentional, lifelong science learners.

Researchers recognized that the culturally diverse audience, along with the complex, systemic nature of science education, necessitated new research methods. Such methods needed to capture the multiple, interacting factors in science instruction and to gather evidence for principles that could guide instructional designers. Methods from sociocultural studies, such as ethnographies and microgenetic analyses, were adopted to characterize the role of social and cultural activities in learning in and out of school (diSessa, Elby, & Hammer, 2002; Engle & Conant, 2002; Hmelo, Holton, & Kolodner, 2000). Design research inspired by architecture, engineering, and computer science guided iterative refinement studies conducted in classrooms (Alexander, Ishikawa, & Silverstein, 1977; A. L. Brown, 1992; Collins, 1992; Cobb, Confrey, diSessa, Lehrer, & Schauble, 2003; Design-Based Research Collective, 2003). Design research conducted in realistic instructional settings with diverse learners allowed investigators to extract principles or patterns to generalize the process (Kali, 2006). It supported the simultaneous evolution of theory and design, and drove the intentional alignment between technology and research-based pedagogy. A theory of intentional learning, for example, evolved from Computer Supported Intentional Learning Environments (CSILE) to Knowledge Forum (Scardamalia & Bereiter, 2006); a theory of knowledge integration evolved from the Knowledge Integration Environment (KIE) to WISE (Linn, 1995; Slotta & Linn, 2009), and theories of learning-by-teaching with teachable agents emerged (Leelawong & Biswas, 2008).

Design research methods benefited from advances in technology that could capture fine-grained impacts on student learning and explore alternative approaches to personalizing instruction. Technology-enhanced learning environments can log student data, capture interactions with modeling environments, and record student collaboration. This rich evidence can inform customization of instruction (Gerard, Spitulnik, et al., 2010), design of personalized guidance (Gerard, Matuk, McElhaney, & Linn, 2015), and design of tools to help teachers diagnose student needs (Hoadley, 2002; Koedinger, McLaughlin, & Heffernan, 2010; Matuk, Linn, & Eylon, 2015). Integration of results from technology-enhanced learning environments strengthened understanding of classroom learning (this topic is discussed primarily in the section "Technology and Science Education").

A major contributor to the integration of new fields was the funding of NSF centers. The Center for Integrating Learning and Technology was founded in 1997 to build a community of cognitive scientists, computer scientists, natural scientists, engineers, classroom teachers, educational researchers, industry leaders, and policy analysts to stimulate the development of technology-enabled solutions to critical educational problems. Starting in 2000, the NSF funded Centers for Teaching and Learning. These centers combined advances in assessment, insights into learning, and innovations in curriculum to build the intellectual infrastructure needed to ensure high-quality STEM (science, technology, engineering, and mathematics) instruction for all students. The Centers for Teaching and Learning enabled participants from diverse fields to collaborate on large-scale efforts to strengthen science education. In 2002, NSF initiated the Mathematics and Science Partnership program that engaged school districts in large-scale collaborations. Then, in 2004, NSF funded Science of Learning centers that integrated knowledge across multiple disciplines to advance learning and instruction.

Syntheses have refuted deficit arguments and begun to clarify the factors contributing to disparities in performance for cultural groups. For gender, declining gaps in opportunity to learn science narrowed the gap in performance on standardized assessments, resulting in Hyde's (2005) argument for gender similarities. These similarities on assessments underpin the argument that disparities in access to science careers reflect cultural stereotypes rather than capability (e.g., D. I. Miller, Eagly, & Linn, 2014; Nosek et al., 2009). Explorations of cultural contributions to performance further clarify both the value of diverse cultural experiences and the factors that lead to patterns of career choice (e.g., Carlone & Johnson, 2007).

Important syntheses captured the interactions among researchers seeking to integrate insights into science instruction (DeBoer, 2014; Duschl, 2008; Lederman & Abell, 2014; Linn & Eylon, 2006; Songer & Kali, 2015). In addition, a series of NRC reports characterized the emerging integration of the field, including *How People Learn* (Bransford, Brown, & Cocking, 1999), *America's Lab Report* (NRC, 2005), *Taking Science to School* (NRC, 2007), *Learning Science in Informal Environments* (NRC, 2009), and *Equity and Diversity in Science and Engineering Education* (NRC, 2012). Furthermore, a growing body of reviews and meta-analyses have captured the integration of insights into effective designs for learning environments (Donnelly, Linn, & Ludvigsen, 2014), scaffolds needed to realize the benefits of scientific visualizations (McElhaney et al., 2015), promising uses of automated guidance in science (Gerard, Matuk, et al., 2015), fruitful ways to promote scientific reasoning (Zimmerman, 2007), and valuable supports for collaboration in all disciplines (Kyndta et al., 2013).

Here, we highlight several salient themes focusing on results that inform our understanding of how to design instruction for a broadening audience: (a) the value of inquiry instruction for promoting identity, (b) the advantages of embedded assessment to develop science practices, and (c) the strengths of peer collaboration to promote lifelong learning.

Value of Inquiry Instruction for Promoting Identity

The NGSS (NGSS Lead States, 2013), initiated in 2011, clarified the definition of inquiry by specifying learning practices such as developing models and designing solutions. They also underscored the importance of knowledge integration by identifying cross-cutting themes and core ideas. Research showed that inquiry can improve science understanding and promote students' identities as science learners (Furtak, Seidel, Iverson, & Briggs, 2012). Detailed analyses of student use of inquiry practices characterized how students with varied perspectives on a science challenge benefit from inquiry (Metz, 1997). Scientific models and simulations embedded in inquiry units can support exploration of phenomena that are too small (atoms), fast (reactions), vast (solar system), or complex (climate science) to observe directly (McElhaney et al., 2015). Careful analysis of successful instruction resulted in more precise recommendations for scaffolding inquiry learning than had emerged in prior research (Quintana et al., 2004). Research-based design guidelines for curriculum designers were synthesized from comprehensive research (Engle & Conant, 2002; Kali, Linn, & Roseman, 2008).

Inquiry instruction has potential to make culturally diverse students feel valued in science courses by encouraging them to test their own ideas (Chiu et al., 2013; Shear, Bell, & Linn, 2004). Research illustrates how inquiry can respect and build on student ideas (diSessa, 2000; Duschl, 2008; Linn & Eylon, 2011; Minstrell & Kraus, 2005). Inquiry activities can garner respect for student ideas by asking students to explain their thinking (Lombrozo, 2010; Rosebery et al., 1992). Thus, engaging students in inquiry takes advantage of their funds of knowledge, can help students distinguish among their ideas, and has the potential for developing intentional learners who identify as science reasoners (Rodriguez, 2013).

Yet some investigators argue for direct instruction based on the view that student ideas have a unified-theory-like character that is not amenable to inquiry instruction (Chi & Slotta, 1993; Gopnik & Wellman, 2012; Vosniadou, 2013). Research comparing inquiry and direct instruction suggests that direct refutation of a science idea motivates students to avoid the intuitive idea in science class but revert back to it on a delayed posttest (e.g., Vitale, McBride, & Linn, 2016). Instead, it is valuable to guide students to distinguish among ideas, consistent with research on desirable difficulties (Bjork & Linn, 2006).

Advantages of Embedded Assessment for Developing Science Practices

Standards and assessment policies gained influence on science education starting with TIMSS (PIRLS International Study Center at Boston College, 1995). International comparisons showed that the United States was behind other developed countries and faulted the proliferation of content standards (Schmidt et al., 1997). Yet the remedy was often to add more tests (Hanushek & Raymond, 2005). High-stakes tests, along with standards that necessitated fleeting coverage of science topics and classroom pacing guides, constrained teachers and schools (Deboer, 2000; Harris et al., 2015; Shavelson, 2007). Multiple-choice assessments reinforced an inadequate model of learning and teaching grounded in memorization (Harris et al., 2015; Hauser, 2004; Sternberg, 2007) and discriminated against language learners and students from nondominant cultures by measuring vocabulary development rather than science reasoning (Carnoy et al., 2013).

Assessments embedded in learning activities are a promising alternative to standardized assessments and end-of-unit tests (Linn, 1996; Pellegrino, 2016; L. B. Resnick & Resnick, 1992; Shepard, 2000). For example, students doing project-based learning document their progress during "pinups" to get guidance during learning (Kolodner et al., 2003). Logs of student interactions allow teachers to monitor student progress, personalize guidance (Ruiz-Primo & Furtak, 2006), and base curricular customizations on valuable evidence (Gerard, Spitulnik, & Linn, 2010).

Instruction featuring embedded assessments that incorporate the Universal Design for Learning perspective (Rose, Meyer, & Hitchcock, 2005) can offer multiple pathways to success to meet the needs of diverse students. For example, students who speak a language other than English at home may represent their scientific arguments more accurately by using a concept-mapping tool than an essay (O. Lee, Penfield, & Maerten-Rivera, 2009; Liu et al., 2014).

Role of Design in Productive Collaboration

Collaborative activities succeed when students consider their peers' ideas and use evidence to negotiate meaning. Structuring interactions is important for fostering generative interactions among culturally diverse students (A. L. Brown & Campione, 1994) and stimulating sustained engagement in science (Engle & Conant, 2002). Inquiry environments can guide students to use scientific evidence to distinguish among alternative ideas held by their peers (Clark & Sampson, 2007; Sato & Linn, 2014; Scardamalia & Bereiter, 2006; Tasker & Herrenkohl, 2016). In a study using the WISE Idea Manager, students who were asked to select peer ideas that differed from their own showed better learning outcomes than students asked to select peer ideas that reinforced their own (Matuk & Linn, 2015). Structuring argumentation by role playing, jigsaw activities, reciprocal teaching, or sentence starters (e.g., "I found that . . .") can promote self-regulation during collaboration but may reduce student motivation to participate by constraining contributions (Dillenbourg, 2002; Kollar, Fischer, & Slotta, 2006). Using technology tools like natural language processing or logs of student interactions to identify ineffective collaborative moves, and providing immediate guidance shows promise for guiding students to learn from each other (e.g., Diziol, Walker, Rummel, & Koedinger, 2010; Rosé et al., 2008).

In summary, research on science instruction has generated promising insights and illustrates ways to meet the needs of increasingly diverse science students. In particular, these studies collectively highlight the promise of engaging students in inquiry instruction featuring interactive models and collaborative activities. Inquiry projects can respect student ideas while also encouraging learners to consider alternatives. They can take advantage of scientific visualizations and provide students with opportunities to generate their own explanations and other scientific artifacts. They offer opportunities for continuous, embedded assessment and personalized guidance. Inquiry projects can promote collaboration in small groups or among whole classes. They can focus on societal issues in local communities and on global problems that resonate with students' interests and experience. By fostering students' identities as scientific thinkers and problem solvers, inquiry instruction imparts practices that have lifelong advantages. Emerging design guidelines can help teachers who are customizing instruction and designers who are creating new units to take advantage of research on science instruction.

SCIENCE TEACHER LEARNING

One hundred years of empirical research has contributed a rich understanding of science teacher learning. Science teacher education has broadened from an early focus primarily on classroom management and pedagogy, to adding specialized science content courses, incorporating cultural and linguistic perspectives, and integrating practices that respond to the variety of student ideas. Our understanding of the teacher as learner has advanced from a view of the teacher as a repository of information, to appreciation that teachers come to the profession with a variety of beliefs about teaching science that are individual and unique, complex, and at times conflicting, based on their prior experience and backgrounds. Teachers face the challenge of combining ideas about the discipline with ideas about how to teach science topics such that they respect and address the alternative conceptions held by their students. The locus of teacher learning has shifted from learning outside of practice (teacher education courses, summer workshops focused on curriculum delivery) to learning within and from practice (guided reflection on classroom video, embedded assessments to inform instructional customizations, learning communities within schools).

Persistent Challenges

During the past 100 years, some science teacher education challenges have persisted. One of the most prominent is the gap between the call for professional development for practicing teachers and the incoherent response. Teachers have called for professional development since 1910. The focus of professional development reflects the instructional focus of each era. In early years, the call was for greater disciplinary and instructional sequencing support (Burnett, 1942). This shifted, with the NSF-funded curricula in the 1960s, to a focus on inquiry teaching strategies (Welch, Klopfer, Aikenhead, & Robinson, 1981). From 1980 to 1995, teachers called for continued support in professional communities (V. E. Lee & Smith, 1996; Little, 1993), particularly to adapt strategies for increasingly diverse learners (National Center for Education Statistics [NCES], 1999). From 1995 to the present, calls for professional development have focused on incorporating student ideas and inquiry practices into instruction (Gerard, Varma, Corliss, & Linn, 2011).

Research demonstrates significant advances in science instruction due to participation in sustained and coherent professional development programs. Outcomes include increased gains in student science learning (e.g., Garet, Porter, Desimone, Birman, & Yoon, 2001), greater numbers of students from groups historically underrepresented in science choosing a science major at the start of college (Bottia, Stearns, Mickelson, Moller, & Valentino, 2015), and reduced teacher turnover (Ingersoll, 2001). However, professional development offerings for teachers have been consistently infrequent and disconnected from what we know about how teachers learn. Researchers have identified, from 1960 to today, teachers' deliberate reflection on artifacts of teaching and learning as an effective mechanism for teacher learning in professional development (e.g., Gerard et al., 2011; Penuel, Fishman, Yamaguchi, & Gallagher, 2007; Sweitzer & Anderson, 1983). Yet most professional development programs neglect opportunities for teachers to test ideas in a classroom and reflect on students' work.

The second persistent challenge concerns science teachers' qualifications and preparation. Throughout the past 100 years, scholars and the general public have called attention to an insufficiently prepared science teacher workforce. In one study, 80% of teachers reported that their job was to bring specialized knowledge to students but that they avoided some science topics due to insufficient knowledge (H. Smith, 1963). Just as today, education leaders noted the high number of secondary teachers working outside their college majors or minors. Furthermore, many complained about inadequate course sequences in science teacher credential programs (Burnett, 1942) and a high teacher turnover rate with vacancies filled by out-of-discipline or uncertified teachers. The response to this problem has largely been to increase the required science courses in preservice education and to invest in science teacher recruitment. These approaches have yielded some positive results. They do not address the challenging problem of preretirement science teacher turnover due primarily to reported dissatisfaction with teaching (Ingersoll, 2001).

A third persistent challenge is the misalignment between effective teaching strategies and the high-stakes student assessments. Teachers have long been held responsible for ensuring both that students have mastered the impossibly long list of topics delineated by standards documents *and* that students engage in inquiry practices to develop integrated understanding and ability to engage in lifelong learning (Davis, Petish, & Smithey, 2006; Eylon & Linn, 1988; Schmidt et al., 1997). The government and public evaluation of teachers rests on their students' ability to recall details on multiple-choice questions. This has resulted in emphasis on practice tests and memorization and undermined efforts to improve science teaching (Shepard, 2000). Since the 1950s, as curriculum designers pushed for inquiry, teachers have reported positive statements about the value of inquiry but felt the need to teach the facts that show up on tests (Marx & Harris, 2006; Welch et al., 1981). Today, technology could enable continuous assessment and automated scoring of generative item types. Yet pacing guides determining how much time to devote to each topic and multiple choice tests that motivate school leaders to require practice tests remain the norm.

1916–1960: Separation of Science Discipline and Pedagogy

In the first era of science teacher education, pedagogy and disciplinary knowledge were treated as separate entities. The teacher was seen as a classroom manager and deliverer of specialized science knowledge, the student as absorbing the information. Research on science teacher preparedness and student science learning foreshadowed recognition of the connections among disciplinary expertise, pedagogy, and student thinking in teacher knowledge.

For both elementary and secondary teacher education, typical courses included educational psychology (emphasizing memorization), history of education, classroom management, and curriculum (Burnett, 1942). The emphasis on pedagogy was due in part to the recent development of teacher preparation colleges as distinct entities from liberal arts colleges. This separated education from science faculty. Some secondary teacher education programs included specialized methods courses. In most states, teachers were required to have some level of college education, but no science major was required.

In the 1920s, newly developed and somewhat undefined science teacher credentialing spurred research surveying the courses provided in teacher education programs. One report noted that more than 60% of the science teachers in California secondary schools lacked college science training in the subject they taught. Subsequently, there was a call for more specialized science courses in teacher preparation programs (H. Smith, 1963). Because science teachers at this time often taught multiple disciplines (chemistry, biology, physics) within a school, there was substantial disagreement as to whether teachers should receive general preparation in all sciences; or education in biology, the most common high school course, and a course in the specialization of their interest; or all courses within a specialization (Curtis, 1930). Meanwhile, teachers were largely determining what science content to teach based on their individual interests and science experiences, administrative pressures due to requisite student achievement expectations (e.g., reading in K–1) and the school community demographics (Piltz, 1958). The National Association of Research in Science Teaching formed in 1928 to provide teacher leadership in instructional decisions.

The period ended with conflict over what science teachers should teach and some encouragement for teacher preparation programs to pursue preparation courses on inquiry. States pushed for more science disciplinary courses in preservice teacher education, yet research indicated that increasing specialized science courses was insufficient to strengthen classroom science teaching (H. Smith, 1963). One study analyzed teacher–student interactions in biology classrooms. Researchers reported a relatively low percentage of student verbal participation, especially student-initiated contributions, and a high percentage of direct verbal teaching procedures employed by most of the teachers. Others reported parallel findings in a study of physics teachers (Bruce, 1969). Researchers found science teaching practices were more closely related to student achievement outcomes than were teachers' preservice education science course experiences (Perkes, 1968).

A distinction hence emerged between whether to prepare teachers to teach science facts or critical thinking skills. Leaders drew on Dewey's (1916) vision for teaching the ways of learning science, rather than teaching science as a body of facts, to alter science teacher preparation. Atkin (1958) found students learned when hypothesizing based on original guesses and experimentation. Based on this finding, he drew the implication that science teachers must be prepared to create an environment that gives students the "right and privilege" to be wrong. This foreshadowed study of interactions between students' prior knowledge and science teaching practices in the next period.

1960–1980: Interaction With Teachers and Evaluators

Natural scientists leading NSF-funded curriculum projects interacted with science teachers and evaluators. Teachers were initially treated as implementers of the NSF reform–oriented curriculum and later recognized as dynamic learners. This shift was due to consistent empirical findings that teachers did not implement curriculum as prescribed. Rather, how teachers implemented the inquiry curriculum materials depended on the interaction of the teacher with multiple factors, including context, beliefs about learning, and prior experiences (Welch, 1979). Surveys such as the Test on Understanding Science, developed by the Educational Testing Service, were used to identify supposed deficiencies in teachers' knowledge of the nature of science and the disciplinary content. Researchers claimed secondary science teachers' knowledge was equivalent to that of high school students or nonscience majors in college (R. L. Carey & Strauss, 1970; Kimball, 1968; P. E. Miller, 1963).

The natural scientists developing the NSF curriculum lamented that teachers were not well enough prepared to effectively teach inquiry (Welch et al., 1981). The NSF funded intensive residential summer institutes to prepare teachers to implement the materials. Teachers came to universities in the summer to learn contemporary science, mathematics, or engineering from science experts. To promote the student-centered approach to inquiry, teachers took the role of students, engaging in investigative practices to test the curriculum materials. Thousands of teachers participated in these institutes. This effort built communities of teachers who appreciated the value of collaboration and who formed strong relationships with expert scientists.

An influential community of science teachers formed, who became leaders in a variety of organizations, including the National Science Teachers Association and the American Association of Physics Teachers (Dow, 1991).

Research involved surveys of teachers' knowledge of science topics and the nature of science, comparison studies of deductive versus inductive teaching methods, and investigations of the impact of professional development on inquiry teaching behaviors. Strengthening teachers' observations of and reflection on the relationship between their teaching practices and students' behaviors was an effective professional development approach to improve inquiry teaching (Sweitzer & Anderson, 1983). The focus on curriculum implementation spurred research on teaching practices. Studies of inductive versus deductive teaching methods (e.g., Boulanger, 1981; Egelston, 1973) showed an advantage for inductive teaching methods at the high school level. Yet surveys showed teachers used primarily deductive or direct instruction. This was most apparent in the use of lectures and recall questions. The curriculum stimulated some new practices, such as teachers using less direct guidance when students struggled (Egelston, 1973).

While at first many had viewed teachers as holding fixed knowledge on content and pedagogy, this view became contested as leaders began to realize that, for inquiry to take hold, teacher learning about practice was necessary (Lederman, 1992). The professional development institutes had focused on preparing teachers to implement the new materials by having them play the roles of students. They neglected opportunities for teachers to create and test new teaching practices with the materials and to distinguish effective strategies (Welch, 1979). Likewise, classroom field experiences, where teachers could test ideas, were included in only some teacher education programs (Sunal, 1980). Meanwhile, consistent evidence suggested that teachers' deliberate examination of their teaching practices relative to student behavior could foster new inquiry teaching practices.

Education researchers used comparison studies to investigate the influence of professional development activities on teacher behavior. Studies of feedback given to teachers after a lesson found, for example, that a supervisory conference coupled with classroom video (of the participating teacher) brought about change in teaching methods. The combination of video and conference was more effective than either a conference or analysis of video alone, or analysis of student data from systematic observations (Sweitzer & Anderson, 1983). A review of 71 studies found that providing teachers with training in systematic observation of class behavior led teachers to change their practice (Balzer, Evans, & Blosser, 1973). Findings were echoed by research on preservice activities such as microteaching. Microteaching was designed to give teachers practice using new teaching strategies with real students. Teachers prepared a short lesson, videotaped their instruction with a small group of students, viewed the video with a mentor who helped the teachers diagnose ways to improve their practice, and then retaught the lesson with a new group of students. A meta-analysis documented a substantial advantage of microteaching (with real students) over a control experience on teacher learning outcomes (Sweitzer & Anderson, 1983).

A comparison study of a preservice program with field experiences including microteaching versus programs without, demonstrated that field experiences led teachers to use significantly more and higher quality inquiry teaching behaviors (Sunal, 1980).

Use of curriculum and likewise the summer institutes dissipated by the late 1970s and in spite of the expenditures of millions of dollars and the involvement of some of the most brilliant scientific minds, the science classroom was not very different. Stake and Easley (1978) conducted case studies of 11 sites using the NSF science materials and noted that the teacher is key to change. While the institutes supported implementation of materials, they neglected support for teacher customization to fit the materials with their teaching and to adjust their teaching to enhance the materials. Nevertheless, the research findings on professional development and teacher education from this era situated teachers as dynamic learners, rather than solely as deliverers of instruction. This emerging view, coupled with the recognition that teacher learning was key to instructional improvement, stimulated the beginning of a paradigm shift to take hold in the next era.

1980–1995: Partnerships Featuring Teacher Communities and Research Collaborations

Starting in the 1980s, appreciation for the relationship between teaching practices and student science learning was at the heart of teacher education efforts. Spurred by Shulman's (1986) articulation of the importance of pedagogical content knowledge (PCK), research focused on identifying the forms of science teacher knowledge that support inquiry instruction, the connections between understanding of inquiry teaching practices and disciplinary knowledge, and the influence of those connections on student learning (Magnusson, Krajcik, & Borko, 1999; D. C. Smith & Neale, 1989). Research involved listening to students' ideas, particularly how their ideas differed from the accepted scientific views, observing teacher strategies, and refining the strategies.

Rich qualitative methods were used to reveal how teachers' integration of ideas across dimensions (e.g., content, instruction, assessment, and learning) was vital to effective science teaching. Clinical interviews, classroom observations, concept maps, and discourse analysis were used to compare PCK between expert and novice science teachers (e.g., Blumenfeld et al., 1991; Clermont, Borko, & Krajcik, 1994) and between teachers who taught familiar versus unfamiliar science topics (e.g., Carlsen, 1993). Teachers identified as having strong PCK were more likely to elicit students' alternative ideas and to build on and challenge students' ideas using varied conceptual representations (Clermont et al., 1994). van Zee and Minstrell's (1997) ethnographic study of an award-winning physics teacher illustrated the dynamic relationship between a teacher's questions during inquiry lesson and the articulation and refinement of students' varied ideas.

A view of the teacher as constructing knowledge within practice by paying close attention to student ideas shifted the locus and structure of professional development. Rather than workshops that provided practice in a new curriculum devoid of students' ideas, programs brought students into the workshops, recognized the importance of contextualized learning, and sought to develop metacognition about teaching practices (e.g., Palincsar & Brown, 1984). Professional development emphasized opportunities for teachers to practice new project-based science or inquiry science–teaching methods in real classrooms, to reflect on their experiences with colleagues and curriculum designers, and to discuss strategies to address the identified challenges (Baird et al., 1991; Krajcik, Blumenfeld, Marx, & Soloway, 1994). Teacher education followed suit. Whereas, initially, natural scientists had believed that a degree in science was essential for secondary teachers, researchers now believed teachers needed guidance to convert accumulated science content knowledge into effective, personalized instruction and to develop teaching strategies that encouraged students to distinguish their specific alternative conceptions from ideas communicated in the curriculum.

Eliciting and building on the ideas that individual students bring to the classroom, particularly students from nonmainstream backgrounds, gained importance (O. Lee, 2005). As researchers recognized the situated nature of students' learning, a majority of science teachers reported they were not adequately prepared to teach English language learners (NCES, 1999). Teachers requested guidance on how to situate science instruction in students' everyday experiences and informal language. The Chèche Konnen Project, one of the most researched science education programs, focused on shaping science curriculum around students' interests and around questions they developed from their everyday experiences outside the formal classroom environment (Rosebery et al., 1992). The teacher's role was to facilitate collaborative student investigation of these questions. Teachers in partnership with researchers identified how to elicit students' questions and observations, and how to incorporate these ideas as resources for science learning. Longitudinal studies demonstrated the benefits of this teaching approach for linguistic minority students' science learning (O. Lee, 2004).

1995–2016: Integration of Science Teaching, Student Learning, and Professional Development

Integrating teacher and student learning characterized this period. Cognitive frameworks used to investigate student learning were applied to teacher learning (e.g., modeling-based inquiry, knowledge integration) and provided rich evidence that teachers integrate ideas about teaching, about the discipline, and about students' alternative conceptions to build expertise (Davis, 2003; Mishra & Koehler, 2006; Schwartz & Gwekwerere, 2006; Talanquer, Tomanek, & Novodvorsky, 2013). Research distinguished the opportunities for teachers to analyze student learning in relation to teaching practices and lesson design as the key professional development mechanism (Gerard et al., 2011). Coherence among teachers' goals, school-wide goals, professional development activities, and research methods were essential to sustaining a community of teacher learners using innovative teaching practices (Garet et al., 2001; Penuel et al., 2007; Wilson & Berne, 1999). NSF-supported centers and partnerships combined disciplines (teacher learning, student learning, curriculum design, technology, cultural studies) and contexts (universities, school districts, science departments) to develop professional development models that integrated teaching, student learning, and school context.

Teacher Learning and Professional Development

Empirical work supported a view of teachers as learners who, like students, build connections among ideas to form an integrated perspective. Studies revealed that science teachers bring beliefs to their science teaching that are individual and unique, complex, and at times conflicting, based on their prior experience and background (Crawford, 2007). Longitudinal studies of teacher beliefs suggest that teachers often develop inquiry-oriented beliefs about instruction during their preservice program but return to a more didactic orientation during their first year in the classroom. This is most often due to a lack of social and intellectual supports for inquiry teaching in the school context (Crawford, 2007; Davis, 2006; Fletcher & Luft, 2011).

Integrating student work into teacher professional development programs has enabled teachers to test and refine their own hypotheses about learning and instruction, which can lead to sustained shifts in teachers' beliefs and practices toward an inquiry teaching model. This resonates with findings about the value of reflection on practice from previous eras (Krajcik et al., 1994; Sweitzer & Anderson, 1983). A synthesis using meta-analysis of professional development in technology-enhanced science demonstrated the value of supporting and encouraging teachers to practice new approaches, gather evidence of the impacts of the new approach from students' work, and reflect on such evidence to distinguish effective strategies (Gerard, Linn, & Liu, 2012). Professional development programs that engaged teachers in using evidence of student work to distinguish among ideas led to significantly greater teacher and student learning outcomes than programs that focused on giving teachers new ideas but lacked activities for teachers to contrast and connect their new ideas with their initial views. Programs that lack opportunities for distinguishing ideas have little impact on the mismatch between teachers' beliefs and what they do in practice.

Professional development models developed and refined in this era shared a common goal of guiding teachers to reflect on students' work from a lesson, distinguish the relationship between their teaching strategy and their students' learning, and refine their approach. Research programs incorporating expertise on curriculum, assessment, teaching, and learning built different versions of this deliberate use of evidence to guide refinement of practice. Lesson Study used collective, iterative teacher development of a science lesson on a predetermined learning challenge (e.g., pendulums), observation and videotaping of a teacher implementing the designed lesson, and collective reflection on the video, observations, and student work artifacts (C. Lewis, Perry, & Murata, 2006). Educative materials embedded generative student assessments, rubrics, and customization prompts into the curriculum to elicit student ideas that could be used to adapt instruction (Bismark, Arias, Davis, & Palincsar,

2015; Davis & Krajcik, 2005). Inquiry learning environments built flexible author-ing tools and visualizations of student assessment information to allow teachers to see a record of student thinking and modify the instruction accordingly (Fishman, Marx, Best, & Tal, 2003; Matuk et al., 2015). Each structure supported teachers to build links between new instructional practices and classroom field experiences. Without this link, teacher beliefs in inquiry remained tenuous (Crawford, 2007). Programs rely on access to generative assessments and rubrics that can give teachers insights into student learning and alignment of assessments with curriculum.

Research shows that successful professional development has goals that resonate with those of the participating teachers and has a duration of one or more years (Garet et al., 2001; Penuel et al., 2007; Wilson & Berne, 1999). Activities that are "packaged and disseminated" to teachers are unlikely to take root in teachers' reper-toires. Professional development programs aim to develop sustained partnerships among stakeholders. This has involved identifying research questions of interest to both the school and research partners (Coburn, Penuel, & Geil, 2013; C. Lewis et al., 2006); ensuring there is a partner teacher or science leader within each school (Diamond & Spillane, 2004; O. Lee et al., 2009); and providing professional devel-opment for administrators as well as teachers (Gerard, Bowyer, & Linn, 2010).

Teaching and Inquiry Learning

Recent research illustrates how teachers integrate inquiry practices and content. Research on the degree of guidance needed to allow students to autonomously engage in science practices and develop coherent understanding has found teachers' roles to be crucial, echoing the case studies of the NSF curricula (Stake & Easley, 1978). A review of 37 comparison studies on inquiry instruction conducted between 1996 and 2006 found that teacher guidance for inquiry added value over unguided student inquiry (Furtak et al., 2012). Teachers' guidance enabled students to more fully expe-rience reform-oriented inquiry activities, whereas student-led inquiry often leads to "deceptive clarity," in which students are engaged but formulate superficial under-standing (Chiu, King Chen, & Linn, 2012). The teacher creates a balance between helping students integrate ideas and giving students the necessary space to flounder and sort out ideas on their own (Engle & Conant, 2002). Balancing support for autonomy and integrated understanding requires teachers to make careful decisions on when to intervene or stand to the side, who to help and who to let work it out on their own, and how to scaffold students' reasoning without giving them the answer.

To guide inquiry, teachers must customize their instruction to the specific alterna-tive conceptions held by their students. This requires teachers to engage in continued informal assessment to shape their practices, as well as to gather information on stu-dents' learning from diagnostic activities to inform instruction (Blumenfeld et al., 1991; Shepard, 2000). Building on the research on questioning of the previous eras (e.g., Boulanger, 1981; van Zee & Minstrell, 1997), design research studies showed the value of eliciting students' ideas and guiding them to integrate those ideas. When teachers explicitly elicited ideas and followed up with adaptive guidance, students learned significantly more science than they did when typical informal assessment approaches were used. Successful practices elicited students' reasoning rather than only eliciting student ideas to evaluate their accuracy (Black & Wiliam, 2006; Minstrell & van Zee, 2000; Ruiz-Primo & Furtak, 2006, 2007; Williams, Linn, Ammon, & Gearhart, 2004). Yet eliciting student ideas to assess accuracy rather than to provide guidance or improve reasoning remains very common (Ruiz-Primo & Furtak, 2006). This is not surprising, given large class sizes and teachers' often limited experience with the wide range of alternative ideas presented by students in an inquiry cycle. While this is a persistent challenge for inquiry teaching (e.g., Welch et al., 1981), new technology tools of this era focus on making students' ideas visible for teachers, so they can spend time adjusting instruction to build on and challenge students' alternative ideas.

Technology and Science Education

Technology is an important driver of scientific advance, often shaping and contributing to evolving methodologies, models, and theories. Many tools developed for professional or military contexts have been adapted for mainstream use. For science education, technologies have helped evolve views of learning, instruction, teaching, and assessment. Over the past century, the role of technology has shifted from an accessory to a partner integrated into practice.

Progress has been disjointed by several persistent challenges. One concerns the typical resistance to innovations. While some embrace technologies as panaceas to educational problems, others fear they will displace teachers or cast doubt on their value. This was the sentiment during the audiovisual movement in the early part of the 20th century and with emerging automated scoring and guidance technologies more recently. A mixture of wariness and enthusiasm has persisted.

Another persistent challenge is the pattern of initially high expectations for new technologies, followed by disappointment in their failure to meet those expectations. For example, in 1922, soon after film was introduced to classrooms, Thomas Edison predicted the obsolescence of school books because "it is possible to teach every branch of human knowledge with the motion picture" (cited by Cuban, 1986, p. 9). More recently, schools invested heavily in interactive whiteboards amid predictions that they would revolutionize classroom teaching and learning, only to be disappointed by their limited functionality. And, as with any innovation, many efforts to leverage technology for learning fail to achieve their promise (e.g., Cordes & Miller, 1999; Healy, 1998; Oppenheimer, 1997; Stoll, 1995). One reason is that teachers generally need both time and support to integrate innovations into their practice. Another is that integration requires designers to customize innovations for science learning. Without support and customization, new technologies become expensive alternatives to traditional ways of teaching, regardless of the intentions behind the design.

An associated challenge concerns sustained funding for technology infrastructure. Even when technologies take hold and enhance learning, they may be abandoned rather than upgraded or sustained. For example, kits developed to accompany hands-on science in the 1960s often fell into disuse due to lack of funds for replacement supplies. And computers are often donated or purchased with grants that do not include the costs of professional development, curriculum materials, software, upgrades, or technical support. They are often embraced by early adopters who move on when they no longer function.

The divide created by individuals' and schools' differential access to technology and technological support is another persistent challenge. At the same time, an important justification for introducing computing into schools is to serve students who lack access in other contexts.

1916–1960: Separation of Technology and Curriculum

In the 1920s and 1930s, teachers lectured at the front of the classroom and led students in rote tasks that emphasized fact recall. Early technologies such as charts, photographs, stereographs, slides, and films were housed in school museums and largely focused on facilitating this process (Saettler, 1968). Similarly, science laboratories featured structured procedures such as for anatomical dissections or chemistry experiments (NRC, 2005). As filmstrip projectors and videotapes entered the classroom, teachers could show educational films and pause to interject with comments and to replay selected segments on demand. Although research could have investigated ways for technology to add value, studies primarily compared typical instruction with film or radio covering the same content and looked at accuracy and efficiency (Rolfe, 1924). Despite the predictions of leading figures of the time (Morgan, 1932), the transformative impacts of technology on education were not realized (Cuban, 1986).

Computers appeared in the 1930s and became increasingly crucial for professional scientists, but were neither affordable nor practical enough for classroom use until the 1980s. Designed on the basis of behaviorist principles, Skinner's (1958) teaching machine addressed the difficulty for teachers of simultaneously monitoring and managing the progress of their many students. It provided students with immediate feedback on written responses and did not allow them to advance until they had answered correctly. Skinner (1958) argued that, unlike lectures, textbooks, and the usual audiovisual aids, the machine induced sustained activity. Skinner advocated for recall and not just recognition, asking students to compose rather than select their responses. In contrast, Pressey's (1926) teaching machine required only recognition.

Thus, technologies generally supported a transmission model of the learner, assuming that students absorb rather than construct knowledge. This debate continues today, with many current technologies being used to transmit information.

1960–1980: Interactions Between Curriculum Design and Technology

Electronic technologies proliferated after the Soviet launch of the Sputnik satellite, underscoring the important role of technology in society. Outside of the classroom, advanced technologies were becoming central to the work of scientists, academics, and other industry professionals. Most continued to be largely impractical for classrooms although Scantron Corporation's scoring of fill-in-the-bubble forms and photocopiers supported existing practices.

Furthermore, television reached most households and increased out-of-school access to science. For example, the Mr. Wizard television show drew 800,000 viewers and led to the establishment of more than 5,000 science clubs (LaFollette, 2008).

The leaders of the NSF-funded curriculum projects commissioned film loops to transmit information that was difficult to explore in high school classrooms. Some, such as molecular motion, were basically demonstrations. Others, such as the collapse of the Tacoma Narrows Bridge, brought a complex event to life. These films remain available today. To support hands-on experimentation, the elementary school leaders designed kits of materials to ensure that teachers could do hands-on experiments. Comparison studies showed overall advantages for the films and kits but did not specify the mechanisms that took advantage of technology (e.g., Shymansky et al., 1990).

The notion of computer literacy emerged as the ability "to 'do computing'—to conceptualize problems algorithmically, to represent them in the syntax of a computer language, to identify conceptual 'bugs,' and to express computational ideas clearly, concisely, and with a degree of organization and readability" (Douglas, 1980, p. 18). Although opportunities to develop this literacy were rare in precollege instruction, a few uses of computer-based instruction were developed (e.g., Suppes & Binford, 1965). For example, the PLATO system for elementary to college students, developed at the University of Illinois, featured an authoring system (the PILOT programming language) and television sets for display. It was purchased by Control Data Corporation and used to deliver instruction remotely. Evaluations found that students enjoyed using the system and that it was as effective as a human teacher (S. G. Smith & Sherwood, 1976).

1980–1995: Partnerships for Learning Technologies

In 1983, *A Nation at Risk*, a report from the National Commission on Excellence in Education, received widespread attention and called for treating computer literacy as equivalent to the three Rs as personal computers and off-the-shelf programs become available. Pioneers in education began to recognize the potential of computers as learning tools, tutors, and resources (Taylor, 1980). Apple spurred experimentation in the 1980s with the Wheels for the Mind competition for school computers. NSF funded high-risk, high-gain innovations with the Advanced Applications of Technology program. Research focused on science practices supported by refinements of expert tools for students (AAAS, 1993b) and on student constructions using tools like Logo (Papert, 1980).

Authentic Practice

Partnerships of natural scientists, science educators, and technologists explored authentic science practices. For example, the ThinkerTools modelling environment enabled students to explore forces affecting a moving object to understand force and motion (B. White & Horwitz, 1987). Microcomputer-based labs used probes for real-time data collection as a valuable way to help students visualize experimental findings in graphs (Mokros & Tinker, 1987). STELLA, a complex-systems thinking tool, enabled students to design models for population growth and ecosystems (Mandinach & Cline, 1994). The WebQuest model (Dodge, 1995) took advantage of content available on the Web to offer students a curated sequence of websites. The KIE team used the emerging Internet to guide students using electronic resources to engage in scientific debate, design, and experimentation (Bell, Davis, & Linn, 1995).

At first, the potential of computer-supported collaborative learning was limited by Internet connectivity (Kay, 1977). CSILE used a communal database to allow students to explore scientific topics using both text and graphics (Scardamalia & Bereiter, 1994). The CoVIS project engaged students to collaboratively investigate local challenges, such as water quality (Pea, 1993).

Research explored whether these technologies helped students investigate and understand emergent patterns in complex systems in biology, chemistry, and physics. Investigations clarified how these tools helped students connect their observations with their prior ideas to develop explanatory models of natural phenomena (e.g., Clark, 1983, 1994; Gordin, Polman, & Pea, 1994; Kozma, 1991; Linn, 1998).

Many tools developed for education drew directly from scientists' practice rather than target citizens' needs and proved difficult to use. Researchers struggled to reconcile what *could* be taught with what *should* be taught with technology (e.g., diSessa, 1995).

Constructionism

Papert proposed the revolutionary idea that computers could allow children to construct understanding of powerful ideas, and his ideas spurred uses of technology to construct understanding. He integrated the Logo programming language to communicate with LEGO's plastic blocks and introduced students to robotics, geometry, and computation through hands-on building projects. DiSessa developed Boxer, an intuitive language intended to entice students to explore personally relevant problems (diSessa & Abelson, 1986). In addition, students who were playing early computer games on Apple computers often found ways to modify the code and became interested in programming. An ongoing debate concerned the value of learning to program, and moreover, whether to learn it separate from or along with science (De Jong & van Joolingen, 1998; Pea & Kurland, 1984).

1995–2015: Integration of Technology and Science Practices

Starting in the mid-1990s, the Internet spread from exclusive use in private and academic sectors to commercial and personal applications. As the cost of devices became more affordable, and Internet use grew, technology was no longer accessible only to wealthy school districts. By 2008, there was an average of one computer for every 3.1 public school students in the United States (NCES, 2014). To support science practices, designers created powerful resources rather than adapting tools of scientists, and technology moved from an accessory to an integral partner in science inquiry, enhancing teachers' roles and guiding students' autonomous learning. Design-based research methods led to exciting refinements of technologies for educational contexts.

Access to the Internet facilitated instructional designs featuring NGSS practices such as creating models of scientific phenomena or testing solutions to design challenges. Access to references, encyclopedias, glossaries, hypertext environments, and multimedia made available by the Internet both promoted autonomy and challenged learners to distinguish, critique, and evaluate information. Among other considerations, users came to be considered not as consumers but as participants and cocreators. Furthermore, licensing options, including open source and Creative Commons, explicitly invited widespread user contributions to building and elaborating electronic resources.

Researchers recognized the literacy skills that such environments foster (e.g., Bryant, Forte, & Bruckman, 2005; Steinkuehler & Duncan, 2008). Reports by the NRC (1999, 2002) noted that technological skills quickly become outdated in the rapidly changing technological landscape. Instead, they urged an emphasis on technological fluency. These reports were critical in distinguishing the kind of fluency emphasized in vocational training from fluency that is more universally valuable for all citizens. Today, the learning of science is entwined with the acquisition of computational thinking (Grover & Pea, 2013; Weintrop, Beheshti, Horn, & Wilensky, 2015).

Refining Authentic Practice for Classroom Learning

Web-based learning environments aligned with the NGSS-supported student-initiated investigations by offering coherent experiences that capitalized on scientific technologies and guided students to engage in authentic inquiry practices (Donnelly et al., 2014; Quintana et al., 2004). For example, the WISE, building on the KIE technology, immersed students in science investigations supported by sophisticated models and simulations designed to merge content with practice and to guide students' autonomous learning (Linn, 1998; Linn & Slotta, 2000). Refinements to ThinkerTools featured scaffolds to guide students through an inquiry cycle that included questioning, prediction, experimentation, modeling, and application (B. Y. White, 1993; B. Y. White & Frederiksen, 1998) and virtual advisors on an Inquiry Island (B. White et al., 2002).

Tools designed for students could promote identity as a scientist by building on students' diverse perspectives and capturing progress to assist teachers. Knowledge Forum refined CSILE in a Web resource where students could view and build on one another's ideas and teachers could monitor progress (Scardamalia & Bereiter, 2006). Visualizations embedded in learning environments were designed to illustrate core science concepts such as density, thermodynamics, photosynthesis, or global climate change. The learning environments logged interactions and tracked learning outcomes (Plass, Homer, & Hayward, 2009; Wilensky & Reisman, 2006). Games and simulations could assess students by tracking progress (Barab, Thomas, Dodge, Carteaux, & Tuzun, 2005; Clark, Sengupta, Brady, Martinez-Garza, & Killingsworth, 2015; Kim & Shute, 2015). For example, students using SimScientists explored a complex ecosystem by performing actions that enabled the software to assess their reasoning strategies (Quellmalz et al., 2007). Students using Newton's Playground revealed their understanding of physics principles while solving complex challenges (Kim & Shute, 2015).

Other environments combined the game genre with mobile and augmented reality technologies, as in the multiuser virtual environment EcoMUVE, where learners collect data from local ecosystems such as ponds and forests, supported by virtual tools (Metcalf, Kamarainen, Tutwiler, Grotzer, & Dede, 2011). For out-of-school users, virtual worlds such as Whyville supported learners to collaborate in investigating a virus epidemic in their online community (Kafai, Feldon, Fields, Giang, & Quintero, 2007).

Constructing Artifacts to Learn Science

Explorations of emerging technologies focused on how they might directly address students' prior understanding and enable them to connect their physical experiences to abstract scientific models. The emphasis on computational fluency as a foundational skill for citizens expanded to include fluency in engineering and design. Student-friendly online platforms such as StarLogo (Wilensky & Resnick, 1999) extended programming to support science modeling and out-of-school use. M. Resnick et al. (2009) developed a large community of learners who used Scratch to explore their creative interests in art and games, alongside exploring important concepts in computing, mathematics, science, and engineering (Brennan, Monroy-Hernández, & Resnick, 2010).

Researchers took notice of the informal science learning that occurred among do-it-yourself communities (Blikstein, 2013). They experimented with school-based fabrication labs, or FabLabs, and makerspaces with the goal of enabling students to develop practices in engineering and experimentation. Using various fabrication technologies, learners could apply advanced science and engineering concepts to projects of personal interest, including videogames (Cooper, Dann, & Pausch, 2000; Millner & Resnick, 2005), and textiles and jewelry (Buechley, Eisenberg, Catchen, & Crockett, 2008; Sylvan, 2005).

Another example featured data-tracking devices. These included wearable personal data-tracking devices to help students understand and communicate patterns in data (e.g., V. R. Lee, Drake, & Williamson, 2015); probeware and handheld devices that helped students explore complex, dynamic relationships (Metcalf & Tinker, 2004); and smart room technologies that embedded phenomena and guidance in students' own classrooms. For example, RoomQuake (Moher, Hussain, Halter, & Kilb, 2005) engaged students in extended investigations of simulated earthquakes. During these investigations, students used Palm Pilots to collect, interpret, and argue about data in order to identify likely fault lines. More recent explorations of emerging technologies, such as stereoscopy (Price, Lee, Plummer, SubbaRao, & Wyatt, 2015) and virtual and mixed reality (Pan et al., 2015), so far show promise to enhance technology-enhanced inquiry.

Technology as Inquiry Teaching Partner

Technology moved from an accessory to an inquiry teaching partner, enhancing teachers' roles and guiding students' autonomous learning. Design-based research documented how school culture, capabilities, and policies affected the integration of technology-enhanced inquiry materials in a science program (Blumenfeld, Fishman, Krajcik, Marx, & Soloway, 2000; Fishman, Marx, Blumenfeld, Krajcik, & Soloway, 2004). Culture concerns the alignment or customizability of the technology-enhanced curriculum with the school goals for science instruction (Cuban, 2001; Penuel, Fishman, Cheng, & Sabelli, 2011); capability refers to the teacher and administrators' conceptual and practical knowledge of the curriculum (Gerard, Bowyer, et al., 2010; Lawless & Pellegrino, 2007); policy refers to the schools' infrastructure, including provision of technology and technical support (Diamond & Spillane, 2004; Zhao, Pugh, Sheldon, & Byers, 2002).

Inquiry learning environments can capture student and teacher interactions. Studies show that teachers can use the insights they gather from student responses to embedded assessments in an inquiry environment to customize instruction (e.g., Gerard, Spitulnik, et al., 2010; Herrenkohl, Tasker, & White, 2011; Williams et al., 2004). Herrenkohl et al. (2011), for example, illustrate how two teachers in different schools used the Web of Inquiry, a Web-based inquiry learning environment to facilitate science investigations of solar energy. The teachers adapted their guidance based on student progress in the inquiry cycle, which was made visible by the learning environment. Teachers' instruction was most salient in helping students distinguish among ideas and make connections across activities.

Automated scoring technologies can support teachers to provide the kind of personalized guidance needed to foster inquiry learning (e.g., Egelston, 1973; van Zee & Minstrell, 1997). Natural language processing techniques and advanced algorithms are used to score students' written essays and drawings embedded in inquiry projects. The computer assigns individualized guidance to the student immediately based on the automated score (Liu et al., 2014; Liu, Rios, Heilman, Gerard, & Linn, 2016). Distinguishing how to guide students during inquiry, given the wide range of ideas elicited by an inquiry project, has been an enduring challenge for teachers (Welch et al., 1981). When teachers analyze a large number of alternative student responses on the same topic, they can refine their guidance based on student thinking and improve student learning (Sisk-Hilton, 2009). Researchers have designed automated guidance that does not provide the right answer but rather promotes student scientific thinking by emulating expert practice (Chin et al., 2010; Gerard, Ryoo, et al., 2015). A meta-analysis of instruction with automated, adaptive guidance found that automated guidance that promoted self-monitoring was more likely to improve learning outcomes than guidance that only addressed content (Gerard, Matuk, et al., 2015). Self-monitoring guidance, triggered by the automated scoring of logged student navigation data, prompted students to reflect on their approach to the problem and distinguish a more successful strategy, such as revisiting relevant evidence in a project before revising (Leelawong & Biswas, 2008).

Technology advances provide other rich forms of evidence of student learning to strengthen inquiry teaching. Classroom video has been used in professional development, echoing research from the 1970s on microteaching (Sweitzer & Anderson, 1983), to strengthen teachers' noticing of student science learning behaviors (Roth et al., 2011; Talanquer et al., 2013). Automated scores of student essays and drawings in an inquiry project can be used to alert the teacher to students who score below a predetermined threshold and need teacher assistance (Gerard & Linn, 2016). Others have provided teachers with real-time visualizations of collective student performance and progress (Tissenbaum, Lui, & Slotta, 2011). How to design these tools to capture the information most useful for teachers to refine instruction remains a rich area for research.

In conclusion, technology for science learning and instruction has undergone vast changes over the past 100 years. It has trended toward lightness, compactness, and mobility. It offers more tools for customizability and expression rather than transmission, finally synchronizing with our evolving views of teaching and learning as creative, reflective practices. Technological advances offer valuable supports for broader, autonomous participation in authentic inquiry practices, including (a) support for students' engagement with disciplinary practices and sensemaking through tools such as interactive simulations and visualizations; (b) scaffolds that break down and guide students through complex inquiry activities; (c) tools for students to monitor and improve their learning, including adaptive guidance, automated feedback, and prompts for refinement; (d) supports for teachers to efficiently allocate their time and to incorporate the rich, diverse ideas students bring to class; and (e) contexts that are relevant to learners and that allow them to build on prior experiences.

At a systemic level, there are the inequities that technology creates and that schools often perpetuate. Rapid advances during the second part of the past century, while beneficial to quality of life in the United States, have also dislocated labor markets and contributed to the hollowing-out of middle-class jobs (Levy & Murname, 2013). Manual labor employment, once abundant for high school graduates in the 1960s, has been mostly eliminated by the computerization or offshoring of routine tasks. Computerization has also changed the nature of work, putting demands on schools that often go unmet. Demands for skills in dealing with complex problems and abstract information—on which humans so far outperform computers—have made emphasis on complex science topics essential. Recent appreciation for learning across contexts, including formal and out-of-school learning, offer opportunities (e.g., Paulsen, 2013).

CONCLUSIONS AND RECOMMENDATIONS

This chapter articulates progress in research programs intended to advance science education. The syntheses of trends toward the integration of ideas, theoretical approaches, and research findings that enrich how researchers view learners, instruction, teaching practice, and technology all contribute to a more coherent and nuanced understanding of science education. Each area has informed ways of educating the changing audience for science education, from preparing future scientists to preparing society's citizens. Each area has benefited from advances in the other areas and contributed to coherence in our understanding of how to make science education more effective. Yet there is still much work to be done to realize the potential of science education for all learners.

Progress in science education has required realignment of the power structure to address the complex, systemic nature of science education. In 1916, natural scientists saw themselves as the leaders, and they gained power during the reforms following Sputnik. With leadership from NSF and other organizations has come a growing respect for each of the fields that contribute to science education. Many partnerships that were formed in the 1980s and beyond involved natural scientists, science educators, classroom teachers, technologists, and, at times, school administrators, who viewed each other as equal participants in these partnerships. Recently, these partnerships have broadened to include cultural studies, linguistics, and other relevant disciplines. Yet more progress is needed to respectfully incorporate the voices and perspectives of groups of people who feel disenfranchised, including those representing nondominant groups. Furthermore, renewed effort is needed to bridge the chasm that still exists between research in science education and educational policy.

Moreover, realizing the full potential of these advances involves scaling innovations that succeed in one context to new and broader instructional, cultural, and social contexts. This requires integrating the perspectives of school and community leaders, who often complain that their voices are not heard by developers, researchers, and policymakers (Coburn, 2003).

The increasing cultural diversification of schools, rapid rate of teacher turnover, and demands of preparing students to deal with global issues present complex challenges specific to science education. These challenges stem from variations in family support, differential access to resources, and sensitivity to the needs of diverse learners and their communities. To make good decisions about health, energy, and policy, citizens need sophisticated strategies for guiding their own learning and teachers who are prepared to help achieve this goal. Only by addressing these challenges systemically can we hope to prepare the next generation of scientifically astute citizens.

The future trajectory for science education is likely to involve reconceiving instruction in a way that combines advances in learning, instruction, professional development, and technology to prepare intentional learners and orchestrate an individualized process of relevant, just-in-time learning. Science education needs to enable learners to address personal dilemmas, prepare for emerging employment opportunities in STEM, and participate in informed decisions about community and global issues concerning health, energy, and the environment. This image of the learner will likely involve typical schooling as only one component (out of many) in an ongoing process of science learning. We need to prepare just-in-time learners who have the capability to attend to their own intellectual development by engaging in authentic science practices; drawing on information resources, social networking, and communication; and leveraging as-yet undeveloped educational opportunities.

Though the growing economic disparities in our society present new challenges for equitable access to powerful learning opportunities, the ubiquitous availability of new learning resources has the potential to mitigate the impact of these disparities. Out-of-school learning opportunities offer promise, and active efforts to create open educational resources and online courses are underway. These resources will contribute to the development of a generation of intentional, autonomous, just-in-time learners. We offer the following recommendations to support the continued integration (and implementation) of important research perspectives into science education.

Science Education Research

Progress in science education reflects effective funding decisions made by public and private foundations, as well as by industry. NSF funding—initially for curriculum materials and professional development, then adding support for research and development of advanced technologies for learning, and recently for broadening participation in science—has advanced the field. Future research funding can build on this success by

1. Creating a generative research enterprise that fosters communication across all stakeholders. This vision can be achieved by promoting research programs that (a) integrate findings from disparate fields; (b) involve diverse stakeholders; (c) take advantage of and refine established and emerging technologies; and (d) include synthesis efforts such as reviews, meta-analyses, and convening activities.
2. Supporting partnerships for research, design, and entrepreneurship, encouraging iterative refinement, and providing incentives for collaboration. Designers of successful environments that share similar goals can collaborate to build customizable tools that can be flexibly used across contexts and platforms, rather than rebuilding many versions of the same tools. Partnerships between researchers and nonprofit entrepreneurs can help achieve the reach and scalability of successful technologies. Such partnerships could address usability and aesthetic appeal, aspects of design that are consequential to learning processes and outcomes.

Science Curriculum and Instruction

Progress in curriculum and instruction has resulted from a plethora of generative research programs using mixed research methods and studying learning in complex settings. Communication of results has benefited from efforts to create frameworks and design guidelines to inform teachers customizing curriculum and future design partnerships. Future work can strengthen instruction by

1. Establishing design guidelines for curriculum materials that prepare students to develop integrated, generative science understanding. Guidelines should inform design of instruction that develops students' ability to self-regulate, set appropriate goals, find and use resources, and leverage fruitful sources of everyday knowledge and skill.
2. Identifying promising ways to help all citizens develop an identity as a science learner. Such learners should feel capable of and responsible for addressing the scientific issues they encounter in their everyday lives.
3. Requiring evidence that instructional materials promote coherent science understanding for diverse students (much like testing the impact of new drugs). Teachers and schools require evidence that published curriculum materials, when implemented as designed or customized for their students, will lead to improved outcomes on meaningful criteria. These materials should be evaluated on their ability to prepare learners who can use science to solve personally relevant problems and identify as able to understand and use science in their lives.

Science Teacher Support

Research shows the importance of teacher learning communities and the value of empowering teachers to customize instruction for their learners. To facilitate these communities, it is important to

1. Modify credentialing requirements to remove dependence on high-stakes standardized tests and, instead, reward teachers for promoting coherent understanding and developing students' identities as science learners. This would involve creating incentives for teachers to try innovative pedagogical approaches with their students, test the impact of those approaches using assessments aligned with instruction, and refine instruction. This shift would empower teachers to take advantage of novel methods of engaging their students in authentic inquiry and continuously monitoring student progress.
2. Provide resources to teacher preparation institutions to develop and support sustained teacher research communities among practicing teachers. These communities could include summer internships with educational mentors and a professional learning community or professional development workshops that

help teachers align curriculum materials with the interests of their communities and use embedded assessments to inform their teaching.

Science Education and Technology

Curriculum materials have integrated promising technologies that can serve as inquiry partners for students and teachers. To sustain this trajectory it is important to

1. Provide institutional support for teachers to adopt, integrate, and sustain the use of established learning technologies in their classrooms. This support would include reliable technology infrastructure and instruction (starting at the preservice level) on how to use technology effectively to promote intentional, autonomous, just-in-time learning.
2. Promote research in which designers focus on leveraging technology's unique affordances to create authentic, integrated, and relevant learning experiences for diverse students. Emerging areas such as mobile technologies, virtual and augmented reality, and interactive rooms show promise for achieving these goals, but they require research from multiple perspectives to provide a strong evidentiary basis for widespread adoption.

ACKNOWLEDGMENTS

This material is based on work supported by the National Science Foundation under NSF Projects 1451604, DRL-1418423, 1119270, 0822388, 0918743, and Department of Education project DOE R305A11782. Any opinions, findings, and conclusions or recommendations expressed in this material are those of the authors and do not necessarily reflect the views of the National Science Foundation.

REFERENCES

Alexander, C., Ishikawa, S., & Silverstein, M. (1977). *A pattern language: Towns, buildings, construction.* New York, NY: Oxford University Press.
American Association for the Advancement of Science. (1993a). *Benchmarks for science literacy.* New York, NY: Oxford University Press.
American Association for the Advancement of Science. (1993b). *Finding aid to the AAAS science: A process approach.* Retrieved from https://www.aaas.org/page/finding-aid-aaas-science-process-approach-records
American Association for the Advancement of Science. (2013). Special Issue: Grand challenges in science education. *Science, 340,* 290–314.
Atkin, J. M. (1958). A study of formulating and suggesting tests for hypotheses in elementary school science experiences. *Science Education, 42,* 414–422.
Baenninger, M., & Newcombe, N. (1989). The role of experience in spatial test performance: A meta-analysis. *Sex Roles, 20,* 327–344. doi:10.1007/BF00287729
Bagno, E., & Eylon, B.-S. (1997). From problem-solving to a knowledge structure: An example from the domain of electromagnetism. *American Journal of Physics, 65,* 726–736.
Baird, J. R., Fensham, P. J., Gunstone, R. F., & White, R. T. (1991). The importance of reflection in improving science teaching and learning. *Journal of Research in Science Teaching, 28,* 163–182. doi:10.1002/tea.3660280207

Balzer, A. L., Evans, T. P., & Blosser, P. E. (1973). *A review of research on teacher behavior.* Columbus, OH: Association for the Education of Teachers in Science.

Barab, S., Thomas, M., Dodge, T., Carteaux, R., & Tuzun, H. (2005). Making learning fun: Quest Atlantis, a game without guns. *Educational Technology Research & Development, 53,* 86–107.

Barton, A. C. (1998). Teaching science with homeless children: Pedagogy, representation, and identity. *Journal of Research in Science Teaching, 35,* 379–394. doi:10.1002/(SICI)1098-2736(199804)35:4<379::AID-TEA8>3.0.CO;2-N

Bell, P., Davis, E. A., & Linn, M. C. (1995). The knowledge integration environment: Theory and design. In J. L. Schnase, & E. L. Cunnius (Eds.), *Proceedings of the Computer Supported Collaborative Learning Conference, CSCL '95* (pp. 14–21). Mahwah, NJ: Lawrence Erlbaum.

Bell, P., & Linn, M. C. (2000). Scientific arguments as learning artifacts: Designing for learning from the Web with KIE. *International Journal of Science Education, 22,* 797–817.

Berkman, M., & Plutzer, E. (2010). *Evolution, creationism, and the battle to control America's classrooms.* Cambridge, England: Cambridge University Press.

Bismark, A. S., Arias, A., Davis, E. A., & Palincsar, A. S. (2015). Examining student work for evidence of teacher uptake of educative curriculum materials. *Journal of Research in Science Teaching, 52,* 816–846.

Bjork, R. A., & Linn, M. C. (2006). The science of learning and the learning of science: Introducing desirable difficulties. *The APS Observer, 19*(3). Retrieved from http://www.psychologicalscience.org/publications/observer/2006/march-06/the-science-of-learning-and-the-learning-of-science.html

Black, P., & Wiliam, D. (2006). Assessment and classroom learning. *Assessment in Education: Principles, Policy & Practice, 5,* 7–74. doi:10.1080/0969595980050102

Blikstein, P. (2013). Digital fabrication and "making" in education: The democratization of invention. In J. W.-H. C. Büching (Ed.), *FabLabs: Of machines, makers and inventors* (pp. 173–180). Bielefeld, Germany: Transcript.

Blumenfeld, P., Fishman, B., Krajcik, J., Marx, R. W., & Soloway, E. (2000). Creating usable innovations in systemic reform: Scaling up technology-embedded project-based science in urban schools. *Educational Psychologist, 35,* 149–164.

Blumenfeld, P., Soloway, E., Marx, R., Krajcik, J., Guzdial, M., & Palincsar, A. (1991). Motivating project-based learning: Sustaining the doing, supporting the learning. *Educational Psychologist, 26,* 369–398.

Bottia, M. C., Stearns, E., Mickelson, R. A., Moller, S., & Valentino, L. (2015, April). Growing the roots of STEM majors: Female math and science high school faculty and the participation of students in STEM. *Economics of Education Review, 45,* 14–27.

Bouillion, L. M., & Gomez, L. M. (2001). Connecting school and community with science learning: Real world problems and school–community partnerships as contextual scaffolds. *Journal of Research in Science Teaching, 38,* 878–898.

Boulanger, F. D. (1981). Instruction and science learning: A quantitative synthesis. *Journal of Research in Science Teaching, 18,* 311–327.

Bowyer, J. B., & Linn, M. C. (1978). Effectiveness of the science curriculum improvement study in teaching scientific literacy. *Journal of Research in Science Teaching, 15,* 209–219.

Bransford, J. D., Brown, A. L., & Cocking, R. (1999). *How people learn: Brain, mind, experience, and school.* Washington, DC: National Academies Press.

Broadbent, D. (1958). *Perception and communication.* London, England: Pergamon Press.

Brown, A. L. (1987). Metacognition, executive control, self-regulation, and other more mysterious mechanisms. In F. E. Weinert, & R. H. Kluwe (Eds.), *Metacognition, motivation, and understanding* (pp. 60–108). Hillsdale, NJ: Lawrence Erlbaum.

Brown, A. L. (1992). Design experiments: Theoretical and methodological challenges in creating complex interventions in classroom settings. *Journal of Learning Sciences, 2,* 141–178.

Brown, A. L., & Campione, J. C. (1994). Guided discovery in a community of learners. In K. McGilly (Ed.), *Classroom lessons: Integrating cognitive theory and classroom practice* (pp. 229–270). Cambridge: MIT Press/Bradford Books.

Brown, B. A. (2006). "It isn't no slang that can be said about this stuff": Language, identity, and appropriating science discourse. *Journal of Research in Science Teaching, 43,* 96–126.

Bruce, M. H. (1969). Teacher education in science. *Review of Educational Research, 39,* 397–427. doi:10.3102/00346543039004415

Bruner, J. S. (1960). *The process of education.* Cambridge, MA: Harvard University Press.

Bryant, S. L., Forte, A., & Bruckman, A. (2005, November). *Becoming Wikipedian: Transformation of participation in a collaborative online encyclopedia.* Paper presented at the Conference on Supporting Group Work, Sanibel Island, FL.

Buechley, L., Eisenberg, M., Catchen, J., & Crockett, A. (2008, April). *The LilyPad Arduino: Using computational textiles to investigate engagement, aesthetics, and diversity in computer science education.* Paper presented at the SIGCHI Conference on Human Factors in Computing Systems, Florence, Italy.

Burbules, N. C., & Linn, M. C. (1991). Science education and the philosophy of science: Congruence or contradiction? *International Journal of Science Education, 13,* 227–241.

Burnett, W. (1942). Teacher education in science and mathematics. *Review of Educational Research, 9,* 443–450.

Carey, R. L., & Strauss, N. G. (1970). An analysis of experienced science teachers' understanding of the nature of science. *School Science and Mathematics, 70,* 366–376. doi:10.1111/j.1949-8594.1970.tb08648.x

Carey, S. (1985). *Conceptual change in childhood.* Cambridge: MIT Press.

Carey, S., & Smith, C. (1993). On understanding the nature of scientific knowledge. *Educational Psychologist, 28,* 235–251.

Carlone, H. B., & Johnson, A. (2007). Understanding the science experiences of successful women of color: Science identity as an analytic lens. *Journal of Research in Science Teaching, 44,* 1187–1218. doi:10.1002/tea.20237

Carlsen, W. S. (1993). Teacher knowledge and discourse control: Quantitative evidence from novice biology teachers' classrooms. *Journal of Research in Science Teaching, 30,* 471–481. doi:10.1002/tea.3660300506

Carnoy, M., Loyalka, P., Dobryakova, M., Dossani, R., Froumin, I., Kuhns, K. M., . . . Wang, R. (2013). *University expansion in a changing global economy: Triumph of the BRICs?* Stanford, CA: Stanford University Press.

Case, R. (1985). *Intellectual development: Birth to adulthood.* Orlando, FL: Academic Press.

Chandler, P., & Sweller, J. (1991). Cognitive load theory and the format of instruction. *Cognition and Instruction, 8,* 293–332.

Chase, W., & Simon, H. A. (1973). Perception in chess. *Cognitive Psychology, 4,* 55–81.

Chemical Education Material Study. (1963). *Chemistry: An experimental science* (G. C. Pimentel, Ed.). San Francisco, CA: W. H. Freeman.

Chi, M. T. H., Bassok, M., Lewis, M. W., Reimann, P., & Glaser, R. (1989). Self-explanations: How students study and use examples in learning to solve problems. *Cognitive Science, 13,* 145–182.

Chi, M. T. H., Feltovich, P. J., & Glaser, R. (1981). Categorization and representation of physics problems by experts and novices. *Cognitive Science, 5,* 121–152.

Chi, M. T. H., & Slotta, J. D. (1993). The ontological coherence of intuitive physics: Commentary on A. diSessa's "Toward an epistemology of physics." *Cognition and Instruction, 10,* 249–260.

Chi, M. T. H., & VanLehn, K. A. (1991). The content of physics self-explanations. *Journal of the Learning Sciences*, *1*, 69–105. doi:10.1207/s15327809jls0101_4

Chin, D. B., Dohmen, I. M., Cheng, B. H., Oppezzo, M. A., Chase, C. C., & Schwartz, D. L. (2010). Preparing students for future learning with teachable agents. *Educational Technology Research & Development*, *58*, 649–669. doi:10.1007/s11423-010-9154-5

Chiu, J. L., Hecht, D., Malcolm, P., DeJaegher, C., Pan, E., Bradley, M., & Burghardt, M. D. (2013). WISEngineering: Supporting precollege engineering design and mathematical understanding. *Computers & Education*, *67*, 142–155.

Chiu, J. L., King Chen, J. Y., & Linn, M. C. (2012). Overcoming deceptive clarity by encouraging metacognition in the web-based inquiry science environment. In R. Azevedo, & V. Aleven (Eds.), *International handbook of metacognition and learning technologies* (pp. 517–531). New York, NY: Springer.

Clark, D. B., & Jorde, D. (2004). Helping students revise disruptive experientially supported ideas about thermodynamics: Computer visualizations and tactile models. *Journal of Research in Science Teaching*, *41*, 1–23.

Clark, D. B., & Sampson, V. (2007). Personally-seeded discussions to scaffold online argumentation. *International Journal of Science Education*, *29*, 253–277.

Clark, D. B., Sengupta, P., Brady, C. E., Martinez-Garza, M. M., & Killingsworth, S. S. (2015). Disciplinary integration of digital games for science learning. *International Journal of STEM Education*, *2*(2). doi:10.1186/s40594-014-0014-4

Clark, R. E. (1983). Reconsidering research on learning from media. *Review of Educational Research*, *53*, 445–459.

Clark, R. E. (1994). Media will never influence learning. *Educational Technology Research & Development*, *42*, 21–29.

Clermont, C. P., Borko, H., & Krajcik, J. S. (1994). Comparative study of the pedagogical content knowledge of experienced and novice chemical demonstrators. *Journal of Research in Science Teaching*, *31*, 419–441. doi:10.1002/tea.3660310409

Cobb, P., Confrey, J., diSessa, A., Lehrer, R., & Schauble, L. (2003). Design experiments in educational research. *Educational Researcher*, *32*(1), 9–13.

Coburn, C. E. (2003). Rethinking scale: Moving beyond numbers to deep and lasting change. *Educational Researcher*, *32*(6), 3–12. doi:10.3102/0013189X032006003

Coburn, C. E., Penuel, W. R., & Geil, K. E. (2013). *Research-practice partnerships: A strategy for leveraging research for educational improvement in school districts.* Retrieved from http://rpp.wtgrantfoundation.org/library/uploads/2016/01/R-P-Partnerships-White-Paper-Jan-2013-Coburn-Penuel-Geil.pdf

Cohen, E. G. (1994). Restructuring the classroom: Conditions for productive small groups. *Review of Educational Research*, *64*, 1–35.

Collins, A. (1992). Toward a design science of education. In E. Scanlon, & T. O'Shea (Eds.), *New directions in educational technology* (pp. 15–22). New York, NY: Springer-Verlag.

Collins, A., & Brown, J. S. (1988). The computer as a tool for learning through reflection. In H. Mandl, & A. M. Lesgold (Eds.), *Learning issues for intelligent tutoring systems* (pp. 1–18). Chicago, IL: Springer-Verlag.

Collins, A., Brown, J. S., & Newman, S. E. (1989). Cognitive apprenticeship: Teaching the crafts of reading, writing, and mathematics. In L. B. Resnick (Ed.), *Knowing, learning and instruction: Essays in honor of Robert Glaser* (pp. 453–494). Hillsdale, NJ: Lawrence Erlbaum.

Conway, E. M., & Oreskes, N. (2010). *Merchants of doubt*. London, England: Bloomsbury.

Cooper, S., Dann, W., & Pausch, R. (2000). Alice: A 3-D tool for introductory programming concepts. *Journal of Computing Sciences in Colleges*, *15*, 107–116.

Cordes, C., & Miller, E. (1999). *Fool's gold: A critical look at computers in childhood*. College Park, MD: Alliance for Childhood.

Crawford, B. (2007). Learning to teach science as inquiry in the rough and tumble of practice. *Journal of Research in Science Teaching, 44,* 613–642.

Cronbach, L. J. (1963). Evaluating course outcomes. *Teacher's College Record, 64,* 672–683.

Cronbach, L. J., & Snow, R. (1977). *Aptitudes and instructional methods: A handbook for research on interactions.* New York, NY: Irvington.

Cuban, L. (1986). *Teachers and machines: The classroom use of technology since 1920.* New York, NY: Teachers College Press.

Cuban, L. (2001). *Oversold and underused: Reforming schools through technology, 1980–2000.* Cambridge, MA: Harvard University Press.

Curtis, F. D. (1930). What constitutes a desirable program of studies in science education for teachers of science in secondary education? *Science Education, 15,* 14–23. doi:10.1002/sce.3730150103

Curtis, F. D. (1963). The evolution of science education research. *Journal of Research in Science Teaching, 1,* 13–14. doi:10.1002/tea.3660010106

Davis, E. A. (2003). Prompting middle school science students for productive reflection: Generic and directed prompts. *Journal of the Learning Sciences, 12,* 91–142.

Davis, E. A. (2006). Preservice elementary teachers' critique of instructional materials for science. *Science Education, 90,* 348–375.

Davis, E. A., & Krajcik, J. (2005). Designing educative curriculum materials to promote teacher learning. *Educational Researcher, 34*(3), 3–14.

Davis, E. A., Petish, D., & Smithey, J. (2006). Challenges new science teachers face. *Review of Educational Research, 76,* 607–651. doi:10.3102/00346543076004607

Deboer, G. E. (2000). Scientific literacy: Another look at its historical and contemporary meanings and its relationship to science education reform. *Journal of Research in Science Teaching, 37,* 582–601. doi:10.1002/1098-2736(200008)37:6<582::AID-TEA5>3.0.CO;2-L

DeBoer, G. E. (2014). The history of science curriculum reform in the United States. In N. G. Lederman, & S. K. Abell (Eds.), *Handbook of research on science education* (Vol. II, pp. 781–806). Abingdon, England: Routledge Handbooks Online. doi:10.4324/9780203097267

De Jong, T., & van Joolingen, W. R. (1998). Scientific discovery learning with computer simulations of conceptual domains. *Review of Educational Research, 68,* 179–201.

Design-Based Research Collective. (2003). Design-based research: An emerging paradigm for educational inquiry. *Educational Researcher, 32*(1), 5–8.

Dewey, J. (1897). John Dewey's famous declaration concerning education. *School Journal, LIV*(3), 77–80.

Dewey, J. (1916). Method in science teaching. *General Science Quarterly, 1*(1), 3–9.

Diamond, J., & Spillane, J. (2004). High-stakes accountability in urban elementary schools: Challenging or reproducing inequality? *Teachers College Record, 106,* 1145–1176.

Dillenbourg, P. (2002). Over-scripting CSCL: The risks of blending collaborative learning with instructional design. In P. A. Kirschner (Ed.), *Three worlds of CSCL: Can we support CSCL* (pp. 61–91). Heerlen, Netherlands: Open Universiteit Nederland.

diSessa, A. A. (1988). Knowledge in pieces. In G. Forman, & P. Pufall (Eds.), *Constructivism in the computer age* (pp. 49–70). Hillsdale, NJ: Lawrence Erlbaum.

diSessa, A. A. (1995). The many faces of a computational medium. In A. diSessa, C. Hoyles, R. Noss, & L. Edwards (Eds.), *Computers and exploratory learning* (pp. 337–359). Berlin, Germany: Springer Verlag.

diSessa, A. A. (2000). *Changing minds: Computers, learning and literacy.* Cambridge: MIT Press.

diSessa, A., & Abelson, A. (1986). Boxer: A reconstructible computational medium. *Communications of the ACM, 29,* 859–868.

diSessa, A. A., Elby, A., & Hammer, D. (2002). J's epistemological stance and strategies. In G. M. Sinatra, & P. R. Pintrich (Eds.), *Intentional conceptual change* (pp. 237–290). Mahwah, NJ: Lawrence Erlbaum.

Diziol, D., Walker, E., Rummel, N., & Koedinger, K. R. (2010). Using intelligent tutor technology to implement adaptive support for student collaboration. *Educational Psychology Review, 22*, 89–102.

Dodge, B. (1995). *Some thoughts about WebQuests*. Retrieved from http://webquest.org/sdsu/about_webquests.html

Donnelly, D. F., Linn, M. C., & Ludvigsen, S. (2014). Impacts and characteristics of computer-based science inquiry learning environments for precollege students. *Review of Educational Research, 84*, 572–608. doi:10.3102/0034654314546954

Douglas, M. E. (1980). Computer literacy: What is it? *Business Education Forum, 34*, 18–22.

Dow, P. B. (1991). *Schoolhouse politics: Lessons from the Sputnik era*. Cambridge, MA: Harvard University Press.

Driver, R., Leach, J., Millar, R., & Scott, P. (1996). *Young people's images of science*. Buckingham, England: Open University Press.

Driver, R., & Oldham, V. (1986). A constructivist approach to curriculum development in science. *Studies in Science Education, 13*, 105–122.

Duckworth, E. (1987). *"The having of wonderful ideas" and Other essays on teaching and learning*. New York, NY: Teachers College Press.

Duncan, R. G., Rogat, A. D., & Yarden, A. (2009). A learning progression for deepening students' understandings of modern genetics across the 5th-10th grades. *Journal of Research in Science Teaching, 46*, 655–674.

Duschl, R. (2008). Science education in three part harmony: Balancing conceptual, epistemic, and social learning goals. *Review of Research in Education, 32*, 269–291.

Egelston, J. (1973). Inductive versus traditional methods of teaching high school biology laboratory experiments. *Science Education, 57*, 467–477.

Engle, R. A., & Conant, F. R. (2002). Guiding principles for fostering productive disciplinary engagement: Explaining an emergent argument in a community of learners classroom. *Cognition and Instruction, 20*, 399–483. doi:10.1207/S1532690XCI2004_1

Eylon, B.-S., & Linn, M. C. (1988). Learning and instruction: An examination of four research perspectives in science education. *Review of Educational Research, 58*, 251–301.

Feynman, R. P., Leighton, R. B., & Sands, M. L. (1995). *Six easy pieces: Essentials of physics, explained by its most brilliant teacher*. Reading, MA: Addison-Wesley.

Fishman, B. J., Marx, R., Best, S., & Tal, R. (2003). Linking teacher and student learning to improve professional development in systemic reform. *Teaching and Teacher Education, 19*, 643–658.

Fishman, B. J., Marx, R., Blumenfeld, P., Krajcik, J. S., & Soloway, E. (2004). Creating a framework for research on systemic technology innovations. *Journal of the Learning Sciences, 13*, 43–76.

Fishman, B. J., Penuel, W. R., Allen, A. R., Cheng, B. H., & Sabelli, N. (2013). Design-based implementation research: An emerging model for transforming the relationship of research and practice. *National Society for the Study of Education, 112*, 136–156.

Flavell, J. H. (1963). *The developmental psychology of Jean Piaget*. Princeton, NJ: Van Nostrand.

Flavell, J. H. (1971). First discussant comments: What is memory development the development of? *Human Development, 14*, 272–278.

Fletcher, S. S., & Luft, J. A. (2011). Early career secondary science teachers: A longitudinal study of beliefs in relation to field experiences. *Science Education, 95*, 1124–1146. doi:10.1002/sce.20450

French, J., Ekstrom, R., & Price, L. (1963). *Kit of reference tests for cognitive factors*. Princeton, NJ: Educational Testing Service.

Furtak, E. M., Seidel, T., Iverson, H., & Briggs, D. C. (2012). Experimental and quasi-experimental studies of inquiry-based science teaching: A meta-analysis. *Review of Educational Research, 82*, 300–329. doi:10.3102/0034654312457206

Fusco, D. (2001). Creating relevant science through urban planning and gardening. *Journal of Research in Science Teaching, 38*, 860–877.

Gardner, H. (1985). *The mind's new science: A history of the cognitive revolution.* New York, NY: Basic Books.

Garet, M., Porter, A., Desimone, L., Birman, B., & Yoon, K. (2001). What makes professional development effective? Analysis of a national sample of teachers. *American Education Research Journal, 38*, 915–945.

Gerard, L. F., Bowyer, J. B., & Linn, M. C. (2010). How does a community of principals develop leadership for technology-enhanced science? *Journal of School Leadership, 20*, 145–183.

Gerard, L. F., & Linn, M. C. (2016). Using automated scores of student essays to support teacher guidance in classroom inquiry. *Journal of Science Teacher Education, 27*, 111–129. doi:10.1007/s10972-016-9455-6

Gerard, L. F., Linn, M. C., & Liu, O. L. (2012, April). *How well can the computer assign feedback on student generated explanations? A Comparison study of computer and teacher adaptive guidance.* Paper presented at the American Education Research Association Annual Meeting, San Francisco, CA.

Gerard, L. F., Matuk, C. F., McElhaney, K. W., & Linn, M. C. (2015). Automated, adaptive guidance for K-12 education. *Educational Research Review, 15*, 41–58. doi:10.1016/j.edurev.2015.04.001

Gerard, L. F., Ryoo, K., McElhaney, K., Liu, L., Rafferty, A. N., & Linn, M. C. (2015). Automated guidance for student inquiry. *Journal of Educational Psychology, 108*, 60–81. doi:10.1037/edu0000052

Gerard, L. F., Spitulnik, M., & Linn, M. C. (2010). Teacher use of evidence to customize inquiry science instruction. *Journal of Research in Science Teaching, 47*, 1037–1063.

Gerard, L. F., Varma, K., Corliss, S. C., & Linn, M. C. (2011). Professional development for technology-enhanced inquiry science. *Review of Educational Research, 81*, 408–448.

Goldin, C. (2008). *The race between education and technology.* Cambridge, MA: Harvard University Press.

Goldstein, J. S. (1992). *A different sort of time: The life of Jerrold R. Zacharias, scientist, engineer, educator.* Cambridge: MIT Press.

Gopnik, A., & Wellman, H. M. (2012). Reconstructing constructivism: Causal models, Bayesian learning mechanisms, and the theory. *Psychological Bulletin, 138*, 1085–1108.

Gordin, D. N., Polman, J. L., & Pea, R. D. (1994). The climate visualizer: Sense-making through scientific visualization. *Journal of Science Education and Technology, 3*, 203–226.

Grosslight, L., Unger, C., Jay, E., & Smith, C. (1991). Understanding models and their use in science: Conceptions of middle and high school students and experts. *Journal of Research in Science Teaching, 28*, 799–822.

Grover, S., & Pea, R. D. (2013). Computational thinking in K–12: A review of the state of the field. *Educational Researcher, 42*, 38–43. doi:10.3102/0013189X12463051

Hanushek, E. A., & Raymond, M. E. (2005). Does school accountability lead to improved student performance? *Journal of Policy Analysis and Management, 24*, 297–327. doi:10.1002/pam.20091

Harle, M., & Towns, M. (1963). A review of spatial ability literature, its connection to chemistry, and implications for instruction *Journal of Research in Science Teaching, 1*, 199–225.

Harris, C. J., Penuel, W. R., D'Angelo, C. M., DeBarger, A. H., Gallagher, L. P., Kennedy, C. A., . . . Krajcik, J. S. (2015). Impact of project-based curriculum materials on student learning in science: Results of a randomized controlled trial. *Journal of Research in Science Teaching, 52,* 1362–1385. doi:10.1002/tea.21263

Haupt, G. W. (1948). First grade concepts of the moon. *Science Education, 24,* 258–262.

Hauser, R. M. (2004, August). *Does anyone really want to know the consequences of high stakes testing?* Paper presented at the American Sociological Association, San Francisco, CA.

Healy, J. (1998). *Failure to connect: How computers affect our children's minds and what we do about it.* New York, NY: Simon & Schuster.

Hegarty, M., Kriz, S., & Cate, C. (2003). The roles of mental animations and external animations in understanding mechanical systems. *Cognition and Instruction, 21,* 325–360.

Herrenkohl, L. R., Tasker, T., & White, B. (2011). Pedagogical practices to support classroom cultures of scientific inquiry. *Cognition and Instruction, 29,* 1–44.

Hmelo, C. E., Holton, D. L., & Kolodner, J. L. (2000). Designing to learn about complex systems. *Journal of the Learning Sciences, 9,* 247–298.

Hoadley, C. (2002). Creating context: Design-based research in creating and understanding CSCL. In G. Stahl (Ed.), *Computer support for collaborative learning* (pp. 453–462). Mahwah, NJ: Lawrence Erlbaum.

Hofer, B. K., & Pintrick, P. R. (1997). The development of epistemological theories: Beliefs about knowledge and knowing and their relation to learning. *Review of Educational Research, 67,* 88–140.

Holland, P., & Wainer, H. (1993). *Differential item functioning.* Hillsdale, NJ: Lawrence Erlbaum.

Howe, C., & Tolmie, A. (2003). Group work in primary school science: Discussion, consensus and guidance from experts. *International Journal of Educational Research, 39*(1–2), 51–72.

Hunt, E., & Minstrell, J. (1994). A cognitive approach to the teaching of physics. In K. McGilly (Ed.), *Classroom lessons: Integrating cognitive theory and classroom practice* (pp. 51–74). Cambridge: MIT Press.

Hyde, J. S. (2005). The gender similarities hypothesis. *American Psychologist, 60,* 581–592. doi:10.1037/0003-066X.60.6.581

Ingersoll, R. M. (2001). Teacher turnover and teacher shortages: An organizational analysis. *American Educational Research Journal, 38,* 499–534. doi:10.3102/00028312038003499

Inhelder, B., & Piaget, J. (1972). *The growth of logical thinking from childhood to adolescence; An essay on the construction of formal operational structures.* New York, NY: Basic Books. (Original work published 1958)

Jones, L. V. (1988). School achievement trends in mathematics and science, and what can be done to improve them. *Review of Research in Education, 15,* 307–341. doi:10.3102/009 1732X015001307

Kafai, Y. B., Feldon, D., Fields, D., Giang, M., & Quintero, M. (2007). Life in the times of Whypox: A virtual epidemic as a community event. In *Communities and technologies* (pp. 171–190). London, England: Springer.

Kali, Y. (2006). Collaborative knowledge-building using the design principles database. *International Journal of Computer Support for Collaborative Learning, 1,* 187–201.

Kali, Y., Linn, M. C., & Roseman, J. E. (Eds.). (2008). *Designing coherent science education: Implications for curriculum, instruction, and policy.* New York, NY: Teachers College Press.

Karplus, R. (1964). The science curriculum improvement study. *Journal of Research in Science Teaching, 22,* 193–303.

Kay, A. C. (1977, September). Microelectronics and the personal computer. *Scientific American,* 231–244.

Kim, Y. J., & Shute, V. J. (2015). The interplay of game elements with psychometric qualities, learning, and enjoyment in game-based assessment. *Computers & Education, 87,* 340–356. doi:10.1016/j.compedu.2015.07.009

Kimball, M. E. (1968). Understanding the nature of science: A comparison of scientists and science teachers. *Journal of Research in Science Teaching, 5*, 110–120. doi:10.1002/tea.3660050204

Koedinger, K. R., McLaughlin, E. A., & Heffernan, N. T. (2010). A quasi-experimental evaluation of an on-line formative assessment and tutoring system. *Journal of Educational Computing Research, 43*, 489–510.

Kollar, I., Fischer, F., & Slotta, J. (2006, April). *Web-based inquiry learning: How internal and external scripts influence collaborative argumentation and individual learning outcomes.* Paper presented at the annual meeting of the American Educational Research Association, San Francisco, CA.

Kolodner, J. L., Camp, P. J., Crismond, D., Fasse, B., Gray, J., Holbrook, J., . . . Ryan, M. (2003). Problem-based learning meets case-based reasoning in the middle-school science classroom: Putting Learning by Design™ into practice. *Journal of the Learning Sciences, 12*, 495–547.

Kozma, R. B. (1991). Learning with media. *Review of Educational Research, 61*, 179–211. doi:10.3102/00346543061002179

Krajcik, J. S., Blumenfeld, P. C., Marx, R. W., & Soloway, E. (1994). A collaborative model for helping middle grade science teachers learn project-based instruction. *Elementary School Journal, 94*, 483–497.

Kuhn, D., Amsel, E., & O'Loughlin, M. (1988). *The development of scientific thinking skills.* Orlando, FL: Academic Press.

Kuhn, T. S. (1962). *The structure of scientific revolutions* (1st ed.). Chicago, IL: University of Chicago Press.

Kyndta, E., Raes, E., Lismont, B., Timmers, F., Cascallar, E., & Dochy, F. (2013). A meta-analysis of the effects of face-to-face cooperative learning. Do recent studies falsify or verify earlier findings? *Educational Research Review, 10*, 133–149. doi:10.1016/j.edurev.2013.02.002

Ladouceur, R. P. (2008). Ella Thea Smith and the lost history of American high school biology textbooks. *Journal of the History of Biology, 41*, 435–471.

LaFollette, M. C. (2008). *Science on the air: Popularizers and personalities on radio and early television.* Chicago, IL: University of Chicago Press.

Lave, J., & Wenger, E. (1991). Situated learning: Legitimate peripheral participation. In R. Pea, & J. S. Brown (Eds.), *Learning in doing: Social, cognitive, and computational perspectives* (pp. 29–129). Cambridge, MA: Cambridge University Press.

Lawless, K. A., & Pellegrino, J. W. (2007). Professional development in integrating technology into teaching and learning: Knowns, unknowns, and ways to pursue better questions and answers. *Review of Educational Research, 77*, 575–614.

Lederman, N. G. (1992). Students' and teachers' conceptions of the nature of science: A review of the research. *Journal of Research in Science Teaching, 29*, 331–359.

Lederman, N. G., & Abell, S. K. (Eds.). (2014). *Handbook of research on science education* (Vol. II). Abingdon, England: Routledge.

Lee, O. (2004). Teacher change in beliefs and practices in science and literacy instruction with English language learners. *Journal of Research in Science Teaching, 41*, 65–93.

Lee, O. (2005). Science education with English language learners: Synthesis and research agenda. *Review of Educational Research, 75*, 491–530. doi:10.3102/00346543075004491

Lee, O., Penfield, R. D., & Maerten-Rivera, J. (2009). Effects of fidelity of implementation on science achievement gains among English language learners. *Journal of Research in Science Teaching, 46*, 836–859.

Lee, V. R., Drake, J., & Williamson, K. (2015). Let's get physical: K-12 students using wearable devices to obtain and learn about data from physical activities. *TechTrends, 59*(4), 46–53.

Lee, V. E., & Smith, J. B. (1996). Collective responsibility for learning and its effects on gains in achievement for early secondary school students. *American Journal of Education, 104,* 103–147. doi:10.1086/444122

Leelawong, K., & Biswas, G. (2008). Designing learning by teaching agents: The Betty's brain system. *International Journal of Artificial Intelligence in Education, 18,* 181–208.

Lehrer, R., Schauble, L., & Petrosino, A. J. (2001). Reconsidering the role of experiment in science education. Designing for science: Implications from everyday, classroom, and professional settings. In K. Crowley, C. D. Schunn, & T. Okada (Ed.), *Designing for science: Implications from everyday, classroom, and professional settings* (pp. 251–278). Mahwah, NJ: Lawrence Erlbaum.

Levy, F., & Murname, R. (2013). *Dancing with robots: Human skills for computerized work.* Washington, DC: Third Way.

Lewis, C., Perry, R., & Murata, A. (2006). How should research contribute to instructional improvement? The case of lesson study. *Educational Researcher, 35*(3), 3–14.

Lewis, E. B. (2008). Content is not enough: A history of secondary earth science teacher preparation with recommendations for today. *Journal of Geoscience Education, 56,* 445–464.

Liben, L. (1974). Operative understanding of horizontality and its relation to long-term memory. *Child Development, 45,* 416–424.

Linn, M. C. (1977). Scientific reasoning: Influences on task performance and response categorization. *Science Education, 61,* 357–363.

Linn, M. C. (1995). Designing computer learning environments for engineering and computer science: The scaffolded knowledge integration framework. *Journal of Science Education and Technology, 4,* 103–126.

Linn, M. C. (1996). From separation to partnership in science education: Students, laboratories, and the curriculum. In R. F. Tinker, & T. Ellermeijer (Eds.), *Microcomputer-based labs: Educational research and standards* (Vol. 156, pp. 13–46). Berlin, Germany: Springer-Verlag.

Linn, M. C. (1998). The impact of technology on science instruction: Historical trends and current opportunities. In K. G. Tobin, & B. J. Fraser (Eds.), *International handbook of science education* (Vol. 1, pp. 265–294). Dordrecht, Netherlands: Kluwer.

Linn, M. C., Clement, C., & Pulos, S. (1983). Is it formal if it's not physics? *Journal of Research in Science Teaching, 20,* 755–770.

Linn, M. C., & Eylon, B.-S. (2006). Science education: Integrating views of learning and instruction. In P. A. Alexander, & P. H. Winne (Eds.), *Handbook of educational psychology* (2nd ed., pp. 511–544). Mahwah, NJ: Lawrence Erlbaum.

Linn, M. C., & Eylon, B.-S. (2011). *Science learning and instruction: Taking advantage of technology to promote knowledge integration.* New York, NY: Routledge.

Linn, M. C., & Hsi, S. (2000). *Computers, teachers, peers: Science learning partners.* Mahwah, NJ: Lawrence Erlbaum.

Linn, M. C., Lewis, C., Tsuchida, I., & Songer, N. B. (2000). Beyond fourth-grade science: Why do U.S. and Japanese students diverge? *Educational Researcher, 29*(3), 4–14.

Linn, M. C., & Muilenburg, L. (1996). Creating lifelong science learners: What models form a firm foundation? *Educational Researcher, 25*(5), 18–24.

Linn, M. C., & Petersen, A. C. (1985). Emergence and characterization of sex differences in spatial ability: A meta-analysis. *Child Development, 56,* 1479–1498.

Linn, M. C., & Slotta, J. D. (2000). WISE science. *Educational Leadership, 58*(2), 29–32.

Linn, M. C., Songer, N. B., & Eylon, B. S. (1996). Shifts and convergences in science learning and instruction. In R. Calfee, & D. Berliner (Eds.), *Handbook of educational psychology* (pp. 438–490). Riverside, NJ: Macmillan.

Linn, M. C., & Thier, H. D. (1975). The effect of experiential science on the development of logical thinking in children. *Journal of Research in Science Teaching, 12,* 49–62.

Little, J. W. (1993). Teachers' professional development in a climate of educational reform. *Education Evaluation and Policy Analysis, 15*, 129–151.

Liu, O. L., Brew, C., Blackmore, J., Gerard, L. F., Madhok, J. J., & Linn, M. C. (2014). Automated scoring of constructed-response science items: Prospects and obstacles. *Educational Measurement, 33*(2), 19–28. doi:10.1111/emip.12028

Liu, O. L., Rios, J. A., Heilman, M., Gerard, L., & Linn, M. C. (2016). Validation of automated scoring of science assessments. *Journal of Research in Science Teaching, 53*, 215–233. doi:10.1002/tea.21299

Lohman, D. F. (1988). Spatial abilities as traits, processes, and knowledge. In R. J. Sternberg (Ed.), *Advances in the psychology of human intelligence* (Vol. 4, pp. 181–248). Hillsdale, NJ: Lawrence Erlbaum.

Lombrozo, T. (2010). Causal-explanatory pluralism: How intentions, functions, and mechanisms influence causal ascriptions. *Cognitive Psychology, 61*, 303–332.

Maccoby, E. E., & Jacklin, C. N. (1974). *The psychology of sex differences*. Stanford, CA: Stanford University Press.

Magnusson, S., Krajcik, J., & Borko, H. (1999). Nature, sources and development of pedagogical content knowledge for science teaching. In J. Gess-Newsome, & N. G. Lederman (Eds.), *Examining pedagogical content knowledge: The construct and its implications for science education* (pp. 95–132). Boston, MA: Kluwer.

Mandinach, E. B., & Cline, H. F. (1994). *Classroom dynamics: Implementing a technology-based learning environment*. Mahwah, NJ: Lawrence Erlbaum.

Markus, H., & Nurius, P. (1986). Possible selves. *American Psychologist, 41*, 954–969. doi:10.1037//0003-066X.41.9.954

Marx, R. W., & Harris, C. J. (2006). No Child Left Behind and science education: Opportunities, challenges, and risks. *Elementary School Journal, 105*, 467–477.

Matuk, C. F., & Linn, M. C. (2015, June). *Examining the real and perceived impacts of a public idea repository on literacy and science inquiry*. Paper presented at the Exploring the Material Conditions of Learning: The Computer Supported Collaborative Learning (CSCL) Conference, Gothenberg, Sweden.

Matuk, C. F., Linn, M. C., & Eylon, B.-S. (2015). Technology to support teachers to use evidence from student work to customize technology-enhanced inquiry units. *Instructional Science, 43*, 229–257. doi:10.1007/s11251-014-9338-1

Mayer, R. E. (1989). Systematic thinking fostered by illustrations in scientific text. *Journal of Educational Psychology, 81*, 240–246.

McCloskey, M. (1983). Naive theories of motion. In D. Gentner, & A. L. Stevens (Eds.), *Mental models* (pp. 299–324). Hillsdale, NJ: Lawrence Erlbaum.

McElhaney, K. W., Chang, H.-Y., Chiu, J. L., & Linn, M. C. (2015). Evidence for effective uses of dynamic visualisations in science curriculum materials. *Studies in Science Education, 51*, 49–85. doi:10.1080/03057267.2014.984506

McNeill, K. L., Lizotte, D. J., Krajcik, J., & Marx, R. W. (2006). Supporting students' construction of scientific explanations by fading scaffolds in instructional materials. *Journal of the Learning Sciences, 15*, 153–191.

Metcalf, S. J., Kamarainen, A., Tutwiler, M. S., Grotzer, T., & Dede, C. (2011). Ecosystem science learning via multi-user virtual environments. *International Journal of Gaming and Computer-Mediated Simulations, 3*, 86–90.

Metcalf, S. J., & Tinker, R. (2004). Probeware and handhelds in elementary and middle school science. *Journal of Science Education and Technology, 13*, 43–49.

Metz, K. E. (1995). Reassessment of developmental constraints on children's science instruction. *Review of Educational Research, 65*, 93–127.

Metz, K. E. (1997). On the complex relation between cognitive developmental research and children's science curricula. *Review of Educational Research, 67*, 151–163.

Millar, R. (1996). Rethinking science education: Meeting the challenge of "science for all." *School Science Review, 93*, 21–30.

Millar, R., & Hunt, A. (2001). Science for public understanding: A different way to teach and learn science. *School Science Review, 83*, 35–42.

Miller, D. I., Eagly, A. H., & Linn, M. C. (2014). Women's representation in science predicts national gender-science stereotypes: Evidence from 66 nations. *Journal of Educational Psychology, 107*, 631–644. doi:10.1037/edu0000005

Miller, P. E. (1963). A comparison of the abilities of secondary teachers and students of biology to understand science. *Iowa Academy of Science, 70*, 510–513.

Millikan, R. A., & Gale, H. G. (1906). *A laboratory course in physics for secondary schools.* Cambridge, MA: Ginn.

Millner, A., & Resnick, M. (2005, June). *Tools for creating custom physical computer interfaces.* Paper presented at the 4th International Conference for Interaction Design for Children, Boulder, CO.

Minstrell, J., & Kraus, P. (2005). Guided inquiry in the science classroom. In M. S. Donovan, & J. D. Bransford (Eds.), *How students learn: History, mathematics, and science in the classroom* (pp. 475–511). Washington, DC: National Academies Press.

Minstrell, J., & van Zee, E. H. (2000). *Inquiring into inquiry learning and teaching in science.* Washington, DC: American Association for the Advancement of Science.

Mishra, P., & Koehler, M. J. (2006). Technological pedagogical content knowledge: A framework for teacher knowledge. *Teachers College Record, 108*, 1017–1054.

Moher, T., Hussain, S., Halter, T., & Kilb, D. (2005, April). *Embedding dynamic phenomena within the physical space of an elementary school classroom.* Paper presented at the ACM Conference on Human Factors in Computing Systems, Portland, OR.

Mokros, J. R., & Tinker, R. F. (1987). The impact of microcomputer-based labs on children's ability to interpret graphs. *Journal of Research in Science Teaching, 24*, 369–383. doi:10.1002/tea.3660240408

Moon, T. J., & Mann, P. B. (1933). *Biology for beginners.* New York, NY: Henry Holt.

Morgan, J. E. (1932). Introduction. In B. H. Darrow (Ed.), *Radio: The assistant teacher.* Columbus, OH: R. H. Adams.

Mousavi, S., Low, R., & Sweller, J. (1995). Reducing cognitive load by mixing auditory and visual presentation modes. *Journal of Educational Psychology, 87*, 319–334.

Mullis, I., Jenkins, V. S., & Lynn, B. (1988). *The science report card: Elements of risk and recovery. Trends and achievement based on the 1986 national assessment.* Princeton, NJ: Educational Testing Service.

National Center for Education Statistics. (1999). *The condition of education, NCES 1999022.* Retrieved from http://nces.ed.gov/pubsearch/pubsinfo.asp?pubid=1999022

National Center for Education Statistics. (2014). *Digest of education statistics.* Retrieved from http://nces.ed.gov/programs/digest/d14/tables/dt14_218.10.asp?current=yes

National Commission on Excellence in Education. (1983). *A nation at risk: The imperative for educational reform.* Retrieved from http://www2.ed.gov/pubs/NatAtRisk/index.html

National Research Council. (1999). *High stakes: Testing for tracking, promotion and graduation.* Washington, DC: Author.

National Research Council. (2002). *Scientific research in education* (R. J. Shavelson & L. Towne, Eds.). Washington, DC: National Academies Press.

National Research Council. (2005). *America's lab report: Investigations in high school science* (S. R. Singer, M. L. Hilton, & H. A. Schweingruber, Eds.). Washington, DC: National Academies Press.

National Research Council. (2007). *Taking science to school: Learning and teaching science in Grades K-8* (R. A. Duschl, H. A. Schweingruber, & A. W. Shouse, Eds.). Washington, DC: National Academies Press.

National Research Council. (2009). *Learning science in informal environments: People, places, and pursuits* (P. Bell, B. Lewenstein, A. W. Shouse, & M. A. Feder, Eds.). Washington, DC: National Academies Press.

National Research Council. (2012). Equity and diversity in science and engineering education. In *A framework for K-12 science education* (pp. 277–296). Washington, DC: National Academies Press.

National Society for the Study of Education. (1932). *The 31st yearbook of the National Society for the Study of Education: Part I—A program for teaching science.* Chicago, IL: University of Chicago Press.

NGSS Lead States. (2013). *Next Generation Science Standards: For states, by states.* Washington, DC: National Academies Press.

Norman, G. R., & Schmidt, H. G. (1992). The psychological basis of problem-based learning: A review of the evidence. *Academic Medicine, 67,* 557–565.

Nosek, B. A., Smyth, F. L., Sriram, N., Lindner, N. M., Devos, T., Ayala, A., . . . Greenwald, A. G. (2009). National differences in gender–science stereotypes predict national sex differences in science and math achievement. *Proceedings of the National Academies of Science, 106,* 10593–10597. doi:10.1073/pnas.0809921106

NSF Taskforce on Cyberlearning. (2008). *Fostering learning in the networked world: The cyberlearning opportunity and challenge.* Washington, DC: National Science Foundation.

Oppenheimer, T. (1997, July). The computer delusion. *The Atlantic.* Retrieved from http://www.theatlantic.com/magazine/archive/1997/07/the-computer-delusion/376899/

Osborne, J., Duschl, R., & Fairbrother, R. (2002). *Breaking the mould? Teaching science for public understanding.* London, England: Nuffield Foundation.

Palincsar, A. S., & Brown, A. (1984). Reciprocal teaching of comprehension-fostering and comprehension monitoring activities. *Cognition and Instruction, 1,* 117–175.

Pan, E., Chiu, J. L., Inkelas, K., Garner, G., Russell, S., & Berger, E. (2015). Affordances and constraints of physical and virtual manipulatives for learning dynamics. *International Journal of Engineering Education, 31,* 1629–1644.

Papert, S. (1980). *Mindstorms: Children, computers, and powerful ideas.* New York, NY: Basic Books.

Paulsen, C. A. (2013). Implementing out-of-school time STEM resources: Best practices from public television. *Afterschool Matters, 17,* 27–35.

Pea, R. D. (1993). The collaborative visualization project. *Communications of the ACM, 36*(5), 60–63.

Pea, R. D., & Kurland, M. D. (1984). On the cognitive effects of learning computer programming. *New Ideas Psychology, 2,* 137–168.

Pellegrino, J. W. (2016). *21st Century science assessment: The future is now.* Menlo Park, CA: SRI International.

Penuel, W. R., Fishman, B., Cheng, B. H., & Sabelli, N. (2011). Organizing research and development at the intersection of learning, implementation, and design. *Educational Researcher, 40,* 331–337. doi:10.3102/0013189X11421826

Penuel, W. R., Fishman, B., Yamaguchi, R., & Gallagher, L. P. (2007). What makes professional development effective? Strategies that foster curriculum implementation. *American Educational Research Journal, 44,* 921–958.

Perkes, V. A. (1968). Junior high school science teacher preparation, teaching behavior and student achievement. *Journal of Research in Science Teaching, 5,* 121–126.

Pew Research Center. (2009). *Fighting over Darwin, state by state.* Retrieved from http://www.pewforum.org/2009/02/04/fighting-over-darwin-state-by-state/

Pfundt, H., & Duit, R. (2009). *Students' and teachers' conceptions and science education.* Retrieved from http://archiv.ipn.uni-kiel.de/stcse/download_stcse.html

Piaget, J. (1930). *The child's conception of physical causality* [La causalite physique chez l'enfant]. London, England: Kegan Paul.

Piaget, J. (1952). *The origins of intelligence in children.* New York, NY: International Universities Press.

Piltz, A. (1958). An investigation of teacher-recognized difficulties encountered in the teaching of science in the elementary schools of Florida. *Science Education, 42,* 440–443. doi:10.1002/sce.3730420518

Pintrich, P. R. (2003). A motivational science perspective on the role of student motivation in learning and teaching contexts. *Journal of Educational Psychology, 95,* 667–686.

Pintrich, P. R., Marx, R. W., & Boyle, R. A. (1993). Beyond cold conceptual change: The role of motivational beliefs and classroom contextual factors in the process of conceptual change. *Review of Educational Research, 63,* 167–199.

PIRLS International Study Center at Boston College. (1995). *Third International Mathematics and Science Study (TIMSS).* Retrieved from http://timss.bc.edu/timss1995.html

Plass, J. L., Homer, B. D., & Hayward, E. O. (2009). Design factors for educationally effective animations and simulations. *Journal of Computing in Higher Education, 21,* 31–61. doi:10.1007/s12528-009-9011-x

Polman, J. L., & Pea, R. D. (2001). Transformative communication as a cultural tool for guiding inquiry science. *Science Education, 85,* 223–238.

Polya, G. (1943). On the zeros of the derivatives of a function and its analytic character. *Bulletin of the American Mathematical Society, 49,* 178–191. doi:10.1090/S0002-9904-1943-07853-6

Pressey, S. L. (1926). A simple apparatus which gives tests and scores—And teaches. *School and Society, 23,* 373–376.

Pribyl, J. R., & Bodner, G. M. (1987). Spatial ability and its role in organic chemistry: A study of four organic courses. *Journal of Research in Science Teaching, 24,* 229–240. doi:10.1002/tea.3660240304

Price, C. A., Lee, H.-S., Plummer, J. D., SubbaRao, M., & Wyatt, R. (2015). Position paper on use of stereoscopy to support science learning: Ten years of research. *Journal of Astronomy & Earth Science Education, 2,* 17–26.

Proctor, R. W., & Vu, K.-P. L. (2006). *Stimulus–response compatibility principles: Data, theory and application.* Boca Raton, FL: CRC Press.

Quellmalz, E. S., DeBarger, A. H., Haertel, G., Schank, P., Buckley, B., Gobert, J., . . . Ayala, C. (2007). *Exploring the role of technology-based simulations in science assessment: The Calipers project.* Retrieved from http://calipers.sri.com/downloads/CalipersAERA07.pdf

Quintana, C., Reiser, B. J., Davis, E. A., Krajcik, J., Fretz, E., Golan, R. D., . . . Soloway, E. (2004). A scaffolding design framework for software to support science inquiry. *Journal of the Learning Sciences, 13,* 337–386.

Resnick, L. B., & Resnick, D. P. (1992). Assessing the thinking curriculum: New tools for educational reform. In B. R. Gifford, & M. C. O'Connor (Eds.), *Changing assessment: Alternative views of aptitude, achievement, and instruction* (pp. 37–75). Boston, MA: Kluwer.

Resnick, M., Maloney, J., Monroy-Hernández, A., Rusk, N., Eastmond, E., Brennan, K., . . . Kafai, Y. (2009). Scratch: Programming for all. *Communications of the ACM, 52*(11), 60–67.

Rodriguez, G. M. (2013). Power and agency in education: Exploring the pedagogical dimensions of funds of knowledge. *Review of Research in Education, 37,* 87–120. doi:10.3102/0091732X12462686

Rolfe, E. C. (1924). A comparison of the effectiveness of a motion picture film and of demonstration in instruction in high school physics. In F. N. Freeman (Ed.), *Visual education* (pp. 335–338). Chicago, IL: University of Chicago Press.

Rosé, C. P., Wang, Y. C., Cui, Y., Arguello, J., Stegmann, K., Weinberger, A., & Fischer, F. (2008). Analyzing collaborative learning processes automatically: Exploiting the advances of computational linguistics in computer-supported collaborative learning. *International Journal of Computer Supported Collaborative Learning, 3,* 237–271.

Rose, D., Meyer, A., & Hitchcock, C. (2005). *The universally designed classroom.* Cambridge, MA: Harvard Education Press.

Rosebery, A. S., Warren, B., & Conant, F. R. (1992). Appropriating scientific discourse: Findings from language minority classrooms. *Journal of the Learning Sciences, 1,* 61–94.

Roth, K., Garnier, H., Chen, C., Lemmens, M., Schwille, K., & Wickler, N. (2011). Video-based lesson analysis: Effective science professional development for teacher and student learning. *Journal of Research in Science Teaching, 48,* 117–148.

Ruiz-Primo, M. A., & Furtak, E. M. (2006). Informal formative assessment and scientific inquiry: Exploring teachers' practices and student learning. *Educational Assessment, 11,* 237–263.

Ruiz-Primo, M. A., & Furtak, E. M. (2007). Exploring teachers' informal formative assessment practices and students' understanding in the context of scientific inquiry. *Journal of Research in Science Teaching, 44,* 57–84.

Saettler, P. (1968). *A history of instructional technology.* New York, NY: McGraw-Hill.

Sandoval, W. A. (2005). Understanding students' practical epistemologies and their influence on learning through inquiry. *Science Education, 89,* 634–656.

Sandoval, W. A. (2012). Situating epistemological development. In J. V. Aalst, K. Thompson, M. J. Jacobson, & P. Reimann (Eds.), *The future of learning: Proceedings of the 10th international conference of the learning sciences* (Vol. 1, pp. 347–354). Sydney, Australia: International Society of the Learning Sciences.

Sandoval, W. A., & Reiser, B. J. (2004). Explanation-driven inquiry: Integrating conceptual and epistemic scaffolds for scientific inquiry. *Science Education, 88,* 345–372.

Sato, E., & Linn, M. C. (2014). Designing critique to improve conceptual understanding. In J. L. Polman, E. A. Kyza, D. K. O'Neill, I. Tabak, W. R. Penuel, A. S. Jurow, & L. . . . D'Amico (Eds.), *Learning and becoming in practice: The International Conference of the Learning Sciences 2014* (Vol. 1, pp. 385–393). Boulder, CO: International Society of the Learning Sciences.

Scardamalia, M., & Bereiter, C. (1994). Computer support for knowledge-building communities. *Journal of the Learning Sciences, 3,* 265–283.

Scardamalia, M., & Bereiter, C. (2006). Knowledge building: Theory, pedagogy, and technology. In K. Sawyer (Ed.), *Cambridge handbook of the learning sciences* (pp. 97–118). New York, NY: Cambridge University Press.

Schauble, L., Glaser, R., Duschl, R. A., Schulze, S., & John, J. (1995). Students' understanding of the objectives and procedures of experimentation in the science classroom. *Journal of the Learning Sciences, 4,* 131–166.

Schauble, L., Glaser, R., Raghavan, K., & Reiner, M. (1992). The integration of knowledge and experimentation strategies in understanding a physical system. *Applied Cognitive Psychology, 6,* 321–343.

Schauble, L., Klopfer, L. E., & Raghavan, K. (1991). Students' transition from an engineering model to a science model of experimentation. *Journal of Research in Science Teaching* (Special Issue: Students' Models and Epistemologies), *28,* 859–882.

Schmidt, W. H., Raizen, S. A., Britton, E. D., Bianchi, L. J., & Wolfe, R. G. (1997). *Many visions, many aims: A cross-national investigation of curricular intentions in school science.* Norwell, MA: Kluwer.

Schwartz, C. V., & Gwekwerere, Y. N. (2006). Using a guided inquiry and modeling instructional framework to support preservice K-8 science teaching. *Science Education, 91,* 158–186.

Sfard, A., & Prusak, A. (2005). Telling identities: In search of an analytic tool for investigating learning as a culturally shaped activity. *Educational Researcher, 34*(4), 14–22. doi:10.3102/0013189X034004014

Shavelson, R. J. (2007). *A brief history of student learning assessment*. Washington, DC: Association of American Colleges and Universities.

Shear, L., Bell, P., & Linn, M. (2004). Partnership models: The case of the deformed frogs. In M. C. Linn, E. A. Davis, & P. Bell (Eds.), *Internet environments for science education* (pp. 289–314). Mahwah, NJ: Lawrence Erlbaum.

Shepard, L. A. (2000). The role of assessment in a learning culture. *Educational Researcher, 29*(7), 4–14. doi:10.3102/0013189X029007004

Sherman, J. A. (1967). Problem of sex differences in space perception and aspects of intellectual functioning. *Psychological Review, 74*, 290–299.

Shulman, L. S. (1986). Those who understand: Knowledge growth in teaching. *Educational Researcher, 15*, 4–14.

Shymansky, J. A., Hedges, L. V., & Woodworth, G. (1990). A reassessment of the effects of inquiry-based science curricula of the 60s on student performance. *Journal of Research in Science Teaching, 27*, 127–144. doi:10.1002/tea.3660270205

Siegler, R. S., & Liebert, R. M. (1975). Acquisition of formal scientific reasoning by 10- and 13-year-olds: Designing a factorial experiment. *Developmental Psychology, 11*, 401–402. doi:10.1037/h0076579

Sisk-Hilton, S. (2009). *Teaching and learning in public: Professional development through shared inquiry*. Columbia, NY: Teachers College Press.

Skinner, B. F. (1938). *The behavior of organisms: An experimental analysis*. New York, NY: Appleton-Century.

Skinner, B. F. (1958). Teaching machines. *Science, 128*, 969–977.

Slamecka, N. J., & Graf, P. (1978). The generation effect: Delineation of a phenomenon. *Journal of Experimental Psychology, 4*, 592–604.

Slotta, J. D., & Linn, M. C. (2009). *WISE science: Web-based inquiry in the classroom*. New York, NY: Teachers College Press.

Smith, D. C., & Neale, D. C. (1989). The Construction of subject matter knowledge in primary science teaching. *Teaching and Teacher Education, 5*, 1–20.

Smith, E. T. (1938). *Exploring biology*. New York, NY: Harcourt.

Smith, H. (1963). Educational research related to science instruction for the elementary and junior high school: A review and commentary. *Journal of Research in Science Teaching, 1*, 199–225.

Smith, J. P., III, diSessa, A. A., & Roschelle, J. (1993). Misconceptions reconceived: A constructivist analysis of knowledge in transition. *Journal of the Learning Sciences, 3*, 115–163.

Smith, S. G., & Sherwood, B. A. (1976). Educational uses of the PLATO computer system. *Science, 192*, 334–352. doi:10.1126/science.769165

Songer, N. B., & Kali, Y. (2015). Science education and the learning sciences as coevolving species. In R. K. Sawyer (Ed.), *Cambridge handbook of the learning sciences* (2nd ed., pp. 565–586). New York, NY: Cambridge University Press.

Songer, N. B., & Linn, M. C. (1991). How do students' views of science influence knowledge integration? *Journal of Research in Science Teaching, 28*, 761–784.

Stake, R. E., & Easley, J. A. (1978). *Case studies in science education. Vol. 2: Design, overview, and general findings*. Washington, DC: U.S. Government Printing Office.

Steele, C. (1997). A threat in the air: How stereotypes shape intellectual identity and performance. *American Psychologist, 52*, 613–629.

Steele, C., & Aronson, J. (1995). Stereotype threat and the intellectual test performance of African Americans. *Journal of Personality and Social Psychology, 69*, 797–811.

Steinkuehler, C., & Duncan, S. (2008). Scientific habits of mind in virtual worlds. *Journal of Science Education and Technology, 17*, 530–543.

Sternberg, R. J. (2007). Assessing what matters. *Educational Leadership, 65*(4), 20–26.

Stoll, C. (1995). *Silicon snake oil: Second thoughts on the information highway*. New York, NY: Doubleday.

Strike, K. A., & Posner, G. J. (1985). A conceptual change view of learning and understanding. In L. H. West, & A. L. Pines (Eds.), *Cognitive structure and conceptual change* (pp. 211–231). Orlando, FL: Academic Press.

Sunal, D. W. (1980). Effect of field experience during elementary methods courses on preservice teacher behavior. *Journal of Research in Science Teaching, 17*, 17–23.

Suppes, P., & Binford, F. (1965). Experimental teaching of mathematical logic in the elementary school. *The Arithmetic Teacher, 12*, 187–195.

Sweitzer, G. L., & Anderson, R. D. (1983). A meta-analysis of research on science teacher education practices associated with inquiry strategy. *Journal of Research in Science Teaching, 20*, 453–466. doi:10.1002/tea.3660200508

Sweller, J. (1988). Cognitive load during problem solving: Effects on learning. *Cognitive Science, 12*, 257–285.

Sylvan, E. (2005, June). *Integrating aesthetic, engineering, and scientific understanding in a hands-on design activity.* Paper presented at the 4th International Conference for Interaction Design for Children, Boulder, CO.

Talanquer, V., Tomanek, D., & Novodvorsky, I. (2013). Assessing students' understanding of inquiry: What do prospective science teachers notice? *Journal of Research in Science Teaching, 50*, 189–208. doi:10.1002/tea.21074

Tasker, T., & Herrenkohl, L. (2016). Using peer feedback to improve students' scientific inquiry. *Journal of Science Teacher Education, 27*, 35–59.

Taylor, R. (Ed.) (1980). *The computer in the school: Tutor, tool, tutee.* Totowa, NJ: Teachers College Press.

Thorndike, E. L. (1912). *Education: A first book.* New York, NY: Macmillan.

Tissenbaum, M., Lui, M., & Slotta, J. D. (2011). Co-designing collaborative smart classroom curriculum for secondary school science. *Journal of Universal Computer Science, 18*, 327–352.

Tschirgi, J. E. (1980). Sensible reasoning: A hypothesis about hypotheses. *Child Development, 51*, 1–10.

Tversky, B., Morrison, J. B., & Betrancourt, M. (2002). Animation: Can it facilitate? *International Journal of Human-Computer Studies, 57*, 247–262.

Tweney, R. D., & Doherty, M. E. (1983). Rationality and the psychology of inference. *Synthese, 57*, 129–138. doi:10.1007/BF01063999

van Zee, E., & Minstrell, J. (1997). Using questioning to guide student thinking. *Journal of the Learning Sciences, 6*, 227–269. doi:10.1207/s15327809jls0602_3

Vitale, J. M., McBride, E., & Linn, M. C. (2016). Distinguishing complex ideas about climate change: Knowledge integration vs. specific guidance. *International Journal of Science Education, 38*, 1548–1569. doi:10.1080/09500693.2016.1198969

Vollmeyer, R., Burns, B. D., & Holyoak, K. J. (1996). The impact of goal specificity on strategy use and the acquisition of problem structure. *Cognitive Science, 20*, 75–100.

Vosniadou, S. (1994). Capturing and modeling the process of conceptual change. *Learning and Instruction, 4*, 45–69.

Vosniadou, S. (Ed.). (2013). *International handbook of research on conceptual change* (2nd ed.). New York, NY: Psychology Press.

Vosniadou, S., & Brewer, W. F. (1992). Mental models of the earth. *Cognitive Psychology, 24*, 123–183.

Vygotsky, L. S. (1978). *Mind in society: The development of higher psychological processes.* Cambridge, MA: Harvard University Press.

Waddington, C. H. (1966). *Principles of development and differentiation.* New York, NY: Macmillan.

Wason, P. C. (1968). Reasoning about a rule. *Quarterly Journal of Experimental Psychology, 20*, 273–281.

Wason, P. C., & Johnson-Laird, P. N. (1972). *Psychology of reasoning: Structure and content.* Cambridge, MA: Harvard University Press.

Watson, J. B. (1913). Psychology as the behaviorist views it. *Psychological Review, 20,* 158–177.

Weintrop, D., Beheshti, E., Horn, M. S., & Wilensky, U. (2015). Defining computational thinking for mathematics and science classrooms. *Journal of Science Education and Technology, 25,* 127–147. doi:10.1007/s10956-015-9581-5

Welch, W. W. (1979). Twenty years of science curriculum development: A look back. In D. C. Berliner (Ed.), *Review of research in education* (Vol. 7, pp. 282–308). Washington, DC: American Educational Research Association.

Welch, W. W., Klopfer, L. E., Aikenhead, G. S., & Robinson, J. T. (1981). The role of inquiry in science education: Analysis and recommendations. *Science Education, 65,* 33–50. doi:10.1002/sce.3730650106.

Welsh, J. R., Kucinkas, S. K., & Curran, L. T. (1990). *Armed Services Vocational Battery (ASVAB): Integrative review of validity studies.* San Antonio, TX: Air Force Systems Command.

White, B., Frederiksen, J., Frederiksen, T., Eslinger, E., Loper, S., & Collins, A. (2002). Inquiry Island: Affordances of a multi-agent environment for scientific inquiry and reflective learning. In P. Bell, R. Stevens, & T. Satwicz (Eds.), *Proceedings of the Fifth International Conference of the Learning Sciences (ICLS).* Retrieved from http://thinkertools.org/Pages/research.html

White, B., & Horwitz, P. (1987). *Thinker tools: Enabling children to understand physical laws.* Cambridge, MA: BBN Technologies.

White, B. Y. (1993). ThinkerTools: Causal models, conceptual change, and science education. *Cognition and Instruction, 10,* 1–100.

White, B. Y., & Frederiksen, J. R. (1998). Inquiry, modeling, and metacognition: Making science accessible to all students. *Cognition and Instruction, 16,* 3–118.

Wilensky, U., & Reisman, K. (2006). Thinking like a wolf, a sheep or a firefly: Learning biology through constructing and testing computational theories—An embodied modeling approach. *Cognition and Instruction, 24,* 171–209.

Wilensky, U., & Resnick, M. (1999). Thinking in levels: A dynamic systems approach to making sense of the world. *Journal of Science Education & Technology, 8,* 3–19.

Williams, M., Linn, M. C., Ammon, P., & Gearhart, M. (2004). Learning to teach inquiry science in a technology-based environment: A case study. *Journal of Science Education and Technology, 13,* 189–206.

Wilson, S. M., & Berne, J. (1999). Teacher learning and the acquisition of professional knowledge: An examination of research on contemporary professional development. In A. Iran-Nejad, & P. D. Pearson (Eds.), *Review of research in education* (pp. 173–209). Washington, DC: American Educational Research Association.

Wiser, M., & Carey, S. (1983). When heat and temperature were one. In D. Gentner, & A. L. Stevens (Eds.), *Mental models* (pp. 267–298). Hillsdale, NJ: Lawrence Erlbaum.

Wollman, W. (1977). Controlling variables: Assessing levels of understanding. *Science Education, 61,* 367–383. doi:10.1002/sce.3730610312

Wu, H.-K., Krajcik, J. S., & Soloway, E. (2001). Promoting conceptual understanding of chemical representations: Students' use of a visualization tool in the classroom. *Journal of Research in Science Teaching, 38,* 821–842.

Young, D. (1958). Atomic energy concepts in third and sixth grade. *School Science and Mathematics, 58,* 535–539. doi:10.1111/j.1949-8594.1958.tb08052.x

Zhao, Y., Pugh, K., Sheldon, S., & Byers, J. (2002). Conditions for classroom technology innovations. *Teachers College Record, 104,* 482–515.

Zimmerman, C. (2007). The development of scientific thinking skills in elementary and middle school. *Developmental Review, 27,* 172–223.

Chapter 16

The Metatheoretical Assumptions of Literacy Engagement: A Preliminary Centennial History

George G. Hruby
Leslie D. Burns
University of Kentucky

Stergios Botzakis
Susan L. Groenke
University of Tennessee, Knoxville

Leigh A. Hall
University of North Carolina, Chapel Hill

Judson Laughter
Richard L. Allington
University of Tennessee, Knoxville

In this review of literacy education research in North America over the past century, the authors examined the historical succession of theoretical frameworks on students' active participation in their own literacy learning, and in particular the metatheoretical assumptions that justify those frameworks. The authors used motivation *and* engagement *as focal topics by which to trace this history because of their conceptual proximity to active literacy participation. They mapped the uses of* motivation *and* engagement *in the major literacy journals and handbooks over the past century, constructed a grounded typology of theoretical assumptions about literate agency and its development to code those uses, and reviewed similar histories of theoretical frameworks in educational, psychological, philosophical, and literary scholarship to draft a narrative history of the emergence of* engaged *literacies.*

I believe that all education proceeds by the participation of the individual in the social consciousness of the race. . . . [T]hat the active side precedes the passive in the development of the child nature; that expression

Review of Research in Education
March 2016, Vol. 40, pp. 588–643
DOI: 10.3102/0091732X16664311
© 2016 AERA. http://rre.aera.net

comes before conscious impression . . . that conscious states tend to project themselves in action. . . . [T]he conditions [in typical classrooms] are such that [the student] is not permitted to follow the law of his nature; the result is friction and waste.

—Dewey (1897, pp. 3, 12, 14)

Active and engaged participation of students in their learning, generally understood, is a theme with a long history in American literacy instruction and developmental research. In recent decades, attention to student activity in literacy education in the United States has markedly increased, with the result that constructs such as *motivation* and *engagement* have become quite focused and distinct. Currently, the term *literacy* is being paired with *engaged* or *engagement* more frequently in English language arts scholarship. Historical surveys of literacy research across the past century reveal an even broader range of terms by which to describe and explain students' active participation in their literacy development (*drive, volition, interest, intention, nature*, etc.). The warrants for these terms seem to be informed by cohesive sets of assumptions relatable across schools of theory, methodology, and philosophy regarding agentive action in learning and development.

Social science scholars often explain related sets of theories, methods, terminologies, and academic motifs by way of sequential histories of theoretical and methodological orientation: that is, as a succession of dominant *theoretical frameworks* (e.g., neoromantic, functionalist, behaviorist, cognitivist, sociocultural, postmodern). These cohering theoretical commitments can purportedly imply distinct and differentiating metatheoretical assumptions about phenomena, as well as about causation, thus playing a central role in justification of theoretical construct, research design, and methodology (Bredo, 2006b; Harré & Gillet, 1994; Harste, Woodward, & Burke, 1984; Johnson, 2011). It may even be the case that general assumptions about causation have a particular relevance for explanations of human development and agency in particular. (Certainly, natural causes are often described as if they had human-like agency, as in expressions such as "governed by the laws of nature." And the concept of "human nature" similarly suggests a categorical connection in the opposite direction.) The question remains open as to whether a close review of particular education research literatures demonstrates the historical succession of theoretical frameworks claimed for larger domains, or whether this idea is helpful in understanding disagreements about learning and instruction within those corpora.

In this chapter, we draft a historical model of metatheoretical framing for education research on instruction for engaged literacy as an exemplary case. We do so not only because of our interest as scholars of literacy but also because of the potential application for such a model across related disciplines. The history of literacy research parallels that of education research more generally and, indeed, of psychology, modern literary criticism, philosophy, and postphilological linguistics (the four most common historical influences on literacy education theory). Thus, such a model could allow for a century-long overview across disciplines contemporaneous with the history of the American Educational Research Association.

As an example, currently there are pointed differences in how the terms *motivation* and *engagement* are used in literacy research, with *motivation* seemingly more popular among cognitive process–oriented reading researchers, and *engagement* seemingly more popular among sociocultural practices–oriented scholars of English language arts and literacy (a supposition verified by this study). In addition, the emerging signifier *engaged literacies* appears poised at the cusp of a new theoretical framework, while owing much of its current articulation to theoretical frameworks past.

To address this line of inquiry, we mapped the use and definition of the terms *motivation* and *engagement* in several of the major literacy research journals and handbooks over the past century. We constructed a typology inspired by well-referenced histories of theoretical frameworks in educational, psychological, and literary scholarship to identify causative assumptions in the literature. With this coded data set and several exemplary histories of framework succession to work from, we drafted a narrative history of causative and agentive assumptions leading up to *engaged literacies* as that construct is used today in literacy education. Our intention was to determine whether empirical evidence supported, refuted, or complicated a historical model of theoretical framework succession in literacy education. We acknowledge that this review can provide only a small piece of the larger puzzle of the history of theoretical change in education research; nevertheless, it may lend clarity to future work on the topic.

A THEORETICAL FRAMEWORK FOR THE STUDY OF THEORETICAL FRAMEWORKS

We draw our account of successive theoretical frameworks in literacy scholarship from similar, previous models in discursive psychology (e.g., Harré & Gillet, 1994), developmental psychology (e.g., Cairns & Cairns, 2006), educational psychology (e.g., Berliner, 2006; Bredo, 2006b), and reading research (e.g., Alexander & Fox, 2013; Chall, 1967; Gaffney & Anderson, 2000; Harris, 1969; Pearson & Cervetti, 2015; Pearson & Stephens, 1993; N. B. Smith, 1934/1965), as well as in English language arts and literacy education (Brass & Burns, 2011; Unrau & Alvermann, 2013) and literary criticism and theory (e.g., Knellwolf & Norris, 2001; Leitch et al., 2010; Litz, Menand, & Rainey, 2000; Selden, 1995). The historiographical value of such scholarly metanarratives is substantiated within the larger domain of intellectual history or genealogy of ideas (Fallace, 2015; Foucault, 1982; Lovejoy, 1964; Monaghan & Hartman, 2000). These historiographical assumptions are grounded in part in influential arguments from philosophy of science on how disciplinarily preferred theoretical framings subsume and direct more specific theoretical models and hypotheses in research, and how these preferences do or should change over time (Cacioppo, Semin, & Bernston, 2004; Godfrey-Smith, 1996; D. L. Hull, 1988; Koltko-Rivera, 2004; Koyré, 1968; Kuhn, 1962/1996; Lakatos, 1978; Medicus, 2005; Peirce, 1923; Pepper, 1948/1972; Popper, 1935/2002).

By *metatheoretical framework* we mean the cohesive set of assumptions about causation and phenomena that guide the generation of pragmatic theoretical models, testable hypotheses, and interpretive lenses in research (cf. Dressman, 2007; Handsfield, 2016; Tracey & Morrow, 2012; Unrau & Alvermann, 2013). A *theoretical framework* is more than a coincident matching of methods, designs, and theories. It is built on a set of cohering, a priori metaphysical assumptions justifying the assembly of those research elements and how they would work together. In this sense, theoretical frameworks are metatheoretical, providing justification for any theory operating within their constraints. As the cognitive philosopher Mark Johnson (2011) noted,

> Frameworks are ways of thinking about, or viewpoints on, a large body of data (Morton and Frith, 1995). Frameworks have testable elements, but primarily serve as a coherent set of assumptions that, taken together, offer an account of a wide range of phenomena. In addition, within a framework more specific and detailed theories can be constructed. Further, [these] general theories guide lines of research and the kinds of hypotheses that are explored. (p. 9)

Notably, Johnson's (2011) "set of assumptions" is "coherent." Theories that address how epistemological and metaphysical assumptions manage to foster coherence also tend to involve an overarching metatheory about how theoretical framings comprise and guide pragmatic and applied theories (i.e., models and hypotheses). Explanations for this include organizing principles or agents such as *worldview* (Koltko-Rivera, 2004), *epistemology* (J. W. Cunningham & Fitzgerald, 1996; Hofer & Pintrich, 1997, 2002), *Weltanschauung* (Freud, 1933), *episteme* (Foucault, 1966/1970), *themata* (Holton, 1973), *thought style* (Fleck, 1935/1979), *tacit theoretical generalization* (Gee, 2012), *conceptual* or *root metaphor* (Lakoff & Johnson, 1980/2003), *world hypothesis* (Pepper, 1948/1972), *species* (Bredo, 2006b), *systems of reason* (Popkewitz, 1997), *research program* (Lakatos, 1978), *theory group* (Kelly, 2006), and *paradigm* (Kuhn, 1962/1996; cf. Cheng, 2015).

Because theoretical frameworks are often grounded in a disciplinarily obligatory metaphor (Lakoff & Johnson, 1980/2003; Pepper, 1948/1972; Ruddell, Ruddell, & Singer, 1994), ideas or scholarship embedded in one theoretical framework are matters of intuitive common sense to adherents but will seem wrongheaded and in defiance of common sense to adherents of other, nonconciliatory theoretical frameworks. This can then give rise to arguments at cross-purposes, a situation often termed *paradigmatic incommensurability*, which has at times afflicted education research in debates about justifications for research methodology and design (D. J. Cunningham, 1992; Donmoyer, 1996; Phillips, 1983).

Granted, there are also arguments against the idea of overarching frameworks for cohering research practices and how they might direct inquiry in science (cf. Feyerabend, 1975/2010; Kelly, 2006; Leahey, 1992; Popper, 1935/2002). We therefore stress that we are employing theoretical frameworks as a widely acknowledged cross-disciplinary convention, and that we do so only for instrumental rather than veridical purposes. We are not claiming that the past actually went through invariant stages of requisite conceptual preference operating on a logic divorced from the intellectual contingencies of historical contexts, nor do we appeal to commandeering zeitgeists. Our experiment in categorizing past epistemological and ontological preferences by underlying metaphysical assumptions is to clarify currently manifest conceptual diversity by way of comparative analysis.

We use the term *metaphysics* in its formal philosophical sense (van Inwagen & Sullivan, 2015), regarding the study of being, the world, the things it comprises, and their tendencies, laws, properties, or potentials. Although metaphysics as the examination of assumptions of causality begins with Aristotle (who termed it *first philosophy*; Falcon, 2015), our interest is in making sense of the varied assumptions that propelled literacy education theory and research through a century of transformation. To avoid either the implication of pseudoscience or the suggestion that we will delve into philosophical analyses, we will refer to this level of assumption only in terms of our intended use, as *metatheoretical framework*.

Literacy education scholarship provides a useful basis for testing whether a historical succession of theoretical frames is helpful for understanding shifts in educational nomenclature. We note that the first literacy study (on readers' eye motions as an indication of mental operations in text processing) was conducted by Javal (1879/1990) in 1879, the very year that Wilhelm Wundt opened the world's first psychological laboratory in Leipzig. By the first decade of the 20th century, reading research was sufficiently abundant to warrant a book-length review (Huey, 1908)—8 years before the founding of the American Educational Research Association. Researchers reviewing reading research at the close of the 20th century, although restricting their efforts to its last four decades (National Institute of Child Health and Human Development, 2000), found themselves facing somewhere in the vicinity of 85,000 studies (Shanahan, 2005, p. 3). Thus, the literacy research database seems sufficiently copious and long-standing to allow testing of any hypothesis about the history of theoretical succession within the field.

In the concept of *literacy research*, we include empirical and theoretical work in reading psychology, reading education, writing education, English language arts education, developmental reading, content area literacy education, disciplinary and new literacy studies, and their foundations in the broader domains of psychology, linguistics, literary theory, sociology, anthropology, and critical theory. Within this multifaceted domain, there are innumerable topics of inquiry; a comprehensive review would be beyond the possible scope of this chapter. We therefore chose a single exemplary topic to focus our history: students' active engagement in literacy learning. We did so because of the renewed advocacy of activity- and inquiry-based instructional practices as next-generation skills for deeper learning (e.g., Bill & Melinda Gates Foundation, n.d.; National Governors Association Center for Best Practices & Council of Chief State School Officers, 2010; University of Kentucky, n.d.). *Reading motivation* and *engaged literacy(ies)* are fairly contemporary ways to describe students' involvement in their own learning (the latter being the much newer term). However, the two terms clearly inhabit distinct theoretical frameworks about human agency and literacy development.

As we shall demonstrate, if we peel away methods, phenomenal foci, theoretical models, descriptive empirical data, and disciplinary habit from previously coined theoretical frameworks, what is left are unique and distinguishing assumptions about causation and, by extension, the development of human agency. These assumptions have a longer pedigree and transdisciplinary reach than the historically situated literacy frameworks they inform, are potentially extendable to other literacy questions and other (at least related) fields, and have a notable relationship to the schools of social, literary, and psychological inquiry that have traditionally informed or inspired theory in literacy education research and practice.

METHODOLOGY AND SOURCES

We began with a fairly basic approach to historical process research (Schutt, 2015) allowing for comparative theoretical analyses through adaptation of the grounded comparative method (Glaser, 1965; Glaser & Strauss, 1967/1999). To start, we ran the search terms *reading motivation, engaged literacy*, and similar phrases through Google Books Ngram Viewer to track appearances in books from 1900 to 2008 (the most recent year data were available), and then from 1800 to present. We did this to locate keyword phrases that demonstrated long-standing trends.

Next, inspired by Guzzetti, Anders, and Neuman (1999), each member of the research team was assigned one or more well-circulated journals of literacy education practice or research, and the task of searching all numbers of said journal on an online archive (JSTOR, journal publisher sites, etc.), seeking research and practice articles on motivation and engagement (using the search stems *motiv-* and *engag-*). One member of the team addressed pertinent chapters in the major literacy handbooks. Another reviewed historical reviews (see Table 1 for list of journals). We coded uses as *central* (C), *substantive* (S), *ancillary* (A), or *trivial* (T). *Central* indicated that the term was the variable under investigation in a study and presumably was defined; *substantive* indicated that the term was formally defined and/or justified with scholarly citations but was not the variable under investigation; *ancillary* indicated that the term was noted as a variable of potential interest but not formally defined; and *trivial* indicated the term was used casually (i.e., not as a variable) and/or not defined.

Uses coded as central or substantive were then categorized by their theoretical framework (see the section "A Metatheoretical Model for Analyzing Theoretical Frameworks"). We coded for theoretical framework based on descriptions or definitions of agentive learning given by the study's authors, by document keywords, or by indicative citation. The articles were categorized as *intentional* (I), *respondent* (R), *constructed* (D), *contingent* (G), or *indeterminate* (N). (See Table 2 for example of handbook coding.) Examples of difficult categorization were cross-checked by at least two other members of the research team. We were prepared to discuss differences of opinion across the group using a modified Delphi methodology (Linstone & Turoff, 1975); however, this was never necessary.

A crucial caveat: All but one of the journals we reviewed began publication within the last half of the past century. We therefore tracked back the citations used to support authors' definitions or theoretical descriptions to locate earlier constructs

TABLE 1
Source Publications for Review

Literacy Journal	Year(s)	Publisher	Online Source	Uses in Studies of M/E	C/S Studies on M/E (Since 1965)
English Education	1969–present	NCTE	JSTOR Arts and Sciences IV (1969–2011), NCTE (2012–2015)	161/183	2/6
Journal of Adolescent & Adult Literacy	1957–present	IRA	ProQuest (1957–2011)/IRA (2012–2015)	414/430	60/88
Journal of Literacy Research	1969–present	LRA	Highwire Press/Sage	338/242	21/32
Language Arts	1923–present	NCTE	JSTOR Arts and Sciences IV (1923–2011), NCTE (2012–2015)	1,044/417	16/30
Research in the Teaching of English	1967–present	NCTE	JSTOR Arts and Sciences IV (1967–2011), NCTE (2012–2015)	236/230	8/20
Reading Research Quarterly	1965–present	IRA	JSTOR Arts and Sciences IV (1965–2011), IRA (2012–2015)	368/252	28/31
Scientific Studies of Reading	1997–present	SSSR	Taylor & Francis	19 in total[a]	10/5
Total				2,580/1,754	145/212

Note. C = central; E = engaged; IRA = International Literacy Association; LRA = Literacy Research Association; M = motivation; NCTE = National Council of Teachers of English; S = substantive; SSSR = Society of the Scientific Study of Reading. This table indicates the number of studies in literacy journals using *motivation* or *engagement*, and the number of studies about *motivation* or *engagement* (central or substantive use), with years of publication and sources.
[a]No electronic access to search (this journal was hand-checked).

for explaining student involvement in literacy learning. In addition, handbooks and handbook chapters relatable to agency in literacy, as well as histories and historical reviews from the early to middle 20th century, were also reviewed to fill in the gap.

We discovered that ranking articles by relevance in the databases often generated erratic results (e.g., article rankings within a journal could change from day to day; inconsequential front matter or reviews could supersede highly relevant articles). Queries to the database companies revealed some of the reasons for these unhelpful results, and we were left to work around the inherent and unresolvable limitations of these search methods by cross-checking corpora using two or more databases by (a) recruiting university staff to duplicate the initial searches through ERIC and/or (b)

TABLE 2

Example of Handbook Analysis

Volume	Chapter	On Motivation	On Engagement	Motivation Is Central
Theoretical Models and Processes of Reading (Singer & Ruddell, 1970)	"Affective Factors in Reading" (Athey, 1970)	Yes	No	No
Theoretical Models and Processes of Reading (2nd ed.; Singer & Ruddell, 1976)	"Developmental Processes and Reading Processes: Invalid Inferences From the Former to the Latter" (Athey, 1976)[a]	Yes	No	No
	*The Function of Attitude in the Reading Process" (Mathewson, 1976)[a]	Yes	No	No
	"Substrata-Factor Patterns Accompanying Development in Power of Reading, Elementary Through College Level" (Singer, 1976)	Yes	No	No
Handbook of Reading Research (Pearson, 1984)	"Readability" (Klare, 1984)	Yes	No	No
	"Classroom Instruction in Reading" (Rosenshine & Stevens, 1984)	No	Yes	No
	"Social and Motivational Influences on Reading" (Wigfield & Asher, 1984)	Yes	No	Yes
Theoretical Models and Processes of Reading (3rd ed.; Singer & Ruddell, 1985)	"Reading Research in the Affective Domain" (Athey, 1985)	Yes	No	No
Handbook of Reading research (Vol. 2; Barr, Kamil, Mosenthal, & Pearson, 1996)	"The Development of Strategic Readers" (Paris, Wasik, & Turner, 1996)	Yes	No	No
	"Teachers' Instructional Actions" (Roehler & Duffy, 1996)	Yes	No	No
Theoretical Models and Processes of Reading (4th ed.; Ruddell, Ruddell, & Singer, 1994)	"Model of Attitude Influence Upon Reading and Learning to Read" (Mathewson, 1994)	Yes	No	No
	"The Development of Children's Comprehension and Motivation During Storybook Discussion" (Ruddell, 1994)	Yes	No	No
Handbook of Reading Research (Vol. 3; Kamil, Mosenthal, Pearson, & Barr, 2000)	"Engagement and Motivation in Reading" (Wigfield & Guthrie, 2000)[a]	Yes	Yes	Yes
Theoretical Models and Processes of Reading (5th ed.; Ruddell & Unrau, 2004b)	"Motivational and Cognitive Predictors of Text Comprehension and Reading Amount" (Guthrie, Wigfield, Metsala, & Cox, 2004)[a]	Yes	No	Yes

(continued)

TABLE 2 (CONTINUED)

Volume	Chapter	On Motivation	On Engagement	Motivation Is Central
	"The Role of Responsive Teaching in Focusing Reader Intention and Developing Reader Motivation" (Ruddell & Unrau, 2004a)	Yes	Yes	Yes
Handbook of Reading Research (Vol. 4; Kamil, Pearson, Moje, & Afflerbach, 2011)	"Supporting Early (and Later) Literacy Development at Home and at School" (Paratore, Cassano, & Schickedanz, 2011)	Yes	Yes	No
	"Adolescents as Readers" (Alexander & Fox, 2011)	No	Yes	No
	"School Reform in Literacy" (B. M. Taylor, Raphael, & Au, 2011)	Yes	No	No
Theoretical Models and Processes of Reading (6th ed.; Alvermann, Unrau, & Ruddell, 2013)	"Literacy Research in the 21st Century: From Paradigms to Pragmatism and Practicality" (Dillon, O'Brien, & Heilman, 2013)	No	Yes	No
	"Reading as a Motivated Meaning-Construction Process: The Reader, the Text, and the Teacher" (Ruddell & Unrau, 2013)	Yes	Yes	Yes
	"Effects of Motivational and Cognitive Variables on Reading Comprehension" (Taboada, Tonks, Wigfield, & Guthrie, 2013)[a]	Yes	No	Yes
	"Toward a More Anatomically Complete Model of Literacy Instruction: A Focus on African-American Male Adolescents and Texts" (Tatum, 2013)	Yes	No	No

Note. This example includes edited general volumes on reading research, with chapters on motivation and engagement indicated.
[a]Chapters were deemed *substantive*.

spot-checking our assigned journals using Google Scholar, ranking by number of citations.

None of these three methods generated exactly similar results, but confirmation of trend patterns across the three methods was evident. As it became clear that a definitive quantitative literature profile was not feasible given our means, the extent to which it should be pursued by hand was weighed against the probability that such rigor would reveal different results. Because we had conducted comprehensive analyses of the databases by two of the three methods, rather than analyses on samples, we judged the evidence of similar patterns in the data sets as an indication of acceptable reliability.

A Metatheoretical Model for Analyzing Theoretical Frameworks

To code the central or substantive journal articles for their respective theoretical frameworks, we needed a category system that addressed three criteria: *parsimony, generalizability*, and *applicability.* Categorical economy required that we group theories into families. We therefore sought a metatheory of theoretical frameworks that was general enough to be inclusive of the multiple disciplinary domains that have influenced literacy theory and thus literacy research (psychology, literary criticism, educational philosophy, linguistics, etc.). At the same time, we needed a metatheory with sufficiently differentiated categories to justify fundamentally different schools of research design, method, and applied theory. Finally, we hoped for a metatheory that was sufficiently nuanced to distinguish individual theorists who putatively shared a similar paradigm, or even to connect parallel strains of theory in adjacent disciplines. Eventually, we decided we would need to devise a unique categorical model for this analysis, but it was clear from our review of available models that we would not lack for high-quality inspiration to guide us.

For instance, in his treatment of education research philosophies, Bredo (2006b) drew from Godfrey-Smith's (1996) distinction between internal and external epistemologies and categorized theoretical frameworks according to whether they were about external or internal relations, adding a third category for dialectical-transactional relations. He "adopted this typology because it is broader and simpler than the familiar distinction[s] . . . [and] because it is more abstract, making it possible to handle recent developments under these wider labels" (Bredo, 2006b, p. 5). On this basis, Bredo grouped empiricism, classical and logical positivism, and postpositivism as treating external relations, and rationalism, Kantian empiricism, transcendentalism, hermeneutics, structuralism, post-structuralism, and postmodernism as treating interior relations. He further grouped Hegelian dialectics (particularly regarding the tension between materialist and idealist ontologies), critical theory, and pragmatism as treating dialectical and transactional relations. We admired the simplicity of this typology and the central epistemological distinction underscored by it, but we sought more nuance.

We turned to Koltko-Rivera's (2004) review of the worldview construct in which he critiqued Pepper's (1948/1972) metatheory of world hypotheses for its singular focus on causation. However, this focus on causes struck us as particularly useful for reviewing research literatures, their designs, choice of method, and theoretical constructs. Although Pepper's metatheory has been influential elsewhere (Lakoff & Johnson, 1980/2003; Morris, 1997; Overton & Reese, 1981), we attended less to its well-known typological features and construct of root metaphors than to its core claims about causation. We extrapolated the distinguishing causative assumptions from Pepper's four major world hypotheses, together with their potential

FIGURE 1
Schematic of Four Metatheoretical Frameworks Regarding Causation
in Development

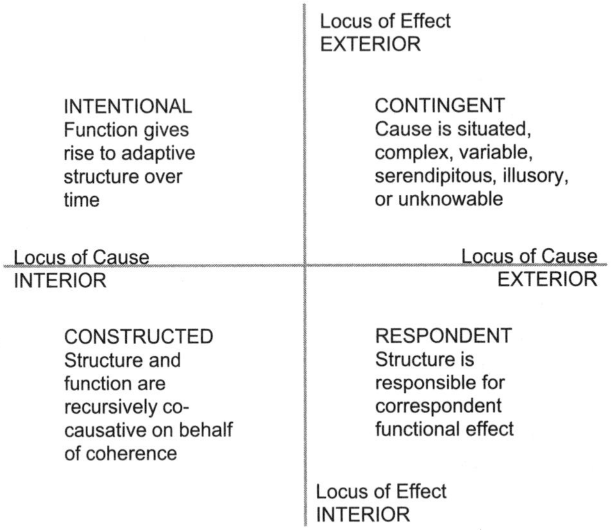

	Locus of Effect EXTERIOR
INTENTIONAL Function gives rise to adaptive structure over time	CONTINGENT Cause is situated, complex, variable, serendipitous, illusory, or unknowable
<u>Locus of Cause</u> INTERIOR	<u>Locus of Cause</u> EXTERIOR
CONSTRUCTED Structure and function are recursively co- causative on behalf of coherence	RESPONDENT Structure is responsible for correspondent functional effect
	Locus of Effect INTERIOR

Source. The schematic is based on the relationships between form and function and between loci of cause and effect.

implications for the relationship of form and function in human development (Lerner, 1992; Overton & Reese, 1981), and reassembled these as theories of human agency in literate activity and literacy development. We then applied Bredo's (2006b) external/internal distinction to the loci of cause and of effect and dovetailed his dialectical/transactional category into our four causes.

The resulting construct (see Figure 1) allowed us to categorize theories of agency and change from psychology, philosophy, literary criticism, linguistics, and educational theory within one of four metatheoretical framework categories: *intentional* (I), *respondent* (R), *constructed* (D), and *contingent* (G). The primary demarcation of each category is the underlying metaphysical assumption about agentive or developmental causation, particularly the relationship of structure and function (respectively, function directs the emergence of structure; structure enacts function; structure and function are developmentally co-causative; causation is complex/historically situated/dynamic). In addition, the locus of cause and the locus of effect may be either typically internal or typically external per framework.

Our categories of causative assumption grant us the theoretical coordinates necessary for aligning metaphysical assumptions or themes within or across adjoining disciplines (e.g., *respondent* generally maps to behaviorism in psychology but also to formalism and New Criticism in literary theory, to structuralism in linguistics, to logical positivism in philosophy, and so forth; see Appendix A for more detailed descriptions of the four main frameworks we drafted). Although traditional framework descriptors seem to indicate assumptions about causation, we found copious examples of atypical causative assumption within these traditional labels, which apparently have allowed individual researchers or research groups useful theoretical wiggle room. This should not be criticized as impiety. If taken too literally as an accurate representation of the world, any metatheoretical framework (or assumption set) would lead a scholar into epistemological grief (Bredo, 2006a).

Data Points and Trends

Our initial Google Books Ngram charts required some thoughtful interpretation. It should be remembered that the term *literacy* was not used to designate a field of education research and practice until the 1990s. (The first use of *literacy* in any sense dates only to 1883; "Literacy," n.d.). Even the phrase *English language arts* emerged in the corpus only in the 1950s (Squire, 2003; see also N. B. Smith, 1952). For this reason, it is not surprising that phrases that include *literacy* do not appear before the end of the 20th century, and so we searched multiple alternative terms to locate similar ideas. We substituted *literary* for *literacy* and searched similar synonyms for *reading, writing, motivation*, and *engagement* to identify phrases that yielded the most use. These were (in rank order, 1800–2008): *engaged reading, reading motivation, literary engagement, reading engagement, engaged writing, motivated reading*, and *engaged literacy*.

We found that uses of *engaged* and *engagement* were far more common in the 1800s than the 1900s, with a marked interest in *literary engagement* in the 1830s and *engaged writing* from 1840 through 1900. The use of *engagement* dampened in the 20th century, apparently displaced to some extent by the construct of *motivation*, which emerged in the 1900s, with increased use in the 1920s through 1940s (when engagement, too, saw increased use). *Motivated reading, engaged reading*, and *engaged writing* were all evident in the 1920s through 1940s, the heyday of progressive education in the United States. Most striking, the use of all seven phrases in aggregate demonstrated a relative depression from the mid-1940s through the mid-1970s, the heart of the Cold War and behaviorist instruction. Thereafter, *motivation* terms resurged, especially in the late 1970s and early 1980s, until the 1990s, when they were superseded by *engagement* terms, even as both terms ascended in use toward the present. (We invite readers to recreate these Ngram charts at https://books.google.com/ngrams.)

Tracking the uses of *motivation* and *engagement* in literacy journals by year generated generally similar results, with *motiv-* being the most common stem across the years of publication, from the mid-1960s until the 1990s, at which time *engag-* became the most common stem, particularly in substantive or central uses (see Table 3, Figures 2 and 3). It was also at this time that both stems increased in prevalence in articles where their use was central or substantive, with a clear upward trend for both.

TABLE 3

Journal Articles Rated Central and/or Substantive for *Motiv** and *Engag*
for All Journals by Decade

Decade	All Articles Published in Journals	All Articles Rated Central and/or Substantive for Motiv* and Engag*	
		N	%
1960–1969	96	3	3
1970–1979	2,413	27	1
1980–1989	2,960	21	0.7
1990–1999	2,945	61	2
2000–2009	2,567	122	5
2010–2015	1,272	91	8

Note. The journals reviewed included *English Education, Journal of Adolescent & Adult Literacy, Journal of Reading Behavior/Journal of Literacy Research, Language Arts, Reading Research Quarterly, Reading Teacher, Research in the Teaching of English*, and *Scientific Studies of Reading.*

FIGURE 2

Prevalence of *Motiv-* and *Engag-* in Analyzed Literacy Journals, 1969–2013,
From ERIC Search With *Motiv-* (Black) or *Engag-* (Gray)

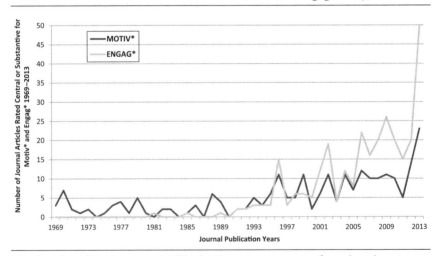

Note. Central or substantive uses are in solid color. Note greater percentage of central or substantive uses in research-focused journals, although there are more uses overall in practitioner journals. The analyzed journals include ***English Education***, *Journal of Adolescent & Adult Literacy, Journal of Reading Behavior/ Journal of Literacy Research*, ***Language Arts***, *Reading Research Quarterly, Reading Teacher*, ***Research in the Teaching of English***, and *Scientific Studies of Reading*. The numbers for 2013 for the journals shown in boldface were extrapolated from the first 6 months of the year because of those journals' shorter range of availability.

FIGURE 3

The Number of Occurrences of the Stems *Motiv-* or *Engag-* in the Analyzed Journals, Either as Central and Substantive, or as Trivial and Ancillary

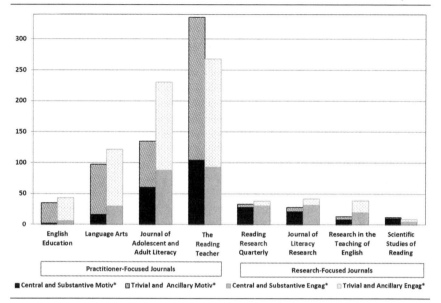

Procedure for Fashioning the Historical Narrative

Drawing on framework histories in psychology and educational psychology, North American philosophy and literary criticism, U.S. reading instruction theory, curricula for literature study and language arts, and literacy education theory, we mapped the succession of terms used to describe dominant frameworks in each of these histories over the past 11 decades, noting evidence of causative assumption. We also noted minor schools of thought in these histories. We then aligned these with our literacy journal and handbook analysis and made connections in particular to what was important for literacy education theory and practice. On the basis of these histories, our coded data set, and our typology of causative assumptions, we crafted the following narrative (see Appendix B for more detail on this process).

Caveats

We must stress that we crafted a historical narrative to determine the utility of our model of metatheoretical frameworks and the validity of common stage theories of theoretical commitment in literacy research. We therefore drew from common scholarly sources for instrumental, not veridical, purposes. We used engaged literacy as an exemplary case, and the metaphysical assumptions we suggest ought to apply equally to other literacy research topics, as well as to related disciplines that have influenced literacy research. Finally, we are describing scholarly, not instructional, practice; we will not parse in detail the debates about models of reading process or "what works" in reading or writing instruction, as current traditions have established.

A PRELIMINARY CENTENNIAL HISTORY OF THE METATHEORETICAL ASSUMPTIONS OF LITERACY ENGAGEMENT

Intentional Assumptions in Early Literacy Research

By the beginning of the 20th century, reading scholarship was impressively advanced, even as education research was only beginning to take shape. The attention to reading was originally meant not to improve instruction, however, but to fortuitously open a window on what Huey (1908) termed "the most intricate workings of the human mind" (p. 6). Reading was eminently observable, displaying the mind in action. Most of the research had been done in Europe (Huey, 1908), but that would change.

Pedagogical debates in North America about best practice in reading instruction had been ongoing since at least the introduction of Noah Webster's popular *Blue Back Speller* in 1783 and his *Compendious Dictionary of the English Language* in 1806 (Balmuth, 2009; N. B. Smith, 1934/1965; Venezky, 1986). These disagreements ranged variously among advocates of by-the-letter versus whole-word reading instruction, sentence-to-word versus alphabetic instruction, what would become synthetic (letter-to-word) versus analytic (word-to-letter) phonics instruction, and rote oral recitation of texts versus silent reading for meaning and cultural enrichment (Pearson, 2000; Walczyk, Tcholakian, Igou, & Dixon, 2014). Early 20th-century reading researchers began to address these debates with the new experimental methods of functional psychology (Chall, 1967; Monaghan, 2007; Pearson & Hamm, 2005).

Early experimental psychologists produced America's first standardized literacy tests, including Thorndike's (1910) handwriting scale and *The Gray Standardized Oral Reading Paragraphs* (N. B. Smith, 1934/1965). (The founding a year later of the American Educational Research Association was itself a contemporaneous acknowledgment of faith in the promise of education research.) The eventual application of this research was a mixed blessing, however. As Pearson (2010) noted, "when psychologists with their new found scientific lenses were put to work creating cheap and efficient tests for beleaguered schools, the course of reading assessment was set" (p. 283). That course, continuing to the present, would prove surprisingly intransigent to subsequent literacy education research, theory, and models.

Consider, as an example, the debate about oral recitation or word calling from texts versus silent reading for thoughtful interpretation. (We select this debate because we assume that reading for meaning and interpretation is more easily related to motivated student engagement than the practicing of automatic letter decoding of texts to recognizable auditory or visual word forms, as in the primary grades; we do not suggest that the latter is not crucial in reading development.) The new research demonstrated that silent reading produced greater speed and comprehension than did oral reading, prompting Gray (1919) to observe, "The results of practically every investigation of this problem [the widespread use of oral reading] indicate clearly the appropriateness of emphasizing the content of what is read, persistently and consistently [and silently], throughout the grades" (p. 29).

The argument for oral performance may have been complicated by a garbled intuition about the importance of activity in learning and its relation to cognitive development. As noted by Parker (1894), "Many of the grossest errors in teaching reading spring from confounding the two processes of attention and expression" (p. 93). And, as observed by Huey (1908), "The consequent attention to reading as an exercise in speaking, and it has usually been a rather bad exercise at that, has been heavily at the expense of reading as the art of thought getting and thought manipulation" (p. 175). Dewey (1913) observed, "To make the idea of activity effective, we must take it broadly enough to cover all the doings that involve growth of power—especially of power to realize the *meaning* of what is done" (p. 66). Judd and Buswell (1922) eventually determined that the relative value of oral and silent reading depended on the level of reading development addressed.

Thoughtful interpretation as the preferred goal of reading was not a new idea (Monaghan, 2005; Venezky, 1987; N. B. Smith, 1961). N. B. Smith (1934/1965) distinguished shifting emphases in 18th- and 19th-century American reading instruction, from Protestant religious inculcation (for spiritually meaningful interpretation), to secular/nationalistic values instruction (for moral evaluation), to meaning making for intelligent citizenship (for independent interpretation on behalf of a functioning democracy), to reading as the means to both acquire and evince a higher cultural sensibility (for self-improvement). Each of these objectives required active meaning making by the reader. Even into the 1920s and 1930s, thoughtful reading was privileged by scholars, often even over text decoding in early reading (Monaghan, 2007; N. B. Smith, 1961). By the time of the cognitive revolution, 20 years later, after a mid-century research hiatus, thoughtful reading would transform into reading comprehension (Pearson, 2010).

However, an emphasis on content or meaning might not necessarily include an emphasis on active and thoughtful engagement in its acquisition (Dewey, 1913; Venezky, 1987). As Dewey (1938/1998) would subsequently reflect, active experience may be the basis of learning, but not all experiences are equally educative. Emphasis on content could refer to traditional rote recollection and eloquent recitation of "the best which has been thought and said in the world" (Arnold, 1869, p. viii.) even as use of this popular phrase from the period neglected the remainder of Arnold's (1869) sentiment: ". . . and, through this knowledge, turning a stream of fresh and free thought upon our stock notions and habits, which we now follow staunchly but mechanically . . ." (p. viii). Educational pioneers Horace Mann (1796–1859) and Col. Francis Parker (1837–1902) both argued for an emphasis on *meaningful* reading rather than mere reading for meaning (Barry, 2008). As Huey (1908) noted, "The child does not want to learn reading as a mechanical tool. He must have a 'personal hunger' for what is read" (pp. 121–122).

The reason for this concern was clear. Regimentation and rote response were widespread in American schools and had precedents in traditions of neoclassical, religious, and Prussian-inspired schooling in America from the 18th century forward (Mathews, 1966; Monaghan, 2005). In the decades around the turn of the century, these didactic approaches were adapted for the newer urban factory model schools (Callahan, 1962; Cuban, 1990; D. W. Moore, Readence, & Rickelman, 1983; see also Bobbitt, 1918; Münsterberg, 1909; F. W. Taylor, 1919). This was the "traditional" form of instruction that the new science of educational psychology, and what loosely became known as progressive education, attempted to improve on through science (Gray, 1924, 1925; Huey, 1908; Thorndike, 1910, 1917).

To understand the metatheoretical assumptions underlying the theories guiding this educational scholarship—those we here term *intentional*—we need to broaden our focus. Historians of education generally agree on the influence of early 20th-century psychology and its relationship to American schooling reform. Both were framed by experimental scientific methods, early functionalist psychological theory, and pragmatist philosophy (Boring, 1950; Buxton, 1985; Cremin, 1964; Walberg & Haertel, 1992). The ostensible goal of scientific education research was to contribute to a tightly managed education system to meet the unprecedented challenges of a newly industrialized, urbanized, and immigrant-engorged democracy (Cremin, 1964; Dewey, 1916; Popkewitz, 2008). Given the Hegel-inspired belief that history advances through the functional development of individuals and collectives, and the modernist conceit that history's course can be made explicit and deliberatively and beneficially directed, it seemed a reasonable and scientific task to redesign American schooling so that children would be prepared to better realize American ideals (Cremin, 1964; Venezky, 1987).

The scientific but radical ideas that most informed these assumptions were provided by the newly emergent life sciences, particularly the insights of Darwin (1859, 1871), Spalding (1872), Haeckel (1876/1914), and others. Darwin (1859) had made the case that evolutionary change could be explained through natural selection. Specifically, he argued that replication with variation in species allowed for the possibility that variants better suited than other variants to their species-specific niche (more functional in the face of environmental contingency for purposes of survival and reproduction) would generally be selected for and propagated over time, thereby changing the characteristics of a species. Notably, he argued that this applied equally to the evolution of human beings (Darwin, 1871). The importance of variation and functional adaptation in relation to environmental conditions for understanding change over time through evolution was soon also recognized as applicable to understanding change over time in human development, learning, history, and even society (e.g., Darwin, 1877; Spencer, 1860; Thorndike, 1909).

The functional assumption shared by all these applications was that *function is responsible for the emergence of effective structure over time*. This is the first element of our *intentional* category of metatheoretical assumption—we take the term from the twinned sense set forth by Brentano (1874/1973). Function driving structure's emergence was, and is, a common theme in theories of human development by functional psychologists (e.g., G. S. Hall, 1894). The motif of selection underscored that children, through trial and error (functional variation), developed effective behaviors in response to their physical, social, and symbolic environments. "The method of learning by the selection of successes from among a lot of acts is the most fundamental method of learning," claimed Thorndike (1901, p. 38; see also Thorndike's *law of effect*, 1905, p. 4). Effective physiological, neurological, and behavioral structures were thought to emerge as a result. The debt to Darwin was openly acknowledged (C. D. Green, 2009; Thorndike, 1909). It was not a great leap to apply this idea to the instruction of skills and knowledge in schools (e.g., Dewey, 1913, 1916; cf. Cziko, 2000).

As an evolved attribute, the child's capacity to be engaged by and to learn from the environment was seen as inherent; that is, the *locus of cause* was *internal* to the learner. But the goal or purpose of the learning was effective engagement with the physical or social environment, and so the *locus of effect* was *external* to the learner. This orientation even carried through to the Harvard relational behaviorists such as James and Tolman (Wozniak, 1997), who construed behavior as "a course of action which the living body executes or is prepared to execute with regard to some object or fact of its environment" (Holt, 1915, p. 56). As Dewey (1913) wrote regarding the debate about the educative value of interest versus effort (which he characterized as an "educational lawsuit" [p. 1]),

Interests . . . are very varied; every impulse and habit that generates a purpose having sufficient force to move a person to strive for its realization, becomes an interest. But in spite of this diversity, interests are one in principle. They all mark an identification in action, and hence in desire, effort, and thought, of self with objects; with, namely, the objects in which the activity terminates (ends) and with the objects by which it is carried forward to its end (means). Interest, in the emotional sense of the word, is the evidence of the way in which the self is engaged, occupied, taken up with, concerned in, absorbed by, carried away by, this objective subject-matter. (p. 90)

Because of human beings' evolved sociality and the altricial nature of human childhood (C. D. Green, 2009; James, 1890/1918), children's inherent facility for engaging with and learning from structured social environments, including from texts, was thought to follow a developmental trajectory with a distinct, increasingly adaptive arc. This developmental trajectory was deemed key to successfully organizing curricula, both for the classroom and for purposes of socialization. Teaching children in developmentally appropriate ways and through engaging activities and environments was stressed. For this reason, reading instruction was not recommended before the age of 6 or 7 (McGill-Franzen, 1993; Teale, 1995).

Relying on the life sciences as an inspirational foundation for psychological theory had limitations. Biology was barely two generations removed from natural philosophy and was still very formative in method and theory. And its implications were generally disturbing to the public at large. Still, thinking of humans as biological kinds allowed direct scientific inquiry and lent weight to animal studies. Moreover, the figurative metaphors that had long been popular among romantic educational naturalists, such as learning as growth, could now be reified with justification. Mental and behavioral change was, in fact, biological change. Finally, the Darwinian stress on variation played well with the romantic and American transcendentalist theme of individualism; differentiated outcomes were to be expected, even encouraged. Progressive education was the result.

Scholars agree that progressivism was not a homogenous social movement but, rather, a combination of overlapping agendas (Labaree, 2005). Historians have variously categorized these as pedagogical and administrative progressivism (Tyack, 1974); social efficiency, child development, and social reconstruction progressivism (Kliebard, 2004); or liberal and conservative progressivism (Church & Sedlak, 1976). Following from Labaree (2005) and others, we believe that what bound these agendas together were adaptive assumptions about child development (e.g., Dewey, 1896; G. S. Hall, 1894; James, 1890/1918). On this, both pedagogical and administrative progressives seemed to agree.

But there the two groups diverged. Pedagogical progressives emphasized the unique developmental needs of the child, arguing for student-centered teaching and classrooms and curricula aligned with the interests of children at given ages, and building on their inborn propensity to be curious and to learn from intriguing phenomena and environments. In this, the pedagogues channeled earlier neoromantic and transcendentalist theorists who had proposed models based on a belief in the inherent goodness of children and their universal predisposition to learn and grow, each in their own but functional way (e.g., Fröbel, 1887; Parker, 1894; Pestalozzi, 1894; Rousseau, 1921; cf. Cuban, 1990; Hirsch, 1999).

Alternatively, administrative progressives arrived at a more institutionally regulated, social utilitarian view of learning informed by assessments of children's intellectual differences and the provision of leveled and appropriate instruction designed to capitalize on those differences (Cremin, 1964; Johnston, 1984; Popkewitz, 2008). The administrative concern was less with the developmental needs of particular children than with the needs of America's modernizing society and its school systems. To this end, administrative progressives ("administratives") channeled social efficiency theorists (e.g., Bobbitt, 1918; Münsterberg, 1909; F. W. Taylor, 1919) and the industrial goal of standardized outcomes, usually combined with a "scientific" notion of genetically determined class, gender, ethnic, and race differences (Fallace, 2015).

The importance of this distinction should not be underemphasized. According to Lagemann (1989), "One cannot understand the history of education in the United States during the twentieth century unless one realizes that Edward L. Thorndike [administrative inspiration] won and John Dewey [pedagogical inspiration] lost" (p. 185). Or, as Labaree (2005) put it, the pedagogues won the air war (the theoretical campaign), but administratives won the ground war (the institutionalization campaign). Labaree further suggested that the rhetoric of pedagogical progressivism was maintained in the teacher education colleges, if not in classroom practice, because it provided air cover for the social impact of administrative progressivism, which,

when examined closely from the perspective of American traditions of democratic equality and individual opportunity, was not an attractive sight. [Social efficiency education] sorted students into ability groups based in part on social origins, provided them with access only to the knowledge deemed within their ability, and then sent them off to particular positions in the pyramid of jobs based on their academic attainments. As an educational process, it was mechanistic, alienating and dull, with a dumbed-down curriculum and a disengaging pedagogy. This was a coldly utilitarian and socially reproductive vision of schooling, and the offer it made to students—learn a skill and take your place in the workforce—was hard to get excited about and easy to refuse. (p. 287)

It is doubtful, then, that elementary reading teachers working within administrative school systems, with their reliance on matched tests and leveled texts (Pearson & Hamm, 2005), actually "discarded basal readers and used materials prepared by children themselves, a wide variety of reference books, and story books which children [chose] to read as a result of their own interests" (N. B. Smith, 1934/1965, p. 197). Even allowing a lag of about 15 years between the high watermark of functional theory in psychology, in the decades around the turn of the 20th century, and the 1919 founding of the Progressive Education Association and the educational activity movement that followed (Cremin, 1964; N. B. Smith, 1952), there was never a golden era of progressive reading instruction.

But clearly, in the years after World War I, university-based teacher education became home for the ideals of pedagogical progressivism and its emphasis on active, meaningful, and educative engagement (Cremin, 1964; N. B. Smith, 1961). Even as behaviorism and operationism were sweeping psychology (see the next subsection, "Flipping the Causative Arrow"), teacher education faculty held that "learning best took place when the child was permitted to carry out his own purposes, meeting and solving attendant problems within the context of his own experiences and needs and through the medium of his own activities" (N. B. Smith, 1934/1965, p. 197). This view was espoused for elementary-grades reading in the 1920s (Monaghan, 2007; N. B. Smith, 1952) and made its way into the secondary English curriculum by the 1930s with *An Experience Curriculum in English* (W. W. Hatfield, 1935), which called for student experience in and through language and literature for "intelligent reading" (Strang & Rose, 1938, p. 28; cf. Rosenblatt, 1938)—an echo of the reading-as-thought-process motif (e.g., Huey, 1908). English educators "began to talk about the project method, about integrating the language arts in 'meaningful' classroom activities, about 'functional teaching' of English" (Squire, 2003, p. 5).

Though not a widespread instructional phenomenon, this approach must have had a tangible impact on educational thinking in the interwar years, as evidenced by the membership and conference attendance numbers of the Progressive Education Association (approximately 25,000 at its height, with conference attendances over 10,000, of whom roughly a third were classroom teachers; Cremin, 1964) and the numerous subsequent critiques of progressive education that followed (Adler, 1940; B. I. Bell, 1949; H. M. Bell, 1938; Bestor, 1953; Dewey, 1938/1998; Flesch, 1955/1986; Hutchins, 1953; Lynd, 1953; Neatby, 1953; M. B. Smith, 1949, 1954; Woodring, 1953). There was also evidence of positive popular culture references from the period (e.g., see "Progressive Education in the 1940s" [n.d.] and *Auntie*

Mame [Dennis, 1955], a best-selling comic novel of the 1950s, whose eccentric 1920s title character was introduced as a partisan in the debate between experimental and traditional approaches to education).

We close this section noting that functional psychology and pragmatist philosophy shared an emphasis on intention, adaptation, and functionality (James and Dewey were major figures in both disciplines). We observe related motifs in the naturalist and realist literary theories of the period, wherein characters' insurmountable propensities were set against social constraints and expectations, leading to comic, tragic, or romantic consequences beyond their full control or understanding (e.g., Cather, 1918/1994; Dreiser, 1900/1994; James, 1888/1911; Pater, 1889; Wharton, 1911/1922). The careless use of this theme—of literary protagonists struggling to overpower environmental or social circumstances—in literary critiques of regional and minority authors whose works were often dismissed as merely indicative of their regional or minority provenance may have contributed to the New Critical backlash on behalf of "the work itself." Many of the writers who would eventually champion New Criticism (e.g., Davidson, Ransom, Warren; see next subsection) first "took a stand" as regional naturalists who resisted the dehumanizing mechanism and conformity of administrative modernism (Twelve Southerners, 1930).

Flipping the Causative Arrow: Respondent Assumptions

Experimental psychologists became ambivalent about functional psychology's theoretical assumptions, mostly due to their often nonscientific cast, the reliance on 19th-century philosophical conceits, and persistent mentalism, vitalism, and dualism (e.g., Bergson, 1907/1911; Berliner, 1993; Glassman, 2004; Kimble, 1994; Manicas, 2002). The resistance on cultural and religious grounds to Darwinian theory, including in the classroom (e.g., the Scopes trial, 1925), and the unfavorable logical-positivist critiques of Pragmatism, such as by Russell (1910, cited in Duran, 1994), may also have contributed to the wane of functional psychology's influence and, more broadly, to the prevalence of what we term *intentionalist* causative assumptions. A more precise mechanistic view of psychological processes emerged as a counterpoint, precociously at first with Watson's (1913) "Psychology as the Behaviorist Views It" and *Behaviorism* (1925), and more comprehensively with the adoption of operationism in the 1930s (J. Moore, 2010).

In terms of metatheoretical assumptions, the early radical behaviorists (e.g., Watson, 1925) externalized the *locus of cause* from the learner to the environment as stimulus (S), which was studied purely in terms of the learner's external response (R); both cause and effect were external to the learner (S → R). Subsequent neobehaviorism, with the adoption of operationism (C. D. Green, 1992) and with support from logical positivism (J. Moore, 2010), internalized the *locus of effect* as drives (C. L. Hull, 1940) or maps (Tolman, 1932), thereby fully inverting the functionalist paradigm. Instead of internal causes resulting in external effects, external causes created internal organismic effects responsible for behavior (S → O → R; for a review, see J. Moore, 2010; for application to educational psychology, see Berliner, 1993; cf. Leahey, 1992; Pearson & Hamm, 2005).

In addition, behaviorists displaced function-over-time as the cause of effective structure, with the temporally closed and mechanistic view of structure as being responsible for function. We identify this alternative set of causative and developmental assumptions as the *respondent* metatheoretical framework. (In this framework, structure is to function as cause is to effect. The framework posits an exterior locus of cause and an interior locus of effect; see Figure 1.) These assumptions are also evident in logical positivist philosophy (e.g., C. L. Hull, 1940; Skinner, 1957; although cf. G. Hatfield, 2002; J. Moore, 1985) and New Criticism literary theory (C. Brooks, 1947; Richards, 1930; Wimsatt & Beardsley, 1946) and so played some role in literacy education theory (Bloom, Engelhart, Furst, Hill, & Krathwohl, 1956; Hilgard, Irvine, & Whipple, 1953; Skinner, 1958; Wellek & Warren, 1956; cf. Catterson & Pearson, in press; Pearson & Cervetti, 2015).

Behaviorism's impact on education and literacy instruction has certainly been acknowledged (e.g., Alexander & Fox, 2013; Pearson, 2000; Pearson & Hamm, 2005), yet this paradigm contributed little to *engaged* or *motivated* literacy instruction as it is understood today. Internal states, such as motivation, desire, or meaning, were not amenable to direct measurement and so were of little scientific interest to behaviorists (Walberg & Haertel, 1992). Insofar as these phenomena could be said to exist, they were attributable to the sequence of experiences that conditioned habits of behavior or drives (e.g., C. L. Hull, 1940; Skinner, 1957; Spence, 1958). In a review of how motivation research was described in handbooks of educational psychology, Weiner (1990) notes that from 1930 to 1960, such motivation research as occurred "had little connection with or relevance for educational psychologists" (p. 618); he cites the use of "the machine metaphor of motivation" (p. 618) as the reason. It may well have been the nadir of educational psychology, as noted by McDonald (1964, cited in Berliner, 1993). In terms of reading research output, Venezky (1984/2002) concurred. No doubt the economic conditions of the Depression and World War II also played a role.

Allowing for our noted 15-year time lag, *respondent* assumptions from psychology, philosophy, and literary criticism from the 1920s to the 1950s became prevalent in literacy education and English language arts research from the 1940s to the 1970s (e.g., Artley, 1977; Beaven, 1972; LaRocque, 1976). Consider Purves and Rippere (1968), who organized 139 elements of students' written responses to literature into 5 categories and 24 subcategories. Notably, their category *engagement-involvement* (p. 10) consisted of the subcategories *1A reaction to literature, 1B reaction to form, 1C reaction to content*, along with *1A1 reaction to author, 1A2 assent to the work, 1A3 moral taste*, and so on. In other words, student engagement was defined as an external text cueing a personal reaction (internal to the student). Notably, the authors justified their schematic by reference to the work of New Critics: C. Brooks and Warren (1960), Richards (1930), and Wellek and Warren (1956). Like the behavioral conditioning models of stimulus-operation-response mechanisms, the New Critics emphasized the text, exterior to the reader, as the proper cause of meaning, the making of which they described, as did the behaviorists, as response or reaction (in the reader). Good reading was a matter of close and careful attention to the text for well-informed response. A simplified and highly structuralist approach to New Criticism was brought into the schools, promulgating what Pearson and Cervetti (2015) described as a "text-centric" (p. 2) view of reading.

Purves and Beach (1972) followed up with an impressively comprehensive annotated review of studies on response to literature, students' reading interests, and teaching of literature. Reading interests were parsed as responses to text (students' preferred subject matter, or their preferred genre/stylistic attributes). In other words, the interests of readers were categorized by text characteristics, rather than texts being categorized by readers' characteristics. None of the categories suggested *active* student engagement. Applebee (1977) questioned the validity and reliability of this taxonomy, but the larger concern for scholars of post–New Critical language arts was the presumption of a hierarchical, factorial model of response (Beach & Hynds, 1996; Cooper & Michalak, 1981; J. D. Williams & Alden, 1983). Nonetheless, it was an impressively ambitious meta-analysis of language arts scholarship, given the constraints of a *respondent* metatheoretical framework.

Other instructional innovations that emerged during this period included standardized assessments, outcome-based learning systems, linear and branched programmatic instruction, learning hierarchies, systematized skill instruction, worksheet-based exercises, and scripted teaching modules (e.g., Bloom et al., 1956; Bruner, 1960; Dibiasio, 1973; Donlan, 1979; Farley & Truog, 1970–1971; Gagné, 1965; Skinner, 1958; see Pearson & Hamm, 2005, for extended review). Many of these mid-century innovations continue in modified form today.

As noted, a systematic, often regimented, approach to instruction had already been evident in reading education during the first decade of the 20th century. Behaviorism, New Criticism, logical positivism, industrial management theory, and modernist structuralism merely gave these traditional forms of didactic instruction renewed intellectual legitimacy (Callahan, 1962; Serafini, 2002). The reasons that similarly didactic instructional preferences persist today are complex (Brown, 1994; Reeve, 2009; Resnick, 1982).

From Respondent to Constructed Assumptions

If *respondent* assumptions, inspired by mechanistic motifs and British empiricist and associationist traditions, dominated North American psychology in the second quarter of the 20th century (Berliner, 2006; Bredo, 2006a; Walberg & Haertel, 1992), a very different set of assumptions was in play in Europe, where psychoanalytic, developmental, ethological, Gestalt, and sociohistorical psychologies were founded on Kantian, Hegelian, and Marxist assumptions. But the work of Freud, Bühler, Piaget, Bartlett, Koffka, Lorenz, and Vygotsky would eventually prove influential in diverse schools of North American psychology after World War II, with subsequent implications for literacy education theory and research.

Indeed, during the era of behaviorist schooling in the United States (1950s–1970s), Freudian, Piagetian, and Gestalt influences began to appear in what was beginning to be called English language arts education and in the teaching of reading (Athey, 1976; C. K. Brooks, 1979; Chall, 1967; J. E. Hartman, 1979; Meade, 1973; Small, 1972; N. B. Smith, 1952), and to a lesser extent in school psychology (Reschly, 1976; Weiner, 1990). For instance, the work of Cofer and Appley (1964) and Young (1961) were of central importance to Mathewson's (1976) reappraisal of motivation in reading. And there seems to have been some theoretical reconsideration of what were still publicly familiar and thus culturally comfortable (if "academically discredited") assumptions about meaningful learning, as suggested by activity-based learning models and humanist psychology (e.g., Maslow, 1943; Mehaffie, Gee, & Larmer, 1978; Rogers, 1951; F. Smith, 1971; Stauffer, 1970).

But the most striking disruption of the North American behaviorist tradition in literacy education research after mid-century was due to the emergence of cognitive psychology (Neisser, 1967) and the putative *cognitive revolution* (Leahey, 1992). In this new theoretical framework, experimental psychologists, who were finding ways to test the mind's structural constraints (e.g., G. A. Miller, 1956), collaborated with psycholinguists, who were studying the deep structure and transformative nature of grammar (e.g., Chomsky, 1957), and information scientists, who had been designing artificial intelligence programs (e.g., Newell & Simon, 1956). The combined result was the view that the mind had a definitive structure, akin to an intelligent data-processing program, which generated behavior and conscious phenomena, and that the structure and processes of this deep program could be back-propagated with carefully constructed experimental (hypothetico-deductive) designs. G. A. Miller (1979) actually gave a precise time and place for this collective inspiration: September 11, 1956, at the Symposium on Information Theory at MIT.

This turn had two major implications. First, thought was treated as representational even beneath the level of language, narrative, gesture, and patterns of multisensory memory, encoded in a type of mental programming language or *mentalese* (Pinker, 1997; cf. Fodor, 2001); the deep syntax of this language restricted what program designs were feasible, thus recasting outcomes as internal program design attributes. Second, the developmental evidence suggested that deep structures were operationalized too quickly by children to be accounted for solely by their environmental experience (Chomsky, 1965); therefore, the deep structures that facilitated the development of cognitive modules (Fodor, 1983) for language and literacy were archetypal, evolved adaptations shared by all members of the human family, as Kant (1781/2008) had argued.

The first of these orientations tied the new cognitive psychology to the logical positivist tradition in analytical philosophy (as behaviorist psychology had been). But the second, with its claim for evolved modules in cognitive architecture, tied the new psychology to the causative assumptions of the functionalists who had preceded the behaviorists. In short, the cognitivists held on to the behaviorist assumption of internal locus of effect but internalized the locus of cause as well. The resulting emphasis on skills and prior knowledge was profound.

We identify this hybridized theoretical frame as the assumption set *constructed*, which posits an internal locus of cause and an internal locus of effect; structure and function are co-causative over time and reciprocally interrelated. The *constructed* assumptions of cognitive psychology and literacy education research can also be found in the postpositivist linguistic turn in North American philosophy (Quine, 1951; Wittgenstein, 1953/2009) and in Chicago School and related literary critique (Booth, 1961; Burke, 1966; Frye, 1957/2015).

The resulting literacy paradigm was epistemologically rationalist, and often ontologically idealist, and allowed earlier European constructivist idioms already grounded in these assumptions to be readily assimilated (e.g., Bartlett, 1932; Koffka, 1935; Piaget, 1947/2003). This assimilation enriched the cognitive movement's theory base and gave its research program a propitious start. It also allowed for the emergence of cognitive constructivist learning theory, including schema theory and radical constructivist views that argued for coherence over correspondence as the basis for truth (Anderson, 1984; Davis & Sumara, 1997; Goodman, 1965; Handsfield, 2016; Otto, 1977; Paris, Lipson, & Wixson, 1983; Von Glasersfeld, 1989).

Alexander and Fox (2013) suggested that the subsequent impact of this cognitive turn on literacy education came in two stages: (a) the era of natural learning (1966–1975), which emphasized the psycholinguistic contribution of children's natural propensity for language and literacy due to archetypal (evolved and hereditary) mental structures (or, as we might say, the assumption of interior cause), and (b) the era of information processing (1976–1985), emphasizing the computational contribution of mental processes as software-like programs for generating output, casting learning as programming (or, as we might say, the assumption of interior effect).

These two orientations were in fact contemporaneous in literacy education. Both Goodman's (1967) "psycholinguistic guessing game" and G. A. Miller's (1956; G. A. Miller, Galanter, & Pribram, 1960) earlier "chunking theory" can be found in a draft typescript of the first edition of Singer and Ruddell's (1970) *Theoretical Models and Processes of Reading* (University of Georgia Library), although the Miller paper was excised from the final print edition. Entwining the two cognitive emphases further, these two views provided the theoretical warrants for the reading wars of the late 20th century—initiating yet another debate on early reading instruction, between advocates of whole language for meaning construction with texts and advocates of systemic training in synthetic phonics skills (Pearson, 2004).

It is during this era of cognitive reading research and constructivist practice that we find a reemergence of *motivation* and *engagement* as topics in literacy research. There were early calls to include affective, attitudinal, and personal aspects of reading in models of literacy in the English language arts (Adkins, Payne, & Ballif, 1972;

Small, 1972), and in reading education, as well (Athey, 1970, 1976; Stauffer, 1970). Cultural memory of progressive instructional traditions from earlier English language arts curricula (e.g., W. W. Hatfield, 1935; N. B. Smith, 1952) is indicated in some subtle counterpoint on behalf of student choice and interests (e.g., Boze, 1968; Emig, 1967, 1972; Farrell, 1978). Athey (1970) made a case for affective variables within prevailing cognitive models of reading (e.g., substrata-factor model; Holmes, 1965). Athey (1976) followed on this quest to define affective factors, contrasting it to the questionable adoption of Piaget's cognitive theories, which, she felt, had obscured the role of motivation by making it "an inherent and inseparable dimension of thought" (p. 739). She questioned this easy adoption, contending that a more nuanced model would require examination of nonintellectual factors and the taking into account of changes in motivation over time, according to age, culture, and social class.

However, most early framings posited student interests and self-perceptions as variables or characteristics of the student (Castenell, 1983; Eccles, Wigfield, & Schiefele, 1998; Wigfield & Asher, 1984). Subsequent work sought to determine the impact of these attributes on student achievement (e.g., Ehrlich, Kurtz-Costes, & Loridant, 1993; Pintrich & Schunk, 1996; Renninger, Hidi, & Krapp, 1992; Schunk & Meece, 1992). Other researchers argued for the inherent social dimensions of these attributes and of their development, demonstrating how social interactions in learning activities actually improved learning (Bergin & LaFave, 1998; Guthrie et al., 1996; Roehler & Duffy, 1996; Ruddell, 1994; Taboada, Tonks, Wigfield, & Guthrie, 2013). Wigfield, Eccles, and Rodriguez (1998) provided a comprehensive review of the motivation research of this period and concluded with a call for fuller study of classroom effects and the need for an integrated account of how all these aspects worked together.

As if reflecting the *constructed* assumption of cognition for organizational coherence, a series of impressive research syntheses were released during this period, beginning with *Becoming a Nation of Readers* (Anderson, Hiebert, Scott, & Wilkinson, 1984), *Beginning to Read: Thinking and Learning About Print* (Adams, 1990), *Comprehension* (Kintsch, 1998), *Teaching Children to Read: An Evidence-Based Assessment of the Scientific Research Literature on Reading and Its Implications for Reading Instruction* (National Reading Panel, 2000), and *Reading for Understanding: Toward an R&D Program in Reading* (RAND Reading Study Group, 2002). The Institute of Education Sciences, U.S. Department of Education, reorganized its website to provide research-based syntheses. Handbooks also began to proliferate (e.g., Barr, Kamil, Mosenthal, & Pearson, 1996; Ruddell et al., 1994), including chapters on motivation and engagement (Guthrie & Wigfield, 2000).

The apparent need to put Humpty Dumpty together again—that is, the need to reintegrate the factors, elements, and processes that had been disambiguated in the earlier mechanistic view of literacy and agency into a more holistic or organic account—became manifest for literacy engagement research in the latter 1990s. Initially, engagement had referred to observable actions by students indicating self-regulation and metacognitive strategies (Meece, Blumenfeld, & Hoyle, 1988), or to how students followed classroom procedures or to when their discussions suggested substantive involvement in the issues and content of a text or literary work (Nystrand & Gamoran, 1991; Reed & Schallert, 1993; Wigfield & Asher, 1984). The turn in the literacy education literature from reading outcomes to the readers themselves was clearly evident (Guzzetti et al., 1999; D. K. Hartman, 1995). But sociality itself was perhaps underarticulated; a richer theory of self was required (Weiner, 1990).

To support the turn to the reader, more comprehensive theories of literacy were devised. Two shifts in metatheoretical assumptions occurred in the literature to allow this. First, although the machine metaphor of behaviorist theory (Weiner, 1990) had been carried into the early cognitive turn with the metaphor of mind as software program—linear flow charts and all—this view was soon displaced by a more recursive and co-causative view of structure and function in development (cf. Alexander, 2005; Kintsch, 1998; Lerner, Hershberg, Hilliard, & Johnson, 2015; RAND Study Group, 2002). Early examples can be found in connectionist neural network models of reading processes (e.g., Adams, 1990; Rumelhart & McClelland, 1981, 1985), in precognitive ecological response models (e.g., Zajonc, 1980), in recursive engagement development models (e.g., Stanovich, 1980, 1986), and in the emergence of psycholinguistic-based whole language pedagogy (Bergin & LaFave, 1998; Goodman, 1967, 1969; F. Smith, 1971), reader response literary theory (Rosenblatt, 1978), and sociocognitive models of literacy instruction (Guthrie et al., 1996; Oldfather & Dahl, 1994).

Second, there was a heightened focus on the self as the central object of psychology, particularly in studies of motivation. Self-efficacy beliefs and self-concept beliefs became highly productive areas of investigation (Wigfield et al., 1998). According to Graham and Weiner (1996, cited in Pajares & Schunk, 2002, p. 4), "It is evident that the self is on the verge of dominating the field of motivation." As Pajares and Schunk (2002) approvingly explained, "The assumption that children's self beliefs are inextricably tied to their thinking and functioning seems so sound, so obvious, so commonsensical" (p. 3). Given the *constructed* metatheoretical assumptions of this period, wherein the loci of both cause and effect were now internal to the learner, it could hardly have seemed otherwise. But as we (and Pajares & Schunk, 2002) have noted, the commonsensical is an alert that metaphysical assumptions are in play. The seemingly obvious would soon be contested.

It was at this point that *engagement* began to supersede *motivation* as the preferred term and focus in research on students' active literacy learning (Alexander & Fox, 2013). Engagement quickly branches into two views, an internal view and an external view. The literacy education research that addressed the internal view was termed *sociocognitive* and emphasized the social dimensions of learning as fostered through educative environments (Almasi & McKeown, 1996; Guthrie et al., 1996; RAND Reading Study Group, 2002). But this research could include a wide range of theoretical models, including study of the social effects on internalized factors (e.g., self-efficacy, motivation), or of the motivation produced in social participation as a necessary component of effective teaching (Allington & Johnston, 2000; Pressley &

Allington, 2015), or of how teachers' need for control could undermine it (Alvermann, O'Brien, & Dillon, 1990). This theme could even be extended into the newer veins of cognitive research (e.g., Spiro, Vispoel, Schmitz, Samaarapungavan, & Boertger, 1987; Spiro & Jehng, 1990).

By contrast, the external view was informed by sociocultural insights (see next subsection), demonstrating how knowledge could be constructed in social collaborations for subsequent possible internalization by students but whose enactment as practice was decidedly external and between social agents (Gavelek & Bresnahan, 2009; New London Group, 1996; Vygotsky, 1978). Some literacy theorists of the late 1990s tapped into the 1970s' ecological turn in psychology (e.g., Bronfenbrenner & Morris, 2006; Gibson, 1979/2015; cf. Heft, 2001). Metatheoretically, the locus of cause began to shift back out of the mind into the social surround, that is, *respondent* regarding causal loci but *constructed* in the co-constructive relationship of structure and function, with a much broader and more ecologically rich sense of the external than the behaviorists had considered, and with a much more nuanced set of implications for mental processes (Bronfenbrenner & Morris, 2006; Perry, 2012; Purcell-Gates, Jacobsen, & Degener, 2004; RAND Reading Study Group, 2002; Weaver-Hightower, 2008).

Contingent Assumptions and the Sociocultural Turn

Beginning in the late 1980s and 1990s, pioneering authors in cultural anthropology and ethnography, psycholinguistics and sociolinguistics, social and cultural-historical psychology, and semiotics were woven together by education researchers into what became known as the sociocultural turn (a bit of bricolage—unlike previous borrowings—with no direct disciplinary inspiration but multiple sources). These authors—including Bleich (1988), Cazden (1988, 1993), Engeström (1987/2015), Fairclough (1989), Gee (2012), Halliday and Hasan (1989), Heath (1983, 1996), Ladson-Billings (1995), Lave and Wegner (1991), Rogoff, Baker-Sennett, Lacasa, and Goldsmith (1995), Scribner and Cole (1981), Street (1984), the New London Group (1996), Vygotsky (1978), and Wertsch (1985), among others—had a profound impact on what was just beginning to be described as *literacy* (which included reading, writing, oral communication, sign systems use, discourses, multimodalities use, enacted identities, and social practices). These scholars rejected the traditions of North American structuralist psychology as a frame of reference, choosing instead to take their theoretical orientations and scholarly insights from work in other fields and other cultural traditions (chiefly continental European). For a concise introduction to sociocultural theory in literacy research, see Enciso and Ryan (2011); for more detailed descriptions of several of the constructs in this domain, see Unrau and Alvermann (2013) or individual chapters in Alvermann, Unrau, and Ruddell (2013).

Although still holding to a coherence (rather than correspondence) epistemology, the sociocultural turn centered on social practices instead of cognitive processes. Simple as such a focal shift might seem, it spawned a drastic metatheoretical shift in literacy education research. In the process, positivist and structural assumptions were displaced by postpositivist, phenomenological, and poststructuralist assumptions (Guba & Lincoln, 1994; St. Pierre, 2014); psychology and psycholinguistics were replaced with sociology and sociolinguistics (e.g., Bloome & Green, 1984; Denzin, 2009; Gee, 1991; Luke, 1995); quantitative methods were exchanged for qualitative methods (Denzin & Lincoln, 1994; J. Green & Bloome, 2004); and cognitive constructivist epistemological themes were displaced by social constructivist and social constructionist themes (Au, 1998; Engeström, Miettenen, & Punamäki, 1999; Gavelek & Bresnahan, 2009; Hruby, 2001; Vygotsky, 1978). Even Goodman's (1967) psycholinguistic guessing game metaphor evolved into the *sociopsycholinguistic guessing game* by the time of publication of the fourth edition of *Theoretical Models and Processes of Reading* (Ruddell et al., 1994; cf. Strauss, Goodman, & Paulson, 2009).

Central to this move were the metatheoretical assumptions that we categorize as *contingent*—external locus of cause, external locus of effect, with both situated in historical and cultural contexts that determine relative and impermanent meanings. (Readers will note that this is an entirely flipped view in comparison with the assumption set *constructed* in just about every way imaginable, perhaps contributing to the acrimony of some of the paradigmatic debate of the turn; Donmoyer, 1996.) Similar assumptions were at work in post-structuralist philosophy, postmodernist literary critique, and cultural-historical psychology, and each had an impact on literacy theory. To draw again from Pearson and Cervetti (2015), literacy was moving from a "reader-centric" to an "activity-centric" perspective (Clark, Chow-Hoy, Herter, & Moss, 2001; Smagorinsky, 1998, 2001; Smagorinsky & O'Donnell-Allen, 1998).

In reviewing self-described *sociocultural* scholarship in American literacy education journals, we found an apparent distinction between scholars who defined the prefix *socio-* as primarily indicating *sociality* (i.e., interpersonal relationship, interaction, and collaboration—typical in sociocognitive or social constructivist theory), those who defined *socio-* as primarily indicating *societal* (i.e., institutional, procedural, employing cultural artifacts—typical in social constructionist, Soviet activity theory), and those who defined *socio-* as signifying both at the same time, with varying degrees of clarity as to the relationship of one to the other (if any). Although all three groups avowed a sociocultural lens and asserted that learning is culturally and historically situated, the writings of the first group implied either *contingent* or *respondent* causative assumptions, while those of the second group implied more emphatic *contingent* assumptions, and the third often retained *constructed* assumptions.

The methodological diversity of this work is similarly impossible to ignore. Sociocognitivist motivation studies were still being done at this time, though often under the sociocultural mantle, and focused on choice or reading preference to describe engaged literacy (e.g., Beck, 2009; Fisher & Frey, 2012; Moje, Overby, Tysvaer, & Morris, 2008; Wilhelm & Smith, 2015; F. Williams, 2013; Worthy, Moorman, & Turner, 1999). Other studies arrived at conciliatory results using alternative methodologies such as constant-comparison analysis and ethnography (e.g., Bailey, 2009; Perry

& Moses, 2011), neo-Marxist Critical Discourse Analysis (e.g., Caughlan & Kelly, 2004; Thein, Guise, & Sloan, 2015), Critical Pedagogy case studies (e.g., Kinloch, 2005; Morrell 2005), and Aesthetic Analysis (Juzwik & Sherry, 2007).

Some scholars inquired into social constructivist and constructionist notions of literacy learning (e.g., DeStigter, 2001; Harste et al., 1984; Hynds, 1989; Moje, 2006; Skerrett, 2009). In these works, literacy motivation is defined as "a feature of the texts and contexts young people experience both in and out of school," rather than as a "static or singular feature of an individual" (Moje, 2006, p. 13). Caughlan, Juzwik, Borsheim-Black, Kelly, and Fine (2013) used Bakhtinian dialogic analysis to study the relations between cognitive motivation and social engagement for learning. Researchers continued to extend concepts of literate self-efficacy to literacy motivation and engagement but, as a result, found that successful instruction relied as much on classroom culture and environment as on individual cognitive abilities, psychologies, and social interactions (e.g., Almasi & Garas-York, 2009; Aukerman & Schuldt, 2015).

A common conclusion from work in this domain is that literacy learning in school may not be a sufficient or accurate indicator of students' actual ability, motivation, and engagement (e.g., Alvermann, 2002). For example, "Third Space" approaches (Gutiérrez, 2008; Gutiérrez & Stone, 2000; Leander & Rowe, 2006; Moje et al., 2004) combined inquiries on both in- and out-of-school learning to envision and design classrooms as new and fundamentally different spaces for learning. These Third Space classrooms operate differently from traditional top-down classrooms, allowing participants to collaborate, co-construct, explore, and use what they already know and do every day to learn literacy content and practices. As a reported result, these students become far more sophisticated communicators and social agents, making new meanings and knowledge about their worlds (Moje, 2008).

Researchers found that teachers consistently identified some students as motivated and engaged but not others (e.g., L. A. Hall, 2009). On closer analysis, however, such identifications were often inaccurate and based on the teachers' unexamined assumptions about their students. As Tatum (2014, p. 35) noted, young people's answers to the question "Who am I?" warranted serious attention because meaningful relationships with texts contributed to intrinsic motivation and prosocial goals, both of which were positively correlated with higher reading achievement. This was seen as a part of identity construction, where identity was framed in schools in terms of advantage and disadvantage relatable to undesirable societal norms (Dutro, 2010; Perry, 2012; Weaver-Hightower, 2008).

One of the unique features of the sociocultural turn was its often outspoken ideological commitment. Stemming mostly from Frankfurt School social critique, many sociocultural theorists held that all research and theory are inherently political. Scholarship that failed to explicitly acknowledge and address its political commitments, from this view, was tacitly accepting the socioeconomic and political status quo. Because the status quo features persistent inequity, injustice, cruelty, and oppression, such acquiescence was said to amount to support and thus culpability for those conditions. This stance was and still is at work in critical education scholarship and much writing on student identities and community (especially regarding marginalization based on race, gender, ethnicity, or sexual orientation; L. A. Bell, 2007; DeStigter, 2001; Heath, 1996; Janks, 2000; Kinloch, 2010; Larson & Marsh, 2004; S. Miller & Burns, in press; Tate, 2012). If the polemical tone of this work has softened in the past two decades, the same cannot be said of its ardency.

It is possible, however, that sociocultural criticality provoked unhelpful political reactions, especially in the face of a rightward swing in U.S. political temperament at the turn of the 21st century. The apparent result was a federal research funding embargo against qualitative studies in literacy education (Shannon & Edmondson, 2011). Complaints by quantitative education researchers that sociocultural work was unduly theoretical and lacked scientific merit or evidence should have tempered their critique with historical hindsight: Cognitive reading research, too, had been highly theoretical in its first decade (the 1960s, e.g., Singer & Ruddell, 1970), and it assembled its impressive research base only in the subsequent decades, thanks largely to plentiful federal research funding (National Reading Panel, 2000). Without similar governmental support for large-scale ethnographic and qualitative research to provide an empirical foundation, the sociocultural turn was prevented from growing much beyond broadly theoretical and small-scale descriptive findings, with a limiting impact on implications (e.g., August & Shanahan, 2006). By the second decade of the 21st century, political reaction began to have a similar effect on sociocognitive research funding (e.g., Congressional elimination of funding for Striving Readers research in 2010).

However, there was a less pronounced form of criticality in this literature that took a high moral road, even as it hewed closely to the familiar beliefs of middle-class liberalism. This view assumed that the central goal of education was to liberate students from their ignorance, their false consciousness, their unexamined and faulty assumptions, so they could realize truths, particularly those that could serve, or be about, themselves. But it also assumed that education was about teaching how the world works in order to be functional in it and thereby become conventionally empowered (Harste, 2003). This more traditional view, with its individualistic intuitions, was a progressivist criticality, one long and comfortably enshrined as a form of folk wisdom among America's professional class (Rorty, 1989).

In any case, the deliberate, quasi-heroic paradigm shattering of the sociocultural turn brought fresh perspectives, methods, and theories to literacy research. Asking similar questions but in different ways, only to arrive at basically similar conclusions on behalf of active, engaged learning, should not be mistaken as a case of wasteful academic turf war or lost opportunity. We believe it should be considered a more thorough confirmation of the value of engagement-oriented literacy instruction.

Engaged Literacies Today

The foregoing review leads us to two presently mainstream but often confluent currents in literacy engagement: one sociocognitive and one sociocultural. The former is grounded in the traditions that emerged out of the cognitive revolution (and the neobehaviorism that preceded it). This view relies on *respondent* and *constructed* metatheoretical assumptions and is attentive to improving the schools we have, generally on behalf of traditional goals. The important empirical contributions of scholars in this tradition continue to inform teacher preparation and professional development, as well as policy and products (tests, textbooks, online materials, etc.). Newer scholars in this vein are continuing to extend and enrich this tradition, often by operationalizing the social factors that socioculturalists have placed on the academic map (e.g., Allington et al., 2010; Cantrell et al., 2016; Guthrie, Wigfield, & You, 2012; Hoffman, 2009; Ivey & Johnston, 2015; Taboada et al., 2013; Thompson, Madhuri, & Taylor, 2008). Much like the early experimental psychologists and administrative progressives at the dawn of the 20th century, scholars in this current have been notably elaborative of best practice within the context of today's policies and programs.

By contrast, the sociocultural current relies on *contingent* or *intentional* assumptions and often deliberately challenges the presumed goals, methods, and organization of today's school systems on behalf of transformational and potentially open-ended objectives. Sociocultural scholarship has been more qualitative and often more theoretical in comparison with sociocognitive work, and thus its effective operationalization is less certain, although clearly possible (e.g., Allington & McGill-Franzen, in press; Ivey & Johnston, 2015; Johnston & Ivey, 2013; Zenkov, Harmon, Bell, Ewaida, & Lynch, 2011). Current sociocultural scholarship transcends earlier sociocultural traditions (e.g., Frankfurt School rhetoric, paradigm wars)—possibly due to radical shifts in the nature of global production and distribution of goods, labor markets, and development of information and communicative technologies— and is seemingly more inspired by current popular movements on behalf of equity and justice (e.g., Black Lives Matter, LGBT and feminist equity, Occupy Wall Street; Kinloch, 2010; Larson & Marsh, 2004; Lewis, Enciso, & Moje, 2007). As with the pedagogical progressives of a century ago, the ideas advocated by these scholars are favored by many teacher educators, but their instructional recommendations are less manifest in the schools.

The two groups share mature and sophisticated views about engagement in literacy development (e.g., Lee, 2012). For both, engaged literacy learning entails *making* and *doing* things that learners view as *authentic* to their lived experiences in terms of *relevance*, and that learners *use* to attain their own goals for their own purposes, both individually and collectively, including but not limited to academic success (with the sociocognitivists emphasizing the "including," and socioculturalists emphasizing the "not limited to"). Successful literacy teaching is thereby understood to engage readers through co-construction of understandings in social interaction, generating identities and agencies in the classroom for potential life use. This approach attends to cultural relevance (from the student vantage) and thereby leads students to motivated learning in ways that they often find more genuine and responsive to their goals. Students taught in these kinds of educative frames are reported as increasingly able and likely to engage in successful literacy learning.

Engagement can be understood in the flow of these twin currents as involving both external and internal dimensions. External dimensions are brought to the fore when engagement is seen as being about the active involvement of students collectively in educative tasks, projects, modalities, and discourses. This is also an important lens for preparing students for success in higher academic institutions, professions, and the modern, often virtual, workplace. Internal dimensions are brought to the fore when engagement is seen as being about a student's personal interests, persistent attentions, social and cognitive goals, and active pursuit of cognitive and affective gratifications. It is eminently important on behalf of effective individuation and meaningful identity within a capitalist democracy.

We conclude that many of these themes are also to be found with different inflections in previous theoretical frames. Yet causative assumptions about literacy learning and development today are more complex, multidirectional, and adaptive. The most current work on multimodal and engaged literacies suggests causal loci shifting from learner-external to learner-internal and back again, depending on how and by whom the research is framed. The relationship of structure and function in this work is similarly treated as a potentially opportune affordance, not as an obligatory and binding metaphysical constraint. Whether this is the new normal or a briefly indeterminate interlude before a disciplinary shift to a *postcontingent* theoretical framework is yet to be determined.

CONCLUSION

In this preliminary centennial review of the metatheoretical assumptions at work in frameworks for addressing literacy education, with a particular focus on active and engaged student participation, we avoided face value reliance on the traditional labels used to mark time periods or paradigms of literacy and education research. We constructed and applied a typology inspired by similar designs, focused on causative assumptions and the role of form and function in development, which guided the drafting of our condensed history of engaged literacies, allowing us to explicate cited and apparent influences.

As noted in the introduction, literacy education research has many parts, and many influences have informed it over the past century. The two main traditions of literacy scholarship are reading research, born of psychology and philosophy, and English language arts research, born of literature theory and critique. Had it not been for the sociocultural turn in the 1980s, their merger would have been unlikely. Yet both had developed within the support of metatheoretical assumptions that held consilience between literary theory, philosophy, psychology, and other social sciences in different ways at different periods in the past. But, too, the different educational needs of early-grades readers mastering decoding/encoding skills and print conventions, and more advanced readers expanding their knowledge of vocabulary, syntactic complexity, text structure, genre, and composition, pulled specialists into distinct clans. The need for professional distinction inspired the building of silos.

Although theoretical frames can seem to succeed one another historically in the literature, older idioms are never entirely displaced but continue to echo in the practitioner literatures and in justifications of classroom practice and school policy (often resurfacing as data in observational studies). In addition, newly preferred theoretical frameworks do not appear de novo but are preceded by formative shifts in academic discourses. The resulting diversity of perspectives can seem openly random or historically coherent, depending on how a review is framed. Rather than merely validating, we hope to have challenged the claim of a readily observed progression of theories with empirical evidence from the research corpus of consistent and cohering metatheoretical assumptions. What is the history of literacy education research? It's complicated.

With the metatheoretical framework we constructed, we were able to track a succession of views about students' active literacy engagement. At the start of the 20th century, students generally were viewed as inherently active organisms developing functional skills for participating in society and for enjoying the best that had been thought and said in their culture through the active practice of literacy and thinking skills. Next came the view of the blank-slate learner, passively conditioned by informal and structured educational experience and by drilling and response, reacting to texts on the basis of internal operations. Next was the active, skilled, strategic reader-writer as a maker of meaning or processor of information working toward internal coherence. And this was followed, at least for many literacy academics, by culturally constructed identities engaged in societally sanctioned semiotics for social positioning and negotiation. In other words, we tracked a general succession of dominant causal assumptions from the *intentional* to the *respondent*, to the *constructed*, to the *contingent* at work in literacy research and practice.

Our impression is that engaged literacies, in all their variety, congregate around the need to place students' interests, meanings, and experiences at the center of instructional designs. This is hardly a new insight, as our historical narrative demonstrates, but it has been articulated in culturally and historically specific ways over the past century. However, during certain periods, this obvious truth was evaded by control-oriented instructional systems and denied through passive models of human development. The research suggests this was a mistake, and current calls for engaged literacy from education reformers, teachers, parents, school administrators, and education researchers intimate that it may, once again, be the next wave in our history of educational efforts. We can only expect ever-increasing technological, economic, and demographic change: thus the great need for creative, adaptive citizens ready for a long life of learning and continual adjustment. Engaged literacy learning may be the sine qua non of both literacy development and social resilience—the things we cannot do without (Graves, 2004).

APPENDIX A

Condensed Description of Metatheoretical Frameworks Model

In the following brief description of these categories, we attempt to justify the demarcations between metatheoretical frameworks by citing illustrative exemplars, retrospective analyses, and historical reference works:

1. *Intentional:* Turn-of-the-20th-century view of the reader/writer/learner as an inherently intentional agent; an organic orientation positing function as the prime cause to explain the emergence of form on behalf of systemic coherence, including in physical, intellectual, and historical development; chiefly demonstrated through early social science scholarship and simple case study as articulated in functional and humanistic psychology (Baldwin, 1897; Brentano, 1874/1973; Dewey, 1896; G. S. Hall, 1894; Huey, 1908; James, 1890/1918; Maslow, 1943; Rogers, 1951); pragmatist philosophy (Dewey, 1938/1998; Peirce, 1923); neoromantic, naturalist, and realist literary criticism (James, 1888/1911; Leitch et al., 2010; Pater, 1889; Singley, 2013); and neoromantic and progressive education (Dewey, 1902, 1916; Gray, 1924; Parker, 1894; N. B. Smith, 1934/1965)

2. *Respondent:* A mid-century emphasis on the reader/writer/learner as a passive object of structured conditioning or textual constraint; a mechanistic orientation with roots in British empiricism, and, most notably, associationism, stressing the idea that structure accounts for functional outcome; chiefly demonstrated through positivist experimentation and metrics, or formalist theories of textual criticism, as articulated in behaviorist psychology (C. L. Hull, 1940; Skinner, 1957; Tolman, 1932; Watson, 1913, 1925); social efficiency theory (F. W. Taylor, 1919); logical positivist philosophy (Russell, 1905; Whitehead & Russell, 1927); New Criticism and formalist literary theory (C. Brooks, 1947; Litz, Menand, & Rainey, 2000; Ransom, 1937, 1941; Richards, 1930; Richards, Ogden, & Wood, 1922; Wimsatt & Beardsley, 1946); and close reading, skill practice, and outcome-based instruction (Bloom et al., 1956; Flesch, 1955/1986; Gagné, 1965; Hilgard, Irvine, & Whipple, 1953; Skinner, 1958; Wellek & Warren, 1956)

3. *Constructed:* A latter 20th-century emphasis, still current, toward the reader/writer/learner as an actively constructed agent; a rationalist orientation extending the idea of causal structure by stressing *structure of process* and the construction of meaning (i.e., constructivism) through componential and hierarchical analyses; relatable to Kantian epistemology and information processing theory, and chiefly demonstrated through theoretical modeling and hypothetico-deductive experiment, or elaborative textual analyses on symbol, narrative, or semantic directionality, as articulated in cognitive psychology (Gardner, 1985; Kintsch, 1998; G. A. Miller, 1956; Neisser, 1967; Piaget, 1937/1957; Weiner, 1990); psycholinguistics (Chomsky, 1959; Goodman, 1967); Chicago school literary criticism (Booth, 1961; Burke, 1945, 1966; Leitch et al., 2010); reader response theory (Langer, 1990; Rosenblatt, 1978); and constructivist, activity-based, and meaning-centered pedagogies (Brown, 1994; Krashen, 2004; McCormick, 1994; F. Smith, 1981; Wood, Bruner, & Ross, 1976)

4. *Contingent:* A late 20th- and early 21st-century emphasis on the importance of sociocultural context in the development of social and cognitive behavioral repertoires or practices, as in research on student identity, ideology, community,

culture, values, and goals related to literate practices; a contextualist (historically situated) orientation with a post-Hegelian, neo-Marxist, or phenomenological stance on causation and its irreducible complexity; chiefly demonstrated by ethnographic inquiry, situated case study, and critical analyses as in sociocultural theory (Berger & Luckmann, 1966/1979; Cushman, Kintgen, Kroll, & Rose, 2001; Heath, 1983, 1996); bio-ecological and cultural-historical psychology (Bronfenbrenner & Morris, 2006; Engeström, 1987/2015; Rogoff, 2003; Vygotsky, 1978); Frankfurt School critical theory and postpositivist philosophy (Foucault, 1982; Habermas, 1985; Rorty, 1979); poststructural and postmodern literary theory (Derrida, 1967/1997; Eagleton, 1996; Halliday & Hasan, 1989; Selden, 1995); educational anthropology (Heath, 1983; Spindler, 1997); and social constructivist theory, culturally responsive education, new literacy studies, disciplinary literacies, and educational identity studies (Davis & Sumara, 1997; Dyson, 2001; Hirtle, 1996; Kinloch, 2011; Ladson-Billings, 1995; New London Group, 1996; St. Pierre, 2000, 2014; Street, 1984)

5. *Indeterminate:* A catchall for uses that could not be easily categorized, or that deliberately blended or defied categories, as in some postmodern positioning and some of the newest literacy and new literacies studies

Although we drew these categories from the theoretical histories of the disciplines that have traditionally influenced theory in literacy education, these framework labels are not meant to map neatly to the better known period designations of historical normal science (Bredo, 2006b; Kuhn, 1962/1996). As we intend these terms, *respondent* should not be read as just another word for *behaviorist*, even though most (not all) self-described behaviorists seemed to hold the assumptions about human agency and development that we group in this category (e.g., C. L. Hull, 1940; Watson, 1913; but cf. Tolman, 1932, who was criticized for his vestigial attachment to what we would identify as *intentional* motifs, especially an internal locus of cause). Similarly, *constructed* should not be read as just another way of indicating cognitive psychology, as there clearly were *constructed* assumptions in reading pedagogy and psychology during earlier periods of functionalist and behaviorist psychology (e.g., Bartlett, 1932; Dewey, 1896; Piaget, 1947/2003), and certainly since.

APPENDIX B
On Our Methods for Drafting a Historical Narrative

In tracking the influences of psychology on literacy instruction, we found multiple historical accounts supporting the succession from functionalist psychology to behaviorist psychology, to cognitive psychology, followed by ecological, social, and cultural-historical psychology. This succession reflects the major themes as filtered through educational psychology into literacy research, however. Psychology proper demonstrates a much broader and richer range of perspectives (e.g., psychoanalysis, developmental psychology, social psychology, personality psychology, positivist psychology, ethology, evolutionary psychology), and periodically pieces of these have been borrowed into literacy research directly (e.g., Gestalt psychology, Piagetian development theory, ecological psychology).

In North American literary theory we similarly found multiple accounts supporting a journey from naturalist and realist criticism to New Criticism and formalism, to Chicago school and structuralist criticism, to postmodern and identity theory criticism, to historicist and "new realist" critique, with minor demonstrations of Freudian, Jungian, Marxist, neuro-, evolutionary, and Big Data (content analysis) analyses along the way. Clearly, not all of these schools were equally influential in literacy education. The greatest impact came from expressive, New Critical, reader response (simplified Chicago school), and identity theory–based criticism.

We observe that these traditional labels have shortcomings. First, as Koyré (1968) and Kuhn (1962/1996) both noted, the requirement that scholars at given times take up the designations of the day in order to be considered members of a particular community of scholarly practice seems occluding. Once a paradigm (or at least its label) becomes dominant, ostensibly designating the normal science paradigm of the era, accepting it becomes obligatory to all who would participate as members of the discipline. Only during periods of abnormal or revolutionary science are fundamental critiques and idiosyncrasy allowed voice (Koyré, 1968). Otherwise, as the physicist Max Planck is purported to have said, science seems to advance one obituary at a time.

It is possible that as a label becomes requisite, it is taken up broadly but without too much scrutiny, becoming shallowly generalized ("Learning is a change in behavior," "Learning is information processing," "Learning is social," etc.). However, within such generalizations, a wider range of more precise epistemological and metatheoretical commitments is possible, often at cross-purposes with (yet contained within) the dominant paradigm. In our review of the literatures we discovered these exceptions to be plentiful, particularly in the scholarship on literacy education practice.

ACKNOWLEDGMENTS

We wish to thank Gail Clark and Jo Davis of the Collaborative Center for Literacy Development at the University of Kentucky for their assistance in collecting cross-check data and tabulating and formatting several of the tables and figures in this manuscript. We also wish to sincerely thank the reviewers and editors for their helpful guidance and critique. Their responses have improved the original manuscript immensely.

REFERENCES

Adams, M. J. (1990). *Beginning to read: Thinking and learning about print.* Cambridge: MIT Press.
Adkins, D. C., Payne, F. D., & Ballif, B. L. (1972). Motivation factor scores and response set scores for ten ethnic-cultural groups of preschool children. *American Educational Research Journal, 9,* 557–572.

Adler, M. J. (1940). *How to read a book: The art of getting a liberal education.* New York, NY: Simon & Schuster.

Alexander, P. A. (2005). The path to competence: A lifespan developmental perspective on reading. *Journal of Literacy Research, 37,* 413–436.

Alexander, P. A., & Fox, E. (2011). Adolescents as readers. In M. L. Kamil, P. D. Pearson, E. B. Moje, & P. P. Afflerbach (Eds.), *Handbook of reading research* (Vol. 4, pp. 157–176). New York, NY: Routledge.

Alexander, P. A., & Fox, E. (2013). A historical perspective on reading research and practice, redux. In D. E. Alvermann, N. J. Unrau, & R. B. Ruddell (Eds.), *Theoretical models and processes of reading* (6th ed., pp. 3–46). Newark, DE: International Reading Association.

Allington, R. L., & Johnston, P. H. (2000). *What do we know about effective fourth-grade teachers and their classrooms?* (Report Series 13010). Albany, NY: National Research Center on English Learning and Achievement. Retrieved from http://www.albany.edu/cela/reports/allington/allington4thgrade13010.pdf

Allington, R. L., & McGill-Franzen, A. M. (in press). Summer reading loss is the basis of almost all the rich/poor reading gap. In R. Horowitz & S. J. Samuels (Eds.), *The achievement gap in reading: Complex causes, persistent issues, and possible solutions.* New York, NY: Routledge.

Allington, R. L., McGill-Franzen, A. M., Camilli, G., Williams, L., Graff, J., Zeig, J., . . . Nowak, R. (2010). Addressing summer reading setback among economically disadvantaged elementary students. *Reading Psychology, 31,* 411–427.

Almasi, J. F., & Garas-York, K. (2009). Comprehension and discussion of text. In S. E. Israel & G. G. Duffy (Eds.), *Handbook of research on reading comprehension* (pp. 470–493). London, England: Routledge.

Almasi, J. F., & McKeown, M. G. (1996). The nature of engaged reading in classroom discussions of literature. *Journal of Literacy Research, 28,* 107–146.

Alvermann, D. A. (Ed.). (2002). *Adolescents and literacies in a digital world.* New York, NY: Peter Lang.

Alvermann, D. A., O'Brien, D. G., & Dillon, D. R. (1990). What teachers do when they say they're having discussions of content area reading assignments: A qualitative analysis. *Reading Research Quarterly, 25,* 296–322.

Alvermann, D. A., Unrau, N. J., & Ruddell, R. B. (Eds.). (2013). *Theoretical models and processes of reading* (6th ed.). Newark, DE: International Reading Association.

Anderson, R. C. (1984). Role of readers' schema in comprehension, learning and memory. In R. Anderson, J. Osbourne, & R. Tierney (Eds.), *Learning to read in American schools: Basal readers and content text* (pp. 243–258). Hillsdale, NJ: Lawrence Erlbaum.

Anderson, R. C., Hiebert, E. H., Scott, J. A., & Wilkinson, I. A. G. (1984). *Becoming a nation of readers: The report of the Commission of Reading.* Washington, DC: National Institute of Education, U.S. Department of Education.

Applebee, A. (1977). The elements of response to a literary work: What we have learned. *Research in the Teaching of English, 11,* 255–271.

Arnold, M. (1869). *Culture and anarchy: An essay in political and social criticism.* Oxford, England: Project Gutenberg.

Artley, A. S. (1977). Putting remediation into remedial reading. *English Education, 8,* 103–110.

Athey, I. (1970). Affective factors in reading. In H. Singer & R. B. Ruddell (Eds.), *Theoretical models and processes of reading* (pp. 98–123). Newark, DE: International Reading Association.

Athey, I. (1976). Developmental processes and reading processes: Invalid inferences from the former to the latter. In H. Singer & R. B. Ruddell (Eds.), *Theoretical models and processes of reading* (2nd ed., pp. 730–742). Newark, DE: International Reading Association.

Athey, I. (1985). Reading research in the affective domain. In H. Singer & R. B. Ruddell (Eds.), *Theoretical models and processes of reading* (3rd ed., pp. 527–557). Newark, DE: International Reading Association.

Au, K. H. (1998). Social constructivism and the school literacy of learning of students of diverse backgrounds. *Journal of Literacy Research, 30,* 297–319.

August, D., & Shanahan, T. (Eds.). (2006). *Developing literacy in second-language learners—Report of the National Literacy Panel on language minority children and youth.* Mahwah, NJ: Lawrence Erlbaum.

Aukerman, M., & Schuldt, L. C. (2015). Children's perceptions of their reading ability and epistemic roles in monologically and dialogically organized bilingual classrooms. *Journal of Literacy Research, 47,* 115–145.

Bailey, N. M. (2009). "It makes it more real": Teaching new literacies in a secondary English classroom. *English Education, 41,* 207–234.

Baldwin, J. M. (1897). *School reading by grades: First[-eighth] year.* New York, NY: American Book.

Balmuth, M. (2009). *The roots of phonics: A historical introduction* (Revised ed.). Baltimore, MD: Paul H. Brookes.

Barr, R., Kamil, M. L., Mosenthal, P., & Pearson, P. D. (1996). *Handbook of reading research* (Vol. 2). Mahwah, NJ: Lawrence Erlbaum.

Barry, A. L. (2008). Reading the past: Historical antecedents to contemporary reading methods and materials. *Reading Horizons, 49,* 31–52.

Bartlett, F. C. (1932). *Remembering: A study in experimental and social psychology.* Cambridge, England: Cambridge University Press.

Beach, R., & Hynds, S. (1996). Research on response to literature. In R. Barr, M. L. Kamil, P. Mosenthal, & P. D. Pearson (Eds.), *Handbook of reading research* (Vol. 2, pp. 453–489). Mahwah, NJ: Lawrence Erlbaum.

Beaven, M. H. (1972). Responses of adolescents to feminine characters in literature. *Research in the Teaching of English, 6,* 48–68.

Beck, S. W. (2009). Individual goals and academic literacy: Integrating authenticity and explicitness. *English Education, 41,* 259–280.

Bell, B. I. (1949). *Crisis in education: A challenge to American complacency.* New York, NY: Whittlesey House.

Bell, H. M. (1938). *Youth tell their story.* Washington, DC: American Council on Education.

Bell, L. A. (2007). Theoretical foundations for social justice education. In M. Adams, L. A. Bell, & P. Griffin (Eds.), *Teaching for diversity and social justice* (pp. 1–14). New York, NY: Routledge.

Berger, P. L., & Luckmann, T. (1979). *The social construction of reality: A treatise in the sociology of knowledge.* New York, NY: Penguin Books. (Original work published 1966)

Bergin, D. A., & LaFave, C. (1998). Continuities between motivation research and whole language philosophy of instruction. *Journal of Literacy Research, 30,* 321–356.

Bergson, H. (1911). *Creative evolution* (A. Mitchell, Trans.). New York, NY: Holt. (Original work published 1907)

Berliner, D. C. (1993). The 100-year journey of educational psychology: From interest to disdain to respect for practice. In T. K. Faigin & G. R. VandenBos (Eds.), *Exploring applied psychology: Origins and critical analyses* (pp. 39–78). Washington, DC: American Psychological Association.

Berliner, D. C. (2006). Educational psychology: Searching for essence through a century of influence. In P. A. Alexander & P. H. Winne (Eds.), *Handbook of educational psychology* (2nd ed., pp. 3–28). Mahwah, NJ: Lawrence Erlbaum.

Bestor, A. (1953). *Educational wastelands.* Urbana: University of Illinois Press.

Bill & Melinda Gates Foundation. (n.d.). *K–12 education.* Retrieved from http://collegeready. gatesfoundation.org/

Bleich, D. (1988). *The double perspective: Language, literacy, and social relations.* New York, NY: Oxford University Press.

Bloom, B. S., Engelhart, M. D., Furst, E. J., Hill, W. H., & Krathwohl, D. R. (1956). *Taxonomy of educational objectives: The classification of educational goals: Handbook 1. Cognitive domain.* New York, NY: Longmans, Green.

Bloome, D., & Green, J. (1984). Directions in the sociolinguistic study of reading. In P. D. Pearson, R. Barr, M. L. Kamil, & P. Mosenthal (Eds.), *Handbook of reading research* (pp. 395–421). Mahwah, NJ: Lawrence Erlbaum.

Bobbitt, J. F. (1918). *The curriculum.* Boston, MA: Houghton Mifflin.

Booth, W. C. (1961). *The rhetoric of fiction.* Chicago, IL: University of Chicago Press.

Boring, E. G. (1950). *A history of experimental psychology* (2nd ed.). New York, NY: Appleton-Century-Crofts.

Boze, N. S. (1968). The proper study. *Research in the Teaching of English, 2,* 115–124.

Brass, J. J., & Burns, L. D. (2011). Research in secondary English, 1912–2011: Historical continuities and discontinuities in the NCTE imprint. *Research in the Teaching of English, 46,* 171–186.

Bredo, E. (2006a). Conceptual confusion and educational psychology. In P. A. Alexander & P. H. Winne (Eds.), *Handbook of educational psychology* (2nd ed., pp. 43–58). New York, NY: Routledge.

Bredo, E. (2006b). Philosophies of educational research. In J. L. Green, G. Camilli, & P. B. Elmore (Eds.), *Handbook of complementary methods in educational research* (pp. 1–32). Washington, DC: American Educational Research Association.

Brentano, F. C. (1973). *Psychology from an empirical standpoint.* New York, NY: Humanities Press. (Original work published 1874)

Bronfenbrenner, U., & Morris, P. A. (2006). The bioecological model of human development. In W. Damon (Series Ed.) & R.M. Lerner (Vol. Ed.), *Handbook of child psychology: Vol. 1. Theoretical models of human development* (pp. 793–828). New York, NY: Wiley.

Brooks, C. (1947). *The well wrought urn: Studies on the structure of poetry.* New York, NY: Harcourt Brace.

Brooks, C., & Warren, R. P. (1960). *Understanding poetry* (3rd ed.). New York, NY: Holt, Rinehart & Winston.

Brooks, C. K. (1979). What beginning English teachers need to know about motivating the unmotivated: These learners "do" have potential. *English Education, 10,* 220–226.

Brown, A. (1994). The advancement of learning. *Educational Researcher, 23,* 4–12.

Bruner, J. (1960). *The process of education.* Cambridge, MA: Harvard University Press.

Burke, K. (1945). *A grammar of motives.* Baltimore, MD: Johns Hopkins Press.

Burke, K. (1966). *Language as symbolic action.* Berkeley: University of California Press.

Buxton, C. (1985). American functionalism. In C. Buxton (Ed.), *Points of view in the modern history of psychology* (pp. 113–140). Cambridge, MA: Academic Press.

Cacioppo, J. T., Semin, G. R., & Bernston, G. G. (2004). Realism, instrumentalism, and scientific symbiosis: Psychological theory as a search for truth and the discovery of solutions. *American Psychologist, 59,* 214–223.

Cairns, R. B., & Cairns, B. D. (2006). The making of developmental psychology. In R. M. Learner (Ed.), *Handbook of child psychology: Vol. 1. Theoretical models of human development* (6th ed., pp. 89–165). Hoboken, NJ: Wiley.

Callahan, R. (1962). *Education and the cult of efficiency.* Chicago, IL: University of Chicago Press.

Cantrell, S. C., Pennington, J., Rintamaa, M., Osborne, M., Parker, C., & Rudd, M. (2016). Supplemental literacy instruction in high school: What students say matters for reading instruction. *Reading & Writing Quarterly.* Advance online publication.

Castenell, L. A. (1983). Achievement motivation: An investigation of adolescents' achievement patterns. *American Educational Research Journal, 20*, 503–510.

Cather, W. (1994). *My Antonia*. New York, NY: Vintage. (Original work published 1918)

Catterson, A. K., & Pearson, P. D. (in press). A close reading of close reading—What does the research tell us about how to promote the thoughtful interrogation of text? In K. A. Hinchmann & D. Appleman (Eds.), *Adolescent literacy: A handbook of practice-based research*. New York, NY: Guilford.

Caughlan, S., Juzwik, M. M., Borsheim-Black, C., Kelly, S., & Fine, J. G. (2013). English teacher candidates developing dialogically organized instructional practices. *Research in the Teaching of English, 47*, 212–246.

Caughlan, S., & Kelly, S. (2004). Bridging methodological gaps: Instructional and institutional effects of tracking in two English classes. *Research in the Teaching of English, 39*, 20–62.

Cazden, C. B. (1988). *Classroom discourse: The language of teaching and learning*. Portsmouth, NH: Heinemann.

Cazden, C. B. (1993). Vygotsky, Hymes, and Bakhtin: From word to utterance and voice. In E. A. Forman, N. Minick, & C. A. Stone (Eds.), *Contexts for learning: Sociocultural dynamics in children's development* (pp. 197–212). New York, NY: Oxford University Press.

Chall, J. S. (1967). *Learning to read: The great debate. An inquiry into the science, art, and ideology of old and new methods of teaching children to read, 1910–1965*. New York, NY: McGraw-Hill.

Cheng, Y. C. (2015). Paradigm shift in education: Toward third-wave research. In L. D. Hill & F. C. Levine (Eds.), *World education research yearbook 2015* (pp. 5–29). New York, NY: Routledge.

Chomsky, N. (1957). *Syntactic structures*. The Hague, Netherlands: Mouton.

Chomsky, N. (1959). A review of B. F. Skinner's *Verbal Behavior. Language, 35*, 26–58.

Chomsky, N. (1965). *Aspects of the theory of syntax*. Cambridge: MIT Press.

Church, R. W., & Sedlak, M. W. (1976). *Education in the United States: An interpretive history*. Ann Arbor, MI: Free Press.

Clark, C., Chow-Hoy, T. K., Herter, R. J., & Moss, P. (2001). Portfolios as sites of learning: Reconceptualizing the connections to motivation and engagement. *Journal of Literacy Research, 33*, 211–241.

Cofer, C. N., & Appley, M. H. (1964). *Motivation: Theory and research*. New York, NY: Wiley.

Cooper, C. A., & Michalak, D. A. (1981). A note on determining response styles in research on response to literature. *Research in the Teaching of English, 15*, 163–169.

Cremin, L. A. (1964). *The transformation of the school: Progressivism in American education, 1876–1957*. New York, NY: Vintage Books.

Cuban, L. (1990). Reforming again, again, and again. *Educational Researcher, 19*(1), 3–13.

Cunningham, D. J. (1992). Beyond educational psychology: Steps toward an educational semiotic. *Educational Psychology Review, 4*, 165–194.

Cunningham, J. W., & Fitzgerald, J. (1996). Epistemology and reading. *Reading Research Quarterly, 31*, 36–60.

Cushman, E., Kintgen, E. R., Kroll, B. M., & Rose, M. (Eds.). (2001). *Literacy: A critical sourcebook*. New York, NY: Bedford/St. Martins.

Cziko, G. (2000). *The things we do: Using the lessons of Bernard and Darwin to understand the what, how, and why of our behavior*. Cambridge: MIT Press. Retrieved from http://faculty.education.illinois.edu/g-cziko/twd/pdf/index.html

Darwin, C. (1859). *On the origin of species by means of natural selection, or the preservation of favored races in the struggle for life*. London, England: John Murray. Retrieved from http://darwin-online.org.uk/converted/pdf/1859_Origin_F373.pdf

Darwin, C. (1871). *The descent of man, and selection in relation to sex.* London, England: John Murray.

Darwin, C. (1877). A biographical sketch of an infant. *Mind, 2,* 285–294.

Davis, B., & Sumara, D. (1997). Cognition, complexity, and teacher education. *Harvard Educational Review, 67,* 105–126.

Dennis, P. (1955). *Auntie Mame: An irreverent escapade.* New York, NY: Broadway Books.

Denzin, N. K. (2009). The elephant in the living room: Or extending the conversation about the politics of evidence. *Qualitative Research, 9,* 139–160.

Denzin, N. K., & Lincoln, Y. S. (1994). *The handbook of qualitative research.* Thousand Oaks, CA: Sage.

Derrida, J. (1997). *Of grammatology* (Corrected ed.). Baltimore, MD: Johns Hopkins University Press. (Original work published 1967)

DeStigter, T. (2001). Affective thought, personalized democracy, and the council's multicultural mission. *English Education, 33,* 290–315.

Dewey, J. (1896). The reflex learning arc concept in psychology. *Psychological Review, 3,* 357–370.

Dewey, J. (1897). *My pedagogic creed.* New York, NY: E. L. Kellogg.

Dewey, J. (1902). *The child and the curriculum.* Chicago, IL: University of Chicago Press.

Dewey, J. (1913). *Interest and effort in education.* Boston, MA: Houghton Mifflin. Retrieved from https://archive.org/details/interestandeffor00deweuoft

Dewey, J. (1916). *Democracy and education.* Chicago, IL: University of Chicago Press.

Dewey, J. (1998). *Experience and education.* West Lafayette, IN: Kappa Delta Pi. (Original work published 1938)

Dibiasio, G. N. (1973). Mastery learning: Implications for the English curriculum. *English Education, 4,* 106–115.

Dillon, D. R., O'Brien, D. G., & Heilman, E. E. (2013). Literacy research in the 21st century: From paradigms to pragmatism and practicality. In D. E. Alvermann, N. J. Unrau, & R. B. Ruddell (Eds.), *Theoretical models and processes of reading* (6th ed., pp. 1104–1132). Newark, DE: International Reading Association.

Donlan, D. (1979). A methodology inventory for composition education. *English Education, 11,* 23–31.

Donmoyer, R. (1996). Educational research in an era of paradigm proliferation: What's a journal editor to do? *Educational Researcher, 25*(2), 19–25.

Dreiser, T. (1994). *Sister Carrie.* New York, NY: Penguin. (Original work published 1900)

Dressman, M. (2007). Theoretically framed: Argument and desire in the production of general knowledge about literacy. *Reading Research Quarterly, 42,* 332–363.

Duran, J. (1994). Russell on pragmatism. *Russell: Journal of the Bertrand Russell Archives, 14,* 31–37.

Dutro, E. (2010). What "hard times" means: Mandated curricula, class-privileged assumptions, and the lives of poor children. *Research in the Teaching of English, 44,* 255–291.

Dyson, A. (2001). Coach Bombay's kids learn to write: Children's appropriation of media material for school literacy. In E. Cushman, E. Kintgen, B. Kroll, & M. Rose (Eds.), *Literacy: A critical sourcebook* (pp. 325–357). New York, NY: Bedford/St. Martins.

Eagleton, T. (1996). *Literary theory: An introduction* (2nd ed.). Minneapolis: University of Minnesota Press.

Eccles, J. S., Wigfield, A., & Schiefele, U. (1998). Motivation to succeed. In W. Damon (Series Ed.) & N. Eisenberg (Ed.), *Handbook of child psychology: Vol 3. Social, emotional, and personality development* (5th ed.). New York, NY: Wiley.

Ehrlich, M., Kurtz-Costes, B., & Loridant, C. (1993). Cognitive and motivational determinants of reading comprehension in good and poor readers. *Journal of Reading Behavior, 25,* 365–381.

Emig, J. (1967). On teaching composition: Some hypotheses as definitions. *Research in the Teaching of English, 1*, 127–135.

Emig, J. (1972). Children and metaphor. *Research in the Teaching of English, 6*, 163–175.

Enciso, P., & Ryan, C. (2011). Sociocultural theory: Expanding the aims and practices of language arts education. In D. Lapp & D. Fischer (Eds.), *Handbook of research on teaching the English language arts* (3rd ed., pp. 132–138). New York, NY: Routledge.

Engeström, Y. (2015). *Learning by expanding: An activity-theoretical approach to developmental research* (2nd ed.). Cambridge, England: Cambridge University Press. (Original work published 1987)

Engeström, Y., Miettinen, R., & Punamäki, R.-L. (Eds.). (1999). *Perspectives on activity theory*. New York, NY: Cambridge University Press.

Fairclough, N. (1989). *Language and power*. London, England: Longman.

Falcon, A. (2015). *Aristotle on causality. The Stanford encyclopedia of philosophy* (E. N. Zalta, Ed.). Retrieved from http://plato.stanford.edu/archives/spr2015/entries/aristotle-causality/

Fallace, T. (2015). The savage origins of child-centered pedagogy, 1971–1913. *American Educational Research Journal, 52*, 73–103.

Farley, F. H., & Truog, A. L. (1970–1971). Individual differences in reading comprehension. *Journal of Reading Behavior, 3*, 29–35.

Farrell, E. J. (1978). The basics: Random reflections on a movement. *English Education, 9*, 199–211.

Feyerabend, P. K. (2010). *Against method: Outline of an anarchistic theory of knowledge* (4th ed.). New York, NY: Verso. (Original work published 1975)

Fisher, D., & Frey, N. (2012). Motivating boys to read: Inquiry, modeling, and choice matter. *Journal of Adolescent & Adult Literacy, 55*, 587–596.

Fleck, L. (1979). *Genesis and development of a scientific fact* (F. Bradley & T. J. Trenn, Trans.). Chicago, IL: University of Chicago Press. (Original work published 1935)

Flesch, R. F. (1986). *Why Johnny can't read: And what you can do about it*. New York, NY: Harper & Row. (Original work published 1955)

Fodor, J. A. (1983). *The modularity of mind*. Cambridge: MIT Press.

Fodor, J. A. (2001). *The mind doesn't work that way: The scope and limits of computational psychology*. Cambridge: MIT Press.

Foucault, M. (1970). *The order of things: An archaeology of the human sciences*. New York, NY: Pantheon. (Original work published 1966)

Foucault, M. (1982). *Archaeology of knowledge*. New York, NY: Vintage.

Freud, S. (1933). *New introductory lectures on psychoanalysis* (W. J. H. Sprott, Trans.). New York, NY: W. W. Norton.

Fröbel, F. (1887). *The education of man* (W. N. Hailmann, Trans.). New York, NY: D. Appleton.

Frye, N. (2015). *Anatomy of criticism: Four essays*. Princeton, NJ: Princeton University Press. (Original work published 1957)

Gaffney, J. S., & Anderson, R. C. (2000). Trends in reading research in the United States: Changing intellectual currents over three decades. In M. L. Kamil, P. B. Mosenthal, P. D. Pearson, & R. Barr (Eds.), *Handbook of reading research* (Vol. 3, pp. 53–74). Mahwah, NJ: Lawrence Erlbaum.

Gagné, R. M. (1965). *The conditions of learning*. New York, NY: Holt, Rinehart & Winston.

Gardner, H. (1985). *The mind's new science: A history of the cognitive revolution*. New York, NY: Basic Books.

Gavelek, J., & Bresnahan, P. (2009). Ways of meaning making: Sociocultural perspectives on reading comprehension. In S. E. Israel & G. G. Duffy (Eds.), *Handbook of research on reading comprehension* (pp. 140–178). New York, NY: Routledge.

Gee, J. P. (1991). Socio-cultural approaches to literacy (literacies). *Annual Review of Applied Linguistics, 12*, 31–48.

Gee, J. P. (2012). *Social linguistics and literacies: Ideology in discourses* (4th ed.). New York, NY: Routledge.

Gibson, J. J. (2015). *The ecological approach to visual perception.* New York, NY: Psychology Press. (Original work published 1979)

Glaser, B. G. (1965). The constant comparative method of qualitative analysis. *Social Problems, 12*, 436–445.

Glaser, B. G., & Strauss, A. L. (1999). *The discovery of grounded theory: Strategies for qualitative research.* New Brunswick, NJ: AldineTransaction. (Original work published 1967)

Glassman, M. (2004). Running in circles: Chasing Dewey. *Educational Theory, 54*, 315–341.

Godfrey-Smith, P. (1996). *Complexity and the function of mind in nature.* Cambridge, England: Cambridge University Press.

Goodman, K. S. (1965). A linguistic study of cues and miscues in reading. *Elementary English, 42*, 639–643.

Goodman, K. S. (1967). Reading: A psycholinguistic guessing game. *Journal of the Reading Specialist, 6*, 126–135.

Goodman, K. S. (1969). Analysis of oral reading miscues: Applied psycholinguistics. *Reading Research Quarterly, 5*, 9–30.

Graves, M. (2004). Theories and constructs that have made a significant difference in adolescent literacy—but have the potential to produce still more positive benefits. In T. Jetton & J. Dole (Eds.), *Adolescent literacy research and practice* (pp. 433–452). New York, NY: Guilford Press.

Gray, W. S. (1919). Principles of method in teaching reading, as derived from scientific investigation. In G. M. Whipple (Ed.), *The eighteenth yearbook of the National Society for the Study of Education, Pt. 2: Fourth report of the Committee on Economy of Time in Education* (pp. 26–51). Bloomington, IL: Public School.

Gray, W. S. (1924). The importance of intelligent silent reading. *Elementary School Journal, 24*, 348–356.

Gray, W. S. (1925). *Summary of investigations relating to reading.* Chicago, IL: University of Chicago Press.

Green, C. D. (1992). Of immortal mythological beasts: Operationism in psychology. *Theory & Psychology, 2*, 291–320.

Green, C. D. (2009). Darwinian theory, functionalism, and the first American psychological revolution. *American Psychologist, 64*, 75–83.

Green, J., & Bloome, D. (2004). Ethnography and ethnographers of and in education: A situated perspective. In J. Flood, S. B. Heath, & D. Lapp (Eds.), *Handbook of research on teaching literacy through the communicative and visual arts* (pp. 181–202). New York, NY: Macmillan.

Guba, E. G., & Lincoln, Y. S. (1994). Competing paradigms in qualitative research. In N. K. Denzin & Y. S. Lincoln (Eds.), *Handbook of qualitative research* (pp. 105–117). Thousand Oaks, CA: Sage.

Guthrie, J. T., Van Meter, P., McCann, A., Wigfield, A., Bennett, L., Poundstone, C., . . . Mitchell, A. (1996). Growth in literacy engagement: Changes in motivations and strategies during concept-oriented reading instruction. *Reading Research Quarterly, 31*, 306–325.

Guthrie, J. T., & Wigfield, A. (2000). Engagement and motivation in reading. In M. L. Kamil, P. B. Mosenthal, P. D. Pearson, & R. Barr (Eds.), *Handbook of reading research* (Vol. 3, pp. 403–422). Mahwah, NJ: Lawrence Erlbaum.

Guthrie, J. T., Wigfield, A., Metsala, J. L., & Cox, K. E. (2004). Motivational and cognitive predictors of text comprehension and reading amount. In R. B. Ruddell & N. J. Unrau

(Eds.), *Theoretical models and processes of reading* (5th ed., pp. 929–953). Newark, DE: International Reading Association.

Guthrie, J. T., Wigfield, A., & You, W. (2012). Instructional contexts for engagement and achievement in reading. In S. L. Christenson, A. L. Reschley, & C. Wiley (Eds.), *Handbook of research on student engagement*. New York, NY: Springer.

Gutiérrez, K. D. (2008). Developing a socioccritical literacy in the third space. *Reading Research Quarterly, 43*, 148–164.

Gutiérrez, K. D., & Stone, L. D. (2000). Synchronic and diachronic dimensions of social practice: An emerging methodology for cultural-historical perspectives on literacy learning. In C. D. Lee & P. Smagorinsky (Eds.), *Vygotskian perspectives on literacy research: Constructing meaning through collaborative inquiry* (pp. 150–164). New York, NY: Cambridge University Press.

Guzzetti, B., Anders, P. L., & Neuman, S. (1999). Thirty years of JRB/JLR: A retrospective of reading/literacy research. *Journal of Literacy Research, 31*, 67–92.

Habermas, J. (1985). *The theory of communicative action: Vol. 1. Reason and the rationalization of society* (T. McCarthy, Trans.). Boston, MA: Beacon Press.

Haeckel, E. (1914). *The history of creation* (6th ed.). New York, NY: D. Appleton. (Original work published 1876)

Hall, G. S. (1894). *How to teach reading and what to read in school*. Boston, MA: D. C. Heath.

Hall, L. A. (2009). Struggling reader, struggling teacher: An examination of student-teacher transactions with reading instruction and texts in social studies. *Research in the Teaching of English, 43*, 286–309.

Halliday, M. A. K., & Hasan, R. (1989). *Language, context, and text: Aspects of language in a social semiotic perspective* (2nd ed.). New York, NY: Oxford University Press.

Handsfield, L. J. (2016). *Literacy theory as practice: Connecting theory and instruction in K–12 classrooms*. New York, NY: Teachers College Press.

Harré, R., & Gillet, G. (1994). *The discursive mind*. Thousand Oaks, CA: Sage.

Harris, T. L. (1969). Reading. In R. L. Ebel (Ed.), *Encyclopedia of educational research* (4th ed., pp. 1069–1108). Toronto, Ontario, Canada: American Educational Research Association/Macmillan.

Harste, J. C. (2003). What do we mean by literacy now? *Voices From the Middle, 10*, 8–12.

Harste, J. C., Woodward, V. A., & Burke, C. L. (1984). Examining our assumptions: A transactional view of literacy and learning. *Research in the Teaching of English, 18*, 84–108.

Hartman, D. K. (1995). Eight readers reading: The intertextual links of proficient readers reading multiple passages. *Reading Research Quarterly, 30*, 520–561.

Hartman, J. E. (1979). Teaching the new students: Their competencies and ours. English explicitness. *English Education, 10*, 259–280.

Hatfield, G. (2002). Psychology, philosophy, and cognitive science: Reflections on the history and philosophy of experimental psychology. *Mind & Language, 17*, 207–232.

Hatfield, W. W. (1935). *An experience curriculum in English*. New York, NY: D. Appleton-Century.

Heath, S. B. (1983). *Ways with words: Language, life, and work in communities and classrooms*. New York, NY: Cambridge University Press.

Heath, S. B. (1996). The sense of being literate: Historical and cross-cultural features. In R. Barr, M. L. Kamil, P. Mosenthal, & P. D. Pearson (Eds.), *Handbook of reading research* (Vol. 2, pp. 3–25). Mahwah, NJ: Lawrence Erlbaum.

Heft, H. (2001). *Psychology in context: James Gibson, Roger Barker, and the legacy of William James's radical empiricism*. Mahwah, NJ: Lawrence Erlbaum.

Hilgard, E. R., Irvine, R. P., & Whipple, J. E. (1953). Rote memorization, understanding, and transfer: An extension of Katona's card trick experiments. *Journal of Experimental Psychology, 46*, 288–292.

Hirsch, E. D. (1999). *The schools we need: And why we don't have them*. New York, NY: Knopf Doubleday.

Hirtle, J. S. (1996). Social constructivism. *English Journal, 85*, 91.

Hofer, B. K., & Pintrich, P. R. (1997). The development of epistemological theories: Beliefs about knowledge and knowing and their relation to learning. *Review of Educational Research, 67*, 88–140.

Hofer, B. K., & Pintrich, P. R. (2002). *Personal epistemology: The psychology of beliefs about knowledge and knowing*. Mahwah, NJ: Lawrence Erlbaum.

Hoffman, J. (2009). In search of a "simple view" of reading comprehension. In S. E. Israel & G. G. Duffy (Eds.), *Handbook of research on reading comprehension* (pp. 54–66). London, England: Routledge.

Holmes, J. A. (1965). Basic assumptions underlying the substrata-factor theory. *Reading Research Quarterly, 1*, 5–28.

Holt, E. B. (1915). *The Freudian wish and its place in ethics*. New York, NY: Holt.

Holton, G. (1973). *Thematic origins of scientific thought: Kepler to Einstein*. Cambridge, MA: Harvard University Press.

Hruby, G. G. (2001). Sociological, postmodern, and "new realism" perspectives in social constructionism: Implications for reading research. *Reading Research Quarterly, 36*, 48–62.

Huey, E. B. (1908). *Psychology and pedagogy of reading, with a review of the history of reading and writing and of methods, texts, and hygiene in reading*. New York, NY: Macmillan.

Hull, C. L. (1940). *The mathematico-deductive theory of rote learning: A study in scientific methodology*. New Haven, CT: Yale University Press.

Hull, D. L. (1988). *Science as process: An evolutionary account of the social and conceptual development of science*. Chicago, IL: University of Chicago Press.

Hutchins, R. M. (1953). *The conflict in education in a democratic society*. New York, NY: Harper.

Hynds, S. (1989). Bringing life to literature and literature to life: Social constructs and contexts of four adolescent readers. *Research in the Teaching of English, 23*, 30–61.

Ivey, G., & Johnston, P. H. (2015). Engaged reading as a collaborative transformative practice. *Journal of Literacy Research, 47*, 297-327.

James, H. (1911). *Partial portraits*. London, England: Macmillan. (Original work published 1888)

James, W. (1918). *The principles of psychology*. New York, NY: Holt. (Original work published 1890)

Janks, H. (2000). Domination, access, diversity and design: A synthesis for critical literacy education. *Educational Review, 52*, 175–186.

Javal, E. (1990). Essay on the physiology of reading (K. J. Ciuffreda & N. Bassil, Trans.). *Ophthalmology and Physiological Optometry, 10*, 381–384. (Original work published 1879)

Johnson, M. H. (2011). Interactive specialization: A domain-general framework for human functional brain development? *Developmental Cognitive Neuroscience, 1*, 7–21.

Johnston, P. H. (1984). Assessment in reading. In P. D. Pearson, R. Barr, M. Kamil, & P. Mosenthal (Eds.), *Handbook of reading research* (pp. 147–182). New York, NY: Longman.

Johnston, P. H., & Ivey, G. (2013). Engagement with young adult literature: Outcomes and processes. *Reading Research Quarterly, 48*, 255–275.

Judd, C. H., & Buswell, G. T. (1922). *Silent reading: A study of the various types* (No. 23). Chicago, IL: University of Chicago.

Juzwik, M. M., & Sherry, M. B. (2007). Expressive language and the art of English teaching: Theorizing the relationship between literature and oral narrative. *English Education, 39*, 226–259.

Kamil, M. L., Mosenthal, P. B., Pearson, P. D., & Barr, D. (Eds.). (2000). *Handbook of reading research* (Vol. 3). Mahwah, NJ: Lawrence Erlbaum.

Kamil, M. L., Pearson, P. D., Moje, E. B., & Afflerbach, P. P. (Eds.). (2011). *Handbook of reading research* (Vol. 4). New York, NY: Routledge

Kant, I. (2008). *Critique of pure reason* (M. Weigelt, Trans.). New York, NY: Penguin. (Original work published 1781)

Kelly, G. J. (2006). Epistemology and educational research. In J. L. Green, G. Camilli, & P. B. Elmore (Eds.), *Handbook of complementary methods in education research* (pp. 33–55). Washington, DC: American Educational Research Association.

Kimble, G. A. (1994). A new formula for behaviorism. *Psychological Review, 101,* 254–258.

Kinloch, V. (2005). Poetry, literacy, and creativity: Fostering effective learning strategies in an urban classroom. *English Education, 37,* 96–114.

Kinloch, V. (2010). *Harlem on our minds: Place, race, and the literacies of urban youth.* New York, NY: Teachers College Press.

Kinloch, V. (Ed.). (2011). *Urban literacies: Critical perspectives on language, learning, and community.* New York, NY: Teachers College Press.

Kintsch, W. (1998). *Comprehension: A paradigm for cognition.* New York, NY: Cambridge University Press.

Klare, G. R. (1984). Readability. In P. D. Pearson (Ed.), *Handbook of reading research* (pp. 681–744). Mahwah, NJ: Lawrence Erlbaum.

Kliebard, H. M. (2004). *The struggle for the American curriculum, 1893–1958* (3rd ed.). New York, NY: RoutledgeFalmer.

Knellwolf, C., & Norris, C. (Eds.). (2001). *The Cambridge history of literary criticism: Vol. 9. Twentieth-century historical, philosophical and psychological perspectives.* New York, NY: Cambridge University Press.

Koffka, K. (1935). *Principles of Gestalt psychology.* New York, NY: Harcourt Brace.

Koltko-Rivera, M. E. (2004). The psychology of worldviews. *Review of General Psychology, 8,* 3–58.

Koyré, A. (1968). *Metaphysics and measurement: Essays in scientific revolution.* Cambridge, MA: Harvard University Press.

Krashen, S. (2004). *The power of reading: Insights from the research* (2nd ed.). Englewood, CA: Libraries Unlimited.

Kuhn, T. (1996). *The structure of scientific revolutions* (3rd ed.). Chicago, IL: University of Chicago Press. (Original work published 1962)

Labaree, D. F. (2005). Progressivism, schools and schools of education: An American romance. *Paedagogica Historica, 41,* 275–288.

Ladson-Billings, G. (1995). Towards a theory of culturally relevant pedagogy. *American Educational Research Journal, 43,* 465–491.

Lagemann, E. C. (1989). The plural worlds of educational research. *History of Education Quarterly, 29,* 183–214.

Lakatos, I. (1978). *The methodology of scientific research programmes: Philosophical papers* (Vol. 1). Cambridge, England: Cambridge University Press.

Lakoff, G., & Johnson, M. (2003). *Metaphors we live by.* Chicago, IL: University of Chicago Press. (Original work published 1980)

Langer, J. A. (1990). The process of understanding: Reading for literary and informative purposes. *Research in the Teaching of English, 24,* 229–260.

LaRocque, G. E. (1976). Nothing new under the sun: Theory and practice in teacher response to literature. *Research in the Teaching of English, 8*(1), 163–169.

Larson, J., & Marsh, J. (2004). *Making literacy real: Theories and practices for learning and teaching.* Thousand Oaks, CA: Sage.

Lave, J., & Wegner, E. (1991). *Situated learning: Legitimate peripheral participation.* New York, NY: Cambridge University Press.

Leahey, T. H. (1992). The mythical revolutions of American psychology. *American Psychologist, 47,* 308–318.

Leander, K. M., & Rowe, D. W. (2006). Mapping literacy spaces in motion: A rhizomatic analysis of a classroom literacy performance. *Reading Research Quarterly, 41*, 428–460.

Lee, C. D. (2012). Conceptual and methodological challenges to a cultural and ecological framework for studying human development. In W. F. Tate IV (Ed.), *Research on schools, neighborhoods, and communities: Towards civic responsibility* (pp. 173–202). Washington, DC: American Educational Research Association.

Leitch, V. B., Cain, W. E., Finke, L. A., Johnson, B. E., McGowan, J., Sharpley-Whiting, T. D., & Williams, J. T. (Eds.). (2010). *The Norton anthology of theory and criticism* (2nd ed.). New York, NY: W. W. Norton.

Lerner, R. M. (1992). Dialectics, developmental contextualism, and the further enhancement of theory about puberty and psychosocial development. *Journal of Early Adolescence, 12*, 366–388.

Lerner, R. M., Hershberg, R. M., Hilliard, L. J., & Johnson, S. K. (2015). Concepts and theories of human development. In M. H. Bornstein & M. E. Lamb (Eds.), *Developmental science: An advanced textbook* (7th ed., pp. 3–42). New York, NY: Taylor & Francis.

Lewis, C., Enciso, P., & Moje, E. B. (Eds.). (2007). *Reframing sociocultural research on literacy: Identity, agency, and power*. Mahwah, NJ: Lawrence Erlbaum.

Linstone, H. A., & Turoff, M. (1975). *The Delphi method: Techniques and applications*. Reading, MA: Addison-Wesley.

Literacy. (n.d.). *Merriam-Webster Online*. Retrieved from http://www.merriam-webster.com/dictionary/literacy

Litz, A. W., Menand, L., & Rainey, L. (Eds.). (2000). *The Cambridge history of literary criticism: Vol. 12. Modernism and the new criticism*. New York, NY: Cambridge University Press.

Lovejoy, A. (1964). *The great chain of being: The history of an idea*. Cambridge, MA: Harvard University Press.

Luke, A. (1995). Text and discourse in education: An introduction to critical discourse analysis. *Review of Research in Education, 21*, 3–48.

Lynd, A. (1953). *Quackery in the public schools*. Boston, MA: Little, Brown.

Manicas, P. T. (2002). John Dewey and American psychology. *Journal for the Theory of Social Behavior. 32*, 267–294.

Maslow, A. H. (1943). A theory of human motivation. *Psychological Review, 50*, 370–396.

Mathews, M. M. (1966). *Teaching to read, historically considered*. Chicago, IL: University of Chicago Press.

Mathewson, G. C. (1976). The function of attitude in the reading process. In H. Singer & R. B. Ruddell (Eds.), *Theoretical models and processes of reading* (2nd ed., pp. 655–676). Newark, DE: International Reading Association.

Mathewson, G. C. (1994). Model of attitude influence upon reading and learning to read. In R. B. Ruddell, M. R. Ruddell, & H. Singer (Eds.), *Theoretical models and processes of reading* (4th ed., pp. 1131–1161). Newark, DE: International Reading Association.

McCormick, K. (1994). *The culture of reading and the teaching of English*. New York, NY: Manchester University Press.

McDonald, F. J. (1964). The influence of learning theories on education (1900–1950). In E. R. Hilgard (Ed.), *Theories of learning and instruction: Sixty-third yearbook of the National Society for the Study of Education* (Pt. 1, pp. 1–26). Chicago, IL: University of Chicago Press.

McGill-Franzen, A. (1993). Literacy for all children: "I could read the words!" Selecting good books for inexperienced readers. *The Reading Teacher, 46*, 424–426.

Meade, R. A. (1973). Accountability for what? *English Education, 4*, 173–180.

Medicus, G. (2005). Mapping transdisciplinarity in human sciences. In J. W. Lee (Ed.), *Focus on gender identity* (pp. 95–114). New York, NY: Nova Science.

Meece, J. L., Blumenfeld, P. C., & Hoyle, R. H. (1988). Students' goal orientations and cognitive engagement in classroom activities. *Journal of Educational Psychology, 80*, 514–523.

Mehaffie, S., Gee, T. C., & Larmer, W. G. (1978). English teachers' use of student-centered approaches in teaching. *English Education, 9*, 111–116.

Miller, G. A. (1956). The magic number seven, plus or minus two: Some limits on our capacity for processing information. *Psychological Review, 63*, 81–97.

Miller, G. A. (1979, June). *A very personal history.* Presentation to the Cognitive Science Workshop, MIT, Cambridge.

Miller, G. A., Galanter, E., & Pribram, K. A. (1960). *Plans and structure of behavior.* New York, NY: Holt, Rinehart & Winston.

Miller, S., & Burns, L. D. (in press). Standard VI: Realizing social justice dispositions in teaching and teacher education. *Scholar-Practitioner Quarterly.*

Moje, E. B. (2006). Motivating texts, motivating contexts, motivating adolescents: An examination of the role of motivation in adolescent literacy practices and development. *Perspectives, Summer 2006*, 10–14.

Moje, E. B. (2008). Responsive literacy teaching in secondary school content areas. In M. W. Conley, J. R. Freidhoff, M. B. Sherry, & S. F. Tuckey (Eds.), *Meeting the challenge of adolescent literacy: Research we have, research we need* (pp. 58–87). New York, NY: Guilford.

Moje, E. B., Ciechanowski, K. M., Kramer, K. E., Ellis, L. M., Carrillo, R., & Collazo, T. (2004). Working toward third space in content area literacy: An examination of everyday funds of knowledge and discourse. *Reading Research Quarterly, 39*, 38–71.

Moje, E. B., Overby, M., Tysvaer, N., & Morris, K. (2008). The complex world of adolescent literacy: Myths, motivations, and mysteries. *Harvard Educational Review, 78*, 107–154.

Monaghan, E. J. (2005). *Learning to read and write in colonial America.* Amherst: University of Massachusetts Press.

Monaghan, E. J. (2007). Scientific research and progressive education: Contexts for the early reading pioneers, 1870–1956. In S. E. Israel & E. J. Monaghan (Eds.), *Shaping the reading field: The impact of early reading pioneers, scientific research, and progressive ideas* (pp. 1–32). Newark, DE: International Reading Association.

Monaghan, E. J., & Hartman, D. K. (2000). Undertaking historical research in literacy. In M. L. Kamil, P. B. Mosenthal, P. D. Pearson, & R. Barr (Eds.), *Handbook of reading research* (Vol. 3, pp. 109–121). Mahwah, NJ: Lawrence Erlbaum.

Moore, D. W., Readence, J. E., & Rickelman, R. J. (1983). An historical exploration of content area reading instruction. *Reading Research Quarterly, 18*, 419–438.

Moore, J. (1985). Some historical and conceptual relations among logical positivism, operationism, and behaviorism. *The Behavior Analyst, 8*, 53–63.

Moore, J. (2010). Philosophy of science, with special consideration given to behaviorism as the philosophy of the science of behavior. *The Psychological Record, 60*, 123–136. Retrieved from http://opensiuc.lib.siu.edu/tpr/vol60/iss1/8

Morrell, E. (2005). Critical English education. *English Education, 37*, 312–321.

Morris, E. K. (1997). Some reflections on contextualism, mechanism, and behavior analysis. *Psychological Record, 47*, 529–542.

Morton, J., & Frith, U. (1995). Causal modeling: A structural approach to developmental psychopathology. In D. Cicchetti & D. Cohen (Eds.), *Manual of developmental psychopathology* (Vol, 1, pp. 357–390). New York, NY: Wiley.

Münsterberg, H. (1909). *Psychology and the teacher.* New York, NY: D. Appleton. Retrieved from https://archive.org/stream/psychologyandte00mngoog#page/n6/mode/2up

National Governors Association Center for Best Practices & Council of Chief State School Officers. (2010). *Common Core State Standards for English language arts and literacy in history/social studies, science, and technical subjects.* Washington, DC: Authors. Retrieved from www.corestandards.org/assets/CCSSI_ELA%20Standards.pdf

National Institute of Child Health and Human Development. (2000). *Report of the National Reading Panel: Teaching Children to Read.* Washington, DC: Author.

National Reading Panel. (2000). *Teaching Children to Read: An evidence-based assessment of the scientific research literature on reading and its implications for reading instruction.* Washington, DC: National Institute of Child Health and Human Development. Retrieved from https://www.nichd.nih.gov/publications/pubs/nrp/Pages/report.aspx

Neatby, H. (1953). *So little for the mind* (2nd ed.). Toronto, Ontario, Canada: Clarke Irwin & Company.

Neisser, U. (1967). *Cognitive psychology.* New York, NY: Appleton-Century Crofts.

Newell, A., & Simon, H. (1956). *The logic theory machine: A complex information processing system.* Santa Monica, CA: RAND.

New London Group. (1996). A pedagogy of multiliteracies: Designing social futures. *Harvard Educational Review, 66,* 60–92.

Nystrand, M., & Gamoran, A. (1991). Instructional discourse, student engagement, and literacy achievement. *Research in the Teaching of English, 25,* 261–290.

Oldfather, P., & Dahl, K. (1994). Toward a social constructivist reconceptualization of intrinsic motivation for literacy learning. *Journal of Reading Behavior, 26,* 139–158.

Otto, W. (1977). The Wisconsin design: A reading program for individually guided elementary education. In R. A. Klausmeier, R. A. Rossmiller, & M. Saily (Eds.), *Individually guided elementary education: Concepts and practices* (216–237). New York, NY: Academic Press.

Overton, W. F., & Reese, H. W. (1981). Conceptual prerequisites for an understanding of stability-change and continuity-discontinuity. *International Journal of Behavioral Development, 4,* 99–123.

Pajares, F., & Schunk, D. H. (2002). Self and self-belief in psychology and education: An historical perspective. In J. Aronson (Ed.), *Improving academic achievement* (pp. 3–25). New York, NY: Academic Press. Retrieved from http://www.uky.edu/~eushe2/Pajares/PSHistoryOfSelf.PDF

Paratore, J. R., Cassano, C. M., & Schickedanz, J. A. (2011). Supporting early (and later) literacy development at home and at school. In M. L. Kamil, P. D. Pearson, E. B. Moje, & P. P. Afflerbach (Eds.), *Handbook of reading research* (Vol. 4, pp. 107–135). New York, NY: Routledge.

Paris, S. G., Lipson, M. Y., & Wixson, K. (1983). Becoming a strategic reader. *Contemporary Educational Psychology, 8,* 293–316.

Paris, S. G., Wasik, B., & Turner, J. C. (1996). The development of strategic readers. In R. Barr, M. L. Kamil, P. B. Mosenthal, & P. D. Pearson (Eds.), *Handbook of reading research* (Vol. 2, pp. 609–640). Mahwah, NJ: Lawrence Erlbaum.

Parker, F. W. (1894). *Talks on pedagogics: An outline of the theory of concentration.* Chicago, IL: Kellogg.

Pater, W. H. (1889). *Appreciations: With an essay on style.* London, England: Macmillan.

Pearson, P. D. (Ed.). (1984). *Handbook of reading research.* New York, NY: Longman.

Pearson, P. D. (2000). Reading in the twentieth century. In T. Good (Ed.), *American education: Yesterday, today, and tomorrow. Yearbook of the National Society for the Study of Education* (pp. 152–208). Chicago, IL: University of Chicago Press. Retrieved from http://www.ciera.org/library/archive/2001-08/0108pdp.pdf

Pearson, P. D. (2004). The reading wars. *Educational Policy, 18,* 216–252.

Pearson, P. D. (2010). The roots of reading comprehension instruction. In K. Ganske & D. Fisher (Eds.), *Comprehension across the curriculum: Perspectives and practices K–12* (pp. 279–321). New York, NY: Guilford Press.

Pearson, P. D., & Cervetti, G. N. (2015). Fifty years of reading comprehension theory and practice. In P. D. Pearson & E. H. Hiebert (Eds.), *Research-based practices for teaching Common Core Literacy.* New York, NY: Teachers College Press.

Pearson, P. D., & Hamm, D. N. (2005). The assessment of reading comprehension: A review of practices: Past, present, and future. In S. G. Paris & S. A. Stahl (Eds.), *Children's reading comprehension and assessment* (pp. 13–69). Mahwah, NJ: Lawrence Erlbaum.

Pearson, P. D., & Stephens, D. (1993). Learning about literacy: A 30-year journey. In C. J. Gordon, G. D. Labercane, & W. R. McEachern (Eds.), *Elementary reading: Process and practice* (pp. 4–18). Boston, MA: Ginn Press.

Peirce, C. S. (1923). The fixation of belief. In M. R. Cohen (Ed.), *Love, chance, and logic* (pp. 7–31). New York, NY: Harcourt, Brace.

Pepper, S. (1972). *World hypotheses: A study in evidence.* Berkeley: University of California Press. (Original work published 1948)

Perry, K. H. (2012). What is literacy? A critical overview of sociocultural perspectives. *Journal of Language and Literacy Education, 8,* 50–71.

Perry, K. H., & Moses, A. M. (2011). Television, language, and literacy practices in Sudanese refugee families: "I learned how to spell English on Channel 18." *Research in the Teaching of English, 45,* 278–307.

Pestalozzi, J. H. (1894). *How Gertrude teaches her children: An attempt to help mothers teach their own children and an account of the method* (L. E. Holland & F. C. Turner, Trans.). Syracuse, NY: C. W. Bardeen. Retrieved from https://archive.org/details/howgertrudeteach00pestuoft

Phillips, D. C. (1983). After the wake: Postpositivistic educational thought. *Educational Researcher, 12*(5), 4–12.

Piaget, J. (1957). *Construction of reality on the child* (M. Cook, Trans.). London, England: Routledge & Kegan Paul. (Original work published 1937)

Piaget, J. (2003). *The psychology of intelligence* (M. Piercy & D. E. Berlyne, Trans.). New York, NY: Routledge. (Original work published 1947)

Pinker, S. (1997). *How the mind works.* New York, NY: W. W. Norton.

Pintrich, P. R., & Schunk, D. H. (1996). *Motivation in education: Theory, research, and applications.* Englewood Cliffs, NJ: Merrill-Prentice Hall.

Popkewitz, T. S. (1997). The production of reason and power: Curriculum history and intellectual traditions. *Journal of Curriculum Studies, 29,* 131–164.

Popkewitz, T. S. (2008). *Cosmopolitanism and the age of school reform: Science, education and making society by making the child.* New York, NY: Routledge.

Popper, K. (2002). *The logic of scientific discovery.* New York, NY: Routledge. (Original work published 1935)

Pressley, M., & Allington, R. L. (2015). *Reading instruction that works: The case for balanced teaching* (4th ed.). New York, NY: Guilford Press.

Progressive Education in the 1940s. (n.d.). [Video]. Retrieved from https://www.youtube.com/watch?v=opXKmwg8VQM

Purcell-Gates, V., Jacobsen, E., & Degener, S. (2004). *Print literacy development: Uniting cognitive and social practice theories.* Cambridge, MA: Harvard University Press.

Purves, A. C., & Beach, R. (1972). *Literature and the reader: Research in response to literature* (Final report to the National Endowment for the Humanities, Project No. H69-0-129). Urbana, IL: National Council of Teachers of English. Retrieved from http://files.eric.ed.gov/fulltext/ED068973.pdf

Purves, A. C., & Rippere, V. (1968). *Elements of writing about a literary work: A study of response to literature* (National Council of Teachers of English, Research Report No. 9). Champaign, IL: National Council of Teachers of English. Retrieved from http://files.eric.ed.gov/fulltext/ED018431.pdf

Quine, W. V. O. (1951). Two dogmas of empiricism. *Philosophical Review, 60,* 20–43.

RAND Reading Study Group. (2002). *Reading for understanding. Toward an R&D program in reading: The report of the RAND Reading Study Group.* Washington, DC: RAND.

Ransom, J. C. (1937). Criticism, Inc. *Virginia Quarterly Review, 13*, 586–603.

Ransom, J. C. (1941). *The new criticism.* Norfolk, CT: New Directions.

Reed, J. H., & Schallert, D. L. (1993). The nature of involvement in academic discourse tasks. *Journal of Educational Psychology, 85*, 253–266.

Reeve, J. (2009). Why teachers adopt a controlling motivating style toward students and how they can become more autonomy supportive. *Educational Psychologist, 44*, 159–175.

Renninger, K. A., Hidi, S., & Krapp, A. (Eds). (1992). *The role of interest in learning and development.* Hillsdale, NJ: Lawrence Erlbaum.

Reschly, D. J. (1976). School psychology consultation: "Frenzied, faddish, or fundamental?" *Journal of School Psychology, 14*, 105–113.

Resnick, D. P. (1982). History of educational testing. In A. K. Wigdor & W. R. Garner (Eds.), Ability testing: Uses, consequences, and controversies (Pt. 2, pp. 173–194). Washington, DC: National Academy Press.

Richards, I. A. (1930). *Practical criticism.* London, England: Kegan Paul, Trench, Trubner.

Richards, I. A., Ogden, C. K., & Wood, J. (1922). *The foundations of aesthetics.* London, England: George Allen and Unwin.

Roehler, L. R., & Duffy, G. G. (1996). Teachers' instructional actions. In R. Barr, M. L. Kamil, P. B. Mosenthal, & P. D. Pearson (Eds.), *Handbook of reading research* (Vol. 2, pp. 861–883). Mahwah, NJ: Lawrence Erlbaum.

Rogers, C. (1951). *Client-centered therapy: Its current practice, implications, and theory.* London, England: Constable Press.

Rogoff, B. (2003). *The cultural nature of human development.* New York, NY: Oxford University Press.

Rogoff, B., Baker-Sennett, J., Lacasa, P., & Goldsmith, D. (1995). Development through participation in sociocultural activity. *New Directions for Child and Adolescent Development, 67*, 45–65. doi:10.1002/cd.23219956707

Rorty, R. (1979). *Philosophy and the mirror of nature.* Princeton, NJ: Princeton University Press.

Rorty, R. (1989). Education, socialization, and individuation. *Liberal Education, 75*(4), 2–9.

Rosenblatt, L. (1938). *Literature as exploration.* New York, NY: Appleton-Century.

Rosenblatt, L. (1978). *The reader, the text, the poem: The transactional theory of the literary work.* Carbondale: Southern Illinois University Press.

Rosenshine, B., & Stevens, R. (1984). Classroom instruction in reading. In P. D. Pearson (Ed.), *Handbook of reading research* (pp. 745–798). Mahwah, NJ: Lawrence Erlbaum.

Rousseau, J. J. (1921). *Emile, or education* (B. Foxley, Trans.). New York, NY: E. P. Dutton.

Ruddell, R. B. (1994). The development of children's comprehension and motivation during storybook discussion. In R. B. Ruddell, M. R. Ruddell, & H. Singer (Eds.), *Theoretical models and processes of reading* (pp. 281–296). Newark, DE: International Reading Association.

Ruddell, R. B., Ruddell, M. R., & Singer, H. (Eds.). (1994). *Theoretical models and processes of reading* (4th ed.). Newark, DE: International Reading Association.

Ruddell, R. B., & Unrau, N. J. (2004a). The role of responsive teaching in focusing reader intention and developing reader motivation. In R. B. Ruddell & N. J. Unrau (Eds.), *Theoretical models and processes of reading* (5th ed., pp. 954–978). Newark, DE: International Reading Association.

Ruddell, R. B., & Unrau, N. J. (Eds.). (2004b). *Theoretical models and processes of reading* (5th ed.). Newark, DE: International Reading Association.

Ruddell, R. B., & Unrau, N. J. (2013). Reading as a motivated meaning-construction process: The reader, the text, and the teacher. In D. E. Alvermann, N. J. Unrau, & R. B. Ruddell (Eds.), *Theoretical models and processes of reading* (6th ed., pp. 1015–1068). Newark, DE: International Reading Association.

Rumelhart, D. E., & McClelland, J. L. (1981). An interactive activation model of context effects in letter perception: Pt 1. An account of basic findings. *Psychological Review, 88,* 375–407.

Rumelhart, D. E., & McClelland, J. L. (1985). *On learning the past tenses of English verbs* (Institute for Cognitive Science Report No. 8507). La Jolla: University of California Press.

Russell, B. (1905). On denoting. *Mind, 56,* 479–493.

Schunk, D. H., & Meece, J. L. (1992). *Student perceptions in the classroom.* New York, NY: Routledge.

Schutt, R. K. (2015). *Investigating the social world: The process and practice of research* (8th ed.). Thousand Oaks, CA: Sage.

Scribner, S., & Cole, M. (1981). *The psychology of literacy.* Cambridge, MA: Harvard University Press.

Selden, R. (Ed.). (1995). *The Cambridge history of literary criticism: Vol. 8. From formalism to poststructuralism.* New York, NY: Cambridge University Press.

Serafini, F. W. (2002). Dismantling the factory model of assessment. *Reading & Writing Quarterly, 18,* 67–85.

Shanahan, T. (2005). *The National Reading Panel report: Practical advice for teachers.* Chicago, IL: Learning Point Associates.

Shannon, P., & Edmondson, J. (2011). The political contexts of reading disabilities. In A. McGill-Franzen & R. L. Allington (Eds.), *Handbook of reading disability research* (pp. 3–12). New York, NY: Routledge.

Singer, H. (1976). Substrata-factor patterns accompanying development in power of reading, elementary through college level. In H. Singer & R. B. Ruddell (Eds.), *Theoretical models and processes of reading* (2nd ed., pp. 619–654). Newark, DE: International Reading Association.

Singer, H., & Ruddell, R. B. (Eds.). (1970). *Theoretical models and processes of reading.* Newark, DE: International Reading Association.

Singer, H., & Ruddell, R. B. (Eds.). (1976). *Theoretical models and processes of reading* (2nd ed.). Newark, DE: International Reading Association.

Singer, H., & Ruddell, R. B. (Eds.). (1985). *Theoretical models and processes of reading* (3rd ed.). Newark, DE: International Reading Association.

Singley, C. J. (2013). American literary realism. In M. A. R. Habib (Ed.), *The Cambridge history of literary criticism: Vol. 11. The nineteenth century c. 1830–1914* (pp. 331–339). New York, NY: Cambridge.

Skerrett, A. (2009). Biographical orientations to secondary English teaching within a mosaic context of diversity. *English Education, 41,* 281–303.

Skinner, B. F. (1957). *Verbal behavior.* Acton, MA: Copley.

Skinner, B. F. (1958). Teaching machines. *Science, 128,* 969–977.

Smagorinsky, P. (1998). Reading as mediated and mediating action: Composing meaning for literature through multimedia interpretive texts. *Reading Research Quarterly, 33,* 198–226.

Smagorinsky, P. (2001). If meaning is constructed, what is it made from? Toward a cultural theory of reading. *Review of Educational Research, 71,* 133–169.

Smagorinsky, P., & O'Donnell-Allen, C. (1998). The depth and dynamics of context: Tracing the sources and channels of engagement and disengagement in students' response to literature. *Journal of Literacy Research, 30,* 515–559.

Small, R. C. (1972). Student authority. *English Education, 3,* 151–161.

Smith, D. V. (Ed.). (1952). *The English language arts.* New York, NY: Appleton-Century-Crofts.

Smith, F. (1971). *Psycholinguistics and reading.* New York, NY: Holt, Rinehart & Winston.

Smith, F. (1981). Demonstrations, engagements and sensitivity: The choice between people and programs. *Language Arts, 58,* 634–642.

Smith, M. B. (1949). *And madly teach.* Chicago, IL: Henry Regnery.

Smith, M. B. (1954). *The diminished mind: A study of planned mediocrity in our public schools.* Chicago, IL: Henry Regnery.

Smith, N. B. (1952). Historical turning points in the teaching of reading. *National Education Association Journal, 41,* 280–283.

Smith, N. B. (1961). What have we accomplished in reading? A review of the past fifty years. *Elementary Education, 38,* 141–150.

Smith, N. B. (1965). *American reading instruction: Its development and its significance in gaining a perspective on current practices in reading.* Newark, DE: International Reading Association. (Original work published 1934)

Spalding, D. A. (1872). On instinct. *Nature, 6,* 485–486.

Spence, K. W. (1958). A theory of emotionally based drive (D) and its relation to performance in simple learning situations. *American Psychologist, 13,* 131–141.

Spencer, H. (1860). The social organism. *Westminster Review, 73,* 90–121.

Spindler, G. D. (1997). *Education and cultural process: Anthropological approaches.* Prospect Heights, IL: Waveland.

Spiro, R., & Jehng, J. (1990). Cognitive flexibility and hypertext: Theory and technology for the linear and nonlinear multidimensional traversal of complex subject matter. In D. Nix & R. Spiro (Eds.), *Cognition, education, and multimedia: Exploring ideas in high technology* (pp. 163–205). Hillsdale, NJ: Lawrence Erlbaum.

Spiro, R. J., Vispoel, W., Schmitz, W., Samaarapungavan, A., & Boertger, A. (1987). Knowledge acquisition for application: Cognitive flexibility and transfer in complex content domains. In B. C. Britton & S. Glynn (Eds.), *Executive control processes* (pp. 177–200). Hillsdale, NJ: Lawrence Erlbaum.

Squire, J. R. (2003). The history of the profession. In J. Flood, D. Lapp, J. R. Squire, & J. M. Jensen (Eds.), *Handbook of research on teaching the English language arts* (2nd ed., pp. 3–17). Mahwah, NJ: Lawrence Erlbaum/International Reading Association and National Council of Teachers of English.

Stanovich, K. E. (1980). Toward an interactive-compensatory model of individual differences in the development of reading fluency. *Reading Research Quarterly, 16,* 32–71.

Stanovich, K. E. (1986). Matthew effects in reading: Some consequences of individual differences in the acquisition of literacy. *Reading Research Quarterly, 21,* 360–407.

Stauffer, R. (1970). *The language experience approach to the teaching of reading.* New York, NY: Harper & Row.

St. Pierre, E. A. (2000). Poststructural feminism in education: An overview. *Qualitative Studies in Education, 13,* 477–515.

St. Pierre, E. A. (2014). A brief and personal history of post qualitative research. *Journal of Curriculum Theorizing, 30,* 2–19.

Strang, R. M., & Rose, F. C. (1938). *Problems in the improvement of reading in high school and college.* New York, NY: Science Press.

Strauss, S. L., Goodman, K. S., & Paulson, E. J. (2009). Brain research and reading: How emerging concepts in neuroscience support a meaning construction view of the reading process. *Educational Research and Review, 4,* 21–33. Retrieved from http://www.academicjournals.org/article/article1379599656_Strauss%20et%20al.pdf?wptouch_preview_theme=enabled

Street, B. V. (1984). *Literacy in theory and practice.* London, England: Cambridge University Press.

Taboada, A., Tonks, S. M., Wigfield, A., & Guthrie, J. T. (2013). Effects of motivational and cognitive variables on reading comprehension. In D. E. Alvermann, N. J. Unrau, & R. B. Ruddell (Eds.), *Theoretical models and processes of reading* (6th ed., pp. 589–610). Newark, DE: International Reading Association.

Tate, W. F., IV (Ed.). (2012). *Research on schools, neighborhoods, and communities: Towards civic responsibility.* Washington, DC: American Educational Research Association.

Tatum, A. W. (2013). Toward a more anatomically complete model of literacy instruction: A focus on African-American male adolescents and texts. In D. E. Alvermann, N. J. Unrau, & R. B. Ruddell (Eds.), *Theoretical models and processes of reading* (6th ed., pp. 611–635). Newark, DE: International Reading Association.

Tatum, A. W. (2014). Orienting African American male adolescents toward meaningful literacy exchanges with texts. *Journal of Education, 194,* 35–47.

Taylor, F. W. (1919). *The principles of scientific management.* New York, NY: Harper & Brothers.

Taylor, B. M., Raphael, T. E., & Au, K. H. (2011). School reform in literacy. In M. L. Kamil, P. D. Pearson, E. B. Moje, & P. P. Afflerbach (Eds.), *Handbook of reading research* (Vol. 4, pp. 594–628). New York, NY: Routledge.

Teale, W. H. (1995). Young children and reading: Trends across the twentieth century. *Journal of Education, 177,* 95–127.

Thein, A. H., Guise, M., & Sloan, D. L. (2015). Examining emotional rules in the English classroom: A critical discourse analysis of one student's literary responses in two academic contexts. *Research in the Teaching of English, 49,* 200–223.

Thompson, G., Madhuri, M., & Taylor, D. (2008). How the Accelerated Reader program can become counter-productive for high school students. *Journal of Adolescent & Adult Literacy, 51,* 550–560.

Thorndike, E. L. (1901). *The human nature club: An introduction to the study of mental life* (2nd ed.). New York, NY: Macmillan.

Thorndike, E. L. (1905). *The psychology of learning.* New York, NY: A. G. Seiler.

Thorndike, E. L. (1909). Darwin's contribution to psychology. *University of California Chronicle, 12,* 65–80.

Thorndike, E. L. (1910). The contribution of psychology to education. *Journal of Educational Psychology, 1,* 5–12.

Thorndike, E. L. (1917). Reading as reasoning: A study of mistakes in paragraph reading. *Journal of Educational Psychology, 8,* 323–332.

Tolman, E. C. (1932). *Purposive behavior in animals and men.* New York, NY: Appleton Century-Crofts.

Tracey, D. H., & Morrow, L. M. (2012). *Lenses on reading: An introduction to theories and models* (2nd ed.). New York, NY: Guilford Press.

Twelve Southerners. (1930). *I'll take my stand: The South and the Agrarian tradition.* New York, NY: Harper and Brothers.

Tyack, D. (1974). *The one best system.* Cambridge, England: Cambridge University Press.

University of Kentucky. (n.d.). *Engagement: National Center for Innovation in Education.* Retrieved from https://education.uky.edu/engagement/national-center-for-innovation-in-education/

Unrau, N. J., & Alvermann, D. A. (2013). Literacies and their investigation through theories and models. In D. A. Alvermann & N. J. Unrau (Eds.), *Theoretical models and processes of reading* (6th ed., pp. 47–90). Newark, DE: International Reading Association.

van Inwagen, P., & Sullivan, M. (Spring 2015). Metaphysics. In E. N. Zalta (Ed.), *Stanford encyclopedia of philosophy.* Retrieved from http://plato.stanford.edu/archives/spr2015/entries/metaphysics/

Venezky, R. L. (1984). The history of reading research. In P. D. Pearson, R. Barr, M. L. Kamil, & P. Mosenthal (Eds.), *Handbook of reading research* (pp. 3–38). Mahwah, NJ: Lawrence Erlbaum.

Venezky, R. L. (1986). Steps toward a modern history of American reading instruction. *Review of Research in Education, 13,* 129–167.

Venezky, R. L. (1987). A history of the American reading textbook. *Elementary School Journal, 87,* 247–265.

Von Glasersfeld, E. (1989). Cognition, construction of knowledge, and teaching. *Synthese, 80,* 121–140.

Vygotsky, L. (1978). *Mind in society.* Cambridge, MA: Harvard University Press.

Walberg, H. J., & Haertel, G. D. (1992). Educational psychology's first century. *Journal of Educational Psychology, 84,* 6–19.

Walczyk, J. J., Tcholakian, T., Igou, F., & Dixon, A. P. (2014). One hundred years of reading research: Successes and missteps of Edmund Burke Huey and other pioneers. *Reading Psychology, 35,* 601–621.

Watson, J. B. (1913). Psychology as the behaviorist views it. *Psychological Review, 20,* 158–177.

Watson, J. B. (1925). *Behaviorism.* New York, NY: W. W. Norton.

Weaver-Hightower, M. B. (2008). An ecology metaphor for educational policy analysis: A call to complexity. *Educational Researcher, 37,* 153–167.

Weiner, B. (1990). History of motivational research in education. *Journal of Educational Psychology, 82,* 616–622.

Wellek, R., & Warren, A. (1956). *Theory of literature.* New York, NY: Harcourt Brace.

Wertsch, J. V. (1985). *Vygotsky and the social formation of mind.* Cambridge, MA: Harvard University Press.

Wharton, E. (1922). *Ethan Frome.* New York, NY: Charles Scribner's Sons. (Original work published 1911)

Whitehead, A. N., & Russell, B. (1927). *Principia mathematica* (2nd ed.). Cambridge, England: Cambridge University Press.

Wigfield, A., & Asher, S. R. (1984). Social and motivational influences on reading. In P. D. Pearson (Ed.), *Handbook of reading research* (pp. 423–452). Mahwah, NJ: Lawrence Erlbaum.

Wigfield, A., Eccles, J. S., & Rodriguez, D. (1998). The development of children's motivation in school contexts. *Review of Research in Education, 23,* 73–118.

Wigfield, A., & Guthrie, J. T. (2000). Engagement and motivation in reading. In M. L. Kamil, P. B. Mosenthal, P. D. Pearson, & D. Barr (Eds.), *Handbook of reading research* (Vol. 3, pp. 403–422). Mahwah, NJ: Lawrence Erlbaum.

Wilhelm, J. D., & Smith, M. W. (2015). Reading don't fix no Chevys (yet!). *Journal of Adolescent & Adult Literacy, 58,* 273–276.

Williams, F. (2013). *Language and poverty: Perspectives on a theme.* New York, NY: Academic Press.

Williams, J. D., & Alden, S. D. (1983). Motivation in the composition class. *Research in the Teaching of English, 17,* 101–112.

Wimsatt, W. K., & Beardsley, M. (1946). The intentional fallacy. *Sewanee Review, 54,* 468–488.

Wittgenstein, L. (2009). *Philosophical investigations* (4th ed.; G. E. M. Anscombe, P. M. S. Hacker, & J. Schulte, Trans.). Malden, MA: Blackwell-Wiley. (Original work published 1953)

Wood, D. J., Bruner, J. S., & Ross, G. (1976). The role of tutoring in problem solving. *Journal of Child Psychiatry and Psychology, 17,* 89–100.

Woodring, P. (1953). *Let's talk sense about our schools.* New York, NY: McGraw Hill.

Worthy, J., Moorman, M., & Turner, M. (1999). What Johnny likes to read is hard to find in school. *Reading Research Quarterly, 34,* 12–27.

Wozniak, R. H. (1997). Behaviorism. In W. G. Bringmann, H. E. Luck, R. Miller, & C. E. Early (Eds.), *A pictorial history of psychology.* Chicago, IL: Quintessence. Retrieved from http://psychclassics.yorku.ca/Watson/commentary.htm

Young, P. T. (1961). *Motivation and emotion: A survey of the determinants of human and animal activity.* Oxford, England: Wiley.

Zajonc, R. B. (1980). Feeling and thinking: Preferences need no inferences. *American Psychologist, 35,* 151–175.

Zenkov, K., Harmon, J., Bell, A., Ewaida, M., & Lynch, M. R. (2011). Seeing our city, students, and school: Using photography to engage diverse youth with our English classes. *English Education, 43,* 369–389.

Chapter 17

Advancing the Science and Practice of Social and Emotional Learning: Looking Back and Moving Forward

DAVID OSHER
YAEL KIDRON
American Institutes for Research

MARC BRACKETT
Yale Center for Emotional Intelligence and Yale Child Study Center

ALLISON DYMNICKI
American Institutes for Research

STEPHANIE JONES
Harvard University

ROGER P. WEISSBERG
Collaborative for Academic, Social, and Emotional Learning, Chicago
University of Illinois at Chicago

This chapter summarizes the results of nearly 100 years of research on school-based social and emotional learning (SEL). The SEL field has grown out of research in many fields and subfields with which educators, researchers, and policymakers are familiar, including the promotion of social competence, bullying prevention, prevention of drug use and abuse, civic and character education, emotional intelligence, conflict resolution, social skills training, and 21st-century skills. The chapter begins with a historical summary of theoretical movements and research trends that have led to today's inclusion of SEL as part of many schools' curricula, policies, and practices. Contemporary approaches that represent current policy and societal concerns are discussed in comparative terms. Based on the converging research evidence, this chapter identifies design elements and implementation quality characteristics of effective approaches to SEL. Recommendations for future practice, policy, and research are provided.

Review of Research in Education
March 2016, Vol. 40, pp. 644–681
DOI: 10.3102/0091732X16673595

Social and emotional learning (SEL) is defined as the processes by which children and adults acquire and apply core competencies to recognize and manage emotions, set and achieve positive goals, appreciate the perspectives of others, establish and maintain supportive relationships, make responsible decisions, and handle personal and interpersonal situations constructively (Elias et al., 1997; Weissberg, Durlak, Domitrovich, & Gullotta, 2015). While the term SEL is only two decades old, the interest of schools and researchers in social and emotional development has been evident for over a century. At the same time, debates about the role of public schools in promoting nonacademic outcomes, such as social and emotional skills, have also occurred (Kidron & Osher, 2012; Kolbe, Collins, & Cortese, 1997; National Research Council, 2012). While some policymakers and researchers have called for developing and supporting SEL, citizenship, and character development, along with teaching academics (e.g., Bridgeland, Bruce, & Hariharan, 2013), others see SEL and other types of nonacademic support as tangential to the core mission of education (Tyack, 1992; Tyack & Cuban, 1995).

SEL-related scholarship traces back to 1900. This work gradually developed over the following decades, expanding dramatically in the 1990s. Building on the growing sophistication of research methods and accumulating evidence on the effectiveness of programs to prevent problem behavior and promote healthy development, research also began highlighting the role of social competence and school climate. Social concerns (e.g., bullying and school shootings) created urgency for school-based programs that aimed to promote safe and supportive school environments (Dwyer, Osher, & Warger, 1998; Dwyer & Osher, 2000). These programs benefited from the identification of common mechanisms underlying methods that prevent problem behavior (e.g., violence, bullying, drug use and abuse) and promote personal and civic growth such as emotional intelligence, civic and character values, deeper learning, health promotion, and 21st-century skills (Consortium on the School-Based Promotion of Social Competence, 1994; Elias et al., 1997; Langdon, 1996).

SEL serves as a coordinating field that aligns other areas with which educators, researchers, and policymakers are familiar. These fields address students' capacities to coordinate cognition, affect, and behavior to navigate daily challenges and succeed in college, careers, and life. There remains a need to delineate how these approaches can be integrated into planned, ongoing, systemic initiatives rather than merely collected as fragmented practices, policies, and programs (Shriver & Weissberg, 1996; Weissberg et al., 2015). SEL scholarship has now come full circle, addressing deep-rooted policy problems (Rittel & Webber, 1973) that were salient in the early 1900s (Gorrell, 1988; Lubove, 1974; Muncy, 1991) including inequality, poverty, delinquency, school disengagement and dropout, and lack of tolerance for diversity (Brackett, Ivcevic-Pringle, Moeller, White, & Stern, 2015; Kann et al., 2013; Weissberg, Walberg, O'Brien, & Kuster, 2003).

This chapter summarizes scholarship that contributed to research and practice in SEL. We focus primarily on school-related approaches to SEL. Following a description of the SEL field, we describe and contextualize interdisciplinary strands of research that set the stage for the emergence of SEL as a research field in the 1990s, including its recent expansion. Next, we analyze contemporary frameworks for understanding SEL, discuss criteria for well-designed SEL approaches and programs, and examine implementation facilitators and challenges. We also identify how challenges can be addressed. We conclude with recommendations for future practice, policy, and research.

WHAT IS SOCIAL AND EMOTIONAL LEARNING?

The field of SEL was introduced and defined in the book *Promoting Social and Emotional Learning: Guidelines for Educators* (Elias et al., 1997), which provided an overview of approaches to teaching both students and adults methods for understanding and managing emotions and social interactions. The fundamental goals of SEL are to (a) promote positive learning environments that are supportive, engaging, and participatory and (b) foster the development of the following five interrelated sets of cognitive, affective, and behavioral competencies:

- *Self-Awareness*—The abilities to recognize one's own emotions and values, to accurately assess weaknesses and strengths, and to possess a well-grounded sense of self-efficacy and optimism
- *Self-Management*—The ability to regulate emotions, thoughts, and behaviors in diverse situations, including the ability to manage stress, control impulses, and set and achieve goals
- *Social Awareness*—The ability to adopt the perspective of those with different backgrounds, understanding social and cultural norms, and recognizing available resources and supports
- *Relationship Skills*—The ability to establish positive relationships with different kinds of people, communicating clearly, listening actively, cooperating, resisting inappropriate peer pressure, negotiating conflict, and seeking help when necessary
- *Responsible Decision Making*—The capacity to make choices based on realistic evaluations of consequences, well-being, ethics, safety, and social norms

A compelling body of research suggests that these core competencies are malleable and can be effectively taught using a variety of approaches and formats. Meta-analytic reviews of this research show that children and adolescents who participate in SEL programs improve their social and emotional skills; attitudes about self, others, and schools; and prosocial behavior, thereby enjoying greater psychological well-being and academic performance (Durlak, Weissberg, Dymnicki, Taylor, & Schellinger, 2011; Sklad, Diekstra, Ritter, Ben, & Gravesteijn, 2012).

SEL intervention strategies evolved over time (Brackett & Rivers, 2013; Jones & Bouffard, 2012; Schonert-Reichl & O'Brien, 2012; Weissberg et al., 2015). SEL has been embedded in schools in a number of forms: as part of a structured curriculum where lessons are taught during time set aside within the school day, as part of a schoolwide approach in which SEL principles are integrated into the fabric of school life, and through after-school and out-of-school opportunities such as service learning or internships for older students (Collaborative for Academic, Social, and Emotional Learning [CASEL], 2013, 2015). Early efforts focused primarily on classroom programs that targeted a single outcome such as peer relationships or bullying (CASEL, 2003). Over the past 10 years, more systemic approaches have involved the implementation and evaluation of coordinated efforts that involved a whole school approach, family connections, and community partnerships (Brackett & Rivers, 2013; Weissberg et al., 2015). Some of these approaches involved explicit skill-building lessons, while other practices were integrated across the curriculum. For example, research conducted by the Center on Great Teachers and Leaders identified 10 instructional strategies that teachers use throughout the school day that can affect students' social and emotional skills. These practices include student-centered discipline, teacher language, cooperative learning, and self-assessment and self-reflection (Yoder, 2014). There is now more focus on local, state, and federal policies that can influence the quality of SEL implementation at the district, school, and classroom levels (Dusenbury et al., 2015; Zaslow, Mackintosh, Mancoll, & Mandell, 2015).

CONTEXTUALIZING THE INTELLECTUAL ROOTS OF SOCIAL AND EMOTIONAL LEARNING

The roots of SEL are intellectually diverse and politically nonpartisan. This section traces these roots to Progressive Education; ecological and transactional perspectives in sociology, criminology, and psychology; school-based promotion of wellness; social learning and cognitive behavioral theory; and developments in studies of personality, emotion, and intelligence.

Engaged Citizenship in Relation to a Democratic Society

The Progressive Era roots trace back to Jane Addams and John Dewey and their promotion of engaged citizenship, the Mental Hygiene Movement and its initial focus on the prevention of mental illness, and Thorndike's (1920) conceptualizations of social intelligence. Addams (1902) and Dewey (1916) addressed the importance of social competence and its relationship to a democratic society and self-directed, socially responsible behavior. Addams (1902) stated that schools should teach students "to direct their own activities and adjust them to those of other people" (p. 42). Dewey (1916) called for schools creating "conditions for growth" (p. 14) where students develop "social dispositions" (p. 13) and develop self-control (as opposed to external control). Both Addams and Dewey understood the power of ecology and viewed group experiences as providing an opportunity for the development of social skills. However, student-centered approaches did not dominate pedagogy, and reforms that worked in lab schools were often diluted in practice (Cuban, 1993; Zilversmit, 1993). A focus on social and emotional development and the factors supporting it was not a part of the grammars of schooling and instruction—those widely held implicit beliefs regarding how schools should be organized and what teachers do (Murphy & Torre, 2013; Scheerens, 1997; Tyack & Cuban, 1995; Tyack & Tobin, 1994). Nonetheless, this line of work contributed to SEL interventions such as the Caring School Communities (CSC; Battistich, Solomon, Watson, & Schaps, 1997) and the Responsive Classroom (Rimm-Kaufman & Chiu, 2007).

The Influence of Ecology and Transactional Models of Development

Four seminal thinkers extended the reach of ecological thinking and influenced the development of SEL. Lewin (1935) suggested that all psychological events are a function of the life space, which he conceptualized as the constellation of interdependent factors associated with the person and environment. Lewin's research demonstrated the impact of social factors on goal setting, conflict, and aspiration (Lewin, 1951) and contributed to research on group dynamics (Lewin, 1947). Bronfenbrenner's "bioecological paradigm" (Bronfenbrenner & Ceci, 1994) influenced research on systemic interventions in the 1980s and 1990s (Elias et al., 1997; Steinberg & Morris, 2001). Vygotsky also focused on how social factors influence learning. His conceptualization of the zone of proximal development was applied successfully to understanding the social origins of self-regulation (Diaz, Neal, & Amaya-Williams, 1990). Finally, Sameroff's transactional model of development emphasized the central role of the interplay between a child and his or her primary relationships and contexts, and the nature and role of risk and protection (Sameroff, 1975). Sameroff introduced a focus on understanding bidirectional relationships between the child and the experiences embedded in the family, school, or community contexts. Together, these approaches contributed to understanding the role of peers, families, teachers, classroom and school climate, and even public policy in fostering social and emotional skills.

Beyond Intervention: The Expansion of Prevention and Promotion Strategies

Ecological thinking was marginalized by many psychologists who focused on reactive and individualized approaches to pathology. In addition, education in the 1960s often focused on compensatory education for disadvantaged learners (Ryan, 1972). Two critiques of these reactive and compensatory approaches to social problems contributed to the development of SEL. The first challenged reactive pathology-focused approaches to mental wellness. Such approaches, Cowen (1971, 1994) argued, could never reach all who needed services and ignored the factors that contribute to psychological wellness (e.g., happiness, life satisfaction, sense of belonging, and sense of purpose in life). Interest in wellness included the study of resilient children (Cowen & Work, 1988). This, in turn, led theorists to see the importance of social awareness and support (Masten, 2013; Werner, 1989) and social competence (Rutter, 1987) in children's ability to overcome adversity.

The second critique attacked the inefficiencies of narrow educational approaches that focused only on academics and reactive treatment of disorders. For example, Comer and Zigler both offered alternatives to educational approaches that attributed academic shortcomings to the disadvantaged students' cognitive deficits. Comer

(2004) focused on the importance of child development and the role that social support and social and emotional competence played in children's success. Zigler and colleagues focused on the whole child more generally and critiqued educational approaches that focused on cognitive abilities alone. In contrast to those approaches, Zigler emphasized the importance of social competence and motivational factors that children develop to adapt to adverse life circumstances such as poverty and neglect (Zigler, 1973; Zigler, Abelson, & Seitz, 1973; Zigler & Trickett, 1978).

Zigler and colleagues' emphases were consistent with social learning theory (SLT) and cognitive behavioral therapy (CBT), which influenced the development of SEL models. SLT leveraged Bandura's (1974, 1977) critique of unidirectional behavioral and trait-based explanations for human behavior and replaced them with "reciprocal determinism." This concept included self-expectancies, which are affected by self-awareness and social awareness, both of which are important to self-monitoring of behavior, its determinants, and its effects (Bandura, 1974, 1977, 1991; Mischel, 1973). Bandura's application of SLT to the prevention and treatment of aggressive behaviors supported the development of classroom and schoolwide approaches to violence prevention, as well to understanding the importance of social modeling in the development of social and emotional competencies (Elias & Clabby, 1992; Elias, Parker, Kash, Weissberg, & O'Brien, 2007).

CBT (Meichenbaum, 1977), which provided a theoretical base for many SEL interventions on social problem solving (Chang, D'Zurilla, & Sanna, 2004; Kazdin & Weisz, 1998) and social information processing (Crick & Dodge, 1994), is, in part, grounded in SLT's focus on modeling, observational learning, and cognitive expectancies. CBT is also grounded in behaviorist theories of classical conditioning and operant learning, as well as in cognitive theory and cognitive therapy, which focus on the thoughts, cognitive schema, beliefs, attitudes, and attributions that influence one's feelings and mediate the relationship between antecedents and behavior. CBT contributed the following pieces to the common SEL problem-solving paradigm:

- Identifying an emotionally challenging or problematic situation
- Identifying and addressing the feelings related to it
- Putting the problem into words and identifying a goal
- Generating multiple options and analyzing their potential short- and long-term consequences for oneself and others
- Making a choice and planning and rehearsing how to carry out that choice
- Taking the necessary action and then reflecting on what happened and what can be learned from it

Understanding the Connection Between Emotions and Cognitive Processing

Affective education reintroduced affect as a domain closely related to student academic performance (Cantor, 1976; Carkhuff, 1982) by simultaneously teaching academics and introducing an affective curriculum to address the affective states and emotional competencies that increase or decrease students' persistence, curiosity, interest, attention, decision making, and other learning-related cognitions and behaviors (Beane, 1985; Martin & Reigeluth, 1992). Affective education recognized that students' feelings about themselves as learners and about their academic interests influence their academic effort and engagement (Lang, Katz, & Menezes, 1998). For example, students who believe that their intellectual abilities are stable rather than malleable are less likely to take on academic challenges and show academic effort, especially in the face of failure (Blackwell, Trzesniewski, & Dweck, 2007; Good, Aronson, & Inzlicht, 2003). Similarly, stereotype threat affects the performance of female students and students of color (Steele, 2003). Affective education research also provided additional support for including experiential, inquiry-based activities in SEL (Buffington & Stilwell, 1981; Thayer, 1976).

A Broader Conceptualization of Intelligence

Research on emotional intelligence (Salovey & Mayer, 1990) began in the 1990s. This work included expanded conceptualizations of intelligence and a renewed interest in emotion, motivation, and social intelligence. It also drew on Gardner's (1983) conceptualization of multiple intelligences, which included inter- and intrapersonal intelligence, as well as Sternberg's (1985) conceptualization of practical intelligence, which included managing self, work, and cooperating with others.

The expanded understanding of emotions moved away from an intrapsychological view of emotions to one that viewed emotions relationally and examined emotion regulation and interpersonal attunement (Campos, Campos, & Barrett, 1989). This work contributed to Salovey and Mayer's (1990) conceptualization of emotional intelligence as "the ability to monitor one's own and others' feelings and emotions, to discriminate among them and to use this information to guide one's thinking and actions" (p. 189). These threads also contributed to a refined conceptualization of social competence as "the capacity to integrate cognition, affect, and behaviors to achieve specified social tasks and positive developmental outcomes" (Consortium on the School-Based Promotion of Social Competence, 1994, p. 275). This development emphasized the role of social and emotional skills in problem solving within the context of one's culture, neighborhood, and interpersonal situation where the interaction occurs.

Research Foundations for Focusing on SEL and Its Relationships to Outcomes That Matter

Although calls for integrating the social and emotional aspects of student learning into academic instruction have been voiced periodically since 1900, funding for SEL research only gained momentum when the definition of school success and quality education was expanded to include nonacademic skills. Two strands of research were important here. The first demonstrated associations between social and emotional skills and academic achievement, as well as other school-related outcomes of interest.

The second demonstrated the relationship between some or all of these skills and postsecondary and vocational success (Deming, 2015; Duckworth & Seligman, 2005; Fergusson, Boden, & Horwood, 2013).

The preponderance of evidence, including implementation studies, revealed at least modest effects of SEL programs when implementation adhered to some key design elements (Faria, Kendziora, Brown, O'Brien, & Osher, 2013; Osher, Kendziora, & Friedman, 2014a, 2014b). A meta-analysis of 207 programs showed effects on social competence, behavior, and academics, for example, an improvement index of 11-percentile-point gain in academic achievement in the 37 studies that assessed it through report card grades and test scores (Durlak et al., 2011).[1] A meta-analysis of 75 universal SEL programs, which included 16 non-U.S. programs (Sklad et al., 2012), provided additional evidence consistent with Durlak et al.'s (2011) findings. Another meta-analysis of programs designed for students presenting a range of social, emotional, and behavioral programs found similar positive impacts of SEL programs on academic outcomes (effect size of 0.53; Dymnicki, Kendziora, & Osher, 2012). Intervention research published subsequent to Durlak et al.'s (2011) meta-analysis supported its conclusion, as does a meta-analysis of longitudinal effects (Taylor, Oberle, Durlak, & Weissberg, in press). For example, randomized controlled trials of a variety of interventions, including Promoting Alternative Thinking Strategies, Responsive Classroom, 4Rs, and Positive Action, showed improved academic effort and achievement using indicators such as reading, writing, and math test scores and absenteeism rates (Bavarian et al., 2013; Jones, Brown & Aber, 2011; Rimm-Kaufman et al., 2014; Schonfeld et al., 2015).

SEL has also been linked to other outcomes of educational interest. For example, one whole school approach to SEL, RULER®, has been shown to influence classroom climate and teacher instructional support (Hagelskamp, Brackett, Rivers, & Salovey, 2013; Rivers, Brackett, Reyes, Elbertson, & Salovey, 2013). Analysis conducted by the What Works Clearinghouse demonstrated that SEL can be an important part of dropout prevention programs (Dynarski et al., 2008). Additional research linked student reports of peer social and emotional competence to graduation rates (Kendziora, Osher, & Chinen, 2008). Similarly, recent approaches to preventing bullying, low-level aggression, and the school-to-prison pipeline emphasized the importance of SEL along with other interventions (Espelage, 2013; Espelage, Rose, & Polanin, 2015; Lewis et al., 2013; Osher, Bear, Sprague, & Doyle, 2010; Osher, Quinn, Poirier, & Rutherford, 2003; Swearer, Espelage, Vaillancourt, & Hymel, 2010). Finally, SEL interventions for teachers (e.g., mindfulness training) may reduce teacher stress, which appears to contribute to exclusionary discipline and discipline disparities (Hart, Wearing, & Conn, 1995; Osher et al., 2012; Roeser et al., 2013).

The broader definition of school success has also been influenced by economists and others who focused on adult outcomes. Heckman and colleagues demonstrated that socioemotional skills and attributes are as important as cognitive competencies and contribute to social performance, job outcomes, and higher education (Almlund, Duckworth, Heckman, & Kautz, 2011; Heckman & LaFontaine, 2010; Heckman,

Stixrud, & Urzua, 2006). The conceptualization of 21st-century skills linked SEL attributes to college and career readiness that includes mastery of nonacademic skills such as flexibility, adaptability, collaboration, and creativity (Dymnicki, Sambolt, & Kidron, 2013; Gabrieli, Ansel, & Krachman, 2015; Partnership for 21st Century Skills, 2008; Trilling & Fadel, 2009).

CONTEMPORARY FRAMEWORKS FOR SOCIAL–EMOTIONAL LEARNING

As noted at the outset of this chapter, SEL has been defined or characterized in a number of ways. This variety is embodied in the large number of frameworks, which represent the diversity of perspectives and disciplinary "takes" on the field. At its core, a framework is an organizing structure that underlies a system, concept, or set of linked ideas and can be broad or narrow. The body of frameworks tied directly and indirectly to SEL include those that are comprehensive in nature (reflecting a broad array of interlinked domains), those that go deep into one particular domain or another (e.g., emotional intelligence, executive function), those that are more narrowly organized around a single concept or construct (e.g., growth mind-set), those that are simply a list of skills, and those that are embodied in state standards (Dusenbury et al., 2015). These frameworks hold a common purpose: to inform and guide research, practice, and policy. Across frameworks, however, terms are often used in different ways, and in some cases, the same skill or competency may have different names, or the same name may be employed to refer to different skills. SEL frameworks also vary in the extent of their focus on school success versus long-term growth and in the degree to which they include social relationships and psychological well-being versus skills that promote college and career readiness and success (Hagen, 2013).

We will provide a brief overview of some major contemporary frameworks for SEL, focusing on those we define as comprehensive (reflecting a broad array of inter-linked domains and typically situating the model in key and influential contexts). However, as noted above, frameworks can take several forms. The nature of any particular framework, and the manner in which it evolved over time, signals its orientation toward practice, research, and policy. Some frameworks (e.g., CASEL, 2013) are organized with an eye toward practice, while others are constructed to guide research (e.g., models of executive function and self-regulation; Diamond, 2013) or policy (e.g., O*Net Online; National Center for O*NET Development, n.d.).

The most ubiquitous and long-standing framework is CASEL's, which builds on SEL research more broadly. It draws on developmental–contextual models, which view human growth and change as taking place in a nested and interactive set of contexts (Bronfenbrenner & Morris, 1998). At the center of this framework are core social and emotional skills or competencies, organized into five domains that are thought to contribute to children's school success and life outcomes. These domains include observable behaviors and internal processes such as perceptions or beliefs. Two domains are self-oriented, two others are relational, and one is behavioral.

Another practice-oriented comprehensive framework, which uses terminology employed in the research literature, applies a developmental lens more elaborately (Jones & Bailey, 2016; Jones & Bouffard, 2012). It arrays skills over time, suggesting that skills are salient at different developmental moments, with early skills laying the foundation for those that come later. It groups social and emotional skills into three overlapping conceptual categories: emotional processes, social/interpersonal skills, and cognitive regulation. Emotional processes include emotional knowledge and expression, emotional and behavioral regulation, and empathy. Social/interpersonal skills include understanding social cues, interpreting others' behaviors and perspective-taking, navigating social situations, interacting positively with peers and adults, and behaving in a prosocial manner. Cognitive regulation includes basic executive functions such as attention control, response inhibition, working memory, and cognitive flexibility or set-shifting.

While the inclusion of cognitive regulation reflects the rapid expansion of research (and intervention) in executive function over the past decade (Diamond, 2013), the idea of the *central capacity for regulation* provides a developmental thread linking the three domains—in order to *use* any of the identified skills to meet the demands of a particular task or context, children should be able to manage themselves in deliberate and goal-oriented ways. Jones's framework also incorporates a general "developmental sequence" organized according to two basic questions: (a) What skills serve as foundations for later ones? (b) What skills must be mastered before moving to the next set? (Jones & Bailey, 2016).

Other comprehensive frameworks include those developed by the Chicago Consortium on School Research and the Wallace Foundation (Farrington et al., 2012; Nagaoka, Farrington, Ehrlich, & Heath, 2015), which directly incorporate a developmental sequencing view and include a more detailed representation of identity, beliefs, values, and mind-sets, and the recently formulated Building Blocks Framework, which requires empirical research to determine the relationships of the individual building blocks and to determine their sequencing. Building Blocks articulates a developmental progression of prerequisite skills or "blocks" (e.g., self-regulation, growth mind-set) that must be cultivated before building higher order skills (e.g., agency, self-direction, resilience) that are common to successful learners (Stafford-Brizard, 2016). These frameworks and others (e.g., Partnership for 21st Century Skills, 2015) represent a growing interest in defining skills that are aligned with the realities of 21st-century education and employment systems, skills that students need if they are to succeed in work, life, and citizenship.

SYNERGY ACROSS FRAMEWORKS

Synergy across contemporary SEL frameworks is possible because key constructs are embedded in some form in most, if not all, frameworks. Self-regulation, including emotional regulation, provides an example of a construct with a deep research base that appears across frameworks, sometimes using different terms, including self-management, self-discipline, self-control, and impulse control.

Emotion regulation involves cognitive, physiological, and behavioral processes that are responsible for monitoring, evaluating, and modifying the experience and expression of emotions in order to accomplish personal goals (Calkins & Hill, 2007; Cole, Martin, & Dennis, 2004; Eisenberg & Spinrad, 2004; Gross & Thompson, 2007). Emotion regulation skills help children organize, enable, or hinder internal psychological processes, such as the deployment of attention, decision making, and the ability to solve complex interpersonal challenges (Fischer, Shaver, & Carnochan, 1990). Research shows that children with more developed emotion regulation skills are more likely to pay attention during class, control their anxiety during tests, and build and maintain friendships (Bradley et al., 2010; Fabes et al., 1999; Graziano, Reavis, Keane, & Calkins, 2007).

SEL frameworks can inform the design of developmentally appropriate emotion regulation programs and practices. For example, research suggests that developmental trajectories of emotion regulation skill acquisition vary across at least five dimensions:

- *Emotion Differentiation*—For example, is anger or disappointment or joy being regulated?
- *Focus of Regulation*—For example, is it the situation that needs to be modified or is it the emotion?
- *The Component of the Emotional System Being Regulated*—For example, are regulation efforts focused on physiological or behavioral responses?
- *Type of Strategy*—For example, does the individual use cognitive or behavioral strategies?
- *Type of Display Rule*—For example, does the individual know when and how to express emotions verbally or nonverbally across contexts? (Torrente, Nathanson, Rivers, & Brackett, 2015)

Developmental research indicates specific patterns of skill acquisition and use across these dimensions. For example, 5-year-olds have a well-developed understanding of basic emotions such as sadness and happiness, but only after age 7 do children come to understand more complex emotions such as shame and pride (Widen & Russell, 2010). Similarly, a 10-year-old can understand that some strategies, such as dampening of expectations, can be useful for preventing a specific emotion such as disappointment, but not other emotions, like frustration (Guttentag & Ferrell, 2008). In general, it is expected that with maturation and experience children expand their repertoire of regulatory strategies. By middle to late childhood, most children can generate a great number of strategies to deal with negative situations and unpleasant emotions, yet there is great variability in the implementation of these strategies (e.g., Blandon, Calkins, Keane, & O'Brien, 2008).

THE MECHANISMS THROUGH WHICH SEL PROGRAMS OPERATE

Contemporary frameworks of SEL elevate essential questions relevant to program design and implementation and challenge program developers and researchers to articulate theories of change and to test explanatory models of the effects of SEL. Framing questions regarding program effects in terms of mediated pathways can expand the scope, rigor, and applicability of SEL research. The limited number of studies on pathways of change notwithstanding, researchers have demonstrated that it is possible to identify the social–cognitive processes and the social and emotional skills, as well as the setting-level characteristics that mediate the effects of SEL programs on desired outcomes, such as reduced problem behavior (Dymnicki, Weissberg, & Henry, 2011; Langeveld, Gundersen, & Svartdal, 2012; Osher, Poirier, Jarjoura, & Haight, 2014).

Such research expands our understanding of developmental trajectories. For example, in early childhood, the effects of self-regulation on academic achievement may be mediated by children's ability to initiate positive interpersonal interactions that facilitate learning (Montroy, Bowles, Skibbe, & Foster, 2014). In early adolescence, social information processing may mediate the relationship between peer experience (e.g., level of popularity or rejection in the peer group) and the use of coping strategies in conflictual situations (Bowker, Bukowski, Hymel, & Sippola, 2000). In addition, such research can also identify program design elements, such as improving classroom management strategies and developing teacher–student relationships, that enhance the effects of SEL programs (Brackett, Rivers, Reyes, & Salovey, 2012; McCormick, Cappella, O'Connor, & McClowry, 2015).

CRITERIA FOR WELL-DESIGNED SEL APPROACHES AND PROGRAMS

The rich body of empirical and descriptive research on universal SEL programs makes it possible to develop criteria for identifying effective SEL programs and practices. Six key criteria for programs are that they be (a) developmentally appropriate, (b) culturally relevant, (c) systemic, (d) comprehensive, (e) evidence-based, and (f) forward thinking.

Developmentally Appropriate SEL Programs

SEL programs must incorporate tools, language, activities, and lessons that are tailored to students' development and align with children's cognitive, social, and emotional skills across multiple grades. Theories of social and emotional development can inform program developers about the skills students tend to have at different ages as well as the type of knowledge and experiences students need to further develop their skills (e.g., Denham, 1998; Jones & Bouffard, 2012; Saarni, 1999). For example, most preschool- and kindergarten-age children understand basic emotion concepts such as happiness and sadness, whereas students in the upper elementary grades can more easily understand complex, self-conscious emotions such as pride and guilt (Harris, 1999). An effective SEL program scaffolds the teaching of different skills accordingly. For example, cognitive reappraisal, a well-researched and effective emotion regulation strategy, is more appropriate for adolescents as opposed to very young children, because of the level of cognitive reframing necessary to employ this strategy (Gross, 1999).

Theories such as social information-processing theory (Crick & Dodge, 1994) and transactional theory (Sameroff, 1975) can help SEL program developers and implementers better understand the psychological needs of students and their interactions with their environment. Understanding child development can also inform our understanding of the number of lessons or experiential opportunities necessary to enhance specific skills at various developmental levels, or the appropriate format or length of a classroom lesson. Dealing with peer pressure, for example, will be more complex for 10th graders than for 3rd graders, and younger students might learn better with 20-minute lessons three times a week that incorporate hands-on activities, whereas high school students might learn better during 45-minute lessons twice a week that incorporate peer teaching methods.

Research and practical experience implementing SEL suggested that key developmental stages, which are related to cognitive and psychological development as well as to changes in a child's social fields, are also connected to SEL development (Kellam & Rebok, 1992). Early childhood is a key time for executive function development, the expansion of simple emotion knowledge and expression, and the emergence of emotion and behavior management and basic social engagement. The transition to school includes the emergence of planning, organizing, and goal setting, as well as basic empathy and perspective taking, as children become more attuned to social cues. Middle childhood includes greater capacity for sophisticated friendships, prosocial behaviors, and conflict resolution strategies.

Theories about adolescent development that highlight the emergence of complex, abstract cognitive reasoning, identity formation, and future aspirations serve as the basis for the design of age-appropriate programs for those age groups. For example, SEL programs for adolescents may include more student voice and choice; students leading SEL activities, including solving moral dilemmas; and service learning. In addition, owing to the rise in risk and criminal behavior in the middle grades, and based on developmental theories that identify precursors for these types of behavior, many SEL programs have been implemented with the primary focus of preventing problem behavior (Jagers, Harris, & Skoog, 2015; Williamson, Modecki, & Guerra, 2015).

Culturally Relevant SEL Programs

Although social and emotional skill development is important for all students (Denham & Weissberg, 2004), the approach to developing these skills, the ways in which they are modeled, and the adults who are teaching them should attend to cultural diversity. This includes considering the cultural relevance of values, attitudes, behavior, and meanings of SEL-related concepts. Considerable research confirms that norms around social and emotional skills vary tremendously by culture. For example, emotions are interpreted, expressed, and regulated differently, and rules governing relationships and social interactions differ depending on culture, including region, socioeconomic status, language, religion, race, and other factors (Hoffman, 2009).

Approaches to SEL must address these cultural differences and adapt approaches to unique environments, beliefs, and behavioral norms. Although insufficiently addressed at this time, this understanding is becoming more widely discussed in the field because of concerns that SEL practices developed and implemented within a Western culture may not address cultural subgroups adequately (CASEL, 2013). Adaptation is possible. For example, the CASEL framework has been adapted by the Association of Alaska Schools Boards in collaboration with First Alaskans to make it consistent with Athabascan, Tlingit, Inuplat, and Yup'ik culture. Self-management, for example, has been operationalized to include self-sufficiency, honesty, patience, humility, and fairness, while relationship skills include sharing, village cooperation, listening, peace, unity, speaking up with care, and holding each other up (Association of Alaska School Boards, 2015). Similarly, Chinese experts have adapted the CASEL framework (and a related one developed by Anchorage Alaska) to be more consistent with Chinese culture. In Chinese culture, there are two kinds of subjects apart from oneself—others and the group—and a person is expected to exhibit different self-regulation and habits when dealing with others than when dealing with the group (Yaqing, 2015). Chinese SEL experts applied this logic to conceptualize and operationalize a Chinese version of SEL. It included the Western focus on understanding and managing oneself and one's relationships with others but also included collective awareness and managing of relationships between oneself and the collective. This conceptualization and its operationalization in a self-report survey informed an initiative of the Chinese Ministry of Education in Collaboration with UNICEF China, which was piloted in five counties in southwest China (Guangxi, Yunnan, Guizhou, Xinjiang, and Chongqing) and included 250 schools, serving approximately 140,000 students (Yaqing, 2015).

Comprehensive and Systemic SEL Programs

SEL is grounded in ecological ideas that center on building social and emotional skills among students and improving the quality of the environments in which learning occurs. Systemic SEL approaches should address the fact that schools are dynamic and complex systems that affect social and emotional outcomes for students (Osher et al., 2014; Tseng & Seidman, 2007). Efforts that align with the roles, personal characteristics, norms, skill levels, and needs of the adults and students within each school will help address the extent to which programs meet this criterion (Garibaldi, Ruddy, Kendziora, & Osher, 2015; Osher & Chasin, 2016; Osher et al., 2014a).

Improving the quality of environments relates to how a school is experienced phenomenologically, which is a product of the relationships between and among students, educators, and staff, and the discipline policies, among many other components (Osher et al., 2008). School climate is also a product of school culture and behavioral norms at both the school and classroom levels, the ways in which the school functions, and the methods by which students are educated. SEL practices also are affected by aspects of school climate that relate to the myriad of interactions that take place between and among members of the school community (Hoy & Miskel, 2012). SEL depends on training and support for all involved in children's lives, including school staff, families, and community members (Brackett & Rivers, 2013; Greenberg et al., 2003). SEL programs are starting to become more explicit about intended outcomes for adults and other members of the school community, given work that suggests the importance of adult modeling, stress management, and coregulation (Jennings & Greenberg, 2009; Osher et al., 2012; Osher et al., 2014b). In addition, systemic SEL programs are starting to include measurement of school-level and adult outcomes, given accumulating research about effects of SEL programs on outcomes such as teacher morale and retention.

Evidence-Based SEL Programs and Practices

The design of many school-based programs and practices has been grounded in developmental and education research, although some of the programs themselves have not yet been subjected to rigorous scientific study (Jones & Bouffard, 2012). As in the case of other types of educational interventions, evaluations of the effects of school-based SEL programs vary in rigor and generalizability. Rigor is necessary for drawing conclusions about relationships of cause and effect, whereas generalizability is necessary for replicating program effects in different school settings and with diverse student populations (Forman, 2015; Hedges, 2013).

A growing number of SEL programs have been reviewed by independent reviewers using systematic research review criteria (e.g., What Works Clearinghouse, 2014) and included in registries of evidence-based programs or published summaries of the strength of the evidence (e.g., CASEL, 2013, 2015; Epstein, Atkins, Cullinan, Kutash, & Weaver, 2008; Mihalic & Elliott, 2015; Osher, Dwyer, & Jackson, 2004; Tolan, 2013).

Comprehensive program reviews have identified evidence-based SEL programs for students at various grade levels to address this need. Registries of the research evidence can be searched online by program and target population characteristics (e.g., the What Works Clearinghouse reviews of interventions under the topic of Student Behavior [http://ies.ed.gov/ncee/wwc/topic.aspx?sid=15] and the National Registry of Evidence-Based Programs and Practices [http://nrepp.samhsa.gov]). The development of standards and tools for examining the research evidence in the context of school-based prevention and intervention programs (e.g., understanding what rigor looks like and what should be the standard expectations for generalizability of research) can support program selection, which must also be attentive to local context and readiness to implement (Dymnicki, Wandersman, Osher, & Pakstis, 2016; Osher et al., 2004).

SEL and New Advancements in Educational Programs

SEL can draw on advances in education. For example, experts have experimented with the use of educational technology for SEL (Stern, Harding, Holzer, & Elbertson,

2015). Schools are increasingly adopting blended learning strategies to incorporate wiki sites, webinars, blogs, and other computer technology innovations into teaching and learning. Blended learning saves schools the costs associated with individualized instruction, including staffing and materials, and can improve learning outcomes for students, as compared with traditional face-to-face instruction (Finn & Achilles, 1990; Staker, 2011; Tamim, Bernard, Borokhovski, Abrami, & Schmid, 2011).

There have been some steps to incorporate technology in SEL interventions (e.g., Enz et al., 2008). Using technology, developers have constructed virtual role-play approaches that provide a safe place for exploring experiences of self and other and reflecting on behavior and attitudes. The use of digital SEL games enables a new kind of assessment. For example, Zoo U is a digital game–based social skills assessment tool in which an avatar created by the student participant is a student in a school for future zookeepers. The avatar encounters common social scenarios similar to those that might be experienced at school, and the student must make dialogue, action, and behavior choices (Craig, DeRosier, & Watanabe, 2015; DeRosier, Craig, & Sanchez, 2012). Computer-based programs are in no way typical of the prevalent school-based SEL approaches, and their efficacy needs to be further established.

Experiential education provides another example. It has been at the forefront of educational innovations in the past three decades. Ranging from art education to service learning, experiential education has been associated with improved social and emotional skills (Celio, Durlak, & Dymnicki, 2011; McKay-Jackson, 2014). Experiential education principles have demonstrated the promise of promoting both social skills and academic learning (Conrad & Hedin, 1982). Student-centered pedagogical approaches such as project-based and inquiry-based learning, self-reflection, and addressing different learning styles promote interest and motivation, which may in turn promote academic effort, engagement, comprehension, and retention of the materials learned (Skelton, Seevers, Dormody, & Hodnett, 2012).

IMPLEMENTATION QUALITY OF SEL PROGRAMS

SEL program design features are important but not sufficient. The quality of implementation also affects outcomes (Durlak & DuPre, 2008; Faria et al., 2013; Osher et al., 2014a; Reyes, Brackett, Rivers, Elbertson, & Salovey, 2012). For example, analyses of evaluation of data from the first cohort of an eight-district collaborating district initiative found that in two of three districts, where a sufficient set of data were available to do rigorous analyses, implementation was significantly related to student outcomes (Osher et al., 2014a).

So far, researchers have most commonly defined implementation quality in terms of fidelity to the original program design or at least to what are defined as its core features. Other aspects of implementation include the extent to which participants are engaged by and involved in the activities (Gottfredson et al., 2015; Mihalic, 2004). Increasingly, definitions of implementation quality have expanded to address conditions that support implementation. Durlak (2015) identified five categories of factors that, according to research reviews, influence quality of implementation: (a) community-level factors, (b) characteristics of staff delivering the program, (c) features of the program to be offered, (d) features of the host school where a program is to be offered, and (e) features of professional development (PD). Under each of these categories, multiple factors may be identified and addressed by program implementers and evaluators.

Syntheses of research and practice wisdom suggest that how implementation fidelity may be operationalized depends on the implementation step. For example, one may not expect a school to reach full program implementation quickly, because of the need to ensure that all the supporting conditions are in place for adequate implementation when the intervention is implemented. Fixsen, Naoom, Blase, Friedman, and Wallace (2005), based on review of the research, identified six key stages of implementation: (a) Exploration and Adoption, (b) Program Installation, (c) Initial Implementation, (d) Full Operation, (e) Innovation, and (f) Sustainability. Each of these stages may require different measures of implementation quality. Nevertheless, some conditions for implementation may be shared by all implementation stages, including PD and technical assistance, educational leadership, and financial and logistical considerations. These conditions are further described below.

Professional Development and Technical Assistance

Many teachers lack prior training in SEL and require PD on SEL in general as well as on the program core components specifically (DeGaston, Jensen, Weed, & Tanas, 1994; Greenberg et al., 2003). In their discussion of factors that influence the outcomes of school-based social skills training programs, Rotheram-Borus, Bickford, and Milburn (2001) argued that implementers need to be socially competent, be able to manage children in small groups, be familiar with the theoretical model underlying the program, and have the opportunity to practice delivering the program.

Research on the association between teacher PD and program outcomes is sparse. For example, Yoon, Duncan, Lee, Scarloss, and Shapley (2007) reviewed more than 1,300 studies of PD in mathematics, science, and English language arts and found only 9 studies that examined the impact of PD on student achievement and met the review's criteria based on What Works Clearinghouse (2014) design standards. Yet the findings suggest that both initial training and follow-up PD are important. For example, a recent rigorous randomized study of PD in reading involving workshops and coaching showed an impact on teachers' knowledge and classroom instruction, although not on student achievement (Garet et al., 2008). Ongoing professional learning and technical assistance supported increased implementation fidelity by teachers with low initial adherence to the program (Dufrene, Noell, Gilbertson, & Duhon, 2005; Mihalic, Fagan, & Argamaso, 2008). A number of studies demonstrated the positive association between teacher training, including the amount of time and the intensity of the training, and the effectiveness of bullying prevention programs (Bradshaw, 2015; Farrington & Ttofi, 2009). In one study of RULER®, students had more positive outcomes, including higher emotional intelligence and better behavior grades, when their teachers participated in more training and coaching (Reyes et al., 2012).

Tools are being developed to help teachers develop these skills. For example, watching videos of themselves teaching SEL lessons can support teachers in developing a reflective practice (Hafen et al., 2012), contribute to student relationships with peers, and reduce disciplinary referrals (Hafen, Ruzek, Gregory, Allen, & Mikami, 2015; Mikami, Gregory, Allen, Pianta, & Lun, 2011).

Educational Leadership

Some key characteristics of the implementation context, such as school leadership, may moderate the relationship between PD and student outcomes. For example, a study of implementation quality of the Responsive Classroom® approach suggested that participation in training on its own may be insufficient to promote teachers' investment in the program and change in their relationships with students (Baroody, Rimm-Kaufman, Larsen, & Curby, 2014). School principals may play an important role in motivating teacher buy-in (Downer et al., 2013), including determining when PD is insufficient and when there are needs for refresher training and one-on-one coaching (Wandersman, Chien, & Katz, 2012). Leaders can create opportunities for teachers' self-reflection on practice, particularly if the leaders nurture relational trust—including teachers' trust in their students, parents' and students' trust in the teachers, and teachers' trust in their colleagues (Schneider, Judy, Ebmeye, & Broda, 2014; Tschannen-Moran & Gareis, 2015).

Leadership entails management, monitoring, and advocacy. Research suggests that school leadership has an important role in the implementation of programs, policies, and practices with fidelity and in ensuring these practices are sustained and institutionalized over time (Osher et al., 2014a). Leaders can advocate for SEL, incorporate goals related to SEL as part of the school's mission and vision to track implementation, troubleshoot challenges to implementation, and hold teachers accountable for SEL outcomes (Elias et al., 1997; Flaspohler, Duffy, Wandersman, Stillman, & Maras, 2008; Han & Weiss, 2005). Research has shown that ongoing communication with staff promotes motivation as well as quality of implementation. Such communication may include opportunities for staff to voice their concerns about the program and joint discussions about how these concerns might be addressed (Freeman, 2014).

Financial and Logistical Considerations

Research suggests that SEL programs produce a strong return on investment. For example, Belfield et al. (2015) determined that six SEL programs produced, on average, a benefit-to-cost ratio of $11 for each dollar invested. SEL programs may reduce the immediate costs associated with aggressive behavior and bullying, such as days of missed school; time of school staff and administrators assigned to handle the behavior incident; resources of mental health and social services; resources for alternative placement of perpetrators; and law enforcement involvement. SEL programs may also reduce long-term costs such as those associated with welfare and incarceration, and increase the amount of state and federal taxes paid by individuals with higher educational attainment and improved job skills (Belfield et al., 2015). However, there is a need for additional studies related to financial and logistical factors associated with the adoption of a school-based program, including the formation of partnerships and the development of an infrastructure to support the technical, financial, administrative, monitoring, evaluative, and logistical needs related to the program (O'Connell, Boat, & Warner, 2009).

Researchers have suggested that anticipating and resolving financial and logistical challenges (e.g., restructuring schedules to add time for SEL instruction and teacher planning time; paying for substitute teachers during staff training) are key responsibilities of the school principal and administrators. Experts have suggested that schools assemble a steering committee or leadership team comprising school staff and other stakeholders from the school and the community to oversee these aspects of implementation. The steering committee can develop implementation plans, develop partnerships with community-based organizations and local businesses with the help of the school district office, and adjust plans and policies based on routine monitoring of implementation (Devaney, O'Brien, Resnik, Keister, & Weissberg, 2006; Fixsen, Blase, Metz, & Van Dyke, 2013).

Program implementation is often at its best during the performance period of grants received from federal, state, or private funding streams. Assuming that it typically takes 2 to 5 years to build full capacity for systemic SEL implementation (Devaney et al., 2006), without sound sustainability plans, schools are at risk of not seeing the full benefits of their investments until after the performance period ends, in spite of the evidence of strong returns on investment (e.g., Clarke, Morreale, Field, Hussein, & Barry, 2015). Sustaining programs after their funding ends depends on teacher, principal, and district commitment to implement SEL practices with quality; implementation support; adequate staffing; and the ability to adapt the program to the local context while minimizing countervailing pressures (Osher et al., 2014a; Tibbits, Bumbarger, Kyler, & Perkins, 2010; Wanless, Groark, & Hatfield, 2015). Sustainability planning should begin with program installation in order to start institutionalizing practices and processes from the outset (Shediac-Rizkallah & Bone, 1998). Long-term, effective implementation of SEL programs requires alignment with other key components of schooling, including learning standards, other programs and services, assessment practices, and teacher PD, as well as the identification of sources for ongoing financial support for implementation (Price, 2015).

DISCUSSION

The rapid accumulation of research evidence over the past two decades indicates that under the right conditions schools can effectively promote the development of students' SEL skills, and that SEL is associated with reduced involvement in risk-taking behaviors and increased success in academic and well-being outcomes. Contributions of SEL research and advancements in statistical methodologies and research design have contributed to researchers' ability to produce valid information about the value of SEL (MacKinnon & Lockwood, 2003; National Research Council, 2009). While the field has come a long way, we need to better understand the complex processes and systems through which SEL programs can be effectively adapted to new cultural, linguistic, and socioeconomic groups and sustained on a large scale (Spoth et al., 2013). Effective universal SEL programs are comprehensive, developmentally and culturally appropriate, evidence-based, systemic, and forward thinking.

Several notable gaps in SEL research remain, which limit investigators' and policymakers' ability to fully utilize the research findings. These gaps include (a) the need for practical, reliable, and valid assessments of specific SEL skills; (b) limited knowledge about effective leadership practices to promote teachers' buy-in and quality of implementation; (c) limited knowledge about how to better align SEL with other school efforts; (d) a need to clarify terminology and align language and frameworks; and (e) a need to translate research into practice, among other issues.

Assessing SEL Development

The field needs practical measures with psychometric evidence that enable comparisons among studies and samples that can replace or supplement self-reports, teacher reports, and indirect measures of social and emotional skills (e.g., disciplinary infractions). As noted by McKown (2015), assessment of social and emotional skills should examine both knowledge (i.e., children's comprehension of social and emotional information; reasoning and decision-making abilities), and children's abilities to execute the skills (i.e., the ability to regulate emotions, expressions, communications, and other behaviors and perform goal-directed behavior). There are few SEL assessments with strong psychometric properties (e.g., reliability, validity) that assess both types of skills. There is also a lack of normed-referenced or standardized measures of social and emotional skills that can be used by trained professionals (e.g., school psychologists and social workers) to compare a student to a specified population (e.g., by age group), with respect to the skill being measured. Although some SEL measures show promise (Atkins-Burnett, Fernandez, Akers, Jacobson, & Smither-Wulsin, 2012; Child Trends, 2014; Denham, Ji, & Hamre, 2010; Haggerty, Elgin, & Woolley, 2011; Humphrey et al., 2010; Lippman, Ryberg, Carney, & Moore, 2015; Philliber Research Associates, 2013a, 2013b; Stecher & Hamilton, 2014), they are limited (Denham, Bassett, Sirotkin, Brown, & Morris, 2015), and typically measure a narrow set of skills, focus on a particular age group, and mostly assess comprehension or execution. These limitations, along with the lack of use of common measures, impede researchers' ability to combine results across studies.

These same limitations, along with the burden of administering assessments, limit practitioners' ability to use formative SEL data to improve their practice. They need tools that enable easy assessment of students and that do not place an undue burden on scarce financial and time resources or reduce students to a "score." Practicality includes the ability of measures to support progress monitoring to effectively guide practice and support teachers' efforts to enhance students' social, emotional, and academic growth. This gap may start to be addressed by the Work Group to Establish Practical Social-Emotional Competence Assessments that is being convened in 2016–2017. It will include over 60 researchers and practitioners who will work together to develop a framework that provides guidance about which intrapersonal and interpersonal competencies are most important to measure, how to best measure them, and how to use data effectively to inform planning and practice (Weissberg et al., 2015).

Leading an SEL School

Limited research exists on effective practices to promote teachers' buy-in and quality of implementation or to promote educational leadership practices that effectively advance quality of implementation. While researchers have established that teachers need training, coaching, and other regular supports in order to effectively implement SEL programs (Davies & Cooper, 2013), there is little information about what school and district administrators should do to ensure successful implementation (Brackett & Patti, 2016). The ongoing evaluation of an eight-district demonstration is developing evidence of how practices and policies of the district and school-level leadership can support SEL implementation in diverse contexts (Osher et al., 2014a, 2014b).

Aligning With School and District Efforts

The third gap involves how SEL can practically align with and support other school, district, and state efforts that involve improving academic performance while reducing the achievement gap and exclusionary discipline practices. There is a competition for both educators' and student's time, and we need to learn which high-leverage strategies or practices can be easily mastered by educators, integrated into their practices, and employed regularly (Jones & Bouffard, 2012). Likewise, tools that have been developed for teachers to use for assessing both their own SEL competencies and methods of integrating SEL strategies into pedagogy also need to be validated (Yoder, 2014). Ways of supporting teachers' effective use of these strategies and tools also need to be researched and validated (Osher, 2012). Research can help determine whether certain practices, strategies, or tools accelerate uptake and institutionalization of SEL, and whether their effective employment helps programs realize larger effect sizes than those already realized by existing programs. Moreover, there is a need to efficiently align widely adopted student support interventions (e.g., Positive Behavioral Interventions and Support and Restorative Practices) in a manner that creates synergies while addressing differences (Bradshaw, Bottiani, Osher, & Sugai, 2013; Osher et al., 2008; Osher et al., 2010).

Aligning Frameworks and Language

Advances in the biological sciences suggest that social and emotional skills are likely to have neurobiological and neuroendocrinal roots that are affected by children's contexts (including epigenetically) and affect children's expression of social and emotional skills (e.g., Blair & Raver, 2014; McEwen, 2016; McEwen et al., 2015). However, these social and emotional skills are expressed differently at different developmental stages as well as in different cultures and contexts.

Social and emotional skills are also conceptualized differently across disciplines. Although specialization is helpful, we also need alignment. We need to align and, where possible, conciliate different frameworks, both in SEL and between SEL and related areas. This alignment should be done through the lens of creating a clear and common language for practitioners. For example, the generic use of the term *noncognitive* to describe factors that include cognitive components (e.g., self-regulation), while grounded in the history of behavioral economics, can be confounding.

It is also necessary to better align related frameworks that interact with SEL, including trauma, resilience, youth development, restorative practices, Positive Behavioral Interventions and Support, character education, cultural competence, school climate, conditions for learning, and deeper learning. Efforts to align these frameworks can also address the fact that discourse and practice sometimes conflate and at other times ignore the relationships between and among many approaches and the dispositional factors that affect the development and expression of social and emotional skills, including the amplification and attenuation of the skills. Examples of the dispositional factors include mindfulness, executive function, self-regulation, grit, perspective taking, and growth mind-sets, as well as aspects of personality and temperament such as impulsivity.

Translating Research Into Practice

Although dissemination of SEL practices and programs is important, risks can occur when nuanced scientific ideas become popularized in a manner that ignores conceptual nuance and when policy fails to address the root causes of social problems (e.g., Nickerson et al., in press; Osher et al., 2015) as well as when practitioners lack the training to implement new practices (Coburn, 2002; Cohen, 1990). Grit and CSC provide examples. While nuanced research on grit suggests that it can be measured and is associated with academic attainment and life success (Credé, Tynan, & Harms, 2016; Duckworth, Peterson, Matthews, & Kelly, 2007; Duckworth & Quinn, 2009, Eskreis-Winkler, Shulman, Beal, & Duckworth, 2014), it has become popularized by nonresearchers as a silver bullet in ways that do not address its relationship to context and to other social and emotional factors. Similarly, although a What Works Clearinghouse (2007) review of CSC found potentially positive effects on student behavior, implementation research suggests that its impact (like that of other interventions) is moderated by whether teachers have a deep understanding of why it works (Coburn, 2002; Cohen, 1990).

Other challenges include cultural insensitivity, devaluing the importance of ecology, and ignoring implementation and dissemination challenges. SEL is not a cure-all for ameliorating educational problems. Similarly, while SEL might help some individuals better navigate the barriers created by institutionalized racism and structural inequality, it does not eliminate them. Failure to address these and other ecological factors such as power, privilege, and hegemony can lead to victim-blaming approaches (Ryan, 1972), which can and will be critiqued (e.g., Hoffman, 2009; Ris, 2015). Culture will affect uptake of interventions, assessment, and outcomes. Although SEL appears to have an appeal that includes Southeast Asia, South Asia, South Africa, and Latin America (e.g., Kam, Wong, & Fung, 2011), it has been conceptualized in an individualized manner that can limit its appeal. In addition, most SEL program evaluations have not disaggregated program effects by race, ethnicity, intersectionality, and context, limiting their ecological validity.

Finally, the successful implementation of evidence-based practices requires individual motivation, individual and organizational capacity (including adult cultural competence social and emotional skills), supportive policies, and attention to the affective and cognitive challenges involved in changing practices as well as addressing the challenges posed by new contexts and the need to adapt programs once implemented (Chambers, Glasgow, & Stange, 2013; Dymnicki et al., 2016).

CONCLUSION

U.S. educators are tackling both promotive and preventive issues that in some ways are similar to those confronted by educators one hundred years ago. Promotive issues include engaging, personalizing, and educating children and youth so that they can (a) succeed academically, socially, and emotionally in what is experienced as a rapidly changing world; (b) be active and responsible citizens; and (c) develop problem-solving, critical-thinking, and social skills (Kliebard, 1986). Prevention efforts include preventing social problems such as school dropout, delinquency, substance abuse, and the extent to which poor education, lack of access to quality education, and disadvantage sustain or amplify inequality (Duncan & Murnane, 2011; Lazerson, 1971; Rothstein, 2004).

The need for SEL may even be greater now owing to the impacts of digital technology on learning, work, and interpersonal relationships, and the increasing challenges associated with inequality, global warming, and population growth. But fortunately, due to multiple developments in the field that have been reviewed in this chapter—including innovations in SEL programs and sustainability, research frameworks and methods, and effective dissemination of data and the knowledge gained from it—the field is in a better place than ever before.

Policy around SEL is also promising due to the dissemination of research on the benefits of SEL for youth and to the lessons learned from the inability of either test-driven improvement or a narrow focus on academic instruction to improve educational outcomes. The new policy environment includes provisions in the revised Elementary and Secondary Education Act, the Organisation for Economic Co-operation and Development's (2015) interest in measuring social and emotional skills, and state and district development of SEL standards (Dusenbury et al., 2015). Both the Elementary and Secondary Education Act and Organisation for Economic Co-operation and Development's Skills for Success work expand the conceptualization of what is counted and reported, while SEL standards provide a focus for integrating academics and SEL.

Finally, a number of ongoing national efforts can focus future research and help make quality SEL part of every child's education. These include The National Commission on Social, Emotional, and Academic Development, which has been convened by the Aspen Institute to create a framework to help accelerate research and practice related to SEL; a national workgroup on SEL assessment that involves many prominent researchers and practitioners, a translational research agenda on SEL and school climate supported by the Robert Wood Johnson Foundation, and an interdisciplinary work group convened by American Educational Research Association to develop a research agenda on schools, rules, and socialization. These efforts and related local, state, national, and even international initiatives provide an opportunity to address and transform the grammars of schooling and instruction, produce more equitable outcomes for students, and most important, better equip all students to handle life's challenges; build and maintain quality relationships; thrive personally, collectively, and professionally; and become engaged citizens.

ACKNOWLEDGMENTS

We would like to thank the editors and reviewers for their very helpful feedback and SooYun Chung for helping with the preparation of this chapter.

NOTE

[1]The improvement index is the expected change in percentile rank for an average comparison-group student if the student had received the intervention (What Works Clearinghouse, 2014).

REFERENCES

Addams, J. (1902). *Democracy and social ethics.* New York, NY: Macmillan.

Almlund, M., Duckworth, A. L., Heckman, J. J., & Kautz, T. D. (2011). Personality psychology and economics. In E. A. Hanushek, S. Machin, & L. Woessmann (Eds.), *Handbook of the economics of education* (Vol. 4, pp. 1–181). Amsterdam, Netherlands: Elsevier.

Association of Alaska School Boards. (2015). *Culturally embedded social and emotional learning.* Retrieved from http://alaskaice.org/wordpress/wp-content/uploads/2015/05/Innovation-Grant.pdf

Atkins-Burnett, S., Fernandez, C., Akers, L., Jacobson, J., & Smither-Wulsin, C. (2012). *Landscape analysis of non-cognitive measures.* Princeton, NJ: Mathematical Policy Research.

Bandura, A. (1974). Behavior theory and the models of man. *The American Psychologist, 29,* 859–869.

Bandura, A. (1977). Self-efficacy: Toward a unifying theory of behavior change. *Psychological Review, 84,* 191–215.

Bandura, A. (1991). Social cognitive theory of self-regulation. *Organizational Behavior and Human Decision Processes, 50*, 248–287.

Baroody, A. E., Rimm-Kaufman, S. E., Larsen, R. A., & Curby, T. W. (2014). The link between responsive classroom training and student-teacher relationship quality in the fifth grade: A study of fidelity of implementation. *School Psychology Review, 43*, 69–85.

Battistich, V., Solomon, D., Watson, M., & Schaps, E. (1997). Caring school communities. *Educational Psychologist, 32*, 137–151.

Bavarian, N., Lewis, K. M., Dubois, D. L., Acock, A., Vuchinich, S., Silverthorn, N., . . . Flay, B. R. (2013). Using social-emotional and character development to improve academic outcomes: A matched-pair, cluster-randomized controlled trial in low-income, urban schools. *Journal of School Health, 83*, 771–779.

Beane, J. A. (1985). The continuing controversy over affective education. *Educational Leadership, 43*(4), 26–31.

Belfield, C., Bowden, B., Klapp, A., Levin, H., Shand, R., & Zander, S. (2015). *The economic value of social and emotional learning.* New York, NY: Center for Benefit-Cost Studies of Education, Teachers College, Columbia University.

Blackwell, L. S., Trzesniewski, K. H., & Dweck, C. S. (2007). Implicit theories of intelligence predict achievement across an adolescent transition: A longitudinal study and an intervention. *Child Development, 78*, 246–263.

Blair, C., & Raver, C. C. (2014, August). School readiness and self-regulation: A developmental psychobiological approach. *Annual Review of Psychology, 66*, 711–731.

Blandon, A. Y., Calkins, S. D., Keane, S. P., & O'Brien, M. (2008). Individual differences in trajectories of emotion regulation processes: The effects of maternal depressive symptomatology and children's physiological regulation. *Developmental Psychology, 44*, 1110–1123.

Bowker, A., Bukowski, W. M., Hymel, S., & Sippola, L. K. (2000). Coping with daily hassles in the peer group during early adolescence: Variations as a function of peer experience. *Journal of Research on Adolescence, 10*, 211–243.

Brackett, M. A., Ivcevic-Pringle, Z., Moeller, J., White, A., & Stern, R. S. (2015). *Emotions matter: High school students' emotions and their relation to school experiences.* Manuscript submitted for publication.

Brackett, M. A., & Patti, J. (2016, April). Creating emotionally intelligent schools: Training in social and emotional skills begins with educators. *School Administrator*, 19–22.

Brackett, M. A., & Rivers, S. E. (2013). Transforming students' lives with social and emotional learning. In R. Pekrun & L. Linnenbrink-Garcia (Eds.), *International handbook of emotions in education* (pp. 368–388). New York, NY: Taylor & Francis.

Brackett, M. A., Rivers, S. E., Reyes, M. R., & Salovey, P. (2012). Enhancing academic performance and social and emotional competence with the RULER feeling words curriculum. *Learning and Individual Differences, 22*, 218–224.

Bradley, R., McCraty, R., Atkinson, M., Tomasino, D., Daugherty, A., & Arguelles, L. (2010). Emotion self-regulation, psychophysiological coherence, and test anxiety: Results from an experiment using electrophysiological measures. *Applied Psychophysiology and Biofeedback, 35*, 261–283.

Bradshaw, C. P. (2015). Translating research to practice in bullying prevention. *The American Psychologist, 70*, 322–332. doi:10.1037/a0039114

Bradshaw, C. P., Bottiani, J., Osher, D., & Sugai, G. (2013). Integrating positive behavioral interventions and supports (PBIS) and social emotional learning. In M. D. Weist, N. A. Lever, C. P. Bradshaw, & J. Owens (Eds.), *Handbook of school mental health: Advancing practice and research* (2nd ed., pp. 101–118). New York, NY: Springer.

Bridgeland, J., Bruce, M., & Hariharan, A. (2013). *The missing piece: A national teacher survey on how social and emotional learning can empower children and transform schools.* Washington, DC: Civic Enterprises/Hart Research Associates.

Bronfenbrenner, U., & Ceci, S. J. (1994). Nature-nurture reconceptualized in developmental perspective: A biological model. *Psychological Review, 101*, 568–586.

Bronfenbrenner, U., & Morris, P. A. (1998). The ecology of developmental processes. In R. M. Lerner (Ed.), *Handbook of child psychology* (5th ed., Vol. 1, pp. 993–1028). New York, NY: Wiley.

Buffington, P. W., & Stilwell, W. E. (1981). Self-competency and affective education. *Education, 102*, 85–90.

Calkins, S. D., & Hill, A. (2007). The emergence of emotion regulation: Biological and behavioral transactions in early development. In J. J. Gross (Ed.), *Handbook of emotion regulation* (pp. 229–248). New York, NY: Guilford.

Campos, J. J., Campos, R. G., & Barrett, K. C. (1989). Emergent themes in the study of emotional development and emotion regulation. *Developmental Psychology, 25*, 394–402.

Cantor, C. L. (1976). Training for affective education: A model for change in the schools. *Journal of Clinical Child & Adolescent Psychology, 5*(2), 5–8.

Carkhuff, R. R. (1982). Affective education in the age of productivity. *Educational Leadership, 39*, 484–487.

Celio, C. I., Durlak, J., & Dymnicki, A. (2011). A meta-analysis of the impact of service-learning on students. *Journal of Experiential Education, 34*, 164–181.

Chambers, D. A., Glasgow, R. E., & Stange, K. C. (2013). The dynamic sustainability framework: Addressing the paradox of sustainment amid ongoing change. *Implementation Science, 8*(1), 117. doi:10.1186/1748-5908-8-117

Chang, E. C., D'Zurilla, T. J., & Sanna, L. J. (2004). *Social problem solving: Theory, research, and training*. Washington, DC: American Psychological Association.

Child Trends. (2014). *Making the grade: Assessing the evidence for integrated student supports*. Retrieved from http://www.childtrends.org/wp-content/uploads/2014/02/2014-07ISSPaper.pdf

Clarke, A. M., Morreale, S., Field, C. A., Hussein, Y., & Barry, M. M. (2015). *What works in enhancing social and emotional skills development during childhood and adolescence? A review of the evidence on the effectiveness of school-based and out-of-school programmes in the UK*. Galway, Ireland: WHO Collaborating Centre for Health Promotion Research, National University of Ireland Galway.

Coburn, C. E. (2002, August). *Beyond decoupling: Rethinking the relationship between the institutional environment and the classroom*. Paper presented at the annual conference of the American Sociological Association, Chicago, IL.

Cohen, D. K. (1990). A revolution in one classroom: The case of Mrs. Oublier. *Educational Evaluation and Policy Analysis, 12*, 311–330.

Cole, P. M., Martin, S. E., & Dennis, T. A. (2004). Emotion regulation as a scientific construct: Methodological challenges and directions for child development research. *Child Development, 75*, 317–333.

Collaborative for Academic, Social, and Emotional Learning. (2003). *Safe and sound: An educational leaders' guide to evidence-based social and emotional learning (SEL) programs*. Chicago, IL: Author.

Collaborative for Academic, Social, and Emotional Learning. (2013). *The 2013 CASEL guide: Effective social and emotional learning programs—Preschool and elementary school edition*. Chicago, IL: Author.

Collaborative for Academic, Social, and Emotional Learning. (2015). *The 2015 CASEL guide: Effective social and emotional learning programs—Middle and high school edition*. Chicago, IL: Author.

Comer, J. P. (2004). *Leave no child behind: Preparing today's youth for tomorrow's world*. New Haven, CT: Yale University Press.

Conrad, D., & Hedin, D. (1982). The impact of experiential education on adolescent development. *Child & Youth Services, 4*(3–4), 57–76.

Consortium on the School-Based Promotion of Social Competence. (1994). The school-based promotion of social competence: Theory, practice, and policy. In R. J. Haggerty, L. R. Sherrod, N. Garmezy, & M. Rutter (Eds.), *Stress, risk, and resilience, in children and adolescents: Processes, mechanisms, and interventions* (pp. 268–316). New York, NY: Cambridge University Press.

Cowen, E. L. (1971). Emergent directions in school mental health: The development and evaluation of a program for early detection and prevention of ineffective school behavior. *The American Scientist, 59,* 723–733.

Cowen, E. L. (1994). The enhancement of psychological wellness: Challenges and opportunities. *American Journal of Community Psychology, 22,* 149–178.

Cowen, E. L., & Work, W. C. (1988). Resilient children, psychological wellness, and primary prevention. *American Journal of Community Psychology, 16,* 591–607.

Craig, A. B., DeRosier, M. E., & Watanabe, Y. (2015). Differences between Japanese and U.S. children's performance on "Zoo U": A game-based social skills assessment. *Games for Health, 4,* 285–294.

Credé, M., Tynan, N. C., & Harms, P. D. (2016, May). Much ado about grit: A meta-analytic synthesis of the grit literature. *Journal of Personality and Social Psychology.* Advance online publication. doi:10.1037/pspp0000102. Retrieved from http://psycnet.apa.org/psycinfo/2016-29674-001/

Crick, N. R., & Dodge, K. A. (1994). A review and reformulation of social information-processing mechanisms in children's social adjustment. *Psychological Bulletin, 115,* 74–101.

Cuban, L. (1993). *How teachers taught: Constancy and change in American classrooms, 1890–1990.* New York, NY: Teachers College Press.

Davies, M., & Cooper, G. (2013). Training teachers to target and develop social skills as an academic enabler. In B. Knight & R. Van Der Zwan (Eds.), *Teaching innovations supporting student outcomes in the 21st century* (pp. 45–55). Tarragindi, Australia: Oxford Global Press.

DeGaston, J. F., Jensen, L., Weed, S. E., & Tanas, R. (1994). Teacher philosophy and program implementation and the impact on sex education outcomes. *Journal of Research and Development in Education, 27,* 265–270.

Deming, D. (2015). *The growing importance of social skills in the labor market* (National Bureau of Economic Research, Working Paper 21473). Retrieved from www.nber.org/papers/w21473

Denham, S. A. (1998). *Emotional development in young children.* New York, NY: Guilford.

Denham, S. A., Bassett, H. H., Sirotkin, Y. S., Brown, C., & Morris, C. S. (2015). "No-ooo peeking": Preschoolers' executive control, social competence, and classroom adjustment. *Journal of Research in Childhood Education, 29,* 212–225.

Denham, S. A., Ji, P., & Hamre, B. (2010). *Compendium of social-emotional learning and associated assessment measures.* Chicago, IL: Collaborative for Academic, Social, and Emotional Learning.

Denham, S. A., & Weissberg, R. P. (2004). Social-emotional learning in early childhood: What we know and where to go from here. In E. Chesebrough, P. King, T. P. Gullotta, & M. Bloom (Eds.), *A blueprint for the promotion of prosocial behavior in early childhood* (pp. 13–50). New York, NY: Kluwer.

DeRosier, M. E., Craig, A. B., & Sanchez, R. P. (2012). Zoo U: A stealth approach to social skills assessments in schools. *Advances in Human-Computer Interaction, 2012,* 654791. doi:10.1155/2012/654791

Devaney, E., O'Brien, M. U., Resnik, H., Keister, S., & Weissberg, R. P. (2006). *Sustainable schoolwide social and emotional learning (SEL): Implementation guide and toolkit.* Chicago, IL: Collaborative for Academic, Social, and Emotional Learning.

Dewey, J. (1916). *Democracy and education: An introduction to the philosophy of education.* New York, NY: Free Press.

Diamond, A. (2013). Executive functions. *Annual Review of Psychology, 64,* 135–168.

Diaz, R. M., Neal, C. J., & Amaya-Williams, M. (1990). The social origins of self-regulation. In L. C. Moll (Ed.), *Vygotsky and education: Instructional implications and applications of sociohistorical psychology* (pp. 127–154). Cambridge, England: Cambridge University Press.

Downer, J., Brown, J., Herrera, M. J., Stuhlman, M., Bourassa, K., Gologor, B., & Wong, P. (2013, March). *Coaching quality and teachers' implementation of the 4Rs social-emotional and literacy curriculum: Testing the link between two levels of intervention fidelity.* Paper presented at the annual conference of the Society for Research on Educational Effectiveness, Washington, DC.

Duckworth, A. L., Peterson, C., Matthews, M. D., & Kelly, D. R. (2007). Grit: Perseverance and passion for long-term goals. *Journal of Personality and Social Psychology, 92,* 1087–1101.

Duckworth, A. L., & Quinn, P. D. (2009). Development and validation of the Short Grit Scale (GRIT-S). *Journal of Personality Assessment, 91,* 166–174.

Duckworth, A. L., & Seligman, M. E. P. (2005). Self-discipline outdoes IQ in predicting academic performance of adolescents. *Psychological Science, 16,* 939–944. doi:10.1111/j.1467-9280.2005.01641.x

Dufrene, B. A., Noell, G. H., Gilbertson, D. N., & Duhon, G. J. (2005). Monitoring implementation of reciprocal peer tutoring: Identifying and intervening with students who do not maintain accurate implementation. *School Psychology Review, 34,* 74–86.

Duncan, G. J., & Murnane, R. J. (2011). *Whither opportunity? Rising inequality, schools, and children's life chances.* New York, NY: Russell Sage Foundation.

Durlak, J. A. (2015). What everyone should know about implementation. In J. A. Durlak, C. E. Domitrovich, R. P. Weissberg, & T. P. Gullotta (Eds.), *Handbook for social and emotional learning: Research and practice* (pp. 395–405). New York, NY: Guilford.

Durlak, J. A., & DuPre, E. P. (2008). Implementation matters: A review of research on the influence of implementation on program outcomes and the factors affecting implementation. *American Journal of Community Psychology, 41,* 327–350.

Durlak, J. A., Weissberg, R. P., Dymnicki, A. B., Taylor, R. D., & Schellinger, K. B. (2011). The impact of enhancing students' social and emotional learning: A meta-analysis of school-based universal interventions. *Child Development, 82,* 405–432.

Dusenbury, L. A., Newman, J. Z., Weissberg, R. P., Goren, P., Domitrovich, C. E., & Mart, A. K. (2015). The case for preschool through high school state learning standards for SEL. In J. A. Durlak, C. E. Domitrovich, R. P. Weissberg, & T. P. Gullotta (Eds.), *Handbook of social and emotional learning: Research and practice* (pp. 532–548). New York, NY: Guilford.

Dwyer, K., & Osher, D. (2000). *Safeguarding our children: An action guide.* Washington, DC: U.S. Departments of Education and Justice and American Institutes for Research.

Dwyer, K., Osher, D., & Warger, C. (1998). *Early warning, timely response: A guide to safe schools.* Washington, DC: U.S. Department of Education.

Dymnicki, A., Kendziora, K., & Osher, D. (2012). Adolescent development for students with learning disabilities and behavioral disorders: The promise of social emotional learning. In B. G. Cook, M. Tankersley, & T. J. Landrum (Eds.), *Classroom behavior, contexts, and interventions: Vol. 25. Advances in learning and behavioral disabilities* (pp. 131–166). Bingley, England: Emerald.

Dymnicki, A., Sambolt, M., & Kidron, Y. (2013). *Improving college and career readiness by incorporating social and emotional learning*. Washington, DC: American Institutes for Research.

Dymnicki, A., Wandersman, A., Osher, D., & Pakstis, A. (2016). Bringing interventions to scale. In M. A. Bond, I. Serrano-Garcia, & C. Keys (Eds.), *Handbook of community psychology*. Washington, DC: American Psychological Association.

Dymnicki, A. B., Weissberg, R. P., & Henry, D. B. (2011). Understanding how programs work to prevent overt aggressive behaviors: A meta-analysis of mediators of elementary school–based programs. *Journal of School Violence, 10*, 315–337. doi:10.1080/1538822 0.2011.602599

Dynarski, M., Clarke, L., Cobb, B., Finn, J., Rumberger, R., & Smink, J. (2008). *Dropout prevention: A practice guide* (NCEE 2008–4025). Washington, DC: National Center for Education Evaluation and Regional Assistance, Institute of Education Sciences, U.S. Department of Education.

Eisenberg, N., & Spinrad, T. L. (2004). Emotion-related regulation: Sharpening the definition. *Child Development, 75*, 334–339.

Elias, M. J., & Clabby, J. F. (1992). *Building social problem-solving skills: Guidelines from a school-based program*. San Francisco, CA: Jossey-Bass/Pfeiffer.

Elias, M. J., Parker, S. J., Kash, V. M., Weissberg, R. P., & O'Brien, M. U. (2007). Social and emotional learning, moral education, and character education: A comparative analysis and a view toward convergence. In L. P. Nucci & D. Narvaez (Eds.), *Handbook of moral and character education* (pp. 248–266). New York, NY: Routledge.

Elias, M. J., Zins, J. E., Weissberg, R. P., Frey, K. S., Greenberg, M. T., Haynes, N. M., . . . Shriver, T. P. (1997). *Promoting social and emotional learning: Guidelines for educators*. Alexandria, VA: Association for Supervision & Curriculum Development.

Enz, S., Zoll, C., Vannini, N., Schneider, W., Hall, L., Paiva, A., & Aylett, R. (2008). E-motional learning in primary schools: FearNot! An anti-bullying intervention based on virtual role-playing with intelligent synthetic characters. *Electronic Journal of e-Learning, 6*, 111–118.

Epstein, M., Atkins, M., Cullinan, D., Kutash, K., & Weaver, R. (2008). *Reducing behavior problems in the elementary school classroom: A practice guide* (NCEE #2008-012). Washington, DC: National Center for Education Evaluation and Regional Assistance.

Eskreis-Winkler, L., Shulman, E. P., Beal, S. A., & Duckworth, A. L. (2014). The grit effect: Predicting retention in the military, the workplace, school and marriage. *Frontiers in Psychology, 5*, 36. doi:10.3389/fpsyg.2014.00036

Espelage, D. L. (2013). Why are bully prevention programs failing in US schools? *Journal of Curriculum and Pedagogy, 10*, 121–124.

Espelage, D. L., Rose, C. A., & Polanin, J. R. (2015). Social-emotional learning program to reduce bullying, fighting, and victimization among middle school students with disabilities. *Remedial and Special Education, 36*, 299–311.

Fabes, R. A., Eisenberg, N., Jones, S., Smith, M., Guthrie, I., Poulin, R., . . . Friedman, J. (1999). Regulation, emotionality, and preschoolers' socially competent peer interactions. *Child Development, 70*, 432–442.

Faria, A. M., Kendziora, K., Brown, L., O'Brien, B., & Osher, D. (2013). *PATHS implementation and outcome study in the Cleveland Metropolitan School District: Final report*. Washington, DC: American Institutes for Research.

Farrington, C. A., Roderick, M., Allensworth, E., Nagaoka, J., Keyes, T. S., Johnson, D. W., & Beechum, N. O. (2012). *Teaching adolescents to become learners. The role of noncognitive factors in shaping school performance: A critical literature review*. Chicago, IL: University of Chicago Consortium on Chicago School Research.

Farrington, D. P., & Ttofi, M. M. (2009). School-based programs to reduce bullying and victimization. *Campbell Systematic Reviews, 6*, 1–147. Retrieved from http://www.campbellcollaboration.org/lib/project/77/

Fergusson, D. M., Boden, J. M., & Horwood, L. J. (2013). Child self-control and adult outcomes: Results from a 30-year longitudinal study. *Journal of the American Academy of Child & Adolescent Psychiatry, 52*, 709–717. doi:10.1016/j.jaac.2013.04.008

Finn, J. D., & Achilles, C. M. (1990). Answers and questions about class size: A statewide experiment. *American Educational Research Journal, 27*, 557–577.

Fischer, K. W., Shaver, P. R., & Carnochan, P. (1990). How emotions develop and how they organise development. *Cognition and Emotion, 4*(2), 81–127.

Fixsen, D., Blase, K., Metz, A., & Van Dyke, M. (2013). Statewide implementation of evidence-based programs. *Exceptional Children, 79*, 213–230.

Fixsen, D. L., Naoom, S. F., Blase, K. A., Friedman, R. M., & Wallace, F. (2005). *Implementation research: A synthesis of the literature*. Tampa: University of South Florida, Louis de la Parte Florida Mental Health Institute, National Implementation Research Network.

Flaspohler, P., Duffy, J., Wandersman, A., Stillman, L., & Maras, M. A. (2008). Unpacking prevention capacity: An intersection of research-to-practice models and community-centered models. *American Journal of Community Psychology, 41*, 182–196.

Forman, S. G. (2015). Implementation evaluation and research. In S. G. Forman (Ed.), *Implementation of mental health programs in schools: A change agent's guide* (pp. 35–53). Washington, DC: American Psychological Association. doi:10.1037/14597-004

Freeman, E. M. (2014). Teacher perspectives on factors facilitating implementation of whole school approaches for resolving conflict. *British Educational Research Journal, 40*, 847–868.

Gabrieli, C., Ansel, D., & Krachman, S. B. (2015). *Ready to be counted: The research case for education policy action on non-cognitive skills*. Boston, MA: Transforming Education.

Gardner, H. (1983). *Frames of mind: The theory of multiple intelligences*. New York, NY: Basic Books.

Garet, M. S., Cronen, S., Eaton, M., Kurki, A., Ludwig, M., Jones, W., . . . Sztejnberg, L. (2008). *The impact of two professional development interventions on early reading instruction and achievement* (NCEE 2008-4030). Washington, DC: National Center for Education Evaluation and Regional Assistance.

Garibaldi, M., Ruddy, S., Kendziora, K., & Osher, D. (2015). Assessment of climate and conditions for learning. In J. Durlak, C. Domitrovich, R. Weissberg, T. Gullotta, & P. Goren (Eds.), *The handbook of social and emotional learning: Research and practice* (pp. 348–358). New York, NY: Guilford.

Good, C., Aronson, J., & Inzlicht, M. (2003). Improving adolescents' standardized test performance: An intervention to reduce the effects of stereotype threat. *Journal of Applied Developmental Psychology, 24*, 645–662.

Gorrell, D. K. (1988). *The age of social responsibility: The social gospel in the Progressive Era, 1900–1920*. Macon, GA: Mercer University Press.

Gottfredson, D. C., Cook, T. D., Gardner, F. M., Gorman-Smith, D., Howe, G. W., Sandler, I. N., & Zafft, K. M. (2015). Standards of evidence for efficacy, effectiveness, and scale-up research in prevention science: Next generation. *Prevention Science, 16*, 893–926.

Graziano, P. A., Reavis, R. D., Keane, S. P., & Calkins, S. D. (2007). The role of emotion regulation in children's early academic success. *Journal of School Psychology, 45*, 3–19.

Greenberg, M. T., Weissberg, R. P., O'Brien, M. U., Zins, J. E., Fredericks, L., Resnik, H., & Elias, M. J. (2003). Enhancing school-based prevention and youth development through coordinated social, emotional, and academic learning. *The American Psychologist, 58*, 466–474.

Gross, J. J. (1999). Emotion regulation: Past, present, and future. *Cognition and Emotion, 13,* 551–573.

Gross, J. J., & Thompson, R. (2007). Emotion regulation: Conceptual foundations. In J. J. Gross (Ed.), *Handbook of emotion regulation* (pp. 3–24). New York, NY: Guilford.

Guttentag, R., & Ferrell, J. (2008). Children's understanding of anticipatory regret and disappointment. *Cognition and Emotion, 22,* 815–832.

Hafen, C. A., Allen, J. P., Gregory, A., Mikami, A. Y., Hamre, B., & Pianta, R. C. (2012, November). *Improving teaching quality in secondary schools through professional development: Evidence from two RCTs of the My Teaching Partner program (Study 1).* Paper presented at Association for Public Policy Analysis and Management Conference, Baltimore, MD. Retrieved from https://appam.confex.com/appam/2012/webprogram/

Hafen, C. A., Ruzek, E. A., Gregory, A., Allen, J. P., & Mikami, A. Y. (2015). Focusing on teacher-student interactions eliminates the negative impact of students' disruptive behavior on teacher perceptions. *International Journal of Behavioral Development, 39,* 426–431. doi:10.1177/0165025415579455

Hagelskamp, C., Brackett, M. A., Rivers, S. E., & Salovey, P. (2013). Improving classroom quality with the ruler approach to social and emotional learning: Proximal and distal outcomes. *American Journal of Community Psychology, 51,* 530–543.

Hagen, E. (2013). *Social and emotional learning: Comparing frameworks.* Minneapolis: University of Minnesota, Extension Center for Youth Development. Retrieved from http://www.extension.umn.edu/youth/research/sel/docs/issue-brief-comparing-frameworks.pdf

Haggerty, K., Elgin, J., & Woolley, A. (2011). *Social-emotional learning assessment measures for middle school youth.* Retrieved from http://www.search-institute.org/sites/default/files/a/DAP-Raikes-Foundation-Review.pdf

Han, S. S., & Weiss, B. (2005). Sustainability of teacher implementation of school-based mental health programs. *Journal of Abnormal Child Psychology, 33,* 665–679.

Harris, P. L. (1999). Individual differences in understanding emotion: The role of attachment status and psychological discourse. *Attachment & Human Development, 1,* 307–324.

Hart, P. M., Wearing, A. J., & Conn, M. (1995). Conventional wisdom is a poor predictor of the relationship between discipline policy, student misbehaviour and teacher stress. *British Journal of Educational Psychology, 65*(1), 27–48.

Heckman, J. J., & LaFontaine, P. A. (2010). The American high school graduation rate: Trends and levels. *Review of Economics and Statistics, 92,* 244–262.

Heckman, J. J., Stixrud, J., & Urzua, S. (2006). The effects of cognitive and noncognitive abilities on labor market outcomes and social behavior. *Journal of Labor Economics, 24,* 411–482.

Hedges, L. l. (2013). Recommendations for practice: Justifying claims of generalizability. *Educational Psychology Review, 25,* 331–337. doi:10.1007/s10648-013-9239-x

Hoffman, D. M. (2009). Reflecting on social emotional learning: A critical perspective on trends in the United States. *Review of Educational Research, 79,* 533–556.

Hoy, W., & Miskel, C. (2012). *Educational administration: Theory, research, and practice.* New York, NY: McGraw-Hill Education.

Humphrey, N., Kalambouka, A., Wigelsworth, M., Lendrum, A., Lennie, C., & Farrell, P. (2010). New beginnings: Evaluation of a short social–emotional intervention for primary-aged children. *Educational Psychology, 30,* 513–532.

Jagers, R. J., Harris, A., & Skoog, A. B. (2015). Social emotional learning in the middle school context. In J. Durlak, R. P. Weissberg, & T. Gullotta (Eds.), *Handbook of social and emotional learning* (pp. 167–180). New York, NY: Guilford.

Jennings, P. A., & Greenberg, M. T. (2009). The prosocial classroom: Teacher social and emotional competence in relation to student and classroom outcomes. *Review of Educational Research, 79,* 491–525.

Jones, S. M., & Bailey, R. (2016). *A developmental model of self-regulation for interventions and applied settings.* Manuscript submitted for publication.

Jones, S. M., & Bouffard, S. (2012). Social and emotional learning in schools: From programs to strategies. *Social Policy Report, 23*(4), 1–33.

Jones, S. M., Brown, J. L., & Aber, J. L. (2011). The longitudinal impact of a universal school-based social-emotional and literacy intervention: An experiment in translational developmental research. *Child Development, 82*, 533–554.

Kam, C. M., Wong, L. W., & Fung, K. (2011). Promoting social-emotional learning in Chinese schools: A feasibility study of PATHS implementation in Hong Kong. *International Journal of Emotional Education, 3*(1), 30–47.

Kann, L., Kinchen, S., Shanklin, S. L., Flint, K. H., Hawkins, J., Harris, W. A., & Zaza, S. (2013). *Youth risk behavior surveillance—United States, 2013.* Washington, DC: Centers for Disease Control and Prevention.

Kazdin, A. E., & Weisz, J. R. (1998). Identifying and developing empirically supported child and adolescent treatments. *Journal of Consulting and Clinical Psychology, 66*, 19–36.

Kellam, S., & Rebok, G. (1992). Building developmental and etiological theory through epidemiological based preventive intervention trials. In J. McCord & R. E. Tremblay (Eds.), *Preventing antisocial behavior: Interventions from birth through adolescence* (pp. 162–195). New York, NY: Neale Watson Academic.

Kendziora, K., Osher, D., & Chinen, M. (2008). *Student connection research: Final narrative report to the Spencer Foundation.* Washington, DC: American Institutes for Research.

Kidron, Y., & Osher, D. (2012). The history and direction of research about prosocial education. In P. M. Brown, A. Higgins-D'Alessandro, & M. Corrigan (Eds.), *Handbook of prosocial education* (pp. 51–70). Lanham, MD: Rowman & Littlefield.

Kliebard, H. M. (1986). *The struggle for the American curriculum: 1893–1958.* Boston, MA: Routledge & Kegan Paul.

Kolbe, L. J., Collins, J., & Cortese, P. (1997). Building the capacity for schools to improve the health of the nation: A call for assistance from psychologists. *The American Psychologist, 52*, 256–265.

Lang, P., Katz, Y., & Menezes, I. (Eds.). (1998). *Affective education: A comparative view.* London, England: Cassell.

Langdon, C. A. (1996). The third annual Phi Delta Kappan poll of teachers' attitudes towards public schools. *Phi Delta Kappan, 3*(78), 244–250.

Langeveld, J. H., Gundersen, K. K., & Svartdal, F. (2012). Social competence as a mediating factor in reduction of behavioral problems. *Scandinavian Journal of Educational Research, 56*, 381–399. doi:10.1080/00313831.2011.594614

Lazerson, M. (1971). *Origins of the urban school: Public education in Massachusetts, 1870–1915.* Cambridge, MA: Harvard University Press.

Lewin, K. (1935). *A dynamic theory of personality.* New York, NY: McGraw-Hill.

Lewin, K. (1947). Frontiers in group dynamics. II: Channels of group life; social planning and action research. *Human Relations, 1*, 143–153.

Lewin, K. (1951). *Field theory in social science.* New York, NY: Harper Torch.

Lewis, K. M., Schure, M. B., Bavarian, N., DuBois, D. L., Day, J., Ji, P., . . . Flay, B. R. (2013). Problem behavior and urban, low-income youth: A randomized controlled trial of Positive Action in Chicago. *American Journal of Preventive Medicine, 44*, 622–630.

Lippman, L. H., Ryberg, R., Carney, R., & Moore, K. A. (2015). *Workforce connections: Key "soft skills" that foster youth workforce success: Toward a consensus across fields.* Bethesda, MD: Child Trends.

Lubove, R. (1974). *The progressives and the slums: Tenement house reform in New York City, 1890–1917.* Westport, CT: Greenwood Press.

MacKinnon, D. P., & Lockwood, C. M. (2003). Advances in statistical methods for substance abuse prevention research. *Prevention Science, 4*, 155–171.

Martin, B. L., & Reigeluth, C. M. (1992). Affective education and the affective domain: Implications for instructional design theories and models. In C. M. Reigeluth (Ed.), *Instructional-design theories and models: A new paradigm of instructional theory* (Vol. 2, pp. 485–511). Hillsdale, NJ: Lawrence Erlbaum.

Masten, A. S. (2013). Risk and resilience in development. In P. D. Zelazo (Ed.), *Oxford handbook of developmental psychology: Vol 2. Self and other* (pp. 579–607). New York, NY: Oxford University Press.

McCormick, M. P., Cappella, E., O'Connor, E. E., & McClowry, S. G. (2015). Context matters for social-emotional learning: Examining variation in program impact by dimensions of school climate. *American Journal of Community Psychology, 56*, 101–119. doi:10.1007/s10464-015-9733-z

McEwen, B. S. (2016). In pursuit of resilience: Stress, epigenetics, and brain plasticity. *Annals of the New York Academy of Sciences, 1373*(1), 56–64. doi:10.1111/nyas.13020

McEwen, B. S., Bowles, N. P., Gray, J. D., Hill, M. N., Hunter, R. G., Karatsoreos, I. N., & Nasca, C. (2015). Mechanisms of stress in the brain. *Nature Neuroscience, 18*, 1353–1363.

McKay-Jackson, C. (2014). A critical approach to social emotional learning instruction through community-based service learning. *Journal of Transformative Education, 12*, 292–312. doi:10.1177/1541344614543191

McKown, C. (2015). Challenges and opportunities in the direct assessment of children's social and emotional comprehension. In J. A. Durlak, C. E. Domitrovich, R. P. Weissberg, & T. P. Gullotta (Eds.), *Handbook for social and emotional learning: Research and practice* (pp. 320–335). New York, NY: Guilford.

Meichenbaum, D. (1977). *Cognitive-behavior modification: An integrative approach.* New York, NY: Plenum.

Mihalic, S. (2004). The importance of implementation fidelity. *Emotional & Behavioral Disorders in Youth, 4*(4), 83–86.

Mihalic, S. F., & Elliott, D. S. (2015). Evidence-based programs registry: Blueprints for healthy youth development. *Evaluation and Program Planning, 48*, 124–131.

Mihalic, S. F., Fagan, A. A., & Argamaso, S. (2008). Implementing the LifeSkills Training Drug Prevention Program: Factors related to implementation fidelity. *Implementation Science, 3*(5), 1–16. doi:10.1186/1748-5908-3-5

Mikami, A. Y., Gregory, A., Allen, J. P., Pianta, R. C., & Lun, J. (2011). Effects of a teacher professional development intervention on peer relationships in secondary classrooms. *School Psychology Review, 40*, 352–366.

Mischel, W. (1973). Toward a cognitive social learning reconceptualization of personality. *Psychological Review, 80*, 252–283.

Montroy, J. J., Bowles, R. P., Skibbe, L. E., & Foster, T. D. (2014). Social skills and problem behaviors as mediators of the relationship between behavioral self-regulation and academic achievement. *Early Childhood Research Quarterly, 29*, 298–309.

Muncy, R. (1991). *Creating a female dominion in American reform, 1890–1935.* New York, NY: Oxford University Press.

Murphy, J., & Torre, D. (2013). Beyond the factors: The threads of school improvement. *International Journal of Education and Research, 1*(10), 1–20.

Nagaoka, J., Farrington, C. A., Ehrlich, S. B., & Heath, R. D. (2015). *Foundations for young adult success: A developmental framework.* Chicago, IL: University of Chicago, Consortium on Chicago School Research.

National Center for O*NET Development. (n.d.). *O*Net online.* Retrieved from https://www.onetonline.org/find/descriptor/browse/Skills/

National Research Council. (2009). *Transforming agricultural education for a changing world.* Washington, DC: National Academies Press.

National Research Council. (2012). *Education for life and work: Developing transferable knowledge and skills in the 21st century.* Retrieved from http://www.p21.org/storage/documents/ Presentations/NRC_Report_Executive_Summary.pdf

Nickerson, A. B., Mayer, M. J., Cornell, D. G., Jimerson, S. R., Osher, D., & Espelage, D. L. (in press). Violence prevention in schools and communities: Multicultural and contextual considerations. In M. Casas, L. Suzuki, C. Alexander, & M. Jackson (Eds.), *Handbook of multicultural counseling* (4th ed.). New York, NY: Sage.

O'Connell, M. E., Boat, T., & Warner, K. E. (Eds.). (2009). *Preventing mental, emotional, and behavioral disorders among young people: Progress and possibilities.* Washington, DC: National Academies Press.

Organisation for Economic Co-operation and Development. (2015). *Skills for social progress: The power of social and emotional skills.* Paris, France: OECD Skills Studies. doi:10.1787/9789264226159-en

Osher, D. (2012). Implementation in busy kitchens and swampy lowlands. *Social Policy Report, 26*(4), 23–24.

Osher, D., Bear, G., Sprague, J., & Doyle, W. (2010). How we can improve school discipline. *Educational Researcher, 39*(1), 48–58.

Osher, D., & Chasin, E. (2016). Bringing together schools and the community: The case of Say Yes to Education. In J. F. Zaff, E. Pufall Jones, A. E. Donlan, & S. A. Anderson (Eds.), *Optimizing child and youth development through comprehensive community initiatives* (pp. 72–104). New York, NY: Psychology Press.

Osher, D., Coggshall, J., Colombi, G., Woodruff, D., Francois, S., & Osher, T. W. (2012). Building school and teacher capacity to eliminate the school-to-prison pipeline. *Teaching Exceptional Children, 32*(2), 30–37.

Osher, D., Dwyer, K., & Jackson, S. (2004). *Safe, supportive, and successful schools step by step.* Longmont, CO: Sopris West.

Osher, D., Fisher, D., Amos, L., Katz, J., Dwyer, K., Duffey, T., & Colombi, G. D. (2015). *Addressing the root causes of disparities in school discipline: An educator's action planning guide.* Washington, DC: National Center on Safe Supportive Learning Environments.

Osher, D., Kendziora, K., & Friedman, L. (2014a). *Cross-district implementation summary: Social and emotional learning in eight school districts.* Washington, DC: American Institutes for Research.

Osher, D., Kendziora, K., & Friedman, L. (2014b). *Cross-district outcome evaluation report: Social and emotional learning in eight school districts.* Washington, DC: American Institutes for Research.

Osher, D., Poirier, J. M., Jarjoura, G. R., & Haight, K. (2014). *Follow-up assessment of conditions for learning in the Cleveland Metropolitan School District.* Washington, DC: American Institutes for Research.

Osher, D., Quinn, M. M., Poirier, J. M., & Rutherford, R. B. (2003). Deconstructing the pipeline: Using efficacy and effectiveness data and cost-benefit analyses to reduce minority youth incarceration. *New Directions for Youth Development, 99*, 91–120.

Osher, D., Sprague, J., Weissberg, R. P., Axelrod, J., Keenan, S., Kendziora, K., & Zins, J. E. (2008). A comprehensive approach to promoting social, emotional, and academic growth in contemporary schools. In A. Thomas & J. Grimes (Eds.), *Best practices in school psychology* (Vol. 4, pp. 1263–1278). Bethesda, MD: National Association of School Psychologists.

Partnership for 21st Century Skills. (2008). *21st Century skills, education, & competitiveness: A resource and policy guide.* Retrieved from http://www.p21.org/storage/documents/21st_ century_skills_education_and_competitiveness_guide.pdf

Partnership for 21st Century Skills. (2015). *21st Century student outcomes and support systems.* Retrieved from http://www.p21.org/storage/documents/1.__p21_framework_2-pager. pdf

Philliber Research Associates. (2013a). *Beyond content: Incorporating social and emotional learning into the strive framework. Volume II: A summary of measures by competency and stage of the cradle to career continuum.* Retrieved from http://www.strivetogether.org/sites/default/ files/images/Strive%20Together%20Volume%20II%20edited_0.pdf

Philliber Research Associates. (2013b). *Beyond content: Incorporating social and emotional learning into the strive framework. Volume III: A compendium of social and emotional competency measures.* Retrieved from http://www.strivetogether.org/sites/default/files/images/ Strive%20Together%20VolumeIII.pdf

Price, O. A. (2015). Financing and funding SEL initiatives. In J. A. Durlak, C. E. Domitrovich, R. P. Weissberg, & T. P. Gullotta (Eds.), *Handbook for social and emotional learning: Research and practice* (pp. 114–131). New York, NY: Guilford.

Reyes, M. R., Brackett, M. A., Rivers, S. E., Elbertson, N. A., & Salovey, P. (2012). The interaction effects of program training, dosage, and implementation quality on targeted student outcomes for the RULER approach to social and emotional learning. *School Psychology Review, 41*(1), 82–99.

Rimm-Kaufman, S. E., & Chiu, Y. I. (2007). Promoting social and academic competence in the classroom: An intervention study examining the contribution of the responsive classroom approach. *Psychology in the Schools, 44*, 397–413.

Rimm-Kaufman, S. E., Larsen, R. A., Baroody, A. E., Curby, T. W., Ko, M., Thomas, J. B., . . . DeCoster, J. (2014). Efficacy of the Responsive Classroom approach results from a 3-year, longitudinal randomized controlled trial. *American Educational Research Journal, 52*, 567–603.

Ris, E. W. (2015). Grit: A short history of a useful concept. *Journal of Educational Controversy, 10*, 1–18. Retrieved from http://cedar.wwu.edu/jec/vol10/iss1/3

Rittel, H. W., & Webber, M. M. (1973). Dilemmas in a general theory of planning. *Policy Sciences, 4*, 155–169.

Rivers, S. E., Brackett, M. A., Reyes, M. R., Elbertson, N. A., & Salovey, P. (2013). Improving the social and emotional climate of classrooms: A clustered randomized controlled trial testing the RULER approach. *Prevention Science, 14*, 77–87.

Roeser, R. W., Schonert-Reichl, K. A., Jha, A., Cullen, M., Wallace, L., Wilensky, R., . . . Harrison, J. (2013). Mindfulness training and reductions in teacher stress and burnout: Results from two randomized, waitlist-control field trials. *Journal of Educational Psychology, 105*, 787–804. doi:10.1037/a0032093

Rotheram-Borus, M. J., Bickford, B., & Milburn, N. (2001). Implementing a classroombased social skills training program in middle childhood. *Journal of Educational and Psychological Consultation, 12*, 91–111.

Rothstein, R. (2004). *Class and schools: Using social, economic, and educational reform to close the achievement gap.* Washington, DC: Economic Policy Institute.

Rutter, M. (1987). Psychosocial resilience and protective mechanisms. *American Journal of Orthopsychiatry, 57*, 316–331.

Ryan, W. (1972). *Blaming the victim.* New York, NY: Random House.

Saarni, C. (1999). *The development of emotional competence.* New York, NY: Guilford.

Salovey, P., & Mayer, J. D. (1990). Emotional intelligence. *Imagination, Cognition and Personality, 9*, 185–211.

Sameroff, A. (1975). Transactional models in early social relations. *Human Development, 18*, 65–79.

Scheerens, J. (1997). Conceptual models and theory-embedded principles on effective schooling. *School Effectiveness and School Improvement, 8*, 269–310.

Schneider, B., Judy, J., Ebmeye, C., & Broda, M. (2014). Trust in elementary and secondary urban schools: A pathway for student success and college ambition. In D. Van Maele, M. Van Houtte, & P. Forsyth (Eds.), *Trust and school life* (pp. 37–56). New York, NY: Springer.

Schonert-Reichl, K. A., & O'Brien, M. U. (2012). Social and emotional learning and prosocial education. In P. M. Brown, M. W. Corrigan, & A. Higgins-D'Alessandro (Eds.), *Handbook of prosocial education* (pp. 311–346). Lanham, MD: Rowman & Littlefield.

Schonfeld, D. J., Adams, R. E., Fredstrom, B. K., Weissberg, R. P., Gilman, R., Voyce, C., & Speese-Linehan, D. (2015). Cluster-randomized trial demonstrating impact on academic achievement of elementary social-emotional learning. *School Psychology Quarterly, 30*, 406–420. doi:10.1037/spq0000099

Shediac-Rizkallah, M. C., & Bone, L. R. (1998). Planning for the sustainability of community-based health programs: Conceptual frameworks and future directions for research, practice and policy. *Health Education Research, 13*, 87–108.

Shriver, T. P., & Weissberg, R. P. (1996, May 15). No new wars! *Education Week*. Retrieved from http://www.edweek.org/ew/articles/1996/05/15/34shrive.h15.html

Skelton, P., Seevers, B., Dormody, T., & Hodnett, F. (2012). A conceptual process model for improving youth science comprehension. *Journal of Extension, 50*(3), Article 3IAW1. Retrieved from http://www.joe.org/joe/2012june/iw1.php

Sklad, M., Diekstra, R., Ritter, M. D., Ben, J., & Gravesteijn, C. (2012). Effectiveness of school-based universal social, emotional, and behavioral programs: Do they enhance students' development in the area of skill, behavior, and adjustment? *Psychology in the Schools, 49*, 892–909. doi:10.1002/pits.21641

Spoth, R., Rohrbach, L. A., Greenberg, M., Leaf, P., Brown, C. H., Fagan, A., . . . Hawkins, J. D. (2013). Addressing core challenges for the next generation of Type 2 translation research and systems: The translation science to population impact (TSci Impact) framework. *Prevention Science, 14*, 319–351. doi:10.1007/s11121-012-0362-6

Stafford-Brizard, K. B. (2016). *Building blocks for learning: A framework for comprehensive student development.* Retrieved from http://www.turnaroundusa.org/wp-content/uploads/2016/03/Turnaround-for-Children-Building-Blocks-for-Learningx-2.pdf

Staker, H. (2011). *The rise of K–12 blended learning: Profiles of emerging models.* Mountain View, CA: Innosight Institute.

Stecher, B. M., & Hamilton, L. S. (2014). *Measuring hard-to-measure student competencies: A research and development plan.* Santa Monica, CA: RAND.

Steele, C. M. (2003). Through the back door to theory. *Psychological Inquiry, 14*, 314–317.

Steinberg, L., & Morris, A. S. (2001). Adolescent development. *Journal of Cognitive Education and Psychology, 2*(1), 55–87.

Stern, R. S., Harding, T. B., Holzer, A. A., & Elbertson, N. A. (2015). Current and potential uses of technology to enhance SEL: What's now and what's next? In J. A. Durlak, C. E. Domitrovich, R. P. Weissberg, & T. P. Gullotta (Eds.), *Handbook for social and emotional learning: Research and practice* (pp. 516–531). New York, NY: Guilford.

Sternberg, R. J. (1985). *Beyond IQ: A triarchic theory of human intelligence.* New York, NY: Cambridge University Press.

Swearer, S. M., Espelage, D. L., Vaillancourt, T., & Hymel, S. (2010). What can be done about school bullying? Linking research to educational practice. *Educational Researcher, 39*(1), 38–47.

Tamim, R. M., Bernard, R. M., Borokhovski, E., Abrami, P. C., & Schmid, R. F. (2011). What forty years of research says about the impact of technology on learning. *Review of Educational Research, 81*, 4–28.

Taylor, R., Oberle, E., Durlak, J. A., & Weissberg, R. P. (in press). *Promoting positive youth development through school-based social and emotional learning interventions: A meta-analysis of follow-up effects*. Chicago: Collaborative for Academic, Social, and Emotional Learning, University of Illinois at Chicago, Loyola University Chicago.

Thayer, L. (1976). *Affective education: Strategies for experiential learning*. Highland, CA: University Associates.

Thorndike, E. L. (1920). Intelligence and its uses. *Harper's Magazine, 140*, 227–235.

Tibbits, M. K., Bumbarger, B. K., Kyler, S. J., & Perkins, D. F. (2010). Sustaining evidence-based interventions under real-world conditions: Results from a large-scale diffusion project. *Prevention Science, 11*, 252–262.

Tolan, P. H. (2013). *Making and using lists of empirically tested programs: Value for violence interventions for progress and impact*. Washington, DC: National Academies Press.

Torrente, C., Nathanson, L., Rivers, S., & Brackett, M. (2015, March). *Testing causal impacts of a school-based SEL intervention using instrumental variable techniques*. Paper presented at the annual meeting of the Society for Research on Educational Effectiveness, Washington, DC.

Trilling, B., & Fadel, C. (2009). *21st Century skills: Learning for life in our times*. San Francisco, CA: Jossey-Bass/Pfeiffer.

Tschannen-Moran, M., & Gareis, C. R. (2015). Principals, trust, and cultivating vibrant schools. *Societies, 5*, 256–276.

Tseng, V., & Seidman, E. (2007). A systems framework for understanding social settings. *American Journal of Community Psychology, 39*, 217–228.

Tyack, D. (1992). Health and social services in public schools: Historical perspectives. *Future of Children, 2*, 19–31.

Tyack, D. B., & Cuban, L. (1995). *Tinkering toward utopia*. Cambridge, MA: Harvard University Press.

Tyack, D. B., & Tobin, W. (1994). The "grammar" of schooling: Why has it been so hard to change? *American Educational Research Journal, 31*, 453–479.

Wandersman, A., Chien, V., & Katz, J. (2012). Toward an evidence-based system for innovation support for implementing innovations with quality: Tools, training, technical assistance, and quality assurance/quality improvement. *American Journal of Community Psychology, 50*, 445–459.

Wanless, S. B., Groark, C. J., & Hatfield, B. E. (2015). Assessing organizational readiness. In J. A. Durlak, C. E. Domitrovich, R. P. Weissberg, & T. P. Gullotta (Eds.), *Handbook for social and emotional learning: Research and practice* (pp. 360–376). New York, NY: Guilford.

Weissberg, R. P., Durlak, J. A., Domitrovich, C. E., & Gullotta, T. P. (2015). Social and emotional learning: Past, present, and future. In J. A. Durlak, C. E. Domitrovich, R. P. Weissberg, & T. P. Gullotta (Eds.), *Handbook for social and emotional learning: Research and practice* (pp. 3–19). New York, NY: Guilford.

Weissberg, R. P., Walberg, H. J., O'Brien, M. U., & Kuster, C. B. (2003). *Long-term trends in the well-being of children and youth*. Washington, DC: Child Welfare League of America Press.

Werner, E. (1989). High-risk children in young adulthood: A longitudinal study from birth to 32 years. *American Journal of Orthopsychiatry, 59*, 72–81.

What Works Clearinghouse. (2007). *WWC intervention report: Caring school community*. Retrieved from http://ies.ed.gov/ncee/wwc/Docs/InterventionReports/WWC_Caring_School_042307.pdf

What Works Clearinghouse. (2014). *What Works Clearinghouse procedures and standards handbook*. Washington, DC: Institute of Education Sciences. Retrieved from http://ies.ed.gov/ncee/wwc/pdf/reference_resources/wwc_procedures_v3_0_draft_standards_handbook.pdf

Widen, S. C., & Russell, J. A. (2010). Children's scripts for social emotions: Causes and consequences are more central than are facial expressions. *British Journal of Developmental Psychology, 28*, 565–581.

Williamson, A. A., Modecki, K. L., & Guerra, N. G. (2015). SEL programs in high school. In J. Durlak, C. Domitrovich, & T. Gullotta (Eds.), *Handbook of social emotional learning* (pp. 181–196). New York, NY: Guilford.

Yaqing, M. (2015, April). *Social and emotional learning in China.* Paper presented at the annual meeting of the American Educational Research Association, Chicago, IL.

Yoder, N. (2014). *Teaching the whole child: Instructional practices that support social-emotional learning in three teacher evaluation frameworks.* Washington, DC: American Institutes for Research.

Yoon, K. S., Duncan, T., Lee, S. W. Y., Scarloss, B., & Shapley, K. (2007). *Reviewing the evidence on how teacher professional development affects student achievement* (Issues & Answers, REL 2007, No. 033). Washington, DC: Institute of Education Sciences.

Zaslow, M., Mackintosh, B., Mancoll, S., & Mandell, S. (2015). Federal policy initiatives and children's SEL. In J. A. Durlak, C. E. Domitrovich, R. P. Weissberg, & T. P. Gullotta (Eds.), *Handbook of social and emotional learning: Research and Practice* (pp. 549–565). New York, NY: Guilford.

Zigler, E. (1973). Motivational factors in the performance of the retarded child. In F. Richardson (Ed.), *Brain and intelligence: The ecology of child development* (pp. 59–69). Hyattsville, MD: National Educational Press.

Zigler, E., Abelson, W. D., & Seitz, V. (1973). Motivational factors in the performance of economically disadvantaged children on the Peabody Picture Vocabulary Test. *Child Development, 44,* 294–303.

Zigler, E., & Trickett, P. K. (1978). IQ, social competence, and evaluation of early childhood intervention programs. *The American Psychologist, 33,* 789–798.

Zilversmit, A. (1993). *Changing schools: Progressive education theory and practice, 1930–1960.* Chicago, IL: University of Chicago Press.

IV. The Changing Attention to Diversity and Differences

Chapter 18

Gender and Education[1]

Lucy E. Bailey
Oklahoma State University

Karen Graves
Denison University

The authors describe broad patterns and key developments in gender and education scholarship to provide an overview of the state of the field. They incorporate historical developments shaping research patterns, broad tensions and shifts, and emerging trajectories in inquiry. Cognizant that reviews are inherently political endeavors in both reflecting—and creating—"the field," the authors suggest that reviews such as this one are inevitably partial and political, even as they provide useful insights into scholarly trends. The dynamic body of work that constitutes what the authors refer to as "gender and education" scholarship (writ large) encompasses diverse inquiries, theoretical investments, sites of analysis, and conceptions of gender that go beyond a straightforward reporting of women's and girls' gradual progress over time in accessing education. The authors argue that gender remains a central force in organizing social relations and educational processes with an array of implications for lived experience that merit sustained scrutiny.

I think it is best to perceive us not as receiving an education, but claiming one.

—Adrienne Rich (1977)

Feminist poet Adrienne Rich's powerful 1977 address to the graduating class of Douglass College, "Claiming an Education," captures her critique of inequitable educational structures and the spirit of feminist advocacy central to the history of gender and education scholarship (see Rich, 1979). Like other feminist scholars active in this period of the women's movement, Rich traced patriarchal practices across the development and evolution of education that shaped girls' and

Review of Research in Education
March 2016, Vol. 40, pp. 682–722
DOI: 10.3102/0091732X16680193
© 2016 AERA. http://rre.aera.net

women's lives and opportunities. While many advocates champion education as an instrument of democracy and a great "social equalizer," feminist activists and scholars in the 1960s and 1970s detailed the array of inequitable practices on the basis of sex (and its gendered assumptions) that were commonplace in education: women's and girls' perceived inferiority, their historical exclusions from schooling, male-dominated teaching and leadership, curricular biases and erasure of women's accomplishments, and schooling practices that constrained female students' development and opportunities. In her address, Rich used the gendered terms "receiving" and "claiming" to urge women to resist their historic positioning as passive subjects and to seize and direct their learning. While gender and education is now a vast, dynamic body of inquiry that transcends its historical focus on women, Rich's critique of constitutive sex- and gender-based inequities and her vision of education as a site of transformative potential remain enduring facets of contemporary analyses. In this view, education is a key site for both reproducing and interrupting inequities.

This chapter describes broad patterns and key developments in gender and education scholarship to provide an overview of the state of the field. It incorporates a feminist perspective in tracing historical developments shaping research patterns, broad tensions and shifts, and current trajectories in inquiry. As we have mentioned elsewhere (e.g., L. E. Bailey & Graves, in press), Lather (1999) suggests that reviews are inherently political endeavors in both reflecting—and creating—"the field." In that spirit, we suggest that reviews such as this one are inevitably partial and political, even as they provide useful insights into scholarly trends. The dynamic body of work that constitutes what we refer to as "gender and education" scholarship (writ large) encompasses diverse inquiries, theoretical investments, sites of analysis, and conceptions of "gender" that morph even as we write. In addition to this conceptual complexity, as Glasser and Smith (2008) indicate, education researchers often use gender in "vague" ways, as if the term were synonymous with sex, or as if its meaning were static and assured (p. 343). As historian Joan Scott (1986) noted regarding the use of gender in research more broadly, the strong associations among the terms *gender, sex,* and, historically, *woman* are apparent in scholars' common and seamless interchanging, but not explicit clarification (Glasser & Smith, 2008), of their terms. Yet concretizing terms or choices in search engines cannot solidify the range of conceptual nuances scholars intend within their research or the contours of the field, given its broad and interdisciplinary reach and its constantly evolving nature. Scholarship that takes up gender issues includes projects such as those analyzing the social implications of biological sex differences between males and females, those focusing on women, and those employing contemporary theories of gender as a fluid, heteroglossic, and always unstable entity. For some, such terms are inherently unstable or hold multiple meanings within the same project. This synthesis primarily uses the term gender as a referent to encompass these diverse expressions in scholarship, which, in their very multiplicity, have cumulatively enriched education research, theory, and practice in significant, if underappreciated, ways.[2]

This chapter is organized into three main sections that discuss the development of "the field," significant transformations, and ongoing sites of research. This introductory section provides a roadmap of the overview and key topics. In the next section, we turn to the development of the field, by first describing general trends and transformations in scholarship and terminology to convey broad shifts, and then examining research on sex and/or gender in several educational journals with a long historical reach. This feminist approach embraces a generous historical view of the roots, scope, and emergence of gender as an animating force in inquiry. Consistent with feminist scholars' critiques of the limits of the "wave" metaphor for capturing the diverse scope and character of women's activism historically (Laughlin et al., 2010), we point to selected education research on women/men, girls/boys, and gender and sex (both terms surface) in the 19th century that suggests diverse origins informing the field.

Next, we address the 1970s development of gender and education as a recognized focus of study fueled by feminist activists invested in women's issues and empowerment, which challenged and transcended disciplinary boundaries. The emergence of women's studies and other interdisciplinary fields of study with commitments to education, advocacy, and justice on behalf of disempowered groups (e.g., African American studies, American Indian studies, ethnic studies) was foundational to this development. While women's and gender studies scholars would argue that education has always been shaped, indeed constituted, by race, class, gender, sexuality, and nationality (among other embodied, theoretical, and epistemological forces), scholarship that intentionally highlighted and traced those forces attained greater visibility during the 1970s. We describe generative critiques of education research and practice (L. Bailey, 2007) and the inquiries undertaken in this vibrant period of social transformation that focused on women and girls, furthered analyses of sex roles that had long characterized gender education research, and examined educational access and equity in the spirit of Rich's classic essay. We highlight key tensions that shaped and expanded research in those decades, from a focus on sex differences and roles rooted in biology to conceptions of gender as socially constructed. Significant for the field's development were the sustained critiques that women of color brought to bear on the homogenous conceptions of "women" dominating White, middle-class research imaginaries to consider how diverse epistemologies, intersecting identities, and social locations—race, sexuality, class, religion, dis/ability, nationality—profoundly shape lived experience and positioning in power relations, the sources of oppression one identifies as most critical, strategies for coalitions and advocacy, and multidimensional understanding of gendered phenomena (e.g., M. L. Anderson & Collins, 1992; Anzaldúa, 1987; Baca Zinn, 1980; Crenshaw, 1989; hooks, 1984; Hull, Scott, & Smith, 1982/1993; Lorde, 1984; Zinn & Dill, 1994). This theorizing influenced many academic fields, including education.

In the second main section, we note a variety of theoretical and topical "turns" fueled by social movements, historical developments, and the crisis of representation in the 1970s and beyond. These late-20th-century shifts expanded scholars' approaches to gender research through broadening conceptions of gender (as well as sex; e.g., Butler, 1990) and the sites in which it is imagined, investigated, and theorized. In addition to the turn from "sex" to "women" to "gender" as conceptual sites of inquiry across the 1970s and 1980s and the deepening of research grounded in intersectionality (Crenshaw, 1989), the expansion to critical men and masculinity studies during the late 1980s and 1990s has shaped research contours, as have the theories and methodologies available for analyzing gendered phenomena (e.g., postcolonial, poststructural; standpoint; affectual; spatial; materialist). We highlight examples of such theoretical productivity and tensions shaping approaches to recurring educational issues.

The third major section of the chapter is devoted to examples of gendered research that display the reach of the field, ranging from the experiences and institutional roles of diverse educational subjects to varied educational practices and processes. Topics include research methodology, body politics, sex education, single-sex education, teen pregnancy and mothering, pedagogy, leadership, corporatization and accountability, extracurricular activities such as sports and beauty pageants, heteronormativity, policy and law, and international and transnational issues. The significance of gendered violence (e.g., Messner, Greenberg, & Peretz, 2015), varied technologies such as social media and the underrepresentation of students and faculty of color and other women/girls in science, technology, engineering, and math (STEM) fields have also garnered attention (e.g., Bystydzienski & Bird, 2006). In addition to analyzing diverse institutional sites, scholars have long noted the power of informal educational vehicles such as reading groups, popular culture, video games, music, and toys (e.g., DuCille, 1994; Peril, 2002; Trier-Bieniek & Leavy, 2014) to teach lessons about social norms and identities. In the latter part of this section, we turn to gendered critiques of neoliberal processes that shape education and conclude with emerging trajectories foundational to rethinking previous work and for moving forward.

As research has expanded, scholars have paused to assess and synthesize the state of educational knowledge related to gender at different points in time. For example, some have conducted meta- or content analyses of gender topics (including women's issues and feminist analysis) in select journals in fields such as adult education (e.g., Clover, 2010; Hayes, 1991, 1992; Hayes & Smith, 1990, 1994) and higher education (e.g., Hart, 2006; Townsend, 1993; Twombly, 1993). Education journals have published special issues to highlight particular dynamics in their fields while feminist journals (e.g., *Signs*) remain instrumental arenas for gendered theorizing of educational practices. The diversity of sites and topics offer insight into the scope of developments. For example, topics range from "Women in Schools and Society" (*Council on Anthropology and Education Quarterly*, 1975, Volume 6, Number 3), to feminist issues in education (*Harvard Educational Review* [*HER*], 1979, Volume 49, Number 4, and 1980, Volume 50, Number 1), engineering (e.g., *European Journal of Engineering Education*, 2005, Volume 30, Number 4), leadership (*Journal of Educational Administration*, 2010, Volume 48, Number 6), broadening opportunities in computer science (e.g., *ACM Transactions on Computing Education*, 2011, Volume 11, Number 2), and writing (*Journal of Writing Research*, 2012, Volume 3, Number 3).[3]

Editors have compiled gender and education dictionaries and encyclopedias (e.g., Bank, 2007; Eisenmann, 1998; Martinez-Alemán & Renn, 2002) and incorporated educational issues, policies, and experiences into encyclopedias focused more broadly on gender and sexuality (e.g., Kramarae & Spender, 2000; Naples, Hoogland, Wickramasinghe, & Wong, in press) and men and masculinities (e.g., Flood, Gardiner, Pease, & Pringle, 2007; Kimmel & Aronson, 2003). In addition, scholars have published collections focused on topical issues (e.g., Arnot & Mac an Ghaill, 2006; Fennell & Arnot, 2008; B. Francis & Skelton, 2001; Jossey-Bass, 2002; C. Skelton, Francis, & Sumulyan, 2006; Woyshner & Gelfond, 1998) as well as handbooks (S. Klein et al., 2007). Some works have also been revised. For example, collaborators revised the *Education Feminism Reader* (Stone, 1994) recently (see Thayer-Bacon, Stone, & Sprecher, 2013) to preserve access to classic readings and expand them to reflect contemporary trends. Gender scholarship is a field in motion.

We began with a general search of the *Education Research Complete* database, as one way to get a sense of the expanse of the field. This initial search revealed patterns in particular journals that we were interested in for this study: *American Educational Research Journal* (*AERJ*), *Educational Researcher*, *Review of Educational Research* (*RER*), and *Review of Research in Education*. This information—combined with a review of the full runs of *Gender and Education, History of Education Quarterly*, the *Journal of Education*, and the *Journal of Negro Education* (*JNE*), as well as surveys of feminist journals in print since the 1970s that were influential for gendered scholarship (e.g., *Signs, Feminist Formations*)—formed the foundation of our work to identify and select themes for this chapter. We supplemented these findings with additional searches of the EBSCOhost, Education Full Text, and Education Research Complete databases to track research on particular lines of inquiry as they emerged, including targeted searches of educational psychology, higher education, and science education journals. Given their prominence in the field, we also ran targeted searches of *Equity & Excellence in Education, HER*, and *Teachers College Record* (*TCR*) and varied journals (e.g., *Race and Ethnicity in Education* and the *NASPA Journal About Women in Higher Education*) that publish articles on women, gender, or intersectional analyses. We found the long runs of the *Journal of Education* and *RER* useful in helping establish a trajectory of research on gender and education and drew from our recent collaborative work on "Gendering History" (Bailey & Graves, in press) to consider a comprehensive historical overview. We analyzed the complete run of *Gender and Education* as a central, dedicated space for tracking contemporary developments in the field post-1989 and selected a variety of monographs and edited collections to represent analyses of issues more detailed than journal articles can provide. Finally, we reviewed online programs for the American Educational Research Association's (AERA) conferences and conference themes, presidential addresses and *Brown* lectures, and the scholarship of colleagues recognized with the AERA Distinguished Contributions to Gender Equity in Education Research Award to track areas of emphasis over time and to determine the extent to which gender analysis has figured into prominent scholarship within the organization. The journals we reviewed were all published in English and focused primarily on American trends.

DEVELOPMENT OF "THE FIELD"

An important characteristic of gender research is the sometimes concurrent, overlapping, and contested rather than solely progressive nature of the topical and theoretical investments the body of work reflects. Particular topics of inquiry, such as sexism, marginalization, sex differences, and inequities or progress in educational access, structure, and practice (e.g., Solomon, 1985) significant to early research recur across the historical landscape and thus endure in scholarship as well. For instance, scholars chart girls' and women's struggles and successes around the globe to access forms of education (L. Cooper, 2013; A. Fuller, Turbin, & Johnston, 2013; Hatoss & Huijser, 2010; Rezai-Rashti, 2015; Tamim, 2013) or professional opportunities (e.g., *Advancing Women in Leadership Journal*; *NASPA Journal About Women in Higher Education*; McNae & Vali, 2015) in male-dominated educational contexts. Alongside these key foci on access, equity, or lived experience, others analyze gendered processes (rather than, or in addition to, individuals or groups) such as discourses, relations, and practices that shape such experiences, education research, and practice (e.g., Davies, 1997; Edwards, 1990; Johannesburg, 1994; Reay, 2002; Thorne, 1993). Indeed, scholars have traced across decades and fields the ideal of the educated subject and the institution as constitutively gendered and/or patriarchal (e.g., Dzuback, 2003; J. R. Martin, 1985; Rich, 1979).

Such inquiries reflect varied theoretical traditions that have been deeply contested in the evolution of feminist, women's, and gender scholarship (e.g., Alcoff, 1988; Butler, 1994; Braidotti & Butler, 1994; Clegg, 2006; Rasmussen, 2009) and capture another key characteristic of the field. The varied frameworks that have been used for theorizing and studying women's and gender issues in education include biological essentialism; Black feminist theory; social constructionism; social reproduction; and standpoint, queer, affect, poststructuralist, postcolonial, and materialist theories, among others. These approaches are sometimes directly at odds, offering conflicting views of the gendered subject with different agendas and aims. Concerns have developed regarding research that displaces women's experiences and the enlightenment subject of "woman" in the service of a theoretical approach that deconstructs the category and furthers gendered discursive investigations even though She has not yet achieved full equity (e.g., Alcoff, 1988; Anyon, 1994; Clegg, 2006). Other research draws out productive tensions regarding intersectional and contextually nuanced analyses for gendered knowledge (e.g., Ali, Mirza, Phoenix, & Ringrose, 2010), the boy turn (Reed, 1999; Weaver-Hightower, 2003), divergent intellectual and political projects that animate philosophically diverse concepts of gender (Butler, 1994; Braidotti & Butler, 1994), and questions regarding the enduring salience of gender, among others. For example, postcolonial theorizing (e.g., McClintock, Mufti, & Shohat, 1997; Mohanty, 1997, 2004; Narayan, 1997; Narayan & Harding, 2000; Spivak, 1988) underscores the insufficiencies of gender as a sole analytic and displaces the Western subject—including the Western feminist/gender theorist—to interrogate the legacies of colonialism and foreground the epistemologies, representations, and experiences of women in postcolonial contexts, including Indigenous women in the United States (e.g., Mihesuah, 1998, 2003).

To add to this complexity, approaches to the study of gender may reflect empirical endeavors with little overt focus on theory, mobilize poststructural conceptions of subjectivity and epistemology (St. Pierre & Pillow, 2000), or apply new materialist conceptions of ontology with gendered implications to education research and practice that rely on conceptions of gender dislodged from bodies, gendered material assemblages, or postgender theorizing (e.g., Coole & Frost, 2010; L. Cooper, 2013; Taylor & Hughes, 2016). Often interdisciplinary endeavors, gendered inquiries invite and nourish research in a range of sites. In the wake of claims that we have arrived in a postracial, postgender, postfeminist era, the robust heterogeneous brew of inquiries and theoretical investments evident across the research landscape reflects productive tensions in a significant, generative site of scholarship.

Theoretically Imbued and Shifting Conceptions of Gender

How scholars have conceptualized the very concept of gender as a site of study and analytic tool has varied theoretically, culturally, and historically. One major shift across the evolution of "gendered" scholarship is disrupting and expanding the units of analysis that scholars view as consequential constructs and sites of inquiry (e.g., biological sex, woman, gender, man, transgender, postgender) on which such scholarship rests. The tapestry of gendered research focused on women/girls and men/boys often proceeded as if the categories captured relatively static, biological, and binary designations. Productive early scholarship, such as Woody's (1929) ambitious historical overview of American women's educational access, exemplifies both investment in "women" as a meaningful category of inquiry and the use of the term as if it held a fixed and self-evident meaning.

During and after the 1970s, feminist interventions in education and research were instrumental for highlighting women's exclusions from educational practice and knowledge and dislodging artificially linked conceptions of biology as "destiny" (sex) from social processes (gender) that constrained and prescribed women's and men's development. They worked to untether the category "sex" as an assumed biological designation based on physicality and physiology from "gender" as a constellation of socially constructed, malleable norms and expectations commonly associated with biological sex. Much research and activism during this period was concerned with building long-neglected knowledge about women, critiquing the patriarchal logics and biological essentialism often used to justify differential treatment of men and women ("nature"), and tracing familial, social, and institutional forces (nurture) that led to gender norms and roles as well as sexism, discrimination, and structural inequities. Simone de Beauvoir's (1949) classic phrase, "One is not *born*, but rather *becomes*, a woman" (italics added), captures this effort to dislodge the social from the biological.

Conceptions of sex and gender (and woman; see Riley, 2003) are thus theoretically imbued. Furthermore, they are always inflected with or interwoven with conceptions of class, sexuality, ethnicity, and race, among other subjectivities, whether or not such categories are explicitly marked. Decades of theoretical developments have produced new conceptions of sex, gender, and the gendered educational subject that have been transformative for how scholars imagine and undertake their inquiries. Scott argued that gender remains a "useful" category of analysis only if its meanings in particular materials, sites, and inquiries remain open, elastic, contextual—and critical (Scott, 1986, 2010a). In her vision, the meaning and salience of gender must emerge in situ, in practice, and in relation. Substantial contemporary scholarship evinces this critical, dynamic, and contextual lens. Some continue to wield "gender" as if synonymous with "sex" (Glasser & Smith, 2008; Scott, 2010a) and, in particular, Woman, while others interrogate and deconstruct binaries to embrace and analyze gendered multiplicities and heteroglossic subjectivities (e.g., Cobbett, 2013; B. Francis, 2010; B. Francis, Burke, & Read, 2014; K. Fuller, 2014; Perry, 2013; Wohlwend, 2012) that have become available through late modernity, neoliberalism, and globalization (e.g., Arnot & Mac an Ghaill, 2006). In Scott's vision, gender is—and should be—endlessly dynamic, potentially transgressive, and/or heteroglossic (B. Francis, 2010) rather than static and essentialized.

Furthermore, varied scholars outside the field of education, such as feminist biologists (e.g., Fausto-Sterling, 1993, 2000) and philosophers (e.g., Butler, 1990), have shaped contemporary theorizing through deconstructing the category "sex" as a biological and binary essence and theorizing it, too, as an entity that humans imagine, create, and through actions and repetition, associate with bodies.

In recent years, scholars have grappled with the public sensibility that we have arrived in a postfeminist/postgender era in which one can "disidentify" (Mayo, 2000) from gender as a social category of belonging because policy and social changes have enabled women and girls (and boys/men) to expand their roles, choices, and life trajectories (McRobbie, 2009) and "have it all" (Pomerantz & Raby, 2011). This postgender discourse suggests that equity initiatives may no longer be necessary if women and girls can freely shed the sexist or gendered constraints of the past to invent, seize, and actualize a range of possible selves and a degree of agency, and educational and social mobility (Arnot & Mac an Ghaill, 2006; McRobbie, 2009). Indeed, by a range of measures, women's inroads into fields previously dominated by men seem to signal multidimensional progress. Yet some suggest the dangers of this postgender "girl power" discourse (A. Brown & Thomas, 2014; Pomerantz & Raby, 2011) because it obscures the limits of individual agency, the material forces that shape the lived realities of diversely positioned people (Thomas, 2011), shifting conceptions of gendered subjectivities, and ever-evolving expressions of the relations of power in a neoliberal era (e.g., Davies, 2007; Ringrose, 2007). The contextual conditions of people's lives, their networks, resources, race, class, ethnicity, sexuality, among other factors, shape and constrain which selves and futures are available.

An Origin Story of Multiplicity

Education research related to sex/gender preceded its concentration as an area of study in the 1970s. Journals such as the *Journal of Education* (founded in 1875), the *RER* (founded in 1931), the *Journal of Higher Education* (founded in 1930), the *JNE* (founded in 1932), and *Science Education* (founded in 1916) reflect a scattered histo-riography focusing on sex and gender as categories of interest in educational phe-nomena. As Schoenfeld (2016) notes in his review of early-20th-century AERA presidential addresses, even as educators set "different proficiency standards for boys and girls" at the time, "the issue of gender differences would take a half century to emerge as a research issue" (p. 106). The intensity of the focus on sex or gender as salient variables in such research varies considerably. Some research analyzes sex dif-ferences between girls and boys on particular measures as their primary units of anal-ysis, while others include sex as only one variable among others in exploring a particular educational matter. Other studies consider the educational implications of particular aspects of sex/gender.

One source that provides insights into early gendered educational concerns is the *Journal of Education*. Our keyword search using the term "gender" surfaced 143 arti-cles across 130 years of circulation, generally declining in number across the century. This decline is at odds with the broader expansion of education research with atten-tion to gender after 1970. The articles falling within search parameters between 1881 and 1899 reflect the conceptions of sex and gender as relatively interchangeable bio-logical designations with social implications, such as emphasizing the responsibility of teachers of both "genders" to serve as role models. The topics appearing before 1900 focus on teacher issues, single-sex education and coeducation, sex or gender differences, gender roles, equity and discrimination, biography, and curriculum. *Science Education* published 59 related articles between 1929 and 1959. The majority focused on sex as one compelling variable among others of interest. Only one explic-itly addressed discrimination against women, specifically, limited opportunities in chemistry (Oppe, 1946).

The existence of coeducational common schools since the first half of the 19th century did not prevent tensions about this institutional structure from emerging in public forums late in the 19th century and seeping into the Progressive Era (Tyack & Hansot, 1990). Tyack and Hansot (1990) tied such tensions to investment in school-ing as a "repository of hopes and anxieties about the gender order of the larger soci-ety" (p. 5). The gender-related topic appearing most frequently across the history of the *Journal of Education* was single-sex/coeducation issues at different levels of school-ing. Most of the 47 articles on this topic were concentrated between 1881 and 1930. The *AERJ* evidenced this topic as well, which surfaced again when debates about single-sex education rekindled in the 1990s (e.g., Arms, 2007; Morse, 1998; Reay, 1990; M. Sadker & Sadker, 1994) and yet again when theoretical or transgender critiques of sex/gender binaries constitutive of schooling structures emerged in the 2010s (Cohen, 2012; Jackson, 2010). Some early-20th-century articles provided brief updates regarding boys' schools or ladies' seminaries or new coeducational trends. Others revealed dialogue about coeducation's growing presence and promise, lurking dangers, implications for learning, or its lack of benefit for either sex, particularly at the high school/college levels ("Segregation in high schools," 1910; "Shameful Wesleyan," 1909; Wells, 1909; "Women's influence not desired," 1910). Some articles framed educational issues explicitly in terms of equity and discrimination. For example, several authors advocated for coeducation on the basis of its common good, reported on "gender" discrimination in pay, or argued that "dedication and commitment" rather than "gender" (Bergen, 1885) should dictate who is entitled to teach.

Teachers were a dominant theme between 1881 and 1930. The idea of Woman as agent of knowledge was slow to gain purchase historically, as Tuana (1993), Munro (1998), and Weiler and Middleton (1999) have argued; however, between 1880 and 1930, the proportion of female teachers in the United States increased from 55% to 75% (Blount, 1998). This "feminization of teaching" prompted articles in the *Journal of Education* focused on teacher salaries, civil rights, preparation and work, marital status, and resistance to the influx of female teachers. None of these articles referred to race. Contemporary scholarship provides essential context for the intersecting economic, racial, and regional influences of these trends (Clifford, 2014; Fultz, 1995; Herbst, 1989; Hoffman, 1981; Rury, 1991; Walker, 2001, 2005, 2013). Some forces propelling the shift are well known, including schooling expansion, the perception that women's nurturing role in the home or community would extend organically to the schools, women's affordability as workers, and men's gravitation to other occupations. Blount (1998) also attributes the increase to women's seizing of opportunities to live independently, earn wages, advance their educations, and contribute to the betterment of others—as A. Cooper (1892) envisioned for African American women's role in social uplift. Articles reflect public support for equal pay for female teachers, as well as social anxieties regarding their feminizing influence in schools. Such concerns about feminization resurfaced in subsequent decades, and in recent years as the numbers of female students increased (Arnot & Mac an Ghaill, 2006; Leathwood & Read, 2009).

Enduring questions regarding which women were "fit" to teach (Blount, 2005), and in which educational spaces, recurred between the 1930s and 1950s—just as they continue today. Of the 39 articles in *RER* focused on sex or gender issues prior to the 1960s, 11 were concerned with teacher issues, particularly debating whether to hire married women and local residents to teach. At times the consequences of these decisions seemed dire, as one author conveyed: Local teachers were "difficult for the board, disastrous to the community, unsatisfactory for teacher's welfare, bad for the children, and a nightmare to the superintendent" (Cooke, 1937, p. 267). This focus was tied to the broader phenomenon that some historians describe as a "masculinity crisis," fueled by the perception that men were losing their traditional claim on political, economic, and social power as women's access to suffrage and higher education increased—a concern echoed today (see "Turns and Transformations" section). In the interwar years, school systems debated whether to drop marriage bans as some challenged the long-held expectation that women teachers remain single (Blount, 1998). Reports variously questioned the mental health of married teachers (Anderson, 1937), dismissed the relevance of marital status for teaching efficacy (Cooke, 1937; Cooke & Simms, 1940), described legal implications of hiring (Cooke, Knox, & Libby, 1943), or advocated for hiring all qualified teachers in a period of teacher shortage (Cooke, Cardwell, & Dark, 1946).

Other topics appearing in early issues of these education journals include sex differences in intelligence, sex discrimination in grading, college women's academic achievement, critiques of the feminine curriculum of high schools, and notable women leaders. In these journals, intersectional perspectives on "women's" experiences were largely absent, conveying historic foci on White, middle-class women without explicit marking of race and class, which are nevertheless constitutive (e.g., Fine, Weis, Powell, & Wong, 1997; Frankenberg, 1993; Morrison, 1992).

The *JNE* represents an important historical intersectional perspective often invisible or excluded in scholarship that, like the journals cited above, render Whiteness invisible and foreground gender as a unidimensional concept rather than a site of intersectional and multidimensional meanings imbued with racialized, classed, and religious standpoints (among others). For example, the journal featured two articles focused on race and gender in its first issue (Daniel, 1932; Hudson, 1932) regarding women's reading interests and personality differences between delinquent and other boys. A search of the full run of the journal from 1932 to 2016 revealed 163 articles addressing gender issues, with the majority focusing on African American girls and women.[4] Articles that address the education of African American boys and men surface throughout and constitute a significant percentage (17%) of the gender-related articles.

Researchers in these early years often expressed the conviction that social factors, including education, can shape differences between men/boys and girls/women. As a brief article concerned with "sissies" and "tomboys" expresses, such gendered "difference is only acquired during childhood through an improper teaching" (Laws, 1938, p. 67). Such wording reflects investment in a binary sex system and increasingly homophobic social norms governing proper behavior, as authors began to attribute such behaviors to social rather than biological factors.

In the early 20th century, psychologists Willystine Goodsell, Helen T. Wooley, and Leta S. Hollingsworth refuted the idea of mental differences between the sexes purported by G. Stanley Hall and Edward L. Thorndike (Graves, 1998; Tyack & Hansot, 1990). As Goodsell (1923) observed,

Obviously Dr. Hall has elevated regard for the sex and maternal functions of woman into a cult which profoundly affects his conception of her entire education. . . . Yet with entire seriousness, the theory is advanced as modern, being garbed in a dubiously scientific dress of biology and psychology. (p. 68)

Over half of the 203 gender articles published in the *Journal of Educational Psychology* from its founding in 1910 until 2016 address human sex differences rooted in learning and achievement. Eight studies published between 1912 and 1941 focused on comparing boys' and girls' learning capacities, interests, and academic success (e.g., Bell, 1918). Interest in this area of study endures, with 14 articles appearing in the 1980s, 33 in the 1990s, and 57 between 2000 and 2016. Studies in this journal that address gender stereotypes, student attitudes, and the importance of self-concept appeared in 1981 and after.

The Emergence of a Sustained Field of Study

While research trends prior to the 1960s demonstrated the gendered imaginaries fueling recurring interest in sex differences, appropriate social roles, and women's educational access and constraints (e.g., Donovan, 1938; Flexner, 1959; Woody, 1929), the strands of gendered inquiry did not coalesce into a sustained focus of study until the mid-20th century. Scholars generally situate the development of the interdisciplinary and transdisciplinary study of "gender and education" during the 1960s and 1970s. In this vibrant period of social activism, change agents within and outside the academy challenged enduring scientific and religious claims that stretched back centuries regarding women's intellectual and corporeal inferiorities (Tuana, 1993). Scholars concerned with widespread social, legal, and educational inequities critiqued claims of "objectivity" and "neutrality" in education research and practice (L. Bailey, 2007) and rallied to develop centers, teaching techniques, policies, academic courses, degrees, programs, journals, and research methodologies to fuel their critical mission.

Working to challenge institutional practices that perceived education as a neutral or inherently liberating force while advancing dominant group interests and marginalizing people of color, other women, and class, sexual, or ethnic minorities, scholars highlighted patterns of inequity to demand that education reflect its democratic ideals. The passage of Title IX (1972) and the development of women's studies as an academic space were among the key outcomes of these social movements. While the tensions between its institutionalization and formative political mission have created enduring challenges for scholar-activists, women's studies was transformational in establishing an intellectual and institutional site (e.g., Wiegman, 2002) for propelling epistemological shifts in the understanding of diverse sociopolitical processes through the lens of gender. Since that generative period, many programs expanded to women's, gender and/or sexuality studies to foreground shifts in the field. Gendered scholarship has informed and been nourished by research and theorizing in a range of fields, including ethnic studies, anthropology, English, history, sociology, psychology, and philosophy, as well as education.

The promise of education as a particularly salient site of gendered analysis and potential transformation is evident in its central role in interdisciplinary feminist scholarship. Scholars analyzed education as a male-dominated and masculine institution, such as the gendered "clockwork" of male careers that shaped expectations for women faculty (Hochschild, 1975). Women's experiential knowledge from their embodied standpoints became a legitimate source of theory and insight into broader social and economic processes (e.g., Collins, 1990, 2004; Harding, 1986, 1987, 1991, 2004; Hartsock, 2004). During this period, analyses of educational issues related to women/girls were often explicitly feminist and disseminated through interdisciplinary women's studies outlets. For example, the first article appearing in the inaugural issue of *Feminist Studies* (1972) provided a literature review of the school's role in sexist stereotyping (Levy, 1972), while the first issue of *Women's Studies: An Interdisciplinary Journal* (1972) included a historical analysis of religious arguments against English women's entry into higher education (Burstyn, 1972). Similarly, such feminist journals as *Frontiers* (1975), *Signs: The Journal of Women in Culture and Society* (1975), *Psychology of Women* (1976), *Women's Studies International Forum* (1978), and *International Journal of Women's Studies* (1978) published articles or special issues on education early in their circulation. Topics included leadership (Estler, 1975), equity issues in part-time academic labor (Reeves, 1975), and psychocognitive and structural elements of American education that led to sexism (Kutner & Brogan, 1976).

Scholarship in such interdisciplinary sites often charted the breadth and particularities of sex inequities and advocated for change in policy and practice based on principles common to liberal feminism—that women, like men, hold inalienable rights to pursue freedom with the support of a just state, which includes rights to participate fully in educational pursuits. The site of scholars' analytic gaze was the category "woman" focused on the practices, policies, or resources that either interfere with her pursuits or propel her development. Detailing inequities involved scrutinizing the pages of textbooks, observing teachers' daily practices, tallying faculty demographics, and analyzing curriculum and resources. The social basis of sex roles attracted particular interest. Levy and others (e.g., Draper, 1975; Frazier & Sadker, 1973; Kutner & Brogan, 1976; Stacey, Béreaud, & Daniels, 1974; Weitzman, 1979; Weitzman, Eifler, Hokada, & Ross, 1972) argued that schools were complicit in reflecting sexist social practices, reinforcing hierarchies and socializing children into rigid roles shaping life outcomes. In 1978, Gould underscored the power of sex designations for shaping gendered treatment in her story *X: A Fabulous Child's Story*, which detailed people's confusion in knowing how to interact with a child who had no clear gender demarcations.

Early research during this period emphasized sex role theories positing and exploring biological, cognitive–developmental, or socialization differences between men and women, which remain an important focus in psychology journals that represent research on learning and achievement. Some education journals reflected similar trends. Reviews of *AERJ* and *RER* uncovered a range of topics. For example, *AERJ* published 25 articles focused broadly on "gender and education" during the 1960s and 1970s, including 14 on sex differences in achievement and cognition and other psychological foci, 5 on curriculum and pedagogy, 3 on teachers, and 2 on STEM issues. The first relevant piece in *AERJ* focused on "teaching boys to read." Few of these articles, however, reflected the shift to conceptualizing gender as a social construction or critiqued structural forces as factors in sex inequalities.

Critiques of structural inequalities in schooling began to surface in varied educational sites in the mid- to late-1970s, influenced by feminist scholarship. Howe (1979) noted that schools of education had been "resistant to the impact of the women's movement" (p. 413), despite the rapid expansion of institutional sites for examining women's issues. The *Council on Anthropology and Education Quarterly* (1975) published a special issue addressing "women in schools and society" that examined such topics as sex roles, schooling structures' influence on occupational choice, and educated and working women's vulnerability to role conflict. *TCR* and *HER* published feminist critiques on sex-role stereotyping, equal employment rights, mathematics anxiety, sex and race discrimination, social movements, school reform, textbooks, curriculum, and strategies to advance women in school administration, among other topics. In 1977, *HER* published Carol Gilligan's classic work "In a Different Voice," and, in 1979 and 1981, the *Journal of Curriculum Theorizing* released Janet Miller's scholarship on gendered silences and feminist pedagogy.

The first publication in *TCR* to address the intersection of race and gender appeared in 1976 (Lightfoot) and in *HER* in 1980 (Baca Zinn) as part of its two-part special issue "Women and Education." Other work focused on challenges women faced in education (Tittle & Denker, 1977), and a 19th-century protest that women led at Cornell University to render visible the history of women students (Haines, 1977). In the 1970s, the *Journal of Higher Education* published work on female faculty status, salaries, and sex discrimination, as well as analyses of affirmative action and Title IX; and the *History of Education Quarterly* published two special issues, "Reinterpreting Women's Education" and "Women's Influence on Education."

TURNS AND TRANSFORMATIONS

The conceptual turn to the term "gender" as socially constructed, malleable, and thus subject to change expanded during the 1980s and 1990s, accompanied by the broadening of gendered and intersectional scholarship. Such analyses appeared in education journals, feminist journals and, later in the 1980s, in new journals focused explicitly on gender and education. *Gender & Society* (1987), and *NWSA Journal* (1988; now *Feminist Formations*) produced articles or special issues on education early in their circulation. *Gender & Society* published 46 articles related to education between 1987 and 2015, while *Signs: The Journal of Women, Culture and Society* published over 50 between 1979 and 2015. In addition, disciplinary journals (e.g., *Psychology of Women Quarterly* [1976]; *Gender & History* [1989]) included educational analyses. Several journals developed as dedicated sites for exploring intersections between gender and education, such as *Feminist Teacher* (1984) and the U.K. journal *Gender and Education* (1989), and, later, journals with educational emphases, such as *Advancing Women in Leadership* (1997). The *Gender and Education* editors recognized the need to create spaces focused on "gender as a category of analysis in education that furthers feminist knowledge, theory, consciousness, action, and debate" ("Editorial," 1989, p. 3).

One significant critique instrumental for shaping gendered research reflected in these interdisciplinary journals centered on the unidimensional conception of gendered analytics that failed to take into account the ways gender varies in salience and the intersectionality of social positioning and identities (see Crenshaw, 1989), for example, how race, class, gender, and sexuality intersect to position people in different networks of power that profoundly shape experience, identities, and roles (e.g., Lorde, 1984). As noted in our overview, scholars critiqued and moved from the "add and stir" approach of adding women of color to existing frameworks to theorizing how intersectionality shapes epistemology, experience, and educational positioning and how racialized/gendered ideologies are structured into the very fibers of educational institutions, pedagogies, interactions, relations, and policies. For example, Fordham (1993) analyzed how African American women resist the White, middle-class constructions of womanhood that shape educational positioning and achievement, while L. Grant's (1994) analysis of African American girls' roles in elementary schools revealed the social rather than academic dimensions of their racialized positioning in class as "helpers, enforcers, and go-betweens." During these years, C. A. Grant and Sleeter (1986) published "Race, Class, and Gender in Education Research: An Argument for Integrative Analysis" in *RER*; and in its first year of publication, *Gender and Education* released a special issue on race, gender, and education (1989).

Varied scholars traced and responded to the absence of socioeconomic class analysis in explicitly gendered research and theory, including Bettie's (1993) ethnography of Mexican American and White females in a California school, as well as the work of hooks (2000), Luttrell (1997), Walkerdine (1990), Weis (1988), and Weis and Fine (1993), which advanced intersectional analysis and knowledge. *Gender and Education* published more than 60 articles focused on or incorporating class as an analytic axis, including over 30 focused on working-class issues, and many on masculinities. The expansive conceptualizing of such intersections during this period also shifted beyond interrogating binaries and static conceptions of identity to theorizing dynamic gendered multiplicities formed in context and in relation. For example, Bhachu's (1991) analysis of Sikh women suggested they formulated identities "continuously in a process of negotiation with a number of economic and political forces that shift over time and space" (p. 45). Lomawaima (1994) highlighted the power of such intersecting forces in her study of one vocational boarding school that the federal government established for Native Americans during the late 19th and early 20th centuries, which, in turn, shaped life opportunities but also fueled resistance. Racist assimilation initiatives forced diverse tribal members to receive vocational training and to provide gender-specific curriculum to teach young men to farm and young women to perform household duties, in part to serve as domestics for Whites.

In addition to exploring gendered aspects of the experiences of gay and lesbian educational subjects (e.g., Garber, 1994; Mac an Ghaill, 1991), scholarship troubled gay/lesbian categories that rely on a stable sexual subject (e.g., Talburt, 2000), explored how homophobia functions as a "weapon" of sexism (Pharr, 1997), considered relations and tensions between gender and sexuality, and traced schools as profoundly heteronormative spaces that establish and police gender and sexuality norms. International turns were visible as well, highlighting the significance of context and culture for shaping gendered meanings and experiences; *Gender and Education* published analyses of education in varied European nations, and later, expanded international theorizing in the Global South exploring policies, equal opportunity, technologies, rurality (e.g., Volume 26, 2014), and higher education (Volume 27, 2015). Analyses focused on enduring effects of colonial power for policies affecting women appeared in the journal in the 1990s (e.g., Gordon, 1994) and expanded with postcolonial and postcolonial feminist theorizing in the 2000s. Scholars from sovereign nations have critiqued colonialist educational legacies to expand knowledge on Native American women (e.g., Mihesuah, 1997, 2003). In addition, some analyzed intersectional gendered educational *processes* and *practices* as well as including "women/girls" as categories of sex/gender analysis or positioning, such as the gendered dynamics of sexuality education (Fine, 1988), prom (Best, 2000), cheerleading (Adams & Bettis, 2003), and, later, beauty pageants on predominantly Black and White college campuses (Tice, 2012).

Widespread attention to the social and schooling disadvantages that girls continue to face emerged in a series of popular and academic publications in the 1980s and 1990s (LaFrance, 1991). Interest surged in the repercussions of sexist socialization for girls' self-esteem and psychological and physical health (Orenstein, 1994; Pipher, 1994), girls' anger (L. M. Brown, 1999, 2003), and their sexuality (Fine, 1988; Tolman, 2002). Reports from the American Association of University Women Educational Foundation—*How Schools Shortchange Girls* (1992) and *Hostile Hallways* (1993)—and M. Sadker and Sadker's (1994) *Failing at Fairness*, among others, focused directly on education. They detailed bias in standardized tests, curriculum and classroom practices, and a hostile climate that supported sexual harassment and "shortchanged" girls—which was a new focus in scholarship on girls (Larkin, 1994)—and that tied directly to equitable conditions for learning that would later become a policy focus under Title IX. Other reports attend to girls' agency, resilience, and promise, such as Ginorio and Huston's (2001) report on Latinas in school and collections such as *Geographies of Girlhood* (Bettis & Adams, 2005). M. Sadker and Sadker (1994) tracked classroom interactions in which teachers provided more resources to boys than girls, such as time and challenging developmental feedback. Similarly, the body as a gendered educational project became a site of study evidenced through, for example, K. Martin's (1998) ethnographic analysis of schooling practices that shaped preschool children's bodies in conventional gendered ways with sobering long-term implications, such as restricting girls' voices and movements, while allowing boys more freedom to move and shout.

At the same time—underscoring the production of vastly different gendered projects occurring simultaneously—Thorne's (1993) classic analysis of children's gender play shifted attention from girls' disadvantages and gender socialization processes to consider gender as dynamic, relational, and formed through girls' and boys' agential interactions. In this sense, gender is not a set of characteristics one possesses.

Curricular analyses reflected these shifts as well. Earlier analyses counted textual representations of women/girls (e.g., Tetreault, 1986; Trecker, 1971; Wolf, 1975), suggesting the cumulative power of these messages, textbook after textbook, alongside other social stereotypes to foster limited imaginaries for girls and women's futures. Later work continued this pattern (e.g., Love, 1993) and also shifted to the gendering of processes, such as E. Martin's (1991) analysis of medical textbooks that infuse even at the cellular reproductive level gendered constructions of women's eggs as passive and men's sperm as active. In the same period, some work disrupted the conception of the female subject as "acted upon" by educational forces, posing an alternative subject who acted, resisted, and extended interpretations of textual messages that she encountered. For example, work on fairy tales (Westland, 1993, p. 237) challenged previous understandings of curricular and classroom stereotyping as inevitably "harmfully reinforcing restrictive images of girlhood and womanhood," to suggest that girls can be "resistant readers," active interpreters, rather than passively absorbing stereotypical messages. Between 1990 and 2015, *Gender and Education* published more than a dozen articles analyzing texts, reflecting different theoretical traditions.

Scholarship that attends to gender has long considered the machinations of masculinity as a consequential construct for shaping social and educational processes and people's lives. For example, publications in the *Journal of Education* (1890s) discussed the value of "masculine teaching" and the dangers of women's overrepresentation as teachers during children's formative years. Echoing late-19th-century arguments about vocational education as a key site to engage boys (Kliebard, 1999), articles surfaced in early issues of the journal focused on concerns about school structures that favored girls, the effects of coeducation on learning proper gender roles, and boys' performance in school. As early as 1900, educators referred to concerns about boys' disengagement and the feminization of teaching as "the boy problem" (Graves, 1998; Rury, 1991; Tyack & Hansot, 1990). Articles in 1934 reported concerns about "mental deficiency [as] commoner in boys than in girls," about girls surpassing boys in academics because of teachers' overuse of texts and insufficient hands-on curricula such as machine work, and about female teachers' giving higher grades to girls than boys. The 1990s trend in gender scholarship that Weaver-Hightower (2003) catchily coined "the boy turn," it turns out, was not without historical precedent.

The 1990s reflected increased analytic attention to men/boys as units of analysis in gendered scholarship that reflected competing perspectives and investments, and inspired fierce debates. Varied social, economic, and educational forces (see Weaver-Hightower, 2003)[5] prompted a wave of attention to a perceived "crisis in masculinity" (Lingard, 2003) and resistance to feminist claims of enduring inequities facing girls/women. Characterized by a degree of media fervor and framed by some as a "war" against boys (Sommers, 2000), the turn led parents, popular figures, and scholars to detail troubling issues facing boys and men that merited social visibility and redress (R. W. Connell, 2000). Research responded to perceptions and concerns regarding patterns of women's advancement, economic displacement of male workers, boys' increasing disaffection with school, and their underachievement, attrition rates, violence and drug use, suspensions, placements in special education, struggles with writing and reading, and anti-intellectualism.

Other profeminist and critical scholars propelled the boy turn (Weaver-Hightower, 2003) through expanding gender research and conceptions of masculinity(ies). Like other important shifts in theorizing gender as co-constituted with other social locations that shape positioning and experiences, scholars questioned undifferentiated groupings of "boys" as essentialist and argued for the importance of analyzing key differences among boys'/men's social positioning on the basis of race, class, nationality, and sexuality (e.g., Baldridge, Hill, & Davis, 2011; J. E. Davis, 2010, 2013; Joe & Davis, 2010). R. W. Connell and Messerschmidt's (2005) concept of hegemonic masculinities has nourished education research in separating masculinity from men and stretching beyond unitary uses to consider its variegated, shifting, hierarchical, and relational nature produced and performed in diverse contexts. In this sense, masculinity is neither biological, held, nor static, but constantly formed and re-formed in relation to other femininities and masculinities with different degrees of power. Gender nonconforming men, gay men, and men of color have different access to the forms of masculinity that carry the most symbolic and cultural capital.

In reviewing *Gender and Education*, we found that more than 100 articles mobilized the concept of "masculinity" as a central focus, and one-fourth of those explored hegemonic masculinity to animate educational dynamics. Engagements with this concept diversify and expand. For example, scholars consider how it governs school cultures (e.g., Farrell, Larsson, & Redelius, 2012; Robinson, 1992; A. Skelton, 1993; C. Skelton, 1994)—sometimes at odds with the messages of the formal curriculum—(Mirembe & Davies, 2001), how individuals "take up" or negotiate masculinities in varied contexts (E. Anderson, 2011; Benjamin, 2001; Davies, 1997; D. Francis, 2014; Heward, 1994), and how acts such as alcohol use (Dempster, 2011) and sexual harassment and abuse (Robinson, 2005; C. Skelton, 1994) mark hegemonic masculinity and cement peer relations. Other examples are works that critique and reconfigure the concept's limits and manifestations (Hanh Thi Do & Brenna, 2015; Haywood & Mac an Ghaill, 2012), as well as 18 articles attending to the pressing educational dynamics of violence or bullying.

Yet scholarship reveals lasting critiques of the turn as well. While feminist scholarship has always invited analyses of males, boys, and masculinity—one reason the editors of *Gender and Education* chose the broad name for the journal ("Editorial," 1989, p. 3)—scholars questioned both the claims that scholarship and schools neglected males and the forces animating those claims. Some feminist scholars read the shift as a backlash against women's successes, an erasure of women's concerns, a false equalizing of the gender issues different people face, and a cooptation of a feminist politic and field dedicated to dismantling male dominance. Some question its longevity as a theoretical line of flight. Contemporary scholarship that focuses on men/masculinity generally rejects sweeping classifications of boys' and men's condition and expressions of masculinities to consider how race, class, gender, and sexualities shape educational processes—and which boys and which men in which contexts enjoy privilege or face systematic disadvantages in the machinations of schooling (e.g., Ferguson, 2000).

In the same generative period, feminist scholars reconsidered core theories, research methodologies, and practice. The work of gendered scholarship has often critiqued previous masculinist theories (e.g., Weiler, 2001), teaching approaches (e.g., *Feminist Teacher*), research methodologies (e.g., Fonow & Cook, 1991; Lather, 1991; Lather & Smithies, 1997; Reinharz, 1992), and concepts, and the knowledge that such approaches have produced. In 1982, for instance, Gilligan critiqued the gendered assumptions underlying Kohlberg's theory of moral development and expanded it to include women. Arnot (1982), working within the tradition of "new" British sociology, extended intersectional attention to class, gender, and education to critique and expand social reproduction theory, while McRobbie (1990) brought similar critiques to bear on British cultural studies scholarship on male adolescents (e.g., Hebdige, 1979; Willis, 1977) to underscore gendered gaps in analyses of adolescent cultures. Similarly, Holland and Eisenhart (1992) traced through ethnography the power of romance culture as a gendered reproductive force to shape and limit women's aspirations on two U.S. college campuses.

A key shift emerged during this period to revisit and disrupt long-accepted premises governing the pursuit of knowledge that remain active trajectories of research today. The research approaches that feminist methodologists introduced at that time were transformative for unsettling dominant beliefs about the nature of knowledge and the techniques deemed most appropriate for wresting that knowledge from social and physical terrain. Scholars and activists raised questions regarding researchers' common distancing stances or claims to "objectivity," asking whether these were possible or even desirable components of inquiry in openly ideological research (see Lather, 1986) exploring gendered phenomena in the lives of marginalized people. They considered how the actual conduct of research—from its guiding assumptions to ethics of practice, to interactions with participants, to the processes of data gathering, analysis, and representation—is a political and power-laden process that merits scrutiny and care to align with feminist goals. Rather than adhering to an "objective" research ethos, researchers embraced the knowledge creation process as necessarily and productively reflexive, political, relational, and emotional (e.g., Fonow & Cook, 1991). They developed collaborative approaches to gathering data and conducting analysis "with" rather than "on" people, and new forms for representing the complexities, challenges, and embodied labor involved in conducting research—particularly with vulnerable subjects. Genre conventions in research typically dictate the production of technical writing in tidy texts that conceal the embodied figures creating the knowledge; in contrast, feminist scholars experimented with fragmented texts, poetic representations, and autobiographical components in their work to trouble and expand what science could look like (e.g., Lather & Smithies, 1997; Richardson, 1997, 2000). It was antithetical to feminist goals, some insisted, to reproduce systems of domination through objectifying and authoritarian research practice. Although scholars undertaking gender research may use any number of methodologies (e.g., Reinharz, 1992) to pursue their inquiries, feminist methodologists emphasized that all research approaches, like other aspects of education, are embedded in relations of power with consequences for the knowledge that is produced and disseminated. Continuing to think critically about research practice, to unsettle conventions, and to imagine new approaches, remains central to the field today.

Feminists also took up key issues in teacher labor, teaching approaches, and philosophies of teaching as sites of intersectional theorizing and potential empowerment (e.g., Omolade, 1987). If schools reproduce power relations by embodying authoritative stances and treating students as passive recipients of knowledge, then teaching, like research, is an act of power and a potential instrument of justice. The journal *Feminist Teacher* explored reflexive and liberating pedagogies, and many other writings (e.g., Lather, 1991) explored forms of resistance. Scholars advocated for the importance of incorporating attention to gender politics into teacher education (M. Sadker & Sadker, 1994; D. M. Sadker, Sadker, & Zittleman, 2009; Sikes, 1991). For Noddings (1984, 1992; Noddings, Katz, & Strike, 1999), educational practices should be relational, based in an ethic of care. Grumet (1988) theorized the pedagogical possibilities of mediating spaces that rely, similarly, on the premise that relationships are a necessary precondition for knowing, noting the complex positioning of female teachers who must negotiate children's transition from the (feminine) home to (masculine) public spaces. Philosopher Jane Roland Martin (1985) constructed a new educational paradigm based on reconsidering the long history of educational thought on women's education. Referencing Rich's classic statement on claiming one's education, Martin redefined the educational realm to bring it into alignment with feminist critique that was transforming education in the last decades of the 20th century.

ONGOING SITES OF RESEARCH

Sociologist Barbara Bank's (2007) two-volume set of essays, *Gender and Education*, addresses key areas in the field of education that point to the breadth and texture of contemporary scholarship. The essays reflect efforts, like this one, to take stock and assess trends in gendered theories, issues, and developments. Gendered scholarship is frequently theoretical and may be oriented to critique and praxis, seeking spaces where gendered subjects can cultivate agency and resistance, challenge dominant discourses and institutional barriers, and consider new conditions of possibility for educational lives. In 1992, Soerensen expressed the need to expand theorizing beyond patriarchal critiques that characterized earlier scholarship, suggesting that we must leave "essential thinking and absolute strategies in order to open up a field of research to plurality and a constructive uncertainty" (p. 201). Yet such plurality met with some resistance (e.g., Anyon, 1994), unleashing generative tensions and dialogue.

Scholarship in recent decades reflects scholars' simultaneous mobilization of diverse theoretical and methodological tools to explore gendered dynamics in a range of sites, as well as to explore the expansive reach of gendered analysis to encompass varied locations, practices, policies, and processes that thicken our understanding of gendered operations in education. For example, articles in *Gender and Education* reference womanist theorizing, feminist theories, masculinity theories, poststructuralist theories (concentrated in the 1990s, though ongoing), and materialist theories, and they make multiple references to Foucault, Bourdieu, and Butler. Additional references address sex role theory; gender egalitarianism; antiviolence, critical, and feminist pedagogies; grounded theory; Cartesian corporeal agency; psychoanalytic theories; leadership theories; and gender reproduction. Dillard (2006) places African American women's narratives, the commitment to research as responsibility, and spirituality at the center of her theorizing in an approach she terms *endarkened feminist epistemology*. Thomas (2011) brings geographical and psychoanalytic theory to bear on critiques of the trend of "banal" and celebratory multiculturalism visible in schools through analyzing how gender and racialized violence is constituted through schooling spaces and heteronormative relationships. Furthermore, new materialities (e.g., Coole & Frost, 2010; Taylor & Hughes, 2016), spatiality (Tamboukou, 1999), postcoloniality (Hughes, 2002), methodologies (Hughes & Lury, 2013), and affect (Åberg & Hedlin, 2015) offer new points of departure, while previous theoretical engagements persist.

Such scholarship also revisits topics from new vantage points. For instance, educators have scrutinized the practice of organizing, sorting, and grouping people by sex to foster gender equity as variously promising or worrisome acts at different points in time: coeducation (late 19th century); single-sex schools, classrooms, or groups (Reay, 1990; M. Sadker & Sadker, 1994); separate spaces for pregnant and mothering teens (Luttrell, 2003; Pillow, 2004); and single-race/sex classrooms or schools (e.g., Metropolitan Center for Urban Education, 2010). Recognizing that, as Susan Franzosa (1993) noted, "more than girls' presence is required to accomplish equality of educational opportunity (p. 334)," widespread concerns about sex discrimination in the schools rekindled interest in forging single-sex schooling spaces and groupings for females during the 1980s and 1990s (Morse, 1998). The surge of interest both appealed and alarmed. A series of studies of single-sex schooling in Australia, Great Britain, Canada, and the United States found promising results from such arrangements, in one case suggesting that context-specific initiatives with skilled teachers could provide "an antidote to a tradition of bias" (Heyward, 1995). Yet Thorne (1993) suggested that schools' marking of sex/gender are forms of "social control" (p. 34), questioning, as have others, why we see "sex" as a sensible, persuasive way to group human beings rather than, for example, height, age, or musical aptitude. In this view, such practices can homogenize and highlight one constructed axis of identity or classification over others, reflect powerful and selective assumptions of difference, reify such assumptions through school structures, and release schools from their responsibility to create equal opportunities for all students in shared spaces.

Recent work (e.g., Cohen, 2012; Jackson, 2010) animates the theoretical and practical implications of sorting and grouping human beings by the designation of biological sex, whether through schools, sports teams, separate bathrooms, or sexual education curriculum, given the fluidity of contemporary gender expressions and decades of conceptual work that troubles gender/sex binaries. Cohen's (2012) work disrupts the single-sex schooling binary by describing how their "girl-only program" grappled with the potentially exclusionary connotations of their mission for intersex, gender-nonconforming, and transgender youth. Allowing student self-identification as the basis for joining the program opened spaces for gender-nonconforming students and transgender youth to participate. Contemporary debates about college dormitories and public school restrooms reflect the historical structure of schooling at odds with more fluid conceptions of gender and of transgender students' needs, identities, and expressions. The 2016 U.S. legal mandate to allow transgender students access to restrooms provides an example of important new areas of policy, theorizing, and research that trouble long taken-for-granted norms.

Such structural separations have also been proposed in the interests of providing focused curriculum, support, and safety. Advocates have created spaces for pregnant and mothering teens, students in special education, "at-risk" students in alternative schools, and sexual minority and gender nonconforming students; and they have created single-sex classrooms/schools for students of color, among others. While policy guidelines require that many arrangements remain "choices" rather than mandates, debates circulate around how to best support the needs of students who struggle with safety issues or race- and gender-based stereotypes that can shape performance. Indeed, the major theme of early research on transgender issues in education focused on how to make campuses more inclusive to serve the educational needs of transgender students (Beemyn, 2003; Lees, 1998; McKinney, 2005). Advocates addressed the importance of providing resources across the curriculum and adopting nondiscrimination policies in research that was driven largely by personal narratives and institutional case studies.

By the end of the first decade of the 21st century, scholarship on transgender issues in education shifted from central concerns regarding access, visibility, and resources in higher education to including studies about the importance of inclusive curricula and pedagogy in primary and secondary schools, and about teacher preparation and medical education (Barozzi & Ojeda, 2014; Rands, 2009; Ryan, Patraw, & Bednar, 2013; Vanderleest & Galper, 2009). Rands argues that responsible teaching should be centered on the concept of gender-complex education, a variant of critical pedagogy described as a basic and pervasive part of all students' education (Rands, 2009, 2013). Articles inform teachers, administrators, school psychologists, and guidance counselors of best practices to support transgender students and document school districts' collective efforts to provide respectful and safe school environments for those who are transitioning (Bowers, Lewandowski, Savage, & Woitaszewski, 2015; Gonzalez & McNulty, 2010; Luecke, 2011). Other research analyzes state and local policies that protect sexual minorities from employment discrimination, noting that LGBT educators remain particularly vulnerable to the threat of dismissal on prejudicial grounds (C. Connell, 2012). Theorizing of transgender issues in interdisciplinary journals (e.g., *Transgender Studies Quarterly*) also can inform educational theory and practice.

Another fertile area of study crosses topics and theoretical traditions that continue earlier patterns of intersectional theorizing, take up the body as a site of study, or have implications for embodiment: sexuality education, eating disorders/problems, pregnant and mothering teens, sports, social activities such as prom and beauty pageants, and important markers of religiosity and piety, such as veiling for Muslim students (e.g., Scott, 2010b), that also function as cultural signifiers in a range of complex gendered and racialized discourses (e.g., Cronin, 2014; Zine, 2006). Such issues can become political sites in which deeply held and conflicting social values become situated. For example, debates about comprehensive versus abstinence education in the late 1990s and 2000s reflected fundamental differences about when and how sexuality should be expressed, what forms it should take, and who should serve as its primary educational vehicles. Fine (1988) raised critical questions about the content, silences, and politics of sexuality curriculum for young women's lives that remain relevant today (Fine & McClelland, 2006, 2007), while others have extended or nuanced her analyses (Allen, 2004; Kendall, 2012; Pillow, 2004; Tolman, 2002) or critiqued a curriculum of abstinence, anatomy, disease, and danger to explore a broader range of racial, social, democratic, and sexuality issues that shape youths' lives (Ashcraft, 2006; Garcia, 2012; Harrison, 2000; Kendall, 2012; Mayo, 2007, 2008, 2011), including the context in which programs are situated (Castro-Vazquez, 2000).

As gender scholars have noted, such curricular initiatives are significant precisely because of their embodied implications for the lived and educational experiences of youth. The reach of Title IX to such embodied experiences casts light on their gendered undercurrents. For example, despite the explicit protection for pregnant and mothering teens in public schools outlined in Title IX, Pillow's ethnographic analysis of high school dynamics demonstrated that even as rates of teen pregnancy *declined*, a degree of racialized urgency animated the "teen pregnancy" crisis as a national problem. Pillow (like Luttrell, 2003) suggests that the pregnant or mothering student is often conceptualized literally and figuratively as an "unfit subject," whose needs for larger chairs or schedule adjustments are at odds with daily schooling practices. Furthermore, Pillow found that school workers are often unaware that Title IX protects the rights of pregnant students to an equal education, are openly disapproving or unprepared to contend with their embodied realities, marginalize or exclude them, or consider them as poor role models. Similar exclusion and readmission struggles in African contexts and in Portugal have been examined as well (Bagele, 2002; Chilisa, 2002; Unterhalter, 2013). And those who pursue their education in alternative schooling spaces, as Luttrell (2003) found in her study of pregnant youth in a separate school, struggle to construct their identities within the larger stigmatizing discourses in which they are situated. Despite the complexities of mothering in school (and as academics; see Ward & Wolf-Wendel, 2012), some have described the role as a significant touchstone and propelling mechanism for educational engagement and return (Luttrell, 1997).

Recent analyses utilize theoretical tools from geography, psychoanalysis, and poststructuralism to demonstrate other embodied aspects of schooling such as the complexity of gendered violence in context (de Lange & Mitchell, 2014; Thomas, 2011). Although analyses of the threat of bullying, sexual harassment, and violence for women, sexual minorities, and other vulnerable populations have long noted the consequences for their educational experiences, a number of highly visible incidents of sexual abuse, bullying, and gun violence in schools and on university campuses have renewed attention to this key area of gendered education. For some, a culture that supports hegemonic masculinities is particularly incendiary in this regard, as it cultivates and reproduces rigid ideas of masculinity and femininity that are reinforced through relations of power in schooling practices (e.g., Cannella & Perez, 2012; Conroy, 2013; Dowler, Cuomo, & Laliberte, 2014; J. Klein, 2012; Meyer, 2009). Katz's (2006, 2013) analyses of representations of cultural violence underscored the tendency of news media to avoid naming the sex of the primary perpetrators—male—a practice that obscured the gendered dimensions of an entrenched cultural practice. Katz's and Foubert's (e.g., 2010) targeted educational programs to combat sexual violence are grounded in gendered analyses of rape and bystander awareness to fuel action and intervention. The power of contextually grounded and theoretical analyses in contemporary gendered scholarship is particularly clear in Thomas's (2011) study of racial and gendered dynamics in a California school site, which traced the family influences, group identifications, social geographies, and psychological investments that fueled school tensions. In *Nabozny v. Podlesny* (1996), *Gebser v. Lago Vista Independent School District* (1998), and *Davis v. Monroe County Board of Education* (1999), courts ruled it the responsibility of schools to protect students from harm. The Campus Sexual Violence Elimination Act (also called the Campus SAVE Act, 2013), as well as new applications of Title IX, reflect renewed attention to and policies for addressing an enduring gendered issue with renewed visibility.

Gendered analysis has extended to educational institutions as sites of violence for particular groups. In a post-9/11 climate, scholars have noted the Islamophobia facing Muslim students, as well as their identity negotiations in diverse schooling spaces (e.g., Cronin, 2014; Fine & Sirin, 2008; Mir, 2014). Carceral analyses of schooling have likened the structure of schools to prisons, noted racial and gendered disparities in school discipline patterns since the 1970s (e.g., Skiba, Michael, Nardo, & Peterson, 2002), and analyzed racialized and gendered educational processes that contribute to profoundly unequal educational outcomes (e.g., Ferguson, 2000) and what critical scholars call "the school-to-prison pipeline." For those incarcerated in the prison-industrial complex (A. Davis, 1979), researchers have also turned to informal education within prisons to consider women's experiences (Sweeney, 2012) and the intersectional contours of women's reading practices in prisons (Sweeney, 2010).

The carceral aspects of schooling and the privatization of prisons that some scholars detail echo recent turns to analysis of neoliberalism visible in gendered scholarship. This term *neoliberalism* is often used in critical ways to refer to a series of economic changes and ideologies that extend or transfer control of particular economic resources from the public to the private sector. In terms of gender scholarship, some analyses have considered the gendered implications of this economic and discursive shift that infuses institutional practices, educational discourses, and the very affects and desires of students and school workers that inhabit those spaces. In this analytic focus, the current audit and testing culture, managerialism, and accountability shaping K–12 schooling and institutions of higher education as increasingly privatized entities are processes gendered masculine (e.g., Arnot & Mac an Ghaill, 2006) with an array of implications for educational practice and a primarily female teaching force.

Neoliberalism has prompted an array of gendered critiques because of its dominant, pervasive, and fundamental effects on educational institutions, priorities, practices, labor, and learning that some argue undermine the democratic, public mission of education (Henry, 2001). Berg and Seeber (2016) mobilize Thornton's striking point regarding the effects of corporatization on the increasing speed of academic processes and the implications for embodied faculty labor and feminist work. Suggesting that "academics are now valued as neoliberal subjects" caught up in increasing production demands, feminists, too, "are expected to serve the new knowledge economy rather than critique it. The homologous relation between feminism and critique means that the contraction of a critical space has also necessarily led to the contraction of feminism within the academy" (Thornton, 2012, as cited in Berg & Seeber, 2016, p. 63). Agendas initiated in the 1960s and 1970s thus remain "unfinished" (Glazer-Raymo, 2008). For example, women of color remain underrepresented in K–12 teaching, higher education, and administration and knowledge about community college faculty remains limited (e.g., Turner, 2008; Twombly, 1993; Twombly & Townsend, 2007). Similarly, while all women remain underrepresented in educational leadership—an enduring focus of feminist efforts—for some faculty who hold such positions, administrative duties within a culture of escalating demands may also have the unfortunate contradictory effect of propelling gender imbalance in producing research knowledge because women's time is consumed elsewhere (e.g., Sannino & Vainio, 2015).

Scholarship has pointed out the limits and illusion of "choice" that is visible in neoliberal discourse: Access to education and employment do not necessarily enable "freedom" when they entangle women within an exploitative global consumerism in which one must purchase commodities to "become somebody." One may feel "free" to choose any major, educational institution, or occupation, to decorate one's body as one wishes, or to experiment with new gendered performances, but people do not in fact have equal structural conditions in which they can access the same mentoring and structural resources and symbolic, cultural, and linguistic capital that enable actualizing such empowering visions (Thomas, 2011) both within and outside of education (e.g., Mullen, 2010). Affect is integrated into such market processes as well, as individual choices may feel empowering—shopping for example—while such choices entangle "choosing" subjects in hegemony. In her work on affective labor in post-Fordism, McRobbie (2010) describes young women's flocking to contemporary popular culture as empowering for creating new forms of identity even as she and others are quick to clarify that despite the construction of endless choices through individual consumerism and competition that neoliberalism normalizes, new forms of power (and agency, e.g., Taylor, 2011) are emerging.

The concept of "choice" as one aspect of contemporary educational practices is also visible in another active research area: gender and STEM. How and why individuals "choose" to enter the sciences, what barriers they face—and what factors help them succeed—has been a particularly robust area of inquiry in the wake of nationalist efforts to attract and retain students in STEM and advance the scientific and technological workforce (e.g., Bystydzienski & Bird, 2006). This focus has encompassed a range of cognitive, pedagogical, cultural, and contextual analyses in K–12 schooling, higher education, and industry (e.g., see *Cultural Studies of Science Education*). For example, using "gender" as a search subject uncovered 281 articles published in the *Journal of Research in Science Teaching*, *Science Education*, the *Journal of Engineering Education*, the *Journal of Science Teacher Education*, and *School Science and Mathematics* between 1939 and 2016. Most articles in the early decades incorporated sex as a factor of analysis in investigations that assumed sex differences regarding knowledge or achievement. In the 1980s, scholars turned to more nuanced understandings of gender, analyzing gender roles, equity issues, and utilizing feminist theory with increasing frequency. For instance, 86 articles published between 2000 and 2016 addressed gender (rather than sex) differences, an additional 23 addressed gender roles, and 29 incorporated gender theory; only 12 articles during this period focused on sex as a factor of analysis. Topics included teachers and teaching, curriculum, classroom dynamics, student preparation, mentoring, tracking, climate issues, and forms of discrimination in educational theory and practice. Despite the claim and sense of science as a male domain, students' preparation in school and teaching strategies shape who studies science, as does self-efficacy (Harding, 1998). Yet others suggest STEM is a thoroughly gendered domain that has only recently created space for women as knowers.

CONCLUSION

There remain persistent absences and "unfinished agendas" (Glazer-Raymo, 2008) in gender and education scholarship and opportunities for theorizing. As Bank (2011) states in her introduction to *Gender and Higher Education*, for those who view gender as a foundational aspect of educational processes,

It always comes as a surprise to discover how many books concerned generally with institutions of higher education, or, more specifically, with college degree programs, declining academic standards, faculty development, student services, academic management, institutional financing, governing policies, and other education-related matters either pay no attention to gender or devote a single chapter [to the given area of focus]. (p. 1)

She argues the same is true of notable education journals and professional conferences as well. This pattern underscores the gendered politics of knowledge production that persists as AERA begins its second century of research in education. The question remains for scholars interested in gender as an axis of analysis in diverse contexts: How, and with what nuances, is gender salient?

A recent special issue of *Educational Researcher* (2016, Volume 45, Number 2), celebrating the AERA centennial and offering reviews of 100 years of AERA presidential addresses, reflects this pattern. While the authors acknowledge the vast scope of the review task and recognize that the presidential addresses inevitably are "a partial lens on the field" (Cochran-Smith, 2016, p. 92), the reviews offer little focused attention on gender. In the 14 articles in which AERA past presidents reflect on education research on diversity and equity in how people learn, educational policy, school reform, research on teaching, teacher education, and curriculum, and more, none *focus* on gender, although 7 of the 14 mention gender in passing as an element in the complex synthesis of educational phenomena in past eras. In five of these essays, the references to gender are restricted to a brief mention of gender bias in Maxine Greene's biography; passing references to women's studies as part of new directions in study or the emergence of gender studies; two references to studies that account for gender as one variable of analysis; and a passing reference to "women's equality protests" in a paragraph offering historical context.

Cochran-Smith's and Cuban's essays incorporate a bit more attention to gender. Cochran-Smith (2016) notes other scholars' critiques of early male authorities in teacher education and their views of women's "limited intellectual capacity" (p. 93). She also notes the role of women in the early years of AERA and mentions Bess Goodykoontz, the first woman president of AERA (1939), whose experience as a teacher likely shaped her views of these male administrators' mandates. Similarly, Cuban notes the number of women who served as AERA presidents, gaps between researchers' social-justice agendas and their limited effects on schooling practices, and Penelope Peterson's "highly personal" 1997 address that reminds researchers and readers of (inevitably gendered) lived experiences.

Contemporary scholarship reflects the simultaneous production of diverse research trajectories building from historical foundations and productive tensions, debates, and disjunctures. As gender is a dynamic, fluid, malleable concept, and as new conceptions of gender and new understandings of the place of gender in society emerge, scholarship shifts and responds. There is a quest for new frameworks that evidence gender, that nourish the conception of gender analytics so scholars can see "anew." As is evident in this overview, the field encompasses far more than a straightforward reporting of women's and girls' gradual "progress" over time in accessing education. The field has become increasingly complex and theoretical as new educational sites and processes emerge that lend themselves to new analyses. As future trajectories unfold, the spirit of Rich's early critiques remain salient: Gender has been a central force in organizing social relations and educational processes, with an array of implications for lived experience that merit sustained scrutiny.

NOTES

[1]Given the intersectional theorizing that characterizes contemporary scholarship, it is in some ways artificial to highlight only gender in the title of this chapter, because gender is always raced, race is always gendered (and classed, etc.), and women of color have long argued

the epistemological issues with highlighting gender over race in lived experience. We thus highlight gender as one axis of social positioning and social organization important to individual/group experience, educational practice, processes, and research, while we also emphasize that its meaning is multidimensional, its degree of salience fluctuates, and its treatment in scholarship as a central or intersectional construct varies considerably (see also Note 2).

²Varied and important intellectual debates surround the terms *women's studies, gender studies,* and *feminist studies* and their use, meaning, and constitutive exclusions. Braidotti and Butler (1994) critiqued the shift to *gender studies* for its "theoretical inadequacy," its "politically amorphous and unfocused nature," its roots in English language and politics that do not translate to other contexts, and the "false symmetry" it suggests between the positions of men and women that occludes the reality of masculine dominance (p. 36).

³Our approach to this essay reflects our own training and work in the field, as it must for any scholar engaged in an endeavor of this scope. The conceptualization of the study has gone through numerous transformations as we wrestled with decisions about which scholarly and historical developments to emphasize in a field as dynamic, encompassing, complex, and sometimes invisible as gender. We signal through the use of "e.g." that many of our in-text citations are offered as instances and examples rather than exhaustive treatments of such scholarship, trends, or approaches.

⁴"The Complete Bibliography of '*The Journal of Negro Education,*' 1932–2006" (*Journal of Negro Education,* 2006, Volume 75, Number 2, pp. 73–318) provided the foundational information for this search. We conducted a supplemental search for 2006 to 2016 on *Education Research Complete.*

⁵Weaver-Hightower mentions a number of forces contributing to the boy turn: (a) media panic and popular books; (b) feminist analysis of gender roles; (c) feminists' initial and too-narrow conceptualizing of indicators of gender equity, such as access, enrollment, and test scores, that rendered them vulnerable to critique by tying notions of progress to numeric increases rather than multidimensional gender forces, effects, and processes; (d) neoliberal forces such as privatization, audit culture, and competition shaping education; (e) "explicit backlash politics" critiquing feminist politics, the feminization of schooling, and the enduring attention to girls, despite their strides in academic success; (f) sweeping economic and workforce changes that feminize the workforce, displace traditionally male jobs in industry, and unsettle men's historic roles as breadwinners; (g) primarily White, middle-class parental concerns about their sons' success; and (h) the "allure" to academics of new trends in scholarship providing niches for publishing. Arnot and Mac an Ghaill (2006) attribute this trend to broader economic patterns.

REFERENCES

Åberg, M., & Hedlin, M. (2015). Happy objects, happy men? Affect and materiality in vocational training. *Gender and Education, 27,* 523–538.

Adams, N., & Bettis, P. (2003). Commanding the room in short skirts: Cheering as the embodiment of ideal girlhood. *Gender & Society, 17,* 73–91.

Alcoff, L. (1988). Cultural feminism vs. poststructuralism: The identity crisis in feminist theory. *Signs: Journal of Women in Culture and Society, 13,* 405–436.

Ali, S., Mirza, H., Phoenix, A., & Ringrose, J. (2010). Intersectionality, Black British feminism and resistance in education: A roundtable discussion. *Gender and Education, 22,* 647–661.

Allen, L. (2004). Beyond the birds and the bees: Constituting a discourse of erotics in sexuality education. *Gender and Education, 16,* 151–167.

American Association of University Women Educational Foundation. (1992). *How schools shortchange girls: The AAUW Report: A study of major findings on girls and education.* New York, NY: Author.

American Association of University Women Educational Foundation. (1993). *Hostile hallways: Bullying, teasing, and sexual harassment in school.* Retrieved from http://www.aauw. org/files/2013/02/hostile-hallways-bullying-teasing-and-sexual-harassment-in-school.pdf

Anderson, E. (2011). Inclusive masculinities of university soccer players in the American Midwest. *Gender and Education, 23*, 729–744.

Anderson, E. W. (1937). Physical and mental health of teachers and administrative adjustments. *Review of Educational Research, 7*, 288–289.

Anderson, M. L., & Collins, P. H. (1992). *Race, class, and gender: An anthology.* Belmont, CA: Wadsworth.

Anyon, J. (1994). The retreat of Marxism and socialist feminism: Postmodern and poststructuralist theories in education. *Curriculum Inquiry, 24*, 115–133.

Anzaldúa, G. E. (1987). *Borderlands/La Frontera: The new Mestiza.* San Francisco, CA: Aunt Lute Books.

Arms, E. (2007). Gender equity in coeducational and single-sex environments. In S. Klein, B. Richardson, D. Grayson, L. Fox, C. Kramarae, D. S. Pollard, & C. A. Dwyer (Eds.), *Handbook for achieving gender equity through education* (2d ed., pp. 171–190). New York, NY: Routledge.

Arnot, M. (1982). Male hegemony, social class, and women's education. *Journal of Education, 164*, 64–89.

Arnot, M., & Mac an Ghaill, M. (Eds.). (2006). *The RoutledgeFalmer reader in gender and education.* London, England: RoutledgeFalmer.

Ashcraft, C. (2006). "Girl, you better go get a condom": Popular culture and teen sexuality as resources for critical multicultural curriculum. *Teachers College Record, 108*, 2145–2186.

Baca Zinn, M. (1980). Employment and education of Mexican-American women: The interplay of modernity and ethnicity in eight families. *Harvard Educational Review, 50*(1), 47–62.

Bagele, C. (2002). National policies on pregnancy in education systems in Sub-Saharan Africa: The case of Botswana. *Gender and Education, 14*, 21–35.

Bailey, L. (2007). Feminist critiques of educational research and practice. In B. J. Bank (Ed.), *Gender and education: An encyclopedia* (pp. 107–116). Westport, CT: Praeger.

Bailey, L. E., & Graves, K. (in press). Gendering history of education. In E. Tamura, & J. Rury (Eds.), *The Oxford handbook of the history of education.* New York, NY: Oxford University Press.

Baldridge, B., Hill, M. L., & Davis, J. E. (2011). New possibilities: (Re)engaging Black male youth within community-based educational spaces. *Race Ethnicity and Education, 14*, 121–136.

Bank, B. J. (Ed.). (2007). *Gender and education: An encyclopedia.* Westport, CT: Praeger.

Bank, B. J. (Ed.). (2011). *Gender and higher education.* Baltimore, MD: Johns Hopkins University Press.

Barozzi, S., & Ojeda, J. R. G. (2014). Discussing sexual identities with pre-service primary school English-language teachers from a Spanish context. *Perspectives in Education, 32*, 131–145.

Beemyn, B. G. (2003). Serving the needs of transgender college students. In J. T. Sears (Ed.), *Gay, lesbian, and transgender issues in education: Programs, policies, and practice* (pp. 105–124). New York, NY: Haworth.

Bell, J. C. (1918). A test in first year chemistry. *Journal of Educational Psychology, 9*, 199–209.

Benjamin, S. (2001). Challenging masculinities: Disability and achievement in testing times. *Gender and Education, 13*, 39–55.

Berg, M., & Seeber, B. K. (2016). *The slow professor: Challenging the culture of speed in the academy.* Toronto, Ontario, Canada: University of Toronto Press.

Bergen, F. D. (1885). Who shall teach? *Journal of Education, 22*(3), 60.

Best, A. (2000). *Prom night: Youth, schools and popular culture.* New York, NY: RoutledgeFalmer.

Bettie, J. (1993). *Women without class: Girls, race and identity.* Oakland: University of California Press.

Bettis, P., & Adams, N. (2005). *Geographies of girlhood: Identities in-between.* New York, NY: Routledge.

Bhachu, P. (1991). Ethnicity constructed and reconstructed: The role of Sikh women in cultural elaboration and educational decision-making in Britain. *Gender and Education, 3,* 45–60.

Blount, J. (1998). *Destined to rule the schools: Women and the superintendency, 1873–1995.* Albany: State University of New York Press.

Blount, J. (2005). *Fit to teach: Same-sex desire, gender, and school work in the twentieth century.* Albany: State University of New York Press.

Bowers, S., Lewandowski, J., Savage, T. A., & Woitaszewski, S. A. (2015). School psychologists' attitudes toward transgender students. *Journal of LGBT Youth, 12*(1), 1–18.

Braidotti, R., & Butler, J. (1994). Interview: Feminism by any other name. *Differences, 6*(2–3), 1–36.

Brown, A., & Thomas, M. (2014). "I just like knowing they can look at it and realize who I really am": Recognition and the limits of girlhood agency on MySpace. *Signs, 39,* 949–972.

Brown, L. M. (1999). *Raising their voices: The politics of girls' anger.* Cambridge, MA: Harvard University Press.

Brown, L. M. (2003). *Girlfighting: Betrayal and rejection among girls.* New York: New York University Press.

Burstyn, J. N. (1972). Religious arguments against higher education for women in England, 1840–1890. *Women's Studies, 1,* 111–132.

Butler, J. (1990). *Gender trouble: Feminism and the subversion of identity.* New York, NY: Routledge.

Butler, J. (1994). Feminism by any other name. *Differences, 6*(2–3), 1–35.

Bystydzienski, J., & Bird, S. R. (2006). *Removing barriers: Women in academic science, technology, engineering, and mathematics.* Bloomington: Indiana University Press.

Cannella, G. S., & Perez, M. S. (2012). Emboldened patriarchy in higher education: Feminist readings of capitalism, violence, and power. *Cultural Studies Critical Methodologies, 12,* 279–286.

Castro-Vazquez, G. (2000). Masculinity and condom use among Mexican teenagers: The Escuela Nacional Preparatoria No. 1's case. *Gender and Education, 12,* 479–492.

Chilisa, B. (2002). National policies on pregnancy in education systems in sub-Saharan Africa: The case of Botswana. *Gender and Education, 14,* 21–35.

Clegg, S. (2006). The problem of agency in feminism: A critical realist approach. *Gender and Education, 18,* 309–324.

Clifford, G. J. (2014). *Those good Gertrudes: A social history of women teachers in America.* Baltimore, MD: Johns Hopkins University Press.

Clover, D. E. (2010). A contemporary review of feminist aesthetic practices in selective adult education journals. *Adult Education Quarterly, 60,* 233–248.

Cobbett, M. C. (2013). "Beauties," "geeks" and "en-john": The possibilities and costs of girls' performances of gender in Antiguan schools. *Gender and Education, 25,* 251–266.

Cochran-Smith, M. (2016). Teaching and teacher education: Absence and presence in AERA presidential addresses. *Educational Researcher, 45,* 92–99.

Cohen, B. D. (2012). Reimagining gender through policy development: The case of a "single-sex" educational organization. *Gender and Education, 24,* 689–705.

Collins, P. H. (1990). *Black feminist thought: Knowledge, consciousness and the politics of empowerment.* New York, NY: Routledge.

Collins, P. H. (2004). Learning from the outsider within: The sociological significance of Black feminist thought. In S. Harding (Ed.), *The feminist standpoint theory reader* (pp. 81–102). New York, NY: Routledge.

Connell, C. (2012). Dangerous disclosures. *Sexuality Research and Social Policy, 9,* 168–177.

Connell, R. W. (2000). *The men and the boys.* Berkeley: University of California Press.

Connell, R. W., & Messerschmidt, J. W. (2005). Hegemonic masculinity: Rethinking the concept. *Gender & Society, 19,* 829–859.

Conroy, A. A. (2013). Gender, power, and intimate partner violence: A study of couples from rural Malawi. *Journal of Interpersonal Violence, 29,* 866–888.

Cooke, D. H. (1937). Local residents and married women as teachers. *Review of Educational Research, 7,* 267–272.

Cooke, D. H., Cardwell, J. F., & Dark, H. J. (1946). Local residents and married women as teachers. *Review of Educational Research, 16,* 233–239.

Cooke, D. H., Knox, W. G., & Libby, R. H. (1943). Local residents and married women as teachers. *Review of Educational Research, 13,* 252–261.

Cooke, D. H., & Simms, C. W. (1940). Local residents and married women as teachers. *Review of Educational Research, 10,* 204–209.

Coole, D., & Frost, S. (Eds.). (2010). *New materialisms: Ontology, agency and politics.* Durham, NC: Duke University Press.

Cooper, A. (1892). *A voice from the South: By a woman from the South.* Xenia, OH: Aldine Printing House.

Cooper, L. (2013). Women and higher education: Perspectives of middle-class, mother-daughter dyads. *Gender and Education, 25,* 624–639.

Crenshaw, K. (1989). Mapping the margins: Intersectionality, identity politics and violence against women of color. *Stanford Law Review, 43,* 1241–1299.

Cronin, S. (Ed.). (2014). *Anti-veiling campaigns in the Muslim world: Gender, modernism and the politics of dress.* New York, NY: Routledge.

Daniel, R. P. (1932). Personality differences between delinquent and non-delinquent Negro boys. *Journal of Negro Education, 1,* 381–387.

Davies, B. (1997). The subject of poststructuralism: A reply to Alison Jones. *Gender and Education, 9,* 271–283.

Davies, B. (2007). Gender economies: Literacy and the gendered production of neo-liberal subjectivities. *Gender and Education, 19,* 1–20.

Davis, A. (1979). The prison industrial complex [CD-ROM audiobook]. San Francisco, CA: AK Press.

Davis, J. E. (2010). Uneasy ties: Race and gender in urban education reform. In V. C. Polite, & E. Zamani (Eds.), *The state of the African American male* (pp. 145–164). East Lansing: Michigan State University Press.

Davis, J. E. (2013). Negotiating masculinity in college: African American males and academic engagement. In M. C. Brown, T. E. Dancy, & J. E. Davis (Eds.), *Educating African American males: Context for consideration, possibilities for practice* (pp. 53–66). New York, NY: Peter Lang.

Davis, v. Monroe County Board of Education, No. 97-843, 526 U.S. 629 (1999) 120 F.3d 1390.

de Beauvoir, S. (1949). *The second sex.* New York, NY: Knopf.

de Lange, N., & Mitchell, C. (2014). Building a future without gender violence: Rural teachers and youth in rural KwaZulu-Natal, South Africa, leading community dialogue. *Gender and Education, 26,* 584–599.

Dempster, S. (2011). I drink, therefore I'm man: Gender discourses, alcohol and the construction of British undergraduate masculinities. *Gender and Education, 23,* 635–653.

Dillard, C. (2006). *On spiritual strivings: Transforming an African American woman's academic life.* Albany: State University of New York Press.

Donovan, F. R. (1938). *The schoolma'am.* New York, NY: Frederic A. Stokes.

Dowler, L., Cuomo, D., & Laliberte, N. (2014). Challenging "The Penn State Way": A feminist response to institutional violence in higher education. *Gender, Place and Culture, 21,* 387–394.

Draper, P. (1975). Sex differences in cognitive styles: Socialization and constitutional variables. *Council on Anthropology & Education Quarterly, 6*(3), 3–6.

DuCille, A. (1994). Dyes and dolls: Multicultural Barbie and the merchandising of difference. *Differences, 6*(1), 46–68.

Dzuback, M. (2003). Gender and the politics of knowledge. *History of Education Quarterly, 43,* 171–195.

Editorial. (1989). *Gender and Education, 1*(1), 3–4.

Edwards, E. (1990). Educational institutions or extended families? The reconstruction of gender in women's colleges in the late-nineteenth and early-twentieth centuries. *Gender and Education, 2,* 17–35.

Eisenmann, L. (Ed.). (1998). *Historical dictionary of women's education in the United States.* Eisenmann Westport, CT: Greenwood.

Estler, S. (1975). Women as leaders in public education. *Signs, 1,* 363–386.

Farrell, B., Larsson, H., & Redelius, K. (2012). The game within the game: Girls' underperforming position in physical education. *Gender and Education, 24,* 101–118.

Fausto-Sterling, A. (1993). The five sexes. *The Sciences, 33*(2), 20–24.

Fausto-Sterling, A. (2000). *Sexing the body: Gender politics and the construction of sexuality.* New York, NY: Basic Books.

Fennell, S., & Arnot, M. (2008). *Gender education and equality in a global context: Conceptual frameworks and policy perspectives.* New York, NY: Routledge.

Ferguson, A. A. (2000). *Bad boys: Public schools in the making of Black masculinity.* Ann Arbor: University of Michigan Press.

Fine, M. (1988). Sexuality, schooling, and adolescent females: The missing discourse of desire. *Harvard Educational Review, 58,* 29–53.

Fine, M., & McClelland, S. (2006). Sexuality education and desire: Still missing after all these years. *Harvard Educational Review, 76,* 297–338.

Fine, M., & McClelland, S. (2007). The politics of teen women's sexuality: Public policy and the adolescent female body, *Emory Law Review, 56,* 993–1038.

Fine, M., & Sirin, S. R. (2008). *Muslim American youth: Understanding hyphenated identities through multiple methods.* New York: New York University Press.

Fine, M., Weis, L., Powell, L., & Wong, L. M. (Eds.). (1997). *Off-white: Readings on power, privilege and resistance.* New York, NY: Routledge.

Flexner, E. (1959). *Century of struggle: The woman's rights movement in the United States.* Cambridge, MA: Belknap Press of Harvard University Press.

Flood, M., Gardiner, J. K., Pease, B., & Pringle, K. (Eds.). (2007). *International encyclopedia of men and masculinities.* London, England: Routledge.

Fonow, M. M., & Cook, J. A. (Eds.). (1991). *Beyond methodology: Feminist scholarship as lived research.* Bloomington: Indiana University Press.

Fordham, S. (1993). "Those loud Black girls": (Black) women, silence and gender "passing" in the academy. *Anthropology & Education Quarterly, 24*(1), 3–32.

Foubert, J. (2010). *The men's and women's programs: Ending rape through peer education.* New York, NY: Routledge.

Francis, B. (2010). Re/theorising gender: Female masculinity and male femininity in the classroom. *Gender and Education, 22,* 477–490.

Francis, B., Burke, P., & Read, B. (2014). The submergence and re-emergence of gender in undergraduate accounts of university experience. *Gender and Education, 26,* 1–17.

Francis, B., & Skelton, C. (2001). Men teachers and the construction of heterosexual masculinity in the classroom. *Sex Education, 1*(1), 9–21.

Francis, D. (2014). "You must be thinking what a lesbian man teacher is doing in a nice place like Dipane Letsie School?" Enacting, negotiating and reproducing dominant understandings of gender in a rural school in the Free State, South Africa. *Gender and Education, 26,* 539–552.

Frankenberg, R. (1993). *White women, race matters: The social construction of Whiteness.* Minneapolis: University of Minnesota Press.

Frazier, N., & Sadker, M. (1973). *Sexism in school and society.* New York, NY: Harper & Row.

Franzosa, S. (1993). Shaking the foundations: How schools shortchange girls. *NWSA Journal, 5,* 325–339.

Fuller, A., Turbin, J., & Johnston, B. (2013). Computer club for girls: The problem with seeing girls as the problem. *Gender and Education, 25,* 499–514.

Fuller, K. (2014). Gendered educational leadership: Beneath the monoglossic façade. *Gender and Education, 26,* 321–337.

Fultz, M. (1995). African American teachers in the South, 1890–1940: Growth, feminization, and salary discrimination. *Teachers College Record, 96,* 544–568.

Garber, L. (Ed.). (1994). *Tilting the tower: Lesbians, teaching, queer subjects.* New York, NY: Routledge.

Garcia, L. (2012). *Respect yourself, protect yourself: Latina girls and sexual identity.* New York: New York University Press.

Gebser, v. Lago Vista Independent School District, No. 96-1866, 106 F.3d 1223, affirmed (1998).

Gilligan, C. (1977). In a different voice: Women's conception of the self and of morality. *Harvard Educational Review, 47,* 481–517.

Gilligan, C. (1982). *In a different voice: Psychological theory and women's development.* Cambridge, MA: Harvard University Press.

Ginorio, A., & Huston, M. (2001). *Si, se puede! Yes, we can: Latinas in school.* Washington, DC: American Association of University Women Educational Foundation.

Glasser, H. M., & Smith, J. P. (2008). On the vague meaning of "gender" in education research: The problem, its sources, and recommendations for practice. *Educational Researcher, 3,* 343–350.

Glazer-Raymo, J. (2008). *Unfinished agendas: New and continuing gender challenges in higher education.* Baltimore, MD: Johns Hopkins University Press.

Gonzalez, M., & McNulty, J. (2010). Achieving competency with transgender youth: School counselors as collaborative advocates. *Journal of LGBT Issues in Counseling, 4,* 176–186.

Goodsell, W. (1923). *The education of women: Its social background and its problems.* New York, NY: Macmillan.

Gordon, R. (1994). Education policy and gender in Zimbabwe. *Gender and Education, 6,* 131–139.

Gould, L. (1978). *X: A fabulous child's story.* New York, NY: Daughters.

Grant, C. A., & Sleeter, C. (1986). Race, class, and gender in education research: An argument for integrative analysis. *Review of Educational Research, 56,* 195–211.

Grant, L. (1994). Helpers, enforcers, and go-betweens: Black females in elementary school classrooms. In M. B. Zinn, & B. T. Dill (Eds.), *Women of color in U.S. society* (pp. 43–64). Philadelphia, PA: Temple University Press.

Graves, K. (1998). *Girls' schooling during the Progressive Era: From female scholar to domesticated citizen.* New York, NY: Garland.

Grumet, M. (1988). *Bittermilk: Women and teaching.* Amherst, MA: Amherst University Press.

Haines, P. F. (1977). For honor and alma mater: Perspectives on coeducation at Cornell University, 1868–1885. *Journal of Education, 159*(3), 25–37.

Hanh Thi Do, V., & Brenna, M. (2015). Complexities of Vietnamese femininities: A resource for rethinking women's university leadership practices. *Gender and Education, 27,* 273–287.

Harding, S. (1986). *The science question in feminism.* Ithaca, NY: Cornell University Press.

Harding, S. (Ed.). (1987). *Feminism and methodology: Social science issues.* Bloomington: Indiana University Press.

Harding, S. (1991). *Whose science? Whose knowledge: Thinking from women's lives.* Ithaca, NY: Cornell University Press.

Harding, S. (1998). *Is science multicultural? Postcolonialisms, feminisms, and epistemologies.* Bloomington: Indiana University Press.

Harding, S. (Ed.). (2004). *The feminist standpoint theory reader.* New York, NY: Routledge.

Harrison, L. (2000). Gender relations and the production of difference in school-based sexuality and HIV/AIDS education in Australia. *Gender and Education, 12,* 5–19.

Hart, J. (2006). Women and feminism in higher education scholarship: An analysis of three core journals. *Journal of Higher Education, 77,* 40–61. doi:10.1353/jhe.2006.0003

Hartsock, N. (2004). The feminist standpoint: Developing the ground for a specifically feminist historical materialism. In S. Harding (Ed.), *The feminist standpoint theory reader* (pp. 35–54). New York, NY: Routledge.

Hatoss, A., & Huijser, H. (2010). Gendered barriers to educational opportunities: Resettlement of Sudanese refugees in Australia. *Gender and Education, 22,* 147–160.

Hayes, E. (1992). The impact of feminism on adult education publications: An analysis of British and American journals. *International Journal of Lifelong Education, 11,* 125–138.

Hayes, E., & Smith, L. (1990, May). *The impact of feminism on adult education literature: An analysis of trends in scholarship.* Paper presented at the proceedings of the 1990 Adult Education Research Conference, Athens, GA.

Hayes, E. R. (1991). Adult education's response to the feminist critique: A comparison of trends in the literature. *Initiatives, 54*(1), 29–38.

Hayes, E. R., & Smith, L. (1994). Women in adult education: An analysis of perspectives in major journals. *Adult Education Quarterly, 44,* 201–221.

Haywood, C., & Mac an Ghaill, M. (2012). "What's next for masculinity?" Reflexive directions for theory and research on masculinity and education. *Gender and Education, 24,* 577–592.

Hebdige, D. (1979). *Subculture: The meaning of style.* London, England: Routledge.

Henry, M. (2001). Globalisation and the politics of accountability: Issues and dilemmas for gender equity in education. *Gender and Education, 13,* 87–100.

Herbst, J. (1989). *And sadly teach: Teacher education and professionalization in American culture.* Madison: University of Wisconsin Press.

Heward, C. (1994). Academic snakes and merit ladders: Reconceptualizing the "glass ceiling." *Gender and Education, 6,* 249–262.

Heyward, C. B. (1995). Catching up: Gender values at a Canadian independent school for girls, 1978–93. *Gender and Education, 7,* 189–203.

Hochschild, A. R. (1975). Inside the clockwork of male careers. In F. Howe (Ed.), *Women and the power to change* (pp. 47–80). New York, NY: McGraw-Hill.

Hoffman, N. (1981). *Women's true profession: Voices from the history of teaching.* Old Westbury, NY: Feminist Press.

Holland, C., & Eisenhart, M. (1992). *Educated in romance: Women, achievement and college culture.* Chicago, IL: University of Chicago Press.

hooks, b. (1984). *Feminist theory: From margin to center.* Boston, MA: South End.

hooks, b. (2000). *Where we stand: Class matters.* New York, NY: Routledge.

Howe, F. (1979). Introduction: The first decade of women's studies. *Harvard Educational Review, 49,* 413–421.

Hudson, A. (1932). Reading achievement, interests, and habits of Negro women. *Journal of Negro Education, 1,* 367–373.

Hughes, C. (2002). Beyond the poststructuralist-modern impasse: The woman-returner as "exile" and "nomad." *Gender and Education, 14,* 411–424.

Hughes, C., & Lury, C. (2013). Re-turning feminist methodologies: From a social to an ecological epistemology. *Gender and Education, 25,* 786–799.

Hull, G. T., Scott, P. B., & Smith, B. (1993). *But some of us are brave: All the women are White, all the Blacks are men: Black Women's studies.* Old Westbury, NY: Feminist Press. (Original work published 1982)

Jackson, J. (2010). "Dangerous presumptions": How single-sex schooling reifies false notions of sex, gender, and sexuality. *Gender and Education, 22*, 227–238.

Joe, E. M., & Davis, J. E. (2010). Parental influence, school readiness and early academic achievement of African American boys. *Journal of Negro Education, 78*, 260–276.

Johannesburg, I. A. (1994). Farm boy from the edge of the Arctic and the seduction of feminist pedagogy in American academia. *Gender and Education, 6*, 293–306.

Jossey-Bass. (2002). *The Jossey-Bass reader on gender and education.* San Francisco, CA: Author.

Katz, J. (2006). *The macho paradox: Why some men hurt women and how all men can help.* Naperville, IL: Sourcebooks.

Katz, J. (2013). Tough Guise II: Violence, manhood and American culture [Film]. Retrieved from http://www.mediaed.org/toughguise2/index.html

Kendall, N. (2012). *The sex education debates.* Chicago, IL: University of Chicago Press.

Kimmel, M., & Aronson, A. (2003). *Men and masculinities: A social, cultural, and historical encyclopedia.* Santa Barbara, CA: ABC-CLIO.

Klein, J. (2012). *The bully society: School shootings and the crisis of bullying in America's schools.* New York: New York University Press.

Klein, S., Richardson, B., Grayson, D., Fox, L., Kramarae, C., Pollard, D. S., & Dwyer, C.A. (2007). *Handbook for achieving gender equity through education.* New York, NY: Routledge.

Kliebard, H. M. (1999). *Schooled to work: Vocationalism and the American curriculum, 1876–1946.* New York, NY: Teachers College Press.

Kramarae, C., & Spender, D. (2000). *Routledge international encyclopedia of women: Global women's issues and knowledge.* New York, NY: Routledge.

Kutner, N. G., & Brogan, D. (1976). Sources of sex discrimination in educational systems: A conceptual model. *Psychology of Women Quarterly, 1*, 50–69. doi:10.1111/j.1471-6402.1976.tb00808.x

LaFrance, M. (1991). School for scandal: Different educational experiences for females and males. *Gender and Education, 3*, 3–13.

Larkin, J. (1994). Walking through walls: The sexual harassment of high school girls. *Gender and Education, 6*, 263–280.

Lather, P. (1986). Research as praxis. *Harvard Educational Review, 56*, 257–278.

Lather, P. (1991). *Getting smart: Feminist research and pedagogy with/in the postmodern.* New York, NY: Routledge.

Lather, P. (1999). To be of use: The work of reviewing. *Review of Educational Research, 69*, 2–7.

Lather, P., & Smithies, C. (1997). *Troubling the angels: Women living with HIV/AIDS.* Boulder, CO: Westview.

Laughlin, K., Gallagher, J., Cobble, D. S., Boris, E., Nadasen, P., Gilmore, S., & Zarnow, L. (2010). Is it time to jump ship? Historians rethink the waves metaphor. *Feminist Formations, 22*, 76–135.

Laws, G. (1938). Vanishing "sissy" and "tomboy" seen in new educational plan. *Journal of Education, 121*(2), 67.

Leathwood, C., & Read, B. (2009). *Gender and the changing face of higher education: A feminized future?* New York, NY: Open University Press.

Lees, L. J. (1998). Transgender students on our campuses. In R. L. Sanlo (Ed.), *Working with lesbian, gay, bisexual, and transgender college students: A handbook for faculty and administrators* (pp. 37–43). Westport, CT: Greenwood.

Levy, B. (1972). The school's role in the sex role stereotyping of girls: A feminist review of literature. *Feminist Studies, 1*(1), 5–23.

Lightfoot, S. L. (1976). Socialization and education of young Black girls in school. *Teachers College Record, 78*, 239–262.

Lingard, B. (2003). Where to in gender policy in education after recuperative masculinity politics? *International Journal of Inclusive Education, 7*(1), 33–56.

Lomawaima, K. T. (1994). *They called it prairie light: The story of Chilocco Indian School.* Lincoln: University of Nebraska Press.

Lorde, A. (1984). *Sister outsider: Essays and speeches.* Berkeley, CA: Crossing Press.

Love, R. (1993). Gender bias: Inequities in the classroom. *IDRA Newsletter, 20*(2), 8, 11–12.

Luecke, J. C. (2011). Working with transgender children and their classmates in pre-adolescence: Just be supportive. *Journal of LGBT Youth, 8,* 116–156.

Luttrell, W. (1997). *School-smart and mother-wise: Working-class women's identity and schooling.* New York, NY: Routledge.

Luttrell, W. (2003). *Pregnant bodies, fertile minds: Gender, race, and the schooling of pregnant teens.* New York, NY: Routledge.

Mac an Ghaill, M. (1991). Schooling, sexuality and male power: Towards an emancipatory curriculum. *Gender and Education, 3,* 291–309.

Martin, E. (1991). The egg and the sperm: How science has constructed a romance based on stereotypical male and female roles. *Signs, 16,* 485–501.

Martin, J. R. (1985). *Reclaiming a conversation: The ideal of the educated woman.* New Haven, CT: Yale University Press.

Martin, K. (1998). Becoming a gendered body: Practices of preschools. *American Sociological Review, 63,* 494–511.

Martinez-Alemán, A. M., & Renn, K. (Eds.). (2002). *Women in higher education: An encyclopedia.* Santa Barbara, CA: ABC-CLIO.

Mayo, C. (2000). Gender disidentification: The perils of the post-gender condition. In R. Curren (Ed.), *Philosophy of education, 1999* (pp. 356–364). Urbana, IL: Philosophy of Education Society.

Mayo, C. (2007). Disruptions of desire: From androgynes to genderqueer. *Philosophy of Education Yearbook,* 49–58. Retrieved from http://ojs.ed.uiuc.edu/index.php/pes/article/view/1435/182

Mayo, C. (2008). Obscene associations: Gay-straight alliances, the Equal Access Act, and abstinence-only policy. *Sexuality Research and Social Policy, 5*(2), 45–55.

Mayo, C. (2011). Sexuality education policy and the educative potentials of risk and rights. *Policy Futures in Education, 9,* 406–415.

McClintock, A., Mufti, A., & Shohat, E. (Eds.). (1997). *Dangerous liaisons: Gender, nation and postcolonial perspectives.* Minneapolis: University of Minnesota Press.

McKinney, J. (2005). On the margins: A study of the experiences of transgender college students. *Journal of Gay & Lesbian Issues in Education, 3,* 63–76.

McNae, R., & Vali, K. (2015). Diverse experiences of women leading in higher education: Locating networks and agency for leadership within a university context in Papua New Guinea. *Gender and Education, 27,* 288–303.

McRobbie, A. (1990). Settling accounts with subcultures. A feminist critique. In S. Frith, & A. Goodwin (Eds.), *On record: Rock, pop, and the written word* (pp. 66–80). London, England: Routledge.

McRobbie, A. (2009). *The aftermath of feminism: Gender, culture, and social change.* Thousand Oaks, CA: Sage.

McRobbie, A. (2010). Reflections on feminism, immaterial labour, and the post-Fordist regime. *New Formations, 70,* 60–76.

Messner, M. A., Greenberg, M. A., & Peretz, T. (2015). *Some men: Feminist allies and the movement to end violence against women.* New York, NY: Oxford University Press.

Metropolitan Center for Urban Education. (2010). *Theories of change among single-sex schools for Black and Latino boys: An intervention in search of theory.* New York: NYU Steinhardt, Steinhardt School of Culture, Education, and Human Development. Retrieved from http://steinhardt.nyu.edu/scmsAdmin/media/users/eaf7/An_Intervention_in_Search_of_Theory_Research_Brief.pdf

Meyer, E. (2009). *Gender, bullying and harassment: Strategies to end sexism and homophobia in schools*. New York, NY: Teachers College Press.

Mihesuah, D. A. (1997). *Cultivating the rosebuds: The education of women at the Cherokee Female Seminary, 1851–1909*. Urbana: University of Illinois Press.

Mihesuah, D. A. (1998). *Natives and academics: Researching and writing about American Indians*. Lincoln: University of Nebraska Press.

Mihesuah, D. A. (2003). *Indigenous American women: Decolonization, empowerment, activism*. Lincoln: University of Nebraska Press.

Miller, J. (1979). Women: the evolving educational consciousness. *Journal of Curriculum Theorizing, 2*, 238–246.

Miller, J. (1981). The sound of silence breaking: Feminist pedagogy and curriculum theory. *Journal of Curriculum Theorizing, 4*, 5–11.

Mir, S. (2014). *Muslim American women on campus: Undergraduate social life and identity*. Chapel Hill: University of North Carolina Press.

Mirembe, R., & Davies, L. (2001). Is schooling a risk? Gender, power relations, and school culture in Uganda. *Gender and Education, 13*, 401–416.

Mohanty, C. T. (1997). *Feminist genealogies, colonial legacies, democratic futures*. New York, NY: Routledge.

Mohanty, C. T. (2004). *Feminism without borders*. Durham, NC: Duke University Press.

Morrison, T. (1992). *Playing in the dark: Whiteness and the literary imagination*. Cambridge, MA: Harvard University Press.

Morse, S. (1998). *Separated by sex: A critical look at single-sex education for girls*. Washington, DC: American Association of University Women Educational Foundation.

Mullen, A. L. (2010). *Degrees of inequality: Culture, class, and gender in American higher education*. Baltimore, MD: Johns Hopkins University Press.

Munro, P. (1998). *Subject to fiction: Women teachers' life history narratives and the cultural politics of resistance*. Philadelphia, PA: Open University Press.

Nabozny v. Podlesny, 92 F.3d 446 (7th Cir. 1996).

Naples, N., Hoogland, R. C., Wickramasinghe, M., & Wong, W. C. A. (in press). *Wiley Blackwell encyclopedia of gender and sexuality studies*. Hoboken, NJ: Wiley Blackwell.

Narayan, U. (1997). *Dislocating cultures: Identities, traditions, and Third World feminism*. New York, NY: Routledge.

Narayan, U., & Harding, S. (2000). *Decentering the centre: Philosophy for a multicultural, postcolonial, and feminist world*. Indianapolis: Indiana University Press.

Noddings, N. (1984). *Caring: A feminine approach to ethics and moral education*. Berkeley: University of California Press.

Noddings, N. (1992). *The challenge to care in schools: An alternative approach to education*. New York, NY: Teachers College Press.

Noddings, N., Katz, M. S., & Strike, K. A. (1999). *Justice and caring: The search for common ground in education* (Professional Ethics in Education Series). New York, NY: Teachers College Press.

Omolade, B. (1987). A Black feminist pedagogy. *Women's Studies Quarterly, 15*(3–4), 32–39.

Oppe, G. (1946). Opportunities for women in chemistry. *Science Education, 30*, 276–278.

Orenstein, P. (1994). *Schoolgirls: Young women, self-esteem, and the confidence gap*. New York, NY: Doubleday.

Peril, L. (2002). *Pink think: Becoming a woman in many uneasy lessons*. New York, NY: W. W. Norton.

Perry, E. (2013). "She's alpha male": Transgressive gender performances in the probation "classroom." *Gender and Education, 25*, 396–412.

Pharr, S. (1997). *Homophobia: A weapon of sexism*. Berkeley, CA: Chardon Press.

Pillow, W. S. (2004). *Unfit subjects: Educational policy and the teen mother*. New York, NY: RoutledgeFalmer.

Pipher, M. (1994). *Reviving Ophelia: Saving the selves of adolescent girls*. New York, NY: Putnam.

Pomerantz, S., & Raby, R. (2011). "Oh, she's so smart": Girls' complex engagements with post/feminist narratives of academic success. *Gender and Education, 23*, 549–564.

Rands, K. (2013). Supporting transgender and gender-nonconforming youth through teaching mathematics for social justice. *Journal of LGBT Youth, 10*(1/2), 106–126.

Rands, K. E. (2009). Considering transgender people in education. *Journal of Teacher Education, 60*, 419–431.

Rasmussen, M. (2009). Beyond gender identity? *Gender and Education, 21*, 431–447.

Reay, D. (1990). Working with boys. *Gender and Education, 2*, 269–282.

Reay, D. (2002). Shaun's story: Troubling discourses of White working-class masculinities. *Gender and Education, 14*, 221–234.

Reed, L. R. (1999). Troubling boys and disturbing discourses on masculinity and schooling: A feminist exploration of current debates and interventions concerning boys in school. *Gender and Education, 11*, 93–110.

Reeves, J. B. (1975). Equity, quality, and cost in higher education. *Frontiers, 1*(1), 53–57.

Reinharz, S. (1992). *Feminist methods in social research*. New York, NY: Oxford University Press.

Rezai-Rashti, G. M. (2015). The politics of gender segregation and women's access to higher education in the Islamic Republic of Iran: The interplay of repression and resistance. *Gender and Education, 27*, 469–486.

Rich, A. (1979). Claiming an education. In *On lies, secrets and silence: Selected prose, 1966–1978* (pp. 231–235). New York, NY: W. W. Norton.

Richardson, L. (1997). *Fields of play: Constructing an academic life*. New Brunswick, NJ: Rutgers University Press.

Richardson, L. (2000). New writing practices in qualitative research. *Sociology of Sport Journal, 17*(1), 5–20.

Riley, D. (2003). *Am I that name? Feminism and the category women in history*. Minneapolis: University of Minnesota Press.

Ringrose, J. (2007). Successful girls? Complicating post-feminist, neoliberal discourses of educational achievement and gender equality. *Gender and Education, 19*, 471–489.

Robinson, K. H. (1992). Class-room discipline: Power, resistance, and gender: A look at teacher perspectives. *Gender and Education, 4*, 273–288.

Robinson, K. H. (2005). Reinforcing hegemonic masculinities through sexual harassment: Issues of identity, power and popularity in secondary schools. *Gender and Education, 17*, 19–37.

Rury, J. (1991). *Education and women's work: Female schooling and the division of labor in urban America, 1870–1930*. Albany: State University of New York Press.

Ryan, C. L., Patraw, J. M., & Bednar, M. (2013). Discussing princess boys and pregnant men: Teaching about gender diversity and transgender experiences within an elementary school curriculum. *Journal of LGBT Youth, 10*, 83–105.

Sadker, D. M., Sadker, M., & Zittleman, K. (2009). *Still failing at fairness: How gender bias cheats girls and boys in school and what we can do about it*. New York, NY: Scribner.

Sadker, M., & Sadker, D. (1994). *Failing at fairness: How America's schools cheat girls*. New York, NY: Charles Scribner's.

Sannino, A., & Vainio, J. (2015). Gendered hegemony and its contradictions among Finnish university physicists. *Gender and Education, 27*, 505–522.

Schoenfeld, A. H. (2016). 100 years of curriculum history, theory, and research. *Educational Researcher, 450*, 105–111.

Scott, J. W. (1986). Gender: A useful category of historical analysis. *American Historical Review, 91*, 1053–1075.

Scott, J. W. (2010a). Gender: Still a useful category of analysis? *Diogenes, 57*(1), 7–14.

Scott, J. W. (2010b). *The politics of the veil*. Princeton, NJ: Princeton University Press.

Segregation in high schools. (1910). *Journal of Education, 71*(3), 42.

Shameful Wesleyan. (1909). *Journal of Education, 69*(15), 413.

Sikes, P. J. (1991). Nature took its course? Student teachers and gender awareness. *Gender and Education, 3,* 145–162.

Skelton, A. (1993). On becoming a male physical education teacher: The informal culture of students and the construction of hegemonic masculinity. *Gender and Education, 5,* 289–303.

Skelton, C. (1994). Sex, male teachers and young children. *Gender and Education, 6,* 87–94.

Skelton, C., Francis, B., & Sumulyan, L. (Eds.). (2006). *The Sage handbook of gender and education.* Thousand Oaks, CA: Sage.

Skiba, R. J., Michael, R. S., Nardo, A. C., & Peterson, R. L. (2002). The color of discipline: Sources of racial and gender disproportionality in school punishment. *Urban Review, 34,* 317–342.

Soerensen, A. S. (1992). The question of representation: Research in gender and education in Scandinavia. *Gender and Education, 1,* 201–212.

Solomon, B. M. (1985). *In the company of educated women: A history of women and higher education in America.* New Haven, CT: Yale University Press.

Sommers, C. H. (2000). *The war against boys: How misguided policies are harming our young men.* New York, NY: Simon & Schuster.

Spivak, G. C. (1988). Can the subaltern speak? In C. Nelson, & L. Grossberg (Eds.), *Marxism and the interpretation of culture* (pp. 271–313). Urbana: University of Illinois Press.

Stacey, J., Béreaud, S., & Daniels, J. (1974). *And Jill came tumbling after: Sexism in American education.* New York, NY: Dell.

Pierre, E., & Pillow, W. (Eds.). (2000). *Working the ruins: Feminist poststructuralism and education.* New York, NY: Routledge.

Stone, L. (Ed.). (1994). *The education feminism reader.* New York, NY: Routledge.

Sweeney, M. (2010). *"Reading is my window": Books and the art of reading in women's prisons.* Chapel Hill: University of North Carolina Press.

Sweeney, M. (2012). *The story within us: Women prisoners reflect on reading.* Urbana, IL: University of Illinois Press.

Talburt, S. (2000). *Subject to identity: Knowledge, sexuality, and academic practices in higher education.* Albany: State University of New York Press.

Tamboukou, M. (1999). Spacing herself: Women in education. *Gender and Education, 11,* 125–139.

Tamim, T. (2013). Higher education, languages, and the persistence of inequitable structures for working-class women in Pakistan. *Gender and Education, 25,* 155–169.

Taylor, C. (2011). "Hope in failure": A level students, discursive agency, post-feminism and feminism. *Gender and Education, 23,* 825–841.

Taylor, C., & Hughes, C. (Eds.). (2016). *Posthuman research practices in education.* New York, NY: Palgrave Macmillan.

Tetreault, M. K. (1986). Integrating women's history: The case of United States history high school textbooks. *The History Teacher, 19,* 211–262.

Thayer-Bacon, B., Stone, L., & Sprecher, K. (2013). *Education feminism: Classic and contemporary readings.* Albany: State University of New York Press.

Thomas, M. (2011). *Multicultural girlhoods: Racism, sexuality and the conflicted spaces of American education.* Philadelphia, PA: Temple University Press.

Thorne, B. (1993). *Gender play: Girls and boys in school.* New Brunswick, NJ: Rutgers University Press.

Thornton, M. (2012). Universities upside down: The impact of the new knowledge economy. In M. Luxton, & M. J. Mossman (Eds.), *Reconsidering knowledge: Feminism and the academy* (pp. 76–95). Halifax Regional Municipality, Nova Scotia, Canada: Fernwood.

Tice, K. (2012). *Queens of academe: Beauty pageantry, student bodies, and college life.* Oxford, England: Oxford University Press.

Tittle, C. K., & Denker, E. R. (1977). Re-entry women: A selective review of the educational process, career choice, and interest measurement. *Review of Educational Research, 47,* 531–584.

Tolman, D. (2002). *Dilemmas of desire: Teenage girls talk about sexuality.* Cambridge, MA: Harvard University Press.

Townsend, B. K. (1993). Feminist scholarship in core higher education journals. *Review of Higher Education, 17,* 21–41.

Trecker, J. L. (1971). Women in U.S. history high school textbooks. *Social Education, 35,* 249–260.

Trier-Bieniek, A., & Leavy, P. (Eds.). (2014). *Gender and pop culture: A text-reader.* Rotterdam, Netherlands: Sense.

Tuana, N. (1993). *The less noble sex: Scientific, religious, and philosophical conceptions of women's nature.* Bloomington: Indiana University Press.

Turner, C. S. V. (2008). Women of color in academe: Experiences of the often invisible. In J. Glazer-Raymo (Ed.), *Unfinished agendas: New and continuing challenges in higher education* (pp. 230–252). Baltimore, MD: Johns Hopkins University Press.

Twombly, S. B. (1993). What we know about women in community colleges. *Journal of Higher Education, 64,* 186–210.

Twombly, S. B., & Townsend, B. K. (2007). *Community college faculty: Overlooked and undervalued.* San Francisco, CA: Jossey-Bass.

Tyack, D. B., & Hansot, E. (1990). *Learning together: A history of coeducation in American schools.* New Haven, CT: Yale University Press.

Unterhalter, E. (2013). Connecting the private and the public: Pregnancy, exclusion, and the expansion of schooling in Africa. *Gender and Education, 25,* 75–90.

Vanderleest, J. G., & Galper, C. Q. (2009). Improving the health of transgender people: Transgender medical education in Arizona. *Journal of the Association of Nurses in AIDS Care, 20,* 411–416.

Walker, V. S. (2001). African American teaching in the South: 1940–1960. *American Educational Research Journal, 38,* 751–779.

Walker, V. S. (2005). Organized resistance and Black educators' quest for school equality, 1878–1938. *Teachers College Record, 107,* 355–388.

Walker, V. S. (2013). Ninth Annual Brown Lecture in Education Research: Black educators as educational advocates in the decades before *Brown v. Board of Education. Educational Researcher, 42,* 207–222.

Walkerdine, V. (1990). *Schoolgirl fictions.* London, England: Verso.

Ward, K., & Wolf-Wendel, L. (2012). *Academic motherhood: How faculty manage work and family.* New Brunswick, NJ: Rutgers University Press.

Weaver-Hightower, M. (2003). The "boy turn" in research on gender and education. *Review of Educational Research, 73,* 471–498.

Weiler, K. (2001). *Feminist engagements: Reading, resisting, and revisioning male theorists in education and cultural studies.* New York, NY: RoutledgeFalmer.

Weiler, K., & Middleton, S. (Eds.). (1999). *Telling women's lives: Narrative inquiries in history of women's education.* Philadelphia, PA: Open University Press.

Weis, L. (1988). *Class, race, and gender in American education.* Albany: State University of New York Press.

Weis, L., & Fine, M. (1993). *Beyond silenced voices: Class, race, and gender in United States schools.* Albany: State University of New York Press.

Weitzman, L. J. (1979). *Sex role socialization: A focus on women.* Palo Alto, CA: Mayfield.

Weitzman, L. J., Eifler, D., Hokada, E., & Ross, C. (1972). Sex-role socialization in picture books for preschool children. *American Journal of Sociology, 77,* 1125–1150.

Wells, K. (1909). Contrast in education. *Journal of Education, 69*(10), 263–264.

Westland, E. (1993). Cinderella in the classroom: Children's responses to gender roles in fairytales. *Gender and Education, 5,* 237–249.

Wiegman, R. (Ed.). (2002). *Women's studies on its own: A next wave reader in institutional change.* Durham, NC: Duke University Press.

Willis, P. E. (1977). *Learning to labor: How working class kids get working class jobs*. New York, NY: Columbia University Press.

Wohlwend, K. E. (2012). The boys who would be princesses: Playing with gender identity intertexts in Disney Princess transmedia. *Gender and Education, 24*, 593–610.

Wolf, C. (1975). Sex roles as portrayed in marriage and the family textbooks: Contributions to the status quo. *Women's Studies: An Interdisciplinary Journal, 3*(1), 45–60.

Women's influence not desired. (1910). *Journal of Education, 71*(25), 724.

Woody, T. (1929). *A history of women's education in the United States* (Vols. 1–2). New York, NY: Science Press.

Woyshner, C. A., & Gelfond, H. S. (1998). *Minding women: Reshaping the educational realm*. Cambridge, MA: Harvard Educational Review.

Zine, J. (2006). Unveiled sentiments: Gendered Islamophobia and experiences of veiling among Muslim girls in a Canadian Islamic school. *Equity & Excellence in Education, 39*, 239–252.

Zinn, M. B., & Dill, B. T. (Eds.). (1994). *Women of color in U.S. society*. Philadelphia, PA: Temple University Press.

JOURNAL LIST OF SPECIAL ISSUES

Bonner, F. B., & Thomas, V. G. (Eds.). (2001). Black women in the academy: Challenges and opportunities. *Journal of Negro Education, 70*(3).

Brickley, L. T., Garfunkel, G., & Hulsizer, D. (Eds.). (1979). Women and education. *Harvard Educational Review, 49*(4).

Cochran-Smith, M., Ladson-Billings, G., & McDonnell, L. (Eds.). (2016). Centennial special issue: A living lens: AERA past presidents reflect on 100 years of education research. *Educational Researcher, 45*, 63–180.

Collier-Thomas, B. (Ed.). (1982). The impact of Black women in education: An historical overview. *Journal of Negro Education, 51*, 173–365.

Fogleman, B. Y. S., & Nihlen, A. S. (Eds.). (1975). Women in schools and society [Special issue]. *Council on Anthropology & Education Quarterly, 6*(3).

Green, L. (1979). Women's influence on education. *History of Education Quarterly, 19*, 93–116.

Jenifer, F. G. (Ed.) (1992). Black males and education [Special issue]. *Journal of Negro Education, 61*, 1–99.

Ladner, R., & VanDeGrift, T. (Eds.). (2011). Introduction to special issue (Part 1): Broadening participation in computing education. *ACM Transactions on Computing Education, 11*(2). doi:10.1145/1993069.1993070

Malcom, S. M., & Malcom, L. E. (Eds.). (2011). The double bind: The next generation. *Harvard Educational Review, 81*, 162–172.

Peterson, S. S., & Parr, J. M. (Eds.). (2012). Gender and writing. *Journal of Writing Research, 3*, 151–277.

Polite, V. C., & Davis, J. E. (Eds.) (1994). Pedagogical and contextual issues affecting African American males in school and society. *Journal of Negro Education, 63*, 505–654.

Reinterpreting women's education. (1974). *History of Education Quarterly, 14*, 1–162.

Sherman, W. H. (Ed.). (2010). Special issue: Globalization: Women's leadership. *Journal of Educational Administration, 48*, 677–786.

Taylor, C. A., & Ivinson, G. (Eds.). (2013). Material feminisms: New directions for education. *Gender and Education, 25*, 665–670.

Theme issue on gender studies in engineering and engineering education. (2005). *European Journal of Engineering Education, 30*, 461.

Chapter 19

Rehumanizing the "Other": Race, Culture, and Identity in Education Research

JENNIFER M. LANGER-OSUNA
Stanford University

NA'ILAH SUAD NASIR
University of California, Berkeley

In this chapter, the authors examine the trajectory of the literature on race, culture, and identity in education research through the past century. The literature is first situated within its historical and conceptual foundations, specifically the dehumanizing legacy of scientific racism, the early efforts by African American scholars to rehumanize marginalized members of society, and the emergence of identity as a construct in the social sciences. The authors then explore the body of education research—from the mid 20th century to today—focused on the relationship between cultural and racial identities and students' experiences with schooling. They close with a vision for the next era of research on this critical topic.

The task of this chapter, and this volume, is to reflect on 100 years of education research: to step back and examine the trends, the overarching themes, and, ultimately, the legacy of the body of scholarship in education. This task is a daunting one, and it presents an immediate challenge around scope and focus. As we reflect specifically on the past century of research on race, culture, and identity, the challenge is perhaps even greater. On one hand, the study of identity draws on and contributes to an understanding of the deep connections between self and society. Given the tremendous changes in U.S. society and schools during the period covered here, as well as several continuing challenges, the study of identity and its intersections with race and culture in education research is vital. On the other hand, the constructs of race, culture, and identity have long been marred by conceptual opacity, making the task of defining clear connections across related bodies of work a challenge.

Review of Research in Education
March 2016, Vol. 40, pp. 723–743
DOI: 10.3102/0091732X16676468
© 2016 AERA. http://rre.aera.net

In almost every quantifiable way, U.S. society has made strides toward being more racially and culturally inclusive (Banks, 1995). One hundred years ago, U.S. racial and cultural minorities[1] had few legal rights (Omi & Winant, 2014). Today, all racial and ethnic groups in the United States are equal in the eyes of the law, which includes the legal right to an education of equal quality (Darling-Hammond, 2015; Kluger, 2004). However, in practice, this legal equality has not resulted in true and full equal access to high-quality education or to societal recognition (Darling-Hammond, 2015; Ladson-Billings & Tate, 1995). Furthermore, over the past 30 years, society has been once again increasingly stratified by race and social class, with grave implications for our democracy. Indeed, the string of killings of unarmed Black men and women by members of law enforcement—many such episodes captured on cell phones and going viral on the Internet—sparked a national protest movement by a multiracial and intergenerational coalition, #BlackLivesMatter (http://blacklivesmatter.com; Hill, 2016; Taylor, 2016). Underlying the protests is the issue of how racial minorities, specifically Black people, are dehumanized in their interactions with the institutional structures of society, including policing and schooling (Leonardo, 2005; Nasir, Ross, McKinney de Royston, Givens, & Bryant, 2013).

We thus situate our chapter in this historical and political context. Research in the social sciences examines and reflects on society and is likewise deeply intertwined with it (Richards, 2003). Any consideration of the role of race, culture, and identity in education research must include how society has, through education, functioned to dehumanize, as well as to humanize, those who have been considered "Other" (Anderson, 1988; Kluger, 2004). In this chapter, we consider the dialectic of dehumanization and humanization, framing strands of education research that served historically to define the Other and strands that served to counter these efforts for learners at the political boundaries of U.S. society.

This chapter explores the research on race, culture, and identity in education. To undertake this exploration, we identified the relevant literature by conducting several literature searches using the keywords each alone with "education" and jointly. One challenge was that the initial literature searches resulted in a large corpus of articles and books (over 8,000). We thus selected articles, books, and chapters that were most relevant to the task of examining the research at the intersections of race, culture, and identity in education, and drew on our own knowledge of the field to add to the corpus of articles with key pieces that provided the theoretical backdrop to the articles selected. We then examined key themes as they emerged across the literature corpus, and engaged in discussion iteratively to identify themes over time.

To make sense of this body of work, we begin by situating this review within the history backdrop to which it responds, specifically the legacy of scientific racism and early efforts by African American scholars to humanize marginalized members of society. We then discuss the emergence of identity as a construct in social science research and its intersections (or, often, lack thereof) with the study of race and culture. With these historical and conceptual foundations laid, we explore the body of work focused on race, culture, and identity in education research. In particular, we describe education research—from the mid 20th century to today—focused on the relationship between cultural and racial identities and students' experiences with schooling. We close with a vision for the next era of research on this critical topic.

THE HISTORY OF SCIENTIFIC RACISM

Research on identity and its intersections with race and culture cannot be understood outside of the legacy of scientific racism. A long history of social science research has framed non–Northern Europeans as inferior, including in their capacity and willingness to learn and participate in society (Long, 1774; Omi & Winant, 2014; White & von Soemmerring, 1799). For instance, early research in psychology framed intelligence as biological, hereditary, and measurable by IQ tests used to compare the (naturalized) intelligence of non-European American and European American children. Social scientists attributed the typically lower scores of non-European children to natural, hereditary differences in intelligence. This interpretation both naturalized differences among races and ethnicities and supported arguments for the inherent intellectual superiority of European children (Burlew, Banks, McAdoo, & Azibo, 1992; Carlson & Henderson, 1950; Garth & Johnson, 1934; Kagan & Zahn, 1975). Francis Galton (1869), whose methodology was rooted in eugenics, offered a 15-point scale of "grades of ability," calculating that the "Negro races" were on average two grades below the "Anglo-Saxon." These calculations were the first attempt to quantify psychological racial differences. Herbert Spencer (1862), a contemporary of Galton, argued that Europeans' neurological evolution had become highly sophisticated, while "primitive" brains were incapable of processing the complex mental relations required for civilization. And G. Stanley Hall, cofounder of the American Psychological Association, stated his views on race in the final chapter of *Adolescence* (Hall, 1904), where he posited a developmental framework of racial hierarchies. Hall characterized the "lower races" as not so much inferior as adolescent in their stage of human development. He attempted to reconcile the nature-nurture dilemma by suggesting that interventions (nurture) nourishing the adolescent races (nature) would support their development. This logic lent support to arguments for segregated education.

Scholarship on race once again ramped up just prior to and after the Civil War and was used in particular to support continuing the racially organized social hierarchy. And U.S. education psychologists in the early 20th century who researched "race differences" in this historical context addressed the issue of whether to maintain segregation for racial minorities, in particular African American, Native American, and Mexican American children (G. O. Ferguson, 1916; Rowe, 1914). For instance, in comparing the intelligence of European American and Native American children, Rowe (1914) argued that "inferior racial ability is the only satisfactory explanation" and concluded that "the type of education suited to the one is not suited to the other" (p. 456).

By the late 1930s, in light of emerging data on the genetic nature of human diversity, the scientific community began contesting the validity of race as a useful construct for informing the debate on education. In turn, a cultural deficit stance emerged. The notion of culture remained linked to biology, though less explicitly (Richards, 2003). With the shift from the biological to the cultural, scholarship also shifted from a focus on inherent intelligence as the capacity to learn to cultural attitudes toward schooling and achievement. Educational achievement was related to values; values were linked to the cultures of different races and ethnicities (e.g., Demos, 1962).

The cultural deficit stance has long dominated scientific interpretations of communities and their members, as well as the design of education interventions for poor and minority children and their families. For example, Demos (1962) examined student experiences in schooling as "attitudes" toward education, finding that Mexican American students expressed significantly more negative attitudes toward education than were expressed by European American students. Interestingly, though 20 items out of the 26-item survey showed no significant differences between the groups and 1 item was significantly more positive for Mexican American students, his conclusions were based on the 5 items where Mexican American students indicated a more negative attitude. A closer look at those five items revealed that Mexican American students provided more negative responses than European American students to questions specifically regarding the helpfulness of school staff and teachers. There was no mention at all that such answers might reflect actual experiences, that is, that teachers and staff were potentially less helpful to Mexican American students than to European American students. Solutions proposed by a cultural deficit stance include interventions that make up for the perceived lack, including cognitive interventions (Blank & Solomon, 1969; Deutsch, 1967; John & Goldstein, 1964).

BLACK SCHOLARS' EFFORTS TO REHUMANIZE THE OTHER

During this time, African American scholars were working with the explicit goal of humanizing African Americans in the eyes of a society that perpetuated racist structures and grave indignities (Morris, 2015). In many ways, these efforts spoke to some of the concerns in psychology and education about the relationship between society and the identity development of marginalized people, and the role of education in that process.

One such scholar was sociologist W. E. B. Du Bois. Born in 1868, Du Bois focused his scholarly career on building an empirical evidence-based body of work to debunk theories stemming from scientific racism (Morris, 2015). His book *The Philadelphia Negro*, published in 1901, was one of the most extensive empirical studies of his day, incorporating observation, interviews, and surveys to study the lives of Blacks in Philadelphia and the role of structural racism in their lives. He was one of the earliest scholars to form a social constructionist view of race (Morris, 2015) and to theorize about the connections among the behavior of Black citizens, lack of opportunity, and the legacy of slavery and Jim Crow racism (Du Bois, 1903/1994). Scholars such as Wright (1969) built on Du Bois and noted,

"The Negro Problem"—that condition which is peculiar to Negroes, and common to them—is rather found in the attitudes of the white race toward the Negro; an attitude of a majority which seeks to shut out a minority from the enjoyment of the whole social and economic life. (pp. 186–187)

Here, Wright (1969) made the point that the real issue is not the characteristics of people of the "Negro" race but rather the way they are treated and regarded by Whites, thus highlighting social structure, not individual characteristics. Du Bois's work also touched on issues of identity. In his 1935 article "Does the Negro Need Separate Schools?" Du Bois (1935) highlighted the critical role of identity in the learning process as he made the argument that what the Negro needs is "neither mixed schools nor segregated schools. What the Negro needs is Education" (p. 329). He elaborated his point:

. . . a separate Negro school, where children are treated like human beings, trained by teachers of their own race, who know what it means to be black in the year of salvation 1935, is infinitely better than making our boys and girls doormats to be spit and trampled upon. (p. 335)

Du Bois's (1903/1994) classic text *The Souls of Black Folk* considered the unique identity position that the legacy of slavery and racism created for Black people, arguing that they faced a double consciousness created by their positioning in society:

It is a peculiar sensation, this double-consciousness, this sense of always looking at one's self through the eyes of others, of measuring one's soul by the tape of a world that looks on in amused contempt and pity. One ever feels his two-ness,—an American, a Negro; two souls, two thoughts, two unreconciled strivings; two warring ideals in one dark body, whose dogged strength alone keeps it from being torn asunder. (p. 3)

Other scholars of the early 20th century took up the project of racial rehumanization through social science, including Carter G. Woodson and Nanny Boroughs. Woodson, a theorist, educator, and institution builder (Givens, 2015a; Goggin, 1993/1997; Romero, 1971), is perhaps best known for *The Mis-Education of the Negro* (Woodson, 1933), in which he made the argument that mainstream education did African Americans a disservice, inasmuch as it perpetuated a notion of Black people as inferior and unaccomplished. He felt strongly that "mainstream educational systems underdeveloped Black students, mystified their subjectivity, and in extreme cases taught them to despise their racial heritage. Schooling, he argued, was a discrete yet proficient technology of White supremacy" (Givens, 2015a, p. 10).

For Woodson, the connection between pride in one's racial heritage, identity as a learner, and the purposes and outcomes of education was paramount. He spent his career writing textbooks, creating schools, and training teachers to teach in ways that acknowledged the contributions of African Americans to U.S. society and the world and that built up a sense of pride in Black students (Brown, 2010; Givens, 2015b).

Borroughs also sought to support the education of Black students, girls in particular, which she did through teaching, advocacy, and institution-building work (Jackson, 2015). Similar to Woodson, she advocated for the central place of Black history in the education of Black students, and she viewed empowering women as in part related to expanding the options that Black women saw for themselves in society. For Borroughs and Woodson, rehumanization was a core function of education, and recognizing the unique contributions and potential of African Americans was a critical aspect of education.

Indeed, Black educators long viewed schools as sites of rehumanization (Walker, 1996, 2009), where it was critical to create an environment that held high expectations for Black students, surrounded students with love and care, and supported them in dealing with the racism of the broader society. This view was true of segregated schools in the South, both immediately after slavery and well into the 20th century (Anderson, 1988; Walker, 1996, 2009).

Central to the idea that school should be a place where students' potential is developed and expanded was the concept of identity—in particular, the human need for social recognition and a positive sense of self. The next section explores the emergence of identity as a construct in the social sciences and the ways in which theories of identity development have or have not reckoned with identity's fundamental intersection with race, culture, and society.

THE EMERGENCE OF IDENTITY AS A CONSTRUCT IN THE SOCIAL SCIENCES

While issues related to identity are often implied in studies focused on race and culture in education, social science research focused explicitly on identity as a construct emerged separately and has often remained disconnected from scholarship on race and culture. In this section, we review major theories of identity and identity development and focus in particular on work that has attempted to bring these theories to bear on issues of race and culture in education.

Identity as a construct in social science research emerged in psychology with James's (1890) focus on the self and in sociology with Cooley's (1902/1972) and Mead's (1934) establishment of symbolic interactionism. Since James, the study of identity has focused on two interrelated aspects: "I" and "me." The "I"—or self as subject—is made up of the mental processes responsible for self-reflection. Research on subtopics such as self-affirmation, self-monitoring, self-awareness, self-esteem, and self-control (Leary & Tangney, 2003), conducted over the course of the subsequent decades, has contributed to a rich body of work on these fundamentally human capacities represented in the linguistic form "I." The "me" is the object of self-reflection. It is at its core a social object, figured within society. It is this aspect of identity—the process of becoming a person-in-society—that is the focus of this chapter. Here we briefly review key theories of identity, both stage model theories and those that focus on identity as constructed through social interaction, and how researchers have elaborated on these theories to take race and culture into account.

Stage Models of Identity Development and Their Relation to Race and Culture

Erikson (1994) offers a psychoanalytic view of the social self, focusing on its development through childhood and adolescence, wherein identity development is about growth into roles and a sense of where one's life is going in adult society. This growth is framed in terms of crises or conflicts that result in new stages of identity development. Although Erikson's stage model does not generally consider the role of power in society, he discusses, in the final chapter of *Identity: Youth and Crisis* (Erikson, 1994), how this process is particularly problematic for marginalized members of society, including Native Americans and African Americans. Erikson concludes that identity development has "two kinds of time: a *developmental stage* in the life of the individual, and a *period* in history" (p. 309).

M. B. Spencer and Markstrom-Adams (1990) built on and connected Erikson to social identity theory (K. B. Clark & Clark, 1939) to argue that minority children face additional precursors to their development that include identification with and beliefs and attitudes about their racial or ethnic group. A primary assertion of social identity theory is that racial or ethnic identity is important to one's self-concept and psychological functions. Several researchers define racial or ethnic identity as a component of social identity (Tajfel, 1981; Tajfel & Turner, 1979). Others have emphasized a sense of belonging, shared values, attitudes toward one's group, shared language, or participation in race- or ethnicity-linked events or practices (Phinney, 1990). Positive racial or ethnic identification is disrupted through experiences of racism. Clark and Clark (1959), for example, found that racial discrimination, undergirding the laws for segregated schools at the time, exacerbated Black students' negative self-esteem, evidenced by a White racial preference bias among Black children.

In later work, Lee, Spencer, and Harpalani (2003) challenged what they framed as enduring misconceptions about the identity development and schooling of nondominant youth. These enduring misconceptions include the assumption of a singular pathway for identity development centered on European and European American children that fundamentally pathologizes the life course challenges of ethnic and racial minorities, as well as a persistent deficit perspective on minority children's home and community experiences. Further misconceptions include, in pathologizing the experiences of minority youth, that minority youth are, "on the whole, homogenous and fundamentally different from the majority" (p. 6) and that attending to race and ethnicity in learning settings is not relevant to majority children. Lee et al. go on to argue,

These assumptions, long held in both human development and cognitive sciences literature, have led researchers, policymakers, and practitioners to view whole communities of children and adolescents as being ill prepared for school and have led them to attribute these students' lack of success in school to problems in their families, communities or to internal problems with them as individuals. (p. 6)

In response, Lee et al. (2003) offered the Phenomenological Variant of Ecological Systems (PVEST) framework, made up of five components that consider the experiences of privilege and marginalization in identity development (M. B. Spencer, 1999; M. B. Spencer, Dupree, Cunningham, Harpalani, & Muñoz-Miller, 2003). The first

component, net vulnerability, consists of stressors—such as race and gender stereotypes and historical processes of racial subordination and discrimination—that can
be offset by protective factors, such as cultural socialization. The second component,
net stress engagement, consists of experiences that harm an individual's well-being
and can be offset by social supports to negotiate those experiences. The third component consists of developmentally appropriate coping strategies in response to stressors
that can lead to adaptive or maladaptive solutions. Over time, they become stable
coping responses that, in aggregate, lead to emergent identities. Emergent identities,
the fourth component, lead to the final component of the PVEST model: the adverse
or productive ways of being for a particular individual.

Identity development, as it relates to race and culture, is framed as part of one's
self-concept and, developmentally, in terms of an affiliation with or a commitment to
one's ethnic or racial group (Phinney, 1989, 1990). Sellers, Smith, Shelton, Rowley,
and Chavous (1998) offered a model of racial identification that takes into account
both the traditional research on racial identity and what they refer to as the "underground" research of the narrative experiences of being African American. Their multidimensional model of racial identity proposes four dimensions of African American
racial identity, including how salient race is to one's sense of self, the extent to which
one normatively defines oneself with respect to race, the positive or negative regard
one has with respect to being Black, and one's ideology with respect to how members
of the race should act.

Identity as Emerging Through (Racialized) Social Interactions

Stage models, such as PVEST, while illuminating trajectories of identity development across the life span do not necessarily explain how the process of identity development occurs at the micro, or moment-to-moment, level of lived experiences. A
symbolic interactionist perspective frames identity development as emerging out of
social interactions within a classified world that designates subject positions (Stets &
Burke, 2003). Through social interactions, people recognize themselves and one
another as occupants of positions. These subject positions become social identities,
coconstructed with others in and reflective of society (Stets & Burke, 2003). This
view frames identity in relation to culture and its ascribed roles but has not typically
considered the role of power in this process and instead has treated "cultures" as relatively neutral. Attributes such as gender, race, and ethnicity function as forms of
master status (Stryker, 1987) but are not framed as components of self (Hogg, Terry,
& White, 1995). Rather, they are framed as indirectly affecting the self by determining the roles people can occupy and the relative social importance of those roles.

Similar to symbolic interactionism, though focusing in particular on discourse,
positioning theory emerged out of social psychology as a way to explain the social
construction of identities (Davies & Harré, 1990). Positioning theory asserts that
(a) human communication is generally mediated by socially constructed and historically situated *story lines*, which give meaning to our words and actions; (b) through

talk (and other forms of nonverbal communication), individuals locate themselves and others—that is, take on *positions*—within story lines; and (c) individuals locate themselves within particular story lines through *acts of positioning*. What makes positioning theory compelling for the study of power relations within classrooms is that the analysis of positioning uncovers the local moral order. That is, not everyone has equal access to the same rights and obligations to perform particular acts (Harré & van Langenhove, 1999; Herbel-Eisenmann, Wagner, Johnson, Suh, & Figueras, 2015). Because access to particular rights and/or particular obligations is a way of framing access to power, positioning theory affords the study of relations of power in the classroom.

In education research concerned with race, culture, and identity, poststructural and critical theories have been applied to theories of identity in order to deepen the focus on how power shapes identity development within schools and society (Denzin, 2001; Hand, Penuel, & Gutiérrez, 2012). Critical race theorists in education research argue that the discourses of schooling typically center on identities of the dominant culture, such that histories of power relations and privilege become invisible and unmarked (Darder, 1991; Dixson & Rousseau, 2005; Gee, 1991; Giroux & McLaren, 1989; Ladson-Billings & Tate, 1995). From a poststructural perspective, such discourses figure identities through subject positions, which the individual takes up or resists. In U.S. schooling (as well as elsewhere), students are racialized through their participation in these discourses; promise lies in rupturing the story lines that organize the typical discourses of schooling by offering alternative story lines centered on students' communities and well-being (Nasir, Snyder, Shah, & Ross, 2012).

REVIEW OF RESEARCH ON RACE, CULTURE, AND IDENTITY IN EDUCATION

So far, we have situated this discussion on both the long-running dialectic between dehumanization and (re)humanization of the "other" and its intersection with the explicit study of identity and identity development in the social sciences. With this background established, we explore here education research—from the mid 20th century to today—focused on the relationship between cultural and racial identities and students' experiences with schooling (e.g., Davidson, 1996; Esmonde & Langer-Osuna, 2013; Fuligni, Witkow, & Garcia, 2005; Gutiérrez & Rogoff, 2003; Howard, 2015; Ladson-Billings, 2009; Langer-Osuna, 2011; Lee, 2007; Roeser et al., 2008; Wortham, 2004; Yip, Seaton, & Sellers, 2006). This research has documented challenges faced by racial and cultural minority students and examined learning spaces designed to support positive identity development and academic achievement. Much of this research offers alternative interpretations and solutions (Ladson-Billings & Tate, 1995), pushing against interpretations of the relationship between race, culture, and schooling that have often positioned minority students as a problem of underachievement (Nasir & Hand, 2008). Scholarship at the intersection of identity, culture, and race blossomed in the late 20th century, when the student body in public schools nationwide became increasingly diverse and as scholars from African American, Latino, Native American, Asian American, and other racial and cultural minority backgrounds joined the ranks of the professoriate. This scholarship emerged, in part, out of critiques of deficit perspectives, and it often argues that differences in schooling outcomes among children of different cultures and races are based not on inherent biological or cultural deficiencies but rather on differences in the norms and practices that make up home and school cultures (e.g., R. M. Clark, 1983; Cole & Bruner, 1971; Jones, 1991). For example, Cole and Bruner (1971) drew on Labov (1969), and troubled the assumption that Ebonics (later called African American English Vernacular) is a less sophisticated mode of communication than Standard English. They argued that all languages are equally functional and that psychological research from a deficit stance reflected ignorance about languages in general and nonstandard dialects in particular. Furthermore, they argued that experimental methods to assess intellectual competence do not consider the importance of context. For example, J. Gay and Cole (1967) showed that Kpelle rice farmers were superior at estimating the number of cups of rice in various bowls compared with Yale sophomores. They argued that, just as Kpelle superiority at this task does not signal a general superior intelligence relative to Yale students, neither does the relative superiority of Yale students on more traditional assessment tasks signal the opposite. Rather, competence is tied to social practices that, for minority communities, are different from those found in mainstream schooling and psychological assessment practices.

This tradition of scholarship examined cultural differences, especially social and linguistic differences, across communities (Bauman & Sherzer, 1974; Gumperz, 1972; Heath, 1983; Hymes, 1974). The culture of schooling was framed both as worthy of critical examination and as linked to Anglo-American, middle-class norms (Cole & Bruner, 1971; Erickson & Mohatt, 1982; Heath, 1983; Michaels, 1981; Van Ness, 1981). In response to these ideas, a "mismatch" theory arose that argued that White, middle-class, affluent children navigate a similar "culture" in school and at home and thus are better aligned for success than minority students who must navigate a culture that is markedly different from their home culture (Au & Mason, 1981; Cazden, John, & Hymes, 1972; Florio & Shultz, 1979; G. Gay & Abrahams, 1972; Genishi, 1979; Heath, 1983; Jordan, 1985; Labov, 1969; Piedstrup, 1973). For example, students whose communicative experiences at home resonate with the communicative expectations of schooling perceive their efforts in the classroom as appropriate and valued (Au & Mason, 1981). This is not necessarily the case for students who experience conflicting communicative expectations at home and at school. Heath (1983) compared patterns of language use at home and school across communities in the southeastern United States, in particular regarding the role of questioning. She found that questions were used differently at home than at school for children in a local African American community. In the home community, children were rarely asked questions because children were not framed as legitimate sources of information among adults. At school, questions served a different function. Rather than to seek information, teachers used questions as requests for children to display their competence. Children from the African American community interpreted teacher questions using the context of their home experiences, leading to confusion as to why teachers would ask questions to which they already knew the answer. Teachers, in turn, interpreted students' confusion as displays of incompetence. These kinds of different interpretations have crucial implications for students' developing identities by racializing particular ways of being (Boykin & Cunningham, 2001). For example, students may learn that "Black" cultural styles or languages other than Standard English are viewed as problematic in the classroom (Nasir, Rowley, & Perez, 2015).

The lack of confluence between the community and schooling practices for children from minority communities has implications for students' identity development. Although positive racial and ethnic identities are associated with better schooling outcomes (Rivas-Drake et al., 2014), this relationship is complicated for students from marginalized communities (Conchas & Vigil, 2010; Darling-Hammond, 2015; Noguera & Wing, 2006; M. B. Spencer, 2006). Research has shown that discourses of schooling often position White and Asian students as "smart," while Black and Latino students are seen as being less capable, as having less parental support, and as presenting behavior problems (Lewis, 2003; Nasir et al., 2012; Pollock, 2009). Interviews with African American and Latino students and teachers illuminate the experience of being racialized in schools as one of marginalization, often through overt discrimination (Martin, 2006; Martinez, 2000). Martin (2006) interviewed African Americans who reported experiences of being ignored, criticized, or pushed into low-track mathematics classes despite interest and achievement in mathematics. Some learners internalized these experiences and began to believe that they were not smart enough. Others recognized that they experienced discrimination, but they were not able to change the consequences of actions by teachers and others in positions of authority. In Martinez (2000), Latino teachers discuss their own (often violent) experiences of discrimination as young students and their personal and professional commitments to teaching their bilingual and immigrant students with care and empathy. Some students respond to the negative stereotypes of their racial group by disidentifying with school as a way to preserve their positive self-esteem in the face of identity challenges (Osborne, 1995). Osborne (1995) showed that as African American students moved from middle school through high school, the correlation between their academic achievement and their self-esteem declined. These and related findings underscore the importance of the development of positive racial and ethnic identities in schools. Research has focused on schools as key sites for racial and ethnic identity development at both the whole-school and classroom levels (Carter, 2012; Davidson, 1996; Lewis, 2003; Nasir et al., 2012; Pollock, 2009). At the whole-school level, structural realities shape opportunities for racial and ethnic identity development. The implication of this work is that limited identity options are available in particular kinds of schooling contexts and that broad identity options are important for healthy racial and academic identity development (Carter, 2012). For example, Nasir (2012) found that students in the higher academic track of an urban high school developed positive racial identities linked to African American history and academic excellence, while students in the lower academic track developed racial identities framed in opposition to schooling. Other work has found that high-achieving non-White students suffer a social cost for participating in higher academic tracks in highly stratified schools. Schools with the greatest stratification across academic tracks have the greatest prevalence of high-achieving African Americans being accused of "acting White" (Fryer & Levitt, 2006; Tyson, Darity, & Castellino, 2005). This trend is most prevalent in schools with the greatest racial stratification across academic tracks and in schools that are less than 20% Black.

At the classroom level, racial identities are shaped through interactions with others and through curricular resources (Esmonde & Langer-Osuna, 2013; Herrenkohl & Mertl, 2010; Langer-Osuna, 2011; Wortham, 2004). How successful these interactions are in fostering both positive racial/ethnic and academic identities varies across classrooms (Varelas, Martin, & Kane, 2013) and depends in large part on the story lines available for students to use to interpret their actions and position themselves as particular kinds of learners (Esmonde & Langer-Osuna, 2013). Turner, Dominguez, Maldonado, and Empson (2013), for example, showed that deliberately centering not only multiple languages but also cross-language communication as part and parcel of what it means to do mathematics positions monolingual Spanish, monolingual English, and Spanish-English bilingual students as legitimate members of the same mathematics learning community.

Curriculum centered on students' lived cultural experiences supports the development of positive racial/ethnic and academic identities (Gutiérrez & Rogoff, 2003; Howard, 2015; Ladson-Billings, 2009; Lee, 2007). Gutiérrez framed such work as social design experiments meant to refigure possible identities in ways that are culturally affirming and productive for all students (Gutiérrez, 2008; Gutiérrez & Vossoughi, 2010; Hand et al., 2012). Rather than remediating students, Guitérrez's work remediates schooling structures that perpetuate failure, transforming learning environments into expansive activity systems termed "third spaces" (Gutiérrez, 2008; Gutiérrez, Rymes, & Larson, 1995). Such spaces focus on heterogeneity as an organizing principle that results from cultural, linguistic, and other social boundary crossings drawn from students' lived realities. Gutiérrez, Morales, and Martinez (2009, p. 235) drew on Engeström (2001) to propose that education researchers should ask the following questions:

1. Who are the subjects of learning, and how are they defined and located?
2. Why do they learn, and what leads them to make the effort?
3. What do they learn, and what are the contents and outcomes of learning?
4. How do they learn, and what are the key actions or processes of learning?

Such questions focus attention on how students' lived experiences can become pedagogical tools rather than on obstacles to be overcome through intensive remedial education. Ladson-Billings (2009) argued that by observing students engaged in community practices, teachers can include aspects of these practices in the organization of the classroom. Lee (2007) similarly argued that teachers can productively use students' cultural and racial identities as pedagogical tools through a process she termed *cultural modeling*. Cultural modeling reframes language and community practices as made up of complex cognitive work that can be productively leveraged in academic activity. Morrell (2002) argued that hip-hop music is a key social practice for pedagogy because the genre was created by and for urban youth (Alim, 2007; George, 2005; Rose, 1994) and can thus be used for the development of critical literacy practices.

Culturally relevant and culturally sustaining pedagogical strategies have expanded to include issues of both epistemology and ontology. With respect to epistemology, Bang and Medin (2010) challenged the implicit valuing of Western modern scientific ways of knowing over native science, typically framed as folk wisdom to be validated by Western science. Their work frames native science as a legitimate epistemological orientation for understanding the natural world, with pedagogical implications for learning contemporary scientific practices in ways that support native students' development of ethnic and academic identities (Nasir & Saxe, 2003). With respect to ontology, Nasir et al. (2013) examined how an all-Black, all-male alternative schooling context offered an alternative to Black male students' experiences with school discipline, wherein dominant notions of race and power were transformed by reframing both discipline practices and students' identities as Black male learners. The alternative space reinterpellated or rehailed (Althusser, 1971) students as learners and as engaged participants in the classroom.

Across the vast and growing body of work is a fundamental respect for the heterogeneity of communities and the transformative and powerful possibilities of using such heterogeneity to support both identity development and educational achievement. The next section offers some possibilities for the next generation of scholarship on identity, race, and culture in education research.

SUGGESTIONS FOR FUTURE RESEARCH

Our review of scholarship on race, culture, and identity reveals that, as the notion of identity has come into focus, scholarship and social conceptions of identity have defined this construct as dynamic, shifting, and malleable rather than as fixed and enduring. Schools are powerful spaces for identity work, including racial and cultural identification and the development of academic identities. As the field of education research moves forward, researchers must continue to ask how schools and classrooms—sites of identity work—can promote healthy development and academic achievement for all students in a pluralistic, yet stratified, society.

Education researchers must continue to examine and develop new ideas that foster social justice in schooling systems at multiple levels, including the state, district, school, and classroom levels. Innovative curricular and structural ideas require theories of learning that take into account the development of academic and racial/cultural identities within discourses of schooling organized around relationships of power.

To engage in such work, researchers must advance insights about learning and human development with explicit attention to relationships of power—in particular, looking at what and how identities and forms of knowledge are generated, where, and by and for whom (Bang & Vossoughi, 2016). This approach will enable the study of innovative forms of learning and supports for identity development. Theories and research methods that attend to relationships of power can support transformative insights (Bang & Vossoughi, 2016; Erickson, 2006; Kirshner, Gaertner, & Pozzoboni, 2010; Mirra, Garcia, & Morrell, 2015). In particular, the coordination of critical perspectives with the study of local activity makes both the epistemological and the ontological aspects of activity analytically visible and thereby available for informing iterative cycles of design, implementation, and analysis. These dimensions must be understood at the microgenetic, ontogenetic, and sociogenetic levels (Nasir & Saxe, 2003).

At the microgenetic level, innovative analytic methods are called for that capture how classroom (and other local) interactions become organized around normative and alternative discursive story lines linked to race, culture, and schooling. So is insight into how classroom interactions position students as particular kinds of learners, both in schools that serve predominantly students of color and in racially, culturally, and linguistically heterogeneous schools and classrooms. At the ontogenetic level, researchers should look at how (agentive) participation in the discourses of schooling and society affect identity development. At the sociogenetic level, a topic of study should be how classrooms, schools, and systems of schooling shift over time as innovative practices transform existing discourses toward increasingly inclusive and developmentally appropriate discourses that support the intellectual thriving and human development of students, teachers, and their communities.

Theories of learning and identity development as they pertain to schooling must be framed by an ethics of caring (Noddings, 2013; Roberts, 2010). It is clear that learning is linked to identity development and that healthy identity development necessitates caring relationships that foster a sense of safety and positive regard. Noddings's (2013) ethics of caring can be expanded to encompass sociopolitical implications, especially in situations where the majority of classroom teachers are White and an increasing proportion of U.S. public school students are not (McKinney de Royston, Vakil, Nasir, Ross, & Givens, in press). What are the sociopolitical dimensions of an ethics of care, and how do they inform theories of learning and schooling practices, as well as teacher education?

In this chapter we reflect on the themes of dehumanization and rehumanization across 100 years of education research on race, culture, and identity. There is much work to build on and much still to do. The study of identity and its intersections with race and culture in education research is more important than ever. As society's demographic shift and stratification by race and income continues, schools are arguably the most important hope for an inclusive society. Education theories and scholarly work must help to actualize this hope and to create learning spaces that are truly inclusive and transformative.

NOTE

[1]We choose the term *racial and cultural minorities* to reflect a political status of nondominance in society rather than a claim of demographic population numbers.

REFERENCES

Alim, H. S. (2007). Critical hip-hop language pedagogies: Combat, consciousness, and the cultural politics of communication. *Journal of Language, Identity, and Education, 6,* 161–176.

Althusser, L. (1971). Ideology and ideological state apparatus (Notes towards an investigation). In "Lenin and Philosophy" and other essays (pp. 127–186). New York, NY: Monthly Review Press.

Anderson, J. D. (1988). *The education of Blacks in the South, 1860–1935.* Chapel Hill: University of North Carolina Press.

Au, K. H. P., & Mason, J. M. (1981). Social organizational factors in learning to read: The balance of rights hypothesis. *Reading Research Quarterly, 17,* 115–152.

Bang, M., & Medin, D. (2010). Cultural processes in science education: Supporting the navigation of multiple epistemologies. *Science Education, 94,* 1008–1026.

Bang, M., & Vossoughi, S. (2016). Participatory design research and educational justice: Studying learning and relations within social change making. *Cognition and Instruction, 34,* 173–193.

Banks, J. (1995). Multicultural education and curriculum transformation. *Journal of Negro Education, 64,* 390–400.

Bauman, R., & Sherzer, J. (1974). *Explorations in the ethnography of speaking.* London, England: Cambridge University Press.

Blank, M., & Solomon, F. (1969). How shall the disadvantaged child be taught? *Child Development, 40,* 47–61.

Boykin, A. W., & Cunningham, R. T. (2001). The effects of movement expressiveness in story content and learning context on the analogical reasoning performance of African American children. *Journal of Negro Education, 70,* 72–83.

Brown, A. L. (2010). Counter-memory and race: An examination of African American scholars' challenges to early twentieth century K–12 historical discourses. *Journal of Negro Education, 79,* 54–65.

Burlew, A. K. H., Banks, W. C., McAdoo, H. P., & Azibo, D. A. (Eds.). (1992). *African American psychology: Theory, research, and practice.* Newbury Park, CA: Sage.

Carlson, H. B., & Henderson, N. (1950). The intelligence of American children of Mexican parentage. *Journal of Abnormal and Social Psychology, 45*(3), 544–551.

Carter, P. L. (2012). *Stubborn roots: Race, culture, and inequality in US and South African schools.* Oxford, England: Oxford University Press.

Cazden, C. B., John, V. P., & Hymes, D. (1972). *Functions of language in the classroom.* New York, NY: Teachers College Press.

Clark, K. B., & Clark, M. K. (1939). The development of consciousness of self and the emergence of racial identification in Negro preschool children. *Journal of Social Psychology, 10,* 591–599.

Clark, R. M. (1983). *Family life and school achievement: Why poor Black children succeed or fail.* Chicago, IL: University of Chicago Press.

Cole, M., & Bruner, J. S. (1971). Cultural differences and inferences about psychological processes. *American Psychologist, 26,* 867–876.

Conchas, G. Q., & Vigil, J. D. (2010). Multiple marginality and urban education: Community and school socialization among low-income Mexican-descent youth. *Journal of Education for Students Placed at Risk, 15*(1–2), 51–65.

Cooley, C. H. (1972). The looking-glass self. In J. G. Manis & B. N. Meltzer (Eds.), *Symbolic interaction: A reader in social psychology* (2nd ed., pp.231–233). Boston, MA: Allyn & Bacon. (Original work published 1902)

Darder, A. (1991). *Culture and power in the classroom: A critical foundation for bicultural education*. Westport, CT: Greenwood.

Darling-Hammond, L. (2015). *The flat world and education: How America's commitment to equity will determine our future*. New York, NY: Teachers College Press.

Davidson, A. L. (1996). *Making and molding identity in schools: Student narratives on race, gender, and academic engagement*. Albany: SUNY Press.

Davies, B., & Harré, R. (1990). Positioning: The discursive production of selves. *Journal for the Theory of Social Behavior, 20*, 43–63.

Demos, G. D. (1962). Attitudes of Mexican-American and Anglo-American groups toward education. *Journal of Social Psychology, 57*, 249–256.

Denzin, N. K. (2001). Symbolic interactionism, poststructuralism, and the racial subject. *Symbolic Interaction, 24*, 243–249.

Deutsch, M. (1967). *The disadvantaged child*. New York, NY: Basic Books.

Dixson, A. D., & Rousseau, C. K. (2005). And we are still not saved: Critical race theory in education ten years later. *Race Ethnicity and Education, 8*, 7–27.

Du Bois, W. E. B. (1935). Does the Negro need separate schools? *Journal of Negro Education, 4*, 328–335.

Du Bois, W. E. B. (1994). *The souls of Black folk*. New York, NY: Gramercy Books. (Original work published 1903)

Engeström, Y. (2001). Expansive learning at work: Toward an activity theoretical reconceptualization. *Journal of Education and Work, 14*, 133–156.

Erikson, E. H. (1994). *Identity: Youth and crisis*. New York, NY: W. W. Norton.

Erickson, F. (2006). Studying side by side: Collaborative action ethnography in educational research. In G. D. Spindler (Ed.), *Innovations in educational ethnography: Theory, methods, and results* (pp. 235–258). Chicago, IL: Psychology Press.

Erickson, F., & Mohatt, G. (1982). Cultural organization of participation structures in two classrooms of Indian students. In G. D. Spindler (Ed.), *Doing the ethnography of schooling* (pp. 131–174). New York, NY: Holt, Rinehart & Winston.

Esmonde, I., & Langer-Osuna, J. M. (2013). Power in numbers: Student participation in mathematical discussions in heterogeneous spaces. *Journal for Research in Mathematics Education, 44*, 288–315.

Ferguson, G. O. (1916). The psychology of the Negro: An experimental study. *Archives of Psychology, 36*, 138–139.

Florio, S., & Shultz, J. (1979). Social competence at home and at school. *Theory Into Practice, 18*, 234–243.

Fryer, R. G., & Levitt, S. D. (2006). The Black-White test score gap through third grade. *American Law and Economics Review, 8*, 249–281.

Fuligni, A. J., Witkow, M., & Garcia, C. (2005). Ethnic identity and the academic adjustment of adolescents from Mexican, Chinese, and European backgrounds. *Developmental Psychology, 41*, 799–811.

Galton, F. (1869). *Hereditary genius: An inquiry into its laws and consequences*. London, England: Macmillan.

Garth, T. R., & Johnson, H. D. (1934). The intelligence and achievement of Mexican children in the United States. *Journal of Abnormal and Social Psychology, 29*, 222–229.

Gay, G., & Abrahams, R. D. (1972). Talking Black in the classroom. In R. D. Abrahams, D. Roger, & R. C. Troike (Eds.), *Language and cultural diversity in American education* (pp. 200–208). Englewood Cliffs, NJ: Prentice Hall.

Gay, J., & Cole, M. (1967). *The new mathematics and an old culture: A study of learning among the Kpelle of Liberia.* New York, NY: Holt, Rinehart & Winston.

Gee, J. (1991). Socio-cultural approaches to literacy (literacies). *Annual Review of Applied Linguistics, 12,* 31–48.

Genishi, C. (1979). Young children communicating in the classroom: Selected research. *Theory Into Practice, 18,* 244–250.

George, N. (2005). *Hip hop America.* New York, NY: Penguin.

Giroux, H. A., & McLaren, P. (1989). Introduction: Schooling, cultural politics, and the struggle for democracy. In H. A. Giroux (Ed.), *Critical pedagogy, the state, and cultural struggle* (pp. xi–xxxv). New York: SUNY Press.

Givens, J. R. (2015a). *Culture, curriculum, and consciousness: Resurrecting the educational praxis of Dr. Carter G. Woodson, 1875–1950* (Unpublished doctoral dissertation). University of California, Berkeley.

Givens, J. R. (2015b). A grammar for Black education beyond borders: Exploring technologies of schooling in the African diaspora. *Race Ethnicity and Education, 19,* 1288–1302.

Goggin, J. (1997). *Carter G. Woodson: A life in Black history* (Reprint ed.). Baton Rouge: LSU Press. (Original work published 1993)

Gumperz, J. J. (1972). The speech community. In P. P. Giglioli (Ed.), *Language and social context* (pp. 219–231). Harmondsworth, England: Penguin Education.

Gutiérrez, K. D. (2008). Developing a sociocritical literacy in the third space. *Reading Research Quarterly, 43,* 148–164.

Gutiérrez, K. D., Morales, P. Z., & Martinez, D. C. (2009). Re-mediating literacy: Culture, difference, and learning for students from nondominant communities. *Review of Research in Education, 33,* 212–245.

Gutiérrez, K. D., & Rogoff, B. (2003). Cultural ways of learning: Individual traits or repertoires of practice. *Educational Researcher, 32*(5), 19–25.

Gutiérrez, K., Rymes, B., & Larson, J. (1995). Script, counterscript, and underlife in the classroom: James Brown versus Brown v. Board of Education. *Harvard Educational Review, 65,* 445–472.

Gutiérrez, K., & Vossoughi, S. (2010). "Lifting off the ground to return anew": Documenting and designing for equity and transformation through social design experiments. *Journal of Teacher Education, 61*(1–2), 100–117.

Hall, G. S. (1904). *Adolescence* (Vols. 1–2). New York, NY: Appleton.

Hand, V., Penuel, W. R., & Gutiérrez, K. D. (2012). (Re)framing educational possibility: Attending to power and equity in shaping access to and within learning opportunities. *Human Development,* 55, 250–268.

Harré, R., & van Langenhove, L. (1999). The dynamics of social episodes. In R. Harré & L. van Langenhove (Eds.), *Positioning theory: Moral contexts of intentional action* (pp. 1–13). Oxford, England: Blackwell.

Heath, S. B. (1983). *Ways with words: Language, life and work in communities and classrooms.* Cambridge, England: Cambridge University Press.

Herbel-Eisenmann, B. A., Wagner, D., Johnson, K. R., Suh, H., & Figueras, H. (2015). Positioning in mathematics education: Revelations on an imported theory. *Educational Studies in Mathematics, 89,* 185–204.

Herrenkohl, L. R., & Mertl, V. (2010). *How students come to be, know, and do: A case for a broad view of learning.* Cambridge, England: Cambridge University Press.

Hill, M. L. (2016). *Nobody: Casualties of America's war on the vulnerable, from Ferguson to Flint and beyond.* New York, NY: Simon & Schuster.

Hogg, M. A., Terry, D. J., & White, K. M. (1995). A tale of two theories: A critical comparison of identity theory with social identity theory. *Social Psychology Quarterly, 58,* 255–269.

Howard, T. C. (2015). *Why race and culture matter in schools: Closing the achievement gap in America's classrooms*. New York, NY: Teachers College Press.

Hymes, D. (1974). Ways of speaking. In R. Bauman & J. Sherzer (Eds.), *Explorations in the ethnography of speaking* (pp. 433–451). New York, NY: Cambridge University Press.

Jackson, S. (2015). *"To struggle and battle and overcome": The educational thought of Nannie Helen Burroughs, 1865–1961* (Unpublished doctoral dissertation). University of California, Berkeley.

James, W. (1890). *The principles of psychology*. New York, NY: Henry Holt.

John, V. P., & Goldstein, L. S. (1964). The social context of language acquisition. *Merrill-Palmer Quarterly of Behavior and Development, 10*, 265–275.

Jones, R. L. (1991). *Black psychology*. Oakland, CA: Cobb & Henry.

Jordan, C. (1985). Translating culture: From ethnographic information to educational program. *Anthropology & Education Quarterly, 16*, 105–123.

Kagan, S., & Zahn, G. L. (1975). Field dependence and the school achievement gap between Anglo-American and Mexican-American children. *Journal of Educational Psychology, 67*, 643–650.

Kirshner, B., Gaertner, M., & Pozzoboni, K. (2010). Tracing transitions: The effect of high school closure on displaced students. *Educational Evaluation and Policy Analysis, 32*(3), 407–429.

Kluger, R. (2004). *Simple justice: The history of Brown v. Board of Education and Black America's struggle for equality*. New York, NY: Vintage Books.

Labov, W. (1969). The logic of non-Standard Negro English. In J. E. Atatis (Ed.), *Linguistics and the teaching of Standard English to speakers of other languages or dialects* (pp. 1–41). Washington, DC: Georgetown University Press.

Ladson-Billings, G. (2009). *The dreamkeepers: Successful teachers of African American children*. San Francisco, CA: John Wiley.

Ladson-Billings, G., & Tate, W. F. (1995). Toward a critical race theory of education. *Teachers College Record, 97*, 47–68.

Langer-Osuna, J. M. (2011). How Brianna became bossy and Kofi came out smart: Understanding the trajectories of identity and engagement for two group leaders in a project-based mathematics classroom. *Canadian Journal of Science, Mathematics and Technology Education, 11*, 207–225.

Leary, M. R., & Tangney, J. P. (2003). The self as an organizing construct in the behavioral and social sciences. In M. R. Leary & J. P. Tangney (Eds.), *Handbook of self and identity* (pp. 3–14).New York, NY: Guilford Press.

Lee, C. D. (2007). *Culture, literacy, and learning: Taking bloom in the midst of the whirlwind* (Multicultural Education Series). New York, NY: Teachers College Press.

Lee, C. D., Spencer, M. B., & Harpalani, V. (2003). "Every shut eye ain't sleep": Studying how people live culturally. *Educational Researcher, 32*(5), 6–13.

Leonardo, Z. (2005). Through the multicultural glass: Althusser, ideology and race relations in post–civil rights America. *Policy Futures in Education, 3*, 400–412.

Lewis, A. (2003). *Race in the schoolyard: Negotiating the color line in classrooms and communities*. New Brunswick, NJ: Rutgers University Press.

Long, E. (1774). *The history of Jamaica: Or, general survey of the ancient and modern state of that island with reflections on its situation settlements, inhabitants, climate, products, commerce, laws, and government* (Vol. 2). London, England: T. Lowndes.

Martin, D. B. (2006). Mathematics learning and participation as racialized forms of experience: African American parents speak on the struggle for mathematics literacy. *Mathematical Thinking and Learning, 8*, 197–229.

Martinez, E. S. (2000). Ideological baggage in the classroom: Resistance and resilience among Latino bilingual students and teachers. In E. T. Trueba & L. I. Bartolome (Eds.),

Immigrant voices: In search of educational equity (pp. 93–106). Lanham, MD: Rowman & Littlefield.

McKinney de Royston, M., Vakil, S., Nasir, N., Ross, K., & Givens, J. (in press). "He's more like a 'brother' than a 'teacher'": Politicized caring in a program for African American males. *Teachers College Record.*

Mead, G. H. (1934). *Mind, self and society.* Chicago, IL: University of Chicago Press.

Michaels, S. (1981). "Sharing time": Children's narrative styles and differential access to literacy. *Language in Society, 10,* 423–442.

Mirra, N., Garcia, A., & Morrell, E. (2015). *Doing youth participatory action research: Transforming inquiry with researchers, educators, and students.* New York, NY: Routledge.

Morrell, E. (2002). Toward a critical pedagogy of popular culture: Literacy development among urban youth. *Journal of Adolescent & Adult Literacy, 46,* 72–77.

Morris, A. (2015). *The scholar denied: W. E. B. Du Bois and the birth of modern sociology.* Berkeley: University of California Press.

Nasir, N. S. (2012). *Racialized identities: Race and achievement for African-American youth.* Redwood City, CA: Stanford University Press.

Nasir, N. S., & Hand, V. (2008). From the court to the classroom: Opportunities for engagement, learning, and identity in basketball and classroom mathematics. *Journal of the Learning Sciences, 17,* 143–179.

Nasir, N. S., Ross, K. M., McKinney de Royston, M., Givens, J., & Bryant, J. (2013). Dirt on my record: Rethinking disciplinary practices in an all-Black, all-male alternative class. *Harvard Educational Review, 83,* 489–512.

Nasir, N. S., Rowley, S. J., & Perez, W. (2015). Cultural, racial/ethnic, and linguistic diversity and identity. In L. Corno & E. M. Anderman (Eds.), *Handbook of educational psychology* (pp. 186–198). New York, NY: Routledge.

Nasir, N. S., & Saxe, G. B. (2003). Ethnic and academic identities: A cultural practice perspective on emerging tensions and their management in the lives of minority students. *Educational Researcher, 32*(5), 14–18.

Nasir, N. S., Snyder, C. R., Shah, N., & Ross, K. (2012). Racial storylines and implications for learning. *Human Development, 55,* 285–301.

Noddings, N. (2013). *Caring: A relational approach to ethics and moral education.* Berkeley: University of California Press.

Noguera, P., & Wing, J. (2006). *Unfinished business: Closing the racial achievement gap in our schools.* San Francisco, CA: Jossey-Bass.

Omi, M., & Winant, H. (2014). *Racial formation in the United States.* New York, NY: Routledge.

Osborne, J. W. (1995). Academics, self-esteem, and race: A look at the underlying assumptions of the disidentification hypothesis. *Personality and Social Psychology Bulletin, 21,* 449–455.

Phinney, J. S. (1989). Stages of ethnic identity development in minority group adolescents. *Journal of Early Adolescence, 9*(1–2), 34–49.

Phinney, J. S. (1990). Ethnic identity in adolescents and adults: Review of research. *Psychological Bulletin, 108,* 499–514.

Piestrup, A. (1973). *Black dialect interference and accommodation of reading instruction in first grade.* Berkeley, CA: Language Behavior Research Laboratory.

Pollock, M. (2009). *Colormute: Race talk dilemmas in an American school.* Princeton, NJ: Princeton University Press.

Richards, G. (2003). *Race, racism and psychology: Towards a reflexive history.* London, England: Routledge.

Rivas-Drake, D., Seaton, E. K., Markstrom, C., Quintana, S., Syed, M., Lee, R. M., . . . Yip, T. (2014). Ethnic and racial identity in adolescence: Implications for psychosocial, academic, and health outcomes. *Child Development, 85*, 40–57.

Roberts, M. A. (2010). Toward a theory of culturally relevant critical teacher care: African American teachers' definitions and perceptions of care for African American students. *Journal of Moral Education, 39*, 449–467.

Roeser, R. W., Galloway, M., Casey-Cannon, S., Watson, C., Keller, L., & Tan, E. (2008). Identity representations in patterns of school achievement and well-being among early adolescent girls: Variable- and person-centered approaches. *Journal of Early Adolescence, 28*, 115–152.

Romero, P. (1971). *Carter G. Woodson: A biography.* Columbus: Ohio State University Press.

Rose, T. (1994). *Black noise: Rap music and black culture in contemporary America.* Middletown, CT: Wesleyan University Press.

Rowe, E. C. (1914). Five hundred forty-seven White and two hundred sixty-eight Indian children tested by the Binet-Simon tests. *The Pedagogical Seminary, 21*, 454–468.

Sellers, R. M., Smith, M. A., Shelton, J. N., Rowley, S. A., & Chavous, T. M. (1998). Multidimensional model of racial identity: A reconceptualization of African American racial identity. *Personality and Social Psychology Review, 2*, 18–39.

Spencer, H. (1862). *First principles of a new system of philosophy.* London, England: Williams & Norgate.

Spencer, M. B. (1999). Social and cultural influences on school adjustment: The application of an identity-focused cultural ecological perspective. *Educational Psychologist, 34*(1), 43–57.

Spencer, M. B. (2006). Phenomenology and ecological systems theory: Development of diverse groups. In W. Damon & R. M. Lerner (Eds.), *Child and adolescent development: An advanced course* (pp. 696–740). Hoboken, NJ: John Wiley.

Spencer, M. B., Dupree, D., Cunningham, M., Harpalani, V., & Muñoz-Miller, M. (2003). Vulnerability to violence: A contextually sensitive, developmental perspective on African American adolescents. *Journal of Social Issues, 59*, 33–49.

Spencer, M. B., & Markstrom-Adams, C. (1990). Identity processes among racial and ethnic minority children in America. *Child Development, 61*, 290–310.

Stets, J. E., & Burke, P. J. (2003). A sociological approach to self and identity. In M. R. Leary & J. P. Tangney (Eds.), *Handbook of self and identity* (pp. 128–152). New York, NY: Guilford Press.

Stryker, S. (1987). Identity theory: Developments and extensions. In K. Yardley & T. Honess (Eds.), *Self and identity: Psychosocial perspectives* (pp. 89–103). Oxford, England: John Wiley.

Tajfel, H. (1981). *Human groups and social categories: Studies in social psychology.* Cambridge, England: Cambridge University Press.

Tajfel, H., & Turner, J. C. (1979). An integrative theory of intergroup conflict. In W. G. Austin & S. Worchel (Eds.), *The social psychology of intergroup relations* (pp. 33–47). Monterey, CA: Brooks/Cole.

Taylor, K. Y. (2016). *From #BlackLivesMatter to Black liberation.* Chicago, IL: Haymarket Books.

Turner, E., Dominguez, H., Maldonado, L., & Empson, S. (2013). English learners' participation in mathematical discussion: Shifting positionings and dynamic identities. *Journal for Research in Mathematics Education, 44*, 199–234.

Tyson, K., Darity, W., & Castellino, D. R. (2005). It's not "a Black thing": Understanding the burden of acting White and other dilemmas of high achievement. *American Sociological Review, 70*, 582–605.

Van Ness, H. (1981). Social control and social organization in an Alaskan Athabaskan classroom: A microethnography of "reading ready" for reading. In H. Trueba, G. Guthrie, & K. Au

(Eds.), *Culture and the bilingual classroom: Studies in classroom ethnography* (pp. 12–138). Rowley, MA: Newbury House.

Varelas, M., Martin, D. B., & Kane, J. M. (2013). Content learning and identity construction: A framework to strengthen African American students' mathematics and science learning in urban elementary schools. *Human Development, 55,* 319–339.

Walker, V. S. (1996). *Their highest potential: An African American school community in the segregated South.* Chapel Hill: University of North Carolina Press.

Walker, V. S. (2009). *Hello professor: A Black principal and professional leadership in the segregated South.* Chapel Hill: University of North Carolina Press.

White, C., & von Soemmerring, S. T. (1799). *An account of the regular gradation in man, and in different animals and vegetables, and from the former to the latter.* London, England: C. Dilly.

Woodson, C. G. (1933). *The mis-education of the American Negro.* New York, NY: AMS Press.

Wortham, S. (2004). From good student to outcast: The emergence of a classroom identity. *Ethos, 32,* 164–187.

Wright, R. R. (1969). *The Negro in Pennsylvania: A study in economic history.* New York, NY: Arno.

Yip, T., Seaton, E. K., & Sellers, R. M. (2006). African American racial identity across the lifespan: Identity status, identity content, and depressive symptoms. *Child Development, 77,* 1504–1517.

Chapter 20

Making the Visible Invisible: Willful Ignorance of Poverty and Social Inequalities in the Research-Policy Nexus

Jeanne M. Powers
Gustavo E. Fischman
David C. Berliner
Arizona State University

The year 2016 marks the 100th anniversary of the American Educational Research Association and the 50th anniversary of the publication of Equality of Educational Opportunity, known as the Coleman Report. These key moments in the field's history ushered in important paradigm shifts in the practice of education research; in how the relationships among poverty, inequality, and schooling were understood; and in the research-policy nexus. This conceptual synthesis of the history of education research in the United States is focused on poverty knowledge in both periods. The authors trace the rise of education as a field of study, the place of poverty in the emergent science of education, and the extent to which leading researchers have acknowledged, analyzed, or contested poverty. The Coleman Report advanced a new paradigm for analysis while being firmly rooted in earlier traditions. Coleman's analytical approach has become common sense in educational policymaking in the form of the accountability movement. The report's fundamental insights about the relationship between poverty and student achievement too often remain unacknowledged by U.S. policymakers.

The year 2016 marks the 100th anniversary of the American Educational Research Association (AERA) and the 50th anniversary of the publication of *Equality of Educational Opportunity*, better known as the Coleman Report (Coleman et al., 1966). These key moments in the field's history ushered in important paradigm shifts in the practice of education research; in how the relationships among poverty, inequality, and schooling were understood; and in the research-policy nexus

Review of Research in Education
March 2016, Vol. 40, pp. 744–776
DOI: 10.3102/0091732X16663703
© 2016 AERA. http://rre.aera.net

(i.e., instances when education research enters the policymaking arena). The first paradigm shift was the replacement of moral philosophy as the primary discipline on which educational practice was based: The new belief was that education could be studied scientifically. Its chief proponents were psychologists whose views were shaped by positivist aspirations, which in turn shaped the zeitgeist within which educational ideas were debated. In the early decades of the 20th century, the ascendance of behaviorist psychological models, along with the emergence of social science approaches to the study of education, also influenced policymaking. The Protestant republicanism that shaped the expansion of the common school was being transformed by the incorporation of nascent scientific methods for achieving efficient education reform. The new tools of the science of education also shaped practices within schools.

AERA was founded in these intellectually tumultuous times. While some peripheral changes occurred in the ways that education was conceptualized and studied, by the 1960s this new research paradigm in education was consolidated and heavily influenced by human capital theory. A second moment of change in how educational issues and, in particular, educational policies were understood occurred in the wake of the Coleman Report. Little heralded at the time of its publication, this monumental study continues to influence contemporary education policy debates because it upended common assumptions about schooling, and it pioneered measurement technologies that have subsequently been embraced by policymakers.

A key thread linking the two periods is that poverty and racial inequality were often considered and recognized but bracketed as irrelevant in shaping educational opportunities and outcomes by policymakers and by researchers who were positioned to engage with the policy community.[1] Moreover, crucial intersectional relationships between economic and class-related dynamics, on one hand, and gender and race/ethnicity, on the other, were largely ignored, even by many of the scholars who advocated for progressive school reform (Rury, 2005).[2] This thread can be considered a blind spot that generated willful avoidance and ignorance of the 600-pound gorilla—the influence of poverty and its intersections with other social inequalities (Berliner, 2006). We use the term *willful ignorance* to highlight how this blind spot is the result of a two-step process whereby researchers and policymakers notice poverty and then ignore it in their substantive conclusions and recommendations.[3] Willful ignorance supports the systematic denial of the dynamics of class-based inequalities in shaping individuals' and groups' life chances. That said, we are not trying to explain or excuse the omissions of those who founded the field. Rather, our goal is to document how, in the research-policy nexus, the inattention to educational inequalities, particularly those associated with poverty, has framed this interchange, with clear negative consequences that extend to the present (Fischman & Tefera, 2014).[4] In our account we highlight positivism and the emphasis on measurement; the use of the White, middle-class male student as the implicit norm against which all other students were assessed and ranked; human capital theory; and culture-of-poverty arguments.

While our primary focus is on poverty and social class, we recognize that there has been a similar inattention to race/ethnicity, gender, and ability, as well as to the inter-sections between them (Artiles, 2011). More specifically, the ways that poverty was understood were shaped in important ways by extant understandings of race, which had long been a focus of the scientific enterprise (Gould, 1996), and later by the emerging social and educational sciences (Baker, 1998; Fass, 1989; Valencia & Suzuki, 2001). Our analysis of the education research–policy nexus is a conceptual synthesis of secondary accounts of the history of education research in the United States (e.g., Cronbach & Suppes, 1969; Lagemann, 2000; Travers, 1983; Vinovskis, 2009; Walters, 2009; Walters & Lareau, 2009) and the history of U.S. social policy (e.g., Katz, 2013; O'Connor, 2001). We consulted disciplinary histories to amplify and refine our analysis when relevant (e.g., H. M. Levin, 1989; Weiner, 1989). In addition, we conducted searches of the major disciplinary history journals and of journals focused on the historiography of education to ensure that we were compre-hensive in our coverage.[5] We also conducted an ERIC search for journal articles using the descriptors *educational policy, educational research*, and *policy research.*

Within this broad framing, we focused on poverty knowledge or the "body of knowledge . . . that has attained a kind of quasi-official status in defining 'the poverty problem' and assessing how social programs affect the poor" (O'Connor, 2001, p. 4).[6] Our goal was to understand the place of poverty in the science of education or, more specifically, the extent to which researchers and policymaking organizations associated with education research have acknowledged, analyzed, or contested poverty. We read and synthesized across secondary accounts, highlighting points of agreement and dis-crepancies, and amplified them with primary documents until we reached saturation.

THE PLACE OF POVERTY IN THE NEW SCIENCE OF EDUCATION

Scientific Management, Measurement, and Positivism in the New Science of Education Research

To anchor our narrative, we begin with the Cleveland School Survey, a massive study of education in Cleveland conducted by a team of 30 researchers led by Leonard Ayres, the head of the Departments of Statistics and Education at the Russell Sage Foundation (Lagemann, 2000). An exemplar of the new emphasis on measurement and scientific management, the Cleveland School Survey provides a window into key cultural and institutional shifts in the American educational system and in the research community that was developing around it. Rooted in progressive-era surveys of com-munities conducted by settlement workers, the Cleveland School Survey was among the most famous of the hundreds of school surveys that were conducted in U.S. public schools between 1911 and 1930, and represented a new phase of education research oriented toward increasing the social efficiency of schools (Lagemann, 2000; Sears, 1922; Tyack & Hansot, 1982). Yet even while the Cleveland Survey provided volumi-nous information about the city's public schools, it made little mention of social class, apart from a brief discussion of the occupations of the inhabitants of the city at the beginning of the report. Most of the report's recommendations were carried out, including a proposal to hire a superintendent of schools charged with overseeing "a system of scientific general supervision" informed by the continual analysis of self-surveys (Ayres, 1917, p. 55; see also Tyack & Hansot, 1982).

The school surveys of this period—large-scale compendiums of data on educational agencies, conducted by education experts using the techniques of social science—reflected the new emphasis on professional models of research and the disciplinary specialization occurring in higher education in the early 20th century. These education researchers were also a key constituency of the "administrative progressives"—the university professors, urban school superintendents, state education leaders, businessmen, lawyers, and elite men and women engaged in reforming elementary and secondary education (Tyack, 1974). Deeply influenced by ideas associated with scientific management, the administrative progressives' goal was to empower experts who would make public schools more efficient and productive by using the data and analyses generated by researchers (Fass, 1989; Mehta, 2013; Tyack & Hansot, 1982).

Institutionalizing the Field

As the field of education gained an institutional presence via the establishment of colleges of education, and a cadre of scholars focused their research on the problems of schooling, two overlapping areas of specialization emerged that shared an emphasis on measurement: educational psychology and educational administration (Clifford, 1986; Labaree, 2004; Lagemann, 2000; White, 1982). Propelled by the work of Edward L. Thorndike, who greatly influenced the field of educational psychology, Teachers College, at Columbia University, became a powerful institutional actor (Lagemann, 2000). In the first decades of the 20th century, Thorndike proposed a behaviorist psychology, experimental research, and statistical measurements to quantify and analyze educational phenomena. Thorndike's ideas were spread by the many Teachers College graduates, who assumed professorships across the United States. For example, at Stanford University, Ellsworth Cubberley built a faculty that was oriented around training school leaders, and he brought the empirical approach that was developing in educational psychology into the nascent field of educational administration (Lagemann, 2000).[7] Inspired by Taylorism and the ideas of scientific management, Cubberley was one of the leading proponents of the school survey as a tool for educational administration. Foundations also began to support education research during this period and conducted their own school surveys (Tyack & Hansot, 1982).

The school survey as a tool for the scientific management of schools helped foster the mass expansion of testing of achievement and intelligence in public schools (P. D. Chapman, 1988). Expert managers needed to know what the students in their schools and districts were learning (Tyack & Hansot, 1982). Thorndike and other education researchers were developing standardized achievement tests aimed at assessing students' performance on school-based tasks (Lagemann, 2000). At Stanford University, Lewis Terman began adapting European intelligence tests and testing methodologies for large-scale administration in U.S. public schools (P. D. Chapman, 1988). An important turning point in this process was the mass administration of IQ tests to screen and sort army recruits during World War I.[8] Terman believed that intelligence was largely inherited, did not change over time, and was measurable, a view that largely dominated the field through the 1940s (P. D. Chapman, 1988; Cronbach & Suppes, 1969; Travers, 1983).[9] This small network of influential White male scholars[10]—among them Ayres, Cubberley, Charles Hubbard Judd, Thorndike, Terman, Guy Montrose Whipple (the longtime editor of the yearbooks of the National Society for the Study of Education), and others—embraced the ideas associated with scientific management and created new tools for measuring and analyzing education phenomena.

While the group linked to Thorndike and behaviorist approaches was consolidating, others were creating and institutionalizing a new field oriented around applied research (Tyack & Hansot, 1982; see also Whipple, 1916). The two groups were tied by informal social networks forged within graduate programs in colleges of education (Clifford, 1986; Tyack & Hansot, 1982). Many were members of the Cleveland Conference, a selective organization of the "leading educators" organized by the researchers involved in the Cleveland School Survey. In the years preceding AERA's founding, many superintendents were establishing research departments in their districts (Martens, 1923; Mershon & Schlossman, 2008). Universities and state governments also established research bureaus aimed at providing technical assistance to public schools.[11] The National Association of Directors of Educational Research (NADER), the organization that became AERA, was founded in 1915 when a small group of research directors convened at a National Education Association (NEA) Department of Superintendence conference to assess the field of survey research (Grinder, 1982; Mershon & Schlossman, 2008).[12] The goal of the founders of NADER was to "create an ongoing forum for discussion and support among the people that were most directly responsible for linking education research to public policy" (Mershon & Schlossman, 2008, p. 317).

From Measuring to Sorting

The promotion of these ideas, tools, and practices, with the promise of addressing the exigencies of organizational expansion in efficient ways, accelerated the process of differentiation and sorting within public schools (Fass, 1989; Labaree, 2010).[13] In the first decades of the 20th century, expanding schooling was a key policy of the overall strategy of economic nationalism, and consequently of the management of the promises of equal opportunity.[14] School enrollments expanded rapidly, spurred by the simultaneous and complex processes of industrialization, immigration, and urbanization (P. D. Chapman, 1988; Cremin, 1955; Fass, 1989). Most of this enrollment growth was concentrated in high schools. Between 1890 and 1915, elementary school enrollment increased by 47%, while high school enrollments increased by 554% (P. D. Chapman, 1988; see also Cubberley, 1919).

As high schools expanded, the administrative progressives advocated for differentiated curricula, which they viewed as better meeting the needs of the new high school students than the classical curriculum offered by the elite high schools of the late 19th century (Labaree, 1997). The NEA's *Cardinal Principles of Secondary Education* (Commission on the Reorganization of Secondary Education, 1918) endorsed the creation of the comprehensive high school, which would offer a traditional curriculum for those "who early manifest[ed] academic interest" (p. 15), alongside a program of vocational training for less academically oriented students (see also Labaree, 2010). In this context, policymakers and university-based researchers promoted the use of intelligence tests to sort students within differentiated school organizations.[15] This approach was driven by the assumption that American schools provided largely similar learning opportunities for all students. As Thorndike wrote in 1921 for a symposium on intelligence:

Consider a score attained by a 12-year old boy in a combination of Stanford Binet, National A and B and Haggerty Delta. . . . If the boy has had ordinary American opportunities, this score will prophesy rather accurately how well he will respond to intellectual demands in the cases of "book learning" and for some years thereafter, and very possibly for all his life. (p. 126; see also Terman et al., 1917, p. 98)

As indicated in P. D. Chapman's (1988) review of Bureau of Education school surveys during the 1920s, many school systems were highly differentiated and used intelligence tests to place students (see also Fass, 1989; Mershon & Schlossman, 2008). In general, these researchers and many of the practitioners they trained shared the belief that the instruments they were developing objectively assessed students for the new opportunity structures in public schools.

Poverty Knowledge in the New Science of Education

One major focus of this "movement for the use of scientific methods in education" was to develop and validate tools for measuring intelligence (Courtis & Packer, 1920, p. 5). Fass (1980) observed that "intelligence testing sharpened and accelerated the cultural awareness of individual and group differences" (p. 439). Given the emphasis on measurement, it is perhaps not surprising that researchers also turned their efforts toward creating objective and reliable measures of social class, using indicators such as home conditions, social status, and economic group (e.g., J. C. Chapman & Sims, 1925; Holley, 1916; Williams, 1918). Researchers quickly linked those goals and used both measures to confirm their assumptions about intelligence and social class, which gave the assumptions the imprimatur of science. For example, Terman et al. (1917) initially drew on Taussig's (1911) division of occupations into five noncompeting and hierarchical groups that ranged from day laborers to the professional classes in order to assess the relationship between students' social status and intelligence.[16]

Subsequent measures allowed Terman and other researchers to quantify and assess the relationship between class status and intelligence. Researchers replaced the more subjective assessments they had been relying on with new, seemingly precise measures of students' class backgrounds.[17] Yet some of the measures were not as rigorous as they appeared. Barr (1918), one of Terman's students, developed a numerical ranking of occupations for use in vocational guidance for his master's thesis project at Stanford University, which Terman later popularized (see Terman, 1926). Barr (1918) selected a list of 100 representative occupations and asked 20 judges—all students in Terman's intelligence testing class at Stanford—to rate the occupations based on their assessment of the "mental ability required for success in the occupation" (p. 28). A statistical analysis of the rankings yielded numeric ratings that ranged between 0.00 (hobo) to 19.62 (surgeon).[18] While Barr viewed his scale as a tool for vocational counselors for determining appropriate occupational choices for advising purposes, education researchers began to use his scale and other indicators to examine the relationship between intelligence and social class. The use of tests for social purposes and the connection between education research and policymaking are discussed by Kett (2013), who noted that researchers involved in intelligence testing for the army during World War I began to analyze the association between intelligence and occupational prestige. The economists of the era engaged in similar analyses.

Most of these analyses did not address poverty per se but legitimized existing patterns of social stratification by documenting and interpreting the association between measures of social class and IQ, which was viewed as an objective and merit-based criterion. In his influential *Genetic Studies of Genius* (1926), a study of 643 children with IQ scores of 130 or higher, Terman used these and other measures including (a) Taussig's five-category ranking of occupations; (b) the Barr scale, which elaborated and quantified Taussig's typology; (c) ratings of students' home and neighborhood conditions; (d) parental education; and (e) the size of students' home libraries as an indicator of the "cultural status" of the home (p. 81). Terman assessed his sample on these measures against comparison groups and concluded that "the heredity of our gifted subjects is much superior to that of the average individual" (p. 83).[19] Because Terman was studying gifted children rather than adults, he inferred that the children's social origins were attributable to "original endowment rather than . . . environmental influences" (p. 66; see also Terman, 1916).

Because it was refracted through scientific racism—one of the dominant racial ideologies of the late 19th and early 20th centuries (Powers & Patton, 2008)—poverty knowledge was also racialized. In the first decades of the 20th century, the mass immigration of southern and eastern Europeans to the eastern United States and of Asians to the western United States complicated the racial order built on slavery, White privilege, and Black subordination (Smedley, 1993). Within this context, intelligence testers also used the new technologies of testing and measurement to rank racial and national groups (e.g., Terman, 1916; see also Stern, 2005; Valencia & Suzuki, 2001). Early researchers found that non-Whites had low IQs and also tended to be poor, and attributed these differences to hereditary factors. While European immigrants did not experience institutionalized boundaries based on race (Fox & Guglielmo, 2012), intelligence testing provided scientific proof of their apparent inferiority to native-born Whites and justified less formalized discrimination and immigration restrictions (Fass, 1989; Ngai, 2007).[20]

The ideas associated with scientific management and intelligence testing were also wedded with eugenics, the science of racial improvement (Baker, 1998; Stern, 2005). Indeed, the intelligence test was translated into English and popularized by a prominent eugenicist, Henry Herbert Goddard, who was one of Terman's early colleagues (Lagemann, 2000). Terman, Thorndike, and other education researchers were active in eugenicist organizations (Barkan, 1992; Stern, 2005), and their psychometric research was also used to rationalize school segregation and the institutionalization and sterilization of juvenile delinquents.[21] While other education researchers may have been more neutral about the relative roles of hereditary and environmental factors in shaping intelligence, Fass (1980) observed that "the clear direction of American interpretation and the construction of experiments with tests were toward the view that intelligence tests were measuring something that was pure and inborn" (p. 441). This legacy left a heavy framing effect on the profession, which in turn shaped how the tests were incorporated into the work and organization of schools in the decades that followed (P. D. Chapman, 1988; Fass, 1980, 1989; Walters, 2009).

Competing Perspectives on the Tools of the Science of Education

During the first four decades of the 20th century, few education researchers questioned how the ideologies and techniques associated with the new science of education facilitated the sorting of students for differentiated school experiences. Because the field was dominated by psychology, most ignored structural issues or how such policies largely reproduced existing class and race inequalities in the guise of objectivity and meritocracy (e.g., Collins, 1928; Goodenough, 1928; Haggerty & Nash, 1924; see also Cohen & Barnes, 1999; Fass, 1989; Kett, 2013; Mehta, 2013; Rury, 2005; Tyack & Hansot, 1982; Valencia & Suzuki, 2001). Only a small cadre of scholars critiqued the relationship between social class and educational outcomes. While their perspective was a minority view among researchers until the Great Society programs of the 1960s, policymakers of the same period were even less concerned about the connection between poverty and educational outcomes (G. Davies, 1996; Katz, 2013; O'Connor, 2001).[22]

One of the critics was Walter Lippman. In a series of articles published in the *New Republic* in 1922, Lippman directly engaged three core tenets of the new science of education: that hereditary intelligence was measurable, that intelligence tests provided a valid measure of intelligence, and that intelligence tests should be used to determine students' access to educational opportunities. To support his claims, Lippman reproduced figures from Terman et al. (1917) that illustrated the association between social class and IQ and argued the results could be interpreted as evidence of the "considerable connection between education and environment" rather than the heritability of IQ (Lippman, 1922, p. 329). Lippman also observed that Terman's finding that the correlation between social class and IQ declined with age could be viewed as "a rather strong argument . . . for the traditional American theory that the public school is an agency for equalizing the opportunities of the privileged and the unprivileged" (p. 329).

John Dewey (1922) also joined the fray in the pages of the *New Republic*. While endorsing Lippman's (1922) argument, Dewey expressed concern that the methodology underlying intelligence tests, which measured students against group averages, obscured the individuality of students. Instead of differentiating students' educational experiences based on a crude measure, Dewey argued for an "inquiring and creative education" as early as elementary school (p. 37). He advocated for an education that expanded the capacities of all students. Until that time, Dewey concluded, "we shall never have any light upon what are the limits of intelligence set by innate qualities" (see also Hlebowitsh & Wraga, 1995).[23]

Among the dissenting voices whose criticism never gained much traction in the field were Stephen S. Colvin and George Counts (Valencia, 1997).[24] Colvin (1922) distinguished between general intelligence, or the "inborn" ability to learn, and acquired intelligence or learning. General intelligence cannot be directly measured; rather, it is "infer[red] from differences in acquired intelligence" (p. 19). In Colvin's view, the appropriate benchmark for assessing the results of individual or group intelligence tests is the results from another group of students who share similar knowledge and experiences. If students are tested on material with which they are not familiar, then the test will not provide an accurate measure of their ability to learn. "Hence children of different social and economic status may score differently in such tests not because of any real difference in native intelligence but because of such differences in home surroundings that some are favored while others are handicapped" (p. 43). Unlike Terman, Colvin also advocated interpreting test results in the context of other information about students, including teachers' assessments of students.

Counts was one of the few education researchers who suggested that access to educational opportunity was a function of social class rather than intelligence. In *The Selective Character of American Secondary Education*, Counts (1922a) analyzed the factors that shaped high school attendance in four large cities. Counts observed that while enrollment in American public high schools had expanded considerably in the 40 years prior to his study, the students attending high schools were a highly select group, and the most important factor determining high school attendance was parental occupation. Children whose parents had lower status occupations were less likely than their more privileged peers to enter and persist in high school. Students were also tracked by parental occupation within high schools: The children of the "laboring classes" were overrepresented in the vocational tracks (p. 142). While there was some degree of selection based on intelligence, Counts observed that there was a considerable overlap in the distribution of ability, such that "there was much excellence out of, as well as much mediocrity in, the high school" (p. 147). While he stopped short of arguing that schools were reproducing class inequalities, Counts viewed the unequal distribution of the opportunity to attend high school as profoundly undemocratic.[25]

During the 1930s, the work of George Stoddard and his colleagues at the Iowa Child Welfare Research Station was also influential in producing a body of research that questioned the assumption that intelligence was fixed and determined primarily by heredity (Beatty, 2012a; Lagemann, 2000). By the mid-1930s, the consensus that the relationship between intelligence and socioeconomic status was rooted in genetics was also beginning to break down, and an increasing number of researchers were attributing the association to environmental factors (e.g., Byrns & Henmon, 1936; Jordan, 1933; Neff, 1938). However, the primary focus of many of these analyses was to document the relationship between socioeconomic status and intelligence. In assessing the significance of their findings, few researchers fundamentally questioned the use of intelligence tests for distributing educational opportunities or the role of schools in sorting, apart from raising relatively mild concerns in passing (e.g., Saltzman, 1940).[26]

Led by W. Lloyd Warner, the Committee on Human Development at the University of Chicago was one of the few research groups that raised more substantive questions about the use of intelligence tests to sort students within schools (Foley, 2010; Lagemann, 2000). For example, in *Who Shall Be Educated* (1944), Warner, Havighurst, and Loeb provided an analysis of the role of schools in perpetuating class-based status hierarchies in U.S. society. Warner et al. observed that although the expansion in access to schooling had promoted a widely held belief that education would provide most children with a path to social mobility, in practice the differentiated educational system sorted and selected students based on their class backgrounds.

Citing a study that examined educational outcomes for a group of students that had IQ scores of 110 or higher, Warner et al. (1944) noted that few students of high ability but below-average socioeconomic status completed high school or college.[27] The authors attributed this phenomenon to the financial and opportunity costs of attending high school and college rather than to a lack of desire on the part of the children and families of the "lower socio-economic levels" (p. 53). When students did attend high school, they were sorted into different curricula, informally or formally, by class background. More specifically, while many people believed that differentiation within schools occurred based on ability, two of the principle methods for determining ability—teachers' assessments and IQ tests—tended to favor middle-class children.[28]

Anticipating the turn toward educational programs in the War on Poverty, Warner et al. (1944) argued for a more fully realized meritocracy that was less dependent on class as a sorting mechanism and, rather, oriented toward identifying and supporting talented students from the lower classes at a young age. While stratification could not be avoided, Warner et al. proposed that the negative effects of stratification could be ameliorated by ensuring that "those from the bottom . . . be given more than a fighting chance to compete with those above them" (p. 146). Warner et al.'s ideas were embraced and promoted by prominent education reformers during this period: James B. Conant, president of Harvard University and later the author of three influential Carnegie Foundation–sponsored reports on American education between 1955 and 1964, and John W. Gardner, president of the Carnegie Foundation (Lagemann, 1989). The dominant view of reformers was that schools needed to more effectively facilitate the mobility of the gifted and talented.

The Zeitgeist of the Coleman Report: The "Culture of Poverty" and Human Capital Theory

Although poverty and other social inequalities were not a primary focus of education researchers' concerns, the work of Warner et al. (1944) exemplifies a broader effort in the social sciences to identify and describe class cultures (O'Connor, 2001). In the 1950s, poverty was "rediscovered" by social scientists and liberal politicians in the United States (Brauer, 1982, p. 99; see also Katz, 2013). While the economy was growing and the middle class was perceived as expanding, John Kenneth Galbraith and others called attention to segments of the country and the population that were experiencing economic dislocation (Galbraith, 1969). As the notion of class cultures was taken up and elaborated by scholars, it offered an appealing explanation for persistent inequalities in "the affluent society."[29]

Highlighting class-related cultural practices and beliefs allowed researchers to explain poverty as a function of deeply ingrained behavioral and psychological traits rather than structural inequalities (O'Connor, 2001; see also Katz, 2013). Most prominently, anthropologist Oscar Lewis argued that the poor adapted to structural dislocation and economic marginalization by developing a culture of poverty that was transmitted to their children through socialization. While originally conceptualized to analyze poverty in underdeveloped countries, the culture of poverty was taken up by social scientists to explain persistent poverty in the United States and introduced to a popular audience by Harrington's (1962) *The Other America*. Riessman's (1962) *The Culturally Disadvantaged Child* provided a detailed analysis of the social psychology of the "culturally deprived child" and a set of strategies aimed at helping schools better address the needs of such children (Beatty, 2012a). In economics, human capital theorists applied market principles to the supply-side of the labor market (O'Connor, 2001) and argued that, much like companies that invest in physical capital, individuals invest in education and training to maximize their returns in the labor market. While the empirical support for human capital theory is not robust (Carnoy, 2009; Karabel & Halsey, 1977; Klees, 2012), it cast the commonsense assumptions of the early school reformers in econometric terms (Labaree, 2010). As we explain below, culture-of-poverty arguments and human capital theory were the conceptual underpinnings for domestic policy initiatives focused on poverty.

This attention to poverty occurred during a period when the Supreme Court's decision in *Brown v. Board of Education* (1954) made segregation and the resistance to desegregation that occurred in its wake a pressing public problem.[30] Yet many prominent educators and researchers, including Conant (a high-profile member of that community), viewed segregation as largely a Southern problem and believed that the major issue facing large metropolitan areas outside the South was the de facto segregation of minority students in urban schools (Urban, 2009; see also Conant, 1961).[31]

The lack of awareness among these researchers of their own politics of expertise and of the sociocultural processes involved in constructing "expert research knowledge" (Walters, 2009) was consistent with a culture of education research that continued to bracket inequality related to poverty and racism. These processes of willful ignorance allowed many education researchers in the late 1950s and early 1960s to pivot from the issue of segregation and its attendant focus on race-based inequalities in educational opportunity, to the more racially neutral problem of the cultural disadvantages of urban youth. For example, in the introduction to *The Educationally Retarded and Disadvantaged*, the 66th yearbook of the National Society for the Study of Education, the yearbook committee noted that "although large numbers of Negro pupils are among the 'disadvantaged,' there are also very large numbers of retarded and 'disadvantaged' white pupils who similarly need 'compensatory' education" (Whitty, 1967, p. 4; see also Artiles, 2011; Martinez & Rury, 2012; Smiley, 1967).

These ideas from the social sciences shaped the perspectives of policymakers, and in particular those of the economists associated with President John F. Kennedy's Council of Economic Advisors, who were also influenced by pragmatic political considerations (O'Connor, 2001). In the early 1960s, the Kennedy administration had begun working on proposals to address poverty (Brauer, 1982). While Kennedy had advocated for civil rights legislation, he also recognized that Southern members of Congress would oppose civil rights but might be more willing to support antipoverty programs because of the high concentration of poverty in the South. Both culture-of-poverty arguments and human capital theory pointed to the benefits of investments in education targeted at youth. Policies aimed at redistributing income to the poor had little political support, so the Kennedy administration focused on targeting a modest amount of funds toward small-scale programs in local communities (Brauer, 1982; Kantor & Lowe, 2006; H. M. Levin, 1989; O'Connor, 2001).

After Kennedy was assassinated, antipoverty proposals, which had not been publicly announced, became key elements of the War on Poverty, the signature initiative of President Lyndon B. Johnson's administration. Johnson also promoted other key policies of the Kennedy administration, including the Civil Rights Act of 1964. *Brown v. Board of Education* and the conflicts it engendered around desegregation also helped focus the Johnson administration's efforts on education policy (Kantor & Lowe, 2006). The Elementary and Secondary Education Act (ESEA) of 1965 funded compensatory education for poor children, although Congress distributed the funds widely and its budgetary appropriations fell short of meeting all students' needs (Kantor & Lowe, 2006). While Johnson's education officials initially saw ESEA as a way to force Southern states to comply with the Civil Rights Act, which prohibited discrimination in schools that received federal dollars, the backlash against efforts to enforce desegregation also threatened the ESEA's political viability. By the late 1960s, government officials began to decouple federal desegregation efforts from Title I of ESEA, which targeted federal funds to low-income schools. Urban (2012) observed that the compensatory education programs of the 1960s, and the researchers that created and championed them, tended to take segregated schools for granted and addressed achievement gaps within that structure rather than engaging in efforts to desegregate schools. While it was unlikely that this approach was motivated by racism, it "reinforce[d] the racism of white educational actors who sought to distance white students from black and other minority students in all settings at all costs" (Urban, 2012, p. 3; see also Beatty, 2012a).

While the War on Poverty was largely framed in color-blind terms, Johnson's June 1965 speech at Howard University signaled a shift in the administration's understanding of Black poverty as a unique problem and in need of targeted policy interventions (G. Davies, 1996; see also Katz, 2013). Drawing on the Moynihan Report, which had not yet been released, Johnson merged a critique of White racism with culture-of-poverty arguments. According to Johnson, the dynamics of Black poverty were fundamentally "the consequence of ancient brutality, past injustice, and present prejudice," which isolated Blacks in ghettos and contributed to the breakdown of the Black family and communities (Johnson, 1965, para. 36). After the Moynihan Report was released and its key arguments and claims were distorted in the national media (Katz, 2013), and as the urban riots of the 1960s unfolded, urban poverty was increasingly understood in racial terms (G. Davies, 1996; Martinez & Rury, 2012).

THE COLEMAN REPORT AND ITS LEGACY

The Genesis of the Coleman Report and Its Findings

Released in 1966, the Coleman Report had a less auspicious reception than its current standing in the field would suggest (G. Grant, 1973). The Civil Rights Act of 1964 required the Commissioner of Education to assess the "lack of availability of equal educational opportunities for individuals by reason of race, color, religion, or national origin in public educational institutions at all levels in the United States" (Section 402). The contract for the project was awarded to sociologist James Coleman, who reframed the goals of the survey required by the legislation from a focus on educational inequalities (i.e., school-based resources) to an analysis of the relationship between educational inputs and outcomes.[32] Coleman and his team of researchers executed the ambitious, state-of-the-art Equality of Educational Opportunity (EEO) survey, which surveyed and tested 645,000 elementary and secondary students at five grade levels attending 4,000 schools, and also surveyed their teachers and principals (Coleman et al., 1966).

Using then cutting-edge statistical techniques, Coleman and his team analyzed the relationships between student achievement and school resources, teacher characteristics, and students' family backgrounds.[33] The latter measures were constructed from students' responses on a set of questions that were aligned with the long-established tradition of measuring socioeconomic status in educational psychology (e.g., J. C. Chapman & Sims, 1925): urbanism, mother's and father's education, family size, items in the home (e.g., telephone, refrigerator, car), and reading material in the home (e.g., books, magazines, encyclopedias).[34] The analysis indicated that while schools were highly segregated, the differences in the characteristics of schools attended by White and Black students were not as large as many of the people involved in the study expected, including Coleman himself (G. Grant, 1973; see also Gamoran & Long, 2007; Mosteller & Moynihan, 1972).

After documenting the substantial achievement gaps between White and Black students, Coleman determined that most of the variation in students' achievement scores occurred within schools rather than between schools and that school characteristics accounted for a small proportion of this within-school variation. Rather, Coleman and his research team found that much of the variation in student achievement was attributable to students' family backgrounds and the backgrounds of the other students attending their schools:[35]

> Schools bring little influence to bear on a child's achievement that is independent of his background and general social context; and . . . this very lack of an independent effect means that the inequalities imposed on children by their home, neighborhood, and peer environment are carried along to become the inequalities with which they confront adult life at the end of school. For equality of educational opportunity through the schools must imply a strong effect of schools that is independent of the child's immediate social environment, and that strong independent effect is not present in American schools. (Coleman et al., 1966, p. 325)

While the Coleman Report's focus on the outcomes of schooling has been widely viewed as shifting scholarly and policy attention from the inputs of schooling to outputs (e.g., Carnoy, 2009; Mosteller & Moynihan, 1972; Walters & Lareau, 2009), we might also see it as both the culmination and extension of long-standing blind spots in education research and the willful ignorance that framed the nexus between education research and policymaking in the first half of the 20th century. These blind spots include positivism and the emphasis on measurement, human capital theory, culture-of-poverty perspectives, and, perhaps more constraining, the systematic willful ignorance that resulted from using the White middle-class male student as the implicit norm and the othering of students who did not conform to "normalized" class, race/ethnicity, gender, and ability categories (Artiles, 2011; Valencia & Suzuki, 2001; Varenne & McDermott, 1999).

The school survey, measures of socioeconomic status, and achievement tests were joined in multivariate analyses of massive nationwide samples of students and schools.[36] To a certain degree, the initial legislative charge to focus the analysis on race-based inequalities in inputs might be viewed as a departure from prior studies, which did not systematically document inequalities in access to educational resources (e.g., Warner et al., 1944). However, Coleman's decision to focus on outputs rather than inputs was a departure only in the context of the heightened awareness of race-based educational and social inequalities fostered by *Brown* and the civil rights movement. His decision can also be read as rooted in early research efforts such as the school survey, even while the report's findings challenged the widely held assumption of early school surveyors that increasing school resources would result in increased efficiency and productivity (Lagemann, 2000; see also Cubberley, 1916).

However, as Mosteller and Moynihan (1972) observed, Coleman and his colleagues did not address social class directly in their analysis. The "presence of social class was implicit in the stated findings that family background, measured in social class terms . . . is apparently a major determinant of educational achievement" (p. 22).

Drawing on another analysis of the EEO data that assessed class differences in achievement within and across racial groups, Mosteller and Moynihan highlighted how some of the racial achievement gaps documented by the Coleman Report were attributable to social class (see Okada, Cohen, & Mayeske, 1969).

Coleman et al. (1966) addressed poverty explicitly only once in the summary of the report, in a discussion of the consistent and widening gaps in achievement between minority and White students across the grade span:

> Whatever may be the combination of non-school factors—poverty, community attitudes, low educational level of parents—which put minority students at a disadvantage in verbal and nonverbal skills when they enter the first grade, the fact is that schools have not overcome it. (p. 21)

Likewise, in an expanded discussion of achievement gaps in the body of the report, Coleman et al. (1966) invoked culture-of-poverty arguments when he noted that the achievement differences suggested that "the ecology of educational disadvantages experienced by particular minority groups in the United States" were largely attributable to "the background cultures from which these groups came" (pp. 273, 275). Coleman noted that if schools provided different opportunities for students, or if they did not address students' cultural disadvantages either by default or by design, these differences would persist and restrict students' opportunities into adulthood.

The Political Impact of the Coleman Report

Coleman et al.'s (1966) central finding that family background was the key factor shaping student outcomes contradicted the common wisdom among officials in the Johnson administration, as well as one of the central myths of American society: that schools are a mechanism for social mobility (Lippman, 1922; Warner et al., 1944). Not incidentally, it also suggested that the billion dollars targeted toward compensatory education programs by the ESEA, which Congress had approved the year before, were being misdirected (G. Grant, 1973). A short summary of the Coleman Report was released on a Friday afternoon prior to a holiday weekend, without a press release. Initial newspaper reports mentioned the findings related to family background but tended to place greater emphasis on the report's findings about segregation and highlighted the areas where there was evidence of school resource gaps between majority-Black and majority-White schools (e.g., Herbers, 1966; see also G. Grant, 1973). The full report was released a month later. Although Congress passed an extension of the ESEA in 1966, few Congressional staff members were aware of the Coleman Report's findings (G. Grant, 1973).

The Coleman Report had relatively little political impact until Daniel Patrick Moynihan, the editor of *The Public Interest*, asked Coleman to write an article for the journal summarizing the findings and their policy implications (G. Grant, 1973). Moynihan also promoted the report's finding in his own speeches and articles. When Moynihan assumed a position in President Richard Nixon's administration, the findings from the Coleman Report were used to justify the administration's unsuccessful attempt to cut funding for education. Four years later, Coleman's results on peer effects and, more specifically, his finding that the family backgrounds of the students attending a school had a strong effect on the achievement of minority students were used to justify federal funding for desegregation by the Nixon administration. Coleman's own advocacy of his findings on Capitol Hill as well as Moynihan's ongoing support were important factors in ensuring that the report gained relevance and momentum as a policy document. While the initial policy impact of the report was to support the Nixon's administration's approach to desegregation, the most enduring findings were that (a) most of the variation in student achievement occurs within rather than between schools, and (b) there is strong relationship between family background and student achievement relative to school factors (see, e.g., Vinovskis, 2009; Walters & Lareau, 2009).

Replications and Extensions: The Coleman Report and Its Influence on Research

Another indicator of the Coleman Report's impact, in addition to the many studies that have engaged its findings,[37] is the repeated analysis of the EEO data, including studies published more than three decades after the report was released (Borman & Dowling, 2010; Konstantopoulos & Borman, 2011). This is striking because there are few replication studies in education research (Makel & Plucker, 2014; Schneider, 2004). Some of the most prominent and early appraisals of Coleman's findings, including the reanalyses of the EEO data, were begun almost immediately after the report was issued in the form of a faculty seminar conducted at Harvard University in 1966–1967, led by Moynihan (Mosteller & Moynihan, 1972). Funded by the Carnegie Corporation, more than 70 faculty members participated in the seminar, including Coleman and some of his coauthors. The seminar generated an edited book addressing the report's findings and their implications for policy and future research (Mosteller & Moynihan, 1972). Most of the reanalyses have tended to confirm the Coleman Report's main conclusions. Here, we highlight those that have addressed social class more directly.

In the Mosteller and Moyhihan (1972) volume, Jencks (1972) and Smith (1972) conducted reanalyses of EEO data that addressed the relationships among social class, school resources, and student achievement more directly than the Coleman Report had. Jencks (1972) focused on Northern elementary schools and found that, on average, poor students (students who had seven or fewer home items) attended schools with resources similar to those of the schools attended by their middle-class peers. Jencks and his colleagues incorporated the analyses of EEO data into a book length treatment of the topic of economic inequality in American society (Jencks et al., 1972). In *Inequality*, Jencks et al. (1972) reached a conclusion that he had hinted at in the Mosteller and Moynihan (1972) volume—that it would be impossible to alter existing patterns of poverty and social inequality through school reform. Rather, Jencks et al. (1972) argued that a more effective way of ending inequality and, in particular, of ameliorating poverty—the goal of the War on Poverty—was to redistribute income. This argument has since been elaborated by education researchers but has had little influence on policymaking (e.g., Anyon, 1997; Apple, 2012; Berliner, 2006; Darling-Hammond, 2010; Kozol, 1992).

Smith (1972) observed that the argument that most of the variation in achievement between schools is attributable to students' family backgrounds rests on the assumption that family background and school characteristics are relatively independent. However, if more advantaged students attend better resourced schools, then the causal claim could be reversed. That is, differences in student achievement would be largely attributable to school resources rather than to family background. Smith suggested that there was little evidence for the latter claim and extended Coleman's conclusions to highlight the sorting function of schools, much like Warner et al. (1944) three decades earlier.

A somewhat different conclusion can be drawn from a school-level reanalysis of the EEO data conducted by Department of Education staff. Mayeske et al. (1969) examined the relationship between indexes constructed from clusters of variables and found that schools' characteristics were highly correlated with the socioeconomic status of their students, and that socioeconomic status and school characteristics had a substantial joint effect on school achievement. Notably, the index of socioeconomic status used in the Mayeske et al. analysis included a survey item that asked students to report their fathers' occupations, whereas Coleman's analyses did not.[38]

While overall the findings from the Mayeske et al. (1969) reanalysis tended to confirm Coleman's initial conclusions, they also highlighted how the "influence of the school is bound up with the social background of the students that they get initially. Very little influence of the schools can be separated from the social background of their students and very little of the influence of social background can be separated from the influence of the schools" (p. 327). In a subsequent analysis of student achievement using the same techniques, Mayeske, Okada, Cohen, Beaton, and Wisler (1973) reached similar conclusions. These findings indicate that students' socioeconomic status was undermeasured in the Coleman report and in reanalyses that used a more limited set of variables to assess it (see also Rury & Saatcioglu, 2015). The undermeasurement of socioeconomic status may explain why the Coleman Report has been less influential in raising public awareness about poverty.

Another influential critique of the Coleman Report came from scholars who argued that schools were not effectively educating the children of the poor (Edmonds, 1979). Studies of "effective schools," including a reanalysis of EEO data (Edmonds & Frederiksen, 1979), focused on analyzing the academic efficacy of schools serving poor children and identifying common practices within the group of higher achieving schools.[39] In the decades that followed, researchers, including Coleman himself, continued to engage the questions raised by the Coleman Report about the relative influence of family background and school factors on student achievement (e.g., Coleman, 1975;[40] Hanushek, 1996; Hedges & Greenwald, 1996; see also Gamoran & Long, 2007, for a review of the school effects literature).

More recent reanalyses of the EEO data using newer and more sophisticated analytical techniques than those available to Coleman and his team have confirmed the Coleman Report's main findings related to family background. They have also indicated that school effects are more substantial than Coleman's analysis suggested (e.g., Konstantopoulos, 2006; Konstantopoulos & Borman, 2011; see also Borman & Dowling, 2010, and the review in Gamoran & Long, 2007). Much like Mayeske et al. (1969) and Mayeske et al. (1973), these newer analyses suggest that it is difficult to disentangle the relationship between students' backgrounds and school resources, at least in the ways that they are conventionally measured (e.g., Konstantopoulos & Borman, 2011). In other words, the effects of school resources are complex and are likely contingent on the social dynamics within schools, or on how resources and opportunities are distributed and engaged by teachers and students (e.g., Bidwell & Kasarda, 1980).

Is the Coleman Report Still Relevant?

If we view the Coleman Report through the lens of the research-policy nexus, it represents a powerful prototypical case of a research study that was legislatively mandated; recognized as rigorous, comprehensive, and connected to what was viewed as the real needs of school reform; and ultimately acknowledged as relevant by the research community, policymakers, and the media. Particularly notable is that a study of this type helped catalyze specific research-based policy recommendations. However, despite all these positive attributes and its enormous potential, the report was constrained by the long-standing blind spots and willful ignorance at the center of the research-policy nexus that we have described.

The six research and policy recommendations outlined by Mosteller and Moynihan (1972) are illustrative in this regard. First, Mosteller and Moynihan argued that "equality of educational achievement for the several racial/ethnic groups, [should be adopted] as a national goal" (p. 52). This is what we would describe in contemporary terms as closing the achievement gap. Second, they pointed to the need for long-term and experimental studies aimed at understanding the effects of educational programs (see also Dyer, 1972; Smith, 1972). Third, they advocated for regular and national-level assessments of student achievement, such as the National Assessment of Educational Progress, which had been initiated recently. Fourth, echoing Jencks (1972), they highlighted the need for employment and income programs aimed at improving children's home environments. They also emphasized the need to evaluate new social programs. Fifth, they recommended supporting the creation of new schools as laboratories for educational innovations. Finally, they exhorted the public and policymakers to embrace "optimism" (Mosteller & Moynihan, 1972, p. 57). They urged the public to pressure elected officials to set educational goals and assess the nation's progress toward meeting those goals. Yet they also noted that gains would be a "rarity" and should be celebrated when they occurred (p. 57). They highlighted the considerable advances that had been made in the 20th century in expanding access to education and reducing inequalities, and pointed to the progress that had been made in desegregating Southern schools since the release of the Coleman Report.

Of Mosteller and Moynihan's (1972) six policy recommendations, some are easily recognizable in contemporary policies such as No Child Left Behind, Race to the Top, and the enshrining of studies using experimental research designs as the "gold standard" (Walters, 2009). Mosteller and Moynihan's first and third recommendations are echoed in the ways that No Child Left Behind institutionalized accountability policies aimed at documenting and closing achievement gaps, annual testing, and the assessment of schools against benchmarks that continued to reverberate in Race to the Top (RTT).[41] The second recommendation, regarding more rigorous and experimental studies, is clearly manifested in the Education Sciences Reform Act of 2002 and the What Works Clearinghouse; the implications of these policies for the research community have been discussed extensively elsewhere (Berliner, 2002; Erickson, 2014; Moss et al., 2009; Pellegrino & Goldman, 2002; Shavelson & Towne, 2002; St. Pierre, 2006).[42] The fifth recommendation is mirrored in the embrace and promotion of charter schools in federal and state policies.

Two of Mosteller and Moynihan's (1972) recommendations have had less resonance for contemporary policymakers. Their sixth recommendation, that the public and policymakers should embrace measured optimism in assessing educational progress, is striking in light of the decades-long perception of crisis in education engendered by *A Nation at Risk* (National Commission on Excellence in Education, 1983; see also Berliner & Biddle, 1995; Mehta, 2013; "Testing Doesn't Measure up," 2015). If their sixth recommendation was rendered irrelevant by the displacement of optimism by crisis-driven pessimism, the fourth (employment, income, and social programs aimed at improving children's home environments) was plainly and willfully ignored. In this regard, it is instructive to reflect on how Mosteller and Moynihan introduced the six recommendations:

No single program can be expected to close the gap in educational achievement between the disadvantaged minorities and the white group. Furthermore, we do not know what school programs might offer the largest improvement for the cost involved. We must also recognize that strengthened educational achievement may not be the most important social reform needed. Indeed, higher income and better occupational changes probably are more immediate targets of reform groups, with educational achievement regarded as part of the means toward such change, as well as having value in itself. (p. 52)[43]

Even with its blind spots, Coleman's analysis gave the relationship between poverty and school outcomes heightened visibility among researchers. As we indicated earlier, a robust "school effects" literature engaged and debated Coleman's findings, using increasingly sophisticated analytical techniques such as multilevel modeling (e.g., Konstantopoulos, 2006). Likewise, as in the founding years of the field, some researchers have consistently addressed issues of poverty, its effects on schools, and access to educational opportunities (e.g., Anyon, 1997; Berliner, 2006; Carter &

Welner, 2013; Darling-Hammond, 2010; Gamoran, 2001, 2008; Kozol, 1992; Oakes, Hunter Quartz, Ryan & Lipton, 2000; and many others), but their arguments have not had the traction they deserve among policymakers, given their empirical robustness and conceptual contributions. Instead, Coleman's analytical approach has become common sense in educational policymaking, in the form of a narrowly conceived and punitive accountability movement (Mehta, 2013). That is, policymakers have tended to embrace the Coleman Report's measurement technologies while ignoring the implications of the findings.[44] It has been more politically expedient for policymakers to implement relatively limited policies that focus on schools rather than redistributive policies aimed at ameliorating poverty. When the more limited policies invariably fail to address poverty or class-based achievement gaps, policymakers tend to blame schools or the poor (Beatty, 2012b). While education research has come full circle to the emphasis on measurement embodied in the early decades of the field, the public seems to have lost faith in schooling as a democratic institution, another hallmark of the administrative progressives' belief system in the early 20th century (Fischman & Haas, 2012).

We are convinced that although many education researchers were instrumental in the development and legitimation of new regimes of research expertise that willfully ignored poverty and other educational inequalities, and their intersectionalities, researchers have also begun to challenge those regimes as the field enters its second century. We are not naive; we understand that in highly polarized and politicized contexts, the biggest challenge in developing a more effective research-policy nexus is not to produce more or better data—the field is already doing that—but to overcome the lack of trust among potential allies and to intervene in the political arena to confront those who manipulate research for political gain.[45] The scenario is complex, and as our own review shows, education researchers do not have a stellar record. Yet we remain cautiously optimistic. There are significant manifestations of communities, teachers, parents, social movements, universities, researchers, and allied groups resisting, denouncing, and demanding changes to the punishing regimes affecting so many children and their schools. A number of foundations, including the William T. Grant and Spencer Foundations, have targeted resources and attention to addressing poverty and improving the connections between education research, policy, and practice.

Even with all the challenges and limitations confronting a professional research organization, AERA has been and remains a key institution in challenging structures and actors that benefit from the visible invisibility of the oppressive effects of unequal educational opportunities. The road to excellent education in democratic societies needs education researchers and allied policymakers who abandon the willful ignorance of poverty and other social inequalities, and instead work together to address the complex relationships between them and the outcomes of education.

ACKNOWLEDGMENTS

We would like to thank the editors and our anonymous reviewers for their detailed and thoughtful feedback, which helped us refine our arguments and analysis.

NOTES

[1]We are not arguing that AERA as an organization was or is ignoring poverty or that there were not critical voices within AERA and the research community but that those voices were not deeply engaged by policymakers.

[2]As Rury (2005) observed,

> It is possible that Dewey and other progressive thinkers did not feel compelled to confront racial issues explicitly simply because relatively few blacks lived in the North at the time. Although his Columbia office was immediately adjacent to Harlem, a vast Black community in 1930, Dewey may have felt that the question of race was part of the larger issue of inequality in the American democracy, a matter he devoted much time and energy to addressing in broader terms. Whatever the cause, issues of race and ethnicity appear to have been something of a blind spot in the progressives' humanitarian campaign to transform the school. It was not a set of problems that they devoted very much time and energy to, and the movement—not to mention the nation's education system—was the poorer for it. (p. 176)

[3]Our understanding of willful ignorance was influenced by Gotanda's (1991) insightful discussion of the racial nonrecognition at the heart of color blindness in social policy.

[4]While a detailed discussion of the research-policy nexus is beyond the scope of this chapter, it has been the subject of a number of studies and reviews (see Cooper, 2013, 2014; P. Davies, 1999; Henig, 2012; Hess, 2008; Honig & Coburn, 2008; Ince, 2008; B. Levin, 2004; Qi & Levin, 2013; Yohalem & Tseng, 2015). We agree with Galway and Sheppard's (2015) observation that "while it has become widely accepted that educational research has improved in volume and quality, difficulties with effective dissemination and integration into practice and underutilization by policy elites remain vexed problems" (p. 4).

[5]An initial search of the *Journal of American History* in JSTOR using the search terms *education, research,* and *poverty* yielded an initial count of 483 potential sources (including many repeated citations), which we narrowed down to five, based on the titles. We searched the *American Educational History Journal* with the term *poverty* and added an additional citation to our preliminary list. We searched *History of Education Quarterly* using the terms *research* and *poverty* and added six additional articles and four books.

[6]Poverty knowledge is generated by experts situated in public agencies, universities, research institutes, and foundations using the techniques of social science research. While the War on Poverty was a key turning point for the production of poverty knowledge, O'Connor (2001) traces its roots to the Progressive Era.

[7]Another important center was the University of Chicago, where Charles Hubbard Judd also helped institutionalize a "science of education" (Lagemann, 2000, p. 68; see also White, 1982).

[8]Terman published the first version of his test, the Stanford-Binet test, in 1916 and a year later joined a committee of the War Department that developed two mass-administered tests. At the end of World War I, the Rockefeller Foundation funded the development of intelligence and achievement tests that could be used in public schools. The Stanford Achievement test was published in 1922, and 3 years later over a million copies of the test were sold annually (Lagemann, 2000). Terman's measure, the intelligence quotient (IQ), was calculated by dividing individuals' mental age by their chronological age and multiplying the result by 100. Mental ages were determined by comparing an individual's score against benchmarks for performance derived from testing large and ostensibly representative samples of students within age-groups (Terman et al., 1917). Terman viewed White, middle-class, American-born students as representative of the average student attending U.S. public schools. Thus the IQ obscures the comparative nature of the assessment process by providing an abstract, statistical

representation of individuals' intellectual capacity against what was in practice a White, middle-class norm (Fass, 1980; see also Valencia & Suzuki, 2001).

[9]The *Twenty-Seventh Yearbook of the National Society for the Study of Education* focused on the relative influence of "nature" versus "nurture" on intelligence. In a review of the volume published in the *Journal of Educational Psychology*, Guy Whipple, the yearbook editor, summarized the volume's studies as providing evidence for the "preponderant role of intelligence in conditioning school achievement" (Whipple, 1928, p. 395). In his own review, Terman (1928) was more oblique but "concluded that IQ does count, that it is not easily influenced by environmental factors, and that it is therefore relatively constant" (p. 370).

[10]For example, women were represented as authors of papers published in the NSSE Yearbooks (e.g., 1922, 1925, 1928, 1931, 1937, 1938, 1940, 1943, 1961, 1967) but, with a few exceptions, did not serve as officers of the society. See also Mershon and Schlossman's (2008) discussion of women's roles in the Educational Research Association of America, the organization that became the National Association of Directors of Educational Research as it expanded its mission to represent a broader range of education researchers.

[11]A half-century later, the National Academy's Committee on Educational Research described their efforts, saying,

> Too many surveyors, relentlessly quantifying, ended up measuring what was measurable. Furthermore, a movement that started out by featuring open-minded questioning soon propagated new orthodoxies. . . . Despite the intention to use local facts as a basis for decision-making, the recommendations of survey teams proved to be remarkably alike in community after community. (Cronbach & Suppes, 1969, pp. 54–55)

[12]NADER's early meetings were focused on the use and application of measurement techniques, the favored tools of the positivist paradigm that was being consolidated in the social sciences.

[13]Fass (1980) observed that even while researchers and educators debated the meaning and relevance of intelligence, intelligence became a central organizing concept within American schools and was taken up by the culture at large.

[14]In the doctrine of economic nationalism, national economic growth was viewed as the principal means for ensuring social progress for workers and their families. The state was viewed as responsible for safeguarding citizens' prosperity, security, and opportunities. The consensus among policymakers and big business was that full employment and opportunity through education, social welfare, and occupational mobility were the most effective ways to facilitate economic growth (Brown, Halsey, Lauder, & Wells, 1997).

[15]For example, in a report for another prominent NEA subcommittee, Terman et al. (1922, *Intelligence Tests and School Reorganization*) observed that students' abilities varied widely within classrooms and that teachers were not able to assess students' abilities objectively. For Terman, the most feasible way to deal with the differences was to use intelligence tests to "classify students more accurately on the basis of native ability" and to group students homogenously by ability within grades (Terman et al., 1922, p. 18; see also Flemming & Rutledge, 1927).

[16]Taussig (1911) viewed the groups as noncompeting because "those born or placed in a given group usually remain there, and don't compete with those of other groups" (p. 134). His descriptions of occupational groups also indexed class standing. For example, he characterized clerical occupations as "lower middle class." While Taussig averred that it was difficult, perhaps impossible, to definitively answer the question of whether social position was a result of "inborn gifts" or environment, he emphasized that mobility between groups was unlikely.

[17]In initial studies, researchers interested in assessing the relationship between socioeconomic status and intelligence had to rely on broader and more clearly subjective measures of class

status, such as school principals' assessments of the class backgrounds of their school populations. One of the earliest quantitative measures, the Whittier Scale for Grading Home Conditions (Williams, 1918), was originally developed to assess the homes of delinquent boys. Williams outlined a method for scoring detailed narrative descriptions of children's homes that influenced the development of subsequent measures of socioeconomic status (e.g., J. C. Chapman & Sims, 1925). Children's homes were rated using a 5-point scale on each of five categories: necessities, neatness, size, parental conditions, and parental supervision. The ratings were summed for a total score of up to 25 points. Williams also developed a supplemental scale for grading children's neighborhoods. For a review and critique of the extant measures, see Loevinger (1940).

[18]Barr (1918) attempted to validate the scale by cross-classifying the intelligence of students attending five schools near Stanford University against the occupations of their parents as ranked by his scale, on the assumption that "the intelligence of the offspring does not vary greatly from their parents when, a large number of cases are considered" (p. 71). Because the correlation between parental occupation and students' IQ scores was high, Barr concluded that the scale was reliable.

[19]As an illustration of the circularity of Terman's argument, the average Barr Scale rating of the occupations of the fathers of his gifted sample was 12.77, compared to 7.92 for the adult male populations in Los Angeles and San Francisco as reported in the 1910 Census.

[20]Restrictions on Asian immigration and naturalization predated mass intelligence testing. In *A Study of American Intelligence* (1923), Carl Brigham analyzed the data from the Army IQ testing program to provide evidence that he interpreted as confirming the conclusions of Madison Grant's (1918) historical analysis in *The Passing of the Great Race*. Madison Grant claimed that northern Europeans were genetically superior to southern and eastern Europeans (see also Leonard, 2016).

[21]For example, Terman (1916) noted that there was a high concentration of the borderline feeble-minded among Blacks and the "Spanish-Indian and Mexican families of the Southwest" (p. 90). He advocated segregated instruction for such groups and also commented that "from a eugenic point of view they constitute a grave problem because of their unusually prolific breeding" (p. 92).

[22]G. Davies (1996) observed that the centerpiece of New Deal social policy, the Social Security Act, "left primary long-term responsibility for ensuring an adequate safety net with the private sector" by creating social insurance that linked benefits to employment (p. 14). Federal programs were narrowly targeted at the "deserving" poor: impoverished senior citizens, the blind, and widows with children (see also Katz, 2013).

[23]Hofstadter (1963) observed that Dewey did not directly address the specific class structure of American society or the role of the educational system within it. Rather, Dewey argued that all students should have the opportunity to engage in active learning experiences.

[24]Franz Boas and his students were the principal proponents of a sustained critique of scientific racism from the discipline of anthropology (Barkan, 1992; Powers & Patton, 2008; see also Burkholder, 2011, for an analysis of their efforts to change how teachers understood race and taught race in U.S. schools). Benedict (1940) and Valencia (1997) highlighted a similar trajectory in the education research community's understanding of the relationship between race and IQ. The work of psychologist Otto Klineberg, who was aligned with the Boasians, was particularly important in challenging hereditarian assumptions about race and intelligence. These perspectives remained a minority view in education research, which was dominated by psychology (Fass, 1989).

[25]In another piece, Counts (1922b) highlighted patterns of income stratification. Anticipating Galbraith's (1969) arguments four decades later, Counts argued that existing proposals for vocational education would not address the problem that a substantial portion of workers were "living on the pauper and poverty levels" in the most developed country in the world during a period of unprecedented expansion of productivity and wealth (p. 502).

[26]The trajectory of the field can be roughly traced by comparing the 1928 and 1940 year-books of the National Society for the Study of Education, both of which focused on assessing the relative influence of nature and nurture on intelligence. In his address discussing the studies in the 1940 yearbook, Whitty (1940) evoked Counts's (1922a) earlier critique of the use of testing as undemocratic. Likewise, in his comments on the implications of the findings from the 1940 yearbook for eugenics, Frederick Osborn of the American Eugenics Society noted,

> Eugenic selection should be based on individual differences, rather than differences between socio-economic groups or racial groups, because the Yearbook confirms the conclusion . . . that if there are differences in the average of organic factors among different socio-economic classes, these differences are small compared with the differences among individuals within each class. (Osborn, 1940, p. 60)

[27]Warner et al. (1944) distinguished between social class, the focus of their analysis, and socioeconomic status, the measure generally used in studies of education. While the former highlighted cultural practices and community members' perceptions of social standing, the latter indexed "economic criteria, such as occupation and income" (p. 176). O'Connor (2001) observed that Warner and his students promoted the idea that "class stratification had a deep-seated cultural dimension that operated independently of economic relationships," a perspective that shaped culture-of-poverty arguments in the 1960s (p. 62). For example, Warner et al. (1944) argued that social inequalities become as deeply ingrained in people as genetic characteristics, so that "it becomes impossible to tell how much of the person is due to heredity and how much to environment" (p. 149).

[28]Allison Davis, one of Warner's students and later a colleague, developed a research program aimed at documenting and eliminating class biases from intelligence tests (Davis, 1961). Davis also examined the effects of race and class on children's educational experiences (Beatty, 2012a).

[29]Galbraith's (1969) analysis highlighted a "peculiar modern form of poverty," insular poverty in rural areas and urban ghettos where masses of people are marginalized from participation in the economy (p. 286; see also O'Connor, 2001). While Galbraith argued that insular poverty would be self-perpetuating without providing a guaranteed income to the poor, he noted that this was not a politically popular proposal. Galbraith also advocated for public sector investments in education, housing, nutrition, and health care to help individuals "overcome the restraints that are imposed by their environment" (p. 294).

[30]Ross (1990) highlighted how the *Brown* decision rejected the practice of "black abstraction," or the "refusal to depict blacks in any real or vividly drawn social context" by acknowledging that racial segregation had very real effects on the hearts and minds of children (p. 2). Yet *Brown* also perpetuated

> the rhetorical theme of white innocence. The segregationist rhetoricians had expressed this theme in their insistence on the absence of racism. On this issue, the *Brown I* opinion offered a howling silence. The Court spoke not at all of the racist motives for segregation. This silence thus left standing the segregationists' insistence on white innocence. (. . .) The price of unanimity was, in effect, the preservation of the rhetoric of white innocence. In this sense, *Brown I* was both a moment of transition and a moment of continuity in our rhetoric of race. Black abstraction was rejected; white innocence was left intact. (Ross, 1990, pp. 24–25)

[31]As Urban (2009) observed, while many of these school attendance patterns were facilitated by the actions of school district officials and other state actors, few questioned the Court's distinction between the two types of segregation.

[32]Coleman (1974) described this focus as a new emphasis on the outcomes of schooling, which he traced to the Supreme Court's decision in *Brown* (1954). When the Court held that "separate but equal" resulted in inequality of educational opportunities for Black and White children, it opened the door to questions about how the effects of schooling may vary. Prior to the Supreme Court's decision, equality of opportunity entailed providing a free education based on a common curriculum within the same schools, and equalizing funding within localities.

[33]Prior to the Coleman Report, a handful of studies used the input-output approach (or the educational production function) to analyze student achievement but on a much smaller scale (see Appendix A in Averch, Carroll, Donaldson, Kiesling, & Pincus, 1972).

[34]Many of the analyses incorporated measures of "subjective background factors," which were students' reports of their parents' interest in and aspirations for their schooling. See Rury and Saatcioglu (2015) for an analysis of how Coleman's measure of family background likely underestimated students' economic status. While Coleman's measures were grounded in a long research tradition of measuring socioeconomic status, it is also possible that, given the genesis of the study in the Civil Rights Act, Coleman did not expect social class–related variables to be important factors in the analysis.

[35]While outside of the scope of the discussion here, another important finding that was significant for subsequent policy debates about desegregation was that students who attended schools with higher percentages of White students had higher achievement than students who attended schools with lower percentages of White students. Coleman et al. (1966) attributed this finding to the "better educational background and the higher educational aspirations that are, on average found among white students" rather than to "racial composition per se" (p. 307; see also Beatty, 2012b, for a discussion of the Coleman Report's findings).

[36]Coleman et al. (1966) noted at the outset of the analysis of test scores that what the tests measured was not intelligence but the "skills which are among the most important in our society for getting a good job and moving up to a better one, and for full participation in an increasingly technical world" (p. 20). This assumes that a student who scored higher on the achievement tests would have a greater array of opportunities after completing high school.

[37]See Gamoran and Long (2007) for a citation analysis of the period between 1966 and 2005.

[38]As others have noted, the parental occupation variable had a substantial number of missing responses (see, e.g., Jencks, 1972). Mayeske et al. (1969) used a criterion scaling technique to address the problem of missing information.

[39]Contemporary "No Excuses" schools draw on claims associated with the effective schools movement. For example, Edmonds (1979) argued,

> [No] notion about schooling is more widely held than the belief that the family is some how the principal determinant of whether or not a child will do well in school. The popularity of this belief continues partly because many social scientists continue to espouse the belief that family background is the chief cause of the quality of pupil performance. Such a belief has the effect of absolving educators of their professional responsibility to be instructionally effective. (p. 21)

[40]In a review of one of the first sets of cross-national studies of student achievement from the International Evaluation Association, Coleman (1975) noted that the effects of family background on student achievement may vary by subject. For example, students are more likely to learn reading in the home than science or mathematics, so the effects of schooling are stronger for the latter subjects (see also Coleman, 1996).

[41]Rury (2005) noted,

Taking a somewhat longer perspective, it is possible to see the rush to institute new regimes of accountability in American education as a corollary of the human capital revolution, and a correspondingly narrow way of viewing the function of schools. The point of systemic reform, after all, was to make schooling more productive in terms of specific curricula. . . . In other words, education was increasingly seen as just another factor of production, subject to measurement and improvement like sources of energy, new machinery, raw material, and waste management. (p. 236)

[42]The What Works Clearinghouse's focus on the average effects of interventions is a narrow and, ultimately, very limited understanding of "what works" (Glass, 2016; Powers & Glass, 2014).

[43]See Jackson, Johnson, and Persico (2016) for an analysis that engages some of these issues. Jackson et al. found that there was a substantial relationship between school spending and educational and economic outcomes, such as reduced rates of adult poverty for poor families. They also point to large-scale social processes outside of schools, such as increased income segregation and mass incarceration, which likely attenuated the effects of increased school spending.

[44]Hanushek (1996) explicitly linked what he viewed as the mixed findings on school effects to the need for performance incentive policies aimed at improving student achievement, even while he admitted that "little is known about how to best structure incentives in this area" (pp. 69–70).

[45]The research on this topic is extensive and robust (see Note 3), yet in our professional experience we have been confronted with several policymakers who find it difficult to accept that there is rigorous, nonpartisan education research. Almost 10 years ago, Henig (2008), perhaps one of the best known analysts of the education research–policy nexus described this ironic situation, which has not changed substantially: "Competing sides in contemporary policy debates typically match one another study for study, and muster equal indignation about their opponents' know-nothing refusal to bow to the power of the cold hard facts" (p. 4). On the other hand, in an essay about the legacy of the Coleman Report, Kane (2016) concluded that in the decades since the Coleman Report, education research has failed to provide meaningful guidance for educational practice and policymakers.

REFERENCES

Anyon, J. (1997). *Ghetto schooling: A political economy of urban educational reform*. New York, NY: Teachers College Press.

Apple, M. W. (2012). *Can education change society?* New York, NY: Routledge.

Artiles, A. (2011). Toward an interdisciplinary understanding of educational equity and difference: The case of the racialization of ability. *Educational Researcher, 40*, 431–445.

Averch, H., Carroll, S. J., Donaldson, T. S., Kiesling, H. J., & Pincus, J. (1972). *How effective is schooling? A critical review and synthesis of research findings*. Santa Monica, CA: RAND.

Ayres, L. (1917). *The Cleveland school survey*. Cleveland, OH: The Survey Committee of the Cleveland Foundation.

Baker, L. D. (1998). *From savage to Negro: Anthropology and the construction of race, 1896–1954*. Berkeley: University of California Press.

Barkan, E. (1992). *The retreat of scientific racism: Changing concepts of race in Britain and the United States between the world wars*. New York, NY: Cambridge University Press.

Barr, F. E. (1918). *A scale for measuring mental ability in vocations and some of its applications* (Unpublished master's thesis). Stanford University, Palo Alto, CA.

Beatty, B. (2012a). The debate over the young "disadvantaged child": Preschool intervention, developmental psychology, and compensatory education in the 1960s and early 1970s. *Teachers College Record, 114*(6), 1–36.

Beatty, B. (2012b). Rethinking compensatory education: Historical perspectives on race, class, culture, language, and the discourse of the "disadvantaged child." *Teachers College Record, 114*(6), 1–11.

Benedict, R. (1940). *Race: Science and politics.* New York, NY: Modern Age Books.

Berliner, D. C. (2002). Educational research: The hardest science of all. *Educational Researcher, 31*(8), 18–20.

Berliner, D. C. (2006). Our impoverished view of educational reform. *Teachers College Record, 108*, 949–995.

Berliner, D. C., & Biddle, B. J. (1995). *The manufactured crisis: Myths, fraud, and the attack on America's public schools.* Reading, MA: Addison-Wesley.

Bidwell, C. E., & Kasarda, J. D. (1980). Conceptualizing and measuring the effects of school and schooling. *American Journal of Education, 88*, 401–430.

Borman, G., & Dowling, M. (2010). Schools and inequality: A multilevel analysis of Coleman's Equality of Educational Opportunity data. *Teachers College Record, 112*, 1201–1246.

Brauer, C. M. (1982). Kennedy, Johnson, and the War on Poverty. *Journal of American History, 69*(1), 98–119.

Brigham, C. C. (1923). *A study of American intelligence.* Princeton, NJ: Princeton University Press.

Brown v. Board of Education, 343 U.S. 483 (1954).

Brown, P. A, Halsey, H., Lauder, H., & Wells, A. S. (1997). The transformation of education and society: An introduction. In H. Halsey, H. Lauder, P. Brown, & A. S. Wells (Eds.), *Education: Culture, economy, and society* (pp. 1–24). New York, NY: Oxford University Press.

Burkholder, Z. (2011). *Color in the classroom: How American schools taught race, 1900–1954.* New York, NY: Oxford University Press.

Byrns, R., & Henmon, V. A. C. (1936). Parental occupation and mental ability. *Journal of Educational Psychology, 27*, 284–291.

Carnoy, M. (2009). Policy research in education: The economic view. In G. Sykes, B. Schneider, & D. J. Plank (Eds.), *Handbook of education policy research* (pp. 27–38). New York, NY: Routledge.

Carter, P., & Welner, K. (Eds.). (2013). *Closing the opportunity gap: What America must do to give every child an even chance.* New York, NY: Oxford University Press.

Chapman, J. C., & Sims, V. M. (1925). The quantitative measurement of certain aspects of socio-economic status. *Journal of Educational Psychology, 16*, 380–390.

Chapman, P. D. (1988). *Schools as sorters: Lewis M. Terman, applied psychology, and the intelligence testing movement, 1890–1930.* New York, NY: New York University Press.

Clifford, G. J. (1986). The formative years of schools of education in America: A five-institution analysis. *American Journal of Education, 94*, 427–446.

Cohen, D. K., & Barnes, C. A. (1999). Research and the purposes of education. In E. C. Lagemann & L. S. Shulman (Eds.), *Issues in education research: Problems and possibilities* (pp. 17–41). San Francisco, CA: Jossey Bass.

Coleman, J. S. (1974). The concept of equality of opportunity. In L. P. Miller & E. W. Gordon (Eds.), *Equality of educational opportunity: A handbook for research* (pp. 3–16). New York, NY: AMS Press.

Coleman, J. S. (1975). Methods and results in the IEA studies of effects of school on learning. *Review of Educational Research, 45*(3), 355–386.

Coleman, J. S. (1996). What is learned in school and what is learned outside? In C. P. Benbow & D. Lubinski (Eds.), *Intellectual talent: Psychometric and social issues* (pp. 211–216). Baltimore, MD: Johns Hopkins University Press.

Coleman, J. S., Campbell, E. Q., Hobson, C. J., McPartland, J., Mood, A. M., Weinfeld, F. D., & York, R. L. (1966). *Equality of Educational Opportunity.* Washington, DC: U.S. Government Printing Office.

Collins, J. E. (1928). The intelligence of school children and paternal occupation. *Journal of Educational Research, 17*, 157–170.

Colvin, S. S. (1922). Principles underlying the construction and use of intelligence tests. In G. M. Whipple (Ed.), *Intelligence tests and their use: The twenty-first yearbook of the National Society for the Study of Education* (pp. 11–44). Bloomington, IL: Public School.

Commission on the Reorganization of Secondary Education. (1918). *Cardinal principles of secondary education.* Washington, DC: National Education Association.

Conant, J. B. (1961). *Slums and suburbs: A commentary on schools in metropolitan areas.* New York, NY: McGraw-Hill.

Cooper, A. (2013). Research mediation in education: A typology of research brokering organizations that exist across Canada. *Alberta Journal of Education Research, 59*, 181–207.

Cooper, A. (2014). The use of online strategies and social media for research dissemination in education. *Education Policy Analysis Archives, 22*(88), 1–26.

Counts, G. S. (1922a). *The selective character of American secondary education.* Chicago, IL: University of Chicago Press.

Counts, G. S. (1922b). Education for vocational efficiency. *The School Review, 30*, 493–513.

Courtis, S. A., & Packer, P. C. (1920). Educational research. *Journal of Educational Research, 1*(1), 5–19.

Cremin, L. A. (1955). The revolution in American secondary education, 1893–1918. *Teachers College Record, 55*, 295–308.

Cronbach, L., & Suppes, P. (Eds.). (1969). *Research for tomorrow's schools: Disciplined inquiry for education* (Report of the Committee of Education Research of the National Academy of Education). Toronto, Ontario, Canada: Macmillan.

Cubberley, E. P. (1916). *The Portland survey: A textbook on city school administration based on a concrete study.* Yonkers-on-Hudson, NY: World Book.

Cubberley, E. P. (1919). *Public education in the United States.* New York, NY: Houghton Mifflin.

Darling-Hammond, L. (2010). *The flat world and education: How America's commitment to equity will determine our future.* New York, NY: Teachers College Press.

Davies, G. (1996). *From opportunity to entitlement: The transformation and decline of Great Society liberalism.* Lawrence: University Press of Kansas.

Davies, P. (1999). What is evidence-based education? *British Journal of Educational Studies, 47*(2), 108–121.

Davis, A. (1961). *Social-class influences on learning.* Cambridge, MA: Harvard University Press.

Dewey, J. (1922, December 6). Mediocrity and individuality. *The New Republic, 33*, 35–37.

Dyer, H. S. (1972). Some thoughts about future studies. In F. Mosteller & D. P. Moynihan (Eds.), *On equality of educational opportunity* (pp. 384–422). New York, NY: Random House.

Edmonds, R. (1979). Effective schools for the urban poor. *Educational Leadership, 37*, 15–24.

Edmonds, R., & Frederiksen, J. R. (1979). *Search for effective schools: The identification and analysis of city schools that are instructionally effective for poor children.* Cambridge, MA: Harvard University Center for Urban Studies.

Erickson, F. (2014). Scaling down: A modest proposal for practice-based policy research in teaching. *Education Policy Analysis Archives, 22*(9), 1-11. Retrieved from http://www.redalyc.org/pdf/2750/275031898040.pdf

Fass, P. S. (1980). The IQ: A cultural and historical framework. *American Journal of Education, 88*, 431–458.

Fass, P. S. (1989). *Outside in: Minorities and the transformation of American education.* New York, NY: Oxford University Press.

Fischman, G. E., & Haas, E. (2012). Beyond "idealized" citizenship education: Embodied cognition, metaphors and democracy. *Review of Research in Education, 36*, 190–217.

Fischman, G. E., & Tefera, A. (2014). Qualitative inquiry in an age of educationalese. *Education Policy Analysis Archives, 22*(7). Retrieved from http://epaa.asu.edu/ojs/article/view/1592/1204

Flemming, C., & Rutledge, S. (1927). The importance of the social and economic quality of the home for pupil guidance. *Teachers College Record, 29,* 202–215.

Foley, D. (2010). The rise of class culture theory in educational anthropology. *Anthropology & Education Quarterly, 41,* 215–227.

Fox, C., & Guglielmo, T. A. (2012). Defining America's racial boundaries: Blacks, Mexicans, and European immigrants, 1890–1945. *American Journal of Sociology, 118,* 327–379.

Galbraith, J. K. (1969). *The affluent society* (2nd ed.). Boston, MA: Houghton Mifflin.

Galway, G., & Sheppard, B. (2015). Research and evidence in education decision-making: A comparison of results from two pan-Canadian studies. *Education Policy Analysis Archives, 23*(109). Retrieved from http://epaa.asu.edu/ojs/article/view/1905/1686

Gamoran, A. (2001). American schooling and educational inequality: A forecast for the 21st century. *Sociology of Education, 74,* 135–153. Retrieved from http://itp.wceruw.org/gamoran%20forecast.pdf

Gamoran, A. (2008). Persisting social class inequality in US education. In L. Weis (Ed.), *The way class works: Readings on school, family, and the economy* (pp. 169–179). New York, NY: Routledge.

Gamoran, A., & Long, D. (2007). Equality of educational opportunity: A 40-year retrospective. In R. Teese, S. Lamb, & M. Duru-Bellat (Eds.), *International studies in educational inequality, theory and policy* (pp. 23–47). New York, NY: Springer.

Glass, G. V. (2016). One hundred years of research: Prudent aspirations. *Educational Researcher, 45,* 69–72.

Goodenough, F. L. (1928). The relation of the intelligence of pre-school children to the occupation of their fathers. *American Journal of Psychology, 40,* 284–294.

Gotanda, N. (1991). A critique of "Our Constitution Is Color-Blind." *Stanford Law Review, 44*(1), 1–68.

Gould, S. J. (1996). *The mismeasure of man.* New York, NY: Norton.

Grant, G. (1973). Shaping social policy: The politics of the Coleman Report. *Teachers College Record, 75*(1), 17–54.

Grant, M. (1918). *The passing of the great race: The racial basis of European history* (2nd ed.). New York, NY: Charles Scribner's Sons.

Grinder, R. E. (1982). The AERA Annual Meeting as reflected in the recent history of the Association. *Educational Researcher, 11*(9), 7–11.

Haggerty, M. E., & Nash, H. B. (1924). Mental capacity of children and paternal occupation. *Journal of Educational Psychology, 15,* 559–572.

Hanushek, E. A. (1996). School resources and school performance. In G. Burtless (Ed.), *Does money matter? The effect of school resources on student achievement and adult success* (pp. 43–73). Washington, DC: Brookings Institution Press.

Harrington, M. (1962). *The other America: Poverty in America.* New York, NY: Macmillan.

Hedges, L. V., & Greenwald, R. (1996). Have times changed? The relation between school resources and school performance. In G. Burtless (Ed.), *Does money matter? The effect of school resources on student achievement and adult success* (pp. 74–92). Washington, DC: Brookings Institution Press.

Henig, J. R. (2008). *Spin cycle: How research gets used in policy debates—The case of charter schools.* New York, NY: Russell Sage Foundation.

Henig, J. R. (2012). The politics of data use. *Teachers College Record, 114*(11), 1–17.

Herbers, J. (1966, July 2). Negro education is found inferior. *New York Times,* p. 18.

Hess, F. (Ed.). (2008). *When research matters: How scholarship influences education policy.* Cambridge, MA: Harvard University Press.

Hlebowitsh, P. S., & Wraga, W. G. (1995). Social class analysis in the early progressive tradition. *Curriculum Inquiry, 25*(1), 7–21.

Hofstadter, R. (1963). *Anti-intellectualism in American life.* New York, NY: Vintage Books.

Holley, C. E. (1916). *The relationship between persistence in school and home conditions: The Fifteenth Yearbook of the National Society for the Study of Education.* Chicago, IL: University of Chicago Press.

Honig, M., & Coburn, C. (2008). Evidence-based decision-making in school district central offices: Toward a policy and research agenda. *Journal of Educational Policy, 22,* 578–608. doi:10.1177/0895904807307067

Ince, M. (2008). Knowledge transformation and impact: A commentary. *Cambridge Journal of Education, 38*(1), 131–134. doi:10.1080/03057640801890038

Jackson, C. K., Johnson, R. C., & Persico, C. (2016). The effects of school spending on educational and economic outcomes: Evidence from school finance reforms. *Quarterly Journal of Economics, 131*(1), 157–218. doi:10.1093/qje/qjv036

Jencks, C. (1972). The Coleman Report and conventional wisdom. In F. Mosteller & D. P. Moynihan (Eds.), *On equality of educational opportunity* (pp. 69–115). New York, NY: Random House.

Jencks, C., Smith, M., Acland, H., Bane, M. J., Cohen, D., Gintis, H., . . . Michelson, S. (1972). *Inequality: A reassessment of the effect of family and schooling in America.* New York, NY: Basic Books.

Johnson, L. B. (1965, June 4). *To fulfill these rights. Commencement address delivered at Howard University.* Retrieved from http://www.lbjlib.utexas.edu/johnson/archives.hom/speeches.hom/650604.asp

Jordan, A. M. (1933). Parental occupations and children's intelligence scores. *Journal of Applied Psychology, 17,* 103–119.

Kane, T. J. (2016). Connecting to practice: How we can put educational research to work. *Education Next, 16,* 80–87.

Kantor, H., & Lowe, R. (2006). From New Deal to no deal: No Child Left Behind and the devolution of responsibility for equal opportunity. *Harvard Educational Review, 76,* 474–502.

Karabel, J., & Halsey, A. H. (1977). Educational research: A review and introduction. In J. Karabel & A. H. Halsey (Eds.), *Power and ideology in education* (pp. 1–77). New York, NY: Oxford University Press.

Katz, M. (2013). *The undeserving poor: America's enduring confrontation with poverty.* New York, NY: Oxford University Press.

Kett, J. F. (2013). *Merit: The history of a founding ideal from the American Revolution to the twenty-first century.* Ithaca, NY: Cornell University Press.

Klees, S. J. (2012). World Bank and education: Ideological premises and ideological conclusions. In C. S. Collins & A. W. Wiseman (Eds.), *Education strategy in the developing world: Revisiting the World Bank's education policy* (pp. 151–171). Bingley, England: Emerald Group.

Konstantopoulos, S. (2006). Trends of school effects on student achievement: Evidence from NLS:72, HSB:82, and NELS:92. *Teachers College Record, 108,* 2550–2581.

Konstantopoulos, S., & Borman, G. D. (2011). Family background and school effects on student achievement: A multilevel analysis of the Coleman data. *Teachers College Record, 113,* 97–132.

Kozol, J. (1992). *Savage inequalities: Children in America's schools.* New York, NY: Basic Books.

Labaree, D. F. (1997). *How to succeed in school without really learning: The credentials race in American education.* New Haven, CT: Yale University Press.

Labaree, D. F. (2004). *The trouble with ed schools.* New Haven, CT: Yale University Press.

Labaree, D. F. (2010). *Someone has to fail: The zero sum game of schooling.* Cambridge, MA: Harvard University Press.

Lagemann, E. C. (1989). *The politics of knowledge: The Carnegie Corporation, philanthropy, and public policy.* Middletown, CT: Wesleyan University Press.

Lagemann, E. C. (2000). *Elusive science: The troubling history of education research.* Chicago, IL: University of Chicago Press.

Leonard, T. C. (2016). *Illiberal reformers.* Princeton, NJ: Princeton University Press.

Levin, B. (2004). Making research matter more. *Education Policy Analysis Archives, 12*(6), 1–21. doi:10.14507/epaa.v12n56.2004

Levin, H. M. (1989). Mapping the economics of education: An introductory essay. *Educational Researcher, 18*(4), 13–73.

Lippman, W. (1922, November 22). Tests of hereditary intelligence. *The New Republic, 32,* 328–330.

Loevinger, J. (1940). Intelligence as related to socio-economic factors. In G. M. Whipple (Ed.), *The thirty-ninth yearbook of the National Society for the Study of Education: Pt. 1. Intelligence: Its nature and nurture* (pp. 159–202). Bloomington, IL: Public School.

Makel, M. C., & Plucker, J. A. (2014). Facts are more important than novelty replication in the education sciences. *Educational Researcher, 43,* 304–316.

Martens, E. (1923). *Organization and functioning of city research bureaus.* Paper presented at the second annual conference on Educational Research and Guidance, San Jose, CA.

Martinez, S., & Rury, J. (2012). From "culturally deprived" to "at risk": The politics of popular expression and educational inequality in the United States, 1960–1985. *Teachers College Record, 114*(6), 1–31.

Mayeske, G. W., Okada, T., Cohen, W. M., Beaton, A. E., Jr., & Wisler, C. E. (1973). *A study of achievement in our nation's schools.* Washington, DC: U.S. Government Printing Office.

Mayeske, G. W., Wisler, C. E., Beaton, A. E., Jr., Weinfeld, F. D., Cohen, W. M., Okada, T., . . . Tabler, K. A. (1969). *A study of our nation's schools* (Working paper). Washington, DC: U.S. Government Printing Office.

Mehta, J. (2013). *The allure of order: High hopes, dashed expectations, and the troubled quest to remake American schooling.* New York, NY: Oxford University Press.

Mershon, S., & Schlossman, S. (2008). Education, science, and the politics of knowledge: The American Educational Research Association, 1915–1940. *American Journal of Education, 114,* 307–340.

Moss, P. A., Phillips, D. C., Erickson, F. D., Floden, R. E., Lather, P. A., & Schneider, B. L. (2009). Learning from our differences: A dialogue across perspectives on quality in education research. *Educational Researcher, 38,* 501–517.

Mosteller, F., & Moynihan, D. P. (1972). A pathbreaking report. In F. Mosteller & D. P. Moynihan (Eds.), *On equality of educational opportunity* (pp. 3–66). New York, NY: Random House.

National Commission on Excellence in Education. (1983). *A nation at risk: The imperative for educational reform.* Washington DC: U.S. Department of Education.

Neff, W. S. (1938). Socioeconomic status and intelligence: A critical survey. *Psychological Bulletin, 35,* 727–757.

Ngai, M. M. (2007). Nationalism, immigration control, and the ethnoracial remapping of America in the 1920s. *OAH Magazine of History, 21*(3), 11–15.

Oakes, J., Hunter Quartz, K., Ryan, S., & Lipton, M. (2000). *Becoming good American schools: The struggle for civic virtue in school reform.* San Francisco, CA: Jossey-Bass.

O'Connor, A. (2001). *Poverty knowledge: Social science, social policy, and the poor in twentieth-century U.S. history.* Princeton, NJ: Princeton University Press.

Okada, T., Cohen, W. M., & Mayeske, G. W. (1969). *Growth in achievement for different regional, racial, and socio-economic groupings of students* (Technical Paper No. 1). Washington, DC: U.S. Department of Health, Education, and Welfare.

Osborn, F. O. (1940). Implications of the Yearbook for eugenics. In G. M. Whipple (Ed.), *Addresses and discussions presenting the Thirty-Ninth Yearbook of the National Society for the Study of Education* (pp. 57–62). Salem, MA: Newcomb & Gauss.

Pellegrino, J. W., & Goldman, S. R. (2002). Be careful what you wish for—You may get it: Educational research in the spotlight. *Educational Researcher, 31*(8), 15–17.

Powers, J. M., & Glass, G. V. (2014). When statistical significance hides more than it reveals. *Teachers College Record*. Retrieved from http://www.tcrecord.org/Content. asp?ContentID=17591

Powers, J. M., & Patton, L. (2008). Between Mendez and Brown: Gonzales v. Sheely (1951) and the legal campaign against segregation. *Law & Social Inquiry, 33*, 127–171.

Qi, J., & Levin, B. (2013). Assessing organizational efforts to mobilize research knowledge in education. *Education Policy Analysis Archives, 21*(2), 2–20.

Riessman, F. (1962). *The culturally deprived child.* New York, NY: Harper & Row.

Ross, T. (1990). The rhetorical tapestry of race: White innocence and Black abstraction. *William & Mary Law Review, 32*, 1–40.

Rury, J. (2005). *Education and social change: Contours in the history of American schooling.* New York, NY: Routledge.

Rury, J., & Saatcioglu, A. (2015). Did the Coleman Report underestimate the effect of economic status on educational outcomes? *Teachers College Record*. Retrieved from http://www.tcrecord.org/content.asp?contentid=17828

Saltzman, S. (1940). The influence of social and economic background on Stanford-Binet performance. *Journal of Social Psychology, 12*, 71–81.

Schneider, B. (2004). Building a scientific community: The need for replication. *Teachers College Record, 106*, 1471–1483.

Sears, J. B. (1922). *Technique of the public school survey. Proceedings of the first annual conference on educational research and guidance.* San Jose, CA: San Jose State Teachers College.

Shavelson, R. J., & Towne, L. (Eds.). (2002). *Scientific research in education.* Washington, DC: National Academies Press.

Smedley, A. (1993). *Race in North America: Origin and evolution of a worldview.* Boulder, CO: Westview Press.

Smiley, M. B. (1967). Objectives of educational programs for the educationally retarded and disadvantaged. In P. Whitty (Ed.), *The educationally retarded and disadvantaged: The sixty-sixth yearbook of the National Society for the Study of Education* (pp. 121–143). Chicago, IL: University of Chicago Press.

Smith, M. S. (1972). Equality of educational opportunity: The basic findings reconsidered. In F. Mosteller & D. P. Moynihan (Eds.), *On equality of educational opportunity* (pp. 230–342). New York, NY: Random House.

Stern, A. M. (2005). *Eugenic nation: Faults and frontiers of better breeding in modern America.* Berkeley: University of California Press.

St. Pierre, E. A. (2006). Scientifically based research in education: Epistemology and ethics. *Adult Education Quarterly, 56*, 239–266.

Taussig, F. W. (1911). *Principles of economics* (Vol. 2). New York, NY: Macmillan.

Terman, L. M. (1916). *The measurement of intelligence.* Boston, MA: Houghton Mifflin.

Terman, L. M. (1926). *Genetic studies of genius: Vol. 1. Mental and physical traits of gifted children.* Palo Alto, CA: Stanford University Press.

Terman, L. M. (1928). The influence of nature and nurture upon intelligence scores: An evaluation of the evidence in Part I of the 1928 Yearbook of the National Society for the Study of Education. *Journal of Educational Psychology, 19*, 362–373.

Terman, L. M., Dickson, V. E., Sutherland, A. H., Franzen, R. H., Tupper, C. R., & Fernald, G. (1922). *Intelligence tests and school organization: Subcommittee report of the Committee on Revision of Elementary Education.* Yonkers-on-Hudson, NY: World Book.

Terman, L. M., Lyman, G., Ordahl, G., Ordahl, L. E., Galbreath, N., & Talbert, W. (1917). *The Stanford revision and extension of the Binet-Simon Scale for measuring intelligence.* Baltimore, MD: Warwick & York.

Testing doesn't measure up for Americans (47th Annual PDK/Gallup Poll). (2015, September). *Phi Delta Kappan, 97*, NP1-NP32.

Thorndike, E. L. (1921). Intelligence and its measurement: A symposium. *Journal of Educational Psychology, 12*, 124–127.

Travers, R. M. (1983). *How research has changed American schools: A history from 1840 to the present.* Kalamazoo, MI: Mythos.

Tyack, D. (1974). *The one best system.* Cambridge, MA: Harvard University Press.

Tyack, D., & Hansot, E. (1982). *Managers of virtue: Public school leadership in America.* New York, NY: Basic Books.

Urban, W. J. (2009). What's in a name: Education and the disadvantaged American (1962). *Paedagogica Historica, 45*, 251–264.

Urban, W. J. (2012). Rethinking "compensatory education." *Teachers College Record, 114*(6), 1–8.

Valencia, R. R. (1997). The genetic pathology model of deficit thinking. In R. R. Valencia (Ed.), *The evolution of deficit thinking* (pp. 41–112). New York, NY: Routledge.

Valencia, R. R., & Suzuki, L. A. (2001). *Intelligence testing and minority students: Foundations, performance factors, and assessment issues.* Thousand Oaks, CA: Sage.

Varenne, H., & McDermott, R. (1999). *Successful failure: The school America builds.* Boulder, CO: Westview Press.

Vinovskis, M. (2009). A history of efforts to improve the quality of federal education research: From Gardner's Task Force to the Institute of Education Sciences. In P. B. Walters, A. Lareau, & S. H. Ranis (Eds.), *Education research on trial: Policy reform and the call for scientific rigo*r (pp. 51–80). New York, NY: Routledge.

Walters, P. B. (2009). The politics of science: Battles for scientific authority in the field of education research. In P. B. Walters, A. Lareau, & S. H. Ranis (Eds.), *Education research on trial: Policy reform and the call for scientific rigor* (pp. 17–50). New York, NY: Routledge.

Walters, P. B., & Lareau, A. (2009). Education research that matters: Influence, scientific rigor, and policymaking. In P. B. Walters, A. Lareau, & S. H. Ranis (Eds*.), Education research on trial: Policy reform and the call for scientific rigor* (pp. 197–220). New York, NY: Routledge.

Warner, W. L., Havighurst, R. J., & Loeb, M. B. (1944). *Who shall be educated?* New York, NY: Harper Brothers.

Weiner, J. M. (1989). Radical historians and the crisis in American history, 1959–1980. *Journal of American History, 76*, 399–434.

Whipple, G. M. (Ed.). (1916). *The fifteenth yearbook of the National Society for the Study of Education: Part 1. Standards and tests for the measurement of the efficiency of schools and school systems.* Chicago, IL: University of Chicago Press.

Whipple, G. M. (1928). Editorial impression of the contribution to knowledge of the *Twenty-Seventh Yearbook. Journal of Educational Psychology, 19*, 389–396.

White, W. T., Jr. (1982). The decline of the classroom and the Chicago study of education, 1909–1929. *American Journal of Education, 90*, 144–174.

Whitty, P. A. (1940). Evidence regarding the nature of intelligence from the study of superior deviates. In G. M. Whipple (Ed.), *Addresses and discussions presenting the Thirty-Ninth Yearbook of the National Society for the Study of Education* (pp. 23–30). Salem, MA: Newcomb & Gauss.

Whitty, P. A. (Ed.). (1967). *The educationally retarded and disadvantaged: The sixty-sixth yearbook of the National Society for the Study of Education.* Chicago, IL: University of Chicago Press.

Williams, J. H. (1918). *A guide to the grading of homes* (Department of Research, Bulletin No. 7). Whittier, CA: Whittier State School Department of Printing Instruction.

Yohalem, N., & Tseng, V. (2015). Commentary: Moving from practice to research and back. *Applied Developmental Science, 19*, 117–120. doi:1080/10888691.2014.983033

Chapter 21

Objects of Protection, Enduring Nodes of Difference: Disability Intersections With "Other" Differences, 1916 to 2016

ALFREDO J. ARTILES
SHERMAN DORN
Arizona State University

AYDIN BAL
University of Wisconsin, Madison

The purpose of this chapter is to contribute a cultural–historical analytical perspective on disability and its intersections. We assume that disability is socially, historically, and spatially constructed. This standpoint enables us to understand and disrupt disparities in education that affect students living at the intersection of disability with race and other identity markers. We trace the evolution of disability as an object of protection and injustice from before 1916 to 2016. The chapter is divided into three sections: disability constructions and intersections before 1960, consolidation of the intersections of difference with disabilities between 1960 and 1990, and the protean nature of disability intersections and fragmentations in contemporary history between 1990 and the present. We review legal, social, and academic discourses and offer interdisciplinary conceptual tools to understand the technical and sociopolitical anatomies of disabilities. We end with a brief discussion of future interdisciplinary research programs, including attention to a biocultural dimension in the study of this complex phenomenon.

The idea of disability has arguably evolved over time from a category of oppression and exclusion to an identity that affords entitlements, programs, and benefits. Indeed, the passage of comprehensive policies such as the Individuals With Disabilities Education Improvement Act (20 U.S.C. §1400 *et seq.* [2004],

Review of Research in Education
March 2016, Vol. 40, pp. 777–820
DOI: 10.3102/0091732X16680606
© 2016 AERA. http://rre.aera.net

reauthorization of the Individuals With Disabilities Education Act of 1990), the Elementary and Secondary Education Act (Pub. L. No. 89-10, 79 Stat. 27 [1965]), and the Americans With Disabilities Act (Pub. L. No. 101-336, 104 Stat. 328 [1990]) have countered discrimination and exclusion while they advance the rights and entitlements of people with disabilities. In this sense, disability has been construed as an *object of protection*,[1] since policies bestow rights that give access to diagnoses, which afford the recognition of needs that precedes access to services and other benefits. At the same time, disability continues to play a central role in the stratification of U.S. society. Historian Douglas Baynton (2001) documented how "disability has functioned historically to justify inequality for disabled people themselves" (p. 33). Eugenics, denial of rights, and segregation were present in the early history of people with disabilities in the United States. More recently, indicators of educational inequality for students with disabilities are reflected in the stigma of these labels, the lower educational opportunities and outcomes of this population compared with their counterparts, and their poor postschool outcomes (Green, Davis, Karshmer, Marsh, & Straight, 2005; Skiba et al., 2008; U.S. Department of Education, 2015). Disability has stigmatizing consequences and deleterious effects in the lives of individuals due to dominant social, political, and institutional arrangements regarding access and participation in the United States (Green et al., 2005). We suggest, therefore, that disability has a dual nature, as a condition that veers people into life trajectories fraught with adversities and discrimination, while it is also an object of protection that recruits state's and communities' resources (e.g., educational and health programs and benefits) to compensate for the impact of impairments and to develop individuals' potential for meaningful participation in society.

The dual nature of disability as an object of protection and a conduit for exclusion and disadvantage appears impervious as we consider its long-standing intersections with racial, language, class, and gender differences, among others. The historical record shows that "not only has it been considered justifiable to treat disabled people unequally, but the concept of disability has been used to justify discrimination against other groups by attributing disability to them" (Baynton, 2001, p. 33). Indeed, when we consider such intersections, classification regimes can compound educational inequities—for example, a special education diagnosis is associated with reduced language supports for English language learners (Zehler et al., 2003). Some disability intersections are associated with biological and medical threats—for example, poverty is correlated with a higher prevalence of health problems that may result in disability. Structural factors mediate these associations—for example, residential racial segregation, which is linked to low economic investments in those communities and lower quality educational opportunities. In other instances, disability intersections have created enduring, systemic crises such as racial disparities in special education. These instances are expressions of the dual nature of disability and the special education paradox (Artiles, 2003). More specifically, this is the case of an educational equity resource created for a marginalized group (i.e., learners with disabilities) that can become a source of inequities for another nondominant group (e.g., racial minorities; Artiles, 2011). For instance, racial minorities are placed in more segregated programs and receive fewer related services and academic opportunities than their White peers *with the same disability diagnosis* (Skiba et al., 2008).

The protective affordances and the perpetuation of injustices stemming from the dual nature of disability pose complex challenges for researchers. How can such injustices be disrupted while civil rights agendas for people with disabilities and other minorities are advanced? How do we explain that even though the entanglements among these vectors of difference date back hundreds of years, the empirical research on disability intersections is relatively young? What robust conceptual resources can be used to theorize the interdependent roles of biology, culture, and power in explanations of disability intersections that afford educational opportunities as well as deepen educational inequalities? We conclude that the dual nature of disability, particularly in the contexts of its intersections with other markers of difference, has been undertheorized and underexamined in the education field. The cultural–historical[2] examination of the construction of disability seeks the possibilities of justice-oriented organizational restructuring and coalition-building activities that promise to transform marginalization mechanisms in educational systems.

This state of affairs calls for an ontological turn and epistemological analyses in future examinations of this complex problem. An ontological turn enables scholars to understand the complex contingencies under which the notion of disability is interpreted and used across spaces; the emphasis is in the study of the nature of disability and its material enactments in particular places with an eye on the patterning of such performances at larger scales. Borrowing from the field of social studies of science,

Probing the ontology of mundane entities [e.g., disability] not only serves to display the multiplicity of realities hidden under everyday and seemingly undisputed signifiers—it is also . . . a method of drawing attention to the failed, unseen, or not-yet-real possibilities hinted at by ordering practices. (Woolgar & Lezaun, 2013, p. 323)

This analytical perspective must be positioned on an interdisciplinary canvas. Specifically, we argue that disability must be examined through historical and intersectional lenses and documented as a boundary object that traverses locales with the plasticity and fluidity to allow for shifting meanings while enabling coordination across institutional practices.[3] In turn, attention to the epistemological dimension of the construction of disability and its intersections with markers of difference sheds light on the assumptions deployed to create knowledge about this construct, how it is represented, what is made visible and invisible, and the consequences—prominent in this line of analysis is the identification of boundaries that demarcate what counts as legitimate knowledge (i.e., boundary work; Artiles et al., 2011).

The purpose of this chapter, therefore, is to engage these questions and issues through a transformative interdisciplinary analytical perspective that helps describe and explain the entanglements of disability with other identity markers across social–historical–spatial contexts. This perspective promises to capture the dual nature of disability—the mechanisms of discrimination as well as protective features, including changes and inconsistencies in the modern definition of disability rights. This line of analysis ought to be situated, for "objects are brought into being, they are *realized* in the course of a certain practical activity, and when that happens, they crystallize, provisionally, a particular reality, they invoke the temporary action of a set of circumstances" (Woolgar & Lezaun, 2013, pp. 323–324). More important, our goal is that this analysis will provide tools and illustrate the challenges and possibilities for transforming disability research and special education. In the end, our analytical framework has implications for the theoretical refinement of educational equity, particularly as it relates to injustices that arise from equity efforts.

An Overview of the Argument and Its Assumptions

Our analysis follows a chronological order from before 1916 to the present, and it is framed from an interdisciplinary standpoint that covers ontological (i.e., cultural mediation, social–historical–spatial and intersectional lenses, and disability as a boundary object) and epistemological considerations about disability. We outline these theoretical threads in this section. We did not craft the chapter in a traditional literature review genre in which systematic searches are conducted covering a time period with specific criteria to select and code research studies. Rather, we drew from our extensive expertise and experience conducting research and synthesizing the empirical literature on the topic of disability intersections and its histories in education (e.g., Artiles, 2003; Artiles, Kozleski, Dorn, & Christensen, 2006; Artiles, Kozleski, Trent, Osher, & Ortiz, 2010; Artiles & Trent, 1994; Artiles, Trent, & Palmer, 2004; Bal & Trainor, 2016; Christensen & Dorn, 1997; Dorn, 2002; Waitoller, Artiles, & Cheney, 2010).

We base our analysis on key theoretical and empirical research sources on the topic and selectively illustrate arguments by citing studies where relevant. The so-called high-incidence disability categories are emphasized throughout the chapter, with particular attention to specific learning disabilities (SLD), intellectual disabilities (ID),[4] and emotional disturbance (ED). These categories not only comprise about half of students with disabilities in the United States (U.S. Department of Education, 2015), but they have also been at the epicenter of debates about the intersections of disability, race, class, gender, and language and the historical evolution of disability in the United States (Artiles & Klingner, 2006).

On the Nature of Disability: Continuities and Variations Then and Now

Historico-spatial considerations. A historical perspective is necessary to understand the changing, seemingly symbiotic intertwining of disability with race and other difference markers and to identify the effects of policies and practices on educational equity for students inhabiting double-bind identities (Artiles, 2011). Space is overlaid in this line of analysis. Attention to space sheds light on the regulation of social and public spaces for people with disabilities, including those from racial-minority backgrounds, in the late 1800s and in the contemporary landscapes of the education field and society (Artiles, 2003; Schweik, 2009). This legacy of state efforts to "cleanse" public space became engraved in bureaucratic behavior. In addition, researchers have documented the spatial distribution of inequities over time that traverse multiple arenas (e.g., public health, education, housing, labor, and health services) and that shape opportunity and social mobility (Artiles et al., 2011; Sampson & Winter, 2016; Tate, 2008). This focus on the structural weight and social uses of space enables researchers to examine technical, social, and ideological dimensions of the intersections of disability with other markers of difference.

The study of disability and its intersections is examined in the present as mediated by the past, which in turn shapes future visions of this idea; thus, a historical understanding of this phenomenon must account for the interdependencies of time scales. Similarly, the notion of disability is shaped by the spaces in which it is examined— local, regional, national, or international levels. This allows us to understand how policies travel across time and space to shape professional and research practices. Moreover, our approach calls for a double analytic focus that examines the connection between local practices and larger sociohistorical processes, which in turn requires a simultaneous focus on multiple time scales, from moment-to-moment histories of human interactions to life histories and histories of groups, communities, populations, and nations. Insights from cultural psychology and critical policy studies inform our work (Artiles, 2003; Cole, 1996; Shore, Wright, & Però, 2011; Ureta, 2014).

Disability as a boundary object. Consistent with our ontological emphasis on the enactment of concepts and ideas in practice, we broaden the analytic focus to account for the sociocultural nature of disability categories and how they are taken up across contexts—what Star and Griesemer (1989) termed "boundary objects."[5] The notion of disability as a boundary object enables us to understand the dual nature of disability as an object of protection and oppression. This means that as a boundary object, disability can shift meanings and uses across settings and communities due in part to local contingencies and group interests. The connections between boundary objects and infrastructures of information and standardization are relevant to this discussion—for example, federal disability definitions are operationalized in states and school districts with various criteria and assessment and identification tools. This helps explain how standard definitions and identification procedures of conditions such as disability produce different prevalence patterns across locales and regions, and disparate (racial, linguistic) groups have different identification risks.

Intersectional perspective of disability. An intersectional lens enables us to understand the complexities of students' social locations and lived experiences in historically stratified communities and institutions. An intersectional analytical perspective illuminates the symbolic and material purposes of social markers (e.g., race, disability) and the consequences (e.g., academic and social opportunities and outcomes) that arise at the intersections of such identities. Thus, intersectionality affords crucial insights about the racialization of disability, compelling us to focus both on the power of assigning categories to individuals and on the authority of those categories "to have social and material consequences" (Crenshaw, 1991, p. 1297). Critical race theory and disability studies literatures inform this perspective.

The role of power plays a central role in the analysis of intersectionality: "Power has clustered around certain [identity] categories and is exercised against others" (Crenshaw, 1991, p. 1297). Therefore, we situate the concept of disability in social, historical, and spatial contexts of power relationships to make visible its long-standing associations with race and other stratifying categories. The hierarchical functions of these intersections have afforded gains to some groups (e.g., access to services) and perpetuated injustices for others (e.g., segregation, denial of rights). The work on White innocence applied to legal decisions and educational reforms illustrates this point, although power can also be examined in practices situated in institutional contexts (i.e., implicit or official regulations, procedures, and practices; Artiles, 2011). Scholarship from critical race theory, critical legal studies, history, and disability studies informs our perspective.

Knowledge Production About Disability: Epistemological Considerations

Empirical findings in a knowledge base are grounded in professional visions (Goodwin, 1994) that entail (often implicit) theoretical framings, logics of action, and methodological approaches situated in unique social, historical, and spatial contexts. Attention to this epistemological dimension enables scholarly communities to infuse a reflexivity that can guide future research programs. An interdisciplinary analysis of the dual nature of disability requires a close attention to the epistemological roots of this knowledge base. That is, it requires a sociological critique of the disciplines that contribute to this literature. Our analysis sheds light on contradictory narratives of progress, as well as critiques of the disciplinary practices that benefit certain groups and particular visions of equity over others. We use the notion of *boundary work* to explain how research communities make categories such as race visible and/or invisible in studies of disabilities (Artiles et al., 2011). Boundary work refers to

the demarcation practices used to maintain a field's identity. Scientific fields invest efforts to demarcate their boundaries through particular practices. For example, funding agencies in medicine create standards so that only individuals with certain kinds of training and credentials have access to financial support; journal editors develop publication criteria for manuscripts to meet agreed-upon requirements and align with the conventions of scholarly reports. Demarcation does not only constitute an analytical problem; there are indeed material and symbolic consequences for the enforcers of boundary work that affirm and enhance their own intellectual authority, afford them professional opportunities, and ensure autonomy to the field. (Artiles et al., 2011, p. 168)

We apply the notion of boundary work to analyze whether and how culture and its historical proxies—race, ethnicity, class, and language differences—have been taken up in the knowledge base about disability. We inform this critique with sociology of science and political philosophy scholarship (Gieryn, 1983, 1995; Latour, 1999; Mills, 1997).

The preceding theoretical threads inform our interdisciplinary analysis. We describe and explain disability intersections with other identity markers across cultural and historical contexts, with particular attention to the paradoxical nature of disability. We organize the chapter following a chronological sequence covering the early period before 1960 and then the periods 1960 to 1990 and 1990 to 2016. We conclude with notes for future research programs.

DISABILITY CONSTRUCTIONS AND INTERSECTIONS BEFORE 1960

The origin of modern intersectionality is partly rooted in the development of the intellectual landscape before 1960, from the expansion of state authority over disability to the development of disability as an object of protection and moral judgment. This earlier history set the stage for civil rights legislation around disability, but that earlier history also contributed to the limits of protective concepts around disability. The early historical construction of disability as an object defined the possible—what was in the universe of definitions for disability and human capacity. That implicit definition was narrow, a limited and constricted ontology. Decades later, disability rights activists actively attempted to dismantle that narrow ontology and institutional definitions of human capacity. Gould's (1996) famous argument about scientific racism and the roles of IQ testing in institutionalization and local public school districts has contributed significantly to our understanding of scientific racism and the ways that bureaucracies such as school systems contain and privilege biases of the day. Yet that focus is insufficient to explain three features of the history of disability as a concept and its intersectionality: the long shadow of Progressive-era disability constructs, the fact that intersectionality became more complicated and paradoxical after post–World War II civil rights struggles over race and disability, and the persistent capacity of schools to convert idealistic initiatives into bureaucratic objects bound to conventional notions of disability. This historical and institutional ontology of disability remains today alongside other definitions of human capacity. To address the persistence of bureaucratic objectification of disability, one first needs to understand the foundation for the (re)generation of disability as a construct in the Progressive era, the early infrastructure of social science expertise, and how that infrastructure privileged and supported a particular set of disability concepts.

The Intellectual History of Disability Is Centuries Old

The intellectual history of disability in the United States is older and more complicated than late 19th-century scientific racism. In stating this, we disagree with the standard history of special education as often portrayed in education, which focuses on the prejudicial attitudes in the late 19th century as the origin of modern disability constructs. It is correct that major actors in the Progressive era often acted on their prejudices (e.g., Franklin, 1994; Gould, 1996). Yet the last few decades of disability studies research have highlighted two important features of the history of disability discourse that have generally been ignored in education: One feature is the older roots of disability discourse, including the racialization of disability discourse. As Baynton (2001) wrote, "Disability has functioned historically to justify inequality for disabled people themselves, but it has also done so for women and minority groups" (p. 33). The second feature is the relationship between constructs of disability and the types of institutional structures discussed later in this section: law, the military, and municipal regulations of behavior.

Racial supremacist thought in the United States has a centuries-long pedigree (e.g., Jordan, 1968), which includes a number of racial myths regarding Africans and their descendants, especially their physical features and inherited moral qualities used to justify slavery. One does not need to resolve various debates over the intellectual history of racism to understand how it intertwined with an evolving discourse of disease and disfigurement. Menchaca (1997) has seen a long strain of racially oriented deficit thinking in British North American colonies and the United States. Not all researchers agree with a long view that emphasizes continuity; Baynton (2001) has located modern definitions of disability in the second half of the 19th century and the ideology of Social Darwinism. Yet Baynton acknowledged that many justifications of American slavery in the first half of the century relied on pseudoscientific claims about the medical fragility of slaves, a feature echoed by other historians (e.g., Barclay, 2011, 2014; Boster, 2015). The late 19th- and early 20th-century intersection of disability discourse and immigration debates in the Progressive era thus built on a much longer history of racism intertwined with medical and other ableist discourses (e.g., Baker, 2002; Baynton, 2005; Molina, 2006).

What was qualitatively different after the Civil War was the growing relationship between institutional authority and ideology, a connection among the uses of disability as a bureaucratic tool of social engineering, the objectification of disability as a concept, and the objectification of individuals labeled as disabled. The growth of private and public bureaucracies at the end of the 19th century encouraged and enabled public officials to experiment in managing armies, veterans, widows benefits, schools, and public health departments (e.g., Graebner, 1977, 1980; Skocpol, 1992; Skowronek, 1982). These experiments paralleled the ways in which businesses had to innovate in the late 19th century in controlling their own affairs (Chandler, 1977; Dorn & Johanningmeier, 1999). The racialization of private and public bureaucracy accompanied their growth and left its mark on the organizations. After the Civil War, disability often became a badge of honor for war veterans, but both the honor and concrete government benefits for war veterans were highly racialized (Logue & Blanck, 2010). Veterans with missing limbs were visible signs of the war, but municipal governments began constructing laws against public display of disability and disfigurement in the late 19th century, trying to cleanse public space of visible "ugliness" (Schweik, 2009). This attempt to cleanse cities of disability came in the same era when city and state governments created racial segregation laws in an attempt to cleanse public spaces of visible interracial interactions (Cell, 1982).[6] Public space became a target of social intervention along intersectional lines. As a gathering place for children and adults, schools were one site of such intervention. In this context of growing bureaucracies, schools served as both a moral agent inherited from earlier decades and the agent of the state, and new constructions of disability found a ready ground for being operationalized as bureaucratic behavior.

In this way across multiple growing organizations, administrative authority became a platform for scientific racism; a critical underpinning of the new discourse of disability was the set of institutional and social networks in support of the new professionals of disability (J. W. Trent, 1994).[7] The construction of recognized knowledge about disability has developed in specific places and networks; the epistemology of disability is inseparable from the social history of administrative authority. In the early 20th century, the premier theorist (and fabulist) of racial and ethnic intellectual differences was the director of research at a residential school for individuals labeled as feebleminded: Henry Goddard of the Vineland Training School. He was not an isolated crank; he was among the first generation of doctoral psychologists in the United States, a student of G. Stanley Hall at Clark University in the 1890s, and enmeshed in a professional network of eugenicists and leaders at residential institutions. The feedback among institutional growth, tools to "manage" a population, and the emergence of disciplinary expertise to study the object of those tools is not an accident: that three-sided relationship was a feature of the era in which special education developed.

Public Authority Over Education, Industrialization, Immigration, and Inequality in the Progressive Era

Progressive-era constructions of disability in education also had their roots in several major changes in American life after the Civil War. First, the Civil War saw the nationalization of the discourse around education as both an object of state power and a right of citizenship. During the war, Congress passed the first land-grant university bill to promote public universities as a resource for economic growth (Veysey, 1965). After the war, the Freedmen's Bureau directly supported hundreds of primary schools across the South, and Reconstruction-era state constitutions in former Confederate states generally guaranteed primary education as a fundamental state obligation, in ways parallel to Northern states from before the war (e.g., Du Bois, 1935). It was also after the Civil War when the passage of compulsory education laws accelerated and states became successful in defending compulsory school laws in state courts (Provasnik, 2006).

While the American discourse around education and state power became nationalized, it was subject to other social and political developments. As post–Civil War industrialization became more mechanized, industrial employment was a significant factor in drawing a new wave of immigration from southern and eastern Europe, a surge that crested between 1890 and 1920 (e.g., Morawska, 2003). In the same decades, the opening of political and social life for African American Southerners during Reconstruction ended brutally with both the suppression of voting rights and the development of segregation in schools, mass transportation, and other parts of public life. As noted earlier, it was also in the same era that public spaces began to be regulated to "cleanse" cities of undesirable sights by elites, whether integrated trolleys in Atlanta or "maimed" or "disfigured" beggars in San Francisco, Chicago, New Orleans, and other cities (Schweik, 2009). Post–Civil War developments ensured that schools across the country maintained or newly acquired a role as moral and economic agents, while the obligations of schools became different by social class, national origin, and race. Schools in many places became responsible for socializing immigrants and limiting the ambitions of African Americans, as well as identifying and excluding children identified as disabled (J. D. Anderson, 1988; Olneck, 1989). These distinctions set the stage for the development of specialization and the incorporation of disability constructs into bureaucratic school routines.

Social Science and Administrative Authority

The desire to assuage the moral panic and other social anxieties around disability in the 19th century was not unique to schools or disability and was intimately connected with the management of public space. One can put the social management of disability in a broader set of social engineering projects in the Progressive era. From the "scientific" organization of charity to public health infrastructures, municipal governments and public agencies sought to expand their capacity to respond to a growing demand for urban development and management. This social management was tied to both the mechanization of industry and the rapid growth of cities and their public spaces. Progressive-era advocates of public authority took pragmatist philosophy's belief in scientific intervention in society and tried to enact it through the objectification and analysis of social problems and intervention in social life (Scott, 1998). For a variety of projects, this search for capacity and tools took advantage of and fed the development of the professional social sciences in the late 19th century. As Ross (1991) has explained, amateur social science in the late 19th century slowly evolved into a more professionalized set of disciplines in the early 20th century, often in service to businesses or social agencies as well as evolving disciplinary notions of scientific objectivity.

Ross (1991) used the early history of the American Social Science Association and economics as her focal point, but the same pattern is true for psychology and especially its relationship with public schooling. In the United States, psychology slowly professionalized in the Progressive era, with a key core of academically trained psychologists defining the field as the science of individual differences and allying themselves with school administrators (e.g., Danziger, 1994). In education, what began as amateur involvement in the field in the child study movement turned into a professional relationship, with consulting and educational ties between educational psychologists such as Edward Thorndike, on the one hand, and school administrators, on the other (e.g., Jonçich, 1968). The colonization of schools by psychology was a development often highly desired by administrators, and it had century-long consequences for both education research and educational practices (e.g., Condliffe Lagemann, 2000; Johanningmeier & Richardson, 2008).

Tools Used in the Creation of Special Education

One of those consequences was that psychology became the most accessible disciplinary ally for Progressive-era school administrators seeking to manage school systems (Tyack & Hansot, 1982). The budding field of psychology claimed to wield the techniques that administrators could use to manage schools. This not only created but changed the nature of the tools administrators had at their disposal. One such tool was testing; while some form of standardized testing has been used in the United States as a vehicle for public accountability on and off since the 1840s (Reese, 2013), the industry of testing became formalized and rationalized in the early 20th century, and its purpose shifted from accountability to sorting. Sorting tools included the IQ test, pushed extensively after World War I, but subject-specific tests played a substantial role as well; Stanford psychologist Louis Terman developed both the Stanford-Binet IQ test and the Stanford Achievement Test, both of which were available to school administrators (Dorn, 2007). The key technique in the process of forming students with disabilities as objects was not tied to a specific test but, rather, the concept of testing students and using the results to classify them and manage their opportunities (Mazzeo, 2001).

One result of the broad use of tests to classify students and stratify the opportunities available to them was the engraving of contemporary prejudices within the bureaucratic routines of schools (Richardson & Parker, 1993). The institutional prejudices of testing and tracking in the early 20th century lasted for decades, and for students judged unable to benefit from schooling on the basis of tests, this routine justified the exclusion of hundreds of thousands of children from schools until the last quarter of the century. For school administrators, the bureaucratic use of testing and stratified education served multiple purposes. It was a tool for managing the reputation of large urban systems (e.g., Labaree, 1988); it justified a broad variety of ways of dividing students and providing limited services to many; it maintained their professional relationships and consulting contracts with many of the faculty who had taught superintendents and other administrators in graduate programs (e.g., Tyack, 1974); and it provided a claim to management expertise for administrators in the early 20th century, a claim that administrators used to buffer themselves from political pressures (Tyack & Hansot, 1982).

The Invention of Special Education and the Triangle of Expertise

This growth of civil administrative power was the essential context for the invention of special education in urban school districts. School administrators were public agents of Progressive social engineering, and they managed both educational opportunities and the largest collection of public buildings and spaces in American cities. Together with new professional, disciplinary expertise, this administrative authority and urban context is often missing from the historical literature on special education. Gould (1996) and Franklin (1994) have pointed to the ideological prejudices in the early days of special education. However, those prejudices would not have persisted without some underlying authority. That authority was a foundation for the 20th-century discourse of disability, a dominant discourse that assumed a universalized study of difference.

The tie between administrative authority and the discourse of special education lay in three connected features: the objects of study in the field, the evangelism of experts embedded in personal and professional networks, and the technical tools that experts and their public partners used in practice. We can call this set a triangle of expertise: objects, experts, and tools. This triangle of expertise appears repeatedly in the Progressive era: Colonized populations were objects studied by White anthropologists in service to European states and the United States (Asad, 1979; Lewis, 1973). Chemical compounds were the objects of study by hundreds of doctorally trained applied chemists hired by industry, with the synthesis of materials as the tool (Bensaude-Vincent & Stengers, 1996). Economies and markets were objects studied by professional economists in the service of the same industrial corporations, with classical economic and later specific market analysis as key tools (Ross, 1991). Poverty was the object studied by the new profession of social work in the service of municipal authorities and wealthy patrons of charity, with casework as the tool (Austin, 1983). Disability and people with disabilities made up an essential object studied by early educational psychologists in service to school authorities, with testing and classification as mediating tools (e.g., Jonçich, 1968).

The object-formation process can only be meaningful in the specific cultural–historical context of nation building in the United States through "the fatally dynamic coupling of power and difference" (Gilmore, 2002, p. 15). Today, nationally and perhaps internationally, the most powerful cultural artifact in the formation of "mental disabilities" is the *Diagnostic and Statistical Manual of Mental Disorders* (DSM). The earliest form of *DSM* was found in the 1840 census under the category of "idiocy/insanity," and it appeared again with a more developed form in the 1880 census with seven categories: mania, melancholia, monomania, paresis, dementia, dipsomania, and epilepsy (American Psychiatric Association, 2016). In the early 20th century, professional psychologists in the American Medico-Psychological Association and the National Commission for Mental Hygiene joined forces with the Bureau of the Census to collect standard information about mental illness, determining its boundaries (American Psychiatric Association, 2016). Altogether, these structures and tools evolved into *DSM*; along the way the process moved from gathering "useful" information for the state to producing uniform diagnostic criteria (demarking mental illness from mental health). *DSM* includes diagnostic criteria for SLD, ID, and the various forms of ED (e.g., oppositional defiant disorder).

Triangles of expertise were the Progressive-era context for the definition of disability within institutional contexts. Across a broad range of fields, these triangles did not blossom simultaneously, neatly, or only in the Progressive era. Nonetheless, the

Progressive era witnessed surprising growth in triangles of expertise connecting new disciplines to system authorities, officials in search of administrative capacity and power. The expansion of administrative power and triangles of expertise can explain the maintenance of prejudices and ideologies in schools, a set of practices that continued long after the heyday of the scientific racists. Social constructions consisted of not just ideological objects but definitions tied closely to institutional structures and practical needs (e.g., Hacking, 1999). With the growth of urban systems in the Progressive era, institutional structures were copied by organizations in the same field—for education, by individual school districts and states. This institutional mimesis carried with it the triangle of expertise (DiMaggio & Powell, 1983). As school administrators copied what they saw as common and useful professional practices, they retained key features—the definition of objects that motivated the mimesis, connections to networks of expertise that expanded with the practice, and the tools that could be described, demonstrated, learned, and replicated.

This was a bureaucratic replication of the triangle of expertise across jurisdictions. The replication of the triangle affirmed the power of individual school districts as administrative regimes. Especially in education, where administrative power carried the authority of the state, disability became an object studied by experts, managed by administrators, and defined with the power of the state (Richardson & Parker, 1993). Psychologists and psychiatrists defined conditions of exclusion and classification for disability, and members of those professions often made individual judgments on classifications. They were hired by superintendents wanting to manage student populations, using the legal authority of the state to shuttle children into different educational experiences and exclude others entirely from school. Institutional routines and tools contained ethnic and racial prejudices embedded in the early 20th-century disability discourse—the easy assumption by mostly White, Protestant school officials that East European immigrants were less intelligent and capable than native Whites. That prejudice had its direct descendant in the later segregation and labeling of Puerto Rican students in New York City and Mexican American students in Riverside, California (Franklin, 1994; Mercer, 1973; Nieto, 2003)—labeling that once again played a role in the management of metropolitan schools and limited the ontological assumptions about children's capacity once they entered public spaces defined as schools. School routines established to identify, label, and separate continued to operate for decades, with key features untouched.

Consequences of the Progressive-Era Creation of Special Education

The invention of special education in the Progressive era thus had long-term consequences for schools and children, not just in transitory bureaucratic routines. Beyond bureaucratic mechanisms, schools became a vehicle for maintaining the Progressive-era discourse of disability. We see this (and all) discourse as a potential license for behavior. This license can exist at either the institutional or individual level. Dominant discourse is often a license for institutional behavior; thus, the intersectional specifics of disability discourse in the early 20th century licensed immigration restrictions, the forced sterilization of poor women, the growth of school segregation, and more. Discourse can also be co-opted—the more humane interpretations of disability thought in the early 20th century gave room for entrepreneurial educators such as Elizabeth Farrell. Farrell's efforts to create ungraded classrooms in New York City carved out a sphere where some children certainly had more educational opportunities than would have existed otherwise (Hendrick & MacMillan, 1989). And yet, that individual action by a humane teacher was co-opted in the early 20th century in a discourse of expertise with an object: disability and individuals labeled as disabled. What Farrell created as a humane educational environment for students in the early 20th century became a tool for restricting the opportunities of students for decades to follow. School practices are the institutional embodiment of ontologies of human capacity. The discourse surrounding those practices both embodies and maintains epistemologies describing how educators learn about and respond to human diversity. In the case of special education, Farrell's humane efforts were islands in an ocean of limited definitions of human capacity and narrow ways of seeing difference. In most of the 20th century, even the most humane "teacherpreneur" (e.g., Berry, Byrd, & Wieder, 2013) could not raise general practice above bureaucratic routines that identified students whose opportunities were to be limited. Even the most avid "cage-busting" teacher (e.g., Hess, 2015) could not fight a discourse embodied in professional training, the courses in colleges of education that defined individual differences as the object of purely psychometric study.

That co-optation of Farrell's invention happened under the guise of expert, objective, and objectified judgment. In the Progressive era, social science and behavioral expertise emerged out of an evangelistic belief in the utility of professional, putatively scientific expertise, on the one hand, and the creation or co-optation of structural and bureaucratic tools, on the other. The first was tied to the constructed ontology of disability, and the second was tied to the official epistemology of difference. That combination of evangelism and tools required an object or objects of study and manipulation. In the first third of the 20th century, disability and individuals labeled as disabled became the objects for the professional class of psychologists and administrators certain that they could manage disability in public education and in other institutional contexts. It would remain for later generations to take the idea of protection, and the legacy of 19th-century social welfare ideology embedded in schools, and use that concept as a hook for civil rights activism to reform school practices.

CHANGES AND CONTINUITIES

Consolidation of the Intersections of Difference With Disabilities (1960s–1990)

Many of the features of the earlier objectified discourse around disability had inverted by the end of the 20th century: Most important, those in the United States who argued for universal education won the battle by the late 1970s. The victory of equal opportunity rhetoric and some institutional structures should not be undersold; it meant access to education for hundreds of thousands of children after 1970 whose counterparts in earlier generations were often excluded from public schooling. On the other hand, other key features of the older discourse remained, especially the links between deficit assumptions and the institutional repertoires of separation and unequal opportunity. The creation of individual rights was layered over the older discourse of problem children as objects of expertise.

This incomplete, messy nature of discourse transitions shows how large paradigm shifts can be leaky. This leakage is common in historical change, and it reflects both the lagging change in what administrators, educators, and others in individual roles understood as disability and the social networks and institutional structures that reinforced preexisting definitions of human capacity and diversity. Courts may have required the desegregation of schools, but the disproportionate placement of African American students in special classes followed. Separate classes for students with disabilities constituted far more access than prior exclusion from schools had, but it became a mechanism for second-generation segregation.[8] One can make similar observations for the intersectional role of disability with regard to social class, gender, language, and other categories of difference. Since the post–World War II civil rights legislation, intersectionality around disability and difference has played havoc with the concept of student rights as the primary reform mechanism in public education. If intersectionality is not the only barrier to effective education for a diverse population, it is an important complicating factor.

The broader discourse around educational inequality in the 1960s was embroiled in debates over poverty, race, and culture. There had long been a tension in the country's social welfare debates about the "worthy" as opposed to the "unworthy" poor, with many social policies attempting to make judgments and regulate the behavior of poor families and poor single adults (Katz, 1996). Through the past half century, a significant strain of writing has targeted poor people's cultures and habits as the main cause of problems for poor children and adults in education, the labor market, and other areas of life (Greenbaum, 2015). The modern version of debates about virtue and poverty implied that government in general is not responsible for addressing poverty. This justification for laissez-faire policies has vied with arguments emerging at the same time that schools are the key lever for addressing poverty and more so that schools must serve the national interest in economic productivity and competitiveness—twin moral panics in which schools and teachers have the major targets of action (Goldstein, 2014). In the same way that the Progressive-era invention of special education emerged from social developments at the time, modern special education practices emerged at a time of vivid debates about the proper role and capacity of schools, with issues of equality, race, and national imperatives in the foreground.

This period was characterized by continued entanglements of disability with other markers of difference. New in the late 20th century was the effort of a broad coalition of individuals with disabilities and other disability rights activists, building on the efforts of the postwar civil rights movement (Fleischer & Zames, 2012; Pelka, 2012; Pfeiffer, 1993; Scotch, 1989; Shapiro, 1994; Winzer, 1993).[9] That development relied in part on the emergence of a discourse on individual rights for racial minorities and individuals with disabilities. This emphasis on individual rights was both a lever and a limitation in the civil rights movement and the fight against segregation (e.g., D. A. Bell, 1987; Ladson-Billings, 2004; see also Tate, 1997). In modern political discourse, disability has a dual nature that reflects the dual nature of children's rights discourse.[10] In the context of disabilities, the construction of rights as *liberatory* (e.g., children's speech rights in *Tinker v. Des Moines*, 393 U.S. 503 [1969]) competed with the construction of children's rights as *protective*, the modern inheritance of views about the innocent and priceless child (Grossberg, 2011; Zelizer, 1985).

Debates about disability rights added a wrinkle with regard to the idealized right to an education. After Congress and the executive branch adopted new federal policy for children and youth with disabilities, other debates ensued over inclusion and the maintenance of separate environments for children with disabilities (e.g., Fleischer & Zames, 2012). This debate among individuals with disabilities and their families, disability rights activists, researchers, and educators overlapped with the postwar tensions in the rhetoric of children's rights. Through this transition and the expansion of special education, the role of disability and individuals with disabilities changed, from an object of expert interaction with schools at the beginning of the century to a boundary object at the end, a conceptual object that was a malleable entity for multiple stakeholders connected to special education. The boundary object of disability exists across spaces in a "virtual community" among school officials, professionals, parents, students with disabilities, researchers, and policy makers. Dumit (2004) explained that virtual communities are "dispersed in space, and although each participant is not necessarily connected directly to every other one, they all interact indirectly with each other via technologies of communication" (p. 11). In this sense, the growing infrastructure of special education, with its attendant technologies of professional standards, policies, technical procedures, and so forth, served a primary role in the creation and maintenance of these virtual communities in which the boundary object of disability has existed.

Civil Rights and Disability Rights

The standard story of the post–World War II disability rights movement is that both inside and outside education, the expansion of disability rights paralleled the primary postwar civil rights movement that focused on race and ethnicity (e.g., Gliedman & Roth, 1980). The earlier wave of efforts by the National Association for the Advancement of Colored People, the American G.I. Forum, the Southern Christian Leadership Conference, and others provided examples of philosophy, tactics, legal structures, and the concept of a broad and inclusive citizenship that supported demands for equal access to education. The modern disability rights movement eventually landed on a combination of individual rights and participation ("Nothing about us without us") and successfully provoked a redefinition of human capacity as well as concrete policy actions (e.g., Pelka, 2012; Shapiro, 1994). This effort pushed back against the ontology of disability created decades ago. The postwar civil rights movement around the rights of individuals with disabilities reached its legislative zenith with the Americans With Disabilities Act of 1990, a broad civil rights statute that expanded on rights embodied in Section 504 of the Rehabilitation Act of 1973 (29 U.S.C. §794) and the Education for All Handicapped Children Act of 1975 (also known as Public Law 94-142, now the Individuals With Disabilities Education Act [IDEA]).[11] Behind those apparent parallel histories, there were important crossing points: the justification of segregation by South Carolina's lawyer on the grounds that desegregation by race would force schools to admit children with disabilities (J. W. Davis, 1952, as quoted in Pelka, 2012, p. 1), the federal court order striking down extreme tracking in the District of Columbia (*Hobson v. Hansen*, 269 F. Supp. 491 [D.D.C. 1967]; Tropea, 1987), and the growing disproportionality of suspensions and placement in special education by race during desegregation (Children's Defense Fund, 1974; Dunn, 1968; Heller, Holtzman, & Messick, 1982; Robert F. Kennedy Memorial & Southern Regional Council, 1973). The result was inconsistent and highly localized educational opportunities that often resulted in the disproportionate placement of children from African American and Latina/o households in special education, disproportionate placement without the appropriate education that federal law putatively promised. This was the local, geographic expression of broader social dynamics and had consequences for specific communities—in the fallout of desegregation, for example, Southern school districts often closed previously all-Black high schools that had served for several decades as keystone institutions of communities (e.g., Cecelski, 1994; Shircliffe, 2006; Siddle-Walker, 1996).

In addition to the high price of racial desegregation that African American communities and educators paid, this expression became disproportionate placement in special education by race. The dual nature of disability discourse is evident in disproportionate placements in special education. With the landmark Supreme Court case of *Brown v. Board of Education of Topeka* and seemingly equity-oriented national policy of racial desegregation, African American students whose neighborhood schools were closed and who were placed in formerly all-White schools were overrepresented in special education classrooms with the label of ID (Dunn, 1968). Disproportionate placement was possible because of bureaucratic routines that still relied on older definitions of human capacity and institutionalized knowledge about children with disabilities as holding deficits within themselves. The expansion of rights for children in the late 20th century added another layer to disability discourse but did not capture all of the discourse.

Legal Discourse and the Messy Legacy of Disability Rights

The standard civil rights framing of the post–World War II legal discourse in education portrays the broader debate as a battle over individual rights in education, rights tied to citizenship and educational justice. It is certainly true that the political uses of the lawsuits commonly focused on an individual right to education tied to citizenship, while defendants tried to persuade the courts and the general public of the limits of school district and state obligations. This legal discourse of rights intersected with race and language in several places where lawsuits challenged the professional authority of school districts in their practices of testing students and placing them in special education. In *Diana v. California State Board of Education* (No. C-70, RFT [N.D. Cal. 1970]), representatives of nine Mexican American students successfully argued that assigning the children to "Educable Mentally Retarded" classes on the basis of English-language testing violated the students' rights when the students' primary language was Spanish. In *Larry P. v. Riles* (343 F. Supp. 1306 [N.D. Cal. 1972]), plaintiffs challenged IQ testing in San Francisco as culturally biased. As Richardson (2000) noted, the court record on such cases is mixed during this period, with a few successful challenges to common practices but frequent court rulings that sided with school districts. In this era, as in prior eras, disability discourse and policy were inextricably intertwined to stress a paradigm that emphasized individual factors and pushed identity intersections to the background. That intersectionality easily accommodated the language of individual rights, even while a rights framework was not an assured method of addressing unequal treatment in schools.

This modern assertion of an individual right to education took as its starting point the 19th-century bundling of education with citizenship: education both prepared students for citizenship and was a right of all children (Katznelson & Weir, 1985). Yet that framework of individual rights to an education was layered onto an older framework of legal discourse that saw rights very differently. The major shift in how courts treated children between 1850 and 1930 focused less on the individual rights of children than on the need to protect the "priceless child" (Zelizer, 1985), the authority of the state to impose compulsory education requirements (Provasnik, 2006), and the countervailing right of parents to guide their children's education, including in private schooling (e.g., *Pierce v. Society of Sisters*, 268 U.S. 510 [1925]; Tyack, 1968).

The result was a postwar discourse that saw two very different meanings of children's rights. On the one hand was the right of children to access education and make important choices including speech—what Grossberg (2011) has called a *liberatory* rights framework. Yet there was also an alternative framework, which Grossberg has termed a *protective* definition of children's rights—the legacy of the "priceless child" ideology. We should remember, however, that the idea of rights had different meanings when applied to immigrants and racial minorities (particularly African Americans), and thus, parallel discourses about rights unfolded in this period. It is already the case that courts are crude and inexact mechanisms for political change (Ladson-Billings, 2004). Given the bifurcated nature of children's rights as discourse after World War II and the disparate meanings that were mediated by race and immigration status, it was inevitable that when advocates pushed for the assertion of civil rights in education, debates followed about what those rights meant in operation. The notion of "policy assemblages" helps us understand that

policies are never the pure application of rational guidelines or the result of powerful individuals but multifaceted processes in which a multitude of entities, all of them carrying different agencies, intervene and are continually reenacted, changing the policy's outcome in accordance with the presence/absence of certain articulations and practices. (Ureta, 2014, p. 303)

Policy assemblages have been at play in the historical trajectories of disability and its intersections, especially in elementary and secondary education where legislated rights have often given discretion to local school districts and school officials, where school districts can win cases if they do not commit egregious violations of process and demonstrate that they followed professional educational standards (Yell & Drasgow, 2000). The consequence was the legal affirmation of what Weatherley and Lipsky (1977) described as "street-level bureaucracy," decision making that educators at the local level had to perform under pressure. It is in that local context that disproportionate placement in special education occurs; the geography of implementation and policy expression matters. Both the local implementation of special education laws and the history of disproportionate placements (e.g., Fleischer & Zames, 2012; Tropea, 1987) make clear that the dual nature of disability can have bureaucratic expressions in different ways that have profound influences on the lives of children. The roots of that expression often lay in older and familiar practices of school systems. The bureaucratic response to expanded educational rights needed techniques with which schools were familiar and which also had the patina of authority, an authority that schools often lacked after 1950 (Tyack & Hansot, 1982).

Classification Schema and Boundary Objects

In their search for authority, school officials and regulators relied on the existing technical tool from the Progressive era: the craft and discourse of classification. By the late 1960s, in the aftermath of unprecedented sociopolitical upheaval,[12] the triangle of expertise that tied psychology to school administrators had been incorporated into school routines and the professional infrastructure of local school systems. When the Education for All Handicapped Children Act passed in 1975, and other legislation and regulations forced states and local districts to change their practices and expand access to education, they turned to that professional infrastructure: pupil personnel offices and school psychologists, for whom classification of children into the various categories of special education service eligibility was an expansion of their prior routines. This mandate for "child find" and classification for services did *not* overturn but, instead, reinforced the authority of school districts and their implicit authority:

Since bureaucracies are themselves elaborate classifications, their work centers on classifying and assigning, with variations in classification *practice* at various levels of government testifying to the political process inherent in officials (the classifiers) exercising power over subjects (the classified) through intermediate agents that apply classificatory rules. (Powell, 2011, p. 79)

Again, geography mattered, as less than two decades before, many school systems in the South had used school psychologists in the bureaucratic routines that maintained segregation through pupil-placement rules throughout Virginia, in Atlanta, and elsewhere (Dorn, 1996). Psychologists in the same roles were in use a short time later, to classify students regarding eligibility for special education services. The intersectionality of disability and special education was embedded in school systems' bureaucratic roles and technical infrastructures. The outcomes of these practices, however, could not be explained simply on technical grounds, as the emerging policy assemblages created contexts that were embedded in unique politico-historical matrices of influence and infrastructures, and as Star and Ruhleder (1996) reminded us, infrastructures are relational.

The ease with which routines became adapted to the new legal protections in special education did not eliminate conflict over the extent of the right to education or the nature of disability as an object. Administrative law hearings and court cases became the civil trench warfare within which lawyers for schools and parents slowly defined and redefined the obligations of school systems after the mid-1970s. The legal battles in special education were matched by questions about the inherent validity of disability categories embedded within federal law. Between 1965 and 1985, the proportion of students identified as having ID declined or remained stable, while a new category, specific learning disabilities, quickly grew to include the plurality of all students receiving special education services (Lyon, 1996). In the 1980s, writers such as Carrier (1986), Sigmon (1987), and Sleeter (1986) asserted that there was no biological or psychological coherence to the SLD category and that its growing use was a result of ideological and social-class maneuvering, the category emerging as a social construction rather than an independently objective category. In particular, Sleeter argued that the category of SLD allowed White middle-class parents to secure resources for struggling children without having the same label ("mentally retarded") that had become much more commonly associated with African American students, at least in the late 1960s and early 1970s.

This critique of SLD as socially constructed and ideological was interesting and provocative in the late 1980s, roughly a decade after the federal government issued regulations to implement the right to an education for all students. And yet, the focus on ideological uses of disability categories omits the connection with school bureaucracies and administrative routines. At the time, African Americans were already disproportionately to be placed in special education for ID, SLD, and ED. Regardless of the potential for the category to be used as a softer, less stigmatizing label than "mental retardation" (Sleeter, 1986), the practice of schools incorporated SLD as a useful tool for declaring eligibility for special education. This development does not make sense if the category is only ideological, but it makes great sense if one understands special education's postwar history as one where the constructs around disability became potentially useful categories for action in schools, a boundary object inhabiting multiple activity systems.

We see special education categories as boundary objects because of the conflicts over their integrity and utility. In part this is the historical working out of epistemology in a field: Special education was embedded in a set of social practices that both required and deepened professional authority. That epistemological practice became contested in the late 20th century, but not just as a set of professional practices; the broader definition of human diversity and value was at stake. If disability was a useful object in the triangle of expertise at the beginning of the 20th century, its role as an object shifted after 1960 as a growing number of groups fought over what the purpose of education was, what equal educational opportunity required, and how special education may or may not serve those goals. With these debates, disability was no longer the focus of a relatively small group—mostly administrators and psychological professionals—and instead disability categories became objects over which many different interest groups met.

The Building Blocks of Disability's Fluid States: Definitions and Classifications

Even if there was no consensus on the definitions of SLD, ID, and ED, the categories and terms around disability provided the raw material for the creation of *boundary objects* (Bowker & Star, 2000; Star & Griesemer, 1989). Classification structures do not have to be coherent or consensual to serve these ends—the infrastructure of classifications grew in the postwar era even while the details were in dispute. The American Psychological Association staked a claim to the process of individual assessment for special education eligibility. The Council for Exceptional Children and advocacy organizations fought for training and professional licensure around categories, and the National Institutes of Health and the U.S. Department of Education provided research and training funding for activities often defined by categorical terms.[13] The machinery of classification ground on during disputes about definitions because disability categories were too useful to discard in a very practical sense—the paradigmatic example of a boundary object. The dilemmas related to the ambiguities of disability definitions have also been evident in other disability arenas such as the Americans With Disabilities Act, which led Crossley (1999) to describe this state of affairs as the disability kaleidoscope.

With the growing use of disability categories as boundary objects, the bureaucratization of special education in the latter 20th century ensured that students with disabilities remained part of objectified routines. Those routines were not neutral in ideology. First, the bureaucratic routines of classification created an inertia around the historical racialization of disability; federal special education laws may have attempted to prohibit discriminatory assessment practices, for example, requiring individualized assessment for special education eligibility in a student's primary language, but the disproportional placement of African American students, students whose first language was not English, and other children from commonly marginalized groups remained an entrenched pattern through the century's end (Donovan & Cross, 2002). In addition, as noted earlier, the broader postwar legal discourse contained an inherent tension between children's rights as liberatory and their rights as protective. With growing debates over inclusion in the 1980s and 1990s, the role of placement routines became part of that debate (Brantlinger, 1997).

At this point, it is important to step away from a narrative focused on organizational structures and ideologies. The histories, laws, procedures, labels, and tools built around disability are experienced directly in the life of individuals with disabilities. As Lefebvre (1988) wrote, "Everyday is a kind of screen, in both senses of the word; it both shows and hides; it reveals both what has and has not changed" (p. 78). In collecting narratives of youth of color educated in New York City with the SLD identification, Connor (2008) has presented how students experience the dual nature of disability. For example, Connor's informant Michael explained how he understood his position within a school bureaucracy:

> Once you are there, it's just like a Hell. For you to get out of special ed., it's not up to your parents, It's up to your teachers. Your teachers have but so much power—it's up to the school and the districts to get you out of special ed. If they don't want to get you out, if they need a certain amount of numbers in that class, your behind is gonna stay in there until you graduate. Any kid can get into special ed. To get out of special ed., it takes Hell to get out of special ed. I think that's the most hardest thing to do, to get out. When you get out of there, you do not want to go back. (p. 149)

Michael's understanding of special education is as a social space that one can reference in physical terms—the difficulty of "getting out" and the desire never to "go back." W. G. captured a very personal sense of disability's dual nature, both protection and permanent labeling (what W. G. sees as empowering):

> My advantage was being put in special ed. One of our classes was resource where you get extra help. You have *nothing to lose* because you have all the time in the world. Wow! I'm *improving* in all my classes. Once you're learning disabled, it's *never ending* because it follows you where ever you go. (p. 264)

In the modern era, the protective side of disability has not prevented schools from being sites of suffering (Dumas, 2014). The dual nature of disability as a both protective and limiting object is embedded in the lived experiences of the students analyzed by Connor (2008); they understand and can articulate it better than most educators and researchers.

THE PROTEAN NATURE OF DISABILITY INTERSECTIONS AND FRAGMENTATIONS IN CONTEMPORARY HISTORY (1990s TO 2016)

At the end of the 20th century, debates about special education and disability continued to evolve. Controversies related to the meanings and roles of special education in an increasingly diverse society mediated debates about educational reform. Scholarship on disability definitions was still highly debated. Notably, student identity intersections played a substantial role in debates about definitions of high-incidence disabilities in this time period. For instance, various versions of the SLD definition were proposed in the late 1980s and early 1990s in which social skill deficits and comorbidity with attention deficit disorders were acknowledged or ignored (Hallahan, Pullen, & Ward, 2013). In the end, however, the definition used in the reauthorization of IDEA (2004) remained largely the same as the one found in the 1975 federal policy. At the same time, growing criticism focused on the achievement–aptitude discrepancy generally used to diagnose SLD. Research showed a weak association between severe discrepancy and the impact of reading interventions—for example, there were minimal differences in the nature and quality of responses to reading interventions among low- and high-aptitude children (Bradley, Danielson, & Hallahan, 2002). In the 1990s, the debates about racial disparities in high-incidence disabilities intensified, which led to the publication of a second National Research Council report in a 20-year period (Donovan & Cross, 2002). This scholarship maintained a trajectory parallel to the research conducted on disability definitions and interventions, thus fragmenting the ways in which disability intersections were engaged in this field. The National Research Council report had a substantial impact in the special education field, contributing to the creation of the first national technical assistance center to address this long-standing problem—the National Center for Culturally Responsive Educational Systems—and the inclusion of racial disproportionality monitoring requirements in the 2004 reauthorization of IDEA. This constituted a rare convergence of policy assemblages in which attention to the intersections of disability, race, and social class crystallized.

In addition, the debate about placement (as a proxy for inclusion) that emerged in the mid-1980s with the regular education initiative and full inclusion movements evolved into the inclusive education movement in the 1990s. The special education placement debate became less polarized, as the inclusive education movement appropriated the notion of diversity to include ability differences, and the vast majority of learners with disabilities were educated in public school buildings (Fuchs & Fuchs, 1994).

In this section, we focus on the research discourse and on a crucial question: Has the advancement of disability rights (including in education) dramatically changed the way that researchers operate? To begin, we note that the scholarship on disability identification, interventions, inclusion, and racial disparities evolved in parallel fashion. Although substantial progress was made in the generation of research knowledge across all of these domains, there was little cross-fertilization across these research communities. Intersections with race, language, and cultural influences were largely invisible in these knowledge bases; this pattern has been present since at least the 1970s in special education, psychology, counseling, and child development research (Artiles, Trent, & Kuan, 1997; Graham, 1992; McLoyd & Randolph, 1985; Ponterotto, 1988). For instance, Artiles et al. (1997) reported that less than 3% of studies published in prominent special education journals between 1972 and 1994 focused on ethnic-minority students. Comparable patterns have been documented for other, subsequent periods—1994 to 2012 (S. Trent et al., 2014) and 1995 to 2009 (Vasquez et al., 2011).

Unfortunately, the invisibility of disability intersections with race, language, and other markers of difference in the empirical knowledge base continued in the most recent decade. We reviewed grants funded by the Institute of Education Sciences (IES) National Center for Special Education Research between 2004 and 2015. We started our review from the most recent reauthorization of IDEA (2004) and aimed to determine the extent to which culturally and linguistically diverse (CLD) individuals were included in funded research projects. We defined CLD as individuals from nondominant racial and linguistic backgrounds (Latina/o, African American, Native American, Asian, and English language learners [ELLs]). This is an admittedly limited way to examine this issue, though it provides a useful indirect indicator of the attention in the research community to disability intersections. We based our analysis on reviews of grant abstracts. We assumed that these abstracts would offer critical information about study samples since research reporting guidelines require clear and specific descriptions of study questions, samples, and research contexts and procedures as means to gauge the rigor of studies and enhance the replicability of research (American Psychological Association, 2006).

We conducted an electronic search of funded research grants on the IES website (https://ies.ed.gov/funding/grantsearch/). We reviewed the reported abstracts that contained information about grant purpose, activities, sample, setting, research design and methods, and outcomes. If a grant included CLD participants or mentioned their cultural or linguistic diversity, we categorized it as a grant that took into account student sociocultural backgrounds.

There were 18 subcategories under special education research grants. We categorized them into three broad categories—(a) intervention research with students and families, (b) workforce research, and (c) other awards including autism spectrum disorder and special education research and development centers. We identified 340 funded projects since 2004 (see Table 1). Four grants under the small business innovation research subcategory did not report abstracts. Therefore, we excluded them from the review. The evidence showed that out of 336 funded projects, 39 special education projects (11.6%) focused on or mentioned CLD individuals. An analysis of the grant categories shows interesting patterns. Two hundred fifteen studies (64%) were intervention research with students and families. Of these 215 intervention studies, 28 (13%) focused on CLD individuals. The second category, workforce research, had 40 funded projects (12%). Of these 40 projects, two (5%) focused on CLD individuals. Last, in the third category, there were 81 projects (24%) funded by IES. Of these projects, only nine projects (11%) focused on CLD individuals.

Overall, since 2004, no IES-funded project specifically focused only on African American and Asian American students. Out of the 39 projects involving CLD individuals, there were five studies (12.8%) that included Latinas/os; one study (2.6%) included Native Americans; three studies (7.7%) included students from different racial backgrounds, including African American learners; and 10 studies (25.6%) included ELLs. Twenty studies (51.3%) mentioned CLD students in their abstracts but did not specify the racial and linguistic backgrounds of participants. Out of the 39 projects, eight funded grants (20.5%) had Spanish-speaking participants. A majority of the projects ($n = 31$; 79.5%) focusing on CLD individuals did not report the language of the participants. In terms of disability categories, about half of the 39 projects ($n = 20$; 51.3%) involving CLD groups focused on SLD, and three studies (7.7%) did not identify a disability category.

TABLE 1

Percentage (and Number) of National Center for Special Education Research–Funded Grants by Sample Demographics and Disability Categories, 2004 to 2015

Demographics	Percentage (Number)
Race and ELL status of targeted population	
Latina/o	12.8 (5)
African American	0
Native American	2.6 (1)
Asian	0
Multiple race categories	7.7 (3)
Not specified	51.3 (20)
ELL	25.6 (10)
Language of targeted population	
Spanish	20.5 (8)
Not stated	79.5 (31)
Type of disability of targeted population	
SLD (general)	7.7 (3)
SLD (math)	10.3 (4)
SLD (reading)	33.3 (13)
Developmental delay	5.1 (2)
Autism spectrum disorder	5.1 (2)
Deafness	2.6 (1)
Language impairment	10.3 (4)
ED	10.3 (4)
SLD/ED/ID	2.6 (1)
All types	5.1 (2)
Not stated	7.7 (3)

Note. The grants funded by the National Center for Special Education Research cover 18 funding programs that include interventions with students and families, workforce research (professional development, postdoctoral training, early career), and other types of grants (e.g., technology, policy, finance). ELL = English language learner; SLD = specific learning disability; ED = emotional disturbance; ID = intellectual disabilities.

Despite small growth, these contemporary findings resemble the aforementioned previous reviews that make apparent the lack of attention to disability intersections with other sociocultural markers. While the disproportionality of placement is now a policy monitoring requirement, no feature of intersectionality is an essential organizing principle for federally sponsored research; meanwhile, "poor diagnostic procedures or discrimination seemingly still play a role in the disproportionate identification of certain groups" (Shifrer, Muller, & Callahan, 2010, p. 304). Peer-reviewed research grants and journal articles constitute the substance of a knowledge base in a scientific field. The knowledge encoded in these publications and grant findings informs professional practices and policies, and thus, researchers leading these efforts play significant gatekeeping roles that define what counts as legitimate knowledge on a topic of study. Thus, these trends suggest that there is a largely color-blind knowledge base on disability and its intersections. This is a troubling contemporary fact given the demographic imperative that the education field faces today in light of the unprecedented growth of non-White, low-income, and linguistic-minority students across the United States.

How do we explain the persistent disregard for recruiting research samples that represent the diversity of the U.S. student population? Or the lack of information in research reports about these key dimensions of study participants? This state of affairs could be interpreted as evidence of boundary work—"the demarcation practices used to maintain a field's identity" (Artiles et al., 2011, p. 168; see also Gieryn, 1995)—in the special education field in which race, ethnicity, language, and other key identity markers are merely considered background variables not deemed essential in sample descriptions. Yet the findings are generalized to all learners. This means that CLD students in special education often receive academic and behavioral interventions that were designed and tested with samples that likely excluded CLD participants. This is a puzzling stance given the evidence against color blindness that reminds us of the structural weight of race (Bobo, 2011), the erosion of hard-fought gains in civil rights and equity agendas such as affirmative action (e.g., Executive Order 11246, Equal Employment Opportunity, September 24, 1965), school racial segregation, the Voting Rights Act (Public Law 89-110, 79 Stat. 437 [1965]), and the requirements to monitor racial inequities in disability identification.

We acknowledge, however, that some of the research on racial disparities in special education has shed light on disability intersections. For instance, while research shows the substantial contribution of poverty to a disability diagnosis, studies also show that race predicts special education placement after controlling for poverty (Skiba, Poloni-Staudinger, Simmons, Feggins-Azziz, & Chung, 2005). The greater risk for African American student disability identification in affluent schools, the lack of national overrepresentation of racial groups with high poverty levels (i.e., Latinas/os), and the disparate treatment (e.g., placement restrictiveness, provision of related services) of racial groups with the same disability labels illustrate the intricacies of disability intersections with social class, race, and location. This complexity reflects an important reality for children in the United States: intersectionality remains deeply embedded within the bureaucratic contexts of schools. In these contexts, school system actions are robust, flexible, and insulated from external accountability. In this way, we find opposition *and* progress on the intersection of disability and race during this historical period. A growing interest in the theorization of culture, space, power, and history promises to situate analyses of this problem in the larger social and economic contexts of inequality in U.S. society (Artiles et al., 2011).

An important insight of the research produced after 2000 is that the complexity of disability intersections is mediated substantially by geography and local contingencies.

TABLE 2
Comparison of States With Highest Risk Indices for African American and Latina/o Students by Disability Category, 1998

Disability Categories	African American Students			Latina/o Students		
	State	Risk Index (RI)	White RI for State	State	RI	White RI for State
Intellectual disabilities	Massachusetts	6.28%	1.32%	Massachusetts	4.48%	1.32%
	Alabama	5.49%	1.80%	Nebraska	2.68%	1.99%
	Arkansas	5.29%	2.06%	Hawaii	2.41%	0.96%
Specific learning disabilities	Delaware	12.19%	7.15%	Delaware	8.93%	7.15%
	Rhode Island	10.38%	10.30%	New York	8.42%	7.03%
	New Mexico	9.99%	6.83%	New Mexico	8.21%	6.83%
Emotional disturbance	Minnesota	3.88%	1.88%	Hawaii	2.68%	2.39%
	Montana	3.58%	0.85%	Vermont	2.16%	1.80%
	Iowa	3.53%	1.05%	Maine	1.99%	1.73%

Note. Adapted from Donovan and Cross (2002).

In some locales, learners from a racial group can have a greater identification risk for a specific disability category at a low-poverty school, but the same racial group could have a lower placement chance in the same disability category at a high-poverty school (Waitoller et al., 2010). In other locales, student race might predict disability placement for ED and discipline disparities, irrespective of income, school demographics, achievement levels, and teacher demographics and education levels (Bal, Betters-Bubon, & Fish, 2016). Yet, in other locations, Skiba et al. (2014) identified several school protective factors (e.g., the percentage of African American enrollment) that buffered the risk for disproportionality. These patterns are related in part to the prevalence variability of disabilities across states and school districts (see Table 2). In this way, the idea of disability as a boundary object becomes visible in local practices across contexts. Since at least the 1990s, researchers have documented the wide unevenness in disability prevalence across states (Bocian, Beebe, MacMillan, & Gresham, 1999; Donovan & Cross, 2002). Factors that explain such variability include eligibility teams' decisions to override state identification criteria for various reasons, resistance from school personnel to apply diagnostic criteria for various (e.g., fiscal, human resource, political) reasons, and manipulations of the assessment and eligibility processes (Reschly & Hosp, 2004). How these practices relate to issues germane to disability intersections with language, class, and race have not been adequately studied.

A subtle, yet potential contributing key factor to the ways in which disability intersections, particularly with race, tend to be ignored in the research community is what we describe as the disguising motility of race as a means of enforcing a color-blind disability ontology. In the process of determining the existence of a disability (SLD, ID, and ED), IDEA (2004) lists "cultural factors," "environmental or economic disadvantage," and "Limited English proficiency" as exclusionary criteria. In other words, following the nature/biology and culture divide, if a learner is identified with a disability, then neither culture, nor class, nor language is supposed to be spoken of in relationship to her or his symptoms. The disguising motility of race describes how this category becomes both vocal and silenced as it moves in time across institutional contexts and practices.[14] The morphing nature of race is mediated in part by ideological assumptions encoded in policies and educational practices. Specifically, as students struggle (academically and/or behaviorally) in general education, their race speaks bureaucratically through the tracking of performance levels by student race, class, and language. Next, there are triggering events/circumstances that lead teachers to refer learners to assessment for disability identification purposes. Sometimes these triggering events are grounded in legitimate concerns about students' developmental/learning difficulties, but we must also acknowledge that student race—among other markers of difference—also plays a substantial role in referral and other remedial practices (Harry & Klingner, 2014; Okonofua & Eberhardt, 2015). At this time, race becomes a sotto voce topic—both spoken and silenced, vocal and ignorable at the same time. Thus, although race is often disguised in the referral reasons noted in institutional records, it is still whispered as it crystallizes ex post facto in reports of racial patterns for discipline referral reasons (e.g., African Americans are referred for more "subjective" reasons [e.g., disrespect] than their White peers) or in the disproportionate referrals of certain racial groups to special education. Once race passes the gate of referrals, a sequence of practices ensues: the assessment process begins, professionals collect evidence, and the team of professionals reaches an official diagnostic decision. Race continues to move through these contexts and practices, sometimes whispered under policy requirements, other times plainly audible. For instance, professional guidelines call for attending to race and other markers of difference (e.g., language) when choosing assessment tools, conducting evaluations, and interpreting assessment results. Yet most professionals tend to ignore these guidelines (Harry & Klingner, 2014). In other words, race breathes through the assessment processes, but it is also silenced.

Next, disability definitions may identify cultural or linguistic differences as exclusionary considerations in diagnostic decisions (e.g., SLD); thus, eligibility teams must assume that although race and language are all over the evidence (audible if whispered), the implicit official admonition is that disability should not be intersectional. Despite the significant advances in special education infrastructures—for example, testing and assessment technologies, conceptual refinement of disability definitions—we must be mindful of the relational nature of infrastructures and that diagnosis is a "communicative practice [that is enacted] across a variety of culturally and situated activities" (Duchan & Kovarsky, 2005, p. 2). As we explain in the following paragraphs, race returns to the stage as contemporary accountability and special education policies require that schools track bodies of color by performance levels, and research shows the differential treatment of individuals with disabilities by race (e.g., White students tend to be placed in more inclusive settings; Skiba et al.,

2008). The disguising motility of race constitutes a key building block of the work that the boundary object of disability does across institutional contexts. It also sheds light on the workings of boundary objects in which intersectionality is at play (e.g., disability and race).

We can see the situational silencing of intersectionality in the relationship between accountability policy in general and special education policy at the federal level. Most prominently, the No Child Left Behind Act of 2001 (NCLB; signed into law in 2002) contributed to the complexities of disability intersections in the educational system. The most visible features of this policy were its accountability requirements and the reliance on student scores from standardized tests. Subgroups defined in statute encoded race and disability as important but separate classifications. Schools were expected to make Adequate Yearly Progress (AYP); otherwise, measures would be taken ranging from publicly labeling schools as "in need of improvement" if they did not meet AYP for two consecutive years to restructuring schools (including closure) after five consecutive years of missing AYP. Assessment results were reported by subgroups of students, including racial groups, low-income students, English learners, and learners with disabilities.

It is beyond the scope of this chapter to present a comprehensive discussion of NCLB. For the purposes of our argument, it suffices to acknowledge that the policy prompted wide protests and opposition, with arguments that NCLB created a "diversity penalty" (Darling-Hammond, 2007), with uneven distribution of qualified teachers across school districts with different socioeconomic levels, deterioration of teacher–student relations, and demoralized teachers (Nichols & Berliner, 2007; Valli & Buese, 2007).

On the other hand, NCLB intersected with other major policies and system-wide programs such as IDEA and Response to Intervention (RTI) in ways that created opportunities while solidifying barriers for subgroups of learners (e.g., Artiles, 2015; Artiles, Bal, & King Thorius, 2010). For instance, some commentators welcomed greater accountability for special education students, while others protested the narrowing of indicators to gauge learning (i.e., test scores) and the weakening of one of the hallmarks of special education, namely, the individualized education plan. Although NCLB allowed for the representation of previously invisible groups in accountability systems, the policy also made some of them invisible as it allowed waivers for achievement reports (e.g., students with disabilities). In other instances, ELLs left this label when they became proficient in English, thus perpetuating an underperforming ELL group. In this sense, NCLB black-boxed the movement of students across subgroups since it only required performance reports of already formed subgroups. In this logic, disability intersectionalities were invisible both in statute and in how the law created incentives for attention to the subgroups defined in an a priori fashion. Over time, despite small changes, the performance gaps among subgroups remained.

The overlap of NCLB and RTI also had important consequences. Contrary to NCLB's a priori definition of subgroups, RTI defines subgroups over time, depending on their responses to interventions as the new way to identify students with

SLD. An interesting paradox is embodied in RTI, however. On the one hand, little systematic attention is given in the design of interventions to cultural issues or to the intersections of student risk or disability status with other identities. At the same time, RTI is assumed to be mindful of such intersectionalities since this model is expected to reduce racial disparities in special education. Of importance, emerging evidence suggests that over time, school districts and states are maintaining racial disparities in disability identification rates while complying with IDEA reporting requirements and, thus, avoiding consequences (Albrecht, Skiba, Losen, Chung, & Middelberg, 2012; Cavendish, Artiles, & Harry, 2014). We do not think that this was inherent in the intellectual construct of RTI. The continuation of older patterns illustrates how sticky school system behavior is, as well as how sticky ontological assumptions about disability and bureaucratic ways of gathering information are. The consequence is that school systems have treated reporting requirements as an object of ritual conformity—certainly not the first time schools have acted in this way. This form of ritual conformity (Artiles & Kozleski, 2016; Scheid & Suchman, 2001) with equity mandates demonstrates how the boundary object of disability navigates policy assemblages while allowing the educational system to communicate about disability across contexts and audiences, but with slightly different and consequential meanings and uses.

This section demonstrates how the last quarter century of research in special education had silenced discussions that effaced and sometimes erased intersectionality in special education. The shift from the No Child Left Behind Act of 2001 to the Every Child Succeeds Act does not change these dynamics sufficiently to eliminate the duality of disability as an object: Schools still must assess children annually in Grades 3 to 8 and must identify schools as low-performing based in a significant way on the results of these tests.

CONCLUSION

We traced a cultural–historical critique of the paradoxes of disability, arguing that its construct has consistently contained a dual nature. From the creation of a triangle of expertise a century ago through the disability rights movement and the modern era of special education law, we see a tension between disability's use as an object of protection and its use as a bureaucratic mechanism embedded in unequal education. In its recent history, it has embodied both protection and inequality. In its bureaucratic and scholarly expressions, disability today is embedded within test-based accountability and a generation of scholarship that too often effaces its intersectional nature. We use the notions of intersectionality and boundary objects to examine the fluid nature of race and disability and document "boundary work" to understand epistemological practices in this field that make race and disability visible and invisible notions. Of importance, we note how a culture- and race-neutral system of disability with an explicit justice agenda (i.e., special education) can morph into a racialized identification system that eventually makes race disappear in its midst.

The startling absence of intersectional frameworks in federally funded special education research concerns us, in part because of the desperate need for new intersectional scholarship. For example, we think that a *rights in action* perspective can help us understand what happens *after* disability identification to learners whose identities are formed at the intersections of disability, race, class, gender, and language in/through multiple activity systems (Artiles, 2014). But our concern is not dependent on our particular epistemological claims. We are also concerned with the decontextualized nature of funded special education research because that invisibility is unnecessary. If the National Institutes of Health has required the inclusion of women and minorities in funded clinical research for almost a quarter century (National Institutes of Health Revitalization Act of 1993, U.S. Public Law 103-43), there is no reason why the Institute of Education Sciences cannot require intersectional research in special education. The prevalence of nonintersectional research is a renewed ontology without social context, risking the continued generation of disability as an intellectual construct apparently knowable primarily as a universal truth, amenable to decontextualized interventions. As we have argued here, disability is a historically contingent object, both protective and risky, with a localized/spatial context and its intersections as objects of protection and inequality.

We broaden the conceptual landscape of this scholarship by taking up a perspective that benefits from developments in the study of health and the body, while it is grounded in interdisciplinary insights from culture theory, social studies of science, critical geography, and cultural psychology, among others (Bowker & Star, 2000; Davis, 2014; Harvey, 2012; Soja, 2010). Our argument is in favor of intersectional scholarship, in favor of acknowledging the dual nature of disability as a boundary object. The fluid view of disability and other difference markers enables us to dispel static notions of people's identities and reenvision (e.g., raced and disabled) individuals as active *makers* and *users* of cultural tools and practices. That argument does not dictate the exact nature of the scholarship that might follow this recognition, but it does suggest a reasonable set of tests for scholarship on disability in the future: Does scholarship on disability avoid an essentialist, context-free definition of disability? Does it avoid reliance on administrative mechanisms as the solitary definition of either disability or knowledge about disability? Does it provide an avenue for contextualized ways of understanding human capacity and diversity?

The standpoint we advance stands in contrast with the biology–culture binary that has pervaded in the study of disability. On the one hand, disability has been historically conceptualized as a fixed, universal, and culture-free condition with biological origins and centered on the individual. Thus, a wealth of evidence has accumulated on the medical deficits of this population, and myriad interventions have been created to address such deficiencies. This perspective is consistent with the dominant paradigm of human development research in Western societies that relies on the biology–culture divide and privileges biology over culture, which is seen as a man-made (unnatural) part of the environment (Cole, 1996). Moreover, this traditional formulation relies on the ontology of self-sufficient, free willing, morally directed individuals as the object of the theories of human development and learning (Popkewitz, 1997).

On the other hand, at least three approaches have taken up the role of culture in disability research (Artiles, Kozleski, et al., 2010). One is conceived from a "diversity" perspective, which tends to be equated with racial, ethnic, linguistic, and other minoritized groups. Both terms (*diversity* and *minority*) are deemed synonyms with culture. Taking "culture" as an external variable in a search for universal truth or "natural" mechanisms for disability and its effect on individuals' thoughts and behaviors, this view tends to construe culture as a demographic factor, and it has permeated the study of disability intersections with race, social class, and language. More important, the idea of culture has evolved to become a proxy for race, which in turn is closely aligned with a deficit orientation—for example, "culture of poverty" and "culturally disadvantaged" are illustrations of these standpoints (Artiles, Kozleski, et al., 2010; Ng & Rury, 2006).

Second, scholars working with a social and political model of disability foreground the role of the social construction of disability. They stress how an ableist world—through its institutions, ideologies, and historical legacies—imposes barriers and silences people with disabilities. Third, a group of scholars has put forward a cultural–historical perspective that focuses on the cultural mediation of human learning and development to account for ideal and material notions of cultural artifacts within object-oriented collective activity systems (Cole, 1996; Engeström, 2015; Rogoff, 2003). This way, cultural dimensions of the actions and thinking of groups (professionals, racial or linguistic communities) and institutions (e.g., rules and division of labor) are brought to bear in studies of disability (Artiles, 2003, 2011; Bal, 2016). Unfortunately, there has been only little cross-fertilization across these three scholarly communities, particularly in the study of disability intersections (Artiles, 2013). Utilizing cultural–historical activity theory and participatory social justice perspective, Bal (2016) conducted a statewide formative intervention study, culturally responsive positive behavioral supports and interventions (CRPBIS). The CRPBIS study aimed to address racial disproportionality in behavioral outcomes by designing inclusive, ecologically valid, adaptive, and sustainable behavioral support systems with local stakeholders in the state of Wisconsin. CRPBIS uses the Learning Lab methodology, an inclusive problem-solving process, bringing together students, family members, educators, school leaders, and community members, specifically those who have been historically excluded from school's decision-making activities (Bal, Kozleski, Schrader, Rodriguez, & Pelton, 2014). Learning Labs have been formed at five public schools. At four Learning Lab schools, members successfully examined outcomes in the existing behavioral support systems, identified systemic problems, and collectively designed culturally responsive schoolwide behavioral systems to be implemented in the subsequent academic years (Bal, 2016). Learning Labs have functioned as research and innovation sites for the schools, districts, state's education agency, and researchers that crafted artifacts and actions such as collective system mapping and interactive data maps (http://crpbis.apl.wisc.edu/) for mediating expansive learning and transformative agency.

More recently, advances in medical and technology research, along with a dose of science envy (e.g., Ross, 1991), have contributed to a biological turn in the social sciences. Researchers have been searching for the genetic and biological roots of certain conditions. For example, aside from a number of genetically determined syndromes (e.g., Fragile X), investigators have reported that

outcomes of brain imaging are viewed as fairly reliable at the group level but not reliable at the level of the single subject. There is strong evidence to support how the central occipitotemporal region underlies development of reading fluency, but there is controversy over the neural mechanisms involved. . . . [Research also shows] that parts of the left-hemispheric posterior brain systems fail to function properly during reading for individuals with dyslexia. Recent studies have begun to focus on age-related changes in the neural system of reading. (Swanson, Harris, & Graham, 2013, p. 13)

Packaged in a discourse of diversity and inclusion, we have witnessed a trend to overlay a biological perspective on scholarship concerned with cultural categories, such as race. For instance, notwithstanding the absence of genetic evidence for the idea of race, some researchers aim to identify and treat race-specific illnesses. Epstein (2007) explained the politics of difference in medical research with the notion of the "inclusion-and-difference" paradigm. This perspective intertwines "the meaning of biological difference [with] the status of socially subordinated groups . . . [through the articulation of] a distinctive way of asking and answering questions about the demarcating of subpopulations of patients and citizens" (p. 18). This line of research responds to the historical underrepresentation of racial minorities in medical research (i.e., it enhances their social visibility), while it increases group representation, thus addressing the political pressure from advocacy groups. There are, however, potential negative repercussions of a biological paradigm of race and other markers of difference. Examples include the perpetuation of essentialist and subhuman views of groups (particularly of racial minorities) that may endorse violence against them, the erasure of social and structural influences in health and educational outcomes across groups, the justification of racial inequities and marginalization (K. Anderson, 2002; Artiles, 2011; Eberhardt, 2005; Goff, Eberhardt, Williams, & Jackson, 2008; Williams & Eberhardt, 2008), and the consolidation of a "new racial geneism" movement in education—that is, "the belief that genes shape the nature of ethnic group achievements and inequities" (Gillborn, 2016, p. 2). We should be reminded that these developments build on a long-standing tradition of biological reinscription of race in science, law, and medicine that, sadly, has been linked to "the broader history of exclusions, hierarchies, and classifications of the living world on which the modern European taxonomies of race were based" (K. Anderson, 2002, p. 27; see also Duster, 2015; Morning, 2014).

Unfortunately, these trends persist in scientific research—particularly in studies of disability intersections—and although efforts are being made to enhance the visibility and political representation of certain marginalized groups, there is an urgent need for a paradigm expansion that disrupts these legacies. This work entails the articulation of a biocultural–historical perspective on human development that recognizes that "cultural history and phylogeny are interwoven *constituents* of ontogenetic development, not merely *influences.* . . . [T]he brain's potential is not simply a matter of preprogrammed specialized modules, but depends crucially on culturally organized experience" (Cole & Packer, 2016, pp. 6–7). Of significance, scholars are advancing a cultural neuroscience approach to the study of cognitive functions and the architecture of the mind to understand the "complex interplay of genetic and experiential processes. . . . [These scholars argue that this line of research will shed light on] how the human mind and brain shape and are shaped by culture-gene coevolutionary processes" (Chiao & Immordino-Yang, 2013, p. 56). A biocultural paradigm requires the examination of embodied identities, for "bodies can be the sum of their biology; the signifying systems in the culture; the historical, social, political surround; the scientific defining points; the symptom pool; the technological add-ons all combined and yet differentiated" (Davis, 2014, p. 7). In short, a biocultural perspective calls for the "study of the scientificized and medicalized body in history, culture and politics" (Davis, 2006, p. 91).

Forging a biocultural paradigm requires an epistemological reflexivity and innovation to question the long-standing differential appreciation of the "hard" and "soft" sciences in understanding complex phenomena such as disability intersections. A biocultural paradigm can benefit from the scholarship on the social dimensions of science and knowledge production to identify theoretical and methodological shortcomings and the limits and affordances of epistemological practices. It calls for a "community of interpreters, across disciplines, willing to learn from each other" (Davis & Morris, 2014, p. 125). Moreover, a biocultural paradigm can rely on a cultural model of human development that accounts for institutional, interpersonal, and individual influences in individuals' experiences. This standpoint aspires to bring forth an integrated understanding of the interplay of biological and cultural notions of disability that torque and traverse other identity markers (e.g., race and class). Future scholarship should not be satisfied with documenting racial gaps in achievement or

race-associated differences in health outcomes[, for] leaving the basis of those differences poorly explained is not benign but has at least three dangerous consequences. It impedes the advance of scientific knowledge, limits efforts at primary prevention, and contributes to ideas of biologic determinism. (Jones, 2001, p. 302)

The same logic applies to the study of racial disparities in special education (Shifrer et al., 2010). But to fulfill that promise, research must remain flexible in its understanding of human capacity and take advantage of the diversity of scholarship on human development. It must embody an understanding that disability intersections ought to be studied from situated perspectives (Artiles, 2011) and shift the analytic gaze to document nondominant groups' cultural repertoires and the learning they do every day in tight circumstances (Dixon-Román, 2014; McDermott, 2010). As Chris Bell (2011) described it, "The work of reading black and disabled bodies is not only recovery work . . . but work that requires a willingness to deconstruct the systems that would keep those bodies in separate spheres" (p. 3). Disability scholarship in the 21st century must take on the challenge to develop adaptive, socially just, locally meaningful, and sustainable systemic solutions to contemporary systemic crises.

ACKNOWLEDGMENTS

The first author acknowledges the support of the Equity Alliance.

NOTES

[1]Building on Star and Griesemer's (1989) work, we use loosely the term *object* to describe what "people act toward and with; it may be a thing but also, for example, a theory [or a policy]" (Timmermans, 2015, p. 4).

[2]We use the term *cultural-historical* in a broad sense to encompass not only the scholarship on human development that falls under this construct (Cole, 1996), but also interdisciplinary traditions to engage notions of culture, identity differences, power, and historical legacies.

[3]We use intersectional in a broad historical sense, understanding that the relationships among categories have been dynamic and extremely consequential. We draw from the seminal critical race theory work of Crenshaw (1991) and other interdisciplinary scholars.

[4]Although the previous label for this disability category was "mental retardation," we use "ID" to be consistent with contemporary practices. The early history covered in this chapter was grounded in the former term, but we use ID for consistency purposes.

[5]These are

> objects which are both plastic enough to adapt to local needs and the constraints of the several parties employing them, yet robust enough to maintain a common identity across sites. They are weakly structured in common use, and become strongly structured in individual-site use. These objects may be abstract or concrete. They have different meanings in different social worlds but their structure is common enough to more than one world to make them recognizable, a means of translation. The creation and management of boundary objects is a key process in developing and maintaining coherence across intersecting social worlds. (Star & Griesemer, 1989, p. 393)

[6]While Cell focuses on the development of legal segregation codes in the American South and South Africa, racist White concerns about the social "pollution" of public space played a significant role as well in efforts to control political power in the South.

[7]This is in contrast with Gould's (1996) focus on the ideology of scientific racist arguments.

[8] The written history of disability rights reflects the importance of institutional behavior in educational change: In a volume dedicated to tracing grassroots activism in the disability rights movement, Fleischer and Zames's (2012) discussion of education focuses on legislation and lawsuits far more than on the voices of individuals with disabilities.

[9]An open question is the relationship between late 20th-century disability rights activism and earlier disability rights efforts, such as the depression-era employment protests documented by Longmore and Goldberger (2000).

[10]Winzer (1993) has framed the history of special education as a broad trend toward inclusion, a narrative of forward progress different from the argument we present.

[11]Martin, Martin, and Terman (1996) have traced the early postwar legislative origins of federal special education law in the United States; Winzer (1993) has provided a broader context.

[12]These events included the assassination of visible leaders (including the president of the United States and Dr. Martin Luther King), the growing struggles surrounding the civil rights movement, the emergence of the War on Poverty, and the Vietnam War, among others.

[13]More narrowly focused groups such as the Association for Children With Learning Disabilities were able to advocate for specific classification slots—leading to consequences such as the legal definition of SLD in the Children With Specific Learning Disabilities Act of 1969.

[14]Fine and Weis (2003) have discussed silencing as an important educational construct inside schools; we think that it is also a prominent (and equally dangerous) phenomenon in research.

REFERENCES

Albrecht, S. F., Skiba, R. J., Losen, D. J., Chung, C. G., & Middelberg, L. (2012). Federal policy on disproportionality in special education: Is it moving us forward? *Journal of Disability Policy Studies, 23*(1), 14–25.

American Psychiatric Association. (2016). *DSM history.* Retrieved from https://www.psychiatry.org/psychiatrists/practice/dsm/history-of-the-dsm

American Psychological Association. (2006). *Publication manual of the American Psychological Association* (6th ed.). Washington, DC: Author.

Anderson, J. D. (1988). *The education of Blacks in the South, 1860–1935.* Charlotte: University of North Carolina Press.

Anderson, K. (2002). The racialization of difference: Enlarging the story field. *The Professional Geographer, 54*(1), 25–30.

Artiles, A. J. (2003). Special education's changing identity: Paradoxes and dilemmas in views of culture and space. *Harvard Educational Review, 73*, 164–202.

Artiles, A. J. (2011). Toward an interdisciplinary understanding of educational equity and difference: The case of the racialization of ability. *Educational Researcher, 40*, 431–445. doi: 10.3102/0013189X11429391

Artiles, A. J. (2013). Untangling the racialization of disabilities: An intersectionality critique across disability models. *Du Bois Review, 10*, 329–347.

Artiles, A. J. (2014, March). *Future research on the intersections of ability, race, and language differences: Re-framing the roles of history and poverty* (Inaugural lecture). University of Birmingham, Birmingham, UK.

Artiles, A. J. (2015). Beyond responsiveness to identity badges: Future research on culture in disability and implications for RTI. *Educational Review, 67*(1), 1–22.

Artiles, A. J., Bal, A., & King Thorius, K. (2010). Back to the future: A critique of response to intervention's social justice views. *Theory Into Practice, 49*, 250–257.

Artiles, A. J., & Klingner, J. (2006). Forging a knowledge base on English language learners with special needs: Theoretical, population, and technical issues. *Teachers College Record, 108*, 2187–2194.

Artiles, A. J., & Kozleski, E. B. (2016). Inclusive education's promises and trajectories: Critical notes about future research on a venerable idea. *Education Policy Analysis Archives, 24*(43). doi:10.14507/epaa.24.1919. Retrieved from http://epaa.asu.edu/ojs/article/viewFile/1919/1766

Artiles, A. J., Kozleski, E. B., Dorn, S., & Christensen, C. (2006). Learning in inclusive education research: Re-mediating theory and methods with a transformative agenda. *Review of Research in Education, 30*, 65–108.

Artiles, A. J., Kozleski, E. B., Trent, S. C., Osher, D., & Ortiz, A. (2010). Justifying and explaining disproportionality, 1968–2008: A critique of underlying views of culture. *Exceptional Children, 76*, 279–299.

Artiles, A. J., Thorius, K. K., Bal, A., Neal, R., Waitoller, F., & Hernandez-Saca, D. (2011). Beyond culture as group traits: Future learning disabilities ontology, epistemology, and inquiry on research knowledge use. *Learning Disability Quarterly, 34*, 167–179.

Artiles, A. J., & Trent, S. C. (1994). Overrepresentation of minority students in special education: A continuing debate. *Journal of Special Education, 27*, 410–437.

Artiles, A. J., Trent, S. C., & Kuan, L. A. (1997). Learning disabilities empirical research on ethnic minority students: An analysis of 22 years of studies published in selected refereed journals. *Learning Disabilities Research and Practice, 12*(2), 82–91.

Artiles, A. J., Trent, S. C., & Palmer, J. (2004). Culturally diverse students in special education: Legacies and prospects. In J. A. Bank, & C. A. McGee Banks (Eds.), *Handbook of research on multicultural education* (2nd ed., pp. 716–735). San Francisco, CA: Jossey-Bass.

Asad, T. (1979). Anthropology and the colonial encounter. In G. Huizer & B. Mannheim (Eds.), *The politics of anthropology: From colonialism and sexism toward a view from below* (pp. 85–94). Paris, France: Mouton.

Austin, D. M. (1983). The Flexner myth and the history of social work. *Social Service Review, 57*, 357–377.

Baker, B. (2002). The hunt for disability: The new eugenics and the normalization of school children. *Teachers College Record, 104*, 663–703. doi:10.1111/1467-9620.00175

Bal, A. (2016). From intervention to innovation: A cultural-historical approach to the racialization of school discipline. *Interchange: A Quarterly Review of Education, 47*, 409–427.

Bal, A., Better-Bubon, J., & Fish, R. (2016). *A multilevel analysis of statewide disproportionality in exclusionary discipline and the identification of emotional disturbance.* Manuscript submitted for publication.

Bal, A., Kozleski, E. B., Schrader, E. M., Rodriguez, E. M., & Pelton, S. (2014). Systemic transformation in school: Using Learning Lab to design culturally responsive schoolwide positive behavioral supports. *Remedial and Special Education, 35*, 327–339. doi:10.1177/0741932514536995

Bal, A., & Trainor, A. A. (2016). Culturally responsive research rubric for experimental intervention studies: The development of a rubric for paradigm expansion. *Review of Educational Research, 86*, 319–359.

Barclay, J. L. (2011). *Cripples all! Or, The mark of slavery: Disability and race in antebellum America, 1820–1860* (Unpublished dissertation). Michigan State University, East Lansing.

Barclay, J. L. (2014). Mothering the "useless": Black motherhood, disability, and slavery. *Women, Gender, and Families of Color, 2*, 115–140. doi:10.5406/womgenfamcol.2.2.0115

Baynton, D. (2001). Disability and the justification of inequality in American history. In P. K. Longmor, & L. Umansky (Eds.), *The new disability history: American perspectives* (pp. 33–57). New York: New York University Press.

Baynton, D. C. (2005). Defectives in the land: Disability and American immigration policy, 1882–1924. *Journal of American Ethnic History, 24*(3), 31–44.

Bensaude-Vincent, B., & Stengers, I. (1996). *A history of chemistry.* Cambridge, MA: Harvard University Press.

Bell, C. M. (Ed.). (2011). *Blackness and disability.* East Lansing: Michigan State University Press.

Bell, D. A. (1987). *And we are not saved: The elusive quest for racial justice.* New York, NY: Basic Books.

Berry, B., Byrd, A., & Wieder, A. (2013). *Teacherpreneurs: Innovative teachers who lead but don't leave.* San Francisco, CA: John Wiley.

Bobo, L. D. (2011). Somewhere between Jim Crow and post-racialism: Reflections on the racial divide in America today. *Daedalus, 140*(2), 11–36.

Bocian, K. M., Beebe, M. E., MacMillan, D. L., & Gresham, F. M. (1999). Competing paradigms in learning disabilities classification by schools and the variations in the meaning of discrepant achievement. *Learning Disabilities Research and Practice, 14*(1), 1–14.

Boster, D. H. (2015). *African American slavery and disability: Bodies, property and power in the antebellum South, 1800–1860*. New York, NY: Routledge.

Bowker, G. C., & Star, S. L. (2000). *Sorting things out*. Cambridge: MIT Press.

Bradley, R., Danielson, L., & Hallahan, D. (Eds.). (2002). *Identification of learning disabilities: Research to practice*. Mahwah, NJ: Lawrence Erlbaum.

Brantlinger, E. (1997). Using ideology: Cases of nonrecognition of the politics of research and practice in special education. *Review of Educational Research, 67*, 425–459.

Carrier, J. G. (1986). *Learning disability: Social class and the construction of inequality in American education*. Westport, CT: Praeger.

Cavendish, W., Artiles, A. J., & Harry, B. (2014). Tracking inequality 60 years after Brown: Does policy legitimize the racialization of disability? *Multiple Voices for Ethnically Diverse Exceptional Learners, 14*(2), 30–40.

Cecelski, D. S. (1994). *Along freedom road: Hyde County, North Carolina, and the fate of Black schools in the South*. Chapel Hill: University of North Carolina Press.

Cell, J. W. (1982). *The highest stage of White supremacy*. New York, NY: Cambridge University Press.

Chandler, A. D. (1977). *The visible hand: The management revolution in American business*. Cambridge, MA: Belknap.

Chiao, J. Y., & Immordino-Yang, M. H. (2013). Modularity and the cultural mind: Contributions of cultural neuroscience to cognitive theory. *Perspectives on Psychological Science, 8*(1), 56–61.

Children's Defense Fund. (1974). *Children out of school in America*. Boston, MA: Author.

Christensen, C., & Dorn, S. (1997). Competing notions of social justice and contradictions in special education reform. *Journal of Special Education, 31*, 181–198.

Condliffe Lagemann, E. (2000). *An elusive science: The troubling history of education research*. Chicago, IL: University of Chicago Press.

Cole, M. (1996). *Cultural psychology*. Cambridge, MA: Harvard University Press.

Cole, M., & Packer, M. (2016). A bio-cultural-historical approach to the study of development. In M. J. Gelfand, C. Chiu, & Y. Hong (Eds.), *Advances in culture and psychology* (Vol. 6, pp. 1–76). Oxford, England: Oxford University Press.

Connor, D. J. (2008). *Urban narratives: Portraits in progress, life at the intersections of learning disability, race, & social class*. New York, NY: Peter Lang.

Crenshaw, K. (1991). Mapping the margins: Intersectionality, identity politics, and violence against women of color. *Stanford Law Review, 43*, 1241–1299.

Crossley, M. (1999). The disability kaleidoscope. *Notre Dame Law Review, 74*, 621–716.

Danziger, K. (1994). *Constructing the subject: Historical origins of psychological research*. New York, NY: Cambridge University Press.

Darling-Hammond, L. (2007). Race, inequality and educational accountability: The irony of "No Child Left Behind". *Race Ethnicity and Education, 10*, 245–260.

Davis, L. J (2006). Stumped by genes: Lingua gataca, DNA and prosthesis. In M. Smith & J. Morra (Eds.), *The prosthetic impulse: From a posthuman present to a biocultural future* (pp. 91–106). Cambridge: MIT Press.

Davis, L. J. (Ed.). (2014). *The end of normal: Identity in a biocultural era*. Ann Arbor: University of Michigan Press.

Davis, L. J., & Morris, D. (2014). The biocultures manifesto. In L. J. Davis (Ed.), *The end of normal: Identity in a biocultural era* (pp. 121–128). Ann Arbor: University of Michigan Press.

DiMaggio, P., & Powell, W. W. (1983). The iron cage revisited: Collective rationality and institutional isomorphism in organizational fields. *American Sociological Review, 48*(2), 147–160.

Dixon-Román, E. J. (2014). Deviance as pedagogy: From nondominant cultural capital to deviantly marked cultural repertoires. *Teachers College Record, 116*, 1–30.

Donovan, M., & Cross, C. T. (Eds.). (2002). *Minority students in special and gifted education.* Washington, DC: National Academies Press.

Dorn, S. (1996). *Creating the dropout: An institutional and social history of school failure.* Westport, CT: Praeger.

Dorn, S. (2002). Public-private symbiosis in Nashville special education. *History of Education Quarterly, 32,* 368–394.

Dorn, S. (2007). *Accountability Frankenstein: Understanding and taming the monster.* Chapel Hill, NC: Information Age.

Dorn, S., & Johanningmeier, E. V. (1999). Dropping out and the military metaphor for schooling. *History of Education Quarterly, 39,* 193–198.

Du Bois, W. E. B. (1935). *Black reconstruction: An essay toward a history of the part which Black folk played in the attempt to reconstruct democracy in America, 1860–1880.* New York, NY: Harcourt, Brace.

Duchan, J. F., & Kovarsky, D. (2005). Introduction. In J. F. Duchan & D. Kovarsky (Eds.), *Diagnosis as cultural practice* (pp. 1–11). New York, NY: Mouton de Gruyter.

Dumas, M. J. (2014). "Losing an arm": Schooling as a site of black suffering. *Race Ethnicity and Education, 17*(1), 1–29.

Dumit, J. (2004). *Picturing personhood: Brain scans and biomedical identity.* Princeton, NJ: Princeton University Press.

Dunn, L. M. (1968). Special education for the mildly retarded: Is much of it justifiable? *Exceptional Children, 35*(1), 5–22.

Duster, T. (2015). A post-genomic surprise: The molecular reinscription of race in science, law and medicine. *British Journal of Sociology, 66,* 1–27.

Eberhardt, J. L. (2005). Imaging race. *American Psychologist, 60,* 181–190.

Engeström, Y. (2015). *Learning by expanding* (2nd. ed.). New York, NY: Cambridge University Press.

Epstein, S. (2007). *Inclusion: The politics of difference in medical research.* Chicago, IL: University of Chicago Press.

Fine, M., & Weis, L. (2003). *Silenced voices and extraordinary conversations: Re-imagining schools.* New York, NY: Teachers College Press.

Fleischer, D. Z., & Zames, F. (2012). *The disability rights movement: From charity to confrontation.* Philadelphia, PA: Temple University Press.

Franklin, B. M. (1994). *From backwardness to "at-risk".* Albany: State University of New York Press.

Fuchs, D., & Fuchs, L. S. (1994). Inclusive schools movement and the radicalization of special education reform. *Exceptional Children, 60,* 294–309.

Gieryn, T. F. (1983). Boundary-work and the demarcation of science from non-science: Strains and interests in professional ideologies of scientists. *American Sociological Review, 48,* 781–795.

Gieryn, T. F. (1995). Boundaries of science. In S. Jasanoff, G. E. Markle, J. C. Peterson, & T. Pinch (Eds.), *Handbook of science and technology studies* (pp. 393–443). Cambridge: MIT Press.

Gillborn, D. (2016). Softly, softly: Genetics, intelligence and the hidden racism of the new geneism. *Journal of Education Policy.* Advance online publication. doi:10.1080/0268093 9.2016.1139189

Gilmore, R. W. (2002). Fatal couplings of power and difference: Notes on racism and geography. *The Professional Geographer, 54*(1), 15–24.

Gliedman, J., & Roth, W. (1980). *The unexpected minority: Handicapped children in America.* New York, NY: Harcourt Brace Jovanovich.

Goff, P. A., Eberhardt, J. L., Williams, M. J., & Jackson, M. C. (2008). Not yet human: Implicit knowledge, historical dehumanization, and contemporary consequences. *Journal of Personality and Social Psychology, 94,* 292–306.

Goldstein, D. (2014). *The teacher wars: A history of America's most embattled profession.* New York, NY: Knopf Doubleday.

Goodwin, C. (1994). Professional vision. *American Anthropologist, 96,* 606–633.

Gould, S. J. (1996). *The mismeasure of man.* New York, NY: W. W. Norton.

Graebner, W. (1977). Federalism in the Progressive Era: A structural interpretation of reform. *Journal of American History, 64,* 331–357.

Graebner, W. (1980). *A history of retirement.* New Haven, CT: Yale University Press.

Graham, S. (1992). "Most of the subjects were White and middle class": Trends in published research on African Americans in selected APA journals, 1970–1989. *American Psychologist, 47,* 629–639. doi:10.1037/0003-066X.47.5.629

Green, S., Davis, C., Karshmer, E., Marsh, P., & Straight, B. (2005). Living stigma: The impact of labeling, stereotyping, separation, status loss, and discrimination in the lives of individuals with disabilities and their families. *Sociological Inquiry, 75,* 197–215.

Greenbaum, S. D. (2015). *Blaming the poor: The long shadow of the Moynihan Report on cruel images about poverty.* New Brunswick, NJ: Rutgers University Press.

Grossberg, M. (2011). Liberation and caretaking: Fighting over children's rights in postwar America. In P. S. Fass & M. Grossberg (Eds.), *Reinventing childhood after World War II* (pp. 19–37). Philadelphia, PA: University of Pennsylvania Press.

Hacking, I. (1999). *The social construction of what?* Cambridge, MA: Harvard University Press.

Hallahan, D. P., Pullen, P. C., & Ward, D. (2013). A brief history of the field of learning disabilities. In H. L. Swanson, K. Harris, & S. Graham (Eds.). *Handbook of learning disabilities* (pp. 15–32). New York, NY: Guilford Press.

Harry, B., & Klingner, J. K. (2014). *Why are so many minority students in special education?* New York, NY: Teachers College Press.

Harvey, D. (2012). *Rebel cities: From the right to the city to the urban revolution.* London, England: Verso.

Heller, K. A., Holtzman, W. H., & Messick, S. (Eds.). (1982). *Placing children in special education: A strategy for equity.* Washington, DC: National Academy Press.

Hendrick, I. G., & MacMillan, D. L. (1989). Selecting children for special education in New York City: William Maxwell, Elizabeth Farrell, and the development of ungraded classes, 1900–1920. *Journal of Special Education, 22,* 395–417.

Hess, F. M. (2015). *The cage-busting teacher.* Cambridge, MA: Harvard Education Press.

Johanningmeier, E. V., & Richardson, T. R. (2008). *Educational research, the national agenda, and educational reform: A history.* Chapel Hill, NC: Information Age.

Jončich, G. M. (1968). *The sane positivist: A biography of Edward L. Thorndike.* Middleton, CT: Wesleyan University Press.

Jones, C. P. (2001). "Race," racism, and the practice of epidemiology. *American Journal of Epidemiology, 154,* 299–304.

Jordan, W. D. (1968). *White over Black: American attitudes towards the Negro, 1550–1812.* Chapel Hill: University of North Carolina Press.

Katz, M. B. (1996). *In the shadow of the poorhouse: A social history of welfare in America.* New York, NY: Basic Books.

Katznelson, I., & Weir, M. (1985). *Schooling for all: Class, race, and the decline of the democratic ideal.* Berkeley: University of California Press.

Labaree, D. F. (1988). *The making of an American high school: The credentials market and the Central High School of Philadelphia, 1838–1939.* New Haven, CT: Yale University Press.

Ladson-Billings, G. (2004). Landing on the wrong note: The price we paid for Brown. *Educational Researcher, 33*(7), 3–13.

Latour, B. (1999). *Pandora's hope.* Cambridge, MA: Harvard University Press.

Lefebvre, H. (1988). Toward a leftist cultural politics: Remarks occasioned by the centenary of Marx's death. In C. Nelson & L. Grossberg (Eds.), *Marxism and the interpretation of culture* (pp. 75–88). Urbana: University of Illinois Press.

Lewis, D. (1973). Anthropology and colonialism. *Current Anthropology, 14*, 581–602.

Logue, L. M., & Blanck, P. (2010). *Race, ethnicity, and disability: Veterans and benefits in post–Civil War America.* New York, NY: Cambridge University Press.

Longmore, P. K., & Goldberger, D. (2000). The league of the physically handicapped and the great depression: A case study in the new disability history. *Journal of American History, 87*, 888–922.

Lyon, G. R. (1996). Learning disabilities. *Future of Children, 6*(1), 54–76.

Martin, E. W., Martin, R., & Terman, D. L. (1996). The legislative and litigation history of special education. *Future of Children, 6*, 25–39.

Mazzeo, C. (2001). Frameworks of state: Assessment policy in historical perspective. *Teachers College Record, 103*, 367–397.

McDermott, R. (2010). The passions of learning in tight circumstances: Toward a political economy of the mind. *National Society for the Study of Education, 109*, 144–159.

McLoyd, V. C., & Randolph, S. M. (1985). Secular trends in the study of Afro-American children: A review of "child development," 1936–1980. *Monographs of the Society for Research in Child Development, 50*, 78–92.

Menchaca, M. (1997). Early racist discourses: Roots of deficit thinking. In R. Valencia (Ed.), *The evolution of deficit thinking: Educational thought and practice* (pp. 13–41). London, England: RoutledgeFarmer.

Mercer, J. R. (1973). *Labeling the mentally retarded.* Berkeley: University of California Press.

Mills, C. W. (1997). *The racial contract.* Ithaca, NY: Cornell University Press.

Molina, N. (2006). Medicalizing the Mexican: Immigration, race, and disability in the early twentieth-century United States. *Radical History Review, 2006*(94), 22–37.

Morawska, E. (2003). *For bread with butter: The life-worlds of East Central Europeans in Johnstown, Pennsylvania, 1890–1940.* Cambridge, England: Cambridge University Press.

Morning, A. (2014). And you thought we had moved beyond all that: Biological race returns to the social sciences. *Ethnic and Racial Studies, 37*, 1676–1685.

Ng, J. C., & Rury, J. (2006, July 18). Poverty and education: A critical analysis of the Ruby Payne phenomenon. *Teachers College Record.* Retrieved from http://www.tcrecord.org/library/Abstract.asp?ContentId=12596

Nichols, S., & Berliner, D. (2007). *Collateral damage. How high-stakes testing corrupts America's schools.* Cambridge, MA: Harvard Education Press.

Nieto, S. (2003). Puerto Rican students in U.S. schools: A troubled past and the search for a hopeful future. In J. A. Banks & C. A. McGee Banks (Eds.), *Handbook of research on multicultural education* (pp. 515–541). San Francisco, CA: Jossey-Bass.

Okonofua, J. A., & Eberhardt, J. L. (2015). Two strikes: Race and the disciplining of young students. *Psychological Science, 26*, 617–624.

Olneck, M. R. (1989). Americanization and the education of immigrants, 1900–1925: An analysis of symbolic action. *American Journal of Education, 97*, 398–423.

Pelka, F. (2012). *What we have done: An oral history of the disability rights movement.* Amherst: University of Massachusetts Press.

Pfeiffer, D. (1993). Overview of the disability movement: History, legislative record, and political implications. *Policy Studies Journal, 21*, 724–734.

Ponterotto, J. G. (1988). Racial/ethnic minority research in the *Journal of Counseling Psychology*: A content analysis and methodological critique. *Journal of Counseling Psychology, 35*, 410–418.

Popkewitz, T. S. (1997). A changing terrain of knowledge and power: A social epistemology of educational research. *Educational Researcher, 26*(9), 18–29.

Powell, J. J. W. (2011). *Barriers to inclusion: Special education in the United States and Germany.* Boulder, CO: Paradigm.

Provasnik, S. (2006). Judicial activism and the origins of parental choice: The court's role in the institutionalization of compulsory education in the United States, 1891–1925. *History of Education Quarterly, 46*, 311–347.

Reese, W. J. (2013). *Testing wars in the public schools.* Cambridge, MA: Harvard University Press.

Reschly, D. J., & Hosp, J. L. (2004). State SLD identification policies and practices. *Learning Disability Quarterly, 27,* 197–213.

Richardson, J. G. (2000). The variable construction of educational risk. In M. T. Hallinan (Ed.), *Handbook of the sociology of education* (pp. 307–323). New York, NY: Springer.

Richardson, J. G., & Parker, T. L. (1993). The institutional genesis of special education: The American case. *American Journal of Education, 101,* 359–392.

Robert F. Kennedy Memorial & Southern Regional Council. (1973). *The student pushout: Victim of continued resistance to desegregation.* Atlanta, GA: Author.

Rogoff, B. (2003). *The cultural nature of human development.* Oxford, England: Oxford University Press.

Ross, D. (1991). *The origins of American social science.* New York, NY: Cambridge University Press.

Sampson, R. J., & Winter, A. S. (2016). The racial ecology of lead poisoning: Toxic inequality in Chicago neighborhoods, 1995–2013. *Du Bois Review, 13,* 261–283. doi:10.1017/S1742058X16000151

Scheid, T. L., & Suchman, M. C. (2001). Ritual conformity to the Americans With Disabilities Act: Coercive and normative isomorphism. In S. W. Hartwell & R. K. Schutt (Eds.), *The organizational response to social problems* (pp. 105–140). Bradford, England: Emerald Group.

Schweik, S. M. (2009). *The ugly laws: Disability in public.* New York: New York University Press.

Scotch, R. K. (1989). Politics and policy in the history of the disability rights movement. *Milbank Quarterly, 67*(Suppl. 3), 380–400.

Scott, J. C. (1998). *Seeing like a state: How certain schemes to improve the human condition have failed.* New Haven, CT: Yale University Press.

Shapiro, J. P. (1994). *No pity: People with disabilities forging a new civil rights movement.* New York, NY: Three Rivers Press.

Shifrer, D., Muller, C., & Callahan, R. (2010). Disproportionality: A sociological perspective of the identification by schools of students with learning disabilities. *Research in Social Science and Disability, 5,* 279–308.

Shircliffe, B. J. (2006). *The best of that world: Historically black high schools and the crisis of desegregation in a southern metropolis.* New York, NY: Hampton Press.

Shore, C., Wright, S., & Però, D. (Eds.). (2011). *Policy worlds: Anthropology and the analysis of contemporary power.* New York, NY: Berghahn Books.

Siddle-Walker, V. (1996). *Their highest potential.* Chapel Hill: University of North Carolina Press.

Sigmon, S. B. (1987). *Radical analysis of special education: Focus on historical development and learning disabilities.* New York, NY: Routledge.

Skiba, R. J., Chung, C. G., Trachok, M., Baker, T. L., Sheya, A., & Hughes, R. L. (2014). Parsing disciplinary disproportionality. *American Educational Research Journal, 51,* 640–670.

Skiba, R. J., Poloni-Staudinger, L., Simmons, A. B., Feggins-Azziz, L. R., & Chung, C. G. (2005). Unproven links: Can poverty explain ethnic disproportionality in special education? *Journal of Special Education, 39*(3), 130–144.

Skiba, R. J., Simmons, A. B., Ritter, S., Gibb, A. C., Rausch, M. K., Cuadrado, J., & Chung, C. G. (2008). Achieving equity in special education: History, status, and current challenges. *Exceptional Children, 74,* 264–288.

Skocpol, T. (1992). *Protecting soldiers and mothers: The political origins of social policy in the United States.* Cambridge, MA: Harvard University Press.

Skowronek, S. (1982). *Building a new American state: The expansion of national administrative capacities, 1877–1920*. New York, NY: Cambridge University Press.

Sleeter, C. E. (1986). Learning disabilities: The social construction of a special education category. *Exceptional Children, 53*(1), 46–54.

Soja, E. W. (2010). *Seeking spatial justice*. Minneapolis: University of Minnesota Press.

Star, S. L., & Griesemer, J. R. (1989). Institutional ecology, "translations" and boundary objects: Amateurs and professionals in Berkeley's Museum of Vertebrate Zoology, 1907–39. *Social Studies of Science, 19*, 387–420.

Star, S. L., & Ruhleder, K. (1996). Steps toward an ecology of infrastructure: Design and access for large information spaces. *Information Systems Research, 7*, 111–134.

Swanson, H. L., Harris, K. R., & Graham, S. (2013). Overview of foundations, causes, instruction, and methodology in the field of learning disabilities. In H. L. Swanson, K. R. Harris, & S. Graham (Eds.), *Handbook of learning disabilities* (pp. 3–14). New York, NY: Guilford Press.

Tate, W. F. (1997). Critical race theory and education: History, theory, and implications. *Review of Research in Education, 22*, 195–247.

Tate, W. F. (2008). "Geography of opportunity": Poverty, place, and educational outcomes. *Educational Researcher, 37*, 397–411.

Timmermans, S. (2015). Introduction: Working with Leigh Star. In G. C. Bowker, S. Timmermans, A. E. Clarke, & E. Balka (Eds.), *Boundary objects and beyond: Working with Leigh Star* (pp. 1–9). Cambridge: MIT Press.

Trent, J. W., Jr. (1994). *Inventing the feeble mind: A history of mental retardation in the United States*. Berkeley: University of California Press.

Trent, S., Driver, M., Rodriguez, D., Oh, K., Stewart, S., Kea, C., . . . Hull, M. (2014). Beyond Brown: Empirical research on culturally and linguistically diverse learners with or at-risk for specific learning disabilities from 1994 to 2012. *Multiple Voices for Ethnically Diverse Exceptional Learners, 14*(2), 12–29.

Tropea, J. L. (1987). Bureaucratic order and special children: Urban schools, 1950s–1960s. *History of Education Quarterly, 27*, 339–361.

Tyack, D. (1968). The perils of pluralism: The background of the Pierce case. *American Historical Review, 74*, 74–98.

Tyack, D. (1974). *The one best system*. Cambridge, MA: Harvard University Press.

Tyack, D., & Hansot, E. (1982). *Managers of virtue: Public school leadership in America, 1820–1980*. New York, NY: Basic Books.

Ureta, S. (2014). Policy assemblages: Proposing an alternative conceptual framework to study public action. *Policy Studies, 35*, 303–318.

U.S. Department of Education. (2015). *The 37th annual report to Congress on the implementation of the Individuals With Disabilities Education Act*. Washington, DC: Author.

Vasquez, E., III, Lopez, A., Straub, C., Powell, S., McKinney, T., Walker, Z., . . . Bedesem, P. L. (2011). Empirical research on ethnic minority students: 1995–2009. *Learning Disabilities Research and Practice, 26*(2), 84–93.

Valli, L., & Buese, D. (2007). The changing roles of teachers in an era of high-stakes accountability. *American Educational Research Journal, 44*, 519–558.

Veysey, L. R. (1965). *The emergence of the American university*. Chicago, IL: University of Chicago Press.

Waitoller, F. R., Artiles, A. J., & Cheney, D. A. (2010). The miner's canary: A review of overrepresentation research and explanations. *Journal of Special Education, 44*, 29–49.

Weatherley, R., & Lipsky, M. (1977). Street-level bureaucrats and institutional innovation: Implementing special-education reform. *Harvard Educational Review, 47*, 171–197.

Williams, M. J., & Eberhardt, J. L. (2008). Biological conceptions of race and the motivation to cross racial boundaries. *Journal of Personality and Social Psychology, 94*, 1033–1047.

Winzer, M. A. (1993). *The history of special education: From isolation to integration.* Washington, DC: Gallaudet University Press.

Woolgar, S., & Lezaun, J. (2013). The wrong bin bag: A turn to ontology in science and technology studies? *Social Studies of Science, 43,* 321–340.

Yell, M. L., & Drasgow, E. (2000). Litigating a free appropriate public education: The Lovaas hearings and cases. *Journal of Special Education, 33,* 205–214.

Zehler, A. M., Fleischman, H. L., Hopstock, P. J., Stephenson, T. G., Pendzick, M. L., & Sapru, S. (2003). *Descriptive study of services to LEP students and LEP students with disabilities. Volume I: Research report.* Arlington, VA: Development Associates, Inc.

Zelizer, V. A. R. (1985). *Pricing the priceless child: The changing social value of children.* Princeton, NJ: Princeton University Press.

Chapter 22

Connecting the Present to the Past: Furthering the Research on Bilingual Education and Bilingualism

DORIS LUFT BAKER
DENI LEE BASARABA
PAUL POLANCO
Southern Methodist University

The authors of this chapter review empirical studies that have been conducted in bilingual education to propose a future research agenda that incorporates the most recent evidence on the effectiveness of bilingual programs, advances in neuroscience, and the body of evidence of the benefits of being bilingual and biliterate. They first describe the historical and sociopolitical precedent of how bilingual education came to play a determinant role in U.S. education. Next, they summarize reviews that have been conducted examining the effects of bilingual education on the academic performance of English learners from 1985 until 2003. They then review the research on bilingual education since 2003. Although the majority of studies reviewed focused on reading, the authors also found studies that compared the effects of bilingual programs on other academic outcomes such as writing, science, and mathematics, inside and outside the United States. In addition, they address the benefits of bilingualism on cognition and discuss the research on cross-linguistic transfer to help the reader better understand the transfer of skills between the native language and the second language within the context of bilingual programs. They end the chapter with recommendations for future research.

Twenty-four years ago, the journal *Educational Researcher* published a special issue on bilingual education. In the introductory article, Pease-Alvarez and Hakuta (1992) suggested that bilingualism was mainly associated with sociocultural theory, implying that learning a second language (L2) was closely connected to personal identity, cultural identification, and communicative effectiveness and was influenced by attitudes toward and beliefs about the native language (L1) and the language being learned. Pease-Alvarez and Hakuta also proposed that education researchers needed to confront practical problems related to the needs of bilingual students and contribute to advances in basic research on bilingual education and bilingualism. Basic research implies including a detailed description of participants and instructional

Review of Research in Education
March 2016, Vol. 40, pp. 821–883
DOI: 10.3102/0091732X16660691
© 2016 AERA. http://rre.aera.net

practices, particularly when examining different bilingual programs (Hakuta, 2011). In addition, basic bilingual education research should focus on measuring how L1 and L2 interact and how the development of language proficiency and content knowledge among bilingual students compares with that of monolingual students. These differences should also be investigated in students with and without learning disabilities (Goldenberg, 2013; Hakuta, 1987).

Twenty years later, Hakuta (2011) called for the continuation of basic research to create a stronger knowledge base investigating the effectiveness of bilingual education in relevant settings. Thus, the purpose of this chapter is to provide a comprehensive review of recent studies examining the effectiveness of bilingual programs, as well as a better understanding of the sociocultural context for conducting bilingual research. This considers (a) the recent proliferation of research studies and books about bilingual education, (b) the apparent increase in bilingual programs across the country, and (c) the evidence suggesting that English-only (EO) policies, such as those advanced by Proposition 227 in California, Proposition 203 in Arizona (Arizona Department of Education, 1998), and Ballot Question 2 in Massachusetts (see Commonwealth of Massachusetts, 2002), do not improve the English language proficiency of English learners (ELs; Guo & Koretz, 2013; F. López, McEneaney, & Neiswandt, 2015; Parrish et al., 2006).

Our chapter is organized as follows. First, we discuss issues with the terminology used in bilingual research and summarize the academic performance of bilingual students in the United States. Second, we briefly review the historical and sociocultural background of bilingual education that has led to the acceptance or rejection of bilingual education in the United States as an anchor for discussing the future of bilingual education. Third, we summarize findings from reviews on bilingual education that have been published since 1985. Fourth, we review selected empirical studies of bilingual programs inside and outside the United States that have been published since 2003. Fifth, we summarize studies on cross-linguistic transfer and cognition as they relate to bilingual education. We conclude with suggestions for future research and practice. Overall, we focus on the effects of bilingual education programs and bilingualism on ELs, as well as studies that include English-only students (EOs) acquiring an L2.

TERMINOLOGY

An issue that has contributed to the controversies surrounding bilingual education has been the terminology used to address a growing population of bilingual students worldwide. As Table 1 illustrates, this group includes students who are labeled *English language learners, dual language learners, English learners, students with limited English proficiency* (*LEP*), and *emergent bilinguals.*

Although these terms, in general, refer to students who speak a language other than English as their L1, each term reflects a somewhat different perspective on how the needs of bilingual students should be addressed and/or the priorities a state

TABLE 1

Labels Referring to Bilingual Students Used in the Chapter or in the Reviewed Studies

Term	Definition
Dual language learner (*DLL*)	Students who are still developing language skills in Spanish at the same time that they are learning how to speak, read, and write in English (Center for Applied Linguistics, 2015)
Emergent bilingual (*EB*)	Children (ages 3–5) who speak a native language other than English and are in the dynamic process of developing bilingual and biliterate competencies with the support of their communities (García, Kleifgen, & Falchi, 2008)
English language learner (*ELL*)/*English learner* (*EL*)	Students whose first language is not English and who are in the process of learning English (Parrish et al., 2006); in this chapter, we use the term *EL*
English-only (*EO*)/*non-LEP*/*non-ELL*	Students who do not speak a language other than English at home (Guo & Koretz, 2013)
Limited English proficient (*LEP*)	Term used to identify students who have insufficient English to succeed in English-only classrooms (Goldenberg, Reese, & Rezaei, 2011)

or school district has established to improve academic outcomes in an environment where the societal language is English. For example, the term *emergent bilingual* refers to children who have the possibility of becoming bilingual if they are instructed in both languages, whether they speak English or another language as their L1 (Garcia, Kleifgen, & Falchi, 2008). The term *limited English proficient* (*LEP*) has been used to refer to students who speak a language other than English as their L1 and who are limited in their English skills and therefore cannot benefit adequately from mainstream English instruction (Goldenberg, Reese, & Rezaei, 2011). The term has been criticized by researchers and practitioners who argue that it emphasizes the deficiencies of students who speak an L1 other than English rather than acknowledging that being bilingual likely increases their cognitive skills and provides them with better educational and economic opportunities (Agirdag, 2014; Calvo & Bialystok, 2013).

It is also difficult to determine the most appropriate term to refer to students who speak only English at home and are attending bilingual programs. These students are most commonly known as English-only (EO), non-LEP, or non–English language learners (non-ELLs; Guo & Koretz, 2013). In this chapter, for consistency and clarity, we use the term *English learner* (*EL*) to refer to U.S. students who do not speak English as their only language at home, and *English-only* (*EO*) to refer to U.S. students who speak only English at home. For studies that include participants outside the United States, we use the terminology used by the authors of those studies.

The terms that define bilingual programs are equally ambiguous. For example, programs where English and an L1 are used have been called *bilingual, dual language, two-way immersion, transitional bilingual* (early and late exit), and *developmental*, among other things. Although these terms describe very different bilingual programs (see Table 2), they are often used in similar ways, which makes it difficult for parents and others to understand the differences among programs and their potential advantages or disadvantages. For example, a transitional bilingual program (TBP) can be defined as a program where students are (a) taught entirely in their L1 for 1 or 2 years, (b) taught in their L1 throughout elementary school with some English language development (ELD) instruction (Slavin & Cheung, 2005), or (c) taught in their L1 for a certain percentage of the time each day (e.g., 30%) and in English for the rest of the time. In other words, in bilingual programs, the amount of time taught in each language in each grade can vary by school, classroom, or even time of year (D. L. Baker, Burns, Kame'enui, Smolkowski, & Baker, & 2015; Umansky et al., 2015). For the purposes of this chapter, we will use the following terminology to discuss the three most common kinds of programs currently in place: English immersion (EI) programs, where students receive mainly instruction in English; TBPs, in which students receive L1 instruction for a few years with some English instruction (e.g., ELD) before they are immersed in EO instruction; and dual language programs (DLPs), where students (ELs, or EOs and ELs) are taught in L1 and L2 from kindergarten with the goal of becoming balanced bilinguals (equally proficient in both languages). In our review of studies on bilingual programs we provide the specific amount of instructional time allocated to each language.

Historically, the question of whether bilingual instruction increases or reduces student learning opportunities has been controversial, and the most serious concerns about this type of instruction were not raised until 50 years ago with the immigration to the United States of large numbers of individuals whose first language is not English (D. L. Baker, Richards-Tutor, Gersten, Baker, & Smith, in press). According to the U.S. Census Bureau (2015), currently more than 400 languages are spoken in the United States; Spanish is by far the most widely spoken other than English (i.e., more than 37 million people speak Spanish), followed by Chinese (2.9 million), Tagalog (the official language of the Philippines, 1.5 million), Vietnamese (1.4 million), Korean (1.1 million), and German (1 million). The main concern in schools responsible for educating large numbers of ELs is the challenge of teaching and learning English in addition to the usual academic content.

To illustrate the problem, examination of recent data from the 2013 National Assessment of Educational Progress (NAEP; Kena et al., 2015) indicates that ELs scored significantly below EOs on the fourth- and eighth-grade assessments of reading (by 38 and 45 points, respectively) and mathematics (by 25 and 41 points, respectively). It is important to point out, however, that language proficiency can be confounded with low socioeconomic status (SES) and immigration status (Umansky & Reardon, 2014). Hispanics, for example, are more likely to live in poverty compared to Whites (33% of Hispanics are poor, compared to 13% of Whites; Kena

TABLE 2
Labels Referring to Bilingual Programs Used in the Chapter or in the Reviewed Studies

Program Label	Definition
50/50 Content model	Mathematics instruction is provided in all grades in English while social studies and science instruction is in Spanish. Language arts instruction is provided in the native language (L1) in pre-K and K and then in the second language (L2) in Grades 1–5. Language of instruction for non–content area–related instruction (announcements, calendar, physical education, etc.) alternates daily from English to Spanish. Students work in bilingual pairs in which English-dominant students are paired with Spanish-dominant students (Gómez, Freeman, & Freeman, 2005).
English as a second language (ESL)	Instruction aims to develop the English skills of students with limited English proficiency. ESL may or may not be content based (Guo & Koretz, 2013).
English for speakers of other languages (ESOL)/ESL	This bilingual model involves individualized instruction focusing on students' acquisition of English language skills (Guo & Koretz, 2013).
ESL pullout	ELs are removed from the mainstream classroom for a portion of the day to receive individualized instruction with an ESL teacher. This method is more common in elementary schools (Guo & Koretz, 2013).
ESL push-in	An ESL teacher works with ELs in the larger mainstream classroom setting (Guo & Koretz, 2013).
Late exit/ developmental/ maintenance	ELs receive a substantial portion of educational instruction in their native language for several years of schooling. The goal is to develop both languages equally so as not to lose the L1 but rather use it to support L2 (Tong, Irby, et al., 2008).
Paired bilingual	Children learn to read in both English and their native language during different time periods each day or on alternating days. Within a few years, the native language reading instruction may be discontinued as children develop the skills to succeed in English (Slavin & Cheung, 2005).
Sheltered English immersion (SEI)	Nearly all classroom instruction is in English but with the curriculum and presentation designed for children who are learning the language. Although teachers may use a minimal amount of the child's native language when necessary, no subject matter is taught in any language other than English, and children in this program learn to read and write solely in English (Commonwealth of Massachusetts, 2002). In the case of structured English immersion models (a form of SEI), teachers have a bilingual education endorsement or ESL credential and understand the students' first language. In the law, SEI and structured English immersion are used interchangeably (Parrish et al., 2006).
Submersion	ELs are not offered any special language services, and instruction is entirely in English. This is often referred to as the "sink or swim" approach (Francis, Lesaux, & August, 2006).

(continued)

TABLE 2 (CONTINUED)

Program Label	Definition
Transitional bilingual program (TBP)	Children are taught to read primarily in their native language through the early elementary grades. Then they transition to instruction in English reading. The hallmark of TBPs is teaching reading in the native language for a period of time. Children in these programs are initially taught mostly in their native language and later are shifted gradually to English instruction (Guo & Koretz, 2013).
TBP early exit	Students transition to English instruction by second or third grade.
TBP late exit	Students receive native language instruction throughout elementary school (Slavin & Cheung, 2005). Late exit programs may use home language instruction 40% of the time or more throughout the elementary school years, even for students who have been reclassified as fluent English proficient (Parrish et al., 2006).
Academic language acquisition (ALA)	Instruction is divided into language blocks throughout the school day. The goal is for students to become proficient in English and in the general curriculum by using the L1. In general, there are three achievement goals of ALA: academic, linguistic, and psychosocial (Hoffstetter, 2004).
Extended foreign language (EFL)	Instruction is about 70% in English and 30% in Spanish. In the study reviewed here, students received 2 hours of English language arts, 30 minutes of independent reading, 30 minutes of social studies in English, 1 hour of mathematics in English, 1 hour of Spanish language arts, and 30 minutes of science in Spanish (M. G. López & Tashakkori, 2004b).
Two-way immersion	Both native English speakers and native speakers of the partner language are enrolled in this dual language program. Neither group makes up more than two thirds of the class. Core academic instruction is provided in both languages (Center for Applied Linguistics, 2015).
Two-way bilingual education	The goal is to facilitate the development of L2 skills while maintaining and enhancing L1 skills and the cultural integrity of students from both the minority and majority language groups (M. G. López & Tashakkori, 2006).

et al., 2015). Hispanics also constitute the majority of ELs at 76.5% (Excelencia in Education, 2015). What is striking, however, is that most ELs who struggle academically are second- and third-generation students who were born in the United States (Hamilton, Martin, & Ventura, 2010). Thus, immigration cannot always fully explain low academic achievement, or English language proficiency. Moreover, NAEP data can also be complex to interpret because they do not adjust for ELs who have been reclassified as EOs (i.e., students who were ELs and are now judged to be fluent English proficient and sufficiently prepared for EO classrooms without EL instructional supports). Once reclassification occurs, it is more difficult to track students and determine, when they struggle, whether their low academic performance is due to continued difficulties in L2 acquisition or to learning difficulties, especially with academic content. Thus, it is possible that more ELs are struggling academically than the numbers indicated by the NAEP assessments (Umansky et al., 2015).

In summary, the diversity of the EL population and the lack of clarity in describing the bilingual programs and the students attending the programs (ELs and EOs) are important to address in future research, particularly considering the rapid increase of the EL population and the increase in the demand for bilingual programs in the country (K. López, 2014; Maxwell, 2012; Reljic, Ferrig, & Martin, 2015). Next, we summarize briefly the history of bilingual education in the United States to anchor our findings from the reviews cited, and to provide guidance for future research.

HISTORICAL AND SOCIOCULTURAL BACKGROUND OF BILINGUAL EDUCATION

Historically, the United States has been a bilingual country (August, Goldenberg, & Rueda, 2010), and bilingual education policies have shifted over time according to changing events (Crawford, 2004). Ovando (2003) argues that the shift in support or rejection of bilingualism through history has occurred not because of a shift in systematic ideas about language, but rather as a consequence of changing localized politics and social and economic forces. In the middle of the 19th century, bilingual education was supported and provided in more than 25 states. For example, schools could teach in Czech in Texas; in Spanish in the Southwest; in German in Colorado, Illinois, Indiana, Maryland, Missouri, Nebraska, Ohio, Oregon, and Pennsylvania; and in Swedish, Norwegian, and Danish in Illinois, Iowa, Minnesota, Nebraska, North Dakota, South Dakota, Washington, and Wisconsin. German was, by far, the most widely spoken language; by 1900, more than 600,000 children were being instructed in German (Kloss, 1977; Ovando, 2003). Stricter enforcement of linguistic assimilation started around 1880 with concerns about linguistic, cultural, and ideological competition between English and other languages (Salomone, 2010).

As a result, attitudes and legislation throughout the United States began to focus more on supporting the development of English language skills in schools. This approach became more widespread during World War I, when teaching in German and other foreign languages during school hours was forbidden because it was considered a threat to the state. The antagonistic attitude toward the teaching in foreign languages (particularly German) led to the Supreme Court case *Meyer v. Nebraska* (1923), in which the Court ruled that the prohibition of teaching in a foreign language in schools prior to eighth grade was unconstitutional. Similar prohibitions were annulled in Iowa and Ohio (Kloss, 1977).

After World War II, with the beginning of the Cold War, the educational focus shifted toward teaching math and science skills because they were essential for military, business, and diplomatic reasons. The lack of emphasis on teaching foreign languages, however, led to the National Defense Education Act of 1958, which had as one of its primary goals increasing foreign language education (Crawford, 2004). This shift in perspective coincided with the Cuban Revolution in 1959 and the Civil Rights Movement in the 1960s. The immigration of Cubans fleeing the revolution led to the creation of a very successful bilingual program at Coral Way Elementary in

Dade County, Florida. Key to its success was the strong support of professional Cuban parents, well-trained Cuban teachers, and federal assistance through the Cuban Refugee Act (Crawford, 2004).

The Civil Rights Movement emboldened Mexican Americans and Puerto Ricans to fight against segregation and lack of educational opportunities for their communities. Although the movement to improve the conditions and opportunities for Hispanics has received less media attention than the movement to end racial segregation and discrimination against African Americans (Dauphine, 2014; Nuñez, 2009), the activities were extensive. An example of Hispanic efforts to end discrimination was Aspira. The movement was started in New York by activists in the Puerto Rican community, and its aim was to improve the living conditions and educational opportunities of Hispanics. Aspira is considered to be the first national educational and leadership development institution in the Puerto Rican community in the United States (Enck-Wanzer, 2006; Nuñez, 2009).

Another important historical event in support of bilingual education was the 1965 Immigration Act, signed into law by President Lyndon B. Johnson. This law revoked previous immigration policies that were based on a quota system with allocations assigned to nationalities according to their representation in past U.S. Census figures. The purposes of the new law were to reunite families whose members were separated by social and political conflicts and to attract skilled labor to the United States. As a result, 18 million immigrants (3 times more than in the preceding 30 years) entered the country, most of them from Asia and Latin America. This large immigration led to a rebirth of bilingual education as most immigrants spoke very little, if any, English (C. Baker, 2011). The same year, Congress also passed the Elementary and Secondary Education Act (ESEA), which provided assistance to educational agencies, through Title I, to support the education of children of low-income families. Although ESEA did not directly support bilingual education programs, it did provide additional funds to schools that served a large number of ELs who were also low-income.

Each of these historical events contributed to the eventual passage of the Bilingual Education Act of 1968, which was intended to assist school districts with the establishment of educational programs for immigrant children who did not speak English (Lyons, 2013). The Bilingual Education Act implied an acknowledgment by the federal government that immigrant children who did not speak English at home experienced unique language-based challenges in meeting educational goals (Gándara, 2015) and that, therefore, federal funding was needed to establish innovative educational programs for them. School districts could apply for the funds through grants intended for (a) purchasing educational programs, (b) training teachers and teacher aides, (c) developing and disseminating educational materials, and (d) involving parents in the education of their children. Funding, however, did not explicitly require schools to provide bilingual instruction (Stewner-Manzanares, 1988).

Nonetheless, bilingual programs began to proliferate, more to reduce social and economic inequalities than to develop the linguistic skills of all children, particularly ELs

(Gándara, 2015). As a result, several civil lawsuits were filed alleging that equal opportunities were being denied to immigrant students. One highly influential case, *Lau vs. Nichols* (1974), was brought against the San Francisco school district alleging that 1,800 Chinese students were being denied equal education because of their limited English skills. The Supreme Court ruled in favor of the children, stating that children who did not understand the language of instruction were being denied equal educational opportunity and that, therefore, the district had violated the civil right of equal treatment for non–English-speaking students. School districts were subsequently required to provide "appropriate action" as evidence that their programs met the academic, linguistic, and sociocultural needs of students. If school districts were not in compliance with the guidelines, they would be denied federal funds (Ovando & Collier, 1998).

The term *appropriate action*, however, was not clearly defined. This lack of specificity led to *Castañeda v. Pickard* (1981), wherein the Fifth Circuit Court of Appeals provided a flexible and practical definition, stating that (a) a school district must use a program informed by education theory, (b) programs and practices need to be implemented with adequate resources and personnel, and (c) if the program implemented fails, or produces English proficiency without overcoming academic deficits, then the program does not constitute appropriate action (Lyons, 2013). The term *appropriate action* left room for later lawsuits focused on issues regarding what adequate instructional programs for bilingual students should entail. For instance, *Gómez v. Illinois Board of Education* (1987) claimed that it was the responsibility of the state to provide language remediation programs. *Horne v. Flores* (2009) involved parents suing the state of Arizona, its state board of education, and its superintendent for not providing adequate services to ELs.

One of the issues regarding the general terminology from the *Castañeda v. Pickard* ruling is that, to a certain extent, many programs can be justified by theory, and that to determine whether a program is adequate requires passage of time for evaluation. It is sometimes difficult to determine why, exactly, a program has failed, and for whom it has failed. The ambiguity in terminology has made it easier for states to implement a wide range of programs, as long as there is a theoretically sound reason, even if there is little or no evidence to support it (Lyons, 2013).

In 2001, Congress passed the No Child Left Behind (NCLB) Act, designed to increase the accountability of states and districts for the education of their students. NCLB required states to develop a set of standards and measurable goals to ensure that public school funding resulted in student performance gains in English. For ELs, NCLB allowed local districts to decide on programs of instruction (e.g., bilingual or EO), but it required high-stakes testing in English for all ELs after they had been in the U.S. education system for 3 years. Schools also had to demonstrate that all of their students, including ELs, were making "adequate yearly progress" in English (Menken, 2010). As a consequence, the test-based accountability system placed stronger emphasis on English acquisition without promoting the L1 of ELs. Thus, many schools decided to eliminate their bilingual programs in the belief that EO instruction was the best way to ensure that ELs would make yearly progress (Menken, 2013).

In December 2015, President Barack Obama signed the Every Student Succeeds Act, which was designed to replace NCLB and the 50-year-old ESEA. The Every Student Succeeds Act does not include any explicit provisions related to bilingual education or the education of bilingual students, and it shifts the responsibility of identifying the interventions and supports for struggling students to the states and local education agencies. Consequently, states and districts need to decide whether to make bilingual education programs available to ELs and EOs (and evaluate the quality of any such programs). Although it is too soon to determine the effects of the law on school programs for bilingual students and on student academic performance, history suggests that bilingual programs may continue to proliferate with or without the support of federal policies.

Recent evidence indicates that ELs *and* EOs can obtain significantly higher scores in reading in fourth grade if they attend schools in states with less restrictive EO rules and more support for bilingual education, including mandated trainings for all teachers (F. López & McEneaney, 2012). Although this study included only eight states, a similar study by F. López, McEneaney, and Nieswandt (2015), which included all 50 states and mathematics and science outcomes, found that Hispanic ELs living in states with higher proportions of Hispanics tended to demonstrate higher academic outcomes when there was a longer history of Hispanic presence in the state and when state-level policies allowed bilingual programs to exist. In addition, studies that have examined the academic performance of ELs in states that passed EO laws (e.g., Proposition 227 in California and the 2002 Massachusetts Act Relative to the Teaching of English in Public Schools; for the latter, see Commonwealth of Massachusetts, 2002) found that academic outcomes of ELs did not improve after these laws were passed (see Gándara & Hopkins, 2010; Guo & Koretz, 2013; Parrish et al., 2006).

In summary, bilingual education in the United States has been a contentious topic in both political and educational arenas. The recent evidence suggests, however, that restrictive policies against bilingual programs, instead of improving outcomes for ELs, can significantly affect their opportunities for educational attainment by reducing the funding and the additional supports and trainings required to address their needs, particularly the needs of ELs at risk for academic failure.

Next, we summarize the results of reviews on bilingual education designed to improve the academic performance of L2 learners. We include one meta-analysis conducted in Europe.

SUMMARY OF REVIEWS ON BILINGUAL EDUCATION

In the past three decades, five meta-analyses (Francis, Lesaux, & August, 2006; Greene, 1998; Reljic et al., 2015; Rolstad, Mahoney, & Glass, 2005; Willig, 1985) and four other systematic reviews (K. Baker & de Kanter, 1981; Genesee, Lindholm-Leary, Saunders, & Christian, 2006; Rossell & Baker, 1996; Slavin & Cheung, 2005) have been conducted to examine the effects of bilingual education on the

TABLE 3

Review Studies in Chronological Order

Review	No. of Studies Reviewed	Types of Program Reviewed	Outcome	Effect Size
Baker and de Kanter (1981)	28	TBPs	EO programs were more beneficial. There was not sufficient evidence to support TBP.	NA
Rossell and Baker (1996)	75	TBP, structured immersion	EO programs were more beneficial.	NA
Slavin and Cheung (2005)	17	English immersion, TBP, paired bilingual model, two-way bilingual	BPs were superior, particularly paired bilingual programs.	*ES* = 0.45
Genesee, Lindholm-Leary, Saunders, and Christian (2006)	200	Two-way bilingual, developmental, ESL, SEI	BPs were more beneficial in oral language, literacy, and academic outcomes.	NA

Note. BP = bilingual program; EO = English-only; *ES* = median effect size; ESL = English as a second language; NA = not applicable; SEI, sheltered English immersion; TBP = transitional bilingual program.

academic achievement of bilingual students. According to Goldenberg (2013), more meta-analyses and reviews have been conducted in bilingual education than in any other field. We summarize findings from these studies in Tables 3 and 4. Although findings from two of the earliest reviews indicated that EO programs produced better English outcomes (K. Baker & de Kanter, 1981) or that bilingual programs did not demonstrate greater effectiveness than EO programs (Rossell & Baker, 1996), each of the other reviews and meta-analyses obtained findings in support of bilingual programs.

In the first meta-analysis of bilingual education research, Willig (1985) analyzed the same studies reviewed by K. Baker and de Kanter (1981) and found that bilingual programs appeared to be as beneficial as EO programs, if not more so, for supporting ELs' English literacy development. Almost 14 years later, Greene (1998) obtained findings that corroborated those obtained by Willig (1985). Results of both meta-analyses favored bilingual programs, with effect sizes of *ES* = 0.21 for reading and *ES* = 0.12 for math. This consistency occurred even though only a few studies were the same in both meta-analyses (Krashen & McField, 2005).

More recent reviews and meta-analyses have obtained similar findings in favor of bilingual programs, and they have provided some additional insights about the benefits of specific bilingual programs in comparison with others (e.g., Francis et al.,

TABLE 4

Meta-Analyses in Chronological Order

Meta-Analysis	No. of Studies Reviewed	Types of Program Reviewed	Outcome	Effect Size
Willig (1985)	23	Transitional bilingual, submersion	BP were as beneficial or sometimes more than EO programs.	ES^a = 0.63 between bilingual programs and submersion
Greene (1998)	11	Transitional bilingual, structured immersion	ELs who are taught using at least some of their native language perform significantly better than similar children who are taught in English.	g = 0.21 for reading and g = 0.12 for math
Rolstad, Mahoney, and Glass (2005)	17	Transitional bilingual program, developmental bilingual	BP programs are favored, particularly developmental bilingual programs in reading, writing, mathematics, and language proficiency.	ES^b = 0.23 bilingual education
Francis, Lesaux, and August (2006)	20	English-only, transitional bilingual, paired bilingual, two-way bilingual	Bilingual education has positive small to moderate effects on English reading outcomes.	d = 0.20 to 0.50
Reljic, Ferrig, and Martin (2015)	5	Bilingual, submersion, dual bilingual, transitional bilingual	Evidence points toward support for BPs as defined by programs that include the home language for the language minority students.	g = 0.23

Note. BP = bilingual program; d = Cohen's d; EO = English-only; *ES* = effect size; g = Hedges's g.
[a]Median effect size. [b]Mean effect size.

2006; Genesee et al., 2006; Rolstad et al., 2005; Slavin & Cheung, 2005). Rolstad et al. (2005) found that developmental bilingual programs, where the goal is bilingualism and biliteracy, produced better results than TBPs, where the primary goal is for students to become proficient in English. Similarly, Genesee et al. (2006) found that bilingual programs with extended instruction in the two languages (e.g., dual language and late exit programs) appeared to be more effective than early exit bilingual programs. In addition, while much of the research in this area has focused on elementary-age students, results from the meta-analysis by Francis et al. (2006) indicated that elementary- *and* secondary-level students instructed in their L1 and English performed better on measures of English language and reading than students instructed only in English ($d = 0.20$ to 0.50). Most recently, Reljic et al. (2015) conducted a meta-analysis examining the effects of bilingual programs versus submersion programs in the societal language for language minority students living in Europe. The results indicated a small positive effect ($g = 0.23$) in favor of bilingual programs over submersion programs on reading outcomes. These findings, however, need to be interpreted cautiously because only five studies met the inclusion criteria and were included in the analysis.

In summary, this collection of evidence appears to indicate that bilingual programs may produce more positive English outcomes for ELs than EO programs. Two limitations, however, must be noted with this body of work as a whole. First, many of the studies included in the reviews and meta-analyses contained methodological problems, such as how students were assigned to experimental and comparison groups, lack of comparability between the two groups (e.g., variability in language proficiency or student background characteristics), and lack of information about the *quality* of the bilingual programs because fidelity of implementation data were not reported (Willig, 1985). Second, few of the studies provided readers with specific details about the bilingual program models that were implemented (e.g., amount of instruction in both languages, length of the bilingual program), and few provided information on how instruction was organized and delivered (Francis et al., 2006; Genesee et al., 2006). Consequently, the results of the meta-analyses and reviews have not allowed researchers and practitioners to determine exactly for whom such programs are the most beneficial and under what circumstances.

Next we review studies published since 2003, the last year of studies included in the Francis et al. (2006) meta-analysis and the Genesee et al. (2006) review. We include any studies that meet our criteria, and that examine the effects of bilingual programs on the academic performance of bilingual students who are learning an L2.

SELECTED EMPIRICAL STUDIES OF BILINGUAL PROGRAMS PUBLISHED SINCE 2003

Selection Criteria

Our initial search for studies was conducted using the search terms *bilingual, bilingual instruction, bilingual education*, and *bilingual program*. First, we searched several electronic databases, including ERIC, PsycINFO, and Google Scholar, for peer-reviewed publications using a combination of the terms above. Second, we conducted "hand searches" (searches of hard copies of the journals) for articles that had been published between 2003 and 2015 in peer-reviewed journals (including those searched by Genesee et al., 2006). Appendix A includes a list of all the journals searched. Third, we examined the reference lists of the articles we located to see if there were any additional articles that focused on bilingual instruction, bilingual interventions, or bilingual education programs. To select appropriate studies for review, we adapted the process suggested by Moher, Liberati, Tetzlaff, Altman, and the PRISMA Group (2009).

Once studies were identified, we read the abstracts using criteria similar to those used by Genesee et al. (2006) in their review. For example, studies had to (a) be empirical and published in peer-reviewed journals, (b) focus on students from pre-K to Grade 12, and (c) either compare programs of instruction or measure academic outcomes in English and/or another language. In total, our search produced 157 articles. Of these, the greatest number of articles (107) were in the reading domain, followed by those in mathematics. We included studies conducted in and outside the United States.

Of the 157 studies whose abstracts we evaluated, 77 met the initial eligibility criteria. These studies were then examined more carefully and coded according to the following inclusion criteria based on components that researchers have noted as being absent from the majority of studies on bilingualism and bilingual education (Goldenberg, 2013; Hakuta, 2011). To be selected, studies had to include (a) a careful description of study participants, including age, language, ethnic background, and SES, by student, school, or district; (b) a detailed description of the program or intervention (e.g., amount of instruction in the two languages, length of the intervention, professional development (PD) requirements); (c) a full description of study methods (including fidelity of implementation, and reliability and validity of measures used); and (d) conclusions clearly linked to data. A total of 59 studies that met our initial criteria were included in the final review. Approximately 20% of the studies were double-coded to establish interrater reliability, and all discrepancies in coding were discussed and resolved at that time.

Findings

In this section we review studies by domain. Effect sizes are included if they were reported by the authors. We decided to summarize the studies in the tables using the more general terminology to describe bilingual programs defined earlier for consistency and clarity. We did, however, include the amount of time spent on each language in bilingual programs and the length of bilingual interventions if applicable. We synthesize the reading studies first, followed by the studies in writing, science, and mathematics. Appendix B lists the measures used in the studies, with their abbreviations.

Reading Studies

Given the large number of studies with reading outcomes that met our inclusion criteria ($n = 48$), we divided them into five types: (a) studies that employed a randomized controlled trial (RCT) design, (b) studies that employed a quasi-experimental or descriptive design, (c) studies that examined the effectiveness of bilingual programs and/or interventions for at-risk students, (d) studies that examined the role of the quality of instruction within the context of bilingual programs and/or interventions, and (e) studies that examined the effectiveness of bilingual programs outside the United States.

Studies comparing bilingual programs using an RCT design. We found five studies published since 2003 that met our inclusion criteria and that compared the effectiveness of different bilingual programs (or interventions) using an RCT design, as indicated in Table 5. Of these, all but one (Slavin, Madden, Calderón, Chamberlain, & Hennessy, 2011) were conducted with students in the preschool/early elementary grades; two (Durán, Roseth, & Hoffman, 2015; Slavin et al., 2011) were longitudinal. The most common comparisons were between a mainly EO program and a DLP or a TBP. All findings from the preschool studies indicated no significant differences in English outcomes between students in the bilingual program (i.e., in either the DLP or the TBP) and students in the EO program. In the longitudinal study by Durán et al. (2015), ELs in the TBP had growth trajectories similar to those of ELs in the mainly EO program in English. In Spanish, however, ELs in the TBP maintained their Spanish advantage compared to ELs in the EO program, corroborating previous findings with ELs in the primary grades, suggesting that bilingual programs present an opportunity for ELs to maintain their L1 without a detriment to their English reading and language development.

The Farver, Lonigan, and Eppe (2009) study compared the effect of an intervention in Spanish for ELs in the TBP program to the effect of the same intervention in English for students in the EO program; ELs in a control group did not receive the intervention. The findings indicated that ELs in the intervention in Spanish or English outperformed ELs in the control group on English vocabulary, blending, elision, and print knowledge tasks, suggesting that even for students at risk, interventions in the L1 can improve English reading skills. Roberts (2008) also found that preschoolers who received storybook reading in English at school, and in the L1 (i.e., either Spanish or Hmong) at home, had significantly higher knowledge of the storybook words than did preschoolers who received storybook reading in only English at home and at school, confirming that providing L1 supports either in preschool or at home is effective in helping children improve their reading skills in English.

Slavin et al. (2011) found that at the end of Grade 1, ELs in the TBP outperformed ELs in the EO programs on all the Spanish measures, but ELs in the EO program outperformed ELs in the TBP on all the English measures. At the end of Grade 4, however, the two groups performed similarly on all the English measures, but ELs in the TBP outperformed ELs in the EO program on Spanish reading comprehension ($ES = 0.39$). In summary, these studies corroborate the findings from the previous meta-analyses suggesting that bilingual programs help maintain and potentially even improve reading skills in students' L1, as well as support their learning of

TABLE 5
Reading Studies Comparing Bilingual Programs Using a Randomized Controlled Design

Study	Grade Level	N	Program Models Compared	Academic Measures	Outcomes
Barnett, Yarosz, Thomas, Jung, and Blanco (2007)	Preschool	131	*Two-way immersion*: Language of instruction alternates weekly; 8 hours/day for 200 school days *English immersion*: 6 hours/day for 180+ school days	*ENG*: PPVT-3, WJ-R *SP*: TVIP, WM-R *Both languages*: phoneme deletion, rhyme recognition	*ENG*: no significant differences *SP*: TWI performed significantly better on TVIP ($ES = 0.61, 0.56$) and rhyme recognition ($ES = 0.45$); significant gains on TVIP, phoneme deletion, and letter recognition for English-dominant in TWI
Durán, Roseth, and Hoffman (2010)	Pre-K	31	*Transitional bilingual*: All instruction in SP during Year 1 *EO*: All instruction in English	*ENG*: PPVT-4, WMLS-R, EL-IGDIs *SP*: TVIP, WMLS-R	*ENG*: No significant differences between groups on ENG measures; both groups demonstrated little growth in letter-word identification *SP*: TBP showed higher rates of growth on oral vocabulary, expressive vocabulary, and letter-word identification
Durán, Roseth, and Hoffman (2014)	Pre-K	28	*Transitional bilingual*: ENG introduced until rate of 70% SP/30% ENG *PE*: SP introduced until 30% SP/70% ENG	*ENG*: PPVT-3, WMLS-R, DIBELS, MAP *SP*: TVIP, WMLS-R	*ENG*: No significant differences *SP*: TBP had significantly higher scores on TVIP ($\eta^2 = 0.41$), WMLS-R letter-word identification ($\eta^2 = 0.30$), WMLS-R picture naming ($\eta^2 = 0.17$), and demonstrated significantly greater growth on DIBELS LNF ($p < .05$)

(continued)

TABLE 5 (CONTINUED)

Study	Grade Level	N	Program Models Compared	Academic Measures	Outcomes
Durán, Roseth, Hoffman, and Robertshaw (2013)	K	31	*Transitional bilingual:* ENG introduced until rate of 70% SP/30% ENG *PE:* SP introduced until 30% SP/70% ENG	*ENG:* PPVT-4, WMLS-R, DIBELS PSF and NWF *SP:* TVIP, WMLS-R, picture naming, letter word	*ENG:* No differences between TBP and PE programs on any measure *SP:* Students in TBP demonstrated significantly greater growth on all Spanish measures
Farver, Lonigan, and Eppe (2009)	Preschool	94	*Transitional bilingual:* High Scope + Literacy Express Preschool Curriculum in SP until Week 9, transitioning to ENG over 3- to 4-week period *EO:* High Scope + Literacy Express Preschool Curriculum in ENG (20 minutes/day, 4× per week) *Control:* High Scope Curriculum	*ENG:* P-CTOPPP *SP:* P-CTOPPP	*ENG:* Students in the TBP intervention and EO intervention had significantly higher vocabulary, blending, elision, and print knowledge scores than control group (*p* < .01); TBP intervention group had significantly higher vocabulary and print knowledge scores than EO intervention group (*p* < .01) *SP:* TBP had significantly higher vocabulary, blending, elision, and print knowledge scores than EO and control groups (*p* < .01)
Roberts (2008)	Preschool	33	*Storybook reading intervention:* Primary language storybook reading at home; English storybook reading at home, plus all instruction and classroom routines in ENG	*ENG:* PPVT-3, pre-IPT, researcher-developed storybook and weekly vocabulary tests *SP:* TVIP	*ENG:* Students who received primary language storybooks at home identified significantly more ENG storybook words than students who received English storybooks at home and at school (*d* = 0.87 to 2.38) *SP:* TVIP scores increased over time, and there were no significant differences in PPVT and TVIP scores

(continued)

TABLE 5 (CONTINUED)

Study	Grade Level	N	Program Models Compared	Academic Measures	Outcomes
Slavin, Madden, Calderón, Chamberlain, and Hennessy (2011)	Grades 1–4	482	*Transitional bilingual:* SP in K + ESL instruction; transition to ENG began, on average, in Grade 2; all ENG by Grade 4	*ENG:* PPVT, WLPB-R	*ENG:* Scores were higher in SEI group across Grades 1–4 (*ES* = 0.08 to 0.31)
			Structured English immersion: All instruction in ENG	*SP:* TVIP, WLPB-R	*SP:* Significantly higher TVIP and WLPB-R scores for TBP students in Grades 1–4 (*ES* = 0.04 to 0.65); differences were not significant in Grade 4 in English, and only significant in Spanish passage comprehension favoring students in TBP (*ES* = 0.39)

Note. DIBELS = Dynamic Indicators of Basic Early Literacy Skills; EL-IGDI = Early Literacy Individual Growth and Development Indicators; ENG = English; EO = English-only; *ES* = effect size; IPT = IDEA Oral Language Proficiency Test; MAP = Measures of Academic Progress; NWF = Nonsense Words Fluency; P-CTOPPP = Preschool Comprehensive Test of Phonological and Print Processing; PE = predominantly English instruction; PPVT = Peabody Picture Vocabulary Test; pre-IPT = preschool IDEA Oral Language Proficiency Test; PSF = Phoneme Segmentation Fluency; SEI = structured English immersion; SP = Spanish; TBP = transitional bilingual program; TVIP = Test de Vocabulario de Imágenes; TWI = two-way immersion; WJ-R = Woodcock Johnson–Revised; WMLS = Woodcock Munoz Language Survey; WLPB-R = Woodcock Language Proficiency Battery–Revised; WM-R = Woodcock Muñoz–Revised; WMLS-R = Woodcock Muñoz Language Survey-Revised.

English. In addition, given that all these studies were RCTs, findings can be causally related to outcomes.

Studies comparing bilingual programs using quasi-experimental or descriptive research designs. As Table 6 indicates, we located 21 studies published since 2003 that met our inclusion criteria and used quasi-experimental research designs (i.e., with comparison groups and/or controlling for pretest performance) or correlational research designs (i.e., where hypothesized causal relations were identified, but research design elements that were needed to make causal inferences, such as pretests or comparison groups, were absent; Shadish, Cook, & Campbell, 2001). Nine of these studies focused on younger students (Grades K–2), eight focused on upper primary students (Grades 2–6), and four focused on longer trajectories (Grades K–5, K–8, or K–11; Hofstetter, 2004; Reese, Gallimore, & Guthrie, 2005; Umansky & Reardon, 2014; Valentino & Reardon, 2015). The majority of the studies conducted in the early grades used primarily measures of phonological awareness, word reading, and vocabulary to determine program effectiveness. Three of the studies in the lower grades found that students receiving bilingual instruction outperformed their peers receiving English instruction with or without minimal ELD supports (Anderberg & McSparran Ruby, 2013; Lindholm-Leary, 2014; M. G. López & Tashakkori, 2004b). Results of the other five studies indicated either no significant differences between bilingual programs and EO programs or higher scores in English for ELs who participated in the English program and higher scores in Spanish for ELs who participated in the bilingual program. Six of the eight studies in the upper primary grades (Grade 2 and above) found that students in bilingual programs significantly outperformed their peers receiving EO instruction on English outcomes. Studies that included Spanish outcomes found, as expected, that Spanish outcomes were higher for students who participated in the bilingual programs than for students who participated in the EO program. Two of the eight studies in the upper primary grades (F. López, Scanlan, & Gorman, 2015; M. G. López & Tashakkori, 2006) found no difference at posttest on English outcomes between the bilingual program and the EO program.

The four longitudinal studies (Hofstetter, 2004; Reese et al., 2005; Umansky & Reardon, 2014; Valentino & Reardon, 2015) examining the effectiveness of bilingual programs over time produced three important findings:

1. Students' initial proficiency levels in Spanish were important for determining their rate of growth in English reading skills when participating in a TBP (Reese et al., 2005).
2. Although students in EI programs may have started with higher skills initially, students in bilingual programs often exhibited faster rates of growth and were able to close the gap and even outperform students in EI programs over time (Umansky & Reardon, 2014; Valentino & Reardon, 2015).
3. The timing of ELs' reclassification as English proficient was often related to the bilingual program models (i.e., students in EI programs were reclassified at

TABLE 6

Reading Studies Comparing Bilingual Programs Using a Quasi-Experimental or Descriptive Design

Study	Grade Level	N	Program Models Compared	Academic Measures	Outcomes
Anderberg and McSparran Ruby (2013)	Preschool	45	*Transitional bilingual:* 20-minute ENG *Dual language:* 50% SP/50% ENG *EO:* All instruction in English	*ENG:* PPVT-3 *SP:* TVIP	*ENG:* Students in all three programs made significant gains from pretest to posttest; 78% of students in TBP made gains from pretest to posttest, compared to 54% in DLP and 51% in EO *SP:* No significant gains for any group
Berens, Kovelman, and Petitto (2013)	Grades 2–3	213	*Dual language:* 50% SP/50% ENG *Dual language:* 90% SP/10% ENG *EO:* All instruction in English	*ENG:* Phonological awareness tasks, CORE regular and irregular word reading, WLPB-R, LCEP *SP:* Phonological awareness tasks, CORE regular and irregular word reading, WLPB-R, LCEP	*ENG:* Students in 90/10 DL significantly outperformed 50/50 DL on phonological awareness and regular word reading tasks ($p < .05$), but 50/50 DL obtained significantly higher scores on irregular word reading ($p < .05$) *SP:* Students in 90/10 DL significantly performed 50/50 DL on all tasks ($\eta^2_p = 0.11$)
Carlo, Barr, August, Calderón, and Artzi (2014)	Grades 3–5	102	*Transitional bilingual (early exit):* All instruction in SP then transitioned to ENG in Grade 3	*ENG:* LAS-O, CAAS, WLPB-R	*ENG:* In Grade 3, EO significantly outperformed TBP-E and TBP-L on reading comprehension ($p < .05$), but by end of Grade 5, EO and TBP-E were performing comparably (and significantly better than the TBP-L group, $p < .05$); EO also significantly outperformed TBP-E and TBP-L on the CAAS and LAS-O (while the bilingual programs did not differ significantly); TBP-E grew at a significantly faster rate than EO on reading comprehension (*ES* for growth were 1.00 for TBP-E when compared to EO and .47 when compared to TBP-L); initial level of SP reading comprehension was a significant predictor after controlling for home language use and SES, indicating that students who started with higher skills demonstrated greater growth ($p = .01$ for TBP-L and $p = .05$ for TBP-E)

(continued)

TABLE 6 (CONTINUED)

Study	Grade Level	N	Program Models Compared	Academic Measures	Outcomes
			Transitional bilingual (late exit): All instruction in SP then transitioned to ENG in Grade 5	*SP:* WLPB-R	*SP:* In Grade 3, both bilingual groups outperformed EOs ($p < .05$), but did not differ significantly from each other
Gómez, Freeman, and Freeman (2005)	Grades 3–5	240	*EO:* All instruction in English *50–50 content model:* Mathematics instruction in ENG; science, and social studies instruction in SP; language arts instruction in native language in pre-K and K and then in students' L2 in Grades 1–5	*ENG:* TAKS	*ENG:* Of 117 Spanish-dominant Grade 3 students tested, 103 (88%) met proficiency standard; of the 56 English-dominant Grade 3 students tested, 51 (91%) met proficiency standard; overall, 154/173 (89%) met Grade 3 proficiency standard on TAKS Reading
Hammer, Lawrence, and Miccio (2007)	Pre-K–K	88	*EO:* ENG primary language of instruction for all students *HEC:* Home ENG communication *SEC:* Students with SP as home language who had no prior ENG experience placed in classrooms where teacher or assistant spoke SP	*ENG:* PPVT-III, TELD-3, TERA-2, WLPB-R *SP:* TVIP, PLS-3, WLPB-R	*ENG:* Although SEC group started significantly lower than HEC group on ENG vocabulary (PPVT-III and TELD-3 component score) with $p < .05$, growth rates were comparable to HEC group; larger growth rates in SP during Head Start resulted in higher reading TERA-2 and ENG and SP WLPB-R letter-word identification scores *SP:* SEC group significantly outperformed HEC group on SP vocabulary tasks at the end of Head Start ($p < .05$); early reading abilities in end of pre-K significantly predicted SP letter-word identification in K

(continued)

TABLE 6 (CONTINUED)

Study	Grade Level	N	Program Models Compared	Academic Measures	Outcomes
Hofstetter (2004)	K–5	441	*ALA:* Instruction in K–1, 70% in L1, 30% in L2; percentage of ENG instruction increases until Grades 4/5, where ratio of instruction is 85% ENG and 15% SP *SEI:* Students receive instruction predominantly in ENG, with 10% to 15% of instruction in ELD, 75% using sheltered ENG strategies	*ENG:* CELDT, SAT-9 *SP:* SABE/2	*ENG:* SEI students earned higher scores on all CELDT subtests, and SAT-9 reading, than ALA students; ALA students who participated in Success for All (SFA) scored higher on SAT-9 than non-SFA *SP:* ALA students scored in upper percentiles on SABE/2 and scored higher on SABE/2 compared to ENG SAT-9; ALA students who participated in SFA scored similarly to non-SFA students in reading.
Lindholm-Leary and Block (2010)	Grades 4–6	Study 1: 193 Study 2: 466	*DLP:* 90% in SP in K–1, 80% in Grade 2, 70% in Grade 3, 60% in Grade 4, and 50% from Grade 5 on *EO:* Control group	*ENG:* ELA *SP:* Aprenda	*ENG:* In Study 1, there were no significant differences between scale scores of EP and EL students by program type; in Study 2, both EP and EL students in a DLP achieved at significantly higher levels than their peers in EO on the ELA CST ($d = 0.71$ for the EP group, and $d = 0.35$ for the EL group). *SP:* EP and EL students in DLP scored above grade level (and the state average) on the Aprenda reading subtest

(continued)

TABLE 6 (CONTINUED)

Study	Grade Level	N	Program Models Compared	Academic Measures	Outcomes
Lindholm-Leary (2014)	K–2	283	*Bilingual:* (pre-K–2) 20% to 50% instruction in ENG *Bilingual/ENG:* Bilingual pre-K (20% to 50% instruction in ENG), ENG in Grades K–1 *ENG/bilingual:* Pre-K, bilingual in Grades 1–2 (20% to 50% instruction in ENG) *English-only:* ENG instruction Pre-K–2	*ENG:* PreLAS/LAS, CELDT *SP:* DRDP, PreLAS/LAS	*ENG:* Students who received bilingual instruction in K–3 did not perform significantly worse than students receiving EO instruction (rather, they showed more *growth* across the grades compared to EO students); the greatest rates of growth were for the bilingual/ENG group; students who were Mostly Proficient in SP scored significantly higher on the CELDT than students who were Mostly Limited in SP ($\eta_p^2 = 0.14$) *SP:* Students receiving ENG instruction who began pre-K with significantly higher SP PreLAS scores performed significantly better ($p < .01$) than students receiving bilingual instruction and maintained higher scores for K and 1 (similar scores by program type in Grade 2); students in bilingual preschool performed comparably (bilingual and bilingual/ENG) and significantly lower than EO but demonstrated significantly greater gains after 1 year of pre-K (compared to the control group)
F. López, Scanlan, and Gorman (2015)	Grades 3–5	995	*Dual bilingual:* 90% SP/10% ENG in K; ENG introduced incrementally through Grade 4 (until 50% SP/50% ENG) *Dual language:* 50% SP/50% ENG starting in K (1 week SP instruction followed by 1 week ENG instruction) *EO:* All instruction in English	*ENG:* State reading assessment (fall/spring)	*ENG:* No significant differences in slopes between dual bilingual and EO classrooms, indicating that the relation between language modeling and reading achievement was the same in these settings; the slope of this relationship was weaker, however, in dual language classrooms

(continued)

TABLE 6 (CONTINUED)

Study	Grade Level	N	Program Models Compared	Academic Measures	Outcomes
M. G. López and Tashakkori (2004a)	K–1	215	*TWI*: 30% SP/70% ENG *English for speakers of other languages*: 10% SP/90% ENG	*ENG*: KAG, ERSA, High Frequency Word List, two writing samples, SRI	*ENG*: In K, students in the ESOL (control) group performed significantly better than students in the TWI (treatment) group on alphabet knowledge ($\eta^2 = 0.31$); in Grade 1, no significant differences were found on any of the measures at posttest.
M. G. López and Tashakkori (2004b)	K–1	66	*EFL*: 30% SP/70% ENG *EO*: All instruction in ENG except 2.5 hours/week of SP language arts	*ENG*: SRI, KAG, High Frequency Word List, OLPSI-R	*ENG*: In K and 1, significant differences were observed on measures of alphabet knowledge, high-frequency word reading, and writing ($\eta_p^2 = 0.001$ to 0.12), but all differences favored the comparison (EO) group; despite being at greater levels of risk at pretest in K, students in the EFL group made sufficient progress, so that there were no statistically significant differences by the end of Grade 1
M. G. López and Tashakkori (2006)	Grade 5	344	*Two-way bilingual*: 40% SP/60% ENG *Transitional bilingual*: SP and ENG until students attained a level 3 in ENG, then option of receiving 2.5 hours/week of SP instruction	*ENG*: FCAT *SP*: EDL	*ENG*: No significant differences in performance on FCAT reading for students in the two groups, but results indicated that students who entered with lower levels of ENG proficiency in K or Grade 1 scored significantly lower than students with higher levels of ENG proficiency ($\eta^2 = 0.11$); the main effect of program type on oral language development was significant, with students in TWBE requiring less time to learn ENG than students in TBP ($\eta^2 = .02$); students with higher initial levels of English proficiency exited ESOL program faster ($\eta^2 = 0.22$), and students with lower levels exited faster in the TWBE program than in the TBP program ($\eta^2 = 0.04$) *SP*: The effect of program type was statistically significant, with TWBE outperforming TBP students on the measure of SP reading fluency ($\eta^2 = 0.26$)

(continued)

TABLE 6 (CONTINUED)

Study	Grade Level	N	Program Models Compared	Academic Measures	Outcomes
Marian, Shook, and Schroeder (2013)	Grades 3–5	2,009	*TWI SP:* SP instruction in Grades K–2, ENG in Grade 3 *TPI:* All instruction in ENG with pull-out ESL instruction as needed *TWI ENG:* ENG instruction in Grades K–2; SP in Grades 3–5 *EO:* All instruction in English	*ENG:* SMAG; SSAT	*ENG:* TWI-SP students showed significant improvements across grade levels in reading ($\eta^2 = 0.24$); similar improvements not observed in the TPI group
Proctor, August, Carlo, and Bar (2010)	Grades 2–5	101	*SpO:* All instruction in SP *EO:* All instruction in ENG *TBP:* Transitioned out of SP into ENG after Grade 2, 3, or 4 (had attained Grade 2 SP literacy proficiency)	*ENG:* WLPB-R *SP:* WLPB-R	*ENG:* EO and TBP students significantly outperformed SpO students in reading comprehension ($p < .05$) *SP:* SpO and TBP students had higher reading comprehension and oral vocabulary scores than EO students ($p < .01$), and SpO had significantly higher scores than TBP ($p < .01$); average reading growth for SpO and EO was comparable (but EO was 2 *SD* below the mean, showing absence of SP proficiency); SpO showed greater growth than TBP ($p < .01$) but no differences in growth for TBP and EO
Reading (2009)	K–1	101	*French immersion:* No ENG instruction in K; 1 hour/day of ENG literacy instruction in Grade 1 *Spanish immersion:* No ENG instruction in K; 1 hour/day of ENG literacy instruction in Grade 1 *EO:* ENG reading instruction using commercially available phonics program	*ENG:* DIBELS ISF, LNF, PSF, NWF, ORF	*ENG:* NWF scores were higher for SP immersion compared to EO ($d = 0.37$, $p < .05$); median subtest scores on all measures were higher for SP immersion than for French immersion at the beginning of Grade 1 (*d* values for LNF, PSF, and NWF are 0.47, 0.44, and 0.46, respectively; $p < .05$ for all); significantly fewer SP immersion students were identified as needing intervention compared to French immersion students

(continued)

845

TABLE 6 (CONTINUED)

Study	Grade Level	N	Program Models Compared	Academic Measures	Outcomes
Reese, Gallimore, and Guthrie (2005)	K–8	91	*TBP*: Move to EO when reading ability in SP is at the third-grade level and have conversational ability in ENG	*ENG*: CTBS, MAT, IDEA Proficiency Task, BSM, ITBS, TAAS, ITAS *SP*: SABE, CTBS-S, Prueba de Lectura Inicial	*ENG*: Students who were identified as high achievers in SP transitioned earlier and, despite experiencing a sharp decline in Grades 2–3 (when the transition occurred) recovered earlier and more quickly; scores for students identified as average or low achievers in SP in K began to decline in SP prior to the transition to ENG and continued to decline after the transition; by Grade 7, grade of transition to ENG was negatively correlated with performance ($r = .48$, $p < .0001$). *SP*: Students who received intensive instruction in K outperformed their peers through Grade 3 ($p < .01$), after which their advantage decreased and was no longer significant
Reese, Goldenberg, and Saunders (2006)	K–2	83	*Transitional bilingual (early)*: Reading/language arts and other content area instruction provided in SP for approximately 1–3 years, then transition to EO *DB*: SP instruction through Grades 2–3, when ENG is added *DLP*: SP instruction in Grades K–1, ENG introduced in Grade 2, then 50% ENG/50% SP in Grades 3–5 *EI*: All instruction in English	*ENG*: WLPB-R *SP*: WLPB-R	*ENG*: Students in programs that emphasized ENG instruction scored higher in ENG *SP*: Students in programs that emphasized SP instruction scored higher in SP

(continued)

TABLE 6 (CONTINUED)

Study	Grade Level	N	Program Models Compared	Academic Measures	Outcomes
Uchikoshi and Maniates (2010)	Grade 2	67	*Transitional bilingual:* 10% Cantonese/90% ENG *Transitional bilingual:* 40% SP/60% ENG	*ENG:* PPVT-3, WLPB-R *SP:* TVIP, WLPB-R *Cantonese:* PPVT-3	*ENG:* Students in Cantonese/ENG TBP performed, on average, similarly to monolingual ENG norms for Grade 1 expressive vocabulary, while SP-speaking students in SP/ENG TBP performed similarly to monolingual norms for ENG kindergarten; students in both TBPs performed about 1 *SD* below the mean on receptive vocabulary and listening comprehension *SP:* Students scored 0.5 *SD* below monolingual SP norms for receptive vocabulary and listening comprehension and had expressive vocabulary scores comparable to those of monolingual SP students in K *Cantonese:* Students scored about 1.5 *SD* lower than monolingual Chinese norms for receptive vocabulary
Umansky and Reardon (2014)	K–11	5,423	*Transitional bilingual:* 80% to 90% SP instruction in K, with amount of ENG instruction increasing each year until Grade 3, when all instruction is in ENG *SP maintenance bilingual:* 80% to 90% SP in K, transitioning to 50% to 60% ENG by Grade 5 *SP DI:* Mainly SP instruction in K to 50% SP/50% ENG by end of elementary; some programs continue through middle/high school *EI:* All instruction in ENG	*ENG:* CELDT, CST (ELA)	*ENG reclassification:* Significantly larger proportions of students in English immersion programs demonstrated ENG proficiency on the CELDT and were reclassified in elementary school than in other programs; however, the proportion of students in transitional bilingual and maintenance programs reclassified as ENG proficient was significantly greater than the proportion of students in EI programs in middle school, and DI surpassed EI by high school *ENG reading:* Students in EI significantly outperformed students in other programs in elementary school, but DI students significantly outperformed EI by Grade 5 (continuing to show advantages throughout middle and high school) and maintenance bilingual students significantly outperformed EI students by Grade 6

(continued)

TABLE 6 (CONTINUED)

Study	Grade Level	N	Program Models Compared	Academic Measures	Outcomes
Valentino and Reardon (2015)	K–8	13,750	*Transitional bilingual: SP* instruction in K and transition to ENG by Grades 2–3 *DB:* In K, 50% to 90% of instruction in target language, proportion of ENG instruction increasing each year *DI:* 80% to 90% of instruction in target language in K–1, transitioning to 50% ENG and 50% target language by Grade 5 *EI:* All instruction in ENG + at least 30 minutes ELD support	*ENG:* State standardized tests of ELA	*ENG:* ELA test scores of students in TBP and DI increased significantly faster (0.064 *SD* faster) than those of students in EI; rates of growth were comparable for DB and EI (conditional on covariates); scores of students in DI (lowest scores in Grade 2) increased at a rate as much as 0.092 *SD* faster per grade than scores of students in other programs

Note. ALA = academic language acquisition; BSM = Bilingual Syntax Measure; CAAS = Computer-Based Academic Assessment System; CELDT = California English Language Development Test; CTBS = Comprehensive Test of Basic Skills; CTBS-S = Comprehensive Test of Basic Skills Spanish; CST = California Standards Test; DB = Developmental Bilingual; DI = Dual Immersion; DIBELS = Dynamic Indicators of Basic Early Literacy Skills; DLP = Dual Language Program; DRDP = Desired Results Developmental Profile; EDL = Español Desarrollo de la Lectura; EFL = Extended Foreign Language; EI = English Immersion; ELA = English language arts; EL = English learner; ELD = English language development; ENG = English; EP = English proficient; EO = English-only; ERSA = Emergent Reader Screening Assessment; ESOL = English for Speakers of Other Languages; FCAT = Florida Comprehensive Assessment Test; HEC = Home English Communication; ISF = Initial Sound Fluency; ITAS = Individual Test of Academic Skills; ITBS = Iowa Test of Basic Skills; KAG = Kindergarten Assessment Guide; LAS = Language Assessment Scales; LAS-O = Language Assessment Scales–Oral; LCEP = Language Competence/Expressive Proficiency Task; LNF = Letter Naming Fluency; MAT = Metropolitan Achievement Test; NWF = Nonsense Word Fluency; OLPSI = Oral Language Proficiency Scale Interview–Revised; ORF = Oral Reading Fluency; PLS = Preschool Language Scale; PPVT = Peabody Picture Vocabulary Test; PreLAS = Preschool Language Assessment Scale; PSF = Phoneme Segmentation Fluency; SABE = Spanish Assessment of Basic Skills; SAT-9 = Stanford Achievement Test; SEC = students with Spanish at home without prior ENG experience; SEI = Structured English Immersion; SFA = Success for All; SMAG = State Measure of Annual Growth in English; SP = Spanish; SpO = Spanish only; SRI = Scholastic Reading Inventory; SSAT = State Standards Achievement Test; TAAS = Texas Assessment of Academic Skills; TAKS = Texas Assessment of Knowledge and Skills; TBP = transitional bilingual program; TBP-E = Transitional bilingual program–early exit; TBP-L = Transitional bilingual program–late exit; TELD-3 = Test of Early Language Development; TERA-2 = Test of Early Reading Ability; TPI = Transitional Program of Instruction; TVIP = Test de Vocabulario en Imágenes; TWI = two-way immersion; TWBI = two-way bilingual education; WLPB = Woodcock Language Proficiency Battery; WLPB-R = Woodcock Language Proficiency Battery–Revised Spanish and English Forms.

greater rates in elementary school, while students in dual immersion, transitional bilingual, and language maintenance programs were more often reclassified in middle school).

The delay in reclassification might have important positive and negative implications for the academic performance of bilingual students. On one hand, reclassification might allow students to participate fully in all course offerings, including those with rigorous content. On the other, delays in reclassification might allow students to receive additional support services, such as ELD, that they would not receive if they were reclassified. The drawback of delayed classification, however, is that students might miss rigorous content because of having to attend ELD classes, which are usually more focused on developing student English language proficiency than building their content knowledge (Umansky & Reardon, 2014).

Studies comparing bilingual programs for at-risk students. We found five studies that disaggregated the data by student risk status or that included students with disabilities. Two studies defined risk status based on academic performance (D. L. Baker, Park, Baker, Basaraba, et al., 2012; Gerber et al., 2004), and two defined it based on the presence of autism spectrum disorders. One study (Kovelman, Baker, & Petito, 2008) examined whether age of acquisition (students are termed *early bilingual, late bilingual,* or *monolingual*) was related to English and Spanish literacy skills. Although this study did not screen students for potential reading disabilities, we included it in Table 7 because bilingual students were disaggregated by age of exposure to Spanish and English, and age of acquisition was found to be a risk factor for later language development.

The study by D. L. Baker, Park, Baker, Basaraba, et al. (2012) compared the effects of two programs on reading outcomes: a paired bilingual program (where students received English and Spanish reading instruction simultaneously in Grades 1–3 at different times of day) and an EO reading program. The results indicated no significant differences in the effects of the two programs on English comprehension outcomes for students not at risk for reading failure in Grades 1 to 3. However, students at risk for reading difficulties appeared to benefit more from the paired bilingual program than from the EO program across the three grades. These findings were significant in Grade 2 ($d = 0.51$). Gerber et al. (2004) also found bilingual instruction favorable for at-risk kindergarten students who received a 30-minute Spanish intervention, in comparison with students who did not receive the intervention on any English measures except Onset Detection ($p < .01$).

Finally, two studies (Hambly & Fombonne, 2012; Ohashi et al., 2012) examined whether the social impairments associated with autism spectrum disorder could cause language delays and/or communication impairments in preschool bilingual children exposed to (a) one language (e.g., English, Spanish, or French), (b) a bilingual language environment prior to 12 months of age (i.e., simultaneous bilingual exposure), or (c) a bilingual language environment after 12 months of age (i.e., sequential bilingual exposure). Results indicated that although there were no statistically significant

TABLE 7

Reading Studies Comparing Bilingual Programs for At-Risk Students

Study	Grade Level	N	Program Models Compared	Academic Measures	Outcomes
D. L. Baker, Park, Baker, Basaraba, et al. (2012)	Grades 1–3	210	*Paired bilingual*: 90 minutes SP + 30–45 minutes ENG in Grades 1–2; 60 minutes SP + 60 minutes ENG in Grade 3 *EO*: 120 minutes ENG instruction	*ENG*: DIBELS ORF, SAT-10	*ENG*: ELs in the paired bilingual program had higher rates of ORF compared to ELs in EO ($d = 0.33$ to 0.53); ELs at risk in the paired bilingual program significantly outperformed ELs at risk in the EO program in reading comprehension in Grade 2 ($d = 0.51$)
Gerber et al. (2004)	K–1	43	*CIM*: SP small group direct instruction in K, transitioned to ENG for all but 14 students who continued to receive SP instruction	*ENG*: Rime/Onset Detection, Phoneme Segmentation, WIAT *SP*: Rime/Onset Detection, Phoneme Segmentation, WIAT	*ENG*: ELs in the SP intervention demonstrated greater gains and closed the achievement gap with comparison students on all ENG measures except Onset Detection ($p < .01$); no significant interactions between group and time *SP*: ELs in the SP intervention made significantly greater gains on SP Rime Detection compared to comparison group ($p < .01$)
Hambly and Fombonne (2012)	Pre-K	75	*MON*: Exposed to one language only (e.g., ENG, French, or SP) *SIM*: Bilingual exposure before 12 months of age *SEQ*: Bilingual exposure after 12 months of age	*ENG*: ADI-R, MCDI, VABS	*ENG*: No significant differences between the bilingual and monolingual groups on measures of expressive vocabulary, receptive language, or early language milestones (e.g., age of first words and phrases; $p > .05$); SIM and MON consistently scored higher than SEQ

(continued)

TABLE 7 (CONTINUED)

Study	Grade Level	N	Program Models Compared	Academic Measures	Outcomes
Kovelman, Baker, and Petito (2008)	Grades 2–3	150	*In California:* Instruction for EOs—ENG in K–2, then SP introduced in Grade 3; for SP-speaking ELs instruction in SP in K–2 and then ENG in Grade 3 *In New Hampshire:* English only	*ENG:* CORE Assessing Reading, LCEP, WLPB-R *SP:* CORE Assessing Reading, LCEP, WLPB-R	*ENG:* Age of first exposure to ENG had significant impact on student's performance in ENG on phonological awareness, reading, and language ($p < 0.01$); students from monolingual ENG homes and early bilinguals significantly outperformed late bilinguals; significant group difference (early vs. late bilingual) for all tasks favoring the early exposure group ($p < .001$); EOs in bilingual program outperformed EOs from monolingual ENG homes on phonemic awareness skills *SP:* Children from monolingual ENG homes performed as well as children from SP-speaking homes on phoneme awareness tasks, but SP early bilinguals significantly outperformed students from monolingual ENG homes on reading tasks ($p <.001$)
Ohashi et al. (2012)[a]	Pre-K	60	*Simultaneous bilingual:* Ongoing exposure at home in two languages (one of which was ENG or FR) *Monolingual exposure:* Exposed to only one language (ENG or FR) from birth to age 3 or 4	*ENG:* ADOS, ADI-R, PLS-4, VABS	*ENG:* No significant differences between simultaneous bilingual and monolingual exposure groups for age of first words or phrases, or for ADOS Total Communication scores

Note. ADI-R = Austim Diagnostic Interview–Revised; ADOS = Autism Diagnostic Observation Schedule; CIM = Core Model Intervention; DIBELS = Dynamic Indicators of Basic Early Literacy Skills; EL = English learner; ENG = English; EO = English-only; FR = French; LCEP = Language Competence/Expressive Proficiency Task; MCDI = MacArthur Communicative Development Inventory; MON = Monolingual; ORF = Oral Reading Fluency; PLS = Preschool Language Scale; SAT = Stanford Achievement Test; SEQ = sequential bilingual exposure; SIM = simultaneous bilingual exposure; SP = Spanish; VABS = Vineland Adaptive Behavior Scales; WIAT = Word Identification/Word Attack; WLPB-R = Woodcock Language Proficiency Battery–Revised.

[a]We included the Ohashi et al. (2012) study here although it was conducted in Canada because we wanted to compare findings from the two studies that included students with autism.

differences in the expressive vocabulary, receptive vocabulary, or language skills of students in the three groups, students who were exposed to only one language or to two languages prior to 12 months of age performed significantly better than students exposed to two languages after 12 months of age.

Ohashi et al. (2012) took a slightly different approach to answering the research question above by examining the age at which students with autism from monolingual (English or French) or simultaneous bilingual language environments (English and French) spoke their first words and phrases and were able to engage in functional communication. Results indicated no statistically significant differences between the two groups, suggesting that bilingual language environments do not cause language delays or disadvantage young children with autism spectrum disorder. In summary, the findings of the studies examining the effects of bilingual programs on students at risk suggest that bilingual programs do not hinder or otherwise impair the development of literacy skills; rather, the results indicate that the programs may support L1 and L2 literacy development for this population of students.

Studies examining the role of quality of instruction within bilingual programs. We found nine studies that examined quality of instruction in the context of bilingual programs and that met our inclusion criteria as indicated in Table 8. All studies were conducted in Grades preK to 2, with the exception of Vaughn et al. (2008), which followed students through Grades 4 and 5 after they had received a bilingual intervention or had been part of a control group in Grade 1. Seven of the eight studies included a detailed description of the high-quality instruction provided during the interventions. High-quality instruction was defined by evidence-based principles of instruction, such as teacher modeling and verbalizations, guided practice, brisk lesson pacing to maintain student engagement, multiple practice opportunities, specific academic feedback, and lessons structured to focus on the core components in reading (Coyne, Kame'enui, & Carnine, 2011). Overall, results of these studies indicated that students who received the high-quality instruction outperformed students in the comparison groups. For example, in the Cena et al. (2013) experimental study, Grade 1 students in a TBP were randomly assigned to receive either a scripted vocabulary intervention or general vocabulary instruction using the standard program and vocabulary routines designed to increase the explicitness of the instruction. Findings indicated that students who received the scripted vocabulary intervention significantly outperformed students who received the general vocabulary instruction, on overall Spanish depth of word knowledge, Spanish vocabulary usage, and Spanish vocabulary definition tasks (η^2 = 0.17, 0.10, and 0.20, respectively). This advantage, however, did not have an effect on English reading and vocabulary outcomes.

The Tong, Irby, Lara-Alecio, and Mathes (2008) experimental study compared two different TBPs (an enhanced TBP and a typical TBP) for Grades K to 2. The enhanced TBP included PD that focused on helping teachers (a) reduce code-switching in the classroom in order to allow ELs to develop their language proficiency in each language without interference from the other language and (b) provide

TABLE 8

Reading Studies Examining the Quality of Instruction in Bilingual Programs

Study	Grade Level	*N*	Program Models Compared	Academic Measures	Outcome
Buysse, Castro, and Peisner-Feimberg (2010)	Pre-K	193	*English-only PD with evidence-based accommodations to support ELs* (visual cues, prereading activities, observing and documenting second language learning) *Treatment: Nuestros Niños PD for 8 weeks in SP*	*ENG:* WLPB-R, PPVT-III, PAT, NL *SP:* WLPB-RS, TVIP, PAT, NL, WMTS-PC	*ENG:* No significant differences between treatment/control on overall PAT score, but treatment students demonstrated significantly greater gains on onset segmentation task (*ES* = 0.61) *SP:* Treatment students demonstrated significantly greater gains on PAT (*ES* = 0.69) and specifically on the rhyme-matching subtask (*ES* = 0.68).
Calhoon, Al Otaiba, Cihak, King, and Avalos (2008)	Grade 1	76	*Two-way immersion with 60 PALS* sessions (30–35 minutes, 3×/ week) *Two-way immersion, no PALS*	*ENG:* DIBELS LNF, PSF, NWF, ORF	*ENG:* Significant time × condition interaction favoring PALS for PSF, NWF, and ORF (*ES* = 0.53, 0.50, 0.51); ELs receiving PALS instruction outperformed control group (*ES* = 1.29, 1.15, and .38 for NWF, LNF, and ORF)
Cena et al. (2013)	Grade 1	50	*Traditional bilingual program (TBP):* Reading in SP with 30 minutes ELD *Vocabulary intervention:* Taught 32 vocabulary words over 8 weeks using scripted lessons	*SP:* DOK SP Vocabulary, TVIP, IDEL FLO, BVAT	*SP:* Students who received vocabulary intervention significantly outperformed control group (TBP only) on DOK definitions (η^2 = 0.20), DOK usage (η^2 = 0.10), and DOK total scores (η^2 = 0.17); no effects on bilingual verbal ability

(continued)

TABLE 8 (CONTINUED)

Study	Grade Level	N	Program Models Compared	Academic Measures	Outcome
Tong, Irby, Lara-Alecio, and Mathes (2008)	K–2	262	*Traditional bilingual program–Enhanced (TBP-E):* 70/30 SP/ENG (70/30 in K, 60/40 in Grade 1, 50/50; all SP instruction in content areas until spring of Grade 2) + tiered intervention (75 minutes K; 90 minutes Grade 1) *Traditional transitional bilingual program (TB):* 80% SP/20% ENG implementing typical practice	*ENG:* Letter naming and letter sound, CTOPP, WLBP-R, DIBELS *SP:* TOPP-S, WLPB-RS, IDEL	*ENG:* Students in TBP-E significantly outperformed students in the "typical" program on Rapid Object Naming (*ES* = 0.12), Blending Phonemes (*ES* = 0.44), Segmenting Phonemes (*ES* = 0.71), Oral Language (*ES* = 0.48), and Reading (*ES* = 0.16 for DIBELS and greater than 0.40 for WLPB-R; after adjusting for initial skill) *SP:* After controlling for initial skill, students in the TBP-E significantly outperformed students in the "typical" program on SP letter naming (*ES* = 0.25), Blending Phonemes (*ES* = 0.38), Segmenting Phonemes (*ES* = 0.21), Listening Comprehension (*ES* = 0.19), and Reading Comprehension (*ES* = 0.38)
Tong, Lara-Alecio, Irby, and Mathes (2011)	K–1	140	Same as above (Tong, Irby, et al., 2008)	*ENG:* WLPB-R, IDEA Oral Proficiency Test *SP:* WLPB-R, IDEA Oral Proficiency Test	*ENG:* ENG oral language skills developed faster from Time 2 to Time 3; students in TB had higher reading comprehension scores than students in TBP-E *SP:* Students demonstrated higher Spanish overall language scores and students in TBP-E had significantly higher scores than students in TB ($\eta_p^2 = 0.41$), with SP developing faster from Time 1 to Time 2; students in TBP-E demonstrated stronger reading skills in SP than ENG and significantly higher scores than students in TB ($\eta_p^2 = 0.08$)

(continued)

TABLE 8 (CONTINUED)

Study	Grade Level	N	Program Models Compared	Academic Measures	Outcome
Tong, Lara-Alecio, Irby, Mathes, and Kwok (2008)	K–1	1,234	Same as above (Tong, Irby, et al., 2008)	*ENG*: WLPB-R, IDEA Oral Proficiency Test	*ENG*: Oral ENG growth was linear regardless of program type, and the rate of growth was significant for each group (.07 through .09); initial levels of performance varied significantly by group, and all but SEI-T showed heterogeneous growth; SEI-T students had significantly higher initial skills (*ES* = 0.40), but SEI-E students demonstrated larger growth (*ES* = 0.71); there were no differences in initial skill between TB and TBP-E, but TBP-E students demonstrated significantly greater growth (*ES* = 1.61); SEI-T students had significantly higher initial skills than TB (*ES* = 1.96), but the two groups grew at comparable rates
Vaughn et al. (2008)	Grade 1	86	*Transitional bilingual program* and intervention in SP. Length of intervention: 32 weeks, 5 days per week, 50 minutes/day in Grade 1. After first grade, core reading instruction was conducted in SP and in ENG, and by Grade 4 all instruction was in ENG.	*ENG*: WLPB-R, TOWRE, Spelling, Aimsweb Mazes, and TOSRE in Grades 4–5.	*ENG*: There were nonsignificant transfer effects favoring the SP treatment group in ENG letter word ID (0.39), ENG word reading (0.34), and ENG sentence reading (0.30).

(continued)

TABLE 8 (CONTINUED)

Study	Grade Level	N	Program Models Compared	Academic Measures	Outcome
Vaughn, Linan-Thompson, et al. (2006)	Grade 1	69	*Transitional bilingual program* and intervention in SP: 32 weeks; 5 days per week; 50 minutes/day	*SP:* WLPB-R, TOWRE-SP, IDEL FLO, spelling *ENG:* WLPB-R, CTOPP, DIBELS ORF, letter naming, sound identification *SP:* WLPB-R, TOPP-S, IDEL FLO, letter naming, sound identification	*SP:* Results were mixed and nonsignificant. However, effects sizes were moderate in FLO (0.32), passage comprehension (0.33), word reading (0.39), and spelling (0.43). *ENG:* No significant differences on reading outcomes between treatment and control groups with the exception of listening comprehension and verbal analogies favoring the control group (*ES* = −0.46 and −0.86, respectively). *SP:* The treatment group significantly outperformed the comparison group on TOPP-S (*d* = 0.73), WLPB-WA (*d* = 0.85), IDEL (*d* = 0.58), WLPB-Reading Comprehension (*d* = 0.55), WLPB-Listening Comprehension (*d* = 0.43)

Note. BVAT = Bilingual Verbal Ability Test; CTOPP = Comprehensive Test of Phonological Processing; DIBELS = Dynamic Indicators of Basic Early Literacy Skills; DOK = Depth of Knowledge; EL = English learner; ELD = English language development; ENG = English; *ES* = effect size; FLO = Fluidez en la Lectura Oral; IDEL = Indicadores Dinámicos del Éxito de la Lectura; LNF = Letter Naming Fluency; NL = Naming Letters; NWF = Nonsense Word Fluency; ORF = Oral Reading Fluency; PALS = Peer-assisted learning strategies; PAT = Phonemic Awareness Task; PD = professional development; PPVT = Peabody Picture Vocabulary Test; PSF = Phoneme Segmentation Fluency; SEI = structured English immersion; SP = Spanish; TOPP-S = Test of Phonological Processing–Spanish; TOSRE = Test of Sentence Reading Efficiency; TOWRE-SP = Test of Word Reading Efficiency FORM B adapted into Spanish; TVIP = Test de Vocabuario de Imágenes; WLPB-R = Woodcock Language Proficiency Battery–Revised; WLPB-RS = Woodcock Language Proficiency Battery–Revised Spanish Form; WMTS-PC = Where's My Teddy Story?–Print Concepts.

differentiated instruction for struggling ELs in a response to intervention model. The findings indicated that ELs in the enhanced TBP outperformed ELs in the typical TBP on almost all the measures in Spanish and English. English oral language proficiency, however, was still below the norm after 3 years, suggesting that students need time to develop their language proficiency in L2 independently of the type of bilingual program they attend (Genesee et al., 2006).

Vaughn, Linan-Thompson, et al. (2006) examined the effectiveness of a researcher-developed Spanish reading intervention that accompanied core instruction in Spanish in a TBP, first when it was implemented with two cohorts of Grade 1 students and then when the same cohorts were assessed again as part of a follow-up study 3 and 4 years later (Vaughn et al., 2008). Findings from the longitudinal study were mixed, and effects of the treatment in first grade in Spanish were mostly nonsignificant three and four years later. Effect sizes, however, ranged from 0.32 in Spanish connected text fluency to 0.43 in Spanish spelling favoring intervention students compared to comparison students in the Spanish study. Moreover, students in the Spanish intervention group appeared to have outscored students in the Spanish comparison group on letter word identification (*ES* = 0.39), on word efficiency (*ES* = 0.34) and on spelling (*ES* = 0.30). These findings are important (even if they were not significant) because they are apparent across decoding, fluency, and comprehension, and they suggest that interventions might have long-lasting effects, particularly if they could be provided across grades.

We could only locate one study that examined the direct effect of a PD program for preschool teachers called Nuestros Niños on Spanish and English student outcomes (Buysse, Castro, & Peisner-Feinberg, 2010). The Nuestros Niños program consists of 3 days of PD followed by classroom support from consultants and biweekly community-of-practice meetings that offer teachers a structured process to develop and refine instructional strategies. ELs in classrooms where teachers received the Nuestros Niños PD demonstrated significantly greater gains on the English onset segmentation task (*ES* = 0.61) and on Spanish phonological awareness tasks (*ES* = 0.69) compared to ELs in classrooms where teachers did not receive the PD.

Altogether, results from these studies confirm what Goldenberg (2013) and other researchers have suggested regarding the importance of providing ELs and EOs with explicit instruction and additional interventions, if necessary, that incorporate evidence-based principles of instructional design (Coyne et al., 2011). Although in Table 8 we described studies that measured quality of instruction, only the Buysse et al. (2010) study in preschool examined the effect of teacher PD in Spanish on EL outcomes in English and in Spanish. Thus, more research is needed to determine whether PD in the primary and upper grades in the language of instruction has a direct effect on student academic outcomes. Moreover, investigating exactly what factors of the PD are directly related to student outcomes (e.g., teacher knowledge of the linguistic systems, pedagogical knowledge, teacher bilingual language proficiency) would greatly benefit the field.

Reading studies comparing bilingual programs outside the United States. We found eight studies that were conducted outside the United States, as indicated in Table 9. The three studies conducted in the Netherlands (Admiraal, Westhoff, & de Bot, 2006; van der Leij, Bekebrede, & Kotterink, 2010; Verspoor, de Bot, & Xu, 2015) examined the effectiveness of different bilingual program models with students of different ages. In all three studies, students in bilingual programs in English and Dutch significantly outperformed their peers on English and Dutch measures in schools where Dutch was the language of instruction and English was taught for 2 hours a week or less.

The Goldenberg et al. (2014) study compared the Spanish reading and language performance of Spanish-speaking ELs in the United States who participated in one of five bilingual programs and Spanish-speaking students in Mexico who received Spanish-only instruction. The results indicated that while U.S. Hispanics who received instruction in either English or Spanish significantly outperformed students in Mexico on phonological awareness tasks ($p < .001$), students from Mexico outperformed students from the United States on picture vocabulary and listening comprehension tasks ($p < .001$). With respect to Spanish reading, Hispanic students receiving primarily Spanish instruction in the United States outperformed Hispanics receiving English instruction and students from Mexico on the Spanish reading tasks in Grade 1. By Grade 2, however, students from Mexico closed the gap and were performing better than Hispanics receiving primarily Spanish instruction in the United States. This result suggests that if the language of instruction is also the societal language, students perform better compared to when students are exposed to two languages in an environment where the societal language is English.

The study by Sailors, Hoffman, Pearson, Beretvas, and Matthee (2010) was conducted in South Africa in rural schools where students were provided with an intervention in their L1 (e.g., Afrikaans, Xhosa, Sotho) and in English in Grades 1 and 2. The findings indicated that ELs in the treatment schools performed better in their L1 and in English than the ELs in control schools. Teachers in the treatment schools were provided with high-quality instructional materials and PD. All of these studies suggest that bilingual programs can also benefit students whose L1 varies significantly from English. Moreover, bilingual instruction appears to provide students the support they need in their L2, as well as help maintain their L1.

Writing Studies

We found only one quasi-experimental study that examined the effects of bilingual programs on writing. As described in Table 10, Bae (2007) compared the effects of an English-Korean two-way immersion program on the writing performance of a bilingual English-Korean group in Grades 1 and 2 versus an EO group in the same grades in the United States. The findings suggested that the English-Korean group had mean scores similar to those of EOs on grammar and coherence by the end of Grade 2. More studies, however, need to be conducted on the effects of bilingual programs on student writing in L1 and L2.

TABLE 9

Reading Studies Comparing Bilingual Programs Outside the United States

Study	Grade Level	N	Program Models Compared	Academic Measures	Outcomes
Admiraal, Westhoff, and de Bot (2006)	Lower secondary (Grades 1–4)	1,305	*Dual immersion:* 50% English; 50% Dutch; *Dutch only*	*ENG:* EFLVT, CITO-Oral, MAVO, content exams (geography and history)	*ENG:* Main effect of bilingual program was large in terms of proportion of variance explained at school level in Vocabulary (R^2 = .48–.97), Reading Comprehension (R^2 = .94), Oral Language (R^2 < .30); bilingual group earned higher scores on content exams in Dutch and ENG
Goldenberg et al. (2014)	Grades 1–2	571	*United States:* English immersion; transitional bilingual education; developmental bilingual; dual language *Mexico:* SP only	*SP:* TOPP-S, WLPB-R	*SP language:* ELs in the United States who received reading instruction in either ENG (ENG ELs) or SP (SP ELs) outperformed students in Mexico on Phonological Awareness tasks (p < .001); students from Mexico outperformed U.S. students on Picture Vocabulary and Listening Comprehension tasks (p < .001)
					SP reading: SP ELs outperformed ENG ELs and students from Mexico on all measures in Grade 1, but students from Mexico closed the gap and outperformed ENG ELs and performed comparably to SP ELs in Grade 2
Lorenzo, Casal, and Moore (2009)	Ages 9–14	1,320	Three content area classes taught in L2 (predetermined by teacher); during bilingual instruction students regroup into bilingual and monolingual groups	Diagnostic tests employed to assess language competencies (reading, listening, writing, speaking)	*ENG, FR, and German:* There were statistically significant differences between bilingual and control groups on reading, listening, writing, and speaking, with means favoring the bilingual group (actual *t*-test values not reported)

(continued)

859

TABLE 9 (CONTINUED)

Study	Grade Level	N	Program Models Compared	Academic Measures	Outcomes
Lyster, Quiroga, and Ballinger (2013)	Grade 2	65	80% FR/20% ENG; 50% FR/50% ENG; 20% FR/80% ENG	*ENG:* PPVT, AAT, MAT *French:* EVIP, AAT, MAT	*ENG:* No significant effects by program type, but significant effects on MAT by group (treatment/control) and language dominance *FR:* No significant effects by program type, but significant effects on MAT by group (treatment/control)
Parsons and Lyddy (2009)	Grade 2	82	*English Reading First:* ENG in 2nd year of schooling and Irish reading during the 3rd year *Irish Reading First:* Irish reading between 1st and 2nd year of schooling and ENG reading toward the end of the 2nd year *Gaeltacht:* Irish reading in Grades 1–2, then ENG in Grades 2–3; Irish reading in Grade 4 English medium	Translational equivalents of single-word reading tasks (50 words, ordered in increasing difficulty)	*ENG:* Accuracy scores of Gaeltacht children were significantly lower than those in the other groups ($p < .01$) *Irish:* ENG medium sample performed significantly lower than other groups ($p < .01$)
Sailors, Hoffman, Pearson, Beretvas, and Matthee (2010)	Grades 1–2	801	*Read Intervention Grade 1 and in Grade 2:* 10 culturally relevant storybooks written in ENG and translated into home languages (used as read-alouds) + 8 picture books to be used during reading instruction	*ENG:* Object Identification, Letter/Sound Identification, Word Identification; Sentence Comprehension, Word Production; Sentence Production, Spelling (All assessments translated into home languages: Afrikaans, Xhosa, Sotho, Zulu, and others)	*ENG:* Students in the READ intervention significantly outperformed students in comparison schools on all language assessment subtests except Sentence Production (Grade 1, $\eta^2 = 0.01$ to 0.03; Grade 2, $\eta^2 = 0.01$ to 0.03); schools that were identified as strong implementers of the intervention performed significantly better on Object Identification, Sentence Comprehension, Word Production, and Spelling In Grade 1, students in strong-implementing schools significantly outperformed "regular" intervention and comparison schools in Coding and Meaning subscales

(continued)

TABLE 9 (CONTINUED)

Study	Grade Level	N	Program Models Compared	Academic Measures	Outcomes
			Comparison: Instruction provided using traditional phonics-based, culturally irrelevant textbooks		*Home language:* Students in the READ intervention significantly outperformed students in comparison schools on all language assessment subtests except Sentence Production in Grade 1 (Grade 1 η^2 = 0.03 to .09; Grade 2, 0.03 to 0.15); "regular" intervention schools significantly outperformed strong implementers and control group on Word Identification task; "regular" intervention and control group scored significantly higher than strong implementers on Word Production and Spelling tasks; in Grade 1, intervention schools significantly outperformed comparison schools on Coding and Meaning subscales; in Grade 2, intervention schools significantly outperformed on Meaning subscale
Van der Leij, Bekebrede, and Kotterink (2010)	Grades 2–3	57	*Bilingual:* Concurrent bilingual instruction from the age of 4 and reading instruction in ENG and Dutch in Grade 1	*ENG:* PPVT, OMT, Loanword Reading Fluency, Orthographic Knowledge and Awareness	*ENG:* Bilingual group performed significantly better on Vocabulary (Grade 2, η_p^2 = 0.12; Grade 3, η_p^2 = 0.53), Word Reading Fluency (OMT; Grade 2, η_p^2 = 0.23; Grade 3, η_p^2 = 0.22), Loanword Reading Fluency (η_p^2 = 0.14), and Orthographic Awareness (η_p^2 = 0.24)

(continued)

TABLE 9 (CONTINUED)

Study	Grade Level	N	Program Models Compared	Academic Measures	Outcomes
			Comparison: Did not receive any instruction or practice in ENG at school	*Dutch:* Similar to English measures	*Dutch:* Bilingual group performed significantly better on Reading Comprehension ($\eta_p^2 = 0.13$) in Grade 2, Multisyllabic Word Fluency (DMT; Grade 2, $\eta_p^2 = 0.08$; Grade 3, $\eta_p^2 = 0.13$), and on Orthographic Knowledge ($\eta_p^2 = 0.10$) in Grade 3
Verspoor, de Bot, and Xu (2015)	Ages 12–14	399	*Bilingual:* 50% (~15 hours/week) of instruction in ENG, 10 hours of which were in content subjects (history, math, art, physical education, etc.) and 5 hours of ENG *Regular:* 2 hours/week ENG instruction *Control:* 2 hours/week ENG instruction	*ENG:* Receptive vocabulary measure, productive informal writing task	*ENG:* Using sum of vocabulary and writing scores, bilinguals had significantly higher scores than regulars and controls in winter and spring ($p < .001$); Year 1 bilinguals had significantly higher ENG proficiency scores than regulars and controls ($\eta^2 = 0.20$) after controlling for initial proficiency, CITO score, out-of-school contact, and motivation); Year 3 bilinguals had significantly higher ENG proficiency scores than regulars ($\eta^2 = 0.16$) but not controls
				Dutch: CITO (scholastic aptitude), Questionnaire (ENG use, motivation, attitudes)	*Dutch:* Bilinguals were significantly more motivated than regulars and controls ($p < .05$), and bilinguals and controls had significantly higher CITO scores than regulars ($p < .001$)

Note. AAT = Auditory Analysis Test; CITO = Dutch National Institute for Test Development; EFLVT = English as a Foreign Language Vocabulary Test; EL = English learner; ENG = English; EVIP = Échelle de vocabulaire en images Peabody; FR = French; MAVO = National Final Examinations for English; MAT = Morphological Awareness Test; OMT = One Minute Test; PPVT = Peabody Picture Vocabulary Test; TOPP-S = Test of Phonological Processing–Spanish; WLPB-R = Woodcock Language Proficiency Battery–Revised.

TABLE 10
Studies Examining the Effectiveness of Bilingual Programs in Supporting Writing Development

Study	Grade Level	*N*	Program Models Compared	Academic Measures	Outcomes
Bae (2007)	Grades 1–2	192	*KETWIP:* 30% of instruction in ENG in K, increasing to 50% ENG in Grade 2 *EO:* All instruction in English	Researcher-developed narrative story task scored with respect to coherence, content, grammar, and text length	*ENG:* Grade 2 KETWIP students performed comparably to students in EO program on indices of grammar and coherence/content; KETWIP students wrote significantly longer narratives than EO students

Note. ENG = English; EO = English-only; KETWIP = Korean-English two-way immersion program.

Science Studies

We found only three quasi-experimental studies that examined science outcomes for ELs and EOs attending bilingual programs as summarized in Table 11. Findings from the Ciechanowski (2014) study indicated that ELs and EOs who attended a DLP that focused on science content made substantial gains in science outcomes in English (the language of science instruction in the DLP) from pretest to posttest. The science language gains were also significantly correlated with science content gains. The Martínez-Alvarez, Bannan, and Peters-Burton (2012) study found no differences in science knowledge in English (the language of science instruction) between students attending a DLP and students attending a TBP ($\eta^2 = 0.07$). However, ELs in the DLP performed significantly better on Spanish reading measures.

Mathematics Studies

Seven of the studies in our review focused on mathematics (see Table 12). One of them took place in Germany (Kempert, Saalbach, & Hardy, 2011). None of them were randomized controlled studies, and only one included pretest data (Valentino & Reardon, 2015). The study by Kempert et al. (2011) indicated that proficiency in the language of testing was more influential than student mathematical problem-solving abilities. In addition, more variance was explained by cognitive abilities, SES, and reading comprehension than by language proficiency or arithmetic skills. This study, however, included only posttest data, so the results should be interpreted with caution.

Valentino and Reardon's (2015) longitudinal study also compared outcomes in mathematics. The only statistically significant outcome was in second grade, favoring the TBP (*ES* = 0.27), but this effect did not last until middle school. Marian, Shook, and Schroeder (2013) found that ELs attending a two-way immersion program

TABLE 11

Studies Examining the Effectiveness of Bilingual Programs in Supporting Student Science Understanding

Study	Grade Level	N	Program Models Compared	Academic Measures	Outcomes
Ciechanowski (2014)	Grade 3	33	*Dual language program:* 50/50 ENG/SP, half of the day taught in ENG, half of the day taught in SP; ELs received an additional 30 min ELD instruction focused on science	*ENG:* FOSS curriculum tests	*ENG:* All emergent bilinguals (ELs and ENG proficient) made significant science gains from pre- to posttest Science language gains were significantly correlated with content gains for both groups ($r = .39–.56$)
M. G. López and Tashakkori (2006)	Grade 5	344	*Two-way bilingual:* 40% SP/60% ENG *Transitional bilingual:* EO with the option of receiving 2.5 hours/week SP instruction	*ENG:* FCAT *SP:* EDL	*ENG:* No significant differences in performance on FCAT science for students in the two groups, but results indicated that students who entered with lower levels of ENG proficiency in K or Grade 1 scored significantly lower than students with higher levels of ENG proficiency ($\eta^2 = 0.09$)
Martinez-Alvarez, Bannan, and Peters-Burton (2012)	Grade 4	78	*InSciRead:* Instructional model based on use of inquiry-based science cognitive strategies and reading comprehension of science texts written in SP *Bilingual model:* 50/50 two-way dual language model in which math, science, and language arts instruction was in SP; social studies and language arts instruction was in ENG	*ENG:* Adapted Detecting Incongruities task *SP:* WMLP	*ENG:* After adjusting for pretest SP reading levels, students in the treatment group had significantly higher adjusted mean scores on total number of sentences correctly identified ($\eta_p^2 = 0.07$)

Note. EL = English learner; EDL = Español Desarrollo de Lectura; ENG = English; EO = English-only; FCAT = Florida Comprehensive Assessment Test; FOSS = Full Option Science System; SP = Spanish; WMLP = Woodcock Muñoz Language Proficiency.

TABLE 12

Studies Examining the Effectiveness of Bilingual Programs in Supporting Student Mathematics Understanding

Study	Grade Level	N	Program Models Compared	Academic Measures	Outcomes
Gómez, Freeman, and Freeman (2005)	Grades 3–5	240	*50–50 Content model:* Mathematics instruction in ENG, science, and social studies instruction in SP; Language Arts instruction in native language in pre-K and K and then in students' L2 in Grades 1–5	*ENG:* TAKS	*ENG:* Of 103 Spanish-dominant Grade 3 students tested, 89 (86%) met the proficiency standard; of the 58 English-dominant Grade 3 students tested, 53 (95%) met the proficiency standard; overall, 142/159 (89%) met the third-grade proficiency standard on TAKS Reading
Hofstetter (2004)	K–3	441	*Academic language acquisition (ALA):* Instruction in K–1, 70% in L1, 30% in L2; percentage of ENG instruction increases until Grades 4/5, where ratio of instruction is 85% ENG and 15% SP *Structured English immersion (SEI):* Students receive instruction predominantly in ENG, with 10% to 15% of instruction in ELD, 75% using sheltered ENG strategies	*ENG:* CELDT, SAT-9 mathematics *SP:* SABE	*ENG:* The percentages of students who achieved the 50th National Percentile Rank on the mathematics test of the SAT-9 were comparable in ALA (38% to 46%) and SEI (40% to 56%)
Kempert, Saalbach, and Hardy (2011)	Grade 3	74	*German only:* Primary language of instruction was German	*German:* BVAT, Mathematical word problems, reading comprehension test, language proficiency test, mathematics test for Grade 2, cognitive ability test (CFT 20)	*German:* Math skills and German language proficiency were the strongest predictors of German mathematics problem solving, accounting for 43.7% of the observed variance

(continued)

TABLE 12 (CONTINUED)

Study	Grade Level	N	Program Models Compared	Academic Measures	Outcomes
			German and Turkish: Children with Turkish backgrounds were offered Turkish language classes	*Turkish:* BVAT, mathematical word problems	*Turkish:* Proficiency in the language of testing (Turkish) was the strongest predictor of Turkish problem solving ($R^2 = .27$) after controlling for SES, cognitive ability, and math skills; no significant change to variance explained after including German language proficiency in the model
Lindholm-Leary and Block (2010)	Grades 4–6	Study 1: 193 Study 2: 466	*DLP:* 90% in SP in K–1, 80% in Grade 2, 70% in Grade 3, 60% in Grade 4, and 50% from Grade 5 on *EO:* Control group	*ENG:* Mathematics California Standards Test	*ENG:* In Study 1, there were no significant differences between scale scores of English proficient (EP) and English learner (EL) students by program type; In Study 2, both EP and EL students in a DLP achieved at significantly higher levels than their peers in EO on the Mathematics CST ($d = 0.77$ for EP group, $d = 0.58$ for EL group)
Marian, Shook, and Schroeder (2013)	Grades 3–5	2,009	*TWI-S:* SP in Grades K–2, ENG in Grades 3–5 (math in SP K–3, ENG in Grades 4–5, social studies/science in SP) *TPI:* ENG with pullout ESL instruction as needed *TWI-E:* ENG in Grades K–2; SP instruction in Grades 3–5 (math in SP in K–3, ENG in Grades 4–5, social studies/science in SP in K–5)	*ENG:* State measure of annual growth in ENG, State Standards Achievement Test	*ENG:* TWI-S students significantly outperformed TPI in math (and showed significant improvements across grade levels); for all grades, TWI-E students outperformed EO students in math

(continued)

TABLE 12 (CONTINUED)

Study	Grade Level	N	Program Models Compared	Academic Measures	Outcomes
Valentino and Reardon (2015)	Grades 2–5	13,750	*Transitional bilingual:* SP instruction in K and transition to ENG by Grades 2–3 *Developmental bilingual:* In K, 50% to 90% of instruction in target language, proportion of ENG instruction increasing each year *Dual immersion:* 80% to 90% of instruction in target language in K–1, transitioning to 50% ENG and 50% target language by Grade 5 *English immersion:* All instruction in ENG plus at least 30 minutes ELD support	*ENG:* State standardized tests in mathematics	*ENG:* Grade 2 math scores were significantly higher for students receiving TB instruction (0.27 *SD* higher), but this difference did not hold to middle school; students receiving DLP instruction grew faster than students receiving English immersion instruction

Note. BVAT = Bilingual Verbal Ability Test; CELDT = California English Language Development Test; CFT = Cognitive ability test; DLP = dual language program; EDL = Español Desarrollo de Lectura; ELD = English language development; ENG = English; EO = English-only; ESL = English as a second language; FCAT = Florida Comprehensive Assessment Test; SABE = Spanish Assessment of Basic Skills; SAT-9 = Stanford Achievement Test; SP = Spanish; TAKS = Texas Assessment of Knowledge and Skills; TPI = Transitional Program of Instruction; TWI-E = two-way immersion–English; TWI-S = two-way immersion–Spanish.

outperformed ELs attending EO programs across grades. Hofstetter (2004), on the other hand, found that ELs performed equally well in a transition program and a structured EI program in Grades K to 3. In summary, ELs attending bilingual programs might not be at a disadvantage in terms of their mathematics performance, but more research is needed to determine the benefits of bilingual programs on mathematics, whether it is taught in L1 or L2.

CROSS-LINGUISTIC TRANSFER AND COGNITION
Cross-Linguistic Transfer

Bilingual programs have been influenced, in part, by two theories about how language and literacy develop in two languages: Cummins's (1979) interdependence hypothesis and Lado's (1964) contrastive analysis hypothesis. Cummins's interdependence hypothesis states that language and reading proficiency in the L1 foster L2 reading acquisition. Lado's contrastive analysis hypothesis states that structural differences and similarities in L1 and L2 can either facilitate the acquisition of L2, if the learner is able to identify the commonalities between the languages, or hinder it if the structures of the L1 and L2 are very different. This is particularly the case when the learner is not able to identify the differences in order to reduce the negative transfer of linguistic structures. Although transfer is often used as an argument in support of bilingual education, according to Snow (2006) the operational definition of transfer and the evidence of its existence is still not clear, given that most studies are only correlational (i.e., they don't explain the causal effect of cross-linguistic transfer).

To better understand cross-linguistic transfer, Melby-Lervåg and Lervåg (2011) conducted a meta-analysis on correlational studies on the topic. Five important findings can be derived from the meta-analysis: (a) there was a small correlation between L1 and L2 oral language skills ($r = .16$); (b) there were moderate to large correlations in phonology and decoding in L1 and L2 ($r = .54$ and $r = .44$); (c) instructional language at school had a moderating effect on decoding skills, suggesting that correlations were higher between decoding in L1 and L2 for students attending bilingual schools than for students attending EO programs; (d) cross-linguistic transfer was more likely to occur when the two writing systems were similar; and (e) decoding in L1was significantly correlated with L2 reading comprehension ($r = .24$). Additional studies that have been conducted since then corroborate these findings (see, e.g., Saiegh-Haddad & Geva, 2008, examining transfer from Arabic to English).

Other recent studies have indicated that, in the early grades, initial levels of decoding and oral reading fluency, as well as growth in those skills, are significant predictors of reading comprehension within the same language but not across languages (D. L. Baker, Park, & Baker, 2012). In other words, the impact of the transfer of beginning reading skills (e.g., phonological awareness and decoding) on more complex reading skills (e.g., comprehension) does not appear to occur naturally from one language to another. An additional RCT study, which examined the effects of an intervention focusing on transition elements intended to help ELs at risk for reading difficulties in the transition from Spanish to English skills, indicated no significant differences in reading outcomes between ELs in the transition intervention and ELs who received a business as usual intervention from the school (D. L. Baker et al., 2015). These findings suggest that providing students in Grade 1 with explicit transition instruction from one language to another might not be necessary.

Results from two other studies also suggest that the level of transfer from beginning reading skills to reading comprehension from Spanish to English depends, in part, on ELs' oral language proficiency in English (D. L. Baker, Park, & Baker, 2013; Nakamoto, Lindsey, & Manis, 2012). Moreover, the level of transfer might also depend on whether students are simultaneous bilinguals (learning two languages simultaneously) or sequential bilinguals (learning foundational skills in L1 first, then transitioning to L2). For example, a study by Grant, Gottardo, and Geva (2011) found that simultaneous bilinguals who spoke Portuguese and English consistently outperformed sequential bilinguals who spoke English and Spanish on measures of phonological awareness, word reading, vocabulary, and nonverbal reasoning tasks in English, suggesting that simultaneous bilinguals transfer their skills from one language to another more effectively than sequential bilinguals.

In summary, given that most studies on cross-linguistic transfer have been correlational, more experimental studies are needed to determine exactly how the relation among reading skills in two languages works, how knowledge and skills in one language might support the development of skills in other domains (e.g., mathematics), and whether language proficiency in two or more languages can be enhanced in the context of different bilingual programs. Research in each of these areas also needs to take into account the linguistic differences among languages, individual student characteristics, and contextual factors (school demographics, language exposure in the home, etc.). This research could also focus on whether the successful transfer of skills requires additional interventions and assessments that specifically address this transfer, or whether the transfer occurs naturally without being taught explicitly. Preliminary studies, such as D. L. Baker et al.'s (2015), suggest that the transfer might not need to be explicitly taught; however, this warrants further exploration.

Cognition

Three major discoveries in neuroscience can significantly influence how bilingual students (ELs and EOs) are taught in schools. The first discovery indicates that bilinguals activate information about both languages when they are using one language alone. This activity can be observed in reading, listening to speech, and preparing to speak one language alone (e.g., Bialystok, Craig, Green, & Gollan, 2009; Kroll, Bobb, & Wodniecka, 2006). The second discovery indicates that the language system is highly adaptive and that emergent bilingualism is not only about acquiring an L2 but also about how the first language changes in response to the L2 (Chang, 2016; Kroll & Bialystok, 2013). The third discovery indicates that bilingualism has significant positive effects on cognition. For example, findings by Abutalebi and Green (2008) and Calvo and Bialystok (2013) suggest that bilinguals outperform monolinguals on cognitive tasks that require ignoring irrelevant information, task switching, and resolving conflict. These findings are particularly important in helping research-ers and practitioners understand how and whether language skills transfer from one language to another and how to use the benefits of the bilingual mind to improve learning of academic content.

Specifically, in a recent meta-analysis examining the correlation between bilin-gualism and cognition (Adesope, Lavin, Thompson, & Ungerleider, 2010), findings indicated small to large weighted mean effect sizes ranging from $g = 0.32$ on metacog-nitive awareness to $g = 0.96$ on attentional control favoring bilinguals when com-pared to monolinguals. Other significant cognitive outcomes were abstract and symbolic representation ($g = 0.57$) and metalinguistic awareness ($g = 0.33$) favoring bilinguals. The largest effect sizes were found when the languages had similar ortho-graphic systems (e.g., English and Spanish, or French and Spanish), when the studies were conducted in the United States or Canada ($g = 1.76$), and when participants were postsecondary students. However, effect sizes did not vary by SES. Although the majority of the studies were conducted in the early elementary grades, and Bialystok et al. (2009) conducted half of them, additional analysis by Adesope et al. (2010) did not indicate researcher bias. Nonetheless, studies varied significantly in their method-ological quality (e.g., the reliability and validity of the measures used were not always reported), and information about how the researchers controlled for biases was missing.

Two recent studies examining the relation between SES and bilingualism on cog-nition can shed more light on how these two variables interact. For example, Calvo and Bialystok (2013) found that low-income bilinguals obtained higher scores on executive functioning tasks that included verbal and nonverbal attention than did low-income and middle-income monolinguals. Esposito and Baker-Ward (2013) found that older low-income bilinguals (i.e., students in fourth grade) attending a DLP outperformed older low-income monolinguals and younger kindergarten and second-grade bilinguals on tasks requiring interference suppression (i.e., on tasks requiring the suppression of interference from an L2, not just the inhibition of a response).

We found only one study since the publication of the meta-analysis by Adesope et al. (2010) that examined the effects of a bilingual program on cognition (Nicolay & Poncelet, 2013). The study compared outcomes on attention and executive con-trol in an EI program and a monolingual French program that taught English as a foreign language. The findings suggest significant differences favoring the bilingual group in reaction times on tasks assessing alertness, auditory attention, divided atten-tion, and flexibility ($ES = 0.44$ to 0.63) but not on response inhibition (suppression of actions that are inappropriate in a given context), interference inhibition (suppres-sion of prior knowledge that interferes with new knowledge), or the Simon effect (wherein stimuli are presented in different locations from the response, even though the location is irrelevant to the task). This study suggests that students attending bilingual programs can also benefit cognitively from learning two languages, particu-larly in the performance of complex tasks that are controlled by executive functioning processes and working memory.

Next, we offer recommendations for future research based on our review of studies of bilingual programs, the historical context for the implementation of bilingual education in the United States, and recent discoveries of how the bilingual mind affects cognitive processes.

FUTURE RESEARCH

As we reflect on the political and scientific activities that have occurred since the publication of *Educational Researcher*'s special issue on bilingual education in 1992, we believe that we may be at a turning point in which bilingual education is viewed increasingly as an asset for ELs and EOs alike. This hypothesis is supported by the rapid rise of bilingual programs in the United States, including in states where EO is mandated, as well as by the large number of publications examining the effects of bilingual policies (Gándara & Hopkins, 2010), bilingual instruction, and bilingualism on economic outcomes (Gándara & Callahan, 2014), academic outcomes, and cognition (Bialystok et al., 2009). However, in 1992, Cziko suggested that instead of asking whether bilingual education works, we should consider the question of what can actually be done to make bilingual education better and accessible to more children. Next, we provide some guidelines on how Cziko's suggestions could be addressed.

Establish Minimum Standards to Conduct Research in Bilingual Education

Given the variation in program labels and the lack of program descriptions, it is important to establish standards to conduct research in this area. The standards should include clear definitions of the terminology used in a study, collect information about instructional practices, and provide a detailed description of the materials and pedagogy used to teach in both languages. In addition, information about teacher language proficiency in the language of instruction, the home environment, the school setting, and the community's support or rejection of bilingual education should be included, to help researchers and practitioners understand how and under what circumstances the program worked.

Conduct More Rigorous Experimental Studies That Examine Specific Variables Within Bilingual Programs

We were able to locate only eight studies that used an RCT design, and most of them were conducted in preschool or in the early grades. Thus, there is a need for more experimental studies that not only compare bilingual programs but also compare specific variables within these programs such as the effect of (a) student level of language proficiency and growth on academic outcomes, (b) academic vocabulary instruction in L1 and L2, (c) writing instruction in L1 and L2, and (d) different configurations of partner practice during bilingual instruction or interventions. Studies of this type should also include EOs attending bilingual programs, given that few studies have examined the academic, cognitive, or potential social benefits of bilingual programs for EOs.

Conduct More Rigorous Studies on the Type of PD Needed to Support Effective Bilingual Instruction

As F. López, McEneaney, and Nieswandt (2015) indicated, students in states that have invested more in PD for bilingual teachers and ESL teachers appear to have higher scores on national assessments than students in states with more restrictive rules. Thus, more studies on how to provide high-quality PD to bilingual teachers, and on tools to accurately assess instructional quality in bilingual programs, are needed. We found only one experimental study that examined the effects of a PD module on student outcomes (Buysse et al., 2010), and we could not locate any studies that examined whether teachers' pedagogical knowledge, and/or their level of language proficiency in the students' L1 and in English, had an effect on student outcomes (Gándara & Hopkins, 2010). These studies should also target the training of preservice and in-service bilingual teachers who work with students who speak English as their L1 and who are also learning an L2.

Examine the Effects of Bilingual Education in Other Domains, Including Writing, Math, Science, and Cognition

Given the rapid advances in neuroscience and the scarcity of research examining outcomes in other domains besides reading, more studies ought to be conducted that examine the effect of bilingual programs on writing, math, science, and cognition. These findings would help practitioners capitalize on the cognitive advantages of bilingualism to improve academic outcomes, not only for ELs but also for EOs learning an L2. Moreover, although we could not find any studies that fit our criteria and that focused on the use of technology to support the academic performance of students attending bilingual programs, we also propose that more studies examine how technology in the context of bilingual programs can enhance instruction and increase student language proficiency in two or more languages. The use of technology in bilingual programs could also provide researchers and practitioners with a better understanding of how the cognitive processes in bilingual students support their academic attainment in two languages.

CONCLUSION

Bilingual education in the United States has been a central part of the culture and identity of many different ethnic groups, particularly of Hispanics. Moreover, our search indicates that bilingual programs, and specifically DLPs, have gained increasing attention from middle-income parents who view bilingual education as an opportunity for their children to obtain a broader view of the world and be more competitive in the job market. Although evidence of the economical and cultural benefits of bilingualism is starting to emerge, additional research targeting the PD of high-quality bilingual teachers and bilingual programs is necessary to create a stronger knowledge base that is well grounded in scientific evidence.

APPENDIX A
Journals Searched by Hand (2003–2015)

American Educational Research Journal
Annual Review of Applied Linguistics[a]
Applied Linguistics[a]
Applied Psycholinguistics[a]
Bilingualism: Language and Cognition
Bilingual Research Journal: The Journal of the National Association of Bilingual Education[a]
Early Childhood Research Quarterly
Educational Researcher[a]
Harvard Education Review[a]
Hispanic Journal of Behavioral Sciences
International Journal of Bilingual Education and Bilingualism[a]
International Journal of Science & Mathematics Education
Intervention in School & Clinic: Journal for Research in Mathematics Education
Journal of Education[a]
Journal of Education for Students Placed at Risk[a]
Journal of Educational Issues of Language Minority Students[a]
Journal of Immersion and Content-Based Language Education
Journal of Learning Disabilities[a]
Journal of Literacy Research (Journal of Reading Behavior[a])
Journal of Multilingual and Multicultural Development
Journal of Research in Science Teaching
Journal of Research on Educational Effectiveness
Language and Education[a]
Language Learning[a]
Language Teaching
Learning Disabilities Research & Practice
Lectura y Vida
Modern Language Journal[a]
NABE Journal of Research and Practice[a]
Peabody Journal of Education[a]
Phi Delta Kappan[a]
Psychology in the Schools
Reading & Writing Quarterly: Overcoming Learning Difficulties
Reading and Writing: An Interdisciplinary Journal
Reading in a Foreign Language
Review of Educational Research
Studies in Second Language Acquisition[a]
TESOL Quarterly[a]
The Elementary School Journal[a]

[a]Journals searched by Genesee, Lindholm-Leary, Saunders, and Christian (2006).

APPENDIX B

Measures Used in Reading and Cross-Linguistic Transfer Studies

Measure Name	Abbreviation
English	
Aimsweb Mazes	Aimsweb Mazes
Auditory Analysis Test	AAT
Autism Diagnostic Interview–Revised	ADI-R
Autism Diagnostic Observation Schedule	ADOS
Bilingual Syntax Measure	BSM
Bilingual Verbal Ability Test	BVAT
California English Language Development Test	CELDT
CITO Oral Proficiency Test for English	CITO
Clinical Evaluation of Language Fundamentals	CELF
Comprehensive Test of Basic Skills	CTBS
Computer-Based Academic Assessment System	CAAS
CORE Assessing Reading	CORE
Desired Results Developmental Profile	DRDP
Developmental Reading Assessment	DRA
DIBELS Letter Naming Fluency	DIBELS LNF
DIBELS Nonsense Word Fluency	DIBELS NWF
DIBELS Oral Reading Fluency	DIBELS ORF
DIBELS Phoneme Segmentation Fluency	DIBELS PSF
Early Childhood Environmental Rating Scale–Revised	ECERS-R
Early Literacy Individual Growth and Development Indicators	EL-IGDIs
Early Phonological Awareness Profile	EPAP
Emergent Literacy Profile	ELP
English as a Foreign Language Vocabulary Test	EFLVT
Expressive One-Word Picture Vocabulary Test	EOWPVT
Florida Comprehensive Assessment Test	FCAT
Gates-MacGinitie Reading	GMR
Get Ready to Read–English	GRR-E
Individual Test of Academic Skills	ITAS
Iowa Test of Basic Skills	ITBS
Kindergarten Assessment Guide	KAG
Language Assessment Scale	LAS
Language Competencies/Expressive Proficiency	LCEP
MacArthur Communicative Development Inventory	MCDI
Matrix Analogies Test	MAT-X
Measures of Academic Progress	MAP
Morphological Awareness Test	MAT
Neale Analysis of Reading Development	Neale
Oral Language Proficiency Scale Interview–Revised	OLPSI-R
Oregon Assessment of Knowledge and Skills	OAKS
Peabody Picture Vocabulary Test	PPVT
Phonological Awareness Tasks	PAT

(continued)

APPENDIX B (CONTINUED)

Measure Name	Abbreviation
Preschool Language Scale	PLS
Rapid Alternating Stimulus	RAS
Rapid Automatizing Naming	RAN
Scholastic Reading Inventory	SRI
Spanish Assessment of Basic Skills	SABE
Stanford Achievement Test (9th and 10th editions)	SAT-9, SAT-10
Stanford English Language Proficiency	SELP
State Measure of Annual Growth	SMAG
State Standards Achievement Test	SSAT
Supports for Early Literacy Assessment	SELA
Support for English Language Learners Classroom Assessment	SELLCA
Test of Early Grammatical Impairment	TEGI
Test of Word Reading Efficiency	TOWRE
Texas Assessment of Academic Skills	TAAS
Texas Assessment of Knowledge and Skills	TAKS
Title Recognition Test	TRT
Vineland Adaptive Behavior Scales	VABS
Weschler Individual Achievement Test	WIAT
Weschler Intelligence Scale for Children	WISC
Woodcock Johnson Psycho-Educational Battery	WJ-R
Woodcock Language Proficiency Battery–Revised Spanish and English Forms	WLPB-R
Woodcock Reading Mastery Test–Revised	WRMT-R
Word List Fluency	WLF
Spanish	
Aprenda: La prueba de logros en Español	Aprenda
Batería Psico-Educativa Revisada de Woodcock Muñoz	WM-R
Comprehensive Test of Basic Skills (Spanish)	CTBS-S
Depth of Knowledge Spanish Vocabulary	DOK-S
Evaluación del desarrollo de la lectura	EDL
Get Ready to Read–Spanish	GRR-S
IDEL Fluidez en la Lectura Oral	IDEL FLO
IDEL Fluidez en las Palabras sin Sentido	IDEL FPS
Phonological Awareness Tasks	PAT
Spanish Assessment of Basic Education	SABE
Stanford Spanish Language Proficiency	SSLP
Test de Vocabulario en Imágenes Peabody	TVIP
Test of Phonological Processing–Spanish	TOPP-S
Test of Spanish Reading Fluency	TOSRE
Woodcock Muñoz Language Proficiency	WMLP
Woodcock Language Proficiency Battery–Revised Spanish Form	WLPB-RS
French	
BEMEL	BEMEL
Test de Vocabulaire en Images	EVIP

ACKNOWLEDGMENT

We would like to acknowledge the contributions of Igone Arteagoitia to an earlier draft of this chapter.

REFERENCES

References marked with an asterisk indicate studies included in the review.

Abutalebi, J., & Green, D. W. (2008). Control mechanisms in bilingual language production: Neural evidence from language switching studies. *Language and Cognitive Processing, 25*, 557–582. doi:10.1080/01690960801920602

Adesope, O. O., Lavin, T., Thompson, T., & Ungerleider, C. (2010). Systematic review and meta-analysis on the cognitive benefits of bilingualism. *Review of Educational Research, 80*, 207–245.

*Admiraal, W., Westhoff, G., & de Bot, K. (2006). Evaluation of bilingual secondary education in the Netherlands: Students' language proficiency in *English*. *Educational Research and Evaluation, 12*, 75–93.

Agirdag, O. (2014). The long-term effects of bilingualism on children of immigration: Student bilingualism and future earnings. *International Journal of Bilingual Education and Bilingualism, 17*, 449–464.

*Anderberg, A., & McSparran Ruby, M. F. (2013). Preschool bilingual learners' receptive vocabulary development in school readiness programs. *NABE Journal of Research and Practice, 4*. Retrieved from https://www2.nau.edu/nabej-p/ojs/index.php/njrp/article/view/15

Arizona Department of Education. (1998). Proposition 203. Retrieved from https://www.azed.gov/wp-content/uploads/pdf/proposition203.pdf

August, D., Goldenberg, C., & Rueda, R. (2010). Restrictive state language policies: Are they scientifically based? In P. Gándara & M. Hopkins (Eds.), *Forbidden language: English learners and restrictive policies* (pp. 139–159). New York, NY: Teachers College Press.

*Bae, J. (2007). Development of English skills need not suffer as a result of immersion: Grades 1 and 2 writing assessment in a Korean/English two-way immersion program. *Language Learning, 57*, 299–332.

Baker, C. (2011). *Foundations of bilingualism and bilingual education* (5th ed.). Bristol, England: Multilingual Matters.

Baker, D. L., Burns, D., Kame'enui, E. J., Smolkowski, K., & Baker, S. K. (2015). Does small group explicit instruction support the transition from Spanish to English reading instruction for first grade English learners at risk for reading difficulties? *Learning Disabilities Quarterly, 1*, 1–14. doi:10.1177/0731948715616757

*Baker, D. L., Park, Y., & Baker, S. K. (2012). The reading performance of English learners in Grades 1–3: The role of initial status and growth on reading fluency in Spanish and English. *Reading and Writing, 25*, 251–281. doi:10.1007/s11145-010-9261-z

Baker, D. L., Park, Y., & Baker, S. K. (2013, July). *Effect of English language proficiency and Spanish and English literacy on English reading comprehension for Spanish-speaking English learners*. Interactive paper presented at the Society for the Scientific Study of Reading conference, Hong Kong, SAR.

Baker, D. L., Park, Y., Baker, S. K., Basaraba, D., Kame'enui, E., & Beck, C. (2012). Effects of a paired bilingual reading program on the reading performance of English learners in Grades 1–3. *Journal of School Psychology, 50*, 737–758. doi:10.1016/j.jsp.2012.09.002

Baker, D. L., Richards-Tutor, C., Gersten, R., Baker, S. K., & Smith, J. (in press). Building literacy for English learners within Response to Intervention. In E. C. López, S. G. Nahari, & S. L. Proctor (Eds.), *The handbook of multicultural school psychology: An interdisciplinary perspective* (2nd ed.). New York, NY: Routledge.

Baker, K., & de Kanter, A. A. (1981). *Effectiveness of bilingual education: A review of the literature* (Final draft report). Washington, DC: Department of Education, Office of Planning, Budget, and Evaluation.

*Barnett, W. S., Yarosz, D. J., Thomas, J., Jung, K., & Blanco, D. (2007). Two-way monolingual English immersion in preschool education: An experimental comparison. *Early Childhood Research Quarterly, 22*, 277–293. doi:10.1016/j.ecresq.2007.03.003

*Berens, M. S., Kovelman, I., & Petitto, L.-A. (2013). Should bilingual children learn reading in two languages at the same time or in sequence? *Bilingual Research Journal, 36*, 35–60. doi:10.1080/15235882.2013.779618

Bialystok, E., Craig, F. I., Green, D. W., & Gollan, T. (2009). Bilingual mind. *Psychological Science in the Public Interest, 10*(3), 89–129. doi:10.1177/1529100610387084

Bilingual Education Act, Pub. L. No. (90-247), 81 Stat. 816 (1968).

*Buysse, V., Castro, D. C., & Peisner-Feinberg, E. (2010). Effects of a professional development program on classroom practices and outcomes for Latino dual language learners. *Early Childhood Research Quarterly, 25*, 194–206. doi:10.1016/j.ecresq.2009.10.001

*Calhoon, M. B., Al Otaiba, S., Cihak, D., King, A., & Avalos, A. (2008). Effects of a peer-mediated program on reading skill acquisition for two bilingual first-grade classrooms. *Learning Disability Quarterly, 30*, 169–184. doi:10.2307/30035562

*Calvo, A., & Bialystok, E. (2013). Independent effects of bilingualism and socioeconomic status on language ability and executive functioning. *Cognition, 130*, 278–288. doi:10.1016/j.cognition.2013.11.015

*Carlo, M. S., Barr, C. D., August, D., Calderón, M., & Artzi, L. (2014). Language of instruction as a moderator for transfer of reading comprehension skills among Spanish-speaking English language learners. *Bilingual Research Journal, 37*, 287–310. doi:10.108/15235882.2014.963739

Castañeda v. Pickard, 648 F.2d 989 (5th Cir. 1981).

*Cena, J., Baker, D. L., Kame'enui, E. J., Baker, S. K., Park, Y., & Smolkowski, K. (2013). The impact of a systematic and explicit vocabulary intervention in Spanish with Spanish-speaking English learners in first grade. *Reading and Writing, 26*, 1289–1316. doi:10.1007/s11145-012-9419-y

Center for Applied Linguistics. (2015). *Resources for two-way immersion and dual language practitioners.* Retrieved from www.cal.org/twi

Chang, C. B. (2016). Bilingual perceptual benefits of experience with a heritage language. *Bilingualism, 19*(4), 791–809. doi:10.1017/S1366728914000261

*Ciechanowski, K. (2014). Weaving together science and English: An interconnected model of language development for emergent bilinguals. *Bilingual Research Journal, 37*, 237–262. doi:10.1080/15235882.2014.963737

Commonwealth of Massachusetts. (2002). *Chapter 386 of the Act of 2002. An act relative to the teaching of English in public schools.* Retrieved from https://malegislature.gov/Laws/SessionLaws/Acts/2002/Chapter386

Coyne, M. D., Kame'enui, E. J., & Carnine, D. W. (2011). *Effective teaching strategies that accommodate diverse learners* (4th ed.). Boston, MA: Pearson.

Crawford, J. (2004). *Educating English learners* (5th ed.). Los Angeles, CA: Bilingual Education Services.

Cummins, J. (1979). Linguistic interdependence and the educational development of bilingual children. *Review of Educational Research, 49*, 222–251.

Cziko, G. A. (1992). The evaluation of bilingual education: From necessity and probability to possibility. *Educational Researcher, 21*(2), 10–15.

Dauphine, N. (2014, May 14). Hispanics are forgotten in civil rights history. *Education Week.* Retrieved from http://www.edweek.org/ew/articles/2014/05/14/31dauphine.h33.html

Durán, L., Roseth, C. J., & Hoffman, P. (2010). An experimental study comparing English-only and transitional bilingual education on Spanish-speaking preschoolers' early literacy development. *Early Childhood Research Quarterly, 25,* 207–217. doi:10.1016/j.ecresq.2009.10.002

Durán, L., Roseth, C. J., & Hoffman, P. (2014). Effects of transitional bilingual education on Spanish-speaking preschoolers' literacy and language development: Year 2 results. *Applied Psycholinguistics, 36,* 921–951. doi:10.107/S014271643000568

Durán, L., Roseth, C. J., Hoffman, P., & Robertshaw, M. B. (2013). Spanish-speaking preschoolers' early literacy development: A longitudinal experimental comparison of predominantly English and transitional bilingual education. *Bilingual Research Journal, 36,* 6–34. doi:10.1080/15235882.2012.735213

Enck-Wanzer, D. (2006). Trashing the system: Social movement, intersectional rhetoric, and collective agency in the young lords' organization's garbage offensive. *Quarterly Journal of Speech, 92,* 174–201. doi:10.1080/00335630600816920

*Esposito, A., & Baker-Ward, L. (2013). Dual-language education for low-income children: Preliminary evidence of benefits for executive function. *Bilingual Research Journal, 36,* 295–310. doi:10.1090/15235882.2013.837848

Excelencia in Education. (2015). *The condition of Latinos in education: 2015 factbook.* Washington, DC: Author.

*Farver, J. M., Lonigan, C. J., & Eppe, S. (2009). Effective early literacy skill development for young Spanish English language learners: An experimental study of two methods. *Child Development, 80,* 703–719. doi:10.1111/j.1467-8624.2009.01292.x

Francis, D., Lesaux, N. K., & August, D. (2006). Language of instruction. In D. L. August & T. Shanahan (Eds.), *Developing literacy in a second language: Report of the National Literacy Panel* (pp. 365–410). Mahwah, NJ: Lawrence Erlbaum.

Gándara, P. (2015). Charting the relationship of English learners and the ESEA: One step forward, two steps back. *RSF: The Russell Sage Foundation Journal of the Sciences, 1,* 112–128.

Gándara, P., & Callahan, R. M. (2014). Looking toward the future: Opportunities in a shifting linguistic landscape. In R. M. Callahan & P. C. Gándara (Eds.), *The bilingual advantage: Language, literacy, and the U.S. labor market* (pp. 286–299). Bristol, England: Multilingual Matters.

Gándara, P., & Hopkins, M. (2010). The changing linguistic landscape of the United States. In P. Gándara & M. Hopkins (Eds.), *Forbidden language: English learners and restrictive policies* (pp. 7–19). New York, NY: Teachers College Press.

García, O., Kleifgen, J. A., & Falchi, L. (2008). *From English language learners to emergent bilinguals. Equity Matters: Research Review No. 1.* New York, NY: Campaign for Educational Equity, Teachers College, Columbia University.

Genesee, F., Lindholm-Leary, K., Saunders, W., & Christian, D. (Eds.). (2006). *Educating English language learners: A synthesis of research evidence.* Cambridge, England: Cambridge University Press.

Gerber, M., Jimenez, T., Leafstedt, J., Villaruz, J., Richards, C., & English, J. (2004). English reading effects of a small-group intensive intervention in Spanish for K–1 English learners. *Learning Disabilities Research & Practice, 19,* 239–251. doi:10.1111/j.1540-5826.2004.00109.x

Goldenberg, C. (2013). Unlocking the research on English learners. *American Educator, Summer,* 4–12.

Goldenberg, C., Reese, L., & Rezaei, A. R. (2011). Contexts for language and literacy development among dual-language learners. In A. Yücesan Durgunoğlu & C. Goldenberg (Eds.), *Language and literacy development in bilingual settings* (pp. 3–28). New York, NY: Guilford Press.

Goldenberg, C., Tolar, T. D., Reese, L., Francis, D. J., Bazán, A. R., & Mejía-Arauz, R. (2014). How important is teaching phonemic awareness to children learning to read in Spanish? *American Educational Research Journal, 51,* 604–633.

Gómez, L., Freeman, D., & Freeman, Y. (2005). Dual-language education: A promising 50–50 model. *Bilingual Research Journal, 29,* 145–164. doi:10.1080/15235882.2005.1 0162828

Gómez v. Illinois State Board of Education, 811 F.2d 1030 (7th Cir. 1987).

Grant, A., Gottardo, A., & Geva, E. (2011). Reading in English as a first or second language: The case of Grade 3 Spanish, Portuguese, and English speakers. *Learning Disabilities Research & Practice, 26,* 67–83. doi:10.1111/j.1540-5826.2011.00327.x

Greene, J. P. (1998). *A meta-analysis of the effectiveness of bilingual education.* Claremont, CA: Thomas Rivera Policy Institute.

Guo, Q., & Koretz, D. (2013). Estimating the impact of the Massachusetts English immersion law on limited English proficient students' reading achievement. *Educational Policy, 27,* 121–149. doi:10.1177/0895904812462776

Hakuta, K. (1987). The second language learner in the context of the study of language acquisition. In P. Homel, M. Palij, & D. Aaronson (Eds.), *Childhood bilingualism: Aspects of cognitive, social and emotional development* (pp. 31–55). Hillsdale, NJ: Lawrence Erlbaum.

Hakuta, K. (2011). The policy context of research on basic processes in bilingual children in the United States. In A. Durgunoğlu & C. Goldenberg (Eds.), *Language and literacy development in bilingual settings* (pp. 335–349). New York, NY: Guilford.

*Hambly, C., & Fombonne, E. (2012). The impact of bilingual environments on language development in children with autism spectrum disorders. *Journal of Autism Development and Disorders, 42,* 1342–1352. doi:10.1007/s10803-011-1365-z

Hamilton, B. E., Martin, J. A., & Ventura, S. J. (2010). Births: Preliminary data for 2008. *National Vital Statistics Reports, 58*(16), 1–18.

*Hammer, C. S., Lawrence, F. R., & Miccio, A. W. (2007). Bilingual children's abilities and early reading outcomes in Head Start and kindergarten. *Language, Speech, and Hearing Services in Schools, 38,* 237–248. doi:0161-1461/07/3803-0237

*Hofstetter, C. H. (2004). Effects of a transitional bilingual education program: Findings, issues, and next steps. *Bilingual Research Journal, 28,* 355–377. doi:10.1080/152358822004.1016261

Horne v. Flores, 129 S. Ct. 2579, 557 U.S. 433, 174 L. Ed. 2d 406 (2009).

*Kempert, S., Saalbach, H., & Hardy, I. (2011). Cognitive benefits and costs of bilingualism in elementary school students: The case of mathematical word problems. *Journal of Educational Psychology, 103,* 547–561. doi:10.1037/a0023619

Kena, G., Musu-Gillette, L., Robinson, J., Wang, X., Rathbun, A., Zhang, J., . . . Dunlop Velez, E. (2015). *The condition of education 2015* (NCES 2015-144). Washington, DC: U.S. Department of Education, National Center for Education Statistics. Retrieved from http://nces.ed.gov/pubs2015/2015144.pdf

Kloss, H. (1977). *The American bilingual tradition.* Rowley, MA: Newbury House.

*Kovelman, I., Baker, S. A., & Petito, L.-A. (2008). Age of first bilingual language exposure as a new window into reading development. *Bilingualism, 11,* 203–223. doi:10.1017. S136678908003386

Krashen, S., & McField, G. (2005). What works? Reviewing the latest evidence on bilingual education. *Language Learner, 1*(2), 7–34.

Kroll, J. F., & Bialystok, E. (2013). Understanding the consequences of bilingualism for language processing and cognition. *Journal of Cognitive Psychology, 25,* 497–514.

Kroll, J. F., Bobb, S. C., & Wodniecka, Z. (2006). Language selectivity is the exception, not the rule: Arguments against a fixed locus of language selection in bilingual speech. *Bilingualism, 9,* 119–135. doi:10.1017/S1366728906002483

Lado, R. (1964). *Language teaching: A scientific approach.* New York, NY: McGraw-Hill.

Lau v. Nichols, 414 U.S. 563, 94 S. Ct. 786, 39 L. Ed. 2d 1 (1974).

*Lindholm-Leary, K. (2014). Bilingual and biliteracy skills in young Spanish-speaking low-SES children: Impact of instructional language and primary language proficiency.

International Journal of Bilingual Education and Bilingualism, 17, 144–159. doi:10.1080 /13670050.2013.866625

*Lindholm-Leary, K., & Block, N. (2010). Achievement in predominantly low-SES/Hispanic dual language schools. *International Journal of Bilingual Education and Bilingualism, 13,* 43–60. doi:10.1080/13670050902777546

López, F., & McEneaney, E. (2012). State implementation of language acquisition policies and reading achievement among Hispanic students. *Educational Policy, 26,* 418–464. doi:10.1177/0895904811417581

López, F., McEneaney, E., & Nieswandt, M. (2015). Language instruction educational programs and academic achievement of Latino English learners: Considerations for states with changing demographics. *American Journal of Education, 121,* 417–450. doi:10.1086/680410

*López, F., Scanlan, M., & Gorman, B. K. (2015). Language modeling and reading achievement: Variations across different types of language instruction programs. *Reading & Writing Quarterly, 31,* 1–29. doi:10.1080/10573569.2013.819187

López, K. (2014, November 9). *Spanish-language immersion schools gain in popularity. NBC News.* Retrieved from http://www.nbcnews.com/news/latino/spanish-language-immersion-schools-gain-popularity-n225776

*López, M. G., & Tashakkori, A. (2004a). Effects of a two-way bilingual program on the literacy development of students in kindergarten and first grade. *Bilingual Research Journal, 28,* 19–34. doi:10.1080/15235882.2004.10162610

*López, M. G., & Tashakkori, A. (2004b). Narrowing the gap: Effects of a two-way bilingual education program on the literacy development of at-risk primary students. *Journal of Education for Students Placed at Risk, 9,* 325–336. doi:10.1207/s15327671espr0904_1

*López, M. G., & Tashakkori, A. (2006). Differential outcomes of two bilingual education programs on English language learners. *Bilingual Research Journal, 30,* 123–145. doi:10. 1080/15235882.2006.10162869

*Lorenzo, F., Casal, S., & Moore, P. (2009). The effects of content and language integrated learning in European education: Key findings from the Andalusian bilingual sections evaluation project. *Applied Linguistics, 31,* 418–442. doi:10.1093/applin/amp041

Lyons, J. (2013). *Opportunity lost: The promise of equal and effective education for emerging bilingual students in the Obama administration.* Boulder, CO: Bueno National Policy Center, University of Colorado, Boulder.

*Lyster, R., Quiroga, J., & Ballinger, S. (2013). The effects of biliteracy instruction on morphological awareness. *Journal of Immersion and Content-Based Language Education, 1,* 169–197. doi:10.1075/jicb/1.2.02lys

*Marian, V., Shook, A., & Schroeder, S. R. (2013). Bilingual two-way immersion programs benefit academic achievement. *Bilingual Research Journal, 36,* 167–186. doi:10.1080/15 235882.2013.818075

*Martínez-Alvarez, P., Bannan, B., & Peters-Burton, E. E. (2012). Effect of strategy instruction on fourth-grade dual language learners' ability to monitor their comprehension of scientific texts. *Bilingual Research Journal, 35,* 331–349. doi:10.1080/15235882.2012.7 34005

Maxwell, L. (2012, March). Dual classes see growth in popularity. *Education Week, 31*(26), 1–3.

Melby-Lervåg, M., & Lervåg, A. (2011). Cross-linguistic transfer of oral language, decoding, phonological awareness, and reading comprehension: A meta-analysis of the correlational evidence. *Journal of Research in Reading, 34,* 114–135. doi:10.1111/j.1467-9817.2010.01477/x

Menken, K. (2010). No Child Left Behind and English language learners: The challenges and consequences of high-stakes testing. *Theory Into Practice, 49,* 121–128.

Menken, K. (2013). Restrictive language education policies and emergent bilingual youth: A perfect storm with imperfect outcomes. *Theory Into Practice, 52,* 160–168.

Meyer v. Nebraska, 262 U.S. 390, 43 S. Ct. 625, 67 L. Ed. 1042 (1923).

Moher, D., Liberati, A., Tetzlaff, J., Altman, D. G., & the PRISMA Group. (2009). Preferred reporting items for systematic reviews and meta-analyses: The PRISMA statement. *Physical Therapy, 89,* 873–880. doi:10.1371/journal.pmed.1000097

Nakamoto, J., Lindsey, K. A., & Manis, F. R. (2012). Development of reading skills from K–3 in Spanish-speaking English language learners following three programs of instruction. *Reading and Writing, 25,* 537–567. doi:10.1007/s11145-010-9285-4

*Nicolay, A., & Poncelet, M. (2013). Cognitive advantage in children enrolled in a second-language immersion elementary school program for three years. *Bilingualism, 16,* 597–607. doi:10.1017/S1366728912000375

No Child Left Behind Act of 2001. Pub. L. No. 107-110, §115, Stat.1425 (2002).

Nuñez, L. (2009). Reflections on Puerto Rican history: Aspira in the sixties and the coming of age of the stateside Puerto Rican community. *CENTRO: Journal of the Center for Puerto Rican Studies, 21*(2), 33–49.

*Ohashi, J. K., Mirenda, P., Marniova-Todd, S., Hambly, C., Fombonne, E., Szatmari, P., . . . Pathways in ASD Study Team. (2012). Comparing early language development in mono-lingual- and bilingual-exposed young children with autism spectrum disorders. *Research in Autism Spectrum Disorders, 6,* 890–897. doi:10.1016/j.rasd.2011.12.002

Ovando, C. J. (2003). Bilingual education in the United States: Historical development and current issues. *Bilingual Research Journal, 27*(1), 1–24. doi:10.1080/15235882.2003.101 62589

Ovando, C. J., & Collier, V. P. (1998). *Bilingual and ESL classrooms: Teaching in multicultural contexts.* Boston, MA: McGraw-Hill.

Parrish, T. B., Merickel, A., Pérez, M., Linquanti, R., Socias, M., Spain, A., . . .Delancey, D. (2006). *Effects of the implementation of Proposition 227 on the education of English learners, K–12: Findings from a five-year evaluation* (Final Report for AB 56 and AB1116). Washington, DC: American Institutes for Research and WestEd.

*Parsons, C. E., & Lyddy, F. (2009). Early reading strategies in Irish and English: Evidence from error types. *Reading in a Foreign Language, 21,* 22–36.

Pease-Alvarez, L., & Hakuta, K. (1992). Enriching our views of bilingualism and bilingual education. *Educational Researcher, 21*(2), 4–19. doi:10.3102/0013189X021002004

*Proctor, C. P., August, D., Carlo, M. S., & Barr, C. (2010). Language maintenance versus language of instruction: Spanish reading development among Latino and Latina bilingual learners. *Journal of Social Issues, 66,* 79–94. doi:10.111/j.1540-4560.2009.01634.x

*Reading, S. (2009). Differential effects of French and Spanish immersion education on English literacy skills. *Bilingual Research Journal, 31,* 115–145. doi:10.1080/15235880802640649

*Reese, L., Gallimore, R., & Guthrie, D. (2005). Reading trajectories of immigrant Latino students in transitional bilingual programs. *Bilingual Research Journal, 29,* 679–697. doi: 10.1080/15235882.2005.10162858

*Reese, L., Goldenberg, C., & Saunders, W. (2006). Variations in reading achievement among Spanish-speaking children in different language programs: Explanations and confounds. *Elementary School Journal, 106,* 363–385.

*Reljic, G., Ferrig, D., & Martin, R. (2015). A meta-analysis on the effectiveness of bilingual programs in Europe. *Review of Educational Research, 85,* 92–128. doi:10.3102/00346543145485414

*Roberts, T. A. (2008). Home storybook reading in primary or secondary language with pre-school children: Evidence of equal effectiveness for second-language vocabulary acquisi-tion. *Reading Research Quarterly, 43,* 103–130. Retrieved from http://dx.doi.org/10.1598/RRQ.43.2.1

Rolstad, K., Mahoney, K., & Glass, G. V. (2005). The big picture: A meta-analysis of program effectiveness on English language learners. *Educational Policy, 19,* 572–594. doi:10.1177/0895904805278067

Rossell, C. H., & Baker, K. (1996). The effectiveness of bilingual education. *Research in the Teaching of English, 30,* 7–74.

*Saiegh-Haddad, E., & Geva, E. (2008). Morphological awareness, phonological awareness, and reading in English-Arabic bilingual children. *Reading and Writing, 21,* 481–504. doi:10.1007/s11145-007-9087-x

*Sailors, M., Hoffman, J. V., Pearson, D. P., Beretvas, S. N., & Matthee, B. (2010). The effects of first- and second-language instruction in rural South African schools. *Bilingual Research Journal, 33,* 21–41. doi:10.1080/15235881003733241

Salomone, R. (2010). *True American: Language, identity, and the education of the immigrant child.* Cambridge, MA: Harvard University Press.

Shadish, W. R., Cook, T. D., & Campbell, D. T. (2001). *Experimental and quasi-experimental designs for generalized causal inference* (2nd ed.). Belmont, CA: Wadsworth.

Slavin, R. E., & Cheung, A. (2005). A synthesis of research on language of reading instruction for English language learners. *Review of Educational Research, 75,* 247–284. doi:10.3102/00346543075002247

*Slavin, R. E., Madden, N., Calderón, M., Chamberlain, A., & Hennessy, M. (2011). Reading and language outcomes of a multiyear randomized evaluation of transitional bilingual education. *Educational Evaluation and Policy Analysis, 33,* 47–58. doi:10.3102/0162373711398127

Snow, K. (2006). Cross-cutting themes and future directions. In D. L. August & T. Shanahan (Eds.), *Developing literacy in a second language: Report of the National Literacy Panel* (pp. 365–410). Mahwah, NJ: Lawrence Erlbaum.

Stewner-Manzanares, G. (1988). *The Bilingual Education Act: Twenty years later.* Washington, DC: National Clearinghouse for Bilingual Education.

*Tong, F., Irby, B. J., Lara-Alecio, R., & Mathes, P. G. (2008). English and Spanish acquisition by Hispanic second graders in developmental bilingual programs: A 3-year longitudinal randomized study. *Hispanic Journal of Behavioral Sciences, 30,* 500–529. doi:10.1177/0739986308324980

*Tong, F., Lara-Alecio, R., Irby, B. J., & Mathes, P. G. (2011). The effects of an instructional intervention on dual language development among first-grade Hispanic English-learning boys and girls: A two-year longitudinal study. *Journal of Educational Research, 104,* 87–99. doi:10.1080/00220670903567364

*Tong, F., Lara-Alecio, R., Irby, B. J., Mathes, P. G., & Kwok, O. (2008). Accelerating early academic oral English development in transitional bilingual and structured English immersion programs. *American Educational Research Journal, 45,* 1011–1044. doi:10.3102/0002831208320790

*Uchikoshi, Y., & Maniates, H. (2010). How does bilingual instruction enhance English achievement? A mixed-method study of Cantonese-speaking and Spanish-speaking bilingual classrooms. *Bilingual Research Journal, 33,* 364–385. doi:10.1080/15235882.2010.5 25294

*Umansky, I. M., & Reardon, S. F. (2014). Reclassification patterns among Latino English learner students in bilingual, dual immersion, and English immersion classrooms. *American Educational Research Journal, 51,* 879–912. doi:10.3102/0002831214534110

Umansky, I. M., Reardon, S. F., Hakuta, K., Thompson, K. D., Estrada, P., Hayes, K., . . . Goldenberg, C. (2015, October). *Improving the opportunities and outcomes of California's students learning English* (PACE Policy Brief 15-1). Stanford, CA: Policy Analysis for California Education.

U.S. Census Bureau. (2015). *Detailed languages spoken at home and ability to speak English for the population 5 years and over: 2009–2013*. Retrieved from http://www.census.gov/data/tables/2013/demo/2009-2013-lang-tables.html

*Valentino, R. A., & Reardon, S. F. (2015). Effectiveness of four instructional programs designed to serve English learners: Variation by ethnicity and initial English proficiency. *Educational Evaluation and Policy Analysis, 37*, 612–637. doi:10.3102/0162373715573310

*Van der Leij, A., Bekebrede, J., & Kotterink, M. (2010). Acquiring reading and vocabulary in Dutch and English: The effect of concurrent instruction. *Reading and Writing, 23*, 415–434. doi:10.1007/s11145-009-9207-5

Vaughn, S., Cirino, P. T., Linan-Thompson, S., Mathes, P., Carlson, C., Cardenas-Hagan, E., . . . Francis, D. J. (2006). Effectiveness of a Spanish intervention and an English intervention for English language learners at risk for reading problems. *American Educational Research Journal, 43*, 449–487. doi:10.3102/00028312043033449

Vaughn, S., Cirino, P. T., Tolar, T. D., Fletcher, J. M., Cardenas-Hagan, E., Carlson, C. D., & Francis, D. J. (2008). Long-term follow-up of Spanish and English interventions for first-grade English language learners at risk for reading problems. *Journal of Research on Educational Effectiveness, 1*, 179–214. doi:10.1080/19345740802114749

*Vaughn, S., Linan-Thompson, S., Mathes, P. G., Cirino, P. T., Carlson, C. D., Pollard-Durodola, S. D., . . . Francis, D. J. (2006). Effectiveness of Spanish intervention for first-grade English language learners at risk for reading difficulties. *Journal of Learning Disabilities, 39*, 56–73. doi:10.1086/510653

*Verspoor, M., de Bot, K., & Xu, X. (2015). The effects of English bilingual education in the Netherlands. *Journal of Immersion and Content-Based Language Education, 3*, 4–27. doi:10.1075/jicb.3.1.01ver

Willig, A. C. (1985). A meta-analysis of selected studies on the effectiveness of bilingual education. *Review of Educational Research, 55*, 269–317. doi:10.3102/00346543055003269

About the Editors

Patricia A. Alexander is the Jean Mullan Professor of Literacy and Distinguished Scholar-Teacher in the Department of Human Development and Quantitative Methodology at the University of Maryland. She served as the president of Division 15 (Educational Psychology) of the American Psychological Association, and vice-president of Division C (Learning and Instruction) of the AERA. Since receiving her PhD in 1981, Alexander has published over 280 articles, books, or chapters in the area of learning and instruction. She has also presented over 400 papers or invited addresses at national and international conferences. She currently serves as the senior editor of *Contemporary Educational Psychology*, was past editor of *Instructional Science* and associate editor of *American Educational Research Journal–Teaching, Learning, and Human Development*, and presently serves on over 10 editorial boards. Alexander is a Fellow of the APA, AERA, and the Society for Text and Discourse. Her honors include the Oscar S. Causey Award for outstanding contributions to literacy research from the National Reading Conference (2001), the E. L. Thorndike Award for Career Achievement in Educational Psychology from APA Division 15 (2006), and the Sylvia Scribner Career Award from AERA Division C (2007).

Felice J. Levine is executive director of the AERA. Her work focuses on research and science policy issues, research ethics, open access and data sharing, the scientific and academic workforce, and higher education. Levine has led initiatives on such issues as *Promoting Diversity and Excellence in Higher Education through Department Change* and, for the National Science Foundation, on *Education and Training in the Social, Behavioral, and Economic Sciences*. She recently served on the National Research Council (NRC) Committee on *Proposed Revisions to the Common Rule for the Protection of Human Subjects in Research in the Behavioral and Social Sciences* and on the NRC panel on *Putting People on the Map: Protecting Confidentiality with Linked Social-Spatial Data*. She currently serves on the NRC Roundtable on the Application of Social and Behavioral Science Research. Levine chairs the Board of the Consortium of Social Science Associations, is past chair and member of the Board of the Council of Professional Associations on Federal Statistics, and is president of the World Education Research Association. In 2014, Levine received a presidential citation from AERA "for creating a presence and fostering sustainability of education research

Review of Research in Education
March 2016, Vol. 40, pp. 884–885
DOI: 10.3102/0091732X16682959
© 2016 AERA. http://rre.aera.net

nationally and internationally." She is a fellow of the American Association for the Advancement of Science, the AERA, and the Association for Psychological Science and an elected member of the International Statistical Institute.

William F. Tate IV is the Edward Mallinckrodt Distinguished University Professor in Arts & Sciences at Washington University in St. Louis. He currently serves as dean of the Graduate School and vice provost for Graduate Education. Tate's research program has focused on the social determinants of mathematics performance. His coedited book titled *Research and Practice Pathways in Mathematics Education: Disrupting Tradition* captures his interest in connecting researchers, policymakers, and practitioners to improve opportunity to learn in mathematics education. Tate has a particular interest in STEM attainment. Ongoing research projects include understanding the distal and social factors that predict STEM doctoral degree attainment broadly defined to include highly quantitative social sciences disciplines (e.g., economics). His coedited book titled *Beyond Stock Stories and Folktales: African Americans' Paths to STEM Fields* captures the direction of this research program. For over a decade, Tate's research has focused on the development of epidemiological and geospatial models to explain the social determinants of educational attainment as well as health and developmental outcomes. His book titled *Research on Schools, Neighborhoods, and Communities: Toward Civic Responsibility* reflects this interest. Professor Tate is a past president of AERA. In 2010, he received a presidential citation from AERA for "his expansive vision of conceptual and methodological tools that can be recruited to address inequities in opportunities to learn." A fellow of AERA, he has received the Distinguished Contributions to Social Contexts in Education Research-Lifetime Achievement Award (AERA-Division G). He is an elected member of the National Academy of Education.

About the Contributors

Richard L. Allington is a professor of education at the University of Tennessee, Knoxville. He has served as president of the International Reading Association (IRA) and the National Reading Conference. He received IRA's Outstanding Dissertation Award, has twice been corecipient of the Albert J. Harris Award from IRA in recognition of his work contributing to the understanding of reading and learning disabilities, received the William S. Gray Award from IRA for his contributions to the profession, and has been named to the Reading Hall of Fame. He serves on the editorial boards of several journals, including *Reading Research Quarterly, Elementary School Journal,* and the *Journal of Educational Psychology*. He is the author of over 100 research articles and has authored or coauthored several books, including *Classrooms That Work: They Can All Read and Write; What Really Matters for Struggling Readers;* and *No Quick Fix: Rethinking Reading Programs in American Elementary Schools*.

Alfredo J. Artiles is the Ryan C. Harris Professor of Special Education and dean of the Graduate College at Arizona State University. His scholarship focuses on understanding and addressing educational inequities related to disability intersections with other sociocultural differences. He directs the Equity Alliance and edits the Teachers College Press book series *Disability, Culture, and Equity*. He was the AERA vice president (2009–2011) and is an AERA fellow. He has been a Spencer Foundation/National Academy of Education postdoctoral fellow (1998–2000) and a resident fellow at Stanford's Center for Advanced Study in the Behavioral Sciences (2008–2009). He received the 2012 Palmer O. Johnson Award for best article published in an AERA journal. He serves on President Obama's Advisory Commission on Educational Excellence for Hispanics. Recent publications include *Keeping the Promise? Contextualizing Inclusive Education in Developing Countries* (Klinkhardt); *World Yearbook of Education 2017: Assessment Inequalities* (Routledge); and *Inclusive Education: Examining Equity on Five Continents* (Harvard Education Press).

Review of Research in Education
March 2016, Vol. 40, pp. 886–903
DOI: 10.3102/0091732X16682474
© 2016 AERA. http://rre.aera.net

Amy Price Azano is an assistant professor of adolescent literacy in the School of Education at Virginia Tech. Her scholarship focuses on rural education, place-based pedagogy, and the literacy needs of special populations. She is the co–principal investigator of Promoting PLACE (Place, Literacy, Achievement, Community, and Engagement) in Rural Schools, a 5-year grant from the U.S. Department of Education designed to support gifted education programs in high-poverty rural communities.

Lucy E. Bailey is an associate professor of social foundations and qualitative inquiry and the director of gender and women's studies at Oklahoma State University. She received graduate degrees in women's studies and in cultural studies of education from the Ohio State University and teaches and conducts research in diversity issues, qualitative methodologies, and American educational history. She is a former president of the Society of Philosophy and History of Education and the current chair of the AERA Biographical and Documentary Research Special Interest Group.

Doris Luft Baker is an assistant professor in the Department of Teaching and Learning, Simmons School of Education and Human Development, at Southern Methodist University. Her research focuses on English learners, including examining the effectiveness of bilingual programs, developing supplemental vocabulary interventions in English and Spanish, improving the quality of instruction in bilingual settings, and engaging Hispanic parents in the education of their children. Her research has been funded by the Institute of Education Sciences, the National Science Foundation, the Knight Foundation, and the Oregon Child Development Coalition, among others. She received her PhD in educational leadership from the University of Oregon. She was born in Brazil and grew up in Brazil, Colombia, and Mexico. She has published extensively in national and international journals.

Eva L. Baker is a Distinguished Professor in the divisions of Psychological Studies in Education and Social Research Methodology at the Graduate School of Education and Information Studies, University of California, Los Angeles, and is the founding director of the National Center for Research on Evaluation, Standards, and Student Testing. Her research is focused on the integration of instruction and measurement, including design and empirical validation of principles for developing both game and simulation instructional systems, and new measures of complex human performance. She is presently involved in the design of technologically sophisticated testing and evaluation systems of assessment in large-scale environments for both military and civilian education.

Aydin Bal is an assistant professor at the University of Wisconsin, Madison, in the Department of Rehabilitation Psychology and Special Education. He studies the racialization of behavioral problems, expansive learning, and systemic transformation across local and national education systems. He has worked with students from historically marginalized communities, trauma survivors, and refugee youth. He developed the

Culturally Responsive Positive Behavioral Interventions and Supports framework. He has been leading a mixed-methods, multisite formative intervention study to address racial disproportionality in school discipline and special education in the state of Wisconsin.

Deni Lee Basaraba is a research affiliate with Southern Methodist University, a courtesy research associate with the University of Oregon, and a data analyst for the Bethel School District 52 in Eugene, Oregon. She has worked on multiple federally funded longitudinal intervention projects and has served as a researcher for a large-scale technical assistance project. She also has prior experience with mathematics assessment development, managing the development of several universal screening and diagnostic assessments of mathematics in Grades preK–8. Her research interests include exploring the relationships among mathematics and language proficiency, assessment and instructional features to support the learning needs of English learners and struggling learners, assessment and observation tool development and validation, and the influence of contextual factors on student performance.

Nancy Beadie is a professor in the College of Education and adjunct professor in the Department of History, College of Arts and Sciences, at the University of Washington. Her research focuses on relationships among education, economics, and state formation at local, state, national, and international levels, as represented in her book *Education and the Creation of Capital in the Early American Republic* (Cambridge University Press, 2010), which won the Outstanding Book Award from the History of Education Society. She has also written extensively on the history of higher schooling and on the history of women in education, work for which she has twice won the History of Education Society Best Article Prize. She is currently senior editor for the *History of Education Quarterly* and previously served as president of the History of Education Society and vice president of AERA for Division F (History and Historiography).

David C. Berliner is Regents' Professor of Education Emeritus at Arizona State University and has taught at many other universities in the United States and abroad. He is a member of the National Academy of Education and the International Academy of Education, and is a past president of both AERA and the Division of Educational Psychology of the American Psychological Association. He has won numerous awards for his work on behalf of the education profession and authored over 200 articles, chapters, and books. Among his best known works are *The Manufactured Crisis*, coauthored with B. J. Biddle; *Collateral Damage: How High-Stakes Testing Corrupts American Education*, coauthored with Sharon Nichols; and *50 Myths and Lies That Threaten America's Public Schools*, coauthored with Gene V Glass. He coedited the first *Handbook of Educational Psychology* and the books *Talks to Teachers; Perspectives on Instructional Time* and *Putting Research to Work in Your School*.

Catharine Biddle is an assistant professor of educational leadership in the College of Education and Human Development at the University of Maine. Her scholarship examines the complexities of school–community relationships, with a focus on rural contexts. She is particularly interested in how schools can more effectively leverage community partnerships to address issues of social inequality and how marginalized groups and voices are included or excluded from these efforts.

Stergios Botzakis is an associate professor in the Theory and Practice in Teacher Education Department at the University of Tennessee, Knoxville. His areas of expertise are content area reading, middle school education, working with struggling adolescent readers, and new literacies. His research interests include middle and secondary education, graphic novels, adolescent literacies, popular culture, and media literacy. He has been published in the *Journal of Adolescent & Adult Literacy*, the *English Journal, Language Arts*, the *ALAN Review*, and the *Teacher Education Quarterly* among other venues.

Marc Brackett is Director of the Yale Center for Emotional Intelligence and a professor at the Child Study Center at Yale University. His research focuses on the role of emotional intelligence in learning, decision making, relationship quality, well-being, performance, and organizational climate. He is the lead developer of RULER, an evidence-based approach to social and emotional learning that has been adopted by over 1,000 public, charter, and private schools across the United States and in other countries. RULER infuses emotional intelligence into the fabric of a school through training for school leaders, educators and staff, students, and families and has been shown to enhance well-being, academic performance, and school climate. He has published over 100 scholarly articles and is the recipient of numerous awards, including the Joseph E. Zins Award. Currently, he works with Facebook to develop tools that help adults and children develop emotional intelligence and resolve online conflict.

Ivar Bråten holds a PhD in educational psychology and is a professor of educational psychology in the Department of Education at the University of Oslo, Norway. He directs the research group TextDIM, which studies text comprehension, including development, instruction, and use of multiple texts. He is currently directing the project Understanding and Promoting Upper-Secondary School Students' Critical Reading and Learning in the 21st Century Information Age, funded by the Norwegian Research Council. In this research, he addresses how critical source evaluation skills develop among students and the importance of such skills to learning processes and learning outcomes. His publication list totals more than 300 titles, including 9 authored or edited books and approximately 125 international peer-reviewed articles and book chapters, coauthored with 50 scholars from 8 countries. He serves on the editorial review boards of the journals *Contemporary Educational Psychology, Learning and Individual Differences, Learning and Instruction*, and *Metacognition and Learning*.

Leslie D. Burns is an associate professor of literacy at the University of Kentucky. His scholarship addresses education policy reform, social justice, adolescent literacies and identities, secondary-level teaching and teacher education, and curriculum studies. His work has appeared in peer-reviewed journals such as the *Harvard Educational Review, Teachers College Record,* the *Journal of Adolescent & Adult Literacy,* and *Research in the Teaching of English* and in books including *Empowering Struggling Readers: Practices for the Middle Grades* (winner of the Edward B. Fry Book Award) and *Teach on Purpose! Responsive Teaching for Student Success.*

Li Cai is a professor in the Advanced Quantitative Methods in Education Research Program in the Graduate School of Education and Information Studies, University of California, Los Angeles (UCLA), where he also serves as director of the National Center for Research on Evaluation, Standards, and Student Testing. In addition, he is affiliated with the UCLA Department of Psychology in the quantitative area. Broadly speaking, his research agenda involves the development, integration, and evaluation of innovative latent variable models that have wide-ranging applications in educational, psychological, and health-related domains of study. A key component on this agenda is statistical computing for psychometric applications, particularly as related to item response theory and multilevel modeling.

Maureen Callanan is a professor of psychology at the University of California, Santa Cruz, Department of Psychology. Her research focuses on how young children develop understanding of the natural world in the context of family conversations. She takes a sociocultural approach, investigating language and cognition in young children, with attention to diversity across families and communities. She has a long-standing research partnership with the Children's Discovery Museum of San Jose, where she has been the principal investigator or co–principal investigator on several National Science Foundation–funded projects investigating children's and families' informal learning about science. She was a coauthor of the 2009 National Academies Press volume *Learning Science in Informal Environments: People, Places, and Pursuits.* She has been an associate editor for *Psychological Bulletin* and the *Journal of Cognition and Development.* She is currently chair of AERA's Informal Learning Environments Research Special Interest Group.

Amy Cassata is a principal research scientist at Outlier Research and Evaluation at UChicago STEM Education at the University of Chicago. She leads Outlier's ongoing work on understanding and measuring the use of educational innovations and exploring the contexts that support or inhibit implementation and the spread of practices to new users. She is currently involved in ongoing development, dissemination, and application of Outlier's implementation conceptual frameworks and measures for educational interventions. She served as the principal investigator or co–principal investigator on three related research studies funded by the National Science Foundation and the Institute of Education Sciences (2011–2015) to validate a suite of instruments for measuring STEM instructional materials implementation and to investigate factors that affect their use and sustainability in different contexts. She received a PhD in education with a specialization in human development from the University of Rochester and completed an Institute of Education Sciences–funded postdoctoral fellowship in experimental education research methods at Vanderbilt University.

Jeanne Century is the director of Outlier Research and Evaluation at UChicago STEM Education at the University of Chicago. Outlier works to empower those who seek to advance and improve education with the knowledge, tools, and support to realize change. She has spent the majority of her 30-year career working in and with urban schools and large urban school districts across the country. She has developed comprehensive science instructional materials and been part of professional development, technical assistance, and strategic planning efforts for teachers and for school, district, and state administrators across the country. Her research and evaluation efforts have focused on the impact of inquiry science instruction, improving utilization of research and evaluation, sustainability of reform, measurement of fidelity and enactment of innovations, STEM schools, and computer science education. She also served on the transition team for the Obama–Biden administration, where she focused on STEM education and education research.

Gregory K. W. K. Chung is the associate director for technology and research innovation at the National Center for Research on Evaluation, Standards, and Student Testing at the University of California, Los Angeles. His research interests are in developing and validating technology-based assessments for learning and assessment purposes. He has developed and validated computer games for instructional and assessment purposes, sensor-based learning and assessment tools, online tools to measure problem solving and conceptual understanding, and computational methods and prototypes for assessment authoring. His current work focuses on designing interaction mechanics and complementary telemetry designs to support measurement of knowledge and skills in game and simulation environments.

Sherman Dorn is a professor at Arizona State University and a historian of education at the Mary Lou Fulton Teachers College. He looks skeptically on our collective definitions of education problems. As individuals we have blind spots, and in a society, those blind spots are reflected in what we think are educational problems and how we try to solve them. He has written about the history of special education in the United States in multiple articles and chapters, the history of the idea of dropping out in *Creating the Dropout* (1996), the modern construction of school accountability in *Accountability Frankenstein* (2007), and the dilemmas of defining schools as communities in *Schools as Imagined Communities* (2006), coedited with Deirdre Cobb-Roberts and Barbara Shircliffe.

Shaun M. Dougherty is an assistant professor of education policy in the Department of Educational Leadership and a faculty member by courtesy in the Department of Public Policy at the University of Connecticut. His work focuses on applied quantitative analysis of education policies and programs and the economics of education. He emphasizes providing causal evidence of the effects of education, including career and technical education, on both short- and long-term student outcomes, with attention to how policies and practices affect educational equity related to race, class, gender, and disability.

Allison Dymnicki is a senior researcher at the American Institutes for Research (AIR), with extensive expertise in social-emotional learning, youth development, evaluation design, measurement and methodology, and mixed-methods longitudinal research. She has led implementation and impact evaluations of school- and community-based initiatives, systematic reviews, and expert panels and has supported schools, districts, and communities in developing safe, supportive environments. At AIR, she has been involved in evaluations focused on understanding the effects of school- and district-wide approaches developed to promote students' social emotional development, to improve school climate, and to decrease involvement in risky behaviors. She has conducted prevention and intervention research at the Institute for Health Research and Policy at the University of Illinois at Chicago; the Collaborative for Academic, Social, and Emotional Learning; and Ounce of Prevention, a home-visiting program. She obtained her master's and doctoral degrees in community psychology and prevention research from the University of Illinois at Chicago.

Frederick Erickson is Inaugural George F. Kneller Professor of Anthropology of Education Emeritus and Professor of Applied Linguistics Emeritus at the University of California, Los Angeles, Graduate School of Education and Information Studies. He is a specialist in the use of video analysis in interactional sociolinguistics and microethnography. His publications include *The Counselor as Gatekeeper: Social Interaction in Interviews* (coauthored with Jeffrey J. Shultz, 1982) and *Talk and Social Theory* (2004), which received AERA's Outstanding Book Award in 2005. He has also written extensively on qualitative methods in educational and social research. In 1998–1999 and 2006–2007 he was a fellow at the Center for Advanced Study in the Behavioral Sciences at Stanford University. He is a fellow of the National Academy of Education and of AERA. In 2014, the Council on Anthropology and Education of the American Anthropological Association named its annual Outstanding Dissertation Award in his honor.

Gustavo E. Fischman is a professor of education policy and director of edXchange, the knowledge mobilization initiative, at Mary Lou Fulton Teachers College, Arizona State University. He advocates for the idea that education research should be considered as a public good, and he focuses his work on understanding and improving the processes of knowledge production and exchange among scholars, educators, activists, practitioners, administrators, media workers, policymakers, and the general public. The main goal of his professional agenda is to promote engaging, responsive, and usable education research aimed at eliminating educational and social inequalities. He has over 100 academic publications and numerous commentaries and interviews. He has been a visiting scholar in graduate programs in Europe and Latin America. He was elected as a fellow of the International Academy of Education in 2013 and of AERA in 2015. He serves on numerous editorial boards and is the editor of the *Education Review*.

David A. Gamson is an associate professor of education in the Department of Education Policy Studies at The Pennsylvania State University. His research focuses on educational policy and school reform, past and present. He has written about the role of school districts in Progressive Era reform, has investigated the changing cognitive demands placed on students by textbooks published over the past century, and is currently working on a history of academic standards. He has been a fellow in the Advanced Studies Fellowship Program at Brown University, a National Academy of Education/Spencer postdoctoral fellow, and a visiting scholar at the Russell Sage Foundation. He recently coedited a special issue of Russell Sage Foundation, "The Elementary and Secondary Education Act at Fifty" (with Kathryn McDermott and Doug Reed). His publications have appeared in *Educational Researcher*, *Paedagogica Historica*; *Mind, Brain, and Education*; *Intelligence*; and the 2007 *Yearbook of the National Society for the Study of Education*.

Libby Gerard is a research scientist at the University of California, Berkeley, Graduate School of Education. Her research examines how innovative learning technologies can capture student ideas and help teachers and principals use those ideas to make decisions about classroom instruction. Her recent projects explore the use of automated scoring of student-written essays and student-created drawings to provide immediate guidance to students as they progress through an inquiry project, and to support the teachers' monitoring of student reasoning. She designs and leads teacher and principal professional development by using embedded student assessment data to inform instructional customization and resource allocation. Prior to being a research scientist, she was a postdoctoral scholar at UC Berkeley. She also taught preschool and elementary school in Oakland, California, and Alessandria, Italy. Her research is published in leading peer-reviewed journals, including *Science* and *Review of Educational Research*.

Karen Graves is a professor and chair in the Department of Education at Denison University. She is a former vice president of AERA's Division F (History and Historiography) and has served on the AERA Committee on Scholars and Advocates for Gender Equity.

Jeffrey A. Greene is an associate professor of learning sciences and psychological studies in the School of Education at the University of North Carolina at Chapel Hill. He holds a doctorate in educational psychology and a Master of Arts degree in educational measurement, statistics, and evaluation, both from the University of Maryland at College Park. His research interests include epistemic cognition, self-regulated learning, and argumentation in science, history, and online contexts. In his most recent work he has focused on digital literacy and argumentation in elementary school literacy classrooms and high school science classrooms. He serves as associate editor of the journal *Contemporary Educational Psychology*, and in 2016 he received the Richard E. Snow Award for early contributions to the field of educational psychology, from Division 15 of the American Psychological Association.

Susan L. Groenke is an associate professor of English education at the University of Tennessee, Knoxville, and the director of the Center for Children's and Young Adult Literature on the UTK campus. Her current scholarship addresses adolescent reading engagement and motivation to read, as well as current trends and issues in young adult literature. Her work has appeared in the *Journal of Adolescent & Adult Literacy, English Education*, and *Qualitative Inquiry*. She is a former editor of the *English Leadership Quarterly*, the journal of the National Council of Teachers of English.

Kris D. Gutiérrez is Carol Liu Professor at the Graduate School of Education, University of California, Berkeley. She is a leader in the learning sciences, literacy, educational policy, and qualitative, design-based approaches to inquiry. She is a member of the National Academy of Education and a fellow of AERA and the Center for Advanced Study in the Behavioral Sciences. She is a past president of AERA and was appointed by President Obama to the National Board for the Institute of Education Sciences. Her research examines learning in designed environments, with attention to students from nondominant communities and English learners. Her work on Third Spaces examines the affordances of syncretic approaches to literacy and learning. Her research has been published widely in premier academic journals, and she is a coauthor of *Learning and Expanding With Activity Theory*. She has won numerous awards, including the AERA Division C Sylvia Scribner Award.

Leigh A. Hall is an associate professor of literacy studies at the University of North Carolina, Chapel Hill. Her scholarship has examined issues of reading identity for adolescents and, in particular, for adolescents who are labeled as struggling readers. She is currently conducting research that examines how youth and adults engage in reading interactive texts on e-readers. Her work has appeared in journals such as *Research in the Teaching of English, Journal of Literacy Research, Reading and Writing Quarterly, Language Arts*, and the *Journal of Adolescent & Adult Literacy*. She blogs about her teaching practices in higher education at leighahall.wordpress.com.

Larry V. Hedges is the Board of Trustees Professor of Statistics, Psychology, in the School of Education and Social Policy, and in the Institute for Policy Research at Northwestern University. He is best known for his work on statistical methods for meta-analysis and its applications to evidence-based policy. He has also worked on the design of social experiments, the assessment of student achievement nationally and cross-nationally, and the role of uncertainty in basic models for cognition in psychology. He has authored or coauthored numerous journal articles and eight books. He is an elected member of the National Academy of Education and is a fellow of the American Academy of Arts and Sciences, the American Statistical Association, the American Psychological Association, and AERA. He also serves on the Board of Directors of the National Board for Education Sciences.

Maarten Hermans is a sociologist and senior research associate at HIVA Research Institute for Work and Society at University of Leuven, Belgium. Previously, he worked as an assistant at the University of Antwerp, teaching courses on research methods. His main research interests are industrial relations, social stratification, and the application of novel analytic methods such as network analysis to large and complex data. Currently, he is finishing a cross-national comparative research project on competitive corporatism and trade union strategies since the financial crisis.

Emily M. Hodge is an assistant professor in the Department of Counseling and Educational Leadership at Montclair State University, in New Jersey. She received her PhD in 2015 from the Department of Education Policy Studies at The Pennsylvania State University. Her research explores the intended and unintended consequences of equity-oriented educational policies in the past and present, including desegregation, detracking, and standards. Her work on federal education policy and desegregation appears in *Educational Policy* and *Education Law & Policy Review*. She and David Gamson are the coeditors of a forthcoming volume on school district history. Her current work focuses on understanding how state educational agencies support the implementation of college- and career-ready standards, including the messages about instruction disseminated through state-provided curricular resources.

Jennifer Jellison Holme is an associate professor of educational policy and planning at the University of Texas at Austin. Her research focuses on the politics and implementation of educational policy, with a particular focus on the relationship between school reform, equity, and diversity in schools. Her specific areas of research include school desegregation policy (currently focusing on interdistrict programs), high-stakes testing, and school choice policy. She earned her BA in sociology from the University of California, Los Angeles; her EdM in administration, planning, and social policy from the Harvard Graduate School of Education; and her PhD in Urban Schooling from the University of California, Los Angeles.

George G. Hruby is an associate research professor of literacy education at the University of Kentucky and the executive director of the university's Collaborative Center for Literacy Development. His scholarship has addressed theories of reading and literacy development, reading difficulties and disorders, and educational neuroscience. His work has appeared in *Reading Research Quarterly* and the *British Journal of Educational Psychology*, among other journals, and in *Theoretical Models and Processes of Reading* and *Handbook of Research on Teaching the English Language Arts*, among other edited volumes.

Stephanie Jones is an associate professor of human development and urban education at Harvard University. She has led multiyear, multisite randomized controlled trials related to the evaluation of a school-based intervention that targeted social and emotional skills. As indicated by her record of publications and research support, she has built extensive expertise in social and emotional development; complex longitudinal studies of social, emotional, and behavioral development; cluster- and place-randomized intervention research; and poverty, exposure to community violence, risk, resilience, and child development.

Yael Kidron, principal researcher at the American Institutes for Research, specializes in safe and supportive school environments and positive youth development. She has extensive experience in conducting rigorous program evaluations and systematic research reviews. Her research has focused on school-based social and emotional programs, school climate, and school leadership. In addition, she has evaluated and consulted for initiatives to promote teacher and leader preparation and professional development. She has developed resources for educators for reducing behavior problems in the classroom for the U.S. Department of Education's Doing What Works Initiative. She has also served as a principal investigator for the Regional Educational Laboratory–Appalachia, as the project director of the U.S. Department of Education's Doing What Works initiative (which was subcontracted to WestEd), and as the deputy project director of the U.S. Department of Education's What Works Clearinghouse.

Stephanie L. Knight is a professor in educational psychology and associate dean for undergraduate and graduate studies in the College of Education, The Pennsylvania State University. Prior to Penn State, she was at Texas A&M University, where she was the Endowed Chair in Urban Education, University Faculty Fellow, and recipient of a university award for outstanding teaching. She teaches courses at Penn State on educational psychology and research methods in teacher education. Her areas of research include the relationships between classroom processes, learning environments, and student outcomes in urban and international settings and preservice and in-service teacher professional development. She has published numerous books, chapters, and journal articles in these areas. She was coeditor of the *American Educational Research Journal* (Section on Teaching, Learning, and Human

Development) from 2004 to 2006, was lead editor of the *Journal of Teacher Education* from 2010 to 2015, and is currently associate editor of *Review of Educational Research*.

Jennifer M. Langer-Osuna is an assistant professor of education at Stanford University's Graduate School of Education and affiliate faculty at Stanford's Center for Comparative Studies in Race and Ethnicity and Chicano/Latino Studies. Her research centers on understanding the role of classroom interactions related to authority and influence on the development of student identities, especially in mathematics classrooms that serve students of color. Her work also examines how race, gender, and language ideologies affect such classroom interactions.

Judson Laughter is an associate professor of English education at the University of Tennessee, Knoxville. His research interests include culturally sustaining pedagogy, critical race theory, and the preparation of preservice teachers for diverse classrooms through dialogue and narrative. He teaches courses in English language arts teaching methods, action research, sociolinguistics, and trends in education. His work has appeared in several peer-reviewed journals, including *Review of Educational Research, Urban Education*, and *Teaching and Teacher Education*. He is an area chair for the Literacy Research Association and an active member of that association and of the National Council of Teachers of English.

Marcia C. Linn is a professor at the Graduate School of Education at the University of California, Berkeley. She is a member of the National Academy of Education and a fellow at the American Association for the Advancement of Science (AAAS) and the American Psychological Association. She was elected chair of the AAAS Education Section and president of the International Society of the Learning Sciences. She directs the Technology-Enhanced Learning in Science community (funded by the National Science Foundation) and serves on the boards of AAAS, the Graduate Record Examination, and the Education and Human Resources Directorate at the National Science Foundation. She received the National Association for Research in Science Teaching Award for Lifelong Distinguished Contributions to Science Education, AERA's Willystine Goodsell Award, and the Council of Scientific Society Presidents' first Award for Excellence in Educational Research. Her most recent book is *Science Learning and Instruction* (2011).

Allison R. Lombardi is an assistant professor in the Department of Educational Psychology at the University of Connecticut. She studies the transition from adolescence to adulthood for students with disabilities and those at risk for school failure, with a particular focus on aligning secondary special education transition services with broader school-wide college- and career-readiness initiatives in high school settings, as well as identifying and testing effective supports for students with disabilities in college settings.

Camillia Matuk is an assistant professor of educational communication and technology at New York University's Steinhardt School of Culture, Education, and Human Development. She designs and studies the role of technology in teaching and learning. Her work examines how online tools can be integrated into inquiry-based environments to enhance students' collaborative learning of science concepts. She also investigates professional development as a context for participatory design, particularly in support of teachers designing tools to support their practice and customizing their instruction to address students' needs. More recently, she has begun to explore processes and supports for learning through codesign within game-based learning environments in after-school and professional development programs.

Kevin W. McElhaney is a science education researcher in the Center for Technology in Learning at SRI International. His research focuses on the design and implementation of instructional innovations and teacher professional development in K–12 science, engineering, and computational thinking. Of central interest are technology-enhanced curriculum materials and assessments that align with emerging frameworks and standards for K–12 science, engineering, and computer science. His work examines how principled design approaches can promote the integration of content knowledge and inquiry practices across these STEM disciplines, as well as alignment between curriculum and assessment. His recent publications address the design of technology-based visualizations, automated guidance, and scaffolding tools for inquiry instruction and the design of classroom-based science assessments that integrate content and practice.

P. Karen Murphy is the Harry and Marion Royer Eberly Fellow and professor of education at The Pennsylvania State University, where she holds a joint appointment in the Educational Psychology program and the Children, Youth, and Families Consortium. Her current research, funded by the Institute of Education Sciences and the National Science Foundation, focuses on the role of classroom discussion in students' critical-analytic thinking and reasoning about, around, and with text and content (see www.qualitytalk.psu.edu). Murphy is a fellow of the American Psychological Association and AERA. She is a past vice president of Division C of AERA, received the Richard E. Snow Early Career Achievement Award from the American Psychological Association, and is presently serving as editor of the *Review of Educational Research*.

Na'ilah Suad Nasir is the Birgeneau Chair in Educational Disparities in the Graduate School of Education at the University of California, Berkeley. She also serves as the second vice chancellor for equity and inclusion for the university. Her research centers on how issues of culture and race influence the learning, achievement, and educational trajectories of African American and other nondominant students in urban school and community settings.

David Osher is a vice president and institute fellow at the American Institutes for Research. He is an expert on violence prevention, school safety, supportive school discipline, conditions for learning and school climate, social and emotional learning, youth development, cultural competence, family engagement, collaboration, mental health services, and implementation science. He has led impact and qualitative evaluations of initiatives and programs, systematic reviews, and expert panels, as well as projects that have developed surveys, and he has supported schools, districts, and states in promoting conditions for learning, including school safety, and in addressing disciplinary disparities. He is a principal investigator of the National Center on Safe and Supportive Learning Environments, the National Resource Center on Mental Health Promotion and Youth Violence Prevention, and the National Evaluation and Technical Assistance Center for the Education of Children and Youth Who Are Neglected, Delinquent, or At Risk.

Terri D. Pigott is dean and professor at Loyola University Chicago, School of Education. She received her PhD in measurement, evaluation, and statistical analysis from the University of Chicago. Her research focuses on methods of meta-analysis, including handling missing data and computing power in meta-analysis. She also studies outcome reporting bias in education research and its implications for systematic review. She has served on a number of editorial boards, including the boards of *Psychological Bulletin, Psychological Methods*, and *Research Synthesis Methods*. She is the former cochair and current coeditor of the Methods Group of the Campbell Collaboration, an international organization that supports the production of systematic reviews of social interventions.

Paul Polanco is a third-year doctoral student in education at Southern Methodist University. His research interests are related to the academic outcomes and economic benefits of bilingual programs for bilingual students. In his fellowship, he works with Doris Baker on a grant from the Institute of Education Sciences, where he develops the science content of a vocabulary intervention for Spanish-speaking English learners. The program focuses on teaching words in depth, using an intelligent tutoring system. He has presented at various conferences on effective teaching practices for bilingual students and for diverse learners in general. Before pursuing his doctorate, he was a science bilingual teacher for 9 years in a large urban school district; before that, he worked as a banker. He was born and raised in the Dominican Republic and is fluent in English and Spanish. He holds an MBA with a concentration in corporate finance from the University of Dallas.

Joshua R. Polanin is a senior research scientist at Development Services Group, Inc. He received his PhD from Loyola University Chicago in 2013 and participated in an Institute of Education Sciences postdoctoral fellowship at Vanderbilt University's Peabody Research Institute from 2013 through 2015. His primary research focuses on the implementation and improvement of systematic review and meta-analysis. In addition, he conducts research on student achievement, safety, and well-being.

Jeanne M. Powers is an associate professor of education policy at the Mary Lou Fulton Teachers College, Arizona State University. She received her PhD in sociology from the University of California, San Diego. Her research focuses on school segregation, school choice, and school finance litigation and on issues of equity and access in education policy more broadly. She has published in the *Review of Research in Education*, the *American Educational Research Journal*, *Educational Policy*, the *American Journal of Education*, *Equity & Excellence in Education*, and *Law and Social Inquiry*. In 2015 she was awarded AERA's Review of Research Award for her article "From Segregation to School Finance: The Legal Context for Language Rights in the United States." She is an associate editor of *Education Policy Analysis Archives*, an open-access peer-reviewed scholarly journal, and a member of the editorial boards of the *American Educational Research Journal; Race, Ethnicity and Education*; and the National Education Policy Center.

Allison Roda is an assistant professor of education in the Molloy College EdD program Educational Leadership for Diverse Learning Communities. Her research and teaching interests are focused on urban education policy, educational stratification, families and schools, and qualitative research methods. She is the author of *Inequality in Gifted and Talented Programs: Parental Choices About Status, School Opportunity, and Second-Generation Segregation* (Palgrave Macmillan, 2015). Her work has appeared in the *American Journal of Education*, the *Journal of Education Policy*, and *Quartz*. Her works have also been published by the Century Foundation and the Hechinger Report. She received her PhD in sociology and education from Teachers College at Columbia University.

Barbara Rogoff is UCSC Foundation Distinguished Professor at the University of California, Santa Cruz, Department of Psychology. She received a Distinguished Lifetime Contributions Award from the Society for Research in Child Development and is a fellow of the National Academy of Education and several international organizations (American Anthropological Association, American Psychological Society, APA, AERA). She held the University of California Presidential Chair and Fellowships of the Center for Advanced Study in the Behavioral Sciences, the Kellogg Foundation, the Spencer Foundation, and the Exploratorium. She served as editor of *Human Development*. Her recent books have received major awards: *Learning Together* (finalist for the Maccoby Award, APA), *The Cultural Nature of Human Development* (APA William James Book Award), and *Developing Destinies: A Mayan Midwife and Town* (Maccoby Award, APA). She recently coedited *Learning by Observing and Pitching in to Family and Community Endeavors* and *Children Learn by Observing and Contributing to Family and Community Endeavors* (see www.learningbyobservingandpitchingin.com).

Ann Marie Ryan is the associate dean of academic programs and an associate professor of teaching and learning in the School of Education at Loyola University Chicago. She received her PhD in curriculum and instruction from the University of Illinois at Chicago in 2004. Her research concentrates on the preparation and professional development of teachers with a particular interest in urban education and the teaching of history. She also has an established research agenda in the field of the history of education, with a focus on the history of Catholic and public education in the Unites States from the early to mid-20th century. Within this field she researches the issue of educational equity and access by examining movements such as standardization, testing, and accreditation.

William A. Sandoval is a professor and head of the Division of Urban Schooling in the Graduate School of Education & Information Studies at the University of California, Los Angeles. His research interests include epistemic cognition, scientific argumentation, classroom interaction and discourse processes, public understanding of science, and educational design research. He serves on the editorial boards of *Cognition & Instruction, Educational Psychologist, Journal of the Learning Sciences*, and *Science Education*. He is a fellow of the International Society for Design and Development in Education and president-elect of the International Society of the Learning Sciences. He earned his PhD in the learning sciences from Northwestern University and a bachelor's degree in computer science from the University of New Mexico.

Alan H. Schoenfeld is the Elizabeth and Edward Conner Professor in the Graduate School of Education and an affiliated professor of mathematics at the University of California, Berkeley. A mathematician by training, he has devoted his career to understanding thinking, teaching, and learning, with the goal of helping students learn to be powerful mathematical thinkers and problem solvers. He is a fellow of AERA and has served as AERA president. He is also a fellow of the American Association for the Advancement of Science, a laureate of the education honor society Kappa Delta Pi, and a member of the National Academy of Education. Among the honors he has received are the International Commission on Mathematical Instruction's Klein Medal, the highest international distinction in mathematics education, and AERA's Distinguished Contributions to Research in Education Award.

Janelle Scott is a Chancellor's Associate Professor at the University of California, Berkeley, in the Graduate School of Education, African American Studies Department, and Goldman School of Public Policy. Her research examines the racial politics of public education with a focus on the role of philanthropy, elite and grassroots advocacy, and research utilization in relation to school choice policies, educational privatization, and charter school reform. She earned her BA in political science from UC Berkeley, and her PhD from the Graduate School of Education and Information Studies at the University of California, Los Angeles.

Charles Tocci is an assistant professor of social studies education at Loyola University Chicago, School of Education. Previously, he taught at South Shore Community Academy in Chicago Public Schools and served as a senior research associate at the National Center for Restructuring Education, Schools, and Teaching at Teachers College, Columbia University. He has published on the history of grading and assessment in American education and is currently investigating the ways that students relate history learned outside of school to history taught in school. He also serves on the leadership team for the National Endowment for the Humanities summer teacher program "Rethinking the Gilded Age and Progressivism: Race, Capitalism, and Democracy 1877–1920."

Frédéric Vandermoere is an assistant professor in the Department of Sociology at the University of Antwerp, Belgium. His research has appeared in publications such as *Public Understanding of Science; Environment and Behavior*, the *Journal of Environmental Planning and Management, Minerva, Science in Context, Risk Analysis*, the *Journal of Nanoparticle Research*, and *Social Science & Medicine*. He is currently completing an edited volume on the importance of imagination at the crossroads of science, technology, and society.

Raf Vanderstraeten is a research professor in the Department of Sociology at Ghent University, Belgium, and visiting researcher in the Department of Sociology at the University of Chicago. He has also worked at universities in the Netherlands, Germany, France, and Finland. His work has appeared in publications such as the *British Journal of Sociology*, the *British Journal of Sociology of Education, Educational Philosophy and Theory, Educational Theory*, the *Journal of Philosophy of Education, Memory Studies, Minerva, Paedagogica Historica, Social Science History, Sociology*, the *Sociological Review, Thesis Eleven, Zeitschrift für Pädagogik*, and *Zeitschrift für Soziologie*. He is currently completing a book on the history of sociology in Belgium.

Roger P. Weissberg is Distinguished Professor of Psychology and Education and NoVo Foundation Endowed Chair in Social and Emotional Learning at the University of Illinois at Chicago. He is also Chief Knowledge Officer of the Collaborative for Academic, Social, and Emotional Learning, an organization committed to making evidence-based social and emotional academic learning an essential part of education. Weissberg has authored 250 publications focusing on preventive interventions with children. He has received several awards, including the American Psychological Association's Award for Distinguished Contributions of Applications of Psychology to Education and Training, the Society for Community Research and Action's Award for Distinguished Contributions to Theory and Research in Community Psychology, and the "Daring Dozen" Award from the George Lucas Educational Foundation for being one of twelve people who are reshaping the future of education. He is also a member of the National Academy of Education for contributions to education research and policy.

Amy Stuart Wells is a professor of sociology and education at Teachers College, Columbia University. She is also the director of the Center for Understanding Race and Education and codirector of Public Good, a nonprofit public school support organization for racially and ethnically diverse schools. Her research and writing have focused broadly on issues of race and education and, more specifically, on educational policies such as school desegregation, school choice, charter schools, and tracking and how they shape and constrain opportunities for students of color. Her ongoing research project "Metro Migrations, Racial Segregation and School Boundaries" examines urban and suburban demographic change and the role that public schools and their boundaries play in who moves where. In February 2016, she and her colleagues published a Century Foundation report titled *How Racially Diverse Schools and Classrooms Can Benefit All Students.*

Ryan T. Williams is a senior researcher at the American Institutes for Research. He leads or coleads a wide range of research and evaluation projects. Much of his work relates to the design and analysis of experimental and quasi-experimental studies. Previously, he worked as an assistant professor of quantitative methods at the University of Memphis, where he taught courses on statistics, measurement, and meta-analysis. His methodological research interests are related to advancing methods for research synthesis and meta-analysis and for improving causal inferences from quasi-experimental research. His recent publications include articles in *Educational Researcher, Educational and Psychological Measurement,* and *Research Synthesis Methods.* He currently serves as coeditor of the Campbell Collaboration methods group. He received his MA and PhD in quantitative research methodology from Loyola University Chicago.